CRITICISM

MAJOR STATEMENTS

Fourth Edition

Edited by

CHARLES KAPLAN

Emeritus, California State University, Northridge

and

WILLIAM DAVIS ANDERSON

California State University, Northridge

Bedford/St. Martin's   Boston ◆ New York

For Bedford/St. Martin's
Developmental Editor: Stephen A. Scipione
Production Editor: Bridget Leahy
Production Supervisor: Cheryl Mamaril
Marketing Manager: Karen Melton
Editorial Assistant: Nicole Simonsen
Copyeditor: Rosemary Winfield
Text Design: Claire Seng-Niemoeller
Cover Design: Trudi Gershenov
Cover Art: Photo © Sean Kernan, Inc.
Composition: Pine Tree Composition, Inc.
Printing and Binding: Haddon Craftsmen, Inc.

President: Charles H. Christensen
Editorial Director: Joan E. Feinberg
Director of Editing, Design, and Production: Marcia Cohen
Managing Editor: Elizabeth M. Schaaf

Library of Congress Catalog Card Number: 99–61998

Manufactured in the United States of America.

4   3   2   1   0   9
f   e   d   c   b   a

For information, write: Bedford/St. Martin's, 75 Arlington Street, Boston, MA 02116
(617-426-7440)

ISBN: 0–312–137451

Acknowledgments

M. M. Bakhtin. "Heteroglossia in the Novel." Excerpt from "Discourse in the Novel," pp. 301–31, in *The Dialogic Imagination: Four Essays* by M. M. Bakhtin, edited by Michael Holquist, translated by Michael Holquist and Caryl Emerson. Copyright © 1981. By permission of the University of Texas Press.
Roland Barthes. "The Structuralist Activity." From *Critical Essays* by Roland Barthes, translated by Richard Howard. Northwestern University Press, 1972. Reprinted by permission of the publisher.

PREFACE

The decades during which this anthology has been in print have seen enormous changes in how criticism is conceived and practiced. Thus, each new edition of *Criticism: Major Statements* presents new challenges to its editors. On the one hand, it is always a pleasure to retain a core of perennially vital statements by such figures as Plato, Aristotle, and Samuel Johnson. On the other hand, the editors must choose responsibly among the works of many important critics whose inclusion must be weighed, at least in part, against the needs of contemporary students, the interests of their instructors, trends in the field, and the time limitations of the course in which *Criticism* is assigned. Given these practical constraints, we have always tried to strike the right balance. Gratifyingly, our colleagues who teach with the book, however much they may rue the omission of particular statements or critics, generally tell us that our choices have served their students well. We trust that this new edition continues to provide an abundance of readings that meet the needs of our colleagues, in a portable form that is neither unwieldy nor too expensive for their students.

Although selections change from edition to edition, some things in *Criticism: Major Statements* have remained constant. As much as possible, we have attempted to include whole essays or at least substantial excerpts that can stand on their own. We have tried to avoid snippets in the belief that students are not well served by heavily edited selections that reduce complex arguments to choppy fragments of text. The selections are arranged chronologically to suggest the scope and advance of criticism and critical dialogues. Students can discover when certain ideas developed and how they evolved over time. (The index should aid them in this endeavor.) Headnotes introduce each selection, but the information they provide does not dictate how students should read the selections or suggest how they should be taught. The selections are lightly footnoted, and at the back of the book we present bibliographies, in case students wish to pursue further their investigations into literary criticism.

New to This Edition

Of the forty-five selections in this fourth edition, seventeen are new. Seven of the new statements (by Dante, Kant, Marx, Nietzsche, Wilde, Freud, and Bakhtin) are recognized classics (although, of course, Bakhtin achieved that status much more recently than Dante!). Among the other ten new texts, we have included major statements representing contemporary Lacanian psychoanalysis (Shoshana Felman), postcolonialism (Homi Bhabha), gay studies (Eve Kosofsky Sedgwick), and hypertextuality (George Landow). Throughout the book, the headnotes have been thoroughly revised and brought up to date. Finally, in recognition of the burgeoning importance of electronic research, we have augmented the Further Readings appendix with annotated links for websites to help students locate resources concerning literary theory and theorists on the Internet. To our knowledge, *Criticism: Major Statements, Fourth Edition,* is the first anthology of literary criticism and theory to provide such assistance. (The Bedford/St. Martin's literature homepage provides additional links to websites on both individual theorists and schools of thought.)

Acknowledgments

We would especially like to thank reviewers of the third edition, who provided us with many helpful suggestions for preparing the fourth edition. They include: Ann Ardis, University of Delaware; Lennard J. Davis, SUNY–Binghamton; Trent Hill, Clemson University; Robert Inchausti, California Polytechnic State University, San Luis Obispo; Steven Shankman, University of Oregon; Gregory Ulmer, University of Florida. A special thanks is due to Professor John Clendenning of California State University, Northridge.

We remain grateful to our colleagues whose opinions, suggestions, and objections were so helpful when we edited earlier editions: Albert R. Baca, California State University, Northridge; Peter Baker, Southern Connecticut State University; John E. Becker, Fairleigh Dickinson University; Alan T. Belsches, Troy State University at Dothan; James R. Bennett, University of Arkansas at Fayetteville; Richard Blakeslee, California State University, Northridge; Joy G. Boyum, New York University; Constance Brown, Barnard College; Lawrence J. Clipper, Indiana University at South Bend; Ancillia Coleman, Jackson State University; Richard Cornelius, Bryan College; Howard Coughlin, Eastern Connecticut State University; Clarence J. Denne, College of New Rochelle; Virginia Doland, Biola University; James Dorrill, University of South Alabama; James Thomas Farrell, College of St. Thomas; Harry Finestone, California State University, Northridge; Christine Gallant, Georgia State University; Robert F. Garratt, University of Puget Sound; Mahlon Gaumer, California State University, Northridge; William A. Geiger, Whittier College; Albert J. Geritz, Fort Hays State University; John Gillen, Castleton State College; Richardson Gray, Montreat-Anderson College; Stephen Hahn, William Paterson College; Eric Heyne, University of Alaska Fairbanks; Eugene Hollahan, Georgia State University; Bernard Kaplan, Clark University; George Kearns, Rutgers University; William P. Keen, Washington and Jefferson College; Benjamin S. Lawson, Albany State College; Thomas M. Leitch, University of Delaware; Joseph Lenz, Drake University; James Livingston, Northern Michigan University; David M. Locke, University of Florida; John B. Mason, Western Washington University; James McKusick, University of Maryland; Fred Misurella, East Stroudsburg University; Bradford Mudge, University of Colorado at Denver; John Paine, Belmont College; Sidney F. Parham, St. Cloud State University; Sue Park, West Texas State University; Elaine Plasberg, California State University, Northridge; Sura P. Rath, Louisiana State University in Shreveport; Frances Restuccia, Boston College; Donald L. Reynolds, Southern Oregon State College; David Richter, Queens College, City University of New York; Terrance Riley, Rutgers University; Bruce Roach, Stephen F. Austin State University; Erik Ryding, Barnard College; Richard Schroeder, Thiel College; Richard Shereikis, Sangamon State University; Phillip J. Sipiora, University of South Florida; Mark Trevor Smith, Southwest Missouri State University; William Snyder, St. Vincent College; Jane W. Stedman, Roosevelt University; Thomas R. Steiner, University of California, Santa Barbara; Ralph S. Stevens, Coppin State College; Robert W. Swords, Elmhurst College; Timea Szell, Barnard College; Stephen L. Tanner, Brigham Young University; Thomas Vargish, University of Maryland; Thomas P. Walsh, University of Nebraska at Omaha; Robert Wilson, University of Missouri–Kansas City; Austin M. Wright, University of Cincinnati.

We are pleased to thank Charles Christensen and Joan Feinberg, respectively President and Editorial Director of Bedford/St. Martin's, and we appreciate the contributions of Donna Erickson and Jason Noe, with whom we worked on the initial stages of this edition, and Steve Scipione, who helped bring it to completion. Bridget Leahy was a tireless and efficient production editor. We are especially grateful to Janet Gardner of the University of Massachusetts, Dartmouth, who helped us revise the headnotes, and Nicole Simonsen, who brought our bibliography into the age of electronic information.

Our many students over the years at California State University, Northridge, have continually rewarded our efforts and refreshed our approaches to teaching through their interest in, and enthusiasm for, the study of literary criticism.

Charles Kaplan
William Davis Anderson

CONTENTS

PLATO

The Republic: Book X

About 370 B.C.

———

It has been said that the history of Western philosophy is a series of footnotes to Plato. If true, then it may also be said that the history of literary criticism is a footnote to Book X of The Republic. *Once Plato (ca. 427–347 B.C.) (or his persona, Socrates) has exiled the poets from the ideal state, the ground rules, many of the issues, and some of the terminology have been established for the two-thousand-year debate that ensues. As you read some of the critics that follow, keep in mind the issues that Plato first raises: the place of the poet in society; the relationship that the form of a literary work bears to its subject matter; the effect of literature on its audience; the proper function of literature; the relative values of literature and science; and, a crucial question, the nature of artistic imitation, or what is being imitated, how it is imitated, and what relationship that thing bears to the "real" world. In* The Ion *(p. 15) Plato raises the question of the nature of the artistic process, which also involves questions about the psychology of the artist. The variations on these themes that have been played since testify to the powerful effect of the Platonic dialogues on later critics, whether these critics write in support, refutation, or modification of Plato's views.*

Because Plato's decision to ban poets from the ideal republic follows from his basic assumptions, it is important to understand just what these assumptions are. In the final analysis, the essence of Plato's philosophy is an idealistic search for metaphysical Truth; for poetry is to be seen not only in its relation to the republic but also as part of the total universe and the means of attaining true knowledge of that universe. Other frames of reference are also employed. Utility is an obvious measure of value for Plato, so he distinguishes among various kinds and degrees of usefulness; poetry is also to be contrasted with other human activities. Plato's analysis of the "parts of the soul" is a psychological model that accounts for the way human beings behave and react and learn. So, given the nature of the universe, the goal of an ideal republic, and the nature of man, where does poetry fit in? And, if you think that Plato dismisses poetry because it is merely an idle and unimportant amusement, can you imagine a political theorist today who would devote serious attention to the subject of poetry?

1

OF THE MANY excellences which I perceive in the order of our State, there is none which upon reflection pleases me better than the rule about poetry.

To what do you refer?

To our refusal to admit the imitative kind of poetry, for it certainly ought not to be received; as I see far more clearly now that the parts of the soul have been distinguished.

What do you mean?

Speaking in confidence, for you will not denounce me to the tragedians and the rest of the imitative tribe, all poetical imitations are ruinous to the understanding of the hearers, unless as an antidote they possess the knowledge of the true nature of the originals.

Explain the purport of your remark.

Well, I will tell you, although I have always from my earliest youth had an awe and love of Homer which even now makes the words falter on my lips, for he seems to be the great captain and teacher of the whole of that noble tragic company; but a man is not to be reverenced more than the truth, and therefore I will speak out.

Very good, he said.

Listen to me then, or rather, answer me.

Put your question.

Can you give me a general definition of imitation? for I really do not myself understand what it professes to be.

A likely thing, then, that I should know.

There would be nothing strange in that, for the duller eye may often see a thing sooner than the keener.

Very true, he said; but in your presence, even if I had any faint notion, I could not muster courage to utter it. Will you inquire yourself?

Well then, shall we begin the inquiry at this point, following our usual method: Whenever a number of individuals have a common name, we assume that there is one corresponding idea or form:[1]—do you understand me?

I do.

Let us take, for our present purpose, any instance of such a group; there are beds and tables in the world—many of each, are there not?

Yes.

But there are only two ideas or forms of such furniture—one the idea of a bed, the other of a table.

True.

And the maker of either of them makes a bed or he makes a table for our use, in accordance with the idea—that is our way of speaking in this and similar instances—but no artificer makes the idea itself: how could he?

Impossible.

---

[1] Or (probably better): 'we have been accustomed to assume that there is one single idea corresponding to each group of particulars; and to these we give the same name (as we give the idea)'.

And there is another artificer,—I should like to know what you would say of him.

Who is he?

One who is the maker of all the works of all other workmen.

What an extraordinary man!

Wait a little, and there will be more reason for your saying so. For this is the craftsman who is able to make not only furniture of every kind, but all that grows out of the earth, and all living creatures, himself included; and besides these he can make earth and sky and the gods, and all the things which are in heaven or in the realm of Hades under the earth.

He must be a wizard and no mistake.

Oh! You are incredulous, are you? Do you mean that there is no such maker or creator, or that in one sense there might be a maker of all these things but in another not? Do you see that there is a way in which you could make them all yourself?

And what way is this? he asked.

An easy way enough; or rather, there are many ways in which the feat might be quickly and easily accomplished, none quicker than that of turning a mirror round and round—you would soon enough make the sun and the heavens, and the earth and yourself, and other animals and plants, and furniture and all the other things of which we were just now speaking, in the mirror.

Yes, he said; but they would be appearances only.

Very good, I said, you are coming to the point now. And the painter too is, as I conceive, just such another—a creator of appearances, is he not?

Of course.

But then I suppose you will say that what he creates is untrue. And yet there is a sense in which the painter also creates a bed? Is there not?

Yes, he said, but here again, an appearance only.

And what of the maker of the bed? were you not saying that he too makes, not the idea which according to our view is the real object denoted by the word bed, but only a particular bed?

Yes, I did.

Then if he does not make a real object he cannot make what *is*, but only some semblance of existence; and if any one were to say that the work of the maker of the bed, or of any other workman, has real existence, he could hardly be supposed to be speaking the truth.

Not, at least, he replied, in the view of those who make a business of these discussions.

No wonder, then, that his work too is an indistinct expression of truth.

No wonder.

Suppose now that by the light of the examples just offered we inquire who this imitator is?

If you please.

Well then, here we find three beds: one existing in nature, which is made by God, as I think that we may say—for no one else can be the maker?

No one, I think.

There is another which is the work of the carpenter?

Yes.

And the work of the painter is a third?

Yes.

Beds, then, are of three kinds, and there are three artists who superintend them: God, the maker of the bed, and the painter?

Yes, there are three of them.

God, whether from choice or from necessity, made one bed in nature and one only; two or more such beds neither ever have been nor ever will be made by God.

Why is that?

Because even if He had made but two, a third would still appear behind them of which they again both possessed the form, and that would be the real bed and not the two others.

Very true, he said.

God knew this, I suppose, and He desired to be the real maker of a real bed, not a kind of maker of a kind of bed, and therefore He created a bed which is essentially and by nature one only.

So it seems.

Shall we, then, speak of Him as the natural author or maker of the bed?

Yes, he replied; inasmuch as by the natural process of creation, He is the author of this and of all other things.

And what shall we say of the carpenter—is not he also the maker of a bed?

Yes.

But would you call the painter an artificer and maker?

Certainly not.

Yet if he is not the maker, what is he in relation to the bed?

I think, he said, that we may fairly designate him as the imitator of that which the others make.

Good, I said; then you call him whose product is third in the descent from nature, an imitator?

Certainly, he said.

And so if the tragic poet is an imitator, he too is thrice removed from the king and from the truth; and so are all other imitators.

That appears to be so.

Then about the imitator we are agreed. And what about the painter?—Do you think he tries to imitate in each case that which originally exists in nature, or only the creations of artificers?

The latter.

As they are or as they appear? you have still to determine this.

What do you mean?

I mean to ask whether a bed really becomes different when it is seen from different points of view, obliquely or directly or from any other point of view? Or does it simply appear different, without being really so? And the same of all things.

Yes, he said, the difference is only apparent.

Now let me ask you another question: Which is the art of painting designed to be—an imitation of things as they are, or as they appear—of appearance or of reality?

Of appearance, he said.

Then the imitator is a long way off the truth, and can reproduce all things because he lightly touches on a small part of them, and that part an image. For example: A painter will paint a cobbler, carpenter, or any other artisan, though he knows nothing of their arts; and, if he is a good painter, he may deceive children or simple persons when he shows them his picture of a carpenter from a distance, and they will fancy that they are looking at a real carpenter.

Certainly.

And surely, my friend, this is how we should regard all such claims: whenever any one informs us that he has found a man who knows all the arts, and all things else that anybody knows, and every single thing with a higher degree of accuracy than any other man—whoever tells us this, I think that we can only retort that he is a simple creature who seems to have been deceived by some wizard or imitator whom he met, and whom he thought all-knowing, because he himself was unable to analyse the nature of knowledge and ignorance and imitation.

Most true.

And next, I said, we have to consider tragedy and its leader, Homer; for we hear some persons saying that these poets know all the arts; and all things human; where virtue and vice are concerned, and indeed all divine things too; because the good poet cannot compose well unless he knows his subject, and he who has not this knowledge can never be a poet. We ought to consider whether here also there may not be a similar illusion. Perhaps they may have come across imitators and been deceived by them; they may not have remembered when they saw their works that these were thrice removed from the truth, and could easily be made without any knowledge of the truth, because they are appearances only and not realities? Or, after all, they may be in the right, and good poets do really know the things about which they seem to the many to speak so well?

The question, he said, should by all means be considered.

Now do you suppose that if a person were able to make the original as well as the image, he would seriously devote himself to the image-making branch? Would he allow imitation to be the ruling principle of his life, as if he had nothing higher in him?

I should say not.

But the real artist, who had real knowledge of those things which he chose also to imitate, would be interested in realities and not in imitations; and would desire to leave as memorials of himself works many and fair; and, instead of being the author of encomiums, he would prefer to be the theme of them.

Yes, he said, that would be to him a source of much greater honour and profit.

Now let us refrain, I said, from calling Homer or any other poet to account regarding those arts to which his poems incidentally refer: we will not ask them, in case any poet has been a doctor and not a mere imitator of medical parlance, to show what patients have been restored to health by a poet, ancient or modern, as they were by Asclepius; or what disciples in medicine a poet has left behind him, like the Asclepiads. Nor shall we press the same question upon them about the other arts. But we have a right to know respecting warfare, strategy, the administration of States and the education of man, which are the chiefest and noblest subjects of his poems, and we may fairly ask him about them. 'Friend Homer,' then we say to him, 'if you are only in the second remove from truth in what you say of virtue, and not in the third—not an image maker, that is, by our definition, an imitator—and if you are able to discern what pursuits make men better or worse in private or public life, tell us what State was ever better governed by your help? The good order of Lacedaemon is due to Lycurgus, and many other cities great and small have been similarly benefited by others; but who says that you have been a good legislator to them and have done them any good? Italy and Sicily boast of Charondas, and there is Solon who is renowned among us; but what city has anything to say about you?' Is there any city which he might name?

I think not, said Glaucon; not even the Homerids themselves pretend that he was a legislator.

Well, but is there any war on record which was carried on successfully owing to his leadership or counsel?

There is not.

Or is there anything comparable to those clever improvements in the arts, or in other operations, which are said to have been due to men of practical genius such as Thales the Milesian or Anacharsis the Scythian?

There is absolutely nothing of the kind.

But, if Homer never did any public service, was he privately a guide or teacher of any? Had he in his lifetime friends who loved to associate with him, and who handed down to posterity an Homeric way of life, such as was established by Pythagoras who was especially beloved for this reason and whose followers are to this day conspicuous among others by what they term the Pythagorean way of life?

Nothing of the kind is recorded of him. For surely, Socrates, Creophylus, the companion of Homer, that child of flesh, whose name always makes us laugh, might be more justly ridiculed for his want of breeding, if what is said is true, that Homer was greatly neglected by him in his own day when he was alive?

Yes, I replied, that is the tradition. But can you imagine, Glaucon, that if Homer had really been able to educate and improve mankind—if he had been capable of knowledge and not been a mere imitator—can you imagine, I say, that he would not have attracted many followers, and been honoured and loved by them? Protagoras of Abdera, and Prodicus of Ceos, and a host of others, have only to whisper to their contemporaries: 'You will never be able to manage either your own house or your own State until you appoint us to be your ministers of education'—and this ingenious device of theirs has such an effect in making men love them that their companions all but carry them about on their shoulders. And is it conceivable that the contemporaries of Homer, or again of Hesiod, would have allowed either of them to go about as rhapsodists, if they had really been able to help mankind forward in virtue? Would they not have been as unwilling to part with them as with gold, and have compelled them to stay at home with them? Or, if the master would not stay, then the disciples would have followed him about everywhere, until they had got education enough?

Yes, Socrates, that, I think, is quite true.

Then must we not infer that all these poetical individuals, beginning with Homer, are only imitators, who copy images of virtue and the other themes of their poetry, but have no contact with the truth? The poet is like a painter who, as we have already observed, will make a likeness of a cobbler though he understands nothing of cobbling; and his picture is good enough for those who know no more than he does, and judge only by colours and figures.

Quite so.

In like manner the poet with his words and phrases[2] may be said to lay on the colours of the several arts, himself understanding their nature only enough to imitate them; and other people, who are as ignorant as he is, and judge only from his words, imagine that if he speaks of cobbling, or of military tactics, or of anything else, in metre and harmony and rhythm, he speaks very well—such is the sweet influence which melody and rhythm by nature have. For I am sure that you know what a poor appearance the works of poets make when stripped of the colours which art puts upon them, and recited in simple prose. You have seen some examples?

Yes, he said.

They are like faces which were never really beautiful, but only blooming, seen when the bloom of youth has passed away from them?

Exactly.

Come now, and observe this point: The imitator or maker of the image knows nothing, we have said, of true existence; he knows appearances only. Am I not right?

Yes.

Then let us have a clear understanding, and not be satisfied with half an explanation.

Proceed.

Of the painter we say that he will paint reins, and he will paint a bit?

---

[2]Or: 'with his nouns and verbs'.

Yes.

And the worker in leather and brass will make them?

Certainly.

But does the painter know the right form of the bit and reins? Nay, hardly even the workers in brass and leather who make them; only the horseman who knows how to use them—he knows their right form.

Most true.

And may we not say the same of all things?

What?

That there are three arts which are concerned with all things: one which uses, another which makes, a third which imitates them?

Yes.

And the excellence and beauty and rightness of every structure, animate or inanimate, and of every action of man, is relative solely to the use for which nature or the artist has intended them.

True.

Then beyond doubt it is the user who has the greatest experience of them, and he must report to the maker the good or bad qualities which develop themselves in use; for example, the flute-player will tell the flute-maker which of his flutes is satisfactory to the performer; he will tell him how he ought to make them, and the other will attend to his instructions?

Of course.

So the one pronounces with knowledge about the goodness and badness of flutes, while the other, confiding in him, will make them accordingly?

True.

The instrument is the same, but about the excellence or badness of it the maker will possess a correct belief, since he associates with one who knows, and is compelled to hear what he has to say; whereas the user will have knowledge?

True.

But will the imitator have either? Will he know from use whether or not that which he paints is correct or beautiful? or will he have right opinion from being compelled to associate with another who knows and gives him instructions about what he should paint?

Neither.

Then an imitator will no more have true opinion than he will have knowledge about the goodness or badness of his models?

I suppose not.

The imitative poet will be in a brilliant state of intelligence about the theme of his poetry?

Nay, very much the reverse.

And still he will go on imitating without knowing what makes a thing good or bad, and may be expected therefore to imitate only that which appears to be good to the ignorant multitude?

Just so.

Thus far then we are pretty well agreed that the imitator has no knowledge worth mentioning of what he imitates. Imitation is only a kind of play or sport, and the tragic poets, whether they write in iambic or in heroic verse, are imitators in the highest degree?

Very true.

And now tell me, I conjure you,—this imitation is concerned with an object which is thrice removed from the truth?

Certainly.

And what kind of faculty in man is that to which imitation makes its special appeal?

What do you mean?

I will explain: The same body does not appear equal to our sight when seen near and when seen at a distance?

True.

And the same objects appear straight when looked at out of the water, and crooked when in the water; and the concave becomes convex, owing to the illusion about colours to which the sight is liable. Thus every sort of confusion is revealed within us; and this is that weakness of the human mind on which the art of painting in light and shadow, the art of conjuring, and many other ingenious devices impose, having an effect upon us like magic.

True.

And the arts of measuring and numbering and weighing come to the rescue of the human understanding—there is the beauty of them—with the result that the apparent greater or less, or more or heavier, no longer have the mastery over us, but give way before the power of calculation and measuring and weighing?

Most true.

And this, surely, must be the work of the calculating and rational principle in the soul?

To be sure.

And often when this principle measures and certifies that some things are equal, or that some are greater or less than others, it is, at the same time, contradicted by the appearance which the objects present?

True.

But did we not say that such a contradiction is impossible—the same faculty cannot have contrary opinions at the same time about the same thing?

We did; and rightly.

Then that part of the soul which has an opinion contrary to measure can hardly be the same with that which has an opinion in accordance with measure?

True.

And the part of the soul which trusts to measure and calculation is likely to be the better one?

Certainly.

And therefore that which is opposed to this is probably an inferior principle in our nature?

No doubt.

This was the conclusion at which I was seeking to arrive when I said that painting or drawing, and imitation in general, are engaged upon productions which are far removed from truth, and are also the companions and friends and associates of a principle within us which is equally removed from reason, and that they have no true or healthy aim.

Exactly.

The imitative art is an inferior who from intercourse with an inferior has inferior offspring.

Very true.

And is this confined to the sight only, or does it extend to the hearing also, relating in fact to what we term poetry?

Probably the same would be true of poetry.

Do not rely, I said, on a probability derived from the analogy of painting; but let us once more go directly to that faculty of the mind with which imitative poetry has converse, and see whether it is good or bad.

By all means.

We may state the question thus:—Imitation imitates the actions of men, whether voluntary or involuntary, on which, as they imagine, a good or bad result has ensued, and they rejoice or sorrow accordingly. Is there anything more?

No, there is nothing else.

But in all this variety of circumstances is the man at unity with himself—or rather, as in the instance of sight there was confusion and opposition in his opinions about the same things, so here also is there not strife and inconsistency in his life? Though I need hardly raise the question again, for I remember that all this has been already admitted; and the soul has been acknowledged by us to be full of these and ten thousand similar oppositions occurring at the same moment?

And we were right, he said.

Yes, I said, thus far we were right; but there was an omission which must now be supplied.

What was the omission?

Were we not saying that a good man, who has the misfortune to lose his son or anything else which is most dear to him, will bear the loss with more equanimity than another?

Yes, indeed.

But will he have no sorrow, or shall we say that although he cannot help sorrowing, he will moderate his sorrow?

The latter, he said, is the truer statement.

Tell me: will he be more likely to struggle and hold out against his sorrow when he is seen by his equals, or when he is alone in a deserted place?

The fact of being seen will make a great difference, he said.

When he is by himself he will not mind saying many things which he would be ashamed of any one hearing, and also doing many things which he would not care to be seen doing?

True.

And doubtless it is the law and reason in him which bids him resist; while it is the affliction itself which is urging him to indulge his sorrow?

True.

But when a man is drawn in two opposite directions, to and from the same object, this, as we affirm, necessarily implies two distinct principles in him?

Certainly.

One of them is ready to follow the guidance of the law?

How do you mean?

The law would say that to be patient under calamity is best, and that we should not give way to impatience, as the good and evil in such things are not clear, and nothing is gained by impatience; also, because no human thing is of serious importance, and grief stands in the way of that which at the moment is most required.

What is most required? he asked.

That we should take counsel about what has happened, and when the dice have been thrown, according to their fall, order our affairs in the way which reason deems best; not, like children who have had a fall, keeping hold of the part struck and wasting time in setting up a howl, but always accustoming the soul forthwith to apply a remedy, raising up that which is sickly and fallen, banishing the cry of sorrow by the healing art.

Yes, he said, that is the true way of meeting the attacks of fortune.

Well then, I said, the higher principle is ready to follow this suggestion of reason?

Clearly.

But the other principle, which inclines us to recollection of our troubles and to lamentation, and can never have enough of them, we may call irrational, useless, and cowardly?

Indeed, we may.

Now does not the principle which is thus inclined to complaint, furnish a great variety of materials for imitation? Whereas the wise and calm temperament, being always nearly equable, is not easy to imitate or to appreciate when imitated, especially at a public festival when a promiscuous crowd is assembled in a theatre. For the feeling represented is one to which they are strangers.

Certainly.

Then the imitative poet who aims at being popular is not by nature made, nor is his art intended, to please or to affect the rational principle in the soul; but he will appeal rather to the lachrymose and fitful temper, which is easily imitated?

Clearly.

And now we may fairly take him and place him by the side of the painter, for he is like him in two ways: first, inasmuch as his creations have an inferior degree of truth—in this, I say, he is like him; and he is also like him in being the associate of an inferior part of the soul; and this is enough to show that we shall be right in refusing to admit him into a State which is to be well ordered, because he awakens and nourishes this part of the soul, and by strengthening it impairs the reason. As in a city when the evil are permitted to wield power and the finer men are put out of the way, so in the soul of each man, as we shall maintain, the imitative poet implants an evil constitution, for he indulges the irrational nature which has no discernment of greater and less, but thinks the same thing at one time great and at another small—he is an imitator of images and is very far removed from the truth.

Exactly.

But we have not yet brought forward the heaviest count in our accusation:—the power which poetry has of harming even the good (and there are very few who are not harmed), is surely an awful thing?

Yes, certainly, if the effect is what you say.

Hear and judge: The best of us, as I conceive, when we listen to a passage of Homer or one of the tragedians, in which he represents some hero who is drawling out his sorrows in a long oration, or singing, and smiting his breast—the best of us, you know, delight in giving way to sympathy, and are in raptures at the excellence of the poet who stirs our feelings most.

Yes, of course I know.

But when any sorrow of our own happens to us, then you may observe that we pride ourselves on the opposite quality—we would fain be quiet and patient; this is considered the manly part, and the other which delighted us in the recitation is now deemed to be the part of a woman.

Very true, he said.

Now can we be right in praising and admiring another who is doing that which any one of us would abominate and be ashamed of in his own person?

No, he said, that is certainly not reasonable.

Nay, I said, quite reasonable from one point of view.

What point of view?

If you consider, I said, that when in misfortune we feel a natural hunger and desire to relieve our sorrow by weeping and lamentation, and that this very feeling which is starved and suppressed in our own calamities is satisfied and delighted by the poets;—the better nature in each of us, not having been sufficiently trained by reason or habit, allows the sympathetic element to break loose because the sorrow is another's; and the spectator fancies that there can be no disgrace to himself in praising and pitying any one who while professing to be a brave man, gives way to untimely lamentation; he thinks that the pleasure is a gain, and is far from wishing to lose it by rejection of the whole poem. Few persons ever reflect, as I should imagine, that the contagion must pass from others to themselves. For the pity which has been nourished and strengthened in the misfortunes of others is with difficulty repressed in our own.

How very true!

And does not the same hold also of the ridiculous? There are jests which you would be ashamed to make yourself, and yet on the comic stage, or indeed in private, when you hear them, you are greatly amused by them, and are not at all disgusted at their unseemliness;—the case of pity is repeated;—there is a principle in human nature which is disposed to raise a laugh, and this, which you once restrained by reason because you were afraid of being thought a buffoon, is now let out again; and having stimulated the risible faculty at the theatre, you are betrayed unconsciously to yourself into playing the comic poet at home.

Quite true, he said.

And the same may be said of lust and anger and all the other affections, of desire and pain and pleasure, which are held to be inseparable from every action—in all of them poetry has a like effect; it feeds and waters the passions instead of drying them up; she lets them rule, although they ought to be controlled if mankind are ever to increase in happiness and virtue.

I cannot deny it.

Therefore, Glaucon, I said, whenever you meet with any of the eulogists of Homer declaring that he has been the educator of Hellas, and that he is profitable for education and for the ordering of human things, and that you should take him up again and again and get to know him and regulate your whole life according to him, we may love and honour those who say these things—they are excellent people, as far as their lights extend; and we are ready to acknowledge that Homer is the greatest of poets and first of tragedy writers; but we must remain firm in our conviction that hymns to the gods and praises of famous men are the only poetry which ought to be admitted into our State. For if you go beyond this and allow the honeyed Muse to enter, either in epic or lyric verse, not law and the reason of mankind, which by common consent have ever been deemed best,[3] but pleasure and pain will be the rulers in our State.

That is most true, he said.

And now since we have reverted to the subject of poetry, let this our defence serve to show the reasonableness of our former judgement in sending away out of our State an art having the tendencies which we have described; for reason constrained us. But that she may not impute to us any harshness or want of politeness, let us tell her that there is an ancient quarrel between philosophy and poetry; of which there are many proofs, such as the saying of 'the yelping hound howling at her lord', or of one 'mighty in the vain talk of fools', and 'the mob of sages circumventing Zeus', and the 'subtle thinkers who are beggars after all';[4] and there are innumerable other signs of ancient enmity between them. Notwithstanding this, let us assure the poetry which aims at pleasure, and the art of imitation, that if she will only prove her title

---

[3] Or: 'law, and the principle which the community in every case has pronounced to be the best'.

[4] Reading and sense uncertain. The origin of all these quotations is unknown.

to exist in a well-ordered State we shall be delighted to receive her—we are very conscious of her charms; but it would not be right on that account to betray the truth. I dare say, Glaucon, that you are as much charmed by her as I am, especially when she appears in Homer?

Yes, indeed, I am greatly charmed.

Shall I propose, then, that she be allowed to return from exile, but upon this condition only—that she make a defence of herself in some lyrical or other metre?

Certainly.

And we may further grant to those of her defenders who are lovers of poetry and yet not poets the permission to speak in prose on her behalf: let them show not only that she is pleasant but also useful to States and to human life, and we will listen in a kindly spirit; for we shall surely be the gainers if this can be proved, that there is a use in poetry as well as a delight?

Certainly, he said, we shall be the gainers.

If her defence fails, then, my dear friend, like other persons who are enamoured of something, but put a restraint upon themselves when they think their desires are opposed to their interests, so too must we after the manner of lovers give her up, though not without a struggle. We too are inspired by that love of such poetry which the education of noble States has implanted in us, and therefore we shall be glad if she appears at her best and truest; but so long as she is unable to make good her defence, this argument of ours shall be a charm to us, which we will repeat to ourselves while we listen to her strains; that we may not fall away into the childish love of her which captivates the many. At all events we are well aware that poetry, such as we have described, is not to be regarded seriously as attaining to the truth; and he who listens to her, fearing for the safety of the city which is within him, should be on his guard against her seductions and make our words his law.

Yes, he said, I quite agree with you.

Yes, I said, my dear Glaucon, for great is the issue at stake, greater than appears, whether a man is to be good or bad. And what will any one be profited if under the influence of honour or money or power, aye, or under the excitement of poetry, he neglect justice and virtue?

Yes, he said; I have been convinced by the argument, as I believe that anyone else would have been.

Translated by Benjamin Jowett.

From *The Ion*

About 390 B.C.

———————

I CANNOT DENY what you say, Socrates. Nevertheless I am conscious in my own self, and the world agrees with me, that I do speak better and have more to say about Homer than any other man; but I do not speak equally well about others. After all, there must be some reason for this; what is it?

I see the reason, Ion; and I will proceed to explain to you what I imagine it to be. The gift which you possess of speaking excellently about Homer is not an art, but, as I was just saying, an inspiration; there is a divinity moving you, like that contained in the stone which Euripides calls a magnet, but which is commonly known as the stone of Heraclea. This stone not only attracts iron rings, but also imparts to them a similar power of attracting other rings; and sometimes you may see a number of pieces of iron and rings suspended from one another so as to form quite a long chain: and all of them derive their power of suspension from the original stone. In like manner the Muse first of all inspires men herself; and from these inspired persons a chain of other persons is suspended, who take the inspiration. For all good poets, epic as well as lyric, compose their beautiful poems not by art, but because they are inspired and possessed. And as the Corybantian revellers when they dance are not in their right mind, so the lyric poets are not in their right mind when they are composing their beautiful strains: but when falling under the power of music and metre they are inspired and possessed; like Bacchic maidens who draw milk and honey from the rivers when they are under the influence of Dionysus but not when they are in their right mind. And the soul of the lyric poet does the same, as they themselves say; for they tell us that they bring songs from honeyed fountains, culling them out of the gardens and dells of the Muses; they, like the bees, winging their way from flower to flower. And this is true. For the poet is a light and winged and holy thing, and there is no invention in him until he has been inspired and is out of his senses, and reason is no longer in him: no man, while he retains that faculty, has the oracular gift of poetry.

Many are the noble words in which poets speak concerning the actions of men; but like yourself when speaking about Homer, they do not speak of them by any rules of art: they are simply inspired to utter that to which the Muse impels them, and that only; and when inspired, one of them will make dithyrambs, another hymns of praise, another choral strains, another epic or iambic verses, but not one of them is of any account in the other kinds. For not by art does the poet sing, but by power divine; had he learned by rules of art, he would have known how to speak not of one theme only, but of all; and therefore God takes away reason from poets, and uses them as his ministers, as he also uses the pronouncers of oracles and holy prophets, in order that we who hear them may know them to be speaking not of themselves, who utter these priceless words while bereft of reason, but that God himself is the speaker, and that through them he is addressing us. And Tynnichus the Chalcidian affords a striking instance of what I am saying: he wrote no poem that anyone would care to remember but the famous paean which is in everyone's mouth, one of the finest lyric poems ever written, simply an invention of the Muses, as he himself says. For in this way God would seem to demonstrate to us and not to allow us to doubt that these beautiful poems are not human, nor the work of man, but divine and the work of God; and that the poets are only the interpreters of the gods by whom they are severally possessed. Was not this the lesson which God intended to teach when by the mouth of the worst of poets he sang the best of songs? Am I not right, Ion?

Yes, indeed, Socrates, I feel that you are; for your words touch my soul, and I am persuaded that in these works the good poets, under divine inspiration, interpret to us the voice of the Gods.

And you rhapsodists are the interpreters of the poets?

There again you are right.

Then you are the interpreters of interpreters?

Precisely.

I wish you would frankly tell me, Ion, what I am going to ask of you: When you produce the greatest effect upon the audience in the recitation of some striking passage, such as the apparition of Odysseus leaping forth on the floor, recognized by the suitors and shaking out his arrows at his feet, or the description of Achilles springing upon Hector, or the sorrows of Andromache, Hecuba, or Priam,— are you in your right mind? Are you not carried out of yourself, and does not your soul in an ecstasy seem to be among the persons or places of which you are speaking, whether they are in Ithaca or in Troy or whatever may be the scene of the poem?

That proof strikes home to me, Socrates. For I must frankly confess that at the tale of pity my eyes are filled with tears, and when I speak of horrors, my hair stands on end and my heart throbs.

Well, Ion, and what are we to say of a man who at a sacrifice or festival, when he is dressed in an embroidered robe, and has golden crowns upon his head, of which nobody has robbed him, appears weeping or panic-stricken in the presence of more than twenty thousand friendly faces, when there is no one despoiling or wronging him;—is he in his right mind or is he not?

No indeed, Socrates, I must say that, strictly speaking, he is not in his right mind.

And are you aware that you produce similar effects on most of the spectators?

Only too well; for I look down upon them from the stage, and behold the various emotions of pity, wonder, sternness, stamped upon their countenances when I am speaking: and I am obliged to give my very best attention to them; for if I make them cry I myself shall laugh, and if I make them laugh I myself shall cry, when the time of payment arrives.

Do you know that the spectator is the last of the rings which, as I am saying, receive the power of the original magnet from one another? The rhapsode like yourself and the actor are intermediate links, and the poet himself is the first of them. Through all these God sways the souls of men in any direction which He pleases, causing each link to communicate the power to the next. Thus there is a vast chain of dancers and masters and under-masters of choruses, who are suspended, as if from the stone, at the side of the rings which hang down from the Muse. And every poet has some Muse from whom he is suspended, and by whom he is said to be possessed, which is nearly the same thing; for he is taken hold of. And from these first rings, which are the poets, depend others, some deriving their inspiration from Orpheus, others from Musaeus; but the greater number are possessed and held by Homer. Of whom, Ion, you are one, and are possessed by Homer; and when anyone repeats the words of another poet you go to sleep, and know not what to say; but when anyone recites a strain of Homer you wake up in a moment, and your soul leaps within you, and you have plenty to say; for not by art or knowledge about Homer do you say what you say, but by divine inspiration and by possession; just as the Corybantian revellers too have a quick perception of that strain only which is appropriated to the god by whom they are possessed, and have plenty of dances and words for that, but take no heed of any other. And you, Ion, when the name of Homer is mentioned have plenty to say, and have nothing to say of others. You ask, 'Why is this?' The answer is that your skill in the praise of Homer comes not from art but from divine inspiration.

Translated by Benjamin Jowett.

ARISTOTLE

The Poetics

About 335–322 B.C.

―――――――
―――――――

Plato's discussion of poetry is a chapter in The Republic, *but Aristotle (384–322 B.C.) devotes a separate treatise to the subject, just as he wrote other treatises on topics such as ethics, politics, physics, and rhetoric. Certain differences in their philosophical views can be gleaned from this fact, as well as from the differences in the kinds of questions that each asks. Where Plato asks, "What good is poetry compared to other things?" Aristotle asks, "What is the good in poetry considered as itself?" When Plato accuses Homer of telling lies skillfully, he stresses the noun; but Aristotle emphasizes the adverb. Of course poets lie, Aristotle grants; now let us analyze the forms and techniques of these fictions to which we respond so powerfully. For Plato, poetry has an instrumental function; for Aristotle, it has a terminal value—that is, it is not to be regarded as a competing medium for information or indoctrination but as creative art. Where Plato is analogical, Aristotle is analytical; where Plato discusses poetry in general terms, Aristotle classifies, divides, and subdivides the kinds of poetry according to their formal differences. Whereas for Plato it is important to know the similarities among all things, for Aristotle it is more crucial to know, for example, how tragedy and epic differ from one another. And, defining tragedy as the highest form of poetry, Aristotle analyzes its component elements in an order and proportion that give the relative importance of each. The process by which he orders the treatise is at least as significant as his conclusions, some of which have been debated and interpreted ever since. His stress on artistic form, instead of subject matter, derives from a conception of imitation that differs from Plato's: for Aristotle, it is not copying but creating. The first formalist critic, he introduces the concept of organic unity, which numerous later critics adapt to their own purposes.*

There are also interesting differences in style between these two critics. Plato, who denounces the poets, is dramatic, eloquent, metaphorical; but Aristotle, who defends them, frequently sounds as though he is writing a technical manual. Though later authors often read Aristotle as a series of commandments, he is not prescribing a formula but describing and analyzing a form.

I

I PROPOSE to treat of Poetry in itself and of its various kinds, noting the essential quality of each; to inquire into the structure of the plot as requisite to a good poem; into the number and nature of the parts of which a poem is composed; and similarly into whatever else falls within the same inquiry. Following, then, the order of nature, let us begin with the principles which come first.

Epic poetry and Tragedy, Comedy also and Dithyrambic poetry, and the music of the flute and of the lyre in most of their forms, are all in their general conception modes of imitation. They differ, however, from one another in three respects,—the medium, the objects, the manner or mode of imitation, being in each case distinct.

For as there are persons who, by conscious art or mere habit, imitate and represent various objects through the medium of colour and form, or again by the voice; so in the arts above mentioned, taken as a whole, the imitation is produced by rhythm, language, or 'harmony,' either singly or combined.

Thus in the music of the flute and of the lyre, 'harmony' and rhythm alone are employed; also in other arts, such as that of the shepherd's pipe, which are essentially similar to these. In dancing, rhythm alone is used without 'harmony'; for even dancing imitates character, emotion, and action, by rhythmical movement.

There is another art which imitates by means of language alone, and that either in prose or verse—which verse, again, may either combine different metres or consist of but one kind—but this has hitherto been without a name. For there is no common term we could apply to the mimes of Sophron and Xenarchus and the Socratic dialogues on the one hand; and, on the other, to poetic imitations in iambic, elegiac, or any similar metre. People do, indeed, add the word 'maker' or 'poet' to the name of the metre, and speak of elegiac poets, or epic (that is, hexameter) poets, as if it were not the imitation that makes the poet, but the verse that entitles them all indiscriminately to the name. Even when a treatise on medicine or natural science is brought out in verse, the name of poet is by custom given to the author; and yet Homer and Empedocles have nothing in common but the metre, so that it would be right to call the one poet, the other physicist rather than poet. On the same principle, even if a writer in his poetic imitation were to combine all metres, as Chaeremon did in his Centaur, which is a medley composed of metres of all kinds, we should bring him too under the general term poet. So much then for these distinctions.

There are, again, some arts which employ all the means above mentioned,—namely, rhythm, tune, and metre. Such are Dithyrambic and Nomic poetry, and also Tragedy and Comedy; but between them the difference is, that in the first two cases these means are all employed in combination, in the latter, now one means is employed, now another.

Such, then, are the differences of the arts with respect to the medium of imitation.

II

Since the objects of imitation are men in action, and these men must be either of a higher or a lower type (for moral character mainly answers to these divisions, goodness and badness being the distinguishing marks of moral differences), it follows that we must represent men either as better than in real life, or as worse, or as they are. It is the same in painting. Polygnotus depicted men as nobler than they are, Pauson as less noble, Dionysius drew them true to life.

Now it is evident that each of the modes of imitation above mentioned will exhibit these differences, and become a distinct kind in imitating objects that are thus distinct. Such diversities may be found even in dancing, flute-playing, and lyre-playing. So again in language, whether prose or verse unaccompanied by music. Homer, for example, makes men better than they are; Cleophon as they are; Hegemon the Thasian, the inventor of parodies, and Nicochares, the author of the Deiliad, worse than they are. The same thing holds good of Dithyrambs and Nomes; here too one may portray different types, as Timotheus and Philoxenus differed in representing their Cyclopes. The same distinction marks off Tragedy from Comedy; for Comedy aims at representing men as worse, Tragedy as better than in actual life.

III

There is still a third difference—the manner in which each of these objects may be imitated. For the medium being the same, and the objects the same, the poet may imitate by narration—in which case he can either take another personality as Homer does, or speak in his own person, unchanged—or he may present all his characters as living and moving before us.

These, then, as we said at the beginning, are the three differences which distinguish artistic imitation,—the medium, the objects, and the manner. So that from one point of view, Sophocles is an imitator of the same kind as Homer—for both imitate higher types of character; from another point of view, of the same kind as Aristophanes—for both imitate persons acting and doing. Hence, some say, the name of 'drama' is given to such poems, as representing action. For the same reason the Dorians claim the invention both of Tragedy and Comedy. The claim to Comedy is put forward by the Megarians,—not only by those of Greece proper, who allege that it originated under their democracy, but also by the Megarians of Sicily, for the poet Epicharmus, who is much earlier than Chionides and Magnes, belonged to that country. Tragedy too is claimed by certain Dorians of the Peloponnese. In each case they appeal to the evidence of language. The outlying villages, they say, are by them called κῶμαι,[1] by the Athenians δῆμοι[2]: and they assume that

[1] *Komai,* villages.
[2] *Demoi,* towns, villages.

Comedians were so named not from κωμάζειν,[3] 'to revel,' but because they wandered from village to village (κατὰ κώμας[4]), being excluded contemptuously from the city. They add also that the Dorian word for 'doing' is δρᾶν,[5] and the Athenian, πράττειν.[6]

This may suffice as to the number and nature of the various modes of imitation.

IV

Poetry in general seems to have sprung from two causes, each of them lying deep in our nature. First, the instinct of imitation is implanted in man from childhood, one difference between him and other animals being that he is the most imitative of living creatures, and through imitation learns his earliest lessons; and no less universal is the pleasure felt in things imitated. We have evidence of this in the facts of experience. Objects which in themselves we view with pain, we delight to contemplate when reproduced with minute fidelity: such as the forms of the most ignoble animals and of dead bodies. The cause of this again is, that to learn gives the liveliest pleasure, not only to philosophers but to men in general; whose capacity, however, of learning is more limited. Thus the reason why men enjoy seeing a likeness is, that in contemplating it they find themselves learning or inferring, and saying perhaps, 'Ah, that is he.' For if you happen not to have seen the original, the pleasure will be due not to the imitation as such, but to the execution, the colouring, or some such other cause.

Imitation, then, is one instinct of our nature. Next, there is the instinct for 'harmony' and rhythm, metres being manifestly sections of rhythm. Persons, therefore, starting with this natural gift developed by degrees their special aptitudes, till their rude improvisations gave birth to Poetry.

Poetry now diverged in two directions, according to the individual character of the writers. The graver spirits imitated noble actions, and the actions of good men. The more trivial sort imitated the actions of meaner persons, at first composing satires, as the former did hymns to the gods and the praises of famous men. A poem of the satirical kind cannot indeed be put down to any author earlier than Homer; though many such writers probably there were. But from Homer onward, instances can be cited,—his own Margites, for example, and other similar compositions. The appropriate metre was also here introduced; hence the measure is still called the iambic or lampooning measure, being that in which people lampooned one another. Thus the older poets were distinguished as writers of heroic or of lampooning verse.

As, in the serious style, Homer is pre-eminent among poets, for he alone combined dramatic form with excellence of imitation, so he too first laid

---

[3] Komazein.
[4] Kata komas.
[5] Dran, to do.
[6] Prattein, to do.

down the main lines of Comedy, by dramatising the ludicrous instead of writing personal satire. His Margites bears the same relation to Comedy that the Iliad and Odyssey do to Tragedy. But when Tragedy and Comedy came to light, the two classes of poets still followed their natural bent: the lampooners became writers of Comedy, and the Epic poets were succeeded by Tragedians, since the drama was a larger and higher form of art.

Whether Tragedy has as yet perfected its proper types or not; and whether it is to be judged in itself, or in relation also to the audience,—this raises another question. Be that as it may, Tragedy—as also Comedy—was at first mere improvisation. The one originated with the authors of the Dithyramb, the other with those of the phallic songs, which are still in use in many of our cities. Tragedy advanced by slow degrees; each new element that showed itself was in turn developed. Having passed through many changes, it found its natural form, and there it stopped.

Aeschylus first introduced a second actor; he diminished the importance of the Chorus, and assigned the leading part to the dialogue. Sophocles raised the number of actors to three, and added scene-painting. Moreover, it was not till late that the short plot was discarded for one of greater compass, and the grotesque diction of the earlier satyric form for the stately manner of Tragedy. The iambic measure then replaced the trochaic tetrameter, which was originally employed when the poetry was of the satyric order, and had greater affinities with dancing. Once dialogue had come in, Nature herself discovered the appropriate measure. For the iambic is, of all measures, the most colloquial: we see it in the fact that conversational speech runs into iambic lines more frequently than into any other kind of verse; rarely into hexameters, and only when we drop the colloquial intonation. The additions to the number of 'episodes' or acts, and the other accessories of which tradition tells, must be taken as already described; for to discuss them in detail would, doubtless, be a large undertaking.

V

Comedy is, as we have said, an imitation of characters of a lower type,—not, however, in the full sense of the word bad, the Ludicrous being merely a subdivision of the ugly. It consists in some defect or ugliness which is not painful or destructive. To take an obvious example, the comic mask is ugly and distorted, but does not imply pain.

The successive changes through which Tragedy passed, and the authors of these changes, are well known, whereas Comedy has had no history, because it was not at first treated seriously. It was late before the Archon granted a comic chorus to a poet; the performers were till then voluntary. Comedy had already taken definite shape when comic poets, distinctively so called, are heard of. Who furnished it with masks, or prologues, or increased the number of actors,—these and other similar details remain unknown. As for the plot, it came originally from Sicily; but of Athenian writers Crates was the first who, abandoning the 'iambic' or lampooning form, generalised his themes and plots.

Epic poetry agrees with Tragedy in so far as it is an imitation in verse of characters of a higher type. They differ, in that Epic poetry admits but one kind of metre, and is narrative in form. They differ, again, in their length: for Tragedy endeavours, as far as possible, to confine itself to a single revolution of the sun, or but slightly to exceed this limit; whereas the Epic action has no limits of time. This, then, is a second point of difference; though at first the same freedom was admitted in Tragedy as in Epic poetry.

Of their constituent parts some are common to both, some peculiar to Tragedy: whoever, therefore, knows what is good or bad Tragedy, knows also about Epic poetry. All the elements of an Epic poem are found in Tragedy, but the elements of a Tragedy are not all found in the Epic poem.

VI

Of the poetry which imitates in hexameter verse, and of Comedy, we will speak hereafter. Let us now discuss Tragedy, resuming its formal definition, as resulting from what has been already said.

Tragedy, then, is an imitation of an action that is serious, complete, and of a certain magnitude; in language embellished with each kind of artistic ornament, the several kinds being found in separate parts of the play; in the form of action, not of narrative; through pity and fear effecting the proper purgation of these emotions. By 'language embellished,' I mean language into which rhythm, 'harmony,' and song enter. By 'the several kinds of separate parts,' I mean, that some parts are rendered through the medium of verse alone, others again with the aid of song.

Now as tragic imitation implies persons acting, it necessarily follows, in the first place, that Spectacular equipment will be a part of Tragedy. Next, Song and Diction, for these are the medium of imitation. By 'Diction' I mean the mere metrical arrangement of the words: as for 'Song,' it is a term whose sense every one understands.

Again, Tragedy is the imitation of an action; and an action implies personal agents, who necessarily possess certain distinctive qualities both of character and thought; for it is by these that we qualify actions themselves, and these—thought and character—are the two natural causes from which actions spring, and on actions again all success or failure depends. Hence, the Plot is the imitation of the action:—for by plot I here mean the arrangement of the incidents. By Character I mean that in virtue of which we ascribe certain qualities to the agents. Thought is required wherever a statement is proved, or, it may be, a general truth enunciated. Every Tragedy, therefore, must have six parts, which parts determine its quality—namely, Plot, Character, Diction, Thought, Spectacle, Song. Two of the parts constitute the medium of imitation, one the manner, and three the objects of imitation. And these complete the list. These elements have been employed, we may say, by the poets to a man; in fact, every play contains Spectacular elements as well as Character, Plot, Diction, Song, and Thought.

But most important of all is the structure of the incidents. For Tragedy is an imitation, not of men, but of an action and of life, and life consists in action, and its end is a mode of action, not a quality. Now character determines men's qualities, but it is by their actions that they are happy or the reverse. Dramatic action, therefore, is not with a view to the representation of character: character comes in as subsidiary to the actions. Hence the incidents and the plot are the end of a tragedy; and the end is the chief thing of all. Again, without action there cannot be a tragedy; there may be without character. The tragedies of most of our modern poets fail in the rendering of character; and of poets in general this is often true. It is the same in painting; and here lies the difference between Zeuxis and Polygnotus. Polygnotus delineates character well: the style of Zeuxis is devoid of ethical quality. Again, if you string together a set of speeches expressive of character, and well finished in point of diction and thought, you will not produce the essential tragic effect nearly so well as with a play which, however deficient in these respects, yet has a plot and artistically constructed incidents. Besides which, the most powerful elements of emotional interest in Tragedy—Peripeteia or Reversal of the Situation, and Recognition scenes—are parts of the plot. A further proof is, that novices in the art attain to finish of diction and precision of portraiture before they can construct the plot. It is the same with almost all the early poets.

The Plot, then, is the first principle, and, as it were, the soul of a tragedy: Character holds the second place. A similar fact is seen in painting. The most beautiful colours, laid on confusedly, will not give as much pleasure as the chalk outline of a portrait. Thus Tragedy is the imitation of an action, and of the agents mainly with a view to the action.

Third in order is Thought,—that is, the faculty of saying what is possible and pertinent in given circumstances. In the case of oratory, this is the function of the political art and of the art of rhetoric: and so indeed the older poets make their characters speak the language of civic life; the poets of our time, the language of the rhetoricians. Character is that which reveals moral purpose, showing what kind of things a man chooses or avoids. Speeches, therefore, which do not make this manifest, or in which the speaker does not choose or avoid anything whatever, are not expressive of character. Thought, on the other hand, is found where something is proved to be or not to be, or a general maxim is enunciated.

Fourth among the elements enumerated comes Diction; by which I mean, as has been already said, the expression of the meaning in words; and its essence is the same both in verse and prose.

Of the remaining elements Song holds the chief place among the embellishments.

The Spectacle has, indeed, an emotional attraction of its own, but, of all the parts, it is the least artistic, and connected least with the art of poetry. For the power of Tragedy, we may be sure, is felt even apart from representation and actors. Besides, the production of spectacular effects depends more on the art of the stage machinist than on that of the poet.

VII

These principles being established, let us now discuss the proper structure of the Plot, since this is the first and most important thing in Tragedy.

Now, according to our definition, Tragedy is an imitation of an action that is complete, and whole, and of a certain magnitude; for there may be a whole that is wanting in magnitude. A whole is that which has a beginning, a middle, and an end. A beginning is that which does not itself follow anything by causal necessity, but after which something naturally is or comes to be. An end, on the contrary, is that which itself naturally follows some other thing, either by necessity, or as a rule, but has nothing following it. A middle is that which follows something as some other thing follows it. A well constructed plot, therefore, must neither begin nor end at haphazard, but conform to these principles.

Again, a beautiful object, whether it be a living organism or any whole composed of parts, must not only have an orderly arrangement of parts, but must also be of a certain magnitude; for beauty depends on magnitude and order. Hence a very small animal organism cannot be beautiful; for the view of it is confused, the object being seen in an almost imperceptible moment of time. Nor, again, can one of vast size be beautiful; for as the eye cannot take it all in at once, the unity and sense of the whole is lost for the spectator; as for instance if there were one a thousand miles long. As, therefore, in the case of animate bodies and organisms a certain magnitude is necessary, and a magnitude which may be easily embraced in one view; so in the plot, a certain length is necessary, and a length which can be easily embraced by the memory. The limit of length in relation to dramatic competition and sensuous presentment, is no part of artistic theory. For had it been the rule for a hundred tragedies to compete together, the performance would have been regulated by the water-clock,—as indeed we are told was formerly done. But the limit as fixed by the nature of the drama itself is this:—the greater the length, the more beautiful will the piece be by reason of its size, provided that the whole be perspicuous. And to define the matter roughly, we may say that the proper magnitude is comprised within such limits, that the sequence of events, according to the law of probability or necessity, will admit of a change from bad fortune to good, or from good fortune to bad.

VIII

Unity of plot does not, as some persons think, consist in the unity of the hero. For infinitely various are the incidents in one man's life which cannot be reduced to unity; and so, too, there are many actions of one man out of which we cannot make one action. Hence the error, as it appears, of all poets who have composed a Heracleid, a Theseid, or other poems of the kind. They imagine that as Heracles was one man, the story of Heracles must also be a unity. But Homer, as in all else he is of surpassing merit, here too—whether from art or natural genius—seems to have happily discerned the truth. In composing the Odyssey he did not include all the adventures of Odysseus—such as his wound on Parnassus, or his feigned madness at the mustering of the host—incidents between which there was no necessary or probable connexion: but he made the Odyssey, and likewise the Iliad, to centre round an action that in our sense of the word is one. As therefore, in the other imitative arts, the imitation is one when the object imitated is one, so the plot, being an imitation of an action, must imitate one action and that a whole, the structural union of the parts being such that, if any one of them is displaced or removed, the whole will be disjointed and disturbed. For a thing whose presence or absence makes no visible difference, is not an organic part of the whole.

IX

It is, moreover, evident from what has been said, that it is not the function of the poet to relate what has happened, but what may happen,—what is possible according to the law of probability or necessity. The poet and the historian differ not by writing in verse or in prose. The work of Herodotus might be put into verse, and it would still be a species of history, with metre no less than without it. The true difference is that one relates what has happened, the other what may happen. Poetry, therefore, is a more philosophical and a higher thing than history: for poetry tends to express the universal, history the particular. By the universal I mean how a person of a certain type will on occasion speak or act, according to the law of probability or necessity; and it is this universality at which poetry aims in the names she attaches to the personages. The particular is—for example—what Alcibiades did or suffered. In Comedy this is already apparent: for here the poet first constructs the plot on the lines of probability, and then inserts characteristic names;—unlike the lampooners who write about particular individuals. But tragedians still keep to real names, the reason being that what is possible is credible: what has not happened we do not at once feel sure to be possible: but what has happened is manifestly possible: otherwise it would not have happened. Still there are even some tragedies in which there are only one or two well known names, the rest being fictitious. In others, none are well known,—as in Agathon's Antheus, where incidents and names alike are fictitious, and yet they give none the less pleasure. We must not, therefore, at all costs keep to the received legends, which are the usual subjects of Tragedy. Indeed, it would be absurd to attempt it; for even subjects that are known are known only to a few, and yet give pleasure to all. It clearly follows that the poet or 'maker' should be the maker of plots rather than of verses; since he is a poet because he imitates, and what he imitates are actions. And even if he chances to take an historical subject, he is none the less a poet; for there is no reason why some events that have actually happened should not conform to the law of the probable and possible, and in virtue of that quality in them he is their poet or maker.

Of all plots and actions the epeisodic are the worst. I call a plot 'epeisodic' in which the episodes or acts succeed one another without probable or necessary sequence. Bad poets compose such pieces by their own fault, good poets, to please the players; for, as they write show pieces for competition, they stretch the plot beyond its capacity, and are often forced to break the natural continuity.

But again, Tragedy is an imitation not only of a complete action, but of events inspiring fear or pity. Such an effect is best produced when the events come on us by surprise; and the effect is heightened when, at the same time, they follow as cause and effect. The tragic wonder will then be greater than if they happened of themselves or by accident; for even coincidences are most striking when they have an air of design. We may instance the statue of Mitys at Argos, which fell upon his murderer while he was a spectator at a festival, and killed him. Such events seem not to be due to mere chance. Plots, therefore, constructed on these principles are necessarily the best.

X

Plots are either Simple or Complex, for the actions in real life, of which the plots are an imitation, obviously show a similar distinction. An action which is one and continuous in the sense above defined, I call Simple, when the change of fortune takes place without Reversal of the Situation and without Recognition.

A Complex action is one in which the change is accompanied by such Reversal, or by Recognition, or by both. These last should arise from the internal structure of the plot, so that what follows should be the necessary or probable result of the preceding action. It makes all the difference whether any given event is a case of *propter hoc* or *post hoc*.

XI

Reversal of the Situation is a change by which the action veers round to its opposite, subject always to our rule of probability or necessity. Thus in the Oedipus, the messenger comes to cheer Oedipus and free him from his alarms about his mother, but by revealing who he is, he produces the opposite effect. Again in the Lynceus, Lynceus is being led away to his death, and Danaus goes with him, meaning to slay him; but the outcome of the preceding incidents is that Danaus is killed and Lynceus saved.

Recognition, as the name indicates, is a change from ignorance to knowledge, producing love or hate between the persons destined by the poet for good or bad fortune. The best form of recognition is coincident with a Reversal of the Situation, as in the Oedipus. There are indeed other forms. Even inanimate things of the most trivial kind may in a sense be objects of recognition. Again, we may recognise or discover whether a person has done a thing or not. But the recognition which is most intimately connected with the plot and action is, as we have said, the recognition of persons. This recognition, combined with Reversal, will produce either pity or fear; and actions producing these effects are those which, by our definition, Tragedy represents. Moreover, it is upon such situations that the issues of good or bad fortune will depend. Recognition, then, being between persons, it may happen that one person only is recognised by the other—when the latter is already known—or it may be necessary that the recognition should be on both sides. Thus Iphigenia is revealed to Orestes by the sending of the letter; but another act of recognition is required to make Orestes known to Iphigenia.

Two parts, then, of the Plot—Reversal of the Situation and Recognition—turn upon surprises. A third part is the Scene of Suffering. The Scene of Suffering is a destructive or painful action, such as death on the stage, bodily agony, wounds and the like.

XII

[The parts of Tragedy which must be treated as elements of the whole have been already mentioned. We now come to the quantitative parts—the separate parts into which Tragedy is divided—namely, Prologue, Episode, Exode, Choric song; this last being divided into Parode and Stasimon. These are common to all plays: peculiar to some are the songs of actors from the stage and the Commoi.

The Prologue is that entire part of a tragedy which precedes the Parode of the Chorus. The Episode is that entire part of a tragedy which is between complete choric songs. The Exode is that entire part of a tragedy which has no choric song after it. Of the Choric part the Parode is the first undivided utterance of the Chorus: the Stasimon is a Choric ode without anapaests or trochaic tetrameters: the Commos is a joint lamentation of Chorus and actors. The parts of Tragedy which must be treated as elements of the whole have been already mentioned. The quantitative parts—the separate parts into which it is divided—are here enumerated.][7]

XIII

As the sequel to what has already been said, we must proceed to consider what the poet should aim at, and what he should avoid, in constructing his plots; and by what means the specific effect of Tragedy will be produced.

[7] The translator's brackets (< > and [ ]) and asterisks, which indicate reconstructed or lost text, have been retained.

A perfect tragedy should, as we have seen, be arranged not on the simple but on the complex plan. It should, moreover, imitate actions which excite pity and fear, this being the distinctive mark of tragic imitation. It follows plainly, in the first place, that the change of fortune presented must not be the spectacle of a virtuous man brought from prosperity to adversity: for this moves neither pity nor fear; it merely shocks us. Nor, again, that of a bad man passing from adversity to prosperity: for nothing can be more alien to the spirit of Tragedy; it possesses no single tragic quality; it neither satisfies the moral sense nor calls forth pity or fear. Nor, again, should the downfall of the utter villain be exhibited. A plot of this kind would, doubtless, satisfy the moral sense, but it would inspire neither pity nor fear; for pity is aroused by unmerited misfortune, fear by the misfortune of a man like ourselves. Such an event, therefore, will be neither pitiful nor terrible. There remains, then, the character between these two extremes, — that of a man who is not eminently good and just, yet whose misfortune is brought about not by vice or depravity, but by some error or frailty. He must be one who is highly renowned and prosperous, — a personage like Oedipus, Thyestes, or other illustrious men of such families.

A well constructed plot should, therefore, be single in its issue, rather than double as some maintain. The change of fortune should be not from bad to good, but, reversely, from good to bad. It should come about as the result not of vice, but of some great error or frailty, in a character either such as we have described, or better rather than worse. The practice of the stage bears out our view. At first the poets recounted any legend that came in their way. Now, the best tragedies are founded on the story of a few houses,—on the fortunes of Alcmaeon, Oedipus, Orestes, Meleager, Thyestes, Telephus, and those others who have done or suffered something terrible. A tragedy, then, to be perfect according to the rules of art should be of this construction. Hence they are in error who censure Euripides just because he follows this principle in his plays, many of which end unhappily. It is, as we have said, the right ending. The best proof is that on the stage and in dramatic competition, such plays, if well worked out, are the most tragic in effect; and Euripides, faulty though he may be in the general management of his subject, yet is felt to be the most tragic of the poets.

In the second rank comes the kind of tragedy which some place first. Like the Odyssey, it has a double thread of plot, and also an opposite catastrophe for the good and for the bad. It is accounted the best because of the weakness of the spectators; for the poet is guided in what he writes by the wishes of his audience. The pleasure, however, thence derived is not the true tragic pleasure. It is proper rather to Comedy, where those who, in the piece, are the deadliest enemies—like Orestes and Aegisthus—quit the stage as friends at the close, and no one slays or is slain.

XIV

Fear and pity may be aroused by spectacular means; but they may also result from the inner structure of the piece, which is the better way, and indicates a superior poet. For the plot ought to be so constructed that, even without the aid of the eye, he who hears the tale told will thrill with horror and melt to pity at what takes place. This is the impression we should receive from hearing the story of the Oedipus. But to produce this effect by the mere spectacle is a less artistic method, and dependent on extraneous aids. Those who employ spectacular means to create a sense not of the terrible but only of the monstrous, are strangers to the purpose of Tragedy; for we must not demand of Tragedy any and every kind of pleasure, but only that which is proper to it. And since the pleasure which the poet should afford is that which comes from pity and fear through imitation, it is evident that this quality must be impressed upon the incidents.

Let us then determine what are the circumstances which strike us as terrible or pitiful.

Actions capable of this effect must happen between persons who are either friends or enemies or indifferent to one another. If an enemy kills an enemy, there is nothing to excite pity either in the act or the intention—except so far as the suffering in itself is pitiful. So again with indifferent persons. But when the tragic incident occurs between those who are near or dear to one another—if, for example, a brother kills, or intends to kill, a brother, a son his father, a mother her son, a son his mother, or any other deed of the kind is done—these are the situations to be looked for by the poet. He may not indeed destroy the framework of the received legends—the fact, for instance, that Clytemnestra was slain by Orestes and Eriphyle by Alcmaeon—but he ought to show invention of his own, and skilfully handle the traditional material. Let us explain more clearly what is meant by skilful handling.

The action may be done consciously and with knowledge of the persons, in the manner of the older poets. It is thus too that Euripides makes Medea slay her children. Or, again, the deed of horror may be done, but done in ignorance, and the tie of kinship or friendship be discovered afterwards. The Oedipus of Sophocles is an example. Here, indeed, the incident is outside the drama proper; but cases occur where it falls within the action of the play: one may cite the Alcmaeon of Astydamas, or Telegonus in the Wounded Odysseus. Again, there is a third case,—<to be about to act with knowledge of the persons and then not to act. The fourth case is> when some one is about to do an irreparable deed through ignorance, and makes the discovery before it is done. These are the only possible ways. For the deed must either be done or not done,—and that wittingly or unwittingly. But of all these ways, to be about to act knowing the persons, and then not to act, is the worst. It is shocking without being tragic, for no disaster follows. It is, therefore, never, or very rarely, found in poetry. One instance, however, is in the Antigone, where Haemon threatens to kill Creon. The next and better way is that the deed should be perpetrated. Still better, that it should be perpetrated in ignorance, and the discovery made afterwards. There is then nothing to shock us, while the discovery produces a startling effect. The last case is the best, as when in the Cresphontes Merope is about to slay her son, but, recognising who he is, spares his life. So in the Iphigenia, the sister recognises the brother just in time. Again in the Helle, the son recognises the mother when on the point of giving her up. This, then, is why a few families only, as has been already observed, furnish the subjects of tragedy. It was not art, but happy chance, that led the poets in search of subjects to impress the tragic quality upon their plots. They are compelled, therefore, to have recourse to those houses whose history contains moving incidents like these.

Enough has now been said concerning the structure of the incidents, and the right kind of plot.

XV

In respect of Character there are four things to be aimed at. First, and most important, it must be good. Now any speech or action that manifests moral purpose of any kind will be expressive of character: the character will be good if the purpose is good. This rule is relative to each class. Even a woman may be good, and also a slave; though the woman may be said to be an inferior being, and the slave quite worthless. The second thing to aim at is propriety. There is a type of manly valour; but valour in a woman, or unscrupulous cleverness, is inappropriate. Thirdly, character must be true to life: for this is a distinct thing from goodness and propriety, as here described. The fourth point is consistency: for though the subject of the imitation, who suggested the type, be inconsistent, still he must be consistently inconsistent. As an example of motiveless degradation of character, we have Menelaus in the Orestes: of character indecorous and inappropriate, the lament of Odysseus in the Scylla, and the speech of Melanippe: of inconsistency, the Iphigenia at Aulis, — for Iphigenia the suppliant in no way resembles her later self.

As in the structure of the plot, so too in the portraiture of character, the poet should always aim either at the necessary or the probable. Thus a person of a given character should speak or act in a given way, by the rule either of necessity or of probability; just as this event should follow that by necessary or probable sequence. It is therefore evident that the unravelling of the plot, no less than the complication, must arise out of the plot itself, it must not be brought about by the *Deus ex Machina* — as in the Medea, or in the Return of the Greeks in the Iliad. The *Deus ex Machina* should be employed only for events external to the drama, — for antecedent or subsequent events, which lie beyond the range of human knowledge, and which require to be reported or foretold; for to the gods we ascribe the power of seeing all things. Within the action there must be nothing irrational. If the irrational cannot be excluded, it should be outside the scope of the tragedy. Such is the irrational element in the Oedipus of Sophocles.

Again, since Tragedy is an imitation of persons who are above the common level, the example of good portrait painters should be followed. They, while reproducing the distinctive form of the original, make a likeness which is true to life and yet more beautiful. So too the poet, in representing men who are irascible or indolent, or have other defects of character, should preserve the type and yet ennoble it. In this way Achilles is portrayed by Agathon and Homer.

These then are rules the poet should observe. Nor should he neglect those appeals to the senses, which, though not among the essentials, are the concomitants of poetry; for here too there is much room for error. But of this enough has been said on our published treatises.

XVI

What Recognition is has been already explained. We will now enumerate its kinds.

First, the least artistic form, which, from poverty of wit, is most commonly employed—recognition by signs. Of these some are congenital,—such as 'the spear which the earth-born race bear on their bodies,' or the stars introduced by Carcinus in his Thyestes. Others are acquired after birth; and of these some are bodily marks, as scars; some external tokens, as necklaces, or the little ark in the Tyro by which the discovery is effected. Even these admit of more or less skilful treatment. Thus in the recognition of Odysseus by his scar, the discovery is made in one way by the nurse, in another by the swineherds. The use of tokens for the express purpose of proof—and, indeed, any formal proof with or without tokens—is a less artistic mode of recognition. A better kind is that which comes about by a turn of incident, as in the Bath Scene in the Odyssey.

Next come the recognitions invented at will by the poet, and on that account wanting in art. For example, Orestes in the Iphigenia reveals the fact that he is Orestes. She, indeed, makes herself known by the letter; but he, by speaking himself, and saying what the poet, not what the plot requires. This, therefore, is nearly allied to the fault above mentioned:—for Orestes might as well have brought tokens with him. Another similar instance is the 'voice of the shuttle' in the Tereus of Sophocles.

The third kind depends on memory when the sight of some object awakens a feeling: as in the Cyprians of Dicaeogenes, where the hero breaks into tears on seeing the picture; or again in the 'Lay of Alcinous,' where Odysseus, hearing the minstrel play the lyre, recalls the past and weeps; and hence the recognition.

The fourth kind is by process of reasoning. Thus in the Choëphori:—'Some one resembling me has come: no one resembles me but Orestes: therefore Orestes has come.' Such too is the discovery made by Iphigenia in the play of Polyidus the Sophist. It was a natural reflexion for Orestes to make, 'So I too must die at the altar like my sister.' So, again, in the Tydeus of Theodectes, the father says, 'I came to find my son, and I lose my own life.' So too in the Phineidae: the women, on seeing the place, inferred their fate:—'Here we are doomed to die, for here we were cast forth.' Again, there is a composite kind of recognition involving false inference on the part of one of the characters, as in the Odysseus Disguised as a Messenger. A said <that no one else was able to bend the bow; . . . hence B (the disguised Odysseus) imagined that A would> recognise the bow which, in fact, he had not seen; and to bring about a recognition by this means—the expectation that A would recognise the bow—is false inference.

But, of all recognitions, the best is that which arises from the incidents themselves, where the startling discovery is made by natural means. Such is that in the Oedipus of Sophocles, and in the Iphigenia; for it was natural that Iphigenia should wish to dispatch a letter. These recognitions alone dispense with the artificial aid of tokens or amulets. Next come the recognitions by process of reasoning.

XVII

In constructing the plot and working it out with the proper diction, the poet should place the scene, as far as possible, before his eyes. In this way, seeing everything with the utmost vividness, as if he were a spectator of the action, he will discover what is in keeping with it, and be most unlikely to overlook inconsistencies. The need of such a rule is shown by the fault found in Carcinus. Amphiaraus was on his way from the temple. This fact escaped the observation of one who did not see the situation. On the stage, however, the piece failed, the audience being offended at the oversight.

Again, the poet should work out his play, to the best of his power, with appropriate gestures; for those who feel emotion are most convincing through natural sympathy with the characters they represent; and one who is agitated storms, one who is angry rages, with the most life-like reality. Hence poetry implies either a happy gift of nature or a strain of madness. In the one case a man can take the mould of any character; in the other, he is lifted out of his proper self.

As for the story, whether the poet takes it ready made or constructs it for himself, he should first sketch its general outline, and then fill in the episodes and amplify in detail. The general plan may be illustrated by the Iphigenia. A young girl is sacrificed; she disappears mysteriously from the eyes of those who sacrificed her; she is transported to another country, where the custom is to offer up all strangers to the goddess. To this ministry she is appointed. Some time later her own brother chances to arrive. The fact that the oracle for some reason ordered him to go there, is outside the general plan of the play. The purpose, again, of his coming is outside the action proper. However, he comes, he is seized, and when on the point of being sacrificed, reveals who he is. The mode of recognition may be either that of Euripides or of Polyidus, in whose play he exclaims very naturally:—'So it was not my sister only, but I too, who was doomed to be sacrificed'; and by that remark he is saved.

After this, the names being once given, it remains to fill in the episodes. We must see that they are relevant to the action. In the case of Orestes, for example, there is the madness which led to his capture, and his deliverance by means of the purificatory rite. In the drama, the episodes are short, but it is these that give extension to Epic poetry. Thus the story of the Odyssey can be stated briefly. A certain man is absent from home for many years; he is jealously watched by Poseidon, and left desolate. Meanwhile his home is in a wretched plight—suitors are wasting his substance and plotting against his son. At length, tempest-tost, he himself arrives; he makes certain persons acquainted with him; he attacks the suitors with his own hand, and is himself preserved while he destroys them. This is the essence of the plot; the rest is episode.

XVIII

Every tragedy falls into two parts,—Complication and Unravelling or *Dénouement*. Incidents extraneous to the action are frequently combined with a portion of the action proper, to form the Complication; the rest is the Unravelling. By the Complication I mean all that extends from the beginning of the action to the part which marks the turning-point to good or bad fortune. The Unravelling is that which extends from the beginning of the change to the end. Thus, in the Lynceus of Theodectes, the Complication consists of the incidents presupposed in the drama, the seizure of the child, and then again * * <The Unravelling> extends from the accusation of murder to the end.

There are four kinds of Tragedy, the Complex, depending entirely on Reversal of the Situation and Recognition; the Pathetic (where the motive is passion),—such as the tragedies on Ajax and Ixion; the Ethical (where the motives are ethical),—such as the Phthiotides and the Peleus. The fourth kind is the Simple. <We here exclude the purely spectacular element>, exemplified by the Phorcides, the Prometheus, and scenes laid in Hades. The poet should endeavour, if possible, to combine all poetic elements; or failing that, the greatest number and those the most important; the more so, in face of the cavilling criticism of the day. For whereas there have hitherto been good poets, each in his own branch, the critics now expect one man to surpass all others in their several lines of excellence.

In speaking of a tragedy as the same or different, the best test to take is the plot. Identity exists where the Complication and Unravelling are the same. Many poets tie the knot well, but unravel it ill. Both arts, however, should always be mastered.

Again, the poet should remember what has been often said, and not make an Epic structure into a Tragedy—by an Epic structure I mean one with a multiplicity of plots—as if, for instance, you were to make a tragedy out of the entire story of the Iliad. In the Epic poem, owing to its length, each part assumes its proper magnitude. In the drama the result is far from answering to the poet's expectation. The proof is that the poets who have dramatised the whole story of the Fall of Troy, instead of selecting portions, like Euripides; or who have taken the whole tale of Niobe, and not a part of her story, like Aeschylus, either fail utterly or meet with poor success on the stage. Even Agathon has been known to fail from this one defect. In his Reversals of the Situation, however, he shows a marvelous skill in the effort to hit the popular taste,—to produce a tragic effect that satisfies the moral sense. This effect is produced when the clever rogue, like Sisyphus, is outwitted, or the brave villain defeated. Such an event is probable in Agathon's sense of the word: 'it is probable,' he says, 'that many things should happen contrary to probability.'

The Chorus too should be regarded as one of the actors; it should be an integral part of the whole, and share in the action, in the manner not of Euripides but of Sophocles. As for the later poets, their choral songs pertain as little to the subject of the piece as to that of any other tragedy. They are, therefore, sung as mere interludes,—a practice first begun by Agathon. Yet what difference is there between introducing such choral interludes, and transferring a speech, or even a whole act, from one play to another?

XIX

It remains to speak of Diction and Thought, the other parts of Tragedy having been already discussed. Concerning Thought, we may assume what is said in the Rhetoric, to which inquiry the subject more strictly belongs. Under Thought is included every effect which has to be produced by speech, the subdivisions being,—proof and refutation; the excitation of the feelings, such as pity, anger, and the like; the suggestion of importance or its opposite. Now, it is evident that the dramatic incidents must be treated from the same points of view as the dramatic speeches, when the object is to evoke the sense of pity, fear, importance, or probability. The only difference is, that the incidents should speak for themselves without verbal exposition; while the effects aimed at in speech should be produced by the speaker, and as a result of the speech. For what were the business of a speaker, if the Thought were revealed quite apart from what he says?

Next, as regards Diction. One branch of the inquiry treats of the Modes of Utterance. But this province of knowledge belongs to the art of Delivery and to the masters of that science. It includes, for instance,—what is a command, a prayer, a statement, a threat, a question, an answer, and so forth. To know or not to know these things involves no serious censure upon the poet's art. For who can admit the fault imputed to Homer by Protagoras,—that in the words, 'Sing, goddess, of the wrath,' he gives a command under the idea that he utters a prayer? For to tell some one to do a thing or not to do it is, he says, a command. We may, therefore, pass this over as an inquiry that belongs to another art, not to poetry.

XX

[Language in general includes the following parts:—Letter, Syllable, Connecting word, Noun, Verb, Inflexion or Case, Sentence or Phrase.

A Letter is an indivisible sound, yet not every such sound, but only which can form part of a group of sounds. For even brutes utter indivisible sounds, none of which I call a letter. The sound I mean may be either a vowel, a semi-vowel, or a mute. A vowel is that which without impact of tongue or lip has an audible sound. A semi-vowel, that which with such impact has an audible sound, as S and R. A mute, that which with such impact has by itself no sound, but joined to a vowel sound becomes audible, as G and D. These are distinguished according to the form assumed by the mouth and the place where they are produced; according as they are aspirated or smooth, long or short; as they are acute, grave, or of an intermediate tone; which inquiry belongs in detail to the writers on metre.

A Syllable is a non-significant sound, composed of a mute and a vowel: for GR without A is a syllable, as also with A,—GRA. But the investigation of these differences belongs also to metrical science.

A Connecting word is a non-significant sound, which neither causes nor hinders the union of many sounds into one significant sound; it may be placed at either end or in the middle of a sentence. Or, a non-significant sound, which out of several sounds, each of them significant, is capable of forming one significant sound,—as ἀμφί,[8] περί,[9] and the like. Or, a non-significant sound, which marks the beginning, end, or division of a sentence; such, however, that it cannot correctly stand by itself at the beginning of a sentence,—as μέν,[10] ἤτοι,[11] δέ.[12]

A Noun is a composite significant sound, not marking time, of which no part is in itself significant: for in double or compound words we do not employ the separate parts as if each were in itself significant. Thus in Theodorus, 'god-given,' the δῶρον[13] or 'gift' is not in itself significant.

A Verb is a composite significant sound, marking time, in which, as in the noun, no part is in itself significant. For 'man,' or 'white' does not express the idea of 'when'; but 'he walks,' or 'he has walked' does connote time, present or past.

Inflexion belongs both to the noun and verb, and expresses either the relation 'of,' 'to,' or the like; or that of number, whether one or many, as 'man' or 'men'; or the modes or tones in actual delivery, e.g., a question or a command. 'Did he go?' and 'go' are verbal inflexions of this kind.

A Sentence or Phrase is a composite significant sound, some at least of whose parts are in themselves significant; for not every such group of words consists of verbs and nouns—'the definition of man,' for example—but it may dispense even with the verb. Still it will always have some significant part, as 'in walking,' or 'Cleon son of Cleon.' A sentence or phrase may form a unity in two ways,—either as signifying one thing, or as consisting of sev-

---

[8] *Amphi*, about.
[9] *Peri*, around.
[10] *Men*, on the one hand.
[11] *Etoi*, surely.
[12] *De*, on the other hand.
[13] *Doron*.

eral parts linked together. Thus the Iliad is one by the linking together of parts, the definition of man by the unity of the thing signified.]

XXI

Words are of two kinds, simple and double. By simple I mean those composed of non-significant elements, such as $\gamma \hat{\eta}$[14] By double or compound, those composed either of a significant and non-significant element (though within the whole word no element is significant), or of elements that are both significant. A word may likewise be triple, quadruple, or multiple in form, like so many Massilian expressions, e.g. 'Hermo-caico-xanthus <who prayed to Father Zeus>.'

Every word is either current, or strange, or metaphorical, or ornamental, or newly-coined, or lengthened, or contracted, or altered.

By a current or proper word I mean one which is in general use among a people; by a strange word, one which is in use in another country. Plainly, therefore, the same word may be at once strange and current, but not in relation to the same people. The word σίγυνον,[15] 'lance,' is to the Cyprians a current term but to us a strange one.

Metaphor is the application of an alien name by transference either from genus to species, or from species to genus, or from species to species, or by analogy, that is, proportion. Thus from genus to species, as: 'There lies my ship'; for lying at anchor is a species of lying. From species to genus, as: 'Verily ten thousand noble deeds hath Odysseus wrought'; for ten thousand is a species of large number, and is here used for a large number generally. From species to species, as: 'With blade of bronze drew away the life,' and 'Cleft the water with the vessel of unyielding bronze.' Here ἀρύσαι,[16] 'to draw away,' is used for ταμεῖιν[17] 'to cleave,' and ταμεῖν again for ἀρύσαι,—each being a species of taking away. Analogy or proportion is when the second term is to the first as the fourth to the third. We may then use the fourth for the second, or the second for the fourth. Sometimes too we qualify the metaphor by adding the term to which the proper word is relative. Thus the cup is to Dionysus as the shield to Ares. The cup may, therefore, be called 'the shield of Dionysus,' and the shield 'the cup of Ares.' Or, again, as old age is to life, so is evening to day. Evening may therefore be called 'the old age of the day,' and old age, 'the evening of life,' or, in the phrase of Empedocles, 'life's setting sun.' For some of the terms of the proportion there is at times no word in existence; still the metaphor may be used. For instance, to scatter seed is called sowing: but the action of the sun in scattering his rays is nameless. Still this process bears to the sun the same relation as sowing to the seed. Hence the expression of the poet 'sowing the god-created light.' There is

[14] Ge, earth. Cf. geology, geometry.
[15] Sigunon.
[16] Arusai.
[17] Tamein.

another way in which this kind of metaphor may be employed. We may apply an alien term, and then deny of that term one of its proper attributes; as if we were to call the shield, not 'the cup of Ares,' but 'the wineless cup.'

<An ornamental word . . . >

A newly-coined word is one which has never been even in local use, but is adopted by the poet himself. Some such words there appear to be: as ἐρνύγες,[18] 'sprouters,' for κέρατα,[19] 'horns,' and ἀρητήρ,[20] 'supplicator,' for ἱερεύς,[21] 'priest.'

A word is lengthened when its own vowel is exchanged for a longer one, or when a syllable is inserted. A word is contracted when some part of it is removed. Instances of lengthening are,—πόληος for πόλεως,[22] and Πηληιάδεω for Πηλείδου:[23] of contraction,—κρῖ,[24] δῶ,[25] and ὄψ,[26] as in μία λίνεται ἀμφοτέρων ὄψ.[27]

An altered word is one in which part of the ordinary form is left unchanged, and part is re-cast; as in δεξιτερὸν κατὰ μαζόν, δεξιτερόν is for δεξιόν.[28]

[Nouns in themselves are either masculine, feminine, or neuter. Masculine are such as end in ν, ρ, ς, or in some letter compounded with ς,—these being two, ψ and ξ. Feminine, such as end in vowels that are always long, namely η and ω, and—of vowels that admit of lengthening—those in α. Thus the number of letters in which nouns masculine and feminine end is the same; for ψ and ξ are equivalent to endings in ς. No noun ends in a mute or a vowel short by nature. Three only end in ι,—μέλι, κόμμι, πέπερι:[29] five end in υ. Neuter nouns end in these two latter vowels; also in ν and ς.]

XXII

The perfection of style is to be clear without being mean. The clearest style is that which uses only current or proper words; at the same time it is mean:—witness the poetry of Cleophon and of Sthenelus. That diction, on the other hand, is lofty and raised above the commonplace which employs unusual words. By unusual, I mean strange (or rare) words, metaphorical, lengthened,—anything, in short, that differs from the normal idiom. Yet a style wholly composed of such words is either a riddle or a jargon; a riddle, if it consists of metaphors; a jargon, if it consists of strange (or rare) words. For the essence of a riddle is to express true facts under impossible combinations.

---

[18] *Ernyges.*
[19] *Kerata.*
[20] *Areter.*
[21] *Hiereus.*
[22] *Poleos* for *poleōs.*
[23] *Pēlēiadeō* for *Pēleidou.*
[24] *Kri,* barley, for *krithe.*
[25] *Do,* house, for *doma.*
[26] *Ops,* voice, appearance, for *opsis.*
[27] *Mia ginetai amphoteron ops,* the voice of both becomes one.
[28] *Dexiteron kata mazon, dexiteron* is for *dexion,* down into the right nipple.
[29] *Meli, kommi, peperi.*

Now this cannot be done by any arrangement of ordinary words, but by the use of metaphor it can. Such is the riddle:—'A man I saw who on another man had glued the bronze by aid of fire,' and others of the same kind. A diction that is made up of strange (or rare) terms is a jargon. A certain infusion, therefore, of these elements is necessary to style; for the strange (or rare) word, the metaphorical, the ornamental, and the other kinds above mentioned, will raise it above the commonplace and mean, while the use of proper words will make it perspicuous. But nothing contributes more to produce a clearness of diction that is remote from commonness than the lengthening, contraction, and alteration of words. For by deviating in exceptional cases from the normal idiom, the language will gain distinction; while, at the same time, the partial conformity with usage will give perspicuity. The critics, therefore, are in error who censure these licenses of speech, and hold the author up to ridicule. Thus Eucleides, the elder, declared that it would be an easy matter to be a poet if you might lengthen syllables at will. He caricatured the practice in the very form of his diction, as in the verse:

Ἐπιχάρην εἶδον Μαραθῶνάδε βαδίζοντα,[30]

or,

οὐκ ἄν γ' ἐράμενος τὸν ἐκείνου ἐλλέβορον.[31]

To employ such license at all obtrusively is, no doubt, grotesque; but in any mode of poetic diction there must be moderation. Even metaphors, strange (or rare) words, or any similar forms of speech, would produce the like effect if used without propriety and with the express purpose of being ludicrous. How great a difference is made by the appropriate use of lengthening, may be seen in Epic poetry by the insertion of ordinary forms in the verse. So, again, if we take a strange (or rare) word, a metaphor, or any similar mode of expression, and replace it by the current or proper term, the truth of our observation will be manifest. For example, Aeschylus and Euripides each composed the same iambic line. But the alteration of a single word by Euripides, who employed the rarer term instead of the ordinary one, makes one verse appear beautiful and the other trivial. Aeschylus in his Philoctetes says:

φαγέδαινα <δ'> ἥ μου σάρκας ἐσθίει ποδός.[32]

Euripides substitutes θοινᾶται[33] 'feasts on' for ἐσθίει[34] 'feeds on.' Again, in the line,

νῦν δέ μ' ἐὼν ὀλίγος τε καὶ οὐτιδανὸς καὶ ἀεικής,[35]

---

[30] *Epicharen eidon Maraphonade badizonta.* I saw Ipichares going to Marathon.

[31] *Ouk an g eramenos ton ekeinou elleboron.* To be sure, I could not like his hellebore.

[32] *Phagedaina <d> e mou sarkas esthiei podos.* A cancer feeds on the flesh of my foot. The word "feeds on" is an ordinary word in the Greek of Æschylus; in the Greek of Euripides, a lofty one.

[33] *Thoinatai.*

[34] *Esthiei.*

[35] *Nun de m eon oligos te kai outidanos kai aeikes.* I that am now little, of no account, nor attractive.

the difference will be felt if we substitute the common words,

νῦν δέ μ' ἐὼν μικρός τε καὶ ἀσθενικὸς καὶ ἀειδής.[36]

Or, if for the line,

δίφρον ἀεικέλιον καταθεὶς ὀλίγην τε τράπεζαν,[37]

we read,

δίφρον μοχθηρὸν καταθεὶς μικράν τε τράπεζαν.[38]

Or, for ἠιόνες βοόωσιν, ἠιόνες κράζουσιν.[39]

Again, Ariphrades ridiculed the tragedians for using phrases which no one would employ in ordinary speech: for example, δωμάτων ἄπο instead of ἀπὸ δωμάτων,[40] σέθεν,[41] ἐγὼ δέ νιν,[42] Ἀχιλλέως πέρι instead of περὶ Ἀχιλλέως,[43] and the like. It is precisely because such phrases are not part of the current idiom that they give distinction to the style. This, however, he failed to see.

It is a great matter to observe propriety in these several modes of expression, as also in compound words, strange (or rare) words, and so forth. But the greatest thing by far is to have a command of metaphor. This alone cannot be imparted by another; it is the mark of genius, for to make good metaphors implies an eye for resemblances.

Of the various kinds of words, the compound are best adapted to dithyrambs, rare words to heroic poetry, metaphors to iambic. In heroic poetry, indeed, all these varieties are serviceable. But in iambic verse, which reproduces, as far as may be, familiar speech, the most appropriate words are those which are found even in prose. These are,— the current or proper, the metaphorical, the ornamental.

Concerning Tragedy and imitation by means of action this may suffice.

XXIII

As to that poetic imitation which is narrative in form and employs a single metre, the plot manifestly ought, as in a tragedy, to be constructed on dramatic principles. It should have for its subject a single action, whole and complete, with a beginning, a middle, and an end. It will thus resemble a living organism in all its unity, and produce the pleasure proper to it. It will differ in structure from historical compositions, which of necessity present not a single action, but a single period, and all that happened within that period to

[36] Nun de m eon mikros te kai asthenikos kai aeides. I that am now small, weak, and ugly.
[37] Diphron aeikelion katatheis oligen te trapezan. He set a stool unseemly and a table small.
[38] Diphron mochtheron katatheis mikran te trapezan. He set a shabby stool and a small table.
[39] Eiones boóosin, eiones krazousin. The seashore is roaring; the seashore is shrieking.
[40] Domaton apo instead of apo domaton. From the houses away instead of from the houses.
[41] Sethen, a rare form of the genitive, meaning "yours."
[42] Ego de nin. Nin is a rarer form for auton. Both mean "him."
[43] Achilleos peri instead of peri Achilleos. Round about Achilles instead of around Achilles.

one person or to many, little connected together as the events may be. For as the sea-fight at Salamis and the battle with the Carthaginians in Sicily took place at the same time, but did not tend to any one result, so in the sequence of events, one thing sometimes follows another, and yet no single result is thereby produced. Such is the practice, we may say, of most poets. Here again, then, as has been already observed, the transcendent excellence of Homer is manifest. He never attempts to make the whole war of Troy the subject of his poem, though that war had a beginning and an end. It would have been too vast a theme, and not easily embraced in a single view. If, again, he had kept it within moderate limits, it must have been over-complicated by the variety of the incidents. As it is, he detaches a single portion, and admits as episodes many events from the general story of the war—such as the Catalogue of the ships and others—thus diversifying the poem. All other poets take a single hero, a single period, or an action single indeed, but with a multiplicity of parts. Thus did the author of the Cypria and of the Little Iliad. For this reason the Iliad and the Odyssey each furnish the subject of one tragedy, or, at most, of two; while the Cypria supplies materials for many, and the Little Iliad for eight—the Award of the Arms, the Philoctetes, the Neoptolemus, the Eurypylus, the Mendicant Odysseus, the Laconian Women, the Fall of Ilium, the Departure of the Fleet.

XXIV

Again, Epic poetry must have as many kinds of Tragedy: it must be simple, or complex, or 'ethical,' or 'pathetic.' The parts also, with the exception of song and spectacle, are the same; for it requires Reversals of the Situation, Recognitions, and Scenes of Suffering. Moreover, the thoughts and the diction must be artistic. In all these respects Homer is our earliest and sufficient model. Indeed each of his poems has a twofold character. The Iliad is at once simple and 'pathetic,' and the Odyssey complex (for Recognition scenes run through it), and at the same time 'ethical.' Moreover, in diction and thought they are supreme.

Epic poetry differs from Tragedy in the scale on which it is constructed, and in its metre. As regards scale or length, we have already laid down an adequate limit:—the beginning and the end must be capable of being brought within a single view. This condition will be satisfied by poems on a smaller scale than the old epics, and answering in length to the group of tragedies presented at a single sitting.

Epic poetry has, however, a great—a special—capacity for enlarging its dimensions, and we can see the reason. In Tragedy we cannot imitate several lines of actions carried on at one and the same time; we must confine ourselves to the action on the stage and the part taken by the players. But in Epic poetry, owing to the narrative form, many events simultaneously transacted can be presented; and these, if relevant to the subject, add mass and dignity to the poem. The Epic has here an advantage, and one that conduces to grandeur of effect, to diverting the mind of the hearer, and relieving the story with varying episodes. For sameness of incident soon produces satiety, and makes tragedies fail on the stage.

As for the metre, the heroic measure has proved its fitness by the test of experience. If a narrative poem in any other metre or in many metres were now composed, it would be found incongruous. For of all measures the heroic is the stateliest and the most massive; and hence it most readily admits rare words and metaphors, which is another point in which the narrative form of imitation stands alone. On the other hand, the iambic and the trochaic tetrameter are stirring measures, the latter being akin to dancing, the former expressive of action. Still more absurd would it be to mix together different metres, as was done by Chaeremon. Hence no one has ever composed a poem on a great scale in any other than heroic verse. Nature herself, as we have said, teaches the choice of the proper measure.

Homer, admirable in all respects, has the special merit of being the only poet who rightly appreciates the part he should take himself. The poet should speak as little as possible in his own person, for it is not this that makes him an imitator. Other poets appear themselves upon the scene throughout, and imitate but little and rarely. Homer, after a few prefatory words, at once brings in a man, or woman, or other personage; none of them wanting in characteristic qualities, but each with a character of his own.

The element of the wonderful is required in Tragedy. The irrational, on which the wonderful depends for its chief effects, has wider scope in Epic poetry, because there the person acting is not seen. Thus, the pursuit of Hector would be ludicrous if placed upon the stage—the Greeks standing still and not joining in the pursuit, and Achilles waving them back. But in the Epic poem the absurdity passes unnoticed. Now the wonderful is pleasing: as may be inferred from the fact that every one tells a story with some addition of his own, knowing that his hearers like it. It is Homer who has chiefly taught other poets the art of telling lies skilfully. The secret of it lies in a fallacy. For, assuming that if one thing is or becomes, a second is or becomes, men imagine that, if the second is, the first likewise is or becomes. But this is a false inference. Hence, where the first thing is untrue, it is quite unnecessary, provided the second be true, to add that the first is or has become. For the mind, knowing the second to be true, falsely infers the truth of the first. There is an example of this in the bath Scene of the Odyssey.

Accordingly, the poet should prefer probable impossibilities to improbable possibilities. The tragic plot must not be composed of irrational parts. Everything irrational should, if possible, be excluded; or, at all events, it should lie outside the action of the play (as, in the Oedipus, the hero's ignorance as to the manner of Laius' death); not within the drama,—as in the Electra, the messenger's account of the Pythian games; or, as in the Mysians, the man who has come from Tegea to Mysia and is still speechless. The plea that otherwise the plot would have been ruined, is ridiculous; such a plot should not in the first instance be constructed. But once the irrational has been introduced and an air of likelihood imparted to it, we must accept it in spite of the absurdity. Take even the irrational incidents in the Odyssey, where Odysseus is left upon the shore of Ithaca. How intolerable even these might have been would be apparent if an inferior poet were to treat the subject. As it is, the absurdity is veiled by the poetic charm with which the poet invests it.

The diction should be elaborated in the pauses of the action, where there is no expression of character or thought. For, conversely, character and thought are merely obscured by a diction that is over brilliant.

XXV

With respect to critical difficulties and their solutions, the number and nature of the sources from which they may be drawn may be thus exhibited.

The poet being an imitator, like a painter or any other artist, must of necessity imitate one of three objects—things as they were or are, things as they are said or thought to be, or things as they ought to be. The vehicle of expression is language,—either current terms or, it may be, rare words or metaphors. There are also many modifications of language, which we concede to the poets. Add to this, that the standard of correctness is not the same in poetry and politics, any more than in poetry and any other art. Within the art of poetry itself there are two kinds of faults,—those which touch its essence, and those which are accidental. If a poet has chosen to imitate something, <but has imitated it incorrectly> through want of capacity, the error is inherent in the poetry. But if the failure is due to a wrong choice—if he has represented a horse as throwing out both his off legs at once, or introduced technical inaccuracies in medicine, for example, or in any other art—the error is not essential to the poetry. These are the points of view from which we should consider and answer the objections raised by the critics.

First as to matters which concern the poet's own art. If he describes the impossible, he is guilty of an error; but the error may be justified, if the end of the art be thereby attained (the end being that already mentioned),—if, that is, the effect of this or any other part of the poem is thus rendered more striking. A case in point is the pursuit of Hector. If, however, the end might have been as well, or better, attained without violating the special rules of the poetic art, the error is not justified: for every kind of error should, if possible, be avoided.

Again, does the error touch the essentials of the poetic art, or some accident of it? For example,—not to know that a hind has no horns is a less serious matter than to paint it inartistically.

Further, if it be objected that the description is not true to fact, the poet may perhaps reply,—'But the objects are as they ought to be': just as Sophocles said that he drew men as they ought to be; Euripides, as they are. In this way the objection may be met. If, however, the representation be of neither kind, the poet may answer,—'This is how men say the thing is.' This applies to tales about the gods. It may well be that these stories are not higher than fact nor yet true to fact: they are, very possibly, what Xenophanes says of them. But anyhow, 'this is what is said.' Again, a description may be no better than the fact; still, it was the fact; as in the passage about the arms: 'Upright upon their butt-ends stood the spears.' This was the custom then, as it now is among the Illyrians.

Again, in examining whether what has been said or done by some one is poetically right or not, we must not look merely to the particular act or saying, and ask whether it is poetically good or bad. We must also consider by whom it is said or done, to whom, when, by what means, or for what end; whether, for instance, it be to secure a greater good, or avert a greater evil.

Other difficulties may be resolved by due regard to the usage of language. We may note a rare word, as in οὐρῆας, μὲν πρῶτον,[44] where the poet perhaps employs οὐρῆας not in the sense of mules, but of sentinels. So, again, of Dolon: 'ill-favoured indeed he was to look upon.' It is not meant that his body was ill-shaped, but that his face was ugly; for the Cretans use the word εὐειδές,[45] 'well-favoured,' to denote a fair face. Again, ζωρότερον δὲ κέραιε,[46] 'mix the drink livelier,' does not mean 'mix it stronger' as for hard drinkers, but 'mix it quicker.'

Sometimes an expression is metaphorical, as 'Now all gods and men were sleeping through the night,'—while at the same time the poet says: 'Often indeed as he turned his gaze to the Trojan plain, he marvelled at the sound of flutes and pipes.' 'All' is here used metaphorically for 'many,' all being a species of many. So in the verse,—'alone she hath no part...,' οἴη,[47] 'alone,' is metaphorical; for the best known may be called the only one.

Again, the solution may depend upon accent or breathing. Thus Hippias of Thasos solved the difficulties in the lines,—δίδομεν (διδόμεν) δέ οἱ, and τὸ μὲν οὗ (οὐ) καταπύθεται ὄμβρῳ.[48]

Or again, the question may be solved by punctuation, as in Empedocles,—'Of a sudden things became mortal that before had learnt to be immortal, and things unmixed before mixed.'

Or again, by ambiguity of meaning,—as παρῴχηκεν δὲ πλέω νύξ,[49] where the word πλέω is ambiguous.

Or by the usage of language. Thus any mixed drink is called οἶνος,[50] 'wine.' Hence Ganymede is said 'to pour the wine to Zeus,' though the gods do not drink wine. So too workers in iron are called χαλκέας,[51] or workers in bronze. This, however, may also be taken as a metaphor.

---

[44] *Oureas, men proton,* first the mules. By "mules" Homer may have meant "Sentinels."

[45] *Eueides.*

[46] *Zoroteron de keraie.*

[47] *Oie.*

[48] *Dídomen (didómen) de oi* and *to men oû (où) kataputhetai ombro.* "And we grant . . . ," to the command form directed to the dream, "Grant to him . . ." A change of meaning from "rots not at all" to "part of it rots."

[49] *Parocheken de pleo nux pleo,* and of the night more than two watches have past. *Pleo* does not mean "full" here, but "full two-thirds."

[50] *Oinos.*

[51] *Chalkeas,* brazen.

Again, when a word seems to involve some inconsistency of meaning, we should consider how many senses it may bear in the particular passage. For example: 'there was stayed the spear of bronze'—we should ask in how many ways we may take 'being checked there.' The true mode of interpretation is the precise opposite of what Glaucon mentions. Critics, he says, jump at certain groundless conclusions; they pass adverse judgment and then proceed to reason on it; and, assuming that the poet has said whatever they happen to think, find fault if a thing is inconsistent with their own fancy. The question about Icarius has been treated in this fashion. The critics imagine he was a Lacedaemonian. They think it strange, therefore, that Telemachus should not have met him when he went to Lacedaemon. But the Cephallenian story may perhaps be the true one. They allege that Odysseus took a wife from among themselves, and that her father was Icadius not Icarius. It is merely a mistake, then, that gives plausibility to the objection.

In general, the impossible must be justified by reference to artistic requirements, or to the higher reality, or to received opinion. With respect to the requirements of art, a probable impossibility is to be preferred to a thing improbable and yet possible. Again, it may be impossible that there should be men such as Zeuxis painted. 'Yes,' we say, 'but the impossible is the higher thing; for the ideal type must surpass the reality.' To justify the irrational, we appeal to what is commonly said to be. In addition to which, we urge that the irrational sometimes does not violate reason; just as 'it is probable that a thing may happen contrary to probability.'

Things that sound contradictory should be examined by the same rules as in dialectical refutation—whether the same thing is meant, in the same relation, and in the same sense. We should therefore solve the question by reference to what the poet says himself, or to what is tacitly assumed by a person of intelligence.

The element of the irrational, and, similarly, depravity of character, are justly censured when there is no inner necessity for introducing them. Such is the irrational element in the introduction of Aegeus by Euripides and the badness of Menelaus in the Orestes.

Thus, there are five sources from which critical objections are drawn. Things are censured either as impossible, or irrational, or morally hurtful, or contradictory, or contrary to artistic correctness. The answers should be sought under the twelve heads above mentioned.

XXVI

The question may be raised whether the Epic or Tragic mode of imitation is the higher. If the more refined art is the higher, and the more refined in every case is that which appeals to the better sort of audience, the art which imitates anything and everything is manifestly most unrefined. The audience is supposed to be too dull to comprehend unless something of their own is thrown in by the performers, who therefore indulge in restless movements.

Bad flute-players twist and twirl, if they have to represent 'the quoit-throw,' or hustle the coryphaeus when they perform the 'Scylla.' Tragedy, it is said, has this same defect. We may compare the opinion that the older actors entertained of their successors. Mynniscus used to call Callippides 'ape' on account of the extravagance of his action, and the same view was held of Pindarus. Tragic art, then, as a whole, stands to Epic in the same relation as the younger to the elder actors. So we are told that Epic poetry is addressed to a cultivated audience, who do not need gesture; Tragedy, to an inferior public. Being then unrefined, it is evidently the lower of the two.

Now, in the first place, this censure attaches not to the poetic but to the histrionic art; for gesticulation may be equally overdone in epic recitation, as by Sosistratus, or in lyrical competition, as by Mnasitheus the Opuntian. Next, all action is not to be condemned—any more than all dancing—but only that of bad performers. Such was the fault found in Callippides, as also in others of our own day, who are censured for representing degraded women. Again, Tragedy like Epic poetry produces its effect even without action; it reveals its power by mere reading. If, then, in all other respects it is superior, this fault, we say, is not inherent in it.

And superior it is, because it has all the epic elements—it may even use the epic metre—with the music and spectacular effects as important accessories; and these produce the most vivid of pleasures. Further, it has vividness of impression in reading as well as in representation. Moreover, the art attains its end within narrower limits; for the concentrated effect is more pleasurable than one which is spread over a long time and so diluted. What, for example, would be the effect of the Oedipus of Sophocles, if it were cast into a form as long as the Iliad? Once more, the Epic imitation has less unity; as is shown by this, that any Epic poem will furnish subjects for several tragedies. Thus if the story adopted by the poet has a strict unity, it must either be concisely told and appear truncated; or, if it conform to the Epic canon of length, it must seem weak and watery. <Such length implies some loss of unity,> if, I mean, the poem is constructed out of several actions, like the Iliad and the Odyssey, which have many such parts, each with a certain magnitude of its own. Yet these poems are as perfect as possible in structure; each is, in the highest degree attainable, an imitation of a single action.

If, then, Tragedy is superior to Epic poetry in all these respects, and, moreover, fulfils its specific function better as an art—for each art ought to produce, not any chance pleasure, but the pleasure proper to it, as already stated—it plainly follows that Tragedy is the higher art, as attaining its end more perfectly.

Thus much may suffice concerning Tragic and Epic poetry in general; their several kinds and parts, with the number of each and their differences; the causes that make a poem good or bad; the objections of the critics and the answers to these objections. * * *

Edited and translated by S. H. Butcher.

LONGINUS

On the Sublime

First Century A.D. *[?]*

Though the authorship of On the Sublime *remains uncertain, most scholars now agree that it was likely written in the first century* A.D. *Whoever he was, "Longinus" (first century* A.D.*) defines his work as a "technical treatise" as early as his second sentence. As such, it will be an examination of the specific methods by which a subject under inquiry may be understood; it will deal with the process by which a particular effect may be achieved. This is certainly a brisk and businesslike attitude toward a subject that might not at first appear to lend itself to such a no-nonsense approach: the heightened emotional response that great literature evokes in us, that ecstasy or transport that results from "eminence and excellence in language" in oratory as well as in poetry. Longinus intends to remove the mystery, confident that Nature "is no creature of random impulse" and that every effect has its discoverable causes. But listing the five sources of the sublime, he assigns the first two to natural gifts. And although this is to be a technical treatise on language, he declares, "Sublimity is the note which rings from a great mind." If this is true, then how can the methods of achieving it be taught?*

The issue confronted is the nature versus art controversy that was to become the central question in the late seventeenth and eighteenth centuries. One aspect of the classical tradition emphasizes the value of the rules, presumably as Aristotle had laid them down; but Longinus here gives the warrant for the doctrine of inspired (though not unlearned) creativity. The debate is between art as the product of knowledge and training or art as self-expression. The analysis of the Sapphic ode in Chapter X shows Longinus as a practical critic, but exactly what is he analyzing? Is he a psychological or a linguistic critic?

In categorizing the other three sources of the sublime, Longinus provides a handbook of rhetorical and grammatical devices that constitute what every writer aspiring to sublimity should know. It is all technique and shop talk, reflecting an attitude similar to that expressed in the twentieth century by Thornton Wilder:

> *I am always uncomfortable, when in "studio" conversation, I hear young artists talking about "truth" and "humanity" and "what is art," and most*

happy when I hear them talking about pigments and the timbre of the flute in
its lower range or the spelling of dialects or James's "center of consciousness."

In what might at first appear to be an irrelevant conclusion, Longinus sur-
veys the contemporary literary situation and states some melancholy facts—the
literary technician turns moralist and bemoans the prevalence of hack or formula
writers.

I

THE TREATISE written by Caecilius 'concerning Sublimity' appeared to us, as you
will remember, dear Postumius Terentianus, when we looked into it together,
to fall below the level of the general subject, failing especially in grasp of vital
points; and to give his readers but little of that assistance which should be the
first aim of every writer. In any technical treatise two points are essential;
the first, that the writer should show what the thing proposed for inquiry is; the
second, but in effect the more important, that he should tell us by what specific
methods that thing may be made our own. Now Caecilius endeavours to show
us by a vast number of instances what the sublime is, as though we did not
know; the process by which we may raise our natural powers to a required advance in scale he unaccountably passed over as unnecessary. So far as he is concerned, perhaps we ought to praise the man for his ingenuity and pains, not to
blame him for the omissions. Since, however, you lay your commands upon
me, that I should take up the subject in my turn, and without fail put something
on paper about Sublimity as a favour to yourself, give me your company; let us
see whether there is anything in the views which I have formed really serviceable to men in public life. You, comrade, will help me by passing judgement,
with perfect frankness, upon all particulars you can and you ought. It was well
answered by one who wished to show wherein we resemble gods: 'in doing
good,' said he, 'and in speaking truth.'

Writing to you, my dear friend, with your perfect knowledge of all liberal study, I am almost relieved at the outset from the necessity of showing at
any length that Sublimity is always an eminence and excellence in language;
and that from this, and this alone, the greatest poets and writers of prose
have attained the first place and have clothed their fame with immortality.
For it is not to persuasion but to ecstasy that passages of extraordinary genius carry the hearer: now the marvellous, with its power to amaze, is always
and necessarily stronger than that which seeks to persuade and to please: to
be persuaded rests usually with ourselves, genius brings force sovereign and
irresistible to bear upon every hearer, and takes its stand high above him.
Again, skill in invention and power of orderly arrangement are not seen from
one passage nor from two, but emerge with effort out of the whole context;
Sublimity, we know, brought out at the happy moment, parts all the matter
this way and that, and like a lightning flash, reveals, at a stroke and in its entirety, the power of the orator. These and suchlike considerations I think, my
dear Terentianus, that your own experience might supply.

II

We, however, must at once raise this further question; is there any art of sublimity or of its opposite? For some go so far as to think all who would bring such terms under technical rules to be entirely mistaken. 'Genius,' says one, 'is inbred, not taught; there is one art for the things of genius, to be born with them.' All natural effects are spoilt, they think, by technical rules, and become miserable skeletons. I assert that the reverse will prove true on examination, if we consider that Nature, a law to herself as she mostly is in all that is passionate and lofty, yet is no creature of random impulse delighting in mere absence of method; that she is indeed herself the first and originating principle which underlies all things, yet rules of degree, of fitting occasion, of unerring practice, and of application can be determined by method and are its contribution; in a sense all greatness is exposed to a danger of its own, if left to itself without science to control, 'unsteadied, unballasted,' abandoned to mere velocity and uninstructed venture; greatness needs the spur often, it also needs the bit. What Demosthenes shows to be true of the common life of men—that of all good things the greatest is good fortune, but a second, not inferior to the first, is good counsel, and that where the latter is wanting the former is at once cancelled—we may properly apply to literature; here Nature fills the place of good fortune, Art of good counsel. Also, and this is most important, it is only from Art that we can learn the very fact that certain effects in literature rest on Nature and on her alone. If, as I said, the critic who finds fault with earnest students, would take all these things into his account, he would in my opinion no longer deem inquiry upon the subjects before us to be unnecessary or unfruitful.

[*Here a portion of the essay has been lost.*]

III

Stay they the furnace! quench the far-flung blaze!
For if I spy one crouching habitant,
I'll twist a lock, one lock of storm-borne flame,
And fire the roof, and char the halls to ash:
Not yet, not now my noble strain is raised.

All this is tragic no longer, but burlesque of tragic; 'locks,' 'to vomit up to heaven,' 'Boreas turned flute player,' and the rest. It is turbid in expression, and confused in imagery, not forcible; and if you examine each detail in clear light, you see a gradual sinking from the terrible to the contemptible. Now when in tragedy, which by its nature is pompous and admits bombast, tasteless rant is found to be unpardonable, I should be slow to allow that it could be in place in true history. Thus we laugh at Gorgias of Leontini for writing 'Xerxes the Zeus of the Persians' and 'vultures, those living tombs,' and at some passages in Callisthenes as being stilted, not sublime, and even more at some in Cleitarchus; he is a mere fantastic, he 'puffs,' to apply the words of

Sophocles, 'on puny pipes, *but* with no mellowing gag.' So with Amphi-crates, Hegesias, and Matris; they often appear to themselves to be pos-sessed, really they are no inspired revellers but children at play. We may take it that turgidity is of all faults perhaps the most difficult to avoid. It is a fact of Nature that all men who aim at grandeur, in avoiding the reproach of being weak and dry, are, we know not how, borne off into turgidity, caught by the adage: — 'To lapse from greatness were a generous fault.' As in bodies, so in writings, all swellings which are hollow and unreal are bad, and very possibly work round to the opposite condition, for 'nothing,' they say, 'so dry as a man with dropsy.'

While tumidity thus tends to overshoot the sublime, puerility is the direct opposite of all that is great; it is in every sense low and small spirited, and es-sentially a most ignoble fault. What then is puerility? Clearly it is a pedantic conceit, which overdoes itself and becomes frigid at the last. Authors glide into this when they make for what is unusual, artificial, above all, agreeable, and so run on the reefs of nonsense and affectation. By the side of these is a third kind of vice, found in passages of strong feeling, and called by Theodorus 'Paren-thyrsus.' This is passion out of place and unmeaning, where there is no call for passion, or unrestrained where restraint is needed. Men are carried aside, as if under strong drink, into expressions of feeling which have nothing to do with the subject, but are personal to themselves and academic: then they play clumsy antics before an audience which has never been moved; it cannot be otherwise, when the speakers are in an ecstasy, and the hearers are not. But we reserve room to speak of the passions elsewhere.

IV

Of the second fault which we mentioned, frigidity, Timaeus is full; an able author in other respects, and not always wanting in greatness of style; learned, acute, but extremely critical of the faults of others, while insensible to his own; often sinking into mere childishness from an incessant desire to start new notions. I will set down one or two instances only from this author, since Caecilius has been before me with most of them. Praising Alexander the Great, he writes: 'who annexed all Asia in fewer years than Isocrates took to write his *Panegyricus* in support of war against the Persians.' Truly a won-derful comparison between the Macedonian and the Sophist: yes, Timaeus, clearly the Lacedaemonians were far out-matched by Isocrates in valour, for they took Messene in thirty years, he composed his *Panegyricus* in ten! Then how he turns upon the Athenians captured in Sicily: 'Because they commit-ted impiety against Hermes, and defaced his images, they suffered punish-ment for it, largely on account of one man, a descendant, on the father's side, of the injured god, Hermocrates, son of Hermon.' This makes me wonder, dear Terentianus, that he does not also write of the tyrant Dionysius: 'He had shown impiety towards Zeus and Heracles; therefore he was deprived of his kingdom by Dion and Heraclides.' What need to speak of Timaeus, when those heroes Xenophon and Plato, although they were of Socrates' own school, sometimes forgot themselves in such paltry attempts to please. Thus Xenophon writes in the *Constitution of the Lacedaemonians:* 'I mean to say that you can no more hear their voices than if they were made of stone, no more draw their eyes aside than if they were made of brass; you might think them more modest than the maiden-pupils in their eyes.' It was worthy of Amphicrates, not of Xenophon, to call the pupils in our eyes 'modest maidens': but what a notion, to believe that the eyes of a whole row were modest, whereas they say that immodesty in particular persons is expressed by nothing so much as by the eyes. Addressing a forward person, 'Wine laden, dog-eyed!' says Homer. Timaeus, however, as if clutching at stolen goods, has not left to Xenophon even this point of frigidity. He says, speaking of Agathocles, that he even carried off his cousin, who had been given in marriage to another man, from the solemnity of Unveiling; 'Now who would have done this, who had maidens, not harlots, in his eyes?' Nay, Plato, the divine, as at other times he is, wishing to mention tablets, says: 'they will write and store in the temples memorials of cypress wood,' and again 'concerning walls, O Megillus, I would take the Spartan view, to allow our walls to sleep on the ground where they lie, and not be raised again.' And Herodotus is hardly clear of this fault, when he calls beautiful women 'pains to the eyes'; though he has some excuse, for the speakers in Herodotus are barbarians and in drink: still, not even through the mouths of such characters is it well, out of sheer pettiness, to cut a clumsy figure before all time.

V

All these undignified faults spring up in literature from a single cause, the craving for intellectual novelties, on which, above all else, our own generation goes wild. It would almost be true to say that the sources of all the good in us are also the sources of all the bad. Thus beauties of expression, and all which is sublime, I will add, all which is agreeable, contribute to success in our writing; and yet every one of these becomes a principle and a foundation, as of success, so of its opposite. Much the same is to be said of changes of construction, hyperboles, plurals for singulars; we will show in the sequel the danger which seems to attend each. Therefore it is necessary at once to raise the question directly, and to show how it is possible for us to escape the vices thus intimately mingled with the sublime.

VI

It is possible, my friend, to do this, if we could first of all arrive at a clear and discriminating knowledge of what true sublimity is. Yet this is hard to grasp: judgement of style is the last and ripest fruit of much experience. Still, if I am to speak in the language of precept, it is perhaps not impossible, from some such remarks as follow, to attain to a right decision upon the matter.

VII

We must, dear friend, know this truth. As in our ordinary life nothing is great which it is a mark of greatness to despise; as fortunes, offices, honours, kingdoms, and such like, things which are praised so pompously from without, could never appear, at least to a sensible man, to be surpassingly good, since actual contempt for them is a good of no mean kind (certainly men admire, more than those who have them, those who might have them, but in greatness of soul let them pass); even so it is with all that is elevated in poetry and prose writings; we have to ask whether it may be that they have that image of greatness to which so much careless praise is attached, but on a close scrutiny would be found vain and hollow, things which it is nobler to despise than to admire. For it is a fact of Nature that the soul is raised by true sublimity, it gains a proud step upwards, it is filled with joy and exultation, as though itself had produced what it hears. Whenever therefore anything is heard frequently by a man of sense and literary experience, but does not dispose his mind to high thoughts, nor leave in it material for fresh reflection, beyond what is actually said; while it sinks, if you look carefully at the whole context, and dwindles away, this can never be true sublimity, being preserved so long only as it is heard. That is really great, which gives much food for fresh reflection; which it is hard, nay impossible, to resist; of which the memory is strong and indelible. You may take it that those are beautiful and genuine effects of sublimity which please always, and please all. For when men of different habits, lives, ambitions, ages, all take one and the same view about the same writings, the verdict and pronouncement of such dissimilar individuals give a powerful assurance, beyond all gainsaying, in favour of that which they admire.

VIII

Now there are five different sources, so to call them, of lofty style, which are the most productive; power of expression being presupposed as a foundation common to all five types, and inseparable from any. First and most potent is the faculty of grasping great conceptions, as I have defined it in my work on Xenophon. Second comes passion, strong and impetuous. These two constituents of sublimity are in most cases native-born, those which now follow come through art: the proper handling of figures, which again seem to fall under two heads, figures of thought, and figures of diction; then noble phraseology, with its subdivisions, choice of words, and use of tropes and of elaboration; and fifthly, that cause of greatness which includes in itself all that preceded it, dignified and spirited composition. Let us now look together at what is included under each of these heads, premising that Caecilius has passed over some of the five, for instance, passion. If he did so under the idea that sublimity and feeling are one and the same thing, coexistent and of common origin, he is entirely wrong. For some passions may be found which are distinct from sublimity and are humble, as those of pity, grief, fear; and again, in many cases, there is sublimity without passion; take, besides countless other instances, the poet's own venturesome lines on the Aloadae:

> Upon Olympus Ossa, leafy Pelion
> On Ossa would they pile, a stair to heaven;

and the yet grander words which follow:

> Now had they worked their will.

In the Orators, again, speeches of panegyric, pomp, display, exhibit on every hand majesty and the sublime, but commonly lack passion: hence Orators of much passion succeed least in panegyric, and again the panegyrists are not strong in passion. Or if, on the other hand, Caecilius did not think that passion ever contributes to sublimity, and, therefore, held it undeserving of mention, he is quite in error. I should feel confidence in maintaining that nothing reaches great eloquence so surely as genuine passion in the right place; it breathes the vehemence of frenzy and divine possession, and makes the very words inspired.

IX

After all, however, the first element, great natural genius, covers far more ground than the others: therefore, as to this also, even if it be a gift rather than a thing acquired, yet so far as is possible we must nurture our souls to all that is great, and make them, as it were, teem with noble endowment. How? you will ask. I have myself written in another place to this effect: — 'Sublimity is the note which rings from a great mind.' Thus it is that, without any utterance, a notion, unclothed and unsupported, often moves our wonder, because the very thought is great; the silence of Ajax in the book of the Lower World is great, and more sublime than any words. First, then, it is quite necessary to presuppose the principle from which this springs: the true Orator must have no low ungenerous spirit, for it is not possible that they who think small thoughts, fit for slaves, and practise them in all their daily life, should put out anything to deserve wonder and immortality. Great words issue, and it cannot be otherwise, from those whose thoughts are weighty. So it is on the lips of men of the highest spirit that words of rare greatness are found. Take the answer of Alexander to Parmenio, who had said 'I were content . . .'

[*Here several pages have been lost.*]

. . . the distance from earth to heaven, a measure one may call it of the stature as well of Homer as of Strife. Unlike this is the passage of Hesiod about Gloom (if *The Shield* is really to be assigned to Hesiod), 'From out her nostrils rheum in streams was poured': he has made the picture hateful, not terrible. But how does Homer make great all that belongs to gods?

> Far as the region of blank air in sight
> Of one who sitting on some beacon height
> Views the long wine-dark barrens of the deep,
> Such space the horses of the realm of light
> Urged by the gods, as on they strain and sweep,
> While their hoofs thunder aloft, bound over at one leap.

He measures their leap by the interval of the boundaries of the world. Who might not justly exclaim, when he marked this extravagance in greatness, that, if the horses of the gods make two leaps, leap after leap, they will no longer find room within the world. Passing great too are the appearances in the Battle of the Gods:—

> Heaven sent its clarion forth: Olympus too:
>
> .   .   .   .
>
> Trembled too Hades in his gloomy reign,
> And leapt up with a scream, lest o'er his head
> Poseidon cleave the solid earth in twain,
> And open the pale kingdom of the dead
> Horrible, foul with blight, which e'en Immortals dread.

You see, comrade, how, when earth is torn up from its foundations, and Tartarus itself laid bare, and the Universe suffers overthrow and dissolution, all things at once, heaven and hell, things mortal and immortal, mingle in the war and the peril of that fight. Yet all this is terrible indeed, though, unless taken as allegory, thoroughly impious and out of proportion. For when Homer presents to us woundings of the gods, their factions, revenges, tears, bonds, sufferings, all massed together, it seems to me that, as he has done his uttermost to make the men of the Trojan war gods, so he has made the gods men. Only for us, when we are miserable, a harbour from our ills is reserved in death; the gods, as he draws them, are everlasting, not in their nature, but in their unhappiness. Far better than the 'Battle of the Gods' are the passages which show us divinity as something undefiled and truly great, with no admixture; for instance, to take a passage which has been worked out by many before us, the lines on Poseidon:

> Tall mountains and wild woods, from height to height,
> The city and the vessels by the main . . .
> Rocked to the immortal feet that, hurrying, bare
> Poseidon in his wrath . . .
> . . . the light wheels along the sea-plain rolled;
> From cave and lair the creatures of the deep
> Flocked to sport round him, and the crystal heap
> Of waters in wild joy disparting know
> Their lord, and as the fleet pair onward sweep . . .

Thus too the lawgiver of the Jews, no common man, when he had duly conceived the power of the Deity, showed it forth as duly. At the very beginning of his Laws, 'God said,' he writes—What? 'Let there be light, and there was light, let there be earth, and there was earth.' Perhaps I shall not seem wearisome, comrade, if I quote to you one other passage from the poet, this time on a human theme, that you may learn how he accustoms his readers to enter with him into majesties which are more than human. Gloom and impenetrable night suddenly cover the battle of the Greeks before him: then Ajax, in his helplessness, says:—

Zeus, sire, do thou the veil of darkness rend,
And make clear daylight, that our eyes may see:
Then in the light e'en slay us—.

Here is the very truth of the passion of Ajax: he does not pray to live—such a petition were too humble for the hero—but when in impracticable darkness he could dispose his valour to no good purpose, chafing that he stands idle for the battle, he prays for light at the speediest, sure of finding therein at the worst a burial worthy of his valour, even if Zeus be arrayed against him. Truly the spirit of Homer goes along with every struggle, in full and carrying gale; he feels the very thing himself, he 'rages;—

Not fire in densest mountain glade,
Nor spear-armed Ares e'er raged dreadfuller:
Foam started from his lips, . . .'

Yet he shows throughout the *Odyssey* (for there are many reasons why we must look closely into passages from that poem also), that, when a great genius begins to decline, the love of story-telling is a mark of its old age. It is clear from many other indications that this work was the second; but more particularly from the fact that he introduces throughout the *Odyssey* remnants of the sufferings before Ilium, as so many additional episodes of the Trojan war; aye, and renders to its heroes fresh lamentations and words of pity, as though awarded in some far distant time. Yes, the *Odyssey* is nothing but an epilogue of the *Iliad*:—

There the brave Aias and Achilleus lie;
Patroclus there, whose wisdom matched the gods on high;
There too Antilochus my son . . .

From the same cause, I think, writing the *Iliad* in the heyday of his spirit, he made the whole structure dramatic and combative; that of the *Odyssey* is in the main narrative, which is the special mark of age. So it is that in the *Odyssey* one might liken Homer to a setting sun; the intensity is gone, but there remains the greatness. Here the tone of those great lays of Ilium is no longer maintained—the passages on one level of sublimity with no sinking anywhere, the same stream of passion poured upon passion, the readiness of turn, the closeness to life, the throng of images all drawn from the truth: as when Ocean retires into himself, and is left lonely around his proper bounds, only the ebbings of his greatness are left to our view, and a wandering among the shallows of the fabulous and the incredible. While I say this, I have not forgotten the storms in the *Odyssey*, nor the story of the Cyclops, nor certain other passages; I am describing an old age, but the old age of Homer. Still in all these, as they follow one another, fable prevails over action. I entered upon this digression, as I said, in order to show how very easily great genius, when the prime is passed, is turned aside to trifling: there are the stories of the wine-skin, of the companions turned by Circe to swine (whom Zoilus called 'porkers in tears'), of Zeus fed by doves like a young bird, of Ulysses ten days without food on the wreck, there are the incredible details of the slaying of the Suitors. What can we call these but in very truth 'dreams of Zeus'? A second reason why the incidents of the *Odyssey* also should be discussed is this; that you may recognize how the decline of passion in great writers and poets passes away into character-drawing; the sketches of the life in the household of Ulysses much resemble a comedy of character.

X

I will now ask you to consider with me whether we may possibly arrive at anything further, which has power to make our writings sublime. Since with all things are associated certain elements, constituents which are essentially inherent in the substance of each, one factor of sublimity must necessarily be the power of choosing the most vital of the included elements, and of making these, by mutual superposition, form as it were a single body. On one side the hearer is attracted by the choice of ideas, on another by the accumulation of those which have been chosen. Thus Sappho, in all cases, takes the emotions incident to the frenzy of love from the attendant symptoms and from actual truth. But wherein does she show her great excellence? In her power of first selecting and then closely combining those which are conspicuous and intense:—

> Blest as the immortal gods is he
> The youth whose eyes may look on thee,
> Whose ears thy tongue's sweet melody
>   May still devour.

> Thou smilest too!—sweet smile, whose charm
> Has struck my soul with wild alarm,
> And, when I see thee, bids disarm
>   Each vital power.

> Speechless I gaze: the flame within
> Runs swift o'er all my quivering skin;
> My eyeballs swim; with dizzy din
>   My brain reels round;

And cold drops fall; and tremblings frail
Seize every limb; and grassy pale
I grow; and then—together fail
    Both sight and sound.[1]

Do you not marvel how she seeks to gather soul and body into one, hearing and tongue, eyes and complexion; all dispersed and strangers before: now, by a series of contradictions, she is cold at once and burns, is irrational, is sensible (for she is either in terror or at the point of death), so that it may not appear to be a single passion which is upon her, but an assemblage of passions? All the symptoms are found severally in lovers; to the choice of those which are conspicuous, and to their concentration into one, is due the pre-eminent merit here. So is it, I think, with the Poet and his storms; he picks out the grimmest of the attendant circumstances. The author of the *Arimaspeia* thinks these lines terrible:—

Here too is mighty marvel for our thought:
Mid seas men dwell, on water, far from land:
Wretches they are, for sorry toil is theirs;
Eyes on the stars, heart on the deep they fix.
Oft to the gods, I ween, their hands are raised,
Their inward parts in evil case upheaved.

Any one, I think, will see that there is more embroidery than terror in it all. Now for Homer; take one instance out of many:—

As when a wave swoln by the wild wind's blore[2]
Down from the clouds upon a ship doth light,
And the whole hulk with scattering foam is white,
And through the sails all tattered and forlorn
Roars the fell blast: the seamen with affright
Shake, out from death a hand-breadth they are borne.

Aratus has attempted to transfer this very notion:—

Tiny the plank which thrusts grim death away.

Only the result is petty and smooth, not terrible. Moreover, he makes the danger limited, by the words 'the plank thrusts death away': and so it does! Again our Poet does not limit the terror to one occurrence; he gives us the picture of men meeting destruction continually, wellnigh in every wave. Yet again, by forcing together prepositions naturally inconsistent, and

---

[1] This ode of Sappho, the great woman-poet of Lesbos (about 600 B.C.), written in the metre which bears her name, has only been preserved to us in this treatise. It has been partly translated by Catullus into Latin, in the same metre. The version in the text is by J. Herman Merivale (1833).
[2] Blore, i.e. blast.

compelling them to combine (I refer to the words 'out from death'), he has so strained the verse as to match the trouble which fell upon them; has so pressed it together as to give the very presentment of that trouble; has stamped, I had almost said, upon the language the form and features of the peril: 'out from death a handbreadth they are borne.' Just so Archilochus in describing the shipwreck, and Demosthenes, when the news of Elateia comes: 'For it was evening,' he says. They chose the expressions of real eminence, looking only to merit (if one may use the word), took them out clean, and placed them one upon another, introducing between them nothing trivial, or undignified, or low. For such things mar the whole effect, much as, in building, massive blocks, intended to cohere and hold together in one, are spoilt by stopgaps and rubble.

XI

Closely connected with the excellencies which I have named is that called Amplification; in which, when the facts and issues admit of several fresh beginnings and fresh halting-places, in periodic arrangement, great phrases come rolling upon others which have gone before, in a continuously ascending order. Whether this be done by way of enlarging upon commonplace topics, or of exaggeration, or of intensifying facts or reasoning, or of handling deeds done or suffering endured (for there are numberless varieties of amplification), the orator must in any case know that none of these can possibly stand by itself without sublimity as a perfect structure. The only exceptions are where pity or depreciation are required; in all other processes of amplification, take away the sublime, and you will take soul out of body; they are effective no longer, and become nerveless and hollow unless braced by passages of sublimity. But, for clearness' sake, I must shortly lay down wherein the difference lies between my present precepts, and what I said above (there I spoke of a sketch embracing the principal ideas and arranging them into one); and the broad difference between Amplification and Sublimity.

XII

I am not satisfied with the definition given by the technical writers. Amplification is, they say, language which invests the subject with greatness. Of course this definition may serve in common for sublimity, and passion, and tropes, since they, too, invest the language with greatness of a particular kind. To me it seems that they differ from one another in this, that Sublimity lies in intensity, Amplification also in multitude; consequently sublimity often exists in a single idea, amplification necessarily implies quantity and abundance. Amplification is—to define it in outline—an accumulation of all the parts and topics inherent in a subject, strengthening the fabric of the argument by insistence; and differs in this from rhetorical proof that the latter seeks to demonstrate the point required. . . .

[*Here several pages have been lost.*]

In richest abundance, like a very sea, Plato often pours into an open expanse of grandeur. Hence it is, I think, that, if we look to style, the Orator, appealing more strongly to passions, has a large element of fire and of spirit aglow; Plato, calm in his stately and dignified magnificence, I will not say, is cold, but is not so intense. It is on these and no other points, as it seems to me, dear Terentianus (that is, if we as Greeks are allowed to form an opinion), that Cicero and Demosthenes differ in their grand passages. Demosthenes' strength is in sheer height of sublimity, that of Cicero in its diffusion. Our countryman, because he burns and ravages all in his violence, swift, strong, terrible, may be compared to a lightning flash or a thunderbolt. Cicero, like a spreading conflagration, ranges and rolls over the whole field; the fire which burns is within him, plentiful and constant, distributed at his will now in one part, now in another, and fed with fuel in relays. These are points on which you can best judge: certainly the moment for the sublimity and tension of Demosthenes is where accumulated invective and strong passion are in play, and generally where the hearer is to be hard struck: the moment for diffusion is where he is to be flooded with detail, as it is always appropriate in enlargement upon commonplaces, in perorations and digressions, and in all passages written for the style and for display, in scientific and physical exposition, and in several other branches of literature.

XIII

That Plato (to return to him) flowing 'in some such noiseless stream', none the less reaches greatness, you will not fail to recognize, since you have read the *Republic,* and know this typical passage: — 'Those who are unversed in wisdom and virtue,' it runs, 'and spend all their days in feastings and the like, are borne downwards, and wander so through life. They never yet raised their eyes to the true world above them, nor were lifted up, nor tasted of solid or pure pleasure; but, like cattle, looking down, and bowed to earth and to the table, they feed and fill themselves and gender; and in the greediness of these desires they kick and butt one another with horns and hoofs of iron, and kill because they cannot be satisfied.'

This author shows us, if we would choose not to neglect the lesson, that there is also another road, besides all that we have mentioned, which leads to the sublime. What, and what manner of road is that? Imitation and emulation of great writers and poets who have been before us. Here is our mark, my friend, let us hold closely to it: for many are borne along inspired by a breath which comes from another; even as the story is that the Pythian prophetess, approaching the tripod, where is a cleft in the ground, inhales, so they say, vapour sent by a god; and then and there, impregnated by the divine power, sings her inspired chants; even so from the great genius of the men of old do streams pass off to the souls of those who emulate them, as though from holy caves; inspired by which, even those not too highly susceptible to the god are possessed by the greatness which was in others.

Was Herodotus alone 'most Homeric'? There was Stesichorus before him, and Archilochus; but more than any, Plato drew into himself from that Homeric fountain countless runlets and channels of water. (Perhaps we ought to have given examples, had not Ammonius drawn up a selection under headings.) Here is no theft, but such a rendering as is made from beautiful spectacles or from carvings or other works of art. I do not think that there would be such a bloom as we find on some of his philosophical dogmas, or that he could have entered so often into poetical matter and expressions, unless he had entered for the first place against Homer, aye, with all his soul, a young champion against one long approved; and striven for the mastery, too emulously perhaps and in the spirit of the lists, yet not without his reward; for 'good,' says Hesiod, 'is this strife for mortals.' Yes, that contest for fame is fair, and its crown worthy of the winning, wherein even to be defeated by our forerunners is not inglorious.

XIV

Therefore even we, when we are working out a theme which requires lofty speech and greatness of thought, do well to imagine within ourselves how, if need were, Homer would have said this same thing, how Plato or Demosthenes, or, in history, Thucydides would have made it sublime. The figures of those great men will meet us on the way while we vie with them, they will stand out before our eyes, and lead our souls upwards towards the measure of the ideal which we have conjured up. Still more so if we add to our mental picture this; how would Homer, were he here, have listened to this phrase of mine? or Demosthenes? how would they have felt at this? Truly great is this competition, where we assume for our own words such a jury, such an audience, and pretend that before judges and witnesses of that heroic build we undergo a scrutiny of what we write. Yet more stimulating than all will it be if you add: 'If I write this, in what spirit will all future ages hear me?' If any man fear this consequence, that he may say something which shall pass beyond his own day and his own life, then needs must all which such a soul can grasp be barren, blunted, dull; for it posthumous fame can bring no fulfilment.

XV

Weight, grandeur, and energy of speaking are further produced in a very high degree, young friend, by appeals to Imagination, called by some 'image making.' Imagination is no doubt a name given generally to anything which suggests, no matter how, a thought which engenders speech; but the word has in our time come to be applied specially to those cases, where, moved by enthusiasm and passion, you seem to see the things of which you speak, and place them under the eyes of your hearers. Imagination means one thing in rhetoric, another with the poets; and you cannot fail to observe that the object of the latter is to amaze, of the former to give distinctness; both, however, seek to stir the mind strongly.

> My mother, never hound these maids on me,
> Of bloody visages and snaky locks:
> Here! here! upon me, nearer yet they leap!

and

> Alas! she'll slay me: whither may I flee?

There the poet saw the Furies with his own eyes, and what his imagination presented he almost compelled his hearers to behold. Now Euripides is most painstaking in employing for the purposes of Tragedy the two passions of madness and love, and is more successful with these than, so far as I know, with any others; not that he lacks boldness in essaying other efforts of imagination. Though his own natural genius was far from being great, he yet forced it in many instances to become tragic: in every detail of his great passages, as the poet has it,

> Sides and loins he lashes to and fro
> With his swift tail, and stirs up battle's thirst.

Thus Helios, handing over the reins to Phaethon, says:—

> But drive thou not within the Libyan clime,
> Th' unmoistened burning air will split thy car.

Then he goes on:—

> Right for the seven Pleiads shape thy course:
> So spake the sire; the son now grasped the reins.
> And lashed the flanks of those winged coursers. They,
> Set free, sped onwards through th' expanse of air:
> The sire, astride great Sirius in the rear,
> Rode, and the boy instructed:—thither drive!
> Here wheel thy car, yea here!

Would you not say that the soul of the writer treads the car with the driver, and shares the peril, and wears wings, as the horses do; such details could never have been imagined by it, if it had not moved in that heavenly display, and kept even pace. So in his Cassandra, 'Ho, ye horse loving Trojans . . .'

Now, whereas Aeschylus hazards the most heroic flights of imagination, as where the Seven chieftains against Thebes, in the play of that name:—

> Seven impetuous warriors, captains bold,
> Slaying the sacred bull o'er black-rimm'd shields

And touching with their hands the victim's gore,
Ares, Enyo, and blood-thirsting Fear
Invoked, and swear . . .

swearing to one another oaths of death, each man of his own, with 'no word
of ruth'; yet sometimes produces thoughts which are not wrought out, but
left in the rough, and harsh; Euripides in emulation forces himself upon the
same perils. Thus in Aeschylus the palace of Lycurgus is troubled by the
Gods in a manner passing strange when Dionysus is made manifest:—

See how the palace is possessed, its halls
Are all a revel . . .

Euripides has smoothed this over and worded it differently—

And all the mountain joined their revelry.

Sophocles has used imagination finely about the dying Oedipus, when he
passes to his own burial amidst elemental portents; and again where
Achilles, as the Greeks are sailing away, appears to them above his tomb, just
when they were standing out to sea, an appearance which no one has expressed with more vivid imagery than Simonides; but it is impossible to put
down all instances. We may, however, say generally, that those found in
poets admit an excess which passes into the mythical and goes beyond all
that is credible; in rhetorical imagination that which has in it reality and truth
is always best. Deviations from this rule become strange and exotic when the
texture of the speech is poetic and mythical, and passes into impossibility of
every sort; surely we need look no further than to our own clever orators,
who, like tragedians, see Furies, and cannot, honest gentlemen, learn so
much as this, that when Orestes says:—

Unhand me; one of my own Furies thou;
Dost grasp my waist, to thrust me down to hell?

he imagines all this because he is mad. What then can imagination in rhetoric
do? It can probably contribute much else to our speeches in energy and passion; but certainly in passages dealing with facts an admixture of it not only
persuades a listener, but makes him its slave. 'Now mark me,' says Demosthenes, 'if at this very moment a cry should be heard in front of our courts,
and then one said that the prison has been opened, and the prisoners are escaping, there is no one, be he old or young, so careless but will help all he
can. But if one were to come forward and say, that the man who released
them is now before you, that man would have no hearing, and would instantly die.' So Hyperides when put on his trial, because he had proposed,
after our defeat, to make the slaves free; 'This proposal,' he said, 'was moved
not by the Orator, but by the battle at Chaeroneia'; here, while he deals with
the facts, he at the same time has used imagination, the audacity of the conception has borne him outside and beyond persuasion. In all such instances it
is a fact of nature that we listen to that which is strongest. We are therefore

drawn away from mere demonstration to that which has in it imagination and surprise, the element of fact being wrapped and lost amid the light which shines around it. This process is only what we might expect; when two forces are combined in one, the stronger always attracts into itself the potency of the other.

What I have now written about the sublime effects which belong to high thoughts, and which are produced by the greatness of man's soul, and secondarily by imitation, or by imagination, will suffice.

XVI

Here comes the place reserved for Figures, our next topic; for these, if handled as they ought to be, should, as I said, form no minor element in greatness. As however it would be a laborious, or rather an unlimited task to give an accurate enumeration of all, we will go through a few of those productive of greatness of speech, in order to make good my assertion, and will begin thus. Demosthenes is offering a demonstration in defending his public acts. Now what was the natural way to deal with it? 'You made no mistake, men of Athens, when you took upon yourselves the struggle for the freedom of the Greeks: you have examples of this near home. For they also made no mistake who fought at Marathon, at Salamis, at Plataea.' But when, as one suddenly inspired and possessed, he breaks out with that oath by the bravest men of Greece: 'It cannot be that you made a mistake; no, by those who bore the brunt at Marathon,' he appears by use of a single figure, that of adjuration (which here I call apostrophe), to have deified those ancestors; suggesting the thought that we ought to swear, as by gods, by men who died so; and implanting in the judges the spirit of the men who there hazarded their lives of old; changing the very nature of demonstration into sublimity and passion of the highest order, and the assured conviction of new and more than natural oaths; and, withal, infusing into the souls of his hearers a plea of sovereign and specific virtue; that so, relieved by the medicine of his words of praise, they should be brought to pride themselves no less on the battle against Philip than on the triumphs won at Marathon and at Salamis. Doing all this, he caught his hearers up and bore them with him, by his use of a figure.

It is said, I know, that the germ of this oath is found in Eupolis: —

I swear by Marathon, the fight, my fight,
No man of them unscathed shall vex my heart.

But then it is not the mere swearing by a name which is great; place, manner, occasion, purpose are all essential. In these lines there is an oath, and that is all; it is addressed to Athenians when prosperous and needing no comfort; besides the poet has not made immortals of the men, and sworn by them, that so he may implant within the hearts of his hearers a worthy record of their valour; he has passed away from the men who bore the brunt to the inanimate thing, the battle. In Demosthenes the oath has been framed to suit beaten men, that so Chaeroneia might appear a failure no longer; it is, as I said, at once a demonstration that they made no mistake, an example, an assurance resting on oaths, a word of praise, an exhortation. And whereas the orator was liable to be met by this objection: 'You are speaking of a defeat under your administration, and yet you swear by victories,' in the next words he squares his phrase by rule, and makes his very words safe, giving us a lesson that 'even in Bacchic transports we must yet be sober.' 'By those who bore the brunt,' are his words, 'at Marathon, by those who fought on sea by Salamis and off Artemisium, by those who stood in the ranks at Plataea!'

Nowhere does he say 'who conquered,' but throughout he has furtively kept back the word which should give the result, because that result was a happy one, the contrary to that of Chaeroneia. Therefore he gives his hearer no time, and at once adds:—'To all of whom the city gave public burial, Aeschines, not to those only who succeeded.'

XVII

At this point I must not omit, my dear friend, to state one of my own conclusions. It shall be given quite concisely, and is this. As though by nature, the figures ally themselves with sublimity, and in turn are marvelously supported by the alliance. Where and how this is so, I will explain. There is a peculiar prejudice against a promiscuous use of the figures: it suggests a suspicion of ambuscade, plot, sophistry; and the more so when the speech is addressed to a judge with absolute powers, above all to tyrants, kings, magistrates of the highest rank: any of these at once becomes indignant, if he feels that there is an attempt to outwit him, like a silly child, by the paltry figure of a skilled orator; he takes the fallacy to be used in contempt for himself, and either rages like a wild beast, or, if he master his wrath, yet is wholly disinclined to be convinced by the arguments. Accordingly a figure is best, when the very fact that it is a figure passes unnoticed. Therefore sublimity and passion are a help against the suspicion attaching to the use of figures, and a resource of marvellous power; because the treacherous art, being once associated with what is beautiful and great, enters and remains, without exciting the least suspicion. This is sufficiently proved in the words quoted above, 'By the men who fought at Marathon!' By what device has the orator concealed the figure? Clearly, by its very light. Much as duller lights are extinguished in the encircling beams of the sun, so the artifices of rhetoric are obscured by the grandeur poured about them. An effect not far removed from this occurs in painting. When colours are used, and the light and the shadow lie upon the same surface beside one another, the light meets the eye before the shadow, and seems not only more prominent, but also much nearer. So it is in speeches; sublimity and passion, lying closer to our souls, always come into view sooner than the figures, because of what I may call natural kinship, and also of brilliance; the artfulness of the figures is thrown into shadow, and, as it were, veiled.

XVIII

What are we to say of the Questions and Interrogations, which come next? Is it not true that, by the very form which this figure takes, our orator gives intensity to his language and makes it much more effective and vehement? 'Or do ye wish (answer me, sir!) to go round and inquire one of another: "is there any news?" What can be greater news than this, that a man of Macedonia is subduing Greece? Is Philip dead? Not dead, Heaven knows, but sick. What matter to you? if anything happen to him, you will quickly make you another Philip.' Again, 'Let us sail to Macedonia. "What harbour shall we ever find to put into?" asked some one. War will discover for itself the weak points in Philip's resources.' The thing put simply would be quite inadequate: as it is, the rush and swift return of question and answer, and the meeting of his own difficulty as if it came from another, make the words not only more sublime by his use of the figure, but actually more convincing. For passionate language is more attractive when it seems to be born of the occasion, rather than deliberately adopted by the speaker: question and answer carried on with a man's self reproduce the spontaneity of passion. Much as those who are questioned by others, when spurred by the sudden appeal, meet the point vigorously and with the plain truth, so it is with the figure of question and answer; it draws the hearer off till he thinks that each point in the inquiry has been raised and put into words without preparation, and so imposes upon him. Again (for the instance from Herodotus has passed for one of the most sublime), if it be this . . .

[*Here several pages have been lost.*]

XIX

The words drop unconnected, and are, so to say, poured forth, almost too fast for the speaker himself. 'Locking their shields,' says Xenophon, 'they pushed, fought, slew, died.' Or take the words of Eurylochus in Homer:—

E'en as thou bad'st, we ranged the thickets through,
We found a house fair fashioned in a glade.

Phrases cut off from one another, yet spoken rapidly, carry the impression of a struggle, where the meaning is at once checked and hurried on. Such an effect Homer has produced by his Asyndeta.

XX

An excellent and stirring effect is often given by the concurrence of figures, when two or three mingled in one company throw into a common fund their force, cogency, beauty. Thus in the speech against Midias we have Asyndeta interwoven with repetitions and vivid presentation. 'There are many things which the striker might do, yet some of which the person struck could never tell another, by gesture, by look, by voice.' Then, in order that the passage may not continue travelling in the same track (for rest shows calm, disarrangement passion, which is a rush and a stirring of the mind), he passes with a bound to fresh Asyndeta and to repetitions: 'by gesture, by look, by voice; when in insult, when in enmity, when with fists, when as slave.' In these phrases the orator does what the striker did, he belabours the intellect of the judges by the speed of blow following blow. Then he goes back from this point, and makes a fresh onset, as gusts of wind do; 'when with fists, when on the face,' he goes on, 'these things stir, these make men frantic, to whom insult is not familiar. No one by telling of these things could possibly represent their atrocity.'

Thus he keeps up in essence throughout the passage his repetitions and Asyndeta, while he continually varies them; so that his order is disorderly, and again his violation of order has in it order of a kind.

XXI

Now insert, if you will, conjunctions, as the school of Isocrates does: 'Again we must not omit this point either, that there are many things which the striker might do, first by gesture, and then by look, and yet further by his very voice': if you rewrite the passage in full sequence, you will recognize how the press and rough effectiveness of passion, when smoothed to one level by conjunctions, fails to pierce the ear, and its fire at once goes out. For as, if one should tie up the limbs of runners, their speed is gone, so passion chafes to be shackled by conjunctions and other additions. The freedom of running is destroyed, and the momentum as of bolt from catapult.

XXII

Under the same head we must set cases of Hyperbaton. This is a disturbance of the proper sequence of phrases or thoughts, and is the surest impress of vehement passion. For as those who are really angry, or in fear, or indignant, or who fall under the influence of jealousy or any other passion (for passions are many, nay countless, past the power of man to reckon), are seen to put forward one set of ideas, then spring aside to another, thrusting in a parenthesis out of all logic, then wheel round to the first, and in their excitement, like a ship before an unsteady gale, drag phrases and thoughts sharply across, now this way, now that, and so divert the natural order into turnings innumerable; so is it in the best writers: imitation of nature leads them by way of Hyperbata to the effects of nature. For art is perfect just when it seems to be nature, and nature successful when the art underlies it unnoticed. Take the speech of Dionysius of Phocaea in Herodotus:—'Our fortunes rest on the edge of a razor, O Ionians, whether we are to be free or slaves, aye runaway slaves. Now, therefore, if you choose to take up hardships, there is toil for you in the present, but you will be able to overcome your enemies.' The natural order was, 'O Ionians, now is the time for you to accept toils, for our fortunes rest on the edge of a razor.' He has transported the words 'Men of Ionia,' starting at once with the mention of the fear, and entirely omitting, in view of the pressing terror, to find time to name his audience. Then he has inverted the order of the thoughts. Before saying that they must endure toil (which is the point of his exhortation) he first assigns the cause why they should do so: 'our fortunes,' he says, 'rest on the edge of a razor': so that his words seem not to have been prepared, but to be forced out of him. Even more marvellous is Thucydides in the skill with which he separates, by the use of Hyperbata, things which nature has made one and inseparable. Demosthenes is not so arbitrary as he; yet he is never tired of the use of this figure in all its applications; the effect of vehemence which he produces by transposition is great, and also that of speaking on the call of the moment; besides all this he draws his hearers with him to face the hazards of his long Hyperbata. For he often leaves suspended the thought with which he began, and interposes, as though he struck into a train of reasoning foreign to it and dissimilar, matter which he rolls upon other matter, all drawn from some source outside, till he strikes his hearer with fear that an entire collapse of the sentence will follow, and forces him by mere vehemence to share the risk with the speaker: then, when you least expect, after a long interval, he makes good the thought which has so long been owing, and works in his own way to a happy conclusion: making the whole a great deal more impressive by the very hazard and imminence of failure which goes with his Hyperbata. Let us spare more instances: there are so many.

XXIII

Next come the figures of many cases, so-called; groupings, changes, gradations, which are very effective, as you know, and work in with ornament, sublimity of every kind, and passion. Only look at variations of case, tense, person, number, gender: how they embroider and enliven our expressions! Of those which are concerned with number, I assert that not only are those instances ornamental where the form is singular, and the meaning, when you look into them, is found to be plural:—

> At once the people in its multitude
> Break man from man, shout 'tunny!' o'er the beach;

but the other class deserves even more attention, because there are cases where plurals fall on the ear with grander effect, and catch our applause by the effect of multitude which the number gives. Take an instance from Sophocles in the *Oedipus*:—

> O marriage rites
> That gave me birth, and having borne me, gave

To me in turn an offspring, and ye showed
Fathers and sons, and brothers, all in one,
Mothers and wives, and daughters, hateful names,
All foulest deeds that men have ever done.

All these express one name, Oedipus, and on the other side Jocasta; but
for all that, the number, spread out into plurals, has made the misfortunes
plural also; or in another case of many for one: 'Forth Hectors issued and
Sarpedons.' And there is the passage of Plato, which I have quoted also in another place, about the Athenians: —

'No Pelopses, nor Cadmuses, nor Aegyptuses, nor Danai, nor other of
the natural-born barbarian dwell here with us; pure Greeks with no cross of
barbarian blood are we that dwell in the land,' and so forth. For things strike
on the ear with more sonorous effect when the names are thus piled upon
one another in groups. Yet this should be done in those cases alone where the
subject admits of enlargement, or multiplication, or hyperbole, or passion, either one of these, or several: for we know that to go everywhere 'hung about
with bells' is a sophist's trick indeed.

XXIV

Yet, on the other hand, contraction from plural to singular sometimes produces an effect conspicuously sublime. 'Then all Peloponnesus was ranged
on different sides,' says the Orator. And look at this, 'when Phrynichus exhibited his drama, the *Taking of Miletus*, the whole theatre fell into tears.'
Where separate individuals are compressed into unity the notion of a single
body is produced. In both cases the cause of the ornamental effect is the
same: where terms are properly singular, to turn them into plurals shows
emotion into which the speaker is surprised; where plural, to bring several
individuals under one sonorous head is a change in the opposite direction,
and equally unexpected.

XXV

Again, where you introduce things past and done as happening in the actual
present, you will make your account no longer a narrative but a living action.
'A man who has fallen under the horse of Cyrus,' says Xenophon, 'and is
being trampled, strikes his sword into the belly of the horse: the horse
plunges and unseats Cyrus, and he falls.' So Thucydides in most instances.

XXVI

Effective also in the same way is the transposition of persons, which often
makes a hearer think that he is moving in the midst of the dangers described: —

> Of toughest kind
> Thou wouldst have called those hosts, so manfully
> Each fought with each.

And Aratus has:—

> Not in that month may seas about thee surge!

In much the same way Herodotus: 'You will sail up stream from the city Elephantina, and then you will come to a level plain. Passing through this tract, you will again embark on another and sail for two days; then you will reach a great city, whose name is Meroe.' You see, comrade, how he takes your spirit with him through the place, and turns hearing into seeing. All such passages, being addressed to the reader in his own person, make him take his place at the very centre of the action. Again, when you speak as though to a single individual, not to all:—

> Nor of the son of Tydeus couldst thou know
> If he with Trojans or Achaians were;

you will render him more moved by the passions and also more attentive; he is filled full of the combat, because he is roused by being himself addressed.

XXVII

Then there are other cases where the writer is giving a narrative about a person, and by a sudden transition himself passes into that person; in this class there is an outburst of passion:—

> But Hector warned the Trojans with loud cry,
> To rush upon the ships, and pass the plunder by:
> 'But whom elsewhere than at the ships I sight,
> Death shall be his that moment.'

Here the poet has assigned the narrative part to himself, as is fitting: the sharp threat he has suddenly, without previous explanation, attached to the angry chieftain: it would have been cold had he inserted 'Hector then said so and so,' whereas now the change of construction has anticipated the poet's change of speaker.

Hence the proper use of the figure is where the occasion is short and sharp, and does not allow the writer to stop, but forces him to hurry from person to person, as in Hecataeus: 'Ceyx, indignant at this, at once commanded the Heraclidae of the later generation to leave the country: "for I have no power to help you; therefore, that you may not perish yourselves, and inflict a wound on me, depart to another people."' Demosthenes, in his Aristogeiton speech, has found a different method to throw passion and swiftness into this change of persons: 'And will none of you be found,' he says, 'to entertain wrath or indignation at the violence of this shameless miscreant; who, thou foulest of mankind, when thy effrontery is stopped, not by barriers nor by gates, such as man might open——'He has not finished what he intended, but passing quickly aside, and, I had almost said, splitting a single sentence between two persons, because he is so angry—'Who, thou foulest of mankind,' he says; with the result that, having turned his speech away from Aristogeiton, and having done with him, you think, he directs it upon him again with far more intensity through the passion.

Much in the same way Penelope:—

What brings thee, herald, thee, the pioneer
Of these imperious suitors? Do they send
To bid the servants of my husband dear
Of their appointed task-work to make end,
And on their lordly revelries attend?
Never elsewhere may they survive to meet!
Here in these halls, while our estates they rend,
May they their latest and their last now eat,
Who thus with outrage foul Telemachus entreat.
Ye to your parents heedful ear lend none,
Nor hearken how Odysseus lived of yore.

XXVIII

No one I think would be in doubt as to Periphrasis being a factor of sublimity. For as in music Paraphones make the principal melody sweeter, so Periphrasis often chimes in with the plain expression, and the concurrence adds to the beauty, more especially if it have not any windy, unmusical effect, but be pleasantly compounded. In proof of this it will be sufficient to quote Plato at the beginning of the Funeral Speech:— 'Of all that we can give, these have now what is rightly theirs, and, having received it, they pass on their appointed journey, escorted publicly by the city, personally each man by those of his kin.' Here he has called death an 'appointed journey,' and the bestowal of the usual rites 'a public escort given by their country.' Is the dignity added to the thought by these turns but a small matter? Or has he rather taken language plain and unadorned, and made it melodious by pouring around it the harmonies which came of periphrasis? Xenophon again:— 'Ye reckon toil to be the guide to happy life, and have received it into your souls as the fairest and the most gallant of all possessions: for ye take more delight in being praised than in any other thing.' By calling toil 'the guide to happy life,' and giving a like expansion to the other points, he has attached to his words of praise a great and definite thought. And that inimitable phrase of Herodotus:— 'On those of the Scythians who plundered the temple the goddess sent a plague which made them women.'

XXIX

Yet Periphrasis is exposed to special risks, more special than any of the figures, if used by a writer without sense of proportion: for it falls feebly on the ear, and savours of trifling and of rank stupidity. So when Plato, (for he always employs the figure with great force, occasionally out of season,) says in the *Laws:* 'we must not allow wealth, either of silver or of gold, to be established in the city and settle there,' mocking critics say that, if he had wanted to forbid them to possess sheep, he would clearly have talked of 'wealth of sheep and wealth of cattle.'

Enough however of this disquisition (which came in by way of parenthesis) on the use of figures in producing sublime effects, all those which we have mentioned make speeches more passionate and stirring; and passion is as large an ingredient in sublimity as sense of character in an agreeable style.

XXX

Next, since the thought and the diction of a speech are in most cases mutually interlaced, I will ask you to consider with me whether any particulars of what concerns expression still remain. That a choice of the right words and of grand words wonderfully attracts and charms hearers — that this stands very high as a point of practice with all orators and all writers, because, of its own inherent virtue, it brings greatness, beauty, raciness, weight, strength, mastery, and an exultation all its own, to grace our words, as though they were the fairest statues — that it imparts to mere facts a soul which has speech — it may perhaps be superfluous to set out at length, for my readers know it. For beautiful words are, in a real and special sense, the light of thought. Yet their majesty is not of service in all places: to apply to trifling details grand and solemn words would appear much the same as if one were to fasten a large mask upon a little child. Yet in poetry . . .

[*Here several pages have been lost.*]

XXXI

. . . very rich and pithy; and this of Anacreon: —

The Thracian filly has no more my care.

So too the novel phrase of Theopompus has merit, from the closeness of the correspondence it appears to me most expressive, yet Caecilius has strangely found fault with it. 'Philip,' he says, 'has a rare power of swallowing down facts perforce.' So vulgar idiom is sometimes much more expressive than ornamental language; it is recognized at once as a touch of common life; and what is familiar is on the way to be credible. Therefore, when applied to a man who patiently puts up with and enjoys what is mean and repulsive in order to better himself, the phrase adopted, 'to swallow down perforce,' is very telling. So in Herodotus:—'Then Cleomenes went mad, and cut his own flesh with the knife into little strips, until he had made collops of himself and so died.' And 'Pythes held on to his ship and fought until he was chopped to pieces.' These scrape the corner of vulgar idiom, but they are not vulgar because they are so expressive.

XXXII

As to number of Metaphors, Caecilius appears to agree with those who lay down a rule allowing two, or at the most three, applied to the same object. About such figures again Demosthenes is the true standard, and the time for their use is, when passions are driven onwards like a torrent, and draw with themselves, as necessary to the passage, the multiplication of metaphors.

'Men foul and flatterers,' he says, 'having mutilated their fatherlands, every one of them, having pledged away their freedom in wine, first to Philip, now to Alexander, measuring happiness by their belly and by the appetites which are most shameful, having thrown to the ground that freedom and that life without a master, wherein the Greeks of old found their very standard and definition of good.' Here the orator's wrath against the traitors screens the number of the metaphors used. Accordingly Aristotle and Theophrastus say that bold metaphors are softened by such devices as the insertion of 'as though,' and 'as it were,' and 'if I may speak thus,' and 'if I am right in using somewhat venturesome phrase'; for 'censure,' they say, 'cures bold expression.' For myself, I accept all these; yet I affirm, as I said in speaking of figures, that bursts of passion, being seasonable and vehement, and sublimity when genuine, are sure specifics for numerous and daring metaphors; because as they surge and sweep, they naturally draw everything their own way, and force it onwards, rather, I would say, they require and exact bold metaphors, and do not allow the hearer leisure to go into questions of their number, because the speaker's excitement is his. Yet further, in speeches about commonplaces and in set descriptions, nothing is so expressive as continued and successive tropes. It is by means of these that in Xenophon the anatomy of man's bodily tabernacle is painted with so much magnificence, and still more admirably in Plato. The head he calls the citadel; between this and the chest an isthmus has been constructed, the neck, to which vertebrae have been attached like hinges; pleasure is a bait tempting men to their hurt, and the tongue supplies the test of taste; the heart is the knot of the veins, and the fountain of the blood which courses violently around, is appointed to be the guard-house. The passages or pores he calls lanes. 'For the beating of the heart, in the expectation of danger or on the summons of wrath, because it is a fiery organ, they devised a resource, introducing the structure of the lungs, which are soft and bloodless, and perforated with cavities like a sponge, in order that, when wrath boils up within it, the heart may beat upon a yielding substance, and so receive no hurt.' The chamber where the appetites dwell he styled the women's chamber, that where the passions, the men's chamber. The spleen is a napkin for the parts within; filled with their purgings it grows large and unsound. 'After this,' he goes on, 'they enshrouded all with fleshy parts, placing the flesh in front, to be a protection from matter outside, like layers of felt.' He called blood the food of the fleshy parts. 'And for the sake of nourishment they made water-courses through the body, like water-courses cut in gardens, that the currents of the veins might run as from an inflowing stream, the body being a narrow canal.' But when the end is at hand, he says that the cables of the souls are loosed, as though of a ship, and it is let go free. Countless similar details follow: those which we have set down suffice to show how grand in their na-ture tropical expressions are, and how metaphors produce sublimity, and that impassioned and descriptive passages admit them most readily. Yet that the use of tropes, like all other beauties of style, leads writers on to neglect proportion, is clear without my saying it. For it is upon these especially that critics pull Plato to pieces, he is so often led on, as though his style were pos-sessed, into untempered and harsh metaphors and portentous allegory. 'For it is not easy to realize,' he says, 'that a city ought to be mixed like a cup, whereinto wine is poured and boils; yet, when chastened by another and a temperate god, in that fair partnership forms an honest and a sober draught.' For to call water 'a temperate god,' they say, and admixture 'chastening,' is the mark of a poet who is anything but sober. Caecilius however, taking up such weak points as this in his pamphlets in praise of Lysias, actually dared to make out Lysias better all round than Plato, mixing up two different feel-ings: for loving Lysias more than he loved himself, he yet hates Plato more thoroughly than he loves Lysias. Only he is carried away by combativeness, nor are his premises admitted as he thought them to be. For he puts forward his orator as without a fault and clear in his record, as against Plato who had made many mistakes. The fact is not so, nor anything like it.

XXXIII

Come now: let us find some writer who is really clear and beyond criticism. Upon this point, is it not worth while to raise the question in a general form, whether in poems and prose writings a greatness with some failings is the better, or a genius which is limited in its successes, but is always sound and never drops? Aye, and this further question; whether the first prize should be carried off by the most numerous excellences in literature or by the greatest? These questions are germane to the subject of Sublimity, and absolutely re-quire a decision. I know, for my own part, that genius of surpassing great-ness has always the least clear record. Precision in every detail comes per-ilously near littleness; in great natures, as in great fortunes, there ought to be something which may even be neglected. Further, this may perhaps be a nec-essary law, that humble or modest genius, which never runs a risk, and never aims at excellence, remains in most cases without a failure and in comparative safety; but that what is great is hazardous by very reason of the greatness. Not that I fail to recognize this second law, that all human things are more easily recognized on their worse side; that the memory of failures remains indelible, while that of the good points passes quickly away. I have myself brought forward not a few failures in Homer and in others of the very greatest, yet never take pleasure in their slips, which I do not call voluntary mistakes, but rather oversights caused by the random, haphazard carelessness of great genius, and passed unmarked by it; and I remain unshaken in my opinion, that in all cases great excellence, although not kept up to one level throughout, should always bear off first award, if for nothing else, yet for the sake of simple intellectual greatness. To take an instance, Apollonius in the *Argonautae* is a poet who never drops, and Theocritus in his *Pastorals* is most successful, except as to a few extraneous matters: now this being so, would you not rather be Homer than Apollonius? Take again Eratosthenes in the *Erigone,* a little poem with nothing in it to blame; is he a greater poet than Archilochus, who drags much ill-arranged matter along in that outpouring of divine inspiration which it is difficult to range under a law? In lyrics again, would you choose to be Bacchylides rather than Pindar, in Tragedy Ion of Chios than Sophocles himself? These poets no doubt never drop, their language is always smooth and the writing beautiful, whereas Pindar and Sophocles at one time set all ablaze in their rush, but the fire is quenched when you least expect it, and they fail most unhappily. Am I not right in saying that no man in his senses, if he put the works of Ion together in a row, would value them against a single play, the *Oedipus*?

XXXIV

If successful passages were to be numbered, not weighed, Hyperides would, on this reckoning, far surpass Demosthenes. He sounds more notes, and has more points of excellence; he wins a second place in pretty well every competition, like the hero of the Pentathlon, being beaten for the first prize by some trained competitor in each, but standing first of the non-professionals. Hyperides certainly, besides matching the successful points in Demosthenes, always excepting composition, has included, over and above these, the virtues and graces of Lysias. He talks with simplicity, when it is required, not in a sustained monotonous manner like Demosthenes, and he shows sense of character, a flavouring added with a light hand; he has indescribable graces, the wit of a man who knows life, good breeding, irony with readiness of fence, jokes not vulgar nor ill-bred as in those great Attic orators, but appropriate, clever raillery, comic power in plenty, the sting which goes with well-aimed fun, and with all this what I may call inimitable charm. He has a strong natural gift for compassion, and also for telling a story fluently, running through a description before a flowing breeze with admirable ease in tacking: for instance, the story of Latona he has treated rather as a poet, the

Funeral Speech as a set, perhaps an unmatched, effort of the oratory of display. Demosthenes has no touches of character, no flowing style; certainly he is not supple, and cannot speak for display: he lacks the whole list of qualities mentioned above: when he is forced to be witty and smart, he raises a laugh against, rather than with himself; when he wants to approach charm of manner he passes farthest from it. We may be sure that if he had attempted to write the little speech on *Phryne* or that on *Athenogenes,* he would have established even more firmly the fame of Hyperides. As I see it, the case stands thus:—The beauties of the latter though they be many, are devoid of greatness, dull 'to a sober man's heart,' and allow the hearer to rest unmoved (who feels fear when he reads Hyperides?); Demosthenes 'taking up the tale,' adds excellences of the highest genius and of consummate perfection, sublimity of tone, passions in living embodiment, copiousness, versatility, speed; also, which is his own prerogative, ability and force beyond approach. Now whereas, I say, he has drawn to himself in one all those marvellous and heaven-sent gifts, for human we may not call them, therefore by the beauties which he has he surpasses all other men and outmatches those which he has not. With his thunder, with his lightning, he bears down the orators of all time; sooner might one open one's eyes in the face of thunderbolts as they rush, than gaze full upon the passions which follow upon passions in Demosthenes.

XXXV

When we come to Plato, there is, as I said, another kind of pre-eminence. For Lysias, who is far below him in the number, as well as in the magnitude of his good points, is yet more in excess of him in faults than in defect as to good points. What then did those immortals see, the writers who aimed at all which is greatest, and scorned the accuracy which lies in every detail? They saw many other things, and they also saw this, that Nature determined man to be no low or ignoble animal; but introducing us into life and this entire universe as into some vast assemblage, to be spectators, in a sort, of her contests, and most ardent competitors therein, did then implant in our souls an invincible and eternal love of that which is great and, by our own standard, more divine. Therefore it is, that for the speculation and thought which are within the scope of human endeavour not all the universe together is sufficient, our conceptions often pass beyond the bounds which limit it; and if one were to look upon life all round, and see how in all things the extraordinary, the great, the beautiful stand supreme, he will at once know for what ends we have been born. So it is that, as by some physical law, we admire, not surely the little streams, transparent though they be, and useful too, but Nile, or Tiber, or Rhine, and far more than all, Ocean; nor are we awed by this little flame of our kindling, because it keeps its light clear, more than by those heavenly bodies, often obscured though they be, nor think it more marvellous than the craters of Etna, whose eruptions bear up stones and entire masses, and sometimes pour forth rivers of that Titanic and unalloyed fire. Regarding all such things we may say this, that what is serviceable or perhaps necessary to man, man can procure; what passes his thought wins wonder.

XXXVI

Hence, when we speak of men of great genius in literature, where the greatness does not necessarily fall outside the needs and service of man, we must at once arrive at the conclusion, that men of this stature, though far removed from flawless perfection, yet all rise above the mortal: other qualities prove those who possess them to be men, sublimity raises them almost to the intellectual greatness of God. No failure, no blame; but greatness has our very wonder. What need still to add, that each of these great men is often seen to redeem all his failures by a single sublimity, a single success; and further, which is most convincing, that if we were to pick out all the failures of Homer, Demosthenes, Plato, and the other greatest writers, and to mass them together, the result would be a small, an insignificant fraction of the successes which men of that heroic build everywhere exhibit. Therefore every age and all time, which envy itself can never prove to be in its dotage, has bestowed upon them the assured prizes of victory; it guards and keeps them to this day safe and inalienable, and will as it seems, keep them

As long as waters flow and poplars bloom.

To the writer, however, who objects that the faulty Colossus is not better work than the Spearman of Polycleitus I might say much, but I say this. In Art the most accurate work is admired, in the works of Nature greatness. Now it is by Nature that man is a being endowed with speech; therefore in statues we seek what is like man, in speech what surpasses, as I said, human standards. Yet it is right (for our precept returns to the early words of this treatise), because the success of never failing is in most cases due to Art, the success of high although not uniform excellence, to Genius; that, therefore, Art should ever be brought in to aid Nature; where they are reciprocal the result should be perfection. It was necessary to go thus far towards a decision upon the points raised: let every one take the view which pleases him, and enjoy it.

XXXVII

In close neighbourhood to Metaphors, for we must go back to them, come Illustrations and Similes, which differ from them in this respect . . .
    [*Here several pages have been lost.*]

XXXVIII

Such Hyperboles as this are also ludicrous, 'unless you wear your brains in your heels to be trampled down.' Hence we ought to know exactly how far each should go, for sometimes to advance beyond these limits destroys the hyperbole; in such cases extreme tension brings relaxation, and even works right round to its opposite. Thus Isocrates fell into a strange puerility owing to his ambition to amplify at all points. The Argument of his *Panegyricus* is that the state of the Athenians surpasses that of the Lacedaemonians in services to the Greeks; but at the very beginning he has this; — 'Moreover words are so potent, that it is possible thereby to make what is great lowly, and to throw greatness about what is small, and to treat old things in a new fashion, and those which have recently happened in an old fashion.' 'What, Isocrates,' some one will say, 'do you mean then to change the parts of the Lacedaemonians and Athenians?' For this set praise of speech goes near to an open warning at the outset not to believe him. Possibly then the best hyperboles, as we said above in speaking of figures, are those which are not noticed as hyperboles at all. This result is obtained when they are uttered in an outburst of strong feeling, and in harmony with a certain grandeur in the crisis described, as where Thucydides is speaking of the men slaughtered in Sicily. 'For the Syracusans,' he says, 'also came down and butchered them, but especially those in the water, which was thus immediately spoiled, but which they went on drinking just the same, mud and all, bloody as it was, even fighting to have it.' That blood and mud were drunk together, and yet were things fought over passes for credible in the intensity of the feeling and in the crisis. The passage in Herodotus about the men of Thermopylae is similar: 'On this spot,' he says, 'while defending themselves with daggers, that is, those who still had them left, and also with hands and with teeth, they were buried alive under the missiles of the Barbarians.' Here 'What sort of thing is it,' you will say, 'to fight with very teeth against armed men,' or what to be 'buried alive under missiles'? But it passes for true like the other; for the fact does not appear to be introduced for the sake of the hyperbole, but the hyperbole to pass because fathered by the fact. For, as I am never tired of saying, every bold experiment in language finds a solvent and a specific in deeds and passions which approach frenzy. So, in Comedy, utterances which approach the incredible pass for true because of the ludicrous: —

He had a field no bigger than the sheet
Which holds a Spartan letter.

For laughter too is a passion, a passion which lies in pleasure. There is an hyperbole on the side of excess, and also one on the side of defect: the common point is a straining of the truth. And, in a manner of speaking, satire is an exaggeration, namely of pettiness.

XXXIX

The fifth of the factors which we mentioned at the outset, as contributing to Sublimity, still remains to be considered, my excellent friend; composition in words, or the precise manner of arranging them. I have already published two treatises on this subject, in which I have rendered full account of such theoretical views as I could form; and need, therefore, only add, as necessary for our present purpose, that melody is not only an instrument natural to man, which produces persuasion and pleasure; it is a marvellous instrument, which produces passion, yet leaves him free. Does not the flute implant within the hearers certain passions, and place them out of their senses, full of wild revelry? Does it not set a certain rhythmical step, and force them to keep step with it, and to conform themselves to the air, though a man have 'no music in him'? Do not the notes of the harp, which in themselves signify nothing, yet by the interchange of sounds, the mutual accompaniment, the mingled harmony, cast upon us a spell, which is, you well know, often marvellous; although these are but images and bastard copies of persuasion, not genuine forces operative upon human nature? And then are we not to think that composition—being as it is, a special melody of words, words which are in man by nature and which reach his very soul, and not his ears alone; stirring, as it does, manifold ideas of words, thoughts, actions, beauty, tunefulness, all of them things born and bred within us; carrying moreover, by the very commixture and multiplicity of its own sounds, the passion which is present to the speaker into the souls of the bystanders, and bringing them into partnership with himself; building phrase on phrase and so shaping whole passages of greatness—that Composition, I say, must by all these means at once soothe us as we hear and also dispose to stateliness, and high mood, and sublimity, and everything which it contains with itself, in each and every direction gaining the mastery over minds? Although it is mere folly to raise problems about things which are so fully admitted, for experience is proof sufficient, I am sure that you will think that a sublime thought, and marvellous indeed it is, which Demosthenes applied to his decree:—'This decree made the danger, which then encompassed the city, to pass away like a vapour.' But the harmony of the thought, no less than the thought itself, has given it voice. For the whole expression rests upon the dactylic rhythms, the most noble and productive of grandeur, which make the structure of heroic metre the noblest known to us. Take any word out of its own place, and transfer it where you will:—'This proposal, like a vapour, made the danger of that day to pass away'; or, again, cut off one syllable only:—'made it to pass like vapour'; and you will learn how closely the rhythm echoes the sublimity. For the actual phrase 'like a vapour' moves with the first rhythm long, if measured by four times. Cut out the one syllable, you have 'as vapour,' the curtailment mutilates the grandeur; as, on the other hand, if you lengthen it out, 'made to pass away like to a vapour,' the sense is the same, but not the effect on the ear, because by the length of the times at the end of the phrase, its sheer sublimity is broken up and unstrung.

XL

Language is made grand in the highest degree by that which corresponds to the collocation of limbs in the body, of which no one, if cut off from another, has anything noticeable in itself, yet all in combination produce a perfect structure. So great passages, when separate and scattered in different parts, scatter also the sublimity; but if they are formed by partnership into a body, and also enclosed by the bond of rhythm, the limits which encircle them give them new voice; one might put it that grand effects within a period contribute to a common fund of grandeur. However it has been already shown that many prose writers and poets of no natural sublimity, possibly themselves altogether wanting in grandeur, and using in general common and popular words, such as contribute nothing remarkable, have yet, by mere arrangement and adjustment, attained a real dignity and distinction of style, in which no pettiness is apparent; so, amongst many others, Philistus, Aristophanes in certain passages, Euripides in most. After the murder of his children Hercules cries:—

I am full fraught with ills—no stowing more.

The phrase is quite popular, but has become sublime because the handling of the words conforms to the subject. If you place the words in other combinations, you will see clearly that Euripides is a poet of composition rather than of intellect.—When Dirce is being dragged away by the bull:—

　　Where'er it chanced,
Rolling around he with him ever drew
Wife, oak-tree, rock, in constant interchange.

The conception in itself is a noble one, but has become more forcible from the rhythm not being hurried, nor borne along as on rollers; the words are solidly attached to one another, and checks caused by the syllabic quantities, which result in stability and grandeur.

XLI

There is nothing which introduces pettiness into sublime passages so much as a broken and excited rhythm, as pyrrhics, trochees, and dichorees, which fall into a thorough dancing measure. For in prose complete rhythm appears dainty and trivial, and entirely lacks passion, because the sameness makes it superficial. The worst point of all about this is, that, as ballad-music draws away the hearers perforce from the subject to itself, so prose which is made over-rhythmical does not give the hearers the effect of the prose but that of the rhythm; so that in some cases, knowing beforehand the endings as they become due, people actually beat time with the speakers, and get before them, and render the movement too soon, as though in a dance. Equally devoid of grandeur are passages which lie too close, cut up into scraps and minute syllables, and bound together by clamps between piece and piece in the way of socket and insertion.

XLII

Another means of lowering sublimity is excessive conciseness of expression; a grand phrase is maimed when it is gathered into too short a compass. I must be understood to refer not to mere undue compression, but to what is absolutely small and comminuted: contraction stunts the sense, a short cut goes straight. In the other direction it is clear that what is spun out is lifeless, all 'which conjures up unseasonable length.'

XLIII

Pettiness of words, again, is strangely potent in making fine passages mean. Thus in Herodotus the storm has been finely described with great spirit, so far as the ideas go, but certain words are included which are surely too ignoble for the subject; this in particular, 'when the sea boiled,' the word 'boiled' greatly spoils the sublimity, being so poor in sound; then he has 'the wind flagged,' and again 'Those who were about the wreck and clutching it met an unwelcome end,' 'flagged' is an undignified vulgarism, and 'unwelcome' is an inadequate word for such a disaster. So also Theopompus, in a brilliant and elaborate account of the descent of the Persian army upon Egypt, by a few paltry words has spoilt the whole passage:—'For what city of Asia, or what tribe, did not send envoys to the King? What beautiful or costly thing which earth grows, or art produces, was not brought as a gift to him? Were there not many and costly coverlets and cloaks, purple, and variegated, and white pieces, and many tents of gold, furnished with all things serviceable; many costly robes and couches? There were also vessels of wrought gold and silver, drinking cups and bowls, of which you might have seen some crusted with precious stones, others worked with elaborate and costly art: besides these were untold quantities of arms, some Greek, some barbarian, beasts of burden in exceedingly great numbers, and victims fatted for slaughter, many bushels of spices, many sacks and bags and sheets of papyrus and all other commodities; and so many pickled carcases of all sorts of animals, that the size of the heaps made those who approached from a distance think that they were mounds and hillocks as they jostled one another.' He runs off from the loftier to the more humble details, whereas he ought to have made his description rise in the other direction. With his marvellous account of the whole provision he has mixed up his bags and spices, and has drawn to the imagination—a cook-shop! Suppose one had really placed among those things of show, in the middle of the gold and the gem-crusted cups and the silver vessels, common bags and sacks, the effects to the eye would have been unseemly; so in a description each of such words placed there out of season is an ugliness and, so to say, a blot where it stands. It was open to him to go through all in broad outline: as he has told us of heaps taken to be hillocks, so he might have given us all the rest of the pageant, camels, a multitude of beasts of burden carrying all supplies for luxury and the enjoyment of the table, or he might have specified heaps of every sort of grain of all that is best for confectionery and daintiness; or, if he meant, at all costs, to put the whole down in an inclusive list, he might have said 'all the dainties known to victuallers and confectioners.' For we ought not in sublime passages to stoop to mean and discredited terms unless we are compelled by some strong necessity; but it would be proper even in words to keep to those which sound worthy of the subject, and to copy Nature who fashioned man; for she did not place our less honourable parts in front, nor the purgings of all gross matter, but hid them away so far as she could, and, as Xenophon tells us, removed the channels of such things to as great a distance as possible, nowhere disfiguring the beauty of the whole animal. But there is no present need to enumerate by their kinds the means of producing pettiness; when we have once shown what things make writings noble and sublime, it is clear that their opposites will make them in most cases low and uncouth.

XLIV

One point remains, which in view of your diligence in learning, I shall not hesitate to add. This is to give a clear answer to a question lately put to me by one of our philosophers: 'I wonder,' he said, 'as assuredly do many others, how it is that in our age we have men whose genius is persuasive and statesman-like in the extreme, keen and versatile; but minds of a high order of sublimity and greatness are no longer produced, or quite exceptionally, such is the world-wide barrenness of literature that now pervades our life. Are we indeed,' he went on, 'to believe the common voice, that democracy is a good nurse of all that is great; that with free government nearly all powerful orators attained their prime, and died with it? For Freedom, they say, has the power of breeding noble spirits; it gives them hopes, and passes hand in hand with them through their eager mutual strife and their ambition to reach the first prizes. Further, because of the prizes offered to competition in commonwealths, the intellectual gifts of orators are kept in exercise and whetted by use; the rub of politics, if I may use the word, kindles them to fire; they shine, as shine they must, with the light of public freedom. But we in our day,' he went on, 'seem to be from our childhood scholars of a dutiful slavery; in its customs and practices we are enwrapped and swathed from the very infancy of our thoughts, never tasting that fairest and most abundant fount of eloquence, I mean Freedom; wherefore we turn out nothing but flatterers of portentous growth.' Other faculties, he asserted, might be the portion of mere household servants, but no slave becomes an orator; for

instantly there surges up the helplessness to speak out, there is the guard on
the lips enforced by the cudgel of habitude. As Homer has it:—

'Half that man's virtue doth Zeus take away,
Whom he surrenders to the servile day.'

'As then,' he went on, 'if what I hear is to be believed, the cages in which the
Pygmies, also called dwarfs, are reared, not only hinder the growth of those
who are shut up in them, but actually shrivel them because of the bonds
lying about their bodies, so one might show that all slavery, though it be
never so dutiful, is a cage of the soul and a public prison.' Here I rejoined:
'Sir,' I said, 'it is easy, and it is man's special habit, always to find fault with
things present: but consider whether it may not be that what spoils noble natures is, not the peace of the universal world, but much rather this war which
masters our desires, and to which no bounds are set, aye, and more than that,
these passions which keep our life a prisoner and make spoil of it altogether?
The love of money, which cannot be satisfied and is a disease with us all, and
the love of pleasure both lead us into slavery, or rather, as one might put it,
thrust our lives and ourselves down into the depths: the love of money, a disease which makes us little, the love of pleasure, which is utterly ignoble. I try
to reckon it up, but I cannot discover how it is possible that we who so
greatly honour boundless wealth, who, to speak more truly, make it a god,
can fail to receive into our souls the kindred evils which enter it. There follows on unmeasured and unchecked wealth, bound to it and keeping step for
step, as they say, costliness of living; which, when wealth opens the way into
cities and houses, enters and settles therein. When these evils have passed
much time in our lives, they build nests, the wise tell us, and soon proceed to
breed and engender boasting, and vapouring, and luxury; no spurious
brood, but all too truly their own. For this must perforce be so; men will no
longer look up, nor otherwise take any account of good reputation; little by
little the ruin of their whole life is effected; all greatness of soul dwindles and
withers, and ceases to be emulated, while men admire their own mortal parts,
and neglect to improve the immortal. A judge bribed for his verdict could
never be a free and sound judge of things just and good, for to the corrupted
judge the side which he is to take must needs appear good and just. Even so,
where bribes already rule our whole lives, and the hunt for other men's
deaths, and the lying in wait for their wills, and where we purchase with our
soul gain from wherever it comes, led captive each by his own luxury, do we
really expect, amidst this ruin and undoing of our life, that any is yet left a
free and uncorrupted judge of great things and things which reads to eternity; and that we are not downright bribed by our desire to better ourselves?
For such men as we are, it may possibly be better to be governed than to be
free; since greed and grasping, if let loose together against our neighbours, as
beasts out of den, would soon deluge the world evils.' I gave the general explanation that what eats up our modern characters is the indolence in which,
with few exceptions, we all now live, never working or undertaking work

save for the sake of praise or of pleasure, instead of that assistance to others which is a thing worthy of emulation and of honour.

'Best leave such things to take their chance,' and pass we to the next topic; this was to be the passions, about which I promised beforehand to write in a separate paper, inasmuch as they cover a side of the general subject of speech, and of sublimity in particular.

Translated by A. O. Prickard.

HORACE

Epistle to the Pisones

The Art of Poetry

About 20 B.C.

At the time he wrote this letter to the wealthy Piso family, Quintus Horatius Flaccus (65–8 B.C.) was regarded in Rome as the greatest living man of letters, a renowned and mature professional author. Assume that you are an aspiring young poet and that you are the recipient of this epistle. What would your reactions be? And do you think that Horace wants you to react in that way? For the tone of this letter is almost as important as the substance: some have characterized it as slick or cool. In the eighteenth century Alexander Pope described it as follows:

> *Horace still charms with graceful negligence,*
> *And without method talks us into sense;*
> *Will, like a friend, familiarly convey*
> *The truest notions in the easiest way.*

Whether Horace wrote without method is debatable, for, despite an apparent lack of organization, the work starts with the sketch of a mad painter and ends with one of a mad poet. His views on poetic inspiration as opposed to painstaking labor are crystal clear. He is full of professional wisdom and practical strategy; he knows the ropes. But is he cynical about literature; does he regard poetry as merely a marketable commodity? His remarks about some of the types that people the world of literature—the arrogant amateurs, the insincere critics—should be noted.

As a professional, Horace regards the audience as a primary source of value. Compare, for example, the bases for his discussion of character with those of Aristotle. Likewise, while Aristotle gives a history of tragedy in terms of the growth of its respective elements, Horace writes another kind of history, one based on the changing nature of the audiences. Three centuries after Aristotle, Horace passes along the Aristotelian observations regarding plot, but they are now rules: Aristotle's discussion of unity and of magnitude becomes Horace's explanation in terms of audience

84

response and the conventions of the time. Another important change to be noted is in the concept of imitation. For Horace, as for other Romans conscious of tradition, imitation means imitation of the Greek models. This interpretation, as you will see later, is to play an important part in future critical debate and form part of the Horatian tradition in English literary criticism.

SUPPOSE A PAINTER meant to attach a horse's neck to the head of a man, and to put fancy-work of many-colored feathers on limbs of creatures picked at random; the kind of thing where the torso of a shapely maiden merges into the dark rear half of a fish; would you smother your amusement, my friends, if you were let in to see the result?

Believe me, Pisones, a book will be very much like that painting if the meaningless images are put together like the dreams of a man in a fever, to the end that the head and the foot do not match the one body. *[there's a method to the madness]*

"Poets and painters have always enjoyed this fair privilege, of experimenting however they will." (10)[1]

I know it; and I claim that privilege as a poet and, as a poet, I grant it to the painter; but not to the extent that vicious creatures mate with gentle ones, that snakes are paired with birds, lambs with tigers.

When a poem has a pretentious introduction, promising great themes, a bright red patch or two is usually stitched on, to achieve an expansive, colorful effect, as when a sacred grove and an altar of Diana are described, or a hurrying rivulet of water wandering through the lovely meadows, or the river Rhine, or a rainbow. All very well; but there was no place for these scenes at this point in the poem.

And perhaps you know how to represent a cypress tree: what good is this when the client who has paid your fee in advance is swimming for his life in the picture from the wreckage of his ship? (20) I have started to mould a two-handled jar to hold wine: why does a pitcher come off the potter's turning wheel? What I am getting at is this: let the work of art be whatever you want, as long as it is simple and has unity.

To you, Piso senior, and to you sons worthy of your father, I admit that the majority of us poets are tricked by our own standards. I work hard to be brief; I turn out to be obscure. When I try to achieve smoothness and polish, I lose punch, the work lacks life; the poet who proposes grandeur is merely pompous; the poet who tries to be too conservative creeps on the ground, afraid of gusts of wind; if he is anxious to lend marvellous variety to a single subject, he paints a dolphin in the forest, a boar in the breakers. (30) The avoidance of mistakes leads to serious defects if one is lacking in artistic sense. The sculptor in the last studio around the [gladiatorial][2] school of *[too much "safety" leads to lack of creativity]*

---

[1] The numbers inserted in parentheses in the translation give the approximate location of every tenth line in the Latin text.

[2] Bracketed material is the translator's.

Aemilius will mould fingernails and imitate wavy hair in bronze, but the net effect of the work will be unfortunate because he will not know how to represent the whole. If I wanted to make a comparison, I would not care to be like him any more than to go through life with an ugly nose but good-looking otherwise, with dark eyes and dark hair.

If you plan to write, adopt material to match your talents, and think over carefully what burdens your shoulders will not carry and how strong they really are. When a writer's chosen material matches his powers, the flow of words will not fail nor will clarity and orderly arrangement. (40) This is the virtue and charm of such arrangement, unless I am mistaken: that one says now what ought to be said and puts off for later and leaves out a great deal for the present. The author of a poem that has been [asked for and] promised likes one thing and rejects another, is sensitive and careful in putting words together.

Again, you will have expressed yourself with distinction if a clever association gives an old word new meaning. If it turns out to be necessary to explain recent discoveries with new terms, you will be allowed to invent words never heard by the Cethegi in their loin-cloths; (50) and licence will be given if you exercise it with due restraint; and new words, recently invented, will win acceptance if they spring from a Greek source with a minor twist in meaning. For that matter, what will a Roman grant to Caecilius and Plautus that he takes away from Vergil and Varius? As for me, why should I be criticized if I add a few words to my vocabulary, when the language of Cato and Ennius enriched the speech of our fathers and produced new names for things? It has always been permissible, and always will be, to mint words stamped with the mark of contemporary coinage. (60)

As the forests change their foliage in the headlong flight of years, as the first leaves fall, so does the old crop of words pass away, and the newly born, like men in the bloom of their youth, come then to the prime of their vigor. We and our works are mortgaged to die. It may be that the land embraces Neptune and diverts the north wind from our navy, the engineering of a king; or a swamp, long unproductive, and good only for boating, now feeds nearby towns and feels the heavy burden of the plow; or it may be that a river, a ravager of fruitful fields, has changed its course, has been taught to follow a better channel: no matter, human accomplishments will pass away, much less does the status of speech endure and popular favor persist. Many things are resurrected which once had passed away, and expressions which are now respected in turn will pass, (70) if usage so decrees—the usage over which the authority and norm of daily speech have final jurisdiction.

The careers of kings and leaders, and sorrow-bringing battles: the meter in which to compose these, Homer has shown us. Laments were first expressed in couplets of unequal lines; later, sentiments of vows fulfilled were included [in this verse] as well. However, what author first published dainty elegiacs, the philologists are arguing, and up to now the dispute rests unresolved. A nasty temper armed Archilochus with his specialty, iambic lines; the sock of comedy and the elevated boot of tragedy took on this meter, (80) just the thing for on-stage conversation, to rise above the noisy audience and quite natural for relations of events. The Muse gave men of wealth and sons of gods, and the victor in the boxing ring and the horse first in the contest, and the heartaches of youth and relaxing wine, to lyric poetry to sing about.

The standard distinctions and overtones of poetic forms: why should I be addressed as a poet if I cannot observe and know nothing about them? Why should I, with a feeble sense of shame, prefer to be ignorant rather than learn them? A comic situation does not want to be treated in tragic verse forms; in the same way, the banquet of Thyestes repudiates a telling in the lines of everyday affairs, close to the level of comedy. (90)

Let each form of poetry occupy the proper place allotted to it.

There are times, however, when comedy raises its voice and an angry Chremes scolds in fury with his swollen cheeks; and, in tragedy, Telephus and Peleus very often express their pain in prose, when the penniless hero and the exile both project inflated lines and complicated compound words, if they are anxious to touch the hearts of the audience with their complaints of deep distress.

It is not enough for poems to be pretty; they must have charm and they must take the heart of the hearer wheresoever they will. (100) Just as the faces of men smile back at those who smile at them, so they join with those who weep. If you want me to weep, you must first feel sorrows yourself; then your misfortunes, Telephus or Peleus, hurt me, too. If you speak your lines badly, I'll go to sleep—or laugh out loud. Sad words fit a mournful face, words full of threats an angry face, playful words a face in fun, words seriously expressed, a sober face. I mean that Nature has already shaped us inwardly for every phase of fortune: fortune makes us happy, or drives us into anger or brings us down to earth with a burden of grief and then torments us. (110) Afterwards it brings out our emotions and our tongue acts as interpreter. If the lines do not correspond to the emotional state of the speaker, the members of the Roman audience will burst out laughing, regardless of their income bracket.

It will make a great deal of difference whether a comedy slave or a tragic hero is speaking, or a man of ripe old age, or a hothead in the flower of youth, or a great lady, or a worrying nursemaid, or a traveling merchant or the farmer of a few flourishing acres, a character from Colchis or an Assyrian, a native of Thebes or of Argos.

You have two choices: either follow the conventions of the stage or invent materials that are self-consistent.

If, as a writer, you happen to bring back on the stage an Achilles (120) whose honor has been satisfied, energetic, hotheaded, ruthless, eager, let him claim that laws were not made for him, that there is nothing not subject to possession by force. Let Medea be wild and untamed, Ino an object of pity and tears, Ixion treacherous, Io a wanderer, Orestes depressed.

If you risk anything new and original on the stage and have the courage to invent a new character, let it maintain to the very end the qualities with which it first appeared—and let it be self-consistent.

It is difficult to develop everyday themes in an original way, and you would do better to present the *Iliad* in dramatic form than if you (130) were the first to produce unknown materials never used before on stage. Material in the public domain will become your private property if you do not waste your time going around in worn-out circles, and do not be a literal translator, faithfully rendering word for word from Greek, and do not be merely an imitator, thereby getting yourself into a hole from which either good conscience, or the laws of the work itself, will forbid you to climb out.

Dont make promises at the start that you cant keep in the end

And do not start off like this, the way a cyclic poet once did: "I shall sing of the fate of Priam and a war of renown." What did this promise produce to match such a wide open mouth? The mountains will go into labor and deliver a silly mouse! How much more properly this poet began who undertook nothing in poor taste: (140) "Sing to me, Muse, of the man who, after the time of the capture of Troy, saw the ways of numbers of men and their cities." He gives thought to producing a light from the smoke, not smoke from the gleam of the firelight, so that he may bring forth beauty thereafter, and wonder, Antiphates and Scylla and with the Cyclops, Charybdis; nor does he in detail relate the return of Diomedes after the passing of Meleager, or the story of the Trojan War, starting with the twin eggs. He speeds always on to the outcome, and rushes his hearer into the midst of the action just as if the setting were known, and the events that he cannot hope to treat with brilliance, he omits. (150) And then, too, his inventions are such that fiction is mingled with fact to the end that the middle may match with the start and the end with the middle.

Listen to me: here is what I look for in a play, and with me, the public.

If you want a fan in the audience who waits for the final curtain and stays in his seat to the very end, when the singer says, "Give us a hand," you must observe the habits and manners of each period in men's lives, and the proper treatment must be given to their quickly changing characters and their years. The little boy who already knows how to talk plants his feet firmly on the ground, and is eager to play with boys of his own age, and loses his temper and for no good reason gets it back, and changes his disposition every hour. (160)

Characters behave in these generalized ways

The adolescent boy with no beard as yet, when [to his relief] he at last is on his own, has fun with hounds and horses and the turf of the sunny Campus, soft as wax to be moulded to folly, resentful of advice, slow to anticipate what is good for him, throwing his money around, high-spirited and eager, quick to change his interests.

The age of maturity brings a change of interests, and the manly character seeks influence and friends, becomes a slave to ambition and is wary of commitments that he will soon have to break off with great difficulty.

Many disagreeable circumstances surround the old man; for example, he still seeks for wealth, and poor fellow, shrinks from spending it, (170) or, again, his management of everything is over-cautious and without any fire, he is indecisive, hopeful without reason, slow to act, grasping for time, hard to get along with, always complaining, always praising the way things were when he was a boy, scolding and correcting the young generation. The years as they come bring with them many advantages, and as they go, take many things away.

Do not by any chance let the character of the elderly be assigned to a younger man, or a man to a boy; we shall always insist upon the qualities of character joined and fitted to the proper age of man.

An event is either acted on the stage or is reported as happening elsewhere. (180) Events arouse our thoughts more slowly when transmitted through the ears than when presented to the accuracy of the eye and reported to the spectator by himself. On the other hand, do not bring out on stage actions that should properly take place inside, and remove from view the many events which the descriptive powers of an actor present on the stage will soon relate. Do not have Medea butcher her sons before the audience, or have the ghoulish Atreus cook up human organs out in public, or Procne turn into a bird, Cadmus into a snake. If you show me anything of this kind, I will not be fooled and I shall resent it.

Do not let a play consist of less than five acts or be dragged out to more than this length, if you want it to enjoy popular demand and have a repeat performance. (190)

Do not have a god intervene unless the complication of the plot turns out to be appropriate to divine solution; and do not have a fourth leading character working hard to get in with his lines.

Have the chorus carry the part of an actor and take a manly role in the play, and do not let them sing anything between the acts which does not contribute to the plot and fit properly into it. The chorus should side with the good and give friendly advice, curb those who are angry and befriend those who fear to do wrong; the chorus should praise a dinner which has but few courses, healthy legal processes and law, and the conditions of peace when the gates of the city stand open; the chorus will keep secrets, entreat the gods and pray that good fortune will come back to the afflicted and desert the overconfident. (200)

The pipes (not, as now, displaced by the brass and their rival the trumpet, but slender in tone and simple, with only a few stops) used to be helpful in accompanying and supporting the chorus and in filling the auditorium (which was not, in those days, overcrowded) with its music—the audience in which the entire community gathered was then such as one could count, what with its small size; it was thrifty, moral and proper.

After the community began to win wars and extend its domain, and the walls of the city enclosed a wider area, and one's guardian spirit was appeased on holidays without reproach with wine in the daytime, (210) greater license in meters and modes came to the theater. This is to say: what critical sense could an ignorant community have when freed from work, the farmer mingling with the townsman, the commoner with the gentleman? And so the flute player added movement and display to the old-fashioned art and trailed his costume about on the platform. And so, again, they invented special notes for the once sober lyre, and the unrestrained speech of the chorus gave rise to a new kind of eloquence, wise in advice on matters of state, and its divine utterances of things to come were quite in the oracular manner of Delphic ambiguities.

The writer who entered the contest for a common goat (220) in tragic verse soon added rustic satyrs with scanty clothing, and crudely tried his hand at humor without loss of tragic dignity, for the reason that the member of the audience had to be kept in his seat by the enticements of novelties, because after taking part in the Bacchic rituals, he was drunk and rowdy. But it is expedient, nonetheless, to sanction the merry, impudent satyrs, to turn solemnity into jest, so that whatever god, whatever hero, may have been but now presented on the stage in gold and royal purple, shall not move into the slums; use vulgar speech, or, while avoiding the ground, grasp at verbal clouds and empty words. (230)

Tragedy is above spouting frivolous lines, like a modest matron told to dance on festive days; the [tragedy] will have little to do, as a respectable woman, with the boisterous satyrs.

As a writer of satyr-plays, my Pisones, I for one will not favor the commonplace and current nouns and verbs, and I shall not try to differ in vocabulary, from the speech that gives tragedy its color; it will make a difference whether Davus is speaking and the saucy Pythias who has swindled a talent out of Simo, or Silenus, the guardian and attendant of a divine foster child.

I shall follow a poetic style from well-known material, just the same as anyone may expect to do himself; (240) and just the same, if he tries it, he will perspire freely and make little progress: that's how difficult the order and connections of words are: that's how much distinction is attached to our everyday vocabulary.

Fauns imported from the woodlands, in my opinion, should be careful not to carouse around in polished lines, like boys reared at the four corners and practically brought up in the Forum, nor shout out dirty words, make scandalous remarks. I mean, they will offend members of the audience who have a house, a distinguished father, and wealth, who will not accept calmly and give the prize to entertainment that pleases the purchaser of dried peas and nuts. (250)

A long syllable following a short is called "iambic," a rapid foot; for this reason, it had the name "three-measure iambic" [trimeter] applied to itself although the beat, the same from first to last, adds up to six per line. Not so very long ago, so that the line might come to the ear more slowly and with a little more weight, the iambic shared its traditional privileges with the steady spondee, accommodating and tolerant, with the reservation that the iambic foot would not, as a partner, move out of its first and fourth position. The spondee, I may add, rarely appears in Accius' "noble" trimeters; and it burdens Ennius' verses, sent ponderously out on the stage, (260) with the charge of overhasty work and the lack of care and attention, or shameful neglect of the principles of art.

No critic whom you may name in Rome can see that a poem is unmusical; and Roman poets have been given unwarranted freedom. Because of that, am I to wander around and write free verse? Or am I to assume that everyone will see my mistakes and play it safe and stay cautiously within the limits of the license I may be granted? No; what I have been saying simply amounts to this: I have merely managed to escape criticism; I have not earned praise.

You—turn our Greek models in your hands at night, turn them in the daytime. But, you say, your forefathers praised the lives and jokes of Plautus; (270) they were much too tolerant of both; they admired him, if I may so, stupidly, assuming that you and I know how to tell the difference between expressions in poor and good taste, and have had enough experience to tell, on our fingers and by ear, when a sound has been produced according to the rules of meter.

Thespis is said to have discovered the form of tragic poetry and to have hauled his plays around on carts: plays sung and acted by those who had smeared their faces with sediment from wine jars.

After Thespis: the discoverer of the mask and colorful costume, Aeschylus, also constructed the stage on a limited scale, and taught how to speak in lofty style and to walk in the high boots of tragedy. (280)

After these came old comedy, not without considerable popular approval; but its freedom of speech fell off into license and a violence that deserved restraint by law: law was acknowledged and the chorus was disgraced into silence when its right to libel was removed.

Our Roman poets have not failed to try all forms of drama; they deserve no honor whatsoever for venturing to desert the trail blazed by the Greeks and attempting to give fame to Roman events—those who presented serious history or comedies of daily life. Nor would the land of the Latins be more mighty in valor and glory in war than in words, if the toil of time and polish did not discourage our poets, every one of them. (290) As for you, who represent the bloodline of Pompilius, see that you are severe in your censure of a poem that many a day and many an erasure has not trimmed down, and not corrected ten times by the test of a newly-cut fingernail.

Because Democritus believed natural talent to contribute more to success than pitiful technical competence, he barred from Helicon all poets who were mentally well-balanced; most poets do not bother to trim their nails, their beards, they look for out-of-the-way places, steer clear of the baths. I mean, one will acquire the title of poet and the reputation, if he never entrusts his head—too crazy to be cured by medicine even from three Anticyras—to Licinus the barber. (300)

Oh, how inept I am! I have myself purged of bile as the spring season comes on! Otherwise no man could write a better poem. But it isn't worth the trouble. I'll play the role of whetstone, which is good enough to put an edge on iron but is out of luck when it comes to cutting. While I write nothing myself, I'll teach the gift, the business of the poet, where he gets his material, what nourishes and forms the poet, what is appropriate, the way of right and wrong.

The origin and source of poetry is the wisdom to write according to moral principles: the Socratic dialogues will be able to clarify your

philosophy, (310) and the words themselves will freely follow the philosophy, once it has been seen before you write. The man who has learned what
he owes to his country, what he owes to his friends, what love is due a father,
how a brother and a family friend are loved, what the duties of a senator are,
what the duties of a judge, what roles a leader sent to war should play: he
knows, as a matter of course, how to assign to each character what is appropriate for it.

I shall tell you to respect the examples of life and of good character—you who have learned the art of imitation—and from this source bring
forth lines that live. Quite often a play which is impressive in spots and portrays good character, but with no particular charm, without real content and
really good writing (320) will give the public more pleasure and hold them
better than lines without ideas and with resounding platitudes.

To the Greeks, genius, the gift of speaking in well-rounded phrases—
these the Muse presented. The Greeks are greedy for nothing save acclaim. The
Roman boys learn to calculate percentages of money by long divison. "Let the
son of Albinus tell me: if one-twelfth is taken from five-twelfths, what's the remainder? You should have been able to tell us by this time." "One-third." "Très
bien! You'll make a good businessman. Add a twelfth, what happens?" "One-
half." (330) When this smut, this worrying about business arithmetic, has permeated our minds, do you think we can expect to put together poems to be
treated with oil of cedar and kept in cypress-wood cases?

Poets aim either to help or to amuse the reader, or to say what is pleasant
and at the same time what is suitable. Whatever you have in the way of a lesson, make it short, so that impressionable minds can quickly grasp your
words and hold them faithfully: every unnecessary word spills over and is
lost to a heart that is already filled up to the brim.

Whatever you invent to please, see that it is close to truth, so your play
does not require belief in anything it wants; do not have it pull a living child
from Lamia's insides just after she has eaten lunch. (340)

The centuries of elders in the audience cannot stand a play that has no
moral; the noble young gentlemen ignore an austere composition; but the
writer who has combined the pleasant with the useful [miscuit utile dulci]
wins on all points, by delighting the reader while he gives advice. This kind
of book makes money for the Sosii [publishers], this kind of book is sold
across the sea and prolongs the famous writer's age.

There are, however, faults which I should like to overlook: I mean that
the string, when plucked, does not give forth the sound that heart and hand
desire; it very often gives back a high note when one calls for a low; and the
arrow does not always hit precisely the mark at which it aimed and threatened. (350) So, when most of the passages are brilliant, I am personally not
bothered by blots, which are spattered here and there by oversight or those
which human nature failed to guard against enough.

Well, what's the point?

If a library copyist keeps on making the same mistake, even though he
has been warned about it, there is no excuse for him, and a lyre player who

always strikes the same sour note is laughed at; so a writer who is consistently sloppy is in a class with Choerilus—you know who I mean—whom I regard with amused admiration if he happens to write two or three good passages. Similarly, I think it's too bad whenever good old Homer dozes off, as he does from time to time, but when all is said and done, it is natural enough for drowsiness to creep up on a long job of writing. (360) A poem is like a painting: you will find a picture which will attract you more if you stand up close, another if you stand farther back. This picture favors shadow, another likes to be viewed in the light—neither has apprehensions about the keen perceptions of the good critic. Here's one that pleases you only once; here's another that you'll like if you come back to it ten times.

And now to address the older of the two of you: ah, even though your tastes have been formed to appreciate the right things by your father (as well as by others), and you have much good sense of your own, acknowledge what I am going to say and remember it: perfectly proper concessions are made to second-raters in certain fields. A second-rate legal authority and member of the bar (370) can be far from having the qualities of Messala, a very able speaker, and not be as learned as Cascellius Aulus, but still he has a certain value—*a second-rate poet gets no advertising posters from either men, gods, or booksellers.*

You know how music off-key grates on your nerves at an otherwise pleasant banquet, and greasy ointment for your hair, and bitter honey from Sardinia mixed with poppy seeds, because the banquet could be carried on without them. That is how it is with poetry: created and developed to give joy to human hearts; but if it takes one step down from the very highest point of merit, it slides all the way back to the bottom.

The lad who does not know how to take part in sports keeps out of the cavalry exercises in the Campus; and if he has not learned how to work with the ball, the disc or the hoop (380)—he sits where he is because he is afraid that the spectators, jammed together, will laugh at his expense—there will be nothing he can do about it. For all of that, the man who has no notion of how to compose poetry has the nerve to go ahead anyhow. Why shouldn't he? After all, he's a free man and born free and what's more to the point, his income is in the top brackets—which puts him beyond criticism.

As for you, my boy, don't do or say anything that Minerva would not approve: that's your standard of judgment, that's your philosophy. However, if you ever do write something, see that it comes into court—to the ears of Maecius as critic, or your father's, or mine, and also see that it is weighted down in storage, put away between the leaves of parchment for revision in the ninth year; you can always edit what you haven't published: the word that is uttered knows no return. (390)

Orpheus, a holy man and spokesman for the gods, forced the wild men of the woods to give up human killing and gruesome feasting; he is said, because of these powers, to soothe tigers and the raging of the lion; yes and Amphion, the builder of the city of Thebes, is said to move rocks with his lyre and with the softness of song to lead them where he will.

I will tell you what was once the poet's wisdom: to decide what were public and what were private suits at law, to say what was sacred and what was not, to enjoin from sexual license, provide a code of conduct for marriage, to build up towns, and carve the laws on wooden tablets. This was the way honor and renown came to god-like poet-preachers and their songs. (400)

After these, Homer gained renown, and Tyrtaeus with his verses whetted the spirits of males for Mars and war; oracles were given in the form of poems and the way of life was shown; the favor of kings was sought in Pierian strains; and dramatic festivals were invented and thus the end of a long task [of development]—in case the Muse in her lyric artistry and Apollo with his song embarrass you.

The question has been asked: is good poetry created by nature or by training?

Personally, I cannot see what good enthusiasm is or uncultivated talent without a rich vein of genius; (410) each requires the help of the other and forms a friendly compact. The would-be poet whose passion is to reach the hoped-for goal in this race for fame, has worked hard in boyhood and endured a great deal, has sweated and shivered, abstained from women and wine; the artist who plays the pipe at the Pythian games has first learned his art and lived in terror of a teacher. Nowadays it's enough to have said, "I beat out wonderful poems; the hell with the rest of the mob; it's a dirty deal for me to be left at the starting line and admit that I obviously don't know what I never learned."

Like a huckster who collects a crowd to buy his wares, the poet with his wealth in land, with wealth resting on coin put out at interest, tells yes-men to come to his readings for gain. (420) Yes, indeed; if there is a man who can set out a really fat banquet, and co-sign notes for irresponsible paupers, and save the neck of the client tangled in a murder trial, I'll be surprised if, for all his wealth, he can tell the difference between a liar and an honest friend! Whether you have already given someone a present or only expect to do so, don't let him near your verses when he's full of joy: I mean, he'll gush "Lovely! Great! Swell!" On top of this, he'll turn pale, he'll even squeeze drops of dew from sympathetic eyes, leap to his feet and stamp on the ground. (430)

The way hired mourners wail at a funeral and—so they say—carry on more painfully than those who sorrow quite sincerely, thus the critic with his tongue in cheek is more deeply moved than the ordinary flatterer. Rich men are said to keep pushing glasses of wine at, and to torment with wine poured straight, the man whom they are trying hard to see through—to see if he is worthy of friendship. If you will put together poems, motives disguised with a foxy expression will never deceive you.

If you were to read anything to Quintilius, "Change this, please," he kept saying, "and this." If you said you couldn't do better, you'd tried twice, three times, with no success, (440) Quintilius used to say to rub it out and put back on the anvil the lines that were spoiled on the lathe. If you preferred to defend your mistake, not revise it, he would not waste another word or go to more useless trouble to keep you from being your only friend, with no competitors.

A true critic and a wise one will scold you for weak lines, blame you for rough ones, he'll indicate unpolished lines with a black cross-mark made with his pen, he'll cut out pretentious embellishments, make you clarify obscure phrases, remove ambiguities, mark things to be changed, he'll turn into an Aristarchus, and he will not say, "Why should I hurt the feelings of a friend over these trifles?" (450) Well, these trifles will get you into serious trouble once you have been laughed down and given a poor reception.

As in the case of a man with a bad attack of the itch or inflammation of the liver or one who's offended Diana—he's moon-struck—everyone with any sense is afraid to touch the madman and keeps out of the way of the poet; small boys pester him and don't know any better than to follow him around. If, while burping out his lines and thinking they're sublime, he goes off the roadway, falls into an excavation or a well, like a hunter intent on his blackbirds—he can yell so you can hear him a mile away, "Help! Hey, neighbors!"—no one would be worried about fishing him out. (460) If someone should get excited about rescuing him and let down a rope, I'll say, "How do you know that he didn't do it on purpose when he threw himself down there, and doesn't want to be rescued?" And I'll tell the story about the death of the Sicilian poet.

While he had a yearning to be regarded as an immortal god, Empedocles was cool enough to jump down into the red-hot crater of Aetna. Let poets have the right to perish; issue them a license! When you rescue a man against his will, you do the same as kill him. This isn't the first time he's done it, either; and if he's hauled out, he still won't behave like a human and give up his love of dying for publicity. And it isn't very clear, either, why he keeps on grinding out his verses, (470) whether he's used his father's funeral urn as a pisspot or whether he's tampered with the boundary markers of a holy plot of ground—an act of sacrilege. He's crazy, that's sure; and like a bear that's powerful enough to break the bars at the front of his cage, this dedicated elocutionist puts to flight the scholar and the layman without discrimination. Yes, and when he catches one, he'll hold on to him and recite him to death. You can be sure he won't let go of the hide of his victim until he's as full of blood as a leech.

Translated by Norman J. DeWitt.

DANTE ALIGHIERI

From the *Letter to Can Grande della Scalla*

1314

In the European Middle Ages, literacy began and ended with the study of the Bible, making biblical exegesis central to theories of reading and literature. According to church doctrine and custom dating back at least to St. Augustine in the sixth century, the Bible—particularly the Old Testament—was meant to be read and interpreted on multiple levels simultaneously. As well as documenting the literal history of the Hebrew people, the Old Testament was believed to prefigure events in the life of Christ and to contain metaphorical and spiritual truths that unlocked religious mysteries for Christians and helped them to lead righteous lives. Thus a single passage of the Bible was understood only when all of its various meanings were known in a single grasp. Because this type of biblical analysis was the centerpiece of medieval semiotics, it is likely that such an interpretive method made the theories of poet Dante Alighieri (1265–1321) more readily accessible to his original audience than to today's readers.

Dante has long been regarded as among the most influential poets of the late Middle Ages. Born and educated in Florence, he lived much of his adult life in political exile, writing on both secular and religious themes. His best-known work, the Comedy (now more usually called the Divine Comedy), is a masterpiece of form and style and the age's best-known expression of Christian sentiment. Since it was important to the poet that the full levels of meaning of his masterwork be understood, he set out to explain his method in a letter to his patron Can Grande della Scalla accompanying Paradiso, the third and final volume of the Comedy. In addition to advocating a polysemous reading strategy (that is, one referring simultaneously to more than one sense of meaning), this letter classifies the work as to its form, genre, and relationship to practical philosophy.

Dante was well trained in the tradition of medieval semiotics and would have learned young this predominant method for reading and interpreting the Bible. (Note his use of biblical examples to clarify his argument.) His literary theory explicitly extends a fourfold interpretive method from sacred to secular texts. Thus, following St.

Augustine, Dante breaks interpretation down into two basic levels—the literal and the allegorical (Augustine used the term spiritual*)—with the latter being further subdivided into three subcategories. Furthermore, the poet takes pains to explain the stylistic and formal divisions of the* Comedy *and the place of the* Paradiso *within it. His analysis, relying heavily on division and classification and the precise definition of terms, places Dante in the classical tradition of Aristotle.*

5. AS THE PHILOSOPHER says in the second book of the *Metaphysics*, "As a thing is with respect to being, so it is with respect to truth";[1] and the reason for this is that the truth concerning a thing, which consists in the truth as its subject, is the perfect image of the thing as it is. And so, of all things which have being, some are such that they have absolute being in themselves, others such that their being is dependent upon a relationship with something else: they exist at the same time with something which is their correlative, as is the case with father and son, master and servant, double and half, the whole and the parts, and many other such things. Because such things depend for their being upon another thing, it follows that their truth would depend upon the truth of the other; not knowing the "half," its "double" could not be understood, and so with the other cases.

6. Therefore, if one should wish to present an introduction to a part of a work, it is necessary to present some conception of the whole work of which it is a part. For this reason I, who wish to present something in the form of an introduction to the above-mentioned part of the whole *Comedy*,[2] have decided to preface it with some discussion of the whole work, in order to make the approach to the part easier and more complete. There are six questions, then, which should be asked at the beginning about any doctrinal work: what is its subject, its form, its agent, its end, the title of the book, and its branch of philosophy. In three cases the answers to these questions will be different for the part of the work I propose to give you than for the whole, that is, in the cases of its subject, form, and title, while in the other three, as will be clear upon inspection, they will be the same. Thus these first three should be specifically asked in a discussion of the whole work, after which the way will be clear for an introduction to the part. Let us, then, ask the last three questions not only about the whole but also about the offered part itself.

7. For the clarification of what I am going to say, then, it should be understood that there is not just a single sense in this work: it might rather be called *polysemous*, that is, having several senses. For the first sense is that which is contained in the letter, while there is another which is contained in what is signified by the letter. The first is called literal, while the second is called allegorical, or moral or anagogical. And in order to make this manner of treatment clear, it can be applied to the following verses: "When Israel

[1] Aristotle, *Metaphysics* 2.1. [Tr.]
[2] His *Divine Comedy*.

went out of Egypt, the house of Jacob from a barbarous people, Judea was made his sanctuary, Israel his dominion."[3] Now if we look at the letter alone, what is signified to us is the departure of the sons of Israel from Egypt during the time of Moses; if at the allegory, what is signified to us is our redemption through Christ; if at the moral sense, what is signified to us is the conversion of the soul from the sorrow and misery of sin to the state of grace; if at the anagogical, what is signified to us is the departure of the sanctified soul from bondage to the corruption of this world into the freedom of eternal glory. And although these mystical senses are called by various names, they may all be called allegorical, since they are all different from the literal or historical. For allegory is derived from the Greek *alleon,* which means in Latin *alienus* ("belonging to another") or *diversus* ("different").

8. This being established, it is clear that the subject about which these two senses play must also be twofold. And thus it should first be noted what the subject of the work is when taken according to the letter, and then what its subject is when understood allegorically. The subject of the whole work, then, taken literally, is the state of souls after death, understood in a simple sense; for the movement of the whole work turns upon this and about this. If on the other hand the work is taken allegorically, the subject is man, in the exercise of his free will, earning or becoming liable to the rewards or punishments of justice.

9. And the form is twofold: the form of the treatise and the form of the treatment. The form of the treatise is threefold, according to its three kinds of divisions. The first division is that which divides the whole work into three canticles. The second is that which divides each canticle into cantos. The third, that which divides the cantos into rhymed units. The form or manner of treatment is poetic, fictive, descriptive, digressive, and transumptive, and it as well consists in definition, division, proof, refutation, and the giving of examples.

10. The title of the work is, "Here begins the Comedy of Dante Alighieri, a Florentine by birth but not in character." To understand the title, it must be known that comedy is derived from *comos,* "a village," and from *oda,* "a song," so that a comedy is, so to speak, "a rustic song." Comedy, then, is a certain genre of poetic narrative differing from all others. For it differs from tragedy in its matter, in that tragedy is tranquil and conducive to wonder at the beginning, but foul and conducive to horror at the end, or catastrophe, for which reason it is derived from *tragos,* meaning "goat," and *oda,* making it, as it were, a "goat song," that is, foul as a goat is foul. This is evident in Seneca's tragedies. Comedy, on the other hand, introduces a situation of adversity, but ends its matter in prosperity, as is evident in Terence's comedies. And for this reason some writers have the custom of saying in their salutations, by way of greeting, "a tragic beginning and a comic ending to you." And, as well, they differ in their manner of speaking. Tragedy uses an elevated and sublime style, while comedy uses an unstudied and low style,

---

[3] Psalm 113:1–2 (114:1–2 in the King James version). [Tr.]

which is what Horace implies in the *Art of Poetry* where he allows comic writers occasionally to speak like the tragic, and also the reverse of this:

> Yet sometimes even comedy elevates its voice,
> and angry Chremes rages in swelling tones;
> and in tragedy Telephus and Peleus often lament
> in prosaic speeches. . . .[4]

So from this it should be clear why the present work is called the *Comedy*. For, if we consider the matter, it is, at the beginning, that is, in Hell, foul and conducive to horror, but at the end, in Paradise, prosperous, conducive to pleasure, and welcome. And if we consider the manner of speaking, it is unstudied and low, since its speech is the vernacular, in which even women communicate. There are, besides these, other genres of poetic narrative, such as pastoral verse, elegy, satire, and the hymn of thanksgiving, as could also be gathered from Horace in his *Art of Poetry*. But there is no purpose to discussing these at this time.

11. Now it can be explained in what manner the part I have offered you may be assigned a subject. For if the subject of the whole work, on the literal level, is the state of souls after death, in an absolute, not in a restricted sense, then the subject of this part is the same state, but restricted to the state of blessed souls after death. And if the subject of the whole work, considered allegorically, is man, through exercise of free will, earning or becoming liable to the rewards or punishments of justice, then it is evident that the subject in this part is restricted to man's becoming eligible, to the extent he has earned them, for the rewards of justice.

12. And in the same manner the form of this part follows from the form ascribed to the whole. For if the form of the whole treatise is threefold, then the form in this part is twofold, that is, the division into cantos and into rhymed units. This part could not have the first division as its form, since this part itself is [a product][5] of the first division.

13. The title of the book also follows; for while the title of the whole book is, as was said earlier, "Here begins the Comedy, etc.," the title of this part is, "Here begins the third canticle of Dante's *Comedy*, etc., which is called *Paradise*."

14. Having settled these three questions, where the answer was different for the part than for the whole, it remains to deal with the other three, where the answers will not be different for either the part or the whole. The agent, then, in the whole and in the part, is he who has been mentioned above; and he is clearly so throughout.

15. The end of the whole and of the part could be multiple, that is, both immediate and ultimate. But, without going into details, it can be briefly stated that the end of the whole as of the part is to remove those living in this life from the state of misery and to lead them to the state of happiness.

[4] Horace, *Art of Poetry*, lines 93–96. [Tr.]
[5] Bracketed material is the translator's.

16. The branch of philosophy which determines the procedure of the work as a whole and in this part is moral philosophy, or ethics, inasmuch as the whole and this part have been conceived for the sake of practical results, not for the sake of speculation. So even if some parts or passages are treated in the manner of speculative philosophy, this is not for the sake of the theory, but for a practical purpose, following that principle which the Philosopher advances in the second book of the *Metaphysics*, that "practical men sometimes speculate about things in their particular and temporal relations."[6]

Translated by Robert S. Haller.

directing the speculation of those who would venture to do so

---

[6] Aristotle, *Metaphysics* 2.1. [Ed.]

SIR PHILIP SIDNEY

An Apology for Poetry[1]

1595

Sir Philip Sidney (1554–1586) slips into his defense of poetry casually, almost apologetically (but contrast this tone to the vigorous eloquence of the conclusion): an anecdote, a story that makes its point indirectly. That is how many stories work, by conveying their moral truths artistically. That poetry delights us even Plato had granted—the pleasure it provides is, in fact, one source of its danger—but Sidney's purpose is to show that it is a better teacher than moral philosophy or history; he attempts to prove that poetry is the very best agent for leading men to act virtuously. But why must men be taught to act virtuously? Sidney's psychological model is the Christian concept of fallen man, possessed of an "erected wit" and an "infected will." In one sense the essay may be regarded as a treatise on educational psychology, for to "move men to virtuous action" is to motivate them to be better than they are. In Sidney's curriculum, neither philosophy nor history can do what poetry does, since poetry combines the precepts of one with the examples of the other, and in addition uses all the pleasurable devices of art to make instruction palatable.

Sidney ranges widely over history for evidence to support his case. In so doing he expands his definition of poetry beyond mere "rhyming and versing," although these too are justified on the grounds of their educational benefits; finally among the ranks of poets he welcomes the historian Herodotus and even Plato, the enemy of poets. What Sidney means by poetry, eventually, is a concept worth examining. It is also instructive to note how Sidney responds to Plato's argument that poetry injures man's moral character. Does he answer Plato's charges or does he shift the terms of the argument?

Like other Renaissance critics, Sidney draws heavily from classical sources; thus, for example, his formal definition of poetry as a speaking picture echoes Horace. (Incidentally, you might consider why this definition is withheld until well into the

---

[1] "An Apology for Poetry," from *Criticism: The Major Texts* by Walter Jackson Bate. Written probably in 1583, and first published in 1595 in two slightly different versions: the *Defense of Poesie* (printed by Ponsonby) and the *Apologie for Poetrie* (printed by Olney). The latter text is used here, and the spelling has been modernized. All the footnotes are Bate's.

essay.) In this same definition, Sidney also cites Aristotle, but in a way that might make Aristotle question the legitimacy of the allusion.

WHEN THE RIGHT virtuous Edward Wotton and I were at the Emperor's Court together, we gave ourselves to learn horsemanship of John Pietro Pugliano, one that with great commendation had the place of an esquire in his stable. And he, according to the fertileness of the Italian wit, did not only afford us the demonstration of his practice, but sought to enrich our minds with the contemplations therein which he thought most precious. But with none I remember mine ears were at any time more loaden, than when (either angered with slow payment, or moved with our learner-like admiration) he exercised his speech in the praise of his faculty. He said, soldiers were the noblest estate of mankind, and horsemen the noblest of soldiers. He said they were the masters of war and ornaments of peace; speedy goers and strong abiders; triumphers both in camps and courts. Nay, to so unbelieved a point he proceeded, as that no earthly thing bred such wonder to a prince as to be a good horseman. Skill of government was but a *pedanteria*[2] in comparison. Then would he add certain praises, by telling what a peerless beast a horse was, the only serviceable courtier without flattery, the beast of most beauty, faithfulness, courage, and such more, that, if I had not been a piece of a logician before I came to him, I think he would have persuaded me to have wished myself a horse. But thus much at least with his no few words he drove into me, that self-love is better than any gilding to make that seem gorgeous wherein ourselves are parties. Wherein, if Pugliano's strong affection and weak arguments will not satisfy you, I will give you a nearer example of myself, who (I know not by what mischance) in these my not old years and idlest times having slipped into the title of a poet, am provoked to say something unto you in the defence of that my unelected vocation, which if I handle with more good will than good reasons, bear with me, since the scholar is to be pardoned that followeth the steps of his master. And yet I must say that, as I have just cause to make a pitiful defence of poor Poetry, which from almost the highest estimation of learning is fallen to be the laughing-stock of children, so have I need to bring some more available proofs, since the former is by no man barred of his deserved credit, the silly latter hath had even the names of philosophers used to the defacing of it, with great danger of civil war among the Muses.

And first, truly, to all them that professing learning inveigh against Poetry may justly be objected, that they go very near to ungratefulness, to seek to deface that which, in the noblest nations and languages that are known, hath been the first light-giver to ignorance, and first nurse, whose milk by little and little enabled them to feed afterwards of tougher knowledges. And will they now play the hedgehog that, being received into the den, drove out

---

[2] That is, mere pedantry, or schoolbook knowledge, in comparison.

his host, or rather the vipers, that with their birth kill their parents? Let learned Greece in any of her manifold sciences be able to show me one book before Musaeus, Homer, and Hesiod, all three nothing else but poets. Nay, let any history be brought that can say any writers were there before them, if they were not men of the same skill, as Orpheus, Linus, and some other are named, who, having been the first of that country that made pens deliverers of their knowledge to their posterity, may justly challenge to be called their fathers in learning, for not only in time they had this priority (although in itself antiquity be venerable) but went before them, as causes to draw with their charming sweetness the wild untamed wits to an admiration of knowledge, so, as Amphion was said to move stones with his poetry to build Thebes, and Orpheus to be listened to by beasts—indeed stony and beastly people. So among the Romans were Livius Andronicus, and Ennius. So in the Italian language the first that made it aspire to be a treasure-house of Science were the poets Dante, Boccaccio, and Petrarch. So in our English were Gower and Chaucer.

After whom, encouraged and delighted with their excellent foregoing, others have followed, to beautify our mother tongue, as well in the same kind as in other arts. This did so notably show itself, that the philosophers of Greece durst not a long time appear to the world but under the masks of poets. So Thales, Empedocles, and Parmenides sang their natural philosophy in verses; so did Pythagoras and Phocylides their moral counsels; so did Tyrtaeus in war matters, and Solon in matters of policy: or rather, they, being poets, did exercise their delightful vein in those points of highest knowledge, which before them lay hid to the world. For that wise Solon was directly a poet it is manifest, having written in verse the notable fable of the Atlantic Island, which was continued by Plato.

And truly, even Plato, whosoever well considereth shall find that in the body of his work, though the inside and strength were Philosophy, the skin as it were and beauty depended most of Poetry: for all standeth upon dialogues, wherein he feigneth many honest burgesses of Athens to speak of such matters, that, if they had been set on the rack, they would never have confessed them, besides his poetical describing the circumstances of their meetings, as the well ordering of a banquet, the delicacy of a walk, with interlacing mere tales, as Gyges' Ring, and others, which who knoweth not to be flowers of poetry did never walk into Apollo's garden.

And even historiographers (although their lips sound of things done, and verity be written in their foreheads) have been glad to borrow both fashion and perchance weight of poets. So Herodotus entitled his history by the name of the nine Muses; and both he and all the rest that followed him either stole or usurped of Poetry their passionate describing of passions, the many particularities of battles, which no man could affirm, or, if that be denied me, long orations put in the mouths of great kings and captains, which it is certain they never pronounced. So that, truly, neither philosopher nor historiographer could at the first have entered into the gates of popular judgements, if they had not taken a great passport of Poetry, which in all nations at this day, where learning flourisheth not, is plain to be seen, in all which they have some feeling of poetry. In Turkey, besides their law-giving divines, they have no other writers but poets. In our neighbour country Ireland, where truly learning goeth very bare, yet are their poets held in a devout reverence. Even among the most barbarous and simple Indians where no writing is, yet have they their poets, who make and sing songs, which they call *Areytos*, both of their ancestors' deeds and praises of their gods—a sufficient probability that, if ever learning come among them, it must be by having their hard dull wits softened and sharpened with the sweet delights of Poetry. For until they find a pleasure in the exercises of the mind, great promises of much knowledge will little persuade them that know not the fruits of knowledge. In Wales, the true remnant of the ancient Britons, as there are good authorities to show the long time they had poets, which they called bards, so through all the conquests of Romans, Saxons, Danes, and Normans, some of whom did seek to ruin all memory of learning from among them, yet do their poets, even to this day, last; so as it is not more notable in soon beginning than in long continuing. But since the authors of most of our sciences were the Romans, and before them the Greeks, let us a little stand upon their authorities, but even so far as to see what names they have given unto this now scorned skill.

Among the Romans a poet was called *Vates*, which is as much as a diviner, foreseer, or prophet, as by his conjoined words *vaticinium* and *vaticinari* is manifest: so heavenly a title did that excellent people bestow upon this heart-ravishing knowledge. And so far were they carried into the admiration thereof, that they thought in the chanceable hitting upon any such verses great foretokens of their following fortunes were placed. Whereupon grew the word of *Sortes Virgilianae*, when, by sudden opening Virgil's book, they lighted upon any verse of his making: whereof the histories of the emperors' lives are full, as of Albinus, the governor of our island, who in his childhood met with this verse,

Arma amens capio nec sat rationis in armis.[3]

and in his age performed it: which, although it were a very vain and godless superstition, as also it was to think that spirits were commanded by such verses—whereupon this word charms, derived of *carmina*, cometh—so yet serveth it to show the great reverence those wits were held in. And altogether not without ground, since both the Oracles of Delphos and Sybilla's prophecies were wholly delivered in verses. For that same exquisite observing of number and measure in words, and that high flying liberty of conceit proper to the poet, did seem to have some divine force in it.

And may not I presume a little further, to show the reasonableness of this word *Vates*, and say that the holy David's Psalms are a divine poem? If I do, I shall not do it without the testimony of great learned men, both ancient and modern. But even the name Psalms will speak for me, which, being interpreted, is nothing but Songs; then that it is fully written in metre, as all

[3] I seize upon arms, while frenzied; nor is there enough reason for arms (*Aeneid*, II, 314).

learned Hebricians agree, although the rules be not yet fully found; lastly and principally, his handling his prophecy, which is merely poetical. For what else is the awaking his musical instruments, the often and free changing of persons, his notable *prosopopeias,* when he maketh you, as it were, see God coming in His majesty, his telling of the beasts' joyfulness, and hills' leaping, but a heavenly poesy, wherein almost he showeth himself a passionate lover of that unspeakable and everlasting beauty to be seen by the eyes of the mind, only cleared by faith? But truly now having named him, I fear me I seem to profane that holy name, applying it to Poetry, which is among us thrown down to so ridiculous an estimation. But they that with quiet judgements will look a little deeper into it, shall find the end and working of it such, as, being rightly applied, deserveth not to be scourged out of the Church of God.

But now, let us see how the Greeks named it, and how they deemed of it. The Greeks called him "a poet," which name hath, as the most excellent, gone through other languages. It cometh of this word *Poiein,* which is "to make": wherein, I know not whether by luck or wisdom, we Englishmen have met with the Greeks in calling him "a maker": which name, how high and incomparable a title it is, I had rather were known by marking the scope of other sciences than by my partial allegation.

There is no art delivered to mankind that hath not the works of Nature for his principal object, without which they could not consist, and on which they so depend, as they become actors and players, as it were, of what Nature will have set forth. So doth the astronomer look upon the stars, and, by that he seeth, setteth down what order Nature hath taken therein. So do the geometrician and arithmetician in their diverse sorts of quantities. So doth the musician in times tell you which by nature agree, which not. The natural philosopher thereon hath his name, and the moral philosopher standeth upon the natural virtues, vices, and passions of man; and "follow Nature" (saith he) "therein, and thou shalt not err." The lawyer saith what men have determined; the historian what men have done. The grammarian speaketh only of the rules of speech; and the rhetorician and logician, considering what in Nature will soonest prove and persuade, thereon give artificial rules, which still are compassed within the circle of a question according to the proposed matter. The physician weigheth the nature of a man's body, and the nature of things helpful or hurtful unto it. And the metaphysic, though it be in the second and abstract notions, and therefore be counted supernatural, yet doth he indeed build upon the depth of Nature. Only the poet, disdaining to be tied to any such subjection, lifted up with the vigour of his own invention, doth grow in effect another nature, in making things either better than Nature bringeth forth, or, quite anew, forms such as never were in Nature, as the Heroes, Demigods, Cyclopes, Chimeras, Furies, and such like: so as he goeth hand in hand with Nature, not enclosed within the narrow warrant of her gifts, but freely ranging only within the zodiac of his own wit.

⌣ 4 Use of personification.   Only the poet "grows" another nature

Nature never set forth the earth in so rich tapestry as divers poets have done—neither with pleasant rivers, fruitful trees, sweet-smelling flowers, nor whatsoever else may make the too much loved earth more lovely. Her world is brazen, the poets only deliver a golden. But let those things alone, and go to man—for whom as the other things are, so it seemeth in him her uttermost cunning is employed—and know whether she have brought forth so true a lover as Theagenes, so constant a friend as Pylades, so valiant a man as Orlando, so right a prince as Xenophon's Cyrus, so excellent a man every way as Virgil's Aeneas. Neither let this be jestingly conceived, because the works of the one be essential, the other in imitation or fiction; for any understanding knoweth the skill of the artificer standeth in that idea or foreconceit of the work, and not in the work itself. And that the poet hath that idea is manifest, by delivering them forth in such excellency as he hath imagined them. Which delivering forth also is not wholly imaginative as, we are wont to say by them that build castles in the air: but so far substantially it worketh, not only to make a Cyrus, which had been but a particular excellency, as Nature might have done, but to bestow a Cyrus upon the world, to make many Cyruses, if they will learn aright why and how that maker made him.

Neither let it be deemed too saucy a comparison to balance the highest point of man's wit with the efficacy of Nature; but rather give right honour to the heavenly Maker of that maker, who, having made man to His own likeness, set him beyond and over all the works of that second nature: which in nothing he showeth so much as in Poetry, when with the force of a divine breath he bringeth things forth far surpassing her doings, with no small argument to the incredulous of that first accursed fall of Adam, since our erected wit maketh us know what perfection is, and yet our infected will keepeth us from reaching unto it. But these arguments will by few be understood, and by fewer granted. Thus much (I hope) will be given me, that the Greeks with some probability of reason gave him the name above all names of learning. Now let us go to a more ordinary opening of him, that the truth may be more palpable: and so I hope, though we get not so unmatched a praise as the etymology of his names will grant, yet his very description, which no man will deny, shall not justly be barred from a principal commendation.

Poesy therefore is an art of imitation, for so Aristotle termeth it in his word *Mimesis*, that is to say, a representing, counterfeiting, or figuring forth—to speak metaphorically, a speaking picture; with this end, to teach and delight. Of this have been three several kinds. The chief, both in antiquity and excellency, were they that did imitate the inconceivable excellencies of God. Such were David in his Psalms; Solomon in his Song of Songs, in his Ecclesiastes, and Proverbs; Moses and Deborah in their Hymns; and the writer of Job, which, beside other, the learned Emanuel Tremellius and Franciscus Junius do entitle the poetical part of the Scripture. Against these none will speak that hath the Holy Ghost in due holy reverence.

In this kind, though in a full wrong divinity, were Orpheus, Amphion, Homer in his Hymns, and many other; both Greeks and Romans, and this poesy must be used by whosoever will follow St. James's counsel in singing psalms when they are merry, and I know is used with the fruit of comfort by some, when, in sorrowful pangs of their death-bringing sins, they find the consolation of the never-leaving goodness.

The second kind is of them that deal with matters philosophical: either moral, as Tyrtaeus, Phocylides, and Cato; or natural, as Lucretius and Virgil's Georgics; or astronomical, as Manilius and Pontanus; or historical, as Lucan; which who mislike, the fault is in their judgements quite out of taste, and not in the sweet food of sweetly uttered knowledge. But because this second sort is wrapped within the fold of the proposed subject, and takes not the course of his own invention, whether they properly be poets or no let grammarians dispute; and go to the third, indeed right poets, of whom chiefly this question ariseth, betwixt whom and these second is such a kind of difference as betwixt the meaner sort of painters, who counterfeit only such faces as are set before them, and the more excellent, who, having no law but wit, bestow that in colours upon you which is fittest for the eye to see, as the constant though lamenting look of Lucretia, when she punished in herself another's fault.

Wherein he painteth not Lucretia whom he never saw, but painteth the outward beauty of such a virtue. For these third be they which most properly do imitate to teach and delight, and to imitate borrow nothing of what is, hath been, or shall be; but range, only reined with learned discretion, into the divine consideration of what may be, and should be. These be they that, as the first and most noble sort may justly be termed *Vates*, so there are waited on in the excellentest languages and best understandings, with the fore-described name of Poets; for these indeed do merely make to imitate, and imitate both to delight and teach, and delight to move men to take that goodness in hand, which without delight they would fly as from a stranger, and teach, to make them know that goodness whereunto they are moved: which being the noblest scope to which ever any learning was directed, yet want there not idle tongues to bark at them. These be subdivided into sundry more special denominations. The most notable be the Heroic, Lyric, Tragic, Comic, Satiric, Iambic, Elegiac, Pastoral, and certain others, some of these being termed according to the matter they deal with, some by the sorts of verses they liked best to write in; for indeed the greatest part of poets have apparelled their poetical inventions in that numbrous kind of writing which is called verse—indeed but apparelled, verse being but an ornament and no cause to Poetry, since there have been many most excellent poets that never versified, and now swarm many versifiers that need never answer to the name of poets. For Xenophon, who did imitate so excellently as to give us *effigiem iusti imperii,* "the portraiture of a just Empire," under name of Cyrus (as Cicero saith of him), made therein an absolute heroical poem.

So did Heliodorus in his sugared invention of that picture of love in Theagenes and Chariclea; and yet both these writ in prose: which I speak to show that it is not rhyming and versing that maketh a poet—no more than a long gown maketh an advocate, who though he pleaded in armour should be an advocate and no soldier. But it is that feigning notable images of virtues,

vices, or what else, with that delightful teaching, which must be the right describing note to know a poet by, although indeed the Senate of Poets hath
chosen verse as their fittest raiment, meaning, as in matter they passed all in
all, so in manner to go beyond them—not speaking (table talk fashion or like
men in a dream) words as they chanceably fall from the mouth, but prizing
each syllable of each word by just proportion according to the dignity of the
subject.

   Now therefore it shall not be amiss first to weigh this latter sort of Poetry
by his works, and then by his parts, and, if in neither of these anatomies he
be condemnable, I hope we shall obtain a more favourable sentence. This pu-
rifying of wit, this enriching of memory, enabling of judgement, and enlarging of conceit, which commonly we call learning, under what name soever it
come forth, or to what immediate end soever it be directed, the final end is to
lead and draw us to as high a perfection as our degenerate souls, made worse
by their clayey lodgings, can be capable of. This, according to the inclination
of the man, bred many formed impressions. For some that thought this felicity principally to be gotten by knowledge and no knowledge to be so high
and heavenly as acquaintance with the stars, gave themselves to Astronomy;
others, persuading themselves to be demigods if they knew the causes of
things, became natural and super-natural philosophers; some an admirable
delight drew to Music; and some the certainty of demonstration to the Mathematics. But all, one and other, having this scope—to know, and by knowledge to lift up the mind from the dungeon of the body to the enjoying his
own divine essence. But when by the balance of experience it was found that
the astronomer looking to the stars might fall into a ditch, that the inquiring
philosopher might be blind in himself, and the mathematician might draw
forth a straight line with a crooked heart, then, lo, did proof, the overruler of
opinions, make manifest that all these are but serving sciences, which, as
they have each a private end in themselves, so yet are they all directed to the
highest end of the mistress-knowledge, by the Greeks called *Architectonike*,
which stands (as I think) in the knowledge of a man's self, in the ethic and
politic consideration, with the end of well doing and not of well knowing
only:—even as the saddler's next end is to make a good saddle, but his farther end to serve a nobler faculty, which is horsemanship; so the horseman's
to soldiery, and the soldier not only to have the skill, but to perform the practice of a soldier. So that, the ending end of all earthly learning being virtuous
action, those skills, that most serve to bring forth that, have a most just title to
be princes over all the rest. Wherein we can show the poet's nobleness, by
setting him before his other competitors, among whom as principal chal-
lengers step forth the moral philosophers, whom, me thinketh, I see coming
towards me with a sullen gravity, as though they could not abide vice by
daylight, rudely clothed for to witness outwardly their contempt of outward
things, with books in their hands against glory, whereto they set their names,
sophistically speaking against sublety, and angry with any man in whom
they see the foul fault of anger. These men casting largesse as they go of definitions, divisions, and distinctions, with a scornful interrogative do soberly

ask whether it be possible to find any path so ready to lead a man to virtue as that which teacheth what virtue is—and teacheth it not only by delivering forth his very being, his causes, and effects, but also by making known his enemy, Vice (which must be destroyed), and his cumbersome servant, Passion (which must be mastered), by showing the generalities that containeth it, and the specialities that are derived from it; lastly, by plain setting down, how it extendeth itself out of the limits of a man's own little world to the government of families, and maintaining of public societies.

The historian scarcely giveth leisure to the moralist to say so much, but that he, laden with old mouse-eaten records, authorizing himself (for the most part) upon other histories, whose greatest authorities are built upon the notable foundation of hearsay; having much ado to accord differing writers and to pick truth out of partiality; better acquainted with a thousand years ago than with the present age, and yet better knowing how this world goeth than how his own wit runneth; curious for antiquities and inquisitive of novelties; a wonder to young folks and a tyrant in table talk, denieth, in a great chafe, that any man for teaching of virtue, and virtuous actions, is comparable to him. "I am *Lux vitae, Temporum magistra, Vita memoriae, Nuncia vetustatis,*" &c.[5]

The philosopher (saith he) "teacheth a disputative virtue, but I do an active. His virtue is excellent in the dangerless Academy of Plato, but mine showeth forth her honourable face in the battles of Marathon, Pharsalia, Poitiers, and Agincourt. He teacheth virtue by certain abstract considerations, but I only bid you follow the footing of them that have gone before you. Old-aged experience goeth beyond the fine-witted philosopher, but I give the experience of many ages. Lastly, if he make the song-book, I put the learner's hand to the lute; and if he be the guide, I am the light."

Then would he allege you innumerable examples, conferring story by story, how much the wisest senators and princes have been directed by the credit of history, as Brutus, Alphonsus of Aragon, and who not, if need be? At length the long line of their disputation maketh a point in this, that the one giveth the precept, and the other the example.

Now, whom shall we find (since the question standeth for the highest form in the School of Learning) to be Moderator? Truly, as me seemeth, the poet; and if not a Moderator, even the man that ought to carry the title from them both, and much more from all other serving sciences. Therefore compare we the poet with the historian, and with the moral philosopher; and, if he go beyond them both, no other human skill can match him. For as for the Divine, with all reverence it is ever to be excepted, not only for having his scope as far beyond any of these as eternity exceedeth a moment, but even for passing each of these in themselves.

And for the lawyer, though Jus be the daughter of Justice, and Justice the chief of virtues, yet because he seeketh to make men good rather *formidine*

---

[5] The light of life, the master of the times, the life of memory, the messenger of antiquity (Cicero, *De Oratore*, II, 9, 36).

poenae than *virtutis amore*,[6] or, to say righter, doth not endeavour to make men good, but that their evil hurt not others, having no care, so he be a good citizen, how bad a man he be: therefore, as our wickedness maketh him necessary, and necessity maketh him honourable, so is he not in the deepest truth to stand in rank with these who all endeavour to take naughtiness away, and plant goodness even in the secretest cabinet of our souls. And these four are all that any way deal in that consideration of men's manners, which being the supreme knowledge, they that best breed it deserve the best commendation.

The philosopher therefore and the historian are they which would win the goal, the one by precept, the other by example. But both, not having both, do both halt. For the philosopher, setting down with thorny argument the bare rule, is so hard of utterance, and so misty to be conceived, that one that hath no other guide but him shall wade in him till he be old before he shall find sufficient cause to be honest. For his knowledge standeth so upon the abstract and general, that happy is that man who may understand him, and more happy that can apply what he doth understand.

On the other side, the historian, wanting the precept, is so tied, not to what should be but to what is, to the particular truth of things and not to the general reason of things, that his example draweth no necessary consequence, and therefore a less fruitful doctrine.

Now doth the peerless poet perform both: for whatsoever the philosopher saith should be done, he giveth a perfect picture of it in some one by whom he presupposeth it was done; so as he coupleth the general notion with the particular example. A perfect picture I say, for he yieldeth to the powers of the mind an image of that whereof the philosopher bestoweth but a wordish description: which doth neither strike, pierce, nor possess the sight of the soul so much as that other doth.

For as in outward things, to a man that had never seen an elephant or a rhinoceros, who should tell him most exquisitely all their shapes, colour, bigness, and particular marks, or of a gorgeous palace the architecture, with declaring the full beauties might well make the hearer able to repeat, as it were by rote, all he had heard, yet should never satisfy his inward conceits with being witness to itself of a true lively knowledge: but the same man, as soon as he might see those beasts well painted, or the house well in model, should straightways grow, without need of any description, to a judicial comprehending of them: so no doubt the philosopher with his learned definition—be it of virtue, vices, matters of public policy or private government—replenisheth the memory with many infallible grounds of wisdom, which notwithstanding, lie dark before the imaginative and judging power, if they be not illuminated or figured forth by the speaking picture of Poesy.

Tully taketh much pains, and many times not without poetical helps, to make us know the force love of our country hath in us. Let us but hear old Anchises speaking in the midst of Troy's flames, or see Ulysses in the fullness

---

[6] By fear of punishment rather than love of virtue.

of all Calypso's delights bewail his absence from barren and beggarly Ithaca. Anger, the Stoics say, was a short madness: let but Sophocles bring you Ajax on a stage, killing and whipping sheep and oxen, thinking them the army of Greeks, with their chieftains Agamemnon and Menelaus, and tell me if you have not a more familiar insight into anger than finding in the Schoolmen his genus and difference. See whether wisdom and temperance in Ulysses and Diomedes, valour in Achilles, friendship in Nisus and Euryalus, even to an ignorant man carry not an apparent shining, and, contrarily, the remorse of conscience in Oedipus, the soon repenting pride of Agamemnon, the self-devouring cruelty in his father Atreus, the violence of ambition in the two Theban brothers, the sour-sweetness of revenge in Medea, and, to fall lower, the Terentian Gnatho and our Chaucer's Pandar so expressed that we now use their names to signify their trades; and finally, all virtues, vices, and passions so in their own natural seats laid to the view, that we seem not to hear of them, but clearly to see through them. But even in the most excellent determination of goodness, what philosopher's counsel can so readily direct a prince, as the feigned Cyrus in Xenophon; or a virtuous man in all fortunes, as Aeneas in Virgil; or a whole Commonwealth, as the way of Sir Thomas More's *Utopia*? I say the way, because where Sir Thomas More erred, it was the fault of the man and not of the poet, for that way of patterning a Commonwealth was most absolute, though he perchance hath not so absolutely performed it. For the question is, whether the feigned image of Poesy or the regular instruction of Philosophy hath the more force in teaching: wherein if the philosophers have more rightly showed themselves philosophers than the poets have attained to the high top of their profession, as in truth,

> *Mediocribus esse poetis,*
> *Non Dii, non homines, non concessere Columnae:*[7]

it is, I say again, not the fault of the art, but that by few men that art can be accomplished.

Certainly, even our Saviour Christ could as well have given the moral commonplaces of uncharitableness and humbleness as the divine narration of Dives and Lazarus; or of disobedience and mercy, as that heavenly discourse of the lost child and the gracious father; but that His through-searching wisdom knew the estate of Dives burning in hell, and of Lazarus being in Abraham's bosom, would more constantly (as it were) inhabit both the memory and judgement. Truly, for myself, meseems I see before my eyes the lost child's disdainful prodigality, turned to envy a swine's dinner: which by the learned Divines are thought not historical acts, but instructing parables. For conclusion, I say the Philosopher teacheth, but he teacheth obscurely, so as the learned only can understand him; that is to say, he teacheth them that are already taught. But the poet is the food for the tenderest stomachs, the poet is indeed the right popular philosopher, whereof Aesop's tales

---

[7] Mediocre poets are not endured by gods, men, or booksellers (Horace, *Art of Poetry*, 372–73).

give good proof: whose pretty allegories, stealing under the formal tales of beasts, make many, more beastly than beasts, begin to hear the sound of virtue from these dumb speakers.

But now may it be alleged that, if this imagining of matters be so fit for the imagination, then must the historian needs surpass, who bringeth you images of true matters, such as indeed were done, and not such as fantastically or falsely may be suggested to have been done. Truly, Aristotle himself, in his discourse of Poesy, plainly determineth this question, saying that Poetry is *Philosophoteron* and *Spoudaioteron*, that is to say, it is more philosophical and more studiously serious than history. His reason is, because Poesy dealeth with *Katholon*, that is to say, with the universal consideration, and the history with *Kathekaston*, the particular "now," saith he, "the universal weighs what is fit to be said or done, either in likelihood or necessity (which the Poesy considereth in his imposed names), and the particular only marks whether Alcibiades did, or suffered, this or that." Thus far Aristotle: which reason of his (as all his) is most full of reason. For indeed, if the question were whether it were better to have a particular act truly or falsely set down, there is no doubt which is to be chosen, no more than whether you had rather have Vespasian's picture right as he was, or at the painter's pleasure nothing resembling. But if the question be for your own use and learning, whether it be better to have it set down as it should be, or as it was, then certainly is more doctrinable the feigned Cyrus in Xenophon than the true Cyrus in Justin, and the feigned Aeneas in Virgil than the right Aeneas in Dares Phrygius.

As to a lady that desired to fashion her countenance to the best grace, a painter should more benefit her to portrait a most sweet face, writing Canidia upon it, than to paint Canidia as she was, who, Horace sweareth, was foul and ill favoured.

If the poet do his part aright, he will show you in Tantalus, Atreus, and such like, nothing that is not to be shunned; in Cyrus, Aeneas, Ulysses, each thing to be followed; where the historian, bound to tell things as things were, cannot be liberal (without he will be poetical) of a perfect pattern, but, as in Alexander or Scipio himself, show doings, some to be liked, some to be misliked. And then how will you discern what to follow but by your own discretion, which you had without reading Quintus Curtius? And whereas a man may say, though in universal consideration of doctrine the poet prevaileth, yet that the history, in his saying such a thing was done, doth warrant a man more in that he shall follow.

The answer is manifest: that if he stand upon that *was*—as if he should argue, because it rained yesterday, therefore it should rain to-day—then indeed it hath some advantage to a gross conceit; but if he know an example only informs a conjectured likelihood, and so go by reason, the poet doth so far exceed him, as he is to frame his example to that which is most reasonable, be it in warlike, politic, or private matters; where the historian in his bare *was* hath many times that which we call fortune to overrule the best wisdom. Many times he must tell events whereof he can yield no cause: or, if he do, it must be poetical. For that a feigned example hath as much force to teach as a true example (for as for to move, it is clear, since the feigned may be tuned to the highest key of passion), let us take one example wherein a poet and a historian do concur.

Herodotus and Justin do both testify that Zopyrus, King Darius's faithful servant, seeing his master long resisted by the rebellious Babylonians, feigned himself in extreme disgrace of his king: for verifying of which, he caused his own nose and ears to be cut off, and so flying to the Babylonians, was received, and for his known valour so far credited, that he did find means to deliver them over to Darius. Much like matter doth Livy record of Tarquinius and his son. Xenophon excellently feigneth such another strategem performed by Abradates in Cyrus's behalf. Now would I fain know, if occasion be presented unto you to serve your prince by such an honest dissimulation, why you do not as well learn it of Xenophon's fiction as of the other's verity—and truly so much the better, as you shall save your nose by the bargain; for Abradates did not counterfeit so far. So then the best of the historian is subject to the poet; for whatsoever action, or faction, whatsoever counsel, policy, or war stratagem the historian is bound to recite, that may the poet (if he list) with his imitation make his own, beautifying it both for further teaching, and more delighting, as it pleaseth him, having all, from Dante's heaven to his hell, under the authority of his pen. Which if I be asked what poets have done so, as I might well name some, yet say I, and say again, I speak of the art, and not of the artificer.

Now, to that which commonly is attributed to the praise of histories, in respect of the notable learning is gotten by marking the success, as though therein a man should see virtue exalted and vice punished—truly that commendation is peculiar to Poetry, and far off from History. For indeed Poetry ever setteth virtue so out in her best colours, making Fortune her well-waiting handmaid, that one must needs be enamoured of her. Well may you see Ulysses in a storm, and in other hard plights; but they are but exercises of patience and magnanimity, to make them shine the more in the near-following prosperity. And of the contrary part, if evil men come to the stage, they ever go out (as the tragedy writer answered to one that misliked the show of such persons) so manacled as they little animate folks to follow them. But the historian, being captived to the truth of a foolish world, is many times a terror from well doing, and an encouragement to unbridled wickedness.

For see we not valiant Miltiades rot in his fetters: the just Phocion and the accomplished Socrates put to death like traitors; the cruel Severus live prosperously; the excellent Severus miserably murdered; Sylla and Marius dying in their beds; Pompey and Cicero slain then when they would have thought exile a happiness?

See we not virtuous Cato driven to kill himself, and rebel Caesar so advanced that his name yet, after 1,600 years, lasteth in the highest honour? And mark but even Caesar's own words of the forenamed Sylla (who in that only did honestly, to put down his dishonest tyranny), *Literas nescivit,*[8] as if want of learning caused him to do well. He meant it not by Poetry, which, not content with earthly plagues, deviseth new punishments in hell for tyrants, nor yet by Philosophy, which teacheth *Occidendos esse;*[9] but no doubt by skill in History, for that indeed can afford your Cypselus, Periander, Phalaris, Dionysius, and I know not how many more of the same kennel, that speed well enough in their abominable injustice or usurpation. I conclude, therefore, that he excelleth History, not only in furnishing the mind with knowledge, but in setting it forward to that which deserveth to be called and accounted good: which setting forward, and moving to well doing, indeed setteth the laurel crown upon the poet as victorious, not only of the historian, but over the philosopher, howsoever in teaching it may be questionable.

For suppose it be granted (that which I suppose with great reason may be denied) that the philosopher, in respect of his methodical proceeding, doth teach more perfectly than the poet, yet do I think that no man is so much *Philophilosophos*[10] as to compare the philosopher, in moving, with the poet.

And that moving is of a higher degree than teaching, it may by this appear, that it is wellnigh the cause and the effect of teaching. For who will be taught, if he be not moved with desire to be taught, and what so much good doth that teaching bring forth (I speak still of moral doctrine) as that it moveth one to do that which it doth teach? For, as Aristotle saith, it is not *Gnosis* but *Praxis*[11] must be the fruit. And how *Praxis* cannot be, without being moved to practise, it is no hard matter to consider.

The philosopher showeth you the way, he informeth you of the particularities, as well of the tediousness of the way, as of the pleasant lodging you shall have when your journey is ended, as of the many by-turnings that may divert you from your way. But this is to no man but to him that will read him, and read him with attentive studious painfulness; which constant desire whosoever hath in him, hath already passed half the hardness of the way, and therefore is beholding to the philosopher but for the other half. Nay truly, learned men have learnedly thought that where once reason hath so much overmastered passion, as that the mind hath a free desire to do well: the inward light each mind hath in itself is as good as a philosopher's book; seeing in nature we know it is well to do well, and what is well and what is evil, although not in the words of art which philosophers bestow upon us. For out of natural conceit the philosophers drew it; but to be moved to do that which we know, or to be moved with desire to know, *Hoc opus, hic labor est.*[12]

Now therein of all sciences (I speak still of human, and according to the humane conceits) is our poet the monarch. For he doth not only show the way, but giveth so sweet a prospect into the way, as will entice any man to

[8] He did not know literature.
[9] They are to be killed.
[10] A lover of the philosopher.
[11] Not mere abstract *knowledge,* that is, but *action.*
[12] This is the work, this the labor (*Aeneid,* VI, 129).

enter into it. Nay, he doth, as if your journey should lie through a fair vine-yard, at the first give you a cluster of grapes, that, full of that taste, you may long to pass further. He beginneth not with obscure definitions, which must blur the margent with interpretations, and load the memory with doubtful-ness; but he cometh to you with words set in delightful proportion, either ac-companied with, or prepared for, the well enchanting skill of music; and with a tale forsooth he cometh unto you, with a tale which holdeth children from play, and old men from the chimney corner. And, pretending no more, doth intend the winning of the mind from wickedness to virtue: even as the child is often brought to take most wholesome things by hiding them in such other as have a pleasant taste: which, if one should begin to tell them the na-ture of aloes or rhubarb they should receive, would sooner take their physic at their ears than at their mouth. So is it in men (most of which are childish in the best things, till they be cradled in their graves): glad they will be to hear the tales of Hercules, Achilles, Cyrus, and Aeneas; and, hearing them, must needs hear the right description of wisdom, valour, and justice; which, if they had been barely, that is to say philosophically, set out, they would swear they be brought to school again.

That imitation whereof Poetry is, hath the most conveniency to Nature of all other, insomuch that, as Aristotle saith, those things which in themselves are horrible, as cruel battles, unnatural monsters, are made in poetical imita-tion delightful. Truly, I have known men, that even with reading *Amadis de Gaule* (which God knoweth wanteth much of a perfect poesy) have found their hearts moved to the exercise of courtesy, liberality, and especially courage.

Who readeth Aeneas carrying old Anchises on his back, that wisheth not it were his fortune to perform so excellent an act? Whom do not the words of Turnus move, the tale of Turnus having planted his image in the imagina-tion? —

> *Fugientem haec terra videbit?*
> *Usque adeone mori miserum est?*[13]

Where the philosophers, as they scorn to delight, so must they be content little to move, saving wrangling whether Virtue be the chief or the only good, whether the contemplative or the active life do excel: which Plato and Boethius well knew, and therefore made Mistress Philosophy very often bor-row the masking raiment of Poesy. For even those hard-hearted evil men who think virtue a school name, and know no other good but *indulgere genio,*[14] and therefore despise the austere admonitions of the philosopher, and feel not the inward reason they stand upon, yet will be content to be de-lighted — which is all the good fellow poet seemeth to promise — and so steal to see the form of goodness, which seen they cannot but love ere themselves

---

[13] Shall this land see [Turnus] fleeing away? Is it so wretched a thing to die as that? (*Aeneid,* XII, 645–46).

[14] To indulge one's nature.

be aware, as if they took a medicine of cherries. Infinite proofs of the strange effects of this poetical invention might be alleged; only two shall serve, which are so often remembered as I think all men know them.

The one of Menenius Agrippa, who, when the whole people of Rome had resolutely divided themselves from the Senate, with apparent show of utter ruin, though he were (for that time) an excellent orator, came not among them upon trust of figurative speeches or cunning insinuations, and much less with farfetched maxims of Philosophy, which (especially if they were Platonic) they must have learned geometry before they could well have conceived; but forsooth he behaves himself like a homely and familiar poet. He telleth them a tale, that there was a time when all the parts of the body made a mutinous conspiracy against the belly, which they thought devoured the fruits of each other's labour: they concluded they would let so unprofitable a spender starve. In the end, to be short (for the tale is notorious, and as notorious that it was a tale), with punishing the belly they plagued themselves. This applied by him wrought such effect in the people, as I never read that ever words brought forth but then so sudden and so good an alteration; for upon reasonable conditions a perfect reconcilement ensued. The other is of Nathan the Prophet, who, when the holy David had so far forsaken God as to confirm adultery with murder, when he was to do the tenderest office of a friend, in laying his own shame before his eyes, sent by God to call again so chosen a servant, how doth he it but by telling of a man whose beloved lamb was ungratefully taken from his bosom?—the application most divinely true, but the discourse itself feigned. Which made David (I speak of the second and instrumental cause) as in a glass to see his own filthiness, as that heavenly Psalm of Mercy well testifieth.

By these, therefore, examples and reasons, I think it may be manifest that the Poet, with that same hand of delight, doth draw the mind more effectually than any other art doth: and so a conclusion not unfitly ensueth, that, as Virtue is the most excellent resting place for all worldly learning to make his end of, so Poetry, being the most familiar to teach it, and most princely to move towards it, in the most excellent work is the most excellent workman. But I am content not only to decipher him by his works (although works in commendation or dispraise must ever hold an high authority), but more narrowly will examine his parts: so that, as in a man, though all together may carry a presence full of majesty and beauty, perchance in some one defectious piece we may find a blemish. Now in his parts, kinds, or species (as you list to term them), it is to be noted that some poesies have coupled together two or three kinds, as tragical and comical, whereupon is risen the tragicomical. Some, in the like manner, have mingled prose and verse, as Sannazzaro and Boethius. Some have mingled matters heroical and pastoral. But that cometh all to one in this question, for, if severed they be good, the conjunction cannot be hurtful. Therefore, perchance forgetting some, and leaving some as needless to be remembered, it shall not be amiss in a word to cite the special kinds, to see what faults may be found in the right use of them.

Is it then the Pastoral Poem which is misliked? For perchance where the hedge is lowest they will soonest leap over. Is the poor pipe disdained, which sometime out of Melibaeus' mouth can show the misery of people under hard lords or ravening soldiers, and again, by Tityrus, what blessedness is derived to them that lie lowest from the goodness of them that sit highest? Sometimes, under the pretty tales of wolves and sheep, can include the whole considerations of wrongdoing and patience; sometimes show that contention for trifles can get but a trifling victory; where perchance a man may see that even Alexander and Darius, when they strave who should be cock of this world's dunghill, the benefit they got was that the afterlivers may say,

> *Haec memini et victum frustra contendere Thirsin;*
> *Ex illo Coridon, Coridon est tempore nobis.*[15]

Or is it the lamenting Elegiac, which in a kind heart would move rather pity than blame, who bewails with the great philosopher Heraclitus the weakness of mankind and the wretchedness of the world; who surely is to be praised, either for compassionate accompanying just causes of lamentation, or for rightly pointing out how weak be the passions of woefulness? Is it the bitter but wholesome Iambic, which rubs the galled mind, in making shame the trumpet of villainy with bold and open crying out against naughtiness? Or the Satiric, who

> *Omne vafer vitium ridenti tangit amico:*[16]

who sportingly never leaveth until he make a man laugh at folly, and, at length ashamed, to laugh at himself, which he cannot avoid, without avoiding the folly; who, while

> *circum praecordia ludit,*[17]

giveth us to feel how many headaches a passionate life bringeth us to; how, when all is done,

> *Est Ulubris animus si nos non deficit aequus?*[18]

No, perchance it is the Comic, whom naughty play-makers and stage-keepers have justly made odious. To the argument of abuse I will answer after. Only thus much now is to be said, that the Comedy is an imitation of the common errors of our life, which he representeth in the most ridiculous and scornful sort that may be, so as it is impossible that any beholder can be content to be such a one.

---

[15] I recall those things, and that the conquered Thyrsis strove in vain: From that time, Corydon for us is Corydon (Virgil, *Eclogue,* VII, 69–70).

[16] The rogue touches every vice while causing his friend to laugh (Persius, *Satires,* I, 116–117).

[17] He plays around the heart-strings (same passage).

[18] Happiness is found in Ulabrae [an extinct or dead city] if we have a sane mind (Horace, *Epistles,* I, 11, 30).

Now, as in Geometry the oblique must be known as well as the right, and in Arithmetic the odd as well as the even, so in the actions of our life who seeth not the filthiness of evil wanteth a great foil to perceive the beauty of virtue. This doth the Comedy handle so in our private and domestical matters, as with hearing it we get as it were an experience, what is to be looked for of a niggardly Demea, of a crafty Davus, of a flattering Gnatho, of a vainglorious Thraso; and not only to know what effects are to be expected, but to know who be such, by the signifying badge given them by the comedian. And little reason hath any man to say that men learn evil by seeing it so set out; since, as I said before, there is no man living but, by the force truth hath in nature, no sooner seeth these men play their parts, but wisheth them in *pistrinum*;[19] although perchance the sack of his own faults lie so behind his back that he seeth not himself dance the same measure; whereto yet nothing can more open his eyes than to find his own actions contemptibly set forth. So that the right use of Comedy will (I think) by nobody be blamed, and much less of the high and excellent Tragedy, that openeth the greatest wounds, and showeth forth the ulcers that are covered with tissue; that maketh kings fear to be tyrants, and tyrants manifest their tyrannical humours; that, with stirring the affects of admiration and commiseration, teacheth the uncertainty of this world, and upon how weak foundations gilden roofs are builded; that maketh us know,

> *Qui sceptra saevus duro imperio regit,*
> *Timet timentes, metus in auctorem redit.*[20]

But how much it can move, Plutarch yieldeth a notable testimony of the abominable tyrant Alexander Pheraeus, from whose eyes a tragedy, well made and represented, drew abundance of tears, who, without all pity, had murdered infinite numbers, and some of his own blood, so as he, that was not ashamed to make matters for tragedies, yet could not resist the sweet violence of a tragedy.

And if it wrought no further good in him, it was that he, in despite of himself, withdrew himself from hearkening to that which might mollify his hardened heart. But it is not the Tragedy they do mislike; for it were too absurd to cast out so excellent a representation of whatsoever is most worthy to be learned. Is it the Lyric that most displeaseth, who with his tuned lyre, and well-accorded voice, giveth praise, the reward of virtue, to virtuous acts, who gives moral precepts, and natural problems, who sometimes raiseth up his voice to the height of the heavens, in singing the lauds of the immortal God? Certainly, I must confess my own barbarousness, I never heard the old song of Percy and Douglas that I found not my heart moved more than with a trumpet; and yet is it sung but by some blind crowder, with no rougher voice than rude style; which, being so evil apparelled in the dust and cobwebs of

---

[19] A Roman mill to which slaves were often condemned as punishment.
[20] The savage ruler who wields the sceptre with a hard hand fears his frightened subjects, and fear thus returns to the author of it (Seneca, *Oedipus*, 705–706).

that uncivil age, what would it work, trimmed in the gorgeous eloquence of Pindar? In Hungary I have seen it the manner at all feasts, and other such meetings, to have songs of their ancestors' valour; which that right soldier-like nation think the chiefest kindlers of brave courage. The incomparable Lacedemonians did not only carry that kind of music ever with them to the field, but even at home, as such songs were made, so were they all content to be the singers of them, when the lusty men were to tell what they did, the old men what they had done, and the young men what they would do. And where a man may say that Pindar many times praiseth highly victories of small moment, matters rather of sport than virtue; as it may be answered, it was the fault of the poet, and not of the poetry, so indeed the chief fault was in the time and custom of the Greeks, who set those toys at so high a price that Philip of Macedon reckoned a horse-race won at Olympus among his three fearful felicities. But as the inimitable Pindar often did, so is that kind most capable and most fit to awake the thoughts from the sleep of idleness, to embrace honourable enterprises.

There rests the Heroical, whose very name (I think) should daunt all backbiters; for by what conceit can a tongue be directed to speak evil of that which draweth with it no less champions than Achilles, Cyrus, Aeneas, Turnus, Tydeus, and Rinaldo? who doth not only teach and move to a truth, but teacheth and moveth to the most high and excellent truth; who maketh magnanimity and justice shine throughout all misty fearfulness and foggy desires; who, if the saying of Plato and Tully be true, that who could see Virtue would be wonderfully ravished with the love of her beauty—this man sets her out to make her more lovely in her holiday apparel, to the eye of any that will deign not to disdain until they understand. But if anything be already said in the defence of sweet Poetry, all concurreth to the maintaining the Heroical, which is not only a kind, but the best and most accomplished kind of Poetry. For as the image of each action stirreth and instructeth the mind, so the lofty image of such worthies most inflameth the mind with desire to be worthy, and informs with counsel how to be worthy. Only let Aeneas be worn in the tablet of your memory, how he governeth himself in the ruin of his country, in the preserving his old father, and carrying away his religious ceremonies, in obeying the god's commandment to leave Dido, though not only all passionate kindness, but even the human consideration of virtuous gratefulness, would have craved other of him; how in storms, how in sports, how in war, how in peace, how a fugitive, how victorious, how besieged, how besieging, how to strangers, how to allies, how to enemies, how to his own; lastly, how in his inward self, and how in his outward government, and I think, in a mind not prejudiced with a prejudicating humour, he will be found in excellency fruitful, yea, even as Horace saith,

Melius Chrysippo et Crantore.[21]

---

[21] Better than do Chrysippus and Crantor (*Epistles*, I, 2, 4). Horace is stating that the knowledge of the good is better learned from Homer than from the above two philosophers.

But truly I imagine it falleth out with these poet-whippers, as with some good women, who often are sick, but in faith they cannot tell where. So the name of Poetry is odious to them, but neither his cause nor effects, neither the sum that contains him nor the particularities descending from him, give any fast handle to their carping dispraise.

Since then Poetry is of all human learning the most ancient and of most fatherly antiquity, as from whence other learnings have taken their beginnings; since it is so universal that no learned nation doth despise it, nor no barbarous nation is without it; since both Roman and Greek gave divine names unto it, the one of "prophesying," the other of "making," and that indeed that name of "making" is fit for him, considering that whereas other Arts retain themselves within their subject, and receive, as it were, their being from it, the poet only bringeth his own stuff, and doth not learn a conceit out of a matter, but maketh matter for a conceit; since neither his description nor his end containeth any evil, the thing described cannot be evil; since his effects be so good as to teach goodness and to delight the learners; since therein (namely in moral doctrine, the chief of all knowledges) he doth not only far pass the historian, but, for instructing, is wellnigh comparable to the philosopher, and, for moving, leaves him behind him; since the Holy Scripture (wherein there is no uncleanness) hath whole parts in it poetical, and that even our Saviour Christ vouchsafed to use the flowers of it; since all his kinds are not only in their united forms but in their severed dissections fully commendable; I think (and think I think rightly) the laurel crown appointed for triumphing captains doth worthily (of all other learnings) honour the poet's triumph. But because we have ears as well as tongues, and that the lightest reasons that may be will seem to weigh greatly, if nothing be put in the counterbalance, let us hear, and, as well as we can, ponder, what objections may be made against this art, which may be worthy either of yielding or answering.

First, truly I note not only in these *Mysomousoi*, poet-haters, but in all that kind of people who seek a praise by dispraising others, that they do prodigally spend a great many wandering words in quips and scoffs, carping and taunting at each thing, which, by stirring the spleen, may stay the brain from a thorough beholding the worthiness of the subject.

Those kind of objections, as they are full of very idle easiness, since there is nothing of so sacred a majesty but that an itching tongue may rub itself upon it, so deserve they no other answer, but, instead of laughing at the jest, to laugh at the jester. We know a playing wit can praise the discretion of an ass, the comfortableness of being in debt, and the jolly commodity of being sick of the plague. So of the contrary side, if we will turn Ovid's verse,

Ut lateat virtus proximitate mali,

that "good lie hid in nearness of the evil," Agrippa will be as merry in showing the vanity of Science as Erasmus was in commending of folly. Neither shall any man or matter escape some touch of these smiling railers. But for Erasmus and Agrippa, they had another foundation than the superficial part would promise. Marry, these other pleasant faultfinders, who will correct the verb before they understand the noun, and confute others' knowledge before they confirm their own, I would have them only remember that scoffing cometh not of wisdom; so as the best title in true English they get with their merriments is to be called good fools, for so have our grave forefathers ever termed that humorous kind of jesters. But that which giveth greatest scope to their scorning humours is rhyming and versing. It is already said (and, as I think, truly said) it is not rhyming and versing that maketh Poesy. One may be a poet without versing, and a versifier without poetry. But yet presuppose it were inseparable (as indeed it seemeth Scaliger judgeth) truly it were an inseparable commendation. For if *Oratio* next to *Ratio*, Speech next to Reason, be the greatest gift bestowed upon mortality, that cannot be praiseless which doth most polish that blessing of speech; which considers each word, not only (as a man may say) by his forcible quality, but by his best measured quantity, carrying even in themselves a harmony (without, perchance, number, measure, order, proportion be in our time grown odious). But lay aside the just praise it hath, by being the only fit speech for Music (Music, I say, the most divine striker of the senses), thus much is undoubtedly true, that if reading be foolish without remembering, memory being the only treasurer of knowledge, those words which are fittest for memory are likewise most convenient for knowledge.

Now, that verse far exceedeth prose in the knitting up of the memory, the reason is manifest, — the words (besides their delight, which hath a great affinity to memory) being so set as one word cannot be lost but the whole work fails; which accuseth itself, calleth the remembrance back to itself, and so most strongly confirmeth it. Besides, one word so, as it were, begetting another, as, be it in rhyme or measured verse, by the former a man shall have a near guess to the follower: lastly, even they that have taught the art of memory have showed nothing so apt for it as a certain room divided into many places well and thoroughly known. Now, that hath the verse in effect perfectly, every word having his natural seat, which seat must needs make the words remembered. But what needeth more in a thing so known to all men? Who is it that ever was a scholar that doth not carry away some verses of Virgil, Horace, or Cato, which in his youth he learned, and even to his old age serve him for hourly lessons? But the fitness it hath for memory is notably proved by all delivery of Arts: wherein for the most part, from Grammar to Logic, Mathematic, Physic, and the rest, the rules chiefly necessary to be borne away are compiled in verses. So that, verse being in itself sweet and orderly, and being best for memory, the only handle of knowledge, it must be in jest that any man can speak against it. Now then go we to the most important imputations laid to the poor poets. For aught I can yet learn, they are these. First, that there being many other more fruitful knowledges, a man might better spend his time in them than in this. Secondly, that it is the mother of lies. Thirdly, that it is the nurse of abuse, infecting us with many pestilent desires, with a siren's sweetness drawing the mind to the serpent's tale of sinful fancy, — and herein, especially, comedies give the largest field to ear (as Chaucer saith), — how both in other nations and in ours, before poets did soften us, we were full of courage, given to martial exercises, the pillars of manlike liberty, and not lulled asleep in shady idleness with poets' pastimes. And lastly, and chiefly, they cry out with an open mouth, as if they outshot Robin Hood, that Plato banished them out of his Commonwealth. Truly, this is much, if there be much truth in it. First, to the first, that a man might better spend his time is a reason indeed: but it doth (as they say) but *petere principium*:[22] for if it be, as I affirm, that no learning is so good as that which teacheth and moveth to virtue, and that none can both teach and move thereto so much as Poetry, then is the conclusion manifest that ink and paper cannot be to a more profitable purpose employed. And certainly, though a man should grant their first assumption, it should follow (methinks) very unwillingly, that good is not good because better is better. But I still and utterly deny that there is sprung out of earth a more fruitful knowledge. To the second therefore, that they should be the principal liars, I answer paradoxically, but truly, I think truly, that of all writers under the sun the poet is the least liar, and, though he would, as a poet can scarcely be a liar. The astronomer, with his cousin the geometrician, can hardly escape, when they take upon them to measure the height of the stars.

How often, think you, do the physicians lie, when they aver things good for sicknesses, which afterwards send Charon a great number of souls drowned in a potion before they come to his ferry? And no less of the rest, which take upon them to affirm. Now, for the poet, he nothing affirms, and therefore never lieth. For, as I take it, to lie is to affirm that to be true which is false; so as the other artists, and especially the historian, affirming many things, can, in the cloudy knowledge of mankind, hardly escape from many lies. But the poet (as I said before) never affirmeth. The poet never maketh any circles about your imagination, to conjure you to believe for true what he writes. He citeth not authorities of other histories, but even for his entry calleth the sweet Muses to inspire into him a good invention; in truth, not labouring to tell you what is, or is not, but what should or should not be. And therefore, though he recount things not true, yet because he telleth them not for true, he lieth not,—without we will say that Nathan lied in his speech, before alleged, to David; which as a wicked man durst scarce say, so think I none so simple would say that Aesop lied in the tales of his beasts: for who thinks that Aesop writ it for actually true were well worthy to have his name chronicled among the beasts he writeth of.

What child is there that, coming to a play, and seeing *Thebes* written in great letters upon an old door, doth believe that it is Thebes? If then a man can arrive, at that child's age, to know that the poets' persons and doings are but pictures what should be, and not stories what have been, they will never give the lie to things not affirmatively but allegorically and figuratively written. And therefore, as in History, looking for truth, they go away full fraught with falsehood, so in Poesy, looking for fiction, they shall use the narration but as an imaginative ground-plot of a profitable invention.

[22] Beg the question.

But hereto is replied, that the poets give names to men they write of, which argueth a conceit of an actual truth, and so, not being true, proves a falsehood. And doth the lawyer lie then, when under the names of "John a Stile" and "John a Noakes" he puts his case? But that is easily answered. Their naming of men is but to make their picture the more lively, and not to build any history; painting men, they cannot leave men nameless. We see we cannot play at chess but that we must give names to our chessmen; and yet, methinks, he were a very partial champion of truth that would say we lied for giving a piece of wood the reverend title of a bishop. The poet nameth Cyrus or Aeneas no other way than to show what men of their fames, fortunes, and estates should do.

Their third is, how much it abuseth men's wit, training it to wanton sinfulness and lustful love: for indeed that is the principal, if not the only, abuse I can hear alleged. They say the Comedies rather teach than reprehend amorous conceits. They say the Lyric is larded with passionate sonnets, the Elegiac weeps the want of his mistress, and that even to the Heroical Cupid hath ambitiously climbed. Alas, Love, I would thou couldst as well defend thyself as thou canst offend others. I would those on whom thou dost attend could either put thee away, or yield good reason why they keep thee. But grant love of beauty to be a beastly fault (although it be very hard, since only man, and no beast, hath that gift to discern beauty); grant that lovely name of Love to deserve all hateful reproaches (although even some of my masters the philosophers spent a good deal of their lamp-oil in setting forth the excellency of it); grant, I say, whatsoever they will have granted; that not only love, but lust, but vanity, but (if they list) scurrility, possesseth many leaves of the poets' books: yet think I, when this is granted, they will find their sentence may with good manners put the last words foremost, and not say that Poetry abuseth man's wit, but that man's wit abuseth Poetry.

For I will not deny but that man's wit may make Poesy, which should be *Eikastike,* which some learned have defined, "figuring forth good things," to be *Phantastike,* which doth, contrariwise, infect the fancy with unworthy objects, as the painter, that should give to the eye either some excellent perspective, or some fine picture, fit for building or fortification, or containing in it some notable example, as Abraham sacrificing his son Isaac, Judith killing Holofernes, David fighting with Goliath, may leave those, and please an ill-pleased eye with wanton shows of better hidden matters. But what, shall the abuse of a thing make the right use odious? Nay truly, though I yield that Poesy may not only be abused, but that being abused, by the reason of his sweet charming force, it can do more hurt than any other army of words, yet shall it be so far from concluding that the abuse should give reproach to the abused, that contrariwise it is a good reason, that whatsoever, being abused, doth most harm, being rightly used (and upon the right use each thing conceiveth his title), doth most good.

Do we not see the skill of Physic (the best rampire to our often assaulted bodies), being abused, teach poison, the most violent destroyer? Doth not knowledge of Law, whose end is to even and right all things, being abused, grow the crooked fosterer of horrible injuries? Doth not (to go to the highest) God's word abused breed heresy, and His Name abused become blasphemy? Truly, a needle cannot do much hurt, and as truly (with leave of ladies be it spoken) it cannot do much good. With a sword thou mayest kill thy father, and with a sword thou mayest defend thy prince and country. So that, as in their calling poets the fathers of lies they say nothing, so in this their argument of abuse they prove the commendation.

They allege herewith, that before poets began to be in price our nation hath set their heart's delight upon action, and not upon imagination, rather doing things worthy to be written, than writing things fit to be done. What that beforetime was, I think scarcely Sphinx can tell, since no memory is so ancient that hath the precedence of Poetry. And certain it is that, in our plainest homeliness, yet never was the Albion nation without Poetry. Marry, this argument, though it be levelled against Poetry, yet is it indeed a chain-shot against all learning, or bookishness, as they commonly term it. Of such mind were certain Goths, of whom it is written that, having in the spoil of a famous city taken a fair library, one hangman, belike, fit to execute the fruits of their wits, who had murdered a great number of bodies, would have set fire on it. "No," said another very gravely, "take heed what you do, for while they are busy about these toys, we shall with more leisure conquer their countries."

This indeed is the ordinary doctrine of ignorance, and many words sometimes I have heard spent in it: but because this reason is generally against all learning, as well as Poetry, or rather, all learning but Poetry; because it were too large a digression to handle, or at least too superfluous (since it is manifest that all government of action is to be gotten by knowledge, and knowledge best by gathering many knowledges, which is reading), I only, with Horace, to him that is of that opinion,

Iubeo stultum esse libenter:[23]

for as for Poetry itself, it is the freest from this objection. For poetry is the companion of the camps.

I dare undertake, Orlando Furioso, or honest King Arthur, will never displease a soldier: but the quiddity of *Ens* and *Prima materia* will hardly agree with a corslet. And therefore, as I said in the beginning, even Turks and Tartars are delighted with poets. Homer, a Greek, flourished before Greece flourished. And if to a slight conjecture a conjecture may be opposed, truly it may seem, that, as by him their learned men took almost their first light of knowledge, so their active men received their first motions of courage. Only Alexander's example may serve, who by Plutarch is accounted of such virtue, that Fortune was not his guide but his footstool; whose acts speak for him, though Plutarch did not,—indeed the Phoenix of warlike princes. This Alexander left his schoolmaster, living Aristotle, behind him, but took dead Homer with him. He put the philosopher Callisthenes to death for his seeming philosophical, indeed mutinous, stubbornness, but the chief thing he ever

---

[23] I ask him to be as much of a fool as he wishes (*Satires,* I, 1, 63).

was heard to wish for was that Homer had been alive. He well found he received more bravery of mind by the pattern of Achilles than by hearing the definition of fortitude: and therefore, if Cato misliked Fulvius for carrying Ennius with him to the field, it may be answered that, if Cato misliked it, the noble Fulvius liked it, or else he had not done it: for it was not the excellent Cato Uticensis (whose authority I would much more have reverenced), but it was the former, in truth a bitter punisher of faults, but else a man that had never well sacrified to the Graces. He misliked and cried out upon all Greek learning, and yet, being 80 years old, began to learn it, belike fearing that Pluto understood not Latin. Indeed, the Roman laws allowed no person to be carried to the wars but he that was in the soldier's roll, and therefore, though Cato misliked his unmustered person, he misliked not his work. And if he had, Scipio Nasica, judged by common consent the best Roman, loved him. Both the other Scipio brothers, who had by their virtues no less surnames than of Asia and Afric, so loved him that they caused his body to be buried in their sepulchre. So as Cato's authority being but against his person, and that answered with so far greater than himself, is herein of no validity. But now indeed my burden is great; now Plato's name is laid upon me, whom, I must confess, of all philosophers I have ever esteemed most worthy of reverence, and with great reason, since of all philosophers he is the most poetical. Yet if he will defile the fountain out of which his flowing streams have proceeded, let us boldly examine with what reasons he did it. First truly, a man might maliciously object that Plato, being a philosopher, was a natural enemy of poets. For indeed, after the philosophers had picked out of the sweet mysteries of Poetry the right discerning true points of knowledge, they forthwith, putting it in method, and making a school art of that which the poets did only teach by a divine delightfulness, beginning to spurn at their guides, like ungrateful prentices, were not content to set up shops for themselves, but sought by all means to discredit their masters; which by the force of delight being barred them, the less they could overthrow them, the more they hated them. For indeed, they found for Homer seven cities strove who should have him for their citizen; where many cities banished philosophers as not fit members to live among them. For only repeating certain of Euripides' verses, many Athenians had their lives saved of the Syracusians, when the Athenians themselves thought many philosophers unworthy to live.

Certain poets, as Simonides and Pindarus, had so prevailed with Hiero the First, that of a tyrant they made him a just king; where Plato could do so little with Dionysius, that he himself of a philosopher was made a slave. But who should do thus, I confess, should requite the objections made against poets with like cavillation against philosophers; as likewise one should do that should bid one read Phaedrus or Symposium in Plato, or the discourse of love in Plutarch, and see whether any poet do authorize abominable filthiness, as they do. Again, a man might ask out of what Commonwealth Plato did banish them. In sooth, thence where he himself alloweth community of women. So as belike this banishment grew not for effeminate wantonness, since little should poetical sonnets be hurtful when a man might have what woman he listed. But I honour philosophical instructions, and bless the wits which bred them: so as they be not abused, which is likewise stretched to Poetry.

St. Paul himself, who yet, for the credit of poets, allegeth twice two poets, and one of them by the name of a prophet, setteth a watchword upon Philosophy,—indeed upon the abuse. So doth Plato upon the abuse, not upon Poetry. Plato found fault that the poets of his time filled the world with wrong opinions of the gods, making light tales of that unspotted essence, and therefore would not have the youth depraved with such opinions. Herein may much be said; let this suffice: the poets did not induce such opinions, but did imitate those opinions already induced. For all the Greek stories can well testify that the very religion of that time stood upon many and many-fashioned gods, not taught so by the poets, but followed according to their nature of imitation. Who list may read in Plutarch the discourses of Isis and Osiris, of the cause why oracles ceased, of the divine providence, and see whether the theology of that nation stood not upon such dreams which the poets indeed superstitiously observed, and truly (since they had not the light of Christ) did much better in it than the philosophers, who, shaking off superstition, brought in atheism. Plato therefore (whose authority I had much rather justly construe than unjustly resist) meant not in general of poets, in those words of which Julius Scaliger saith, *Qua authoritate barbari quidam atque hispidi abuti velint ad poetas e republica exigendos;*[24] but only meant to drive out those wrong opinions of the Deity (whereof now, without further law, Christianity hath taken away all the hurtful belief), perchance (as he thought) nourished by the then esteemed poets. And a man need go no further than to Plato himself to know his meaning: who, in his Dialogue called *Ion,* giveth high and rightly divine commendation to Poetry. So as Plato, banishing the abuse, not the thing, not banishing it, but giving due honour unto it, shall be our patron and not our adversary. For indeed I had much rather (since truly I may do it) show their mistaking of Plato (under whose lion's skin they would make an ass-like braying against Poesy) than go about to overthrow his authority; whom, the wiser a man is, the more just cause he shall find to have in admiration; especially since he attributeth unto Poesy more than myself do, namely, to be a very inspiring of a divine force, far above man's wit, as in the aforenamed Dialogue is apparent.

Of the other side, who would show the honours have been by the best sort of judgements granted them, a whole sea of examples would present themselves: Alexanders, Caesars, Scipios, all favourers of poets; Laelius, called the Roman Socrates, himself a poet, so as part of *Heautontimorumenos* in Terence was supposed to be made by him, and even the Greek Socrates, whom Apollo confirmed to be the only wise man, is said to have spent part of his old time in putting Aesop's fables into verses. And therefore, full evil should it become his scholar Plato to put such words in his master's mouth

[24] The rude and barbarous would abuse such an authority in order to drive the poets out of the state (*Poetice*, 1, 2).

against poets. But what need more? Aristotle writes the Art of Poesy: and why, if it should not be written? Plutarch teacheth the use to be gathered of them, and how, if they should not be read? And who reads Plutarch's either history or philosophy, shall find he trimmeth both their garments with guards of Poesy. But I list not to defend Poesy with the help of her underling Historiography. Let it suffice that it is a fit soil for praise to dwell upon; and what dispraise may set upon it, is either easily overcome, or transformed into just commendation. So that, since the excellencies of it may be so easily and so justly confirmed, and the low-creeping objections so soon trodden down; it not being an art of lies, but of true doctrine; not of effeminateness, but of notable stirring of courage; not of abusing man's wit, but of strengthening man's wit; not banished, but honoured by Plato; let us rather plant more laurels for to engarland our poets' heads (which honour of being laureate, as besides them only triumphant captains wear, is a sufficient authority to show the price they ought to be had in) than suffer the ill-favouring breath of such wrong-speakers once to blow upon the clear springs of Poesy.

But since I have so long a career in this matter, methinks, before I give my pen a full stop, it shall be but a little more lost time to inquire why England (the mother of excellent minds) should be grown so hard a stepmother to poets, who certainly in wit ought to pass all other, since all only proceedeth from their wit, being indeed makers of themselves, not takers of others. How can I but exclaim,

Musa, mihi causas memora, quo numine laeso![25]

Sweet Poesy, that hath anciently had kings, emperors, senators, great captains, such as, besides a thousand others, David, Adrian, Sophocles, Germanicus, not only to favour poets, but to be poets; and of our nearer times can present for her patrons a Robert, king of Sicily, the great King Francis of France, King James of Scotland; such cardinals as Bembus and Bibbiena: such famous preachers and teachers as Beza and Melancthon; so learned philosophers as Fracastorius and Scaliger; so great orators as Pontanus and Muretus; so piercing wits as George Buchanan; so grave counsellors as, besides many, but before all, that Hospital of France, than whom (think) that realm never brought forth a more accomplished judgement, more firmly builded upon virtue—I say these, with numbers of others, not only to read others' poesies, but to poetize for others' reading—that Poesy, thus embraced in all other places, should only find in our time a hard welcome in England, I think the very earth lamenteth it, and therefore decketh our soil with fewer laurels than it was accustomed. For heretofore poets have in England also flourished, and, which is to be noted, even in those times when the trumpet of Mars did sound loudest. And now that an overfaint quietness should seem to strew the house for poets, they are almost in as good reputation as the mountebanks at Venice. Truly even that, as of the one side it giveth great praise to Poesy, which like Venus (but to better purpose) hath rather be troubled in the

[25] Tell me, O Muse, in what way was her divinity injured (*Aeneid*, I, 8).

net with Mars than enjoy the homely quiet of Vulcan; so serves it for a piece of a reason why they are less grateful to idle England, which now can scarce endure the pain of a pen. Upon this necessarily followeth, that base men with servile wits undertake it, who think it enough if they can be rewarded of the printer. And so as Epaminondas is said, with the honour of his virtue, to have made an office, by his exercising it, which before was contemptible, to become highly respected, so these, no more but setting their names to it, by their own disgracefulness disgrace the most graceful Poesy. For now, as if all the Muses were got with child, to bring forth bastard poets, without any commission they do post over the banks of Helicon, till they make the readers more weary than posthorses, while, in the meantime, they,

> *Queis meliore luto finxit praecordia Titan,*[26]

are better content to suppress the outflowing of their wit, than, by publishing them, to be accounted knights of the same order. But I that, before ever I durst aspire unto the dignity, am admitted into the company of the paper-blurrers, do find the very true cause of our wanting estimation is want of desert, taking upon us to be poets in despite of Pallas. Now, wherein we want desert were a thankworthy labour to express: but if I knew, I should have mended myself. But I, as I never desired the title, so have I neglected the means to come by it. Only, overmastered by some thoughts, I yielded an inky tribute unto them. Marry, they that delight in Poesy itself should seek to know what they do, and how they do, and, especially, look themselves in an unflattering glass of reason, if they be inclinable unto it. For Poesy must not be drawn by the ears; it must be gently led, or rather it must lead; which was partly the cause that made the ancient-learned affirm it was a divine gift, and no human skill; since all other knowledges lie ready for any that hath strength of wit; a poet no industry can make, if his own genius be not carried unto it; and therefore is it an old proverb, *Orator fit, Poeta nascitur.*[27] Yet confesse I always that as the fertilest ground must be manured, so must the highest-flying wit have a Daedalus to guide him. That Daedalus, they say, both in this and in other, hath three wings to bear itself up into the air of due commendation: that is, Art, Imitation, and Exercise. But these, neither artificial rules nor imitative patterns, we much cumber ourselves withal. Exercise indeed we do, but that very fore-backwardly: for where we should exercise to know, we exercise as having known: and so is our brain delivered of much matter which never was begotten by knowledge. For, there being two principal parts—matter to be expressed by words and words to express the matter—in neither we use Art or Imitation rightly. Our matter is *Quodlibet* indeed, though wrongly performing Ovid's verse,

> *Quicquid conabar dicere, versus erat;*[28]

never marshalling it into an assured rank, that almost the readers cannot tell where to find themselves. Chaucer, undoubtedly, did excellently in his

---

[26] Whose hearts Titan has fashioned of finer clay (Juvenal, *Satires,* XIV, 35).
[27] The orator is made, the poet is born.
[28] Whatever I shall try to say will be verse (*Tristia,* IV, 10, 26).

Troilus and Cressida; of whom, truly, I know not whether to marvel more, either that he in that misty time could see so clearly, or that we in this clear age walk so stumblingly after him. Yet had he great wants, fit to be forgiven in so reverent antiquity. I account the *Mirrour of Magistrates* meetly furnished of beautiful parts, and in the Earl of Surrey's *Lyrics* many things tasting of a noble birth, and worthy of a noble mind. The *Shepheard's Calendar* hath much poetry in his Eclogues, indeed worthy the reading, if I be not deceived. That same framing of his style to an old rustic language I dare not allow, since neither Theocritus in Greek, Virgil in Latin, nor Sannazzaro in Italian did affect it. Besides these, do I not remember to have seen but few (to speak boldly) printed, that have poetical sinews in them: for proof whereof, let but most of the verses be put in prose, and then ask the meaning; and it will be found that one verse did but beget another, without ordering at the first what should be at the last; which becomes a confused mass of words, with a tingling sound of rhyme, barely accompanied with reason.

Our Tragedies and Comedies (not without cause cried out against), observing rules neither of honest civility nor of skilful Poetry, excepting *Gorboduc* (again, I say, of those that I have seen), which notwithstanding, as it is full of stately speeches and well-sounding phrases, climbing to the height of Seneca's style, and as full of notable morality, which it doth most delightfully teach, and so obtain the very end of Poesy, yet in truth it is very defectious in the circumstances, which grieveth me, because it might not remain as an exact model of all Tragedies. For it is faulty both in place and time, the two necessary companions of all corporal actions. For where the stage should always represent but one place, and the uttermost time presupposed in it should be, both by Aristotle's precept and common reason, but one day, there is both many days, and many places, inartificially imagined. But if it be so in *Gorboduc,* how much more in all the rest, where you shall have Asia of the one side, and Afric of the other, and so many other under-kingdoms, that the player, when he cometh in, must ever begin with telling where he is, or else the tale will not be conceived? Now ye shall have three ladies walk to gather flowers and then we must believe the stage to be a garden. By and by we hear news of shipwreck in the same place, and then we are to blame if we accept it not for a rock.

Upon the back of that comes out a hideous monster, with fire and smoke, and then the miserable beholders are bound to take it for a cave. While in the meantime two armies fly in, represented with four swords and bucklers, and then what hard heart will not receive it for a pitched field? Now, of time they are much more liberal, for ordinary it is that two young princes fall in love. After many traverses, she is got with child, delivered of a fair boy; he is lost, groweth a man, falls in love, and is ready to get another child; and all this in two hours' space: which, how absurd it is in sense, even sense may imagine, and Art hath taught, and all ancient examples justified, and, at this day, the ordinary players in Italy will not err in. Yet will some bring in an example of Eunuchus in Terence,[29] that containeth matter of two days, yet far short of

---

[29] The *Heautontimorumenos* (or *Self-Punisher*) of Terence, not the *Eunuchus.*

twenty years. True it is, and so was it to be played in two days, and so fitted to the time it set forth. And though Plautus hath in one place done amiss, let us hit with him, and not miss with him. But they will say, How then shall we set forth a story, which containeth both many places and many times? And do they not know that a Tragedy is tied to the laws of Poesy, and not of History; not bound to follow the story, but, having liberty, either to feign a quite new matter, or to frame the history to the most tragical conveniency? Again, many things may be told which cannot be showed, if they know the difference betwixt reporting and representing. As, for example, I may speak (though I am here) of Peru, and in speech digress from that to the description of Calicut; but in action I cannot represent it without Pacolet's horse. And so was the manner the ancients took, by some Nuncius[30] to recount things done in former time or other place. Lastly, if they will represent an history, they must not (as Horace saith) begin *ab ovo*,[31] but they must come to the principal point of that one action which they will represent. By example this will be best expressed. I have a story of young Polydorus, delivered for safety's sake, with great riches, by his father Priam to Polymnestor, king of Thrace, in the Trojan war time. He, after same years, hearing the overthrow of Priam, for to make the treasure his own, murdereth the child. The body of the child is taken up by Hecuba. She, the same day, findeth a slight to be revenged most cruelly of the tyrant. Where now would one of our tragedy writers begin, but with the delivery of the child? Then should he sail over into Thrace, and so spend I know not how many years, and travel numbers of places. But where doth Euripides? Even with the finding of the body, leaving the rest to be told by the spirit of Polydorus. This need no further to be enlarged; the dullest wit may conceive it. But besides these gross absurdities, how all their plays be neither right tragedies, nor right comedies, mingling kings and clowns, not because the matter so carrieth it, but thrust in clowns by head and shoulders, to play a part in majestical matters, with neither decency[32] nor discretion, so as neither the admiration and commiseration, nor the right sportfulness, is by their mongrel tragi-comedy obtained. I know Apuleius did somewhat so, but that is a thing recounted with space of time, not represented in one moment: and I know the ancients have one or two examples of tragi-comedies, as Plautus hath *Amphitrio*. But, if we mark them well, we shall find, that they never, or very daintily, match hornpipes and funerals. So falleth it out that, having indeed no right comedy, in that comical part of our tragedy we have nothing but scurrility, unworthy of any chaste ears, or some extreme show of doltishness, indeed fit to lift up a loud laughter, and nothing else: where the whole tract of a comedy should be full of delight, as the tragedy should be still maintained in a well-raised admiration. But our comedians think there is no delight without laughter; which is very wrong, for though laughter may come with delight, yet cometh it not of delight, as though delight should be

---

[30] Messenger.
[31] From the egg (or beginning); *Art of Poetry*, 1, 147.
[32] Decorum (what is suitable or fitting).

the cause of laughter; but well may one thing breed both together. Nay, rather in themselves they have, as it were, a kind of contrariety: for delight we scarcely do but in things that have a conveniency to ourselves or to the general nature: laughter almost ever cometh of things most disproportioned to ourselves and nature. Delight hath a joy in it, either permanent or present. Laughter hath only a scornful tickling.

For example, we are ravished with delight to see a fair woman, and yet are far from being moved to laughter. We laugh at deformed creatures, wherein certainly we cannot delight. We delight in good chances, we laugh at mischances; we delight to hear the happiness of our friends, or country, at which he were worthy to be laughed at that would laugh. We shall, contrarily, laugh sometimes to find a matter quite mistaken and go down the hill against the bias, in the mouth of some such men, as for the respect of them one shall be heartily sorry, yet he cannot choose but laugh; and so is rather pained than delighted with laughter. Yet deny I not but that they may go well together. For as in Alexander's picture well set out we delight without laughter, and in twenty mad antics we laugh without delight, so in Hercules, painted with his great beard and furious countenance, in woman's attire, spinning at Omphale's commandment, it breedeth both delight and laughter. For the representing of so strange a power in love procureth delight: and the scornfulness of the action stirreth laughter. But I speak to this purpose, that all the end of the comical part be not upon such scornful matters as stirreth laughter only, but, mixed with it, that delightful teaching which is the end of Poesy. And the great fault even in that point of laughter, and forbidden plainly by Aristotle, is that they stir laughter in sinful things, which are rather execrable than ridiculous; or in miserable, which are rather to be pitied than scorned. For what is it to make folks gape at a wretched beggar, or a beggarly clown; or, against law of hospitality, to jest at strangers, because they speak not English so well as we do? What do we learn, since it is certain

> Nil habet infelix paupertas durius in se,
> Ouam quod ridiculos homines facit?[33]

But rather a busy loving courtier, a heartless threatening Thraso, a self-wise-seeming schoolmaster, an awry-transformed traveller — these if we saw walk in stage names, which we play naturally, therein were delightful laughter, and teaching delightfulness: as in the other, the tragedies of Buchanan do justly bring forth a divine admiration. But I have lavished out too many words of this play matter. I do it because, as they are excelling parts of Poesy, so is there none so much used in England, and none can be more pitifully abused; which, like an unmannerly daughter showing a bad education, causeth her mother Poesy's honesty to be called in question. Other sorts of Poetry almost have we none, but that lyrical kind of songs and sonnets: which, Lord, if He gave us so good minds, how well it might be employed,

---

[33] Unhappy poverty has nothing worse than that it makes men ridiculous (Juvenal, *Satires*, III, 152–153).

and with how heavenly fruit, both private and public, in singing the praises of the immortal beauty, the immortal goodness of that God who giveth us hands to write and wits to conceive; of which we might well want words, but never matter; of which we could turn our eyes to nothing, but we should ever have new budding occasions. But truly many of such writings as come under the banner of unresistible love, if I were a mistress, would never persuade me they were in love; so coldly they apply fiery speeches, as men that had rather read lovers' writings and so caught up certain swelling phrases (which hang together like a man which once told me the wind was at northwest, and by south, because he would be sure to name winds enough), than that in truth they feel those passions, which easily (as I think) may be betrayed by that same forcibleness or *Energia* (as the Greeks call it) of the writer. But let this be a sufficient short note, that we miss the right use of the material point of Poesy.

Now, for the outside of it, which is words, or (as I may term it) Diction, it is even well worse. So is that honey-flowing matron Eloquence apparelled, or rather disguised, in a courtesan-like painted affectation: one time with so far-fetched words, they may seem monsters, but must seem strangers, to any poor Englishman; another time, with coursing of a letter, as if they were bound to follow the method of a dictionary; another time, with figures and flowers, extremely winter-starved. But I would this fault were only peculiar to versifiers, and had not as large possession among prose-printers, and (which is to be marvelled) among many scholars, and (which is to be pitied) among some preachers. Truly I could wish, if at least I might be so bold to wish in a thing beyond the reach of my capacity, the diligent imitators of Tully and Demosthenes (most worthy to be imitated) did not so much keep Nizolian paper-books of their figures and phrases, as by attentive translation (as it were) devour them whole, and make them wholly theirs. For now they cast sugar and spice upon every dish that is served to the table, like those Indians, not content to wear earrings at the fit and natural place of the ears, but they will thrust jewels through their nose and lips, because they will be sure to be fine.

Tully, when he was to drive out Catiline, as it were with a thunderbolt of eloquence, often used that figure of repetition, *Vivit. Vivit? Imo in Senatum venit*, &c.[34] Indeed, inflamed with a well-grounded rage, he would have his words (as it were) double out of his mouth, and so do that artificially which we see men do in choler naturally. And we, having noted the grace of those words, hale them in sometime to a familiar epistle, when it were too much choler to be choleric. Now for similitudes in certain printed discourses, I think all Herberists, all stories of beasts, fowls, and fishes are rifled up, that they come in multitudes to wait upon any of our conceits; which certainly is as absurd a surfeit to the ears as is possible: for the force of a similitude not being to prove anything to a contrary disputer, but only to explain to a will-

---

[34] He lives. Lives? — He even comes into the senate.

ing hearer; when that is done, the rest is a most tedious prattling, rather over-swaying the memory from the purpose whereto they were applied, than any whit informing the judgment, already either satisfied, or by similitudes not to be satisfied. For my part, I do not doubt, when Antonius and Crassus, the great forefathers of Cicero in eloquence, the one (as Cicero testifieth of them) pretended not to know art, the other not to set by it, because with a plain sensibleness they might win credit of popular ears; which credit is the nearest step to persuasion; which persuasion is the chief mark of Oratory—I do not doubt (I say) that but they used these knacks very sparingly; which, who doth generally use, any man may see doth dance to his own music; and so be noted by the audience more careful to speak curiously than to speak truly.

Undoubtedly (at least to my opinion undoubtedly) I have found in divers small-learned courtiers a more sound style than in some professors of learning: of which I can guess no other cause, but that the courtier, following that which by practice he findeth fittest to nature, therein (though he know it not) doth according to Art, though not by Art: where the other, using Art to show Art, and not to hide Art (as in these cases he should do), flieth from na-ture, and indeed abuseth Art.

But what? Methinks I deserve to be pounded for straying from Poetry to Oratory: but both have such an affinity in this wordish consideration, that I think this digression will make my meaning receive the fuller understand-ing—which is not to take upon me to teach poets how they should do, but only, finding myself sick among the rest, to show some one or two spots of the common infection grown among the most part of writers: that, acknowl-edging ourselves somewhat awry, we may bend to the right use both of mat-ter and manner; whereto our language giveth us great occasion, being indeed capable of any excellent exercising of it. I know some will say it is a mingled language. And why not so much the better, taking the best of both the other? Another will say it wanteth grammar. Nay truly, it hath that praise, that it wanteth grammar: for grammar it might have, but it needs it not; being so easy of itself, and so void of those cumbersome differences of cases, genders, moods, and tenses, which I think was a piece of the Tower of Babylon's curse, that a man should be put to school to learn his mother-tongue. But for the uttering sweetly and properly the conceits of the mind, which is the end of speech, that hath it equally with any other tongue in the world: and is par-ticularly happy in compositions of two or three words together, near the Greek, far beyond the Latin: which is one of the greatest beauties can be in a language.

Now, of versifying there are two sorts, the one ancient, the other mod-ern: the ancient marked the quantity of each syllable, and according to that framed his verse; the modern observing only number (with some regard of the accent), the chief life of it standeth in that like sounding of the words, which we call rhyme. Whether of these be the most excellent, would bear many speeches. The ancient (no doubt) more fit for music, both words and tune observing quantity, and more fit lively to express divers passions, by the low and lofty sound of the well-weighed syllable. The latter likewise, with his rhyme, striketh a certain music to the ear: and, in fine, since it doth delight, though by another way, it obtains the same purpose: there being in either sweetness, and wanting in neither majesty. Truly the English, before any other vulgar language I know, is fit for both sorts: for, for the ancient, the Italian is so full of vowels that it must ever be cumbered with elisions; the Dutch so, of the other side, with consonants, that they cannot yield the sweet sliding fit for a verse; the French, in his whole language, hath not one word that hath his accent in the last syllable saving two, called *Antepenultima*; and little more hath the Spanish: and, therefore, very gracelessly may they use dactyls. The English is subject to none of these defects.

Now, for the rhyme, though we do not observe quantity, yet we observe the accent very precisely: which other languages either cannot do, or will not do so absolutely. That *caesura,* or breathing place in the midst of the verse, neither Italian nor Spanish have, the French, and we, never almost fail of. Lastly, even the very rhyme itself the Italian cannot put in the last syllable, by the French named the "masculine rhyme," but still in the next to the last, which the French call the "female," or the next before that, which the Italians term *sdrucciola*. The example of the former is *buono: suono,* of the *sdrucciola, femina: semina*. The French, of the other side, hath both the male, as *bon: son,* and the female, as *plaise: taise* but the *sdrucciola* he hath not: where the English hath all three, as *due: true, father: rather, motion: potion,* with much more which might be said, but that I find already the triflingness of this discourse is much too much enlarged. So that since the ever-praise-worthy Poesy is full of virtue-breeding delightfulness, and void of no gift that ought to be in the noble name of learning; since the blames laid against it are either false or feeble; since the cause why it is not esteemed in England is the fault of poet-apes, not poets; since, lastly, our tongue is most fit to honour Poesy, and to be honoured by Poesy; I conjure you all that have had the evil luck to read this ink-wasting toy of mine, even in the name of the Nine Muses, no more to scorn the sacred mysteries of Poesy, no more to laugh at the name of "poets," as though they were next inheritors to fools, no more to jest at the reverent title of a "rhymer"; but to believe, with Aristotle, that they were the ancient treasurers of the Grecians' Divinity; to believe, with Bernbus, that they were first bringers-in of all civility; to believe, with Scaliger, that no philosopher's precepts can sooner make you an honest man than the reading of Virgil; to believe, with Clauserus, the translator of Cornutus, that it pleased the heavenly Deity, by Hesiod and Homer, under the veil of fables, to give us all knowledge, Logic, Rhetoric, Philosophy, natural and moral, and *Quid non?*,[35] to believe, with me, that there are many mysteries contained in Poetry, which of purpose were written darkly, lest by profane wits it should be abused; to believe, with Landino, that they are so beloved of the gods that whatsoever they write proceeds of a divine fury; lastly, to believe themselves, when they tell you they will make you immortal by their verses.

[35] What not?

Thus doing, your name shall flourish in the printers' shops; thus doing, you shall be of kin to many a poetical preface; thus doing, you shall be most fair, most rich, most wise, most all; you shall dwell upon superlatives. Thus doing, though you be *libertino patre natus,* you shall suddenly grow *Herculea proles,*

> *Si quid mea carmina possunt.*[36]

Thus doing, your soul shall be placed with Dante's Beatrix, or Virgil's Anchises. But if (fie of such a but) you be born so near the dull-making cataract of Nilus that you cannot hear the planet-like music of Poetry, if you have so earth-creeping a mind that it cannot lift itself up to look to the sky of Poetry, or rather, by a certain rustical disdain, will become such a Mome as to be a Momus of Poetry; then, though I will not wish unto you the ass's ears of Midas, nor to be driven by a poet's verses (as Bubonax was) to hang himself, nor to be rhymed to death, as is said to be done in Ireland; yet thus much curse I must send you, in the behalf of all poets, that while you live, you live in love, and never get favour for lacking skill of a Sonnet, and, when you die, your memory die from the earth for want of an Epitaph.

---

[36] The whole sentence may be rendered, "Thus doing, though you be the son of a former slave, you shall suddenly grow Herculean offspring, if my poems are able to do anything." The Latin phrases are, in order, from Horace, Ovid, and Virgil.

JOHN DRYDEN

An Essay of Dramatic Poesy

1668

John Dryden's (1631–1700) artistry calls attention to itself: the essay, which is really
a dramatization of a debate, is set in a narrative framework. Why this day, of all days
(it happens to be June 3, 1665), do the characters engage in an urbane literary argument on a barge floating in the Thames River in London? Dryden's first sentence indicates his purpose, "to vindicate the honour of our English writers," including the
redemption of the then-somewhat-tarnished reputation of Shakespeare; so the larger
naval battle in which the English defeat the Dutch serves to prefigure the outcome of
the debate aboard the barge. The form of the dialogue allows Dryden to present four
critical perspectives on key issues of late seventeenth-century literary theory: the
value of the unities, the ancients versus the moderns, the neoclassical French versus
the Elizabethan English, narrative versus action, Shakespeare versus Jonson, rhyme
versus blank verse, and so forth. Throughout, the basic contraries are art versus nature; although each speaker uses nature as an anesthetic norm and the basis of his argument, each attaches a different meaning to that term. During the course of the debate we see alliances formed, based on the assumptions each holds; we also hear
practical as well as theoretical criticism, rebuttal as well as formulation of theory.

Despite this lively and varied argument, the essay is not finally inconclusive.
The dialectical form allows for the gradual development of principles that will apply
to all poetic drama, for Dryden is attempting to establish universal principles, not
merely to defend his own age. As the concluding speaker in the first round, Neander
("the new man") introduces the new criterion of the imagination: the nature of the
human mind, which includes the mind of the audience as well as that of the poet.
This leads directly to the "entr'acte," the Shakespeare–Ben Jonson comparison and
the analysis of "The Silent Woman," in which art and nature are combined. Incidentally, Jonson plays an important symbolic role in this essay; note the various uses the
speakers make of him.

The shorter debate on rhyme may be thought of as a separate issue; however,
seen as a second act in this drama, it is logically coherent with what has gone before.
It is worthwhile considering why now only Crites and Neander speak and how their

136

arguments here relate to what they have said earlier. It should also be remembered that Dryden was a playwright, concerned with the question of where he himself would be placed among the ranks of great dramatists that already included Shakespeare, Jonson, and Corneille.

To the Reader

THE DRIFT of the ensuing Discourse was chiefly to vindicate the honour of our English writers, from the censure of those who unjustly prefer the French before them. This I intimate, lest any should think me so exceeding vain, as to teach others an art which they understand much better than myself. But if this incorrect Essay, written in the country without the help of books, or advice of friends, shall find any acceptance in the world, I promise to myself a better success of the second part, wherein the virtues and faults of the English poets, who have written either in this, the epic, or the lyric way, will be more fully treated of, and their several styles impartially imitated.

It was that memorable day, in the first summer of the late war, when our navy engaged the Dutch; a day wherein the two most mighty and best appointed fleets which any age had ever seen, disputed the command of the greater half of the globe, the commerce of nations, and the riches of the universe. While these vast floating bodies, on either side, moved against each other in parallel lines, and our countrymen, under the happy conduct of his Royal Highness, went breaking, by little and little, into the line of the enemies; the noise of the cannon from both navies reached our ears about the City, so that all men being alarmed with it, and in a dreadful suspense of the event which we knew was then deciding, every one went following the sound as his fancy led him; and leaving the town almost empty, some took towards the park, some cross the river, others down it; all seeking the noise in the depth of silence.

Among the rest, it was the fortune of Eugenius, Crites, Lisideius, and Neander, to be in company together; three of them persons whom their wit and quality have made known to all the town; and whom I have chose to hide under these borrowed names, that they may not suffer by so ill a relation as I am going to make of their discourse.

Taking then a barge which a servant of Lisideius had provided for them, they made haste to shoot the bridge, and left behind them that great fall of waters which hindered them from hearing what they desired: after which, having disengaged themselves from many vessels which rode at anchor in the Thames, and almost blocked up the passage towards Greenwich, they ordered the watermen to let fall their oars more gently; and then, every one favouring his own curiosity with a strict silence, it was not long ere they perceived the air break about them like the noise of distant thunder, or of

swallows in a chimney: those little undulations of sound, though almost vanishing before they reached them, yet still seeming to retain somewhat of their
first horror, which they had betwixt the fleets. After they had attentively
listened till such time as the sound by little and little went from them,
Eugenius, lifting up his head, and taking notice of it, was the first who congratulated to the rest that happy omen of our Nation's victory: adding, we
had but this to desire in confirmation of it, that we might hear no more of
that noise, which was now leaving the English coast. When the rest had concurred in the same opinion, Crites, a person of a sharp judgment, and somewhat too delicate a taste in wit, which the world have mistaken in him for ill-
nature, said, smiling to us, that if the concernment of this battle had not been
so exceeding great, he could scarce have wished the victory at the price he
knew he must pay for it, in being subject to the reading and hearing of so
many ill verses as he was sure would be made upon it. Adding, that no argument could scape some of those eternal rhymers, who watch a battle with
more diligence than the ravens and birds of prey; and the worst of them
surest to be first in upon the quarry: while the better able either out of modesty writ not at all, or set that due value upon their poems, as to let them be
often called for and long expected! 'There are some of those impertinent
people you speak of,' answered Lisideius, 'who to my knowledge are already
so provided, either way, that they can produce not only a Panegyric upon the
victory, but, if need be, a Funeral Elegy on the Duke; and after they have
crowned his valour with many laurels, at last deplore the odds under which
he fell, concluding that his courage deserved a better destiny.' All the company smiled at the conceit of Lisideius; but Crites, more eager than before,
began to make particular exceptions against some writers, and said, the public magistrate ought to send betimes to forbid them; and that it concerned the
peace and quiet of all honest people, that ill poets should be as well silenced
as seditious preachers. 'In my opinion,' replied Eugenius, 'you pursue your
point too far; for as to my own particular, I am so great a lover of poesy, that I
could wish them all rewarded, who attempt but to do well; at least, I would
not have them worse used than Sylla the Dictator did one of their brethren
heretofore:—*Quem in concione vidimus* (says Tully) *cum ei libellum malus poeta
de populo subjecisset, quod epigramma in eum fecisset tantummodo alternis versibus
longiusculis, statim ex iis rebus quas tunc vendebat jubere ei præmium tribui, sub ea
conditione ne quid postea scriberet.*[1] 'I could wish with all my heart,' replied
Crites, 'that many whom we know were as bountifully thanked upon the
same condition,—that they would never trouble us again. For amongst
others, I have a mortal apprehension of two poets, whom this victory, with
the help of both her wings, will never be able to escape.' ''Tis easy to guess
whom you intend,' said Lisideius; 'and without naming them, I ask you, if

---

[1] When in the assembly we saw (*says Tully*) that a bad poet from the crowd offered him
a complimentary poem in rough elegiacs, he immediately ordered that a reward from the
goods he was now selling should be given to him on condition that he should never afterwards write.

one of them does not perpetually pay us with clenches upon words, and a certain clownish kind of raillery? if now and then he does not offer at a catachresis or Clevelandism, wresting and torturing a word into another meaning: in fine, if he be not one of those whom the French would call *un mauvais buffon;* one that is so much a well-willer to the satire, that he spares no man; and though he cannot strike a blow to hurt any, yet ought to be punished for the malice of the action, as our witches are justly hanged, because they think themselves so; and suffer deservedly for believing they did mischief, because they meant it.' 'You have described him,' said Crites, 'so exactly, that I am afraid to come after you with my other extremity of poetry. He is one of those who, having had some advantage of education and converse, knows better than the other what a poet should be, but puts it into practice more unluckily than any man; his style and matter are everywhere alike: he is the most calm, peaceable writer you ever read: he never disquiets your passions with the lest concernment, but still leaves you in as even a temper as he found you; he is a very Leveller in poetry: he creeps along with ten little words in every line, and helps out his numbers with *For to,* and *Unto,* and all the pretty expletives he can find, till he drags them to the end of another line; while the sense is left tired half way behind it: he doubly starves all his verses, first for want of thought, and then of expression; his poetry neither has wit in it, nor seems to have it; like him in Martial:

> *Pauper videri Cinna vult, et est pauper.*[2]

'He affects plainness, to cover his want of imagination: when he writes the serious way, the highest flight of his fancy is some miserable antithesis, or seeming contradiction; and in the comic he is still reaching at some thin conceit, the ghost of a jest, and that too flies before him, never to be caught; these swallows which we see before us on the Thames are the just resemblance of his wit: you may observe how near the water they stoop, how many proffers they make to dip, and yet how seldom they touch it; and when they do, 'tis but the surface: they skim over it but to catch a gnat, and then mount into the air and leave it.'

'Well, gentlemen,' said Eugenius, 'you may speak your pleasure of these authors; but though I and some few more about the town may give you a peaceable hearing, yet assure yourselves, there are multitudes who would think you malicious and them injured: especially him whom you first described; he is the very Withers of the city: they have bought more editions of his works than would serve to lay under all their pies at the Lord Mayor's Christmas. When his famous poem first came out in the year 1660, I have seen them reading it in the midst of 'Change time; nay so vehement they were at it, that they lost their bargain by the candles' ends; but what will you say, if he has been received amongst the great ones? I can assure you he is, this day, the envy of a great Person who is lord in the art of quibbling; and who does not take it well, that any man should intrude so far into his

---

[2] Cinna pretends to be poor —and, in fact, he is poor.

province.' 'All I would wish,' replied Crites, 'is that they who love his writings, may still admire him, and his fellow poet: *Qui Bavium non odit, &c.*,[3] is curse sufficient.' 'And farther,' added Lisideius, 'I believe there is no man who writes well, but would think himself very hardly dealt with, if their admirers should praise anything of his: *Nam quos contemnimus, eorum quoque laudes contemnimus.*'[4] 'There are so few who write well in this age,' says Crites, 'that methinks any praises should be welcome; they neither rise to the dignity of the last age, nor to any of the Ancients: and we may cry out of the writers of this time, with more reason than Petronius of his, *Pace vestra liceat dixisse, primi omnium eloquentiam perdidistis*[5]: you have debauched the true old poetry so far, that Nature, which is the soul of it, is not in any of your writings.'

'If your quarrel,' said Eugenius, 'to those who now write, be grounded only on your reverence to antiquity, there is no man more ready to adore those great Greeks and Romans than I am: but on the other side, I cannot think so contemptibly of the age I live in, or so dishonourably of my own country, as not to judge we equal the Ancients in most kinds of poesy, and in some surpass them; neither know I any reason why I may not be as zealous for the reputation of our age, as we find the Ancients themselves in reference to those who lived before them. For you hear your Horace saying,

> *Indignor quidquam reprehendi, non quia crasse*
> *Compositum, illepidève putetur, sed quia nuper.*[6]

And after:

> *Si meliora dies, ut vina, poemata reddit,*
> *Scire velim, pretium chartis quotus arroget annus?*[7]

'But I see I am engaging in a wide dispute, where the arguments are not like to reach close on either side; for Poesy is of so large an extent, and so many both of the Ancients and Moderns have done well in all kinds of it, that in citing one against the other, we shall take up more time this evening than each man's occasions will allow him: therefore I would ask Crites to what part of Poesy he wound confine his arguments, and whether he would defend the general cause of the Ancients against the Moderns, or oppose any age of the Moderns against this of ours?'

Crites, a little while considering upon this demand, told Eugenius he approved his propositions, and if he pleased, he would limit their dispute to Dramatic Poesy; in which he thought it not difficult to prove, either that the Ancients were superior to the Moderns, or the last age to this of ours.

---

[3] Who does not hate Bavius.

[4] For we despise the praise of people whom we despise.

[5] With your permission, let me say that you were the first of all to lose your eloquence.

[6] I resent anything's being condemned merely because it is new and not because it is considered to be crudely or coarsely written.

[7] If time improves poems, as it does wines, I should like to know how many years give value to literature.

Eugenius was somewhat surprised, when he heard Crites make choice of that subject. 'For ought I see,' said he, 'I have undertaken a harder province than I imagined; for though I never judged the plays of the Greek or Roman poets comparable to ours, yet, on the other side, those we now see acted come short of many which were written in the last age: but my comfort is, if we are o'ercome, it will be only by our own countrymen: and if we yield to them in this one part of poesy, we more surpass them in all the other: for in the epic or lyric way, it will be hard for them to show us one such amongst them, as we have many now living, or who lately were so: they can produce nothing so courtly writ, or which expresses so much the conversation of a gentleman, as Sir John Suckling; nothing so even, sweet, and flowing, as Mr. Waller; nothing so majestic, so correct, as Sir John Denham; nothing so elevated, so copious, and full of spirit, as Mr. Cowley; as for the Italian, French, and Spanish plays, I can make it evident, that those who now write surpass them; and that the Drama is wholly ours.'

All of them were thus far of Eugenius his opinion, that the sweetness of English verse was never understood or practised by our fathers; even Crites himself did not much oppose it: and every one was willing to acknowledge how much our poesy is improved by the happiness of some writers yet living; who first taught us to mould our thoughts into easy and significant words; to retrench the superfluities of expression, and to make our rhyme so properly a part of the verse, that it should never mislead the sense, but itself be led and governed by it.

Eugenius was going to continue this discourse, when Lisideius told him it was necessary, before they proceeded further, to take a standing measure of their controversy; for how was it possible to be decided who writ the best plays, before we know what a play should be? But, this once agreed on by both parties, each might have recourse to it, either to prove his own advantages, or to discover the failings of his adversary.

He had no sooner said this, but all desired the favour of him to give the definition of a play; and they were the more importunate, because neither Aristotle, nor Horace, nor any other, who writ of that subject, had ever done it.

Lisideius, after some modest denials, at last confessed he had a rude notion of it; indeed, rather a description than a definition; but which served to guide him in his private thoughts, when he was to make a judgment of what others writ: that he conceived a play ought to be, *A just and lively image of human nature, representing its passions and humours, and the changes of fortune to which it is subject, for the delight and instruction of mankind.*

This definition, though Crites raised a logical objection against it; that it was only *a genere at fine,* and so not altogether perfect; was yet well received by the rest: and after they had given order to the watermen to turn their barge, and row softly, that they might take the cool of the evening in their return, Crites, being desired by the company to begin, spoke on behalf of the Ancients, in this manner:

'If confidence presage a victory, Eugenius, in his own opinion, has already triumphed over the Ancients: nothing seems more easy to him, than to overcome those whom it is our greatest praise to have imitated well; for we do not only build upon their foundation, but by their models. Dramatic Poesy had time enough, reckoning from Thespis (who first invented it) to Aristophanes, to be born, to grow up, and to flourish in maturity. It has been observed of arts and sciences, that in one and the same century they have arrived to a great perfection; and no wonder, since every age has a kind of universal genius, which inclines those that live in it to some particular studies: the work then being pushed on by many hands, must of necessity go forward.

'Is it not evident, in these last hundred years (when the study of philosophy has been the business of all the Virtuosi in Christendom), that almost a new Nature has been revealed to us?—that more errors of the school have been detected, more useful experiments in philosophy have been made, more noble secrets in optics, medicine, anatomy, astronomy, discovered, than in all those credulous and doting ages from Aristotle to us?—so true it is, that nothing spreads more fast than science, when rightly and generally cultivated.

'Add to this, the more than common emulation that was in those times of writing well; which though it be found in all ages and all persons that pretend to the same reputation, yet Poesy, being then in more esteem than now it is, had greater honours decreed to the professors of it, and consequently the rivalship was more high between them; they had judges ordained to decide their merit, and prizes to reward it; and historians have been diligent to record of Eschylus, Euripides, Sophocles, Lycophron, and the rest of them, both who they were that vanquished in these wars of the theatre, and how often they were crowned: while the Asian kings and Grecian commonwealths scarce afforded them a nobler subject than the unmanly luxuries of a debauched court, or giddy intrigues of a factious city. *Alit æmulatio ingenia,* (says Paterculus,) *et nunc invidia, nunc admiratio incitationem accendit:* Emulation is the spur of wit; and sometimes envy, sometimes admiration, quickens our endeavours.

'But now, since the rewards of honour are taken away, that virtuous emulation is turned into direct malice; yet so slothful, that it contents itself to condemn and cry down others, without attempting to do better: 'tis a reputation too unprofitable, to take the necessary pains for it; yet, wishing they had it is incitement enough to hinder others from it. And this, in short, Eugenius, is the reason why you have now so few good poets, and so many severe judges. Certainly, to imitate the Ancients well, much labour and long study is required; which pain, I have already shown, our poets would want encouragement to take, if yet they had ability to go through with it. Those Ancients have been faithful imitators and wise observers of that Nature which is so torn and ill represented in our plays; they have handed down to us a perfect resemblance of her; which we, like ill copiers, neglecting to look on, have rendered monstrous, and disfigured. But, that you may know how much you are indebted to those your masters, and be ashamed to have so ill requited them, I must remember you, that all the rules by which we practise the

Drama at this day, (either such as relate to the justness and symmetry of the plot, or the episodical ornaments, such as descriptions, narrations and other beauties, which are not essential to the play,) were delivered to us from the observations which Aristotle made, of those poets, which either lived before him, or were his contemporaries: we have added nothing of our own, except we have the confidence to say our wit is better; of which none boast in this our age, but such as understand not theirs. Of that book which Aristotle has left us, περὶ τῆς Ποιητικῆς,[8] Horace his *Art of Poetry* is an excellent comment, and, I believe, restores to us that Second Book of his concerning *Comedy*, which is wanting in him.

'Out of these two have been extracted the famous Rules, which the French call *Des Trois Unitez*, or, the Three Unities, which ought to be observed in every regular play; namely, of Time, Place, and Action.

'The Unity of Time they comprehend in twenty-four hours, the compass of a natural day, or as near as it can be contrived; and the reason of it is obvious to every one,—that the time of the feigned action, or fable of the play, should be proportioned as near as can be to the duration of that time in which it is represented: since therefore, all plays are acted on the theatre in a space of time much within the compass of twenty-four hours, that play is to be thought the nearest imitation of nature, whose plot or action is confined within that time; and, by the same rule which concludes this general proportion of time, it follows, that all the parts of it are to be equally subdivided; as namely, that one act take not up the supposed time of half a day, which is out of proportion to the rest; since the other four are then to be straitened within the compass of the remaining half: for it is unnatural that one act, which being spoke or written is not longer than the rest, should be supposed longer by the audience; 'tis therefore the poet's duty, to take care that no act should be imagined to exceed the time in which it is represented on the stage; and that the intervals and inequalities of time be supposed to fall out between the acts.

'This rule of time, how well it has been observed by the Ancients, most of their plays will witness; you see them in their tragedies, (wherein to follow this rule, is certainly most difficult,) from the very beginning of their plays, falling close into that part of the story which they intend for the action or principal object of it, leaving the former part to be delivered by narration: so that they set the audience, as it were, at the post where the race is to be concluded; and, saving them the tedious expectation of seeing the poet set out and ride the beginning of the course, you behold him not till he is in sight of the goal, and just upon you.

'For the second Unity, which is that of Place, the Ancients meant by it, that the scene ought to be continued through the play, in the same place where it was laid in the beginning: for the stage on which it is represented being but one and the same place, it is unnatural to conceive it many; and

---

[8] *Peri tes Poietikes*, "The Poetics."

those far distant from one another. I will not deny but, by the variation of painted scenes, the fancy, which in these cases will contribute to its own deceit, may sometimes imagine it several places, with some appearance of probability; yet it still carries the greater likelihood of truth, if those places be supposed so near each other, as in the same town or city; which may all be comprehended under the larger denomination of one place; for a greater distance will bear no proportion to the shortness of time which is allotted in the acting, to pass from one of them to another; for the observation of this, next to the Ancients, the French are to be most commended. They tie themselves so strictly to the Unity of Place, that you never see in any of their plays, a scene changed in the middle of an act: if the act begins in a garden, a street, or chamber, 'tis ended in the same place; and that you may know it to be the same, the stage is so supplied with persons, that it is never empty all the time: he that enters the second, has business with him who was on before; and before the second quits the stage, a third appears who has business with him. This Corneille calls *la liaison des scènes,* the continuity or joining of the scenes; and 'tis a good mark of a well-contrived play, when all the persons are known to each other, and everyone of them has some affairs with all the rest.

'As for the third Unity, which is that of Action, the Ancients meant no other by it than what the logicians do by their *finis,* the end or scope of any action; that which is the first in intention, and last in execution: now the poet is to aim at one great and complete action, to the carrying on of which all things in his play, even the very obstacles, are to be subservient; and the reason of this is as evident as any of the former.

'For two actions, equally laboured and driven on by the writer, would destroy the unity of the poem; it would be no longer one play, but two: not but that there may be many actions in a play, as Ben Jonson has observed in his *Discoveries;* but they must be all subservient to the great one, which our language happily expresses in the name of *under-plots:* such as in Terence's *Eunuch* is the difference and reconcilement of Thais and Phædria, which is not the chief business of the play, but promotes the marriage of Chærea and Chremes's sister, principally intended by the poet. There ought to be but one action, says Corneille, that is, one complete action which leaves the mind of the audience in a full repose; but this cannot be brought to pass but by many other imperfect actions, which conduce to it, and hold the audience in a delightful suspence of what will be.

'If by these rules (to omit many other drawn from the precepts and practice of the Ancients) we should judge our modern plays, 'tis probable that few of them would endure the trial: that which should be the business of a day, takes up in some of them an age; instead of one action, they are the epitomes of a man's life; and for one spot of ground (which the stage should represent) we are sometimes in more countries than the map can show us.

'But if we will allow the Ancients to have contrived well, we must acknowledge them to have writ better; questionless we are deprived of a great stock of wit in the loss of Menander among the Greek poets, and of Cæcilius,

Afranius, and Varius, among the Romans; we may guess at Menander's excellency by the plays of Terence, who translated some of his; and yet wanted
so much of him, that he was called by C. Caesar the half-Menander; and may
judge of Varius, by the testimonies of Horace, Martial, and Velleius Paterculus. 'Tis probable that these, could they be recovered, would decide the
controversy; but so long as Aristophanes in the old Comedy, and Plautus in
the new are extant, while the tragedies of Euripides, Sophocles, and Seneca,
are to be had, I can never see one of those plays which are now written, but it
increases my admiration of the Ancients. And yet I must acknowledge farther, that to admire them as we ought, we should understand them better
than we do. Doubtless many things appear flat to us, whose wit depended on
some custom or story, which never came to our knowledge; or perhaps on
some criticism in their language, which being so long dead, and only remaining in their books, 'tis not possible they should make us know it perfectly. To
read Macrobius, explaining the propriety and elegancy of many words in
Virgil, which I had before passed over without consideration, as common
things, is enough to assure me that I ought to think the same of Terence; and
that in the purity of his style (which Tully so much valued that he ever carried his works about him) there is yet left in him great room for admiration, if
I knew but where to place it. In the mean time I must desire you to take notice, that the greatest man of the last age (Ben Jonson) was willing to give
place to them in all things: he was not only a professed imitator of Horace,
but a learned plagiary of all the others; you track him every where in their
snow: if Horace, Lucan, Petronius Arbiter, Seneca, and Juvenal, had their
own from him, there are few serious thoughts which are new in him: you
will pardon me, therefore, if I presume he loved their fashion, when he wore
their clothes. But since I have otherwise a great veneration for him, and you,
Eugenius, prefer him above all other poets, I will use no farther argument to
you than his example: I will produce Father Ben to you, dressed in all the ornaments and colours of the Ancients; you will need no other guide to our
party, if you follow him; and whether you consider the bad plays of our age,
or regard the good ones of the last, both the best and worst of the modern
poets will equally instruct you to esteem the Ancients.'

Crites had no sooner left speaking, but Eugenius, who had waited with
some impatience for it, thus began:

'I have observed in your speech, that the former part of it is convincing
as to what the Moderns have profited by the rules of the Ancients; but in the
latter you are careful to conceal how much they have excelled them; we own
all the helps we have from them, and want neither veneration nor gratitude
while we acknowledge that to overcome them we must make use of the advantages we have received from them: but to these assistances we have
joined our own industry; for, had we sat down with a dull imitation of them,
we might then have lost somewhat of the old perfection, but never acquired
any that was new. We draw not therefore after their lines, but those of Nature; and having the life before us, besides the experience of all they knew, it
is wonder if we hit some airs and features which they have missed. I deny

not what you urge of arts and sciences, that they have flourished in some ages more than others; but your instance in philosophy makes for me: for if natural causes be more known now than in the time of Aristotle, because more studied, it follows that poesy and other arts may, with the same pains, arrive still nearer to perfection; and, that granted, it will rest for you to prove that they wrought more perfect images of human life than we; which seeing in your discourse you have avoided to make good, it shall now be my task to show you some part of their defects, and some few excellencies of the Moderns. And I think there is none among us can imagine I do it enviously, or with purpose to detract from them; for what interest of fame or profit can the living lose by the reputation of the dead? On the other side, it is a great truth which Velleius Paterculus affirms: *Audita visis libentius laudamus; et præsentia invidia, præterita admiratione prosequimur; et his nos obrui, illis instrui credimus*[9]: that praise or censure is certainly the most sincere, which unbribed posterity shall give us.

'Be pleased then in the first place to take notice, that the Greek poesy, which Crites has affirmed to have arrived to perfection in the reign of the Old Comedy, was so far from it, that the distinction of it into acts was not known to them; or if it were, it is yet so darkly delivered to us that we cannot make it out.

'All we know of it is, from the singing of their Chorus; and that too is so uncertain, that in some of their plays we have reason to conjecture they sung more than five times. Aristotle indeed divides the integral parts of play into four. First, the *Protasis*, or entrance, which gives light only to the characters of the persons, and proceeds very little into any part of the action. Secondly, the *Epitasis*, or working up of the plot; where the play grows warmer, the design or action of it is drawing on, and you see something promising that it will come to pass. Thirdly, the *Catastasis*, or counterturn, which destroys that expectation, imbroils the action in new difficulties, and leaves you far distant from that hope in which it found you; as you may have observed in a violent stream resisted by a narrow passage,—it runs round to an eddy, and carries back the waters with more swiftness than it brought them on. Lastly, the *Catastrophe*, which the Grecians called λύσις [lysis], the French *le dénouement*, and we the discovery or unravelling of the plot: there you see all things settling again upon their first foundations; and, the obstacles which hindered the design or action of the play once removed, it ends with that resemblance of truth and nature, that the audience are satisfied with the conduct of it. Thus this great man delivered to us the image of a play; and I must confess it is so lively, that from thence much light has been derived to the forming it more perfectly into acts and scenes: but what poet first limited to five the number of the acts, I know not; only we see it so firmly established in the time of Horace, that he gives it for a rule in comedy; *Neu brevior quinto, neu sit productior actu.*[10] So that you see the Grecians cannot be said to have consummated

[9] What is heard we praise more willingly than what is seen, and we follow the present with envy, the past with admiration; and we believe ourselves harmed by the former but edified by the latter.
[10] Let it be neither shorter than five acts, nor longer.

this art; writing rather by entrances, than by acts, and having rather a general indigested notion of a play, than knowing how and where to bestow the particular graces of it.

'But since the Spaniards at this day allow but three acts, which they call *Jornadas,* to a play, and the Italians in many of theirs follow them, when I condemn the Ancients, I declare it is not altogether because they have not five acts to every play, but because they have not confined themselves to one certain number: it is building an house without a model; and when they succeeded in such undertakings, they ought to have sacrificed to Fortune, not to the Muses.

'Next, for the plot, which Aristotle called τὸ μυθος,[11] and often τῶν πραγμάτων σύνθεσις,[12] and from him the Romans *Fabula,* it has already been judiciously observed by a late writer, that in their tragedies it was only some tale derived from Thebes or Troy, or at least something that happened in those two ages; which was worn so threadbare by the pens of all the epic poets, and even by tradition itself of the talkative Greeklings, (as Ben Jonson calls them,) that before it came upon the stage, it was already known to all the audience: and the people, so soon as ever they heard the name of Œdipus, knew as well as the poet, that he had killed his father by a mistake, and committed incest with his mother, before the play; that they were now to hear of a great plague, an oracle, and the ghost of Laius: so that they sat with a yawning kind of expectation, till he was to come with his eyes pulled out, and speak a hundred or two of verses in a tragic tone, in complaint of his misfortunes. But one Œdipus, Hercules, or Medea, had been tolerable: poor people, they scaped not so good cheap; they had still the *chapon bouillé*[13] set before them, till their appetites were cloyed with the same dish, and, the novelty being gone, the pleasure vanished; so that one main end of Dramatic Poesy in its definition, which was to cause delight, was of consequence destroyed.

'In their comedies, the Romans generally borrowed their plots from the Greek poets; and theirs was commonly a little girl stolen or wandered from her parents, brought back unknown to the same city, there got with child by some lewd young fellow, who, by the help of his servant, cheats his father; and when her time comes, to cry *Juno Lucina, fer opem,*[14] one or other sees a little box or cabinet which was carried away with her, and so discovers her to her friends, if some god do not prevent it, by coming down in a machine, and take the thanks of it to himself.

'By the plot you may guess much of the characters of the persons. An old father, who would willingly, before he dies, see his son well married; his debauched son, kind in his nature to his wench, but miserably in want of money; a servant or slave, who has so much wit to strike in with him, and help to dupe his father; a braggadochio captain, a parasite, and a lady of pleasure.

[11] *To mythos;* compare English *myth.*
[12] *Ton pragmaton synthesis,* the putting together of the action.
[13] Boiled capon, *literally. Probably meaning* a luxury.
[14] Juno, goddess of childbirth, bring help.

'As for the poor honest maid, whom all the story is built upon, and who ought to be one of the principal actors in the play, she is commonly a mute in it: she has the breeding of the old Elizabeth way, for maids to be seen and not to be heard; and it is enough you know she is willing to be married, when the fifth act requires it.

'These are plots built after the Italian mode of houses; you see through them all at once: the characters are indeed the imitations of Nature, but so narrow, as if they had imitated only an eye or an hand, and did not dare to venture on the lines of a face, or the proportion of a body.

[handwritten margin note: One dimensional characters no risk taken]

'But in how strait a compass soever they have bounded their plots and characters, we will pass it by, if they have regularly pursued them, and perfectly observed those three Unities of Time, Place, and Action; the knowledge of which you say is derived to us from them. But in the first place give me leave to tell you, that the Unity of Place, however it might be practised by them, was never any of their rules: we neither find it in Aristotle, Horace, or any who have written of it, till in our age the French poets first made it a precept of the stage. The Unity of Time, even Terence himself (who was the best and most regular of them) has neglected: his *Heautontimorumenos,* or *Self-Punisher,* takes up visibly two days; therefore, says Scaliger, the two first acts concluding the first day were acted overnight; the three last on the ensuing day; and Euripides, in tying himself to one day, has committed an absurdity never to be forgiven him; for in one of his tragedies he has made Theseus go from Athens to Thebes, which was about forty English miles, under the walls of it to give battle, and appear victorious in the next act; and yet, from the time of his departure to the return of the Nuntius, who gives the relation of his victory, Æthra and the Chorus have but thirty-six verses; that is not for every mile a verse.

'The like error is as evident in Terence his *Eunuch,* when Laches, the old man, enters in a mistake the house of Thais; where, betwixt his exit and the entrance of Pythias, who comes to give an ample relation of the garboyles he has raised within, Parmeno, who was left upon the stage, has not above five lines to speak. *C'est bien employer un temps si court,*[15] says the French poet, who furnished me with one of the observations: and almost all their tragedies will afford us examples of the like nature.

''Tis true, they have kept the continuity, or, as you called it, *liaison des scènes,* somewhat better: two do not perpetually come in together, talk, and go out together; and other two succeed them, and do the same throughout the act, which the English call by the name of single scenes; but the reason is, because they have seldom above two or three scenes, properly so called, in every act; for it is to be accounted a new scene, not every time the stage is empty; but every person who enters, though to others, makes it so; because he introduces a new business. Now the plots of their plays being narrow, and the persons few, one of their acts was written in a less compass than one of

---

[15] So short a time is well used.

our well-wrought scenes; and yet they are often deficient even in this. To go no further than Terence; you find in the *Eunuch* Antipho entering single in the midst of the third act, after Cremes and Pythias were gone off; in the same play you have likewise Dorias beginning the fourth act alone; and after she had made a relation of what was done at the Soldier's entertainment (which by the way was very inartificial, because she was presumed to speak directly to the audience, and to acquaint them with what was necessary to be known, but yet should have been so contrived by the poet as to have been told by persons of the drama to one another, and so by them to have come to the knowledge of the people), she quits the stage, and Phædria enters next, alone likewise: he also gives you an account of himself, and of his returning from the country, in monologue; to which unnatural way of narration Terence is subject in all his plays. In his *Adelphi,* or Brothers, Syrus and Demea enter after the scene was broken by the departure of Sostrata, Geta, and Canthara; and indeed you can scarce look into any of his comedies, where you will not presently discover the same interruption.

'But as they have failed both in laying of their plots, and managing of them, swerving from the rules of their own art by misrepresenting Nature to us, in which they have ill satisfied one intention of a play, which was delight; so in the instructive part they have erred worse: instead of punishing vice and rewarding virtue, they have often shown a prosperous wickedness, and an unhappy piety: they have set before us a bloody image of revenge in Medea, and given her dragons to convey her safe from punishment; a Priam and Astyanax murdered, and Cassandra ravished, and the lust and murder ending in the victory of him who acted them: in short, there is no indecorum in any of our modern plays, which if I would excuse, I could not shadow with some authority from the Ancients.

'And one farther note of them let me leave you: tragedies and comedies were not writ then as they are now, promiscuously, by the same person; but he who found his genius bending to the one, never attempted the other way. This is so plain, that I need not instance to you, that Aristophanes, Plautus, Terence, never any of them writ a tragedy; Æschylus, Euripides, Sophocles, and Seneca, never meddled with comedy: the sock and buskin were not worn by the same poet. Having then so much care to excel in one kind, very little is to be pardoned them, if they miscarried in it; and this would lead me to the consideration of their wit, had not Crites given me sufficient warning not to be too bold in my judgment of it; because, the languages being dead, and many of the customs and little accidents on which it depended lost to us, we are not competent judges of it. But though I grant that here and there we may miss the application of a proverb or a custom, yet a thing well said will be wit in all languages; and though it may lose something in the translation, yet to him who reads it in the original, 'tis still the same: he has an idea of its excellency, though it cannot pass from his mind into any other expression or words than those in which he finds it. When Phædria, in the *Eunuch,* had a command from his mistress to be absent two days, and, encouraging himself to go through with it, said, *Tandem ego non illa caream, si sit opus, vel totum triduum?*[16]—Parmeno, to mock the softness of his master, lifting up his hands and eyes, cries out, as it were in admiration, *Hui! universum triduum!*[17] the elegancy of which *universum,* though it cannot be rendered in our language, yet leaves an impression on our souls: but this happens seldom in him; in Plautus oftener, who is infinitely too bold in his metaphors and coining words, out of which many times his wit is nothing; which questionless was one reason why Horace falls upon him so severely in those verses:—

> *Sed proavi nostri Plautinos et nummeros et*
> *Laudavere sales, nimium patienter utrumque,*
> *Ne dicam stolidè.*[18]

For Horace himself was cautious to obtrude a new word on his readers, and makes custom and common use the best measure of receiving it into our writings:

> *Multa renascentur quae nunc cecidere cadentque*
> *Quae nunc sunt honore vocabula, si volet usus,*
> *Quem penes arbitrium est, et jus, et norma loquendi.*[19]

'The not observing this rule is that which the world has blamed in our satyrist, Cleveland: to express a thing hard and unnaturally, is his new way of elocution. 'Tis true, no poet but may sometimes use a catachresis: Virgil does it—

> *Mistaque ridenti colocasia fundet acantho*— [20]

in his eclogue of *Pollio;* and in his 7th *Æneid,*

> *. . . mirantur et undae,*
> *Miratur nemus insuetum fulgentia longe*
> *Scuta virum fluvio pictasque innare carinas.*[21]

And Ovid once so modestly, that he asks leave to do it:

> *. . . quem, si verbo audacia detur,*
> *Haud metuam summi dixisse Palatia caeli;*[22]

calling the court of Jupiter by the name of Augustus his palace; though in another place he is more bold, where he says,—*et longas visent Capitolia pompas.*[23] But to do this always, and never be able to write a line without it,

---

[16] Shall I not do without her for even three days if necessary?

[17] Alas, all of three days!

[18] Our ancestors praised the meter and wit of Plautus all too tolerantly, if not stupidly.

[19] Many words now disused will revive, and many now esteemed will wither, if custom demands; for custom determines the right usage in language.

[20] And the colocasia shall flower, joined with the smiling acanthus.

[21] The woods and waters wonder at the gleam/Of shields, and painted ships, that stem the stream. (Dryden)

[22] If I may be allowed a bold metaphor, I should not fear to call it the imperial palace.

[23] The capitol will see long processions.

though it may be admired by some few pedants, will not pass upon those who know that wit is best conveyed to us in the most easy language; and is most to be admired when a great thought comes dressed in words so commonly received, that it is understood by the meanest apprehensions, as the best meat is the most easily digested: but we cannot read a verse of Cleveland's without making a face at it, as if every word were a pill to swallow: he gives us many times a hard nut to break our teeth, without a kernel for our pains. So that there is this difference betwixt his *Satires* and doctor Donne's; that the one gives us deep thoughts in common language, though rough cadence; the other gives us common thoughts in abstruse words: 'tis true, in some places his wit is independent of his words, as in that of the *Rebel Scot*:

Had *Cain* been *Scot*, God would have chang'd his doom;
Not forc'd him wander, but confin'd him home.

'*Si sic omnia dixisset!*[24] This is wit in all languages: 'tis like Mercury, never to be lost or killed:—and so that other—

For beauty, like white powder, makes no noise,
And yet the silent hypocrite destroys.

You see, the last line is highly metaphorical, but it is so soft and gentle, that it does not shock us as we read it.

'But, to return from whence I have digressed, to the consideration of the Ancients' writing, and their wit; of which by this time you will grant us in some measure to be fit judges. Though I see many excellent thoughts in Seneca, yet he of them who had a genius most proper for the stage, was Ovid; he had a way of writing so fit to stir up a pleasing admiration and concernment, which are the objects of a tragedy, and to show the various movements of a soul combating betwixt two different passions, that, had he lived in our age, or in his own could have writ with our advantages, no man but must have yielded to him; and therefore I am confident the *Medea* is none of his: for, though I esteem it for the gravity and sententiousness of it, which he himself concludes to be suitable to a tragedy,—*Omne genus scripti gravitate tragaedia vincit*,[25]—yet it moves not my soul enough to judge that he, who in the epic way wrote things so near the drama as the story of Myrrha, of Caunus and Biblis, and the rest, should stir up no more concernment where he most endeavoured it. The master-piece of Seneca I hold to be that scene in the *Troades*, where Ulysses is seeking for Astyanax to kill him; there you see the tenderness of a mother so represented in Andromache, that it raises compassion to a high degree in the reader, and bears the nearest resemblance of any thing in their tragedies to the excellent scenes of passion in Shakespeare, or in Fletcher: for love-scenes, you will find few among them; their tragic poets dealt not with that soft passion, but with lust, cruelty, revenge, ambi-

[24] If only he had said everything thus.
[25] Tragedy exceeds every other kind of writing in gravity.

tion, and those bloody actions they produced; which were more capable of raising horror than compassion in an audience: leaving love untouched, whose gentleness would have tempered them, which is the most frequent of all the passions, and which, being the private concernment of every person, is soothed by viewing its own image in a public entertainment.

'Among their comedies, we find a scene or two of tenderness, and that where you would least expect it, in Plautus; but to speak generally, their lovers say little, when they see each other, but *anima mea, vita mea; ζωη και ψυχη*,[26] as the women in Juvenal's time used to cry out in the fury of their kindness: then indeed to speak sense were an offence. Any sudden gust of passion (as an extasy of love in an unexpected meeting) cannot better be expressed than in a word and a sigh, breaking one another. Nature is dumb on such occasions; and to make her speak, would be to represent her unlike herself. But there are a thousand other concernments of lovers, as jealousies, complaints, contrivances, and the like, where not to open their minds at large to each other, were to be wanting to their own love, and to the expectation of the audience; who watch the movements of their minds, as much as the changes of their fortunes. For the imaging of the first is properly the work of a poet; the latter he borrows of the historian.'

Eugenius was proceeding in that part of his discourse, when Crites interrupted him. 'I see,' said he, 'Eugenius and I are never like to have this question decided betwixt us; for he maintains the Moderns have acquired a new perfection in writing; I can only grant they have altered the mode of it. Homer described his heroes men of great appetites, lovers of beef broiled upon the coals, and good fellows; contrary to the practice of the French Romances, whose heroes neither eat, nor drink, nor sleep, for love. Virgil makes Æneas a bold avower of his own virtues:

Sum pius Æneas, fama super aethera notus:[27]

which in the civility of our poets is the character of a fanfaron or Hector: for with us the knight takes occasion to walk out, or sleep, to avoid the vanity of telling his own story, which the trusty squire is ever to perform for him. So in their love-scenes, of which Eugenius spoke last, the Ancients were more hearty, we more talkative: they writ love as it was then the mode to make it; and I will grant thus much to Eugenius, that perhaps one of their poets, had he lived in our age, *si foret hoc nostrum fato delapsus in ævum*[28] (as Horace says of Lucilius), he had altered many things; not that they were not as natural before, but that he might accommodate himself to the age he lived in. Yet in the mean time, we are not to conclude any thing rashly against those great men, but preserve to them the dignity of masters, and give that honour to their memories, *quos Libitina sacravit*,[29] part of which we expect may be paid to us in future times.'

[26] *Zoe kai psyche,* my soul, my life.
[27] I am pious Aeneas, whose fame is known above the heavens.
[28] If he had been dropped into our age by fate.
[29] Which Libitina has consecrated.

This moderation of Crites, as it was pleasing to all the company, so it put an end to that dispute; which Eugenius, who seemed to have the better of the argument, would urge no farther: but Lisideius, after he had acknowledged himself of Eugenius his opinion concerning the Ancients, yet told him, he had forborne, till his discourse were ended, to ask him why he preferred the English plays above those of other nations? and whether we ought not to submit our stage to the exactness of our neighbours?

'Though,' said Eugenius, 'I am at all times ready to defend the honour of my country against the French, and to maintain, we are as well able to vanquish them with our pens, as our ancestors have been with their swords; yet, if you please,' added he, looking upon Neander, 'I will commit this cause to my friend's management; his opinion of our plays is the same with mine: and besides, there is no reason, that Crites and I, who have now left the stage, should re-enter so suddenly upon it; which is against the laws of comedy.'

'If the question had been stated,' replied Lisideius, 'who had writ best, the French or English, forty years ago, I should have been of you opinion, and adjudged the honour to our own nation; but since that time' (said he, turning towards Neander) 'we have been so long together bad Englishmen, that we had not leisure to be good poets. Beaumont, Fletcher, and Jonson (who were only capable of bringing us to that degree of perfection which we have) were just then leaving the world; as if (in an age of so much horror) wit, and those milder studies of humanity, had no farther business among us. But the Muses, who ever follow peace, went to plant in another country: it was then that the great Cardinal of Richelieu began to take them into his production; and that, by his encouragement, Corneille, and some other Frenchmen, reformed their theatre, which before was as much below ours, as it now surpasses it and the rest of Europe. But because Crites in his discourse for the Ancients has prevented me, by touching upon many rules of the stage which the Moderns have borrowed from them, I shall only, in short, demand of you, whether you are not convinced that of all nations the French have best observed them? In the Unity of Time you find them so scrupulous, that it yet remains a dispute among their poets, whether the artificial day of twelve hours, more or less, be not meant by Aristotle, rather than the natural one of twenty-four; and consequently, whether all plays ought not to be reduced into that compass. This I can testify, that in all their dramas writ within these last twenty years and upwards, I have not observed any that have extended the time to thirty hours: in the Unity of Place they are full as scrupulous; for many of their critics limit it to that very spot of ground where the play is supposed to begin; none of them exceed the compass of the same town or city. The Unity of Action in all plays is yet more conspicuous; for they do not burden them with underplots, as the English do: which is the reason why many scenes of our tragi-comedies carry on a design that is nothing of kin to the main plot; and that we see two distinct webs in a play, like those in ill-wrought stuffs; and two actions, that is, two plays, carried on together, to the confounding of the audience; who, before they are warm in their concernments for one part, are diverted to another; and by that means espouse the interest of neither. From hence likewise it arises, that the one half of our actors are not known to the other. They keep their distances, as if they were Montagues and Capulets, and seldom begin an acquaintance till the last scene of the fifth act, when they are all to meet upon the stage. There is no theatre in the world has any thing so absurd as the English tragi-comedy; 'tis a drama of our own invention, and the fashion of it is enough to proclaim it so; here a course of mirth, there another of sadness and passion, a third of honour, and fourth a duel: thus, in two hours and a half, we run through all the fits of Bedlam. The French affords you as much variety on the same day, but they do it not so unseasonably, or *mal à propos*, as we: our poets present you the play and the farce together; and our stages still retain somewhat of the original civility of the *Red Bull:*

> *Atque ursum et pugiles media inter carmina poscunt.*[30]

The end of tragedies or serious plays, says Aristotle, is to beget admiration, compassion, or concernment; but are not mirth and compassion things incompatible? and is it not evident that the poet must of necessity destroy the former by intermingling of the latter? that is, he must ruin the sole end and object of his tragedy, to introduce somewhat that is forced in, and is not of the body of it. Would you not think that physician mad, who, having prescribed a purge, should immediately order you to take restringents upon it?

But to leave our plays, and return to theirs. I have noted one great advantage they have had in the plotting of their tragedies; that is, they are always grounded upon some known history: according to that of Horace, *Ex noto fictum carmen sequar*[31]; and in that they have so imitated the Ancients, that they have surpassed them. For the Ancients, as was observed before, took for the foundation of their plays some poetical fiction, such as under that consideration could move but little concernment in the audience, because they already knew the event of it. But the French goes farther:

> *Atque ita mentitur, sic veris falsa remiscet,*
> *Primo ne medium, medio ne discrepet imum.*[32]

He so interweaves truth with probable fiction, that he puts a pleasing fallacy upon us; mends the intrigues of fate, and dispenses with the severity of history, to reward that virtue which has been rendered to us there unfortunate. Sometimes the story has left the success so doubtful, that the writer is free, by the privilege of a poet, to take that which of two or more relations will best suit with his design: as for example, the death of Cyrus, whom Justin and some others report to have perished in the Scythian war, but Xenophon affirms to have died in his bed of extreme old age. Nay more, when the event is past dispute, even then we are willing to be deceived, and the poet, if he con-

---

[30] In the middle of plays they ask for a bear and boxers.

[31] From a well-known story, I should bring a poem.

[32] He so lies, and mixes the false with the true, that you cannot tell apart the beginning, middle, or end.

trives it with appearance of truth, has all the audience of his party; at least during the time his play is acting: so naturally we are kind to virtue, when our own interest is not in question, that we take it up as the general concernment of mankind. On the other side, if you consider the historical plays of Shakespeare, they are rather so many chronicles of kings, or the business many times of thirty or forty years, cramped into a representation of two hours and an half; which is not to imitate or paint Nature, but rather to draw her in miniature, to take her in little; to look upon her through the wrong end of a perspective, and receive her images not only much less, but infinitely more imperfect than the life: this, instead of making a play delightful, renders it ridiculous:—

> *Quodcunque ostendis mihi sic, incredulus odi.*[33]

For the spirit of man cannot be satisfied but with truth, or at least verisimility; and a poem is to contain, if not τὰ ἔτυμα, yet ἐτύμοισιν ὁμοῖα,[34] as one of the Greek poets has expressed it.

'Another thing in which the French differ from us and from the Spaniards, is, that they do not embarrass, or cumber themselves with too much plot; they only represent so much of a story as will constitute one whole and great action sufficient for a play; we, who undertake more, do but multiply adventures; which, not being produced from one another, as effects from causes, but barely following, constitute many actions in the drama, and consequently make it many plays.

'But by pursuing close one argument, which is not cloyed with many turns, the French have gained more liberty for verse, in which they write; they have leisure to dwell on a subject which deserves it; and to represent the passions (which we have acknowledged to be the poet's work), without being hurried from one thing to another, as we are in the plays of Calderon, which we have seen lately upon our theatres, under the name of Spanish plots. I have taken notice but of one tragedy of ours, whose plot has that uniformity and unity of design in it, which I have commended in the French; and that is *Rollo*, or rather, under the name of Rollo, the story of Bassianus and Geta in Herodian: there indeed the plot is neither large nor intricate, but just enough to fill the minds of the audience, not to cloy them. Besides, you see it founded upon the truth of history, only the time of the action is not reduceable to the strictness of the rules; and you see in some places a little farce mingled, which is below the dignity of the other parts; and in this all our poets are extremely peccant: even Ben Jonson himself, in *Sejanus* and *Catiline*, has given us this oleo of a play, this unnatural mixture of comedy and tragedy; which to me sounds just as ridiculously as the history of David with the merry humours of Golias. In *Sejanus* you may take notice of the scene betwixt Livia and the physician, which is a pleasant satire upon the artificial helps of beauty: in *Catiline* you may see the

---

[33] Whatever you show me in this way I find unbelievable and disgusting.
[34] *Ta etuma; etumoisin omoia.* True things; things like the truth.

parliament of women; the little envies of them to one another; and all that passes betwixt Curio and Fulvia: scenes admirable in their kind, but of an ill mingle with the rest.

'But I return again to the French writers, who, as I have said, do not burden themselves too much with plot, which has been reproached to them by an *ingenious person* of our nation as a fault; for, he says, they commonly make but one person considerable in a play; they dwell on him, and his concernments, while the rest of the persons are only subservient to set him off. If he intends this by it, that there is one person in the play who is of greater dignity than the rest, he must tax, not only theirs, but those of the Ancients, and which he would be loth to do, the best of ours; for it is impossible but that one person must be more conspicuous in it than any other, and consequently the greatest share in the action must devolve on him. We see it so in the management of all affairs; even in the most equal aristocracy, the balance cannot be so justly poised, but some one will be superior to the rest, either in parts, fortune, interest, or the consideration of some glorious exploit; which will reduce the greatest part of business into his hands.

'But, if he would have us to imagine, that in exalting one character the rest of them are neglected, and that all of them have not some share or other in the action of the play, I desire him to produce any of Corneille's tragedies, wherein every person, like so many servants in a well-governed family, has not some employment, and who is not necessary to the carrying on of the plot, or at least to your understanding it.

'There are indeed some protatick persons in the Ancients, whom they make use of in their plays, either to hear or give the relation: but the French avoid this with great address, making their narrations only to, or by such, who are some way interested in the main design. And now I am speaking of relations, I cannot take a fitter opportunity to add this in favour of the French, that they often use them with better judgment and more *à propos* than the English do. Not that I commend narrations in general,—but there are two sorts of them. One, of those things which are antecedent to the play, and are related to make the conduct of it more clear to us. But 'tis a fault to choose such subjects for the stage as will force us on that rock, because we see they are seldom listened to by the audience, and that is many times the ruin of the play; for, being once let pass without attention, the audience can never recover themselves to understand the plot: and indeed it is somewhat unreasonable that they should be put to so much trouble, as that, to comprehend what passes in their sight, they must have recourse to what was done, perhaps, ten or twenty years ago.

'But there is another sort of relations, that is, of things happening in the action of the play, and supposed to be done behind the scenes; and this is many times both convenient and beautiful; for by it the French avoid the tumult which we are subject to in England, by representing duels, battles, and the like; which renders our stage too like the theatres where they fight prizes. For what is more ridiculous than to represent an army with a drum and five men behind it; all which the hero of the other side is to drive in before him; or to see a duel fought, and one slain with two or three thrusts of the foils, which we know are so blunted, that we might give a man an hour to kill another in good earnest with them.

'I have observed that in all our tragedies, the audience cannot forbear laughing when the actors are to die; it is the most comic part of the whole play. All *passions* may be lively represented on the stage, if to the well-writing of them the actor supplies a good commanded voice, and limbs that move easily, and without stiffness; but there are many *actions* which can never be imitated to a just height: dying especially is a thing which none but a Roman gladiator could naturally perform on the stage, when he did not imitate or represent, but naturally do it; and therefore it is better to omit the representation of it.

'The words of a good writer, which describe it lively, will make a deeper impression of belief in us than all the actor can persuade us to, when he seems to fall dead before us; as a poet in the description of a beautiful garden, or a meadow, will please our imagination more than the place itself can please our sight. When we see death represented, we are convinced it is but fiction; but when we hear it related, our eyes, the strongest witnesses, are wanting, which might have undeceived us; and we are all willing to favour the sleight, when the poet does not too grossly impose on us. They therefore who imagine these relations would make no concernment in the audience, are deceived, by confounding them with the other, which are of things antecedent to the play: those are made often in cold blood, as I may say, to the audience; but these are warmed with our concernments, which were before awakened in the play. What the philosophers say of motion, that, when it is once begun, it continues of itself, and will do so to eternity, without some stop put to it, is clearly true on this occasion: the soul, being already moved with the characters and fortunes of those imaginary persons, continues going of its own accord; and we are no more weary to hear what becomes of them when they are not on the stage, than we are to listen to the news of an absent mistress. But it is objected, that if one part of the play may be related, then why not all? I answer, some parts of the action are more fit to be represented, some to be related. Corneille says judiciously, that the poet is not obliged to expose to view all particular actions which conduce to the principal: he ought to select such of them to be seen, which will appear with the greatest beauty, either by the magnificence of the show, or the vehemence of passions which they produce, or some other charm which they have in them; and let the rest arrive to the audience by narration. 'Tis a great mistake in us to believe the French present no part of the action on the stage; every alteration or crossing of a design, every new-sprung passion, and turn of it, is a part of the action, and much the noblest, except we conceive nothing to be action till they come to blows; as if the painting of the hero's mind were not more properly the poet's work than the strength of his body. Nor does this anything contradict the opinion of Horace, where he tells us,

Segnius irritant animos demissa per aurem,
Quam quae sunt oculis subjecta fidelibus.[35]

For he says immediately after,

. . . . . *Non tamen intus*
Digna geri promes in scenam; multaque *tolles*
Ex oculis, quae mox narret facundia præsens.[36]

Among which many he recounts some:

Nec pueros coram populo Medea trucidet,
Aut in avem Procne mutetur, Cadmus in anguem: &c.[37]

That is, those actions which by reason of their cruelty will cause aversion in us, or by reason of their impossibility, unbelief, ought either wholly to be avoided by a poet, or only delivered by narration. To which we may have leave to add such as to avoid tumult (as was before hinted), or to reduce the plot into a more reasonable compass of time, or for defect of beauty in them, are rather to be related than presented to the eye. Examples of all these kinds are frequent, not only among all the Ancients, but in the best received of our English poets. We find Ben Jonson using them in his *Magnetick Lady,* where one comes out from dinner, and relates the quarrels and disorders of it, to save the undecent appearance of them on the stage, and to abbreviate the story; and this in express imitation of Terence, who had done the same before him in his *Eunuch,* where Pythias makes the like relation of what had happened within at the Soldier's entertainment. The relations likewise of Sejanus's death, and the prodigies before it, are remarkable; the one of which was hid from sight, to avoid the horror and tumult of the representation; the other, to shun the introducing of things impossible to be believed. In that excellent play, *The King and no King,* Fletcher goes yet farther; for the whole unravelling of the plot is done by narration in the fifth act, after the manner of the Ancients; and it moves great concernment in the audience, though it be only a relation of what was done many years before the play. I could multiply other instances, but these are sufficient to prove that there is no error in choosing a subject which requires this sort of narrations; in the ill managing of them, there may.

'But I find I have been too long in this discourse, since the French have many other excellencies not common to us; as that you never see any of their plays end with a conversion, or simple change of will, which is the ordinary way which our poets use to end theirs. It shows little art in the conclusion of a dramatic poem, when they who have hindered the felicity during the four

---

[35] What we hear through our ears stirs us less strongly than what we see through our eyes.

[36] You should not bring on stage what should be done off it: many things should be kept out of sight, and instead told with a vivid eloquence.

[37] Medea should not cut up her children in front of the audience, Procne should not be changed into a bird there, nor Cadmus into a snake, etc.

acts, desist from it in the fifth, without some powerful cause to take them off; and though I deny not but such reasons may be found, yet it is a path that is cautiously to be trod, and the poet is to be sure he convinces the audience that the motive is strong enough. As for example, the conversion of the Usurer in *The Scornful Lady*, seems to me a little forced; for, being an Usurer, which implies a lover of money to the highest degree of covetousness (and such the poet has represented him), the account he gives for the sudden change is, that he has been duped by the wild young fellow; which in reason might render him more wary another time, and make him punish himself with harder fare and coarser clothes, to get it up again: but that he should look on it as a judgment, and so repent, we may expect to hear of in a sermon, but I should never endure it in a play.

'I pass by this; neither will I insist on the care they take, that no person after his first entrance shall ever appear, but the business which brings him upon the stage shall be evident; which, if observed, must needs render all the events in the play more natural; for there you see the probability of every accident, in the cause that produced it; and that which appears chance in the play, will seem so reasonable to you, that you will there find it almost necessary: so that in the exits of the actors you have a clear account of their purpose and design in the next entrance (though, if the scene be well wrought, the event will commonly deceive you), for there is nothing so absurd, says Corneille, as for an actor to leave the stage, only because he has no more to say.

'I should now speak of the beauty of their rhyme, and the just reason I have to prefer that way of writing in tragedies before ours in blank verse; but because it is partly received by us, and therefore not altogether peculiar to them, I will say no more of it in relation to their plays. For our own, I doubt not but it will exceedingly beautify them; and I can see but one reason why it should not generally obtain, that is, because our poets write so ill in it. This indeed may prove a more prevailing argument than all others which are used to destroy it, and therefore I am only troubled when great and judicious poets, and those who are acknowledged such, have writ or spoke against it: as for others, they are to be answered by that one sentence of an accident author:—*Sed ut primo ad consequendos eos quos priores ducimus, accendimur, ita ubi aut præteriri, aut æquari eos posse desperavimus, studium cum spe senescit: quod, scilicet, assequi non potest, sequi desinit; . . . præteritoque eo in quo eminere non possumus, aliquid in quo nitamur, conquirimus.*'[38]

Lisideius concluded in this manner; and Neander, after a little pause, thus answered him:

'I shall grant Lisideius, without much dispute, a great part of what he has urged against us; for I acknowledge that the French contrive their plots more regularly, and observe the laws of comedy, and decorum of the stage (to speak generally), with more exactness than the English. Farther, I deny

---

[38] Just as we are inspired to follow those we consider most worthy, so—when we despair of excelling or equaling them—our enthusiasm and hope diminish. For what it cannot attain, it ceases to follow; . . . after we have abandoned what we are unable to excel in, we look for something else for which to strive. (Velleius Paterculus, I, 17)

not but he has taxed us justly in some irregularities of ours, which he has mentioned; yet, after all, I am of opinion that neither our faults nor their virtues are considerable enough to place them above us.

'For the lively imitation of Nature being in the definition of a play, those which best fulfil that law ought to be esteemed superior to the others. 'Tis true, those beauties of the French poesy are such as will raise perfection higher where it is, but are not sufficient to give it where it is not: they are indeed the beauties of a statue, but not of a man, because not animated with the soul of Poesy, which is imitation of humour and passions: and this Lisideius himself, or any other, however biassed to their party, cannot but acknowledge, if he will either compare the humours of our comedies, or the characters of our serious plays, with theirs. He that will look upon theirs which have been written till these last ten years, or thereabouts, will find it an hard matter to pick out two or three passable humours amongst them. Corneille himself, their arch-poet, what has he produced except *The Liar,* and you know how it was cried up in France; but when it came upon the English stage, though well translated, and that part of Dorant acted to so much advantage by Mr. Hart as I am confident it never received in its own country, the most favourable to it would not put it in competition with many of Fletcher's or Ben Jonson's. In the rest of Corneille's comedies you have little humour; he tells you himself, his way is, first to show two lovers in good intelligence with each other; in the working up of the play to embroil them by some mistake, and in the latter end to clear it, and reconcile them.

'But of late years Molière, the younger Corneille, Quinault, and some others, have been imitating afar off the quick turns and graces of the English stage. They have mixed their serious plays with mirth, like our tragicomedies, since the death of Cardinal Richelieu; which Lisideius and many others not observing, have commended that in them for a virtue which they themselves no longer practice. Most of their new plays are, like some of ours, derived from the Spanish novels. There is scarce one of them without a veil, and a trusty Diego, who drolls much after the rate of the *Adventures.* But their humours, if I may grace them with that name, are so thin-sown, that never above one of them comes up in any play. I dare take upon me to find more variety of them in some one play of Ben Jonson's, than in all theirs together; as he who has seen *The Alchemist, The Silent Woman,* or *Bartholomew-Fair,* cannot but acknowledge with me.

'I grant the French have performed what was possible on the groundwork of the Spanish plays; what was pleasant before, they have made regular: but there is not above one good play to be writ on all those plots; they are too much alike to please often; which we need not the experience of our own stage to justify. As for their new way of mingling mirth with serious plot, I do not, with Lisideius, condemn the thing, though I cannot approve their manner of doing it. He tells us, we cannot so speedily recollect ourselves after a scene of great passion and concernment, as to pass to another of mirth and humour, and to enjoy it with any relish: but why should he imagine the soul of man more heavy than his senses? Does not the eye pass from an unpleasant object to a pleasant in a much shorter time than is required to this?

and does not the unpleasantness of the first commend the beauty of the latter? The old rule of logic might have convinced him, that contraries, when placed near, set off each other. A continued gravity keeps the spirit too much bent; we must refresh it sometimes, as we bait in a journey, that we may go on with greater ease. A scene of mirth, mixed with tragedy, has the same effect upon us which our music has betwixt the acts; and that we find a relief to us from the best plots and language of the stage, if the discourses have been long. I must therefore have stronger arguments, ere I am convinced that compassion and mirth in the same subject destroy each other; and in the mean time cannot but conclude, to the honour of our nation, that we have invented, increased, and perfected a more pleasant way of writing for the stage, than was ever known to the ancients or moderns of any nation, which is tragi-comedy.

'And this leads me to wonder why Lisideius and many others should cry up the barrenness of the French plots, above the variety and copiousness of the English. Their plots are single; they carry on one design, which is pushed forward by all the actors, every scene in the play contributing and moving towards it. Our plays, besides the main design, have underplots or by-concernments, of less considerable persons and intrigues, which are carried on with the motion of the main plot: just as they say the orb of the fixed stars, and those of the planets, though they have motions of their own, are whirled about by the motion of the *Primum Mobile,* in which they are contained. That similitude expresses much of the English stage; for if contrary motions may be found in nature to agree; if a planet can go east and west at the same time, one way by virtue of his own motion, the other by the force of the First Mover, it will not be difficult to imagine how the under-plot, which is only different, not contrary to the great design, may naturally be conducted along with it.

'Eugenius has already shown us, from the confession of the French poets, that the Unity of Action is sufficiently preserved, if all the imperfect actions of the play are conducing to the main design; but when those petty intrigues of a play are so ill ordered, that they have no coherence with the other, I must grant that Lisideius has reason to tax that want of due connexion; for co-ordination in a play is as dangerous and unnatural as in a state. In the mean time he must acknowledge, our variety, if well ordered, will afford a greater pleasure to the audience.

'As for his other argument, that by pursuing one single theme they gain an advantage to express and work up the passions, I wish any example he could bring from them would make it good; for I confess their verses are to me the coldest I have ever read. Neither, indeed, it is possible for them, in the way they take, so to express passion, as that the effects of it should appear in the concernment of an audience, their speeches being so many declamations, which tire us with the length; so that instead of persuading us to grieve for their imaginary heroes, we are concerned for our own trouble, as we are in the tedious visits of bad company; we are in pain till they are gone. When the French stage came to be reformed by Cardinal Richelieu, those long harangues were introduced, to comply with the gravity of a churchman. Look upon the

Cinna and the *Pompey*; they are not so properly to be called plays, as long discourses of reason of state; and *Polieucte* in matters of religion is as solemn as the
long stops upon our organs. Since that time it is grown into a custom, and their
actors speak by the hour-glass, as our parsons do; nay, they account it the
grace of their parts, and think themselves disparaged by the poet, if they may
not twice or thrice in a play entertain the audience with a speech of an hundred
or two hundred lines. I deny not but this may suit well enough with the
French; for as we, who are a more sullen people, come to be diverted at our
plays, so they, who are of an airy and gay temper, come thither to make themselves more serious: and this I conceive to be one reason why comedy is more
pleasing to us, and tragedies to them. But to speak generally: it cannot be denied that short speeches and replies are more apt to move the passions and
beget concernment in us, than the other; for it is unnatural for any one in a gust
of passion to speak long together, or for another in the same condition to suffer
him, without interruption. Grief and passion are like floods raised in little
brooks by a sudden rain; they are quickly up; and if the concernment be
poured unexpectedly in upon us, it overflows us: but a long sober shower
gives them leisure to run out as they came in, without troubling the ordinary
current. As for Comedy, repartee is one of its chiefest graces; the greatest pleasure of the audience is a chace of wit, kept up on both sides, and swiftly managed. And this our forefathers, if not we, have had in Fletcher's plays, to a
much higher degree of perfection than the French poets can arrive at.

'There is another part of Lisideius his discourse, in which he has rather
excused our neighbours, than commended them; that is, for aiming only to
make one person considerable in their plays. 'Tis very true what he has
urged, that one character in all plays, even without the poet's care, will have
advantage of all the others; and that the design of the whole drama will
chiefly depend on it. But this hinders not that there may be more shining
characters in the play: many persons of a second magnitude, nay, some so
very near, so almost equal to the first, that greatness may be opposed to
greatness, and all the persons be made considerable, not only by their quality, but their action. 'Tis evident that the more the persons are, the greater
will be the variety of the plot. If then the parts are managed so regularly, that
the beauty of the whole be kept entire, and that the variety become not a perplexed and confused mass of accidents, you will find it infinitely pleasing to
be led in a labyrinth of design, where you see some of your way before you,
yet discern not the end till you arrive at it. And that all this is practicable, I
can produce for examples many of our English plays: as *The Maid's Tragedy,
The Alchemist, The Silent Woman*: I was going to have named *The Fox*, but that
the unity of design seems not exactly observed in it; for there appear two actions in the play; the first naturally ending with the fourth act; the second
forced from it in the fifth: which yet is the less to be condemned in him, because the disguise of Volpone, though it suited not with his character as a
crafty or covetous person, agreed well enough with that of a voluptuary; and
by it the poet gained the end he aimed at, the punishment of vice, and the reward of virtue, which that disguise produced. So that to judge equally of it, it
was an excellent fifth act, but not so naturally proceeding from the former.

'But to leave this, and pass to the latter part of Lisideius his discourse, which concerns relations: I must acknowledge with him, that the French have reason when they hide that part of the action which would occasion too much tumult on the stage, and choose rather to have it made known by narration to the audience. Farther, I think it very convenient, for the reasons he has given, that all incredible actions were removed; but, whether custom has so insinuated itself into our countrymen, or nature has so formed them to fierceness, I know not; but they will scarcely suffer combats and other objects of horror to be taken from them. And indeed, the indecency of tumults is all which can be objected against fighting: for why may not our imagination as well suffer itself to be deluded with the probability of it, as with any other thing in the play? For my part, I can with as great ease persuade myself that the blows which are struck, are given in good earnest, as I can, that they who strike them are kings or princes, or those persons which they represent. For objects of incredibility, I would be satisfied from Lisideius, whether we have any so removed from all appearance of truth, as are those of Corneille's *Andromède;* a play which has been frequented the most of any he has writ. If the Perseus, or the son of an heathen god, the Pegasus, and the Monster, were not capable to choke a strong belief, let him blame any representation of ours hereafter. Those indeed were objects of delight; yet the reason is the same as to the probability: for he makes it not a Ballet or masque, but a play, which is to resemble truth. But for death, that it ought not to be represented, I have, besides the arguments alleged by Lisideius, the authority of Ben Jonson, who has forborn it in his tragedies; for both the death of Sejanus and Catiline are related: though in the latter I cannot but observe one irregularity of that great poet; he has removed the scene in the same act from Rome to Catiline's army, and from thence again to Rome; and besides, has allowed a very inconsiderable time, after Catiline's speech, for the striking of the battle, and the return of Petreius, who is to relate the event of it to the senate: which I should not animadvert on him, who was otherwise a painful observer of τὸ πρέπον,[39] or the *decorum* of the stage, if he had not used extreme severity in his judgment on the incomparable Shakespeare for the same fault.—To conclude on this subject of relations; if we are to be blamed for showing too much of the action, the French are as faulty for discovering too little of it: a mean betwixt both should be observed by every judicious writer, so as the audience may neither be left unsatisfied by not seeing what is beautiful, or shocked by beholding what is either incredible or undecent.

'I hope I have already proved in this discourse, that though we are not altogether so punctual as the French, in observing the laws of Comedy, yet our errors are so few, and little, and those things wherein we excel them so considerable, that we ought of right to be preferred before them. But what will Lisideius say, if they themselves acknowledge they are too strictly tied up by those laws, for breaking which he has blamed the English? I will allege Corneille's words, as I find them in the end of his Discourse of the Three

---

[39] *To prepon.*

Unities:—*Il est facile aux spéculatifs d'estre sévères, etc.* "'Tis easy for speculative persons to judge severely; but if they would produce to public view ten
or twelve pieces of this nature, they would perhaps give more latitude to the
rules than I have done, when, by experience, they had known how much we
are bound up and constrained by them, and how many beauties of the stage
they banished from it." To illustrate a little what he has said: by their servile
observations of the Unities of Time and Place, and integrity of scenes, they
have brought on themselves that dearth of plot, and narrowness of imagination, which may be observed in all their plays. How many beautiful accidents
might naturally happen in two or three days, which cannot arrive with any
probability in the compass of twenty-four hours? There is time to be allowed
also for maturity of design, which, amongst great and prudent persons, such
as are often represented in Tragedy, cannot, with any likelihood of truth, be
brought to pass at so short a warning. Farther; by tying themselves strictly to
the Unity of Place, and unbroken scenes, they are forced many times to omit
some beauties which cannot be shown where the act began; but might, if the
scene were interrupted, and the stage cleared for the persons to enter in another place; and therefore the French poets are often forced upon absurdities;
for if the act begins in a chamber, all the persons in the play must have some
business or other to come thither, or else they are not to be shown that act;
and sometimes their characters are very unfitting to appear there. As, suppose it were the king's bed-chamber; yet the meanest man in the tragedy
must come and dispatch his business there, rather than in the lobby or court-
yard (which is fitter for him), for fear the stage should be cleared, and the
scenes broken. Many times they fall by it in a greater inconvenience; for they
keep their scenes unbroken, and yet change the place; as in one of their
newest plays, where the act begins in the street. There a gentleman is to meet
his friend; he sees him with his man, coming out from his father's house; they
talk together, and the first goes out: the second, who is a lover, has made an
appointment with his mistress; she appears at the window, and then we are
to imagine the scene lies under it. This gentleman is called away, and leaves
his servant with his mistress; presently her father is heard from within; the
young lady is afraid the servingman should be discovered, and thrusts him
in through a door, which is supposed to be her closet. After this, the father
enters to the daughter, and now the scene is in a house; for he is seeking from
one room to another for this poor Philipin, or French Diego, who is heard
from within, drolling and breaking many a miserable conceit upon his sad
condition. In this ridiculous manner the play goes on, the stage being never
empty all the while: so that the street, the window, the houses, and the closet,
are made to walk about, and the persons to stand still. Now what, I beseech
you, is more easy than to write a regular French play, or more difficult than
to write an irregular English one, like those of Fletcher, or of Shakespeare?

'If they content themselves, as Corneille did, with some flat design, which,
like an ill riddle, is found out ere it be half proposed, such plots we can make
every way regular, as easily as they; but whene'er they endeavour to rise to
any quick turns and counterturns of plot, as some of them have attempted,

since Corneille's plays have been less in vogue, you see they write as irregularly as we, though they cover it more speciously. Hence the reason is perspicuous, why no French plays, when translated, have, or ever can succeed on the English stage. For, if you consider the plots, our own are fuller of variety; if the writing, ours are more quick and fuller of spirit; and therefore 'tis a strange mistake in those who decry the way of writing plays in verse, as if the English therein imitated the French. We have borrowed nothing from them; our plots are weaved in English looms: we endeavour therein to follow the variety and greatness of characters which are derived to us from Shakespeare and Fletcher; the copiousness and well-knitting of the intrigues we have from Jonson; and for the verse itself we have English precedents of elder date than any of Corneille's plays. Not to name our old comedies before Shakespeare, which were all writ in verse of six feet, or Alexandrines, such as the French now use, I can show in Shakespeare, many scenes of rhyme together, and the like in Ben Jonson's tragedies: in *Catiline* and *Sejanus* sometimes thirty or forty lines, I mean besides the Chorus, or the monologues; which, by the way, showed Ben no enemy to this way of writing, especially if you look upon his *Sad Shepherd,* which goes sometimes on rhyme, sometimes on blank verse, like an horse who eases himself on trot and amble. You find him likewise commending Fletcher's pastoral of *The Faithful Shepherdess,* which is for the most part rhyme, though not refined to that purity to which it hath since been brought. And these examples are enough to clear us from a servile imitation of the French.

'But to return from whence I have digressed: I dare boldly affirm these two things of the English drama;—First, that we have many plays of ours as regular as any of theirs, and which, besides, have more variety of plot and characters; and secondly, that in most of the irregular plays of Shakespeare or Fletcher (for Ben Jonson's are for the most part regular) there is a more masculine fancy and greater spirit in the writing, than there is in any of the French. I could produce, even in Shakespeare's and Fletcher's works, some plays which are almost exactly formed; as *The Merry Wives of Windsor,* and *The Scornful Lady:* but because (generally speaking) Shakespeare, who writ first, did not perfectly observe the laws of Comedy, and Fletcher, who came nearer to perfection, yet through carelessness made many faults; I will take the pattern of a perfect play from Ben Jonson, who was a careful and learned observer of the dramatic laws, and from all his comedies I shall select *The Silent Woman;* of which I will make a short examen, according to those rules which the French observe.'

As Neander was beginning to examine *The Silent Woman,* Eugenius, looking earnestly upon him; 'I beseech you, Neander,' said he, 'gratify the company, and me in particular, so far, as before you speak of the play, to give us a character of the author; and tell us frankly your opinion, whether you do not think all writers, both French and English, ought to give place to him.'

'I fear,' replied Neander, 'that in obeying your commands I shall draw a little envy on myself. Besides, in performing them, it will be first necessary to speak somewhat of Shakespeare and Fletcher, his rivals in poesy; and one of them, in my opinion, at least his equal, perhaps his superior.

'To begin, then, with Shakespeare. He was the man who of all modern, and perhaps ancient poets, had the largest and most comprehensive soul. All the images of Nature were still present to him, and he drew them, not laboriously, but luckily; when he describes any thing, you more than see it, you feel it too. Those who accuse him to have wanted learning, give him the greater commendation: he was naturally learned; he needed not the spectacles of books to read Nature; he looked inwards, and found her there. I cannot say he is everywhere alike; were he so, I should do him injury to compare him with the greatest of mankind. He is many times flat, insipid; his comic wit degenerating into clenches, his serious swelling into bombast. But he is always great, when some great occasion is presented to him; no man can say he ever had a fit subject for his wit, and did not then raise himself as high above the rest of poets,

     Quantum lenta solent inter viburna cupressi.[40]

The consideration of this made Mr. Hales of Eaton say, that there was no subject of which any poet ever writ, but he would produce it much better treated of in Shakespeare; and however others are not generally preferred before him, yet the age wherein he lived, which had contemporaries with him Fletcher and Jonson, never equalled them to him in their esteem: and in the last King's court, when Ben's reputation was at highest, Sir John Suckling, and with him the greater part of the courtiers, set our Shakespeare far above him.

'Beaumont and Fletcher, of whom I am next to speak, had, with the advantage of Shakespeare's wit, which was their precedent, great natural gifts, improved by study: Beaumont especially being so accurate a judge of plays, that Ben Jonson, while he lived, submitted all his writings to his censure, and, 'tis thought, used his judgment in correcting, if not contriving, all his plots. What value he had for him, appears by the verses he writ to him; and therefore I need speak no farther of it. The first play that brought Fletcher and him in esteem was their *Philaster:* for before that, they had written two or three very unsuccessfully, as the like is reported of Ben Jonson, before he writ *Every Man in his Humour.* Their plots were generally more regular than Shakespeare's, especially those which were made before Beaumont's death; and they understood and imitated the conversation of gentlemen much better; whose wild debaucheries, and quickness of wit in repartees, no poet can ever paint as they have done. Humour, which Ben Jonson derived from particular persons, they made it not their business to describe: they represented all the passions very lively, but above all, love. I am apt to believe the English language in them arrived to its highest perfection: what words have since been taken in, are rather superfluous than ornamental. Their plays are now the most pleasant and frequent entertainments of the stage; two of theirs being acted through the year for one of Shakespeare's or Jonson's: the reason is, because there is a certain gaiety in their comedies, and pathos in their more serious plays, which suits generally with all men's humours. Shake-

---

[40] As cypresses raise themselves above scraggly shrubs.

speare's language is likewise a little obsolete, and Ben Jonson's wit comes short of theirs.

'As for Jonson, to whose character I am now arrived, if we look upon him while he was himself (for his last plays were but his dotages), I think him the most learned and judicious writer which any theatre ever had. He was a most severe judge of himself, as well as others. One cannot say he wanted wit, but rather that he was frugal of it. In his works you find little to retrench or alter. Wit, and language, and humour also in some measure, we had before him; but something of art was wanting to the Drama, till he came. He managed his strength to more advantage than any who preceded him. You seldom find him making love in any of his scenes, or endeavouring to move the passions; his genius was too sullen and saturnine to do it gracefully, especially when he knew he came after those who had performed both to such an height. Humour was his proper sphere; and in that he delighted most to represent mechanic people. He was deeply conversant in the Ancients, both Greek and Latin, and he borrowed boldly from them: there is scarce a poet or historian among the Roman authors of those times whom he has not translated in *Sejanus* and *Catiline*. But he has done his robberies so openly, that one may see he fears not to be taxed by any law. He invades authors like a monarch; and what would be theft in other poets, is only victory in him. With the spoils of these writers he so represents old Rome to us, in its rites, ceremonies, and customs, that if one of their poets had written either of his tragedies, we had seen less of it than in him. If there was any fault in his language, 'twas that he weaved it too closely and laboriously, in his serious plays: perhaps too, he did a little too much Romanize our tongue, leaving the words which he translated almost as much Latin as he found them: wherein, though he learnedly followed the idiom of their language, he did not enough comply with the idiom of ours. If I would compare him with Shakespeare, I must acknowledge him the more correct poet, but Shakespeare the greater wit. Shakespeare was the Homer, or father of our dramatic poets; Jonson was the Virgil, the pattern of elaborate writing; I admire him, but I love Shakespeare. To conclude of him; as he has given us the most correct plays, so in the precepts which he has laid down in his *Discoveries,* we have as many and profitable rules for perfecting the stage, as any wherewith the French can furnish us.

'Having thus spoken of the author, I proceed to the examination of his comedy, *The Silent Woman.*

'Examen of *The Silent Woman*

'To begin first with the length of the action; it is so far from exceeding the compass of a natural day, that it takes not up an artificial one. 'Tis all included in the limits of three hours and an half, which is no more than is required for the presentment on the stage. A beauty perhaps not much observed; if it had, we should not have looked on the Spanish translation of *Five*

Hours with so much wonder. The scene of it is laid in London; the latitude of place is almost as little as you can imagine; for it lies all within the compass of two houses, and after the first act, in one. The continuity of scenes is observed more than in any of our plays, except his own *Fox* and *Alchemist*. They are not broken above twice or thrice at most in the whole comedy; and in the two best of Corneille's plays, the *Cid* and *Cinna,* they are interrupted once apiece. The action of the play is entirely one; the end or aim of which is the settling Morose's estate on Dauphine. The intrigue of it is the greatest and most noble of any pure unmixed comedy in any language; you see in it many persons of various characters and humours, and all delightful: as first, Morose, or an old man, to whom all noise but his own talking is offensive. Some who would be thought critics, say this humour of his is forced: but to remove that objection, we may consider him first to be naturally of a delicate hearing, as many are, to whom all sharp sounds are unpleasant; and secondly, we may attribute much of it to the peevishness of his age, or the wayward authority of an old man in his own house, where he may make himself obeyed; and this the poet seems to allude to in his name Morose. Besides this, I am assured from divers persons, that Ben Jonson was actually acquainted with such a man, one altogether as ridiculous as he is here represented. Others say, it is not enough to find one man of such an humour; it must be common to more, and the more common the more natural. To prove this, they instance in the best of comical characters, Falstaff: there are many men resembling him; old, fat, merry, cowardly, drunken, amorous, vain, and lying. But to convince these people, I need but tell them, that humour is the ridiculous extravagance of conversation, wherein one man differs from all others. If then it be common, or communicated to many, how differs it from other men's? or what indeed causes it to be ridiculous so much as the singularity of it? As for Falstaff, he is not properly one humour, but a miscellany of humours or images, drawn from so many several men: that wherein he is singular is his wit, or those things he says *præter expectatum,* unexpected by the audience; his quick evasions, when you imagine him surprised, which, as they are extremely diverting of themselves, so receive a great addition from his person; for the very sight of such an unwieldy old debauched fellow is a comedy alone. And here, having a place so proper for it, I cannot but enlarge somewhat upon this subject of humour into which I am fallen. The ancients had little of it in their comedies; for the τὸ γελοῖον[41] of the Old Comedy, of which Aristophanes was chief, was not so much to imitate a man, as to make the people laugh at some odd conceit, which had commonly somewhat of unnatural or obscene in it. Thus, when you see Socrates brought upon the stage, you are not to imagine him made ridiculous by the imitation of his actions, but rather by making him perform something very unlike himself; something so childish and absurd, as by comparing it with the gravity of the true Socrates, makes a ridiculous object for the spectators. In their New Com-

---

[41] *To geloion,* the laughable.

edy which succeeded, the poets sought indeed to express the $\hat{\eta}\theta o s$,[42] as in their tragedies the $\pi\acute{\alpha}\theta o s$[43] of mankind. But this $\hat{\eta}\theta o s$ contained only the general characters of men and manners; as old men, lovers, serving-men, courtezans, parasites, and such other persons as we see in their comedies; all which they made alike: that is, one old man or father, one lover, one courtezan, so like another, as if the first of them had begot the rest of every sort: *Ex homine hunc natum dicas*.[44] The same custom they observed likewise in their tragedies. As for the French, though they have the word *humeur* among them, yet they have small use of it in their comedies or farces; they being but ill imitations of the *ridiculum,* or that which stirred up laughter in the Old Comedy. But among the English 'tis otherwise: where by humour is meant some extravagant habit, passion, or affection, particular (as I said before) to some one person, by the oddness of which, he is immediately distinguished from the rest of men; which being lively and naturally represented, most frequently begets that malicious pleasure in the audience which is testified by laughter; as all things which are deviations from common customs are ever the aptest to produce it: though by the way this laughter is only accidental, as the person represented is fantastic or bizarre; but pleasure is essential to it, as the imitation of what is natural. The description of these humours, drawn from the knowledge and observation of particular persons, was the peculiar genius and talent of Ben Jonson; to whose play I now return.

'Besides Morose, there are at least nine or ten different characters and humours in *The Silent Woman;* all which persons have several concernments of their own, yet are all used by the poet, to the conducting of the main design to perfection. I shall not waste time in commending the writing of this play; but I will give you my opinion, that there is more wit and acuteness of fancy in it than in any of Ben Jonson's. Besides, that he has here described the conversation of gentlemen in the persons of True-Wit, and his friends, with more gaiety, air, and freedom, than in the rest of his comedies. For the contrivance of the plot, 'tis extreme elaborate, and yet withal easy; for the $\lambda\acute{\upsilon}\sigma\iota s$,[45] or untying of it, 'tis so admirable, that when it is done, no one of the audience would think the poet could have missed it; and yet it was concealed so much before the last scene, that any other way would sooner have entered into your thoughts. But I dare not take upon me to commend the fabric of it, because it is altogether so full of art, that I must unravel every scene in it to commend it as I ought. And this excellent contrivance is still the more to be admired, because 'tis comedy, where the persons are only of common rank, and their business private, not elevated by passions or high concernments, as in serious plays. Here every one is a proper judge of all he sees, nothing is represented but that with which he daily converses: so that by consequence all faults lie open to discovery, and few are pardonable. 'Tis this which Horace has judiciously observed:

[42] *Ethos*, character.
[43] *Pathos*, emotion.
[44] You would say that one was born from another.
[45] *Lysis.*

Creditur, ex medio quia res arcessit, habere
Sudoris minimum: sed habet Comedia tanto
Plus oneris, quanto veniæ minus.[46]

But our poet who was not ignorant of these difficulties, had prevailed himself of all advantages; as he who designs a large leap takes his rise from the highest ground. One of these advantages is that which Corneille has laid down as the greatest which can arrive to any poem, and which he himself could never compass above thrice in all his plays; viz. the making choice of some signal and long-expected day, whereon the action of the play is to depend. This day was that designed by Dauphine for the settling of his uncle's estate upon him; which to compass, he contrives to marry him. That the marriage had been plotted by him long beforehand, is made evident by what he tells True-Wit in the second act, that in one moment he had destroyed what he had been raising many months.

'There is another artifice of the poet, which I cannot here omit, because by the frequent practice of it in his comedies he has left it to us almost as a rule; that is, when he has any character or humour wherein he would show a *coup de Maistre,* or his highest skill, he recommends it to your observation by a pleasant description of it before the person first appears. Thus, in *Bartholomew-Fair* he gives you the pictures of Numps and Cokes, and in this those of Daw, Lafoole, Morose, and the Collegiate Ladies; all which you hear described before you see them. So that before they come upon the stage, you have a longing expectation of them, which prepares you to receive them favourably; and when they are there, even from their first appearance you are so far acquainted with them, that nothing of their humour is lost to you.

'I will observe yet one thing further of this admirable plot; the business of it rises in every act. The second is greater than the first; the third than the second; and so forward to the fifth. There too you see, till the very last scene, new difficulties arising to obstruct the action of the play; and when the audience is brought into despair that the business can naturally be effected, then, and not before, the discovery is made. But that the poet might entertain you with more variety all this while, he reserves some new characters to show you, which he opens not till the second and third act. In the second Morose, Daw, the Barber, and Otter; in the third the Collegiate Ladies: all which he moves afterwards in by-walks, or under-plots, as diversions to the main design, lest it should grow tedious, though they are still naturally joined with it, and somewhere or other subservient to it. Thus, like a skilful chess-player, by little and little he draws out his men, and makes his pawns of use to his greater persons.

'If this comedy and some others of his were translated into French prose (which would now be no wonder to them, since Moliere has lately given them plays out of verse, which have not displeased them), I believe the controversy would soon be decided betwixt the two nations, even making them

---

[46]Comedy is thought to demand the least work; for it draws its subjects from ordinary life. But the less indulgence it has, the more work it requires.

the judges. But we need not call our heroes to our aid; be it spoken to the honour of the English, our nation can never want in any age such who are able to dispute the empire of wit with any people in the universe. And though the fury of a civil war, and power for twenty years together abandoned to a barbarous race of men, enemies of all good learning, had buried the Muses under the ruins of monarchy; yet, with the restoration of our happiness, we see revived Poesy lifting up its head, and already shaking off the rubbish which lay so heavy on it. We have seen since his Majesty's return, many dramatic poems which yield not to those of any foreign nation; and which deserve all laurels but the English. I will set aside flattery and envy: it cannot be denied but we have had some little blemish either in the plot or writing of all those plays which have been made within these seven years (and perhaps there is no nation in the world so quick to discern them, or so difficult to pardon them, as ours): yet if we can persuade ourselves to use the candour of that poet, who, though the most severe of critics, has left us this caution by which to moderate our censures—

> . . . *ubi plura nitent in carmine, non ego paucis*
> *Offendar maculis:* —[47]

if, in consideration of their many and great beauties, we can wink at some slight and little imperfections, if we, I say, can be thus equal to ourselves, I ask no favour from the French. And if I do not venture upon any particular judgment of our late plays, 'tis out of the consideration which an ancient writer gives me: *vivorum, ut magna admiratio, ita censura difficilis:*[48] betwixt the extremes of admiration and malice, 'tis hard to judge uprightly of the living. Only I think it may be permitted me to say, that as it is no lessening to us to yield to some plays, and those not many, of our own nation in the last age, so can it be no addition to pronounce of our present poets, that they have far surpassed all the Ancients, and the modern writers of other countries.'

This, my Lord, was the substance of what was then spoke on that occasion; and Lisideius, I think, was going to reply, when he was prevented thus by Crites: 'I am confident,' said he, 'that the most material things that can be said have been already urged on either side; if they have not, I must beg of Lisideius that he will defer his answer till another time: for I confess I have a joint quarrel to you both, because you have concluded, without any reason given for it, that rhyme is proper for the stage. I will not dispute how ancient it hath been among us to write this way; perhaps our ancestors knew no better till Shakespeare's time. I will grant it was not altogether left by him, and that Fletcher and Ben Jonson used if frequently in their Pastorals, and sometimes in other plays. Farther, I will not argue whether we received it originally from our own countrymen, or from the French; for that is an inquiry of as little benefit, as theirs who, in the midst of the great Plague, were not so solicitous to provide against it as to know whether we had it from the

---

[47] When many beauties shine out in a poem, I shall not be offended at small faults.
[48] Just as admiration for the living is great, it is difficult to criticize them.

malignity of our own air, or by transportation from Holland. I have therefore only to affirm, that it is not allowable in serious plays; for comedies, I find you already concluding with me. To prove this, I might satisfy myself to tell you, how much in vain it is for you to strive against the stream of the people's inclination; the greatest part of which are prepossessed so much with those excellent plays of Shakespeare, Fletcher, and Ben Jonson, which have been written out of rhyme, that except you could bring them such as were written better in it, and those too by persons of equal reputation with them, it will be impossible for you to gain your cause with them, who will still be judges. This it is to which, in fine, all your reasons must submit. The unanimous consent of an audience is so powerful, that even Julius Cæsar (as Macrobius reports of him), when he was perpetual dictator, was not able to balance it on the other side. But when Laberius, a Roman Knight, at his request contended in the Mime with another poet, he was forced to cry out, *Etiam favente me victus es, Laberi.*[49] But I will not on this occasion take the advantage of the greater number, but only urge such reasons against rhyme, as I find in the writings of those who have argued for the other way. First then, I am of opinion, that rhyme is unnatural in a play, because dialogue there is presented as the effect of sudden thought: for a play is the imitation of Nature; and since no man without premeditation speaks in rhyme, either ought he to do it on the stage. This hinders not but the fancy may be there elevated to an higher pitch of thought than it is in ordinary discourse; for there is a probability that men of excellent and quick parts may speak noble things *ex tempore:* but those thoughts are never fettered with the numbers or sound of verse without study, and therefore it cannot be but unnatural to present the most free way of speaking in that which is the most constrained. For this reason, says Aristotle, 'tis best to write tragedy in that kind of verse which is the least such, or which is nearest prose: and this amongst the Ancients was the iambic, and with us is blank verse, or the measure of verse kept exactly without rhyme. These numbers therefore are fittest for a play; the others for a paper of verses, or a poem; blank verse being as much below them, as rhyme is improper for the Drama. And if it be objected that neither are blank verses made *ex tempore,* yet, as nearest nature, they are still to be preferred.—But there are two particular exceptions, which many besides myself have had to verse; by which it will appear yet more plainly how improper it is in plays. And the first of them is grounded on that very reason for which some have commended rhyme; they say, the quickness of repartees in argumentative scenes receives an ornament from verse. Now what is more unreasonable than to imagine that a man should not only light upon the wit, but the rhyme too, upon the sudden? This nicking of him who spoke before both in sound and measure, is so great an happiness, that you must at least suppose the persons of your play to be born poets: *Arcades omnes, et cantare pares, et respondere parati*[50]: they must have arrived to the degree of *quicquid conabar*

---

[49] You are defeated even with me on your side, Laberius.
[50] All Arcadians, prepared to sing on equal terms and reply.

dicere[51];—to make verses almost whether they will or no. If they are any thing below this, it will look rather like the design of two, than the answer of one: it will appear that your actors hold intelligence together; that they perform their tricks like fortune-tellers, by confederacy. The hand of art will be too visible in it, against that maxim of all professions, *Ars est celare artem,*[52] that it is the greatest perfection of art to keep itself undiscovered. Nor will it serve you to object, that however you manage it, 'tis still known to be a play; and, consequently, the dialogue of two persons understood to be the labour of one poet. For a play is still an imitation of Nature; we know we are to be deceived, and we desire to be so; but no man ever was deceived but with a probability of truth; for who will suffer a gross lie to be fastened on him? Thus we sufficiently understand, that the scenes which represent cities and countries to us are not really such, but only painted on boards and canvas; but shall that excuse the ill painture or designment of them? Nay, rather ought they not to be laboured with so much the more diligence and exactness, to help the imagination? since the mind of man does naturally tend to, and seek after truth; and therefore the nearer any thing comes to the imitation of it, the more it pleases.

'Thus, you see, your rhyme is uncapable of expressing the greatest thoughts naturally, and the lowest it cannot with any grace: for what is more unbefitting the majesty of verse, than to call a servant, or bid a door be shut in rhyme? And yet this miserable necessity you are forced upon. But verse, you say, circumscribes a quick and luxuriant fancy, which would extend itself too far on every subject, did not the labour which is required to well-turned and polished rhyme, set bounds to it. Yet this argument, if granted, would only prove that we may write better in verse, but not more naturally. Neither is it able to evince that; for he who wants judgment to confine his fancy in blank verse, may want it as much in rhyme: and the who has it will avoid errors in both kinds. Latin verse was as great a confinement to the imagination of those poets, as rhyme to ours; and yet you find Ovid saying too much on every subject. *Nescivit* (says Seneca) *quod bene cessit relinquere*[53]: of which he gives you one famous instance in his description of the deluge:

> *Omnia pontus erat, deerant quoque litora ponto.*
> Now all was sea, nor had that sea a shore.

Thus Ovid's fancy was not limited by verse, and Virgil needed not verse to have bounded his.

'In our own language we see Ben Jonson confining himself to what ought to be said, even in the liberty of blank verse; and yet Corneille, the most judicious of the French poets, is still varying the same sense an hundred ways, and dwelling eternally on the same subject, though confined by rhyme. Some other exceptions I have to verse; but being these I have named are for the

---

[51] Of singing whatever they attempted.
[52] It is an art to conceal art.
[53] He did not know how to end when he should have.

most part already public, I conceive it reasonable they should first be answered.'

'It concerns me less than any,' said Neander (seeing he had ended), 'to reply to this discourse; because when I should have proved that verse may be natural in plays, yet I should always be ready to confess, that those which I have written in this kind come short of that perfection which is required. Yet since you are pleased I should undertake this province, I will do it, though with all imaginable respect and deference, both to that person from whom you have borrowed your strongest arguments, and to whose judgment, when I have said all, I finally submit. But before I proceed to answer your objections, I must first remember you, that I exclude all Comedy from my defence; and next that I deny not but blank verse may be also used; and content myself only to assert, that in serious plays where the subject and characters are great, and the plot unmixed with mirth, which might allay or divert these concernments which are produced, rhyme is there as natural and more effectual than blank verse.

'And now having laid down this as a foundation,—to begin with Crites, I must crave leave to tell him, that some of his arguments against rhyme reach no farther than, from the faults or defects of ill rhyme, to conclude against the use of it in general. May not I conclude against blank verse by the same reason? If the words of some poets who write in it, are either ill chosen, or ill placed, which makes not only rhyme, but all kind of verse in any language unnatural, shall I, for their vicious affectation, condemn those excellent lines of Fletcher, which are written in that kind? Is there any thing in rhyme more constrained than this line in blank verse, *I heaven invoke, and strong resistance make?* where you see both the clauses are placed unnaturally, that is, contrary to the common way of speaking, and that without the excuse of a rhyme to cause it: yet you would think me very ridiculous, if I should accuse the stubbornness of blank verse for this, and not rather the stiffness of the poet. Therefore, Crites, you must either prove that words, though well chosen, and duly placed, yet render not rhyme natural in itself; or that, however natural and easy the rhyme may be, yet it is not proper for a play. If you insist on the former part, I would ask you, what other conditions are required to make rhyme natural in itself, besides an election of apt words, and a right disposing of them? For the due choice of your words expresses your sense naturally, and the due placing them adapts the rhyme to it. If you object that one verse may be made for the sake of another, though both the words and rhyme be apt, I answer, it cannot possibly so fall out; for either there is a dependance of sense betwixt the first line and the second, or there is none: if there be that connection, then in the natural position of the words the latter line must of necessity flow from the former; if there be no dependance, yet still the due ordering of words makes the last line as natural in itself as the other: so that the necessity of a rhyme never forces any but bad or lazy writers to say what they would not otherwise. 'Tis true, there is both care and art required to write in verse. A good poet never concludes upon the first line, till he has sought out such a rhyme as may fit the sense, already prepared to heighten the second: many times the close of the sense falls into the middle of the next verse, or farther off, and he may often prevail himself of the same advantages in English which Virgil had in Latin; he may break off in the hemistich, and begin another line. Indeed, the not observing these two last things, makes plays which are writ in verse so tedious: for though, most commonly, the sense is to be confined to the couplet, yet nothing that does *perpetuo tenore fluere*, run in the same channel, can please always. 'Tis like the murmuring of a stream, which not varying in the fall, causes at first attention, at last drowsiness. Variety of cadences is the best rule; the greatest help to the actors, and refreshment to the audience.

'If then verse may be made natural in itself, how becomes it improper to a play? You say the stage is the representation of Nature, and no man in ordinary conversation speaks in rhyme. But you foresaw when you said this, that it might be answered—neither does any man speak in blank verse, or in measure without rhyme. Therefore you concluded, that which is nearest Nature is still to be preferred. But you took no notice that rhyme might be made as natural as blank verse, by the well placing of the words, &c. All the difference between them, when they are both correct, is, the sound in one, which the other wants; and if so, the sweetness of it, and all the advantage resulting from it, which are handled in the Preface to *The Rival Ladies*, will yet stand good. As for that place of Aristotle, where he says, plays should be writ in that kind of verse which is nearest prose, it makes little for you; blank verse being properly but measured prose. Now measure alone, in any modern language, does not constitute verse; those of the Ancients in Greek and Latin consisted in quantity of words, and a determinate number of feet. But when, by the inundation of the Goths and Vandals into Italy, new languages were brought in, and barbarously mingled with the Latin, of which the Italian, Spanish, French, and ours (made out of them and the Teutonic) are dialects, a new way of poesy was practised; new, I say, in those countries, for in all probability it was that of the conquerors in their own nations. This new way consisted in measure or number of feet, and rhyme; the sweetness of rhyme, and observation of accent, supplying the place of quantity in words, which could neither exactly be observed by those Barbarians, who knew not the rules of it, neither was it suitable to their tongues, as it had been to the Greek and Latin. No man is tied in modern poesy to observe any farther rule in the feet of his verse, but that they be dissyllables; whether spondee, trochee, or iambic, it matters not; only he is obliged to rhyme. Neither do the Spanish, French, Italian, or Germans, acknowledge at all, or very rarely, any such kind of poesy as blank verse amongst them. Therefore, at most 'tis but a poetic prose, a *sermo pedestris*; and as such, most fit for comedies, where I acknowledge rhyme to be improper. Farther; as to that quotation of Aristotle, our couplet verses may be rendered as near prose as blank verse itself, by using those advantages I lately named, as breaks in a hemistich, or running the sense into another line, thereby making art and order appear as loose and free as nature: or not tying ourselves to couplets strictly, we may use the benefit of the Pindaric way practised in *The Siege of Rhodes;* where the numbers vary, and the rhyme is disposed carelessly, and far from often chiming. Neither is that other advantage of the Ancients to be despised, of changing the kind of verse when they please, with the change of the scene, or some new entrance; for they confine not themselves always to iambics, but extend their liberty to all lyric numbers, and sometimes even to hexameter. But I need not go so far to prove that rhyme, as it succeeds to all other offices of Greek and Latin verse, so especially to this of plays, since the custom of all nations at this day confirms it, all the French, Italian, and Spanish tragedies are generally writ in it; and sure the universal consent of the most civilized parts of the world ought in this, as it doth in our customs, to include the rest.

'But perhaps you may tell me, I have proposed such a way to make rhyme natural, and consequently proper to plays, as is unpracticable; and that I shall scarce find six or eight lines together in any play, where the words are so placed and chosen as is required to make it natural. I answer, no poet need constrain himself at all times to it. It is enough he makes it his general rule; for I deny not but sometimes there may be a greatness in placing the words otherwise; and sometimes they may sound better, sometimes also the variety itself is excuse enough. But if, for the most part, the words be placed as they are in the negligence of prose, it is sufficient to denominate the way practicable; for we esteem that to be such, which in the trial oftener succeeds than misses. And thus far you may find the practice made good in many plays: where you do not, remember still, that if you cannot find six natural rhymes together, it will be as hard for you to produce as many lines in blank verse, even among the greatest of our poets, against which I cannot make some reasonable exception.

'And this, Sir, calls to my remembrance the beginning of your discourse, where you told us we should never find the audience favourable to this kind of writing, till we could produce as good plays in rhyme, as Ben Jonson, Fletcher, and Shakespeare, had writ out of it. But it is to raise envy to the living, to compare them with the dead. They are honoured, and almost adored by us, as they deserve; neither do I know any so presumptuous of themselves as to contend with them. Yet give me leave to say thus much, without injury to their ashes; that not only we shall never equal them, but they could never equal themselves, were they to rise and write again. We acknowledge them our fathers in wit; but they have ruined their estates themselves, before they came to their children's hands. There is scarce an humour, a character, or any kind of plot, which they have not blown upon. All comes sullied or wasted to us: and were they to entertain this age, they could not make so plenteous treatments out of such decayed fortunes. This therefore will be a good argument to us, either not to write at all, or to attempt some other way. There is no bays to be expected in their walks: *tentanda via est, qua me quoque possum tollere humo.*[54]

---

[54] I must explore new ways in which to raise my name aloft.

'This way of writing in verse they have only left free to us; our age is arrived to a perfection in it, which they never knew; and which (if we may guess by what of theirs we have seen in verse, as *The Faithful Shepherdess*, and *Sad Shepherd*) 'tis probable they never could have reached. For the genius of every age is different; and though ours excel in this, I deny not but that to imitate Nature in that perfection which they did in prose, is a greater commendation than to write in verse exactly. As for what you have added, that the people are not generally inclined to like this way; if it were true, it would be no wonder, that betwixt the shaking off an old habit, and the introducing of a new, there should be difficulty. Do we not see them stick to Hopkins' and Sternhold's psalms, and forsake those of David, I mean Sandys his translation of them? If by the people you understand the multitude, ὃι πολλοί,[55] 'tis no matter what they think; they are sometimes in the right, sometimes in the wrong: their judgment is a mere lottery. *Est ubi plebs recte putat, est ubi peccat.*[56] Horace says it of the vulgar, judging poesy. But if you mean the mixed audience of the populace and the noblesse, I dare confidently affirm that a great part of the latter sort are already favourable to verse; and that no serious plays written since the King's return have been more kindly received by them, than *The Siege of Rhodes*, the *Mustapha*, *The Indian Queen*, and *Indian Emperor*.

'But I come now to the inference of your first argument. You said the dialogue of plays is presented as the effect of sudden thought, but no man speaks suddenly, or *ex tempore*, in rhyme; and you inferred from thence, that rhyme, which you acknowledge to be proper to epic poesy, cannot equally be proper to dramatic, unless we could suppose all men born so much more than poets, that verses should be made in them, not by them.

'It has been formerly urged by you, and confessed by me, that since no man spoke any kind of verse *ex tempore*, that which was nearest Nature was to be preferred. I answer you, therefore, by distinguishing betwixt what is nearest to the nature of Comedy, which is the imitation of common persons and ordinary speaking, and what is nearest the nature of a serious play: this last is indeed the representation of Nature, but 'tis Nature wrought up to an higher pitch. The plot, the characters, the wit, the passions, the descriptions, are all exalted above the level of common converse, as high as the imagination of the poet can carry them, with proportion to verisimility. Tragedy, we know, is wont to image to us the minds and fortunes of noble persons, and to portray these exactly; heroic rhyme is nearest Nature, as being the noblest kind of modern verse.

Indignatur enim privatis et prope socco
Dignis carminibus narrari cæna Thyestæ,[57]

---

[55] *Hoi polloi*, the many, the masses.
[56] Sometimes the people think rightly, sometimes not.
[57] The banquet of Thyestes should not be told in the familiar verses appropriate to comedy.

says Horace: and in another place,

> *Effutire leves indigna tragœdia versus.*[58]

Blank verse is acknowledged to be too low for a poem, nay more, for a paper of verses; but if too low for an ordinary sonnet, how much more for Tragedy, which is by Aristotle, in the dispute betwixt the epic poesy and the dramatic, for many reasons he there alleges, ranked above it?

'But setting this defence aside, your argument is almost as strong against the use of rhyme in poems as in plays; for the epic way is every where interlaced with dialogue, or discoursive scenes; and therefore you must either grant rhyme to be improper there, which is contrary to your assertion, or admit it into plays by the same title which you have given it to poems. For though Tragedy be justly preferred above the other, yet there is a great affinity between them, as may easily be discovered in that definition of a play which Lisideius gave us. The *genus* of them is the same, a just and lively image of human nature, in its actions, passions, and traverses of fortune: so is the end, namely, for the delight and benefit of mankind. The characters and persons are still the same, viz. the greatest of both sorts; only the manner of acquainting us with those actions, passions, and fortunes, is different. Tragedy performs it *viva voce*, or by action, in dialogue; wherein it excels the Epic Poem, which does it chiefly by narration, and therefore is not so lively an image of human nature. However, the agreement betwixt them is such, that if rhyme be proper for one, it must be for the other. Verse, 'tis true, is not the effect of sudden thought; but this hinders not that sudden thought may be represented in verse, since those thoughts are such as much be higher than Nature can raise them without premeditation, especially to a continuance of them, even out of verse; and consequently you cannot imagine them to have been sudden either in the poet or in the actors. A play, as I have said, to be like Nature, is to be set above it; as statues which are placed on high are made greater than the life, that they may descend to the sight in their just proportion.

'Perhaps I have insisted too long on this objection; but the clearing of it will make my stay shorter on the rest. You tell us, Crites, that rhyme appears most unnatural in repartees, or short replies: when he who answers, it being presumed he knew not what the other would say, yet makes up that part of the verse which was left incomplete, and supplies both the sound and measure of it. This, you say, looks rather like the confederacy of two, than the answer of one.

'This, I confess, is an objection which is in every one's mouth, who loves not rhyme: but suppose, I beseech you, the repartee were made only in blank verse, might not part of the same argument be turned against you? for the measure is as often supplied there, as it is in rhyme; the latter half of the hemistich as commonly made up, or a second line subjoined as a reply to the former; which any one leaf in Jonson's plays will sufficiently clear to you.

---

[58] It is not proper for tragedy to babble forth light verse.

You will often find in the Greek tragedians, and in Seneca, that when a scene grows up into the warmth of repartees, which is the close fighting of it, the latter part of the trimeter is supplied by him who answers; and yet it was never observed as a fault in them by any of the ancient or modern critics. The case is the same in our verse, as it was in theirs; rhyme to us being in lieu of quantity to them. But if no latitude is to be allowed a poet, you take from him not only his licence of *quidlibet audendi*,[59] but you tie him up in a straiter compass than you would a philosopher. This is indeed *Musas colere severiores*.[60] You would have him follow Nature, but he must follow her on foot: you have dismounted him from his Pegasus. But you tell us, this supplying the last half of a verse, or adjoining a whole second to the former, looks more like the design of two, than the answer of one. Supposing we acknowledge it: how comes this confederacy to be more displeasing to you, than in a dance which is well contrived? You see there the united design of many persons to make up one figure: after they have separated themselves in many petty divisions, they rejoin one by one into a gross: the confederacy is plain amongst them, for chance could never produce any thing so beautiful; and yet there is nothing in it, that shocks your sight. I acknowledge the hand of art appears in repartee, as of necessity it must in all kinds of verse. But there is also the quick and poynant brevity of it (which is an high imitation of Nature in those sudden gusts of passion) to mingle with it; and this, joined with the cadency and sweetness of the rhyme, leaves nothing in the soul of the hearer to desire. 'Tis an art which appears; but it appears only like the shadowings of painture, which being to cause the rounding of it, cannot be absent; but while that is considered, they are lost: so while we attend to the other beauties of the matter, the care and labour of the rhyme is carried from us, or at least drowned in its own sweetness, as bees are sometimes buried in their honey. When a poet has found the repartee, the last perfection he can add to it, is to put it into verse. However good the thought may be, however apt the words in which 'tis couched, yet he finds himself at a little unrest, while rhyme is wanting: he cannot leave it till that comes naturally, and then is at ease, and sits down contented.

'From replies, which are the most elevated thoughts of verse, you pass to the most mean ones, those which are common with the lowest of household conversation. In these, you say, the majesty of verse suffers. You instance in the calling of a servant, or commanding a door to be shut, in rhyme. This, Crites, is a good observation of yours, but no argument: for it proves no more but that such thoughts should be waved, as often as may be, by the address of the poet. But suppose they are necessary in the places where he uses them, yet there is no need to put them into rhyme. He may place them in the beginning of a verse, and break it off, as unfit, when so debased, for any other use; or granting the worst,—that they require more room than the hemistich will allow, yet still there is a choice to be made of the best words, and least vulgar

---

[59] Of taking any liberty he wishes.
[60] To cultivate the more serious Muses.

(provided they be apt) to express such thoughts. Many have blamed rhyme in general, for this fault, when the poet with a little care might have re-dressed it. But they do it with no more justice, than if English Poesy should be made ridiculous for the sake of the Water Poet's rhymes. Our language is noble, full, and significant; and I know not why he who is master of it may not clothe ordinary things in it as decently as the Latin, if he use the same diligence in his choice of words. *Delectus verborum origo est eloquentiae.*[61] It was the saying of Julius Cæsar, one so curious in his, that none of them can be changed but for a worse. One would think, *unlock the door,* was a thing as vulgar as could be spoken; and yet Seneca could make it sound high and lofty in his Latin:

Reserate clusos regii postes laris.
Set wide the palace gates.

'But I turn from this exception, both because it happens not above twice or thrice in any play that those vulgar thoughts are used; and then too, were there no other apology to be made, yet the necessity of them which is alike in all kind of writing, may excuse them. Besides that the great eagerness and precipitation with which they are spoken makes us rather mind the sub-stance than the dress; that for which they are spoken, rather than what is spoken. For they are always the effect of some hasty concernment, and some-thing of consequence depends on them.

'Thus, Crites, I have endeavoured to answer your objections; it remains only that I should vindicate an argument for verse, which you have gone about to overthrow. It had formerly been said, that the easiness of blank verse renders the poet too luxuriant, but that the labour of rhyme bounds and circumscribes an overfruitful fancy; the sense there being commonly confined to the couplet, and the words so ordered that the rhyme naturally follows them, not they the rhyme. To this you answered, that it was no argu-ment to the question in hand; for the dispute was not which way a man may write best, but which is most proper for the subject on which he writes.

'First, give me leave, Sir, to remember you, that the argument against which you raised this objection, was only secondary: it was built on this hy-pothesis, that to write in verse was proper for serious plays. Which supposi-tion being granted (as it was briefly made out in that discourse, by showing how verse might be made natural), it asserted, that this way of writing was an help to the poet's judgment, by putting bounds to a wild overflowing fancy. I think, therefore, it will not be hard for me to make good what it was to prove. But you add, that were this let pass, yet he who wants judgment in the liberty of his fancy, may as well show the defect of it when he is confined to verse; for he who has judgment will avoid errors, and he who has it not, will commit them in all kinds of writing.

'This argument, as you have taken it from a most acute person, so I con-fess it carries much weight in it: but by using the word judgment here indefi-

[61] The origin of eloquence is the proper choice of words.

nitely, you seem to have put a fallacy upon us. I grant, he who has judgment, that is, so profound, so strong, so infallible a judgment, that he needs no helps to keep it always poised and upright, will commit no faults either in rhyme or out of it. And on the other extreme, he who has a judgment so weak and crazed that no helps can correct or amend it, shall write scurvily out of rhyme, and worse in it. But the first of these judgments is no where to be found, and the latter is not fit to write at all. To speak therefore of judgment as it is in the best poets; they who have the greatest proportion of it, want other helps than from it, within. As for example, you would be loth to say, that he who was endued with a sound judgment had no need of History, Geography, or Moral Philosophy, to write correctly. Judgment is indeed the master-workman in a play; but he requires many subordinate hands, many tools to his assistance. And verse I affirm to be one of these; 'tis a rule and line by which he keeps his building compact and even, which otherwise lawless imagination would raise either irregularly or loosely. At least, if the poet commits errors with this help, he would make greater and more without it: 'tis, in short, a slow and painful, but the surest kind of working. Ovid, whom you accuse for luxuriancy in verse, had perhaps been farther guilty of it, had he writ in prose. And for your instance of Ben Jonson, who, you say, writ exactly without the help of rhyme; you are to remember, 'tis only an aid to a luxuriant fancy, which his was not: as he did not want imagination, so none ever said he had much to spare. Neither was verse then refined so much to be an help to that age, as it is to ours. Thus then the second thoughts being usually the best, as receiving the maturest digestion from judgment, and the last and most mature product of those thoughts being artful and laboured verse, it may well be inferred, that verse is a great help to a luxuriant fancy; and this is what that argument which you opposed was to evince.'

Neander was pursuing this discourse so eagerly, that Eugenius had called to him twice or thrice, ere he took notice that the barge stood still, and that they were at the foot of Somerset Stairs, where they had appointed it to land. The company were all sorry to separate so soon, though a great part of the evening was already spent; and stood a while looking back on the water, which the moon-beams played upon, and made it appear like floating quicksilver: at last they went up through a crowd of French people, who were merrily dancing in the open air, and nothing concerned for the noise of guns which had alarmed the town that afternoon. Walking thence together to the Piazze, they parted there; Eugenius and Lisideius to some pleasant appointment they had made, and Crites and Neander to their several lodgings.

ALEXANDER POPE

An Essay on Criticism

1711

In writing an essay in the form of a poem, young Alexander Pope (1688–1744) (he was twenty-three when the work was published, and he may have written it at nineteen) was not being deliberately perverse but conscientiously traditional. The poem is in a genre that had the sanction of both classical precedent (Horace's Art of Poetry, p. 84, being only one instance) and many seventeenth-century examples; thus Pope's poem is an imitation of a classical model. But Pope's subject matter is not poetry; it is criticism itself, a shift in emphasis that reflects the period's self-consciousness about literary standards. Again, however, Pope's originality is limited: the substance of his verse essay consists of familiar neoclassical critical values and doctrines. Taking the doctrines for granted, he codified and condensed them into witty and memorable language so that many of his lines have become aphorisms with the weight of proverbial wisdom. To use his own words, the essay is "what oft was thought but ne'er so well expressed." And for an example of his virtuoso versification, study lines 137 to 173 in Part II, which illustrate the doctrine of "representative meter."

At the heart of the essay is the same nature-versus-art controversy found in Dryden's Essay of Dramatic Poesy (p. 136). Consider which of the four critics in that debate most nearly states the views that Pope expounds. To answer this question is to establish one distinction between Dryden and Pope. Pope, too, has to allow for the "Great Wits," those who deviate from the rules and yet achieve greatness; but can you imagine that he would say with Neander, "I admire Jonson but I love Shakespeare"? In connection with this perplexing problem, two of Pope's statements on nature should be studied: "The rules of old are Nature methodiz'd" and also "True Wit is Nature to advantage dress'd." What, then, is the relationship between the rules and true wit? How can tradition and natural gifts be reconciled? Watch for the recurrence of this question, even though it may be stated in different terms by future critics.

The three-part organization of the poem is also worth studying for its internal structure, both for the subject matter in each part and for the sequence in which these *topics are presented. In Part III, Pope's history of criticism consists of a gallery of great critics; are his criteria for greatness spelled out explicitly?*

Part I

'T IS HARD to say if greater want of skill
Appear in writing or in judging ill;
But of the two less dangerous is th' offence
To tire our patience than mislead our sense:
Some few in that, but numbers err in this;
Ten censure wrong for one who writes amiss;
A fool might once himself alone expose;
Now one in verse makes many more in prose.
   'T is with our judgments as our watches, none
Go just alike, yet each believes his own.   10
In Poets as true Genius is but rare,
True Taste as seldom is the Critic's share;
Both must alike from Heav'n derive their light,
These born to judge, as well as those to write.
Let such teach others who themselves excel,
And censure freely who have written well;
Authors are partial to their wit, 'tis true,
But are not Critics to their judgment too?
   Yet if we look more closely, we shall find
Most have the seeds of judgment in their mind: 20
Nature affords at least a glimm'ring light;
The lines, tho' touch'd but faintly, are drawn right:
But as the slightest sketch, if justly traced,
Is by ill col'ring but the more disgraced,
So by false learning is good sense defaced:
Some are bewilder'd in the maze of schools,
And some made coxcombs Nature meant but fools:
In search of wit these lose their common sense,
And then turn Critics in their own defence:
Each burns alike, who can or cannot write,   30
Or with a rival's or an eunuch's spite.
All fools have still an itching to deride,
And fain would be upon the laughing side.
If Mævius scribble in Apollo's spite,
There are who judge still worse than he can write.
   Some have at first for Wits, then Poets pass'd;
Turn'd Critics next, and prov'd plain Fools at last.
Some neither can for Wits nor Critics pass,

[Handwritten annotations in right margin:]
- relationship between writing and judging
- bad poetry is annoying, but bad criticism misleads
- everyone is writing criticism, opposite as now as far as poetry is concerned anyway

As heavy mules are neither horse nor ass.
Those half-learn'd witlings, numerous in our isle,　　　　　　40
As half-form'd insects on the banks of Nile;
Unfinish'd things, one knows not what to call,
Their generation's so equivocal;
To tell them would a hundred tongues require,
Or one vain Wit's, that might a hundred tire.
    But you who seek to give and merit fame,
And justly bear a Critic's noble name,
Be sure yourself and your own reach to know,
How far your Genius, Taste, and Learning go,
Launch not beyond your depth, but be discreet,　　　　　　50
And mark that point where Sense and Dulness meet.
    Nature to all things fix'd the limits fit,
And wisely curb'd proud man's pretending wit.
As on the land while here the ocean gains,
In other parts it leaves wide sandy plains;
Thus in the soul while Memory prevails,
The solid power of Understanding fails;
Where beams of warm Imagination play,
The Memory's soft figures melt away.
One Science only will one genius fit;　　　　　　60
So vast is Art, so narrow human wit:
Not only bounded to peculiar arts,
But oft in those confin'd to single parts.
Like Kings we lose the conquests gain'd before,
By vain ambition still to make them more:
Each might his sev'ral province well command,
Would all but stoop to what they understand.
    First follow Nature, and your judgment frame
By her just standard, which is still the same;
Unerring Nature, still divinely bright,　　　　　　70
One clear, unchanged, and universal light,
Life, force, and beauty must to all impart,
At once the source, and end, and test of Art.
Art from that fund each just supply provides,
Works without show, and without pomp presides.
In some fair body thus th' informing soul
With spirits feeds, with vigour fills the whole;
Each motion guides, and every nerve sustains,
Itself unseen, but in th' effects remains.
Some, to whom Heav'n in wit has been profuse,　　　　　　80
Want as much more to turn it to its use;
For Wit and Judgment often are at strife,
Tho' meant each other's aid, like man and wife.
'T is more to guide than spur the Muse's steed,

Restrain his fury than provoke his speed:
The winged courser, like a gen'rous horse,
Shows most true mettle when you check his course.
   Those rules of old, discover'd, not devised,
Are Nature still, but Nature methodized;
Nature, like Liberty, is but restrain'd   90
By the same laws which first herself ordain'd.
   Hear how learn'd Greece her useful rules indites
When to repress and when indulge our flights:
High on Parnassus' top her sons she show'd,
And pointed out those arduous paths they trod;
Held from afar, aloft, th' immortal prize,
And urged the rest by equal steps to rise.
Just precepts thus from great examples giv'n,
She drew from them what they derived from Heav'n.
The gen'rous Critic fann'd the poet's fire,   100
And taught the world with reason to admire.
Then Criticism the Muse's handmaid prov'd,
To dress her charms, and make her more belov'd:
But following Wits from that intention stray'd:
Who could not win the mistress woo'd the maid;
Against the Poets their own arms they turn'd,
Sure to hate most the men from whom they learn'd.
So modern 'pothecaries, taught the art
By doctors' bills to play the doctor's part,
Bold in the practice of mistaken rules,   110
Prescribe, apply, and call their masters fools.
Some on the leaves of ancient authors prey;
Nor time nor moths e'er spoil'd so much as they;
Some drily plain, without invention's aid,
Write dull receipts how poems may be made;
These leave the sense their learning to display,
And those explain the meaning quite away.
   You then whose judgment the right course would steer,
Know well each ancient's proper character;
His fable, subject, scope in every page;   120
Religion, country, genius of his age:
Without all these at once before your eyes,
Cavil you may, but never criticise.
Be Homer's works your study and delight,
Read them by day, and meditate by night;
Thence form your judgment, thence your maxims bring,
And trace the Muses upward to their spring.
Still with itself compared, his text peruse;
And let your comment be the Mantuan Muse.
   When first young Maro in his boundless mind   130

A work t' outlast immortal Rome design'd,
Perhaps he seem'd above the critic's law,
And but from Nature's fountains scorn'd to draw;
But when t' examine ev'ry part he came, *relationship between*
Nature and Homer were, he found, the same. *art & nature*
Convinced, amazed, he checks the bold design,
And rules as strict his labour'd work confine
As if the Stagyrite o'erlook'd each line.
Learn hence for ancient rules a just esteem;
To copy Nature is to copy them.   140
    Some beauties yet no precepts can declare,
For there 's a happiness as well as care.
Music resembles poetry; in each
Are nameless graces which no methods teach,
And which a master-hand alone can reach.
If, where the rules not far enough extend,
(Since rules were made but to promote their end)
Some lucky license answer to the full
Th' intent proposed, that license is a rule.
Thus Pegasus, a nearer way to take,   150
May boldly deviate from the common track.
Great Wits sometimes may gloriously offend,
And rise to faults true Critics dare not mend;
From vulgar bounds with brave disorder part,
And snatch a grace beyond the reach of Art,
Which, without passing thro' the judgment, gains
The heart, and all its end at once attains.
In prospects thus some objects please our eyes,
Which out of Nature's common order rise,
The shapeless rock, or hanging precipice.   160
But tho' the ancients thus their rules invade,
(As Kings dispense with laws themselves have made)
Moderns, beware! or if you must offend
Against the precept, ne'er transgress its end;
Let it be seldom, and compell'd by need;
And have at least their precedent to plead;
The Critic else proceeds without remorse,
Seizes your fame, and puts his laws in force.
    I know there are to whose presumptuous thoughts
Those freer beauties, ev'n in them, seem faults.   170
Some figures monstrous and misshaped appear,
Consider'd singly, or beheld too near,
Which, but proportion'd to their light or place,
Due distance reconciles to form and grace.
A prudent chief not always must display
His powers in equal ranks and fair array,

But with th' occasion and the place comply,
Conceal his force, nay, seem sometimes to fly.
Those oft are stratagems which errors seem,
Nor is it Homer nods, but we that dream. 180
   Still green with bays each ancient altar stands
Above the reach of sacrilegious hands,
Secure from flames, from Envy's fiercer rage,
Destructive war, and all-involving Age.
See from each clime the learn'd their incense bring!
Hear in all tongues consenting pæans ring!
In praise so just let ev'ry voice be join'd,
And fill the gen'ral chorus of mankind.
Hail, Bards triumphant! born in happier days,
Immortal heirs of universal praise! 190
Whose honours with increase of ages grow,
As streams roll down, enlarging as they flow;
Nations unborn your mighty names shall sound,
And worlds applaud that must not yet be found!
O may some spark of your celestial fire
The last, the meanest of your sons inspire,
(That on weak wings, from far, pursues your flights,
Glows while he reads, but trembles as he writes)
To teach vain Wits a science little known,
T' admire superior sense, and doubt their own. 200

Part II

Of all the causes which conspire to blind
Man's erring judgment, and misguide the mind,
What the weak head with strongest bias rules,
Is Pride, the never failing vice of fools.
Whatever Nature has in worth denied
She gives in large recruits of needful Pride:
For as in bodies, thus in souls, we find
What wants in blood and spirits swell'd with wind:
Pride, where Wit fails, steps in to our defence,
And fills up all the mighty void of Sense: 10
If once right Reason drives that cloud away,
Truth breaks upon us with resistless day.
Trust not yourself; but your defects to know,
Make use of ev'ry friend—and ev'ry foe.
   A little learning is a dangerous thing;
Drink deep, or taste not the Pierian spring:
There shallow draughts intoxicate the brain,
And drinking largely sobers us again.

[handwritten marginal notes:]
disagrees w/ Emerson who says "trust thyself"
- be the opposite of proud
- Pride is impediment to good critic
- learn alot or not at all

Fired at first sight with what the Muse imparts,
In fearless youth we tempt the heights of arts,   20
While from the bounded level of our mind
Short views we take, nor see the lengths behind:
But more advanc'd, behold with strange surprise
New distant scenes of endless science rise!
So pleas'd at first the tow'ring Alps we try,
Mount o'er the vales, and seem to tread the sky;
Th' eternal snows appear already past,
And the first clouds and mountains seem the last:
But those attain'd, we tremble to survey
The growing labours of the lengthen'd way;   30
Th' increasing prospect tires our wand'ring eyes,
Hills peep o'er hills, and Alps on Alps arise!
   A perfect judge will read each work of wit
With the same spirit that its author writ;
Survey the whole, nor seek slight faults to find
Where Nature moves, and Rapture warms the mind:
Nor lose, for that malignant dull delight,
The gen'rous pleasure to be charm'd with wit.
But in such lays as neither ebb nor flow,
Correctly cold, and regularly low,   40
That shunning faults one quiet tenor keep,
We cannot blame indeed—but we may sleep.
In Wit, as Nature, what affects our hearts
Is not th' exactness of peculiar parts;
'T is not a lip or eye we beauty call,
But the joint force and full result of all.
Thus when we view some well proportion'd dome,
(The world's just wonder, and ev'n thine, O Rome!)
No single parts unequally surprise,
All comes united to th' admiring eyes;   50
No monstrous height, or breadth, or length, appear;
The whole at once is bold and regular.
   Whoever thinks a faultless piece to see,
Thinks what ne'er was, nor is, nor e'er shall be.
In every work regard the writer's end,
Since none can compass more than they intend;
And if the means be just, the conduct true,
Applause, in spite of trivial faults, is due.
As men of breeding, sometimes men of wit,
T' avoid great errors must the less commit;   60
Neglect the rules each verbal critic lays,
For not to know some trifles is a praise.
Most critics, fond of some subservient art,
Still make the whole depend upon a part:

They talk of Principles, but Notions prize,
And all to one lov'd folly sacrifice.
　　Once on a time La Mancha's Knight, they say,
A certain bard encount'ring on the way,
Discours'd in terms as just, with looks as sage,
As e'er could Dennis, of the Grecian Stage;   70
Concluding all were desperate sots and fools
Who durst depart from Aristotle's rules.
Our author, happy in a judge so nice,
Produced his play, and begg'd the knight's advice;
Made him observe the Subject and the Plot,
The Manners, Passions, Unities; what not?
All which exact to rule were brought about,
Were but a combat in the lists left out.
'What! leave the combat out?' exclaims the knight.
'Yes, or we must renounce the Stagyrite.'   80
'Not so, by Heaven! (he answers in a rage)
Knights, squires, and steeds must enter on the stage.'
'So vast a throng the stage can ne'er contain.'
'Then build a new, or act it in a plain.'
　　Thus critics of less judgment than caprice,
Curious, not knowing, not exact, but nice,
Form short ideas, and offend in Arts
(As most in Manners), by a love to parts.
　　Some to Conceit alone their taste confine,
And glitt'ring thoughts struck out at every line;   90
Pleas'd with a work where nothing 's just or fit,
One glaring chaos and wild heap of wit.
Poets, like painters, thus unskill'd to trace
The naked nature and the living grace,
With gold and jewels cover every part,
And hide with ornaments their want of Art.
True Wit is Nature to advantage dress'd,
What oft was thought, but ne'er so well express'd;
Something whose truth convinced at sight we find,
That gives us back the image of our mind.   100
As shades more sweetly recommend the light,
So modest plainness sets off sprightly wit:
For works may have more wit than does them good,
As bodies perish thro' excess of blood.
　　Others for language all their care express,
And value books, as women men, for dress:
Their praise is still—the Style is excellent;
The Sense they humbly take upon content.
Words are like leaves; and where they most abound,
Much fruit of sense beneath is rarely found.   110

False eloquence, like the prismatic glass,
Its gaudy colours spreads on every place;
The face of Nature we no more survey,
All glares alike, without distinction gay;
But true expression, like th' unchanging sun,
Clears and improves whate'er it shines upon;
It gilds all objects, but it alters none.
Expression is the dress of thought, and still
Appears more decent as more suitable.
A vile Conceit in pompous words express'd   120
Is like a clown in regal purple dress'd.
For diff'rent styles with diff'rent subjects sort,
As sev'ral garbs with country, town, and court.
Some by old words to fame have made pretence,
Ancients in phrase, mere moderns in their sense;
Such labour'd nothings, in so strange a style,
Amaze th' unlearn'd, and make the learned smile;
Unlucky as Fungoso in the play,
These sparks with awkward vanity display
What the fine gentleman wore yesterday;   130
And but so mimic ancient wits at best,
As apes our grandsires in their doublets drest.
In words as fashions the same rule will hold,
Alike fantastic if too new or old:
Be not the first by whom the new are tried,
Nor yet the last to lay the old aside.
   But most by Numbers judge a poet's song,
And smooth or rough with them is right or wrong.
In the bright Muse tho' thousand charms conspire,
Her voice is all these tuneful fools admire;   140
Who haunt Parnassus but to please their ear,
Not mend their minds; as some to church repair,
Not for the doctrine, but the music there.
These equal syllables alone require,
Tho' oft the ear the open vowels tire,
While expletives their feeble aid do join,
And ten low words oft creep in one dull line:
While they ring round the same unvaried chimes,
With sure returns of still expected rhymes;
Where'er you find 'the cooling western breeze,'   150
In the next line, it 'whispers thro' the trees;'
If crystal streams 'with pleasing murmurs creep,'
The reader 's threaten'd (not in vain) with 'sleep;'
Then, at the last and only couplet, fraught
With some unmeaning thing they call a thought,
A needless Alexandrine ends the song,

language should fit your subject
—compare with Longinus
pg 50

That, like a wounded snake, drags its slow length along.
Leave such to tune their own dull rhymes, and know
What 's roundly smooth, or languishingly slow;
And praise the easy vigour of a line   160
Where Denham's strength and Waller's sweetness join.
True ease in writing comes from Art, not Chance,
As those move easiest who have learn'd to dance.
'T is not enough no harshness gives offence;
The sound must seem an echo to the sense.
Soft is the strain when zephyr gently blows,
And the smooth stream in smoother numbers flows;
But when loud surges lash the sounding shore,
The hoarse rough verse should like the torrent roar.
When Ajax strives some rock's vast weight to throw,   170
The line, too, labours, and the words move slow:
Not so when swift Camilla scours the plain,
Flies o'er th' unbending corn, and skims along the main.
Hear how Timotheus' varied lays surprise,
And bid alternate passions fall and rise!
While at each change the son of Libyan Jove
Now burns with glory, and then melts with love;
Now his fierce eyes with sparkling fury glow,
Now sighs steal out, and tears begin to flow:
Persians and Greeks like turns of nature found,   180
And the world's Victor stood subdued by sound!
The power of music all our hearts allow
And what Timotheus was is Dryden now.
   Avoid extremes, and shun the fault of such
Who still are pleas'd too little or too much.
At ev'ry trifle scorn to take offence;
That always shows great pride or little sense:
Those heads, as stomachs, are not sure the best
Which nauseate all, and nothing can digest.
Yet let not each gay turn thy rapture move;   190
For fools admire, but men of sense approve:
As things seem large which we thro' mist descry,
Dulness is ever apt to magnify.
   Some foreign writers, some our own despise;
The ancients only, or the moderns prize.
Thus Wit, like Faith, by each man is applied
To one small sect, and all are damn'd beside.
Meanly they seek the blessing to confine,
And force that sun but on a part to shine,
Which not alone the southern wit sublimes,   200
But ripens spirits in cold northern climes;
Which from the first has shone on ages past,

Enlights the present, and shall warm the last;
Tho' each may feel increases and decays,
And see now clearer and now darker days.
Regard not then if wit be old or new,
But blame the False and value still the True.
   Some ne'er advance a judgment of their own,
But catch the spreading notion of the town;
They reason and conclude by precedent,   210
And own stale nonsense which they ne'er invent.
Some judge of authors' names, not works, and then
Nor praise nor blame the writings, but the men.
Of all this servile herd, the worst is he
That in proud dulness joins with quality;
A constant critic at the great man's board,
To fetch and carry nonsense for my lord.
What woful stuff this madrigal would be
In some starv'd hackney sonneteer or me!
But let a lord once own the happy lines,   220
How the Wit brightens! how the Style refines!
Before his sacred name flies every fault,
And each exalted stanza teems with thought!
   The vulgar thus thro' imitation err,
As oft the learn'd by being singular;
So much they scorn the crowd, that if the throng
By chance go right, they purposely go wrong.
So schismatics the plain believers quit,
And are but damn'd for having too much wit.
Some praise at morning what they blame at night,   230
But always think the last opinion right.
A Muse by these is like a mistress used,
This hour she 's idolized, the next abused;
While their weak heads, like towns unfortified,
'Twixt sense and nonsense daily change their side.
Ask them the cause; they 're wiser still they say;
And still to-morrow's wiser than to-day.
We think our fathers fools, so wise we grow;
Our wiser sons no doubt will think us so.
Once school-divines this zealous isle o'erspread;   240
Who knew most sentences was deepest read.
Faith, Gospel, all seem'd made to be disputed,
And none had sense enough to be confuted.
Scotists and Thomists now in peace remain
Amidst their kindred cobwebs in Duck-lane.
If Faith itself has diff'rent dresses worn,
What wonder modes in Wit should take their turn?
Oft, leaving what is natural and fit,

The current Folly proves the ready Wit;
And authors think their reputation safe,   250
Which lives as long as fools are pleas'd to laugh.
    Some, valuing those of their own side or mind,
Still make themselves the measure of mankind:
Fondly we think we honour merit then,
When we but praise ourselves in other men.
Parties in wit attend on those of state,
And public faction doubles private hate.
Pride, Malice, Folly, against Dryden rose,
In various shapes of parsons, critics, beaux:
But sense survived when merry jests were past;   260
For rising merit will buoy up at last.
Might he return and bless once more our eyes,
New Blackmores and new Milbournes must arise.
Nay, should great Homer lift his awful head,
Zoilus again would start up from the dead.
Envy will Merit as its shade pursue,
But like a shadow proves the substance true;
For envied Wit, like Sol eclips'd, makes known
Th' opposing body's grossness, not its own.
When first that sun too powerful beams displays,   270
It draws up vapours which obscure its rays;
But ev'n those clouds at last adorn its way,
Reflect new glories, and augment the day.
    Be thou the first true merit to befriend;
His praise is lost who stays till all commend.
Short is the date, alas! of modern rhymes,
And 't is but just to let them live betimes.
No longer now that Golden Age appears,
When patriarch wits survived a thousand years:
Now length of fame (our second life) is lost,   280
And bare threescore is all ev'n that can boast:
Our sons their fathers' failing language see,
And such as Chaucer is shall Dryden be.
So when the faithful pencil has design'd
Some bright idea of the master's mind,
Where a new world leaps out at his command,
And ready Nature waits upon his hand;
When the ripe colours soften and unite,
And sweetly melt into just shade and light;
When mellowing years their full perfection give,   290
And each bold figure just begins to live,
The treach'rous colours the fair art betray,
And all the bright creation fades away!
    Unhappy Wit, like most mistaken things,

Atones not for that envy which it brings:
In youth alone its empty praise we boast,
But soon the short-lived vanity is lost;
Like some fair flower the early Spring supplies,
That gaily blooms, but ev'n in blooming dies.
What is this Wit, which must our cares employ?   300
The owner's wife that other men enjoy;
Then most our trouble still when most admired,
And still the more we give, the more required;
Whose fame with pains we guard, but lose with ease,
Sure some to vex, but never all to please,
'T is what the vicious fear, the virtuous shun;
By fools 't is hated, and by knaves undone!
    If Wit so much from Ignorance undergo,
Ah, let not Learning too commence its foe!
Of old those met rewards who could excel,   310
And such were prais'd who but endeavour'd well;
Tho' triumphs were to gen'rals only due,
Crowns were reserv'd to grace the soldiers too.
Now they who reach Parnassus' lofty crown
Employ their pains to spurn some others down;
And while self-love each jealous writer rules,
Contending wits become the sport of fools;
But still the worst with most regret commend,
For each ill author is as bad a friend.
To what base ends, and by what abject ways,   320
Are mortals urged thro' sacred lust of praise!
Ah, ne'er so dire a thirst of glory boast,
Nor in the critic let the man be lost!
Good nature and good sense must ever join;
To err is human, to forgive divine.
    But if in noble minds some dregs remain,
Not yet purged off, of spleen and sour disdain,
Discharge that rage on more provoking crimes,
Nor fear a dearth in these flagitious times.
No pardon vile obscenity should find,   330
Tho' Wit and Art conspire to move your mind;
But dulness with obscenity must prove
As shameful sure as impotence in love.
In the fat age of pleasure, wealth, and ease
Sprung the rank weed, and thrived with large increase:
When love was all an easy monarch's care,
Seldom at council, never in a war;
Jilts ruled the state, and statesmen farces writ;
Nay wits had pensions, and young lords had wit;
The Fair sat panting at a courtier's play,   340

And not a mask went unimprov'd away;
The modest fan was lifted up no more,
And virgins smil'd at what they blush'd before.
The following license of a foreign reign
Did all the dregs of bold Socinus drain;
Then unbelieving priests reform'd the nation,
And taught more pleasant methods of salvation;
Where Heav'n's free subjects might their rights dispute,
Lest God himself should seem too absolute;
Pulpits their sacred satire learn'd to spare,   350
And vice admired to find a flatt'rer there!
Encouraged thus, Wit's Titans braved the skies,
And the press groan'd with licens'd blasphemies.
These monsters, Critics! with your darts engage,
Here point your thunder, and exhaust your rage!
Yet shun their fault, who, scandalously nice,
Will needs mistake an author into vice:
All seems infected that th' infected spy,
As all looks yellow to the jaundic'd eye.

Critic can't see good because of critical self

Part III

Learn then what morals Critics ought to show,
For 't is but half a judge's task to know.
'T is not enough Taste, Judgment, Learning join;
In all you speak let Truth and Candour shine;
That not alone what to your Sense is due
All may allow, but seek your friendship too.
  Be silent always when you doubt your Sense,
And speak, tho' sure, with seeming diffidence.
Some positive persisting fops we know,
Who if once wrong will needs be always so;   10
But you with pleasure own your errors past,
And make each day a critique on the last.
  'T is not enough your counsel still be true;
Blunt truths more mischief than nice falsehoods do.
Men must be taught as if you taught them not,
And things unknown proposed as things forgot.
Without good breeding truth is disapprov'd;
That only makes superior Sense belov'd.
  Be niggards of advice on no pretence,
For the worst avarice is that of Sense.   20
With mean complacence ne'er betray your trust,
Nor be so civil as to prove unjust.
Fear not the anger of the wise to raise;

Those best can bear reproof who merit praise.
   'T were well might critics still this freedom take,
But Appius reddens at each word you speak,
And stares tremendous, with a threat'ning eye,
Like some fierce tyrant in old tapestry.
Fear most to tax an honourable fool,
Whose right it is, uncensured to be dull: 30
Such without Wit, are poets when they please,
As without Learning they can take degrees.
Leave dangerous truths to unsuccessful satires,
And flattery to fulsome dedicators;
Whom, when they praise, the world believes no more
Than when they promise to give scribbling o'er.
'T is best sometimes your censure to restrain,
And charitably let the dull be vain;
Your silence there is better than your spite,
For who can rail so long as they can write?   40
Still humming on their drowsy course they keep,
And lash'd so long, like tops, are lash'd asleep.
False steps but help them to renew the race,
As, after stumbling, jades will mend their pace.
What crowds of these, impenitently bold,
In sounds and jingling syllables grown old,
Still run on poets, in a raging vein,
Ev'n to the dregs and squeezings of the brain,
Strain out the last dull dropping of their sense,
And rhyme with all the rage of impotence!   50
   Such shameless bards we have; and yet 't is true
There are as mad abandon'd critics too.
The bookful blockhead ignorantly read,
With loads of learned lumber in his head,
With his own tongue still edifies his ears,
And always list'ning to himself appears.
All books he reads, and all he reads assails,
From Dryden's Fables down to Durfey's Tales.
With him most authors steal their works, or buy;
Garth did not write his own Dispensary.   60
Name a new play, and he's the poet's friend;
Nay, show'd his faults—but when would poets mend?
No place so sacred from such fops is barr'd,
Nor is Paul's church more safe than Paul's churchyard:
Nay, fly to altars, there they'll talk you dead;
For fools rush in where angels fear to tread.
Distrustful sense with modest caution speaks,
It still looks home, and short excursions makes;
But rattling nonsense in full volleys breaks

And never shock'd, and never turn'd aside,   70
Bursts out, resistless, with a thund'ring tide.
    But where's the man who counsel can bestow,
Still pleas'd to teach, and yet not proud to know?
Unbiass'd or by favour or by spite;
Not dully prepossess'd nor blindly right;
Tho' learn'd, well bred, and tho' well bred sincere;
Modestly bold, and humanly severe;
Who to a friend his faults can freely show,
And gladly praise the merit of a foe;
Bless'd with a taste exact, yet unconfin'd,   80
A knowledge both of books and humankind;
Gen'rous converse; a soul exempt from pride;
And love to praise, with reason on his side?
Such once were critics; such the happy few
Athens and Rome in better ages knew.
The mighty Stagyrite first left the shore,
Spread all his sails, and durst the deeps explore;
He steer'd securely, and discover'd far,
Led by the light of the Mæonian star.
Poets, a race long unconfin'd and free,   90
Still fond and proud of savage liberty,
Receiv'd his laws, and stood convinc'd 't was fit
Who conquer'd Nature should preside o'er Wit.
    Horace still charms with graceful negligence,
And without method talks us into sense;
Will, like a friend, familiarly convey
The truest notions in the easiest way.
He who, supreme in judgment as in wit,
Might boldly censure as he boldly writ,
Yet judg'd with coolness, though he sung with fire;   100
His precepts teach but what his works inspire.
Our critics take a contrary extreme,
They judge with fury, but they write with phlegm;
Nor suffers Horace more in wrong translations
By Wits, than Critics in as wrong quotations.
See Dionysius Homer's thoughts refine,
And call new beauties forth from ev'ry line!
Fancy and art in gay Petronius please,
The Scholar's learning with the courtier's ease.
    In grave Quintilian's copious work we find   110
The justest rules and clearest method join'd.
Thus useful arms in magazines we place,
All ranged in order, and disposed with grace;
But less to please the eye then arm the hand,
Still fit for use, and ready at command.

Thee, bold Longinus! all the Nine inspire,
And bless their critic with a poet's fire:
An ardent judge, who, zealous in his trust,
With warmth gives sentence, yet is always just;
Whose own example strengthens all his laws,   120
And is himself that great sublime he draws.
    Thus long succeeding critics justly reign'd,
License repress'd, and useful laws ordain'd:
Learning and Rome alike in empire grew,
And arts still follow'd where her eagles flew;
From the same foes at last both felt their doom,
And the same age saw learning fall and Rome.
With tyranny then superstition join'd,
As that the body, this enslaved the mind;
Much was believ'd, but little understood,   130
And to be dull was construed to be good;
A second deluge learning thus o'errun,
And the monks finish'd what the Goths begun.
    At length Erasmus, that great injur'd name,
(The glory of the priesthood and the shame!)
Stemm'd the wild torrent of a barb'rous age,
And drove those holy Vandals off the stage.
    But see! each Muse in Leo's golden days
Starts from her trance, and trims her wither'd bays.
Rome's ancient genius, o'er its ruins spread,   140
Shakes off the dust, and rears his rev'rend head.
Then sculpture and her sister arts revive;
Stones leap'd to form, and rocks began to live;
With sweeter notes each rising temple rung;
A Raphael painted and a Vida sung:
Immortal Vida! on whose honour'd brow
The poet's bays and critic's ivy grow:
Cremona now shall ever boast thy name,
As next in place to Mantua, next in fame!
    But soon by impious arms from Latium chased,   150
Their ancient bounds the banish'd Muses pass'd;
Thence arts o'er all the northern world advance,
But critic learning flourish'd most in France;
The rules a nation born to serve obeys,
And Boileau still in right of Horace sways.
But we, brave Britons, foreign laws despised,
And kept unconquer'd and uncivilized;
Fierce for the liberties of wit, and bold,
We still defied the Romans, as of old.
Yet some there were, among the sounder few   160
Of those who less presumed and better knew,

Who durst assert the juster ancient cause,
And here restor'd Wit's fundamental laws.
Such was the Muse whose rules and practice tell
'Nature's chief masterpiece is writing well.'
Such was Roscommon, not more learn'd than good,
With manners gen'rous as his noble blood;
To him the wit of Greece and Rome was known,
And every author's merit but his own.
Such late was Walsh—the Muse's judge and friend,   170
Who justly knew to blame or to commend;
To failings mild but zealous for desert,
The clearest head, and the sincerest heart.
This humble praise, lamented Shade! receive;
This praise at least a grateful Muse may give:
The Muse whose early voice you taught to sing,
Prescribed her heights, and pruned her tender wing,
(Her guide now lost), no more attempts to rise,
But in low numbers short excursions tries;
Content if hence th' unlearn'd their wants may view,   180
The learn'd reflect on what before they knew;
Careless of censure, nor too fond of fame;
Still pleas'd to praise, yet not afraid to blame;
Averse alike to flatter or offend;
Not free from faults, nor yet too vain to mend.

Always make self better at whatever one does

SAMUEL JOHNSON

Preface to Shakespeare

1765

The sonorous diction and the sculptured syntax of Dr. Johnson's (1709–1784) first paragraph may suggest that he is a magisterial defender of the classical rules, the classicist par excellence. But that picture of him surely vanishes when we later read: "That this is a practice contrary to the rules of criticism will be readily allowed; but there is always an appeal open from criticism to nature." (Or, elsewhere, in his essay on Dryden: "Reason wants not Horace to support it.") Despite his classicism, he is not a mere formalist following or issuing arbitrary edicts about literature, so it comes as no surprise that in the conflict between the "three unities" and the "irregularities" of Shakespeare, it is the validity of the rules that loses out. (In 1822, when the novelist Stendhal was attacking French neoclassicism, he cited Johnson as the authority for his argument.) Examining the concepts of time, place, and action, Johnson works his way back by common sense to the same conclusion that Aristotle reached as to the only essential unity in the drama.

The long-sustained experience of humankind, not an antiquarian worship of the past, is Johnson's test for older writers, and Shakespeare is preeminent because he is the poet of "general nature." Opposed to the general—or which we may read universal and therefore "truthful"—is the particular, the special, the individual. Shakespeare's appeal rests on his ability to portray human nature, not kings or Romans; this is Shakespeare's "mirrour of life" that has stood the test of time and that narrower critics have misunderstood. Johnson likewise defends Shakespeare against the objection that he mixed comedy and tragedy; again, Johnson regards the differentiation of Shakespeare's plays into formal genres as merely a critical convenience, useful neither to the audience nor to Shakespeare, "who never fails to attain his purpose." It is the end and not the means that Johnson values.

About that end he is unambiguous: it is "to instruct, by pleasing." The moral criterion is another measurement for evaluating Shakespeare, and Johnson's discussion of how the plays instruct, as well as when and why they do not, should be studied as an example of a firm critical mind drawing distinctions and making judgments based on a clearly defined system of values.

THAT PRAISES are without reason lavished on the dead, and that the honours due only to excellence are paid to antiquity, is a complaint likely to be always continued by those, who, being able to add nothing to truth, hope for eminence from the heresies of paradox; or those, who, being forced by disappointment upon consolatory expedients, are willing to hope from posterity what the present age refuses, and flatter themselves that the regard which is yet denied by envy, will be at last bestowed by time.

Antiquity, like every other quality that attracts the notice of mankind, has undoubtedly votaries that reverence it, not from reason, but from prejudice. Some seem to admire indiscriminately whatever has been long preserved, without considering that time has sometimes co-operated with chance; all perhaps are more willing to honour past than present excellence; and the mind contemplates genius through the shades of age, as the eye surveys the sun through artificial opacity. The great contention of criticism is to find the faults of the moderns, and the beauties of the ancients. While an author is yet living we estimate his powers by his worst performance, and when he is dead, we rate them by his best.

To works, however, of which the excellence is not absolute and definite, but gradual and comparative; to works not raised upon principles demonstrative and scientific, but appealing wholly to observation and experience, no other test can be applied than length of duration and continuance of esteem. What mankind have long possessed they have often examined and compared; and if they persist to value the possession, it is because frequent comparisons have confirmed opinion in its favour. As among the works of nature no man can properly call a river deep, or a mountain high, without the knowledge of many mountains, and many rivers; so in the productions of genius, nothing can be stiled excellent till it has been compared with other works of the same kind. Demonstration immediately displays its power, and has nothing to hope or fear from the flux of years; but works tentative and experimental must be estimated by their proportion to the general and collective ability of man, as it is discovered in a long succession of endeavours. Of the first building that was raised, it might be with certainty determined that it was round or square; but whether it was spacious or lofty must have been referred to time. The Pythagorean scale of numbers was at once discovered to be perfect; but the poems of Homer we yet know not to transcend the common limits of human intelligence, but by remarking, that nation after nation, and century after century, has been able to do little more than transpose his incidents, new-name his characters, and paraphrase his sentiments.

The reverence due to writings that have long subsisted arises therefore not from any credulous confidence in the superior wisdom of past ages, or gloomy persuasion of the degeneracy of mankind, but is the consequence of acknowledged and indubitable positions, that what has been longest known has been most considered, and what is most considered is best understood.

The Poet, of whose works I have undertaken the revision, may now begin to assume the dignity of an ancient, and claim the privilege of established fame and prescriptive veneration. He has long outlived his century, the term commonly fixed as the test of literary merit. Whatever advantages he might once derive from personal allusions, local customs, or temporary opinions, have for many years been lost; and every topick of merriment, or motive of sorrow, which the modes of artificial life afforded him, now only obscure the scenes which they once illuminated. The effects of favour and competition are at the end; the tradition of his friendships and his enmities has perished; his works support no opinion with arguments, nor supply any faction with invectives; they can neither indulge vanity nor gratify malignity; but are read without any other reason than the desire of pleasure, and are therefore praised only as pleasure is obtained; yet, thus unassisted by interest or passion, they have passed through variations of taste and changes of manners, and, as they devolved from one generation to another, have received new honours at every transmission.

But because human judgment, though it be gradually gaining upon certainty, never becomes infallible; and approbation, though long continued may yet be only the approbation of prejudice or fashion, it is proper to inquire, by what peculiarities of excellence Shakespeare has gained and kept the favour of his countrymen.

Nothing can please many, and please long, but just representations of general nature. Particular manners can be known to few, and therefore few only can judge how nearly they are copied. The irregular combinations of fanciful invention may delight a-while, by that novelty of which the common satiety of life sends us all in quest; but the pleasures of sudden wonder are soon exhausted, and the mind can only repose on the stability of truth.

Shakespeare is above all writers, at least above all modern writers, the poet of nature; the poet that holds up to his readers a faithful mirrour of manners and of life. His characters are not modified by the customs of particular places, unpractised by the rest of the world; by the peculiarities of studies or professions, which can operate but upon small numbers; or by the accidents of transient fashions or temporary opinions: they are the genuine progeny of common humanity, such as the world will always supply, and observation will always find. His persons act and speak by the influence of those general passions and principles by which all minds are agitated, and the whole system of life is continued in motion. In the writings of other poets a character is too often an individual; in those of Shakespeare is commonly a species.

It is from this wide extension of design that so much instruction is derived. It is this which fills the plays of Shakespeare with practical axioms and domestick wisdom. It was said of Euripides, that every verse was a precept; and it may be said of Shakespeare, that from his works may be collected a system of civil and oeconomical prudence. Yet his real power is not shewn in the splendour of particular passages, but by the progress of his fable, and the tenour of his dialogue; and he that tries to recommend him by select quotations, will succeed like the pedant in Hierocles, who, when he offered his house to sale, carried a brick in his pocket as a specimen.

It will not easily be imagined how much Shakespeare excells in accommodating his sentiments to real life, but by comparing him with other authours. It was observed of the ancient schools of declamation, that the more diligently they were frequented, the more was the student disqualified for the world, because he found nothing there which he should ever meet in any other place. The same remark may be applied to every stage but that of Shakespeare. The theatre, when it is under any other direction, is peopled by such characters as were never seen, conversing in a language which was never heard, upon topicks which will never arise in the commerce of mankind. But the dialogue of this authour is often so evidently determined by the incident which produces it, and is pursued with so much ease and simplicity, that it seems scarcely to claim the merit of fiction, but to have been gleaned by diligent selection out of common conversation, and common occurrences.

Upon every other stage the universal agent is love, by whose power all good and evil is distributed, and every action quickened or retarded. To bring a lover, a lady and a rival into the fable; to entangle them in contradictory obligations, perplex them with oppositions of interest, and harass them with violence of desires inconsistent with each other; to make them meet in rapture and part in agony; to fill their mouths with hyperbolical joy and outrageous sorrow; to distress them as nothing human ever was distressed; to deliver them as nothing human ever was delivered; is the business of a modern dramatist. For this probability is violated, life is misrepresented, and language is depraved. But love is only one of many passions; and as it has no great influence upon the sum of life, it has little operation in the dramas of a poet, who caught his ideas from the living world, and exhibited only what he saw before him. He knew, that any other passion, as it was regular or exorbitant, was a cause of happiness or calamity.

Characters thus ample and general were not easily discriminated and preserved, yet perhaps no poet ever kept his personages more distinct from each other. I will not say with Pope, that every speech may be assigned to the proper speaker, because many speeches there are which have nothing characteristical; but perhaps, though some may be equally adapted to every person, it will be difficult to find, any that can be properly transferred from the present possessor to another claimant. The choice is right, when there is reason for choice.

Other dramaticks can only gain attention by hyperbolical or aggravated characters, by fabulous and unexampled excellence or depravity, as the writers of barbarous romances invigorated the reader by a giant and a dwarf; and he that should form his expectations of human affairs from the play, or from the tale, would be equally deceived. Shakespeare has no heroes; his scenes are occupied only by men, who act and speak as the reader thinks that he should himself have spoken or acted on the same occasion: Even where the agency is supernatural the dialogue is level with life. Other writers disguise the most natural passions and most frequent incidents; so that he who contemplates them in the book will not know them in the world: Shakespeare

'What oft was thought, n'er so well expressed'

approximates the remote, and familiarizes the wonderful; the event which he represents will not happen, but if it were possible, its effects would probably be such as he has assigned; and it may be said, that he has not only shewn human nature as it acts in real exigencies, but as it would be found in trials, to which it cannot be exposed.

This therefore is the praise of Shakespeare, that his drama is the mirrour of life; that he who has mazed his imagination, in following the phantoms which other writers raise up before him, may here be cured of his delirious extasies, by reading human sentiments in human language, by scenes from which a hermit may estimate the transactions of the world, and a confessor predict the progress of the passions.

His adherence to general nature has exposed him to the censure of criticks, who form their judgments upon narrower principles. Dennis and Rhymer think his Romans not sufficiently Roman; and Voltaire censures his kings as not completely royal. Dennis is offended, that Menenius, a senator of Rome, should play the buffoon; and Voltaire perhaps thinks decency violated when the Danish Usurper is represented as a drunkard. But Shakespeare always makes nature predominate over accident; and if he preserves the essential character, is not very careful of distinctions superinduced and adventitious. His story requires Romans or kings, but he thinks only on men. He knew that Rome, like every other city, had men of all dispositions; and wanting a buffoon, he went into the senate-house for that which the senate-house would certainly have afforded him. He was inclined to shew an usurper and a murderer not only odious but despicable, he therefore added drunkenness to his other qualities, knowing that kings love wine like other men, and that wine exerts its natural power upon kings. These are the petty cavils of petty minds; a poet overlooks the casual distinction of country and condition, as a painter, satisfied with the figure, neglects the drapery.

The censure which he has incurred by mixing comick and tragick scenes, as it extends to all his works, deserves more consideration. Let the fact be first stated, and then examined.

Shakespeare's plays are not in the rigorous and critical sense either tragedies or comedies, but compositions of a distinct kind; exhibiting the real state of sublunary nature, which partakes of good and evil, joy and sorrow, mingled with endless variety of proportion and innumerable modes of combination; and expressing the course of the world, in which the loss of one is the gain of another; in which, at the same time, the reveller is hasting to his wine, and the mourner burying his friend; in which the malignity of one is sometimes defeated by the frolick of another; and many mischiefs and many benefits are done and hindered without design.

Out of this chaos of mingled purposes and casualties the ancient poets, according to the laws which custom had prescribed, selected some the crimes of men, and some their absurdities; some the momentous vicissitudes of life, and some the lighter occurrences; some the terrours of distress, and some the gayeties of prosperity. Thus rose the two modes of imitation, known by the names of tragedy and comedy, compositions intended to promote different

ends by contrary means, and considered as so little allied, that I do not recollect among the Greeks or Romans a single writer who attempted both.

Shakespeare has united the powers of exciting laughter and sorrow not
only in one mind, but in one composition. Almost all his plays are divided
between serious and ludicrous characters, and, in the successive evolutions
of the design, sometimes produce seriousness and sorrow, and sometimes
levity and laughter.

That this is a practice contrary to the rules of criticism will be readily allowed; but there is always an appeal open from criticism to nature. The end
of writing is to instruct; the end of poetry is to instruct by pleasing. That the
mingled drama may convey all the instruction of tragedy or comedy cannot
be denied, because it includes both in its alternations of exhibition and approaches nearer than either to the appearance of life, by shewing how great
machinations and slender designs may promote or obviate one another, and
the high and the low co-operate in the general system by unavoidable con-
catenation. *(linking together)*

[margin: Horace Sidney always should be a lesson]

It is objected, that by this change of scenes the passions are interrupted in
their progression, and that the principal event, being not advanced by a due
gradation of preparatory incidents, wants at last the power to move, which
constitutes the perfection of dramatick poetry. This reasoning is so specious,
that it is received as true even by those who in daily experience feel it to be false.
The interchanges of mingled scenes seldom fail to produce the intended vicissitudes of passion. Fiction cannot move so much, but that the attention may be
easily transferred; and though it must be allowed that pleasing melancholy be
sometimes interrupted by unwelcome levity, yet let it be considered likewise,
that melancholy is often not pleasing, and that the disturbance of one man may
be the relief of another; that different auditors have different habitudes; and
that, upon the whole, all pleasure consists in variety.

The players, who in their edition divided our authour's works into
comedies, histories, and tragedies, seem not to have distinguished the three
kinds by any very exact or definite ideas.

An action which ended happily to the principal persons, however serious or distressful through its intermediate incidents, in their opinion, constituted a comedy. This idea of a comedy continued long amongst us; and plays
were written, which, by changing the catastrophe, were tragedies to-day, and
comedies to-morrow.

Tragedy was not in those times a poem of more general dignity or elevation than comedy; it required only a calamitous conclusion, with which the
common criticism of that age was satisfied, whatever lighter pleasure it afforded in its progress.

History was a series of actions, with no other than chronological succession, independent on each other, and without any tendency to introduce or
regulate the conclusion. It is not always very nicely distinguished from
tragedy. There is not much nearer approach to unity of action in the tragedy
of *Antony and Cleopatra*, than in the history of *Richard the Second.* But a history
might be continued through many plays; as it had no plan, it had no limits.

Through all these denominations of the drama, Shakespeare's mode of composition is the same; an interchange of seriousness and merriment, by which the mind is softened at one time, and exhilarated at another. But whatever be his purpose, whether to gladden or depress, or to conduct the story, without vehemence or emotion, through tracts of easy and familiar dialogue, he never fails to attain his purpose; as he commands us, we laugh or mourn, or sit silent with quiet expectation, in tranquillity without indifference.

When Shakespeare's plan is understood, most of the criticisms of Rhymer and Voltaire vanish away. The play of *Hamlet* is opened, without impropriety, by two sentinels; Iago bellows at Brabantio's window, without injury to the scheme of the play, though in terms which a modern audience would not easily endure; the character of Polonius is seasonable and useful; and the Grave-diggers themselves may be heard with applause.

Shakespeare engaged in dramatick poetry with the world open before him; the rules of the ancients were yet known to few; the publick judgment was unformed; he had no example of such fame as might force him upon imitation, nor criticks of such authority as might restrain his extravagance: He therefore indulged his natural disposition, and his disposition, as Rhymer has remarked, led him to comedy. In tragedy he often writes, with great appearance of toil and study, what is written at last with little felicity; but in his comick scenes, he seems to produce without labour, what no labour can improve. In tragedy he is always struggling after some occasion to be comick; but in comedy he seems to repose, or to luxuriate, as in a mode of thinking congenial to his nature. In his tragick scenes there is always something wanting, but his comedy often surpasses expectation or desire. His comedy pleases by the thoughts and the language, and his tragedy for the greater part by incident and action. His tragedy seems to be skill, his comedy to be instinct.

The force of his comick scenes has suffered little diminution from the changes made by a century and a half, in manners or in words. As his personages act upon principles arising from genuine passion, very little modified by particular forms, their pleasures and vexations are communicable to all times and to all places; they are natural, and therefore durable; the adventitious peculiarities of personal habits, are only superficial dies, bright and pleasing for a little while, yet soon fading to a dim tinct, without any remains of former lustre; but the discriminations of true passion are the colours of nature; they pervade the whole mass, and can only perish with the body that exhibits them. The accidental compositions of heterogeneous modes are dissolved by the chance which combined them; but the uniform simplicity of primitive qualities neither admits increase, nor suffers decay. The sand heaped by one flood is scattered by another, but the rock always continues in its place. The stream of time, which is continually washing the dissoluble fabricks of other poets, passes without injury by the adamant of Shakespeare.

If there be, what I believe there is, in every nation, a stile which never becomes obsolete, a certain mode of phraseology so consonant and congenial to the analogy and principles of its respective language as to remain settled and unaltered; this style is probably to be sought in the common intercourse of life, among those who speak only to be understood, without ambition of elegance. The polite are always catching modish innovations, and the learned depart from established forms of speech, in hope of finding or making better; those who wish for distinction forsake the vulgar, when the vulgar is right; but there is a conversation above grossness and below refinement, where propriety resides, and where this poet seems to have gathered his comick dialogue. He is therefore more agreeable to the ears of the present age than any other authour equally remote, and among his other excellencies deserves to be studied as one of the original masters of our language.

These observations are to be considered not as unexceptionably constant, but as containing general and predominant truth. Shakespeare's familiar dialogue is affirmed to be smooth and clear, yet not wholly without ruggedness or difficulty; as a country may be eminently fruitful, though it has spots unfit for cultivation: His characters are praised as natural, though their sentiments are sometimes forced, and their actions improbable; as the earth upon the whole is spherical, though its surface is varied with protuberances and cavities.

Shakespeare with his excellencies has likewise faults, and faults sufficient to obscure and overwhelm any other merit. I shall shew them in the proportion in which they appear to me, without envious malignity or superstitious veneration. No question can be more innocently discussed than a dead poet's pretensions to renown; and little regard is due to that bigotry which sets candour higher than truth.

His first defect is that to which may be imputed most of the evil in books or in men. He sacrifices virtue to convenience, and is so much more careful to please than to instruct, that he seems to write without any moral purpose. From his writings indeed a system of social duty may be selected, for he that thinks reasonably must think morally; but his precepts and axioms drop casually from him; he makes no just distribution of good or evil, nor is always careful to shew in the virtuous a disapprobation of the wicked; he carries his persons indifferently through right and wrong, and at the close dismisses them without further care, and leaves their examples to operate by chance. This fault the barbarity of his age cannot extenuate; for it is always a writer's duty to make the world better, and justice is a virtue independant on time or place.

The plots are often so loosely formed, that a very slight consideration may improve them, and so carelessly pursued, that he seems not always fully to comprehend his own design. He omits opportunities of instructing or delighting which the train of his story seems to force upon him, and apparently rejects those exhibitions which would be more affecting, for the sake of those which are more easy.

It may be observed, that in many of his plays the latter part is evidently neglected. When he found himself near the end of his work, and, in view of his reward, he shortened the labour to snatch the profit. He therefore remits his efforts where he should most vigorously exert them, and his catastrophe is improbably produced or imperfectly represented.

r/t probability

He had no regard to distinction of time or place, but gives to one age or nation, without scruple, the customs, institutions, and opinions of another, at the expence not only of likelihood, but of possibility. These faults Pope has endeavoured, with more zeal than judgment, to transfer to his imagined interpolators. We need not wonder to find Hector quoting Aristotle, when we see the loves of Theseus and Hippolyta combined with the Gothick mythology of fairies. Shakespeare, indeed, was not the only violator of chronology, for in the same age Sidney, who wanted not the advantages of learning, has, in his *Arcadia*, confounded the pastoral with the feudal times, the days of innocence, quiet and security, with those of turbulence, violence, and adventure.

In his comick scenes he is seldom very successful, when he engages his characters in reciprocations of smartness and contests of sarcasm; their jests are commonly gross, and their pleasantry licentious; neither his gentlemen nor his ladies have much delicacy, nor are sufficiently distinguished from his clowns by any appearance of refined manners. Whether he represented the real conversation of his time is not easy to determine; the reign of Elizabeth is commonly supposed to have been a time of stateliness, formality and reserve; yet perhaps the relaxations of that severity were not very elegant. There must, however, have been always some modes of gayety preferable to others, and a writer ought to chuse the best.

In tragedy his performance seems constantly to be worse, as his labour is more. The effusions of passion which exigence forces out are for the most part striking and energetick; but whenever he solicits his invention, or strains his faculties, the offspring of his throes is tumour, meanness, tediousness, and obscurity.

In narration he affects a disproportionate pomp of diction, and a wearisome train of circumlocution, and tells the incident imperfectly in many words, which might have been more plainly delivered in few. Narration in dramatick poetry is naturally tedious, as it is unanimated and inactive, and obstructs the progress of the action; it should therefore always be rapid, and enlivened by frequent interruption. Shakespeare found it an encumbrance, and instead of lightening it by brevity, endeavoured to recommend it by dignity and splendour.

His declamations or set speeches are commonly cold and weak, for his power was the power of nature; when he endeavoured, like other tragick writers, to catch opportunities of amplification, and instead of inquiring what the occasion demanded, to show how much his stores of knowledge could supply, he seldom escapes without the pity or resentment of his reader.

It is incident to him to be now and then entangled with an unwieldy sentiment, which he cannot well express, and will not reject; he struggles with it a while, and if it continues stubborn, comprises it in words such as occur, and leaves it to be disentangled and evolved by those who have more leisure to bestow upon it.

Not that always where the language is intricate the thought is subtle, or the image always great where the line is bulky; the equality of words to things is very often neglected, and trivial sentiments and vulgar ideas disappoint the attention, to which they are recommended by sonorous epithets and swelling figures.

But the admirers of this great poet have never less reason to indulge their hopes of supreme excellence, than when he seems fully resolved to sink them in dejection, and mollify them with tender emotions by the fall of greatness, the danger of innocence, or the crosses of love. He is not long soft and pathetick without some idle conceit, or contemptible equivocation. He no sooner begins to move, than he counteracts himself; and terrour and pity, as they are rising in the mind, are checked and blasted by sudden frigidity.

A quibble is to Shakespeare, what luminous vapours are to the traveller; he follows it at all adventures; it is sure to lead him out of his way, and sure to engulf him in the mire. It has some malignant power over his mind, and its fascinations are irresistible. Whatever be the dignity or profundity of his disquisition, whether he be enlarging knowledge or exalting affection, whether he be amusing attention with incidents, or enchaining it in suspense, let but a quibble spring up before him, and he leaves his work unfinished. A quibble is the golden apple for which he will always turn aside from his career, or stoop from his elevation. A quibble, poor and barren as it is, gave him such delight, that he was content to purchase it, by the sacrifice of reason, propriety and truth. A quibble was to him the fatal Cleopatra for which he lost the world, and was content to lose it.

It will be thought strange, that, in enumerating the defects of this writer, I have not yet mentioned his neglect of the unities; his violation of those laws which have been instituted and established by the joint authority of poets and of criticks.

For his other deviations from the art of writing, I resign him to critical justice, without making any other demand in his favour, than that which must be indulged to all human excellence: that his virtues be rated with his failings: But, from the censure which this irregularity may bring upon him, I shall, with due reverence to that learning which I must oppose, adventure to try how I can defend him.

His histories, being neither tragedies nor comedies are not subject to any of their laws; nothing more is necessary to all the praise which they expect, than that the changes of action be so prepared as to be understood, that the incidents be various and affecting, and the characters consistent, natural, and distinct. No other unity is intended, and therefore none is to be sought.

In his other works he has well enough preserved the unity of action. He has not, indeed, an intrigue regularly perplexed and regularly unravelled: he does not endeavour to hide his design only to discover it, for this is seldom the order of real events, and Shakespeare is the poet of nature: But his plan has commonly what Aristotle requires, a beginning, a middle, and an end; one event is concatenated with another, and the conclusion follows by easy consequence. There are perhaps some incidents that might be spared, as in other poets there is much talk that only fills up time upon the stage; but the general system makes gradual advances, and the end of the play is the end of expectation.

To the unities of time and place he has shewn no regard; and perhaps a nearer view of the principles on which they stand will diminish their value, and withdraw from them the veneration which, from the time of Corneille, they have very generally received, by discovering that they have given more trouble to the poet, than pleasure to the auditor.

The necessity of observing the unities of time and place arises from the supposed necessity of making the drama credible. The criticks hold it impossible, that an action of months or years can be possibly believed to pass in three hours; or that the spectator can suppose himself to sit in the theatre, while ambassadors go and return between distant kings, while armies are levied and towns besieged, while an exile wanders and returns, or till he whom they saw courting his mistress, shall lament the untimely fall of his son. The mind revolts from evident falsehood, and fiction loses its force when it departs from the resemblance of reality.

From the narrow limitation of time necessarily arises the contraction of place. The spectator, who knows that he saw the first act at Alexandria, cannot suppose that he sees the next at Rome, at a distance to which not the dragons of Medea could, in so short a time, have transported him; he knows with certainty that he has not changed his place, and he knows that place cannot change itself; that what was a house cannot become a plain; that what was Thebes can never be Persepolis.

Such is the triumphant language with which a critick exults over the misery of an irregular poet, and exults commonly without resistance or reply. It is time therefore to tell him by the authority of Shakespeare, that he assumes, as an unquestionable principle, a position, which, while his breath is forming it into words, his understanding pronounces to be false. It is false, that any representation is mistaken for reality; that any dramatick fable in its materiality was ever credible, or, for a single moment, was ever credited.

The objection arising from the impossibility of passing the first hour at Alexandria, and the next at Rome, supposes, that when the play opens, the spectator really imagines himself at Alexandria, and believes that his walk to the theatre has been a voyage to Egypt, and that he lives in the days of Antony and Cleopatra. Sure he that imagines this may imagine more. He that can take the stage at one time for the palace of the Ptolemies, may take it in half an hour for the promontory of Actium. Delusion, if delusion be admitted, has no certain limitation; if the spectator can be once persuaded, that his old acquaintance are Alexander and Cæsar, that a room illuminated with candles is the plain of Pharsalia, or the bank of Granicus, he is in a state of elevation above the reach of reason, or of truth, and from the heights of empyrean poetry, may despise the circumscriptions of terrestrial nature. There is no reason why a mind thus wandering in extasy should count the clock, or why an hour should not be a century in that calenture of the brains that can make the stage a field.

The truth is, that the spectators are always in their senses, and know, from the first act to the last, that the stage is only a stage, and that the players are only players. They came to hear a certain number of lines recited with just gesture and elegant modulation. The lines relate to some action, and an action must be in some place; but the different actions that compleat a story may be in places very remote from each other; and where is the absurdity of allowing that space to represent first Athens, and then Sicily, which was always known to be neither Sicily nor Athens, but a modern theatre?

By supposition, as place is introduced, time may be extended; the time required by the fable elapses for the most part between the acts; for, of so much of the action as is represented, the real and poetical duration is the same. If, in the first act, preparations for war against Mithridates are represented to be made in Rome, the event of the war may, without absurdity, be represented in the catastrophe, as happening in Pontus; we know that there is neither war, nor preparation for war; we know that we are neither in Rome nor Pontus; that neither Mithridates nor Lucullus are before us. The drama exhibits successive imitations of successive actions; and why may not the second imitation represent an action that happened years after the first, if it be so connected with it, that nothing but time can be supposed to intervene? Time is, of all modes of existence, most obsequious to the imagination; a lapse of years is as easily conceived as a passage of hours. In contemplation we easily contract the time of real actions, and therefore willingly permit it to be contracted when we only see their imitation.

It will be asked, how the drama moves, if it is not credited. It is credited with all the credit due to a drama. It is credited, whenever it moves, as a just picture of a real original; as representing to the auditor what he would himself feel, if he were to do or suffer what is there feigned to be suffered or to be done. The reflection that strikes the heart is not, that the evils before us are real evils, but that they are evils to which we ourselves may be exposed. If there be any fallacy, it is not that we fancy the players, but that we fancy ourselves unhappy for a moment; but we rather lament the possibility than suppose the presence of misery, as a mother weeps over her babe, when she remembers that death may take it from her. The delight of tragedy proceeds from our consciousness of fiction; if we thought murders and treasons real, they would please no more.

Imitations produce pain or pleasure, not because they are mistaken for realities, but because they bring realities to mind. When the imagination is recreated by a painted landscape, the trees are not supposed capable to give us shade, or the fountains coolness; but we consider, how we should be pleased with such fountains playing beside us, and such woods waving over us. We are agitated in reading the history of *Henry the Fifth,* yet no man takes his book for the field of Agencourt. A dramatick exhibition is a book recited with concomitants that encrease or diminish its effect. Familiar comedy is often more powerful on the theatre, than in the page; imperial tragedy is always less. The humour of Petruchio may be heightened by grimace; but what voice or what gesture can hope to add dignity or force to the soliloquy of Cato.

A play read, affects the mind like a play acted. It is therefore evident, that the action is not supposed to be real; and it follows, that between the acts a longer or shorter time may be allowed to pass, and that no more account of space or duration is to be taken by the auditor of a drama, than by the reader of a narrative, before whom may pass in an hour the life of a hero, or the revolution of an empire.

Whether Shakespeare knew the unities, and rejected them by design, or deviated from them by happy ignorance, it is, I think, impossible to decide, and useless to enquire. We may reasonably suppose, that, when he rose to notice, he did not want the counsels and admonitions of scholars and cricks, and that he at last deliberately persisted in a practice, which he might have begun by chance. As nothing is essential to the fable, but unity of action, and as the unities of time and place arise evidently from false assumptions, and, by circumscribing the extent of the drama, lessen its variety, I cannot think it much to be lamented, that they were not known by him, or not observed: Nor, if such another poet could arise, should I very vehemently reproach him, that his first act passed at Venice, and his next in Cyprus. Such violations of rules merely positive, become the comprehensive genius of Shakespeare, and such censures are suitable to the minute and slender criticism of Voltaire:

> Non usque adea permiscuit imis
> Longus summa dies, ut non, si voce Metelli
> Serventur leges, malint a Cæsare tolli.[1]

Yet when I speak thus slightly of dramatick rules, I cannot but recollect how much wit and learning may be produced against me; before such authorities I am afraid to stand, not that I think the present question one of those that are to be decided by mere authority, but because it is to be suspected, that these precepts have not been so easily received but for better reasons than I have yet been able to find. The result of my enquiries, in which it would be ludicrous to boast of impartiality, is, that the unities of time and place are not essential to a just drama, that though they may sometimes conduce to pleasure, they are always to be sacrificed to the nobler beauties of variety and instruction; and that a play, written with nice observation of critical rules, is to be contemplated as an elaborate curiosity, as the product of superfluous and ostentatious art, by which is shewn, rather what is possible, than what is necessary.

He, that, without diminution of any other excellence, shall preserve all the unities unbroken, deserves the like applause with the architect, who shall display all the orders of architecture in a citadel, without any deduction from its strength; but the principal beauty of a citadel is to exclude the enemy; and the greatest graces of a play, are to copy nature and instruct life.

Perhaps, what I have here not dogmatically but deliberately written, may recall the principles of the drama to a new examination. I am almost frighted at my own temerity; and when I estimate the fame and the strength of those that maintain the contrary opinion, am ready to sink down in rever-

---

[1] A long period of time does not bring such confusion that the laws made by Metellus should need to be abolished by Caesar.

ential silence; as Æneas withdrew from the defence of Troy, when he saw Neptune shaking the wall, and Juno heading the besiegers.

Those whom my arguments cannot persuade to give their approbation to the judgment of Shakespeare, will easily, if they consider the condition of his life, make some allowance for his ignorance.

Every man's performances, to be rightly estimated, must be compared with the state of the age in which he lived, and with his own particular opportunities; and though to the reader a book be not worse or better for the circumstances of the authour, yet as there is always a silent reference of human works to human abilities, and as the enquiry, how far man may extend his designs, or how high he may rate his native force, is of far greater dignity than in what rank we shall place any particular performance, curiosity is always busy to discover the instruments, as well as to survey the workmanship, to know how much is to be ascribed to original powers, and how much to casual and adventitious help. The palaces of Peru or Mexico were certainly mean and incommodious habitations, if compared to the houses of European monarchs; yet who could forbear to view them with astonishment, who remembered that they were built without the use of iron?

The English nation, in the time of Shakespeare, was yet struggling to emerge from barbarity. The philology of Italy had been transplanted hither in the reign of Henry the Eighth; and the learned languages had been successfully cultivated by Lilly, Linacer, and More; by Pole, Cheke, and Gardiner; and afterwards by Smith, Clerk, Haddon, and Ascham. Greek was now taught to boys in the principal schools; and those who united elegance with learning, read, with great diligence, the Italian and Spanish poets. But literature was yet confined to professed scholars, or to men and women of high rank. The publick was gross and dark; and to be able to read and write, was an accomplishment still valued for its rarity.

Nations, like individuals, have their infancy. A people newly awakened to literary curiosity, being yet unacquainted with the true state of things, knows not how to judge of that which is proposed as its resemblance. Whatever is remote from common appearances is always welcome to vulgar as to childish credulity; and of a country unenlightened by learning, the whole people is the vulgar. The study of those who then aspired to plebeian learning was laid out upon adventures, giants, dragons, and enchantments. *The Death of Arthur* was the favourite volume.

The mind, which has feasted on the luxurious wonders of fiction, has no taste of the insipidity of truth. A play which imitated only the common occurrences of the world, would, upon the admirers of *Palmerin* and *Guy of Warwick*, have made little impression; he that wrote for such an audience was under the necessity of looking round for strange events and fabulous transactions, and that incredibility, by which maturer knowledge if offended, was the chief recommendation of writings, to unskilful curiosity.

Our authour's plots are generally borrowed from novels, and it is reasonable to suppose, that he chose the most popular, such as were read by many, and related by more; for his audience could not have followed him through the intricacies of the drama, had they not held the thread of the story in their hands.

The stories, which we now find only in remoter authours, were in his time accessible and familiar. The fable of *As you like it,* which is supposed to be copied from Chaucer's *Gamelyn,* was a little pamphlet of those times; and old Mr. Cibber remembered the tale of *Hamlet* in plain English prose, which the criticks have now to seek in Saxo Grammaticus.

His English histories he took from English chronicles and English ballads; and as the ancient writers were made known to his countrymen by versions, they supplied him with new subjects; he dilated some of Plutarch's lives into plays, when they had been translated by North.

His plots, whether historical or fabulous, are always crouded with incidents, by which the attention of a rude people was more easily caught than by sentiment or argumentation; and such is the power of the marvellous even over those who despise it, that every man finds his mind more strongly seized by the tragedies of Shakespeare than of any other writer; others please us by particular speeches, but he always makes us anxious for the event, and has perhaps excelled all but Homer in securing the first purpose of a writer, by exciting restless and unquenchable curiosity and compelling him that reads his work to read it through.

The shows and bustle with which his plays abound have the same original. As knowledge advances, pleasure passes from the eye to the ear, but returns, as it declines, from the ear to the eye. Those to whom our authour's labours were exhibited had more skill in pomps or processions than in poetical language, and perhaps wanted some visible and discriminated events, as comments on the dialogue. He knew how he should most please; and whether his practice is more agreeable to nature, or whether his example has prejudiced the nation, we still find that on our stage something must be done as well as said, and inactive declamation is very coldly heard, however musical or elegant, passionate or sublime.

Voltaire expresses his wonder, that our authour's extravagances are endured by a nation, which has seen the tragedy of *Cato.* Let him be answered, that Addison speaks the language of poets, and Shakespeare, of men. We find in *Cato* innumerable beauties which enamour us of its authour, but we see nothing that acquaints us with human sentiments or human actions; we place it with the fairest and the noblest progeny which judgment propagates by conjunction with learning, but *Othello* is the vigorous and vivacious offspring of observation impregnated by genius. *Cato* affords a splendid exhibition of artificial and fictitious manners, and delivers just and noble sentiments, in diction easy, elevated and harmonious, but its hopes and fears communicate no vibration to the heart; the composition refers us only to the writer; we pronounce the name of *Cato,* but we think on Addison.

The work of a correct and regular writer is a garden accurately formed and diligently planted, varied with shades, and scented with flowers; the composition of Shakespeare is a forest, in which oaks extend their branches, and pines tower in the air, interspersed sometimes with weeds and brambles, and sometimes giving shelter to myrtles and to roses; filling the eye with awful pomp, and gratifying the mind with endless diversity. Other poets display cabinets of precious rarities, minutely finished, wrought into shape, and polished unto brightness. Shakespeare opens a mine which contains gold and diamonds in unexhaustible plenty, though clouded by incrustations, debased by impurities, and mingled with a mass of meaner minerals.

It has been much disputed, whether Shakespeare owed his excellence to his own native force, or whether he had the common helps of scholastick education, the precepts of critical science, and the examples of ancient authours.

There has always prevailed a tradition, that Shakespeare wanted learning, that he had no regular education, nor much skill in the dead languages. Jonson, his friend, affirms, that *he had small Latin, and no Greek;* who, besides that he had no imaginable temptation to falsehood, wrote at a time when the character and acquisitions of Shakespeare were known to multitudes. His evidence ought therefore to decide the controversy, unless some testimony of equal force could be opposed.

Some have imagined, that they have discovered deep learning in many imitations of old writers; but the examples which I have known urged, were drawn from books translated in his time; or were such easy coincidencies of thought, as will happen to all who consider the same subjects; or such remarks on life or axioms of morality as float in conversation, and are transmitted through the world in proverbial sentences.

I have found it remarked, that, in this important sentence, *Go before, I'll follow,* we read a translation of, *I prae, sequar.* I have been told, that when *Caliban,* after a pleasing dream, says, *I cry'd to sleep again,* the authour imitates Anacreon, who had, like every other man, the same wish on the same occasion.

There are a few passages which may pass for imitations, but so few, that the exception only confirms the rule; he obtained them from accidental quotations, or by oral communication, and as he used what he had, would have used more if he had obtained it.

The *Comedy of Errors* is confessedly taken from the *Menæchmi* of Plautus; from the only play of Plautus which was then in English. What can be more probable, than that he who copied that, would have copied more; but that those which were not translated were inaccessible?

Whether he knew the modern languages is uncertain. That his plays have some French scenes proves but little; he might easily procure them to be written, and probably, even though he had known the language in the common degree, he could not have written it without assistance. In the story of *Romeo and Juliet* he is observed to have followed the English translation, where it deviates from the Italian; but this on the other part proves nothing against his knowledge of the original. He was to copy, not what he knew himself, but what was known to his audience.

It is most likely that he had learned Latin sufficiently to make him acquainted with construction, but that he never advanced to an easy perusal of the Roman authours. Concerning his skill in modern languages, I can find no sufficient ground of determination; but as no imitations of French or Italian authours have been discovered, though the Italian poetry was then high in esteem, I am inclined to believe, that he read little more than English, and chose for his fables only such tales as he found translated.

That much knowledge is scattered over his works is very justly observed by Pope, but it is often such knowledge as books did not supply. He that will understand Shakespeare, must not be content to study him in the closet, he must look for his meaning sometimes among the sports of the field, and sometimes among the manufactures of the shop.

There is however proof enough that he was a very diligent reader, nor was our language then so indigent of books, but that he might very liberally indulge his curiosity without excursion into foreign literature. Many of the Roman authours were translated, and some of the Greek; the reformation had filled the kingdom with theological learning; most of the topicks of human disquisition had found English writers; and poetry had been culti-vated, not only with diligence, but success. This was a stock of knowledge sufficient for a mind so capable of appropriating and improving it.

But the greater part of his excellence was the product of his own genius. He found the English stage in a state of the utmost rudeness; no essays either in tragedy or comedy had appeared, from which it could be discovered to what degree of delight either one or other might be carried. Neither character nor dialogue were yet understood. Shakespeare may be truly said to have in-troduced them both amongst us, and in some of his happier scenes to have carried them both to the utmost height.

By what gradations of improvement he proceeded, is not easily known; for the chronology of his works is yet unsettled. Rowe is of opinion, that *per-haps we are not to look for his beginning, like those of other writers, in his least per-fect works; art had so little, and nature so large a share in what he did, that for ought I know,* says he, *the performances of his youth, as they were the most vigorous, were the best.* But the power of nature is only the power of using to any certain purpose the materials which diligence procures, or opportunity supplies. Na-ture gives no man knowledge, and when images are collected by study and experience, can only assist in combining or applying them. Shakespeare, however favoured by nature, could impart only what he had learned; and as he must increase his ideas, like other mortals, by gradual acquisition, he, like them, grew wiser as he grew older, could display life better, as he knew it more, and instruct with more efficacy, as he was himself more amply in-structed.

There is a vigilance of observation and accuracy of distinction which books and precepts cannot confer; from this almost all original and native ex-cellence proceeds. Shakespeare must have looked upon mankind with per-spicacity, in the highest degree curious and attentive. Other writers borrow their characters from preceding writers, and diversify them only by the acci-dental appendages of present manners; the dress is a little varied, but the body is the same. Our authour had both matter and form to provide; for except the characters of Chaucer, to whom I think he is much indebted, there were no writers in English, and perhaps not many in other modern languages, which shewed life in its native colours.

The contest about the original benevolence or malignity of man had not yet commenced. Speculation had not yet attempted to analyse the mind, to trace the passions to their sources, to unfold the seminal principles of vice and virtue, or sound the depths of the heart for the motives of action. All those enquiries, which from that time that human nature became the fashionable study, have been made sometimes with nice discernment, but often with idle subtilty, were yet unattempted. The tales, with which the infancy of learning was satisfied, exhibited only the superficial appearances of action, related the events but omitted the causes, and were formed for such as delighted in wonders rather than in truth. Mankind was not then to be studied in the closet; he that would know the world, was under the necessity of gleaning his own remarks, by mingling as he could in its business and amusements.

Boyle congratulated himself upon his high birth, because it favoured his curiosity, by facilitating his access. Shakespeare had no such advantage; he came to London a needy adventurer, and lived for a time by very mean employments. Many works of genius and learning have been performed in states of life, that appear very little favourable to thought or to enquiry; so many, that he who considers them is inclined to think that he sees enterprise and perseverance predominating over all external agency, and bidding help and hindrance vanish before them. The genius of Shakespeare was not to be depressed by the weight of poverty, nor limited by the narrow conversation to which men in want are inevitably condemned; the incumbrances of his fortune were shaken from his mind, *as dewdrops from a lion's mane.*

Though he had so many difficulties to encounter, and so little assistance to surmount them, he has been able to obtain an exact knowledge of many modes of life, and many casts of native dispositions; to vary them with great multiplicity; to mark them by nice distinctions; and to shew them in full view by proper combinations. In this part of his performance he had none to imitate, but has himself been imitated by all succeeding writers; and it may be doubted, whether from all his successors more maxims of theoretical knowledge, or more rules of practical prudence, can be collected, than he alone has given to his country.

Nor was his attention confined to the actions of men; he was an exact surveyor of the inanimate world; his descriptions have always some peculiarities, gathered by contemplating things as they really exist. It may be observed, that the oldest poets of many nations preserve their reputation, and that the following generations of wit, after a short celebrity, sink into oblivion. The first, whoever they be, must take their sentiments and descriptions immediately from knowledge; the resemblance is therefore just, their descriptions are verified by every eye, and their sentiments acknowledged by every breast. Those whom their fame invites to the same studies, copy partly them, and partly nature, till the books of one age gain such authority, as to stand in the place of nature to another, and imitation, always deviating a little, becomes at last capricious and casual. Shakespeare, whether life or nature be his subject, shews plainly, that he has seen with his own eyes; he gives the image which he receives, not weakened or distorted by the intervention of any other mind; the ignorant feel his representations to be just, and the learned see that they are compleat.

Perhaps it would not be easy to find any authour, except Homer, who invented so much as Shakespeare, who so much advanced the studies which he cultivated, or effused so much novelty upon his age or country. The form, the characters, the language, and the shows of the English drama are his. *He seems,* says Dennis, *to have been the very original of our English tragical harmony, that is, the harmony of blank verse, diversified often by dissyllable and trissyllable terminations. For the diversity distinguishes it from heroick harmony, and by bringing it nearer to common use makes it more proper to gain attention, and more fit for action and dialogue. Such verse we make when we are writing prose; we make such verse in common conversation.*

I know not whether this praise is rigorously just. The dissyllable termination, which the critick rightly appropriates to the drama, is to be found, though, I think, not in *Gorboduc* which is confessedly before our authour; yet in *Hieronnymo,* of which the date is not certain, but which there is reason to believe at least as old as his earliest plays. This however is certain, that he is the first who taught either tragedy or comedy to please, there being no theatrical piece of any older writer, of which the name is known, except to antiquaries and collectors of books, which are sought because they are scarce, and would not have been scarce, had they been much esteemed.

To him we must ascribe the praise, unless Spenser may divide it with him, of having first discovered to how much smoothness and harmony the English language could be softened. He has speeches, perhaps sometimes scenes, which have all the delicacy of Rowe, without his effeminacy. He endeavours indeed commonly to strike by the force and vigour of his dialogue, but he never executes his purpose better, than when he tries to sooth by softness.

Yet it must be at last confessed, that as we owe every thing to him, he owes something to us; that, if much of his praise is paid by perception and judgement, much is likewise given by custom and veneration. We fix our eyes upon his graces, and turn them from his deformities, and endure in him what we should in another loath or despise. If we endured without praising, respect for the father of our drama might excuse us; but I have seen, in the book of some modern critick, a collection of anomalies, which shew that he has corrupted language by every mode of depravation, but which his admirer has accumulated as a monument of honour.

He has scenes of undoubted and perpetual excellence, but perhaps not one play, which, if it were now exhibited as the work of a contemporary writer, would be heard to the conclusion. I am indeed far from thinking, that his works were wrought to his own ideas of perfection; when they were such as would satisfy the audience, they satisfied the writer. It is seldom that authours, though more studious of fame than Shakespeare, rise much above the standard of their own age; to add a little of what is best will always be sufficient for present praise, and those who find themselves exalted into fame, are willing to credit their encomiasts, and to spare the labour of contending with themselves.

It does not appear, that Shakespeare thought his works worthy of posterity, that he levied any ideal tribute upon future times, or had any further prospect, than of present popularity and present profit. When his plays had been acted, his hope was at an end; he solicited no addition of honour from the reader. He therefore made no scruple to repeat the same jests in many dialogues, or to entangle different plots by the same knot of perplexity, which may be at least forgiven him, by those who recollect, that of Congreve's four comedies, two are concluded by a marriage in a mask, by a deception, which perhaps never happened, and which, whether likely or not, he did not invent.

So careless was this great poet of future fame, that, though he retired to ease and plenty, while he was yet little *declined into the vale of years,* before he could be disgusted with fatigue, or disabled by infirmity, he made no collection of his works, nor desired to rescue those that had been already published from the depravations that obscured them, or secure to the rest a better destiny, by giving them to the world in their genuine state.

Of the plays which bear the name of Shakespeare in the late editions, the greater part were not published till about seven years after his death, and the few which appeared in his life are apparently thrust into the world without the care of the authour, and therefore probably without his knowledge.

Of all the publishers, clandestine or professed, their negligence and unskilfulness has by the late revisers been sufficiently shewn. The faults of all are indeed numerous and gross, and have not only corrupted many passages perhaps beyond recovery, but have brought others into suspicion, which are only obscured by obsolete phraseology, or by the writer's unskilfulness and affectation. To alter is more easy than to explain, and temerity is a more common quality than diligence. Those who saw that they must employ conjecture to a certain degree, were willing to indulge it a little further. Had the author published his own works, we should have sat quietly down to disentangle his intricacies, and clear his obscurities; but now we tear what we cannot loose, and eject what we happen not to understand.

The faults are more than could have happened without the concurrence of many causes. The stile of Shakespeare was in itself ungrammatical, perplexed and obscure; his works were transcribed for the players by those who may be supposed to have seldom understood them; they were transmitted by copiers equally unskilful, who still multiplied errours; they were perhaps sometimes mutilated by the actors, for the sake of shortening the speeches; and were at last printed without correction of the press.

In this state they remained, not as Dr. Warburton supposes, because they were unregarded, but because the editor's art was not yet applied to modern languages, and our ancestors were accustomed to so much negligence of

English printers, that they could very patiently endure it. At last an edition was undertaken by Rowe; not because a poet was to be published by a poet, for Rowe seems to have thought very little on correction or explanation, but that our authour's works might appear like those of his fraternity, with the appendages of a life and recommendatory preface. Rowe has been clamorously blamed for not performing what he did not undertake, and it is time that justice be done him, by confessing, that though he seems to have had no thought of corruption beyond the printer's errours, yet he has made many emendations, if they were not made before, which his successors have received without acknowledgement, and which, if they had produced them, would have filled pages and pages with censures of the stupidity by which the faults were committed, with displays of the absurdities which they involved, with ostentatious expositions of the new reading, and self congratulations on the happiness of discovering it.

Of Rowe, as of all the editors, I have preserved the preface, and have likewise retained the authour's life, though not written with much elegance or spirit; it relates however what is now to be known, and therefore deserves to pass through all succeeding publications.

The nation has been for many years content enough with Mr. Rowe's performance, when Mr. Pope made them acquainted with the true state of Shakespeare's text, shewed that it was extremely corrupt, and gave reason to hope that there were means of reforming it. He collated the old copies, which none had thought to examine before, and restored many lines to their integrity; but, by a very compendious criticism, he rejected whatever he disliked, and thought more of amputation than of cure.

I know not why he is commended by Dr. Warburton for distinguishing the genuine from the spurious plays. In this choice he exerted no judgement of his own; the plays which he received, were given by Hemings and Condel, the first editors; and those which he rejected, though, according to the licentiousness of the press in those times, they were printed during Shakespeare's life, with his name, had been omitted by his friends, and were never added to his works before the edition of 1664, from which they were copied by the later printers.

This was a work which Pope seems to have thought unworthy of his abilities, being not able to suppress his contempt of *the dull duty of an editor.* He understood but half his undertaking. The duty of a collator is indeed dull, yet, like other tedious tasks, is very necessary; but an emendatory critick would ill discharge his duty, without qualities very different from dullness. In perusing a corrupted piece, he must have before him all possibilities of meaning, with all possibilities of expression. Such must be his comprehension of thought, and such his copiousness of language. Out of many readings possible, he must be able to select that which best suits with the state of opinions, and modes of language prevailing in every age, and with his authour's particular cast of thought, and turn of expression. Such must be his knowledge, and such his taste. Conjectural criticism demands more than humanity possesses, and he that exercises it with most praise has very frequent need of indulgence. Let us now be told no more of the dull duty of an editor.

Confidence is the common consequence of success. They whose excellence of any kind has been loudly celebrated, are ready to conclude, that their powers are universal. Pope's edition fell below his own expectations, and he was so much offended, when he was found to have left any thing for others to do, that he past the latter part of his life in a state of hostility with verbal criticism.

I have retained all his notes, that no fragment of so great a writer may be lost; his preface, valuable alike for elegance of composition and justness of remark, and containing a general criticism on his authour, so extensive that little can be added, and so exact, that little can be disputed, every editor has an interest to suppress, but that every reader would demand its insertion.

Pope was succeeded by Theobald, a man of narrow comprehension and small acquisitions, with no native and intrinsick splendour of genius, with little of the artificial light of learning, but zealous for minute accuracy, and not negligent in pursuing it. He collated the ancient copies, and rectified many errors. A man so anxiously scrupulous might have been expected to do more, but what little he did was commonly right.

In his report of copies and editions he is not to be trusted, without examination. He speaks sometimes indefinitely of copies, when he has only one. In his enumeration of editions, he mentions the two first folios as of high, and the third folio as of middle authority; but the truth is, that the first is equivalent to all others, and that the rest only deviate from it by the printer's negligence. Whoever has any of the folios has all, excepting those diversities which mere reiteration of editions will produce. I collated them all at the beginning, but afterwards used only the first.

Of his notes I have generally retained those which he retained himself in his second edition, except when they were confuted by subsequent annotators, or were too minute to merit preservation. I have sometimes adopted his restoration of a comma, without inserting the panegyrick in which he celebrated himself for his atchievement. The exuberant excrescence of his diction I have often lopped, his triumphant exultations over Pope and Rowe I have sometimes suppressed, and his contemptible ostentation I have frequently concealed; but I have in some places shewn him, as he would have shewn himself, for the reader's diversion, that the inflated emptiness of some notes may justify or excuse the contraction of the rest.

Theobald, thus weak and ignorant, thus mean and faithless, thus petulant and ostentatious, by the good luck of having Pope for his enemy, has escaped, and escaped alone, with reputation, from this undertaking. So willingly does the world support those who solicite favour, against those who command reverence; and so easily is he praised, whom no man can envy.

Our authour fell then into the hands of Sir Thomas Hanmer, the Oxford editor, a man, in my opinion, eminently qualified by nature for such studies. He had, what is the first requisite to emendatory criticism, that intuition by which the poet's intention is immediately discovered, and that dexterity of intellect which despatches its work by the easiest means. He had undoubtedly read much; his acquaintance with customs, opinions, and traditions, seems to have been large; and he is often learned without shew. He seldom passes what he does not understand, without an attempt to find or to make a meaning, and sometimes hastily makes what a little more attention would have found. He is solicitous to reduce to grammar, what he could not be sure that his authour intended to be grammatical. Shakespeare regarded more the series of ideas, than of words; and his language, not being designed for the reader's desk, was all that he desired it to be, if it conveyed his meaning to the audience.

Hanmer's care of the metre has been too violently censured. He found the measures reformed in so many passages, by the silent labours of some editors, with the silent acquiescence of the rest, that he thought himself allowed to extend a little further the license, which had already been carried so far without reprehension; and of his corrections in general, it must be confessed, that they are often just, and made commonly with the least possible violation of the text.

But, by inserting his emendations, whether invented or borrowed, into the page, without any notice of varying copies, he has appropriated the labour of his predecessors, and made his own edition of little authority. His confidence indeed, both in himself and others, was too great; he supposes all to be right that was done by Pope and Theobald; he seems not to suspect a critick of fallibility, and it was but reasonable that he should claim what he so liberally granted.

As he never writes without careful enquiry and diligent consideration, I have received all his notes, and believe that every reader will wish for more.

Of the last editor it is more difficult to speak. Respect is due to high place, tenderness to living reputation, and veneration to genius and learning; but he cannot be justly offended at that liberty of which he has himself so frequently given an example, nor very solicitous what is thought of notes, which he ought never to have considered as part of his serious employments, and which, I suppose, since the ardour of composition is remitted, he no longer numbers among his happy effusions.

The original and predominant errour of his commentary, is acquiescence in his first thoughts; that precipitation which is produced by consciousness of quick discernment; and that confidence which presumes to do, by surveying the surface, what labour only can perform, by penetrating the bottom. His notes exhibit sometimes perverse interpretations, and sometimes improbable conjectures; he at one time gives the authour more profundity of meaning, than the sentence admits, and at another discovers absurdities, where the sense is plain to every other reader. But his emendations are likewise often happy and just; and his interpretation of obscure passages learned and sagacious.

Of his notes, I have commonly rejected those, against which the general voice of the publick has exclaimed, or which their own incongruity immediately condemns, and which, I suppose, the authour himself would desire to be forgotten. Of the rest, to part I have given the highest approbation, by inserting the offered reading in the text; part I have left to the judgment of the reader, as doubtful, though specious; and part I have censured without reserve, but I am sure without bitterness of malice, and, I hope, without wantonness of insult.

It is no pleasure to me, in revising my volumes, to observe how much paper is wasted in confutation. Whoever considers the revolutions of learning, and the various questions of greater or less importance, upon which wit and reason have exercised their powers, must lament the unsuccessfulness of enquiry, and the slow advances of truth, when he reflects, that great part of the labour of every writer is only the destruction of those that went before him. The first care of the builder of a new system, is to demolish the fabricks which are standing. The chief desire of him that comments an authour, is to shew how much other commentators have corrupted and obscured him. The opinions prevalent in one age, as truths above the reach of controversy, are confuted and rejected in another, and rise again to reception in remoter times. Thus the human mind is kept in motion without progress. Thus sometimes truth and errour, and sometimes contrarieties of errour, take each other's place by reciprocal invasion. The tide of seeming knowledge which is poured over one generation, retires and leaves another naked and barren; the sudden meteors of intelligence which for a while appear to shoot their beams into the regions of obscurity, on a sudden withdraw their lustre, and leave mortals again to grope their way.

These elevations and depressions of renown, and the contradictions to which all improvers of knowledge must for ever be exposed, since they are not escaped by the highest and brightest of mankind, may surely be endured with patience by criticks and annotators, who can rank themselves but as the satellites of their authours. How canst thou beg for life, says Achilles to his captive, when thou knowest that thou art now to suffer only what must another day be suffered by Achilles?

Dr. Warburton had a name sufficient to confer celebrity on those who could exalt themselves into antagonists, and his notes have raised a clamour too loud to be distinct. His chief assailants are the authours of *the Canons of criticism* and of the *Review of Shakespeare's text;* of whom one ridicules his errours with airy petulance, suitable enough to the levity of the controversy; the other attacks them with gloomy malignity, as if he were dragging to justice an assassin or incendiary. The one stings like a fly, sucks a little blood, takes a gay flutter, and returns for more; the other bites like a viper, and would be glad to leave inflammations and gangrene behind him. When I think on one, with his confederates, I remember the danger of Coriolanus, who was afraid that *girls with spits, and boys with stones, should slay him in puny battle;* when the other crosses my imagination, I remember the prodigy in *Macbeth,*

An eagle tow'ring in his pride of place,
Was by a mousing owl hawk'd at and kill'd.

Let me however do them justice. One is a wit, and one a scholar. They have both shown acuteness sufficient in the discovery of faults, and have both advanced some probable interpretations of obscure passages; but when they aspire to conjecture and emendation, it appears how falsely we all estimate our own abilities, and the little which they have been able to perform might have taught them more candour to the endeavours of others.

Before Dr. Warburton's edition, *Critical observations on Shakespeare* had been published by Mr. Upton, a man skilled in languages, and acquainted with books, but who seems to have had no great vigour of genius or nicety of taste. Many of his explanations are curious and useful, but he likewise, though he professed to oppose the licentious confidence of editors, and adhere to the old copies, is unable to restrain the rage of emendation, though his ardour is ill seconded by his skill. Every cold empirick, when his heart is expanded by a successful experiment, swells into a theorist, and the laborious collator at some unlucky moment frolicks in conjecture.

Critical, historical and explanatory notes have been likewise published upon Shakespeare by Dr. Grey, whose diligent perusal of the old English writers has enabled him to make some useful observations. What he undertook he has well enough performed, but as he neither attempts judicial nor emendatory criticism, he employs rather his memory than his sagacity. It were to be wished that all would endeavour to imitate his modesty who have not been able to surpass his knowledge.

I can say with great sincerity of all my predecessors, what I hope will hereafter be said of me, that not one has left Shakespeare without improvement, nor is there one to whom I have not been indebted for assistance and information. Whatever I have taken from them it was my intention to refer to its original authour, and it is certain, that what I have not given to another, I believed when I wrote it to be my own. In some perhaps I have been anticipated; but if I am ever found to encroach upon the remarks of any other commentator, I am willing that the honour, be it more or less, should be transferred to the first claimant, for his right, and his alone, stands above dispute; the second can prove his pretensions only to himself, nor can himself always distinguish invention, with sufficient certainty, from recollection.

They have all been treated by me with candour, which they have not been careful of observing to one another. It is not easy to discover from what cause the acrimony of a scholiast can naturally proceed. The subjects to be discussed by him are of very small importance; they involve neither property nor liberty; nor favour the interest of sect or party. The various readings of copies, and different interpretations of a passage, seem to be questions that might exercise the wit, without engaging the passions. But, whether it be, that *small things make mean men proud,* and vanity catches small occasions; or that all contrariety of opinion, even in those that can defend it no longer, makes proud men angry; there is often found in commentaries a spontaneous strain of invective and contempt, more eager and venomous than is vented by the most furious controvertist in politicks against those whom he is hired to defame.

Perhaps the lightness of the matter may conduce to the vehemence of the agency; when the truth to be investigated is so near to inexistence, as to escape attention, its bulk is to be enlarged by rage and exclamation: That to which all would be indifferent in its original state, may attract notice when the fate of a name is appended to it. A commentator has indeed great temptations to supply by turbulence what he wants of dignity, to beat his little gold to a spacious surface, to work that to foam which no art or diligence can exalt to spirit.

The notes which I have borrowed or written are either illustrative, by which difficulties are explained; or judicial, by which faults and beauties are remarked; or emendatory, by which depravations are corrected.

The explanations transcribed from others, if I do not subjoin any other interpretation, I suppose commonly to be right, at least I intend by acquiescence to confess, that I have nothing better to propose.

After the labours of all the editors, I found many passages which appeared to me likely to obstruct the greater number of readers, and thought it my duty to facilitate their passage. It is impossible for an expositor not to write too little for some, and too much for others. He can only judge what is necessary by his own experience; and how long soever he may deliberate, will at last explain many lines which the learned will think impossible to be mistaken, and omit many for which the ignorant will want his help. These are censures merely relative, and must be quietly endured. I have endeavoured to be neither superfluously copious, nor scrupulously reserved, and hope that I have made my authour's meaning accessible to many who before were frighted from perusing him, and contributed something to the publick, by diffusing innocent and rational pleasure.

The compleat explanation of an authour not systematick and consequential, but desultory and vagrant, abounding in casual allusions and light hints, is not to be expected from any single scholiast. All personal reflections, when names are suppressed, must be in a few years irrecoverably obliterated; and customs, too minute to attract the notice of law, such as modes of dress, formalities of conversation, rules of visits, disposition of furniture, and practices of ceremony, which naturally find places in familiar dialogue, are so fugitive and unsubstantial, that they are not easily retained or recovered. What can be known, will be collected by chance, from the recesses of obscure and obsolete papers, perused commonly with some other view. Of this knowledge every man has some, and none has much; but when an authour has engaged the publick attention, those who can add any thing to his illustration, communicate their discoveries, and time produces what had eluded diligence.

To time I have been obliged to resign many passages, which, though I did not understand them, will perhaps hereafter be explained, having, I hope, illustrated some, which others have neglected or mistaken, sometimes by short remarks, or marginal directions, such as every editor has added at his will, and often by comments more laborious than the matter will seem to deserve; but that which is most difficult is not always most important, and to an editor nothing is a trifle by which his authour is obscured.

The poetical beauties or defects I have not been very diligent to observe. Some plays have more, and some fewer judicial observations, not in proportion to their difference of merit, but because I gave this part of my design to chance and to caprice. The reader, I believe, is seldom pleased to find his opinion anticipated; it is natural to delight more in what we find or make, than in what we receive. Judgment, like other faculties, is improved by practice, and its advancement is hindered by submission to dictatorial decisions, as the memory grows torpid by the use of a table book. Some initiation is however necessary; of all skill, part is infused by precept, and part is obtained by habit; I have therefore shewn so much as may enable the candidate of criticism to discover the rest.

To the end of most plays, I have added short strictures, containing a general censure of faults, or praise of excellence; in which I know not how much I have concurred with the current opinion; but I have not, by any affectation of singularity, deviated from it. Nothing is minutely and particularly examined, and therefore it is to be supposed, that in the plays which are condemned there is much to be praised, and in those which are praised much to be condemned.

The part of criticism in which the whole succession of editors has laboured with the greatest diligence, which has occasioned the most arrogant ostentation, and excited the keenest acrimony, is the emendation, of corrupted passages, to which the publick attention having been first drawn by the violence of contention between Pope and Theobald, has been continued by the persecution, which, with a kind of conspiracy, has been since raised against all the publishers of Shakespeare.

That many passages have passed in a state of depravation through all the editions is indubitably certain; of these the restoration is only to be attempted by collation of copies or sagacity of conjecture. The collator's province is safe and easy, the conjecturer's perilous and difficult. Yet as the greater part of the plays are extant only in one copy, the peril must not be avoided, nor the difficulty refused.

Of the readings which this emulation of amendment has hitherto produced, some from the labours of every publisher I have advanced into the text; those are to be considered as in my opinion sufficiently supported; some I have rejected without mention, as evidently erroneous; some I have left in the notes without censure or approbation, as resting in equipoise between objection and defence; and some, which seemed specious but not right, I have inserted with a subsequent animadversion.

Having classed the observations of others, I was at last to try what I could substitute for their mistakes, and how I could supply their omissions. I collated such copies as I could procure, and wished for more, but have not found the collectors of these rarities very communicative. Of the editions which chance or kindness put into my hands I have given an enumeration, that I may not be blamed for neglecting what I had not the power to do.

By examining the old copies, I soon found that the later publishers, with all their boasts of diligence, suffered many passages to stand unauthorised, and contented themselves with Rowe's regulation of the text, even where they knew it to be arbitrary, and with a little consideration might have found it to be wrong. Some of these alterations are only the ejection of a word for one that appeared to him more elegant or more intelligible. These corruptions I have often silently rectified; for the history of our language, and the true force of our words, can only be preserved, by keeping the text of authours free from adulteration. Others, and those very frequent, smoothed the cadence, or regulated the measure; on these I have not exercised the same rigour; if only a word was transposed, or a particle inserted or omitted, I have sometimes suffered the line to stand; for the inconstancy of the copies is such, as that some liberties may be easily permitted. But this practice I have not suffered to proceed far, having restored the primitive diction wherever it could for any reason be preferred.

The emendations, which comparison of copies supplied, I have inserted in the text; sometimes where the improvement was slight, without notice, and sometimes with an account of the reasons of the change.

Conjecture, though it be sometimes unavoidable, I have not wantonly nor licentiously indulged. It has been my settled principle, that the reading of the ancient books is probably true, and therefore is not to be disturbed for the sake of elegance, perspicuity, or mere improvement of the sense. For though much credit is not due to the fidelity, nor any to the judgement of the first publishers, yet they who had the copy before their eyes were more likely to read it right, than we who read it only by imagination. But it is evident that they have often made strange mistakes by ignorance or negligence, and that therefore something may be properly attempted by criticism, keeping the middle way between presumption and timidity.

Such criticism I have attempted to practice, and where any passage appeared inextricably perplexed, have endeavoured to discover how it may be recalled to sense, with least violence. But my first labour is, always to turn the old text on every side, and try if there be any interstice, through which light can find its way; nor would Huetius himself condemn me, as refusing the trouble of research, for the ambition of alteration. In this modest industry I have not been unsuccessful. I have rescued many lines from the violations of temerity, and secured many scenes from the inroads of correction. I have adopted the Roman sentiment, that it is more honourable to save a citizen, than to kill an enemy, and have been more careful to protect than to attack.

I have preserved the common distribution of the plays into acts, though I believe it to be in almost all the plays void of authority. Some of those which are divided in the later editions have no division in the first folio, and some that are divided in the folio have no division in the preceding copies. The settled mode of the theatre requires four intervals in the play, but few, if any, of our authour's compositions can be properly distributed in that manner. An act is so much of the drama as passes without intervention of time or change of place. A pause makes a new act. In every real, and therefore in every imitative action, the intervals may be more or fewer, the restriction of five acts being accidental and arbitrary. This Shakespeare knew, and this he practiced; his plays were written, and at first printed in one unbroken continuity, and ought now to be exhibited with short pauses, interposed as often as the scene is changed, or any considerable time is required to pass. This method would at once quell a thousand absurdities.

In restoring the authour's works to their integrity, I have considered the punctuation as wholly in my power; for what could be their care of colons and commas, who corrupted words and sentences. Whatever could be done by adjusting points is therefore silently performed, in some plays with much diligence, in others with less; it is hard to keep a busy eye steadily fixed upon evanescent atoms, or a discursive mind upon evanescent truth.

The same liberty has been taken with a few particles, or other words of slight effect. I have sometimes inserted or omitted them without notice. I have done that sometimes, which indeed the state of the text may sufficiently justify.

The greater part of readers, instead of blaming us for passing trifles, will wonder that on mere trifles so much labour is expended, with such importance of debate, and such solemnity of diction. To these I answer with confidence, that they are judging of an art which they do not understand; yet cannot much reproach them with their ignorance, nor promise that they would become in general, by learning criticism, more useful, happier or wiser.

As I practised conjecture more, I learned to trust it less; and after I had printed a few plays, resolved to insert none of my own readings in the text. Upon this caution I now congratulate myself, for every day encreases my doubt of my emendations.

Since I have confined my imagination to the margin, it must not be considered as very reprehensible, if I have suffered it to play some freaks in its own dominion. There is no danger in conjecture, if it be proposed as conjecture; and while the text remains uninjured, those changes may be safely offered, which are not considered even by him that offers them as necessary or safe.

If my readings are of little value, they have not been ostentatiously displayed or importunately obtruded. I could have written longer notes, for the art of writing notes is not of difficult attainment. The work is performed, first by railing at the stupidity, negligence, ignorance, and asinine tastelessness of the former editors, and shewing, from all that goes before and all that follows, the inelegance and absurdity of the old reading; then by proposing something, which to superficial readers would seem specious, but which the editor rejects with indignation; then by producing the true reading, with a long paraphrase, and concluding with loud acclamations on the discovery, and a sober wish for the advancement and prosperity of genuine criticism.

All this may be done, and perhaps done sometimes without impropriety. But I have always suspected that the reading is right, which requires many words to prove it wrong; and the emendation wrong, that cannot without so much labour appear to be right. The justness of a happy restoration strikes at once, and the moral precept may be well applied to criticism, *quod dubitas ne feceris*.[2]

To dread the shore which he sees spread with wrecks, is natural to the sailor. I had before my eye, so many critical adventures ended in miscarriage, that caution was forced upon me. I encountered in every page Wit struggling with its own sophistry, and Learning confused by the multiplicity of its views. I was forced to censure those whom I admired, and could not but reflect, while I was dispossessing their emendations, how soon the same fate might happen to my own, and how many of the readings which I have corrected may be by some other editor defended and established.

> *Criticks, I saw, that other's names efface,*
> *And fix their own, with labour, in the place;*
> *Their own, like others, soon their place resign'd,*
> *Or disappear'd, and left the first behind.* — Pope.

That a conjectural critick should often be mistaken, cannot be wonderful, either to others or himself, if it be considered, that in his art there is no system, no principal and axiomatical truth that regulates subordinate positions. His chance of errour is renewed at every attempt; an oblique view of the passage, a slight misapprehension of a phrase, a casual inattention to the parts connected, is sufficient to make him not only fail, but fail ridiculously; and when he succeeds best, he produces perhaps but one reading of many probable, and he that suggests another will always be able to dispute his claims.

It is an unhappy state, in which danger is hid under pleasure. The allurements of emendation are scarcely resistible. Conjecture has all the joy and all the pride of invention, and he that has once started a happy change, is too much delighted to consider what objections may rise against it.

Yet conjectural criticism has been of great use in the learned world; nor is it my intention to depreciate a study, that has exercised so many mighty minds, from the revival of learning to our own age, from the Bishop of Aleria to English Bentley. The criticks on ancient authors have, in the exercise of their sagacity, many assistances, which the editor of Shakespeare is condemned to want. They are employed upon grammatical and settled languages, whose construction contributes so much to perspicuity, that Homer has fewer passages unintelligible than Chaucer. The words have not only a known regimen, but invariable quantities, which direct and confine the choice. There are commonly more manuscripts than one; and they do not often conspire in the same mistakes. Yet Scaliger could confess to Salmasius how little satisfaction his emendations gave him. *Illudunt nobis conjecturæ nostræ, quarum nos pudet, posteaquam in meliores codices incidimus.*[3] And Lipsius

---

[2] When in doubt, refrain.

[3] Our conjectures make fools of us, putting us to shame, when we later discover better manuscripts.

could complain, that criticks were making faults, by trying to remove them, *Ut olim vitiis, ita nunc remediis laboratur.*[4] And indeed, where mere conjecture is to be used, the emendations of Scaliger and Lipsius, notwithstanding their wonderful sagacity and erudition, are often vague and disputable, like mine or Theobald's.

Perhaps I may not be more censured for doing wrong, than for doing little; for raising in the publick expectations, which at last I have not answered. The expectation of ignorance is indefinite, and that of knowledge is often tyrannical. It is hard to satisfy those who know not what to demand, or those who demand by design what they think impossible to be done. I have indeed disappointed no opinion more than my own; yet I have endeavoured to perform my task with no slight solicitude. Not a single passage in the whole work has appeared to me corrupt, which I have not attempted to restore; or obscure, which I have not endeavoured to illustrate. In many I have failed like others; and from many, after all my efforts, I have retreated, and confessed the repulse. I have not passed over, with affected superiority, what is equally difficult to the reader and to myself, but where I could not instruct him, have owned my ignorance. I might easily have accumulated a mass of seeming learning upon easy scenes; but it ought not to be imputed to negligence, that, where nothing was necessary, nothing has been done, or that, where others have said enough, I have said no more.

Notes are often necessary, but they are necessary evils. Let him, that is yet unacquainted with the powers of Shakespeare, and who desires to feel the highest pleasure that the drama can give, read every play from the first scene to the last, with utter negligence of all his commentators. When his fancy is once on the wing, let it not stoop at correction or explanation. When his attention is strongly engaged, let it disdain alike to turn aside to the name of Theobald and of Pope. Let him read on through brightness and obscurity, through integrity and corruption; let him preserve his comprehension of the dialogue and his interest in the fable. And when the pleasures of novelty have ceased, let him attempt exactness, and read the commentators.

Particular passages are cleared by notes, but the general effect of the work is weakened. The mind is refrigerated by interruption; the thoughts are diverted from the principal subject; the reader is weary, he suspects not why; and at last throws away the book, which he has too diligently studied.

Parts are not to be examined till the whole has been surveyed; there is a kind of intellectual remoteness necessary for the comprehension of any great work in its full design and its true proportions; a close approach shews the smaller niceties, but the beauty of the whole is discerned no longer.

It is not very grateful to consider how little the succession of editors has added to this author's power of pleasing. He was read, admired, studied, and imitated, while he was yet deformed with all the improprieties which ignorance and neglect could accumulate upon him; while the reading was yet not rectified, nor his allusions understood; yet then did Dryden pronounce

[4] As before we toiled over corruptions, now we struggle with corrections.

"that Shakespeare was the man, who, of all modern and perhaps ancient poets, had the largest and most comprehensive soul. All the images of nature were still present to him, and he drew them not laboriously, but luckily: When he describes any thing, you more than see it, you feel it too. Those who accuse him to have wanted learning, give him the greater commendation: he was naturally learned: he needed not the spectacles of books to read nature; he looked inwards, and found her there. I cannot say he is every where alike; were he so, I should do him injury to compare him with the greatest of mankind. He is many times flat and insipid; his comick wit degenerating into clenches, his serious swelling into bombast. But he is always great, when some great occasion is presented to him: No man can say, he ever had a fit subject for his wit, and did not then raise himself as high above the rest of poets,

> *Quantum lenta solent inter viburna cupressi.*"[5]

It is to be lamented, that such a writer should want a commentary; that his language should become obsolete, or his sentiments obscure. But it is vain to carry wishes beyond the condition of human things; that which must happen to all, has happened to Shakespeare, by accident and time; and more than has been suffered by any other writer since the use of types, has been suffered by him through his own negligence of fame, or perhaps by that superiority of mind, which despised its own performances, when it compared them with its powers, and judged those works unworthy to be preserved, which the criticks of following ages were to contend for the fame of restoring and explaining.

Among these candidates of inferiour fame, I am now to stand the judgment of the publick; and wish that I could confidently produce my commentary as equal to the encouragement which I have had the honour of receiving. Every work of this kind is by its nature deficient, and I should feel little solicitude about the sentence, were it to be pronounced only by the skilful and the learned.

[5] As cypresses raise themselves above scraggly shrubs.

IMMANUEL KANT

From *Critique of Judgment*

1790

In humanity's ongoing search to understand itself, the eighteenth-century German philosopher Immanuel Kant (1724–1804) plays an important role, for he is responsible for a major shift in how we comprehend human perception and consciousness. He believed that experience is ordered by the preexisting perceptual categories of time and space and that thought is likewise ordered by such broad and generally applicable categories as quality, quantity, relation, and causation. Our minds process the raw data of experience using these categories, and our knowledge base thus grows out of a synthesis of sensual perception and understanding. As we process our experience to build knowledge, the individual human mind actually creates the world as we understand it.

Kant's most direct influence on literary theory and criticism comes from his work in the field of aesthetics, the study of beauty. For him, there is a central flaw in the common belief that beauty must somehow be related either to rational understanding or to moral goodness and therefore must serve a useful purpose in the world. Beauty has no purpose; it simply is. Furthermore, the experience of beauty is inherently subjective, occurring at a spontaneous and intuitive level in each individual. In the excerpt from the Critique of Judgment that follows, Kant discusses this subjectivity and its necessary separation from what he terms "interest." The interest he describes is of two types: interest in the agreeable and interest in the good. We seek the agreeable because it affords us pleasurable sensations and is thus useful to us personally, and we seek the ethically or morally good because it is useful to humanity collectively. The experience of beauty, though, is disconnected from such utility. A pure or free aesthetic response arises directly from the experience of beauty in the imagination and is unconnected with desires, rational concerns, or purposes.

Kant's aesthetics, positioned in direct opposition to most previous theories of art, had far-reaching consequences for literary theory. The Roman poet Horace (see p. 84) articulated the idea that poetry (and, by association, all art) had the dual purpose to delight and to instruct, a position reiterated and expanded by generations of later writers including Sir Philip Sydney in the Renaissance (p. 101) and Samuel Johnson closer to Kant's own time (p. 200). In divorcing art from these higher purposes, Kant pointed toward the coming Romantic movement with its focus on subjective experience as supe-

rior to reason. Samuel Taylor Coleridge's literary theories, for instance, owe much to Kant. In Chapter XIV of Biographia Literaria *(p. 257), Coleridge asserts that "A poem is that species of composition, which is opposed to works of science by proposing for its immediate object pleasure, not truth." Kant's influence continued into the twentieth century in the doctrines of formalism and New Criticism, which insist that a literary work is a free-standing object, existing separate from such "external" issues as biography, psychology, economics, politics, and religion.*

[handwritten margin notes: sensations are what you feel / sense is information you get from an object, characteristics are senses]

1. A Judgment of Taste Is Aesthetic

IF WE WISH to decide whether something is beautiful or not, we do not use understanding to refer the presentation[1] to the object so as to give rise to cognition;[2] rather, we use imagination (perhaps in connection with understanding) to refer the presentation to the subject and his feeling of pleasure or displeasure. Hence a judgment of taste is not a cognitive judgment and so is not a logical judgment but an aesthetic one, by which we mean a judgment whose determining basis *cannot be other* than *subjective*. But any reference of presentations, even of sensations, can be objective (in which case it signifies what is real [rather than formal] in an empirical presentation); excepted is a reference to the feeling of pleasure and displeasure—this reference designates nothing whatsoever in the object, but here the subject feels himself, [namely] how he is affected by the presentation.

To apprehend a regular, purposive building with one's cognitive power[3] (whether the presentation is distinct or confused) is very different from being conscious of this presentation with a sensation of liking. Here the presentation is referred only to the subject, namely, to his feeling of life, under the name feeling of pleasure or displeasure, and this forms the basis of a very special power of discriminating and judging.[4] This power does not contribute anything to cognition, but merely compares the given presentation in the subject with the entire presentational power, of which the mind becomes conscious when it feels its own state. The presentations given in a judgment may be empirical (and hence aesthetic[5]), but if we refer them to the object, the judgment we make by means of them is logical. On the other hand, even if the given presentations were rational, they would still be aesthetic if, and to the extent that, the subject referred them, in his judgment, solely to himself (to his feeling).

[1] *Vorstellung,* traditionally rendered as 'representation.' (See above, Ak. 175 br. n. 17.) 'Presentation' is a generic term referring to such objects of our direct awareness as sensations, intuitions, perceptions, concepts, cognitions, ideas, and schemata. Cf. the *Critique of Pure Reason,* A 320 = B 376–77 and A 140 = B 179. [All notes are the translator's unless otherwise indicated. Ed.]

[2] *Erkenntnis.* Cf. above, Ak. 167 br. n. 2.

[3] For my use of 'power,' rather than 'faculty,' see above, Ak. 167 br. n. 3.

[4] *Beurteilung.* On Kant's attempt to make a terminological distinction between '*beurteilen*' and '*urteilen*,' see above, Ak. 169 br. n. 9.

[5] From Greek αἰσθέσθαι (aisthésthai), 'to sense.'

2. The Liking That Determines a Judgment
of Taste Is Devoid of All Interest

Interest is what we call the liking we connect with the presentation of an object's existence. Hence such a liking always refers at once to our power of desire, either as the basis that determines it, or at any rate as necessarily connected with that determining basis. But if the question is whether something is beautiful, what we want to know is not whether we or anyone cares, or so much as might care, in any way, about the thing's existence, but rather how we judge it in our mere contemplation of it (intuition or reflection). Suppose someone asks me whether I consider the palace I see before me beautiful. I might reply that I am not fond of things of that sort, made merely to be gaped at. Or I might reply like that Iroquois *sachem* who said that he liked nothing better in Paris than the eating-houses.[6] I might even go on, as *Rousseau* would, to rebuke the vanity of the great who spend the people's sweat on such superfluous things. I might, finally, quite easily convince myself that, if I were on some uninhabited island with no hope of ever again coming among people, and could conjure up such a splendid edifice by a mere wish, I would not even take that much trouble for it if I already had a sufficiently comfortable hut. The questioner may grant all this and approve of it; but it is not to the point. All he wants to know is whether my mere presentation of the object is accompanied by a liking, no matter how indifferent I may be about the existence of the object of this presentation. We can easily see that, in order for me to say that an object is *beautiful*, and to prove that I have taste, what matters is what I do with this presentation within myself, and not the [respect] in which I depend on the object's existence. Everyone has to admit that if a judgment about beauty is mingled with the least interest then it is very partial and not a pure judgment of taste. In order to play the judge in matters of taste, we must not be in the least biased in favor of the thing's existence but must be wholly indifferent about it.

There is no better way to elucidate this proposition, which is of prime importance, than by contrasting the pure disinterested[7] liking that occurs in a

---

[6] Wilhelm Windelband, editor of the *Akademie* edition of the *Critique of Judgment*, notes (Ak. V, 527) that Kant's reference has been traced to (Pierre François Xavier de) Charlevoix (1682–1761, French Jesuit traveler and historian), *Histoire et déscription générale de la Nouvelle-France (History and General Description of New France* [in eastern Canada]) (Paris, 1744). Windelband quotes a passage (from III, 322) in French, which translates: "Some Iroquois went to Paris in 1666 and were shown all the royal mansions and all the beauties of that great city. But they did not admire anything in these, and would have preferred the villages to the capital of the most flourishing kingdom of Europe if they had not seen the *rue de la Huchette* where they were delighted with the rotisseries that they always found furnished with meats of all sorts." (All translations given in footnotes are my own, and this fact is not indicated in each such footnote individually.)

[7] A judgment we make about an object of our liking may be wholly *disinterested* but still very *interesting*, i.e., it is not based on any interest but it gives rise to an interest; all pure moral judgments are of this sort. But judgments of taste, of themselves, do not even give rise to any interest. Only in society does it become *interesting* to have taste; the reason for this will be indicated later. [Kant's note.] See esp. Ak. 275–76 and 296–98.

judgment of taste with a liking connected with interest, especially if we can also be certain that the kinds of interest I am about to mention are the only ones there are.

3. A Liking *for the Agreeable* Is Connected with Interest

Agreeable is what the senses like in sensation. Here the opportunity arises at once to censure and call attention to a quite common confusion of the two meanings that the word sensation can have. All liking (so it is said or thought) is itself sensation (of a pleasure). Hence whatever is liked, precisely inasmuch as it is liked, is agreeable (and, depending on the varying degrees or on the relation to other agreeable sensations, it is *graceful, lovely, delightful, gladdening, etc.*). But if we concede this, then sense impressions that determine inclination, or principles of reason that determine the will, or mere forms of intuition that we reflect on [and] that determine the power of judgment, will all be one and the same insofar as their effect on the feeling of pleasure is concerned, since pleasure would be the agreeableness [found] in the sensation of one's state. And since, after all, everything we do with our powers must in the end aim at the practical and unite in it as its goal, we could not require them to estimate things and their value in any other way than by the gratification they promise; how they provided it would not matter at all in the end. And since all that could make a difference in that promised gratification would be what means we select, people could no longer blame one another for baseness and malice, but only for foolishness and ignorance, since all of them, each according to his own way of viewing things, would be pursuing one and the same goal: gratification.

When [something determines the feeling of pleasure or displeasure and this] determination of that feeling is called sensation, this term means something quite different from what it means when I apply it to the presentation of a thing (through the senses, a receptivity that belongs to the cognitive power). For in the second case the presentation is referred to the object, but in the first it is referred solely to the subject and is not used for cognition at all, not even for that by which the subject *cognizes* himself.

As I have just explicated it [i.e., for the second case], the word sensation means an objective presentation of sense; and, to avoid constantly running the risk of being misinterpreted, let us call what must always remain merely subjective, and cannot possibly be the presentation of an object, by its other customary name: feeling.[8] The green color of meadows belongs to *objective* sensation, i.e., to the perception of an object of sense; but the color's agreeableness belongs to *subjective* sensation, to feeling, through which no object is presented, but through which the object is regarded as an object of our liking (which is not a cognition of it).

----

[8] Kant does not, however, consistently adhere to this stipulation, and the inconsistency has been left intact in the translation.

Now, that a judgment by which I declare an object to be agreeable expresses an interest in that object is already obvious from the fact that, by
means of sensation, the judgment arouses a desire for objects of that kind, so
that the liking presupposes something other than my mere judgment about
the object: it presupposes that I have referred the existence of the object to my
state insofar as that state is affected by such an object. This is why we say of
the agreeable not merely that we *like* it but that it *gratifies* us. When I speak of
the agreeable, I am not granting mere approval: the agreeable produces an
inclination. Indeed, what is agreeable in the liveliest way requires no judgment at all about the character of the object, as we can see in people who aim
at nothing but enjoyment (this is the word we use to mark the intensity of the
gratification): they like to dispense with all judging.

4. A Liking *for the Good* Is Connected
with Interest[9]

Good is what, by means of reason, we like through its mere concept. We call
something (viz., if it is something useful) *good for* [this or that] if we like it
only as a means. But we call something *intrinsically good* if we like it for its
own sake. In both senses of the term, the good always contains the concept of
a purpose, consequently a relation of reason to a volition (that is at least possible), and hence a liking for the existence of an object or action. In other
words, it contains some interest or other.

In order to consider something good, I must always know what sort of
thing the object is [meant] to be, i.e., I must have a [determinate] concept of it.
But I do not need this in order to find beauty in something. Flowers, free designs, lines aimlessly intertwined and called foliage: these have no significance, depend on no determinate concept, and yet we like [*gefallen*] them. A
liking [*Wohlgefallen*[10]] for the beautiful must depend on the reflection, regarding an object, that leads to some concept or other (but it is indeterminate
which concept this is). This dependence on reflection also distinguishes the
liking for the beautiful from [that for] the agreeable, which rests entirely on
sensation.

It is true that in many cases it seems as if the agreeable and the good are
one and the same. Thus people commonly say that all gratification (especially if it lasts) is intrinsically good, which means roughly the same as to be
(lastingly) agreeable and to be good are one and the same. Yet it is easy to see
that in talking this way they are merely substituting one word for another by
mistake, since the concepts that belong to these terms are in no way inter-

---

[9] Cf., in this section, the *Critique of Practical Reason*, Ak. V, 22–26.

[10] The only noun Kant had for the verb *'gefallen'* ('to be liked') was *'Wohlgefallen,'* and
'wohl' does not add anything. Grammar aside, Kant uses the two interchangeably. Moreover, he uses them just as much concerning the good and the agreeable as concerning the
beautiful, and what is special about the liking for the beautiful lies in what else Kant says
about it, not in the word *'Wohlgefallen'* itself.

changeable. Insofar as we present an object as agreeable, we present it solely in relation to sense; but if we are to call the object good [as well], and hence an object of the will, we must first bring it under principles of reason, using the concept of a purpose. [So] if something that gratifies us is also called *good*, it has a very different relation to our liking. This is [also] evident from the fact that in the case of the good there is always the question whether it is good merely indirectly or good directly[11] (i.e., useful, or intrinsically good), whereas in the case of the agreeable this question cannot even arise, since this word always signifies something that we like directly. (What we call beautiful is also liked directly.)

Even in our most ordinary speech we distinguish the agreeable from the good. If a dish stimulates [*erheben*] our tasting by its spices and other condiments, we will not hesitate to call it agreeable while granting at the same time that it is not good; for while the dish is directly *appealing* to our senses, we dislike it indirectly, i.e., as considered by reason, which looks ahead to the consequences. Even when we judge health, this difference is still noticeable. To anyone who has it, health is directly agreeable (at least negatively, as the absence of all bodily pain). But in order to say that health is good, we must also use reason and direct this health toward purposes: we must say that health is a state that disposes us to [attend to] all our tasks. [Perhaps in the case of happiness, at least, the agreeable and the good are the same?] Surely everyone believes that happiness, the greatest sum (in number as well as duration) of what is agreeable in life, may be called a true good, indeed the highest good[?] And yet reason balks at this too. Agreeableness is enjoyment. But if our sole aim were enjoyment, it would be foolish to be scrupulous about the means for getting it, [i.e.,] about whether we got it passively, from nature's bounty, or through our own activity and our own doing. But reason can never be persuaded that there is any intrinsic value in the existence of a human being who lives merely for *enjoyment* (no matter how industrious he may be in pursuing that aim), even if he served others, all likewise aiming only at enjoyment, as a most efficient means to it because he participated in their gratification by enjoying it through sympathy. Only by what he does without concern for enjoyment, in complete freedom and independently of whatever he could also receive passively from nature, does he give his existence [*Dasein*] an absolute value, as the existence [*Existenz*[12]] of a person. Happiness, with all its abundance of agreeableness, is far from being an unconditioned good.[13]

---

[11] '*Mittelbar*,' '*unmittelbar*.' The more literal rendering of these as 'mediately' and 'immediately' has been avoided in this translation because 'immediately' has also its temporal sense, which would frequently be misleading.

[12] In the *Critique of Judgment* Kant uses '*Dasein*' and '*Existenz*' synonymously, and they will both be rendered as 'existence.' Moreover, rendering '*Dasein*' as '*being*' or '*Being*' leads to serious trouble in the contexts where Kant also refers to the original being (*Wesen*); see esp. Ak. 475.

[13] An obligation to enjoy oneself is a manifest absurdity. So, consequently, must be an alleged obligation to any acts that aim merely at enjoyment, no matter how intellectually subtle (or veiled) that enjoyment may be, indeed, even if it were a mystical, so-called heavenly, enjoyment. [Kant's note.]

But despite all this difference between the agreeable and the good, they do agree in this: they are always connected with an interest in their object. This holds not only for the agreeable—see section 3—and for what is good indirectly (useful), which we like as the means to something or other that is agreeable, but also for what is good absolutely and in every respect, i.e., the moral good, which carries with it the highest interest. For the good is the object of the will (a power of desire that is determined by reason). But to will something and to have a liking for its existence, i.e., to take an interest in it, are identical.

5. Comparison of the Three Sorts of Liking, Which Differ in Kind

Both the agreeable and the good refer to our power of desire and hence carry a liking with them, the agreeable a liking that is conditioned pathologically by stimuli (*stimuli*), the good a pure practical liking that is determined not just by the presentation of the object but also by the presentation of the subject's connection with the existence of the object; i.e., what we like is not just the object but its existence as well. A judgment of taste, on the other hand, is merely *contemplative*, i.e., it is a judgment that is indifferent to the existence of the object:[14] it [considers] the character of the object only by holding it up to[15] our feeling of pleasure and displeasure. Nor is this contemplation, as such, directed to concepts, for a judgment of taste is not a cognitive judgment (whether theoretical or practical) and hence is neither *based* on concepts, nor directed to them as *purposes*.

Hence the agreeable, the beautiful, and the good designate three different relations that presentations have to the feeling of pleasure and displeasure, the feeling by reference to which we distinguish between objects or between ways of presenting them. The terms of approbation which are appropriate to each of these three are also different. We call *agreeable* what GRATIFIES us, *beautiful* what we just LIKE, *good* what we ESTEEM, or *endorse* [*billigen*], i.e., that to which we attribute [*setzen*] an objective value. Agreeableness holds for nonrational animals too; beauty only for human beings, i.e., beings who are animal and yet rational, though it is not enough that they be rational (e.g., spirits) but they must be animal as well; the good, however, holds for every rational being as such, though I cannot fully justify and explain this proposition until later. We may say that, of all these three kinds of liking, only the liking involved in taste for the beautiful is disinterested and *free*, since we are not compelled to give our approval by any interest, whether of

[14]Cf. the *Metaphysics of Morals*, Ak. VI, 212.
[15]For comparison: i.e., the feeling, as we shall see shortly (Ak. 222), is a nonconceptual awareness of a harmony (with a certain indeterminate form) between imagination and understanding; in an aesthetic judgment of reflection we hold, for comparison, a *given* form up to the form of that harmony.

sense or of reason. So we might say that [the term] liking, in the three cases mentioned, refers to *inclination,* or to *favor,* or to *respect.* For FAVOR is the only free liking. Neither an object of inclination, nor one that a law of reason enjoins on us as an object of desire, leaves us the freedom to make an object of pleasure for ourselves out of something or other. All interest either presupposes a need or gives rise to one; and, because interest is the basis that determines approval, it makes the judgment about the object unfree.

Consider, first, the interest of inclination, [which occurs] with the agreeable. Here everyone says: Hunger is the best sauce; and to people with a healthy appetite anything is tasty provided it is edible. Hence if people have a liking of this sort, that does not prove that they are selecting [*Wahl*] by taste. Only when their need has been satisfied can we tell who in a multitude of people has taste and who does not. In the same way, second, one can find manners (*conduite*) without virtue, politeness without benevolence, propriety without integrity, and so on.[16] For where the moral law speaks we are objectively no longer free to select what we must do; and to show taste in our conduct (or in judging other people's conduct) is very different from expressing our moral way of thinking. For this contains a command and gives rise to a need, whereas moral taste[17] only plays with the objects of liking without committing itself to any of them.

Translated by Werner S. Pluhar.

---

[16] I.e., taste, which is free, can manifest itself in manners, politeness, and propriety only where virtue, benevolence, and integrity, with the moral interest they involve, are absent.

[17] As displayed in one's conduct: in manners, politeness, or propriety.

WILLIAM WORDSWORTH

Preface to *Lyrical Ballads*

1800

The most immediately striking aspect of Wordsworth's (1770–1850) essay is the disappearance of the critical terminology of the eighteenth century. The older issues have not been finally settled; Wordsworth is simply not interested in the struggle between the ancients and the moderns or the relative claims of genius against learning.

Wordsworth's attack on both the subject matter and the "poetic diction" of the preceding age has psychological, sociological, and moral frames of reference. The aim of poetry, which is the communication of pleasure, is not to be achieved by inducing stereotyped reactions and stock responses; modern people, already suffering from the psychosocial pressures imposed upon them by urban life, are prevented from realizing themselves and their relation to nature by this "artificial" literature. What Wordsworth is proposing is nothing less than revivifying the human mind through poetry by insisting on the primacy of the imagination as a moral agent. The key words repeated throughout are "relationship" and "association." By portraying and exemplifying the psychological laws that govern human nature, even in the most humble, commonplace persons, the poet "binds together by passion and knowledge the vast empire of human society." This is the "moral purpose" of his poems twice referred to. The poet, "a man speaking to men" in "the language of men," records his own sensations, observations, reflections, and conclusions, creating a pleasurable imaginative response that is inseparable from the highest kind of knowledge. The scientist provides information, but the poet provides insight.

The conjunction of the terms knowledge *and* pleasure *may remind you of the Platonic challenge that poetry must be useful as well as delightful. Does Wordsworth mean the same thing by* knowledge *that Plato does? Also note, in this connection, Wordsworth's discussion of the relationship between poetry and prose (unfortunately relegated to a footnote). The distinctions he makes here lead him later in the essay to some conclusions about the function of metrical language—conclusions to be challenged by his erstwhile collaborator on the* Lyrical Ballads, *Samuel Taylor Coleridge.*

THE FIRST volume of these Poems has already been submitted to general perusal. It was published, as an experiment, which, I hoped, might be of some use to ascertain, how far, by fitting to metrical arrangement a selection of the real language of men in a state of vivid sensation, that sort of pleasure and that quantity of pleasure may be imparted, which a Poet may rationally endeavour to impart.

I had formed no very inaccurate estimate of the probable effect of those Poems: I flattered myself that they who should be pleased with them would read them with more than common pleasure: and, on the other hand, I was well aware, that by those who should dislike them, they would be read with more than common dislike. The result had differed from my expectation in this only, that a greater number have been pleased than I ventured to hope I should please.

. . . .

Several of my Friends are anxious for the success of these Poems, from a belief, that if the views with which they were composed were indeed realized, a class of Poetry would be produced, well adapted to interest mankind permanently, and not unimportant in the quality, and in the multiplicity of its moral relations: and on this account they have advised me to prefix a systematic defense of the theory upon which the Poems were written. But I was unwilling to undertake the task, knowing that on this occasion the Reader would look coldly upon my arguments, since I might be suspected of having been principally influenced by the selfish and foolish hope of *reasoning* him into an approbation of these particular Poems: and I was still more unwilling to undertake the task, because, adequately to display the opinions, and fully to enforce the arguments, would require a space wholly disproportionate to a preface. For, to treat the subject with the clearness and coherence of which it is susceptible, it would be necessary to give a full account of the present state of the public taste in this country, and to determine how far this taste is healthy or depraved; which, again, could not be determined, without pointing out in what manner language and the human mind act and re-act on each other, and without retracing the revolutions, not of literature alone, but likewise of society itself. I have therefore altogether declined to enter regularly upon this defence; yet I am sensible, that there would be something like impropriety in abruptly obtruding upon the Public, without a few words of introduction, Poems so materially different from those upon which general approbation is at present bestowed.

It is supposed, that by the act of writing in verse an Author makes a formal engagement that he will gratify certain known habits of association; that he not only thus apprises the Reader that certain classes of ideas and expressions will be found in his book, but that others will be carefully excluded. This exponent or symbol held forth by metrical language must in different eras of literature have excited very different expectations: for example, in the age of Catullus, Terence, and Lucretius, and that of Statius or Claudian; and in our own country, in the age of Shakespeare and Beaumont and Fletcher, and that of Donne and Cowley, or Dryden, or Pope. I will not take upon me to determine the exact import of the promise which, by the act of writing in verse, an Author in the present day makes to his reader: but it will undoubtedly appear to many persons that I have not fulfilled the terms of an engagement thus voluntarily contracted. They who have been accustomed to the gaudiness and inane phraseology of many modern writers, if they persist in reading this book to its conclusion, will, no doubt, frequently have to struggle with feelings of strangeness and awkwardness: they will look round for poetry, and will be induced to inquire by what species of courtesy these attempts can be permitted to assume that title. I hope therefore the reader will not censure me for attempting to state what I have proposed to myself to perform; and also (as far as the limits of a preface will permit) to explain some of the chief reasons which have determined me in the choice of my purpose: that at least he may be spared any unpleasant feeling of disappointment, and that I myself may be protected from one of the most dishonourable accusations which can be brought against an Author; namely, that of an indolence which prevents him from endeavouring to ascertain what is his duty, or, when his duty is ascertained, prevents him from performing it.

The principal object, then, proposed in these Poems was to choose incidents and situations from common life, and to relate or describe them, throughout, as far as was possible in a selection of language really used by men, and, at the same time, to throw over them a certain colouring of imagination, whereby ordinary things should be presented to the mind in an unusual aspect; and, further, and above all, to make these incidents and situations interesting by tracing in them, truly though not ostentatiously, the primary laws of our nature: chiefly, as far as regards the manner in which we associate ideas in a state of excitement. Humble and rustic life was generally chosen, because, in that condition, the essential passions of the heart find a better soil in which they can attain their maturity, are less under restraint, and speak a plainer and more emphatic language; because in that condition of life our elementary feelings coexist in a state of greater simplicity, and, consequently, may be more accurately contemplated, and more forcibly communicated; because the manners of rural life germinate from those elementary feelings, and, from the necessary character of rural occupations, are more easily comprehended, and are more durable; and, lastly, because in that condition the passions of men are incorporated with the beautiful and permanent forms of nature. The language, too, of these men has been adopted (purified indeed from what appear to be its real defects, from all lasting and rational causes of dislike or disgust) because such men hourly communicate with the best objects from which the best part of language is originally derived; and because, from their rank in society and the sameness and narrow circle of their intercourse, being less under the influence of social vanity, they convey their feelings and notions in simple and unelaborated expressions. Accordingly, such a language, arising out of repeated experience and regular feelings, is a more permanent, and a far more philosophical language, than that which is frequently substituted for it by Poets, who think that they are conferring honour upon themselves and their art, in proportion as they separate themselves from the sympathies of men, and indulge in arbitrary and capricious habits of expression, in order to furnish food for fickle tastes, and fickle appetites, of their own creation.[1]

I cannot, however, be insensible to the present outcry against the triviality and meanness, both of thought and language, which some of my contemporaries have occasionally introduced into their metrical compositions; and I acknowledge that this defect, where it exists, is more dishonourable to the Writer's own character than false refinement or arbitrary innovation, though I should contend at the same time, that it is far less pernicious in the sum of its consequences. From such verses the Poems in these volumes will be found distinguished at least by one mark of difference, that each of them has a worthy *purpose*. Not that I always began to write with a distinct purpose formally conceived; but habits of meditation have, I trust, so prompted and regulated my feelings, that my descriptions of such objects as strongly excite those feelings, will be found to carry along with them a *purpose*. If this opinion be erroneous, I can have little right to the name of a Poet. For all good poetry is the spontaneous overflow of powerful feelings: and though this be true, Poems to which any value can be attached were never produced on any variety of subjects but by a man who, being possessed of more than usual organic sensibility, had also thought long and deeply. For our continued influxes of feeling are modified and directed by our thoughts, which are indeed the representatives of all our past feelings; and, as by contemplating the relation of these general representatives to each other, we discover what is really important to men, so, by the repetition and continuance of this act, our feelings will be connected with important subjects, till at length, if we be originally possessed of much sensibility, such habits of mind will be produced, that, by obeying blindly and mechanically the impulses of those habits, we shall describe objects, and utter sentiments, of such a nature, and in such connexion with each other, that the understanding of the Reader must necessarily be in some degree enlightened, and his affections strengthened and purified.

It has been said that each of these poems has a purpose. Another circumstance must be mentioned which distinguishes these Poems from the popular Poetry of the day; it is this, that the feeling therein developed gives importance to the action and situation, and not the action and situation to the feeling.

A sense of false modesty shall not prevent me from asserting, that the Reader's attention is pointed to this mark of distinction, far less for the sake of these particular Poems than from the general importance of the subject. The subject is indeed important! For the human mind is capable of being excited without the application of gross and violent stimulants; and he must have a very faint perception of its beauty and dignity who does not know this, and who does not further know, that one being is elevated above

[1] It is worth while here to observe, that the affecting parts of Chaucer are almost always expressed in language pure and universally intelligible even to this day. [All notes are Wordsworth's. Ed.]

another, in proportion as he possesses this capability. It has therefore appeared to me, that to endeavour to produce or enlarge this capability is one of the best services in which, at any period, a Writer can be engaged; but this service, excellent at all times, is especially so at the present day. For a multitude of causes, unknown to former times, are now acting with a combined force to blunt the discriminating powers of the mind, and, unfitting it for all voluntary exertion, to reduce it to a state of almost savage torpor. The most effective of these causes are the great national events which are daily taking place, and the increasing accumulation of men in cities, where the uniformity of their occupations produces a craving for extraordinary incident, which the rapid communication of intelligence hourly gratifies. To this tendency of life and manners the literature and theatrical exhibitions of the country have conformed themselves. The invaluable works of our elder writers, I had almost said the works of Shakespeare and Milton, are driven into neglect by frantic novels, sickly and stupid German Tragedies, and deluges of idle and extravagant stories in verse.—When I think upon this degrading thirst after outrageous stimulation, I am almost ashamed to have spoken of the feeble endeavour made in these volumes to counteract it; and, reflecting upon the magnitude of the general evil, I should be oppressed with no dishonourable melancholy, had I not a deep impression of certain inherent and indestructible qualities of the human mind, and likewise of certain powers in the great and permanent objects that act upon it, which are equally inherent and indestructible; and were there not added to this impression a belief, that the time is approaching when the evil will be systematically opposed, by men of greater powers, and with far more distinguished success.

Having dwelt thus long on the subjects and aim of these Poems, I shall request the Reader's permission to apprise him of a few circumstances relating to their *style*, in order, among other reasons, that he may not censure me for not having performed what I never attempted. The Reader will find that personifications of abstract ideas rarely occur in these volumes; and are utterly rejected, as an ordinary device to elevate the style, and raise it above prose. My purpose was to imitate, and, as far as possible, to adopt the very language of men; and assuredly such personifications do not make any natural or regular part of that language. They are, indeed, a figure of speech occasionally prompted by passion, and I have made use of them as such; but have endeavoured utterly to reject them as a mechanical device of style, or as a family language which Writers in metre seem to lay claim to by prescription. I have wished to keep the Reader in the company of flesh and blood, persuaded that by so doing I shall interest him. Others who pursue a different track will interest him likewise; I do not interfere with their claim, but wish to prefer a claim of my own. There will also be found in these volumes little of what is usually called poetic diction; as much pains has been taken to avoid it as is ordinarily taken to produce it; this has been done for the reason already alleged, to bring my language near to the language of men; and further, because the pleasure which I have proposed to myself to impart, is of a kind very different from that which is supposed by many persons to be the proper object of poetry. Without being culpably particular, I do not know how to give my Reader a more exact notion of the style in which it was my wish and intention to write, than by informing him that I have at all times endeavoured to look steadily at my subject; consequently, there is I hope in these Poems little falsehood of description, and my ideas are expressed in language fitted to their respective importance. Something must have been gained by this practice, as it is friendly to one property of all good poetry, namely, good sense: but it has necessarily cut me off from a large portion of phrases and figures of speech which from father to son have long been regarded as the common inheritance of Poets. I have also thought it expedient to restrict myself still further, having abstained from the use of many expressions, in themselves proper and beautiful, but which have been foolishly repeated by bad Poets, till such feelings of disgust are connected with them as it is scarcely possible by any art of association to overpower.

[handwritten marginal note: Breaking with tradition]

If in a poem there should be found a series of lines, or even a single line, in which the language, though naturally arranged, and according to the strict laws of metre, does not differ from that of prose, there is a numerous class of critics, who, when they stumble upon these prosaisms, as they call them, imagine that they have made a notable discovery, and exult over the Poet as over a man ignorant of his own profession. Now these men would establish a canon of criticism which the Reader will conclude he must utterly reject, if he wishes to be pleased with these volumes. And it would be a most easy task to prove to him, that not only the language of a large portion of every good poem, even of the most elevated character, must necessarily, except with reference to the metre, in no respect differ from that of good prose, but likewise that some of the most interesting parts of the best poems will be found to be strictly the language of prose when prose is well written. The truth of this assertion might be demonstrated by innumerable passages from almost all the poetical writings, even of Milton himself. To illustrate the subject in a general manner, I will here adduce a short composition of Gray, who was at the head of those who, by their reasonings, have attempted to widen the space of separation betwixt Prose and Metrical composition, and was more than any other man curiously elaborate in the structure of his own poetic diction.

> In vain to me the smiling mornings shine,
> And reddening Phœbus lifts his golden fire:
> The birds in vain their amorous descant join,
> Or cheerful fields resume their green attire.
> These ears, alas! for other notes repine;
> *A different object do these eyes require:*
> *My lonely anguish melts no heart but mine:*
> *And in my breast the imperfect joys expire:*
> Yet morning smiles the busy race to cheer,
> And new-born pleasure brings to happier men;
> The fields to all their wonted tribute bear;
> To warm their little loves the birds complain.
> *I fruitless mourn to him that cannot hear,*
> *And weep the more because I weep in vain.*

It will easily be perceived, that the only part of this Sonnet which is of any value is the lines printed in Italics; it is equally obvious, that, except in the rhyme, and in the use of the single word 'fruitless' for fruitlessly, which is so far a defect, the language of these lines does in no respect differ from that of prose.

By the foregoing quotation it has been shown that the language of Prose may yet be well adapted to Poetry; and it was previously asserted, that a large portion of the language of every good poem can in no respect differ from that of good Prose. We will go further. It may be safely affirmed, that there neither is, nor can be, any *essential* difference between the language of prose and metrical composition. We are fond of tracing the resemblance between Poetry and Painting, and, accordingly, we call them Sisters: but where shall we find bonds of connexion sufficiently strict to typify the affinity betwixt metrical and prose composition? They both speak by and to the same organs; the bodies in which both of them are clothed may be said to be of the same substance, their affections are kindred, and almost identical, not necessarily differing even in degree; Poetry[2] sheds no tears 'such as Angels weep,' but natural and human tears; she can boast of no celestial ichor that distinguishes her vital juices from those of prose; the same human blood circulates through the veins of them both.

If it be affirmed that rhyme and metrical arrangements of themselves constitute a distinction which overturns what has just been said on the strict affinity of metrical language with that of prose, and paves the way for other artificial distinctions which the mind voluntarily admits, I answer that the language of such Poetry as is here recommended is, as far as is possible, a selection of the language really spoken by men; that this selection, wherever it is made with true taste and feeling, will of itself form a distinction far greater than would at first be imagined, and will entirely separate the composition from the vulgarity and meanness of ordinary life; and, if metre be superadded thereto, I believe that a dissimilitude will be produced altogether sufficient for the gratification of a rational mind. What other distinction would we have? Whence is it to come? And where is it to exist? Not, surely, where the Poet speaks through the mouths of his characters: it cannot be necessary here, either for elevation of style, or any of its supposed ornaments: for, if the Poet's subject be judiciously chosen, it will naturally, and upon fit occasion, lead him to passions the language of which, if selected truly and judiciously, must necessarily be dignified and variegated, and alive with metaphors and figures. I forbear to speak of an incongruity which would shock the intelligent Reader, should the Poet interweave any foreign splendour of his own

---

[2] I here use the word 'Poetry' (though against my own judgment) as opposed to the word Prose, and synonymous with metrical composition. But much confusion has been introduced into criticism by this contradistinction of Poetry and Prose, instead of the more philosophical one of Poetry and Matter of Fact, or Science. The only strict antithesis to Prose is Metre; nor is this, in truth, a *strict* antithesis, because lines and passages of metre so naturally occur in writing prose, that it would be scarcely possible to avoid them, even were it desirable.

with that which the passion naturally suggests: it is sufficient to say that such addition is unnecessary. And, surely, it is more probable that those passages, which with propriety abound with metaphors and figures, will have their due effect, if, upon other occasions where the passions are of a milder character, the style also be subdued and temperate.

But, as the pleasure which I hope to give by the Poems now presented to the Reader must depend entirely on just notions upon this subject, and, as it is in itself of high importance to our taste and moral feelings, I cannot content myself with these detached remarks. And if, in what I am about to say, it shall appear to some that my labour is unnecessary, and that I am like a man fighting a battle without enemies, such persons may be reminded, that, whatever be the language outwardly holden by men, a practical faith in the opinions which I am wishing to establish is almost unknown. If my conclusions are admitted, and carried as far as they must be carried if admitted at all, our judgments concerning the works of the greatest Poets both ancient and modern will be far different from what they are at present, both when we praise, and when we censure: and our moral feelings influencing and influenced by these judgements will, I believe, be corrected and purified.

——Taking up the subject, then, upon general grounds, let me ask, what is meant by the word Poet? What is a Poet? To whom does he address himself? And what language is to be expected from him?—He is a man speaking to men: a man, it is true, endowed with more lively sensibility, more enthusiasm and tenderness, who has a greater knowledge of human nature, and a more comprehensive soul, than are supposed to be common among mankind; a man pleased with his own passions and volitions, and who rejoices more than other men in the spirit of life that is in him; delighting to contemplate similar volitions and passions as manifested in the goings-on of the Universe, and habitually impelled to create them where he does not find them. To these qualities he has added a disposition to be affected more than other men by absent things as if they were present; an ability of conjuring up in himself passions, which are indeed far from being the same as those produced by real events, yet (especially in those parts of the general sympathy which are pleasing and delightful) do more nearly resemble the passions produced by real events, than anything which, from the motions of their own minds merely, other men are accustomed to feel in themselves:—whence, and from practice, he has acquired a greater readiness and power in expressing what he thinks and feels, and especially those thoughts and feelings which, by his own choice, or from the structure of his own mind, arise in him without immediate external excitement.

But whatever portion of this faculty we may suppose even the greatest Poet to possess, there cannot be a doubt that the language which it will suggest to him, must often, in liveliness and truth, fall short of that which is uttered by men in real life, under the actual pressure of those passions, certain shadows of which the Poet thus produces, or feels to be produced, in himself.

However exalted a notion we would wish to cherish of the character of a Poet, it is obvious, that while he describes and imitates passions, his employment is in some degree mechanical, compared with the freedom and power of real and substantial action and suffering. So that it will be the wish of the Poet to bring his feelings near to those of the persons whose feelings he describes, nay, for short spaces of time, perhaps, to let himself slip into an entire delusion, and even confound and identify his own feelings with theirs; modifying only the language which is thus suggested to him by a consideration that he describes for a particular purpose, that of giving pleasure. Here, then, he will apply the principle of selection which has been already insisted upon. He will depend upon this for removing what would otherwise be painful or disgusting in the passion; he will feel that there is no necessity to trick out or to elevate nature: and, the more industriously he applies this principle, the deeper will be his faith that no words, which *his* fancy or imagination can suggest, will be to be compared with those which are the emanations of reality and truth.

But it may be said by those who do not object to the general spirit of these remarks, that, as it is impossible for the Poet to produce upon all occasions language as exquisitely fitted for the passion as that which the real passion itself suggests, it is proper that he should consider himself as in the situation of a translator, who does not scruple to substitute excellencies of another kind for those which are unattainable by him; and endeavours occasionally to surpass his original, in order to make some amends for the general inferiority to which he feels that he must submit. But this would be to encourage idleness and unmanly despair. Further, it is the language of men who speak of what they do not understand; who talk of Poetry as of a matter of amusement and idle pleasure; who will converse with us as gravely about a *taste* for Poetry, as they express it, as if it were a thing as indifferent as a taste for rope-dancing, or Frontiniac of Sherry. Aristotle, I have been told, has said, that Poetry is the most philosophic of all writing: it is so: its object is truth, not individual and local, but general, and operative; not standing upon external testimony, but carried alive into the heart by passion; truth which is its own testimony, which gives competence and confidence to the tribunal to which it appeals, and receives them from the same tribunal. Poetry is the image of man and nature. The obstacles which stand in the way of the fidelity of the Biographer and Historian, and of their consequent utility, are incalculably greater than those which are to be encountered by the Poet who comprehends the dignity of his art. The Poet writes under one restriction only, namely, the necessity of giving immediate pleasure to a human Being possessed of that information which may be expected from him, not as a lawyer, a physician, a mariner, an astronomer, or a natural philosopher, but as a Man. Except this one restriction, there is no object standing between the Poet and the image of things; between this, and the Biographer and Historian, there are a thousand.

Nor let this necessity of producing immediate pleasure be considered as a degradation of the Poet's art. It is far otherwise. It is an acknowledgement of the beauty of the universe, an acknowledgement the more sincere, because not formal, but indirect; it is a task light and easy to him who looks at the world in the

"Be at one w/ the universe, man."

spirit of love: further, it is a homage paid to the native and naked dignity of man, to the grand elementary principle of pleasure, by which he knows, and feels, and lives, and moves. We have no sympathy but what is propagated by pleasure: I would not be misunderstood; but wherever we sympathize with pain, it will be found that the sympathy is produced and carried on by subtle combinations with pleasure. We have no knowledge, that is, no general principles drawn from the contemplation of particular facts, but what has been built up by pleasure, and exists in us by pleasure alone. The Man of science, the Chemist and Mathematician, whatever difficulties and disgusts they may have had to struggle with, know and feel this. However painful may be the objects with which the Anatomist's knowledge is connected, he feels that his knowledge is pleasure; and where he has no pleasure he has no knowledge. What then does the Poet? He considers man and the objects that surround him as acting and re-acting upon each other, so as to produce an infinite complexity of pain and pleasure; he considers man in his own nature and in his ordinary life as contemplating this with a certain quantity of immediate knowledge, with certain convictions, intuitions, and deductions, which from habit acquire the quality of intuitions; he considers him as looking upon this complex scene of ideas and sensations, and finding everywhere objects that immediately excite in him sympathies which, from the necessities of his nature, are accompanied by an overbalance of enjoyment.

To this knowledge which all men carry about with them, and to these sympathies in which, without any other discipline than that of our daily life, we are fitted to take delight, the Poet principally directs his attention. He considers man and nature as essentially adapted to each other, and the mind of man as naturally the mirror of the fairest and most interesting properties of nature. And thus the Poet, prompted by this feeling of pleasure, which accompanies him through the whole course of his studies, converses with general nature, with affections akin to those, which, through labour and length of time, the Man of science has raised up in himself, by conversing with those particular parts of nature which are the objects of his studies. The knowledge both of the Poet and the Man of science is pleasure; but the knowledge of the one cleaves to us as a necessary part of our existence, our natural and unalienable inheritance; the other is a personal and individual acquisition, slow to come to us, and by no habitual and direct sympathy connecting us with our fellow-beings. The Man of science seeks truth as a remote and unknown benefactor; he cherishes and loves it in his solitude: the Poet, singing a song in which all human beings join with him, rejoices in the presence of truth as our visible and hourly companion. Poetry is the breath and finer spirit of all knowledge; it is the impassioned expression which is in the countenance of all Science. Emphatically may it be said of the Poet, as Shakespeare hath said of man, 'that he looks before and after.' He is the rock of defense for human nature; an upholder and preserver, carrying everywhere with him relationship and love. In spite of difference of soil and climate, of language and manners, of laws and customs: in spite of things silently gone out of mind, and things violently destroyed; the Poet binds together by passion and knowledge the vast empire of human society, as it is spread over the whole earth, and over all time. The objects of the Poet's thoughts are everywhere; though the eyes and senses of man are, it is true, his favourite guides, yet he will follow wheresoever he can find an atmosphere of sensation in which to move his wings. Poetry is the first and last of all knowledge—it is as immortal as the heart of man. If the labours of Men of science should ever create any material revolution, direct or indirect, in our condition, and in the impressions which we habitually receive, the Poet will sleep then no more than at present; he will be ready to follow the steps of the Man of science, not only in those general indirect effects, but he will be at his side, carrying sensation into the midst of the objects of the science itself. The remotest discoveries of the Chemist, the Botanist, or Mineralogist, will be as proper objects of the Poet's art as any upon which it can be employed, if the time should ever come when these things shall be familiar to us, and the relations under which they are contemplated by the followers of these respective sciences shall be manifestly and palpably material to us as enjoying and suffering beings. If the time should ever come when what is now called science, thus familiarized to men, shall be ready to put on, as it were, a form of flesh and blood, the Poet will lend his divine spirit to aid the transfiguration, and will welcome the Being thus produced, as a dear and genuine inmate of the household of man.—It is not, then, to be supposed that any one, who holds that sublime notion of Poetry which I have attempted to convey, will break in upon the sanctity and truth of his pictures by transitory and accidental ornaments, and endeavour to excite admiration of himself by arts, the necessity of which must manifestly depend upon the assumed meanness of his subject.

What has been thus far said applies to Poetry in general; but especially to those parts of composition where the Poet speaks through the mouths of his characters; and upon this point it appears to authorize the conclusion that there are few persons of good sense, who would not allow that the dramatic parts of composition are defective, in proportion as they deviate from the real language of nature, and are coloured by a diction of the Poet's own, either peculiar to him as an individual Poet or belonging simply to Poets in general; to a body of men who, from the circumstance of their compositions being in metre, it is expected will employ a particular language.

It is not, then, in the dramatic parts of composition that we look for this distinction of language; but still it may be proper and necessary where the Poet speaks to us in his own person and character. To this I answer by referring the Reader to the description before given of a Poet. Among the qualities there enumerated as principally conducing to form a Poet, is implied nothing differing in kind from other men, but only in degree. The sum of what was said is, that the Poet is chiefly distinguished from other men by a greater promptness to think and feel without immediate external excitement, and a greater power in expressing such thoughts and feelings as are produced in him in that manner. But these passions and thoughts and feelings are the general passions and thoughts and feelings of men. And with what are they connected? Undoubtedly with our moral sentiments and animal sensations, and with the causes which excite these; with the operations of the elements, and the appearances of the visible universe; with storm and sunshine, with the revolutions of the seasons, with cold and heat, with loss of friends and kindred, with injuries and resentments, gratitude and hope, with fear and sorrow. These, and the like, are the sensations and objects which the Poet describes, as they are the sensations of other men, and the objects which interest them. The Poet thinks and feels in the spirit of human passions. How, then, can his language differ in any material degree from that of all other men who feel vividly and see clearly? It might be *proved* that it is impossible. But supposing that this were not the case, the Poet might then be allowed to use a peculiar language when expressing his feelings for his own gratification, or that of men like himself. But Poets do not write for Poets alone, but for men. Unless therefore we are advocates for that admiration which subsists upon ignorance, and that pleasure which arises from hearing what we do not understand, the Poet must descend from this supposed height; and, in order to excite rational sympathy, he must express himself as other men express themselves. To this it may be added, that while he is only selecting from the real language of men, or, which amounts to the same thing, composing accurately in the spirit of such selection, he is treading upon safe ground, and we know what we are to expect from him. Our feelings are the same with respect to metre; for, as it may be proper to remind the Reader, the distinction of metre is regular and uniform, and not, like that which is produced by what is usually called POETIC DICTION, arbitrary, and subject to infinite caprices upon which no calculation whatever can be made. In the one case, the Reader is utterly at the mercy of the Poet, respecting what imagery or diction he may choose to connect with the passion; whereas, in the other, the metre obeys certain laws, to which the Poet and Reader both willingly submit because they are certain, and because no interference is made by them with the passion, but such as the concurring testimony of ages has shown to heighten and improve the pleasure which co-exists with it.

It will now be proper to answer an obvious question, namely, Why, professing these opinions, have I written in verse? To this, in addition to such answer as is included in what has been already said, I reply, in the first place, Because, however I may have restricted myself, there is still left open to me what confessedly constitutes the most valuable object of all writing, whether in prose or verse; the great and universal passions of men, the most general and interesting of their occupations, and the entire world of nature before me—to supply endless combinations of forms and imagery. Now, supposing for a moment that whatever is interesting in these objects may be as vividly described in prose, why should I be condemned for attempting to superadd to such description the charm which, by the consent of all nations, is acknowledged to exist in metrical language? To this, by such as are yet unconvinced, it may be answered that a very small part of the pleasure given by Poetry depends upon the metre, and that it is injudicious to write in metre, unless it be accompanied with the other artificial distinctions of style with which metre is usually accompanied, and that, by such deviation, more will be lost from the shock which will thereby be given to the Reader's associations than will be counterbalanced by any pleasure which he can derive from the general power of numbers. In answer to those who still contend for the necessity of accompanying metre with certain appropriate colours of style in order to the accomplishment of its appropriate end, and who also, in my opinion, greatly underrate the power of metre in itself, it might, perhaps, as far as relates to these Volumes, have been almost sufficient to observe, that poems are extant, written upon more humble subjects, and in a still more naked and simple style, which have continued to give pleasure from generation to generation. Now, if nakedness and simplicity be a defect, the fact here mentioned affords a strong presumption that poems somewhat less naked and simple are capable of affording pleasure at the present day; and, what I wished *chiefly* to attempt, at present, was to justify myself for having written under the impression of this belief.

But various causes might be pointed out why, when the style is manly, and the subject of some importance, words metrically arranged will long continue to impart such a pleasure to mankind as he who proves the extent of that pleasure will be desirous to impart. The end of Poetry is to produce excitement in co-existence with an overbalance of pleasure; but, by the supposition, excitement is an unusual and irregular state of the mind; ideas and feelings do not, in that state, succeed each other in accustomed order. If the words, however, by which this excitement is produced be in themselves powerful, or the images and feelings have an undue proportion of pain connected with them, there is some danger that the excitement may be carried beyond its proper bounds. Now the co-presence of something regular, something to which the mind has been accustomed in various moods and in a less excited state, cannot but have great efficacy in tempering and restraining the passion by an intertexture of ordinary feeling, and of feeling not strictly and necessarily connected with the passion. This is unquestionably true; and hence, though the opinion will at first appear paradoxical, from the tendency of metre to divest language, in a certain degree, of its reality, and thus to throw a sort of half-consciousness of unsubstantial existence over the whole composition, there can be little doubt but that more pathetic situations and sentiments, that is, those which have a greater proportion of pain connected with them, may be endured in metrical composition, especially in rhyme, than in prose. The metre of the old ballads is very artless; yet they contain many passages which would illustrate this opinion; and, I hope, if the following Poems be attentively perused, similar instances will be found in them. This opinion may be further illustrated by appealing to the Reader's own experience of the reluctance with which he comes to the re-perusal of the distressful parts of *Clarissa Harlowe*, or *The Gamester*; while Shakespeare's writings, in the most pathetic scenes, never act upon us, as pathetic, beyond the bounds of pleasure—an effect which, in a much greater degree than might at first be imagined, is to be ascribed to small, but continual and regular impulses of pleasurable surprise from the metrical arrangement.—On the other hand (what it must be allowed will much more frequently happen) if the

Poet's words should be incommensurate with the passion, and inadequate to raise the Reader to a height of desirable excitement, then (unless the Poet's choice of his metre has been grossly injudicious), in the feelings of pleasure which the Reader has been accustomed to connect with metre in general, and in the feeling, whether cheerful or melancholy, which he has been accustomed to connect with that particular movement of metre, there will be found something which will greatly contribute to impart passion to the words, and to effect the complex end which the Poet proposes to himself.

If I had undertaken a SYSTEMATIC defense of the theory here maintained, it would have been my duty to develop the various causes upon which the pleasure received from metrical language depends. Among the chief of these causes is to be reckoned a principle which must be well known to those who have made any of the Arts the object of accurate reflection; namely, the pleasure which the mind derives from the perception of similitude in dissimilitude. This principle is the great spring of the activity of our minds, and their chief feeder. From this principle the direction of the sexual appetite, and all the passions connected with it, take their origin: it is the life of our ordinary conversation; and upon the accuracy with which similitude in dissimilitude, and dissimilitude in similitude are perceived, depend our taste and our moral feelings. It would not be a useless employment to apply this principle to the consideration of metre, and to show that metre is hence enabled to afford much pleasure, and to point out in what manner that pleasure is produced. But my limits will not permit me to enter upon this subject, and I must content myself with a general summary.

I have said that poetry is the spontaneous overflow of powerful feelings: it takes its origin from emotion recollected in tranquillity: the emotion is contemplated till, by a species of reaction, the tranquillity gradually disappears, and an emotion, kindred to that which was before the subject of contemplation, is gradually produced, and does itself actually exist in the mind. In this mood successful composition generally begins, and in a mood similar to this it is carried on; but the emotion, of whatever kind, and in whatever degree, from various causes, is qualified by various pleasures, so that in describing any passions whatsoever, which are voluntarily described, the mind will, upon the whole, be in a state of enjoyment. If Nature be thus cautious to preserve in a state of enjoyment a being so employed, the Poet ought to profit by the lesson held forth to him, and ought especially to take care, that, whatever passions he communicates to his Reader, those passions, if his Reader's mind be sound and vigorous, should always be accompanied with an overbalance of pleasure. Now the music of harmonious metrical language, the sense of difficulty overcome, and the blind association of pleasure which has been previously received from works of rhyme or metre of the same or similar construction, an indistinct perception perpetually renewed of language closely resembling that of real life, and yet, in the circumstance of metre, differing from it so widely—all these imperceptibly make up a complex feeling of delight, which is of the most important use in tempering the painful feeling always found intermingled with powerful descriptions of the deeper

[handwritten marginalia, left margin:] Wordsworth creates "built in" arguments against his critics — "if poems are attentively pursued" / "if his Reader's mind be sound and vigorous — makes him seem arrogant

[handwritten marginalia, right margin:] Thinking back, in a moment of tranquillity a time of strong emotion — until that emotion seems to exist again, writing while in that state

passions. This effect is always produced in pathetic and impassioned poetry; while, in lighter compositions, the ease and gracefulness with which the Poet manages his numbers are themselves confessedly a principal source of the gratification of the Reader. All that it is *necessary* to say, however, upon this subject, may be effected by affirming, what few persons will deny, that, of two descriptions, either of passions, manners, or characters, each of them equally well executed, the one in prose and the other in verse, the verse will be read a hundred times where the prose is read once.

Having thus explained a few of my reasons for writing in verse, and why I have chosen subjects from common life, and endeavoured to bring my language near to the real language of men, if I have been too minute in pleading my own cause, I have at the same time been treating a subject of general interest; and for this reason a few words shall be added with reference solely to these particular poems, and to some defects which will probably be found in them. I am sensible that my associations must have sometimes been particular instead of general, and that, consequently, giving to things a false importance, I may have sometimes written upon unworthy subjects; but I am less apprehensive on this account, than that my language may frequently have suffered from those arbitrary connexions of feelings and ideas with particular words and phrases, from which no man can altogether protect himself. Hence I have no doubt, that, in some instances, feelings, even of the ludicrous, may be given to my Readers by expressions which appeared to me tender and pathetic. Such faulty expressions, were I convinced they were faulty at present, and that they must necessarily continue to be so, I would willingly take all reasonable pains to correct. But it is dangerous to make these alterations on the simple authority of a few individuals, or even of certain classes of men; for where the understanding of an Author is not convinced, or his feelings altered, this cannot be done without great injury to himself: for his own feelings are his stay and support; and, if he set them aside in one instance, he may be induced to repeat this act till his mind shall lose all confidence in itself, and become utterly debilitated. To this it may be added, that the critic ought never to forget that he is himself exposed to the same errors as the Poet, and, perhaps, in a much greater degree: for there can be no presumption in saying of most readers, that it is not probable they will be so well acquainted with the various stages of meaning through which words have passed, or with the fickleness or stability of the relations of particular ideas to each other; and, above all, since they are so much less interested in the subject, they may decide lightly and carelessly.

Long as the Reader has been detained, I hope he will permit me to caution him against a mode of false criticism which has been applied to Poetry, in which the language closely resembles that of life and nature. Such verses have been triumphed over in parodies, of which Dr. Johnson's stanza is a fair specimen: —

I put my hat upon my head
And walked into the Strand,

And there I met another man
Whose hat was in his hand.

Immediately under these lines let us place one of the most justly admired stanzas of the 'Babes in the Wood.'

These pretty Babes with hand in hand
Went wandering up and down;
But never more they saw the Man
Approaching from the Town.

In both these stanzas the words, and the order of the words, in no respect differ from the most unimpassioned conversation. There are words in both, for example, 'the Strand,' and 'the Town,' connected with none but the most familiar ideas; yet the one stanza we admit as admirable, and the other as a fair example of the superlatively contemptible. Whence arises this difference? Not from the metre, not from the language, not from the order of the words; but the _matter_ expressed in Dr. Johnson's stanza is contemptible. The proper method of treating trivial and simple verses, to which Dr. Johnson's stanza would be a fair parallelism, is not to say, this is a bad kind of poetry, or, this is not poetry; but, this wants sense; it is neither interesting in itself, nor can _lead_ to anything interesting; the images neither originate in that sane state of feeling which arises out of thought, nor can excite thought or feeling in the Reader. This is the only sensible manner of dealing with such verses. Why trouble yourself about the species till you have previously decided upon the genus? Why take pains to prove that an ape is not a Newton, when it is self-evident that he is not a man?

One request I must make of my reader, which is, that in judging these Poems he would decide by his own feelings genuinely, and not by reflection upon what will probably be the judgement of others. How common is it to hear a person say, I myself do not object to this style of composition, or this or that expression, but, to such and such classes of people it will appear mean or ludicrous! This mode of criticism, so destructive of all sound unadulterated judgement, is almost universal: let the Reader then abide, independently, by his own feelings, and, if he finds himself affected, let him not suffer such conjectures to interfere with his pleasure.

If an Author, by any single composition, has impressed us with respect for his talents, it is useful to consider this as affording a presumption, that on other occasions where we have been displeased, he, nevertheless, may not have written ill or absurdly; and further, to give him so much credit for this one composition as may induce us to review what has displeased us, with more care than we should otherwise have bestowed upon it. This is not only an act of justice, but, in our decisions upon poetry especially, may conduce, in a high degree, to the improvement of our own taste; for an _accurate_ taste in poetry, and in all the other arts, as Sir Joshua Reynolds has observed, is an _acquired_ talent, which can only be produced by thought and a long continued intercourse with the best models of composition. This is mentioned, not with so ridiculous a purpose as to prevent the most inexperienced Reader from judging for himself (I have already said that I wish him to judge for himself), but merely to temper the rashness of decision, and to suggest, that, if Poetry be a subject on which much time has not been bestowed, the judgement may be erroneous; and that, in many cases, it necessarily will be so.

Nothing would, I know, have so effectually contributed to further the end which I have in view, as to have shown of what kind the pleasure is, and how that pleasure is produced, which is confessedly produced by metrical composition essentially different from that which I have here endeavoured to recommend: for the Reader will say that he has been pleased by such composition; and what more can be done for him? The power of any art is limited; and he will suspect, that, if it be proposed to furnish him with new friends, that can be only upon condition of his abandoning his old friends. Besides, as I have said, the Reader is himself conscious of the pleasure which he has received from such composition, composition to which he has peculiarly attached the endearing name of Poetry; and all men feel an habitual gratitude, and something of an honourable bigotry, for the objects which have long continued to please them: we not only wish to be pleased, but to be pleased in that particular way in which we have been accustomed to be pleased. There is in these feelings enough to resist a host of arguments; and I should be the less able to combat them successfully, as I am willing to allow, that, in order entirely to enjoy the Poetry which I am recommending, it would be necessary to give up much of what is ordinarily enjoyed. But, would my limits have permitted me to point out how this pleasure is produced, many obstacles might have been removed, and the Reader assisted in perceiving that the powers of language are not so limited as he may suppose; and that it is possible for poetry to give other enjoyments, of a purer, more lasting, and more exquisite nature. This part of the subject has not been altogether neglected, but it has not been so much my present aim to prove, that the interest excited by some other kinds of poetry is less vivid, and less worthy of the nobler powers of the mind, as to offer reasons for presuming, that if my purpose were fulfilled, a species of poetry would be produced, which is genuine poetry; in its nature well adapted to interest mankind permanently, and likewise important in the multiplicity and quality of its moral relations.

From what has been said, and from a perusal of the Poems, the Reader will be able clearly to perceive the object which I had in view: he will determine how far it has been attained; and, what is a much more important question, whether it be worth attaining: and upon the decision of these two questions will rest my claim to the approbation of the Public.

SAMUEL TAYLOR COLERIDGE

From *Biographia Literaria*

1817

Coleridge's (1772–1834) definition of "a legitimate poem" in Chapter XIV of his Biographia Literaria *stresses the idea of its organic unity, harkening back to Aristotle. In his "Shakespeare Lectures," Coleridge distinguishes "organic" from "mechanic" form: "The form is mechanic, when on any given material we impress a predetermined form, not necessarily arising out of the properties of the material;—as when to a mass of wet clay we give whatever shape we wish it to retain when hardened. The organic form, on the other hand, is innate; it shapes, as it develops, itself from within, and the fulness of its development is one and the same with the perfection of its outward form. Such as the life is, such is the form."*

Given this theory, it is easy to understand Coleridge's objection to Wordsworth's statement that meter is a "super-added" element. Concerned with questions of form, Coleridge also takes issue with Wordsworth's blurring of the distinction between poetry and prose, for what makes a poem is the immediate pleasure that it communicates, not its ultimate truth. (He raises a further objection, to Wordsworth's theories about diction, in Chapter XVII.) Thus far, Coleridge is a formal critic, defining and differentiating the particular qualities of a poem.

But when he equates the questions, "What is poetry?" and "What is a poet?" he moves into the realm of psychological criticism. The discussion of Fancy and Imagination in Chapter XIII is his attempt to distinguish and define those "faculties" that are the source of all mental activity, including the creative. It should be said here that Coleridge scholars and critics are still not in unanimous agreement over the interpretation of some of the knottier passages. However, these terms and others, such as "the poetic genius" and "the whole soul of man," imply a psychological model in which various faculties are arranged in a hierarchy of value, all in their totality, represented and subordinated, comprising the whole soul. Ideally, a legitimate poem is an externalization of the poetic genius; the poet's soul is expressed in poetry: "Such as the life is, such is the form."

Coleridge as the practical critic is seen at work in Chapter XV, and the obvious question to be considered is the extent to which the specific comments on Shakespeare derive from his theories. But even here Coleridge introduces some new theoretical considerations, such as the necessary "aloofness" of the poet from the poem's subject matter (a concept developed further by later critics). Despite the rather disordered and rambling sequence of the Biographia Literaria, *Coleridge clearly exemplifies the shift in critical focus in the early nineteenth century, from the poem to the character of the poet, from the rules and the conventions of poetry to the activity of poem-making.*

XIV

Occasion of the Lyrical Ballads, and the objects originally proposed — Preface to the second edition — The ensuing controversy, its causes and acrimony — Philosophic definitions of a poem and poetry with scholia.

DURING THE first year that Mr. Wordsworth and I were neighbours, our conversations turned frequently on the two cardinal points of poetry, the power of exciting the sympathy of the reader by a faithful adherence to the truth of nature, and the power of giving the interest of novelty by the modifying colors of imagination. The sudden charm, which accidents of light and shade, which moon-light or sun-set diffused over a known and familiar landscape, appeared to represent the practicability of combining both. These are the poetry of nature. The thought suggested itself (to which of us I do not recollect) that a series of poems might be composed of two sorts. In the one, the incidents and agents were to be, in part at least, supernatural; and the excellence aimed at was to consist in the interesting of the affections by the dramatic truth of such emotions, as would naturally accompany such situations, supposing them real. And real in *this* sense they have been to every human being who, from whatever source of delusion, has at any time believed himself under supernatural agency. For the second class, subjects were to be chosen from ordinary life; the characters and incidents were to be such, as will be found in every village and its vicinity, where there is a meditative and feeling mind to seek after them, or to notice them, when they present themselves.

In this idea originated the plan of the "Lyrical Ballads"; in which it was agreed, that my endeavours should be directed to persons and characters supernatural, or at least romantic; yet so as to transfer from our inward nature a human interest and a semblance of truth sufficient to procure for these shadows of imagination that willing suspension of disbelief for the moment, which constitutes poetic faith. Mr. Wordsworth, on the other hand, was to propose to himself as his object, to give the charm of novelty to things of every day, and to excite a feeling analogous to the supernatural, by awakening the mind's attention from the lethargy of custom, and directing it to the loveliness and the wonders of the world before us; an inexhaustible treasure, but for which, in consequence of the film of familiarity and selfish solicitude we have eyes, yet see not, ears that hear not, and hearts that neither feel nor understand.

With this view I wrote "The Ancient Mariner," and was preparing among other poems, "The Dark Ladie," and the "Christabel," in which I should have more nearly realized my ideal, than I had done in my first attempt. But Mr. Wordsworth's industry had proved so much more successful, and the number of his poems so much greater, that my compositions, instead of forming a balance, appeared rather an interpolation of heterogeneous matter. Mr. Wordsworth added two or three poems written in his own character, in the impassioned, lofty, and sustained diction, which is characteristic of his genius. In this form the "Lyrical Ballads" were published; and were presented by him, as an *experiment,* whether subjects, which from their nature rejected the usual ornaments and extra-colloquial style of poems in general, might not be so managed in the language of ordinary life as to produce the pleasureable interest, which it is the peculiar business of poetry to impart. To the second edition he added a preface of considerable length; in which, notwithstanding some passages of apparently a contrary import, he was understood to contend for the extension of this style to poetry of all kinds, and to reject as vicious and indefensible all phrases and forms of style that were not included in what he (unfortunately, I think, adopting an equivocal expression) called the language of *real* life. From this preface, prefixed to poems in which it was impossible to deny the presence of original genius, however mistaken its direction might be deemed, arose the whole long-continued controversy. For from the conjunction of perceived power with supposed heresy I explain the inveteracy and in some instances, I grieve to say, the acrimonious passions, with which the controversy has been conducted by the assailants.

Had Mr. Wordsworth's poems been the silly, the childish things, which they were for a long time described as being; had they been really distinguished from the compositions of other poets merely by meanness of language and inanity of thought; had they indeed contained nothing more than what is found in the parodies and pretended imitations of them; they must have sunk at once, a dead weight, into the slough of oblivion, and have dragged the preface along with them. But year after year increased the number of Mr. Wordsworth's admirers. They were found too not in the lower classes of the reading public, but chiefly among young men of strong sensibility and meditative minds; and their admiration (inflamed perhaps in some degree by opposition) was distinguished by its intensity, I might almost say, by its *religious* fervor. These facts, and the intellectual energy of the author, which was more or less consciously felt, where it was outwardly and even boisterously denied, meeting with sentiments of aversion to his opinions, and of alarm at their consequences, produced an eddy of criticism, which would of itself have borne up the poems by the violence, with which it whirled them round and round. With many parts of this preface, in the sense attributed to them, and which the words undoubtedly seem to authorize, I never concurred; but on the contrary objected to them as erroneous in principle, and as contradictory (in appearance at least) both to other parts of the same preface, and to the author's own practice in the greater number of the poems themselves. Mr. Wordsworth in his recent collection has, I find, degraded this prefatory disquisition to the end of his second volume, to be read or not at the reader's choice. But he has not, as far as I can discover, announced any change in his poetic creed. At all events, considering it as the source of a controversy, in which I have been honored more than I deserve by the frequent conjunction of my name with his, I think it expedient to declare once for all, in what points I coincide with his opinions, and in what points I altogether differ. But in order to render myself intelligible I must previously, in as few words as possible, explain my ideas, first, of a POEM; and secondly, of POETRY itself, in *kind,* and in *essence.*

The office of philosophical *disquisition* consists in just *distinction;* while it is the priviledge of the philosopher to preserve himself constantly aware, that distinction is not division. In order to obtain adequate notions of any truth, we must intellectually separate its distinguishable parts; and this is the technical *process* of philosophy. But having so done, we must then restore them in our conceptions to the unity, in which they actually co-exist; and this is the *result* of philosophy. A poem contains the same elements as a prose composition; the difference therefore must consist in a different combination of them, in consequence of a different object being proposed. According to the difference of the object will be the difference of the combination. It is possible, that the object may be merely to facilitate the recollection of any given facts or observations by artificial arrangement; and the composition will be a poem, merely because it is distinguished from prose by metre, or by rhyme, or by both conjointly. In this, the lowest sense, a man might attribute the name of a poem to the well known enumeration of the days in the several months;

> "Thirty days hath September,
> April, June, and November," &c.

and others of the same class and purpose. And as a particular pleasure is found in anticipating the recurrence of sounds and quantities, all compositions that have this charm super-added, whatever be their contents, *may* be entitled poems.

So much for the superficial *form.* A difference of object and contents supplies an additional ground of distinction. The immediate purpose may be the communication of truths; either of truth absolute and demonstrable, as in works of science; or of facts experienced and recorded, as in history. Pleasure, and that of the highest and most permanent kind, may *result* from the *attainment* of the end; but it is not itself the immediate end. In other works the communication of pleasure may be the immediate purpose; and though truth, either moral or intellectual, ought to be the *ultimate* end, yet this will distinguish the character of the author, not the class to which the work belongs. Blest indeed is that state of society, in which the immediate purpose would be baffled by the perversion of the proper ultimate end; in which no charm of diction or imagery could exempt the Bathyllus even of an Anacreon, or the Alexis of Virgil, from disgust and aversion!

But the communication of pleasure may be the immediate object of a work not metrically composed; and that object may have been in a high degree attained, as in novels and romances. Would then the mere superaddition of metre, with or without rhyme, entitle *these* to the name of poems? The answer is, that nothing can permanently please, which does not contain in itself the reason why it is so, and not otherwise. If metre be superadded, all other parts must be made consonant with it. They must be such, as to justify the perpetual and distinct attention to each part, which an exact correspondent recurrence of accent and sound are calculated to excite. The final definition then, so deduced, may be thus worded. A poem is that species of composition, which is opposed to works of science by proposing for its *immediate* object pleasure, not truth; and from all other species (having *this* object in common with it) it is discriminated by proposing to itself such delight from the *whole*, as is compatible with a distinct gratification from each component *part*.

Controversy is not seldom excited in consequence of the disputants attaching each a different meaning to the same word; and in few instances has this been more striking, than in disputes concerning the present subject. If a man chooses to call every composition a poem, which is in rhyme, or measure, or both, I must leave his opinion uncontroverted. The distinction is at least competent to characterize the writer's intention. If it were subjoined, that the whole is likewise entertaining or affecting, as a tale, or as a series of interesting reflections, I of course admit this as another fit ingredient of a poem, and an additional merit. But if the definition sought for be that of a *legitimate* poem, I answer, it must be one, the parts of which mutually support and explain each other; all in their proportion harmonizing with, and supporting the purpose and known influences of metrical arrangement. The philosophic critics of all ages coincide with the ultimate judgement of all countries, in equally denying the praises of a just poem, on the one hand, to a series of striking lines or distiches, each of which, absorbing the whole attention of the reader to itself, disjoins it from its context, and makes it a separate whole, instead of an harmonizing part; and on the other hand, to an unsustained composition, from which the reader collects rapidly the general result, unattracted by the component parts. The reader should be carried forward, not merely or chiefly by the mechanical impulse of curiosity, or by a restless desire to arrive at the final solution; but by the pleasureable activity of mind excited by the attractions of the journey itself. Like the motion of a serpent, which the Egyptians made the emblem of intellectual power; or like the path of sound through the air; at every step he pauses and half recedes, and from the retrogressive movement collects the force which again carries him onward. "Praecipitandus est *liber* spiritus,"[1] says Petronius Arbiter most happily. The epithet, *liber,* here balances the preceding verb; and it is not easy to conceive more meaning condensed in fewer words.

[1] "A free spirit should be cast down headlong." [All notes are Coleridge's. Ed.]

But if this should be admitted as a satisfactory character of a poem, we have still to seek for a definition of poetry. The writings of PLATO, and Bishop TAYLOR, and the "Theoria Sacra" of BURNET, furnish undeniable proofs that poetry of the highest kind may exist without metre, and even without the contra-distinguishing objects of a poem. The first chapter of Isaiah (indeed a very large portion of the whole book) is poetry in the most emphatic sense; yet it would be not less irrational than strange to assert, that pleasure, and not truth, was the immediate object of the prophet. In short, whatever *specific* import we attach to the word, poetry, there will be found involved in it, as a necessary consequence, that a poem of any length neither can be, or ought to be, all poetry. Yet if an harmonious whole is to be produced, the remaining parts must be preserved *in keeping* with the poetry; and this can be no otherwise effected than by such a studied selection and artificial arrangement, as will partake of *one,* though not a *peculiar* property of poetry. And this again can be no other than the property of exciting a more continuous and equal attention than the language of prose aims at, whether colloquial or written.

My own conclusions on the nature of poetry, in the strictest use of the word, have been in part anticipated in the preceding disquisition on the fancy and imagination.[2] What is poetry? is so nearly the same question with, what is a poet? that the answer to the one is involved in the solution of the other. For it is a distinction resulting from the poetic genius itself, which sustains and modifies the images, thoughts, and emotions of the poet's own mind.

The poet, described in *ideal* perfection, brings the whole soul of man into activity, with the subordination of its faculties to each other, according to their relative worth and dignity. He diffuses a tone and spirit of unity, that blends, and (as it were) *fuses,* each into each, by that synthetic and magical power, to which we have exclusively appropriated the name of imagination. This power, first put in action by the will and understanding, and retained under their irremissive, though gentle and unnoticed, control (*laxis effertur habenis*) reveals itself in the balance or reconciliation of opposite or discordant qualities: of sameness, with difference; of the general, with the concrete; the idea, with the image; the individual, with the representative; the sense of novelty and freshness, with old and familiar objects; a more than usual state of emotion, with more than usual order; judgement ever awake and steady self-possession, with enthusiasm and feeling profound or vehement; and while it blends and harmonizes the natural and the artificial, still subordinates art to nature; the manner to the matter; and our admiration of the poet to our sympathy with the poetry. "Doubtless," as Sir John Davies observes of the soul (and his words may with slight alteration be applied, and even more appropriately, to the poetic IMAGINATION)

"Doubtless this could not be, but that she turns
    Bodies to spirit by sublimation strange,
As fire converts to fire the things it burns,
    As we our food into our nature change.

[2] See the selection from Chapter XIII, following.

From their gross matter she abstracts their forms,
    And draws a kind of quintessence from things;
Which to her proper nature she transforms,
    To bear them light on her celestial wings.

Thus does she, when from individual states
    She doth abstract the universal kinds;
Which then re-clothed in divers names and fates
    Steal access through our senses to our minds."

Finally, GOOD SENSE is the body of poetic genius, FANCY its DRAPERY, MOTION its LIFE, and IMAGINATION the SOUL that is everywhere, and in each: and forms all into one graceful and intelligent whole.

From XIII

The IMAGINATION then, I consider either as primary, or secondary. The primary IMAGINATION I hold to be the living Power and prime Agent of all human Perception, and as a repetition in the finite mind of the eternal act of creation in the infinite I AM. The secondary Imagination I consider as an echo of the former, co-existing with the conscious will, yet still as identical with the primary in the *kind* of its agency, and differing only in *degree*, and in the *mode* of its operation. It dissolves, diffuses, dissipates, in order to recreate; or where this process is rendered impossible, yet still at all events it struggles to idealize and to unify. It is essentially *vital*, even as all objects (*as objects*) are essentially fixed and dead.

FANCY, on the contrary, has no other counters to play with, but fixities and definites. The Fancy is indeed no other than a mode of Memory emancipated from the order of time and space; while it is blended with, and modified by that empirical phenomenon of the will, which we express by the word CHOICE. But equally with the ordinary memory the Fancy must receive all its materials ready made from the law of association.

Whatever more than this, I shall think it fit to declare concerning the powers and privileges of the imagination in the present work, will be found in the critical essay on the uses of the Supernatural in poetry, and the principles that regulate its introduction: which the reader will find prefixed to the poem of "The Ancient Mariner."

XV

The specific symptoms of poetic power elucidated in a critical analysis of Shakespeare's "Venus and Adonis," and "Lucrece."

In the application of these principles to purposes of practical criticism as employed in the appraisal of works more or less imperfect, I have endeavoured to discover what the qualities in a poem are, which may be deemed promises and specific symptoms of poetic power, as distinguished from general talent determined to poetic composition by accidental motives, by an act of the will, rather than by the inspiration of a genial and productive nature. In this investigation, I could not, I thought, do better, than keep before me the earliest work of the greatest genius, that perhaps human nature has yet produced, our *myriad-minded* Shakespeare. I mean the "Venus and Adonis," and the "Lucrece"; works which give at once strong promises of the strength, and yet obvious proofs of the immaturity, of his genius. From these I abstracted the following marks, as characteristics of original poetic genius in general.

1. In the "Venus and Adonis," the first and most obvious excellence is the perfect sweetness of the versification; its adaptation to the subject; and the power displayed in varying the march of the words without passing into a loftier and more majestic rhythm than was demanded by the thoughts, or permitted by the propriety of preserving a sense of melody predominant. The delight in richness and sweetness of sound, even to a faulty excess, if it be evidently original, and not the result of an easily imitable mechanism, I regard as a highly favourable promise in the compositions of a young man. "The man that hath not music in his soul" can indeed never be a genuine poet. Imagery (even taken from nature, much more when transplanted from books, as travels, voyages, and works of natural history); affecting incidents; just thoughts; interesting personal or domestic feelings; and with these the art of their combination or intertexture in the form of a poem; may all by incessant effort be acquired as a trade, by a man of talents and much reading, who, as I once before observed, has mistaken an intense desire of poetic reputation for a natural poetic genius; the love of the arbitrary end for a possession of the peculiar means. But the sense of musical delight, with the power of producing it, is a gift of imagination; and this together with the power of reducing multitude into unity of effect, and modifying a series of thoughts by some one predominant thought or feeling, may be cultivated and improved, but can never be learned. It is in these that "poeta nascitur non fit."

2. A second promise of genius is the choice of subjects very remote from the private interests and circumstances of the writer himself. At least I have found, that where the subject is taken immediately from the author's personal sensations and experiences, the excellence of a particular poem is but an equivocal mark, and often a fallacious pledge, of genuine poetic power. We may perhaps remember the tale of the statuary, who had acquired considerable reputation for the legs of his goddesses, though the rest of the statue accorded but indifferently with ideal beauty; till his wife, elated by her husband's praises, modestly acknowledged that she herself had been his constant model. In the "Venus and Adonis" this proof of poetic power exists even to excess. It is throughout as if a superior spirit more intuitive, more intimately conscious, even than the characters themselves, not only of very outward look and act, but of the flux and reflux of the mind in all its subtlest thoughts and feelings, were placing the whole before our view; himself meanwhile unparticipating in the passions, and actuated only by that plea-

sureable excitement, which had resulted from the energetic fervor of his own spirit in so vividly exhibiting, what it had so accurately and profoundly contemplated. I think, I should have conjectured from these poems, that even then the great instinct, which impelled the poet to the drama, was secretly working in him, prompting him by a series and never broken chain of imagery, always vivid and, because unbroken, often minute; by the highest effort of the picturesque in words, of which words are capable, higher perhaps than was ever realized by any other poet, even Dante not excepted; to provide a substitute for that visual language, that constant intervention and running comment by tone, look and gesture, which in his dramatic works he was entitled to expect from the players. His "Venus and Adonis" seem at once the characters themselves, and the whole representation of those characters by the most consummate actors. You seem to be told nothing, but to see and hear everything. Hence it is, that from the perpetual activity of attention required on the part of the reader; from the rapid flow, the quick change, and the playful nature of the thoughts and images; and above all from the alienation, and, if I may hazard such an expression, the utter *aloofness* of the poet's own feelings, from those of which he is at once the painter and the analyst; that though the very subject cannot but detract from the pleasure of a delicate mind, yet never was poem less dangerous on a moral account. Instead of doing as Ariosto, and as, still more offensively, Wieland has done, instead of degrading and deforming passion into appetite, the trials of love into the struggles of concupiscence; Shakespeare has here represented the animal impulse itself, so as to preclude all sympathy with it, by dissipating the reader's notice among the thousand outward images, and now beautiful, now fanciful circumstances, which form its dresses and its scenery; or by diverting our attention from the main subject by those frequent witty or profound reflections, which the poet's ever active mind has deduced from, or connected with, the imagery and the incidents. The reader is forced into too much action to sympathize with the merely passive of our nature. As little can a mind thus roused and awakened be brooded on by mean and distinct emotion, as the low, lazy mist can creep upon the surface of a lake, while a strong gale is driving it onward in waves and billows.

3. It has been before observed that images, however beautiful, though faithfully copied from nature, and as accurately represented in words, do not of themselves characterize the poet. They become proofs of original genius only as far as they are modified by a predominant passion; or by associated thoughts or images awakened by that passion; or when they have the effect of reducing multitude to unity, or succession to an instant; or lastly, when a human and intellectual life is transferred to them from the poet's own spirit,

"Which shoots its being through earth, sea, and air."

In the two following lines for instance, there is nothing objectionable, nothing which would preclude them from forming, in their proper place, part of a descriptive poem:

"Behold yon row of pines, that shorn and bow'd
Bend from the sea-blast, seen at twilight eve."

But with a small alteration of rhythm, the same words would be equally in their place in a book of topography, or in a descriptive tour. The same image will rise into semblance of poetry if thus conveyed:

"Yon row of bleak and visionary pines,
By twilight glimpse discerned, mark! how they flee
From the fierce sea-blast, all their tresses wild
Streaming before them."

I have given this as an illustration, by no means as an instance, of that particular excellence which I had in view, and in which Shakespeare even in his earliest, as in his latest, works surpasses all other poets. It is by this, that he still gives a dignity and a passion to the objects which he presents. Unaided by any previous excitement, they burst upon us at once in life and in power.

"Full many a glorious morning have I seen
Flatter the mountain tops with sovereign eye."

Shakespeare, Sonnet 33rd.

"Not mine own fears, nor the prophetic soul
Of the wide world dreaming on things to come—

.   .   .   .

The mortal moon hath her eclipse endur'd,
And the sad augurs mock their own presage;
Incertainties now crown themselves assur'd,
And Peace proclaims olives of endless age.
Now with the drops of this most balmy time
My Love looks fresh, and DEATH to me subscribes!
Since spite of him, I'll live in this poor rhyme,
While he insults o'er dull and speechless tribes.
And thou in this shalt find thy monument,
When tyrants' crests, and tombs of brass are spent."

Sonnet 107.

As of higher worth, so doubtless still more characteristic of poetic genius does the imagery become, when it moulds and colors itself to the circumstances, passion, or character, present and foremost in the mind. For unrivalled instances of this excellence, the reader's own memory will refer him to the LEAR, OTHELLO, in short to which not of the *"great, ever living, dead man's"* dramatic works? "Inopem me copia fecit."[3] How true it is to nature, he has himself finely expressed in the instance of love in Sonnet 98.

"From you have I been absent in the spring,
When proud pied April drest in all its trim

---

[3] Wealth has rendered me poor.

Hath put a spirit of youth in every thing,
That heavy Saturn laugh'd and leap'd with him.
Yet nor the lays of birds, nor the sweet smell
Of different flowers in odour and in hue,
Could make me any summer's story tell,
Or from their proud lap pluck them, where they grew:
Nor did I wonder at the lilies white,
Nor praise the deep vermilion in the rose;
They were, tho' sweet, but figures of delight,
Drawn after you, you pattern of all those.
Yet seem'd it winter still, and, you away,
As with your shadow I with these did play!"

Scarcely less sure, or if a less valuable, not less indispensable mark

Γονίμου μὲν ποιητοῦ——
——ὅστις ῥῆμα γενναῖον λάκοι,[4]

will the imagery supply, when, with more than the power of the painter, the poet gives us the liveliest image of succession with the feeling of simultaneousness!

"With this, he breaketh from the sweet embrace
Of those fair arms, that held him to her heart,
And homeward through the dark lawns runs apace:
Look! How a bright star shooteth from the sky,
So glides he in the night from Venus' eye."

4. The last character I shall mention, which would prove indeed but little, except as taken conjointly with the former; yet without which the former could scarce exist in a high degree, and (even if this were possible) would give promises only of transitory flashes and a meteoric power; is DEPTH, and ENERGY of THOUGHT. No man was ever yet a great poet, without being at the same time a profound philosopher. For poetry is the blossom and the fragrancy of all human knowledge, human thoughts, human passions, motions, language. In Shakespeare's *poems* the creative power and the intellectual energy wrestle as in a war embrace. Each in its excess of strength seems to threaten the extinction of the other. At length in the DRAMA they were reconciled, and fought each with its shield before the breast of the other. Or like two rapid streams, that, at their first meeting within narrow and rocky banks, mutually strive to repel each other and intermix reluctantly and in tumult; but soon finding a wider channel and more yielding shores blend, and dilate, and flow on in one current and with one voice. The "Venus and Adonis" did not perhaps allow the display of the deeper passions. But the story of Lucretia seems to favor and even demand their intensest

---

[4] *Gonimou men poietou—ostis rema gennaion lakoi.* A creative poet . . . who gives vent to a single noble thought.

workings. And yet we find in *Shakespeare's* management of the tale neither pathos, nor any other *dramatic* quality. There is the same minute and faithful imagery as in the former poem, in the same vivid colors, inspirited by the same impetuous vigor of thought, and diverging and contracting with the same activity of the assimilative and of the modifying faculties; and with a yet larger display, a yet wider range of knowledge and reflection; and lastly, with the same perfect dominion, often *domination,* over the whole world of language. What then shall we say? even this; that Shakespeare, no mere child of nature; no automaton of genius; no passive vehicle of inspiration possessed by the spirit, not possessing it; first studied patiently, meditated deeply, understood minutely, till knowledge, become habitual and intuitive, wedded itself to his habitual feelings, and at length gave birth to that stupendous power, by which he stands alone, with no equal or second in his own class; to that power which seated him on one of the two glory-smitten summits of the poetic mountain, with Milton as his compeer, not rival. While the former darts himself forth, and passes into all the forms of human character and passion, the one Proteus of the fire and the flood; the other attracts all forms and things to himself, into the unity of his own IDEAL. All things and modes of action shape themselves anew in the being of MILTON; while SHAKESPEARE becomes all things, yet for ever remaining himself. O what great men hast thou not produced, England! my country! truly indeed—

> "Must *we* be free or die, who speak the tongue,
> Which SHAKESPEARE spake; the faith and morals hold,
> Which MILTON held. In every thing we are sprung
> Of earth's first blood, have titles manifold!"

WORDSWORTH.

XVII

Examination of the tenets peculiar to Mr. Wordsworth—Rustic life (above all, low and rustic life) especially unfavorable to the formation of a human diction—The best parts of language the product of philosophers, not of clowns or shepherds—Poetry essentially ideal and generic—The language of Milton as much the language of real life, yea, incomparably more so than that of the cottager.

As far then as Mr. Wordsworth in his preface contended, and most ably contended, for a reformation in our poetic diction, as far as he has evinced the truth of passion, and the *dramatic* propriety of those figures and metaphors in the original poets, which, stripped of their justifying reasons, and converted into mere artifices of connection or ornament, constitute the characteristic falsity in the poetic style of the moderns; and as far as he has, with equal acuteness and clearness, pointed out the process by which this change was effected, and the resemblances between that state into which the reader's mind is thrown by the pleasureable confusion of thought from an unaccustomed train of words and images; and that state which is induced by the natural language of empassioned feeling; he undertook a useful task, and deserves all praise, both for the attempt and for the execution. The provocations to this remonstrance in behalf of truth and nature were still of perpetual recurrence before and after the publication of this preface. I cannot likewise but add, that the comparison of such poems of merit, as have been given to the public within the last ten or twelve years, with the majority of those produced previously to the appearance of that preface, leave no doubt on my mind, that Mr. Wordsworth is fully justified in believing his efforts to have been by no means ineffectual. Not only in the verses of those who have professed their admiration of his genius, but even of those who have distinguished themselves by hostility to his theory, and depreciation of his writings, are the impressions of his principles plainly visible. It is possible, that with these principles others may have been blended, which are not equally evident; and some which are unsteady and subvertible from the narrowness or imperfection of their basis. But it is more than possible, that these errors of defect or exaggeration, by kindling and feeding the controversy, may have conduced not only to the wider propagation of the accompanying truths, but that, by their frequent presentation to the mind in an excited state, they may have won for them a more permanent and practical result. A man will borrow a part from his opponent the more easily, if he feels himself justified in continuing to reject a part. While there remain important points in which he can still feel himself in the right, in which he still finds firm footing for continued resistance, he will gradually adopt those opinions, which were the least remote from his own convictions, as not less congruous with his own theory than with that which he reprobates. In like manner with a kind of instinctive prudence, he will abandon by little and little his weakest posts, till at length he seems to forget that they had ever belonged to him, or affects to consider them at most as accidental and "petty annexments," the removal of which leaves the citadel unhurt and unendangered.

My own differences from certain supposed parts of Mr. Wordsworth's theory ground themselves on the assumption that his words had been rightly interpreted, as purporting that the proper diction for poetry in general consists altogether in a language taken, with due exceptions, from the mouths of men in real life, a language which actually constitutes the natural conversation of men under the influence of natural feelings. My objection is, first, that in *any* sense this rule is applicable only to *certain* classes of poetry; secondly, that even to these classes it is not applicable, except in such a sense, as hath never by any one (as far as I know or have read) been denied or doubted; and lastly, that as far as, and in that degree in which it is *practicable,* yet as a *rule* it is useless if not injurious, and therefore either need not, or ought not to be practised. The poet informs his reader, that he had generally chosen *low and rustic* life; but not *as* low and rustic, or in order to repeat that pleasure of doubtful moral effect, which persons of elevated rank and of superior refinement oftentimes derive from a happy *imitation* of the rude unpolished manners and discourse of their inferiors. For the pleasure so derived may be traced to three exciting causes. The first is the naturalness, in *fact*, of the things represented. The second is the apparent naturalness of the *representation*, as raised and qualified by an imperceptible infusion of the author's own knowledge and talent, which infusion does, indeed, constitute it an *imitation* as distinguished from a mere *copy*. The third cause may be found in the reader's conscious feeling of his superiority awakened by the contrast presented to him; even as for the same purpose the kings and great barons of yore retained sometimes *actual* clowns and fools, but more frequently shrewd and witty fellows in that *character*. These, however, were not Mr. Wordsworth's objects. He chose low and rustic life, "because in that condition the essential passions of the heart find a better soil, in which they can attain their maturity, are less under restraint, and speak a plainer and more emphatic language; because in that condition of life our elementary feelings coexist in a state of greater simplicity, and consequently may be more accurately contemplated, and more forcibly communicated; because the manners of rural life germinate from those elementary feelings; and from the necessary character of rural occupations are more easily comprehended, and are more durable; and lastly, because in that condition the passions of men are incorporated with the beautiful and permanent forms of nature."

Now it is clear to me, that in the most interesting of the poems, in which the author is more or less dramatic, as "the Brothers," "Michael," "Ruth," "the Mad Mother," &c., the persons introduced are by no means taken *from low or rustic life* in the common acceptation of those words; and it is not less clear, that the sentiments and languages, as far as they can be conceived to have been really transferred from the minds and conversation of such persons, are attributable to causes and circumstances not necessarily connected with "their occupations and abode." The thoughts, feelings, language, and manner of the shepherd-farmers in the vales of Cumberland and Westmoreland, as far as they are actually adopted in those poems, may be accounted for from causes, which will and do produce the same results in *every* state of life, whether in town or country. As the two principal I rank that INDEPENDENCE, which raises a man above servitude, or daily toil for the profit of others, yet not above the necessity of industry and a frugal simplicity of domestic life; and the accompanying unambitious, but solid and religious, EDUCATION, which has rendered few books familiar, but the Bible, and the liturgy or hymn book. To this latter cause, indeed, which is so far *accidental*, that it is the blessing of particular countries and a particular age, not the product of particular places or employments, the poet owes the show of probability, that his personages might really feel, think, and talk with any tolerable resemblance to his representation. It is an excellent remark of Dr. Henry More's, (Enthusiasmus triumphatus, Sec. XXXV), that "a man of confined education, but of good parts, by constant reading of the Bible will naturally form a more winning and commanding rhetoric than those that are learned; the intermixture of tongues and of artificial phrases debasing *their* style."

It is, moreover, to be considered that to the formation of healthy feelings, and a reflecting mind, *negations* involve impediments not less formidable than sophistication and vicious intermixture. I am convinced, that for the human soul to prosper in rustic life a certain vantage-ground is pre-requisite. It is not every man that is likely to be improved by a country life or by country labors. Education, or original sensibility, or both, must pre-exist, if the changes, forms, and incidents of nature are to prove a sufficient stimulant. And where these are not sufficient, the mind contracts and hardens by want of stimulants: and the man becomes selfish, sensual, gross, and hard-hearted. Let the management of the POOR LAWS in Liverpool, Manchester, or Bristol be compared with the ordinary dispensation of the poor rates in agricultural villages, where the *farmers* are the overseers and guardians of the poor. If my own experience had not been particularly unfortunate, as well as that of the many respectable country clergymen with whom I have conversed on the subject, the result would engender more than scepticism concerning the desireable influences of low and rustic life in and for itself. Whatever may be concluded on the other side, from the stronger local attachments and enterprising spirit of the Swiss, and other mountaineers, applies to a particular mode of pastoral life, under forms of property that permit and beget manners truly republican, not to rustic life in general, or to the absence of artificial cultivation. On the contrary the mountaineers, whose manners have been so often eulogized, are in general better educated and greater readers than men of equal rank elsewhere. But where this is not the case, as among the peasantry of North Wales, the ancient mountains, with all their terrors and all their glories, are pictures to the blind, and music to the deaf.

I should not have entered so much into detail upon this passage, but here seems to be the point, to which all the lines of difference converge as to their source and centre. (I mean, as far as, and in whatever respect, my poetic creed *does* differ from the doctrines promulged in this preface.) I adopt with full faith the principle of Aristotle, that poetry as poetry is essentially[5] *ideal*,

---

[5] Say not that I am recommending abstractions; for these class-characteristics which constitute the instructiveness of a character, are so modified and particularized in each person of the Shakespearean Drama, that life itself does not excite more distinctly that sense of individuality which belongs to real existence. Paradoxical as it may sound, one of the essential properties of Geometry is not less essential to dramatic excellence; and Aristotle has accordingly required of the poet an involution of the universal in the individual. The chief differences are, that in Geometry it is the universal truth, which is uppermost in the consciousness; in poetry the individual form, in which the truth is clothed. With the ancients, and not less with the elder dramatists of England and France, both comedy and tragedy were considered as kinds of poetry. They neither sought in comedy to make us laugh merely; much less to make us laugh by wry faces, accidents of jargon, *slang* phrases for the day, or the clothing of common-place morals drawn from the shops or mechanic occupations of their characters. Nor did they condescend in tragedy to wheedle away the applause of the spectators, by representing before them facsimiles of their own mean selves in all their existing meanness, or to work on the sluggish sympathies by a pathos not a whit more respectable than the maudlin tears of drunkenness. Their tragic scenes were meant to *affect* us indeed; but yet within the bounds of pleasure, and in union with the activity both of our understanding and imagination. They wished to transport the mind to a sense of its possible greatness, and to implant the germs of that greatness, during the temporary oblivion of the worthless "thing we are," and of the peculiar state in which each man *happens* to be, suspending our individual recollections and lulling them to sleep amid the music of nobler thoughts.

FRIEND, Pages 251, 252.

that it avoids and excludes all *accident*; that its apparent individualities of rank, character, or occupation must be *representative* of a class; and that the *persons* of poetry must be clothed with *generic* attributes, with the *common* attributes of the class: not with such as one gifted individual might *possibly* possess, but such as from his situation it is most probable before-hand that he *would* possess. If my premises are right and my deductions legitimate, it follows that there can be no *poetic* medium between the swains of Theocritus and those of an imaginary golden age.

The characters of the vicar and the shepherd-mariner in the poem of "The Brothers," that of the shepherd of Greenhead Ghyll in the "MICHAEL," have all the verisimilitude and representative quality, that the purposes of poetry can require. They are persons of a known and abiding class, and their manners and sentiments the natural product of circumstances common to the class. Take "MICHAEL" for instance:

"An old man stout of heart, and strong of limb:
His bodily frame had been from youth to age
Of an unusual strength: his mind was keen,
Intense, and frugal, apt for all affairs,
And in his shepherd's calling he was prompt
And watchful more than ordinary men.
Hence he had learnt the meaning of all winds,
Of blasts of every tone; and oftentimes
When others heeded not, he heard the South
Make subterraneous music, like the noise
Of bagpipers on distant Highland hills.
The shepherd, at such warning, of his flock
Bethought him, and he to himself would say,
The winds are now devising work for me!
And truly at all times the storm, that drives
The traveller to a shelter, summon'd him
Up to the mountains. He had been alone
Amid the heart of many thousand mists,
That came to him and left him on the heights.
So liv'd he, till his eightieth year was pass'd.
And grossly that man errs, who should suppose
That the green vallies, and the streams and rocks,
Were things indifferent to the shepherd's thoughts.
Fields, where with chearful spirits he had breath'd
The common air; the hills, which he so oft
Had climb'd with vigorous steps; which had impress'd
So many incidents upon his mind
Of hardship, skill or courage, joy or fear;
Which, like a book, preserved the memory
Of the dumb animals, whom he had sav'd,
Had fed or shelter'd, linking to such acts,

So grateful in themselves, the certainty
Of honorable gain; these fields, these hills
Which were his living being, even more
Than his own blood — what could they less?   had laid
Strong hold on his affections, were to him
A pleasureable feeling of blind love,
The pleasure which there is in life itself."

On the other hand, in the poems which are pitched at a lower note, as the "HARRY GILL," "IDIOT BOY," the *feelings* are those of human nature in general; though the poet has judiciously laid the *scene* in the country, in order to place *himself* in the vicinity of interesting images, without the necessity of ascribing a sentimental perception of their beauty to the persons of his drama. In the "Idiot Boy," indeed, the mother's character is not so much a real and native product of a "situation where the essential passions of the heart find a better soil, in which they can attain their maturity and speak a plainer and more emphatic language," as it is an impersonation of an instinct abandoned by judgement. Hence the two following charges seem to me not wholly ground-less: at least, they are the only plausible objections, which I have heard to that fine poem. The one is, that the author has not, in the poem itself, taken suffi-cient care to preclude from the reader's fancy the disgusting images of *ordi-nary morbid idiocy*, which yet it was by no means his intention to represent. He has even by the "burr, burr, burr," uncounteracted by any preceding de-scription of the boy's beauty, assisted in recalling them. The other is, that the idiocy of the *boy* is so evenly balanced by the folly of the *mother*, as to pre-sent to the general reader rather a laughable burlesque on the blindness of anile dotage, than an analytic display of maternal affection in its ordinary workings.

In the "Thorn" the poet himself acknowledges in a note the necessity of an introductory poem, in which he should have portrayed the character of the person from whom the words of the poem are supposed to proceed: a su-perstitious man moderately imaginative, of slow faculties and deep feelings, "a captain of a small trading vessel, for example, who, being past the middle age of life, had retired upon an annuity, or small independent income, to some village or country town of which he was not a native, or in which he had not been accustomed to live. Such men having nothing to do become credulous and talkative from indolence." But in a poem, still more in a lyric poem (and the NURSE in Shakespeare's Romeo and Juliet alone prevents me from extending the remark even to dramatic *poetry*, if indeed the Nurse itself can be deemed altogether a case in point) it is not possible to imitate truly a dull and garrulous discourser, without repeating the effects of dullness and garrulity. However this may be, I dare assert, that the parts (and these form the far larger portion of the whole) which might as well or still better have proceeded from the poet's own imagination, and have been spoken in his own character, are those which have given, and which will continue to give, universal delight; and that the passages exclusively appropriate to the supposed narrator, such as the last couplet of the third stanza;⁶ the seven last lines of the tenth;⁷ and the five following stanzas, with the exception of the four admirable lines at the commencement of the fourteenth, are felt by many unprejudiced and unsophisticated hearts, as sudden and unpleasant sinkings from the height to which the poet had previously lifted them, and to which he again re-elevates both himself and his reader.

⁶ I've measured it from side to side;
　'Tis three feet long, and two feet wide.
⁷ Nay, rack your brain—'tis all in vain,
　I'll tell you every thing I know;
　But to the Thorn, and to the Pond
　Which is a little step beyond,
　I wish that you would go:
　Perhaps when you are at the place,
　You something of her tale may trace.
　I'll give you the best help I can:
　Before you up the mountain go,
　Up to the dreary mountain-top,
　I'll tell you all I know.
　'Tis now some two-and-twenty years
　Since she (her name is Martha Ray)
　Gave, with a maiden's true good will,
　Her company to Stephen Hill;
　And she was blithe and gay,
　And she was happy, happy still
　Whene'er she thought of Stephen Hill.

　And they had fix'd the wedding-day,
　The morning that must wed them both;
　But Stephen to another maid
　Had sworn another oath;
　And, with this other maid, to church
　Unthinking Stephen went—
　Poor Martha! on that woeful day
　A pang of pitiless dismay
　Into her soul was sent;
　A fire was kindled in her breast,

　Which might not burn itself to rest.
　They say, full six months after this,
　While yet the summer leaves were green,
　She to the mountain-top would go,
　And there was often seen.
　'Tis said a child was in her womb,
　As now to any eye was plain;
　She was with child, and she was mad;
　Yet often she was sober sad
　From her exceeding pain.
　Oh me! ten thousand times I'd rather
　That he had died, that cruel father!

　Last Christmas when we talked of this,
　Old farmer Simpson did maintain,
　That in her womb the infant wrought
　About its mother's heart, and brought
　Her senses back again:
　And, when at last her time drew near,
　Her looks were calm, her senses clear.

If then I am compelled to doubt the theory, by which the choice of *characters* was to be directed, not only *a priori*, from grounds of reason, but both from the few instances in which the poet himself *need* be supposed to have been governed by it, and from the comparative inferiority of those instances; still more must I hesitate in my assent to the sentence which immediately follows the former citation; and which I can neither admit as particular fact, or as general rule. "The language too of these men is adopted (purified indeed from what appear to be its real defects, from all lasting and rational causes of dislike or disgust) because such men hourly communicate with the best objects from which the best part of language is originally derived; and because, from their rank in society and the sameness and narrow circle of their intercourse, being less under the action of social vanity, they convey their feelings and notions in simple and unelaborated expressions." To this I reply; that a rustic's language, purified from all provincialism and grossness, and so far reconstructed as to be made consistent with the rules of grammar (which are in essence no other than the laws of universal logic, applied to psychological materials) will not differ from the language of any other man of common-sense, however learned or refined he may be, except as far as the notions, which the rustic has to convey, are fewer and more indiscriminate. This will become still clearer, if we add the consideration (equally important though less obvious) that the rustic, from the more imperfect development of his faculties, and from the lower state of their cultivation, aims almost solely to convey *insulated facts,* either those of his scanty experience or his traditional belief; while the educated man chiefly seeks to discover and express those *connections* of things, or those relative *bearings* of fact to fact, from which some more or less general law is deducible. For *facts* are valuable to a wise man, chiefly as they lead to the discovery of the indwelling *law,* which is the true *being* of things, the sole solution of their modes of existence, and in the knowledge of which consists our dignity and our power.

As little can I agree with the assertion, that from the objects with which the rustic hourly communicates the best part of language is formed. For first, if to communicate with an object implies such an acquaintance with it, as renders it capable of being discriminately reflected on; the distinct knowledge of an uneducated rustic would furnish a very scanty vocabulary. The few things, and modes of action, requisite for his bodily conveniences, would

---

No more I know, I wish I did,
And I would tell it all to you:
For what became of this poor child
There's none that ever knew:
And if a child was born or no,
There's no one that could ever tell;
And if 'twas born alive or dead,
There's no one knows, as I have said:
But some remember well,
That Martha Ray about this time
Would up the mountain often climb.

alone be individualized; while all the rest of nature would be expressed by a small number of confused general terms. Secondly, I deny that the words and combinations of words derived from the objects, with which the rustic is familiar, whether with distinct or confused knowledge, can be justly said to form the *best* part of language. It is more than probable, that many classes of the brute creation possess discriminating sounds, by which they can convey to each other notices of such objects as concern their food, shelter, or safety. Yet we hesitate to call the aggregate of such sounds a language, otherwise than metaphorically. The best part of human language, properly so called, is derived from reflection on the acts of the mind itself. It is formed by a voluntary appropriation of fixed symbols to internal acts, to processes and results of imagination, the greater part of which have no place in the consciousness of uneducated man; though in civilized society, by imitation and passive remembrance of what they hear from their religious instructors and other superiors, the most uneducated share in the harvest which they neither sowed or reaped. If the history of the phrases in hourly currency among our peasants were traced, a person not previously aware of the fact would be surprised at finding so large a number, which three or four centuries ago were the exclusive property of the universities and the schools; and, at the commencement of the Reformation, had been transferred from the school to the pulpit, and thus gradually passed into common life. The extreme difficulty, and often the impossibility, of finding words for the simplest moral and intellectual processes of the languages of uncivilized tribes has proved perhaps the weightiest obstacle to the progress of our most zealous and adroit missionaries. Yet these tribes are surrounded by the same nature as our peasants are; but in still more impressive forms; and they are, moreover, obliged to *particularize* many more of them. When, therefore, Mr. Wordsworth adds, "accordingly, such a language" (meaning, as before, the language of rustic life purified from provincialism) "arising out of repeated experience and regular feelings, is a more permanent, and a far more philosophical language, than that which is frequently substituted for it by poets, who think they are conferring honor upon themselves and their art in proportion as they indulge in arbitrary and capricious habits of expression:" it may be answered, that the language, which he has in view, can be attributed to rustics with no greater right, than the style of Hooker or Bacon to Tom Brown or Sir Roger L'Estrange. Doubtless, if what is peculiar to each were omitted in each, the result must needs be the same. Further, that the poet, who uses an illogical diction, or a style fitted to excite only the low and changeable pleasure of wonder by means of groundless novelty, substitutes a language of *folly* and *vanity*, not for that of the *rustic*, but for that of *good* sense and *natural feeling.*

Here let me be permitted to remind the reader, that the positions, which I controvert, are contained in the sentences—"*a selection of the* REAL *language of men;*"—"*the language of these men*" (i.e., men in low and rustic life) "*I propose to myself to imitate, and, as far as is possible, to adopt the very language of men.*" "*Between the language of prose and that of metrical composition, there neither is, nor can be any essential difference.*" It is against these exclusively that my opposition is directed.

I object, in the very first instance, to an equivocation in the use of the word "real." Every man's language varies, according to the extent of his knowledge, the activity of his faculties, and the depth or quickness of his feelings. Every man's language has, first, its *individualities;* secondly, the common properties of the *class* to which he belongs; and thirdly, words and phrases of *universal* use. The language of Hooker, Bacon, Bishop Taylor, and Burke differs from the common language of the learned class only by the superior number and novelty of the thoughts and relations which they had to convey. The language of Algernon Sidney differs not at all from that, which every well-educated gentleman would wish to write, and (with due allowances for the undeliberateness, and less connected train, of thinking natural and proper to conversation) such as he would wish to talk. Neither one nor the other differ half so much from the general language of cultivated society, as the language of Mr. Wordsworth's homeliest composition differs from that of a common peasant. For "real" therefore, we must substitute *ordinary,* or *lingua communis.* And this, we have proved is no more to be found in the phraseology of low and rustic life than in that of any other class. Omit the peculiarities of each, and the result of course must be common to all. And assuredly the omissions and changes to be made in the language of rustics, before it could be transferred to any species of poem, except the drama or other professed imitation, are at least as numerous and weighty, as would be required in adapting to the same purpose the ordinary language of tradesmen and manufactures. Not to mention, that the language so highly extolled by Mr. Wordsworth varies in every county, nay in every village, according to the accidental character of the clergyman, the existence or non-existence of schools; or even, perhaps, as the exciseman, publican, or barber, happen to be, or not to be, zealous politicians, and readers of the weekly newspaper *pro bono publico.* Anterior to cultivation, the lingua communis of every country, as Dante has well observed, exists every where in parts, and no where as a whole.

Neither is the case rendered at all more tenable by the addition of the words, *in a state of excitement.* For the nature of a man's words, where he is strongly affected by joy, grief, or anger, must necessarily depend on the number and quality of the general truths, conceptions and images, and of the words expressing them, with which his mind had been previously stored. For the property of passion is not to *create;* but to set in increased activity. At least, whatever new connections of thoughts or images, or (which is equally, if not more than equally, the appropriate effect of strong excitement) whatever generalizations of truth or experience, the heat of passion may produce; yet the terms of their conveyance must have pre-existed in his former conversations, and are only collected and crowded together by the unusual stimulation. It is indeed very possible to adopt in a poem the unmeaning repetitions, habitual phrases, and other blank counters, which an unfurnished or confused understanding interposes at short intervals, in order to keep hold of his subject which is still slipping from him, and to give him time for recollection; or in mere aid of vacancy, as in the scanty companies of a country stage the same player pops backwards and forwards, in order to prevent the appearance of empty spaces, in the procession of Macbeth, or Henry VIIIth. But what assistance to the poet, or ornament to the poem, these can supply, I am at a loss to conjecture. Nothing assuredly can differ either in origin or in mode more widely from the *apparent* tautologies of intense and turbulent feeling, in which the passion is greater and of longer endurance than to be exhausted or satisfied by a single representation of the image or incident exciting it. Such repetitions I admit to be a beauty of the highest kind; as illustrated by Mr. Wordsworth himself from the song of Deborah. *"At her feet he bowed, he fell, he lay down; at her feet he bowed, he fell; where he bowed, there he fell down dead."*

John Keats

Four Letters

1817–1818

What is the poetical "self"? How does the poet differ from other people? Is the poet's poetry only the expression of that self? The twenty-two-year-old John Keats (1795–1821), at the threshold of his most productive poetic year, had a head full of ideas about the poetic character, the creative process, the nature of the imagination, and the meaning of beauty—ideas that came tumbling out in a disorganized fashion in a series of personal letters to friends and family. These are not essayistic letters written with a larger audience in mind. Reading Keats, we sense the pressure and the feverishness of an excited young poet scribbling about personal matters and gossip but unable to keep his ideas on poetry from forcing their way through. We see Keats observing himself in the process of forming his own conclusions, the most notable instance in Letter 45. Notice how his various activities, culminating in a fashionable dinner party, make things "dovetail" in his mind.

The true poet has no identity and no nature; "he is certainly the most unpoetical of all God's creatures," Keats declares. The poetical character "is every thing and nothing." Seeing the sparrow picking at the gravel, a poet feels himself becoming that sparrow through an empathetic identification: and he delights "in conceiving an Iago as an Imogen" (allusions to a Shakespearean villain and heroine). But to achieve these feats of the imagination one must possess Negative Capability, which is the central concept in Keats's definition of the poet: the faculty of not having to force one's observations into doctrinaire systems, philosophies, or opinions. Nor must a poet allow ego to interfere with sensations; Keats everywhere rejects the ego in art, as in the "wordsworthian or egotistical sublime." (Elsewhere, he objects to being "bullied into a certain Philosophy engendered in the whims of an Egotist"—Wordsworth again.) Truth is attained not by thought or logic but by the "silent working" of the imagination; what it "seizes as Beauty must be truth." Keats uses the paradoxical phrase "diligent indolence" to refer to the necessary receptivity and openness to experience that marks a great writer like Shakespeare, whose own ego is nowhere to be found in his works.

We speak today of cognitive and affective ways of learning, a distinction that Keats seems to be making when he exclaims (Letter 43), "O for a Life of Sensations

279

*rather than of Thoughts!" It is worthwhile to raise the issue of whether Keats's posi-
tion is, fundamentally, an anti-intellectual one.*

Letter 43.　　To Benjamin Bailey.　　22 November 1817

MY DEAR BAILEY,

I will get over the first part of this (*un*said)[1] Letter as soon as possible for
it relates to the affair of poor Crips—To a Man of your nature, such a Letter
as Haydon's must have been extremely cutting—What occasions the greater
part of the World's Quarrels? simply this, two Minds meet and do not understand each other time enough to p[r]aevent[2] any shock or surprise at the conduct of either party—As soon as I had known Haydon three days I had got
enough of his character not to have been surp[r]ised at such a Letter as he has
hurt you with. Nor when I knew it was it a principle with me to drop his acquaintance although with you it would have been an imperious feeling. I
wish you knew all that I think about Genius and the Heart—and yet I think
you are thoroughly acquainted with my innermost breast in that respect or
you could not have known me even thus long and still hold me worthy to be
your dear friend. In passing however I must say of one thing that has pressed
upon me lately and encreased my Humility and capability of submission and
that is this truth—Men of Genius are great as certain ethereal Chemicals operating on the Mass of neutral intellect—by[3] they have not any individuality,
any determined Character. I would call the top and head of those who have a
proper self Men of Power—

But I am running my head into a Subject[4] which I am certain I could not
do justice to under five years s[t]udy and 3 vols octavo—and moreover long
to be talking about the Imagination—so my dear Bailey do not think of this
unpleasant affair if possible—do not—I defy any ha[r]m to come of it—I
defy—I'll shall write to Crips this Week and reque[s]t him to tell me all his
goings on from time to time by Letter wherever I may be—it will all go on
well—so don't because you have suddenly discover'd a Coldness in Haydon
suffer yourself to be teased. Do not my dear fellow. O I wish I was as certain
of the end of all your troubles as that of your momentary start about the authenticity of the Imagination. I am certain of nothing but of the holiness of
the Heart's affections and the truth of Imagination—What the imagination
seizes as Beauty must be truth—whether it existed before or not—for I have
the same Idea of all our Passions as of Love they are all in their sublime, creative of essential Beauty—In a Word, you may know my favorite Specula-

[1] A pun on the legal use of "said": " 'This said letter' . . . would be Haydon's to Bailey:
'this *un*said letter' " the present one.

[2] Letters in brackets indicate an addition by Hyder E. Rollins, the editor of *The Letters of
John Keats, 1814–1821,* to clarify Keats's spelling.

[3] *For* but.

[4] See Letter 118.

tion by my first Book and the little song I sent in my last—which is a representation from the fancy of the probable mode of operating in these Matters—The Imagination may be compared to Adam's dream—he awoke and
found it truth. I am the more zealous in this affair, because I have never yet
been able to perceive how any thing can be known for truth by consequitive
reasoning—and yet it must be—Can it be that even the greatest Philosopher
ever <when>[5] arrived at his goal without putting aside numerous objections—However it may be, O for a Life of Sensations rather than of
Thoughts! It is 'a Vision in the form of Youth' a Shadow of reality to
come—and this consideration has further conv[i]nced me for it has come as
auxiliary to another favorite Speculation of mine, that we shall enjoy ourselves here after by having what we called happiness on Earth repeated in a
finer tone and so repeated—And yet such a fate can only befall those who
delight in sensation rather than hunger as you do after Truth—Adam's
dream will do here and seems to be a conviction that Imagination and its
empyreal reflection is the same as human Life and its spiritual repetition. But
as I was saying—the simple imaginative Mind may have its rewards in the
repeti[ti]on of its own silent Working coming continually on the spirit with a
fine suddenness—to compare great things with small—have you never by
being surprised with an old Melody—in a delicious place—by a delicious
voice, fe[l]t over again your very speculations and surmises at the time it first
operated on your soul—do you not remember forming to yourself the
singer's face more beautiful that[6] it was possible and yet with the elevation of
the Moment you did not think so—even then you were mounted on the
Wings of Imagination so high—that the Prototype must be here after—that
delicious face you will see—What a time! I am continually running away
from the subject—sure this cannot be exactly the case with a complex
Mind—one that is imaginative and at the same time careful of its
fruits—who would exist partly on sensation partly on thought—to whom it
is necessary that years should bring the philosophic Mind—such an one I
consider your's and therefore it is necessary to your

drink

eternal Happiness that you not only <have> this old Wine of Heaven which I
shall call the redigestion of our most ethereal Musings on Earth; but also increase in knowledge and know all things. I am glad to hear you are in a fair
Way for Easter—you will soon get through your unpleasant reading and
then!—but the world is full of troubles and I have not much reason to think
myself pestered with many—I think Jane or Marianne has a better opinion of
me than I deserve—for really and truly I do not think my Brothers illness connected with mine—you know more of the real Cause than they do—nor have
I any chance of being rack'd as you have been—you perhaps at one time
thought there was such a thing as Worldly Happiness to be arrived at, at certain

---

[5]<...> indicates a word struck through by Keats. [...] indicates an editorial addition by
Rollins to clarify words.
   [6]*For* than.

[margin handwritten notes: seeking sensations rather than thoughts or truths or expectations]

periods of time marked out—you have of necessity from your disposition been thus led away—I scarcely remember counting upon any Happiness—I look not for it if it be not in the present hour—nothing startles me beyond the Moment. The setting sun will always set me to rights—or if a Sparrow come before my Window I take part in its existence and pick about the Gravel. The first think that strikes me on hea[r]ing a Misfortune having befalled another is this 'Well it cannot be helped.—he will have the pleasure of trying the resources of his spirit, and I beg now my dear Bailey that hereafter should you observe any thing cold in me not to but[7] it to the account of heartlessness but abstraction—for I assure you I sometimes feel not the influence of a Passion or Affection during a whole week—and so long this sometimes continues I begin to suspect myself and the genuiness of my feelings at other times—thinking them a few barren Tragedy-tears}—My Brother Tom is much improved—he is going to Devonshire—whither I shall follow him—at present I am just arrived at Dorking to change the Scene—change the Air and give me a spur to wind up my Poem, of which there are wanting 500 Lines. I should have been here a day sooner but the Reynoldses persuaded me to spop[8] in Town to meet your friend Christie—There were Rice and Martin—we talked about Ghosts—I will have some talk with Taylor and let you know—when please God I come down a[t] Christmas—I will find that Examiner if possible. My best regards to Gleig—My Brothers to you and Mrs Bentley.

Your affectionate friend
JOHN KEATS—

I want to say much more to you—a few hints will set me going
Direct Burford Bridge near dorking

Letter 45.   To George and Tom Keats.
21, 27 [?] December 1817

Hampstead Sunday
22 December 1817

MY DEAR BROTHERS

I must crave your pardon for not having written ere this & & I saw Kean return to the public in Richard III, & finely he did it, & at the request of Reynolds I went to criticise his Luke in Riches—the critique is in todays champion, which I send you with the Examiner in which you will find very proper lamentation on the obsoletion of christmas Gambols & pastimes: but it was mixed up with so much egotism of that drivelling nature that pleasure is entirely lost. Hone the publisher's trial, you must find very amusing; & as Englishmen very <amusing> encouraging—his *Not Guilty* is a thing, which not to have been, would have dulled still more Liberty's Emblazoning—Lord Ellenborough has been paid in his own coin—Wooler & Hone have

---

[7] *For* put.
[8] *For* stop.

done us an essential service—I have had two very pleasant evenings with
Dilke yesterday & today; & am at this moment just come from him & feel in
the humour to go on with this, began in the morning, & from which he came
to fetch me. I spent Friday evening with Wells & went the next morning to
see *Death on the Pale horse*. It is a wonderful picture, when West's age is considered; But there is nothing to be intense upon; no women one feels mad to
kiss; no face swelling into reality. the excellence of every Art is its intensity,
capable of making all disagreeables evaporate, from their being in close relationship with Beauty & Truth—Examine King Lear & you will find this ex-
amplified throughout; but in this picture we have unpleasantness without
any momentous depth of speculation excited, in which to bury its repulsive-
ness—The picture is larger than Christ rejected—I dined with Haydon the
sunday after you left, & had a very pleasant day, I dined too (for I have been
out too much lately) with Horace Smith & met his two Brothers with Hill &
Kingston & one Du Bois, they only served to convince me, how superior humour is to wit in respect to enjoyment—These men say things which make
one start, without making one feel, they are all alike; their manners are alike;
they all know fashionables; they have a mannerism in their very eating &
drinking, in their mere handling a Decanter—They talked of Kean & his low
company—Would I were with that company instead of yours said I to myself! I know such like acquaintance will never do for me & yet I am going to
Reynolds, on wednesday—Brown & Dilke walked with me & back from the
Christmas pantomime. I had not a dispute but a disquisition with Dilke, on
various subjects; several things dovetailed in my mind, & at once it struck
me, what quality went to form a Man of Achievement especially in Literature
& which Shakespeare posessed so enormously—I mean *Negative Capability*,
that is when man is capable of being in uncertainties, Mysteries, doubts,
without any irritable reaching after fact & reason—Coleridge, for instance,
would let go by a fine isolated verisimilitude caught from the Penetralium of
mystery, from being incapable of remaining content with half knowledge.
This pursued through Volumes would perhaps take us no further than this,
that with a great poet the sense of Beauty overcomes every other consideration, or rather obliterates all consideration.

    Shelley's poem is out & there are words about its being objected too, as
much as Queen Mab was. Poor Shelley I think he has his Quota of good qualities, in sooth la!! Write soon to your most sincere friend & affectionate Brother
                                    (Signed) JOHN

Messrs Keats
Teignmouth Devonshire

Letter 62. To J. H. Reynolds.
19 February 1818

MY DEAR REYNOLDS,
    I have an idea that a Man might pass a very pleasant life in this man-
ner—let him on any certain day read a certain Page of full Poesy or distilled

[Marginalia, left: No feeling in what is said, no feeling results— (echo of pleasure principle in Wordsw.?) Men seeking answers, unable to live w/ questions is un- appealing to others]

[Marginalia, right: What art does to observer / these guys were witty & Keats amused / prefers humor / not seeking truth through the frustration involved, but being comfortable with close uncertainties, questions lingering / Coleridge wants concrete answers, by rules, can't handle "half knowledge"]

Prose and let him wander with it, and muse upon it, and reflect from it, and bring home to it, and prophesy upon it, and dream upon it—untill it becomes stale—but when will it do so? Never—When Man has arrived at a certain ripeness in intellect any one grand and spiritual passage serves him as a starting post towards all "the two-and thirty Pallaces" How happy is such a "voyage of conception," what delicious diligent Indolence! A doze upon a Sofa does not hinder it, and a nap upon Clover engenders ethereal finger-pointings—the prattle of a child gives it wings, and the converse of middle age a strength to beat them—a strain of musick conducts to 'an odd angle of the Isle' and when the leaves whisper it puts a 'girdle round the earth. Nor will this sparing touch of noble Books be any irreverance to their Writers—for perhaps the honors paid by Man to Man are trifles in comparison to the Benefit done by great Works to the 'Spirit and pulse of good' by their mere passive existence. Memory should not be called knowledge—Many have original Minds who do not think it—they are led away by Custom—Now it appears to me that almost any Man may like the Spider spin from his own inwards his own airy Citadel—the points of leaves and twigs on which the Spider begins her work are few and she fills the Air with a beautiful circuiting: man should be content with as few points to tip with the fine Webb of his Soul and weave a tapestry empyrean—full of Symbols for his spiritual eye, of softness for his spiritual touch, of space for his wandering of distinctness for his Luxury—But the Minds of Mortals are so different and bent on such diverse Journeys that it may at first appear impossible for any common taste and fellowship to exist <bettween> between two or three under these suppositions—It is however quite the contrary—Minds would leave each other in contrary directions, traverse each other in Numberless points, and all[9] last greet each other at the Journeys end—A old Man and a child would talk together and the old Man be led on his Path, and the child left thinking—Man should not dispute or assert but whisper results to his neighbour, and thus by every germ of Spirit sucking the Sap from mould ethereal every human might become great, and Humanity instead of being a wide heath of Furse and Briars with here and there a remote Oak or Pine, would become a grand democracy of Forest Trees. It has been an old Comparison for our urging on—the Bee hive—however it seems to me that we should rather be the flower than the Bee—for it is a false notion that more is gained by receiving than giving—no the receiver and the giver are equal in their benefits—The f[l]ower I doubt not receives a fair guerdon from the Bee—its leaves blush deeper in the next spring—and who shall say between Man and Woman which is the most delighted? Now it is more noble to sit like Jove that[10] to fly like Mercury—let us not therefore go hurrying about and collecting honey-bee like, buzzing here and there impatiently from a knowledge of what is to be arrived at: but let us open our leaves like a flower and be passive and receptive—budding patiently under the eye of Apollo

[9] For at.
[10] For than.

and taking hints from evey noble insect that favors us with a visit—sap will be given us for Meat and dew for drink—I was led into these thoughts, my dear Reynolds, by the beauty of the morning operating on a sense of Idleness—I have not read any Books—the Morning said I was right—I had no Idea but of the Morning and the Thrush said I was right—seeming to say—

'O thou whose face hath felt the Winter's wind;
   Whose eye has seen the Snow clouds hung in Mist
And the black-elm tops 'mong the freezing Stars
To thee the Spring will be a harvest-time—
O thou whose only book has been the light
Of supreme darkness which thou feddest on
Night after night, when Phœbus was away
To thee the Spring shall be a tripple morn—
O fret not after knowledge—I have none
And yet my song comes native with the warmth
O fret not after knowledge—I have none
And yet the Evening listens—He who saddens
At thought of Idleness cannot be idle,
And he's awake who thinks himself asleep.'

Now I am sensible all this is a mere sophistication, however it may neighbour to any truths, to excuse my own indolence—so I will not deceive myself that Man should be equal with jove—but think himself very well off as a sort of scullion-Mercury or even a humble Bee—It is not[11] matter whether I am right or wrong either one way or another, if there is sufficient to lift a little time from your Shoulders.

Your affectionate friend
JOHN KEATS—

Letter 118. To Richard Woodhouse.
27 October 1818

MY DEAR WOODHOUSE,

    Your Letter gave me a great satisfaction; more on account of its freindliness, than any relish of that matter in it which is accounted so acceptable in the 'genus irritabile.' The best answer I can give you is in a clerklike manner to make some observations on two principle points, which seem to point like indices into the midst of the whole pro and con, about genius, and views and atchievements and ambition and cœtera. 1st As to the poetical Character itself, (I mean that sort of which, if I am any thing, I am a Member) that sort distinguished from the wordsworthian or egotistical sublime; which is a thing per se and stands alone) it is not itself—it has no self—it is every thing and nothing—It has no character—it enjoys light and shade; it lives in

[11] For no.

Poet & Keats himself have no "self" no individuality

gusto, be it foul or fair, high or low, rich or poor, mean or elevated—It has as much delight in conceiving an Iago as an Imogen. What shocks the virtuous philosop[h]er, delights the camelion Poet. It does no harm from its relish of the dark side of things any more than from its taste for the bright one; because they both end in speculation. A Poet is the most unpoetical of any thing in existence; because he has no Identity—he is continually in for— and filling some other Body—The Sun, the Moon, the Sea and Men and Women who are creatures of impulse are poetical and have about them an unchangeable attribute—the poet has none; no identity—he is certainly the most unpoetical of all God's Creatures. If then he has no self, and if I am a Poet,

where is the Wonder that I should say I would <right> write no more? Might I not at that very instant [have] been cogitating on the Characters of saturn and Ops? It is a wretched thing to confess; but is a very fact that not one word I ever utter can be taken for granted as an opinion growing out of my identical nature—how can it, when I have no nature? When I am in a room with People if I ever am free from speculating on creations of my own brain, then not myself goes home to myself: but the identity of every one in the room begins [to] to press upon me that, I am in a very little time annihilated—not only among Men; it would be the same in a Nursery of children: I know not whether I make myself wholly understood: I hope enough so to let you see that no dependence is to be placed on what I said that day.

In the second place I will speak of my views, and of the life I purpose to myself—I am ambitious of doing the world some good: if I should be spared that may be the work of maturer years—in the interval I will assay to reach to as high a summit in Poetry as the nerve bestowed upon me will suffer. The faint conceptions I have of Poems to come brings the blood frequently into my forehead—All I hope is that I may not lose all interest in human affairs—that the solitary indifference I feel for applause even from the finest Spirits, will not blunt any acuteness of vision I may have. I do not think it will—I feel assured I should write from the mere yearning and fondness I have for the Beautiful even if my night's labours should be burnt every morning and no eye ever shine upon them. But even now I am perhaps not speaking from myself; but from some character in whose soul I now live. I am sure however that this next sentence is from myself. I feel your anxiety, good opinion and friendliness in the highest degree, and am

Your's most sincerely
JOHN KEATS

PERCY BYSSHE SHELLEY

A Defence of Poetry

1821; published 1840

Shelley's (1792–1822) impassioned and at times rhapsodic defense might bring to mind Sidney's apology for poetry (p. 101), and, like Sidney, he too *vindicates poetry on moral grounds*. But he goes far beyond Sidney in his *conception of who poets are, what they do, and how their creations effect improvements in people and in society*. Shelley arrives at the often-quoted climactic metaphor, "Poets are the unacknowledged legislators of the world," by assuming a Platonic conception of the universe. But although he accepts Plato's idealistic premises, and his psychological model as well, he completely reverses Plato's conclusion about the place of poets in society (see The Republic, Book X, p. 1). Not through reason (analysis) but through the imagination (synthesis) do we perceive the "indestructible order" and harmony of the universe. Poets perceive the existing but unrecognized relationships and either express their perceptions in language or embody them in ideal social, legal, or religious orders. To reveal the ideal is to reveal the good, the true, and the beautiful as a harmonious One. (Note how metrical language is justified on these grounds.) Thus the imaginative mind is creative and unifying; the *"reasoners," who analyze and dissect, can never inspire the human mind as poets do*. Plato had said that poets were useless; but, re-defining utility, Shelley tells us (sounding strikingly modern) that we have accumulated more facts than we can digest and that we need the large unifying views that the great imaginative thinkers (or "poets") can provide and that enable us to find meaning in our lives.

But *how does poetry teach? It is important to distinguish between Sidney's conception of poetry as teaching specific moral doctrines and Shelley's view in which the imagination itself becomes the teaching agent;* in fact, Shelley praises the poet John Milton for boldly neglecting "a direct moral purpose" in his portrayal of Satan in Paradise Lost (1667). Poetry works indirectly by *awakening our ability to identify and empathize*. Shelley calls this "a going out of our own nature" and even implies that the difference between good and bad people is the degree to which they have active imaginations. Poetry creates a broadened range of sympathy and an enlargement of the circumference of the mind; therefore, the poetic effect is associated with a beneficial awakening and change in ideas and institutions.

Shelley devotes about two-thirds of the essay to a history that is rather more polemical than factual. He was replying to Thomas Love Peacock's charge in The Four Ages of Poetry *that poetry was and always had been useless and irrelevant; in rebutting Peacock, Shelley employs a theory of history that should be analyzed in relation to the ideas in the first part of his essay.*

Part I

ACCORDING TO one mode of regarding those two classes of mental action, which are called reason and imagination, the former may be considered as mind contemplating the relations borne by one thought to another, however produced; and the latter, as mind acting upon those thoughts so as to colour them with its own light, and composing from them, as from elements, other thoughts, each containing within itself the principle of its own integrity. The one is the τὸ ποιεῖν,[1] or the principle of synthesis, and has for its objects those forms which are common to universal nature and existence itself; the other is the τὸ λογίζειν,[2] or principle of analysis, and its action regards the relations of things, simply as relations; considering thoughts, not in their integral unity, but as the algebraical representations which conduct to certain general results. Reason is the enumeration of quantities already known; imagination is the perception of the value of those quantities, both separately and as a whole. Reason respects the differences, and imagination the similitudes of things. Reason is to the imagination as the instrument to the agent, as the body to the spirit, as the shadow to the substance.

Poetry, in a general sense, may be defined to be 'the expression of the imagination': and poetry is connate with the origin of man. Man is an instrument over which a series of external and internal impressions are driven, like the alternations of an ever-changing wind over an Aeolian lyre, which move it by their motion to ever-changing melody. But there is a principle within the human being, and perhaps within all sentient beings, which acts otherwise than in the lyre, and produces not melody alone, but harmony, by an internal adjustment of the sounds or motions thus excited to the impressions which excite them. It is as if the lyre could accommodate its chords to the motions of that which strikes them, in a determined proportion of sound; even as the musician can accommodate his voice to the sound of the lyre. A child at play by itself will express its delight by its voice and motions; and every inflexion of tone and every gesture will bear exact relation to a corresponding antitype in the pleasurable impressions which awakened it; it will be the reflected image of that impression; and as the lyre trembles and sounds after the wind has died away, so the child seeks, by prolonging in its voice and motions the duration of the effect, to prolong also a consciousness of the

---

[1] *To poiein.*
[2] *To logizein.*

cause. In relation to the objects which delight a child, these expressions are, what poetry is to higher objects. The savage (for the savage is to ages what the child is to years) expresses the emotions produced in him by surrounding objects in a similar manner; and language and gesture, together with plastic or pictorial imitation, become the image of the combined effect of those objects, and of his apprehension of them. Man in society, with all his passions and his pleasures, next becomes the object of the passions and pleasures of man; an additional class of emotions produces an augmented treasure of expressions; and language, gesture, and the imitative arts, become at once the representation and the medium, the pencil and the picture, the chisel and the statue, the chord and the harmony. The social sympathies, or those laws from which, as from its elements, society results, begin to develop themselves from the moment that two human beings coexist; the future is contained within the present, as the plant within the seed; and equality, diversity, unity, contrast, mutual dependence, become the principles alone capable of affording the motives according to which the will of a social being is determined to action, inasmuch as he is social; and constitute pleasure in sensation, virtue in sentiment, beauty in art, truth in reasoning, and love in the intercourse of kind. Hence men, even in the infancy of society, observe a certain order in their words and actions, distinct from that of the objects and the impressions represented by them, all expression being subject to the laws of that from which it proceeds. But let us dismiss those more general considerations which might involve an inquiry into the principles of society itself, and restrict our view to the manner in which the imagination is expressed upon its forms.

In the youth of the world, men dance and sing and imitate natural objects, observing in these actions, as in all others, a certain rhythm or order. And, although all men observe a similar, they observe not the same order, in the motions of the dance, in the melody of the song, in the combinations of language, in the series of their imitations of natural objects. For there is a certain order or rhythm belonging to each of these classes of mimetic representation, from which the hearer and the spectator receive an intenser and purer pleasure than from any other; the sense of an approximation to this order has been called taste by modern writers. Every man in the infancy of art observes an order which approximates more or less closely to that from which this highest delight results: but the diversity is not sufficiently marked, as that its gradations should be sensible, except in those instances where the predominance of this faculty of approximation to the beautiful (for so we may be permitted to name the relation between this highest pleasure and its cause) is very great. Those in whom it exists in excess are poets, in the most universal sense of the word; and the pleasure resulting from the manner in which they express the influence of society or nature upon their own minds, communicates itself to others, and gathers a sort of reduplication from that community. Their language is vitally metaphorical; that is, it marks the before unapprehended relations of things and perpetuates their apprehension, until the words which represent them become, through time, signs for portions or classes of thoughts instead of pictures of integral thoughts; and then if no new poets should arise to create afresh the associations which have been thus disorganized, language will be dead to all the nobler purposes of human intercourse. These similitudes or relations are finely said by Lord Bacon to be 'the same footsteps of nature impressed upon the various subjects of the world'; and he considers the faculty which perceives them as the storehouse of axioms common to all knowledge. In the infancy of society every author is necessarily a poet, because language itself is poetry; and to be a poet is to apprehend the true and the beautiful, in a world, the good which exists in the relation, subsisting, first between existence and perception, and secondly between perception and expression. Every original language near to its source is in itself the chaos of a cyclic poem: the copiousness of lexicography and the distinctions of grammar are the works of a later age, and are merely the catalogue and the form of the creations of poetry.

But poets, or those who imagine and express this indestructible order, are not only the authors of language and of music, of the dance, and architecture, and statuary, and painting; they are the institutions of laws, and the founders of civil society, and the inventors of the arts of life, and the teachers, who draw into a certain propinquity with the beautiful and the true, that partial apprehension of the agencies of the invisible world which is called religion. Hence all original religions are allegorical, or susceptible of allegory, and, like Janus, have a double face of false and true. Poets, according to the circumstances of the age and nation in which they appeared, were called, in the earlier epochs of the world, legislators, or prophets: a poet essentially comprises and unites both these characters. For he not only beholds intensely the present as it is, and discovers those laws according to which present things ought to be ordered, but he beholds the future in the present, and his thoughts are the germs of the flower and the fruit of latest time. Not that I assert poets to be prophets in the gross sense of the word, or that they can foretell the form as surely as they foreknow the spirit of events: such is the pretence of superstition, which would make poetry an attribute of prophecy, rather than prophecy an attribute of poetry. A poet participates in the eternal, the infinite, and the one; as far as relates to his conceptions, time and place and number are not. The grammatical forms which express the moods of time, and the difference of persons, and the distinction of place, are convertible with respect to the highest poetry without injuring it as poetry; and the choruses of Aeschylus, and the book of *Job,* and Dante's *Paradise,* would afford, more than any other writings, examples of this fact, if the limits of this essay did not forbid citation. The creations of sculpture, painting, and music, are illustrations still more decisive.

Language, colour, form, and religious and civil habits of action, are all the instruments and materials of poetry; they may be called poetry by that figure of speech which considers the effect as a synonym of the cause. But poetry in a more restricted sense expresses those arrangements of language, and especially metrical language, which are created by that imperial faculty, whose throne is curtained within the invisible nature of man. And this springs from the nature itself of language, which is a more direct representation of the actions and passions of our internal being, and is susceptible of more various and delicate combinations, than colour, form, or motion, and is more plastic and obedient to the control of that faculty of which it is the creation. For language is arbitrarily produced by the imagination, and has relation to thoughts alone; but all other materials, instruments, and conditions of art, have relations among each other, which limit and interpose between conception and expression. The former is as a mirror which reflects, the latter as a cloud which enfeebles, the light of which both are mediums of communication. Hence the fame of sculptors, painters, and musicians, although the intrinsic powers of the great masters of these arts may yield in no degree to that of those who have employed language as the hieroglyphic of their thoughts, has never equaled that of poets in the restricted sense of the term; as two performers of equal skill will produce unequal effects from a guitar and a harp. The fame of legislators and founders of religions, so long as their institutions last, alone seems to exceed that of poets in the restricted sense; but it can scarcely be a question, whether, if we deduct the celebrity which their flattery of the gross opinions of the vulgar usually conciliates, together with that which belonged to them in their higher character of poets, any excess will remain.

We have thus circumscribed the word poetry within the limits of that art which is the most familiar and the most perfect expression of the faculty itself. It is necessary, however, to make the circle still narrower, and to determine the distinction between measured and unmeasured language; for the popular division into prose and verse is inadmissible in accurate philosophy.

Sounds as well as thoughts have relation both between each other and towards that which they represent, and a perception of the order of those relations has always been found connected with a perception of the order of the relations of thoughts. Hence the language of poets has ever affected a certain uniform and harmonious recurrence of sound, without which it were not poetry, and which is scarcely less indispensable to the communication of its influence, than the words themselves, without reference to that peculiar order. Hence the vanity of translation; it were as wise to cast a violet into a crucible that you might discover the formal principle of its colour and odour, as seek to transfuse from one language into another the creations of a poet. The plant must spring again from its seed, or it will bear no flower—and this is the burthen of the curse of Babel.

An observation of the regular mode of the recurrence of harmony in the language of poetical minds, together with its relation to music, produced metre, or a certain system of traditional forms of harmony and language. Yet it is by no means essential that a poet should accommodate his language to this traditional form, so that the harmony, which is its spirit, be observed. The practice is indeed convenient and popular, and to be preferred, especially in such composition as includes much action: but every great poet must inevitably innovate upon the example of his predecessors in the exact structure of his peculiar versification. The distinction between poets and prose writers is a vulgar error. The distinction between philosophers and poets has been anticipated. Plato was essentially a poet—the truth and splendour of his imagery, and the melody of his language, are the most intense that it is possible to conceive. He rejected the measure of the epic, dramatic, and lyrical forms, because he sought to kindle a harmony in thoughts divested of shape and action, and he forbore to invent any regular plan of rhythm which would include, under determinate forms, the varied pauses of his style. Cicero sought to imitate the cadence of his periods, but with little success. Lord Bacon was a poet. His language has a sweet and majestic rhythm, which satisfies the sense, no less than the almost superhuman wisdom of his philosophy satisfies the intellect; it is a strain which distends, and then bursts the circumference of the reader's mind, and pours itself forth together with it into the universal element with which it has perpetual sympathy. All the authors of revolutions in opinion are not only necessarily poets as they are inventors, nor even as their words unveil the permanent analogy of things by images which participate in the life of truth; but as their periods are harmonious and rhythmical, and contain in themselves the elements of verse; being the echo of the eternal music. Nor are those supreme poets, who have employed traditional forms of rhythm on account of the form and action of their subjects, less capable of perceiving and teaching the truth of things, than those who have omitted that form. Shakespeare, Dante, and Milton (to confine ourselves to modern writers) are philosophers of the very loftiest power.

A poem is the very image of life expressed in its eternal truth. There is this difference between a story and a poem, that a story is a catalogue of detached facts, which have no other connexion than time, place, circumstance, cause and effect; the other is the creation of actions according to the unchangeable forms of human nature, as existing in the mind of the Creator, which is itself the image of all other minds. The one is partial, and applies only to a definite period of time; and a certain combination of events which can never again recur; the other is universal, and contains within itself the germ of a relation to whatever motives or actions have place in the possible varieties of human nature. Time, which destroys the beauty and the use of the story of particular facts, stripped of the poetry which should invest them, augments that of poetry, and for ever develops new and wonderful applications of the eternal truth which it contains. Hence epitomes have been called the moths of just history; they eat out the poetry of it. A story of particular facts is as a mirror which obscures and distorts that which should be beautiful: poetry is a mirror which makes beautiful that which is distorted.

The parts of a composition may be poetical, without the composition as a whole being a poem. A single sentence may be considered as a whole, though it may be found in the midst of a series of unassimilated portions: a single word even may be a spark of inextinguishable thought. And thus all the great historians, Herodotus, Plutarch, Livy, were poets; and although the plan of these writers, especially that of Livy, restrained them from developing this faculty in its highest degree, they made copious and ample amends for their subjection, by filling all the interstices of their subjects with living images.

Having determined what is poetry, and who are poets, let us proceed to estimate its effects upon society.

Poetry is ever accompanied with pleasure: all spirits on which it falls open themselves to receive the wisdom which is mingled with its delight. In the infancy of the world, neither poets themselves nor their auditors are fully aware of the excellence of poetry: for it acts in a divine and unapprehended manner, beyond and above consciousness; and it is reserved for future generations to contemplate and measure the mighty cause and effect in all the strength and splendour of their union. Even in modern times, no living poet ever arrived at the fullness of his fame; the jury which sits in judgment upon a poet, belonging as he does to all time, must be composed of his peers: it must be impanelled by Time from the selectest of the wise of many generations. A poet is a nightingale, who sits in darkness and sings to cheer its own solitude with sweet sounds; his auditors are as men entranced by the melody of an unseen musician, who feel that they are moved and softened, yet know not whence or why. The poems of Homer and his contemporaries were the delight of infant Greece; they were the elements of that social system which is the column upon which all succeeding civilization has reposed. Homer embodied the ideal perfection of his age in human character; nor can we doubt that those who read his verses were awakened to an ambition of becoming like to Achilles, Hector, and Ulysses: the truth and beauty of friendship, patriotism, and persevering devotion to an object, were unveiled to the depths in these immortal creations: the sentiments of the auditors must have been refined and enlarged by a sympathy with such great and lovely impersonations, until from admiring they imitated, and from imitation they identified themselves with the objects of their admiration. Nor let it be objected, that these characters are remote from moral perfection, and that they can by no means be considered as edifying patterns for general imitation. Every epoch, under names more or less specious, has deified its peculiar errors; Revenge is the naked idol of the worship of a semi-barbarous age; and Self-deceit is the veiled image of unknown evil, before which luxury and satiety lie prostrate. But a poet considers the vices of his contemporaries as a temporary dress in which his creations must be arrayed, and which cover without concealing the eternal proportions of their beauty. An epic or dramatic personage is understood to wear them around his soul, as he may the ancient armour or the modern uniform around his body; whilst it is easy to conceive a dress more graceful than either. The beauty of the internal nature cannot be so far concealed by its accidental vesture, but that the spirit of its form shall communicate itself to the very disguise, and indicate the shape it hides from the manner in which it is worn. A majestic form and graceful motions will express themselves through the most barbarous and tasteless costume. Few poets of the highest class have chosen to exhibit the beauty of their conceptions in its naked truth and splendour; and it is doubtful whether the alloy of costume, habit, &c., be not necessary to temper this planetary music for mortal ears.

The whole objection, however, of the immorality of poetry rests upon a misconception of the manner in which poetry acts to produce the moral improvement of man. Ethical science arranges the elements which poetry has created, and propounds schemes and proposes examples of civil and domestic life: nor is it for want of admirable doctrines that men hate, and despise, and censure, and deceive, and subjugate one another. But poetry acts in another and diviner manner. It awakens and enlarges the mind itself by rendering it the receptacle of a thousand unapprehended combinations of thought. Poetry lifts the veil from the hidden beauty of the world, and makes familiar objects be as if they were not familiar; it reproduces all that it represents, and the impersonations clothed in its Elysian light stand thenceforward in the minds of those who have once contemplated them, as memorials of that gentle and exalted content which extends itself over all thoughts and actions with which it coexists. The great secret of morals is love; or a going out of our own nature, and an identification of ourselves with the beautiful which exists in thought, action, or person, not our own. A man, to be greatly good, must imagine intensely and comprehensively; he must put himself in the place of another and of many others; the pains and pleasures of his species must become his own. The great instrument of moral good is the imagination; and poetry administers to the effect by acting upon the cause. Poetry enlarges the circumference of the imagination by replenishing it with thoughts of ever new delight, which have the power of attracting and assimilating to their own nature all other thoughts, and which form new intervals and interstices whose void for ever craves fresh food. Poetry strengthens the faculty which is the organ of the moral nature of man, in the same manner as exercise strengthens a limb. A poet therefore would do ill to embody his own conceptions of right and wrong, which are usually those of his place and time, in his poetical creations which participate in neither. By this assumption of the inferior office of interpreting the effect, in which perhaps after all he might acquit himself but imperfectly, he would resign a glory in a participation in the cause. There was little danger that Homer, or any of the eternal poets, should have so far misunderstood themselves as to have abdicated this throne of their widest dominion. Those in whom the poetical faculty, though great, is less intense, as Euripides, Lucan, Tasso, Spenser, have frequently affected a moral aim, and the effect of their poetry is diminished in exact proportion to the degree in which they compel us to advert to this purpose.

Homer and the cyclic poets were followed at a certain interval by the dramatic and lyrical poets of Athens, who flourished contemporaneously with all that is most perfect in the kindred expressions of the poetical faculty; architecture, painting, music, the dance, sculpture, philosophy, and, we may add, the forms of civil life. For although the scheme of Athenian society was deformed by many imperfections which the poetry existing in chivalry and Christianity has erased from the habits and institutions of modern Europe; yet never at any other period has so much energy, beauty, and virtue, been developed; never was blind strength and stubborn form so disciplined and rendered subject to the will of man, or that will less repugnant to the dictates of the beautiful and the true, as during the century which preceded the death of Socrates. Of no other epoch in the history of our species have we records and fragments stamped so visibly with the image of the divinity in man. But it is poetry alone, in form, in action, or in language, which has rendered this epoch memorable above all others, and the storehouse of examples to everlasting time. For written poetry existed at that epoch simultaneously with the other arts, and it is an idle inquiry to demand which gave and which received the light, which all, as from a common focus, have scattered over the darkest periods of succeeding time. We know no more of cause and effect than a constant conjunction of events: poetry is ever found to coexist with whatever other arts contribute to the happiness and perfection of man. I appeal to what has already been established to distinguish between the cause and the effect.

It was at the period here adverted to, that the drama had its birth; and however a succeeding writer may have equalled or surpassed those few great specimens of the Athenian drama which have been preserved to us, it is indisputable that the art itself never was understood or practised according to the true philosophy of it, as at Athens. For the Athenians employed language, action, music, painting, the dance, and religious institutions, to produce a common effect in the representation of the highest idealisms of passion and of power; each division in the art was made perfect in its kind by artists of the most consummate skill, and was disciplined into a beautiful proportion and unity one towards the other. On the modern stage a few only of the elements capable of expressing the image of the poet's conception are employed at once. We have tragedy without music and dancing; and music and dancing without the highest impersonations of which they are the fit accompaniment, and both without religion and solemnity. Religious institution has indeed been usually banished from the stage. Our system of divesting the actor's face of a mask, on which the many expressions appropriated to his dramatic character might be moulded into one permanent and unchanging expression, is favourable only to a partial and inharmonious effect; it is fit for nothing but a monologue, where all the attention may be directed to some great master of ideal mimicry. The modern practice of blending comedy with tragedy, though liable to great abuse in point of practice, is undoubtedly an extension of the dramatic circle; but the comedy should be as in *King Lear*, universal, ideal, and sublime. It is perhaps the intervention of this principle which determines the balance in favour of *King Lear* against the *Oedipus Tyrannus* or the *Agamemnon*, or, if you will, the trilogies with which they are connected; unless the intense power of the choral poetry, especially that of the latter, should be considered as restoring the equilibrium. *King Lear*, if it can sustain this comparison, may be judged to be the most perfect specimen of the dramatic art existing in the world; in spite of the narrow conditions to which the poet was subjected by the ignorance of the philosophy of the drama which has prevailed in modern Europe. Calderon, in his religious *Autos*, has attempted to fulfill some of the high conditions of dramatic representation neglected by Shakespeare; such as the establishing a relation between the drama and religion, and the accommodating them to music and dancing; but he omits the observation of conditions still more important, and more is lost than gained by the substitution of the rigidly-defined and ever-repeated idealisms of a distorted superstition for the living impersonations of the truth of human passion.

But I digress. — The connexion of scenic exhibitions with the improvement or corruption of the manners of men, has been universally recognized: in other words, the presence or absence of poetry in its most perfect and universal form, has been found to be connected with good and evil in conduct or habit. The corruption which has been imputed to the drama as an effect, begins, when the poetry employed in its constitution ends: I appeal to the history of manners whether the periods of the growth of the one and the decline of the other have not corresponded with an exactness equal to any example of moral cause and effect.

The drama at Athens, or wheresoever else it may have approached to its perfection, ever co-existed with the moral and intellectual greatness of the age. The tragedies of the Athenian poets are as mirrors in which the spectator beholds himself, under a thin disguise of circumstance, stripped of all but that ideal perfection and energy which every one feels to be the internal type of all that he loves, admires, and would become. The imagination is enlarged by a sympathy with pains and passions so mighty, that they distend in their conception the capacity of that by which they are conceived; the good affections are strengthened by pity, indignation, terror, and sorrow; and an exalted calm is prolonged from the satiety of this high exercise of them into the tumult of familiar life: even crime is disarmed of half its horror and all its contagion by being represented as the fatal consequence of the unfathomable agencies of nature; error is thus divested of its wilfulness; men can no longer cherish it as the creation of their choice. In a drama of the highest order there is little food for censure or hatred; it teaches rather self-knowledge and self-respect. Neither the eye nor the mind can see itself, unless reflected upon that which it resembles. The drama, so long as it continues to express poetry, is as a prismatic and many-sided mirror, which collects the brightest rays of human nature and divides and reproduces them from the simplicity of these elementary forms, and touches them with majesty and beauty, and multiplies all that it reflects, and endows it with the power of propagating its like wherever it may fall.

But in periods of the decay of social life, the drama sympathizes with that decay. Tragedy becomes a cold imitation of the form of the great masterpieces of antiquity, divested of all harmonious accompaniment of the kindred arts; and often the very form misunderstood, or a weak attempt to teach certain doctrines, which the writer considers as moral truths; and which are usually no more than specious flatteries of some gross vice or weakness, with which the author, in common with his auditors, are infected. Hence what has been called the classical and domestic drama. Addison's *Cato* is a specimen of the one; and would it were not superfluous to cite examples of the other! To such purposes poetry cannot be made subservient. Poetry is a sword of lightning, ever unsheathed, which consumes the scabbard that would contain it. And thus we observe that all dramatic writings of this nature are unimaginative in a singular degree; they affect sentiment and passion, which, divested of imagination, are other names for caprice and appetite. The period in our own history of the grossest degradation of the drama is the reign of Charles II, when all forms in which poetry had been accustomed to be expressed became hymns to the triumph of kingly power over liberty and virtue. Milton stood alone illuminating an age unworthy of him. At such periods the calculating principle pervades all the forms of dramatic exhibition, and poetry ceases to be expressed upon them. Comedy loses its ideal universality: wit succeeds to humour; we laugh from self-complacency and triumph, instead of pleasure; malignity, sarcasm, and contempt, succeed to sympathetic merriment; we hardly laugh, but we smile. Obscenity, which is ever blasphemy against the divine beauty in life, becomes, from the very veil which it assumes, more active if less disgusting: it is a monster for which the corruption of society for ever brings forth new food, which it devours in secret.

The drama being that form under which a greater number of modes of expression of poetry are susceptible of being combined than any other, the connexion of poetry and social good is more observable in the drama than in whatever other form. And it is indisputable that the highest perfection of human society has ever corresponded with the highest dramatic excellence; and that the corruption or the extinction of the drama in a nation where it has once flourished, is a mark of a corruption of manners, and an extinction of the energies which sustain the soul of social life. But, as Machiavelli says of political institutions, that life may be preserved and renewed, if men should arise capable of bringing back the drama to its principles. And this is true with respect to poetry in its most extended sense: all language, institution and form require not only to be produced but to be sustained: the office and character of a poet participates in the divine nature as regards providence, no less than as regards creation.

Civil war, the spoils of Asia, and the fatal predominance first of the Macedonian, and then of the Roman arms, were so many symbols of the extinction or suspension of the creative faculty in Greece. The bucolic writers, who found patronage under the lettered tyrants of Sicily and Egypt, were the latest representatives of its most glorious reign. Their poetry is intensely melodius; like the odour of the tuberose, it overcomes and sickens the spirit with excess of sweetness; whilst the poetry of the preceding age was as a meadow-gale of June, which mingles the fragrance of all the flowers of the field, and adds a quickening and harmonizing spirit of its own, which endows the sense with a power of sustaining its extreme delight. The bucolic and erotic delicacy in written poetry is correlative with that softness in statuary, music, and the kindred arts, and even in manners and institutions, which distinguished the epoch to which I now refer. Nor is it the poetical faculty itself, or any misapplication of it, to which this want of harmony is to be imputed. An equal sensibility to the influence of the senses and the affections is to be found in the writings of Homer and Sophocles: the former, especially, has clothed sensual and pathetic images with irresistible attractions. Their superiority over these succeeding writers consists in the presence of those thoughts which belong to the inner faculties of our nature, not in the absence of those which are connected with the external: their incomparable perfection consists in a harmony of the union of all. It is not what the erotic poets have, but what they have not, in which their imperfection consists. It is not inasmuch as they were poets, but inasmuch as they were not poets, that they can be considered with any plausibility as connected with the corruption of their age. Had that corruption availed so as to extinguish in them the sensibility to pleasure, passion, and natural scenery, which is imputed to them as an imperfection, the last triumph of evil would have been achieved. For the end of social corruption is to destroy all sensibility to pleasure; and, therefore, it is corruption. It begins at the imagination and the intellect as at the core, and distributes itself thence as a paralysing venom, through the affections into the very appetites, until all become a torpid mass in which hardly sense survives. At the approach of such a period, poetry ever addresses itself to those faculties which are the last to be destroyed, and its voice is heard, like the footsteps of Astraea, departing from the world. Poetry ever communicates all the pleasure which men are capable of receiving: it is ever still the light of life; the source of whatever of beautiful or generous or true can have place in an evil time. It will readily be confessed that those among the luxurious citizens of Syracuse and Alexandria, who were delighted with the poems of Theocritus, were less cold, cruel, and sensual than the remnant of their tribe. But corruption must utterly have destroyed the fabric of human society before poetry can ever cease. The sacred links of that chain have never been entirely disjoined, which descending through the minds of many men is attached to those great minds, whence as from a magnet the invisible effluence is sent forth, which at once connects, animates, and sustains the life of all. It is the faculty which contains within itself the seeds at once of its own and of social renovation. And let us not circumscribe the effects of the bucolic and erotic poetry within the limits of the sensibility of those to whom it was addressed. They may have perceived the beauty of those immortal compositions, simply as fragments and isolated portions: those who are more finely organized, or born in a happier age, may recognize them as episodes to that great poem, which all poets, like the co-operating thoughts of one great mind, have built up since the beginning of the world.

The same revolutions within a narrower sphere had place in ancient Rome; but the actions and forms of its social life never seem to have been perfectly saturated with the poetical element. The Romans appear to have considered the Greeks as the selectest treasuries of the selectest forms of manners and of nature, and to have abstained from creating in measured language, sculpture, music, or architecture, anything which might bear a particular relation to their own condition, whilst it should bear a general one to the universal constitution of the world. But we judge from partial evidence, and we judge perhaps partially. Ennius, Varro, Pacuvius, and Accius, all great poets, have been lost. Lucretius is in the highest, and Virgil in a very high sense, a creator. The chosen delicacy of expressions of the latter, are as a mist of light which conceal from us the intense and exceeding truth of his conceptions of nature. Livy is instinct with poetry. Yet Horace, Catullus, Ovid, and generally the other great writers of the Virgilian age, saw man and nature in the mirror of Greece. The institutions also, and the religion of Rome were less poetical than those of Greece, as the shadow is less vivid than the substance. Hence poetry in Rome, seemed to follow, rather than accompany, the perfection of political and domestic society. The true poetry of Rome lived in its institutions; for whatever of beautiful, true, and majestic, they contained, could have sprung only from the faculty which creates the order in which they consist. The life of Camillus, the death of Regulus; the expectation of the senators, in their godlike state, of the victorious Gauls: the refusal of the republic to make peace with Hannibal, after the battle of Cannae, were not the consequences of a refined calculation of the probable personal advantage to result from such a rhythm and order in the shows of life, to those who were at once the poets and the actors of these immortal dramas. The imagination beholding the beauty of this order, created it out of itself according to its own idea; the consequence was empire, and the reward everliving fame. These things are not the less poetry *quia carent vate sacro*.[3] They are the episodes of that cyclic poem written by Time upon the memories of men. The Past, like an inspired rhapsodist, fills the theatre of everlasting generations with their harmony.

At length the ancient system of religion and manners had fulfilled the circle of its revolutions. And the world would have fallen into utter anarchy and darkness, but that there were found poets among the authors of the Christian and chivalric systems of manners and religion, who created forms of opinion and action never before conceived; which, copied into the imaginations of men, become as generals to the bewildered armies of their thoughts. It is foreign to the present purpose to touch upon the evil produced by these systems: except that we protest, on the ground of the principles already established, that no portion of it can be attributed to the poetry they contain.

It is probable that the poetry of Moses, Job, David, Solomon, and Isaiah, had produced a great effect upon the mind of Jesus and his disciples. The scattered fragments preserved to us by the biographers of this extraordinary person, are all instinct with the most vivid poetry. But his doctrines seem to have been quickly distorted. At a certain period after the prevalence of a system of opinions founded upon those promulgated by him, the three forms into which Plato had distributed the faculties of mind underwent a sort of apotheosis, and became the object of the worship of the civilized world. Here it is to be confessed that 'Light seems to thicken,' and

> The crow makes wing to the rooky wood,
> Good things of day begin to droop and drowse,
> And night's black agents to their preys do rouze.

---

[3] "Because they lack the divine bard" (Horace).

But mark how beautiful an order has sprung from the dust and blood of this fierce chaos! how the world, as from a resurrection, balancing itself on the golden wings of knowledge and of hope, has reassumed its yet unwearied flight into the heaven of time. Listen to the music, unheard by outward ears, which is as a ceaseless and invisible wind, nourishing its everlasting course with strength and swiftness.

The poetry in the doctrines of Jesus Christ, and the mythology and institutions of the Celtic conquerors of the Roman empire, outlived the darkness and the convulsions connected with their growth and victory, and blended themselves in a new fabric of manners and opinion. It is an error to impute the ignorance of the dark ages to the Christian doctrines or the predominance of the Celtic nations. Whatever of evil their agencies may have contained sprang from the extinction of the poetical principle, connected with the progress of despotism and superstition. Men, from causes too intricate to be here discussed, had become insensible and selfish: their own will had become feeble, and yet they were its slaves, and thence the slaves of the will of others: lust, fear, avarice, cruelty, and fraud, characterized a race amongst whom no one was to be found capable of *creating* in form, language, or institution. The moral anomalies of such a state of society are not justly to be charged upon any class of events immediately connected with them, and those events are most entitled to our approbation which could dissolve it most expeditiously. It is unfortunate for those who cannot distinguish words from thoughts, that many of these anomalies have been incorporated into our popular religion.

It was not until the eleventh century that the effects of the poetry of the Christian and chivalric systems began to manifest themselves. The principle of equality had been discovered and applied by Plato in his *Republic,* as the theoretical rule of the mode in which the materials of pleasure and of power, produced by the common skill and labour of human beings, ought to be distributed among them. The limitations of this rule were asserted by him to be determined only by the sensibility of each, or the utility to result to all. Plato, following the doctrines of Timaeus and Pythagoras, taught also a moral and intellectual system of doctrine, comprehending at once the past, the present, and the future condition of man. Jesus Christ divulged the sacred and eternal truths contained in these views to mankind, and Christianity, in its abstract purity, became the exoteric expression of the esoteric doctrines of the poetry and wisdom of antiquity. The incorporation of the Celtic nations with the exhausted population of the south, impressed upon it the figure of the poetry existing in their mythology and institutions. The result was a sum of the action and reaction of all the causes included in it; for it may be assumed as a maxim that no nation or religion can supersede any other without incorporating into itself a portion of that which it supersedes. The abolition of personal and domestic slavery, and the emancipation of women from a great part of the degrading restraints of antiquity, were among the consequences of these events.

all the ways we *limit ourselves*
morality

The abolition of personal slavery is the basis of the highest political hope
that it can enter into the mind of man to conceive. The freedom of women
produced the poetry of sexual love. Love became a religion, the idols of
whose worship were ever present. It was as if the statues of Apollo and the
Muses had been endowed with life and motion, and had walked forth among
their worshippers; so that earth became peopled by the inhabitants of a diviner world. The familiar appearance and proceedings of life became wonderful and heavenly, and a paradise was created as out of the wrecks of
Eden. And as this creation itself is poetry, so its creators were poets; and language was the instrument of their art: 'Galeotto fù il libro, e chi lo scrisse.'[4]
The Provençal Trouveurs, or inventors, preceded Petrarch, whose verses are
as spells, which unseal the inmost enchanted fountains of the delight which
is in the grief of love. It is impossible to feel them without becoming a portion
of that beauty which we contemplate: it were superfluous to explain how the
gentleness and the elevation of mind connected with these sacred emotions
can render men more amiable, more generous and wise, and lift them out of
the dull vapours of the little world of self. Dante understood the secret things
of love even more than Petrarch. His *Vita Nuova* is an inexhaustible fountain
of purity of sentiment and language: it is the idealized history of that period,
and those intervals of his life which were dedicated to love. His apotheosis of
Beatrice in Paradise, and the gradations of his own love and her loveliness,
by which as by steps he feigns himself to have ascended to the throne of the
Supreme Cause, is the most glorious imagination of modern poetry. The
acutest critics have justly reversed the judgement of the vulgar, and the order
of the great acts of the 'Divine Drama,' in the measure of the admiration
which they accord to the Hell, Purgatory, and Paradise. The latter is a perpetual hymn of everlasting love. Love, which found a worthy poet in Plato alone
of all the ancients, has been celebrated by a chorus of the greatest writers of
the renovated words; and the music has penetrated the caverns of society,
and its echoes still drown the dissonance of arms and superstition. At successive intervals, Ariosto, Tasso, Shakespeare, Spenser, Calderon, Rousseau,
and the great writers of our own age, have celebrated the dominion of love,
planting as it were trophies in the human mind of that sublimest victory over
sensuality and force. The true relation borne to each other by the sexes into
which human kind is distributed, has become less misunderstood; and if the
error which confounded diversity with inequality of the powers of the two
sexes has been partially recognized in the opinions and institutions of modern Europe, we owe this great benefit to the worship of which chivalry was
the law, and poets the prophets.

The poetry of Dante may be considered as the bridge thrown over the
stream of time, which unites the modern and ancient world. The distorted
notions of invisible things which Dante and his rival Milton have idealized,
are merely the mask and the mantle in which these great poets walk through

---

[4] "Galeotto was the book and he that wrote it" (Dante).

eternity enveloped and disguised. It is a difficult question to determine how far they were conscious of the distinction which must have subsisted in their minds between their own creeds and that of the people. Dante at least appears to wish to mark the full extent of it by placing Riphaeus, whom Virgil calls *justissimus unus*, in Paradise, and observing a most heretical caprice in his distribution of rewards and punishments. And Milton's poem contains within itself a philosophical refutation of that system, of which, by a strange and natural antithesis, it has been a chief popular support. Nothing can exceed the energy and magnificence of the character of Satan as expressed in *Paradise Lost*. It is a mistake to suppose that he could ever have been intended for the popular personification of evil. Implacable hate, patient cunning, and a sleepless refinement of device to inflict the extremest anguish on an enemy, these things are evil; and, although venial in a slave, are not to be forgiven in a tyrant; although redeemed by much that ennobles his defeat in one subdued, are marked by all that dishonours his conquest in the victor. Milton's Devil as a moral being is as far superior to his God, as one who perseveres in some purpose which he has conceived to be excellent in spite of adversity and torture, is to one who in the cold security of undoubted triumph inflicts the most horrible revenge upon his enemy, not from any mistaken notion of inducing him to repent of a perseverance in enmity, but with the alleged design of exasperating him to deserve new torments. Milton has so far violated the popular creed (if this shall be judged to be a violation) as to have alleged no superiority of moral virtue to his God over his Devil. And this bold neglect of a direct moral purpose is the most decisive proof of the supremacy of Milton's genius. He mingled as it were the elements of human nature as colours upon a single pallet, and arranged them in the composition of his great picture according to the laws of epic truth; that is, according to the laws of that principle by which a series of actions of the external universe and of intelligent and ethical beings is calculated to excite the sympathy of succeeding generations of mankind. The *Divina Commedia* and *Paradise Lost* have conferred upon modern mythology a systematic form; and when change and time shall have added one more superstition to the mass of those which have arisen and decayed upon the earth, commentators will be learnedly employed in elucidating the religion of ancestral Europe, only not utterly forgotten because it will have been stamped with the eternity of genius.

Homer was the first and Dante the second epic poet: that is, the second poet, the series of whose creations bore a defined and intelligible relation to the knowledge and sentiment and religion of the age in which he lived, and of the ages which followed it: developing itself in correspondence with their development. For Lucretius had limed the wings of his swift spirit in the dregs of the sensible world; and Virgil, with a modesty that ill became his genius, had affected the fame of an imitator, even whilst he created anew all that he copied; and none among the flock of mock-birds, though their notes were sweet, Apollonius Rhodius, Quintus Calaber, Nonnus, Lucan, Statius, or Claudian, have sought even to fulfil a single condition of epic truth. Milton was the third epic poet. For if the title of epic in its highest sense be refused to the *Aeneid*, still less can it be conceded to the *Orlando Furioso*, the *Gerusalemme Liberata*, the *Lusiad*, or the *Fairy Queen*.

Dante and Milton were both deeply penetrated with the ancient religion of the civilized world; and its spirit exists in their poetry probably in the same proportion as its forms survived in the unreformed worship of modern Europe. The one preceded and the other followed the Reformation at almost equal intervals. Dante was the first religious reformer, and Luther surpassed him rather in the rudeness and acrimony than in the boldness of his censures of papal usurpation. Dante was the first awakener of entranced Europe; he created a language, in itself music and persuasion, out of a chaos of inharmonious barbarisms. He was the congregator of those great spirits who presided over the resurrection of learning; the Lucifer of that starry flock which in the thirteenth century shone forth from republican Italy, as from a heaven, into the darkness of the benighted world. His very words are instinct with spirit; each is as a spark, a burning atom of inextinguishable thought; and many yet lie covered in the ashes of their birth, and pregnant with a lightning which has yet found no conductor. All high poetry is infinite; it is as the first acorn, which contained all oaks potentially. Veil after veil may be undrawn, and the inmost naked beauty of the meaning never exposed. A great poem is a fountain for ever overflowing with the waters of wisdom and delight; and after one person and one age has exhausted all its divine effluence which their peculiar relations enable them to share, another and yet another succeeds, and new relations are ever developed, the source of an unforeseen and an unconceived delight.

The age immediately succeeding to that of Dante, Petrarch, and Boccaccio, was characterized by a revival of painting, sculpture, and architecture. Chaucer caught the sacred inspiration, and the superstructure of English literature is based upon the materials of Italian invention.

But let us not be betrayed from a defence into a critical history of poetry and its influence on society. Be it enough to have pointed out the effects of poets, in the large and true sense of the word, upon their own and all succeeding times.

But poets have been challenged to resign the civic crown to reasoners and mechanists, on another plea. It is admitted that the exercise of the imagination is most delightful, but it is alleged that that of reason is more useful. Let us examine as the grounds of this distinction, what is here meant by utility. Pleasure or good, in a general sense, is that which the consciousness of a sensitive and intelligent being seeks, and in which, when found, it acquiesces. There are two kinds of pleasure, one durable, universal and permanent; the other transitory and particular. Utility may either express the means of producing the former or the latter. In the former sense, whatever strengthens and purifies the affections, enlarges the imagination, and adds spirit to sense, is useful. But a narrower meaning may be assigned to the word utility, confining it to express that which banishes the importunity of the wants of our animal nature the surrounding men with security of life, the dispersing the grosser delusions of superstition, and the conciliating such a degree of

idea of utility & pleasure, meeting needs

mutual forbearance among men as may consist with the motives of personal advantage.

Undoubtedly the promoters of utility, in this limited sense, have their appointed office in society. They follow the footsteps of poets, and copy the sketches of their creations into the book of common life. They make space, and give time. Their exertions are of the highest value, so long as they confine their administration of the concerns of the inferior powers of our nature within the limits due to the superior ones. But whilst the sceptic destroys gross superstitions, let him spare to deface, as some of the French writers have defaced, the eternal truths charactered upon the imagination of men. Whilst the mechanist abridges, and the political economist combines labour, let them beware that their speculations, for want of correspondence with those first principles which belong to the imagination, do not tend, as they have in modern England, to exasperate at once the extremes of luxury and want. They have exemplified the saying, 'To him that hath, more shall be given; and from him that hath not, the little that he hath shall be taken away.' The rich have become richer, and the poor have become poorer; and the vessel of the state is driven between the Scylla and Charybdis of anarchy and despotism. Such are the effects which must ever flow from an unmitigated exercise of the calculating faculty.

It is difficult to define pleasure in its highest sense; the definition involving a number of apparent paradoxes. For, from an inexplicable defect of harmony in the constitution of human nature, the pain of the inferior is frequently connected with the pleasures of the superior portions of our being. Sorrow, terror, anguish, despair itself, are often the chosen expressions of an approximation to the highest good. Our sympathy in tragic fiction depends on this principle; tragedy delights by affording a shadow of the pleasure which exists in pain. This is the source also of the melancholy which is inseparable from the sweetest melody. The pleasure that is in sorrow is sweeter than the pleasure of pleasure itself. And hence the saying, 'It is better to go to the house of mourning, than to the house of mirth.' Not that this highest species of pleasure is necessarily linked with pain. The delight of love and friendship, the ecstasy of the admiration of nature, the joy of the perception and still more of the creation of poetry, is often wholly unalloyed.

The production and assurance of pleasure in this highest sense is true utility. Those who produce and preserve this pleasure are poets or poetical philosophers.

The exertions of Locke, Hume, Gibbon, Voltaire, Rousseau,[5] and their disciples, in favour of oppressed and deluded humanity, are entitled to the gratitude of mankind. Yet it is easy to calculate the degree of moral and intellectual improvement which the world would have exhibited, had they never lived. A little more nonsense would have been talked for a century or two; and perhaps a few more men, women, and children, burnt as heretics. We

---

[5] Although Rousseau has been thus classed, he was essentially a poet. The others, even Voltaire, were mere reasoners. [Shelley's note.]

might not at this moment have been congratulating each other on the abolition of the Inquisition in Spain. But it exceeds all imagination to conceive
what would have been the moral condition of the world if neither Dante,
Petrarch, Boccaccio, Chaucer, Shakespeare, Calderon, Lord Bacon, nor Milton, had ever existed; if Raphael and Michael Angelo had never been born; if
the Hebrew poetry had never been translated; if a revival of the study of
Greek literature had never taken place; if no monuments of ancient sculpture
had been handed down to us; and if the poetry of the religion of the ancient
world had been extinguished together with its belief. The human mind could
never, except by the intervention of these excitements, have been awakened
to the invention of the grosser sciences, and that application of analytical reasoning to the aberrations of society, which it is now attempted to exalt over
the direct expression of the inventive and creative faculty itself.

We have more moral, political and historical wisdom, than we know
how to reduce into practice; we have more scientific and economical knowledge than can be accommodated to the just distribution of the produce which
it multiplies. The poetry in these systems of thought, is concealed by the accumulation of facts and calculating processes. There is no want of knowledge respecting what is wisest and best in morals, government, and political
economy, or at least, what is wiser and better than what men now practice
and endure. But we let 'I dare not wait upon I would, like the poor cat in the
adage.' We want the creative faculty to imagine that which we know; we
want the generous impulse to act that which we imagine; we want the poetry
of life: our calculations have outrun conception; we have eaten more than we
can digest. The cultivation of those sciences which have enlarged the limits of
the empire of man over the external world, has, for want of the poetical faculty, proportionally circumscribed those of the internal world; and man, having enslaved the elements, remains himself a slave. To what but a cultivation
of the mechanical arts in a degree disproportioned to the presence of the creative faculty, which is the basis of all knowledge, is to be attributed the abuse
of all invention for abridging and combining labour, to the exasperation of
the inequality of mankind? From what other cause has it arisen that the discoveries which should have lightened, have added a weight to the curse
imposed on Adam? Poetry, and the principle of Self, of which money is the
visible incarnation, are the God and Mammon of the world.

The function of the poetical faculty are two-fold; by one it creates new
materials of knowledge and power and pleasure; by the other it engenders in
the mind a desire to reproduce and arrange them according to a certain
rhythm and order which may be called the beautiful and the good. The cultivation of poetry is never more to be desired than at periods when, from an
excess of the selfish and calculating principle, the accumulation of the materials of external life exceed the quantity of the power of assimilating them to
the internal laws of human nature. The body has then become too unwieldy
for that which animates it.

Poetry is indeed something divine. It is at once the centre and circumference of knowledge; it is that which comprehends all science, and that to

language epiphanal, almost religious

which all science must be referred. It is at the same time the root and blossom of all other systems of thought; it is that from which all spring, and that which adorns all; and that which, if blighted, denies the fruit and the seed, and withholds from the barren world the nourishment and the succession of the scions of the tree of life. It is the perfect and consummate surface and bloom of all things; it is as the odour and the colour of the rose to the texture of the elements which compose it, as the form and splendour of unfaded beauty to the secrets of anatomy and corruption. What were virtue, love, patriotism, friendship—what were the scenery of this beautiful universe which we inhabit; what were our consolations on this side of the grave—and what were our aspirations beyond it, if poetry did not ascend to bring light and fire from those eternal regions where the owl-winged faculty of calculation dare not ever soar? Poetry is not like reasoning, a power to be exerted according to the determination of the will. A man cannot say, 'I will compose poetry.' The greatest poet even cannot say it; for the mind in creation is as a fading coal, which some invisible influence, like an inconstant wind, awakens to transitory brightness; this power arises from within, like the color of a flower which fades and changes as it is developed, and the conscious portions of our natures are unprophetic either of its approach or its departure. Could this influence be durable in its original purity and force, it is impossible to predict the greatness of the results; but when composition begins, inspiration is already on the decline, and the most glorious poetry that has ever been communicated to the world is probably a feeble shadow of the original conceptions of the poet. I appeal to the greatest poets of the present day, whether it is not an error to assert that the finest passages of poetry are produced by labour and study. The toil and the delay recommended by critics, can be justly interpreted to mean no more than a careful observation of the inspired moments, and an artificial connexion of the spaces between their suggestions by the intertexture of conventional expressions; a necessity only imposed by the limitedness of the poetical faculty itself; for Milton conceived the *Paradise Lost* as a whole before he executed it in portions. We have his own authority also for the muse having 'dictated' to him the 'unpremeditated song.' And let this be an answer to those who would allege the fifty-six various readings of the first line of the *Orlando Furioso*. Compositions so produced are to poetry what mosaic is to painting. This instinct and intuition of the poetical faculty is still more observable in the plastic and pictorial arts; a great statue or picture grows under the power of the artist as a child in the mother's womb; and the very mind which directs the hands in formation is incapable of accounting to itself for the origin, the gradations, or the media of the process.

Poetry is the record of the best and happiest moments of the happiest and best minds. We are aware of evanescent visitations of thought and feeling sometimes associated with place or person, sometimes regarding our own mind alone, and always arising unforeseen and departing unbidden, but elevating and delightful beyond all expression: so that even in the desire and regret they leave, there cannot but be pleasure, participating as it does in the nature of its object. It is as it were the interpenetration of a diviner nature through our own; but its footsteps are like those of a wind over the sea, which the coming calm erases, and whose traces remain only, as on the wrinkled sand which paves it. These and corresponding conditions of being are experienced principally by those of the most delicate sensibility and the most enlarged imagination; and the state of mind produced by them is at war with every base desire. The enthusiasm of virtue, love, patriotism, and friendship, is essentially linked with such emotions; and whilst they last, self appears as what it is, an atom to a universe. Poets are not only subject to these experiences as spirits of the most refined organization, but they can colour all that they combine with the evanescent hues of this ethereal world; a word, a trait in the representation of a scene or a passion, will touch the en-chanted chord, and reanimate, in those who have ever experienced these emotions, the sleeping, the cold, the buried image of the past. Poetry thus makes immortal all that is best and most beautiful in the world; it arrests the vanishing apparitions which haunt the interlunations of life, and veiling them, or in language or in form, sends them forth among mankind, bearing sweet news of kindred joy to those with whom their sisters abide — abide, because there is no portal of expression from the caverns of the spirit which they inhabit into the universe of things. Poetry redeems from decay the visi-tations of the divinity in man.

Poetry turns all things to loveliness; it exalts the beauty of that which is most beautiful, and it adds beauty to that which is most deformed; it marries exultation and horror, grief and pleasure, eternity and change; it subdues to union under its light yoke, all irreconcilable things. It transmutes all that it touches, and every form moving within the radiance of its presence is changed by wondrous sympathy to an incarnation of the spirit which it breathes: its secret alchemy turns to potable gold the poisonous waters which flow from death through life; it strips the veil of familiarity from the world, and lays bare the naked and sleeping beauty, which is the spirit of its forms.

All things exist as they are perceived; at least in relation to the percipient. 'The mind is its own place, and of itself can make a heaven of hell, a hell of heaven.' But poetry defeats the curse which binds us to be subjected to the accident of surrounding impressions. And whether it spreads its own figured curtain, or withdraws life's dark veil from before the scene of things, it equally creates for us a being within our being. It makes us the inhabitants of a world to which the familiar world is a chaos. It reproduces the common universe of which we are portions and percipients, and it purges from our in-ward sight the film of familiarity which obscures from us the wonder of our being. It compels us to feel that which we perceive, and to imagine that which we know. It creates anew the universe, after it has been annihilated in our minds by the recurrence of impressions blunted by reiteration. It justifies the bold and true words of Tasso: *Non merita nome di creatore, se non Iddio ed il Poeta.*[6]

---

[6] None but God and the poet deserve the name of creator.

⌐A poet, as he is the author to others of the highest wisdom, pleasure, virtue and glory, so he ought personally to be the happiest, the best, the wisest, and the most illustrious of men. As to his glory, let time be challenged to declare whether the fame of any other institutor of human life be comparable to that of a poet. That he is the wisest, the happiest, and the best, inasmuch as he is a poet, is equally incontrovertible: the greatest poets have been men of the most spotless virtue, of the most consummate prudence, and, if we would look into the interior of their lives, the most fortunate of men: and the exceptions, as they regard those who possessed the poetic faculty in a high yet inferior degree, will be found on consideration to confine rather than destroy the rule. Let us for a moment stoop to the arbitration of popular breath, and usurping and uniting in our own persons the incompatible characters of accuser, witness, judge, and executioner, let us decide without trial, testimony, or form, that certain motives of those who are 'there sitting where we dare not soar,' are reprehensible. Let us assume that Homer was a drunkard, that Virgil was a flatterer, that Horace was a coward, that Tasso was a madman, that Lord Bacon was a peculator, that Raphael was a libertine, that Spenser was a poet laureate. It is inconsistent with this division of our subject to cite living poets, but posterity has done ample justice to the great names now referred to. Their errors have been weighed and found to have been dust in the balance; if their sins 'were as scarlet, they are now white as snow': they have been washed in the blood of the mediator and redeemer, Time. Observe in what a ludicrous chaos the imputations of real or fictitious crime have been confused in the contemporary calumnies against poetry and poets; consider how little is, as it appears—or appears, as it is; look to your own motives, and judge not, lest ye be judged.

⌐Poetry, as has been said, differs in this respect from logic, that it is not subject to the control of the active powers of the mind, and that its birth and recurrence have no necessary connexion with the consciousness or will. It is presumptuous to determine that these are the necessary conditions of all mental causation, when mental effects are experienced unsusceptible of being referred to them. The frequent recurrence of the poetical power, it is obvious to suppose, may produce in the mind a habit of order and harmony correlative with its own nature and with its effects upon other minds. But in the intervals of inspiration, and they may be frequent without being durable, a poet becomes a man, and is abandoned to the sudden reflux of the influences under which others habitually live. But as he is more delicately organized than other men, and sensible to pain and pleasure, both his own and that of others, in a degree unknown to them, he will avoid the one and pursue the other with an ardour proportioned to this difference. And he renders himself obnoxious to calumny, when he neglects to observe the circumstances under which these objects of universal pursuit and flight have disguised themselves in one another's garments.

But there is nothing necessarily evil in this error, and thus cruelty, envy, revenge, avarice, and the passions purely evil, have never formed any portion of the popular imputations on the lives of poets.

I have thought it most favourable to the cause of truth to set down these remarks according to the order in which they were suggested to my mind, by a consideration of the subject itself, instead of observing the formality of a polemical reply; but if the view which they contain be just, they will be found to involve a refutation of the arguers against poetry, so far at least as regards the first division of the subject. I can readily conjecture what should have moved the gall of some learned and intelligent writers who quarrel with certain versifiers; I confess myself, like them, unwilling to be stunned by the Theseids of the hoarse Codri of the day. Bavius and Maevius undoubtedly are, as they ever were, insufferable persons. But it belongs to a philosophical critic to distinguish rather than confound.

The first part of these remarks has related to poetry in its elements and principles; and it has been shown, as well as the narrow limits assigned them would permit, that what is called poetry, in a restricted sense, has a common source with all other forms of order and of beauty, according to which the materials of human life are susceptible of being arranged, and which is poetry in a universal sense.

The second part will have for its object an application of these principles to the present state of the cultivation of poetry, and a defence of the attempt to idealize the modern forms of manners and opinions, and compel them into a subordination to the imaginative and creative faculty. For the literature of England, an energetic development of which has ever preceded or accompanied a great and free development of the national will, has arisen as it were from a new birth. In spite of the low-thoughted envy which would undervalue contemporary merit, our own will be a memorable age in intellectual achievements, and we live among such philosophers and poets as surpass beyond comparison any who have appeared since the last national struggle for civil and religious liberty. The most unfailing herald, companion, and follower of the awakening of a great people to work a beneficial change in opinion or institution, is poetry. At such periods there is an accumulation of the power of communicating and receiving intense and impassioned conceptions respecting man and nature. The persons in whom this power resides may often, as far as regards many portions of their nature, have little apparent correspondence with that spirit of good of which they are the ministers. But even whilst they deny and abjure, they are yet compelled to serve, the power which is seated on the throne of their own soul. It is impossible to read the compositions of the most celebrated writers of the present day without being startled with the electric life which burns within their words. They measure the circumference and sound the depths of human nature with a comprehensive and all-penetrating spirit, and they are themselves perhaps the most sincerely astonished at its manifestations; for it is less their spirit than the spirit of the age. Poets are the hierophants of an unapprehended inspiration; the mirrors of the gigantic shadows which futurity casts upon the present; the words which express what they understand not; the trumpets which sing to battle, and feel not what they inspire; the influence which is moved not, but moves. Poets are the unacknowledged legislators of the world.

KARL MARX

From *The German Ideology*

1846

Karl Marx (1818–1883) perceived the vast inequalities of the class structure against which his writings argue so forcibly, even though he was born into a well-off German family, received a good education in law, and was expected to live a traditional upper-middle-class life. Horrified by the excesses of the nineteenth-century industrial revolution, he took to journalism and political agitation and lived much of his later life in poverty and exile in London. There he refined his theories and produced some of his best-known writings, including The Communist Manifesto (1848) and Das Kapital (1867). In these and other works, Marx set himself in opposition to those philosophers who sought merely to interpret the world around them. Marx, and his frequent collaborator and sometimes patron Friedrich Engels, wanted to change that world.

In contrast to idealist philosophy, which concerns itself primarily with the world of the mind, ideas, and the transcendent, Marx's philosophy is materialist, empirically grounded in the concrete world of work and economic relationships, rejecting metaphysical explanations. Few would dispute that such things as housing, clothing, and consumption of material goods are determined in large part by economic factors. But according to Marx, even more abstract concerns such as history and culture are likewise so determined. He discusses the stages of history—a move from tribal and communal ownership through feudal organization to the modern state of industrial capitalism—as based on the increasing fragmentation of class and concentration of production and ownership. Indeed, what we think of as culture—laws, religion, philosophy, art, ideas—Marx saw as a superstructure that rests on and grows out of a base of socioeconomic power relations and class struggle. Thus, for instance, the structure of the family is a product of the need to produce and train workers for the next generation and not solely an indication of altruistic parental affection. Because Marx believed that language and its uses are socially and economically conditioned, he became an important figure for literary theorists and critics.

If Marx's tone in this excerpt seems at times defensive, we should remember that he sets himself in opposition to the whole history of philosophy, particularly the *idealist philosophy of his German predecessors, such as Immanuel Kant (p. 232). It also becomes clear in this excerpt that just as Marx saw the external world as influencing cultural production, his writings too are a product of his particular time and circumstances. As such, some of his ideas and stylistic conventions can strike contemporary readers as naively old-fashioned or even offensive. Later critics have faulted, for example, his unfailing belief in "progress" and his ethnocentric reliance on European history as his only model. Neither Marx nor his original audience, however, was in a position to notice or critique these things, and despite them (and the general skepticism about communism that pervaded America and Western Europe) his work has remained enormously influential. Terry Eagleton, in the selection beginning on page 525, explores some of the ways Marxist theory has influenced literary criticism.*

The Premisses of the Materialist Method

THE PREMISSES from which we begin are not arbitrary ones, not dogmas, but real premisses from which abstraction can only be made in the imagination. They are the real individuals, their activity and the material conditions under which they live, both those which they find already existing and those produced by their activity. These premisses can thus be verified in a purely empirical way.

The first premiss of all human history is, of course, the existence of living human individuals. Thus the first fact to be established is the physical organization of these individuals and their consequent relation to the rest of nature. Of course, we cannot here go either into the actual physical nature of man, or into the natural conditions in which man finds himself—geological, oro-hydrographical, climatic, and so on. The writing of history must always set out from these natural bases and their modification in the course of history through the action of men.

Men can be distinguished from animals by consciousness, by religion, or anything else you like. They themselves begin to distinguish themselves from animals as soon as they begin to produce their means of subsistence, a step which is conditioned by their physical organization. By producing their means of subsistence men are indirectly producing their actual material life.

The way in which men produce their means of subsistence depends first of all on the nature of the actual means of subsistence they find in existence and have to reproduce. This mode of production must not be considered simply as being the production of the physical existence of the individuals. Rather it is a definite form of activity of these individuals, a definite form of expressing their life, a definite mode of life on their part. As individuals express their life, so they are. What they are, therefore, coincides with their production, both with *what* they produce and with *how* they produce. The nature of individuals thus depends on the material conditions determining their production.

This production only makes its appearance with the increase of population. In its turn this presupposes the intercourse of individuals with one another. The form of this intercourse is again determined by production.

The relations of different nations among themselves depend upon the extent to which each has developed its productive forces, the division of labour, and internal intercourse. This statement is generally recognized. But not only the relation of one nation to others, but also the whole internal structure of the nation itself depends on the stage of development reached by its production and its internal and external intercourse. How far the productive forces of a nation are developed is shown most manifestly by the degree to which the division of labour has been carried. Each new productive force, in so far as it is not merely a quantitative extension of productive forces already known (for instance the bringing into cultivation of fresh land), causes a further development of the division of labour.

The division of labour inside a nation leads at first to the separation of industrial and commercial from agricultural labour, and hence to the separation of town and country and to the conflict of their interests. Its further development leads to the separation of commercial from industrial labour. At the same time, through the division of labour inside these various branches there develop various divisions among the individuals co-operating in definite kinds of labour. The relative position of these individual groups is determined by the methods employed in agriculture, industry, and commerce (patriarchalism, slavery, estates, classes). These same conditions are to be seen (given a more developed intercourse) in the relations of different nations to one another.

The various stages of development in the division of labour are just so many different forms of ownership, i.e. the existing stage in the division of labour determines also the relations of individuals to one another with reference to the material, instrument, and product of labour.

The first form of ownership is tribal ownership. It corresponds to the undeveloped stage of production, at which a people lives by hunting and fishing, by the rearing of beasts, or, in the highest stage, agriculture. In the latter case it presupposes a great mass of uncultivated stretches of land. The division of labour is at this stage still very elementary and is confined to a further extension of the natural division of labour existing in the family. The social structure is, therefore, limited to an extension of the family; patriarchal family chieftains, below them the members of the tribe, finally slaves. The slavery latent in the family only develops gradually with the increase of population, the growth of wants, and with the extension of external relations, both of war and of barter.

The second form is the ancient communal and State ownership which proceeds especially from the union of several tribes into a city by agreement or by conquest, and which is still accompanied by slavery. Beside communal ownership we already find movable, and later also immovable, private property developing, but as an abnormal form subordinate to communal ownership. The citizens hold power over their labouring slaves only in their community, and on this account alone, therefore, they are bound to the form of communal ownership. It is the communal private property which compels the active citizens to remain in this spontaneously derived form of association over against their slaves. For this reason the whole structure of society based on this communal ownership, and with it the power of the people, decays in the same measure as, in particular, immovable private property evolves. The division of labour is already more developed. We already find the antagonism of town and country; later the antagonism between those states which represent town interests and those which represent country interests, and inside the towns themselves the antagonism between industry and maritime commerce. The class relation between citizens and slaves is now completely developed.

With the development of private property, we find here for the first time the same conditions which we shall find again, only on a more extensive scale, with modern private property. On the one hand, the concentration of private property, which began very early in Rome (as the Licinian agrarian law proves) and proceeded very rapidly from the time of the civil wars and especially under the Emperors; on the other hand, coupled with this, the transformation of the plebeian small peasantry into a proletariat, which, however, owing to its intermediate position between propertied citizens and slaves, never achieved an independent development.

The third form of ownership is feudal or estate property. If antiquity started out from the town and its little territory, the Middle Ages started out from the country. This differing starting-point was determined by the sparseness of the population at that time, which was scattered over a large area and which received no large increase from the conquerors. In contrast to Greece and Rome, feudal development at the outset, therefore, extends over a much wider territory, prepared by the Roman conquests and the spread of agriculture at first associated with it. The last centuries of the declining Roman Empire and its conquest by the barbarians destroyed a number of productive forces; agriculture had declined, industry had decayed for want of a market, trade had died out or been violently suspended, the rural and urban population had decreased. From these conditions and the mode of organization of the conquest determined by them, feudal property developed under the influence of the Germanic military constitution. Like tribal and communal ownership, it is based again on a community; but the directly producing class standing over against it is not, as in the case of the ancient community, the slaves, but the enserfed small peasantry. As soon as feudalism is fully developed, there also arises antagonism towards the towns. The hierarchical structure of landownership, and the armed bodies of retainers associated with it, gave the nobility power over the serfs. This feudal organization was, just as much as the ancient communal ownership, an association against a subjected producing class; but the form of association and the relation to the direct producers were different because of the different conditions of production.

This feudal system of landownership had its counterpart in the towns in the shape of corporative property, the feudal organization of trades. Here

property consisted chiefly in the labour of each individual person. The necessity for association against the organized robber barons, the need for communal covered markets in an age when the industrialist was at the same time a
merchant, the growing competition of the escaped serfs swarming into the
rising towns, the feudal structure of the whole country: these combined to
bring about the guilds. The gradually accumulated small capital of individual craftsmen and their stable numbers, as against the growing population,
evolved the relation of journeyman and apprentice, which brought into being
in the towns a hierarchy similar to that in the country.

Thus the chief form of property during the feudal epoch consisted on the
one hand of landed property with serf labour chained to it, and on the other
of the labour of the individual with small capital commanding the labour of
journeymen. The organization of both was determined by the restricted conditions of production—the small-scale and primitive cultivation of the land
and the craft type of industry. There was little division of labour in the heyday of feudalism. Each country bore in itself the antithesis of town and country; the division into estates was certainly strongly marked; but apart from
the differentiation of princes, nobility, clergy, and peasants in the country,
and masters, journeymen, apprentices, and soon also the rabble of casual
labourers in the towns, no division of importance took place. In agriculture it
was rendered difficult by the strip-system, beside which the cottage industry
of the peasants themselves emerged. In industry there was no division of
labour at all in the individual trades themselves, and very little between
them. The separation of industry and commerce was found already in existence in older towns; in the newer it only developed later, when the towns
entered into mutual relations.

The grouping of larger territories into feudal kingdoms was a necessity
for the landed nobility as for the towns. The organization of the ruling class,
the nobility, had, therefore, everywhere a monarch at its head.

The fact is, therefore, that definite individuals who are productively active in a definite way enter into these definite social and political relations.
Empirical observation must in each separate instance bring out empirically,
and without any mystification and speculation, the connection of the social
and political structure with production. The social structure and the State are
continually evolving out of the life-process of definite individuals, but of individuals, not as they may appear in their own or other people's imagination,
but as they really are, i.e. as they operate, produce materially, and hence as
they work under definite material limits, presuppositions, and conditions independent of their will.

The production of ideas, of conceptions, of consciousness, is at first directly interwoven with the material activity and the material intercourse of
men, the language of real life. Conceiving, thinking, the mental intercourse of
men, appear at this stage as the direct efflux of their material behaviour. The
same applies to mental production as expressed in the language of politics,
laws, morality, religion, metaphysics, etc. of a people. Men are the producers
of their conceptions, ideas, etc.—real, active men, as they are conditioned by

a definite development of their productive forces and of the intercourse corresponding to these, up to its furthest forms. Consciousness can never be anything else than conscious existence, and the existence of men is their actual life-process. If in all ideology men and their circumstances appear upside-down as in a *camera obscura*, this phenomenon arises just as much from their historical life-process as the inversion of objects on the retina does from their physical life-process.

In direct contrast to German philosophy which descends from heaven to earth, here we ascend from earth to heaven. That is to say, we do not set out from what men say, imagine, conceive, nor from men as narrated, thought of, imagined, conceived, in order to arrive at men in the flesh. We set out from real, active men, and on the basis of their real life-process we demonstrate the development of the ideological reflexes and echoes of this life-process. The phantoms formed in the human brain are also, necessarily, sublimates of their material life-process, which is empirically verifiable and bound to material premises. Morality, religion, metaphysics, all the rest of ideology and their corresponding forms of consciousness, thus no longer retain the semblance of independence. They have no history, no development; but men, developing their material production and their material intercourse, alter, along with this their real existence, their thinking and the products of their thinking. Life is not determined by consciousness, but consciousness by life. In the first method of approach the starting-point is consciousness taken as the living individual; in the second method, which conforms to real life, it is the real living individuals themselves, and consciousness is considered solely as their consciousness.

This method of approach is not devoid of premises. It starts out from the real premises and does not abandon them for a moment. Its premises are men, not in any fantastic isolation and rigidity, but in their actual, empirically perceptible process of development under definite conditions. As soon as this active life-process is described, history ceases to be a collection of dead facts as it is with the empiricists (themselves still abstract), or an imagined activity of imagined subjects, as with the idealists.

Where speculation ends—in real life—there real, positive science begins: the representation of the practical activity, of the practical process of development of men. Empty talk about consciousness ceases, and real knowledge has to take its place. When reality is depicted, philosophy as an independent branch of knowledge loses its medium of existence. At the best its place can only be taken by a summing-up of the most general results, abstractions which arise from the observation of the historical development of men. Viewed apart from real history, these abstractions have in themselves no value whatsoever. They can only serve to facilitate the arrangement of historical material, to indicate the sequence of its separate strata. But they by no means afford a recipe or schema, as does philosophy, for neatly trimming the epochs of history. On the contrary, our difficulties begin only when we set about the observation and the arrangement—the real depiction—of our historical material, whether of a past epoch or of the present. The removal of these difficulties is governed by premisses which it is quite impossible to state here, but which only the study of the actual life-process and the activity of the individuals of each epoch will make evident. We shall select here some of these abstractions, which we use in contradistinction to the ideologists, and shall illustrate them by historical examples.

Since we are dealing with the Germans, who are devoid of premisses, we must begin by stating the first premiss of all human existence and, therefore, of all history, the premiss, namely, that men must be in a position to live in order to be able to 'make history'. But life involves before everything else eating and drinking, a habitation, clothing, and many other things. The first historical act is thus the production of the means to satisfy these needs, the production of material life itself. And indeed this is an historical act, a fundamental condition of all history, which today, as thousands of years ago, must daily and hourly be fulfilled merely in order to sustain human life. Even when the sensuous world is reduced to a minimum, to a stick as with Saint Bruno, it presupposes the action of producing the stick. Therefore in any interpretation of history one has first of all to observe this fundamental fact in all its significance and all its implications and to accord it its due importance. It is well known that the Germans have never done this, and they have never, therefore, had an earthly basis for history and consequently never an historian. The French and the English, even if they have conceived the relation of this fact with so-called history only in an extremely one-sided fashion, particularly as long as they remained in the toils of political ideology, have nevertheless made the first attempts to give the writing of history a materialistic basis by being the first to write histories of civil society, of commerce and industry.

The second point is that the satisfaction of the first need (the action of satisfying, and the instrument of satisfaction which has been acquired) leads to new needs; and this production of new needs is the first historical act. Here we recognize immediately the spiritual ancestry of the great historical wisdom of the Germans who, when they run out of positive material and when they can serve up neither theological nor political nor literary rubbish, assert that this is not history at all, but the 'prehistoric era'. They do not, however, enlighten us as to how we proceed from this nonsensical 'prehistory' to history proper; although, on the other hand, in their historical speculation they seize upon this 'prehistory' with especial eagerness because they imagine themselves safe there from interference on the part of 'crude facts', and, at the same time, because there they can give full rein to their speculative impulse and set up and knock down hypotheses by the thousand.

The third circumstance which, from the very outset, enters into historical development, is that men, who daily remake their own life, begin to make other men, to propagate their kind: the relation between man and woman, parents and children, the family. The family, which to begin with is the only social relationship, becomes later, when increased needs create new social relations and the increased population new needs, a subordinate one (except in Germany), and must then be treated and analysed according to the existing empirical data, not according to 'the concept of the family', as is the custom in Germany. These three aspects of social activity are not of course to be taken as three different stages, but just as three aspects or, to make it clear to the Germans, three 'moments', which have existed simultaneously since the dawn of history and the first men, and which still assert themselves in history today.

The production of life, both of one's own in labour and of fresh life in procreation, now appears as a double relationship: on the one hand as a natural, on the other as a social, relationship. By social we understand the co-operation of several individuals, no matter under what conditions, in what manner, and to what end. It follows from this that a certain mode of production, or industrial stage, is always combined with a certain mode of co-operation, or social stage, and this mode of co-operation is itself a 'productive force'. Further, that the multitude of productive forces accessible to men determines the nature of society, hence, that the 'history of humanity' must always be studied and treated in relation to the history of industry and exchange. But it is also clear how in Germany it is impossible to write this sort of history, because the Germans lack not only the necessary power of comprehension and the material but also the 'evidence of their senses', for across the Rhine you cannot have any experience of these things since history has stopped happening. Thus it is quite obvious from the start that there exists a materialistic connection of men with one another, which is determined by their needs and their mode of production, and which is as old as men themselves. This connection is ever taking on new forms, and thus presents a 'history' independently of the existence of any political or religious nonsense which in addition may hold men together.

Only now, after having considered four moments, four aspects of the primary historical relationships, do we find that man also possesses 'consciousness', but, even so, not inherent, not 'pure' consciousness. From the start the 'spirit' is afflicted with the curse of being 'burdened' with matter, which here makes its appearance in the form of agitated layers of air, sounds, in short, of language. Language is as old as consciousness, language is practical consciousness that exists also for other men, and for that reason alone it really exists for me personally as well; language, like consciousness, only arises from the need, the necessity, of intercourse with other men. Where there exists a relationship, it exists for me: the animal does not enter into 'relations' with anything, it does not enter into any relation at all. For the animal, its relation to others does not exist as a relation. Consciousness is, therefore, from the very beginning a social product, and remains so as long as men exist at all. Consciousness is at first, of course, merely consciousness concerning the immediate sensuous environment and consciousness of the limited connection with other persons and things outside the individual who is growing self-conscious. At the same time it is consciousness of nature, which first appears to men as a completely alien, all-powerful, and unassailable force, with which men's relations are purely animal and by which they are overawed like beasts; it is thus a purely animal consciousness of nature (natural religion) just because nature is as yet hardly modified historically. (We see here immediately that this natural religion or this particular relation of men to nature is determined by the form of society and vice versa. Here, as everywhere, the identity of nature and man appears in such a way that the restricted relation of men to nature determines their restricted relation to one another, and their restricted relation to one another determines men's restricted relation to nature.) On the other hand, man's consciousness of the necessity of associating with the individuals around him is the beginning of the consciousness that he is living in society at all. This beginning is as animal as social life itself at this stage. It is mere herd-consciousness, and at this point man is only distinguished from sheep by the fact that with him consciousness takes the place of instinct or that his instinct is a conscious one. This sheep-like or tribal consciousness receives its further development and extension through increased productivity, the increase of needs, and, what is fundamental to both of these, the increase of population. With these there develops the division of labour, which was originally nothing but the division of labour in the sexual act, then that division of labour which develops spontaneously or 'naturally' by virtue of natural predisposition (e.g. physical strength), needs, accidents, etc. etc. Division of labour only becomes truly such from the moment when a division of material and mental labour appears. (The first form of ideologists, priests, is concurrent.) From this moment onwards consciousness can really flatter itself that it is something other than consciousness of existing practice, that it really represents something without representing something real; from now on consciousness is in a position to emancipate itself from the world and to proceed to the formation of 'pure' theory, theology, philosophy, ethics, etc. But even if this theory, theology, philosophy, ethics, etc. comes into contradiction with the existing relations, this can only occur because existing social relations have come into contradiction with existing forces of production; this, moreover, can also occur in a particular national sphere of relations through the appearance of the contradiction, not within the national orbit, but between this national consciousness and the practice of other nations, i.e. between the national and the general consciousness of a nation (as we see it now in Germany).

Moreover, it is quite immaterial what consciousness starts to do on its own: out of all such muck we get only the one inference that these three moments, the forces of production, the state of society, and consciousness, can and must come into contradiction with one another, because the division of labour implies the possibility, nay the fact, that intellectual and material activity—enjoyment and labour, production and consumption—devolve on different individuals, and that the only possibility of their not coming into contradiction lies in the negation in its turn of the division of labour. It is self-evident, moreover, that 'spectres', 'bonds', 'the higher being', 'concept', 'scruple', are merely the idealistic, spiritual expression, the conception apparently of the isolated individual, the image of very empirical fetters and limitations, within which the mode of production of life and the form of intercourse coupled with it move.

                                          Translated by S. Ryazanskaya.

FRIEDRICH NIETZSCHE

From *The Birth of Tragedy*

1874

═══════════
═══════════

German philosopher Friedrich Nietzsche (1844–1900) was not primarily a literary critic (though it is obvious from the following excerpt that he was well read in the classics), but he is important in the history of literary theory for having turned on its head one of the key components of Aristotle's Poetics *(p. 18). He saw tragedy, indeed all drama, as consisting of interplay between the two forces he named* Dionysian *and* Apollonian. *Named for the Greek god of the sun, the Apollonian spirit is individual, rational, and calm and is seen most clearly in the dramatic elements of plot and language. The Dionysian spirit, named for the god of wine and revelry, is communal, irrational, and frenzied and is embodied on stage in spectacle and music. The (rarely used) full title of Nietzsche's first book,* The Birth of Tragedy from the Spirit of Music, *suggests the primacy he gives to the Dionysian, in direct opposition to Aristotle's privileging of plot and language. Nietzsche was interested in the irrational power of tragic spectacle, which allowed civilized people to "lose" themselves through "the shattering of the individual and his fusion with primal being."*

In the excerpt that follows, Nietzsche concerns himself with two elements of Greek tragedy, one historical and the other formal. First, he posits the origins of drama in the religious festival of Dionysus, a theory that has since been confirmed and further developed by drama historians. This origin leads directly to the form of the drama, with a chorus playing a central role in the action and in our interpretation of that action. The key to understanding the role of the chorus is the spectacle of the satyr dances from which it arose. The first edition of The Birth of Tragedy *was dedicated to Richard Wagner, whose grand, mythic operas, Nietzsche thought, satisfied modern audiences by dramatizing for them an apocalyptic musical spectacle as Greek tragedy once had done.*

Nietzsche's belief that the human soul constantly hungers for knowledge and transcendence set him against the complacency that many consider the predominant spirit of the Victorian age. For a number of years after World War II his work fell out of favor because his ideas were taken up and used to support Nazi ideology in ways that no doubt would have appalled the philosopher himself. However, his questioning of commonly held beliefs, his overturning of previous hierarchies, and his insistence on the primacy of interpretations over facts helped Nietzsche's works find new currency with the poststructuralists of the late twentieth century, including Jacques Derrida (p. 493) and Paul de Man (p. 559).

7

WE MUST NOW avail ourselves of all the principles of art considered so far, in order to find our way through the labyrinth, as we must call it, of *the origin of Greek tragedy.* I do not think I am unreasonable in saying that the problem of this origin has as yet not even been seriously posed, to say nothing of solved, however often the ragged tatters of ancient tradition have been sewn together in various combinations and torn apart again. This tradition tells us quite unequivocally *that tragedy arose from the tragic chorus,* and was originally only chorus and nothing but chorus. Hence we consider it our duty to look into the heart of this tragic chorus as the real proto-drama, without resting satisfied with such arty clichés as that the chorus is the "ideal spectator" or that it represents the people in contrast to the aristocratic region of the scene. This latter explanation has a sublime sound to many a politician—as if the immutable moral law had been embodied by the democratic Athenians in the popular chorus, which always won out over the passionate excesses and extravagances of kings. This theory may be ever so forcibly suggested by one of Aristotle's observations; still, it has no influence on the original formation of tragedy, inasmuch as the whole opposition of prince and people—indeed the whole politico-social sphere—was excluded from the purely religious origins of tragedy. But even regarding the classical form of the chorus in Aeschylus and Sophocles, which is known to us, we should deem it blasphemy to speak here of intimations of "constitutional popular representation." From this blasphemy, however, others have not shrunk. Ancient constitutions knew of no constitutional representation of the people in *praxi,* and it is to be hoped that they did not even "have intimations" of it in tragedy.

Much more famous than this political interpretation of the chorus is the idea of A. W. Schlegel,[1] who advises us to regard the chorus somehow as the essence and extract of the crowd of spectators—as the "ideal spectator." This view, when compared with the historical tradition that originally tragedy was only chorus, reveals itself for what it is—a crude, unscientific, yet brilliant claim that owes its brilliancy only to its concentrated form of expression, to the typically Germanic bias in favor of anything called "ideal," and to our momentary astonishment. For we are certainly astonished the moment we compare our familiar theatrical public with this chorus, and ask ourselves whether it could ever be possible to idealize from such a public something

[1]One of the leading spirits of the early German romantic movement, especially renowned for his translations of about half of Shakespeare's plays; born 1767, died 1845. [All notes are the translator's.]

analogous to the Greek tragic chorus. We tacitly deny this, and now wonder as much at the boldness of Schlegel's claim as at the totally different nature of the Greek public. For we had always believed that the right spectator, whoever he might be, must always remain conscious that he was viewing a work of art and not an empirical reality. But the tragic chorus of the Greeks is forced to recognize real beings in the figures on the stage. The chorus of the Oceanides really believes that it sees before it the Titan Prometheus, and it considers itself as real as the god of the scene. But could the highest and purest type of spectator regard Prometheus as bodily present and real, as the Oceanides do? Is it characteristic of the ideal spectator to run onto the stage and free the god from his torments? We had always believed in an aesthetic public and considered the individual spectator the better qualified the more he was capable of viewing a work of art as art, that is, aesthetically. But now Schlegel tells us that the perfect, ideal spectator does not at all allow the world of the drama to act on him aesthetically, but corporally and empirically. Oh, these Greeks! we sigh; they upset all our aesthetics! But once accustomed to this, we repeated Schlegel's saying whenever the chorus came up for discussion.

Now the tradition, which is quite explicit, speaks against Schlegel. The chorus as such, without the stage—the primitive form of tragedy—and the chorus of ideal spectators do not go together. What kind of artistic genre could possibly be extracted from the concept of the spectator, and find its true form in the "spectator as such"? The spectator without the spectacle is an absurd notion. We fear that the birth of tragedy is to be explained neither by any high esteem for the moral intelligence of the masses nor by the concept of the spectator without a spectacle; and we consider the problem too deep to be even touched by such superficial considerations.

An infinitely more valuable insight into the significance of the chorus was displayed by Schiller in the celebrated Preface to his *Bride of Messina*, where he regards the chorus as a living wall that tragedy constructs around itself in order to close itself off from the world of reality and to preserve its ideal domain and its poetical freedom.

With this, his chief weapon, Schiller combats the ordinary conception of the natural, the illusion usually demanded in dramatic poetry. Although the stage day is merely artificial, the architecture only symbolical, and the metrical language ideal in character, nevertheless an erroneous view still prevails in the main, as he points out: it is not sufficient that one merely tolerates as poetic license what is actually the essence of all poetry. The introduction of the chorus, says Schiller, is the decisive step by which war is declared openly and honorably against all naturalism in art.

It would seem that to denigrate this view of the matter our would-be superior age has coined the disdainful catchword "pseudo-idealism." I fear, however, that we, on the other hand, with our present adoration of the natural and the real, have reached the opposite pole of all idealism, namely, the region of wax-work cabinets. There is an art in these, too, as there is in certain novels much in vogue at present; but we really should not be plagued with the claim that such art has overcome the "pseudo-idealism" of Goethe and Schiller.

It is indeed an "ideal" domain, as Schiller correctly perceived, in which the Greek satyr chorus, the chorus of primitive tragedy, was wont to dwell. It is a domain raised high above the actual paths of mortals. For this chorus the Greek built up the scaffolding of a fictitious *natural state* and on it placed fictitious *natural beings*. On this foundation tragedy developed and so, of course, it could dispense from the beginning with a painstaking portrayal of reality. Yet it is no arbitrary world placed by whim between heaven and earth; rather it is a world with the same reality and credibility that Olympus with its inhabitants possessed for the believing Hellene. The satyr, as the Dionysian chorist, lives in a religiously acknowledged reality under the sanction of myth and cult. That tragedy should begin with him, that he should be the voice of the Dionysian wisdom of tragedy, is just as strange a phenomenon for us as the general derivation of tragedy from the chorus.

Perhaps we shall have a point of departure for our inquiry if I put forward the proposition that the satyr, the fictitious natural being, bears the same relation to the man of culture that Dionysian music bears to civilization. Concerning the latter, Richard Wagner says that it is nullified[2] by music just as lamplight is nullified by the light of day. Similarly, I believe, the Greek man of culture felt himself nullified in the presence of the satyric chorus; and this is the most immediate effect of the Dionysian tragedy, that the state and society and, quite generally, the gulfs between man and man give way to an overwhelming feeling of unity leading back to the very heart of nature. The metaphysical comfort—with which, I am suggesting even now, every true tragedy leaves us—that life is at the bottom of things, despite all the changes of appearances, indestructibly powerful and pleasurable—this comfort appears in incarnate clarity in the chorus of satyrs, a chorus of natural beings who live ineradicably, as it were, behind all civilization and remain eternally the same, despite the changes of generations and of the history of nations.

With this chorus the profound Hellene, uniquely susceptible to the tenderest and deepest suffering, comforts himself, having looked boldly right into the terrible destructiveness of so-called world history as well as the cruelty of nature, and being in danger of longing for a Buddhistic negation of the will.[3] Art saves him, and through art—life.

For the rapture of the Dionysian state with its annihilation of the ordinary bounds and limits of existence contains, while it lasts, a *lethargic* element in which all personal experiences of the past become immersed. This chasm of oblivion separates the worlds of everyday reality and of Dionysian reality.

---

[2] *Aufgehoben:* one of Hegel's favorite words, which can also mean lifted up or preserved.

[3] Here Nietzsche's emancipation from Schopenhauer becomes evident, and their difference from each other concerns the central subject of the whole book: the significance of tragedy. Nietzsche writes about tragedy as the great life-affirming alternative to Schopenhauer's negation of the will. One can be as honest and free of optimistic illusions as Schopenhauer was, and still celebrate life as fundamentally powerful and pleasurable as the Greeks did.

But as soon as this everyday reality re-enters consciousness, it is experienced as such, with nausea: an ascetic, will-negating mood is the fruit of these states.

In this sense the Dionysian man resembles Hamlet: both have once looked truly into the essence of things, they have *gained knowledge*, and nausea inhibits action; for their action could not change anything in the eternal nature of things; they feel it to be ridiculous or humiliating that they should be asked to set right a world that is out of joint. Knowledge kills action; action requires the veils of illusion: that is the doctrine of Hamlet, not that cheap wisdom of Jack the Dreamer who reflects too much and, as it were, from an excess of possibilities does not get around to action. Not reflection, no—true knowledge, an insight into the horrible truth, outweighs any motive for action, both in Hamlet and in the Dionysian man.

Now no comfort avails any more; longing transcends a world after death, even the gods; existence is negated along with its glittering reflection in the gods or in an immortal beyond. Conscious of the truth he has once seen, man now sees everywhere only the horror or absurdity of existence; now he understands what is symbolic in Ophelia's fate; now he understands the wisdom of the sylvan god, Silenus: he is nauseated.

Here, when the danger to his will is greatest, *art* approaches as a saving sorceress, expert at healing. She alone knows how to turn these nauseous thoughts about the horror or absurdity of existence into notions with which one can live: these are the *sublime* as the artistic taming of the horrible, and the *comic* as the artistic discharge of the nausea of absurdity. The satyr chorus of the dithyramb is the saving deed of Greek art; faced with the intermediary world of these Dionysian companions, the feelings described here exhausted themselves.[4]

8

The satyr, like the idyllic shepherd of more recent times, is the offspring of a longing for the primitive and the natural; but how firmly and fearlessly the Greek embraced the man of the woods, and how timorously and mawkishly modern man dallied with the flattering image of a sentimental, flute-playing, tender shepherd! Nature, as yet unchanged by knowledge, with the bolts of culture still unbroken—that is what the Greek saw in his satyr who nevertheless was not a mere ape. On the contrary, the satyr was the archetype of man, the embodiment of his highest and most intense emotions, the ecstatic reveler enraptured by the proximity of his god, the sympathetic companion

[4] Having finally broken loose from Schopenhauer, Nietzsche for the first time shows the brilliancy of his own genius. It is doubtful whether anyone before him had illuminated *Hamlet* so extensively in so few words: the passage invites comparison with Freud's great footnote on *Hamlet* in the first edition of *Die Traumdeutung* (interpretation of dreams), 1900. Even more obviously, the last three paragraphs invite comparison with existentialist literature, notably, but by no means only, Sartre's *La Nausée* (1938).

in whom the suffering of the god is repeated, one who proclaims wisdom from the very heart of nature, a symbol of the sexual omnipotence of nature which the Greeks used to contemplate with reverent wonder.

The satyr was something sublime and divine: thus he had to appear to the painfully broken vision of Dionysian man. The contrived shepherd in his dress-ups would have offended him: on the unconcealed and vigorously magnificent characters of nature, his eye rested with sublime satisfaction; here the true human being was disclosed, the bearded satyr jubilating to his god. Confronted with him, the man of culture shriveled into a mendacious caricature.

Schiller is right about these origins of tragic art, too: the chorus is a living wall against the assaults of reality because it—the satyr chorus—represents existence more truthfully, really, and completely than the man of culture does who ordinarily considers himself as the only reality. The sphere of poetry does not lie outside the world as a fantastic impossibility spawned by a poet's brain: it desires to be just the opposite, the unvarnished expression of the truth, and must precisely for that reason discard the mendacious finery of that alleged reality of the man of culture.

The contrast between this real truth of nature and the lie of culture that poses as if it were the only reality is similar to that between the eternal core of things, the thing-in-itself, and the whole world of appearances:[5] just as tragedy, with its metaphysical comfort, points to the eternal life of this core of existence which abides through the perpetual destruction of appearances, the symbolism of the satyr chorus proclaims this primordial relationship between the thing-in-itself and appearance.[6] The idyllic shepherd of modern man is merely a counterfeit of the sum of cultural illusions that are allegedly nature; the Dionysian Greek wants truth and nature in their most forceful form—and sees himself changed, as by magic, into a satyr.

The reveling throng, the votaries of Dionysus jubilate under the spell of such moods and insights whose power transforms them before their own eyes till they imagine that they are beholding themselves as restored geniuses of nature, as satyrs. The later constitution of the chorus in tragedy is the artistic imitation of this natural phenomenon, though, to be sure, at this point the separation of Dionysian spectators and magically enchanted Dionysians became necessary. Only we must always keep in mind that the public at an Attic tragedy found itself in the chorus of the *orchestra*,[7] and there was at bottom no opposition between public and chorus: everything is

---

[5] The word translated as "appearances" in this passage is *Erscheinungen*.

[6] Here Nietzsche returns to Schopenhauer's perspective.

[7] "The Greek theatre appears to have been originally designed for the performance of dithyrambic choruses in honour of Dionysus. The centre of it was the *orchēstrā* ('dancing-place'), a circular space, in the middle of which stood the *thumelē* or altar of the god. Round more than half of the *orchestra*, forming a kind of horse-shoe, was the *theātron* ('seeing-place') proper, circular tiers of seats, generally cut out of the side of a hill . . . Behind the orchestra and facing the audience was the *skēnē* [called "scene" in the above translation], originally a wooden structure, a façade with three doors, through which, when the drama had developed from the dithyrambic chorus, the actors made their entrances" (*The Oxford Companion to Classical Literature*, ed. Sir Paul Harvey, revised edition, 1946, pp. 422f.).

merely a great sublime chorus of dancing and singing satyrs or of those who permit themselves to be represented by such satyrs.

Now we are ready to understand Schlegel's formulation in a deeper sense. The chorus is the "ideal spectator"[8] insofar as it is the only beholder, the beholder of the visionary world of the scene.[9] A public of spectators as we know it was unknown to the Greeks: in their theaters the terraced structure of concentric arcs made it possible for everybody to actually *overlook*[10] the whole world of culture around him and to imagine, in absorbed contemplation, that he himself was a chorist.

In the light of this insight we may call the chorus in its primitive form, in proto-tragedy, the mirror image in which the Dionysian man contemplates himself. This phenomenon is best made clear by imagining an actor who, being truly talented, sees the role he is supposed to play quite palpably before his eyes. The satyr chorus is, first of all, a vision of the Dionysian mass of spectators, just as the world of the stage, in turn, is a vision of this satyr chorus: the force of this vision is strong enough to make the eye insensitive and blind to the impression of "reality," to the men of culture who occupy the rows of seats all around. The form of the Greek theater recalls a lonely valley in the mountains: the architecture of the scene appears like a luminous cloud formation that the Bacchants swarming over the mountains behold from a height—like the splendid frame in which the image of Dionysus is revealed to them.

In the face of our learned views about elementary artistic processes, this artistic proto-phenomenon which we bring up here to help explain the tragic chorus is almost offensive, although nothing could be more certain than the fact that a poet is a poet only insofar as he sees himself surrounded by figures who live and act before him and into whose inmost nature he can see. Owing to a peculiar modern weakness, we are inclined to imagine the aesthetic proto-phenomenon in a manner much too complicated and abstract.

For a genuine poet, metaphor is not a rhetorical figure but a vicarious image that he actually beholds in place of a concept. A character is for him not a whole he has composed out of particular traits, picked up here and there, but an obtrusively alive person before his very eyes, distinguished from the otherwise identical vision of a painter only by the fact that it continually goes on living and acting. How is it that Homer's descriptions are so much more vivid than those of any other poet? Because he visualizes so much more vividly. We talk so abstractly about poetry because all of us are usually bad poets. At bottom, the aesthetic phenomenon is simple: let anyone

---

[8] *Der "idealische Zuschauer."*

[9] *Der einzige Schauer ist, der Schauer der Visionswelt der Scene.* The word *Schauer* could also mean shudder, the shudder of holy awe; and while this is certainly not the primary meaning intended here, it somehow enters into the coloring of the sentence.

[10] *Übersehen,* like overlook, can mean both survey and ignore. Francis Golffing, in his translation, opts for "quite literally survey," which makes nonsense of the passage. The context unequivocally requires oblivion of the whole world of culture: nothing is between the beholder and the chorus. Golffing's translation is altogether more vigorous than it is reliable.

have the ability to behold continually a vivid play and to live constantly surrounded by hosts of spirits, and he will be a poet; let anyone feel the urge to
transform himself and to speak out of other bodies and souls, and he will be
a dramatist.

The Dionysian excitement is capable of communicating this artistic gift
to a multitude, so they can see themselves surrounded by such a host of spirits while knowing themselves to be essentially one with them. This process of
the tragic chorus is the *dramatic* proto-phenomenon: to see oneself transformed before one's own eyes and to begin to act as if one had actually entered into another body, another character. This process stands at the beginning of the origin of drama. Here we have something different from the
rhapsodist who does not become fused with his images but, like a painter,
sees them outside himself as objects of contemplation. Here we have a surrender of individuality and a way of entering into another character. And
this phenomenon is encountered epidemically: a whole throng experiences
the magic of this transformation.

The dithyramb is thus essentially different from all other choral odes.
The virgins who proceed solemnly to the temple of Apollo, laurel branches in
their hands, singing a processional hymn, remain what they are and retain
their civic names: the dithyrambic chorus is a chorus of transformed characters whose civic past and social status have been totally forgotten: they have
become timeless servants of their god who live outside the spheres of society.
All the other choral lyric poetry of the Hellenes is merely a tremendous in-
tensification of the Apollinian solo singer, while in the dithyramb we confront a community of unconscious actors who consider themselves and one
another transformed.

Such magic transformation is the presupposition of all dramatic art. In
this magic transformation the Dionysian reveler sees himself as a satyr, *and as
a satyr, in turn, he sees the god,* which means that in his metamorphosis he beholds another vision outside himself, as the Apollinian complement of his
own state. With this new vision the drama is complete.

In the light of this insight we must understand Greek tragedy as the
Dionysian chorus which ever anew discharges itself in an Apollinian world
of images. Thus the choral parts with which tragedy is interlaced are, as it
were, the womb that gave birth to the whole of the so-called dialogue, that is,
the entire world of the stage, the real drama. In several successive discharges
this primal ground of tragedy radiates this vision of the drama which is by
all means a dream apparition and to that extent epic in nature; but on the
other hand, being the objectification of a Dionysian state, it represents not
Apollinian redemption through mere appearance but, on the contrary, the
shattering of the individual and his fusion with primal being. Thus the
drama is the Dionysian embodiment of Dionysian insights and effects and
thereby separated, as by a tremendous chasm, from the epic.

The *chorus* of the Greek tragedy, the symbol of the whole excited
Dionysian throng, is thus fully explained by our conception. Accustomed as
we are to the function of our modern stage chorus, especially in operas, we

could not comprehend why the tragic chorus of the Greeks should be older, more original and important than the "action" proper, as the voice of tradition claimed unmistakably. And with this traditional primacy and originality we could not reconcile the fact that the chorus consisted only of humble beings who served—indeed, initially only of goatlike satyrs. Finally, there remained the riddle of the orchestra in front of the scene. But now we realize that the scene, complete with the action, was basically and originally thought of merely as a *vision;* the chorus is the only "reality" and generates the vision, speaking of it with the entire symbolism of dance, tone, and words. In its vision this chorus beholds its lord and master Dionysus and is therefore eternally the *serving* chorus: it sees how the god suffers and glorifies himself and therefore does not itself *act.* But while its attitude toward the god is wholly one of service, it is nevertheless the highest, namely the Dionysian, expression of *nature* and therefore pronounces in its rapture, as nature does, oracles and wise sayings: *sharing his suffering* it also shares something of his *wisdom* and proclaims the truth from the heart of the world. That is the origin of the fantastic and seemingly so offensive figure of the wise and rapturous satyr who is at the same time "the simple man" as opposed to the god—the image of nature and its strongest urges, even their symbol, and at the same time the proclaimer of her wisdom and art—musician, poet, dancer, and seer of spirits in one person.

Dionysus, the real stage hero and center of the vision, was, according both to this insight and to the tradition, not actually present at first, in the very oldest period of tragedy; he was merely imagined as present, which means that originally tragedy was only "chorus" and not yet "drama." Later the attempt was made to show the god as real and to represent the visionary figure together with its transfiguring frame as something visible for every eye—and thus "drama" in the narrower sense began. Now the dithyrambic chorus was assigned the task of exciting the mood of the listeners to such a Dionysian degree that, when the tragic hero appeared on the stage, they did not see the awkwardly masked human being but rather a visionary figure, born as it were from their own rapture.

Consider Admetus as he is brooding over the memory of his recently departed wife Alcestis, consuming himself in her spiritual contemplation, when suddenly a similarly formed, similarly walking woman's figure is led toward him, heavily veiled; let us imagine his sudden trembling unrest, his tempestuous comparisons, his instinctive conviction—and we have an analogy with what the spectator felt in his Dionysian excitement when he saw the approach on the stage of the god with whose sufferings he had already identified himself. Involuntarily, he transferred the whole magic image of the god that was trembling before his soul to that masked figure and, as it were, dissolved its reality into the unreality of spirits.

This is the Apollinian state of dreams in which the world of the day becomes veiled, and a new world, clearer, more understandable, more moving than the everyday world and yet more shadowy, presents itself to our eyes in continual rebirths. Accordingly, we recognize in tragedy a sweeping opposition of styles: the language, color, mobility, and dynamics of speech fall apart into the Dionysian lyrics of the chorus and, on the other hand, the Apollinian dream world, and become two utterly different spheres of expression. The Apollinian appearances in which Dionysus objectifies himself are no longer "an eternal sea, changeful strife, a glowing life,"[11] like the music of the chorus, no longer those forces, merely felt and not condensed into images, in which the enraptured servant of Dionysus senses the nearness of the god: now the clarity and firmness of epic form addresses him from the scene; now Dionysus no longer speaks through forces but as an epic hero, almost in the language of Homer.

9

Everything that comes to the surface in the Apollinian part of Greek tragedy, in the dialogue, looks simple, transparent, and beautiful. In this sense, the dialogue is an image of the Hellene whose nature is revealed in the dance because in the dance the greatest strength remains only potential but betrays itself in the suppleness and wealth of movement. Thus the language of Sophocles' heroes amazes us by its Apollinian precision and lucidity, so we immediately have the feeling that we are looking into the inner-most ground of their being, with some astonishment that the way to this ground should be so short. But suppose we disregard the character of the hero as it comes to the surface, visibly—after all, it is in the last analysis nothing but a bright image projected on a dark wall, which means appearance[12] through and through; suppose we penetrate into the myth that projects itself in these lucid reflections: then we suddenly experience a phenomenon that is just the opposite of a familiar optical phenomenon. When after a forceful attempt to gaze on the sun we turn away blinded, we see dark-colored spots before our eyes, as a cure, as it were. Conversely, the bright image projections of the Sophoclean hero—in short, the Apollinian aspect of the mask—are necessary effects of a glance into the inside and terrors of nature; as it were, luminous spots to cure eyes damaged by gruesome night. Only in this sense may we believe that we properly comprehend the serious and important concept of "Greek cheerfulness." The misunderstanding of this concept as cheerfulness in a state of unendangered comfort is, of course, encountered everywhere today.

Sophocles understood the most sorrowful figure of the Greek stage, the unfortunate Oedipus, as the noble human being who, in spite of his wisdom, is destined to error and misery but who eventually, through his tremendous suffering, spreads a magical power of blessing that remains effective even beyond his decease. The noble human being does not sin, the profound poet wants to tell us: though every law, every natural order, even the moral world

---

[11] Quoted from Goethe's *Faust*, lines 505–507.
[12] *Erscheinung.*

may perish through his actions, his actions also produce a higher magical circle of effects which found a new world on the ruins of the old one that has been overthrown. That is what the poet wants to say to us insofar as he is at the same time a religious thinker. As a poet he first shows us a marvelously tied knot of a trial, slowly unraveled by the judge, bit by bit, for his own undoing. The genuinely Hellenic delight at this dialectical solution is so great that it introduces a trait of superior cheerfulness into the whole work, everywhere softening the sharp points of the gruesome presuppositions of this process.

In *Oedipus at Colonus* we encounter the same cheerfulness, but elevated into an infinite transfiguration. The old man, struck by an excess of misery, abandoned solely to *suffer* whatever befalls him, is confronted by the supraterrestrial cheerfulness that descends from the divine sphere and suggests to us that the hero attains his highest activity, extending far beyond his life, through his purely passive posture, while his conscious deeds and desires, earlier in his life, merely led him into passivity. Thus the intricate legal knot of the Oedipus fable that no mortal eye could unravel is gradually disentangled—and the most profound human joy overcomes us at this divine counterpart of the dialectic.

If this explanation does justice to the poet one may yet ask whether it exhausts the contents of the myth—and then it becomes evident that the poet's whole conception is nothing but precisely that bright image which healing nature projects before us after a glance into the abyss. Oedipus, the murderer of his father, the husband of his mother, the solver of the riddle of the Sphinx! What does the mysterious triad of these fateful deeds tell us?

There is a tremendously old popular belief, especially in Persia, that a wise magus can be born only from incest. With the riddle-solving and mother-marrying Oedipus in mind, we must immediately interpret this to mean that where prophetic and magical powers have broken the spell of present and future, the rigid law of individuation, and the real magic of nature, some enormously unnatural event—such as incest—must have occurred earlier, as a cause. How else could one compel nature to surrender her secrets if not by triumphantly resisting her, that is, by means of something unnatural? It is this insight that I find expressed in that horrible triad of Oedipus' destinies: the same man who solves the riddle of nature—that Sphinx of two species[13]—also must break the most sacred natural orders by murdering his father and marrying his mother. Indeed, the myth seems to wish to whisper to us that wisdom, and particularly Dionysian wisdom, is an unnatural abomination; that he who by means of his knowledge plunges nature into the abyss of destruction must also suffer the dissolution of nature in his own person. "The edge of wisdom turns against the wise: wisdom is a crime against

---

[13] Lion and human. Actually, the Sphinx also has wings in ancient Greek representations.

Nietzsche's comments on incest are influenced by Wagner and should be compared with *The Case of Wagner*, section 4.

nature": such horrible sentences are proclaimed to us by the myth; but the Hellenic poet touches the sublime and terrible Memnon's Column of myth like a sunbeam, so that it suddenly begins to sound—in Sophoclean melodies.[14]

Let me now contrast the glory of activity, which illuminates Aeschylus' *Prometheus*, with the glory of passivity. What the thinker Aeschylus had to say to us here, but what as a poet he only allows us to sense in his symbolic image, the youthful Goethe was able to reveal to us in the audacious words of his Prometheus:

> Here I sit, forming men
> in my own image,
> a race to be like me,
> to suffer, to weep,
> to delight and to rejoice,
> and to defy you,
> as I do.[15]

Man, rising to Titanic stature, gains culture by his own efforts and forces the gods to enter into an alliance with him because in his very own wisdom he holds their existence and their limitations in his hands. But what is most wonderful in this Prometheus poem, which in its basic idea is the veritable hymn of impiety, is the profoundly Aeschylean demand for *justice*. The immeasurable suffering of the bold "individual" on the one hand and the divine predicament and intimation of a twilight of the gods on the other, the way the power of these two worlds of suffering compels a reconciliation, a metaphysical union—all this recalls in the strongest possible manner the center and main axiom of the Aeschylean view of the world which envisages Moira enthroned above gods and men as eternal justice.

In view of the astonishing audacity with which Aeschylus places the Olympian world on the scales of his justice, we must call to mind that the profound Greek possessed an immovably firm foundation for metaphysical thought in his mysteries, and all his skeptical moods could be vented against the Olympians. The Greek artist in particular had an obscure feeling of mutual dependence when it came to the gods; and precisely in the *Prometheus* of Aeschylus this feeling is symbolized. In himself the Titanic artist found the defiant faith that he had the ability to create men and at least destroy Olympian gods, by means of his superior wisdom which, to be sure, he had

---

[14] Memnon's Column was an ancient name given to one of the two colossal statues of the pharaoh Amenophis III, near the Egyptian Thebes between the Nile and the valley of the kings, across the river from Karnak. When the first rays of the sun struck the weathered statue in the morning, it is said to have produced a musical sound—a phenomenon that stopped when an earthquake damaged the statue still further. The "statue of Memnon" also appears in Ibsen's *Peer Gynt* (1867), in Act IV.

[15] Goethe's poem—original text and verse translation on facing pages—is included in *Twenty German Poets*, trans. W. Kaufmann.

to atone for with eternal suffering. The splendid "ability" of the great genius for which even eternal suffering is a slight price, the stern pride of the *artist*—that is the content and soul of Aeschylus' poem, while Sophocles in his *Oedipus* sounds as a prelude the *holy man's* song of triumph.

But Aeschylus' interpretation of the myth does not exhaust the astounding depth of its terror. Rather the artist's delight in what becomes, the cheerfulness of artistic creation that defies all misfortune, is merely a bright image of clouds and sky mirrored in a black lake of sadness. The Prometheus story is an original possession of the entire Aryan community of peoples and evidences their gift for the profoundly tragic. Indeed, it does not seem improbable that this myth has the same characteristic significance for the Aryan character which the myth of the fall has for the Semitic character, and that these two myths are related to each other like brother and sister.[16] The presupposition of the Prometheus myth is to be found in the extravagant value which a naïve humanity attached to *fire* as the true palladium of every ascending culture. But that man should freely dispose of fire without receiving it as a present from heaven, either as a lightning bolt or as the warming rays of the sun, struck these reflective primitive men as sacrilege, as a robbery of divine nature. Thus the very first philosophical problem immediately produces a painful and irresolvable contradiction between man and god and moves it before the gate of every culture, like a huge boulder. The best and highest possession mankind can acquire is obtained by sacrilege and must be paid for with consequences that involve the whole flood of sufferings and sorrows with which the offended divinities have to afflict the nobly aspiring race of men. This is a harsh idea which, by the *dignity* it confers on sacrilege, contrasts strangely with the Semitic myth of the fall in which curiosity, mendacious deception, susceptibility to seduction, lust—in short, a series of preeminently feminine affects was considered the origin of evil. What distinguishes the Aryan notion is the sublime view of *active sin* as the characteristically Promethean virtue. With that, the ethical basis for pessimistic tragedy has been found: the justification of human evil, meaning both human guilt and the human suffering it entails.

The misfortune in the nature of things, which the contemplative Aryan is not inclined to interpret away—the contradiction at the heart of the world reveals itself to him as a clash of different worlds, e.g., of a divine and human one, in which each, taken as an individual, has right on its side, but nevertheless has to suffer for its individuation, being merely a single one beside another. In the heroic effort of the individual to attain universality, in the attempt to transcend the curse of individuation and to become the *one* world-being, he suffers in his own person the primordial contradiction that is concealed in things, which means that he commits sacrilege and suffers.

[16] After his emancipation from Wagner, Nietzsche came to consider the terms "Aryan" and "Semitic" more problematic. See, e.g., his note: "Contra Aryan and Semitic. Where races are mixed, there is the source of great cultures" (*Werke, Musarion* edition, vol. XVI, pp. 373f.).

Thus the Aryans understand sacrilege as something masculine,[17] while the Semites understand sin as feminine,[18] just as the original sacrilege is committed by a man, the original sin by a woman. Also, the witches' chorus says:

If that is so, we do not mind it:
With a thousand steps the women find it;
But though they rush, we do not care:
With one big jump the men get there.[19]

Whoever understands this innermost kernel of the Prometheus story—namely, the necessity of sacrilege imposed upon the titanically striving individual—must also immediately feel how un-Apollinian this pessimistic notion is. For Apollo wants to grant repose to individual beings precisely by drawing boundaries between them and by again and again calling these to mind as the most sacred laws of the world, with his demands for self-knowledge and measure.

Lest this Apollinian tendency congeal the form to Egyptian rigidity and coldness, lest the effort to prescribe to the individual wave its path and realm might annul the motion of the whole lake, the high tide of the Dionysian destroyed from time to time all those little circles in which the one-sidedly Apollinian "will" had sought to confine the Hellenic spirit. The suddenly swelling Dionysian tide then takes the separate little wave-mountains of individuals on its back, even as Prometheus' brother, the Titan Atlas, does with the earth. This Titanic impulse to become, as it were, the Atlas for all individuals, carrying them on a broad back, higher and higher, farther and farther, is what the Promethean and the Dionysian have in common.

In this respect, the Prometheus of Aeschylus is a Dionysian mask, while in the aforementioned profound demand for justice Aeschylus reveals to the thoughtful his paternal descent from Apollo, the god of individuation and of just boundaries. So the dual nature of Aeschylus' Prometheus, his nature which is at the same time Dionysian and Apollinian, might be expressed thus in a conceptual formula: "All that exists is just and unjust and equally justified in both."

That is your world! A world indeed!—[20]

Translated by Walter Kaufmann.

---

[17] *Der Frevel.*
[18] *Die Sünde.*
[19] Goethe's *Faust,* lines 3982–85.
[20] Goethe's *Faust,* line 409.

MATTHEW ARNOLD

The Study of Poetry

1880

When established beliefs are brought into question, when all creeds, dogmas, and traditions seem to be failing, where can one turn for consolation and support? Matthew Arnold's (1822–1888) essay restates what he had been saying for a decade about the social, religious, and cultural questions of his day; like other writers during the Victorian era — which has become, in the popular myths of our times, the epitome of assurance, solidity, and permanence — Arnold saw the central issue of his own day as a crisis of faith. Writing a preface for an anthology called The English Poets, Arnold seizes the opportunity to offer what is, in effect, another defense of poetry. As such, it should be compared with the essays by Sidney (p. 101) and Shelley (p. 287), both of whom justify poetry on moral grounds and claim for it an important role in shaping human minds and values. Like Wordsworth, too, Arnold attempts to correct misconceptions about the relative importance of science and poetry in terms of the kind of knowledge that each provides. What this adds up to is Arnold's notion of poetry as "a criticism of life," an interpretation and evaluation of the meaning of human existence — a substitute for what religion can no longer do.

Because he believes that only the best poetry can perform this high function, Arnold deals not only with the question of "Why study poetry?" but also with the question of how to study poetry so as to be able to distinguish the very best. Therefore, most of the essay is a discussion of his criteria for making a judgment and of three possible approaches to poetry. Arnold gives the theoretical bases and exemplifies his principles in a series of specific thumbnail judgments that amount to a brief survey of the English poets from Chaucer to Burns. He rejects two of the customary academic criteria by which poetry has commonly been judged, the historical and the impressionistic, on grounds that students of literature today might still find valid. Arnold proposes instead a technique for making objective evaluations and permanent classifications: This is his "touchstone" theory, by which a poet's work may be measured by comparing it to selected passages from the tradition of the "classic" writers. It is not difficult to find the logical fallacy in Arnold's distinction between the personal and the real estimates or to see how his own personal values keep cropping up *(as in his judgments about Chaucer and Burns); but the comparative method as a way of developing one's taste and judgment should not therefore be slighted.*

'THE FUTURE of poetry is immense, because in poetry, where it is worthy of its high destinies, our race, as time goes on, will find an ever surer and surer stay. There is not a creed which is not shaken, not an accredited dogma which is not shown to be questionable, not a received tradition which does not threaten to dissolve. Our religion has materialised itself in the fact, in the supposed fact; it has attached its emotion to the fact, and now the fact is failing it. But for poetry the idea is everything; the rest is a world of illusion, of divine illusion. Poetry attaches its emotion to the idea; the idea *is* the fact. The strongest part of our religion to-day is its unconscious poetry.'

Let me be permitted to quote these words of my own, as uttering the thought which should, in my opinion, go with us and govern us in all our study of poetry. In the present work it is the course of one great contributory stream to the world-river of poetry that we are invited to follow. We are here invited to trace the stream of English poetry. But whether we set ourselves, as here, to follow only one of the several streams that make the mighty river of poetry, or whether we seek to know them all, our governing thought should be the same. We should conceive of poetry worthily, and more highly than it has been the custom to conceive of it. We should conceive of it as capable of higher uses, and called to higher destinies, than those which in general men have assigned to it hitherto. More and more mankind will discover that we have to turn to poetry to interpret life for us, to console us, to sustain us. Without poetry, our science will appear incomplete; and most of what now passes with us for religion and philosophy will be replaced by poetry. Science, I say, will appear incomplete without it. For finely and truly does Wordsworth call poetry 'the impassioned expression which is in the countenance of all science'; and what is a countenance without its expression? Again, Wordsworth finely and truly calls poetry 'the breath and finer spirit of all knowledge': our religion, parading evidences such as those on which the popular mind relies now; our philosophy, pluming itself on its reasonings about causation and finite and infinite being; what are they but the shadows and dreams and false shows of knowledge? The day will come when we shall wonder at ourselves for having trusted to them, for having taken them seriously; and the more we perceive their hollowness, the more we shall prize 'the breath and finer spirit of knowledge' offered to us by poetry.

But if we conceive thus highly of the destinies of poetry, we must also set our standard for poetry high, since poetry, to be capable of fulfilling such high destinies, must be poetry of a high order of excellence. We must accustom ourselves to a high standard and to a strict judgment. Sainte-Beuve relates that Napoleon one day said, when somebody was spoken of in his presence as a charlatan: 'Charlatan as much as you please; but where is there *not* charlatanism?'—'Yes,' answers Sainte-Beuve, 'in politics, in the art of governing mankind, that is perhaps true. But in the order of thought, in art, the glory, the eternal honour is that charlatanism shall find no entrance; herein lies the inviolableness of that noble portion of man's being.' It is admirably said, and let us hold fast to it. In poetry, which is thought and art in one, it is the glory, the eternal honour, that charlatanism shall find no entrance; that this noble sphere be kept inviolate and inviolable. Charlatanism is for confusing or obliterating the distinctions between excellent and inferior, sound and unsound or only half-sound, true and untrue or only half-true. It is charlatanism, conscious or unconscious, whenever we confuse or obliterate these. And in poetry, more than anywhere else, it is unpermissible to confuse or obliterate them. For in poetry the distinction between excellent and inferior, sound and unsound or only half-sound, true and untrue or only half-true, is of paramount importance. It is of paramount importance because of the high destinies of poetry. In poetry, as a criticism of life under the conditions fixed for such a criticism by the laws of poetic truth and poetic beauty, the spirit of our race will find, we have said, as time goes on and as other helps fail, its consolation and stay. But the consolation and stay will be of power in proportion to the power of the criticism of life. And the criticism of life will be of power in proportion as the poetry conveying it is excellent rather than inferior, sound rather than unsound or half-sound, true rather than untrue or half-true.

The best poetry is what we want; the best poetry will be found to have a power of forming, sustaining, and delighting us, as nothing else can. A clearer, deeper sense of the best in poetry, and of the strength and joy to be drawn from it, is the most precious benefit which we can gather from a poetical collection such as the present. And yet in the nature and conduct of such a collection there is inevitably something which tends to obscure in us the consciousness of what our benefit should be, and to distract us from the pursuit of it. We should therefore steadily set it before our minds at the outset, and should compel ourselves to revert constantly to the thought of it as we proceed.

Yes; constantly in reading poetry, a sense for the best, the really excellent, and of the strength and joy to be drawn from it, should be present in our minds and should govern our estimate of what we read. But this real estimate, the only true one, is liable to be superseded, if we are not watchful, by two other kinds of estimate, the historic estimate and the personal estimate, both of which are fallacious. A poet or a poem may count to us historically, they may count to us on grounds personal to ourselves, and they may count to us really. They may count to us historically. The course of development of a nation's language, thought, and poetry, is profoundly interesting; and by regarding a poet's work as a stage in this course of development we may easily bring ourselves to make it of more importance as poetry than in itself it really is, we may come to use a language of quite exaggerated praise in criticising it; in short, to over-rate it. So arises in our poetic judgments the fallacy caused by the estimate which we may call historic. Then, again, a poet or a poem may count to us on grounds personal to ourselves. Our personal affinities, likings, and circumstances, have great power to sway our estimate of this or that poet's work, and to make us attach more importance to it as poetry than in itself it really possesses, because to us it is, or has been, of high importance. Here also we over-rate the object of our interest, and apply to it a language of praise which is quite exaggerated. And thus we get the source of a second fallacy in our poetic judgments—the fallacy caused by an estimate which we may call personal.

Both fallacies are natural. It is evident how naturally the study of the history and development of a poetry may incline a man to pause over reputations and works once conspicuous but now obscure, and to quarrel with a careless public for skipping, in obedience to mere tradition and habit, from one famous name or work in its national poetry to another, ignorant of what it misses, and of the reason for keeping what it keeps, and of the whole process of growth in its poetry. The French have become diligent students of their own early poetry, which they long neglected; the study makes many of them dissatisfied with their so-called classical poetry, the court-tragedy of the seventeenth century, a poetry which Pellisson long ago reproached with its want of the true poetic stamp, with its *politesse stérile et rampante*,[1] but which nevertheless has reigned in France as absolutely as if it had been the perfection of classical poetry indeed. The dissatisfaction is natural; yet a lively and accomplished critic, M. Charles d'Héricault, the editor of Clément Margot, goes too far when he says that 'the cloud of glory playing round a classic is a mist as dangerous to the future of a literature as it is intolerable for the purposes of history.' 'It hinders,' he goes on, 'it hinders us from seeing more than one single point, the culminating and exceptional point; the summary, fictitious and arbitrary, of a thought and of a work. It substitutes a halo for a physiognomy, it puts a statue where there was once a man, and hiding from us all trace of the labour, the attempts, the weaknesses, the failures, it claims not study but veneration; it does not show us how the thing is done, it imposes upon us a model. Above all, for the historian this creation of classic personages is inadmissible; for it withdraws the poet from his time, from his proper life, it breaks historical relationships, it blinds criticism by conventional admiration, and renders the investigation of literary origins unacceptable. It gives us a human personage no longer, but a God seated immovable amidst His perfect work, like Jupiter on Olympus; and hardly will it be possible for the young student, to whom such work is exhibited at such a distance from him, to believe that it did not issue ready made from that divine head.'

All this is brilliantly and tellingly said, but we must plead for a distinction. Everything depends on the reality of a poet's classic character. If he is a dubious classic, let us sift him; if he is a false classic, let us explode him. But if he is a real classic, if his work belongs to the class of the very best (for this is the true and right meaning of the word *classic, classical*), then the great thing for us is to feel and enjoy his work as deeply as ever we can, and to appreciate the wide difference between it and all work which has not the same high

---

[1] Sterile and overstriding polish.

character. This is what is salutary, this is what is formative; this is the great
benefit to be got from the study of poetry. Everything which interferes with
it, which hinders it, is injurious. True, we must read our classic with open
eyes, and not with eyes blinded with superstition; we must perceive when
his work comes short, when it drops out of the class of the very best, and we
must rate it, in such cases, at its proper value. But the use of this negative
criticism is not in itself, it is entirely in its enabling us to have a clearer sense
and a deeper enjoyment of what is truly excellent. To trace the labour, the attempts, the weaknesses, the failures of a genuine classic, to acquaint oneself
with his time and his life and his historical relationships, is mere literary
dilettantism unless it has that clear sense and deeper enjoyment for its end. It
may be said that the more we know about a classic the better we shall enjoy
him; and, if we lived as long as Methuselah and had all of us heads of perfect
clearness and wills of perfect steadfastness, this might be true in fact as it is
plausible in theory. But the case here is much the same as the case with the
Greek and Latin studies of our schoolboys. The elaborate philological
groundwork which we require them to lay is in theory an admirable preparation for appreciating the Greek and Latin authors worthily. The more thoroughly we lay the groundwork, the better we shall be able, it may be said, to
enjoy the authors. True, if time were not so short, and schoolboys' wits not so
soon tired and their power of attention exhausted; only, as it is, the elaborate
philological preparation goes on, but the authors are little known and less enjoyed. So with the investigator of 'historic origins' in poetry. He ought to
enjoy the true classic all the better for his investigations; he often is distracted
from the enjoyment of the best, and with the less good he overbusies himself,
and is prone to over-rate it in proportion to the trouble which it has cost him.

The idea of tracing historic origins and historical relationships cannot be
absent from a compilation like the present. And naturally the poets to be exhibited in it will be assigned to those persons for exhibition who are known
to prize them highly, rather than to those who have no special inclination towards them. Moreover the very occupation with an author, and the business
of exhibiting them, disposes us to affirm and amplify his importance. In the
present work, therefore, we are sure of frequent temptation to adopt the historic estimate, or the personal estimate, and to forget the real estimate; which
latter, nevertheless, we must employ if we are to make poetry yield us its full
benefit. So high is that benefit, the benefit of clearly feeling and of deeply enjoying the really excellent, the truly classic in poetry, that we do well, I say, to
set it fixedly before our minds as our object in studying poets and poetry,
and to make the desire of attaining it the one principle to which, as the *Imitation* says, whatever we may read or come to know, we always return. *Cum
multa legeris et cognoveris, ad unum semper oportet redire principium.*[2]

The historic estimate is likely in especial to affect our judgment and our
language when we are dealing with ancient poets; the personal estimate

---

[2] Although you have read and are acquainted with much, you should return to the one
principle.

when we are dealing with poets our contemporaries, or at any rate modern. The exaggerations due to the historic estimate are not in themselves, perhaps, of very much gravity. Their report hardly enters the general ear; probably they do not always impose even on the literary men who adopt them. But they lead to a dangerous abuse of language. So we hear Cædmon, amongst our own poets, compared to Milton. I have already noticed the enthusiasm of one accomplished French critic for 'historic origins.' Another eminent French critic, M. Vitet, comments upon that famous document of the early poetry of his nation, the *Chanson de Roland.* It is indeed a most interesting document. The *joculator* or *jongleur* Taillefer, who was with William the Conqueror's army at Hastings, marched before the Norman troops, so said the tradition, singing 'of Charlemagne and of Roland and of Oliver, and of the vassals who died at Roncevaux'; and it is suggested that in the *Chanson de Roland* by one Turoldis or Théroulde, a poem preserved in a manuscript of the twelfth century in the Bodleian Library at Oxford, we have certainly the matter, perhaps even some of the words, of the chant which Taillefer sang. The poem has vigour and freshness; it is not without pathos. But M. Vitet is not satisfied with seeing in it a document of some poetic value, and of very high historic and linguistic value; he sees in it a grand and beautiful work, a monument of epic genius. In its general design he finds the grandiose conception, in its details he finds the constant union of simplicity with greatness, which are the marks, he truly says, of the genuine epic, and distinguish it from the artificial epic of literary ages. One thinks of Homer; this is the sort of praise which is given to Homer, and justly given. Higher praise there cannot well be, and it is the praise due to epic poetry of the highest order only, and to no other. Let us try, then the *Chanson de Roland* at its best. Roland, mortally wounded, lays himself down under a pine-tree, with his face turned towards Spain and the enemy—

> 'De plusurs choses à remembrer li prist,
> De tantes teres cume li bers cunquist,
> De dulce France, des humes de sun lign,
> De Carlemagne sun seignor ki l'nurrit.'[3]

That is primitive work, I repeat, with an undeniable poetic quality of its own. It deserves such praise, and such praise is sufficient for it. But now turn to Homer—

> ʽΩς φάτο· τοὺς δ᾽ ἤδη κατέχεν φυσίζοος αἶα
> ἐν Λακεδαίμονι αὖθι, φίλῃ ἐν πατρίδι γαίῃ.[4]

---

[3] Then began he to call many things to remembrance,—all the lands which his valour conquered, and pleasant France, and the men of his lineage, and Charlemagne his liege lord who nourished him.—*Chanson de Roland,* iii. 939–942.

[4] *Os phato; tous d ede katechen physizoos aia en Lakedaimoni authi phile en patridi gaie.*

So said she; they long since in Earth's soft arms were reposing,
There, in their own dear land, their fatherland, Lacedæmon.
                                        Iliad, iii. 243, 244 (translated by Dr. Hawtrey).

We are here in another world, another order of poetry altogether; here is rightly due such supreme praise as that which M. Vitet gives to the *Chanson de Roland*. If our words are to have any meaning, if our judgments are to have any solidity, we must not heap that supreme praise upon poetry of an order immeasurably inferior.

Indeed there can be no more useful help for discovering what poetry belongs to the class of the truly excellent, and can therefore do us most good, than to have always in one's mind lines and expressions of the great masters, and to apply them as a touchstone to other poetry. Of course we are not to require this other poetry to resemble them; it may be very dissimilar. But if we have any tact we shall find them, when we have lodged them well in our minds, an infallible touchstone for detecting the presence or absence of high poetic quality, and also the degree of this quality, in all other poetry which we may place beside them. Short passages, even single lines, will serve our turn quite sufficiently. Take the two lines which I have just quoted from Homer, the poet's comment on Helen's mention of her brothers;—or take his

> Ἀ δειλώ, τί σφῶϊ δόμεν Πηλῆϊ ἄνακτι
> θανητᾳ̂ ; ὑμεῖς δ ἐστὸν ἀγήρω τ᾽ ἀθανάτω τε.
> ἦ ἵνα δυστήνοισι μετ᾽ ἀνδράσιν ἄλγε ἔχητον;[5]

the address of Zeus to the horses of Peleus;—or take finally his

> Καὶ σέ, λέρον, τὸ πρὶν μὲν ἀκούομεν ὄλβιον εἶναι·[6]

the words of Achilles to Priam, a suppliant before him. Take that incomparable line and a half of Dante, Ugolino's tremendous words—

> 'Io no piangeva; sì dentro impietrai.
> Piangevan elli…'[7]

take the lovely words of Beatrice to Virgil—

> 'Io son fatta da Dio, sua mercè, tale,
> Che la vostra miseria non mi tange,
> Nè fiamma d'esto incendio non m'assale…'[8]

take the simple, but perfect, single line—

[5] *A deilo ti sphoi domen Pelei anakti*
  thaneta; umeis d eston agero t athanato te
  e ina dystenoisi met andrasin alge echeton.

Ah, unhappy pair, why gave we you to King Peleus, to a mortal? but ye are without old age, and immortal. Was it that with men born to misery ye might have sorrow?—*Iliad*, xvii. 443–445.

[6] *Kai se, geron, to prin men akouomen olbion einai.* Nay, and thou too, old man, in former days wast, as we hear, happy.—*Iliad*, xxiv. 543.

[7] I wailed not, so of stone grew I within;—*they* wailed.—*Inferno*, xxxiii. 39, 40.

[8] Of such sort hath God, thanked be His mercy, made me, that your misery toucheth me not, neither doth the flame of this fire strike me.—*Inferno*, ii. 91–93.

'In la sua volontade è nostra pace.'[9]

Take of Shakespeare a line or two of Henry the Fourth's expostulation with
sleep—

> 'Wilt thou upon the high and giddy mast
> Seal up the ship-boy's eyes, and rock his brains
> In cradle of the rude imperious surge...'

and take, as well, Hamlet's dying request to Horatio—

> 'If thou didst ever hold me in thy heart,
> Absent thee from felicity awhile,
> And in this harsh world draw thy breath in pain
> To tell my story...'

Take of Milton that Miltonic passage—

> 'Darken'd so, yet shone
> Above them all the archangel; but his face
> Deep scars of thunder had intrench'd, and care
> Sat on his faded cheek...'

add two such lines as—

> 'And courage never to submit or yield
> And what is else not to be overcome...'

and finish with the exquisite close to the loss of Proserpine, the loss

> '...which cost Ceres all that pain
> To seek her through the world.'

These few lines, if we have tact and can use them, are enough even of themselves to keep clear and sound our judgments about poetry, to save us from
fallacious estimates of it, to conduct us to a real estimate.

The specimens I have quoted differ widely from one another, but they
have in common this: the possession of the very highest poetical quality. If
we are thoroughly penetrated by their power, we shall find that we have acquired a sense enabling us, whatever poetry may be laid before us, to feel the
degree in which a high poetical quality is present or wanting there. Critics
give themselves great labour to draw out what in the abstract constitutes the
characters of a high quality of poetry. It is much better simply to have recourse to concrete examples;—to take specimens of poetry of the high, the
very highest quality, and to say: The characters of a high quality of poetry are
what is expressed *there*. They are far better recognised by being felt in the
verse of the master, than by being perused in the prose of the critic. Nevertheless if we are urgently pressed to give some critical account of them, we
may safely, perhaps, venture on laying down, not indeed how and why the
characters arise, but where and in what they arise. They are in the matter and
substance of the poetry, and they are in its manner and style. Both of these,

[9] In His will is our peace.—*Paradiso*, iii. 85.

the substance and matter on the one hand, the style and manner on the other, have a mark, an accent, of high beauty, worth, and power. But if we are asked to define this mark and accent in the abstract, our answer must be: No, for we should thereby be darkening the question, not clearing it. The mark and accent are as given by the substance and matter of that poetry, by the style and manner of that poetry, and of all other poetry which is akin to it in quality.

Only one thing we may add as to the substance and matter of poetry, guiding ourselves by Aristotle's profound observation that the superiority of poetry over history consists in its possessing a higher truth and a higher seriousness (φιλοσοφώτερον καὶ σπουδαιότερον).[10] Let us add, therefore, to what we have said, this: that the substance and matter of the best poetry acquire their special character from possessing, in an eminent degree, truth and seriousness. We may add yet further, what is in itself evident, that to the style and manner of the best poetry their special character, their accent, is given by their diction, and, even yet more, by their movement. And though we distinguish between the two characters, the two accents, of superiority, yet they are nevertheless vitally connected one with the other. The superior character of truth and seriousness, in the matter and substance of the best poetry, is inseparable from the superiority of diction and movement marking its style and manner. The two superiorities are closely related, and are in steadfast proportion one to the other. So far as high poetic truth and seriousness are wanting to a poet's matter and substance, so far also, we may be sure, will a high poetic stamp of diction and movement be wanting to his style and manner. In proportion as this high stamp of diction and movement, again, is absent from a poet's style and manner, we shall find, also, that high poetic truth and seriousness are absent from his substance and matter.

So stated, these are but dry generalities; their whole force lies in their application. And I could wish every student of poetry to make the application of them for himself. Made by himself, the application would impress itself upon his mind far more deeply than made by me. Neither will my limits allow me to make any full application of the generalities above propounded; but in the hope of bringing out, at any rate, some significance in them, and of establishing an important principle more firmly by their means, I will, in the space which remains to me, follow rapidly from the commencement the course of our English poetry with them in my view.

Once more I return to the early poetry of France, with which our own poetry, in its origins, is indissolubly connected. In the twelfth and thirteenth centuries, that seed-time of all modern language and literature, the poetry of France had a clear predominance in Europe. Of the two divisions of that poetry, its productions in the *langue d'oil* and its productions in the *langue d'oc*,[11] the poetry of the *langue d'oc,* of southern France, of the troubadours, is of

---

[10] *Philosophoteron kai spoudaioteron.*

[11] The words *oc* (*hoc*) and *oil* (*oui*) mean *yes.* The phrases mean *the language of—,* the forms of *yes* identifying the dialects.

importance because of its effect on Italian literature;—the first literature of modern Europe to strike the true and grand note, and to bring forth, as in Dante and Petrarch it brought forth, classics. But the predominance of French poetry in Europe, during the twelfth and thirteenth centuries, is due to its poetry of the *langue d'oil*, the poetry of northern France and of the tongue which is now the French language. In the twelfth century the bloom of this romance-poetry was earlier and stronger in England, at the court of our Anglo-Norman kings, than in France itself. But it was a bloom of French poetry; and as our native poetry formed itself, it formed itself out of this. The romance-poems which took possession of the heart and imagination of Europe in the twelfth and thirteenth centuries are French; 'they are,' as Southey justly says, 'the pride of French literature, nor have we anything which can be placed in competition with them.' Themes were supplied from all quarters; but the romance-setting which was common to them all, and which gained the ear of Europe, was French. This constituted for the French poetry, literature, and language, at the height of the Middle Age, an unchallenged predominance. The Italian Brunetto Latini, the master of Dante, wrote his *Treasure* in French because, he says, 'la parleure en est plus délitable et plus commune à toutes gens.'[12] In the same century, the thirteenth, the French romance-writer, Christian of Troyes, formulates the claims, in chivalry and letters, of France, his native country, as follows.—

> 'Or vous ert par ce livre apris,
> Que Gresse ot de chevalerie
> Le premier los et de clergie;
> Puis vint chevalerie à Rome,
> Et de la clergie la some,
> Qui ore est en France venue.
> Diex doinst qu'ele i soit retenue,
> Et que li lius li abelisse
> Tant que de France n'isse
> L'onor qui s'i est arestée!'

'Now by this book you will learn that first Greece had the renown for chivalry and letters: then chivalry and the primacy in letters passed to Rome, and now it is come to France. God grant it may be kept there; and that the place may please it so well, that the honour which has come to make stay in France may never depart thence!'

Yet it now all gone, this French romance-poetry, of which the weight of substance and the power of style are not unfairly represented by this extract from Christian of Troyes. Only by means of the historic estimate can we persuade ourselves now to think that any of it is of poetical importance.

But in the fourteenth century there comes an Englishman nourished on this poetry, taught his trade by this poetry, getting words, rhyme, metre from this poetry; for even of that stanza which the Italians used, and which

[12] The speaking of it is most delectable and most common to all peoples.

Chaucer derived immediately from the Italians, the basis and suggestion was probably given in France. Chaucer (I have already named him) fascinated his contemporaries, but so too did Christian of Troyes and Wolfram of Eschenbach. Chaucer's power of fascination, however, is enduring; his poetical importance does not need the assistance of the historic estimate; it is real. He is a genuine source of joy and strength, which is flowing still for us and will flow always. He will be read, as time goes on, far more generally than he is read now. His language is a cause of difficulty for us; but so also, and I think in quite as great a degree, is the language of Burns. In Chaucer's case, as in that of Burns, it is a difficulty to be unhesitatingly accepted and overcome.

If we ask ourselves wherein consists the immense superiority of Chaucer's poetry over the romance-poetry—why it is that in passing from this to Chaucer we suddenly feel ourselves to be in another world, we shall find that his superiority is both in the substance of his poetry and in the style of his poetry. His superiority in substance is given by his large, free, simple, clear yet kindly view of human life,—so unlike the total want, in the romance-poets, of all intelligent command of it. Chaucer has not their helplessness; he has gained the power to survey the world from a central, a truly human point of view. We have only to call to mind the Prologue to *The Canterbury Tales*. The right comment upon it is Dryden's: 'It is sufficient to say, according to the proverb, that *here is God's plenty*.' And again: 'He is a perpetual fountain of good sense.' It is by a large, free, sound representation of things, that poetry, this high criticism of life, has truth of substance; and Chaucer's poetry has truth of substance.

Of his style and manner, if we think first of the romance-poetry and then of Chaucer's divine liquidness of diction, his divine fluidity of movement, it is difficult to speak temperately. They are irresistible, and justify all the rapture with which his successors speak of his 'gold dew-drops of speech.' Johnson misses the point entirely when he finds fault with Dryden for ascribing to Chaucer the first refinement of our numbers, and says that Gower also can show smooth numbers and easy rhymes. The refinement of our numbers means something far more than this. A nation may have versifiers with smooth numbers and easy rhymes, and yet may have no real poetry at all. Chaucer is the father of our splendid English poetry; he is our 'well of English undefiled,' because by the lovely charm of his diction, the lovely charm of his movement, he makes an epoch and founds a tradition. In Spenser, Shakespeare, Milton, Keats, we can follow the tradition of the liquid diction, the fluid movement, of Chaucer; at one time it is his liquid diction of which in these poets we feel the virtue, and at another time it is his fluid movement. And the virtue is irresistible.

Bounded as is my space, I must yet find room for an example of Chaucer's virtue, as I have given examples to show the virtue of the great classics. I feel disposed to say that a single line is enough to show the charm of Chaucer's verse; that merely one line like this—

'O martyr souded[13] in virginitee!'

[13] The French *soudé;* soldered, fixed fast.

has a virtue of manner and movement such as we shall not find in all the verse of romance-poetry;—but this is saying nothing. The virtue is such as we shall not find, perhaps, in all English poetry, outside the poets whom I have named as the special inheritors of Chaucer's tradition. A single line, however, is too little if we have not the strain of Chaucer's verse well in our memory; let us take a stanza. It is from *The Prioress's Tale*, the story of the Christian child murdered in a Jewry—

> 'My throte is cut unto my nekke-bone
> Saidè this child, and as by way of kinde
> I should have deyd, yea, longè time agone;
> But Jesu Christ, as ye in bookès finde,
> Will that his glory last and be in minde,
> And for the worship of his mother dere
> Yet may I sing *O Alma* loud and clere.'

Wordsworth has modernised this Tale, and to feel how delicate and evanescent is the charm of verse, we have only to read Wordsworth's first three lines of this stanza after Chaucer's—

> 'My throat is cut unto the bone, I trow,
> Said this young child, and by the law of kind
> I should have died, yea, many hours ago.'

The charm is departed. It is often said that the power of liquidness and fluidity in Chaucer's verse was dependent upon a free, a licentious dealing with language, such as is now impossible; upon a liberty, such as Burns too enjoyed, of making words like *neck, bird*, into a dissyllable by adding to them, and words like *cause, rhyme*, into a dissyllable by sounding the *e* mute. It is true that Chaucer's fluidity is conjoined with this liberty, and is admirably served by it; but we ought not to say that it was dependent upon it. It was dependent upon his talent. Other poets with a like liberty do not attain to the fluidity of Chaucer; Burns himself does not attain to it. Poets, again, who have a talent akin to Chaucer's, such as Shakespeare or Keats, have known how to attain to his fluidity without the like liberty.

And yet Chaucer is not one of the great classics. His poetry transcends and effaces, easily and without effort, all the romance-poetry of Catholic Christendom; it transcends and effaces all the English poetry contemporary with it, it transcends and effaces all the English poetry subsequent to it down to the age of Elizabeth. Of such avail is poetic truth of substance, in its natural and necessary union with poetic truth of style. And yet, I say, Chaucer is not one of the great classics. He has not their accent. What is wanting to him is suggested by the mere mention of the name of the first great classic of Christendom, the immortal poet who died eighty years before Chaucer,—Dante. The accent of such verse as

> 'In la sua volontade è nostra pace...'

is altogether beyond Chaucer's reach; we praise him, but we feel that this accent is out of the question for him. It may be said that it was necessarily out of the reach of any poet in the England of that stage of growth. Possibly; but we are to adopt a real, not a historic, estimate of poetry. However we may account for its absence, something is wanting, then, to the poetry of Chaucer, which poetry must have before it can be placed in the glorious class of the best. And there is no doubt what that something is. It is the σπουδαιότης,[14] the high and excellent seriousness, which Aristotle assigns as one of the grand virtues of poetry. The substance of Chaucer's poetry, his view of things and his criticism of life, has largeness, freedom, shrewdness, benignity; but it has not this high seriousness. Homer's criticism of life has it, Dante's has it, Shakespeare's has it. It is this chiefly which gives to our spirits what they can rest upon; and with the increasing demands of our modern ages upon poetry, this virtue of giving us what we can rest upon will be more and more highly esteemed. A voice from the slums of Paris, fifty or sixty years after Chaucer, the voice of poor Villon out of his life of riot and crime, has at its happy moments (as, for instance, in the last stanza of *La Belle Heaulmière*)[15] more of this important poetic virtue of seriousness than all the productions of Chaucer. But its apparition in Villon, and in men like Villon, is fitful; the greatness of the great poets, the power of their criticism of life, is that their virtue is sustained.

To our praise, therefore, of Chaucer as a poet there must be this limitation; he lacks the high seriousness of the great classics, and therewith an important part of their virtue. Still, the main fact for us to bear in mind about Chaucer is his sterling value according to that real estimate which we firmly adopt for all poets. He has poetic truth of substance, though he has not high poetic seriousness, and corresponding to his truth of substance he has an exquisite virtue of style and manner. With him is born our real poetry.

For my present purpose I need not dwell on our Elizabethan poetry, or on the continuation and close of this poetry in Milton. We all of us profess to be agreed in the estimate of this poetry; we all of us recognise it as great poetry, our greatest, and Shakespeare and Milton as our poetical classics. The real estimate, here, has universal currency. With the next age of our poetry

---

[14] *Spoudaiotes.*

[15] The name *Heaulmière* is said to be derived from a headdress (helm) worn as a mark by courtesans. In Villon's ballad, a poor old creature of this class laments her days of youth and beauty. The last stanza of the ballad runs thus —

'Ainsi le bon temps regretons
Entre nous, pauvres vieilles sottes,
Assises bas, à croppetons,
Tout en ung tas comme pelottes:
A petit feu de chenevottes
Tost allumées, tost estainctes.
Et jadis fusmes si mignottes!
Ainsi en prend à maintz et maintes.'

'Thus amongst ourselves we regret the good time, poor silly old things, low-seated on our heels, all in a heap like so many balls; by a little fire of hemp-stalks, soon lighted, soon spent. And once we were such darlings! So fares it with many and many a one.'

divergency and difficulty begin. An historic estimate of that poetry has established itself; and the question is, whether it will be found to coincide with the
real estimate.

The age of Dryden, together with our whole eighteenth century which
followed it, sincerely believed itself to have produced poetical classics of its
own, and even to have made advance, in poetry, beyond all its predecessors.
Dryden regards as not seriously disputable the opinion 'that the sweetness of
English verse was never understood or practised by our fathers.' Cowley
could see nothing at all in Chaucer's poetry. Dryden heartily admired it, and,
as we have seen, praised its matter admirably; but of its exquisite manner
and movement all he can find to say is that 'there is the rude sweetness of a
Scotch tune in it, which is natural and pleasing, though not perfect.' Addison,
wishing to praise Chaucer's numbers, compares them with Dryden's own.
And all through the eighteenth century, and down even into our own times,
the stereotyped phrase of approbation for good verse found in our early poetry has been, that it even approached the verse of Dryden, Addison, Pope,
and Johnson.

Are Dryden and Pope poetical classics? Is the historic estimate, which
represents them as such, and which has been so long established that it cannot easily give way, the real estimate? Wordsworth and Coleridge, as is well
known, denied it; but the authority of Wordsworth and Coleridge does not
weigh much with the young generation, and there are many signs to show
that the eighteenth century and its judgments are coming into favour again.
Are the favourite poets of the eighteenth century classics?

It is impossible within my present limits to discuss the question fully.
And what man of letters would not shrink from seeming to dispose dictatori-
ally of the claims of two men who are, at any rate, such masters in letters as
Dryden and Pope; two men of such admirable talent, both of them, and one
of them, Dryden, a man, on all sides, of such energetic and genial power?
And yet, if we are to gain the full benefit from poetry, we must have the real
estimate of it. I cast about for some mode of arriving, in the present case, at
such an estimate without offence. And perhaps the best way is to begin, as it
is easy to begin, with cordial praise.

When we find Chapman, the Elizabethan translator of Homer, expressing himself in his preface thus: 'Though truth in her very nakedness sits in
so deep a pit, that from Gades to Aurora and Ganges few eyes can sound her,
I hope yet those few here will so discover and confirm that, the date being
out of her darkness in this morning of our poet, he shall now gird his temples
with the sun,'—we pronounce that such a prose is intolerable. When we find
Milton writing: 'And long it was not after, when I was confirmed in this
opinion, that he, who would not be frustrate of his hope to write well hereafter in laudable things, ought himself to be a true poem,'—we pronounce
that such a prose has its own grandeur, but that it is obsolete and inconve-
nient. But when we find Dryden telling us: 'What Virgil wrote in the vigour
of his age, in plenty and at ease, I have undertaken to translate in my declining years; struggling with wants, oppressed with sickness, curbed in my ge-

nius, liable to be misconstrued in all I write,'—then we exclaim that here at last we have the true English prose, a prose such as we would all gladly use if we only knew how. Yet Dryden was Milton's contemporary.

But after the Restoration the time had come when our nation felt the imperious need of a fit prose. So, too, the time had likewise come when our nation felt the imperious need of freeing itself from the absorbing preoccupation which religion in the Puritan age had exercised. It was impossible that this freedom should be brought about without some negative excess, without some neglect and impairment of the religious life of the soul; and the spiritual history of the eighteenth century shows us that the freedom was not achieved without them. Still, the freedom was achieved; the preoccupation, an undoubtedly baneful and retarding one if it had continued, was got rid of. And as with religion amongst us at that period, so it was also with letters. A fit prose was a necessity; but it was impossible that a fit prose should establish itself amongst us without some touch of frost to the imaginative life of the soul. The needful qualities for a fit prose are regularity, uniformity, precision, balance. The men of letters, whose destiny it may be to bring their nation to the attainment of a fit prose, must of necessity, whether they work in prose or in verse, give a predominating, an almost exclusive attention to the qualities of regularity, uniformity, precision, balance. But an almost exclusive attention to these qualities involves some repression and silencing of poetry.

We are to regard Dryden as the puissant and glorious founder, Pope as the splendid high priest, of our age of prose and reason, of our excellent and indispensable eighteenth century. For the purposes of their mission and destiny their poetry, like their prose, is admirable. Do you ask me whether Dryden's verse, take it almost where you will, is not good?

'A milk-white Hind, immortal and unchanged,
Fed on the lawns and in the forest ranged.'

I answer: Admirable for the purposes of the inaugurator of an age of prose and reason. Do you ask me whether Pope's verse, take it almost where you will, is not good?

'To Hounslow Heath I point, and Banstead Down;
Thence comes your mutton, and these chicks my own.'

I answer: Admirable for the purposes of the high priest of an age of prose and reason. But do you ask me whether such verse proceeds from men with an adequate poetic criticism of life, from men whose criticism of life has a high seriousness, or even, without that high seriousness, has poetic largeness, freedom, insight, benignity? Do you ask me whether the application of ideas to life in the verse of these men, often a powerful application, no doubt, is a powerful *poetic* application? Do you ask me whether the poetry of these men has either the matter or the inseparable manner of such an adequate poetic criticism; whether it has the accent of

'Absent thee from felicity awhile...'

or of

> 'And what is else not to be overcome...'

or of

> 'O martyr souded in virginitee!'

I answer: It has not and cannot have them; it is the poetry of the builders of an age of prose and reason. Though they may write in verse, though they may in a certain sense be masters of the art of versification, Dryden and Pope are not classics of our poetry, they are classics of our prose.

Gray is our poetical classic of that literature and age; the position of Gray is singular, and demands a word of notice here. He has not the volume or the power of poets who, coming in times more favourable, have attained to an independent criticism of life. But he lived with the great poets, he lived, above all, with the Greeks, through perpetually studying and enjoying them; and he caught their poetic point of view for regarding life, caught their poetic manner. The point of view and the manner are not self-sprung in him, he caught them of others; and he had not the free and abundant use of them. But whereas Addison and Pope never had the use of them, Gray had the use of them at times. He is the scantiest and frailest of classics in our poetry, but he is a classic.

And now, after Gray, we are met, as we draw towards the end of the eighteenth century, we are met by the great name of Burns. We enter now on times where the personal estimate of poets begins to be rife, and where the real estimate of them is not reached without difficulty. But in spite of the disturbing pressures of personal partiality, of national partiality, let us try to reach a real estimate of the poetry of Burns.

By his English poetry Burns in general belongs to the eighteenth century, and has little importance for us.

> 'Mark ruffian Violence, distain'd with crimes,
> Rousing elate in these degenerate times;
> View unsuspecting Innocence a prey,
> As guileful Fraud points out the erring way;
> While subtle Ligitation's pliant tongue
> The life-blood equal sucks of Right and Wrong!'

Evidently this is not the real Burns, or his name and fame would have disappeared long ago. Nor is Clarinda's love-poet, Sylvander, the real Burns either. But he tells us himself: 'These English songs gravel me to death. I have not the command of the language that I have of my native tongue. In fact, I think that my ideas are more barren in English than in Scotch. I have been at *Duncan Gray* to dress it in English, but all I can do is desperately stupid.' We English turn naturally, in Burns, to the poems in our own language, because we can read them easily; but in those poems we have not the real Burns.

The real Burns is of course is his Scotch poems. Let us boldly say that of much of his poetry, a poetry dealing perpetually with Scotch drink, Scotch religion, and Scotch manners, a Scotchman's estimate is apt to be personal. A Scotchman is used to this world of Scotch drink, Scotch religion, and Scotch manners; he has a tenderness for it; he meets its poets half way. In this tender mood he reads pieces like the *Holy Fair* or *Halloween*. But this world of Scotch drink, Scotch religion, and Scotch manners is against a poet, not for him, when it is not a partial countryman who reads him; for in itself it is not a beautiful world, and no one can deny that it is of advantage to a poet to deal with a beautiful world. Burns's world of Scotch drink, Scotch religion, and Scotch manners, is often a harsh, a sordid, a repulsive world: even the world of his *Cotter's Saturday Night* is not a beautiful world. No doubt a poet's criticism of life may have such truth and power that it triumphs over its world and delights us. Burns may triumph over his world, often he does triumph over his world, but let us observe how and where. Burns is the first case we have had where the bias of the personal estimate tends to mislead; let us look at him closely, he can bear it.

Many of his admirers will tell us that we have Burns, convivial, genuine, delightful, here—

'Leeze me on drink! it gies us mair
    Than either school or college;
It kindles wit, it waukens lair,
    It pangs us fou o' knowledge.
Be 't whisky gill or penny wheep
    Or ony stronger portion,
It never fails, on drinking deep,
    To kittle up our notion
        By night or day.'

There is a great deal of that sort of thing in Burns, and it is unsatisfactory, not because it is bacchanalian poetry, but because it has not that accent of sincerity which bacchanalian poetry, to do it justice, very often has. There is something in it of bravado, something which makes us feel that we have not the man speaking to us with his real voice; something, therefore, poetically unsound.

With still more confidence will his admirers tell us that we have the genuine Burns, the great poet, when his strain asserts the independence, equality, dignity, of men, as in the famous song *For a' that and a' that*—

'A prince can mak' a belted knight,
    A marquis, duke, and a' that;
But an honest man's aboon his might,
    Guid faith he mauna fa' that!
      For a' that, and a' that,
        Their dignities, and a' that,
      The pith o' sense, and pride o' worth,
        Are higher rank than a' that.'

Here they find his grand, genuine touches; and still more, when this puissant genius, who so often set morality at defiance, falls moralising—

> 'The sacred lowe o' weel-placed love
>   Luxuriantly indulge it;
> But never tempt th' illicit rove,
>   Tho' naething should divulge it.
> I waive the quantum o' the sin,
>   The hazard o' concealing,
> But och! it hardens a' within,
>   And petrifies the feeling.'

Or in a higher strain—

> 'Who made the heart, 'tis He alone
>   Decidedly can try us;
> He knows each chord, its various tone;
>   Each spring, its various bias.
> Then at the balance let's be mute,
>   We never can adjust it;
> What's *done* we partly may compute,
>   But know not what's resisted.'

Or in a better strain yet, a strain, his admirers will say, unsurpassable—

> 'To make a happy fire-side clime
>   To weans and wife,
> That's the true pathos and sublime
>   Of human life.'

There is criticism of life for you, the admirers of Burns will say to us; there is the application of ideas to life! There is, undoubtedly. The doctrine of the last-quoted lines coincides almost exactly with what was the aim and end, Xenophon tells us, of all the teaching of Socrates. And the application is a powerful one; made by a man of vigorous understanding, and (need I say?) a master of language.

But for supreme poetical success more is required than the powerful application of ideas to life; it must be an application under the conditions fixed by the laws of poetic truth and poetic beauty. Those laws fix as an essential condition, in the poet's treatment of such matters as are here in question, high seriousness;—the high seriousness which comes from absolute sincerity. The accent of high seriousness, born of absolute sincerity, is what gives to such verse as

> 'In la sua volontade è nostra pace...'

to such criticism of life as Dante's, its power. Is this accent felt in the passages which I have been quoting from Burns? Surely not; surely, if our sense is quick, we must perceive that we have not in those passages a voice from the very inmost soul of the genuine Burns; he is not speaking to us from these depths, he is more or less preaching. And the compensation for admiring such passages less, from missing the perfect poetic accent in them, will be that we shall admire more the poetry where that accent is found.

No: Burns, like Chaucer, comes short of the high seriousness of the great classics, and the virtue of matter and manner which goes with that high seriousness is wanting to his work. At moments he touches it in a profound and passionate melancholy, as in those four immortal lines taken by Byron as a motto for *The Bride of Abydos,* but which have in them a depth of poetic quality such as resides in no verse of Byron's own—

'Had we never loved sae kindly,
Had we never loved sae blindly,
Never met, or never parted,
We had ne'er been broken-hearted.'

But a whole poem of what quality Burns cannot make; the rest, in the *Farewell to Nancy,* is verbiage.

We arrive best at the real estimate of Burns, I think, by conceiving his work as having truth of matter and truth of manner, but not the accent or the poetic virtue of the highest masters. His genuine criticism of life, when the sheer poet in him speaks, is ironic; it is not—

'Thou Power Supreme, whose mighty scheme
    These woes of mine fulfil,
Here firm I rest, they must be best
    Because they are Thy will!'

It is far rather: *Whistle owre the lave o't!* Yet we may say of him as of Chaucer, that of life and the world, as they come before him, his view is large, free, shrewd, benignant,—truly poetic, therefore; and his manner of rendering what he sees is to match. But we must note, at the same time, his great difference from Chaucer. The freedom of Chaucer is heightened, in Burns, by a fiery, reckless energy; the benignity of Chaucer deepens, in Burns, into an overwhelming sense of the pathos of things;—of the pathos of human nature, the pathos, also, of non-human nature. Instead of the fluidity of Chaucer's manner, the manner of Burns has spring, bounding swiftness. Burns is by far the greater force, though he has perhaps less charm. The world of Chaucer is fairer, richer, more significant than that of Burns; but when the largeness and freedom of Burns get full sweep, as in *Tam o' Shanter,* or still more in that puissant and splendid production, *The Jolly Beggars,* his world may be what it will, his poetic genius triumphs over it. In the world of *The Jolly Beggars* there is more than hideousness and squalor, there is bestiality; yet the piece is a superb poetic success. It has a breadth, truth, and power which make the famous scene in Auerbach's Cellar, of Goethe's *Faust,* seem artificial and tame beside it, and which are only matched by Shakespeare and Aristophanes.

Here, where his largeness and freedom serve him so admirably, and also in those poems and songs where to shrewdness he adds infinite archness and wit, and to benignity infinite pathos, where his manner is flawless, and a perfect poetic whole is the result,—in things like the address to the mouse whose home he had ruined, in things like *Duncan Gray, Tam Glen, Whistle and I'll come to you my Lad, Auld Lang Syne* (this list might be made much longer),—here we have the genuine Burns, of whom the real estimate must be high indeed. Not a classic, nor with the excellent σπουδαιότης[16] of the great classics, nor with a verse rising to a criticism of life and virtue like theirs; but a poet with thorough truth of substance and an answering truth of style, giving us a poetry sound to the core. We all of us have a leaning towards the pathetic, and may be inclined perhaps to prize Burns most for his touches of piercing, sometimes almost intolerable, pathos; for verse like—

> 'We twa hae paidl't i' the burn
>   From mornin' sun till dine;
> But seas between us braid hae roar'd
>   Sin auld lang syne...'

where he is as lovely as he is sound. But perhaps it is by the perfection of soundness of his lighter and archer masterpieces that he is poetically most wholesome for us. For the votary misled by a personal estimate of Shelley, as so many of us have been, are, and will be,—of that beautiful spirit building his many-coloured haze of words and images

> 'Pinnacled dim in the intense inane'—

no contact can be wholesomer than the contact with Burns at his archest and soundest. Side by side with the

> 'On the brink of the night and the morning
>   My coursers are wont to respire,
> But the Earth has just whispered a warning
>   That their flight must be swifter than fire...'

of *Prometheus Unbound,* how salutary, how very salutary, to place this from *Tam Glen*—

> 'My minnie does constantly deave me
>   And bids me beware o' young men;
> They flatter, she says, to deceive me;
>   But wha can think sae o' Tam Glen?'

But we enter on burning ground as we approach the poetry of times so near to us—poetry like that of Byron, Shelley, and Wordsworth—of which the estimates are so often not only personal, but personal with passion. For my purpose, it is enough to have taken the single case of Burns, the first poet we come to of whose work the estimate formed is evidently apt to be personal, and to have suggested how we may proceed, using the poetry of the great classics as a sort of touchstone, to correct this estimate, as we had previ-

---

[16] *Spoudaiotes,* "high and excellent seriousness."

ously corrected by the same means the historic estimate where we met with it. A collection like the present, with its succession of celebrated names and celebrated poems, offers a good opportunity to us for resolutely endeavouring to make our estimates of poetry real. I have sought to point out a method which will help us in making them so, and to exhibit it in use so far as to put any one who likes in a way of applying it for himself.

At any rate the end to which the method and the estimate are designed to lead and from leading to which, if they do lead to it, they get their whole value,—the benefit of being able clearly to feel and deeply to enjoy the best, the truly classic, in poetry,—is an end, let me say it once more at parting, of supreme importance. We are often told that an era is opening in which we are to see multitudes of a common sort of readers, and masses of a common sort of literature; that such readers do not want and could not relish anything better than such literature, and that to provide it is becoming a vast and profitable industry. Even if good literature entirely lost currency with the world, it would still be abundantly worth while to continue to enjoy it by oneself. But it never will lose currency with the world, in spite of momentary appearances; it never will lose supremacy. Currency and supremacy are insured to it, not indeed by the world's deliberate and conscious choice, but by something far deeper,—by the instinct of self-preservation in humanity.

Walter Pater

From *Studies in the History of the Renaissance*

1888 (Third Edition)

Like other familiar expressions, the phrase "art for art's sake" deserves a closer look. When readers find it as the culmination of Pater's (1839–1894) essay, it carries the accumulated burden of everything that has preceded it and is far from being a glib comment about the limitations of art. But this brief essay is not primarily about art (for its own sake), let alone literature: Pater offers no literary theory, is not concerned with formal problems, and discusses neither authors nor works. His purpose may be inferred from his use of the Greek epigraph and the repetition of the words "impressions" and "we," "us," and "our": Pater's focus is on individual subjectivity—how one perceives and should live in the world. If, as science has taught us, this is a world of perpetual process and change, characterized by flux both within and without, the apparent solidity of external objects is merely an illusion; what is real is the swarm of sharp but fleeting impressions registered on the mind of each solitary observer. All experience is merely subjective, and our lives consist of only a limited number of moments: how then is one to live successfully? For Pater, the answer is to crowd as many impressions as possible into our lives—to make each moment count, to experience directly and intensely, to "burn always with this hard, gemlike flame." Firsthand experience, not abstractions about experience, is what is needed.

As T. S. Eliot said, Pater is fundamentally a moralist, despite his association with the so-called aesthetic movement in England. (For more on the aesthetic movement, see the introductory note to Oscar Wilde, p. 374.) In urging us to wake up, to live intensely, moment by moment, Pater is hardly concerned with art as a unique activity or creation; it is a means of providing "the highest quality to [our] moments as they pass." In the fourth paragraph, Pater lists various kinds of pleasures, apparently indiscriminately. In seeming to imply that "a curious odour" is intrinsically as valuable as any work of art, is Pater urging a "do your own thing" or "whatever turns you on" lifestyle?

It is useful to contrast Pater with Arnold on the question of individual subjectivity. How do their conceptions of the function of poetry affect their attitudes on what Arnold calls the "personal estimate"? Finally, what does the subjective approach do to any possibility of establishing critical standards? Anatole France defined criticism as "the adventures of a soul among masterpieces." Does the impressionistic approach make for a useful way of talking about literature, or does it lead merely to another familiar credo: "I don't know anything about art, but I know what I like"?

Λέγει που ʽΗράκλειτος ʼότι πάντα χωρεῖ καὶ οὐδὲν μένει[1]

TO REGARD all things and principles of things as inconstant modes or fashions has more and more become the tendency of modern thought. Let us begin with that which is without—our physical life. Fix upon it in one of its more exquisite intervals, the moment, for instance of delicious recoil from the flood of water in summer heat. What is the whole physical life in that moment but a combination of natural elements to which science gives their names? But these elements, phosphorus and lime and delicate fibres, are present not in the human body alone: we detect them in places most remote from it. Our physical life is a perpetual motion of them—the passage of the blood, the wasting and repairing of the lenses of the eye, the modification of the tissues of the brain by every ray of light and sound—processes which science reduces to simpler and more elementary forces. Like the elements of which we are composed, the action of these forces extends beyond us; it rusts iron and ripens corn. Far out on every side of us those elements are broadcast, driven by many forces; and birth and gesture and death and the springing of violets from the grave are but a few out of ten thousand resultant combinations. That clear, perpetual outline of face and limb is but an image of ours, under which we group them—a design in a web, the actual threads of which pass out beyond it. This at least of flamelike our life has, that it is but the concurrence, renewed from moment to moment, of forces parting sooner or later on their ways.

Or if we begin with the inward world of thought and feeling, the whirlpool is still more rapid, the flame more eager and devouring. There it is no longer the gradual darkening of the eye and fading of colour from the wall,—the movement of the shore-side, where the water flows down indeed, though in apparent rest,—but the race of the midstream, a drift of momentary acts of sight and passion and thought. At first sight experience seems to bury us under a flood of external objects, pressing upon us with a sharp and importunate reality, calling us out of ourselves in a thousand forms of action. But when reflexion begins to act upon those objects they are dissipated under its influence; the cohesive force seems suspended like a trick of magic; each object is loosed into a group of impressions—colour, odour, texture—in the mind of the observer. And if we continue to dwell in thought on this world,

[1] *Legei pou Herakleitos oti panta chorei kai ouden menei.* Heraclitus says that all things move and nothing remains.

not of objects in the solidity with which language invests them, but of impressions unstable, flickering, inconsistent, which burn and are extinguished with our consciousness of them, it contracts still further; the whole scope of observation is dwarfed to the narrow chamber of the individual mind. Experience, already reduced to a swarm of impressions, is ringed round for each one of us by that thick wall of personality through which no real voice has ever pierced on its way to us, or from us to that which we can only conjecture to be without. Every one of those impressions is the impression of the individual in his isolation, each mind keeping as a solitary prisoner its own dream of a world. Analysis goes a step farther still, and assures us that those impressions of the individual mind to which, for each one of us, experience dwindles down, are in perpetual flight; that each of them is limited by time, and that as time is infinitely divisible, each of them is infinitely divisible also; all that is actual in it being a single moment, gone while we try to apprehend it, of which it may ever be more truly said that it has ceased to be than that it is. To such a tremulous wisp constantly reforming itself on the stream, to a single sharp impression, with a sense in it, a relic more or less fleeting, of such moments gone by, what is real in our life fines itself down. It is with this movement, with the passage and dissolution of impressions, images, sensations, that analysis leaves off—that continual vanishing away, that strange, perpetual weaving and unweaving of ourselves.

Philosophiren, says Novalis, *ist dephlegmatisiren, vivificiren.*[2] The service of philosophy, of speculative culture, towards the human spirit is to rouse, to startle it into sharp and eager observation. Every moment some form grows perfect in hand or face; some tone on the hills or the sea is choicer than the rest; some mood of passion or insight or intellectual excitement is irresistibly real and attractive for us,—for that moment only. Not the fruit of experience, but experience itself, is the end. A counted number of pulses only is given to us of a variegated, dramatic life. How may we see in them all that is to be seen in them by the finest senses? How shall we pass most swiftly from point to point, and be present always at the focus where the greatest number of vital forces unite in their purest energy?

To burn always with this hard, gemlike flame, to maintain this ecstasy, is success in life. In a sense it might even be said that our failure is to form habits: for, after all, habit is relative to a stereotyped world, and meantime it is only the roughness of the eye that makes any two persons, things, situations, seem alike. While all melts under our feet we may well catch at any exquisite passion, or any contribution to knowledge that seems by a lifted horizon to set the spirit free for a moment, or any stirring of the senses, strange dyes, strange colours, and curious odours, or work of the artist's hands, or the face of one's friend. Not to discriminate every moment some passionate attitude in those about us, and in the brilliancy of their gifts some tragic dividing of forces on their ways, is, on this short day of frost and sun, to sleep before evening. With this sense of the splendour of our experience and of its

---

[2] To philosophize is to rouse from inertia, to come alive.

awful brevity, gathering all we are into one desperate effort to see and touch, we shall hardly have time to make theories about the things we see and touch. What we have to do is to be for ever curiously testing new opinions and courting new impressions, never acquiescing in a facile orthodoxy of Comte, or of Hegel, or of our own. Philosophical theories or ideas, as points of view, instruments of criticism, may help us to gather up what might otherwise pass unregarded by us. "Philosophy is the microscope of thought." The theory or idea or system which requires of us the sacrifice of any part of this experience, in consideration of some interest into which we cannot enter, or some abstract theory we have not identified with ourselves, or what is only conventional, has no real claim upon us.

One of the most beautiful passages in the writings of Rousseau is that in the sixth book of the *Confessions*, where he describes the awakening in him of the literary sense. An undefinable taint of death had always clung about him, and now in early manhood he believed himself smitten by mortal disease. He asked himself how he might make as much as possible of the interval that remained; and he was not biassed by anything in his previous life when he decided that it must be by intellectual excitement, which he found just then in the clear, fresh writings of Voltaire. Well! we are all *condamnés*, as Victor Hugo says: we are all under sentence of death but with a sort of indefinite reprieve—*les hommes sont tous condamnés à mort avec des sursis indéfinis:* we have an interval, and then our place knows us no more. Some spend this interval in listlessness, some in high passions, the wisest, at least among "the children of this world," in art and song. For our one chance lies in expanding that interval, in getting as many pulsations as possible into the given time. Great passions may give us this quickened sense of life, ecstasy and sorrow of love, the various forms of enthusiastic activity, disinterested or otherwise, which come naturally to many of us. Only be sure it is passion—that it does yield you this fruit of a quickened, multiplied consciousness. Of this wisdom, the poetic passion, the desire of beauty, the love of art for art's sake, has most; for art comes to you professing frankly to give nothing but the highest quality to your moments as they pass, and simply for those moments' sake.

HENRY JAMES

The Art of Fiction

1884

Here is another "defense" of art, but this time it is the novel, a relatively recent genre, that in James's (1843–1916) view needs some serious discussion. Because Walter Besant's then influential pamphlet on "the art of fiction" is both conventional and superficial, James here will "edge in a few words" on the subject and in so doing rebut Besant's position point for point. This rebuttal, James's best-known essay on the theory of fiction, touches on various issues amplified and developed in his extensive critical writing: the relationship between fiction and life, the freedom and responsibilities of the novelist, the task of the critic, the relationship between plot and character, the importance of technique, the place of subject matter in fiction, the morality of fiction, and the character of the novelist. How James deals with these topics should be studied, for in his essays we find the beginnings of modern fictional theory. The basic assumption is that fiction, like any other art form, must be taken seriously by authors, readers, and critics alike.

The word "free" occurs so often in the essay that it directs our attention to a major point. James rejects conventional critical labels and distinctions; he rejects a priori prescriptions and rules about how to write a novel; he rejects limitations on the artist's freedom of choice in respect to subject matter and technique; he rejects traditional concepts of plot; and, climactically, he rejects Besant's formulation concerning "the conscious moral purpose" of the novel. If "the province of art is all life, all feeling; all observation, all vision . . . all experience," novelists cannot be handcuffed in their attempts to represent life. Throughout, James stresses the artist's necessary sensitivity to experience and the transformation of that experience by the imagination; as critics and readers, we can judge a novelist only by the "execution," the "treatment," the rendering of the raw multitudinous materials of life into a unified work of art.

When James declares that the novel is "a living thing, all one and continuous, like any other organism," the very simile reminds us of Aristotle and how his discussion of character merges back into a discussion of plot, the two being inseparable. James's theory of fictional form is equally organic, but for him a flawed structure and a failure of execution are symptomatic of either intellectual or moral failures on the

358

part of the novelist: the integrity of a work is a reflection of the artist's integrity. In this view, James denies that the novel must have a conscious moral purpose. On the contrary, what is commonly thought of as morality he defines as timidity—that is, the avoidance of certain "improper" but nevertheless real subjects. To insist that a novel be morally didactic is to restrict the artist's freedom from another direction. The requisite "moral energy" liberates the novelist; thus James connects total artistic freedom, the "search for form," and morality in the interest of rendering life in fiction.

I SHOULD not have affixed so comprehensive a title to these few remarks, necessarily wanting in any completeness upon a subject the full consideration of which would carry us far, did I not seem to discover a pretext for my temerity in the interesting pamphlet lately published under this name by Mr. Walter Besant. Mr. Besant's lecture at the Royal Institution—the original form of his pamphlet—appears to indicate that many persons are interested in the art of fiction, and are not indifferent to such remarks, as those who practise it may attempt to make about it. I am therefore anxious not to lose the benefit of this favourable association, and to edge in a few words under cover of the attention which Mr. Besant is sure to have excited. There is something very encouraging in his having put into form certain of his ideas on the mystery of story-telling.

It is a proof of life and curiosity—curiosity on the part of the brotherhood of novelists as well as on the part of their readers. Only a short time ago it might have been supposed that the English novel was not what the French call *discutable*. It had no air of having a theory, a conviction, a consciousness of itself behind it—of being the expression of an artistic faith, the result of choice and comparison. I do not say it was necessarily the worse for that: it would take much more courage than I possess to intimate that the form of the novel as Dickens and Thackeray (for instance) saw it had any taint of incompleteness. It was, however, *naïf* (if I may help myself out with another French word); and evidently if it be destined to suffer in any way for having lost its *naïveté* it has now an idea of making sure of the corresponding advantages. During the period I have alluded to there was a comfortable, good-humoured feeling abroad that a novel is a novel, as a pudding is a pudding, and that our only business with it could be to swallow it. But within a year or two, for some reason or other, there have been signs of returning animation—the era of discussion would appear to have been to a certain extent opened. Art lives upon discussion, upon experiment, upon curiosity, upon variety of attempt, upon the exchange of views and the comparison of standpoints; and there is a presumption that those times when no one has anything particular to say about it, and has no reason to give for practice or preference, though they may be times of honour, are not times of development—are times, possibly even, a little of dulness. The successful application of any art is a delightful spectacle, but the theory too is interesting; and though there is a great deal of the latter without the former I suspect there has never been a genuine success that has not had a latent core of conviction. Discussion, suggestion, formulation, these things are fertilising when they are frank and sincere. Mr. Besant has set an excellent example in saying what he thinks, for his part, about the way in which fiction should be written, as well as about the way in which it should be published; for his view of the "art," carried on into an appendix, covers that too. Other labourers in the same field will doubtless take up the argument, they will give it the light of their experience, and the effect will surely be to make our interest in the novel a little more what it had for some time threatened to fail to be—a serious, active, inquiring interest, under protection of which this delightful study may, in moments of confidence, venture to say a little more what it thinks of itself.

It must take itself seriously for the public to take it so. The old superstition about fiction being "wicked" has doubtless died out in England; but the spirit of it lingers in a certain oblique regard directed toward any story which does not more or less admit that it is only a joke. Even the most jocular novel feels in some degree the weight of the proscription that was formerly directed against literary levity: the jocularity does not always succeed in passing for orthodoxy. It is still expected, though perhaps people are ashamed to say it, that a production which is after all only a "make-believe" (for what else is a "story"?) shall be in some degree apologetic—shall renounce the pretension of attempting really to represent life. This, of course, any sensible, wide-awake story declines to do, for it quickly perceives that the tolerance granted to it on such a condition is only an attempt to stifle it disguised in the form of generosity. The old evangelical hostility to the novel, which was as explicit as it was narrow, and which regarded it as little less favourable to our immortal part than a stage-play, was in reality far less insulting. The only reason for the existence of a novel is that it does attempt to represent life. When it relinquishes this attempt, the same attempt that we see on the canvas of the painter, it will have arrived at a very strange pass. It is not expected of the picture that it will make itself humble in order to be forgiven; and the analogy between the art of the painter and the art of the novelist is, so far as I am able to see, complete. Their inspiration is the same, their process (allowing for the different quality of the vehicle), is the same, their success is the same. They may learn from each other, they may explain and sustain each other. Their cause is the same, and the honour of one is the honour of another. The Mahometans think a picture an unholy thing, but it is a long time since any Christian did, and it is therefore the more odd that in the Christian mind the traces (dissimulated though they may be) of a suspicion of the sister art should linger to this day. The only effectual way to lay it to rest is to emphasise the analogy to which I just alluded—to insist on the fact that as the picture is reality, so the novel is history. That is the only general description (which does it justice) that we may give of the novel. But history also is allowed to represent life; it is not, any more than painting, expected to apologise. The subject-matter of fiction is stored up likewise in documents and records, and if it will not give itself away, as they say in California, it must speak with assurance, with the tone of the historian. Certain accomplished novelists have a habit of giving themselves away which must often bring tears to the eyes of people who take their fiction seriously. I was lately struck, in reading over many pages of Anthony Trollope, with his want of discretion in this particular. In a digression, a parenthesis or an aside, he concedes to the reader that he and this trusting friend are only "making believe." He admits that the events he narrates have not really happened, and that he can give his narrative any turn the reader may like best. Such a betrayal of a sacred office seems to me, I confess, a terrible crime; it is what I mean by the attitude of apology, and it shocks me every whit as much in Trollope as it would have shocked me in Gibbon or Macaulay. It implies that the novelist is less occupied in looking for the truth (the truth, of course I mean, that he assumes, the premises that we must grant him, whatever they may be), than the historian, and in doing so it deprives him at a stroke of all his standing-room. To represent and illustrate the past, the actions of men, is the task of either writer, and the only difference that I can see is, in proportion as he succeeds, to the honour of the novelist, consisting as it does in his having more difficulty in collecting his evidence, which is so far from being purely literary. It seems to me to give him a great character, the fact that he has at once so much in common with the philosopher and the painter; this double analogy is a magnificent heritage.

It is of all this evidently that Mr. Besant is full when he insists upon the fact that fiction is one of the *fine* arts, deserving in its turn of all the honours and emoluments that have hitherto been reserved for the successful profession of music, poetry, painting, architecture. It is impossible to insist too much on so important a truth, and the place that Mr. Besant demands for the work of the novelist may be represented, a trifle less abstractly, by saying that he demands not only that it shall be reputed artistic, but that it shall be reputed very artistic indeed. It is excellent that he should have struck this note, for his doing so indicates that there was need of it, that his proposition may be to many people a novelty. One rubs one's eyes at the thought; but the rest of Mr. Besant's essay confirms the revelation. I suspect in truth that it would be possible to confirm it still further, and that one would not be far wrong in saying that in addition to the people to whom it has never occurred that a novel ought to be artistic, there are a great many others who, if this principle were urged upon them, would be filled with an indefinable mistrust. They would find it difficult to explain their repugnance, but it would operate strongly to put them on their guard. "Art," in our Protestant communities, where so many things have got so strangely twisted about, is supposed in certain circles to have some vaguely injurious effect upon those who make it an important consideration, who let it weigh in the balance. It is assumed to be opposed in some mysterious manner to morality, to amusement, to instruction. When it is embodied in the work of the painter (the sculptor is another affair!) you know what it is: it stands there before you, in the honesty of pink and green and a gilt frame; you can see the worst of it at a glance, and you can be on your guard. But when it is introduced into literature it becomes more insidious—there is danger of its hurting you before you know it. Literature should be either instructive or amusing, and there is in many minds an impression that these artistic preoccupations, the search for form, contribute to neither end, interfere indeed with both. They are too frivolous to be edifying, and too serious to be diverting; and they are moreover priggish and paradoxical and superfluous. That, I think, represents the manner in which the latent thought of many people who read novels as an exercise in skipping would explain itself if it were to become articulate. They would argue, of course, that a novel ought to be "good," but they would interpret this term in a fashion of their own, which indeed would vary considerably from one critic to another. One would say that being good means representing virtuous and aspiring characters, placed in prominent positions; another would say that it depends on a "happy ending," on a distribution at the last of prizes, pensions, husbands, wives, babies, millions, appended paragraphs, and cheerful remarks. Another still would say that it means being full of incident and movement, so that we shall wish to jump ahead, to see who was the mysterious stranger, and if the stolen will was ever found, and shall not be distracted from this pleasure by any tiresome analysis or "description." But they would all agree that the "artistic" idea would spoil some of their fun. One would hold it accountable for all the description, another would see it revealed in the absence of sympathy. Its hostility to a happy ending would be evident, and it might even in some cases render any ending at all impossible. The "ending" of a novel is, for many persons, like that of a good dinner, a course of dessert and ices, and the artist in fiction is regarded as a sort of meddlesome doctor who forbids agreeable aftertastes. It is therefore true that this conception of Mr. Besant's of the novel as a superior form encounters not only a negative but a positive indifference. It matters little that as a work of art it should really be as little or as much of its essence to supply happy endings, sympathetic characters, and an objective tone, as if it were a work of mechanics: the association of ideas, however incongruous, might easily be too much for it if an eloquent voice were not sometimes raised to call attention to the fact that it is at once as free and as serious a branch of literature as any other.

Certainly this might sometimes be doubted in presence of the enormous number of works of fiction that appeal to the credulity of our generation, for it might easily seem that there could be no great character in a commodity so quickly and easily produced. It must be admitted that good novels are much compromised by bad ones, and that the field at large suffers discredit from overcrowding. I think, however, that this injury is only superficial, and that the superabundance of written fiction proves nothing against the principle itself. It has been vulgarised, like all other kinds of literature, like everything else to-day, and it has proved more than some kinds accessible to vulgarisation. But there is as much difference as there ever was between a good novel and a bad one: the bad is swept with all the daubed canvases and spoiled marble into some unvisited limbo, or infinite rubbish-yard beneath the back-windows of the world, and the good subsists and emits its light and stimulates our desire for perfection. As I shall take the liberty of making but a single criticism of Mr. Besant, whose tone is so full of the love of his art, I may as well have done with it at once. He seems to me to mistake in attempting to say so definitely beforehand what sort of an affair the good novel will be. To indicate the danger of such an error as that has been the purpose of these few pages; to suggest that certain traditions on the subject, applied *a priori,* have already had much to answer for, and that the good health of an art which undertakes so immediately to reproduce life must demand that it be perfectly free. It lives upon exercise, and the very meaning of exercise is freedom. The only obligation to which in advance we may hold a novel, without incurring the accusation of being arbitrary, is that it be interesting. That general responsibility rests upon it, but it is the only one I can think of. The ways in which it is at liberty to accomplish this result (of interesting us) strike me as innumerable, and such as can only suffer from being marked out or fenced in by prescription. They are as various as the temperament of man, and they are successful in proportion as they reveal a particular mind, different from others. A novel is in its broadest definition a personal, a direct impression of life: that, to begin with, constitutes its value, which is greater or less according to the intensity of the impression. But there will be no intensity at all, and therefore no value, unless there is freedom to feel and say. The tracing of a line to be followed, of a tone to be taken, of a form to be filled out, is a limitation of that freedom and a suppression of the very thing that we are most curious about. The form, it seems to me, is to be appreciated after the fact: then the author's choice has been made, his standard has been indicated; then we can follow lines and directions and compare tones and resemblances. Then in a word we can enjoy one of the most charming of pleasures, we can estimate quality, we can apply the test of execution. The execution belongs to the author alone; it is what is most personal to him, and we measure him by that. The advantage, the luxury, as well as the torment and responsibility of the novelist, is that there is no limit to what he may attempt as an executant—no limit to his possible experiments, efforts, discoveries, successes. Here it is especially that he works, step by step, like his brother of the brush, of whom we may always say that he has painted his picture in a manner best known to himself. His manner is his secret, not necessarily a jealous one. He cannot disclose it as a general thing if he would; he would be at a loss to teach it to others. I say this with a due recollection of having insisted on the community of method of the artist who paints a picture and the artist who writes a novel. The painter *is* able to teach the rudiments of his practice, and it is possible, from the study of good work (granted the aptitude), both to learn how to paint and to learn how to write. Yet it remains true, without injury to the *rapprochement,* that the literary artist would be obliged to say to his pupil much more than the other, "Ah, well, you must do it as you can!" It is a question of degree, a matter of delicacy. If there are exact sciences, there are also exact arts, and the grammar of painting is so much more definite that it makes the difference.

I ought to add, however, that if Mr. Besant says at the beginning of his essay that the "laws of fiction may be laid down and taught with as much precision and exactness as the laws of harmony, perspective, and proportion," he mitigates what might appear to be an extravagance by applying his remark to "general" laws, and by expressing most of these rules in a manner with which it would certainly be unaccommodating to disagree. That the novelist must write from his experience, that his "characters must be real and such as might be met with in actual life," that "a young lady brought up in a quiet country village should avoid descriptions of garrison life," and "a writer whose friends and personal experiences belong to the lower middle-class should carefully avoid introducing his characters into society;" that one should enter one's notes in a common-place book; that one's figures should be clear in outline; that making them clear by some trick of speech or of carriage is a bad method and "describing them at length" is a worse one; that English Fiction should have a "conscious moral purpose;" that "it is almost impossible to estimate too highly the value of careful workmanship—that is, of style;" that "the most important point of all is the story," that "the story is everything": these are principles with most of which it is surely impossible not to sympathise. That remark about the lower middle-class writer and his knowing his place is perhaps rather chilling; but for the rest I should find it difficult to dissent from any one of these recommendations. At the same time, I should find it difficult positively to assent to them, with the exception, perhaps, of the injunction as to entering one's notes in a common-place book. They scarcely seem to me to have the quality that Mr. Besant attributes to the rules of the novelist—the "precision and exactness" of "the laws of harmony, perspective, and proportion." They are suggestive, they are even inspiring, but they are not exact, though they are doubtless as much so as the case admits of: which is a proof of that liberty of interpretation for which I just contended. For the value of these different injunctions—so beautiful and so vague—is wholly in the meaning one attaches to them. The characters, the situation, which strike one as real will be those that touch and interest one most, but the measure of reality is very difficult to fix. The reality of Don Quixote or of Mr. Micawber is a very delicate shade; it is a reality so coloured by the author's vision that, vivid as it may be, one would hesitate to propose it as a model: one would expose one's self to some very embarrassing questions on the part of a pupil. It goes without saying that you will not write a good novel unless you possess the sense of reality; but it will be difficult to give you a recipe for calling that sense into being. Humanity is immense, and reality has a myriad forms; the most one can affirm is that some of the flowers of fiction have the odour of it, and others have not; as for telling you in advance how your nosegay should be composed, that is another affair. It is equally excellent and inconclusive to say that one must write from experience; to our suppositious aspirant such a declaration might savour of mockery. What kind of experience is intended, and where does it begin and end? Experience is never limited, and it is never complete; it is an immense sensibility, a kind of huge spider-web of the finest silken threads suspended in the chamber of consciousness, and catching every airborne particle in its tissue. It is the very atmosphere of the mind; and when the mind is imaginative—much more when it happens to be that of a man of genius—it takes to itself the faintest hints of life, it converts the very pulses of the air into revelations. The young lady living in a village has only to be a damsel upon whom nothing is lost to make it quite unfair (as it seems to me) to declare to her that she shall have nothing to say about the military. Greater miracles have been seen than that, imagination assisting, she should speak the truth about some of these gentlemen. I remember an English novelist, a woman of genius, telling me that she was much commended for the impression she had managed to give in one of her tales of the nature and way of life of the French Protestant youth. She had been asked where she learned so much about this recondite being, she had been congratulated on her peculiar opportunities. These opportunities consisted in her having once, in Paris, as she ascended a staircase, passed an open door where, in the household of a *pasteur*, some of the young Protestants were seated at table round a finished meal. The glimpse made a picture; it lasted only a moment, but that moment was experience. She had got her direct personal impression, and she turned out her type. She knew what youth was, and what Protestantism; she also had the advantage of having seen what it was to be French, so that she converted these ideas into a concrete image and produced a reality. Above all, however, she was blessed with the faculty which when you give it an inch takes an ell, and which for the artist is a much greater source of strength than any accident of residence or of place in the social scale. The power to guess the unseen from the seen, to trace the implication of things, to judge the whole piece by the pattern, the condition of feeling life in general so completely that you are well on your way to knowing any particular corner of it—this cluster of gifts may almost be said to constitute experience, and they occur in country and in town, and in the most differing stages of education. If experience consists of impressions, it may be said that impressions *are* experience, just as (have we not seen it?) they are the very air we breathe. Therefore, if I should certainly say to a novice, "Write from experience and experience only," I should feel that this was rather a tantalising monition if I were not careful immediately to add, "Try to be one of the people on whom nothing is lost!"

I am far from intending by this to minimise the importance of exactness—of truth of detail. One can speak best from one's own taste, and I may therefore venture to say that the air of reality (solidity of specification) seems to me to be the supreme virtue of a novel—the merit on which all its other merits (including that conscious moral purpose of which Mr. Besant speaks) helplessly and submissively depend. If it be not there they are all as nothing, and if these be there, they owe their effect to the success with which the author has produced the illusion of life. The cultivation of this success, the study of this exquisite process, form, to my taste, the beginning and the end of the art of the novelist. They are his inspiration, his despair, his reward, his torment, his delight. It is here in very truth that he competes with life; it is here that he competes with his brother the painter in *his* attempt to render the look of things, the look that conveys their meaning, to catch the colour, the relief, the expression, the surface, the substance of the human spectacle. It is in regard to this that Mr. Besant is well inspired when he bids him take notes. He cannot possibly take too many, he cannot possibly take enough. All life solicits him, and to "render" the simplest surface, to produce the most momentary illusion, is a very complicated business. His case would be easier, and the rule would be more exact, if Mr. Besant had been able to tell him what notes to take. But this, I fear, he can never learn in any manual; it is the business of his life. He has to take a great many in order to select a few, he has to work them up as he can, and even the guides and philosophers who might have most to say to him must leave him alone when it comes to the application of precepts, as we leave the painter in communion with his palette. That his characters "must be clear in outline," as Mr. Besant says—he feels that down to his boots; but how he shall make them so is a secret between his good angel and himself. It would be absurdly simple if he could be taught that a great deal of "description" would make them so, or that on the contrary the absence of description and the cultivation of dialogue, or the absence of dialogue and the multiplication of "incident," would rescue him from his difficulties. Nothing, for instance, is more possible than that he be of a turn of mind for which this odd, literal opposition of description and dialogue, incident and description, has little meaning and light. People often talk of these things as if they had a kind of internecine distinctness, instead of melting into each other at every breath, and being intimately associated parts of one general effort of expression. I cannot imagine composition existing in a series of blocks, nor conceive, in any novel worth discussing at all, of a passage of description that is not in its intention narrative, a passage of dialogue that is not in its intention descriptive, a touch of truth of any sort that does not partake of the nature of incident, or an incident that derives its interest from any other source than the general and only source of the success of a work of art—that of being illustrative. A novel is a living thing, all one and continuous, like any other organism, and in proportion as it lives will it be found, I think, that in each of the parts there is something of each of the other parts. The critic who over the close texture of a finished work shall pretend to trace a geography of items will mark some frontiers as artificial, I fear, as any that have been known to history. There is an old-fashioned distinction between the novel of character and the novel of incident which must have cost many a smile to the intending fabulist who was keen about his work. It appears to me as little to the point as the equally celebrated distinction between the novel and the romance—to answer as little to any reality. There are bad novels and good novels, as there are bad pictures and good pictures; but that is the only distinction in which I see any meaning, and I can as little imagine speaking of a novel of character as I can imagine speaking of a picture of character. When one says picture one says of character, when one says novel one says of incident, and the terms may be transposed at will. What is character but the determination of incident? What is incident but the illustration of character? What is either a picture or a novel that is *not* of character? What else do we seek in it and find in it? It is an incident for a woman to stand up with her hand resting on a table and look out at you in a certain way; or if it be not an incident I think it will be hard to say what it is. At the same time it is an expression of character. If you say you don't see it (character in *that — allons donc!*[1]), this is exactly what the artist who has reasons of his own for thinking he *does* see it undertakes to show you. When a young man makes up his mind that he has not faith enough after all to enter the church as he intended, that is an incident, though you may not hurry to the end of the chapter to see whether perhaps he doesn't change once more. I do not say that these are extraordinary or startling incidents. I do not pretend to estimate the degree of interest proceeding from them, for this will depend upon the skill of the painter. It sounds almost puerile to say that some incidents are instrinsically much more important than others, and I need not take this precaution after having professed my sympathy for the major ones in remarking that the only classification of the novel that I can understand is into that which has life and that which has it not.

The novel and the romance, the novel of incident and that of character — these clumsy separations appear to me to have been made by critics and readers for their own convenience, and to help them out of some of their occasional queer predicaments, but to have little reality or interest for the producer, from whose point of view it is of course that we are attempting to consider the art of fiction. The case is the same with another shadowy category which Mr. Besant apparently is disposed to set up — that of the "modern English novel"; unless indeed it be that in this matter he has fallen into an accidental confusion of standpoints. It is not quite clear whether he intends the remarks in which he alludes to it to be didactic or historical. It is as difficult to suppose a person intending to write a modern English as to suppose him writing an ancient English novel: that is a label which begs the question. One writes the novel, one paints the picture, of one's language and of one's time, and calling it modern English will not, alas! make the difficult task any easier. No more, unfortunately, will calling this or that work of one's fellow-artist a romance — unless it be, of course, simply for the pleasantness of the thing, as for instance when Hawthorne gave this heading to his story of *Blithedale*. The French, who have brought the theory of fiction to remarkable completeness, have but one name for the novel, and have not attempted smaller things in it, that I can see, for that. I can think of no obligation to which the "romancer" would not be held equally with the novelist; the standard of execution is equally high for each. Of course it is of execution that we are talking — that being the only point of a novel that is open to contention. This is perhaps too often lost sight of, only to produce interminable confusions and cross-purposes. We must grant the artist his subject, his idea, his *donnée:* our criticism is applied only to what he makes of it. Naturally I do not mean that we are bound to like it or find it interesting: in case we do not our

[1] Oh, come now!

course is perfectly simple—to let it alone. We may believe that of a certain idea even the most sincere novelist can make nothing at all, and the event may perfectly justify our belief; but the failure will have been a failure to execute, and it is in the execution that the fatal weakness is recorded. If we pretend to respect the artist at all, we must allow him his freedom of choice, in the face, in particular cases, of innumerable presumptions that the choice will not fructify. Art derives a considerable part of its beneficial exercise from flying in the face of presumptions, and some of the most interesting experiments of which it is capable are hidden in the bosom of common things. Gustave Flaubert has written a story about the devotion of a servant girl to a parrot, and the production, highly finished as it is, cannot on the whole be called a success. We are perfectly free to find it flat, but I think it might have been interesting; and I, for my part, am extremely glad he should have written it; it is a contribution to our knowledge of what can be done—or what cannot. Ivan Turgénieff has written a tale about a deaf and dumb serf and a lap-dog, and the thing is touching, loving, a little masterpiece. He struck the note of life where Gustave Flaubert missed it—he flew in the face of a presumption and achieved a victory.

Nothing, of course, will ever take the place of the good old fashion of "liking" a work of art or not liking it: the most improved criticism will not abolish that primitive, that ultimate test. I mention this to guard myself from the accusation of intimating that the idea, the subject, of a novel or a picture, does not matter. It matters, to my sense, in the highest degree, and if I might put up a prayer it would be that artists should select none but the richest. Some, as I have already hastened to admit, are much more remunerative than others, and it would be a world happily arranged in which persons intending to treat them should be exempt from confusions and mistakes. This fortunate condition will arrive only, I fear, on the same day that critics become purged from error. Meanwhile, I repeat, we do not judge the artist with fairness unless we say to him, "Oh, I grant you your starting-point, because if I did not I should seem to prescribe to you, and heaven forbid I should take that responsibility. If I pretend to tell you what you must not take, you will call upon me to tell you then what you must take; in which case I shall be prettily caught. Moreover, it isn't till I have accepted your data that I can begin to measure you. I have the standard, the pitch; I have no right to tamper with your flute and then criticise your music. Of course I may not care for your idea at all; I may think it silly, or stale, or unclean; in which case I wash my hands of you altogether. I may content myself with believing that you will not have succeeded in being interesting, but I shall, of course, not attempt to demonstrate it, and you will be as indifferent to me as I am to you. I needn't remind you that there are all sorts of tastes: who can know it better? Some people, for excellent reasons, don't like to read about carpenters; others, for reasons even better, don't like to read about courtesans. Many object to Americans. Others (I believe they are mainly editors and publishers) won't look at Italians. Some readers don't like quiet subjects; others don't like bustling ones. Some enjoy a complete illusion, others the consciousness of large concessions. They choose their novels accordingly, and if they don't care about your idea they won't, *a fortiori,* care about your treatment."

So that it comes back very quickly, as I have said, to the liking: in spite of M. Zola, who reasons less powerfully than he represents, and who will not reconcile himself to this absoluteness of taste, thinking that there are certain things that people ought to like, and that they can be made to like. I am quite at a loss to imagine anything (at any rate in this matter of fiction) that people *ought* to like or to dislike. Selection will be sure to take care of itself, for it has a constant motive behind it. That motive is simply experience. As people feel life, so they will feel the art that is most closely related to it. This closeness of relation is what we should never forget in talking of the effort of the novel. Many people speak of it as a factitious, artificial form, a product of ingenuity, the business of which is to alter and arrange the things that surround us, to translate them into conventional, traditional moulds. This, however, is a view of the matter which carries us but a very short way, condemns the art to an eternal repetition of a few familiar *clichés,* cuts short its development, and leads us straight up to a dead wall. Catching the very note and trick, the strange irregular rhythm of life, that is the attempt whose strenuous force keeps Fiction upon her feet. In proportion as in what she offers us we see life *without* rearrangement do we feel that we are touching the truth; in proportion as we see it *with* rearrangement do we feel that we are being put off with a substitute, a compromise and convention. It is not uncommon to hear an extraordinary assurance of remark in regard to this matter of rearranging, which is often spoken of as if it were the last word of art. Mr. Besant seems to me in danger of falling into the great error with his rather unguarded talk about "selection." Art is essentially selection, but it is a selection whose main care is to be typical, to be inclusive. For many people art means rose-coloured window-panes, and selection means picking a bouquet for Mrs. Grundy. They will tell you glibly that artistic considerations have nothing to do with the disagreeable, with the ugly; they will rattle off shallow commonplaces about the province of art and the limits of art till you are moved to some wonder in return as to the province and the limits of ignorance. It appears to me that no one can ever have made a seriously artistic attempt without becoming conscious of an immense increase—a kind of revelation—of freedom. One perceives in that case—by the light of a heavenly ray—that the province of art is all life, all feeling, all observation, all vision. As Mr. Besant so justly intimates, it is all experience. That is a sufficient answer to those who maintain that it must not touch the sad things of life, who stick into its divine unconscious bosom little prohibitory inscriptions on the end of sticks, such as we see in public gardens—"It is forbidden to walk on the grass; it is forbidden to touch the flowers; it is not allowed to introduce dogs or to remain after dark; it is requested to keep to the right." The young aspirant in the line of fiction whom we continue to imagine will do nothing without taste, for in that case his freedom would be of little use to him; but the first advantage of his taste will be to reveal to him the absurdity of the little sticks and tickets. If he have taste, I must add, of course he will have ingenuity, and my disrespectful reference to that quality just now was not meant to imply that it is useless in fiction. But it is only a secondary aid; the first is a capacity for receiving straight impressions.

Mr. Besant has some remarks on the question of "the story" which I shall not attempt to criticise, though they seem to me to contain a singular ambiguity, because I do not think I understand them. I cannot see what is meant by talking as if there were a part of a novel which is the story and part of it which for mystical reasons is not—unless indeed the distinction be made in a sense in which it is difficult to suppose that any one should attempt to convey anything. "The story," if it represents anything, represents the subject, the idea, the *donné* of the novel; and there is surely no "school"—Mr. Besant speaks of a school—which urges that a novel should be all treatment and no subject. There must assuredly be something to treat; every school is intimately conscious of that. This sense of the story being the idea, the starting-point, of the novel, is the only one that I see in which it can be spoken of as something different from its organic whole; and since in proportion as the work is successful the idea permeates and penetrates it, informs and animates it, so that every word and every punctuation-point contribute directly to the expression, in that proportion do we lose our sense of the story being a blade which may be drawn more or less out of its sheath. The story and the novel, the idea and the form, are the needle and thread, and I never heard of a guild of tailors who recommended the use of the thread without the needle, or the needle without the thread. Mr. Besant is not the only critic who may be observed to have spoken as if there were certain things in life which constitute stories, and certain others which do not—I find the same odd implication in an entertaining article in the *Pall Mall Gazette,* devoted, as it happens, to Mr. Besant's lecture. "The story is the thing!" says this graceful writer, as if with a tone of opposition to some other idea. I should think it was, as every painter who, as the time for "sending in" his picture looms in the distance, finds himself still in quest of a subject—as every belated artist not fixed about his theme will heartily agree. There are some subjects which speak to us and others which do not, but he would be a clever man who should undertake to give a rule—an index expurgatorius—by which the story and the no-story should be known apart. It is impossible (to me at least) to imagine any such rule which shall not be altogether arbitrary. The writer in the *Pall Mall* opposes the delightful (as I suppose) novel of *Margot la Balafrée* to certain tales in which "Bostonian nymphs" appear to have "rejected English dukes for psychological reasons." I am not acquainted with the romance just designated, and can scarcely forgive the *Pall Mall* critic for not mentioning the name of the author, but the title appears to refer to a lady who may have received a scar in some heroic adventure. I am inconsolable at not being acquainted with this episode, but am utterly at a loss to see why it is a story when the rejection (or acceptance) of a duke is not, and why a reason, psychological or other, is not a subject when a cicatrix is. They are all particles of the multitudinous life with which the novel deals, and surely no dogma which pretends to make it lawful to touch the one and unlawful to touch the other will stand for a moment on its feet. It is the special picture that must stand or fall, according as it seem to possess truth or to lack it. Mr. Besant does not, to my sense, light up the subject by intimating that a story must, under penalty of not being a story, consist of "adventures." Why of adventures more than of green spectacles? He mentions a category of impossible things, and among them he places "fiction without adventure." Why without adventure, more than without matrimony, or celibacy, or parturition, or cholera, or hydropathy, or Jansenism? This seems to me to bring the novel back to the hapless little rôle of being an artificial, ingenious thing—bring it down from its large, free character of an immense and exquisite correspondence with life. And what *is* adventure, when it comes to that, and by what sign is the listening pupil to recognise it? It is an adventure—an immense one—for me to write this little article; and for a Bostonian nymph to reject an English duke is an adventure only less stirring, I should say, than for an English duke to be rejected by a Bostonian nymph. I see dramas within dramas in that, and innumerable points of view. A psychological reason is, to my imagination, an object adorably pictorial; to catch the tint of its complexion—I feel as if that idea might inspire one to Titianesque efforts. There are few things more exciting to me, in short, than a psychological reason, and yet, I protest, the novel seems to me the most magnificent form of art. I have just been reading, at the same time, the delightful story of *Treasure Island,* by Mr. Robert Louis Stevenson and, in a manner less consecutive, the last tale from M. Edmond de Goncourt, which is entitled *Chérie.* One of these works treats of murders, mysteries, islands of dreadful renown, hairbreadth escapes, miraculous coincidences and buried doubloons. The other treats of a little French girl who lived in a fine house in Paris, and died of wounded sensibility because no one would marry her. I call *Treasure Island* delightful, because it appears to me to have succeeded wonderfully in what it attempts; and I venture to bestow no epithet upon *Chérie,* which strikes me as having failed deplorably in what it attempts—that is in tracing the development of the moral consciousness of a child. But one of these productions strikes me as exactly as much of a novel as the other, and as having a "story" quite as much. The moral consciousness of a child is as much a part of life as the islands of the Spanish Main, and the one sort of geography seems to me to have those "surprises" of which Mr. Besant speaks quite as much as the other. For myself (since it comes back in the last resort, as I say, to the preference of the individual), the picture of the child's experience has the advantage that I can at successive steps (an immense luxury, near to the "sensual pleasure" of which Mr. Besant's critic in the *Pall Mall* speaks) say Yes or No, as it may be, to what the artist puts before me. I have been a child in fact, but I have been on a quest for a buried treasure only in supposition, and it is a simple accident that with M. de Goncourt I should have for the most part to say No. With George Eliot, when she painted that country with a far other intelligence, I always said Yes.

The most interesting part of Mr. Besant's lecture is unfortunately the briefest passage—his very cursory allusion to the "conscious moral purpose" of the novel. Here again it is not very clear whether he be recording a fact or laying down a principle; it is a great pity that in the latter case he should not have developed his idea. This branch of the subject is of immense importance, and Mr. Besant's few words point to considerations of the widest reach, not to be lightly disposed of. He will have treated the art of fiction but superficially who is not prepared to go every inch of the way that these considerations will carry him. It is for this reason that at the beginning of these remarks I was careful to notify the reader that my reflections on so large a theme have no pretension to be exhaustive. Like Mr. Besant, I have left the question of the morality of the novel till the last, and at the last I find I have used up my space. It is a question surrounded with difficulties, as witness the very first that meets us, in the form of a definite question, on the threshold. Vagueness, in such a discussion, is fatal, and what is the meaning of your morality and your conscious moral purpose? Will you not define your terms and explain how (a novel being a picture) a picture can be either moral or immoral? You wish to paint a moral picture or carve a moral statue: will you not tell us how you would set about it? We are discussing the Art of Fiction; questions of art are questions (in the widest sense) of execution; questions of morality are quite another affair, and will you not let us see how it is that you find it so easy to mix them up? These things are so clear to Mr. Besant that he has deduced from them a law which he sees embodied in English Fiction, and which is "a truly admirable thing and a great cause for congratulation." It is a great cause for congratulation indeed when such thorny problems become as smooth as silk. I may add that in so far as Mr. Besant perceives that in point of fact English Fiction has addressed itself preponderantly to these delicate questions he will appear to many people to have made a vain discovery. They will have been positively struck, on the contrary, with the moral timidity of the usual English novelist; with his (or with her) aversion to face the difficulties with which on every side the treatment of reality bristles. He is apt to be extremely shy (whereas the picture that Mr. Besant draws is a picture of boldness), and the sign of his work, for the most part, is a cautious silence on certain subjects. In the English novel (by which of course I mean the American as well), more than in any other, there is a traditional difference between that which people know and that which they agree to admit that they know, that which they see and that which they speak of, that which they feel to be a part of life and that which they allow to enter into literature. There is the great difference, in short, between what they talk of in conversation and what they talk of in print. The essence of moral energy is to survey the whole field, and I should directly reverse Mr. Besant's remark and say not that the English novel has a purpose, but that it has a diffidence. To what degree a purpose in a work of art is a source of corruption I shall not attempt to inquire; the one that seems to me least dangerous is the purpose of making a perfect work. As for our novel, I may say lastly on this score that as we find it in England to-day it strikes me as addressed in a large degree to "young people," and that this in itself constitutes a presumption that it will be rather shy. There are certain things which it is generally agreed not to discuss, not even to mention, before young people. That is very well, but the absence of discussion is not a symptom of the moral passion. The purpose of the English novel—"a truly admirable thing, and a great cause for congratulation"—strikes me therefore as rather negative.

There is one point at which the moral sense and the artistic sense lie very near together; that is in the light of the very obvious truth that the deepest quality of a work of art will always be the quality of the mind of the producer. In proportion as that intelligence is fine will the novel, the picture, the statue partake of the substance of beauty and truth. To be constituted of such elements is, to my vision, to have purpose enough. No good novel will ever proceed from a superficial mind; that seems to me an axiom which, for the artist in fiction, will cover all needful moral ground: if the youthful aspirant take it to heart it will illuminate for him many of the mysteries of "purpose." There are many other useful things that might be said to him, but I have come to the end of my article, and can only touch them as I pass. The critic in the *Pall Mall Gazette,* whom I have already quoted, draws attention to the danger, in speaking of the art of fiction, of generalising. The danger that he has in mind is rather, I imagine, that of particularising, for there are some comprehensive remarks which, in addition to those embodied in Mr. Besant's suggestive lecture, might without fear of misleading him be addressed to the ingenuous student. I should remind him first of the magnificence of the form that is open to him, which offers to sight so few restrictions and such innumerable opportunities. The other arts, in comparison, appear confined and hampered; the various conditions under which they are exercised are so rigid and definite. But the only condition that I can think of attaching to the composition of the novel is, as I have already said, that it be sincere. This freedom is a splendid privilege, and the first lesson of the young novelist is to learn to be worthy of it. "Enjoy it as it deserves," I should say to him; "take possession of it, explore it to its utmost extent, publish it, rejoice in it. All life belongs to you, and do not listen either to those who would shut you up into corners of it and tell you that it is only here and there that art inhabits, or to those who would persuade you that this heavenly messenger wings her way outside of life altogether, breathing a superfine air, and turning away her head from the truth of things. There is no impression of life, no manner of seeing it and feeling it, to which the plan of the novelist may not offer a place; you have only to remember that talents so dissimilar as those of Alexandre Dumas and Jane Austen, Charles Dickens and Gustave Flaubert have worked in this field with equal glory. Do not think too much about optimism and pessimism; try and catch the colour of life itself. In France to-day we see a prodigious effort (that of Emile Zola, to whose solid and serious work no explorer of the capacity of the novel can allude without respect), we see an extraordinary effort vitiated by a spirit of pessimism on a narrow basis. M. Zola is magnificent, but he strikes an English reader as ignorant; he has an air of working in the dark; if he had as much light as energy, his results would be of the highest value. As for the aberrations of a shallow optimism, the ground (of English fiction especially) is strewn with their brittle particles as with broken glass. If you must indulge in conclusions, let them have the taste of a wide knowledge. Remember that your first duty is to be as complete as possible—to make as perfect a work. Be generous and delicate and pursue the prize."

Oscar Wilde

From *The Critic as Artist*

1891

Even before the sexual scandal for which he became infamous, Anglo-Irish poet, play-wright, journalist, and critic Oscar Wilde (1854–1900) had gained wide notoriety in Europe and America as a prominent and eccentric proponent of what came to be called the aesthetic movement. The aesthetes, who were active in Europe in the 1880s and 1890s, were known to value "art for art's sake" and to hold in contempt those who sought a moral or social function in literature and the other arts. This attitude spoke in direct opposition to such contemporary luminaries as Matthew Arnold (see "The Study of Poetry," p. 333) and Leo Tolstoy (What Is Art? p. 382). As a writer and speaker, Wilde was known for his witty one-liners and clever turns of phrase, as well as for his flippant demeanor, which challenged the traditional morality of late Victorian society. His critical attitude and epigrammatic style are exemplified in the preface to the 1891 novel **The Picture of Dorian Gray**, where he lays out many of his ideas about writing, including "There is no such thing as a moral or an immoral book" and "All art is quite useless."

Nowadays, Wilde's life story has become far better known than his critical atti-tudes. Recent biographies and films — which have usually concentrated on his trial, imprisonment, and public disgrace for "crimes" of homosexuality — tend to portray him as a man misunderstood and ahead of his time. The astute and ever-wry Wilde would likely have been both fascinated and pleased by such a turn of events, since he considered his own life inseparable from his art. Indeed, it has been said that he worked as diligently on the creation of his flamboyant public persona, which ironi-cally both flouted and created style, as he did on his writing. As much as anything he wrote, the act of self-fashioning has made him a popular subject of contemporary scholarship in gender studies.

The selection that follows is from the essay entitled "The Critic as Artist." As the title implies, it argues that literary and other art criticism is itself a form of artistry, indeed a more advanced and more necessary form than the creative arts, which are generally more venerated. While Wilde is being deliberately provocative with this stance, he nonetheless has serious intent — to challenge the entrenched tru-isms of Victorian criticism. To defend his somewhat unorthodox views, Wilde in-

*vokes, among others, Walter Pater (see p. 354), a teacher who had a profound influ-
ence on Wilde's developing ideas about art when the younger man was a student at
Oxford. He also returns to the Greeks for evidence of the primacy of literary criticism, and even here he overturns the then widely held preference for Platonic criticism. Wilde prefers Aristotle's criticism over Plato's, since the former focuses more
on form and the latter on function and morality. Also notable is the dialogue form of
the piece (perhaps not a surprising choice for a playwright), a style whose precedents
include Dryden's* Essay of Dramatic Poesy *(p. 136) and of course many of the
works of Plato himself.*

ERNEST: . . . You have said that the Greeks were a nation of art-critics. What
art-criticism have they left us?

GILBERT: My dear Ernest, even if not a single fragment of art-criticism had
come down to us from Hellenic or Hellenistic days, it would be none the
less true that the Greeks were a nation of art-critics, and that they invented the criticism of art just as they invented the criticism of everything else. For, after all, what is our primary debt to the Greeks? Simply
the critical spirit. And, this spirit, which they exercised on questions of
religion and science, of ethics and metaphysics, of politics and education,
they exercised on questions of art also, and, indeed, of the two supreme
and highest arts, they have left us the most flawless system of criticism
that the world has ever seen.

ERNEST: But what are the two supreme and highest arts?

GILBERT: Life and Literature, life and the perfect expression of life. The principles of the former, as laid down by the Greeks, we may not realise in an
age so marred by false ideals as our own. The principles of the latter, as
they laid them down, are, in many cases, so subtle that we can hardly
understand them. Recognising that the most perfect art is that which
most fully mirrors man in all his infinite variety, they elaborated the criticism of language, considered in the light of the mere material of that art,
to a point to which we, with our accentual system of reasonable or emotional emphasis, can barely if at all attain; studying, for instance, the metrical movements of a prose as scientifically as a modern musician studies
harmony and counterpoint, and, I need hardly say, with much keener
aesthetic instinct. In this they were right, as they were right in all things.
Since the introduction of printing, and the fatal development of the habit
of reading amongst the middle and lower classes of this country, there
has been a tendency in literature to appeal more and more to the eye,
and less and less to the ear which is really the sense which, from the
standpoint of pure art, it should seek to please, and by whose canons of
pleasure it should abide always. Even the work of Mr. Pater, who is, on
the whole, the most perfect master of English prose now creating
amongst us, is often far more like a piece of mosaic than a passage in
music, and seems, here and there, to lack the true rhythmical life of

words and the fine freedom and richness of effect that such rhythmical life produces. We, in fact, have made writing a definite mode of composition, and have treated it as a form of elaborate design. The Greeks, upon the other hand, regarded writing simply as a method of chronicling. Their test was always the spoken word in its musical and metrical relations. The voice was the medium, and the ear the critic. I have sometimes thought that the story of Homer's blindness might be really an artistic myth, created in critical days, and serving to remind us, not merely that the great poet is always a seer, seeing less with the eyes of the body than he does with the eyes of the soul, but that he is a true singer also, building his song out of music, repeating each line over and over again to himself till he has caught the secret of its melody, chaunting in darkness the words that are winged with light. Certainly, whether this be so or not, it was to his blindness, as an occasion, if not as a cause, that England's great poet owed much of the majestic movement and sonorous splendour of his later verse. When Milton could no longer write he began to sing. Who would match the measures of *Comus* with the measures of *Samson Agonistes,* or of *Paradise Lost* or *Regained*? When Milton became blind he composed, as every one should compose, with the voice purely, and so the pipe or reed of earlier days became that mighty many-stopped organ whose rich reverberant music has all the stateliness of Homeric verse, if it seeks not to have its swiftness, and is the one imperishable inheritance of English literature sweeping through all the ages, because above them, and abiding with us ever, being immortal in its form. Yes: writing has done much harm to writers. We must return to the voice. That must be our test, and perhaps then we shall be able to appreciate some of the subtleties of Greek art-criticism.

As it now is, we cannot do so. Sometimes, when I have written a piece of prose that I have been modest enough to consider absolutely free from fault, a dreadful thought comes over me that I may have been guilty of the immoral effeminacy of using trochaic and tribrachic movements, a crime for which a learned critic of the Augustan age censures with most just severity the brilliant if somewhat paradoxical Hegesias.[1] I grow cold when I think of it, and wonder to myself if the admirable ethical effect of the prose of that charming writer, who once in a spirit of reckless generosity towards the uncultivated portion of our community proclaimed the monstrous doctrine that conduct is three-fourths of life, will not some day be entirely annihilated by the discovery that the paeons have been wrongly placed.

ERNEST: Ah! now you are flippant.

GILBERT: Who would not be flippant when he is gravely told that the Greeks had no art-critics? I can understand it being said that the constructive genius of the Greeks lost itself in criticism, but not that the race to whom

---

[1] Hegesias (ca. 300 or 250 B.C.), Greek orator and historian whose inflated oratory was deplored by ancient critics.

we owe the critical spirit did not criticise. You will not ask me to give
you a survey of Greek art criticism from Plato to Plotinus. The night is
too lovely for that, and the moon, if she heard us, would put more ashes
on her face than are there already. But think merely of one perfect little
work of aesthetic criticism, Aristotle's *Treatise on Poetry*. It is not perfect
in form, for it is badly written, consisting perhaps of notes dotted down
for an art lecture, or of isolated fragments destined for some larger book,
but in temper and treatment it is perfect, absolutely. The ethical effect of
art, its importance to culture, and its place in the formation of character,
had been done once for all by Plato; but here we have art treated, not
from the moral, but from the purely aesthetic point of view. Plato had, of
course, dealt with many definitely artistic subjects, such as the importance of unity in a work of art, the necessity for tone and harmony, the
aesthetic value of appearances, the relation of the visible arts to the external world, and the relation of fiction to fact. He first perhaps stirred in
the soul of man that desire that we have not yet satisfied, the desire to
know the connection between Beauty and Truth, and the place of Beauty
in the moral and intellectual order of the Kosmos. The problems of idealism and realism, as he sets them forth, may seem to many to be somewhat barren of result in the metaphysical sphere of abstract being in
which he places them, but transfer them to the sphere of art, and you
will find that they are still vital and full of meaning. It may be that it is as
a critic of Beauty that Plato is destined to live, and that by altering the
name of the sphere of his speculation we shall find a new philosophy.
But Aristotle, like Goethe, deals with art primarily in its concrete manifestations, taking Tragedy, for instance, and investigating the material it
uses, which is language, its subject-matter, which is life, the method by
which it works, which is action, the conditions under which it reveals itself, which are those of theatric presentation, its logical structure, which
is plot, and its final aesthetic appeal, which is to the sense of beauty re-
alised through the passions of pity and awe. That purification and spiri-
tualising of the nature which he calls κάθαρσις[2] is, as Goethe saw, essentially aesthetic, and is not moral, as Lessing fancied. Concerning himself
primarily with the impression that the work of art produces, Aristotle
sets himself to analyse that impression, to investigate its source, to see
how it is engendered. As a physiologist and psychologist, he knows that
the health of a function resides in energy. To have a capacity for a passion and not to realise it, is to make oneself incomplete and limited. The
mimic spectacle of life that Tragedy affords cleanses the bosom of much
"perilous stuff," and by presenting high and worthy objects for the exercise of the emotions purifies and spiritualises the man; nay, not merely
does it spiritualise him, but it initiates him also into noble feelings of
which he might else have known nothing, the word κάθαρσις having, it
has sometimes seemed to me, a definite allusion to the rite of initiation, if

[2] Catharsis.

indeed that be not, as I am occasionally tempted to fancy, its true and only meaning here. This is of course a mere outline of the book. But you see what a perfect piece of aesthetic criticism it is. Who indeed but a Greek could have analysed art so well? After reading it, one does not wonder any longer that Alexandria devoted itself so largely to art-criticism, and that we find the artistic temperaments of the day investigating every question of style and manner discussing the great Academic schools of painting, for instance, such as the school of Sicyon, that sought to preserve the dignified traditions of the antique mode, or the realistic and impressionist schools, that aimed at reproducing actual life, or the elements of ideality in portraiture, or the artistic value of the epic form in an age so modern as theirs, or the proper subject-matter for the artist. Indeed, I fear that the inartistic temperaments of the day busied themselves also in matters of literature and art, for the accusations of plagiarism were endless, and such accusations proceed either from the thin colourless lips of impotence, or from the grotesque mouths of those who, possessing nothing of their own, fancy that they can gain a reputation for wealth by crying out that they have been robbed. And I assure you, my dear Ernest, that the Greeks chattered about painters quite as much as people do nowadays, and had their private views, and shilling exhibitions, and Arts and Crafts guilds, and Pre-Raphaelite movements, and movements toward realism, and lectured about art, and wrote essays on art, and produced their art-historians, and their archaeologists, and all the rest of it. Why, even the theatrical managers of travelling companies brought their dramatic critics with them when they went on tour, and paid them very handsome salaries for writing laudatory notices. Whatever, in fact, is modern in our life we owe to the Greeks. Whatever is an anachronism is due to mediaevalism. It is the Greeks who have given us the whole system of art-criticism, and how fine their critical instinct was, may be seen from the fact that the material they criticised with most care was, as I have already said, language. For the material that painter or sculptor uses is meagre in comparison with that of words. Words have not merely music as sweet as that of viol and lute, colour as rich and vivid as any that makes lovely for us the canvas of the Venetian or the Spaniard, and plastic form no less sure and certain than that which reveals itself in marble or in bronze but thought and passion and spirituality are theirs also, are theirs indeed alone. If the Greeks had criticised nothing but language, they would still have been the great art-critics of the world. To know the principles of the highest art is to know the principles of all the arts.

But I see that the moon is hiding behind a sulphur-coloured cloud. Out of a tawny mane of drift she gleams like a lion's eye. She is afraid that I will talk to you of Lucian and Longinus, of Quintilian and Dionysius, of Pliny and Fronto and Pausanias, of all those who in the antique world wrote or lectured upon art matters. She need not be afraid. I am tired of my expedition into the dim, dull abyss of facts. There is nothing left for me now but the divine μονόχρονος ἡδονή[3] of another cigarette. Cigarettes have at least the charm of leaving one unsatisfied.

ERNEST: Try one of mine. They are rather good. I get them direct from Cairo. The only use of our *attachés* is that they supply their friends with excellent tobacco. And as the moon has hidden herself, let us talk a little longer. I am quite ready to admit that I was wrong in what I said about the Greeks. They were, as you have pointed out, a nation of art-critics. I acknowledge it, and I feel a little sorry for them. For the creative faculty is higher than the critical. There is really no comparison between them.

GILBERT: The antithesis between them is entirely arbitrary. Without the critical faculty, there is no artistic creation at all, worthy of the name. You spoke a little while ago of that fine spirit of choice and delicate instinct of selection by which the artist realises life for us, and gives to it a momentary perfection. Well, that spirit of choice, that subtle tact of omission, is really the critical faculty in one of its most characteristic moods, and no one who does not possess this critical faculty can create anything at all in art. Arnold's definition of literature as a criticism of life, was not very felicitous in form, but it showed how keenly he recognised the importance of the critical element in all creative work.

ERNEST: I should have said that great artists worked unconsciously, that they were "wiser than they knew," as, I think, Emerson remarks somewhere.

GILBERT: It is really not so, Ernest. All fine imaginative work is self-conscious and deliberate. No poet sings because he must sing. At least, no great poet does. A great poet sings because he chooses to sing. It is so now, and it has always been so. We are sometimes apt to think that the voices that sounded at the dawn of poetry were simpler, fresher and more natural than ours, and that the world which the early poets looked at, and through which they walked, had a kind of poetical quality of its own, and almost without changing could pass into song. The snow lies thick now upon Olympus, and its steep scarped sides are bleak and barren, but once, we fancy, the white feet of the Muses brushed the dew from the anemones in the morning, and at evening came Apollo to sing to the shepherds in the vale. But in this we are merely lending to other ages what we desire, or think we desire, for our own. Our historical sense is at fault. Every century that produces poetry is, so far, an artificial century, and the work that seems to us to be the most natural and simple product of its time is always the result of the most self-conscious effort. Believe me, Ernest, there is no fine art without self-consciousness, and self-consciousness and the critical spirit are one.

ERNEST: I see what you mean, and there is much in it. But surely you would admit that the great poems of the early world, the primitive, anonymous collective poems, were the result of the imagination of races, rather than of the imagination of individuals?

---

[3] Undivided pleasure.

GILBERT: Not when they became poetry. Not when they received a beautiful
    form. For there is no art where there is no style, and no style where there
    is no unity, and unity is of the individual. No doubt Homer had old bal-
    lads and stories to deal with, as Shakespeare had chronicles and plays
    and novels from which to work, but they were merely his rough mate-
    rial. He took them, and shaped them into song. They became his, be-
    cause he made them lovely. They were built out of music,

> "And so not built at all,
> And therefore built for ever."

The longer one studies life and literature, the more strongly one feels
that behind everything that is wonderful stands the individual, and that
it is not the moment that makes the man, but the man who creates the
age. Indeed, I am inclined to think that each myth and legend that seems
to us to spring out of the wonder, or terror, or fancy of tribe and nation,
was in its origin the invention of one single mind. The curiously limited
number of the myths seems to me to point to this conclusion. But we
must not go off into questions of comparative mythology. We must keep
to criticism. And what I want to point out is this. An age that has no criticism is either an age in which art is immobile, hieratic, and confined to
the reproduction of formal types, or an age that possesses no art at all.
There have been critical ages that have not been creative, in the ordinary
sense of the word, ages in which the spirit of man has sought to set in
order the treasures of his treasure-house, to separate the gold from the
silver, and the silver from the lead, to count over the jewels, and to give
names to the pearls. But there has never been a creative age that has not
been critical also. For it is the critical faculty that invents fresh forms. The
tendency of creation is to repeat itself. It is to the critical instinct that we
owe each new school that springs up, each new mould that art finds
ready to its hand. There is really not a single form that art now uses that
does not come to us from the critical spirit of Alexandria, where these
forms were either stereotyped or invented or made perfect. I say Alexandria, not merely because it was there that the Greek spirit became most
self-conscious, and indeed ultimately expired in scepticism and theology, but because it was to that city, and not to Athens, that Rome turned
for her models, and it was through the survival, such as it was, of the
Latin language that culture lived at all. When, at the Renaissance, Greek
literature dawned upon Europe, the soil had been in some measure prepared for it. But, to get rid of the details of history, which are always
wearisome and usually inaccurate, let us say generally, that the forms of
art have been due to the Greek critical spirit. To it we owe the epic, the
lyric, the entire drama in every one of its developments, including burlesque, the idyll, the romantic novel, the novel of adventure, the essay,
the dialogue, the oration, the lecture, for which perhaps we should not
forgive them, and the epigram, in all the wide meaning of that word. In
fact, we owe it everything, except the sonnet, to which, however, some

curious parallels of thought-movement may be traced in the Anthology, American journalism, to which no parallel can be found anywhere, and the ballad in sham Scotch dialect, which one of our most industrious writers has recently proposed should be made the basis for a final and unanimous effort on the part of our second-rate poets to make themselves really romantic. Each new school, as it appears, cries out against criticism, but it is to the critical faculty in man that it owes its origin. The mere creative instinct does not innovate, but reproduces.

LEO TOLSTOY

What Is Art?

1898

———————

Of the various critics encountered thus far, none places a greater emphasis on the instrumental nature of art than the Russian novelist Count Leo Tolstoy (1828–1910). The words "purpose" and "function" seem to echo throughout, and concerning that purpose Tolstoy is redundantly emphatic: the purpose of art is to promote universal understanding among humanity. "Good" art promotes that unity; "bad" art serves to divide people from one another. Insisting that art is and always must be an instrument for reform and progress, Tolstoy stands at a 180-degree remove from Henry James, as may be seen, for example, by contrasting their views on the issues of the morality of art and the importance of artistic technique. But even when compared with a critic like Shelley, with whom Tolstoy has many striking points of similarity, Tolstoy's views seem extreme. In Chapter 20, sounding very Arnoldian, Tolstoy declares, "The task of art is enormous." But would Arnold agree with Tolstoy's definition of the means by which this task is to be accomplished? We have to go all the way back to Plato, with his directive that the imagination be employed in the interests of shaping human values and directing human conduct, to find Tolstoy's parallel. It is instructive to discover the many ways in which their positions are alike, particularly their awareness of the powerful emotional responses that art can evoke, the importance each attaches to subject matter, and the value they place on artistic technique as such. It is also useful to compare Plato and Tolstoy on what the latter calls the "infectiousness" of art (are they talking about the same kinds of feelings to be transmitted?) and to set them both against the Aristotelian theory of the catharsis evoked by tragedy.

Although the basic frame of reference is moralistic, Tolstoy also specifies an aesthetic theory. His categorizing of works of art as either "universal" or "exclusive" gives precedence to art that has the greatest popular appeal over art that appeals to a limited or restricted audience. The consequence of this theory is illustrated in Tolstoy's references to particular works. What makes for the widest appeal is familiar subject matter and easy comprehensibility; thus bad art is marked by complexity, allusiveness, indirection, formalism, "artificiality"—any quality that interferes with the immediate apprehension of the message. Two passages in particular should be

noted: his discussions of the drawing by Kramskoy and of Beethoven's Ninth Sym-
phony. Also, do not overlook the footnote in which Tolstoy ruthlessly examines his
own works.

XVI

HOW IN the subject-matter of art are we to decide what is good and what is
bad?

Art like speech is a means of communication and therefore of progress,
that is, of the movement of humanity forward towards perfection. Speech
renders accessible to men of the latest generations all the knowledge discovered by the experience and reflection both of preceding generations and of
the best and foremost men of their own times; art renders accessible to men
of the latest generations all the feelings experienced by their predecessors and
also those felt by their best and foremost contemporaries. And as the evolution of knowledge proceeds by truer and more necessary knowledge dislodg-
ing and replacing what was mistaken and unnecessary, so the evolution of
feeling proceeds by means of art—feelings less kind and less necessary for
the well-being of mankind being replaced by others kinder and more needful
for that end. That is the purpose of art. And speaking now of the feelings
which are its subject-matter, the more art fulfils that purpose the better the
art, and the less it fulfils it the worse the art.

The appraisement of feelings (that is, the recognition of one or other set
of feelings as more or less good, more or less necessary for the well-being of
mankind) is effected by the religious perception of the age.

In every period of history and in every human society there exists an understanding of the meaning of life, which represents the highest level to
which men of that society have attained—an understanding indicating the
highest good at which that society aims. This understanding is the religious
perception of the given time and society. And this religious perception is always clearly expressed by a few advanced men and more or less vividly perceived by members of the society generally. Such a religious perception and
its corresponding expression always exists in every society. If it appears to us
that there is no religious perception in our society, this is not because there
really is none, but only because we do not wish to see it. And we often wish
not to see it because it exposes the fact that our life is inconsistent with that
religious perception.

Religious perception in a society is like the direction of a flowing river. If
the river flows at all it must have a direction. If a society lives, there must be
a religious perception indicating the direction in which, more or less consciously, all its members tend.

And so there always has been, and is, a religious perception in every society. And it is by the standard of this religious perception that the feelings
transmitted by art have always been appraised. It has always been only on

the basis of this religious perception of their age, that men have chose from amid the endlessly varied spheres of art that art which transmitted feelings making religious perception operative in actual life. And such art has always been highly valued and encouraged, while art transmitting feelings already outlived, flowing from the antiquated religious perceptions of a former age, has always been condemned and despised. All the rest of art transmitting those most diverse feelings by means of which people commune with one another was not condemned and was tolerated if only it did not transmit feelings contrary to religious perception. Thus for instance among the Greeks, art transmitting feelings of beauty, strength, and courage (Hesiod, Homer, Phidias) was chosen, approved, and encouraged, while art transmitting feelings of rude sensuality, despondency, and effeminacy, was condemned and despised. Among the Jews, art transmitting feelings of devotion and submission to the God of the Hebrews and to His will (the epic of Genesis, the prophets, the Psalms) was chosen and encouraged, while art transmitting feelings of idolatry (the Golden Calf) was condemned and despised. All the rest of art—stories, songs, dances, ornamentation of houses, of utensils, and of clothes—which was not contrary to religious perception, was neither distinguished nor discussed. Thus as regards its subject-matter has art always and everywhere been appraised and thus it should be appraised, for this attitude towards art proceeds from the fundamental characteristics of human nature, and those characteristics do not change.

I know that according to an opinion current in our times religion is a superstition humanity has outgrown, and it is therefore assumed that no such thing exists as a religious perception common to us all by which art in our time can be appraised. I know that this is the opinion current in the pseudo-cultured circles of today. People who do not acknowledge Christianity in its true meaning because it undermines their social privileges, and who therefore invent all kinds of philosophic and aesthetic theories to hide from themselves the meaninglessness and wrongfulness of their lives, cannot think otherwise. These people intentionally, or sometimes unintentionally, confuse the notion of a religious cult with the notion of religious perception, and think that by denying the cult they get rid of the perception. But even the very attacks on religion and the attempts to establish an idea of life contrary to the religious perception of our times, most clearly demonstrate the existence of a religious perception condemning the lives that are not in harmony with it.

If humanity progresses, that is, moves forward, there must inevitably be a guide to the direction of that movement. And religions have always furnished that guide. All history shows that the progress of humanity is accomplished no otherwise than under the guidance of religion. But if the race cannot progress without the guidance of religion,—and progress is always going on, and consequently goes on also in our own times,—then there must be a religion of our times. So that whether it pleases or displeases the so-called cultured people of to-day, they must admit the existence of religion—not of a religious cult, Catholic, Protestant, or another, but of religious perception—which even in our times is the guide always present where there is any progress. And if a religious perception exists amongst us, then the feelings dealt with by our art should be appraised on the basis of that religious perception; and as has been the case always and everywhere, art transmitting feelings flowing from the religious perception of our time should be chosen from amid all the indifferent art, should be acknowledged, highly valued, and encouraged, while art running counter to that perception should be condemned and despised, and all the remaining, indifferent, art should neither be distinguished nor encouraged.

The religious perception of our time in its widest and most practical application is the consciousness that our well-being, both material and spiritual, individual and collective, temporal and eternal, lies in the growth of brotherhood among men—in their loving harmony with one another. This perception is not only expressed by Christ and all the best men of past ages, it is not only repeated in most varied forms and from most diverse sides by the best men of our times, but it already serves as a clue to all the complex labour of humanity, consisting as this labour does on the one hand in the destruction of physical and moral obstacles to the union of men, and on the other hand in establishing the principles common to all men which can and should unite them in one universal brotherhood. And it is on the basis of this perception that we should appraise all the phenomena of our life and among the rest our art also: choosing from all its realms and highly prizing and encouraging whatever transmits feelings flowing from this religious perception, rejecting whatever is contrary to it, and not attributing to the rest of art an importance that does not properly belong to it.

The chief mistake made by people of the upper classes at the time of the so-called Renaissance,—a mistake we still perpetuate,—was not that they ceased to value and attach importance to religious art (people of that period could not attach importance to it because, like our own upper classes, they could not believe in what the majority considered to be religion), but their mistake was that they set up in place of the religious art that was lacking, an insignificant art which aimed merely at giving pleasure, that is, they began to choose, to value, and to encourage, in place of religious art, something which in any case did not deserve such esteem and encouragement.

One of the Fathers of the Church said that the great evil is not that men do not know God, but that they have set up instead of God, that which is not God. So also with art. The great misfortune of the people of the upper classes of our time is not so much that they are without a religious art as that, instead of a supreme religious art chosen from all the rest as being specially important and valuable, they have chosen a most insignificant and, usually, harmful art, which aims at pleasing certain people and which therefore, if only by its exclusive nature, stands in contradiction to that Christian principle of universal union which forms the religious perception of our time. Instead of religious art, an empty and often vicious art is set up, and this hides from men's notice the need of that true religious art which should be present in life to improve it.

It is true that art which satisfies the demands of the religious perception of our time is quite unlike former art, but notwithstanding this dissimilarity, to a man who does not intentionally hide the truth from himself, what forms the religious art of our age is very clear and definite. In former times when the highest religious perception united only some people (who even if they formed a large society were yet but one society among others—Jews, or Athenian or Roman citizens), the feelings transmitted by the art of that time flowed from a desire for the might, greatness, glory, and prosperity, of that society, and the heroes of art might be people who contributed to that prosperity by strength, by craft, by fraud, or by cruelty (Ulysses, Jacob, David, Samson, Hercules, and all the heroes). But the religious perception of our times does not select any one society of men; on the contrary it demands the union of all—absolutely of all people without exception—and above every other virtue it sets brotherly love of all men. And therefore the feelings transmitted by the art of our time not only cannot coincide with the feelings transmitted by former art, but must run counter to them.

Christian, truly Christian, art has been so long in establishing itself, and has not yet established itself, just because the Christian religious perception was not one of those small steps by which humanity advances regularly, but was an enormous revolution which, if it has not already altered, must inevitably alter the entire conception of life of mankind, and consequently the whole internal organization of that life. It is true that the life of humanity, like that of an individual, moves regularly; but in that regular movement come, as it were, turning-points which sharply divide the preceding from the subsequent life. Christianity was such a turning-point; such at least it must appear to us who live by the Christian perception of life. Christian perception gave another, a new, direction to all human feelings, and therefore completely altered both the content and the significance of art. The Greeks could make use of Persian art and the Romans could use Greek art, or, similarly, the Jews could use Egyptian art—the fundamental ideals were one and the same. Now the ideal was the greatness and prosperity of the Greeks, now that of the Romans. The same art was transferred to other conditions and served new nations. But the Christian ideal changed and reversed everything, so that, as the Gospel puts it, 'That which was exalted among men has become an abomination in the sight of God.' The ideal is no longer the greatness of Pharaoh or of a Roman emperor, not the beauty of a Greek nor the wealth of Phœnicia, but humility, purity, compassion, love. The hero is no longer Dives, but Lazarus the beggar; not Mary Magdalene in the day of her beauty but in the day of her repentance; not those who acquire wealth but those who have abandoned it; not those who dwell in palaces but those who dwell in catacombs and huts; not those who rule over others, but those who acknowledge no authority but God's. And the greatest work of art is no longer a cathedral of victory with statues of conquerors, but the representation of a human soul so transformed by love that a man who is tormented and murdered, yet pities and loves his persecutors.

And the change is so great that men of the Christian world find it difficult to resist the inertia of the heathen art to which they have been accustomed all their lives. The subject-matter of Christian religious art is so new to them, so unlike the subject-matter of former art, that it seems to them as though Christian art were a denial of art, and they cling desperately to the old art. But this old art, having no longer in our day any source in religious perception, has lost its meaning, and we shall have to abandon it whether we wish to or not.

The essence of the Christian perception consists in the recognition by every man of his sonship to God and of the consequent union of men with God and with one another, as is said in the Gospel (John xvii. 21[1]). Therefore the subject-matter of Christian art is of a kind that feeling can unite men with God and with one another.

The expression *unite men with God and with one another* may seem obscure to people accustomed to the misuse of these words that is so customary, but the words have a perfectly clear meaning nevertheless. They indicate that the Christian union of man (in contradiction to the partial, exclusive, union of only certain men) is that which unites all without exception.

Art, all art, has this characteristic, that it unites people. Every art causes those to whom the artist's feeling is transmitted to unite in soul with the artist and also with all who receive the same impression. But non-Christian art while uniting some people, makes that very union a cause of separation between these united people and others; so that union of this kind is often a source not merely of division but even of enmity towards others. Such is all patriotic art, with its anthems, poems, and monuments; such is all Church art, that is, the art of certain cults, with their images, statues, processions, and other local cere-monies. Such art is belated and non-Christian, uniting the people of one cult only to separate them yet more sharply from the members of other cults, and even to place them in relations of hostility to one another. Christian art is such only as tends to unite all without exception, either by evoking in them the per-ception that each man and all men stand in a like relation towards God and to-wards their neighbour, or by evoking in them identical feelings, which may even be the very simplest, provided that they are not repugnant to Christianity and are natural to every one without exception.

Good Christian art of our time may be unintelligible to people because of imperfections in its form or because men are inattentive to it, but it must be such that all men can experience the feelings it transmits. It must be the art not of some one group of people, or of one class, or of one nationality, or of one religious cult; that is, it must not transmit feelings accessible only to a man educated in a certain way, or only to an aristocrat, or a merchant, or only to a Russian, or a native of Japan, or a Roman Catholic, or a Buddhist, and so on, but it must transmit feelings accessible to every one. Only art of this kind can in our time be acknowledged to be good art, worthy of being chose out from all the rest of art and encouraged.

Christian art, that is, the art of our time, should be catholic in the original meaning of the word, that is, universal, and therefore it should unite all men.

---

[1] 'That they may all be one; even as thou, Father, art in me, and I in Thee, that they also may be in us.' [The notes are Tolstoy's unless otherwise indicated. Ed.]

And only two kinds of feeling unite all men: first, feelings flowing from a perception of our sonship to God and of the brotherhood of man; and next, the simple feelings of common life accessible to every one without exception—such as feelings of merriment, of pity, of cheerfulness, of tranquillity, and so forth. Only these two kinds of feelings can now supply material for art good in its subject-matter.

And the action of these two kinds of art apparently so dissimilar, is one and the same. The feelings flowing from the perception of our sonship to God and the brotherhood of man—such as a feeling of sureness in truth, devotion to the will of God, self-sacrifice, respect for and love of man—evoked by Christian religious perception; and the simplest feelings, such as a softened or a merry mood caused by a song or an amusing jest intelligible to every one, or by a touching story, or a drawing, or a little doll: both alike produce one and the same effect—the loving union of man with man. Sometimes people who are together, if not hostile to one another, are at least estranged in mood and feeling, till perhaps a story, a performance, a picture, or even a building, but oftenest of all music, unites them all as by an electric flash, and in place of their former isolation or even enmity they are conscious of union and mutual love. Each is glad that another feels what he feels; glad of the communion established not only between him and all present, but also with all now living who will yet share the same impression; and more than that, he feels the mysterious gladness of a communion which, reaching beyond the grave, unites us with all men of the past who have been moved by the same feelings and with all men of the future who will yet be touched by them. And this effect is produced both by religious art which transmits feelings of love of God and one's neighbour, and by universal art transmitting the very simplest feelings common to all men.

The art of our time should be appraised differently from former art chiefly in this, that the art of our time, that is, Christian art (basing itself on a religious perception which demands the union of man), excludes from the domain of art good in its subject-matter, everything transmitting exclusive feelings which do not unite men but divide them. It relegates such work to the category of art that is bad in its subject-matter; while on the other hand it includes in the category of art that is good in subject-matter a section not formerly admitted as deserving of selection and respect, namely, universal art transmitting even the most trifling and simple feelings if only they are accessible to all men without exception, and therefore unite them. Such art cannot but be esteemed good in our time, for it attains the end which Christianity the religious perception of our time, sets before humanity.

Christian art either evokes in men feelings which through love of God and of one's neighbour draw them to closer and ever closer union and make them ready for, and capable of, such union; or evokes in them feelings which show them that they are already united in the joys and sorrows of life. And therefore the Christian art of our time can be and is of two kinds: first, art transmitting feelings flowing from a religious perception of man's position in the world in relation to God and to his neighbour—religious art in the limited meaning of the term; and secondly, art transmitting the simplest feelings of common life, but such always as are accessible to all men in the whole world—the art of common life—the art of the people—universal art. Only these two kinds of art can be considered good art in our time.

The first, religious art—transmitting both positive feelings of love of God and one's neighbour, and negative feelings of indignation and horror at the violation of love—manifests itself chiefly in the form of words, and to some extent also in painting and sculpture: the second kind, universal art, transmitting feelings accessible to all, manifests itself in words, in painting, in sculpture, in dances, in architecture, and most of all in music.

If I were asked to give modern examples of each of these kinds of art, then as examples of the highest art flowing from love of God and man (both of the higher, positive, and of the lower, negative kind), in literature I should name *The Robbers* by Schiller; Victor Hugo's *Les Pauvres Gens* and *Les Misérables;* the novels and stories of Dickens—*The Tale of Two Cities, The Christmas Carol, The Chimes,* and others—*Uncle Tom's Cabin;* Dostoévski's works—especially his *Memoirs from the House of Death*—and *Adam Bede* by George Eliot.

In modern painting, strange to say, works of this kind, directly transmitting the Christian feeling of love of God and of one's neighbour, are hardly to be found, especially among the works of the celebrated painters. There are plenty of pictures treating of the Gospel stories; these however, while depicting historical events with great wealth of detail, do not and cannot transmit religious feelings not possessed by their painters. There are many pictures treating of the personal feelings of various people, but of pictures representing great deeds of self-sacrifice and Christian love there are very few, and what there are are principally by artists who are not celebrated, and they are for the most part not pictures but merely sketches. Such for instance is the drawing by Kramskóy (worth many of his finished pictures), showing a drawing-room with a balcony past which troops are marching in triumph on their return from the war. On the balcony stands a wet-nurse holding a baby, and a boy. They are admiring the procession of the troops, but the mother, covering her face with a handkerchief, has fallen back on the sofa sobbing. Such also is the picture by Walter Langley to which I have already referred, and such again is a picture by the French artist Morlon, depicting a lifeboat hastening in a heavy storm to the relief of a steamer that is being wrecked. Approaching these in kind are pictures which represent the hard-working peasant with respect and love. Such are the pictures by Millet and particularly his drawing, 'The Man with the Hoe,' also pictures in this style by Jules Breton, Lhermitte, Defregger, and others. As examples of pictures evoking indignation and horror at the violation of love of God and man, Gay's picture 'Judgment' may serve, and also Leizen-Mayer's 'Signing the Death Warrant.' But there are very few of this kind also. Anxiety about the technique and the beauty of the picture for the most part obscures the feeling. For instance,

Gérôme's 'Pollice Verso' expresses, not so much horror as what is being perpetrated as attraction by the beauty of the spectacle.[2]

To give examples from the modern art of our upper classes, of art of the
second kind: good universal art, or even of the art of a whole people, is yet
more difficult, especially in literature and music. If there are some works
which by their inner contents might be assigned to this class (such as *Don
Quixote*, Molière's comedies, *David Copperfield* and *The Pickwick Papers* by
Dickens, Gógol's and Púshkin's tales, and some things of Maupassant's),
these works for the most part—owing to the exceptional nature of the feelings they transmit, and the superfluity of special details of time and locality,
and above all on account of the poverty of their subject-matter in comparison
with examples of universal ancient art (such, for instance, as the story of
Joseph)—are comprehensible only to people of their own circle. That
Joseph's brethren, being jealous of his father's affection, sell him to the mer-
chants; that Potiphar's wife wishes to tempt the youth; that having attained
to highest station he takes pity on his brothers, including Benjamin the
favourite—these and all the rest are feelings accessible alike to a Russian
peasant, a Chinese, an African, a child, or an old man, educated or uneducated; and it is all written with such restraint, is so free from any superfluous
detail, that the story may be told to any circle and will be equally comprehensible and touching to everyone. But not such are the feelings of Don Quixote
or of Molière's heroes (though Molière is perhaps the most universal, and
therefore the most excellent, artist of modern times), nor of Pickwick and his
friends. These feelings are not common to all men but very exceptional, and
therefore to make them contagious the authors have surrounded them with
abundant details of time and place. And this abundance of detail makes the
stories difficult of comprehension to all who do not live within reach of the
conditions described by the author.

The author of the novel of Joseph did not need to describe in detail, as
would be done nowadays, the blood-stained coat of Joseph, the dwelling and
dress of Jacob, the pose and attire of Potiphar's wife, and how adjusting the
bracelet on her left arm she said, 'Come to me,' and so on, because the content of feeling in this novel is so strong that all details except the most essential—such as that Joseph went out into another room to weep—are superfluous and would only hinder the transmission of emotion. And therefore this
novel is accessible to all men, touches people of all nations and classes young
and old, and has lasted to our times and will yet last for thousands of years to
come. But strip the best novels of our time of their details and what will remain?

It is therefore impossible in modern literature to indicate works fully satisfying the demands of universality. Such works as exist are to a great extent
spoilt by what is usually called 'realism,' but would be better termed 'provincialism', in art.

In music the same occurs as in verbal art, and for similar reasons. In
consequence of the poorness of the feeling they contain, the melodies of

---

[2] In this picture the spectators in the Roman Amphitheatre are turning down their
thumbs to show that they wish the vanquished gladiator to be killed. [Tr.]

the modern composers are amazingly empty and insignificant. And to strengthen the impression produced by these empty melodies the new musicians pile complex modulations on each trivial melody, not only in their own national manner, but also in the way characteristic of their own exclusive circle and particular musical school. Melody—every melody—is free and may be understood of all men; but as soon as it is bound up with a particular harmony, it ceases to be accessible except to people trained to such harmony, and it becomes strange, not only to common men of another nationality, but to all who do not belong to the circle whose members have accustomed themselves to certain forms of harmonization. So that music, like poetry, travels in a vicious circle. Trivial and exclusive melodies, in order to make them attractive, are laden with harmonic, rhythmic, and orchestral complications and thus become yet more exclusive, and far from being universal are not even national, that is, they are not comprehensible to the whole people, but only to some people.

In music, besides marches and dances by various composers which satisfy the demands of universal art, one can indicate very few works of this class: Bach's famous violin *aria*, Chopin's nocturne in E flat major, and perhaps a dozen bits (not whole pieces, but parts) selected from the works of Haydn, Mozart, Schubert, Beethoven, and Chopin.[3]

Although in painting the same thing is repeated as in poetry and in music—namely, that in order to make them more interesting, works weak in conception are surrounded by minutely studied accessories of time and place which give them a temporary and local interest but make them less universal—still in painting more than in other spheres of art may be found works satisfying the demands of universal Christian art; that is to say, there are more works expressing feelings in which all men may participate.

In the arts of painting and sculpture, all pictures and statues in so-called genre style, representations of animals, landscapes, and caricatures with subjects comprehensible to every one, and also all kinds of ornaments, are universal in subject-matter. Such productions in painting and sculpture are very numerous (for instance, china dolls), but for the most part such objects (for instance, ornaments of all kinds) are either not considered to be art or are considered to be art of low quality. In reality all such objects if only they transmit a true feeling experienced by the artist and comprehensible to every one (however insignificant it may seem to us to be), are works of real, good, Christian, art.

I fear it will here be urged against me that having denied that the conception of beauty can supply a standard for works of art, I contradict myself

---

[3] While offering as examples of art those that seem to me best, I attach no special importance to my selection; for, besides being insufficiently informed in all branches of art, I belong to the class of people whose taste has been perverted by false training. And therefore my old, inured habits may cause me to err, and I may mistake for absolute merit the impression a work produced on me in my youth. My only purpose in mentioning examples of works of this or that class is to make by meaning clearer and to show how, with my present views, I understand excellence in art in relation to its subject-matter. I must moreover mention that I consign my own artistic productions to the category of bad art, excepting the story *God Sees the Truth but Waits*, which seeks a place in the first class, and *A Prisoner of the Caucasus*, which belongs to the second.

by acknowledging ornaments to be works of good art. The reproach is unjust, for the subject-matter of all kinds of ornamentation consists not in the beauty but in the feeling (of admiration at, and delight in, the combination of lines and colours) which the artist has experienced and with which he infects the spectator. Art remains what it was and what it must be: nothing but the infection by one man of another or of others with the feelings experienced by the artist. Among these feelings is the feeling of delight at what pleases the sight. Objects pleasing the sight may be such as please a small or a large number of people, or such as please all men—and ornaments for the most part are of the latter kind. A landscape representing a very unusual view, or a genre picture of a special subject, may not please every one, but ornaments, from Yakútsk ornaments to Greek ones, are intelligible to every one and evoke a similar feeling of admiration in all, and therefore this despised kind of art should in Christian society be esteemed far above exceptional, pretentious, pictures and sculptures.

So that in relation to feelings conveyed, there are only two kinds of good Christian art, all the rest of art not comprised in these two divisions should be acknowledged to be bad art, deserving not to be encouraged but to be driven out, denied, and despised, as being art not uniting but dividing people. Such in literary art are all novels and poems which transmit ecclesiastical or patriotic feelings, and also exclusive feelings pertaining only to the class of the idle rich: such as aristocratic honour, satiety, spleen, pessimism, and refined and vicious feelings flowing from sex-love—quite incomprehensible to the great majority of mankind.

In painting we must similarly place in the class of bad art all ecclesiastical, patriotic, and exclusive pictures; all pictures representing the amusements and allurements of a rich and idle life; all so-called symbolic pictures in which the very meaning of the symbol is comprehensible only to those of a certain circle; and above all pictures with voluptuous subjects—all that odious female nudity which fills all the exhibitions and galleries. And to this class belongs almost all the chamber and opera music of our times,—beginning especially with Beethoven (Schumann, Berlioz, Liszt, Wagner),—by its subject-matter devoted to the expression of feelings accessible only to people who have developed in themselves an unhealthy nervous irritation evoked by this exclusive, artificial, and complex music.

'What! the *Ninth Symphony* not a good work of art!' I hear exclaimed by indignant voices.

And I reply: Most certainly it is not. All that I have written I have written with the sole purpose of finding a clear and reasonable criterion by which to judge the merits of works of art. And this criterion, coinciding with the indications of plain and sane sense, indubitably shows me that that symphony of Beethoven's is not a good work of art. Of course to people educated in the worship of certain productions and of their authors, to people whose taste has been perverted just by being educated in such a worship, the acknowledgment that such a celebrated work is bad, is amazing and strange. But how are we to escape the indications of reason and common sense?

Beethoven's *Ninth Symphony* is considered a great work of art. To verify its claim to be such I must first ask myself whether this work transmits the highest religious feeling? I reply in the negative, since music in itself cannot transmit those feelings; and therefore I ask myself next: Since this work does not belong to the highest kind of religious art, has it the other characteristic of the good art of our time—the quality of uniting all men in one common feeling—does it rank as Christian universal art? And again I have no option but to reply in the negative; for not only do I not see how the feelings transmitted by this work could unite people not specially trained to submit themselves to its complex hypnotism, but I am unable to imagine to myself a crowd of normal people who could understand anything of this long, confused, and artificial production, except short snatches which are lost in a sea of what is incomprehensible. And therefore, whether I like it or not, I am compelled to conclude that this work belongs to the rank of bad art. It is curious to note in this connexion, that attached to the end of this very symphony is a poem of Schiller's which (though somewhat obscurely) expresses this very thought, namely that feeling (Schiller speaks only of the feeling of gladness) unites people and evokes love in them. But though this poem is sung at the end of the symphony, the music does not accord with the thought expressed in the verses; for the music is exclusive and does not unite all men, but unites only a few, dividing them off from the rest of mankind.

And just in this same way, in all branches of art, many and many works considered great by the upper classes of our society will have to be judged. By this one sure criterion we shall have to judge the celebrated *Divine Comedy* and *Jerusalem Delivered*; and a great part of Shakespeare's and Goethe's work, and in painting every representation of miracles, including Raphael's Transfiguration, etc.

Whatever the work may be and however it may have been extolled, we have first to ask whether this work is one of real art, or a counterfeit. Having acknowledged, on the basis of the indication of its infectiousness even to a small class of people, that a certain production belongs to the realm of art, it is necessary on this basis to decide the next question. Does this work belong to the category of bad exclusive art opposed to religious perception, or of Christian art uniting people? And having acknowledged a work to belong to real Christian art, we must then, according to whether it transmits feelings flowing from love of God and man, or merely the simple feelings uniting all men, assign it a place in the ranks of religious art, or in those of universal art.

Only on the basis of such verification shall we find it possible to select from the whole mass of what in our society claims to be art, those works which form real, important, necessary, spiritual food, and to separate them from all the harmful and useless art and from the counterfeits of art which surround us. Only on the basis of such verification shall we be able to rid ourselves of the pernicious results of harmful art and avail ourselves of that beneficent action which is the purpose of true and good art, and which is indispensable for the spiritual life of man and of humanity.

                                             Translated by Aylmer Maude.

SIGMUND FREUD

The Theme of the Three Caskets

1913

─────────

Sigmund Freud (1856–1939), the Viennese founder of psychoanalysis, profoundly changed the way we think about human motivation by theorizing that we are all susceptible to childhood memories and desires, unknown even to ourselves, to which many of our actions can be attributed. In The Interpretation of Dreams (1900), he suggested that dreams are symbolic wish fulfillments and that by analyzing them we can begin to uncover a lexicon of the unconscious mind. For Freud and his followers, then, dream symbols have a common meaning; a cigar, for instance is a phallic symbol, and a box, with its enclosed, womblike space, represents a woman. Literary critics quickly saw the applicability of psychoanalytic theory in explaining previously inexplicable aspects of literature and art. If the Freudian interpretation of symbolic material was true, it would provide a key to additional meanings in poems, plays, and fiction.

The application of Freud to literature has typically taken one of three approaches. First, on the assumption that artists, often unconsciously, encode their own psyches in their creative work, some critics believe that they can come to a better understanding of an author by analyzing interesting or recurrent symbols in his or her work. (In her essay "The Case of Poe," p. 662, Shoshana Felman takes exception to this approach.) Second, psychoanalytic theory has often been applied to characters in literature to understand their motivations. Several critics, for instance, have suggested that Hamlet is motivated in part by a fixation on his mother. Finally, psychoanalysis of the public at large might account for why particular works or particular themes achieve enduring popularity.

It is this third type of analysis that forms the basis of "The Theme of Three Caskets," one of Freud's few examples of direct literary criticism. In it, Freud examines the recurring theme in myth and literature of a hero choosing between three boxes. Interpreting the stories as he would a patient's dreams, Freud considers boxes to represent women, silence to be equivalent to death, and various reversals within stories to suggest unfulfilled wishes. That so many cultures have found the same theme compelling he attributes not to the idea that myths and stories descend from "the heavens" but rather that they are "projected onto the heavens after having arisen ... under purely human conditions."

Many of Freud's theories came under attack in the late twentieth century. Not only did they prove to be of limited medical value and fail to be scientifically verified, but they also suggested to his most orthodox followers that Freud's insights about his well-to-do, nineteenth-century, Viennese patients can be universally applied to all humanity with equal success. He has also received severe criticism for sexist and patriarchal attitudes toward his women and homosexual patients. Despite all of this, though, his theories have retained considerable influence over both psychological theory and literary criticism.

I

TWO SCENES from Shakespeare, one from a comedy and the other from a tragedy, have lately given me occasion for posing and solving a small problem.

The first of these scenes is the suitors' choice between the three caskets in *The Merchant of Venice*. The fair and wise Portia is bound at her father's bidding to take as her husband only that one of her suitors who chooses the right casket from among the three before him. The three caskets are of gold, silver and lead: the right casket is the one that contains her portrait. Two suitors have already departed unsuccessful: they have chosen gold and silver. Bassanio, the third, decides in favour of lead; thereby he wins the bride, whose affection was already his before the trial of fortune. Each of the suitors gives reasons for his choice in a speech in which he praises the metal he prefers and depreciates the other two. The most difficult task thus falls to the share of the fortunate third suitor; what he finds to say in glorification of lead as against gold and silver is little and has a forced ring. If in psycho-analytic practice we were confronted with such a speech, we should suspect that there were concealed motives behind the unsatisfying reasons produced.

Shakespeare did not himself invent this oracle of the choice of a casket; he took it from a tale in the *Gesta Romanorum*,[1] in which a girl has to make the same choice to win the Emperor's son.[2] Here too the third metal, lead, is the bringer of fortune. It is not hard to guess that we have here an ancient theme, which requires to be interpreted, accounted for and traced back to its origin. A first conjecture as to the meaning of this choice between gold, silver and lead is quickly confirmed by a statement of Stucken's,[3] who has made a study of the same material over a wide field. He writes: 'The identity of Portia's three suitors is clear from their choice: the Prince of Morocco chooses the gold casket—he is the sun; the Prince of Arragon chooses the silver casket—he is the moon; Bassanio chooses the leaden casket—he is the star youth.' In support of this explanation he cites an episode from the Estonian

---

[1] [A mediaeval collection of stories of unknown authorship.] (Bracketed notes are the translator's. All other notes are Freud's. Ed.)

[2] Brandes (1896).

[3] Stucken (1907, 655).

folk-epic 'Kalewipoeg', in which the three suitors appear undisguisedly as the sun, moon and star youths (the last being 'the Pole-star's eldest boy') and once again the bride falls to the lot of the third.

Thus our little problem has led us to an astral myth! The only pity is that with this explanation we are not at the end of the matter. The question is not exhausted, for we do not share the belief of some investigators that myths were read in the heavens and brought down to earth; we are more inclined to judge with Otto Rank[4] that they were projected on to the heavens after having arisen elsewhere under purely human conditions. It is in this human content that our interest lies.

Let us look once more at our material. In the Estonian epic, just as in the tale from the *Gesta Romanorum*, the subject is a girl choosing between three suitors; in the scene from *The Merchant of Venice* the subject is apparently the same, but at the same time something appears in it that is in the nature of an inversion of the theme: a *man* chooses between three—caskets. If what we were concerned with were a dream, it would occur to us at once that caskets are also women, symbols of what is essential in woman, and therefore of a woman herself—like coffers, boxes, cases, baskets, and so on.[5] If we boldly assume that there are symbolic substitutions of the same kind in myths as well, then the casket scene in *The Merchant of Venice* really becomes the inversion we suspected. With a wave of the wand, as though we were in a fairy tale, we have stripped the astral garment from our theme; and now we see that the theme is a human one, *a man's choice between three women.*

This same content, however, is to be found in another scene of Shakespeare's, in one of his most powerfully moving dramas; not the choice of a bride this time, yet linked by many hidden similarities to the choice of the casket in *The Merchant of Venice*. The old King Lear resolves to divide his kingdom while he is still alive among his three daughters, in proportion to the amount of love that each of them expresses for him. The two elder ones, Goneril and Regan, exhaust themselves in assseverations and laudations of their love for him; the third, Cordelia, refuses to do so. He should have recognized the unassuming, speechless love of his third daughter and rewarded it, but he does not recognize it. He disowns Cordelia, and divides the kingdom between the other two, to his own and the general ruin. Is not this once more the scene of a choice between three women, of whom the youngest is the best, the most excellent one?

There will at once occur to us other scenes from myths, fairy tales, and literature, with the same situation as their content. The shepherd Paris has to choose between three goddesses, of whom he declares the third to be the most beautiful. Cinderella, again, is a youngest daughter, who is preferred by the prince to her two elder sisters. Psyche, in Apuleius's story, is the youngest and fairest of three sisters. Psyche is, on the one hand, revered as Aphrodite in human form; on the other, she is treated by that goddess as Cin-

[4] Rank (1909, 8 ff.).
[5] [See *The Interpretation of Dreams* (1900a), *Standard Ed.*, 5, 354.]

derella was treated by her stepmother and is set the task of sorting a heap of mixed seeds, which she accomplishes with the help of small creatures (doves in the case of Cinderella, ants in the case of Psyche).[6] Anyone who cared to make a wider survey of the material would undoubtedly discover other versions of the same theme preserving the same essential features.

Let us be content with Cordelia, Aphrodite, Cinderella and Psyche. In all the stories the three women, of whom the third is the most excellent one, must surely be regarded as in some way alike if they are represented as sisters. (We must not be led astray by the fact that Lear's choice is between three *daughters*; this may mean nothing more than that he has to be represented as an old man. An old man cannot very well choose between three women in any other way. Thus they become his daughters.)

But who are these three sisters and why must the choice fall on the third? If we could answer this question, we should be in possession of the interpretation we are seeking. We have once already made use of an application of psycho-analytic technique, when we explained the tree caskets symbolically as three women. If we have the courage to proceed in the same way, we shall be setting foot on a path which will lead us first to something unexpected and incomprehensible, but which will perhaps, by a devious route, bring us to a goal.

It must strike us that this excellent third woman has in several instances certain peculiar qualities besides her beauty. They are qualities that seem to be tending towards some kind of unity; we must certainly not expect to find them equally well marked in every example. Cordelia makes herself unrecognizable, inconspicuous like lead, she remains dumb, she 'loves and is silent'.[7] Cinderella hides so that she cannot be found. We may perhaps be allowed to equate concealment and dumbness. These would of course be only two instances out of the five we have picked out. But there is an intimation of the same thing to be found, curiously enough, in two other cases. We have decided to compare Cordelia, with her obstinate refusal, to lead. In Bassanio's short speech while he is choosing the casket, he says of lead (without in any way leading up to the remark):

'Thy paleness[8] moves me more than eloquence.'

That is to say: 'Thy plainness moves me more than the blatant nature of the older two.' Gold and silver are 'loud'; lead is dumb — in fact like Cordelia, who 'loves and is silent'.[9]

In the ancient Greek accounts of the Judgement of Paris, nothing is said of any such reticence on the part of Aphrodite. Each of the three goddesses

---

[6] I have to thank Dr. Otto Rank for calling my attention to these similarities. [Cf. a reference to this in Chapter XII of *Group Psychology* (1921c), *Standard Ed.*, 18, 136.]

[7] [From an aside of Cordelia's, Act I, Scene 1.]

[8] 'Plainness' according to another reading.

[9] In Schlegel's translation this allusion is quite lost; indeed it is given the opposite meaning: 'Dein schlichtes Wesen spricht beredt mich an.' ['Thy plainness speaks to me with eloquence.']

speaks to the youth and tries to win him by promises. But, oddly enough, in a quite modern handling of the same scene this characteristic of the third one which has struck us makes its appearance again. In the libretto of Offenbach's *La Belle Hélène*, Paris, after telling of the solicitations of the other two goddesses, describes Aphrodite's behaviour in this competition for the beauty-prize:

> La troisième, ah! la troisième . . .
> La troisième ne dit rien.
> Elle eut le prix tout de même . . .[10]

If we decided to regard the peculiarities of our 'third one' as concentrated in her 'dumbness', then psycho-analysis will tell us that in dreams dumbness is a common representation of death.[11]

More than ten years ago a highly intelligent man told me a dream which he wanted to use as evidence of the telepathic nature of dreams. In it he saw an absent friend from whom he had received no news for a very long time, and reproached him energetically for his silence. The friend made no reply. It afterwards turned out that he had met his death by suicide at about the time of the dream. Let us leave the problem of telepathy on one side:[12] there seems, however, not to be any doubt that here the dumbness in the dream represented death. Hiding and being unfindable—a thing which confronts the prince in the fairly tale of Cinderella three times, is another unmistakable symbol of death in dreams; so, too, is a marked pallor, of which the 'paleness' of the lead in one reading of Shakespeare's text is a reminder.[13] It would be very much easier for us to transpose these interpretations from the language of dreams to the mode of expression used in the myth that is now under consideration if we could make it seem probable that dumbness must be interpreted as a sign of being dead in productions other than dreams.

At this point I will single out the ninth story in Grimm's *Fairy Tales*, which bears the title 'The Twelve Brothers'.[14] A king and a queen have twelve children, all boys. The king declares that if the thirteenth child is a girl, the boys will have to die. In expectation of her birth he has twelve coffins made. With their mother's help the twelve sons take refuge in a hidden wood, and swear death to any girl they may meet. A girl is born, grows up, and learns one day from her mother that she has had twelve brothers. She decides to seek them out, and in the wood she finds the youngest; he recognizes her, but is anxious to hide her on account of the brothers' oath. The sister says: 'I will gladly die, if by so doing I can save my twelve brothers.' The

---

[10] [Literally: 'The third one, ah! the third one . . . the third one said nothing. She won the prize all the same.'—The quotation is from Act I, Scene 7, of Meilhac and Halévy's libretto. In the German version used by Freud 'the third one' *'blieb stumm'*— 'remained dumb'.]

[11] In Stekel's *Sprache des Traumes*, too, dumbness is mentioned among the 'death' symbols (1911*a*, 351). [Cf. *The Interpretation of Dreams* (1900*a*), *Standard Ed.*, 5, 357.]

[12] [Cf. Freud's later paper on 'Dreams and Telepathy' (1922*a*).]

[13] Stekel (1911*a*), loc. cit.

[14] ['Die zwölf Brüder.' Grimm, 1918, 1, 42.]

brothers welcome her affectionately, however, and she stays with them and looks after their house for them. In a little garden beside the house grow twelve lilies. The girl picks them and gives one to each brother. At that moment the brothers are changed into ravens, and disappear, together with the house and garden. (Ravens are spirit-birds; the killing of the twelve brothers by their sister is represented by the picking of the flowers, just as it is at the beginning of the story by the coffins and the disappearance of the brothers.) The girl, who is once more ready to save her brothers from death, is now told that as a condition she must be dumb for seven years, and not speak a single word. She submits to the test, which brings her herself into mortal danger. She herself, that is, dies for her brothers, as she promised to do before she met them. By remaining dumb she succeeds at last in setting the ravens free.

In the story of 'The Six Swans'[15] the brothers who are changed into birds are set free in exactly the same way—they are restored to life by their sister's dumbness. The girl has made a firm resolve to free her brothers, 'even if it should cost her her life'; and once again (being the wife of the king) she risks her own life because she refuses to give up her dumbness in order to defend herself against evil accusations.

It would certainly be possible to collect further evidence from fairy tales that dumbness is to be understood as representing death. These indications would lead us to conclude that the third one of the sisters between whom the choice is made is a dead woman. But she may be something else as well—namely, Death itself, the Goddess of Death. Thanks to a displacement that is far from infrequent, the qualities that a deity imparts to men are ascribed to the deity himself. Such a displacement will surprise us least of all in relation to the Goddess of Death, since in modern versions and representations, which these stories would thus be forestalling, Death itself is nothing other than a dead man.

But if the third of the sisters is the Goddess of Death, the sisters are known to us. They are the Fates, the Moerae, the Parcae or the Norns, the third of whom is called Atropos, the inexorable.

II

We will for the time being put aside the task of inserting the interpretation that we have found into our myth, and listen to what the mythologists have to teach us about the role and origin of the Fates.[16]

The earliest Greek mythology (in Homer) only knew a single Μοῖρα, personifying inevitable fate. The further development of this one Moera into a company of three (or less often two) sister-goddesses probably came about on the basis of other divine figures to which the Moerae were closely related—the Graces and the Horae [the Seasons].

---

[15] ['Die sechs Schwäne.' Grimm, 1918, 1, 217. (No. 49.)]
[16] What follows is taken from Roscher's lexicon [1884–1937], under the relevant headings.

The Horae were originally goddesses of the waters of the sky, dispensing rain and dew, and of the clouds from which rain falls; and, since the clouds were conceived of as something that has been spun, it came about that these goddesses were looked upon as spinners, an attribute that then became attached to the Moerae. In the sun-favoured Mediterranean lands it is the rain on which the fertility of the soil depends, and thus the Horae became vegetation goddesses. The beauty of flowers and the abundance of fruit was their doing, and they were accredited with a wealth of agreeable and charming traits. They became the divine representatives of the Seasons, and it is possibly owing to this connection that there were three of them, if the sacred nature of the number three is not a sufficient explanation. For the peoples of antiquity at first distinguished only three seasons: winter, spring and summer. Autumn was only added in late Graeco-Roman times, after which the Horae were often represented in art as four in number.

The Horae retained their relation to time. Later they presided over the times of day, as they did at first over the times of the year; and at last their name came to be merely a designation of the hours (*heure, ora*). The Norns of German mythology are akin to the Horae and the Moerae and exhibit this time-signification in their names.[17] It was inevitable, however, that a deeper view should come to be taken of the essential nature of these deities, and that their essence should be transposed on to the regularity with which the seasons change. The Horae thus became the guardians of natural law and of the divine Order which causes the same thing to recur in Nature in an unalterable sequence.

This discovery of Nature reacted on the conception of human life. The nature-myth changed into a human myth: the weather-goddesses became goddesses of Fate. But this aspect of the Horae found expression only in the Moerae, who watch over the necessary ordering of human life as inexorably as do the Horae over the regular order of nature. The ineluctable severity of Law and its relation to death and dissolution, which had been avoided in the charming figures of the Horae, were now stamped upon the Moerae, as though men had only perceived the full seriousness of natural law when they had to submit their own selves to it.

The names of the three spinners, too, have been significantly explained by mythologists. Lachesis, the name of the second, seems to denote 'the accidental that is included in the regularity of destiny'[18]—or, as we should say, 'experience'; just as Atropos stands for 'the ineluctable'—Death. Clotho would then be left to mean the innate disposition with its fateful implications.

But now it is time to return to the theme which we are trying to interpret—the theme of the choice between three sisters. We shall be deeply disappointed to discover how unintelligible the situations under review become and what contradictions of their apparent content result, if we apply to them

---

[17] [Their names may be rendered: 'What was', 'What is', 'What shall be'.]
[18] Roscher [ibid.], quoting Preller, ed. Robert (1894).

the interpretation that we have found. On our supposition the third of the sisters is the Goddess of Death, Death itself. But in the Judgement of Paris she is the Goddess of Love, in the tale of Apuleius she is someone comparable to the goddess for her beauty, in *The Merchant of Venice* she is the fairest and wisest of women, in *King Lear* she is the one loyal daughter. We may ask whether there can be a more complete contradiction. Perhaps, improbable though it may seem, there is a still more complete one lying close at hand. Indeed, there certainly is; since, whenever our theme occurs, the choice between the women is free, and yet it falls on death. For, after all, no one chooses death, and it is only by a fatality that one falls a victim to it.

However, contradictions of a certain kind—replacements by the precise opposite—offer no serious difficulty to the work of analytic interpretation. We shall not appeal here to the fact that contraries are so often represented by one and the same element in the modes of expression used by the unconscious, as for instance in dreams.[19] But we shall remember that there are motive forces in mental life which bring about replacement by the opposite in the form of what is known as reaction-formation; and it is precisely in the revelation of such hidden forces as these that we look for the reward of this enquiry. The Moerae were created as a result of a discovery that warned man that he too is a part of nature and therefore subject to the immutable law of death. Something in man was bound to struggle against this subjection, for it is only with extreme unwillingness that he gives up his claim to an exceptional position. Man, as we know, makes use of his imaginative activity in order to satisfy the wishes that reality does not satisfy. So his imagination rebelled against the recognition of the truth embodied in the myth of the Moerae, and constructed instead the myth derived from it, in which the Goddess of Death was replaced by the Goddess of Love and by what was equivalent to her in human shape. The third of the sisters was no longer Death; she was the fairest, best, most desirable and most lovable of women. Nor was this substitution in any way technically difficult: it was prepared for by an ancient ambivalence, it was carried out along a primaeval line of connection which could not long have been forgotten. The Goddess of Love herself, who now took the place of the Goddess of Death, had once been identical with her. Even the Greek Aphrodite had not wholly relinquished her connection with the underworld, although she had long surrendered her chthonic role to other divine figures, to Persephone, or to the tri-form Artemis-Hecate. The great Mother-goddesses of the oriental peoples, however, all seem to have been both creators and destroyers—both goddesses of life and fertility and goddesses of death. Thus the replacement by a wishful opposite in our theme harks back to a primaeval identity.

The same consideration answers the question how the feature of a choice came into the myth of the three sisters. Here again there has been a wishful reversal. Choice stands in the place of necessity, of destiny. In this way man overcomes death, which he has recognized intellectually. No greater triumph

---

[19] [Cf. *The Interpretation of Dreams* (1900a), *Standard Ed.*, 4, 318.]

of wish-fulfilment is conceivable. A choice is made where in reality there is obedience to a compulsion; and what is chosen is not a figure of terror, but the fairest and most desirable of women.

On closer inspection we observe, to be sure, that the original myth is not so thoroughly distorted that traces of it do not show through and betray its presence. The free choice between the three sisters is, properly speaking, no free choice, for it must necessarily fall on the third if every kind of evil is not to come about, as it does in *King Lear*. The fairest and best of women, who has taken the place of the Death-goddess, has kept certain characteristics that border on the uncanny, so that from them we have been able to guess at what lies beneath.[20]

So far we have been following out the myth and its transformation, and it is to be hoped that we have correctly indicated the hidden causes of the transformation. We may now turn our interest to the way in which the dramatist has made use of the theme. We get an impression that a reduction of the theme to the original myth is being carried out in his work, so that we once more have a sense of the moving significance which had been weakened by the distortion. It is by means of this reduction of the distortion, this partial return to the original, that the dramatist achieves his more profound effect upon us.

To avoid misunderstandings, I should like to say that it is not my purpose to deny that King Lear's dramatic story is intended to inculcate two wise lessons: that one should not give up one's possessions and rights during one's lifetime, and that one must guard against accepting flattery at its face value. These and similar warnings are undoubtedly brought out by the play; but it seems to me quite impossible to explain the overpowering effect of *King Lear* from the impression that such a train of thought would produce, or to suppose that the dramatist's personal motives did not go beyond the intention of teaching these lessons. It is suggested, too, that his purpose was to present the tragedy of ingratitude, the sting of which he may well have felt in his own heart, and that the effect of the play rests on the purely formal element of its artistic presentation; but this cannot, so it seems to me, take the place of the understanding brought to us by the explanation we have reached of the theme of the choice between the three sisters.

Lear is an old man. It is for this reason, as we have already said, that the three sisters appear as his daughters. The relationship of a father to his chil-

---

[20] The Psyche of Apuleius's story has kept many traits that remind us of her relation with death. Her wedding is celebrated like a funeral, she has to descend into the underworld, and afterwards she sinks into a death-like sleep (Otto Rank).—On the significance of Psyche as goddess of the spring and as 'Bride of Death', cf. Zinzow (1881).—In another of Grimm's Tales ('The Goose-girl at the Fountain' ['Die Gänsehirtin am Brunnen', 1918, 2, 300], No. 179) there is, as in 'Cinderella', an alternation between the beautiful and the ugly aspect of the third sister, in which one may no doubt see an indication of her double nature—before and after the substitution. This third daughter is repudiated by her father, after a test which is almost the same as the one in *King Lear*. Like her sisters, she has to declare how fond she is of their father, but can find no expression for her love but a comparison with salt. (Kindly communicated by Dr. Hanns Sachs.)

dren, which might be a fruitful source of many dramatic situations, is not turned to further account in the play. But Lear is not only an old man: he is a dying man. In this way the extraordinary premiss of the division of his inheritance loses all its strangeness. But the doomed man is not willing to renounce the love of women; he insists on hearing how much he is loved. Let us now recall the moving final scene, one of the culminating points of tragedy in modern drama. Lear carries Cordelia's dead body on to the stage. Cordelia is Death. If we reverse the situation it becomes intelligible and familiar to us. She is the Death-goddess who, like the Valkyrie in German mythology, carries away the dead hero from the battlefield. Eternal wisdom, clothed in the primaeval myth, bids the old man renounce love, choose death and make friends with the necessity of dying.

The dramatist brings us nearer to the ancient theme by representing the man who makes the choice between the three sisters as aged and dying. The regressive revision which he has thus applied to the myth, distorted as it was by wishful transformation, allows us enough glimpses of its original meaning to enable us perhaps to reach as well a superficial allegorical interpretation of the three female figures in the theme. We might argue that what is represented here are the three inevitable relations that a man has with a woman—the woman who bears him, the woman who is his mate and the woman who destroys him; or that they are the three forms taken by the figure of the mother in the course of a man's life—the mother herself, the beloved one who is chosen after her pattern, and lastly the Mother Earth who receives him once more. But it is in vain that an old man yearns for the love of woman as he had it first from his mother; the third of the Fates alone, the silent Goddess of Death, will take him into her arms.

Translated by James Strachey.

T. S. ELIOT

Tradition and the Individual Talent

1920

The two apparently opposed terms in the title of Eliot's (1888–1965) best-known essay immediately bring to mind an issue for critical debate that we have encountered many times before. Whether the opposing terms are ancients and moderns, or art and nature, or learning and genius, or rules and originality, the question has often been (and particularly for a critic who is also a poet), "Where and how does a new poet fit into the pantheon?" Differentiating mere novelty from the truly new, Eliot asks, in effect, how original can a poet ever be? Eliot redefines "old" and "new," and his apparently paradoxical conclusion rests upon a theory of literary history that is nonchronological. Starting with the debatable commonplace that all art continues to live in a timeless present, he proposes a "simultaneous existence" and a "simultaneous order" of all the "existing monuments." The image of monuments may be unfortunate, for what Eliot stresses is their permanent vitality, so that the works of an earlier period are always being altered by the introduction of later works. Eliot's comparative approach, which is aesthetic and not merely historical, should be compared and contrasted with Arnold's "touchstone" method: do they start with the same assumptions?

Stressing the poet's inevitable and necessary consciousness of history leads Eliot to another formulation that has profoundly influenced twentieth-century criticism—the theory of the depersonalization of art. When he declares that poetry "is only a medium and not a personality" and that it "is not a turning loose of emotions, but an escape from emotion," against what theories and what critics is he arguing? Understanding why he rejects Wordsworth's definition of poetry as "emotion recollected in tranquillity" will also enable you to grasp why Eliot, in other essays, expresses unqualified enthusiasm for Keats as a critic.

The theory of history and the theory of impersonality combined have far-reaching implications for the practice of criticism. In this essay Eliot succinctly states the critic's task: "to divert interest from the poet to the poetry." With this phrase, Eliot is identified as one of the progenitors of the twentieth century's "New Criticism," which has as its principal tenet the close examination of the poem as poem, without regard for biographical, social, ethical, or other frames of reference as sources *of judgment; the poem has its own intrinsic value. (For a fuller description of New Criticism and its influence, see the introductory notes to John Crowe Ransom, p. 448, and Cleanth Brooks, p. 465.) That this is not a totally new, exclusively modern approach, however, will become apparent if you recall one of the oldest of the existing critical monuments—Aristotle's* Poetics *(p. 18).*

IN ENGLISH writing we seldom speak of tradition, though we occasionally apply its name in deploring its absence. We cannot refer to "the tradition" or to "a tradition"; at most, we employ the adjective in saying that the poetry of So-and-so is "traditional" or even "too traditional." Seldom, perhaps, does the word appear except in a phrase of censure. If otherwise, it is vaguely approbative, with the implication, as to the work approved, of some pleasing archaeological reconstruction. You can hardly make the word agreeable to English ears without this comfortable reference to the reassuring science of archaeology.

Certainly the word is not likely to appear in our appreciations of living or dead writers. Every nation, every race, has not only its own creative, but its own critical turn of mind; and is even more oblivious of the shortcomings and limitations of its critical habits than of those of its creative genius. We know, or think we know, from the enormous mass of critical writing that has appeared in the French language the critical method or habit of the French; we only conclude (we are such unconscious people) that the French are "more critical" than we, and sometimes even plume ourselves a little with the fact, as if the French were the less spontaneous. Perhaps they are; but we might remind ourselves that criticism is as inevitable as breathing, and that we should be none the worse for articulating what passes in our minds when we read a book and feel an emotion about it, for criticizing our own minds in their work of criticism. One of the facts that might come to light in this process is our tendency to insist, when we praise a poet, upon those aspects of his work in which he least resembles any one else. In these aspects or parts of his work we pretend to find what is individual, what is the peculiar essence of the man. We dwell with satisfaction upon the poet's difference from his predecessors, especially his immediate predecessors; we endeavour to find something that can be isolated in order to be enjoyed. Whereas if we approach a poet without this prejudice we shall often find that not only the best, but the most individual parts of his work may be those in which the dead poets, his ancestors, assert their immortality most vigorously. And I do not mean the impressionable period of adolescence, but the period of full maturity.

Yet if the only form of tradition, of handing down, consisted in following the ways of the immediate generation before us in a blind or timid adherence to its successes, "tradition" should positively be discouraged. We have seen many such simple currents soon lost in the sand; and novelty is better than repetition. Tradition is a matter of much wider significance. It cannot be inherited, and if you want it you must obtain it by great labour. It involves, in the first place, the historical sense, which we may call nearly indispensable to any one who would continue to be a poet beyond his twenty-fifth year; and the historical sense involves a perception, not only of the pastness of the past, but of its presence; the historical sense compels a man to write not merely with his own generation in his bones, but with a feeling that the whole of the literature of Europe from Homer and within it the whole of the literature of his own country has a simultaneous existence and composes a simultaneous order. This historical sense, which is a sense of the timeless as well as the temporal and of the timeless and of the temporal together, is what makes a writer traditional. And it is at the same time what makes a writer most acutely conscious of his place in time, of his own contemporaneity.

No poet, no artist of any art, has his complete meaning alone. His significance, his appreciation is the appreciation of his relation to the dead poets and artists. You cannot value him alone; you must set him, for contrast and comparison, among the dead. I mean this as a principle of aesthetic, not merely historical, criticism. The necessity that he shall conform, that he shall cohere, is not one-sided; what happens when a new work of art is created is something that happens simultaneously to all the works of art which preceded it. The existing monuments form an ideal order among themselves, which is modified by the introduction of the new (the really new) work of art among them. The existing order is complete before the new work arrives; for order to persist after the supervention of novelty, the *whole* existing order must be, if ever so slightly, altered; and so the relations, proportions, values of each work of art toward the whole are readjusted; and this is conformity between the old and the new. Whoever has approved this idea of order, of the form of European, of English literature will not find it preposterous that the past should be altered by the present as much as the present is directed by the past. And the poet who is aware of this will be aware of great difficulties and responsibilities.

In a peculiar sense he will be aware also that he must inevitably be judged by the standards of the past. I say judged, not amputated, by them; not judged to be as good as, or worse or better than, the dead; and certainly not judged by the canons of dead critics. It is a judgment, a comparison, in which two things are measured by each other. To conform merely would be for the new work not really to conform at all; it would not be new, and would therefore not be a work of art. And we do not quite say that the new is more valuable because it fits in; but its fitting in is a test of its value—a test, it is true, which can only be slowly and cautiously applied, for we are none of us infallible judges of conformity. We say: it appears to conform, and is perhaps individual, or it appears individual, and may conform; but we are hardly likely to find that it is one and not the other.

To proceed to a more intelligible exposition of the relation of the poet to the past: he can neither take the past as a lump, an indiscriminate bolus, nor can he form himself wholly on one or two private admirations, nor can he form himself wholly upon one preferred period. The first course is inadmissible, the second is an important experience of youth, and the third is a pleasant and highly desirable supplement. The poet must be very conscious of the main current, which does not at all flow invariably through the most distinguished reputations. He must be quite aware of the obvious fact that art never improves, but that the material of art is never quite the same. He must be aware that the mind of Europe—the mind of his own country—a mind which he learns in time to be much more important than his own private mind—is a mind which changes, and that this change is a development which abandons nothing *en route*, which does not superannuate either Shakespeare, or Homer, or the rock drawing of the Magdalenian draughtsmen. That this development, refinement perhaps, complication certainly, is not, from the point of view of the artist, any improvement. Perhaps not even an improvement from the point of view of the psychologist or not to the extent which we imagine; perhaps only in the end based upon a complication in economics and machinery. But the difference between the present and the past is that the conscious present is an awareness of the past in a way and to an extent which the past's awareness of itself cannot show.

Some one said: "The dead writers are remote from us because we *know* so much more than they did." Precisely, and they are that which we know.

I am alive to a usual objection to what is clearly part of my programme for the *métier* of poetry. The objection is that the doctrine requires a ridiculous amount of erudition (pedantry), a claim which can be rejected by appeal to the lives of poets in any pantheon. It will even be affirmed that much learning deadens or perverts poetic sensibility. While, however, we persist in believing that a poet ought to know as much as will not encroach upon his necessary receptivity and necessary laziness, it is not desirable to confine knowledge to whatever can be put into a useful shape for examinations, drawing-rooms, or the still more pretentious modes of publicity. Some can absorb knowledge, the more tardy must sweat for it. Shakespeare acquired more essential history from Plutarch than most men could from the whole British Museum. What is to be insisted upon is that the poet must develop or procure the consciousness of the past and that he should continue to develop this consciousness throughout his career.

What happens is a continual surrender of himself as he is at the moment to something which is more valuable. The progress of an artist is a continual self-sacrifice, a continual extinction of personality.

There remains to define this process of depersonalization and its relation to the sense of tradition. It is in this depersonalization that art may be said to approach the condition of science. I, therefore, invite you to consider, as a suggestive analogy, the action which takes place when a bit of finely filiated platinum is introduced into a chamber containing oxygen and sulphur dioxide.

II

Honest criticism and sensitive appreciation are directed not upon the poet but upon the poetry. If we attend to the confused cries of the newspaper critics and the *susurrus* of popular repetition that follows, we shall hear the names of poets in great numbers; if we seek not Blue-book knowledge but the enjoyment of poetry, and ask for a poem, we shall seldom find it. I have tried to point out the importance of the relation of the poem to other poems by other authors, and suggested the conception of poetry as a living whole of all the poetry that has ever been written. The other aspect of this Impersonal theory of poetry is the relation of the poem to its author. And I hinted, by an analogy, that the mind of the mature poet differs from that of the immature one not precisely in any valuation of "personality," not being necessarily more interesting, or having "more to say," but rather by being a more finely perfected medium in which special, or very varied, feelings are at liberty to enter into new combinations.

The analogy was that of the catalyst. When the two gases previously mentioned are mixed in the presence of a filament of platinum, they form sulphurous acid. This combination takes place only if the platinum is present; nevertheless the newly formed acid contains no trace of platinum, and the platinum itself is apparently unaffected; has remained inert, neutral, and unchanged. The mind of the poet is the shred of platinum. It may partly or exclusively operate upon the experience of the man himself; but, the more perfect the artist, the more completely separate in him will be the man who suffers and the mind which creates; the more perfectly will the mind digest and transmute the passions which are its material.

The experience, you will notice, the elements which enter the presence of the transforming catalyst, are of two kinds: emotions and feelings. The effect of a work of art upon the person who enjoys it is an experience different in kind from any experience not of art. It may be formed out of one emotion, or may be a combination of several; and various feelings, inhering for the writer in particular words or phrases or images, may be added to compose the final result. Or great poetry may be made without the direct use of any emotion whatever: composed out of feelings solely. Canto XV of the *Inferno* (Brunetto Latini) is a working up of the emotion evident in the situation; but the effect, though single as that of any work of art, is obtained by considerable complexity of detail. The last quatrain gives an image, a feeling attaching to an image, which "came," which did not develop simply out of what precedes, but which was probably in suspension in the poet's mind until the proper combination arrived for it to add itself to. The poet's mind is in fact a receptacle for seizing and storing up numberless feelings, phrases, images, which remain there until all the particles which can unite to form a new compound are present together.

If you compare several representative passages of the greatest poetry you see how great is the variety of types of combination, and also how completely any semi-ethical criterion of "sublimity" misses the mark. For it is not the "greatness," the intensity, of the emotions, the components, but the intensity of the artistic process, the pressure, so to speak, under which the fusion takes place, that counts. The episode of Paolo and Francesca employs a definite emotion, but the intensity of the poetry is something quite different from whatever intensity in the supposed experience it may give the impression of.

It is no more intense, furthermore, than Canto XXVI, the voyage of Ulysses, which has not the direct dependence upon an emotion. Great variety is possible in the process of transmutation of emotion: the murder of Agamemnon, or the agony of Othello, gives an artistic effect apparently closer to a possible original than the scenes from Dante. In the *Agamemnon*, the artistic emotion approximates to the emotion of an actual spectator; in *Othello* to the emotion of the protagonist himself. But the difference between art and the event is always absolute; the combination which is the murder of Agamemnon is probably as complex as that which is the voyage of Ulysses. In either case there has been a fusion of elements. The ode of Keats contains a number of feelings which have nothing particular to do with the nightingale, but which the nightingale, partly, perhaps, because of its attractive name, and partly because of its reputation, served to bring together.

The point of view which I am struggling to attack is perhaps related to the metaphysical theory of the substantial unity of the soul: for my meaning is, that the poet has, not a "personality" to express, but a particular medium, which is only a medium and not a personality, in which impressions and experiences combine in peculiar and unexpected ways. Impressions and experiences which are important for the man may take no place in the poetry, and those which become important in the poetry may play quite a negligible part in the man, the personality.

I will quote a passage which is unfamiliar enough to be regarded with fresh attention in the light—or darkness—of these observations:

> And now methinks I could e'en chide myself
> For doating on her beauty, though her death
> Shall be revenged after no common action.
> Does the silkworm expend her yellow labours
> For thee? For thee does she undo herself?
> Are lordships sold to maintain ladyships
> For the poor benefit of a bewildering minute?
> Why does yon fellow falsify highways,
> And put his life between the judge's lips,
> To refine such a thing — keeps horse and men
> To beat their valours for her? . . .

In this passage (as is evident if it is taken in its context) there is a combination of positive and negative emotions: an intensely strong attraction toward beauty and an equally intense fascination by the ugliness which is contrasted with it and which destroys it. This balance of contrasted emotion is in the dramatic situation to which the speech is pertinent, but that situation alone is inadequate to it. This is, so to speak, the structural emotion, provided by the drama. But the whole effect, the dominant tone, is due to the fact that a number of floating feelings, having an affinity to this emotion by no means superficially evident, have combined with it to give us a new art emotion.

It is not in his personal emotions, the emotions provoked by particular events in his life, that the poet is in any way remarkable or interesting. His

particular emotions may be simple, or crude, or flat. The emotion in his poetry will be a very complex thing, but not with the complexity of the emotions of people who have very complex or unusual emotions in life. One
error, in fact, of eccentricity in poetry is to seek for new human emotions to
express; and in this search for novelty in the wrong place it discovers the perverse. The business of the poet is not to find new emotions, but to use the ordinary ones and, in working them up into poetry, to express feelings which
are not in actual emotions at all. And emotions which he has never experienced will serve his turn as well as those familiar to him. Consequently, we
must believe that "emotion recollected in tranquillity" is an inexact formula.
For it is neither emotion, nor recollection, nor, without distortion of meaning,
tranquillity. It is a concentration, and a new thing resulting from the concentration, of a very great number of experiences which to the practical and active person would not seem to be experiences at all; it is a concentration
which does not happen consciously or of deliberation. These experiences are
not "recollected," and they finally unite in an atmosphere which is "tranquil"
only in that it is a passive attending upon the event. Of course this is not
quite the whole story. There is a great deal, in the writing of poetry, which
must be conscious and deliberate. In fact, the bad poet is usually unconscious
where he ought to be conscious, and conscious where he ought to be unconscious. Both errors tend to make him "personal." Poetry is not a turning loose
of emotion, but an escape from emotion; it is not the expression of personality, but an escape from personality. But, of course, only those who have personality and emotions know what it means to want to escape from these
things.

III

ὁ δὲ νοῦς ἴσως Θειότερόν τι χαὶ ἀπαθές ἐστιν.[1]

This essay proposes to halt at the frontier of metaphysics or mysticism, and
confine itself to such practical conclusions as can be applied by the responsible person interested in poetry. To divert interest from the poet to the
poetry is a laudable aim: for it would conduce to a juster estimation of actual
poetry, good and bad. There are many people who appreciate the expression
of sincere emotion in verse, and there is a smaller number of people who can
appreciate technical excellence. But very few know when there is an expression of *significant* emotion, emotion which has its life in the poem and not in
the history of the poet. The emotion of art is impersonal. And the poet cannot
reach this impersonality without surrendering himself wholly to the work to
be done. And he is not likely to know what is to be done unless he lives in
what is not merely the present, but the present moment of the past, unless he
is conscious, not of what is dead, but of what is already living.

---

[1] *O de nous isos Theioteron ti chai apathes estin.* For the mind is something both divine and
impassive. [Eliot's note.]

Virginia Woolf

Shakespeare's Sister

From *A Room of One's Own*

1929

In 1928, Virginia Woolf (1882–1941) delivered two lectures at Girton and Newn-ham Colleges of Cambridge University, expanding them for publication in 1929 as the six chapters of A Room of One's Own. Invited to speak on "Women in Fic-tion," Woolf indicates in the first chapter that although she found the subject global and endless, she can state one fundamental point: "A woman must have money and a room of her own if she is to write fiction." Instead of keeping to a narrow treatment of women writers, or the portrayal of women in fiction, Woolf's lectures examine the larger historical issues of why women do not have, and have not had, money of their own and rooms of their own.

In Chapter 3, Woolf considers the question of why no women writers are repre-sented in the canon of Elizabethan drama. To explore the issue, Woolf invents a mythical sister, Judith, for William Shakespeare and compares the barriers brother and sister would have encountered in achieving success as playwrights. Woolf must resort to anecdotal narrative because the history books, virtually all written by males, tell her practically nothing about the lives of women before the eighteenth century.

Imaginatively, Woolf despairs of Judith's having possessed a genius equal to her brother's, for her lack of education would have denied its flowering. The debate over education for women in the Victorian period often favored a special training for them to improve domestic skills and the ability to serve as a husband's helpmate. Although Girton College, founded in 1869, was the first to admit women students to Cam-bridge University, the women's colleges did not receive full university status until 1948. At Oxford, the first women's college, Lady Margaret Hall, was founded in 1878, but full university status was granted only in 1959.

As to the issue of "money of her own," only in 1882 were married women in England allowed to own property in their own right. In attaining a voice in the gov-ernance of England, certainly connected with achieving economic independence, women over the age of thirty gained the vote in 1918, while total suffrage was achieved only in 1928, the year of Woolf's lectures. Certainly these facts must have

411

*resonated in the lecture hall as Woolf exhorted the students of Girton and Newnham
to correct the omission of women from the learned histories.*

*Another insidious prejudice that Shakespeare's hypothetical sister would have
encountered continued to assail women as late as Woolf's own time and place;
namely, the belief that the female mind is always inferior to that of a male. Woolf offers a graceful satire of the prejudice by characterizing it as the quaint notion of dod-
dering buffoons. Nevertheless, Woolf knew the power of the men she satirizes. And
the prejudice went far beyond the examples Woolf names: Freud, for example, found a
rational, focused intelligence in women to be masculine and unnatural.*

*Given these historical circumstances, Woolf spins a tale contrasting William's
theatrical adventures in London leading to his golden career with the possible careers
of his ill-fated sister. And like the great writer of fiction that she is, Woolf convinces
us of the truth of her tale.*

*Besides being the first practical and theoretical exposition of a feminist literary
history,* A Room of One's Own *is a rallying image in the feminist project to attain
an identity other than the one defined by rooms that specified the inherently submis-
sive roles of women—kitchen, bedroom, and nursery. Among the increasing number
of scholarly books and articles produced each year on the subject of women in history
and in literature (some of which are represented in the essays by Adrienne Rich,
p. 511; Nina Baym, p. 586; Elaine Showalter, p. 615; and Sandra M. Gilbert and
Susan Gubar, p.683), Woolf's writings are the object of great and devoted attention.*

IT WAS disappointing not to have brought back in the evening some important
statement, some authentic fact. Women are poorer than men because—this or
that. Perhaps now it would be better to give up seeking for the truth, and receiving on one's head an avalanche of opinion hot as lava, discolored as dish-
water. It would be better to draw the curtains; to shut out distractions; to light
the lamp; to narrow the enquiry and to ask the historian, who records not opinions but facts, to describe under what conditions women lived, not throughout
the ages, but in England, say in the time of Elizabeth.

For it is a perennial puzzle why no woman wrote a word of that extraordinary literature when every other man, it seemed, was capable of song or sonnet. What were the conditions in which women lived, I asked myself; for fiction, imaginative work that is, is not dropped like a pebble upon the ground, as
science may be; fiction is like a spider's web, attached ever so lightly perhaps,
but still attached to life at all four corners. Often the attachment is scarcely perceptible; Shakespeare's plays, for instance, seem to hang there complete by
themselves. But when the web is pulled askew, hooked up at the edge, torn in
the middle, one remembers that these webs are not spun in midair by incorpo-
real creatures, but are the work of suffering human beings, and are attached to
grossly material things, like health and money and the houses we live in.

I went, therefore, to the shelf where the histories stand and took down
one of the latest, Professor Trevelyan's *History of England*.[1] Once more I

---

[1] George Macaulay Trevelyan (1876–1962). British historian, known for numerous
works, including a one-volume *History of England*, 1926.

looked up Women, found "position of," and turned to the pages indicated. "Wife-beating," I read, "was a recognised right of man, and was practised without shame by high as well as low. . . . Similarly," the historian goes on, "the daughter who refused to marry the gentleman of her parents' choice was liable to be locked up, beaten and flung about the room, without any shock being inflicted on public opinion. Marriage was not an affair of personal affection, but of family avarice, particularly in the 'chivalrous' upper classes. . . . Betrothal often took place while one or both of the parties was in the cradle, and marriage when they were scarcely out of the nurses' charge." That was about 1470, soon after Chaucer's time. The next reference to the position of women is some two hundred years later, in the time of the Stuarts. "It was still the exception for women of the upper and middle class to choose their own husbands, and when the husband had been assigned, he was lord and master, so far at least as law and custom could make him. Yet even so," Professor Trevelyan concludes, "neither Shakespeare's women nor those of authentic seventeenth-century memoirs, like the Verneys and the Hutchinsons, seem wanting in personality and character." Certainly, if we consider it, Cleopatra must have had a way with her; Lady Macbeth, one would suppose, had a will of her own; Rosalind, one might conclude, was an attractive girl. Professor Trevelyan is speaking no more than the truth when he remarks that Shakespeare's women do not seem wanting in personality and character. Not being a historian, one might go even further and say that women have burnt like beacons in all the works of all the poets from the beginning of time—Clytemnestra, Antigone, Cleopatra, Lady Macbeth, Phèdre, Cressida, Rosalind, Desdemona, the Duchess of Malfi, among the dramatists; then among the prose writers: Millamant, Clarissa, Becky Sharp, Anna Karenine, Emma Bovary, Madame de Guermantes—the names flock to mind, nor do they recall women "lacking in personality and character." Indeed, if woman had no existence save in the fiction written by men, one would imagine her a person of the utmost importance; very various; heroic and mean; splendid and sordid; infinitely beautiful and hideous in the extreme; as great as a man, some think even greater.[2] But this is woman in fiction. In fact, as Professor Trevelyan points out, she was locked up, beaten and flung about the room.

---

[2] "It remains a strange and almost inexplicable fact that in Athena's city, where women were kept in almost Oriental suppression as odalisques or drudges, the stage should have yet produced figures like Clytemnestra and Cassandra, Atossa and Antigone, Phèdre and Medea, and all the other heroines who dominate play after play of the 'misogynist' Euripides. But the paradox of this world where in real life a respectable woman could hardly show her face alone in the street, and yet on the stage woman equals or surpasses man, has never been satisfactorily explained. In modern tragedy the same predominance exists. At all events, a very cursory survey of Shakespeare's work (similarly with Webster, though not with Marlowe or Jonson) suffices to reveal how this dominance, this initiative of women, persists from Rosalind to Lady Macbeth. So too in Racine; six of his tragedies bear their heroines' names; and what male characters of his shall we set against Hermione and Andromaque, Bérénice and Roxane, Phèdre and Athalie? So again with Ibsen; what men shall we match with Solveig and Nora, Hedda and Hilda Wangel and Rebecca West?"—F. L. Lucas, *Tragedy,* pp. 114–15. [Woolf's note.]

A very queer, composite being thus emerges. Imaginatively she is of the highest importance; practically she is completely insignificant. She pervades poetry from cover to cover; she is all but absent from history. She dominates the lives of kings and conquerors in fiction; in fact she was the slave of any boy whose parents forced a ring upon her finger. Some of the most inspired words, some of the most profound thoughts in literature fall from her lips; in real life she could hardly read, could scarcely spell, and was the property of her husband.

It was certainly an odd monster that one made up by reading the historians first and the poets afterwards—a worm winged like an eagle; the spirit of life and beauty in a kitchen chopping up suet. But these monsters, however amusing to the imagination, have no existence in fact. What one must do to bring her to life was to think poetically and prosaically at one and the same moment, thus keeping in touch with fact—that she is Mrs. Martin, aged thirty-six, dressed in blue, wearing a black hat and brown shoes; but not losing sight of fiction either—that she is a vessel in which all sorts of spirits and forces are coursing and flashing perpetually. The moment, however, that one tries this method with the Elizabethan woman, one branch of illumination fails; one is held up by the scarcity of facts. One knows nothing detailed, nothing perfectly true and substantial about her. History scarcely mentions her. And I turned to Professor Trevelyan again to see what history meant to him. I found by looking at his chapter headings that it meant—

"The Manor Court and the Methods of Open-field Agriculture . . . The Cistercians and Sheep-farming . . . The Crusades . . . The University . . . The House of Commons . . . The Hundred Years' War . . . The Wars of the Roses . . . The Renaissance Scholars . . . The Dissolution of the Monasteries . . . Agrarian and Religious Strife . . . The Origin of English Sea-power . . . The Armada . . ." and so on. Occasionally an individual woman is mentioned, an Elizabeth, or a Mary; a queen or a great lady. But by no possible means could middle-class women with nothing but brains and character at their command have taken part in any one of the great movements which, brought together, constitute the historian's view of the past. Nor shall we find her in any collection of anecdotes. Aubrey[3] hardly mentions her. She never writes her own life and scarcely keeps a diary; there are only a handful of her letters in existence. She left no plays or poems by which we can judge her. What one wants, I thought—and why does not some brilliant student at Newnham or Girton supply it?—is a mass of information; at what age did she marry; how many children had she as a rule; what was her house like; had she a room to herself; did she do the cooking; would she be likely to have a servant? All these facts lie somewhere, presumably, in parish registers and account books; the life of the average Elizabethan woman must be scattered about somewhere, could one collect it and make a book of it. It would be ambitious beyond my daring, I thought, looking about the shelves for books that were not there, to suggest to the students of those famous colleges

[3]John Aubrey (1626–1697), author of *Lives of Eminent Men,* first printed in 1813.

that they should re-write history, though I own that it often seems a little queer as it is, unreal, lop-sided; but why should they not add a supplement to history? calling it, of course, by some inconspicuous name so that women might figure there without impropriety? For one often catches a glimpse of them in the lives of the great, whisking away into the background, concealing, I sometimes think, a wink, a laugh, perhaps a tear. And, after all, we have lives enough of Jane Austen; it scarcely seems necessary to consider again the influence of the tragedies of Joanna Baillie upon the poetry of Edgar Allan Poe; as for myself, I should not mind if the homes and haunts of Mary Russell Mitford were closed to the public for a century at least. But what I find deplorable, I continued, looking about the bookshelves again, is that nothing is known about women before the eighteenth century. I have no model in my mind to turn about this way and that. Here am I asking why women did not write poetry in the Elizabethan age, and I am not sure how they were educated; whether they were taught to write; whether they had sitting-rooms to themselves; how many women had children before they were twenty-one; what, in short, they did from eight in the morning till eight at night. They had no money evidently; according to Professor Trevelyan they were married whether they liked it or not before they were out of the nursery, at fifteen or sixteen very likely. It would have been extremely odd, even upon this showing, had one of them suddenly written the plays of Shakespeare, I concluded, and I thought of that old gentleman, who is dead now, but was a bishop, I think, who declared that it was impossible for any woman, past, present, or to come, to have the genius of Shakespeare. He wrote to the papers about it. He also told a lady who applied to him for information that cats do not as a matter of fact go to heaven, though they have, he added, souls of a sort. How much thinking those old gentlemen used to save one! How the borders of ignorance shrank back at their approach! Cats do not go to heaven. Women cannot write the plays of Shakespeare.

Be that as it may, I could not help thinking, as I looked at the works of Shakespeare on the shelf, that the bishop was right at least in this; it would have been impossible, completely and entirely, for any woman to have written the plays of Shakespeare in the age of Shakespeare. Let me imagine, since facts are so hard to come by, what would have happened had Shakespeare had a wonderfully gifted sister, called Judith, let us say. Shakespeare himself went, very probably—his mother was an heiress—to the grammar school, where he may have learnt Latin—Ovid, Virgil and Horace—and the elements of grammar and logic. He was, it is well known, a wild boy who poached rabbits, perhaps shot a deer, and had, rather sooner than he should have done, to marry a woman in the neighbourhood, who bore him a child rather quicker than was right. That escapade sent him to seek his fortune in London. He had, it seemed, a taste for the theatre; he began by holding horses at the stage door. Very soon he got work in the theatre, became a successful actor, and lived at the hub of the universe, meeting everybody, knowing everybody, practising his art on the boards, exercising his wits in the streets, and even getting access to the palace of the queen. Meanwhile his extraordinarily gifted sister, let us suppose, remained at home. She was as adventurous, as imaginative, as agog to see the world as he was. But she was not sent to school. She had no chance of learning grammar and logic, let alone of reading Horace and Virgil. She picked up a book now and then, one of her brother's perhaps, and read a few pages. But then her parents came in and told her to mend the stockings or mind the stew and not moon about with books and papers. They would have spoken sharply but kindly, for they were substantial people who knew the conditions of life for a woman and loved their daughter—indeed, more likely than not she was the apple of her father's eye. Perhaps she scribbled some pages up in an apple loft on the sly, but was careful to hide them or set fire to them. Soon, however, before she was out of her teens, she was to be betrothed to the son of a neighbouring wool-stapler. She cried out that marriage was hateful to her, and for that she was severely beaten by her father. Then he ceased to scold her. He begged her instead not to hurt him, not to shame him in this matter of her marriage. He would give her a chain of beads or a fine petticoat, he said; and there were tears in his eyes. How could she disobey him? How could she break his heart? The force of her own gift alone drove her to it. She made up a small parcel of her belongings, let herself down by a rope one summer's night and took the road to London. She was not seventeen. The birds that sang in the hedge were not more musical than she was. She had the quickest fancy, a gift like her brother's, for the tune of words. Like him, she had a taste for the the-atre. She stood at the stage door; she wanted to act, she said. Men laughed in her face. The manager—a fat, loose-lipped man—guffawed. He bellowed something about poodles dancing and women acting—no woman, he said, could possibly be an actress. He hinted—you can imagine what. She could get no training in her craft. Could she even seek her dinner in a tavern or roam the streets at midnight? Yet her genius was for fiction and lusted to feed abundantly upon the lives of men and women and the study of their ways. At last—for she was very young, oddly like Shakespeare the poet in her face, with the same grey eyes and rounded brows—at last Nick Greene the actor-manager took pity on her; she found herself with child by that gentleman and so—who shall measure the heat and violence of the poet's heart when caught and tangled in a woman's body?—killed herself one win-ter's night and lies buried at some cross-roads where the omnibuses now stop outside the Elephant and Castle.[4]

That, more or less, is how the story would run, I think, if a woman in Shakespeare's day had had Shakespeare's genius. But for my part, I agree with the deceased bishop, if such he was—it is unthinkable that any woman in Shakespeare's day should have had Shakespeare's genius. For genius like Shakespeare's is not born among labouring, uneducated, servile people. It was not born in England among the Saxons and the Britons. It is not born today among the working classes. How, then, could it have been born among women whose work began, according to Professor Trevelyan, almost before

[4] A location in London south of the River Thames.

they were out of the nursery, who were forced to it by their parents and held to it by all the power of law and custom? Yet genius of a sort must have existed among women as it must have existed among the working classes. Now and again an Emily Brontë or a Robert Burns blazes out and proves its presence. But certainly it never got itself on to paper. When, however, one reads of a witch being ducked, of a woman possessed by devils, of a wise woman selling herbs, or even of a very remarkable man who had a mother, then I think we are on the track of a lost novelist, a suppressed poet, of some mute and inglorious Jane Austen, some Emily Brontë who dashed her brains out on the moor or mopped and mowed about the highways crazed with the torture that her gift had put her to. Indeed, I would venture to guess that Anon, who wrote so many poems without signing them, was often a woman. It was a woman Edward Fitzgerald, I think, suggested who made the ballads and the folk-songs, crooning them to her children, beguiling her spinning with them, or the length of the winter's night.

This may be true or it may be false—who can say?—but what is true in it, so it seemed to me, reviewing the story of Shakespeare's sister as I had made it, is that any woman born with a great gift in the sixteenth century would certainly have gone crazed, shot herself, or ended her days in some lonely cottage outside the village, half witch, half wizard, feared and mocked at. For it needs little skill in psychology to be sure that a highly gifted girl who had tried to use her gift for poetry would have been so thwarted and hindered by other people, so tortured and pulled asunder by her own contrary instincts, that she must have lost her health and sanity to a certainty. No girl could have walked to London and stood at a stage door and forced her way into the presence of actor-managers without doing herself a violence and suffering an anguish which may have been irrational—for chastity may be a fetish invented by certain societies for unknown reasons—but were none the less inevitable. Chastity had then, it has even now, a religious importance in a woman's life, and has so wrapped itself round with nerves and instincts that to cut it free and bring it to the light of day demands courage of the rarest. To have lived a free life in London in the sixteenth century would have meant for a woman who was a poet and a playwright a nervous stress and dilemma which might well have killed her. Had she survived, whatever she had written would have been twisted and deformed, issuing from a strained and morbid imagination. And undoubtedly, I thought, looking at the shelf where there are no plays by women, her work would have gone unsigned. That refuge she would have sought certainly. It was the relic of the sense of chastity that dictated anonymity to women even so late as the nineteenth century. Currer Bell, George Eliot, George Sand, all the victims of inner strife as their writings prove, sought ineffectively to veil themselves by using the name of a man. Thus they did homage to the convention, which if not implanted by the other sex was liberally encouraged by them (the chief glory of a woman is not to be talked of, said Pericles, himself a much-talked-of man), that publicity in women is detestable. Anonymity runs in their blood. The desire to be veiled still possesses them. They are not even now as concerned about the health of their fame as men are, and, speaking generally, will pass a tombstone or a signpost without feeling an irresistible desire to cut their names on it, as Alf, Bert or Chas. must do in obedience to their instinct, which murmurs if it sees a fine woman go by, or even a god, Ce chien est à moi.[5] And, of course, it may not be a dog, I thought, remembering Parliament Square, the Sieges Allee and other avenues; it may be a piece of land or a man with curly black hair. It is one of the great advantages of being a woman that one can pass even a very fine negress without wishing to make an Englishwoman of her.

That woman, then, who was born with a gift of poetry in the sixteenth century, was an unhappy woman, a woman at strife against herself. All the conditions of her life, all her own instincts, were hostile to the state of mind which is needed to set free whatever is in the brain. But what is the state of mind that is most propitious to the act of creation, I asked? Can one come by any notion of the state that furthers and makes possible that strange activity? Here I opened the volume containing the Tragedies of Shakespeare. What was Shakespeare's state of mind, for instance, when he wrote *Lear* and *Antony and Cleopatra*? It was certainly the state of mind most favourable to poetry that there has ever existed. But Shakespeare himself said nothing about it. We only know casually and by chance that he "never blotted a line." Nothing indeed was ever said by the artist himself about his state of mind until the eighteenth century perhaps. Rousseau perhaps began it. At any rate, by the nineteenth century self-consciousness had developed so far that it was the habit for men of letters to describe their minds in confessions and autobiographies. Their lives also were written, and their letters were printed after their deaths. Thus, though we do not know what Shakespeare went through when he wrote *Lear*, we do know what Carlyle went through when he wrote *The French Revolution*; what Flaubert went through when he wrote *Madame Bovary*; what Keats was going through when he tried to write poetry against the coming of death and the indifference of the world.

And one gathers from this enormous modern literature of confession and self-analysis that to write a work of genius is almost always a feat of prodigious difficulty. Everything is against the likelihood that it will come from the writer's mind whole and entire. Generally material circumstances are against it. Dogs will bark; people will interrupt; money must be made; health will break down. Further, accentuating all these difficulties and making them harder to bear is the world's notorious indifference. It does not ask people to write poems and novels and histories; it does not need them. It does not care whether Flaubert finds the right word or whether Carlyle scrupulously verifies this or that fact. Naturally, it will not pay for what it does not want. And so the writer, Keats, Flaubert, Carlyle, suffers, especially in the creative years of youth, every form of distraction and discouragement. A curse, a cry of agony, rises from those books of analysis and confession. "Mighty poets in their misery dead"—that is the burden of their song. If

[5] "That dog is mine."

anything comes through in spite of all this, it is a miracle, and probably no book is born entire and uncrippled as it was conceived.

But for women, I thought, looking at the empty shelves, these difficulties were infinitely more formidable. In the first place, to have a room of her own, let alone a quiet room or a sound-proof room, was out of the question, unless her parents were exceptionally rich or very noble, even up to the beginning of the nineteenth century. Since her pin money, which depended on the good will of her father, was only enough to keep her clothed, she was debarred from such alleviations as came even to Keats or Tennyson or Carlyle, all poor men, from a walking tour, a little journey to France, from the separate lodging which, even if it were miserable enough, sheltered them from the claims and tyrannies of their families. Such material difficulties were formidable; but much worse were the immaterial. The indifference of the world which Keats and Flaubert and other men of genius have found so hard to bear was in her case not indifference but hostility. The world did not say to her as it said to them, Write if you choose; it makes no difference to me. The world said with a guffaw, Write? What's the good of your writing? Here the psychologists of Newnham and Girton might come to our help. I thought, looking again at the blank spaces on the shelves. For surely it is time that the effect of discouragement upon the mind of the artist should be measured, as I have seen a dairy company measure the effect of ordinary milk and Grade A milk upon the body of the rat. They set two rats in cages side by side, and of the two one was furtive, timid and small, and the other was glossy, bold and big. Now what food do we feed women as artists upon? I asked, remembering, I suppose, that dinner of prunes and custard. To answer that question I had only to open the evening paper and to read that Lord Birkenhead is of opinion—but really I am not going to trouble to copy out Lord Birkenhead's opinion upon the writing of women. What Dean Inge says I will leave in peace.[6] The Harley Street specialist may be allowed to rouse the echoes of Harley Street with his vociferations without raising a hair on my head. I will quote, however, Mr. Oscar Browning, because Mr. Oscar Browning was a great figure in Cambridge at one time, and used to examine the students at Girton and Newnham. Mr. Oscar Browning was wont to declare "that the impression left on his mind, after looking over any set of examination papers, was that, irrespective of the marks he might give, the best woman was intellectually the inferior of the worst man." After saying that Mr. Browning went back to his rooms—and it is this sequel that endears him and makes him a human figure of some bulk and majesty—he went back to his rooms and found a stable-boy lying on the sofa—"a mere skeleton, his cheeks were cavernous and sallow, his teeth were black, and he did not appear to have the full use of his limbs. . . . 'That's Arthur' [said Mr. Browning]. 'He's a dear boy really and most high-minded.'" The two pictures always seem to me to complete each other. And happily in this age of biography the two pictures often

⁶William Ralph Inge (1860–1954). Dean of St. Paul's, London, who contributed a column to the London *Evening Standard*.

do complete each other, so that we are able to interpret the opinions of great men not only by what they say, but by what they do.

But though this is possible now, such opinions coming from the lips of important people must have been formidable enough even fifty years ago. Let us suppose that a father from the highest motives did not wish his daughter to leave home and become writer, painter or scholar. "See what Mr. Oscar Browning says," he would say; and there was not only Mr. Oscar Browning; there was the *Saturday Review;* there was Mr. Greg—the "essentials of a woman's being," said Mr. Greg emphatically, "are that *they are supported by, and they minister to, men"*—there was an enormous body of masculine opinion to the effect that nothing could be expected of women intellectually. Even if her father did not read out loud these opinions, any girl could read them for herself; and the reading, even in the nineteenth century, must have lowered her vitality, and told profoundly upon her work. There would always have been that assertion—you cannot do this, you are incapable of doing that—to protest against, to overcome. Probably for a novelist this germ is no longer of much effect; for there have been women novelists of merit. But for painters it must still have some sting in it; and for musicians, I imagine, is even now active and poisonous in the extreme. The woman composer stands where the actress stood in the time of Shakespeare. Nick Greene, I thought, remembering the story I had made about Shakespeare's sister, said that a woman acting put him in mind of a dog dancing. Johnson repeated the phrase two hundred years later of women preaching. And here, I said, opening a book about music, we have the very words used again in this year of grace, 1928, of women who try to write music. "Of Mlle. Germaine Tailleferre one can only repeat Dr. Johnson's dictum concerning a woman preacher, transposed into terms of music. 'Sir, a woman's composing is like a dog's walking on his hind legs. It is not done well, but you are surprised to find it done at all.'"[7] So accurately does history repeat itself.

Thus, I concluded, shutting Mr. Oscar Browning's life and pushing away the rest, it is fairly evident that even in the nineteenth century a woman was not encouraged to be an artist. On the contrary, she was snubbed, slapped, lectured and exhorted. Her mind must have been strained and her vitality lowered by the need of opposing this, of disproving that. For here again we come within range of that very interesting and obscure masculine complex which has had so much influence upon the woman's movement; that deep-seated desire, not so much that *she* shall be inferior as that *he* shall be superior, which plants him wherever one looks, not only in front of the arts, but barring the way to politics too, even when the risk to himself seems infinitesimal and the suppliants humble and devoted. Even Lady Bessborough, I remembered, with all her passion for politics, must humbly bow herself and write to Lord Granville Leveson-Gower: ". . . notwithstanding all my violence in politics and talking so much on that subject, I perfectly agree with you that no woman has any business to meddle with that or any other serious business,

---

[7] *A Survey of Contemporary Music,* Cecil Gray, p. 246. [Woolf's note.]

farther than giving her opinion (if she is ask'd)." And so she goes on to spend her enthusiasm where it meets with no obstacle whatsoever upon that immensely important subject, Lord Granville's maiden speech in the House of Commons. The spectacle is certainly a strange one, I thought. The history of men's opposition to women's emancipation is more interesting perhaps than the story of that emancipation itself. An amusing book might be made of it if some young student at Girton or Newnham would collect examples and deduce a theory—but she would need thick gloves on her hands, and bars to protect her of solid gold.

But what is amusing now, I recollected, shutting Lady Bessborough, had to be taken in desperate earnest once. Opinions that one now pastes in a book labelled cock-a-doodle-dum and keeps for reading to select audiences on summer nights once drew tears, I can assure you. Among your grandmothers and great-grandmothers there were many that wept their eyes out. Florence Nightingale shrieked aloud in her agony.[8] Moreover, it is all very well for you, who have got yourselves to college and enjoy sitting-rooms—or is it only bed-sitting-rooms?—of your own to say that genius should disregard such opinions; that genius should be above caring what is said of it. Unfortunately, it is precisely the men or women of genius who mind most what is said of them. Remember Keats. Remember the words he had cut on his tombstone. Think of Tennyson; think—but I need hardly multiply instances of the undeniable, if very unfortunate, fact that it is the nature of the artist to mind excessively what is said about him. Literature is strewn with the wreckage of men who have minded beyond reason the opinions of others.

And this susceptibility of theirs is doubly unfortunate, I thought, returning again to my original enquiry into what state of mind is most propitious for creative work, because the mind of an artist, in order to achieve the prodigious effort of freeing whole and entire the work that is in him, must be incandescent, like Shakespeare's mind, I conjectured, looking at the book which lay open at *Antony and Cleopatra*. There must be no obstacle in it, no foreign matter unconsumed.

For though we say that we know nothing about Shakespeare's state of mind, even as we say that, we are saying something about Shakespeare's state of mind. The reason perhaps why we know so little of Shakespeare—compared with Donne or Ben Jonson or Milton—is that his grudges and spites and antipathies are hidden from us. We are not held up by some "revelation" which reminds us of the writer. All desire to protest, to preach, to proclaim an injury, to pay off a score, to make the world the witness of some hardship or grievance was fired out of him and consumed. Therefore his poetry flows from him free and unimpeded. If ever a human being got his work expressed completely, it was Shakespeare. If ever a mind was incandescent, unimpeded, I thought, turning again to the bookcase, it was Shakespeare's mind.

[8] See *Cassandra*, by Florence Nightingale, printed in *The Cause*, by R. Strachey. [Woolf's note.]

MIKHAIL BAKHTIN

Heteroglossia in the Novel

From *Discourse in the Novel*

1934–1935

Though an acutely sensitive reader and a prolific and thought-provoking writer, the Russian professor and critic Mikhail Bakhtin (1895–1975) was not well known until almost fifty years after his most influential works were first written. His work both draws on and critiques the Russian formalists and Marxists of his era, but his anti-authoritarian attitude clashed with Soviet-era politics and kept him out of favor with the academy and the authorities for many years. He spent many of his most productive years exiled from prestigious academic centers in Russia, where he found it difficult to publish or otherwise disseminate his ideas. Not until the 1980s, after his work began to be widely translated and read in Europe and America, did his theories gain currency among literary critics and theorists worldwide. He is best known for popularizing the concept of heteroglossia *("the voice of the other") and for describing literature as existing on a continuum between* monologic, *expressing one controlling voice and viewpoint, and* dialogic, *suggesting a dialogue between various perspectives.*

As the following excerpt illustrates, Bakhtin found fault with the prevailing view of the novel, which saw the form as necessarily authoritarian and single-voiced. For him, the novel, and particularly the comic novel, was the site of some of the most radical examples of dialogism to be found in literature. He saw a clever critique of accepted social order in the "parodic stylization" of various voices in prose fiction, voices representing particular classes, professions, or other special interests. Here he explains three particular types of dialogism: the narrator standing in dialogic relationship to the author, often expressing sentiments with which the author disagrees; the heteroglossic language of (and surrounding) particular characters; and the use of "incorporated genres" within fiction, as when a newspaper article or a song lyric is reproduced within a novel. By analyzing examples from Dickens's Little Dorritt, *among other novels, Bakhtin demonstrates how parodies of ceremonial speech and oratory enter descriptive passages written in otherwise plain style, creating dissonance in readers and leading them to see the hypocrisy of "official" sentiments concerning the rich and powerful.*

At a time when most formal criticism was examining works of lyric poetry and the American New Critics particularly were extolling the virtues of poetic complexity and ambiguity (see Cleanth Brooks, p. 465, and John Crowe Ransom, p. 448), Bakhtin swam against the critical tide. He proclaimed lyric poetry to be the most authoritarian and monologic form of literature, for the ambiguities and uncertainties within it are most often worked out within the internal discourse of a single, controlling authorial consciousness, leaving readers little room for their own interpretations. Railing against the "poetic absolutism" he loathed, Bakhtin elevated prose fiction within his criticism and even went so far as to claim that works of poetry demonstrating heteroglossia were really more like prose. Bakhtin's theory is the reverse of Ransom's later dictum that "A poem is . . . a democratic state, whereas a prose discourse . . . is a totalitarian state" (p. 456).

THE COMPOSITIONAL forms for appropriating and organizing heteroglossia in the novel, worked out during the long course of the genre's historical development, are extremely heterogeneous in their variety of generic types. Each such compositional form is connected with particular stylistic possibilities, and demands particular forms for the artistic treatment of the heteroglot "languages" introduced into it. We will pause here only on the most basic forms that are typical for the majority of novel types.

The so-called comic novel makes available a form for appropriating and organizing heteroglossia that is both externally very vivid and at the same time historically profound: its classic representatives in England were Fielding, Smollett, Sterne, Dickens, Thackeray and others, and in Germany Hippel and Jean Paul.

In the English comic novel we find a comic-parodic re-processing of almost all the levels of literary language, both conversational and written, that were current at the time. Almost every novel we mentioned above as being a classic representative of this generic type is an encyclopedia of all strata and forms of literary language: depending on the subject being represented, the story-line parodically reproduces first the forms of parliamentary eloquence, then the eloquence of the court, or particular forms of parliamentary protocol, or court protocol, or forms used by reporters in newspaper articles, or the dry business language of the City, or the dealings of speculators, or the pedantic speech of scholars, or the high epic style, or Biblical style, or the style of the hypocritical moral sermon or finally the way one or another concrete and socially determined personality, the subject of the story, happens to speak.

This usually parodic stylization of generic, professional and other strata of language is sometimes interrupted by the direct authorial word (usually as an expression of pathos, of Sentimental or idyllic sensibility), which directly embodies (without any refracting) semantic and axiological intentions of the author. But the primary source of language usage in the comic novel is a highly specific treatment of "common language." This "common language"—usually the average norm of spoken and written language for a given social group—is taken by the author precisely as the *common view*, as the verbal approach to people and things normal for a given sphere of society, as the *going point of view* and the going *value*. To one degree or another, the author distances himself from this common language, he steps back and objectifies it, forcing his own intentions to refract and diffuse themselves through the medium of this common view that has become embodied in language (a view that is always superficial and frequently hypocritical).

The relationship of the author to a language conceived as the common view is not static—it is always found in a state of movement and oscillation that is more or less alive (this sometimes is a rhythmic oscillation): the author exaggerates, now strongly, now weakly, one or another aspect of the "common language," sometimes abruptly exposing its inadequacy to its object and sometimes, on the contrary, becoming one with it, maintaining an almost imperceptible distance, sometimes even directly forcing it to reverberate with his own "truth," which occurs when the author completely merges his own voice with the common view. As a consequence of such a merger, the aspects of common language, which in the given situation had been parodically exaggerated or had been treated as mere things, undergo change. The comic style demands of the author a lively to-and-fro movement in his relation to language, it demands a continual shifting of the distance between author and language, so that first some, then other aspects of language are thrown into relief. If such were not the case, the style would be monotonous or would require a greater individualization of the narrator—would, in any case, require a quite different means for introducing and organizing heteroglossia.

Against this same backdrop of the "common language," of the impersonal, going opinion, one can also isolate in the comic novel those parodic stylizations of generic, professional and other languages we have mentioned, as well as compact masses of direct authorial discourse—pathos-filled, moral-didactic, sentimental-elegiac or idyllic. In the comic novel the direct authorial word is thus realized in direct, unqualified stylizations of poetic genres (idyllic, elegiac, etc.) or stylizations of rhetorical genres (the pathetic, the moral-didactic). Shifts from common language to parodying of generic and other languages and shifts to the direct authorial word may be gradual, or may be on the contrary quite abrupt. Thus does the system of language work in the comic novel.

We will pause for analysis on several examples from Dickens, from his novel *Little Dorrit*.

(1) The conference was held at four or five o'clock in the afternoon, when all the region of Harley Street, Cavendish Square, was resonant of carriage-wheels and double-knocks. It had reached this point when Mr. Merdle came home *from his daily occupation of causing the British name to be more and more respected in all parts of the civilized globe capable of appreciation of wholewide commercial enterprise and gigantic combinations of skill and capital.* For, though nobody knew with the least precision what Mr. Merdle's business was, except that it

was to coin money, these were the terms in which everybody defined it on all ceremonious occasions, and which it was the last new
polite reading of the parable of the camel and the needle's eye to accept without inquiry. [book 1, ch. 33]

The italicized portion represents a parodic stylization of the language of
ceremonial speeches (in parliaments and at banquets). The shift into this style
is prepared for by the sentence's construction, which from the very beginning is kept within bounds by a somewhat ceremonious epic tone. Further
on—and already in the language of the author (and consequently in a different style)—the parodic meaning of the ceremoniousness of Merdle's labors becomes apparent: such a characterization turns out to be "another's
speech," to be taken only in quotation marks ("these were the terms in which
everybody defined it on all ceremonious occasions").

Thus the speech of another is introduced into the author's discourse (the
story) in *concealed form,* that is, without any of the *formal* markers usually accompanying such speech, whether direct or indirect. But this is not just another's speech in the same "language"—it is another's utterance in a language that is itself "other" to the author as well, in the archaicized language
of oratorical genres associated with hypocritical official celebrations.

(2) In a day or two it was announced to all the town, that Edmund
Sparkler, Esquire, son-in-law of the eminent Mr. Merdle of world-
wide renown, was made one of the Lords of the Circumlocution Office; and proclamation was issued, to all true believers, that this admirable *appointment was to be hailed as a graceful and gracious mark of
homage, rendered by the graceful and gracious Decimus, to that commercial
interest which must ever in a great commercial country—and all the rest
of it, with blast of trumpet.* So, bolstered by this mark of Government
homage, the *wonderful* Bank and all the other *wonderful* undertakings
went on and went up; and gapers came to Harley Street, Cavendish
Square, only to look at the house where the golden wonder lived.
[book 2, ch. 12]

Here, in the italicized portion, another's speech in another's (official-
ceremonial) language is openly introduced as indirect discourse. But it is surrounded by the hidden, diffused speech of another (in the same official-
ceremonial language) that clears the way for the introduction of a form more
easily perceived *as* another's speech and that can reverberate more fully as
such. The clearing of the way comes with the word "Esquire," characteristic
of official speech, added to Sparkler's name; the final confirmation that this is
another's speech comes with the epithet "wonderful." This epithet does not
of course belong to the author but to that same "general opinion" that had
created the commotion around Merdle's inflated enterprises.

(3) It was a dinner to provoke an appetite, though he had not had
one. The rarest dishes, sumptuously cooked and sumptuously
served; the choicest fruits, the most exquisite wines; marvels of

workmanship in gold and silver, china and glass; innumerable things delicious to the senses of taste, smell, and sight, were insinuated into its composition. *O, what a wonderful man this Merdle, what a great man, what a master man, how blessedly and enviably endowed*—in one word, what a rich man! [book 2, ch. 12]

The beginning is a parodic stylization of high epic style. What follows is an enthusiastic glorification of Merdle, a chorus of his admirers in the form of the concealed speech of another (the italicized portion). The whole point here is to expose the real basis for such glorification, which is to unmask the chorus' hypocrisy: "wonderful," "great," "master," "endowed" can all be replaced by the single word "rich." This act of authorial unmasking, which is openly accomplished within the boundaries of a single simple sentence, merges with the unmasking of another's speech. The ceremonial emphasis on glorification is complicated by a second emphasis that is indignant, ironic, and this is the one that ultimately predominates in the final unmasking words of the sentence.

We have before us a typical double-accented, double-styled *hybrid construction.*

What we are calling a hybrid construction is an utterance that belongs, by its grammatical (syntactic) and compositional markers, to a single speaker, but that actually contains mixed within it two utterances, two speech manners, two styles, two "languages," two semantic and axiological belief systems. We repeat, there is no formal—compositional and syntactic—boundary between these utterances, styles, languages, belief systems; the division of voices and languages takes place within the limits of a single syntactic whole, often within the limits of a simple sentence. It frequently happens that even one and the same word will belong simultaneously to two languages, two belief systems that intersect in a hybrid construction—and, consequently, the word has two contradictory meanings, two accents (examples below). As we shall see, hybrid constructions are of enormous significance in novel style.[1]

(4) But Mr. Tite Barnacle was a buttoned-up man, and *consequently* a weighty one. [book 2, ch. 12]

The above sentence is an example of *pseudo-objective motivation,* one of the forms for concealing another's speech—in this example, the speech of "current opinion." If judged by the formal markers above, the logic motivating the sentence seems to belong to the author, i.e., he is formally at one with it; but in actual fact, the motivation lies within the subjective belief system of his characters, or of general opinion.

Pseudo-objective motivation is generally characteristic of novel style,[2] since it is one of the manifold forms for concealing another's speech in hybrid

[1] For more detail on hybrid constructions and their significance, see ch. 4 of the present essay. [All notes are Bakhtin's unless otherwise indicated.]
[2] Such a device is unthinkable in the epic.

constructions. Subordinate conjunctions and link words ("thus," "because," "for the reason that," "in spite of" and so forth), as well as words used to maintain a logical sequence ("therefore," "consequently," etc.) lose their direct authorial intention, take on the flavor of someone else's language, become refracted or even completely reified.

Such motivation is especially characteristic of comic style, in which someone else's speech is dominant (the speech of concrete persons, or, more often, a collective voice).[3]

> (5) As a vast fire will fill the air to a great distance with its roar, so the sacred flame which the mighty Barnacles had fanned caused the air to resound more and more with the name of Merdle. It was deposited on every lip, and carried into every ear. There never was, there never had been, there never again should be, such a man as Mr. Merdle. Nobody, as aforesaid, knew what he had done; but *everybody knew him to be the greatest that had appeared.* [book 2, ch. 13]

Here we have an epic, "Homeric" introduction (parodic, of course) into whose frame the crowd's glorification of Merdle has been inserted (concealed speech of another in another's language). We then get direct authorial discourse; however, the author gives an objective tone to this "aside" by suggesting that "everybody knew" (the italicized portion). It is as if even the author himself did not doubt the fact.

> (6) That illustrious man and great national ornament, Mr. Merdle, continued his shining course. It began to be widely understood that one who had done society the admirable service *of making so much money out of it,* could not be suffered to remain a commoner. A baronetcy was spoken of with confidence; a peerage was frequently mentioned. [book 2, ch. 24]

We have here the same fictive solidarity with the hypocritically ceremonial general opinion of Merdle. All the epithets referring to Merdle in the first sentences derive from general opinion, that is, they are the concealed speech of another. The second sentence—"it began to be widely understood," etc.—is kept within the bounds of an emphatically objective style, representing not subjective opinion but the admission of an objective and completely indisputable fact. The epithet "who had done society the admirable service" is completely at the level of common opinion, repeating its official glorification, but the subordinate clause attached to that glorification ("of making so much money out of it") are the words of the author himself (as if put in parentheses in the quotation). The main sentence then picks up again at the level of common opinion. We have here a typical hybrid construction, where the subordinate clause is in direct authorial speech and the main clause in someone else's speech. The main and subordinate clauses are constructed in different semantic and axiological conceptual systems.

---

[3] Cf. the grotesque pseudo-objective motivations in Gogol.

The whole of this portion of the novel's action, which centers around Merdle and the persons associated with him, is depicted in the language (or more accurately, the languages) of hypocritically ceremonial common opinion about Merdle, and at the same time there is a parodic stylization of that everyday language of banal society gossip, or of the ceremonial language of official pronouncements and banquet speeches, or the high epic style or Biblical style. This atmosphere around Merdle, the common opinion about him and his enterprises, infects the positive heroes of the novel as well, in particular the sober Pancks, and forces him to invest his entire estate—his own, and Little Dorrit's—in Merdle's hollow enterprises.

> (7) Physician had engaged to break the intelligence in Harley Street. Bar could not at once return to his inveiglements of the most enlightened and remarkable jury he had ever seen in that box, with whom, he could tell his learned friend, no shallow sophistry would go down, and no unhappily abused professional tact and skill prevail (this was the way he meant to begin with them); so he said he would go too, and would loiter to and fro near the house while his friend was inside. [book 2, ch. 25, mistakenly given as ch. 15 in Russian text, tr.]

Here we have a clear example of hybrid construction where within the frame of authorial speech (informative speech)—the beginning of a speech prepared by the lawyer has been inserted, "The Bar could not at once return to his inveiglements . . . of the jury . . . so he said he would go too. . . ." etc.—while this speech is simultaneously a fully developed epithet attached to the subject of the author's speech, that is, "jury." The word "jury" enters into the context of informative authorial speech (in the capacity of a necessary object to the word "inveiglements") as well as into the context of the parodic-stylized speech of the lawyer. The author's word "inveiglement" itself emphasizes the parodic nature of the re-processing of the lawyer's speech, the hypocritical meaning of which consists precisely in the fact that it would be impossible to inveigle such a remarkable jury.

> (8) It followed that Mrs. Merdle, as a woman of fashion and good breeding *who had been sacrificed to wiles of a vulgar barbarian* (for Mr. Merdle was found out from the crown of his head to the sole of his foot, the moment he was found out in his pocket), must be actively championed by her order for her order's sake. [book 2, ch. 33]

This is an analogous hybrid construction, in which the definition provided by the general opinion of society—"a sacrifice to the wiles of a vulgar barbarian"—merges with authorial speech, exposing the hypocrisy and greed of common opinion.

So it is throughout Dickens' whole novel. His entire text is, in fact, everywhere dotted with quotation marks that serve to separate out little islands of scattered direct speech and purely authorial speech, washed by heteroglot waves from all sides. But it would have been impossible actually to insert such marks, since, as we have seen, one and the same word often figures both as the speech of the author and as the speech of another—and at the same time.

Another's speech—whether as storytelling, as mimicking, as the display of a thing in light of a particular point of view, as a speech deployed first in compact masses, then loosely scattered, a speech that is in most cases impersonal ("common opinion," professional and generic languages)—is at none of these points clearly separated from authorial speech: the boundaries are deliberately flexible and ambiguous, often passing through a single syntactic whole, often through a simple sentence, and sometimes even dividing up the main parts of a sentence. This varied *play with the boundaries of speech types,* languages and belief systems is one most fundamental aspects of comic style.

Comic style (of the English sort) is based, therefore, on the stratification of common language and on the possibilities available for isolating from these strata, to one degree or another, one's own intentions, without ever completely merging with them. *It is precisely the diversity of speech, and not the unity of a normative shared language, that is the ground of style.* It is true that such speech diversity does not exceed the boundaries of literary language conceived as a linguistic whole (that is, language defined by abstract linguistic markers), does not pass into an authentic heteroglossia and is based on an abstract notion of language as unitary (that is, it does not require knowledge of various dialects or languages). However a mere concern for language is but the abstract side of the concrete and active (i.e., dialogically engaged) understanding of the living heteroglossia that has been introduced into the novel and artistically organized within it.

In Dickens' predecessors, Fielding, Smollett and Sterne, the men who founded the English comic novel, we find the same parodic stylization of various levels and genres of literary language, but the distance between these levels and genres is greater than it is in Dickens and the exaggeration is stronger (especially in Sterne). The parodic and objectivized incorporation into their work of various types of literary language (especially in Sterne) penetrates the deepest levels of literary and ideological thought itself, resulting in a parody of the logical and expressive structure of any ideological discourse as such (scholarly, moral and rhetorical, poetic) that is almost as radical as the parody we find in Rabelais.

Literary parody understood in the narrow sense plays a fundamental role in the way language is structured in Fielding, Smollett and Sterne (the Richardsonian novel is parodied by the first two, and almost all contemporary novel-types are parodied by Sterne). Literary parody serves to distance the author still further from language, to complicate still further his relationship to the literary language of his time, especially in the novel's own territory. The novelistic discourse dominating a given epoch is itself turned into an object and itself becomes a means for refracting new authorial intentions.

Literary parody of dominant novel-types plays a large role in the history of the European novel. One could even say that the most important novelistic models and novel-types arose precisely during this parodic destruction of preceding novelistic worlds. This is true of the work of Cervantes, Mendoza, Grimmelshausen, Rabelais, Lesage and many others.

In Rabelais, whose influence on all novelistic prose (and in particular the comic novel) was very great, a parodic attitude toward almost all forms of ideological discourse—philosophical, moral, scholarly, rhetorical, poetic and in particular the pathos-charged forms of discourse (in Rabelais, pathos almost always is equivalent to lie)—was intensified to the point where it became a parody of the very act of conceptualizing anything in language. We might add that Rabelais taunts the deceptive human word by a parodic destruction of syntactic structures, thereby reducing to absurdity some of the logical and expressively accented aspects of words (for example, predication, explanations and so forth). Turning away from language (by means of language, of course), discrediting any direct or unmediated intentionality and expressive excess (any "weighty" seriousness) that might adhere in ideological discourse, presuming that all language is conventional and false, maliciously inadequate to reality—all this achieves in Rabelais almost the maximum purity possible in prose. But the truth that might oppose such falsity receives almost no direct intentional and verbal expression in Rabelais, it does not receive its *own* word—it reverberates only in the parodic and unmasking accents in which the lie is present. Truth is restored by reducing the lie to an absurdity, but truth itself does not seek words; she is afraid to entangle herself in the word, to soil herself in verbal pathos.

Rabelais' "philosophy of the word"—a philosophy expressed not as much in direct utterances as in stylistic practice—has had enormous influence on all consequent novel prose and in particular of the great representative forms of the comic novel; with that in mind we bring forward the purely Rabelaisian formulation of Sterne's Yorick, which might serve as an epigraph to the history of the most important stylistic lines of development in the European novel:

> For aught I know there might be some mixture of unlucky wit at the bottom of such Fracas:—For, to speak the truth, Yorick had an invincible dislike and opposition in his nature to gravity;—not to gravity as such;—for where gravity was wanted, he would be the most grave or serious of mortal men for days and weeks together;—but he was an enemy to the affectation of it, and declared open war against it, only as it appeared a cloak for ignorance, or for folly; and then, whenever it fell his way, however sheltered and protected, he seldom gave it much quarter.
>
> Sometimes, in his wild way of talking, he would say, That gravity was an errant scoundrel; and he would add,—of the most dangerous kind too,—because a sly one; and that, he verily believed, more honest, well-meaning people were bubbled out of their goods and money by it in one twelve-month, than by pocket-picking and shop-lifting in seven. In the naked temper which a merry heart discovered, he would say, There was no danger,—but to itself:—whereas the very essence of gravity was design, and conse-

quently decit;—'twas a taught trick to gain credit of the world for more sense and knowledge than a man was worth; and that, with all its pretensions,—it was no better, but often worse, than what a French wit had long ago defined it,—viz. A mysterious carriage of the body to cover the defects of the mind;—which definition of gravity, Yorick, with great imprudence, would say, deserved to be wrote in letters of gold. [Bakhtin does not locate citation; it is from *Tristram Shandy*, vol. 1, ch. 11, tr.]

Close to Rabelais, but in certain respects even exceeding him in the decisive influence he had on all of novelistic prose, is Cervantes. The English comic novel is permeated through and through with the spirit of Cervantes. It is no accident that this same Yorick, on his deathbed, quotes the words of Sancho Panza.

While the attitude toward language and toward its stratification (generic, professional and otherwise) among the German comic writers, in Hippel and especially in Jean Paul, is basically of the Sternean type, it is raised—as it is in Sterne himself—to the level of a purely philosophical problem, the very possibility of literary and ideological speech as such. The philosophical and ideological element in an author's attitude toward his own language forces into the background the play between intention and the concrete, primarily generic and ideological levels of literary language (cf. the reflection of just this in the aesthetic theories of Jean Paul).[4]

Thus the stratification of literary language, its speech diversity, is an indispensable prerequisite for comic style, whose elements are projected onto different linguistic planes while at the same time the intention of the author, refracted as it passes through these planes, does not wholly give itself up to any of them. It is as if the author has no language of his own, but does possess his own style, his own organic and unitary law governing the way he plays with languages and the way his own real semantic and expressive intentions are refracted within them. Of course this play with languages (and frequently the complete absence of a direct discourse of his own) in no sense degrades the general, deep-seated intentionality, the overarching ideological conceptualization of the work as a whole.

In the comic novel, the incorporation of heteroglossia and its stylistic utilization is characterized by two distinctive features:

(1) Incorporated into the novel are a multiplicity of "language" and verbal-ideological belief systems—generic, professional, class-and-interest-group (the language of the nobleman, the farmer, the merchant, the peasant); tendentious, everyday (the languages of rumour, of society chatter, servants' language) and so forth, but these languages are, it is true, kept primarily within the limits of the literary written and conversational language; at the

---

[4] Intellect as embodied in the forms and the methods of verbal and ideological thought (i.e., the linguistic horizon of normal human intellectual activity) becomes in Jean Paul something infinitely petty and ludicrous when seen in the light of "reason." His humor results from play with intellectual activity and its forms.

same time these languages are not, in most cases, consolidated into fixed persons (heroes, storytellers) but rather are incorporated in an impersonal form "from the author," alternating (while ignoring precise formal boundaries) with direct authorial discourse.

(2) The incorporated languages and socio-ideological belief systems, while of course utilized to refract the author's intentions, are unmasked and destroyed as something false, hypocritical, greedy, limited, narrowly rationalistic, inadequate to reality. In most cases these languages—already fully formed, officially recognized, reigning languages that are authoritative and reactionary—are (in real life) doomed to death and displacement. Therefore what predominates in the novel are various forms and degrees of *parodic stylization* of incorporated languages, a stylization that, in the most radical, most Rabelaisian[5] representatives of this novel-type (Sterne and Jean Paul), verges on a rejection of any straightforward and unmediated seriousness (true seriousness is the destruction of all false seriousness, not only in its pathos-charged expression but in its Sentimental one as well);[6] that is, it limits itself to a principled criticism of the word as such.

There is a fundamental difference between this comic form for incorporating and organizing heteroglossia in the novel and other forms that are defined by their use of a personified and concretely posited author (written speech) or teller (oral speech).

Play with a posited author is also characteristic of the comic novel (Sterne, Hippel, Jean Paul), a heritage from *Don Quixote*. But in these examples such play is purely a compositional device, which strengthens the general trend toward relativity, objectification and the parodying of literary forms and genres.

The posited author and teller assume a completely different significance where they are incorporated as carriers of a particular verbal-ideological linguistic belief system, with a particular point of view on the world and its events, with particular value judgments and intonations—"particular" both as regards the author, his real direct discourse, and also as regards "normal" literary narrative and language.

This particularity, this distancing of the posited author or teller from the real author and from conventional literary expectations, may occur in differing degrees and may vary in its nature. But in every case a particular belief system belonging to someone else, a particular point of view on the world belonging to someone else, is used by the author because it is highly productive, that is, it is able on the one hand to show the object of representation in a new light (to reveal new sides or dimensions in it) and on the other hand to illuminate in a new way the "expected" literary horizon, that horizon against which the particularities of the teller's tale are perceivable.

---

[5] It is of course impossible in the strict sense to include Rabelais himself—either chronologically or in terms of his essential character—among the representatives of comic novelists.

[6] Nevertheless sentimentality and "high seriousness" is not completely eliminated (especially in Jean Paul).

For example: Belkin was chosen (or better, created) by Pushkin because of his particular "unpoetic" point of view on objects and plots that are traditionally poetic (the highly characteristic and calculated use of the *Romeo and Juliet* plot in "Mistress into Maid" or the romantic "Dances of Death" in "The Coffinmaker"). Belkin, who is on the same level with those narrators-at-third-remove out of whose mouths he has taken his stories, is a "prosaic" man, a man without a drop of poetic pathos. The successful "prosaic" resolutions of the plots and the very means of the story's telling destroy any expectation of traditional poetic effects. The fruitfulness of the prosaic quality in Belkin's point of view consists in just this failure to understand poetic pathos.

Maxim Maximych in *A Hero of Our Time,* Rudy Panko, the narrators of "Nose" and "Overcoat," Dostoevsky's chroniclers, folkloric narrators and storytellers who are themselves characters in Melnikov-Pechersky and Mamin-Sibiryak, the folkloric and down-to-earth storytellers in Leskov, the character-narrators in populist literature and finally the narrators in Symbolist and post-Symbolist prose (in Remizov, Zamyatin and others)—with all their widely differing forms of narration (oral and written), with all their differing narrative languages (literary, professional, social-and-special-interest-group language, everyday, slang, dialects and others)—everywhere, they recommend themselves as specific and limited verbal ideological points of view, belief systems, opposed to the literary expectations and points of view that constitute the background needed to perceive them; but these narrators are productive precisely *because* of this very limitedness and specificity.

The speech of such narrators is always *another's speech* (as regards the real or potential direct discourse of the author) and in *another's language* (i.e., insofar as it is a particular variant of the literary language that clashes with the language of the narrator).

Thus we have in this case "nondirect speaking"—not *in* language but *through* language, through the linguistic medium of another—and consequently through a refraction of authorial intentions.

The author manifests himself and his point of view not only in his effect on the narrator, on his speech and his language (which are to one or another extent objectivized, objects of display) but also in his effect on the subject of the story—as a point of view that differs from the point of view of the narrator. Behind the narrator's story we read a second story, the author's story; he is the one who tells us how the narrator tells stories, and also tells us about the narrator himself. We acutely sense two levels at each moment in the story; one, the level of the narrator, a belief system filled with his objects, meanings and emotional expressions, and the other, the level of the author, who speaks (albeit in a refracted way) by means of this story and through this story. The narrator himself, with *his* own discourse, enters into this authorial belief system along with what is actually being told. We puzzle out the author's emphases that overlie the subject of the story, while we puzzle out the story itself and the figure of the narrator as he is revealed in the process of telling his tale. If one fails to sense this second level, the intentions and accents of the author himself, then one has failed to understand the work.

As we have said above, the narrator's story or the story of the posited author is structured against the background of normal literary language, the expected literary horizon. Every moment of the story has a conscious relationship with this normal language and its belief system, is in fact set against them, and set against them *dialogically*: one point of view opposed to another, one evaluation opposed to another, one accent opposed to another (i.e., they are not contrasted as two abstractly linguistic phenomena). This interaction, this dialogic tension between two languages and two belief systems, permits authorial intentions to be realized in such a way that we can acutely sense their presence at every point in the work. The author is not to be found in the language of the narrator, not in the normal literary language to which the story opposes itself (although a given story may be closer to a given language)—but rather, the author utilizes now one language, now another, in order to avoid giving himself up wholly to either of them; he makes use of this verbal give-and-take, this dialogue of languages at every point in his work, in order that he himself might remain as it were neutral with regard to language, a third party in a quarrel between two people (although he might be a *biased* third party).

All forms involving a narrator or a posited author signify to one degree or another by their presence the author's freedom from a unitary and singular language, a freedom connected with the relativity of literary and language systems; such forms open up the possibility of never having to define oneself in language, the possibility of translating one's own intentions from one linguistic system to another, of fusing "the language of truth" with "the language of the everyday," of saying "I am me" in someone else's language, and in my own language, "I am other."

Such a refracting of authorial intentions takes place in all these forms (the narrator's tale, the tale of a posited author or that of one of the characters); it is therefore possible to have in them, as in the comic novel, a variety of different distances between distinct aspects of the narrator's language and the author's language: the refraction may be at times greater, at times lesser, and in some aspects of language there may be an almost complete fusion of voices.

The next form for incorporating and organizing heteroglossia in the novel—a form that every novel without exception utilizes—is the language used by characters.

The language used by characters in the novel, how they speak, is verbally and semantically autonomous; each character's speech possesses its own belief system, since each is the speech of another in another's language; thus it may also refract authorial intentions and consequently may to a certain degree constitute a second language for the author. Moreover, the character speech almost always influences authorial speech (and sometimes powerfully so), sprinkling it with another's words (that is, the speech of a character perceived as the concealed speech of another) and in this way introducing into it stratification and speech diversity.

Thus even where there is no comic element, no parody, no irony and so forth, where there is no narrator, no posited author or narrating character, speech diversity and language stratification still serve as the basis for style in the novel. Even in those places where the author's voice seems at first glance to be unitary and consistent, direct and unmediately intentional, beneath that smooth single-languaged surface we can nevertheless uncover prose's three-dimensionality, its profound speech diversity, which enters the project of style and is its determining factor.

Thus the language and style of Turgenev's novels have the appearance of being single-languaged and pure. Even in Turgenev, however, this unitary language is very far from poetic absolutism. Substantial masses of this language are drawn into the battle between points of view, value judgments and emphases that the characters introduce into it; they are infected by mutually contradictory intentions and stratifications; words, sayings, expressions, definitions and epithets are scattered throughout it, infected with others' intentions with which the author is to some extent at odds, and through which his own personal intentions are refracted. We sense acutely the various distances between the author and various aspects of his language, which smack of the social universes and belief systems of others. We acutely sense in various aspects of his language varying degrees of the presence of the author and of his *most recent semantic instantiation.* In Turgenev, heteroglossia and language stratification serve as the most fundamental factors of style, and orchestrate an authorial truth of their own; the author's linguistic consciousness, his consciousness as a writer of prose, is thereby relativized.

In Turgenev, social heteroglossia enters the novel primarily in the direct speeches of his characters, in dialogues. But this heteroglossia, as we have said, is also diffused throughout the authorial speech that surrounds the characters, creating highly particularized *character zones* [*zony geroev*]. These zones are formed from the fragments of character speech [*polureč'*], from various forms for hidden transmission of someone else's word, from scattered words and sayings belonging to someone else's speech, from those invasions into authorial speech of others' expressive indicators (ellipsis, questions, exclamations). Such a character zone is the field of action for a character's voice, encroaching in one way or another upon the author's voice.

However—we repeat—in Turgenev, the novelistic orchestration of the theme is concentrated in direct dialogues; the characters do not create around themselves their own extensive or densely saturated zones, and in Turgenev fully developed, complex stylistic hybrids are relatively rare.

We pause here on several examples of diffuse heteroglossia in Turgenev.[7]

> (1) His name is Nikolai Petrovich Kirsanov. Some ten miles from the coaching-inn stands a respectable little property of his consisting of a couple of hundred serfs—or five thousand acres, as he expresses it now that he has divided up his land and let it to the peasants, and started a "farm." [*Fathers and Sons*, ch. 1]

Here the new expressions, characteristic of the era and in the style of the liberals, are put in quotation marks or otherwise "qualified."

---

[7] Citations from *Fathers and Sons* are from: Ivan Turgenev, *Fathers and Sons*, tr. Rosemary Edmonds (London: Penguin, 1965). [Note by Michael Holquist, Bakhtin's editor.]

(2) He was secretly beginning to feel irritated. Bazarov's complete indifference exasperated his aristocratic nature. *This son of a medico was not only self-assured: he actually returned abrupt and reluctant answers, and there was a churlish, almost insolant note in his voice.* [*Fathers and Sons*, ch. 4]

The third sentence of this paragraph, while being a part of the author's speech if judged by its formal syntactic markers, is at the same time in its choice of expressions ("this son of a medico") and in its emotional and expressive structure the hidden speech of someone else (Pavel Petrovich).

(3) Pavel Petrovich sat down at the table. He was wearing an elegant suit cut in the English fashion, and a gay little fez graced his head. The fez and the carelessly knotted cravat carried a suggestion of the more free life in the country but the stiff collar of his shirt—not white, it is true, but striped *as is correct for morning wear*—stood up as inexorably as ever against his well-shaven chin. [*Fathers and Sons*, ch. 5]

This ironic characterization of Pavel Petrovich's morning attire is consistent with the tone of a gentleman, precisely in the style of Pavel Petrovich. The statement "as is correct for morning wear" is not, of course, a simple authorial statement, but rather the norm of Pavel Petrovich's gentlemanly circle, conveyed ironically. One might with some justice put it in quotation marks. This is an example of a pseudo-objective underpinning.

(4) *Matvei Ilyich's suavity of demeanour was equalled only by his stately manner.* He had a gracious word for everyone—with an added shade of disgust in some cases and deference in others; he was gallant, "un vrai chevalier français," to all the ladies, and was continually bursting into hearty resounding laughter, in which no one else took part, as befits a high official. [*Fathers and Sons*, ch. 14]

Here we have an analogous case of an ironic characterization given from the point of view of the high official himself. Such is the nature of this form of pseudo-objective underpinning: "as befits a high official."

(5) The following morning Nezhdanov betook himself to Sipyagin's town residence, and there, in a magnificent study, filled with furniture of a severe style, *in full harmony with the dignity of a liberal politician and modern gentleman.* . . . [*Virgin Soil*, ch. 4]

This is an analogous pseudo-objective construction.

(6) Semyon Petrovich was in the ministry of the Court, he had the title of a *kammeryunker. He was prevented by his patriotism from joining the diplomatic service,* for which he seemed destined by everything, his education, his knowledge of the world, his popularity with women, and his very appearance. . . . [*Virgin Soil*, ch. 5][8]

---

[8]Citations from *Virgin Soil* are from: Ivan Turgenev, *Virgin Soil*, tr. Constance Garnett (New York: Grove Press, n.d.). [Note by Michael Holquist, Bakhtin's editor.]

The motivation for refusing a diplomatic career is pseudo-objective. The entire characterization is consistent in tone and given from the point of view of Kallomyetsev himself, fused with his direct speech, being—at least judging by its syntactic markers—a subordinate clause attached to authorial speech ("for which he seemed destined by everything . . . mais quitter la Russie!" and so forth).

> (7) Kallomyetsev had come to S—— Province on a two months' leave to look after his property, that is to say, "to scare some and squeeze others." *Of course, there's no doing anything without that.* [*Virgin Soil*, ch. 5]

The conclusion of the paragraph is a characteristic example of a pseudo-objective statement. Precisely in order to give it the appearance of an objective authorial judgment, it is not put in quotation marks, as are the preceding words of Kallomyetsev himself; it is incorporated into authorial speech and deliberately placed directly after Kallomyetsev's own words.

> (8) But Kallomyetsev deliberately stuck his round eyeglass between his nose and his eyebrow, and stared at the [snit of a] *student who dared not share* his "apprehensions." [*Virgin Soil*, ch. 7]

This is a typical hybrid construction. Not only the subordinate clause but also the direct object ("the [snit of a] student") of the main authorial sentence is rendered in Kallomyetsev's tone. The choice of words ("snit of a student," "dared not share") are determined by Kallomyetsev's irritated intonation, and at the same time, in the context of authorial speech, these words are permeated with the ironic intonation of the author; therefore the construction has two accents (the author's ironic transmission, and a mimicking of the irritation of the character).

Finally, we adduce examples of an intrusion of the emotional aspects of someone else's speech into the syntactic system of authorial speech (ellipsis, questions, exclamations).

> (9) Strange was the state of his mind. In the last two days so many new sensations, new faces. . . . For the first time in his life he had come close to a girl, whom, in all probability, he loved; he was present at the beginning of the thing to which, in all probability, all his energies were consecrated. . . . Well? was he rejoicing? No. Was he wavering, afraid, confused? Oh, certainly not. Was he at least, feeling that tension of his whole being, that impulse forward into the front ranks of the battle, to be expected as the struggle grew near? No again. Did he believe, then, in this cause? Did he believe in his own love? "Oh, damned artistic temperament! sceptic!" his lips murmured inaudibly. Why this weariness, this disinclination to speak even, without shrieking and raving? What inner voice did he want to stifle with those ravings? [*Virgin Soil*, ch. 18]

Here we have, in essence, a form of a character's quasi-direct discourse [*nesobstvenno-prjamaja reč'*]. Judging by its syntactic markers, it is authorial speech, but its entire emotional structure belongs to Nezhdanov. This is his inner speech, but transmitted in a way regulated by the author, *with provocative questions from the author and with ironically debunking reservations* ("in all probability"), although Nezhdanov's emotional overtones are preserved.

Such a form for transmitting inner speech is common in Turgenev (and is generally one of the most widespread forms for transmitting inner speech in the novel). This form introduces order and stylistic symmetry into the disorderly and impetuous flow of a character's internal speech (a disorder and impetuosity would otherwise have to be re-processed into direct speech) and, moreover, through its syntactic (third-person) and basic stylistic markers (lexicological and other), such a form permits another's inner speech to merge, in an organic and structured way, with a context belonging to the author. But at the same time it is precisely this form that permits us to preserve the expressive structure of the character's inner speech, its inability to exhaust itself in words, its flexibility, which would be absolutely impossible within the dry and logical form of indirect discourse [*kosvennaja reč'*]. Precisely these features make this form the most convenient for transmitting the inner speech of characters. It is of course a hybrid form, for the author's voice may be present in varying degrees of activity and may introduce into the transmitted speech a second accent of its own (ironic, irritated and so on).

The same hybridization, mixing of accents and erasing of boundaries between authorial speech and the speech of others is also present in other forms for transmitting characters' speech. With only three templates for speech transcription (direct speech [*prjamaja reč'*], indirect speech [*kosvennaja reč'*] and quasi-direct speech [*nesobstvenno-prjamaja reč'*]) a great diversity is nevertheless made possible in the treatment of character speech—i.e., the way characters overlap and infect each other—the main thing being how the authorial context succeeds in exploiting the various means for replicating frames and re-stratifying them.

The examples we have offered from Turgenev provide a typical picture of the character's role in stratifying the language of the novel and incorporating heteroglossia into it. A character in a novel always has, as we have said, a zone of his own, his own sphere of influence on the authorial context surrounding him, a sphere that extends—and often quite far—beyond the boundaries of the direct discourse allotted to him. The area occupied by an important character's voice must in any event be broader than his direct and "actual" words. This zone surrounding the important characters of the novel is stylistically profoundly idiosyncratic: the most varied hybrid constructions hold sway in it, and it is always, to one degree or another, dialogized; inside this area a dialogue is played out between the author and his characters—not a dramatic dialogue broken up into statement-and-response, but that special type of novelistic dialogue that realizes itself within the boundaries of constructions that externally resemble monologues. The potential for such dialogue is one of the most fundamental privileges of novelistic prose, a privilege available neither to dramatic nor to purely poetic genres.

Character zones are a most interesting object of study for stylistic and linguistic analysis: in them one encounters constructions that cast a completely new light on problems of syntax and stylistics.

Let us pause finally on one of the most basic and fundamental forms for incorporating and organizing heteroglossia in the novel—"incorporated genres."

The novel permits the incorporation of various genres, both artistic (inserted short stories, lyrical songs, poems, dramatic scenes, etc.) and extra-artistic (everyday, rhetorical, scholarly, religious genres and others). In principle, any genre could be included in the construction of the novel, and in fact it is difficult to find any genres that have not at some point been incorporated into a novel by someone. Such incorporated genres usually preserve within the novel their own structural integrity and independence, as well as their own linguistic and stylistic peculiarities.

There exists in addition a special group of genres that play an especially significant role in structuring novels, sometimes by themselves even directly determining the structure of a novel as a whole—thus creating novel-types named after such genres. Examples of such genres would be the confession, the diary, travel notes, biography, the personal letter and several others. All these genres may not only enter the novel as one of its essential structural components, but may also determine the form of the novel as a whole (the novel-confession, the novel-diary, the novel-in-letters, etc.). Each of these genres possesses its own verbal and semantic forms for assimilating various aspects of reality. The novel, indeed, utilizes these genres precisely because of their capacity, as well-worked-out forms, to assimilate reality in words.

So great is the role played by these genres that are incorporated into novels that it might seem as if the novel is denied any primary means for verbally appropriating reality, that it has no approach of its own, and therefore requires the help of other genres to re-process reality; the novel itself has the appearance of being merely a secondary syncretic unification of other seemingly primary verbal genres.

All these genres, as they enter the novel, bring into it their own languages, and therefore stratify the linguistic unity of the novel and further intensify its speech diversity in fresh ways. It often happens that the language of a nonartistic genre (say, the epistolary), when introduced into the novel, takes on a significance that creates a chapter not only in the history of the novel, but in the history of literary language as well.

The languages thus introduced into a novel may be either directly intentional or treated completely as objects, that is, deprived of any authorial intentions—not as a word that has been spoken, but as a word to be displayed, like a thing. But more often than not, these languages do refract, to one degree or another, authorial intentions—although separate aspects of them may in various ways *not* coincide with the semantic operation of the work that immediately precedes their appearance.

Thus poetic genres of verse (the lyrical genres, for example) when introduced into the novel may have the direct intentionality, the full semantic charge, of poetry. Such, for example, are the versus Goethe introduced into *Wilhelm Meister*. In such a way did the Romantics incorporate their own verses into their prose—and, as is well known, the Romantics considered the presence of verses in the novel (verses taken as directly intentional expressions of the author) one of its constitutive features. In other examples, incorporated verses refract authorial intentions; for example, Lensky's poem in *Evgenij Onegin*, "Where, o where have you gone. . . ." Although the verses from *Wilhelm Meister* may be directly attributed to Goethe (which is actually done), then "Where, o where have you gone. . . ." can in no way be attributed to Pushkin, or if so, only as a poem belonging to a special group comprising "parodic stylizations" (where we must also locate Grinev's poem in *The Captain's Daughter*). Finally, poems incorporated into a novel can also be completely objectified, as are, for example, Captain Lebyadkins' verses in Dostoevsky's *The Possessed*.

A similar situation is the novel's incorporation of every possible kind of maxim and aphorism; they too may oscillate between the purely objective (the "word on display") and the directly intentional, that is, the fully conceptualized philosophical dicta of the author himself (unconditional discourse spoken with no qualifications or distancing). Thus we find, in the novels of Jean Paul—which are so rich in aphorisms—a broad scale of gradations between the various aphorisms, from purely objective to directly intentional, with the author's intentions refracted in varying degrees in each case.

In *Evgenij Onegin* aphorisms and maxims are present either on the plane of parody or of irony—that is, authorial intentions in these dicta are to a greater or lesser extent refracted. For example, the maxim

> He who has lived and thought can never
> Look on mankind without disdain;
> He who has felt is haunted ever
> By days that will not come again;
> No more for him enchantments semblance,
> On him the serpent of remembrance
> Feeds, and remorse corrodes his heart.[9]

is given us on a lighthearted, parodic plane, although one can still feel throughout a close proximity, almost a fusion with authorial intentions. And yet the lines that immediately follow:

> All this is likely to impart
> An added charm to conversation

---

[9]Citations from *Eugene Onegin* are from the Walter Arndt translation (New York: Dutton, 1963), slightly modified to correspond with Bakhtin's remarks about particulars. [Note by Michael Holquist, Bakhtin's editor.]

(a conversation of the posited author with Onegin) strengthen the parodic-ironic emphasis, make the maxim more of an inert thing. We sense that the maxim is constructed in a field of activity dominated by Onegin's voice, in his—Onegin's—belief system, with his—Onegin's—emphases.

But this refraction of authorial intentions, in the field that resounds with Onegin's voice, in Onegin's zone—is different than the refraction in, say, Lensky's zone (cf. the almost objective parody on his poems).

This example may also serve to illustrate the influence of a character's language on authorial speech, something discussed by us above: the aphorism in question here is permeated with Onegin's (fashionably Byronic) intentions, therefore the author maintains a certain distance and does not completely merge with him.

The question of incorporating those genres fundamental to the novel's development (the confession, the diary and others) is much more complicated. Such genres also introduce into the novel their own languages, of course, but these languages are primarily significant for making available points of view that are generative in a material sense, since they exist outside literary conventionality and thus have the capacity to broaden the horizon of language available to literature, helping to win for literature new worlds of verbal perception, worlds that had been already sought and partially subdued in other—extraliterary—spheres of linguistic life.

A comic playing with languages, a story "not from the author" (but from a narrator, posited author or character), character speech, character zones and lastly various introductory or framing genres are the basic forms for incorporating and organizing heteroglossia in the novel. All these forms permit languages to be used in ways that are indirect, conditional, distanced. They all signify a relativizing of linguistic consciousness in the perception of language borders—borders created by history and society, and even the most fundamental borders (i.e., those between languages as such)—and permit expression of a feeling for the materiality of language that defines such a relativized consciousness. This relativizing of linguistic consciousness in no way requires a corresponding relativizing in the semantic intentions themselves: even within a prose linguistic consciousness, intentions themselves can be unconditional. But because the idea of a singular language (a sacrosanct, unconditional language) is foreign to prose, prosaic consciousness must orchestrate its *own*—even though unconditional—semantic intentions. Prose consciousness feels cramped when it is confined to only *one* out of a multitude of heteroglot languages, for one linguistic timbre is inadequate to it.

We have touched upon only those major forms typical of the most important variants of the European novel, but in themselves they do not, of course, exhaust all the possible means for incorporating and organizing heteroglossia in the novel. A combination of all these forms in separate given novels, and consequently in various generic types generated by these novels, is also possible. Of such a sort is the classic and purest model of the novel as genre—Cervantes' *Don Quixote*, which realizes in itself, in extraordinary depth and breadth, all the artistic possibilities of heteroglot and internally dialogized novelistic discourse.

Heteroglossia, once incorporated into the novel (whatever the forms for its incorporation), is *another's speech in another's language,* serving to express authorial intentions but in a refracted way. Such speech constitutes a special type of *double-voiced discourse.* It serves two speakers at the same time and expresses simultaneously two different intentions: the direct intention of the character who is speaking, and the refracted intention of the author. In such discourse there are two voices, two meanings and two expressions. And all the while these two voices are dialogically interrelated, they — as it were — know about each other (just as two exchanges in a dialogue know of each other and are structured in this mutual knowledge of each other); it is as if they actually hold a conversation with each other. Double-voiced discourse is always internally dialogized. Examples of this would be comic, ironic or parodic discourse, the refracting discourse of a narrator, refracting discourse in the language of a character and finally the discourse of a whole incorporated genre — all these discourses are double-voiced and internally dialogized. A potential dialogue is embedded in them, one as yet unfolded, a concentrated dialogue of two voices, two world views, two languages.

Double-voiced, internally dialogized discourse is also possible, of course, in a language system that is hermetic, pure and unitary, a system alien to the linguistic relativism of prose consciousness; it follows that such discourse is also possible in the purely poetic genres. But in those systems there is no soil to nourish the development of such discourse in the slightest meaningful or essential way. Double-voiced discourse is very widespread in rhetorical genres, but even there — remaining as it does within the boundaries of a single language system — it is not fertilized by a deep-rooted connection with the forces of historical becoming that serve to stratify language, and therefore rhetorical genres are at best merely a distanced echo of this becoming, narrowed down to an individual polemic.

Such poetic and rhetorical double-voicedness, cut off from any process of linguistic stratification, may be adequately unfolded into an individual dialogue, into individual argument and conversation between two persons, even while the exchanges in the dialogue are immanent to a single unitary language: they may not be in agreement, they may even be opposed, but they are diverse neither in their speech nor in their language. Such double-voicing, remaining within the boundaries of a single hermetic and unitary language system, without any underlying fundamental socio-linguistic orchestration, may be only a stylistically secondary accompaniment to the dialogue and forms of polemic.[10] The internal bifurcation (double-voicing) of discourse, sufficient to a single and unitary language and to a consistently monologic style, can never be a fundamental form of discourse: it is merely a game, a tempest in a teapot.

[10] In neoclassicism, this double-voicing becomes crucial only in the low genres, especially in satire.

The double-voicedness one finds in prose is of another sort altogether. There — on the rich soil of novelistic prose — double-voicedness draws its energy, its dialogized ambiguity, not from *individual* dissonances, misunderstandings or contradictions (however tragic, however firmly grounded in individual destinies);[11] in the novel, this double-voicedness sinks its roots deep into a fundamental, socio-linguistic speech diversity and multi-languagedness. True, even in the novel heteroglossia is by and large always personified, incarnated in individual human figures, with disagreements and oppositions individualized. But such oppositions of individual wills and minds are submerged in *social* heteroglossia, they are reconceptualized through it. Oppositions between individuals are only surface upheavals of the untamed elements in social heteroglossia, surface manifestations of those elements that play *on* such individual oppositions, make them contradictory, saturate their consciousness and discourses with a more fundamental speech diversity.

Therefore the internal dialogism of double-voiced prose discourse can never be exhausted thematically (just as the metaphoric energy of language can never be exhausted thematically); it can never be developed into the motivation or subject for a manifest dialogue, such as might fully embody, with no residue, the internally dialogic potential embedded in linguistic heteroglossia. The internal dialogism of authentic prose discourse, which grows organically out of a stratified and heteroglot language, cannot fundamentally be dramatized or dramatically resolved (brought to an authentic end); it cannot ultimately be fitted into the frame of any manifest dialogue, into the frame of a mere conversation between persons; it is not ultimately divisible into verbal exchanges possessing precisely marked boundaries.[12] This double-voicedness in prose is prefigured in language itself (in authentic metaphors, as well as in myth), in language as a social phenomenon that is becoming in history, socially stratified and weathered in this process of becoming.

The relativizing of linguistic consciousness, its crucial participation in the social multi- and vari-languagedness of evolving languages, the various wanderings of semantic and expressive intentions and the trajectory of this consciousness through various languages (languages that are all equally well conceptualized and equally objective), the inevitable necessity for such a consciousness to speak indirectly, conditionally, in a refracted way — these are all indispensable prerequisites for an authentic double-voiced prose discourse. This double-voicedness makes its presence felt by the novelist in the living heteroglossia of language, and in the multi-languagedness surrounding and nourishing his own consciousness; it is not invented in superficial, isolated rhetorical polemics with another person.

If the novelist loses touch with this linguistic ground of prose style, if he is unable to attain the heights of a relativized, Galilean linguistic

---

[11] Within the limits of the world of poetry and a unitary language, everything important in such disagreements and contradictions can and must be laid out in a direct and pure dramatic dialogue.

[12] The more consistent and unitary the language, the more acute, dramatic and "finished" such exchanges generally are.

consciousness, if he is deaf to organic double-voicedness and to the internal dialogization of living and evolving discourse, then he will never comprehend, or even realize, the actual possibilities and tasks of the novel as a genre. He may, of course, create an artistic work that compositionally and thematically will be similar to a novel, will be "made" exactly as a novel is made, but he will not thereby have created a novel. The style will always give him away. We will recognize the naively self-confident of obtusely stubborn unity of a smooth, pure single-voiced language (perhaps accompanied by a primitive, artificial, worked-up double-voicedness). We quickly sense that such an author finds it easy to purge his work of speech diversity: he simply does not listen to the fundamental heteroglossia inherent in actual language; he mistakes social overtones, which create the timbres of words, for irritating noises that it is his task to eliminate. The novel, when torn out of authentic linguistic speech diversity, emerges in most cases as a "closet drama," with detailed, fully developed and "artistically worked out" stage directions (it is, of course, bad drama). In such a novel, divested of its language diversity, authorial language inevitably ends up in the awkward and absurd position of the language of stage directions in plays.[13]

The double-voiced prose word has a double meaning. But the poetic word, in the narrow sense, also has a double, even a multiple, meaning. It is this that basically distinguishes it from the word as concept, or the word as term. The poetic word is a trope, requiring a precise feeling for the two meanings contained in it.

But no matter how one understands the interrelationship of meanings in a poetic symbol (a trope), this interrelationship is never of the dialogic sort; it is impossible under any conditions or at any time to imagine a trope (say, a metaphor) being unfolded into the two exchanges of a dialogue, that is, two meanings parceled out between two separate voices. For this reason the dual meaning (or multiple meaning) of the symbol never brings in its wake dual accents. On the contrary, one voice, a single-accent system, is fully sufficient to express poetic ambiguity. It is possible to interpret the interrelationships of different meanings in a symbol logically (as the relationship of a part or an individual to the whole, as for example a proper noun that has become a symbol, or the relationship of the concrete to the abstract and so on); one may grasp this relationship philosophically and ontologically, as a special kind of representational relationship, or as a relationship between essence and appearance and so forth, or one may shift into the foreground the emotional and evaluative dimension of such relationship—but all these types of relationships between various meanings do not and cannot go beyond the boundaries of the relationship between a word and its object, or the boundaries of various aspects in the object. The entire event is played out between

[13] In his well-known works on the theory and technique of the novel, Spielhagen focuses on precisely such unnovelistic novels, and ignores precisely the kind of potential specific to the novel as a genre. As a theoretician Spielhagen was deaf to heteroglot language and to that which it specifically generates: double-voiced discourse.

the word and its object; all of the play of the poetic symbol is in that space. A symbol cannot presuppose any fundamental relationship to another's word, to another's voice. The polysemy of the poetic symbol presupposes the unity of a voice with which it is identical, and it presupposes that such a voice is completely alone within its own discourse. As soon as another's voice, another's accent, the possibility of another's point of view breaks through this play of the symbol, the poetic plane is destroyed and the symbol is translated onto the plane of prose.

To understand the difference between ambiguity in poetry and double-voicedness in prose, it is sufficient to take any symbol and give it an ironic accent (in a correspondingly appropriate context, of course), that is, to introduce into it one's own voice, to refract within it one's own fresh intention.[14] In this process the poetic symbol—while remaining, of course, a symbol—is at one and the same time translated onto the plane of prose and becomes a double-voiced word: in the space between the word and its object another's word, another's accent intrudes, a mantle of materiality is cast over the symbol (an operation of this sort would naturally result in a rather simple and primitive double-voiced structure).

An example of this simplest type of prosification of the poetic symbol in *Evgenij Onegin* is the stanza on Lensky:

> Of love he [Lensky] sang, love's service choosing,
> And timid was his simple tune
> As ever artless maiden's musing,
> As babes aslumber, as the moon. . . .[15]

The poetic symbols of this stanza are organized simultaneously at two levels: the level of Lensky's lyrics themselves—in the semantic and expressive system of the "Göttigen Geist"—and on the level of Pushkin's speech, for whom the "Göttigen Geist" with its language and its poetics is merely an instantiation of the literary heteroglossia of the epoch, but one that is already becoming typical: a fresh tone, a fresh voice amid the multiple voices of literary language, literary world views and the life these world views regulate. Some other voices in this heteroglossia—of literature and of the real life contemporaneous with it—would be Onegin's Byronic-Chateaubriandesque language, the Richardsonian language and world of the provincial Tatiana, the down-to-earth rustic language spoken at the Larins' estate, the language and the world of Tatiana in Petersburg and other languages as

---

[14] Alexei Alexandrovich Karenin had the habit of avoiding certain words, and expressions connected with them. He made up double-voiced constructions outside any context, exclusively on the intonational plane: "'Well, yes, as you see, your devoted husband, as devoted as in the first year of marriage, is burning with impatience to see you,' he said in his slow high-pitched voice and in the tone in which he almost always addressed her, a tone of derision for anyone who could really talk like that" (*Anna Karenina* [New York: Signet, 1961] part 1, ch. 30; translation by David Magarshack).

[15] We offer an analysis of this example in the essay "From the Prehistory of Novelistic Discourse."

well—including the indirect languages of the author—which undergo change in the course of the work. The whole of this heteroglossia (*Evgenij Onegin* is an encyclopedia of the styles and languages of the epoch) orchestrates the intentions of the author and is responsible for the authentically novelistic style of this work.

Thus the images in the above-cited stanza, being ambiguous (metaphorical) poetic symbols serving Lensky's intentions in Lensky's belief system, become double-voiced prose symbols in the system of Pushkin's speech. These are, of course, authentic prose symbols, arising from the heteroglossia inherent in the epoch's evolving literary language, not a superficial, rhetorical parody or irony.

Such is the distinction between true double-voicedness in fictive practice, and the *single-voiced* double or multiple meaning that finds expression in the purely poetic symbol. The ambiguity of double-voiced discourse is internally dialogized, fraught with dialogue, and may in fact even give birth to dialogues comprised of truly separate voices (but such dialogues are not dramatic; they are, rather, interminable prose dialogues). What is more, double-voicedness is never exhausted in these dialogues, it cannot be extracted fully from the discourse—not by a rational, logical counting of the individual parts, nor by drawing distinctions between the various parts of a monologic unit of discourse (as happens in rhetoric), nor by a definite cut-off between the verbal exchanges of a finite dialogue, such as occurs in the theater. Authentic double-voicedness, although it generates novelistic prose dialogues, is not exhausted in these dialogues and remains in the discourse, in language, like a spring of dialogism that never runs dry—for the internal dialogism of discourse is something that inevitably accompanies the social, contradictory historical becoming of language.

If the central problem in poetic theory is the problem of the poetic symbol, then the central problem in prose theory is the problem of the double-voiced, internally dialogized word, in all its diverse types and variants.

For the novelist working in prose, the object is always entangled in someone else's discourse about it, it is already present with qualifications, an object of dispute that is conceptualized and evaluated variously, inseparable from the heteroglot social apperception of it. The novelist speaks of this "already qualified world" in a language that is heteroglot and internally dialogized. Thus both object and language are revealed to the novelist in their historical dimension, in the process of social and heteroglot becoming. For the novelist, there is no world outside his socioheteroglot perception—and there is no language outside the heteroglot intentions that stratify that world. Therefore it is possible to have, even in the novel, that profound but unique unity of a language (or more precisely, of languages) with its own object, with its own world, unity of the sort one finds in poetry. Just as the poetic image seems to have been born out of language itself, to have sprung organically from it, to have been pre-formed in it, so also novelistic images seem to be grafted organically on to their own double-voiced language, pre-formed, as it were, within it, in the innards of the distinctive multi-speechedness organic to that language. In the novel, the "already bespoke quality" [*ogovoren-nost'*] of the world is woven together with the "already uttered" quality [*pere-govorennost'*] of language, into the unitary event of the world's heteroglot becoming, in both social consciousness and language.

Even the poetic word (in the narrow sense) must break through to its object, penetrate the alien word in which the object is entangled; it also encounters heteroglot language and must break through in order to create a unity and a pure intentionality (which is neither given nor ready-made). But the trajectory of the poetic word toward its own object and toward the unity of language is a path along which the poetic word is continually encountering someone else's word, and each takes new bearings from the other; the records of the passage remain in the slag of the creative process, which is then cleared away (as scaffolding is cleared away once construction is finished), so that the finished work may rise as unitary speech, one co-extensive with its object, as if it were speech about an "Edenic" world. This single-voiced purity and unqualified directness that intentions possess in poetic discourse so crafted is purchased at the price of a certain conventionality in poetic language.

If the art of poetry, as a utopian philosophy of genres, gives rise to the conception of a purely poetic, extrahistorical language, a language far removed from the petty rounds of everyday life, a language of the gods—then it must be said that the art of prose is close to a conception of languages as historically concrete and living things. The prose art presumes a deliberate feeling for the historical and social concreteness of living discourse, as well as its relativity, a feeling for its participation in historical becoming and in social struggle; it deals with discourse that is still warm from that struggle and hostility, as yet unresolved and still fraught with hostile intentions and accents; prose art finds discourse in this state and subjects it to the dynamic-unity of its own style.

Translated by Caryl Emerson.

JOHN CROWE RANSOM

Criticism as Pure Speculation

1941

What may appear to be only a conventionally graceful personal tribute in the first paragraphs of Ransom's (1888–1974) essay is the real clue to his approach: if "the authority of criticism" rests on a reconciliation of criticism and philosophical aesthetics, Ransom's own critical theory is to be grounded in certain assumptions about the nature of reality. What Ransom means by his key term "ontology" is the nature of a poem's being—namely, as a symbolic yet concrete representation of human experience, differing from scientific discourse in its avoidance of and resistance to abstract concepts. The critic's task is to approach a poem not in terms of its "meaning" but in terms of its "icons" or images—"to attend to the poetic object." Recall, at this point, Eliot's influential statement of what he hoped his criticism would do: "to divert interest from the poet to the poetry." As one of the main progenitors of the New Criticism, Ransom distinguishes between science and poetry and then dismisses two traditional approaches to poetry, the "psychologistic" and the "moralistic."

Ransom's insistence on "a structural understanding of poetry" derives from his premise that poetry is not to be confused with the poet's biography or intentions, the audience response to the poem, or the uses to which it may be put. As an autonomous object, a poem is a special kind of verbal structure that must be read closely for the complex meaning that is there only because it is inherent in style, technique, and form. Despite some considerable differences in emphases, other formalists and New Critics also take this as their starting point.

In order to solve the perplexing philosophical problem of how a poem can be both universal and concrete, Ransom formulates a distinction of great importance to him: the relationship between structure and texture, each having a particular function. Although he rejects the poetry of abstract ideas, to what extent does his concept of a "paraphrasable core" in a poem resemble what might also be thought of as the "content"? In this connection, study his own analogy of poetry with architecture: Is wallpaper organic?

Ransom's essays greatly influenced many younger New Critics. His book The New Criticism (1941) even gave the name to this new way of studying and teaching literature, a mode that was the dominant critical approach of the mid-twentieth cen-

tury. The essay by Cleanth Brooks (see p. 465) demonstrates the application of the theory to a particular poem and exemplifies the kind of analytical close reading that characterizes the New Criticism.

I

I WILL TESTIFY to the weight of responsibility felt by the critic who enters a serial discussion with such other lecturers as Mr. Wilson, Mr. Auden, and Mr. Foerster; and delivers his opinion to an audience at Princeton, where live at least two eminent critics, in Mr. Tate and Mr. Blackmur, and one eminent esthetician, in Mr. Greene.

Indeed, Mr. Blackmur and Mr. Greene have recently published books which bear on this discussion. Mr. Blackmur's essays are probably all that can be expected of a critic who has not explicitly submitted them to the discipline of general esthetics; but with that limitation the best critic in the world might expose himself to review and reproach. Mr. Greene's esthetic studies, in turn, may have wonderful cogency as philosophical discourse; but if throughout them he should fail to maintain intimate contact with the actual works of art he would invite damaging attentions from the literary critics. I am far from suggesting such proceedings against them. Mr. Blackmur has his native philosophical sense to keep his critical foundations from sliding into the sea. Mr. Greene is in a very strong position: recognizing the usual weakness of formal esthetics, he tries to device to secure his own studies against it; for when he needs them he uses reports from reputable actual critics upon the practices in the several arts. A chasm, perhaps an abyss, separates the critic and the esthetician ordinarily, if the books in the library are evidence. But the authority of criticism depends on its coming to terms with esthetics, and the authority of literary esthetics depends on its coming to terms with criticism. Mr. Greene is an esthetician, and his department is philosophy, but he has subscribed in effect to this thesis. I am a sort of critic, and my department is English poetry, so that I am very much in Mr. Blackmur's position: and I subscribe to the thesis, and am altogether disposed to solicit Mr. Greene's philosophical services.

When we inquire into the "intent of the critic," we mean: the intent of the generalized critic, or critic as such. We will concede that any professional critic is familiar with the technical practices of poets so long as these are conventional, and is expert in judging when they perform them brilliantly and when only fairly, or badly. We expect a critical discourse to cover that much, but we know that more is required. The most famous poets of our own time, for example, make wide departures from conventional practices: how are they to be judged? Innovations in poetry, or even conventions when pressed to their logical limits, cause the ordinary critic to despair. They cause the good critic to review his esthetic principles; perhaps to re-formulate his esthetic principles. He tries the poem against his best philosophical conception of the peculiar character that a poem should have.

Mr. T. S. Eliot is an extraordinarily sensitive critic. But when he discusses the so-called "metaphysical" poetry, he surprises us by refusing to study the so-called "conceit" which is its reputed basis; he observes instead that the metaphysical poets of the seventeenth century are more like their immediate predecessors than the latter are like the eighteenth and nineteenth century poets, and then he goes into a very broad philosophical comparison between two whole "periods" or types of poetry. I think it has come to be understood that his comparison is unsound; it has not proved workable enough to assist critics who have otherwise borrowed liberally from his critical principles. (It contains the famous dictum about the "sensibility" of the earlier poets, it imputes to them a remarkable ability to "feel their thought," and to have a kind of "experience" in which the feeling cannot be differentiated from the thinking.) Now there is scarcely another critic equal to Eliot at distinguishing the practices of two poets who are closely related. He is supreme as a comparative critic when the relation in question is delicate and subtle; that is, when it is a matter of close perception and not a radical difference in kind. But this line of criticism never goes far enough. In Eliot's own range of criticism the line does not always answer. He is forced by discontinuities in the poetic tradition into sweeping theories that have to do with esthetics, the philosophy of poetry; and his own philosophy probably seems to us insufficient, the philosophy of the literary man.

The intent of the critic may well be, then, first to read his poem sensitively, and make comparative judgments about its technical practice, or, as we might say, to emulate Eliot. Beyond that, it is to read and remark the poem knowingly; that is, with an esthetician's understanding of what a poem generically "is."

Before I venture, with inadequate argument, to describe what I take to be the correct understanding of poetry, I would like to describe two other understandings which, though widely professed, seem to me misunderstandings. First, there is a smart and belletristic theory of poetry which may be called "psychologistic." Then there is an altogether staid and commonplace theory which is moralistic. Of these in their order.

II

It could easily be argued about either of these untenable conceptions of poetry that it is an act of despair to which critics resort who cannot find for the discourse of poetry any precise differentia to remove it from the category of science. Psychologistic critics hold that poetry is addressed primarily to the feelings and motor impulses; they remind us frequently of its contrast with the coldness, the unemotionality, of science, which is supposed to address itself to the pure cognitive mind. Mr. Richards came out spectacularly for the doctrine, and furnished it with detail of the greatest ingenuity. He very nearly severed the dependence of poetic effect upon any standard of objective knowledge or belief. But the feelings and impulses which he represented as gratified by the poem were too tiny and numerous to be named. He never identified them; they seemed not so much psychological as infrapsychological. His was an esoteric poetic: it could not be disproved. But neither could it be proved, and I think it is safe at this distance to say that eventually his readers, and Richards himself, lost interest in it as being an improvisation, much too unrelated to the public sense of a poetic experience.

With other critics psychologism of some sort is an old story, and one that will probably never cease to be told. For, now that all of us know about psychology, there must always be persons on hand precisely conditioned to declare that poetry is an emotional discourse indulged in resentment and compensation for science, the bleak cognitive discourse in its purity. It becomes less a form of knowledge than a form of "expression." The critics are willing to surrender the honor of objectivity to science if they may have the luxury of subjectivity for poetry. Science will scarcely object. But one or two things have to be said about that. In every experience, even in science, there is feeling. No discourse can sustain itself without interest, which is feeling. The interest, or the feeling, is like an automatic index to the human value of the proceeding—which would not otherwise proceed. Mr. Eliseo Vivas is an esthetician who might be thought to reside in the camp of the enemy, for his affiliations are positivist; yet in a recent essay he writes about the "passion" which sustains the heroic labors of the scientist as one bigger and more intense than is given to most men.

I do not mean to differ with that judgment at all in remarking that we might very well let the passions and the feelings take care of themselves; it is precisely what we do in our pursuit of science. The thing to attend to is the object to which they attach. As between two similar musical phrases, or between two similar lines of poetry, we may often defy the most proficient psychologist to distinguish the one feeling—response from the other; unless we permit him to say at long last that one is the kind of response that would be made to the first line, and the other is the kind of response that would be made to the second line. But that is to do, after much wasted motion, what I have just suggested: to attend to the poetic object and let the feelings take care of themselves. It is their business to "respond." There may be a feeling correlative with the minutest alteration in an object, and adequate to it, but we shall hardly know. What we do know is that the feelings are grossly inarticulate if we try to abstract them and take their testimony in their own language. Since it is not the intent of the critic to be inarticulate, his discriminations must be among the objects. We understand this so well intuitively that the critic seems to us in possession of some esoteric knowledge, some magical insight, if he appears to be intelligent elsewhere and yet refers confidently to the "tone" or "quality" or "value" of the feeling he discovers in a given line. Probably he is bluffing. The distinctness resides in the cognitive or "semantical" objects denoted by the words. When Richards bewilders us by reporting affective and motor disturbances that are too tiny for definition, and other critics by reporting disturbances that are too massive and gross, we cannot fail to grow suspicious of this whole way of insight as incompetent.

Eliot has a special version of psychologist theory which looks extremely fertile, though it is broad and nebulous as his psychologistic terms require it to be. He likes to regard the poem as a structure of emotion and feeling. But the emotion is singular, there being only one emotion per poem, or at least per passage: it is the central emotion or big emotion which attaches to the main theme or situation. The feeling is plural. The emotion combines with many feelings; these are our little responses to the single words and phrases, and he does not think of them as being parts of the central emotion or even related to it. The terminology is greatly at fault, or we should recognize at once, I think, a principle that might prove very valuable. I would not answer for the conduct of a technical philosopher in assessing this theory; he might throw it away, out of patience with its jargon. But a lay philosopher who respects his Eliot and reads with all his sympathy might salvage a good thing from it, though I have not heard of anyone doing so. He would try to escape from the affective terms, and translate Eliot into more intelligible language. Eliot would be saying in effect that a poem has a central logic or situation or "paraphrasable core" to which an appropriate interest doubtless attaches, and that in this respect the poem is like a discourse of science behind which lies the sufficient passion. But he would be saying at the same time, and this is the important thing, that the poem has also a context of lively local details to which other and independent interests attach; and that in this respect it is unlike the discourse of science. For the detail of scientific discourse intends never to be independent of the thesis (either objectively or affectively) but always functional, and subordinate to the realization of the thesis. To say that is to approach to a structural understanding of poetry, and to the kind of understanding that I wish presently to urge.

III

As for the moralistic understanding of poetry, it is sometimes the specific moralists, men with moral axes to grind, and incidentally men of unassailable public position, who cherish that; they have a "use" for poetry. But not exclusively, for we may find it held also by critics who are more spontaneous and innocent: apparently they fall back upon it because it attributes some special character to poetry, which otherwise refuses to yield up to them a character. The moral interest is so much more frequent in poetry than in science that they decide to offer its moralism as a differentia.

This conception of poetry is of the greatest antiquity—it antedates the evolution of close esthetic philosophy, and persists beside it too. Plato sometimes spoke of poetry in this light—perhaps because it was recommended to him in this light—but nearly always scornfully. In the *Gorgias,* and other dialogues, he represents the poets as moralizing, and that is only what he, in the person of Socrates, is doing at the very moment, and given to doing; but he considers the moralizing of poets as mere "rhetoric," or popular philosophy, and unworthy of the accomplished moralist who is the real or technical philosopher. Plato understood very well that the poet does not conduct a technical or an original discourse like that of the scientist—and the term includes here the moral philosopher—and that close and effective moralizing is scarcely to be had from him. It is not within the poet's power to offer that if his intention is to offer poetry; for the poetry and the morality are so far from being identical that they interfere a little with each other.

Few famous estheticians in the history of philosophy have cared to bother with the moralistic conception; many critics have, in all periods. Just now we have at least two schools of moralistic critics contending for the official possession of poetry. One is the Neo-Humanist, and Mr. Foerster has identified himself with that. The other is the Marxist, and I believe it is represented in some degree and shade by Mr. Wilson, possibly by Mr. Auden. I have myself taken profit from the discussions by both schools, but recently I have taken more—I suppose this is because I was brought up in a scholastic discipline rather like the Neo-Humanist—from the writings of the Marxist critics. One of the differences is that the Neo-Humanists believe in the "respectable" virtues, but the Marxists believe that respectability is the greatest of vices, and equate respectable with "genteel." That is a very striking difference, and I think it is also profound.

But I do not wish to be impertinent; I can respect both these moralities, and appropriate moral values from both. The thing I wish to argue is not the comparative merits of the different moralities by which poetry is judged, but their equal inadequacy to the reading of the poet's intention. The moralistic critics wish to isolate and discuss the "ideology" or theme or paraphrase of the poem and not the poem itself. But even to the practitioners themselves, if they are sophisticated, comes sometimes the apprehension that this is moral rather than literary criticism. I have not seen the papers of my colleagues in this discussion, for that was against the rules, but it is reported to me that both Mr. Wilson and Mr. Foerster concede in explicit words that criticism has both the moral and the esthetic branches; Mr. Wilson may call them the "social" and esthetic branches. And they would hold the critical profession responsible for both branches. Under these circumstances the critics cease to be mere moralists and become dualists; that is better. My feel about such a position would be that the moral criticism we shall have with us always, and have had always, and that it is easy—comparatively speaking—and that what is hard, and needed, and indeed more and more urgent after all the failures of poetic understanding, is a better esthetic criticism. This is the branch which is all but invariably neglected by the wise but morally zealous critics; they tend to forget their dual responsibility. I think I should go so far as to think that, in strictness, the business of the literary critic is exclusively with an esthetic criticism. The business of the moralist will naturally, and properly, be with something else.

If we have the patience to read for a little while in the anthology, paying some respect to the varieties of substance actually in the poems, we cannot logically attribute ethical character by definition to poetry; for that character is not universal in the poems. And if we have any faith in a community of character among the several arts, we are stopped quickly from risking such a definition for art at large. To claim a moral content for most of sculpture, painting, music, or architecture, is to plan something dialectically very roundabout and subtle, or else to be so arbitrary as to invite instant exposure. I should think the former alternative is impractical, and the latter, if it is not stupid, is masochistic.

The moralistic critics are likely to retort upon their accusers by accusing them in turn of the vapid doctrine known as Art for Art's Sake. And with frequent justice; but again we are likely to receive the impression that it is first because Art for Art's Sake, the historic doctrine, proved empty, and availed them so little esthetically, like all the other doctrines that came into default, that they have fled to their moralism. Moralism does at least impute to poetry a positive substance, as Art for Art's Sake does not. It asserts an autonomy for art, which is excellent; but autonomy to do what? Only to be itself, and to reduce its interpreters to a tautology? With its English adherents in the 'nineties the doctrine seemed to make only a negative requirement of art, that is, that it should be anti-Victorian as we should say today, a little bit naughty and immoral perhaps, otherwise at least non-moral, or carefully squeezed dry of moral substance. An excellent example of how two doctrines, inadequate equally but in opposite senses, may keep themselves alive by abhorring each other's errors.

It is highly probable that the poem considers an ethical situation, and there is no reason why it should repel this from its consideration. But, if I may say so without being accused of verbal trifling, the poetic consideration of the ethical situation is not the same as the ethical consideration of it. The straight ethical consideration would be prose; it would be an act of interested science, or an act of practical will. The poetic consideration, according to Schopenhauer, is the objectification of this act of will; that is, it is our contemplation and not our exercise of will, and therefore qualitatively a very different experience; knowledge without desire. That doctrine also seems too negative and indeterminate. I will put the point as I see it in another way. It should be a comfort to the moralist that there is ordinarily a moral composure in the poem, as if the poet had long known good and evil, and made his moral choice between them once and for all. Art is post-ethical rather than unethical. In the poem there is an increment of meaning which is neither the ethical content nor opposed to the ethical content. The poetic experience would have to stop for the poet who is developing it, or for the reader who is following it, if the situation which is being poetically treated should turn back into a situation to be morally determined; if, for example, the situation were not a familiar one, and one to which we had habituated our moral wills; for it would rouse the moral will again to action, and make the poetic treatment impossible under its heat. Art is more cool than hot, and a moral fervor is as disastrous to it as a burst of passion itself. We have seen Marxists recently so revolted by Shakespeare's addiction to royal or noble personae that they cannot obtain esthetic experience from the plays; all they get is moral agitation. In another art, we know, and doubtless we approve, the scruple of the college authorities in not permitting the "department of fine arts" to direct the collegians in painting in the nude. Doctor Hanns Sachs, successor to Freud, in a recent number of his *American Imago*, gives a story from a French author as follows:

"He tells that one evening strolling along the streets of Paris he noticed a row of slot machines which for a small coin showed pictures of women in full or partial undress. He observed the leering interest with which men of all kind and description, well dressed and shabby, boys and old men, enjoyed the peep show. He remarked that they all avoided one of these machines, and wondering what uninteresting pictures it might show, he put his penny in the slot. To his great astonishment the generally shunned picture turned out to be the Venus of Medici. Now he begins to ponder: Why does nobody get excited about her? She is decidedly feminine and not less naked than the others which hold such strong fascination for everybody. Finally he finds a satisfactory answer: They fight shy of her because she is beautiful."

And Doctor Sachs, though in his own variety of jargon, makes a number of wise observations about the psychic conditions precedent to the difficult apprehension of beauty. The experience called beauty is beyond the powerful ethical will precisely as it is beyond the animal passion, and indeed these last two are competitive, and coordinate. Under the urgency of either we are incapable of appreciating the statue or understanding the poem.

IV

The ostensible substance of the poem may be anything at all which words may signify: an ethical situation, a passion, a train of thought, a flower or landscape, a thing. This substance receives its poetic increment. It might be safer to say it receives some subtle and mysterious alteration under poetic treatment, but I will risk the cruder formula: the ostensible substance is increased by an x, which is an increment. The poem actually continues to contain its ostensible substance, which is not fatally diminished from its prose state: that is its logical core or paraphrase. The rest of the poem is x, which we are to find.

We feel the working of this simple formula when we approach a poetry with our strictest logic, provided we can find deliverance from certain inhibiting philosophical prepossessions into which we have been conditioned by the critics we have had to read. Here is Lady Macbeth planning a murder with her husband:

When Duncan is asleep—
Whereto the rather shall his hard day's journey

Soundly invite him — his two chamberlains
Will I with wine and wassail so convince,
That memory, the warder of the brain,
Shall be a fume, and the receipt of reason
A limbec only; when in swinish sleep
Their drenched natures lie as in a death,
What cannot you and I perform upon
The unguarded Duncan? what not put upon
His spongy officers, who shall bear the guilt
Of our great quell?

It is easy to produce the prose argument or paraphrase of this speech; it has one upon which we shall all agree. But the passage is more than its argument. Any detail, with this speaker, seems capable of being expanded in some direction which is not that of the argument. For example, Lady Macbeth says she will make the chamberlains drunk so that they will not remember their charge, nor keep their wits about them. But it is indifferent to this argument whether memory according to the old psychology is located at the gateway to the brain, whether it is to be disintegrated into fume as of alcohol, and whether the whole receptacle of the mind is to be turned into a still. These are additions to the argument both energetic and irrelevant — though they do not quite stop or obscure the argument. From the point of view of the philosopher they are excursions into particularity. They give, in spite of the argument, which would seem to be perfectly self-sufficient, a sense of the real density and contingency of the world in which arguments and plans have to be pursued. They bring out the private character which the items of an argument can really assume if we look at them. This character spreads out in planes at right angles to the course of the argument, and in effect gives to the discourse another dimension, not present in a perfectly logical prose. We are expected to have sufficient judgment not to let this local character take us too far or keep us too long from the argument.

All this would seem commonplace remark, I am convinced, but for those philosophically timid critics who are afraid to think that the poetic increment is local and irrelevant, and that poetry cannot achieve its own virtue and keep undiminished the virtues of prose at the same time. But I will go a little further in the hope of removing the sense of strangeness in the analysis. I will offer a figurative definition of a poem.

A poem is, so to speak, a democratic state, whereas a prose discourse — mathematic, scientific, ethical, or practical and vernacular — is a totalitarian state. The intention of a democratic state is to perform the work of state as effectively as it can perform it, subject to one reservation of conscience; that it will not despoil its members, the citizens, of the free exercise of their own private and independent characters. But the totalitarian state is interested solely in being effective, and regards the citizens as no citizens at all; that is, regards them as functional members whose existence is totally defined by their allotted contributions to its ends; it has no use for their private characters, and therefore no provision for them. I indicate of course the extreme or polar opposition between two polities, without denying that a polity may come to us rather mixed up.

In this trope the operation of the state as a whole represents of course the logical paraphrase or argument of the poem. The private character of the citizens represents the particularity asserted by the parts in the poem. And this last is our x.

For many years I had seen—as what serious observer has not—that a poem as a discourse differentiated itself from prose by its particularity, yet not to the point of sacrificing its logical cogency or universality. But I could get no further. I could not see how real particularity could get into a universal. The object of esthetic studies became for me a kind of discourse, or a kind of natural configuration, which like any other discourse or configuration claimed universality, but which consisted actually, and notoriously, of particularity. The poem was concrete, yet universal, and in spite of Hegel I could not see how the two properties could be identified as forming in a single unit the "concrete universal." It is usual, I believe, for persons at this stage to assert that somehow the apparent diffuseness of particularity in the poem gets itself taken up or "assimilated" into the logic, to produce a marvellous kind of unity called a "higher unity," to which ordinary discourse is not eligible. The belief is that the "idea" or theme proves itself in poetry to be even more dominating than in prose by overcoming much more energetic resistance than usual on the part of the materials, and the resistance, as attested in the local development of detail, is therefore set not to the debit but to the credit of the unifying power of the poetic spirit. A unity of that kind is one which philosophers less audacious and more factual than Hegel would be loath to claim. Critics incline to call it, rather esoterically, an "imaginative" rather than a logical unity, but one supposes they mean a mystical, an ineffable, unity. I for one could neither grasp it nor deny it. I believe that is not an uncommon situation for poetic analysts to find themselves in.

It occurred to me at last that the solution might be very easy if looked for without what the positivists call "metaphysical prepossessions." Suppose the logical substance remained there all the time, and was in no way specially remarkable, while the particularity came in by accretion, so that the poem turned out partly universal, and partly particular, but with respect to different parts. I began to remark the dimensions of a poem, or other work of art. The poem was not a mere moment in time, nor a mere point in space. It was sizeable, like a house. Apparently it had a "plan," or a central frame of logic, but it had also a huge wealth of local detail, which sometimes fitted the plan functionally or served it, and sometimes only subsisted comfortably under it; in either case the house stood up. But it was the political way of thinking which gave me the first analogy which seemed valid. The poem was like a democratic state, in action, and observed both macroscopically and microscopically.

The house occurred also, and provided what seems to be a more negotiable trope under which to construe the poem. A poem is a *logical structure* having a *local texture*. These terms have been actually though not

systematically employed in literary criticism. To my imagination they are architectural. The walls of my room are obviously structural; the beams and
boards have a function; so does the plaster, which is the visible aspect of the
final wall. The plaster might have remained naked, aspiring to no character,
and purely functional. But actually it has been painted, receiving color; or it
has been papered, receiving color and design, though these have no structural value; and perhaps it has been hung with tapestry, or with paintings,
for "decoration." The paint, the paper, the tapestry are texture. It is logically
unrelated to structure. But I indicate only a few of the textural possibilities in
architecture. There are not fewer of them in poetry.

The intent of the good critic becomes therefore to examine and define the
poem with respect to its structure and its texture. If he has nothing to say
about its texture he has nothing to say about it specifically as a poem, but is
treating it only insofar as it is prose.

I do not mean to say that the good critic will necessarily employ my
terms.

V

Many critics today are writing analytically and with close intelligence, in
whatever terms, about the logical substance or structure of the poem, and its
increment of irrelevant local substance or texture. I believe that the understanding of the ideal critic has to go even further than that. The final desider-
atum is an ontological insight, nothing less. I am committed by my title to
representation of criticism as, in the last resort, a speculative exercise. But my
secret committal was to speculative in the complete sense of — ontological.

There is nothing especially speculative or ontological in reciting, or even
appraising, the logical substance of the poem. This is its prose core — its science perhaps, or its ethics if it seems to have an ideology. Speculative interest
asserts itself principally when we ask why we want the logical substance to
be compounded with the local substance, the good lean structure with a
great volume of texture that does not function. It is the same thing as asking
why we want the poem to be what it is.

It has been a rule, having the fewest exceptions, for estheticians and great
philosophers to direct their speculations by the way of overstating and over-
valuing the logical substance. They are impressed by the apparent obedience of
material nature, whether in fact or in art, to definable form or "law" imposed
upon it. They like to suppose that in poetry, as in chemistry, everything that figures in the discourse means to be functional, and that the poem is imperfect in
the degree that it contains items, whether by accident or intention, which manifest a private independence. It is a bias with which we are entirely familiar,
and reflects the extent to which our philosophy hitherto has been impressed by
the successes of science in formulating laws which would "govern" their objects. Probably I am here reading the state of mind of yesterday rather than of
today. Nevertheless we know it. The world-view which ultimately forms itself

in the mind so biased is that of a world which is rational and intelligible. The view is sanguine, and naïve. Hegel's world-view, I think it is agreed, was a subtle version of this, and if so, it was what determined his view of art. He seemed to make the handsomest concession to realism by offering to knowledge a kind of universal which was not restricted to the usual abstracted aspects of the material, but included all aspects, and was a concrete universal. The concreteness in Hegel's handling was not honestly, or at any rate not fairly, defended. It was always represented as being in process of pointing up and helping out the universality. He could look at a work of art and report all its substance as almost assimilated to a ruling "idea." But at least Hegel seemed to distinguish what looked like two ultimate sorts of substance there, and stated the central esthetic problem as the problem of relating them. And his writings about art are speculative in the sense that he regarded the work of art not as of great intrinsic value necessarily, but as an object-lesson or discipline in the understanding of the world-process, and as its symbol.

I think of two ways of construing poetry with respect to its ultimate purpose; of which the one is not very handsome nor speculatively interesting, and the other will appear somewhat severe.

The first construction would picture the poet as a sort of epicure, and the poem as something on the order of a Christmas pudding, stuffed with what dainties it will hold. The pastry alone, or it may be the cake, will not serve; the stuffing is wanted too. The values of the poem would be intrinsic, or immediate, and they would include not only the value of the structure but also the incidental values not only the value of the structure but also the incidental values to be found in the texture. If we exchange the pudding for a house, they would include not only the value of the house itself but also the value of the furnishings. In saying intrinsic or immediate, I mean that the poet is fond of the precise objects denoted by the words, and writes the poem for the reason that he likes to dwell upon them. In talking about the main value and the incidental values I mean to recognize the fact that the latter engage the affections just as truly as the former. Poetic discourse therefore would be more agreeable than prose to the epicure or the literally acquisitive man; for prose has but a single value, being about one thing only; its parts have no values of their own, but only instrumental values, which might be reckoned as fractions of the single value proportionate to their contributions to it. The prose is one-valued and the poem is many-valued. Indeed, there will certainly be poems whose texture contains many precious objects, and aggregates a greater value than the structure.

So there would be a comfortable and apparently eligible view that poetry improves on prose because it is a richer diet. It causes five or six pleasures to appear, five or six good things, where one had been before; an alluring consideration for robustious, full-blooded, bourgeois souls. The view will account for much of the poem, if necessary. But it does not account for all of it, and sometimes it accounts for less than at other times.

The most impressive reason for the bolder view of art, the speculative one, is the existence of the "pure," or "abstractionist," or nonrepresentational works of art; though these will probably occur to us in other arts than poetry. There is at least one art, music, whose works are all of this sort. Tones are not words, they have no direct semantical function, and by themselves they mean nothing. But they combine to make brilliant phrases, harmonies, and compositions. In these compositions it is probable that the distinction between structure or functional content, on the one hand, and texture or local variation and departure, on the other, is even more determinate than in an impure art like poetry. The world of tones seems perfectly inhuman and impracticable; there is no specific field of experience "about which" music is telling us. Yet we know that music is powerfully affective. I take my own musical feelings, and those attested by other audients, as the sufficient index to some overwhelming human importance which the musical object has for us. At the same time it would be useless to ask the feelings precisely what they felt; we must ask the critic. The safest policy is to take the simplest construction, and try to improvise as little fiction as possible. Music is not music, I think, until we grasp its effects both in structure and in texture. As we grow in musical understanding the structures become always more elaborate and sustained, and the texture which interrupts them and sometimes imperils them becomes more bold and unpredictable. We can agree in saying about the works of music that these are musical structures, and they are richly textured; we can identify these elements, and perhaps precisely. To what then do our feelings respond? To music as structural composition itself; to music as manifesting the structural principles of the world; to modes of structure which we feel to be ontologically possible, or even probable. Schopenhauer construed music very much in that sense. Probably it will occur to us that musical compositions bear close analogy therefore to operations in pure mathematics. The mathematicians confess that their constructions are "nonexistential"; meaning, as I take it, that the constructions testify with assurance only to the structural principles, in the light of which they are possible but may not be actual, or if they are actual may not be useful. This would define the mathematical operations as speculative; as motivated by an interest so generalized and so elemental that no word short of ontological will describe it.

But if music and mathematics have this much in common, they differ sharply in their respective world-views or ontological biasses. That of music, with its prodigious display of texture, seems the better informed about the nature of the world, the more realistic, the less naïve. Perhaps the difference is between two ontological educations. But I should be inclined to imagine it as rising back of that point; in two ontological temperaments.

There are also, operating a little less successfully so far as the indexical evidences would indicate, the abstractionist paintings, of many schools, and perhaps also works of sculpture; and there is architecture. These arts have tried to abandon direct representational intention almost as heroically as music. They exist in their own materials and indicate no other specific materials; structures of color, light, space, stone—the cheapest of materials. They too can symbolize nothing of value unless it is structure or composition itself. But that is precisely the act which denotes will and intelligence; which becomes the act of fuller intelligence if it carefully accompanies its structures with their material textures; for then it understands better the ontological nature of materials.

Returning to the poetry. It is not all poems, and not even all "powerful" poems, having high index-ratings, whose semantical meanings contain situations important in themselves or objects precious in themselves. There may be little correlation between the single value of the poem and the aggregate value of its contents—just as there is no such correlation whatever in music. The "effect" of the poem may be astonishingly disproportionate to our interest in its materials. It is true, of course, that there is no art employing materials of equal richness with poetry, and that it is beyond the capacity of poetry to employ indifferent materials. The words used in poetry are the words the race has already formed, and naturally they call attention to things and events that have been thought to be worth attending to. But I suggest that any poetry which is "technically" notable is in part a work of abstractionist art, concentrating upon the structure and the texture, and the structure-texture relation, out of a pure speculative interest.

At the end of *Love's Labour's Lost* occurs a little diversion which seems proportionately far more effective than that laborious play as a whole. The play is over, but Armado stops the principals before they disperse to offer them a show:

> ARM: But, most esteemed greatness, will you hear the dialogue that the two learned men have compiled in praise of the owl and the cuckoo? It should have followed in the end of our show.
> KING: Call them forth quickly; we will do so.
> ARM: Holla! approach.

Re-enter Holofernes, etc.

This side is Hiems, Winter, this Ver, the Spring; the one maintained by the owl, the other by the cuckoo. Ver, begin.

The Song

SPRING.
> When daisies pied and violets blue
> And lady-smocks all silver-white
> And cuckoo-buds of yellow hue
> Do paint the meadows with delight,
> The cuckoo then, on every tree,
> Mocks married men; for thus sings he,
>   Cuckoo;
> Cuckoo, cuckoo: O word of fear,
> Unpleasing to a married ear!

When shepherds pipe on oaten straws,
And merry larks are ploughmen's clocks,
When turtles tread, and rooks, and daws,
And maidens bleach their summer smocks,
The cuckoo then, on every tree,
Mocks married men; for thus sings he,
    Cuckoo;
Cuckoo, cuckoo: O word of fear,
Unpleasing to a married ear!

WINTER.
When icicles hang by the wall,
And Dick the shepherd blows his nail,
And Tom bears logs into the hall,
And milk comes frozen home in pail,
When blood is nipp'd and ways be foul,
Then nightly sings the staring owl,
    Tu-who;
Tu-whit, tu-who, a merry note,
While greasy Joan doth keel the pot.

When all aloud the wind doth blow,
And coughing drowns the parson's saw,
And birds sit brooding in the snow,
And Marian's nose looks red and raw,
When roasted crabs hiss in the bowl,
Then nightly sings the staring owl,
    Tu-who;
Tu-whit, tu-who, a merry note,
While greasy Joan doth keel the pot.

ARM: The words of Mercury are harsh after the songs of Apollo. You
    that way, — we this way.

                                                    (Exeunt.)

The feeling-index registers such strong approval of this episode that a
critic with ambition is obliged to account for it. He can scarcely account for it
in terms of the weight of its contents severally.

At first glance Shakespeare has provided only a pleasant little caricature
of the old-fashioned (to us, medieval) debate between personified characters.
It is easygoing, like nonsense; no labor is lost here. Each party speaks two
stanzas and concludes both stanzas with the refrain about his bird, the
cuckoo or the owl. There is next to no generalized argument, or dialectic
proper. Each argues by citing his characteristic exhibits. In the first stanza
Spring cites some flowers; in the second stanza, some business by country
persons, with interpolation of some birds that make love. Winter in both

stanzas cites the country business of the season. In the refrain the cuckoo, Spring's symbol, is used to refer the love-making to more than the birds; and this repeats itself though it is naughty. The owl is only a nominal symbol for Winter, an "emblem" that is not very emblematic, but the refrain manages another reference to the kitchen, and repeats itself, as if Winter's pleasures focussed in the kitchen.

In this poem texture is not very brilliant, but it eclipses structure. The argument, we would say in academic language, is concerned with "the relative advantages of Spring and Winter." The only logical determinateness this structure has is the good coordination of the items cited by Spring as being really items peculiar to Spring, and of the Winter items as peculiar to Winter. The symbolic refrains look like summary or master items, but they seem to be a little more than summary and in fact to mean a little more than they say. The argument is trifling on the whole, and the texture from the point of view of felt human importance lacks decided energy; both which observations are to be made, and most precisely, of how many famous lyrics, especially those before that earnest and self-conscious nineteenth century! The value of the poem is greater than the value of its parts: that is what the critic is up against.

Unquestionably it is possible to assemble very fine structures out of ordinary materials. The good critic will study the poet's technique, in confidence that here the structural principles will be discovered at home. In this study he will find as much range for his activities as he desires.

Especially must he study the metrics, and their implications for structural composition. In this poem I think the critic ought to make good capital of the contrast between the amateurishness of the pleasant discourse as meaning and the hard determinate form of it phonetically. The meter on the whole is out of relation to the meaning of the poem or to anything else specifically; it is a musical material of low grade, but plastic and only slightly resistant material, and its presence in every poem is that of an abstractionist element that belongs to the art.

And here I will suggest another analogy, this one between Shakespeare's poem and some ordinary specimen of painting. It does not matter how old-fashioned or representational the painting is, we shall all, if we are instructed in the tradition of this art, require it to exhibit along with its represented object an abstract design in terms of pure physical balance or symmetry. We sense rather than measure the success of this design, but it is as if we had drawn a horizontal axis and a vertical axis through the center of the picture, and required the painted masses to balance with respect to each of these two axes. This is an over-simple statement of a structural requirement by which the same details function in two worlds that are different, and that do not correlate with each other. If the painting is of the Holy Family, we might say that this object has a drama, or an economy, of its own; but that the physical masses which compose it must enter also into another economy, that of abstract design; and that the value of any unit mass for the one economy bears no relation to its value for the other. The painting is of great ontological interest because it embodies this special dimension of abstract form. And turning to the poem we should find that its represented "meaning" is analogous to the represented object in the painting, while its meter is analogous to the pure design.

A number of fascinating speculative considerations must follow upon this discovery. They will have to do with the most fundamental laws of this world's structure. They will be profoundly ontological, though I do not mean that they must be ontological in some recondite sense; ontological in such a homely and compelling sense that perhaps a child might intuit the principles which the critic will arrive at analytically, and with much labor.

I must stop at this point, since I am desired not so much to anticipate the critic as to present him. In conclusion I will remark that the critic will doubtless work empirically, and set up his philosophy only as the drift of his findings compel him. But ultimately he will be compelled. He will have to subscribe to an ontology. If he is a sound critic his ontology will be that of his poets; and what is that? I suggest that the poetic world-view is Aristotelian and "realistic" rather than Platonic and "idealistic." He cannot follow the poets and still conceive himself as inhabiting the rational or "tidy" universe that is supposed by the scientists.

CLEANTH BROOKS

Keats's Sylvan Historian: History without Footnotes

From *The Well Wrought Urn*

1942

"It was possible to know everything about a literary work except why it was litera-ture," an essayist once complained, reflecting on his university education in English. Indeed, until the early 1940s the typical academic approaches were historical, social, biographical, philosophical, psychological, mimetic, and moral, in any combination. The New Criticism seemed to be a liberation, a fresh new way of studying literature by returning to the words on the printed page, to the text itself. Although various of the New Critics differed from one another in particulars, the general direction was clear. The task of the critic and the teacher of literature was to analyze and describe objectively the formal properties of a literary text by a close, detailed reading, without regard to extrinsic considerations.

The principal exponents of this critical movement were American university professors such as John Crowe Ransom (see p. 448), Cleanth Brooks (1906–1994), Robert Penn Warren, W. K. Wimsatt, and Allen Tate, whose influential essays and books (including textbooks) redirected the study and teaching of literature for more than a generation. They rejected the idea of the work as an expression of a specific time and place; they rejected the idea of authorial intention, considered a Romantic fallacy; and they rejected the idea that a literary work was to be studied as an expres-sion of its author's personality. As formalist critics, they were concerned only with the poem as poem, with an analysis of its form, structure, and imagery. The only rel-evant history was the historical meanings of words, including their connotations. (It should be noted that New Criticism applied more effectively to the analysis of poetry than to fiction or drama.)

New terms were introduced into the critical vocabulary. By "structure," the New Critics referred to the interrelationships between the parts of a poem, how the complex organization of its parts created coherent meaning not of a logical kind, such as would be found in the propositions in expository writing, but of a kind peculiar to

poems, thus distinguishing poems from other verbal structures. Unity, ambiguity,
irony, integrity, and paradox were some of the new terms describing desirable liter-
ary qualities.

    Eventually overcoming the entrenched opposition of the more traditional aca-
demics, New Criticism by the 1950s had become the principal mode of criticism in
American and British universities. Less interested in evaluation than in analysis and
description, the New Critics nevertheless enunciated principles that purportedly dis-
tinguished good poetry from bad and that brought about a revaluation of literary his-
tory by upgrading seventeenth-century metaphysical poetry and largely downgrad-
ing Romantic poetry. However, by the end of the 1960s, despite the significant
change of direction it had given to the study of literature, the New Criticism was be-
coming old hat. It was to decline into overingenious, self-enclosed exercises in expli-
cation, as ambiguities, ironies, and paradoxes were discovered to flourish everywhere.
But its influence is still strong today, and essays by some of its original practitioners
retain their capacity to illuminate, as Brooks's exemplary article demonstrates.

THERE IS MUCH in the poetry of Keats which suggests that he would have approved of Archibald MacLeish's dictum, "A poem should not mean/ But
be." There is even some warrant for thinking that the Grecian urn (real or
imagined) which inspired the famous ode was, for Keats, just such a poem,
"palpable and mute," a poem in stone. Hence it is the more remarkable that
the "Ode" itself differs from Keats's other odes by culminating in a statement—a statement even of some sententiousness in which the urn itself is
made to say that beauty is truth, and—more sententious still—that this bit
of wisdom sums up the whole of mortal knowledge.[1]

    This is "to mean" with a vengeance—to violate the doctrine of the objec-
tive correlative, not only by stating truths, but by defining the limits of truth.
Small wonder that some critics have felt that the unravished bride of quietness protests too much.

    T. S. Eliot, for example, says that "this line ["Beauty is truth," etc.] strikes
me as a serious blemish on a beautiful poem; and the reason must be either
that I fail to understand it, or that it is a statement which is untrue." But even
for persons who feel that they do understand it, the line may still constitute a
blemish. Middleton Murry, who, after a discussion of Keats's other poems

---

[1] This essay had been finished some months before I came upon Kenneth Burke's brilliant essay on Keats's "Ode" ("Symbolic Action in a Poem by Keats," *Accent*, Autumn,
1943). I have decided not to make any alterations, though I have been tempted to adopt
some of Burke's insights, and, in at least one case, his essay has convinced me of a point
which I had considered but rejected—the pun on "breed" and "Brede."

    I am happy to find that two critics with methods and purposes so different should
agree so thoroughly as we do on the poem. I am pleased, for my part, therefore, to acknowledge the amount of duplication which exists between the two essays, counting it as rather
important corroboration of a view of the poem which will probably seem to some critics
overingenious. In spite of the common elements, however, I feel that the emphasis of my
essay is sufficiently different from Burke's to justify my going on with its publication.
[Brooks's note.]

and his letters, feels that he knows what Keats meant by "beauty" and what he meant by "truth," and that Keats used them in senses which allowed them to be properly bracketed together, still, is forced to conclude: "My own opinion concerning the value of these two lines *in the context of the poem itself* is not very different from Mr. T. S. Eliot's." The troubling assertion is apparently an intrusion upon the poem—does not grow out of it—is not dramatically accommodated to it.

This is essentially Garrod's objection, and the fact that Garrod does object indicates that a distaste for the ending of the "Ode" is by no means limited to critics of notoriously "modern" sympathies.

But the question of real importance is not whether Eliot, Murry, and Garrod are right in thinking that "Beauty is truth, truth beauty" injures the poem. The question of real importance concerns beauty and truth in a much more general way: what is the relation of the beauty (the goodness, the perfection) of a poem to the truth or falsity of what it seems to assert? It is a question which has particularly vexed our own generation—to give it I. A. Richards' phrasing, it is the problem of belief.

The "Ode," by its bold equation of beauty and truth, raises this question in its sharpest form—the more so when it becomes apparent that the poem itself is obviously intended to be a parable on the nature of poetry, and of art in general. The "Ode" has apparently been an enigmatic parable, to be sure: one can emphasize *beauty* is truth and throw Keats into the pure-art camp, the usual procedure. But it is only fair to point out that one could stress *truth* is beauty, and argue with the Marxist critics of the 'thirties for a propaganda art. The very ambiguity of the statement, "Beauty is truth, truth beauty" ought to warn us against insisting very much on the statement in isolation, and to drive us back to a consideration of the context in which the statement is set.

It will not be sufficient, however, if it merely drives us back to a study of Keats's reading, his conversation, his letters. We shall not find our answer there even if scholarship does prefer on principle investigations of Browning's ironic question, "What porridge had John Keats?" For even if we knew just what porridge he had, physical and mental, we should still not be able to settle the problem of the "Ode." The reason should be clear: our specific question is not what did Keats the man perhaps want to assert here about the relation of beauty and truth; it is rather: was Keats the poet able to exemplify that relation in this particular poem? Middleton Murry is right: the relation of the final statement in the poem to the total context is all-important.

Indeed, Eliot, in the very passage in which he attacks the "Ode" has indicated the general line which we are to take in its defense. In that passage, Eliot goes on to contrast the closing lines of the "Ode" with a line from *King Lear*, "Ripeness is all." Keats's lines strike him as false; Shakespeare's, on the other hand, as not clearly false, and as possibly quite true. Shakespeare's generalization, in other words, avoids raising the question of truth. But is it really a question of truth and falsity? One is tempted to account for the difference of effect which Eliot feels in this way: "Ripeness is all" is a statement put in the mouth of a dramatic character and a statement which is governed and qualified by the whole context of the play. It does not directly challenge an examination into its truth because its relevance is pointed up and modified by the dramatic context.

Now, suppose that one could show that Keats's lines, *in quite the same way,* constitute a speech, a consciously riddling paradox, put in the mouth of a particular character, and modified by the total context of the poem. If we could demonstrate that the speech was "in character," was dramatically appropriate, was properly prepared for—then would not the lines have all the justification of "Ripeness is all"? In such case, should we not have waived the question of the scientific or philosophic truth of the lines in favor of the application of a principle curiously like that of dramatic propriety? I suggest that some such principle is the only one legitimately to be invoked in any case. Be this as it may, the "Ode on a Grecian Urn" provides us with as neat an instance as one could wish in order to test the implications of such a maneuver.

It has seemed best to be perfectly frank about procedure: the poem is to be read in order to see whether the last lines of the poem are not, after all, dramatically prepared for. Yet there are some claims to be made upon the reader too, claims which he, for his part, will have to be prepared to honor. He must not be allowed to dismiss the early characterizations of the urn as merely so much vaguely beautiful description. He must not be too much surprised if "mere decoration" turns out to be meaningful symbolism—or if ironies develop where he has been taught to expect only sensuous pictures. Most of all, if the teasing riddle spoken finally by the urn is not to strike him as a bewildering break in tone, he must not be too much disturbed to have the element of paradox latent in the poem emphasized, even in those parts of the poem which have none of the energetic crackle of wit with which he usually associates paradox. This is surely not too much to ask of the reader—namely, to assume that Keats meant what he said and that he chose his words with care. After all, the poem begins on a note of paradox, though a mild one: for we ordinarily do not expect an urn to speak at all; and yet, Keats does more than this: he begins his poem by emphasizing the apparent contradiction.

The silence of the urn is stressed—it is a "bride of quietness"; it is a "foster-child of silence," but the urn is a "historian" too. Historians tell the truth, or are at least expected to tell the truth. What is a "Sylvan historian"? A historian who is like the forest rustic, a woodlander? Or, a historian who writes histories of the forest? Presumably, the urn is sylvan in both senses. True, the latter meaning is uppermost: the urn can "express/ A flowery tale more sweetly than our rhyme," and what the urn goes on to express is a "leaf-fring'd legend" of "Tempe or the dales of Arcady." But the urn, like the "leaf-fring'd legend" which it tells, is covered with emblems of the fields and forests: "Overwrought,/ With forest branches and the trodden weed." When we consider the way in which the urn utters its history, the fact that it must be sylvan in both senses is seen as inevitable. Perhaps too the fact that it is a rural historian, a rustic, a peasant historian, qualifies in our minds the dignity and the "truth" of the histories which it recites. Its histories, Keats has already conceded, may be characterized as "tales"—not formal history at all.

The sylvan historian certainly supplies no names and dates—"What men or gods are these?" the poet asks. What it does give is action—of men *or* gods, of godlike men or of superhuman (though not daemonic) gods—action, which is not the less intense for all that the urn is cool marble. The words "mad" and "ecstasy" occur, but it is the quiet, rigid urn which gives the dynamic picture. And the paradox goes further: the scene is one of violent love-making, a Bacchanalian scene, but the urn itself is like a "still unravish'd bride," or like a child, a child "of silence and slow time." It is not merely like a child, but like a "foster-child." The exactness of the term can be defended. "Silence and slow time," it is suggested, are not the true parents, but foster-parents. They are too old, one feels, to have borne the child themselves. Moreover, they dote upon the "child" as grandparents do. The urn is fresh and unblemished; it is still young, for all its antiquity, and time which destroys so much has "fostered" it.

With Stanza II we move into the world presented by the urn, into an examination, not of the urn as a whole—as an entity with its own form—but of the details which overlay it. But as we enter that world, the paradox of silent speech is carried on, this time in terms of the objects portrayed on the vase.

The first lines of the stanza state a rather bold paradox—even the dulling effect of many readings has hardly blunted it. At least we can easily revive its sharpness. Attended to with care, it is a statement which is preposterous, and yet true—true on the same level on which the original metaphor of the speaking urn is true. The unheard music is sweeter than any audible music. The poet has rather cunningly enforced his conceit by using the phrase, "ye soft pipes." Actually, we might accept the poet's metaphor without being forced to accept the adjective "soft." The pipes might, although "unheard," be shrill, just as the action which is frozen in the figures on the urn can be violent and ecstatic as in Stanza I and slow and dignified as in Stanza IV (the procession to the sacrifice). Yet, by characterizing the pipes as "soft," the poet has provided a sort of realistic basis for his metaphor: the pipes, it is suggested, are playing very softly; if we listen carefully, we can hear them; their music is just below the threshold of normal sound.

The general paradox runs through the stanza: action goes on though the actors are motionless; the song will not cease; the lover cannot leave his song; the maiden, always to be kissed, never actually kissed, will remain changelessly beautiful. The maiden is, indeed, like the urn itself, a "still unravished bride of quietness"—not even ravished by a kiss; and it is implied, perhaps, that her changeless beauty, like that of the urn, springs from this fact.

The poet is obviously stressing the fresh, unwearied charm of the scene itself which can defy time and is deathless. But, at the same time, the poet is being perfectly fair to the terms of his metaphor. The beauty portrayed is deathless because it is lifeless. And it would be possible to shift the tone easily and ever so slightly by insisting more heavily on some of the phrasings so as to give them a darker implication. Thus, in the case of "thou canst not leave/ Thy song," one could interpret: the musician cannot leave the song even if he would: he is fettered to it, a prisoner. In the same way, one could enlarge on the hint that the lover is not wholly satisfied and content: "never canst thou kiss,/ . . . *yet, do not grieve*." These items are mentioned here, not because one wishes to maintain that the poet is bitterly ironical, but because it is important for us to see that even here the paradox is being used fairly, particularly in view of the shift in tone which comes in the next stanza.

This third stanza represents, as various critics have pointed out, a recapitulation of earlier motifs. The boughs which cannot shed their leaves, the unwearied melodist, and the ever-ardent lover reappear. Indeed, I am not sure that this stanza can altogether be defended against the charge that it represents a falling-off from the delicate but firm precision of the earlier stanzas. There is a tendency to linger over the scene sentimentally: the repetition of the word "happy" is perhaps symptomatic of what is occurring. Here, if anywhere, in my opinion, is to be found the blemish on the ode—not in the last two lines. Yet, if we are to attempt a defense of the third stanza, we shall come nearest success by emphasizing the paradoxical implications of the repeated items; for whatever development there is in the stanza inheres in the increased stress on the paradoxical element. For example, the boughs cannot "bid the Spring adieu," a phrase which repeats "nor ever can those trees be bare," but the new line strengthens the implications of speaking: the falling leaves are a gesture, a word of farewell to the joy of spring. The melodist of Stanza II played sweeter music because unheard, but here, in the third stanza, it is implied that he does not tire of his song for the same reason that the lover does not tire of his love—neither song nor love is consummated. The songs are "for ever new" because they cannot be completed.

The paradox is carried further in the case of the lover whose love is "For ever warm and still to be enjoy'd." We are really dealing with an ambiguity here, for we can take "still to be enjoy'd" as an adjectival phrase on the same level as "warm"—that is, "still virginal and warm." But the tenor of the whole poem suggests that the warmth of the love depends upon the fact that it has not been enjoyed—that is, "warm and still to be enjoy'd" may mean also "warm *because* still to be enjoy'd."

But though the poet has developed and extended his metaphors furthest here in this third stanza, the ironic counterpoise is developed furthest too. The love which a line earlier was "warm" and "panting" becomes suddenly in the next line, "All breathing human passion far above." But if it is *above* all breathing passion, it is, after all, outside the realm of breathing passion, and therefore, not human passion at all.

(If one argues that we are to take "All breathing human passion" as qualified by "That leaves a heart high-sorrowful and cloy'd"—that is, if one argues that Keats is saying that the love depicted on the urn is above only that human passion which leaves one cloyed and not above human passion in general, he misses the point. For Keats in the "Ode" is stressing the ironic fact that all human passion *does* leave one cloyed; hence the superiority of art.)

The purpose in emphasizing the ironic undercurrent in the foregoing lines is not at all to disparage Keats—to point up implications of his poem of which he was himself unaware. Far from it: the poet knows precisely what he is doing. The point is to be made simply in order to make sure that we are completely aware of what he *is* doing. Garrod, sensing this ironic undercurrent, seems to interpret it as an element over which Keats was not able to exercise full control. He says: "Truth to his main theme [the fixity given by art to forms which in life are impermanent] has taken Keats farther than he meant to go. The pure and ideal art of this 'cold Pastoral,' this 'silent form,' *has* a cold silentness which in some degree saddens him. In the last lines of the fourth stanza, especially the last three lines . . . every reader is conscious, I should suppose, of an undertone of sadness, of disappointment." The undertone is there, but Keats has not been taken "farther than he meant to go." Keats's attitude, even in the early stanzas, is more complex than Garrod would allow: it is more complex and more ironic, and a recognition of this is important if we are to be able to relate the stanza to the rest of the "Ode." Keats is perfectly aware that the frozen moment of loveliness is more dynamic than is the fluid world of reality *only* because it is frozen. The love depicted on the urn remains warm and young because it is not human flesh at all but cold, ancient marble.

With Stanza IV, we are still within the world depicted by the urn, but the scene presented in this stanza forms a contrast to the earlier scenes. It emphasizes, not individual aspiration and desire, but communal life. It constitutes another chapter in the history that the "Sylvan historian" has to tell. And again, names and dates have been omitted. We are not told to what god's altar the procession moves, nor the occasion of the sacrifice.

Moreover, the little town from which the celebrants come is unknown; and the poet rather goes out of his way to leave us the widest possible option in locating it. It may be a mountain town, or a river town, or a tiny seaport. Yet, of course, there is a sense in which the nature of the town—the essential character of the town—is actually suggested by the figured urn. But it is not given explicitly. The poet is willing to leave much to our imaginations; and yet the stanza in its organization of imagery and rhythm does describe the town clearly enough; it is small, it is quiet, its people are knit together as an organic whole, and on a "pious morn" such as this, its whole population has turned out to take part in the ritual.

The stanza has been justly admired. Its magic of effect defies reduction to any formula. Yet, without pretending to "account" for the effect in any mechanical fashion, one can point to some of the elements active in securing the effect: there is the suggestiveness of the word "green" in "green altar"—something natural, spontaneous, living; there is the suggestion that the little town is caught in a curve of the seashore, or nestled in a fold of the mountains—at any rate, is something secluded and something naturally related to its terrain; there is the effect of the phrase "peaceful citadel," a phrase which involves a clash between the ideas of war and peace and resolves it in the sense of stability and independence without imperialistic ambition—the sense of stable repose.

But to return to the larger pattern of the poem: Keats does something in this fourth stanza which is highly interesting in itself and thoroughly relevant to the sense in which the urn is a historian. One of the most moving passages in the poem is that in which the poet speculates on the strange emptiness of the little town which, of course, has not been pictured on the urn at all.

The little town which has been merely implied by the procession portrayed on the urn is endowed with a poignance beyond anything else in the poem. Its streets "for evermore/ Will silent be," its desolation forever shrouded in a mystery. No one in the figured procession will ever be able to go back to the town to break the silence there, not even one to tell the stranger there why the town remains desolate.

If one attends closely to what Keats is doing here, he may easily come to feel that the poet is indulging himself in an ingenious fancy, an indulgence, however, which is gratuitous and finally silly; that is, the poet has created in his own imagination the town implied by the procession of worshipers, has given it a special character of desolation and loneliness, and then has gone on to treat it as if it were a real town to which a stranger might actually come and be puzzled by its emptiness. (I can see no other interpretation of the lines, "and not a soul to tell/ Why thou art desolate can e'er return.") But, actually, of course, no one will ever discover the town except by the very same process by which Keats has discovered it: namely, through the figured urn, and then, of course, he will not need to ask why it is empty. One can well imagine what a typical eighteenth-century critic would have made of this flaw in logic.

It will not be too difficult, however, to show that Keats's extension of the fancy is not irrelevant to the poem as a whole. The "reality" of the little town has a very close relation to the urn's character as a historian. If the earlier stanzas have been concerned with such paradoxes as the ability of static carving to convey dynamic action, of the soundless pipes to play music sweeter than that of the heard melody, of the figured lover to have a love more warm and panting than that of breathing flesh and blood, so in the same way the town implied by the urn comes to have a richer and more important history than that of actual cities. Indeed, the imagined town is to the figured procession as the unheard melody is to the carved pipes of the unwearied melodist. And the poet, by pretending to take the town as real—so real that he can imagine the effect of its silent streets upon the stranger who chances to come into it—has suggested in the most powerful way possible its essential reality for him—and for us. It is a case of the doctor's taking his own medicine: the poet is prepared to stand by the illusion of his own making.

With Stanza V we move back out of the enchanted world portrayed by the urn to consider the urn itself once more as a whole, as an object. The shift in point of view is marked with the first line of the stanza by the apostrophe, "O Attic shape . . ." It is the urn itself as a formed thing, as an autonomous world, to which the poet addresses these last words. And the rich, almost breathing world which the poet has conjured up for us contracts and hardens into the decorated motifs on the urn itself: "with brede/ Of marble men and maidens overwrought." The beings who have a life above life—"All breathing human passion far above"—are marble, after all.

This last is a matter which, of course, the poet has never denied. The recognition that the men and maidens are frozen, fixed, arrested, has, as we have already seen, run through the second, third, and fourth stanzas as an ironic undercurrent. The central paradox of the poem, thus, comes to conclusion in the phrase, "Cold Pastoral." The word "pastoral" suggests warmth, spontaneity, the natural and the informal as well as the idyllic, the simple, and the informally charming. What the urn tells is a "flowery tale," a "leaf-fring'd legend," but the "sylvan historian" works in terms of marble. The urn itself is cold, and the life beyond life which it expresses is life which has been formed, arranged. The urn itself is a "silent form," and it speaks, not by means of statement, but by "teasing us out of thought." It is as enigmatic as eternity is, for, like eternity, its history is beyond time, outside time, and for this very reason bewilders our time-ridden minds: it teases us.

The marble men and maidens of the urn will not age as flesh-and-blood men and women will: "When old age shall this generation waste." (The word "generation," by the way, is very rich. It means on one level "that which is generated"—that which springs from human loins—Adam's breed; and yet, so intimately is death wedded to men, the word "generation" itself has become, as here, a measure of time.) The marble men and women lie outside time. The urn which they adorn will remain. The "Sylvan historian" will recite its history to other generations.

What will it say to them? Presumably, what it says to the poet now: that "formed experience," imaginative insight, embodies the basic and fundamental perception of man and nature. The urn is beautiful, and yet its beauty is based—what else is the poem concerned with?—on an imaginative perception of essentials. Such a vision is beautiful but it is also true. The sylvan historian presents us with beautiful histories, but they are true histories, and it is a good historian.

Moreover, the "truth" which the sylvan historian gives is the only kind of truth which we are likely to get on this earth, and, furthermore, it is the only kind that we *have* to have. The names, dates, and special circumstances, the wealth of data—these the sylvan historian quietly ignores. But we shall never get all the facts anyway—there is no end to the accumulation of facts. Moreover, mere accumulations of facts—a point our own generation is only beginning to realize—are meaningless. The sylvan historian does better than that: it takes a few details and so orders them that we have not only beauty but insight into essential truth. Its "history," in short, is a history without footnotes. It has the validity of myth—not myth as a pretty but irrelevant make-believe, an idle fancy, but myth as a valid perception into reality.

So much for the "meaning" of the last lines of the "Ode." It is an interpretation which differs little from past interpretations. It is put forward here with no pretension to novelty. What is important is the fact that it can be derived from the context of the "Ode" itself.

And now, what of the objection that the final lines break the tone of the poem with a display of misplaced sententiousness? One can summarize the answer already implied thus: throughout the poem the poet has stressed the paradox of the speaking urn. First, the urn itself can tell a story, can give a history. Then, the various figures depicted upon the urn play music or speak or sing. If we have been alive to these items, we shall not, perhaps, be too much surprised to have the urn speak once more, not in the sense in which it tells a story—a metaphor which is rather easy to accept—but, to have it speak on a higher level, to have it make a commentary on its own nature. If the urn has been properly dramatized, if we have followed the development of the metaphors, if we have been alive to the paradoxes which work throughout the poem, perhaps then, we shall be prepared for the enigmatic, final paradox which the "silent form" utters. But in that case, we shall not feel that the generalization, unqualified and to be taken literally, is meant to march out of its context to compete with the scientific and philosophical generalizations which dominate our world.

"Beauty is truth, truth beauty" has precisely the same status, and the same justification as Shakespeare's "Ripeness is all." It is a speech "in character" and supported by a dramatic context.

To conclude thus may seem to weight the principle of dramatic propriety with more than it can bear. This would not be fair to the complexity of the problem of truth in art nor fair to Keats's little parable. Granted; and yet the principle of dramatic propriety may take us further than would first appear. Respect for it may at least insure our dealing with the problem of truth at the level on which it is really relevant to literature. If we can see that the assertions made in a poem are to be taken as part of an organic context, if we can resist the temptation to deal with them in isolation, then we may be willing to go on to deal with the world-view, or "philosophy," or "truth" of the *poem as a whole* in terms of its dramatic wholeness: that is, we shall not neglect the maturity of attitude, the dramatic tension, the emotional *and* intellectual coherence in favor of some statement of theme abstracted from it by paraphrase. Perhaps, best of all, we might learn to distrust our ability to represent any poem adequately by paraphrase. Such a distrust is healthy. Keats's sylvan historian, who is not above "teasing" us, exhibits such a distrust, and perhaps the point of what the sylvan historian "says" is to confirm us in our distrust.

NORTHROP FRYE

The Archetypes
of Literature

1951

To see and to study the principles of optics are obviously different kinds of experiences; to enjoy a novel and to criticize it are equally different. Seeing and enjoying cannot be taught, but physics and criticism can be. Nobody mistakes the expression "I feel cold" for a statement about the nature of heat, but similar statements applied to literature are called criticism. Literature, like the physical world, is "an inexhaustible source" of new discoveries; and criticism, like physics, can be assumed to be a "totally intelligible" science, an organized body of knowledge.

This basic assumption underlies Northrop Frye's (1912–1991) prodigious output of essays and books; this early essay is representative of and wholly consistent with his theory of archetypes, dealt with more fully in his Anatomy of Criticism (1957). Like Aristotle, Frye is a supreme systematizer, attempting nothing less than the creation of a new and comprehensive poetics of criticism, "a systematic structure of knowledge" to replace the "leisure-class conversation" that passes for critical discourse. His intention is to supply the missing organizing principle for criticism, a "central hypothesis" that will put into perspective various partial or fragmentary critical approaches.

To study the principles of literary form, Frye relies heavily on both the insights and the methods of anthropology; indeed, he calls the search for archetypes "a kind of literary anthropology." As a literary anthropologist, he relates narrative to the creation of rituals, imagery to moments of instantaneous insights, rhythm to natural cycles, and so forth. The central myth of all literature he identifies as the quest-myth, seen in four distinct phases that correspond to four aspects of cyclical recurrence. In his reordering of all literature from epics to comic strips according to this classification, Frye's system is clearly not bound by any sense of historical continuity or development; his ideas on literary history should be compared with those of Eliot, who also posits a nonchronological view of the "existing monuments" of literature.

Because Frye's attempts to organize a systematic and comprehensive critical theory involve him in schematics, charts, and maps, with classifications and subclassifications that tend to get increasingly baroque, he has himself been called a *poetic myth-maker and not a scientist; and indeed his work, which is both bold and imaginative, has had a strong and continuing influence on criticism as much for the strikingly suggestive quality of his style as his ideas. A frequently voiced criticism of the archetypal approach is that it ultimately tends to wash out the specifics of individual works in favor of the universals charted in the larger patterns. It is worth considering whether, in actual practice, his classification does tend to stress the system at the expense of particular uniquenesses.*

EVERY ORGANIZED body of knowledge can be learned progressively; and experience shows that there is also something progressive about the learning of literature. Our opening sentence has already got us into a semantic difficulty. Physics is an organized body of knowledge about nature, and a student of it says that he is learning physics, not that he is learning nature. Art, like nature, is the subject of a systematic study, and has to be distinguished from the study itself, which is criticism. It is therefore impossible to "learn literature": one learns about it in a certain way, but what one learns, transitively, is the criticism of literature. Similarly, the difficulty often felt in "teaching literature" arises from the fact that it cannot be done: the criticism of literature is all that can be directly taught. So while no one expects literature itself to behave like a science, there is surely no reason why criticism, as a systematic and organized study, should not be, at least partly, a science. Not a "pure" or "exact" science, perhaps, but these phrases form part of a nineteenth century cosmology which is no longer with us. Criticism deals with the arts and may well be something of an art itself, but it does not follow that it must be unsystematic. If it is to be related to the sciences too, it does not follow that it must be deprived of the graces of culture.

Certainly criticism as we find it in learned journals and scholarly monographs has every characteristic of a science. Evidence is examined scientifically; previous authorities are used scientifically; fields are investigated scientifically; texts are edited scientifically. Prosody is scientific in structure; so is phonetics; so is philology. And yet in studying this kind of critical science the student becomes aware of a centrifugal movement carrying him away from literature. He finds that literature is the central division of the "humanities," flanked on one side by history and on the other by philosophy. Criticism so far ranks only as a subdivision of literature; and hence, for the systematic mental organization of the subject, the student has to turn to the conceptual framework of the historian for events, and to that of the philosopher for ideas. Even the more centrally placed critical sciences, such as textual editing, seem to be part of a "background" that recedes into history or some other non-literary field. The thought suggests itself that the ancillary critical disciplines may be related to a central expanding pattern of systematic comprehension which has not yet been established, but which, if it were established, would prevent them from being centrifugal. If such a pattern exists, then criticism would be to art what philosophy is to wisdom and history to action.

Most of the central area of criticism is at present, and doubtless always will be, the area of commentary. But the commentators have little sense, unlike the researchers, of being contained within some sort of scientific discipline: they are chiefly engaged, in the words of the gospel hymn, in brightening the corner where they are. If we attempt to get a more comprehensive idea of what criticism is about, we find ourselves wandering over quaking bogs of generalities, judicious pronouncements of value, reflective comments, perorations to works of research, and other consequences of taking the large view. But this part of the critical field is so full of pseudo-propositions, sonorous nonsense that contains no truth and no falsehood, that it obviously exists only because criticism, like nature, prefers a waste space to an empty one.

The term "pseudo-proposition" may imply some sort of logical positivist attitude on my own part. But I would not confuse the significant proposition with the factual one; nor should I consider it advisable to muddle the study of literature with a schizophrenic dichotomy between subjective-emotional and objective-descriptive aspects of meaning, considering that in order to produce any literary meaning at all one has to ignore this dichotomy. I say only that the principles by which one can distinguish a significant from a meaningless statement in criticism are not clearly defined. Our first step, therefore, is to recognize and get rid of meaningless criticism: that is, talking about literature in a way that cannot help to build up a systematic structure of knowledge. Casual value-judgments belong not to criticism but to the history of taste, and reflect, at best, only the social and psychological compulsions which prompted their utterance. All judgments in which the values are not based on literary experience but are sentimental or derived from religious or political prejudice may be regarded as casual. Sentimental judgments are usually based either on nonexistent categories or antitheses ("Shakespeare studied life, Milton books") or on a visceral reaction to the writer's personality. The literary chit-chat which makes the reputations of poets boom and crash in an imaginary stock exchange is pseudo-criticism. That wealthy investor Mr. Eliot, after dumping Milton on the market, is now buying him again; Donne has probably reached his peak and will begin to taper off; Tennyson may be in for a slight flutter but the Shelley stocks are still bearish. This sort of thing cannot be part of any systematic study, for a systematic study can only progress: whatever dithers or vacillates or reacts is merely leisure-class conversation.

We next meet a more serious group of critics who say: the foreground of criticism is the impact of literature on the reader. Let us, then, keep the study of literature centripetal, and base the learning process on a structural analysis of the literary work itself. The texture of any great work of art is complex and ambiguous, and in unravelling the complexities we may take in as much history and philosophy as we please, if the subject of our study remains at the center. If it does not, we may find that in our anxiety to write about literature we have forgotten how to read it.

The only weakness in this approach is that it is conceived primarily as the antithesis of centrifugal or "background" criticism, and so lands us in a somewhat unreal dilemma, like the conflict of internal and external relations in philosophy. Antitheses are usually resolved, not by picking one side and refuting the other, or by making eclectic choices between them, but by trying to get past the antithetical way of stating the problem. It is right that the first effort of critical apprehension should take the form of a rhetorical or structural analysis of a work of art. But a purely structural approach has the same limitation in criticism that it has in biology. In itself it is simply a discreet series of analyses based on the mere existence of the literary structure, without developing any explanation of how the structure came to be what it was and what its nearest relatives are. Structural analysis brings rhetoric back to criticism, but we need a new poetics as well, and the attempt to construct a new poetics out of rhetoric alone can hardly avoid a mere complication of rhetorical terms into a sterile jargon. I suggest that what is at present missing from literary criticism is a coordinating principle, a central hypothesis which, like the theory of evolution in biology, will see the phenomena it deals with as parts of a whole. Such a principle, though it would retain the centripetal perspective of structural analysis, would try to give the same perspective to other kinds of criticism too.

The first postulate of this hypothesis is the same as that of any science: the assumption of total coherence. The assumption refers to the science, not to what it deals with. A belief in an order of nature is an inference from the intelligibility of the natural sciences; and if the natural sciences ever completely demonstrated the order of nature they would presumably exhaust their subject. Criticism, as a science, is totally intelligible; literature, as the subject of a science, is, so far as we know, an inexhaustible source of new critical discoveries, and would be even if new works of literature ceased to be written. If so, then the search for a limiting principle in literature in order to discourage the development of criticism is mistaken. The assertion that the critic should not look for more in a poem than the poet may safely be assumed to have been conscious of putting there is a common form of what may be called the fallacy of premature teleology. It corresponds to the assertion that a natural phenomenon is as it is because Providence in its inscrutable wisdom made it so.

Simple as the assumption appears, it takes a long time for a science to discover that it is in fact a totally intelligible body of knowledge. Until it makes this discovery it has not been born as an individual science, but remains an embryo within the body of some other subject. The birth of physics from "natural philosophy" and of sociology from "moral philosophy" will illustrate the process. It is also very approximately true that the modern sciences have developed in the order of their closeness to mathematics. Thus physics and astronomy assumed their modern form in the Renaissance, chemistry in the eighteenth century, biology in the nineteenth, and the social sciences in the twentieth. If systematic criticism, then, is developing only in our day, the fact is at least not an anachronism.

We are now looking for classifying principles lying in an area between two points that we have fixed. The first of these is the preliminary effort of criticism, the structural analysis of the work of art. The second is the assumption that there is such a subject as criticism, and that it makes, or could make, complete sense. We may next proceed inductively from structural analysis, associating the data we collect and trying to see larger patterns in them. Or we may proceed deductively, with the consequences that follow from postulating the unity of criticism. It is clear, of course, that neither procedure will work indefinitely without correction from the other. Pure induction will get us lost in haphazard guessing; pure deduction will lead to inflexible and over-simplified pigeon-holing. Let us now attempt a few tentative steps in each direction, beginning with the inductive one.

II

The unity of a work of art, the basis of structural analysis, has not been produced solely by the unconditioned will of the artist, for the artist is only its efficient cause: it has form, and consequently a formal cause. The fact that revision is possible, that the poet makes changes not because he likes them better but because they are better, means that poems, like poets, are born and not made. The poet's task is to deliver the poem in as uninjured a state as possible, and if the poem is alive, it is equally anxious to be rid of him, and screams to be cut loose from his private memories and associations, his desire for self-expression, and all the other navel-strings and feeding tubes of his ego. The critic takes over where the poet leaves off, and criticism can hardly do without a kind of literary psychology connecting the poet with the poem. Part of this may be a psychological study of the poet, though this is useful chiefly in analysing the failures in his expression, the things in him which are still attached to his work. More important is the fact that every poet has his private mythology, his own spectroscopic band or peculiar formation of symbols, of much of which he is quite unconscious. In works with characters of their own, such as dramas and novels, the same psychological analysis may be extended to the interplay of characters, though of course literary psychology would analyse the behavior of such characters only in relation to literary convention.

There is still before us the problem of the formal cause of the poem, a problem deeply involved with the question of genres. We cannot say much about genres, for criticism does not know much about them. A good many critical efforts to grapple with such words as "novel" or "epic" are chiefly interesting as examples of the psychology of rumor. Two conceptions of the genre, however, are obviously fallacious, and as they are opposite extremes, the truth must lie somewhere between them. One is the pseudo-Platonic conception of genres as existing prior to and independently of creation, which confuses them with mere conventions of form like the sonnet. The other is that pseudo-biological conception of them as evolving species which turns up in so many surveys of the "development" of this or that form.

We next inquire for the origin of the genre, and turn first of all to the social conditions and cultural demands which produced it—in other words to the material cause of the work of art. This leads us into literary history, which differs from ordinary history in that its containing categories, "Gothic," "Baroque," "Romantic," and the like are cultural categories, of little use to the ordinary historian. Most literary history does not get as far as these categories, but even so we know more about it than about most kinds of critical scholarship. The historian treats literature and philosophy historically; the philosopher treats history and literature philosophically; and the so-called "history of ideas" approach marks the beginning of an attempt to treat history and philosophy from the point of view of an autonomous criticism.

But still we feel there is something missing. We say that every poet has his own peculiar formation of images. But when so many poets use so many of the same images, surely there are much bigger critical problems involved than biographical ones. As Mr. Auden's brilliant essay *The Enchafèd Flood* shows, an important symbol like the sea cannot remain within the poetry of Shelley or Keats or Coleridge: it is bound to expand over many poets into an archetypal symbol of literature. And if the genre has a historical origin, why does the genre of drama emerge from medieval religion in a way so strikingly similar to the way it emerged from Greek religion centuries before? This is a problem of structure rather than origin, and suggests that there may be archetypes of genres as well as of images.

It is clear that criticism cannot be systematic unless there is a quality in literature which enables it to be so, an order of words corresponding to the order of nature in the natural sciences. An archetype should be not only a unifying category of criticism, but itself a part of a total form, and it leads us at once to the question of what sort of total form criticism can see in literature. Our survey of critical techniques has taken us as far as literary history. Total literary history moves from the primitive to the sophisticated, and here we glimpse the possibility of seeing literature as a complication of a relatively restricted and simple group of formulas that can be studied in primitive culture. If so, then the search for archetypes is a kind of literary anthropology, concerned with the way that literature is informed by pre-literary categories such as ritual, myth and folktale. We next realize that the relation between these categories and literature is by no means purely one of descent, as we find them reappearing in the greatest classics—in fact there seems to be a general tendency on the part of great classics to revert to them. This coincides with a feeling that we have all had: that the study of mediocre works of art, however energetic, obstinately remains a random and peripheral form of critical experience, whereas the profound masterpiece seems to draw us to a point at which we can see an enormous number of converging patterns of significance. Here we begin to wonder if we cannot see literature, not only as complicating itself in time, but as spread out in conceptual space from some unseen center.

This inductive movement towards the archetype is a process of backing up, as it were, from structural analysis, as we back up from a painting if we want to see composition instead of brushwork. In the foreground of the grave-digger scene in *Hamlet,* for instance, is an intricate verbal texture, ranging from the puns of the first clown to the *danse macabre* of the Yorick soliloquy, which we study in the printed text. One step back, and we are in the Wilson Knight and Spurgeon group of critics, listening to the steady rain of images of corruption and decay. Here too, as the sense of the place of this scene in the whole play begins to dawn on us, we are in the network of psychological relationships which were the main interest of Bradley. But after all, we say, we are forgetting the genre: *Hamlet* is a play, and an Elizabethan play. So we take another step back into the Stoll and Shaw group and see the scene conventionally as part of its dramatic context. One step more, and we can begin to glimpse the archetype of the scene, as the hero's *Liebestod* and first unequivocal declaration of his love, his struggle with Laertes and the sealing of his own fate, and the sudden sobering of his mood that marks the transition to the final scene, all take shape around a leap into and return from the grave that has so weirdly yawned open on the stage.

At each stage of understanding this scene we are dependent on a certain kind of scholarly organization. We need first an editor to clean up the text for us, then the rhetorician and philologist, then the literary psychologist. We cannot study the genre without the help of the literary social historian, the literary philosopher and the student of the "history of ideas," and for the archetype we need a literary anthropologist. But now that we have got our central pattern of criticism established, all these interests are seen as converging on literary criticism instead of receding from it into psychology and history and the rest. In particular, the literary anthropologist who chases the source of the Hamlet legend from the pre-Shakespeare play to Saxo, and from Saxo to nature-myths, is not running away from Shakespeare: he is drawing closer to the archetypal form which Shakespeare recreated. A minor result of our new perspective is that contradictions among critics, and assertions that this and not that critical approach is the right one, show a remarkable tendency to dissolve into unreality. Let us now see what we can get from the deductive end.

III

Some arts move in time, like music; others are presented in space, like painting. In both cases the organizing principle is recurrence, which is called rhythm when it is temporal and pattern when it is spatial. Thus we speak of the rhythm of music and the pattern of painting; but later, to show off our sophistication, we may begin to speak of the rhythm of painting and the pattern of music. In other words, all arts may be conceived both temporally and spatially. The score of a musical composition may be studied all at once; a picture may be seen as the track of an intricate dance of the eye. Literature seems to be intermediate between music and painting: its words form rhythms which approach a musical sequence of sounds at one of its boundaries, and form patterns which approach the hieroglyphic or pictorial image at the other. The attempts to get as near to these boundaries as possible form the main body of what is called experimental writing. We may call the rhythm of literature the narrative, and the pattern, the simultaneous mental grasp of the verbal structure, the meaning or significance. We hear or listen to a narrative, but when we grasp a writer's total pattern we "see" what he means.

The criticism of literature is much more hampered by the representational fallacy than even the criticism of painting. That is why we are apt to think of narrative as a sequential representation of events in an outside "life," and of meaning as a reflection of some external "idea." Properly used as critical terms, an author's narrative is his linear movement; his meaning is the integrity of his completed form. Similarly an image is not merely a verbal replica of an external object, but any unit of a verbal structure seen as part of a total pattern or rhythm. Even the letters an author spells his words with form part of his imagery, though only in special cases (such as alliteration) would they call for critical notice. Narrative and meaning thus become respectively, to borrow musical terms, the melodic and harmonic contexts of the imagery.

Rhythm, or recurrent movement, is deeply founded on the natural cycle, and everything in nature that we think of as having some analogy with works of art, like the flower or the bird's song, grows out of a profound synchronization between an organism and the rhythms of its environment, especially that of the solar year. With animals some expressions of synchronization, like the mating dances of birds, could almost be called rituals. But in human life a ritual seems to be something of a voluntary effort (hence the magical element in it) to recapture a lost rapport with the natural cycle. A farmer must harvest his crop at a certain time of year, but because this is involuntary, harvesting itself is not precisely a ritual. It is the deliberate expression of a will to synchronize human and natural energies at that time which produces the harvest songs, harvest sacrifices and harvest folk customs that we call rituals. In ritual, then, we may find the origin of narrative, a ritual being a temporal sequence of acts in which the conscious meaning or significance is latent: it can be seen by an observer, but is largely concealed from the participators themselves. The pull of ritual is toward pure narrative, which, if there could be such a thing, would be automatic and unconscious repetition. We should notice too the regular tendency of ritual to become encyclopedic. All the important recurrences in nature, the day, the phases of the moon, the seasons and solstices of the year, the crises of existence from birth to death, get rituals attached to them, and most of the higher religions are equipped with a definitive total body of rituals suggestive, if we may put it so, of the entire range of potentially significant actions in human life.

Patterns of imagery, on the other hand, or fragments of significance, are oracular in origin, and derive from the epiphanic moment, the flash of instantaneous comprehension with no direct reference to time, the importance of which is indicated by Cassirer in *Language and Myth*. By the time we get them, in the form of proverbs, riddles, commandments and etiological folk-tales, there is already a considerable element of narrative in them. They too are encyclopedic in tendency, building up a total structure of significance, or doctrine, from random and empiric fragments. And just as pure narrative would be an unconscious act, so pure significance would be an incommunicable state of consciousness, for communication begins by constructing narrative.

The myth is the central informing power that gives archetypal significance to the ritual and archetypal narrative to the oracle. Hence the myth *is* the archetype, though it might be convenient to say myth only when referring to narrative, and archetype when speaking of significance. In the solar cycle of the day, the seasonal cycle of the year, and the organic cycle of human life, there is a single pattern of significance, out of which myth constructs a central narrative around a figure who is partly the sun, partly vegetative fertility and partly a god or archetypal human being. The crucial importance of this myth has been forced on literary critics by Jung and Frazer in particular, but the several books now available on it are not always systematic in their approach, for which reason I supply the following table of its phases:

1. The dawn, spring and birth phase. Myths of the birth of the hero, of revival and resurrection, of creation and (because the four phases are a cycle) of the defeat of the powers of darkness, winter and death. Subordinate characters: the father and the mother. The archetype of romance and of most dithyrambic and rhapsodic poetry.
2. The zenith, summer, and marriage or triumph phase. Myths of apotheosis, of the sacred marriage, and of entering into Paradise. Subordinate characters: the companion and the bride. The archetype of comedy, pastoral and idyll.
3. The sunset, autumn and death phase. Myths of fall, of the dying god, of violent death and sacrifice and of the isolation of the hero. Subordinate characters: the traitor and the siren. The archetype of tragedy and elegy.
4. The darkness, winter and dissolution phase. Myths of the triumph of these powers; myths of floods and the return of chaos, of the defeat of the hero, and Götterdämmerung myths. Subordinate characters: the ogre and the witch. The archetype of satire (see, for instance, the conclusion of *The Dunciad*).

The quest of the hero also tends to assimilate the oracular and random verbal structures, as we can see when we watch the chaos of local legends that results from prophetic epiphanies consolidating into a narrative mythology of departmental gods. In most of the higher religions this in turn has become the same central quest-myth that emerges from ritual, as the Messiah myth became the narrative structure of the oracles of Judaism. A local flood may beget a folktale by accident, but a comparison of flood stories will show how quickly such tales become examples of the myth of dissolution. Finally, the tendency of both ritual and epiphany to become encyclopedic is realized in the definitive body of myth which constitutes the sacred scriptures of religions. These sacred scriptures are consequently the first documents that the literary critic has to study to gain a comprehensive view of his subject. After he has understood their structure, then he can descend from archetypes to genres, and see how the drama emerges from the ritual side of myth and lyric from the epiphanic or fragmented side, while the epic carries on the central encyclopedic structure.

Some words of caution and encouragement are necessary before literary criticism has clearly staked out its boundaries in these fields. It is part of the critic's business to show how all literary genres are derived from the quest-myth, but the derivation is a logical one within the science of criticism: the quest-myth will constitute the first chapter of whatever future handbooks of criticism may be written that will be based on enough organized critical knowledge to call themselves "introductions" or "outlines" and still be able to live up to their titles. It is only when we try to expound the derivation chronologically that we find ourselves writing pseudo-prehistorical fictions and theories of mythological contact. Again, because psychology and anthropology are more highly developed sciences, the critic who deals with this kind of material is bound to appear, for some time, a dilettante of those subjects. These two phases of criticism are largely undeveloped in comparison with literary history and rhetoric, the reason being the later development of the sciences they are related to. But the fascination which *The Golden Bough* and Jung's book on libido symbols have for literary critics is not based on dilettantism, but on the fact that these books are primarily studies in literary criticism, and very important ones.

In any case the critic who is studying the principles of literary form has a quite different interest from the psychologist's concern with states of mind or the anthropologist's with social institutions. For instance: the mental response to narrative is mainly passive; to significance mainly active. From this fact Ruth Benedict's *Patterns of Culture* develops a distinction between "Apollonian" cultures based on obedience to ritual and "Dionysiac" ones based on a tense exposure of the prophetic mind to epiphany. The critic would tend rather to note how popular literature which appeals to the inertia of the untrained mind puts a heavy emphasis on narrative values, whereas a sophisticated attempt to disrupt the connection between the poet and his environment produces the Rimbaud type of *illumination,* Joyce's solitary epiphanies, and Baudelaire's conception of nature as a source of oracles. Also how literature, as it develops from the primitive to the self-conscious, shows a gradual shift of the poet's attention from narrative to significant values, this shift of attention being the basis of Schiller's distinction between naive and sentimental poetry.

The relation of criticism to religion, when they deal with the same documents, is more complicated. In criticism, as in history, the divine is always treated as a human artifact. God for the critic, whether he finds him in *Paradise Lost* or the Bible, is a character in a human story; and for the critic all epiphanies are explained, not in terms of the riddle of a possessing god or devil, but as mental phenomena closely associated in their origin with dreams. This once established, it is then necessary to say that nothing in criticism or art compels the critic to take the attitude of ordinary waking consciousness towards the dream or the god. Art deals not with the real but with the conceivable; and criticism, though it will eventually have to have some theory of conceivability, can never be justified in trying to develop, much less assume, any theory of actuality. It is necessary to understand this before our next and final point can be made.

We have identified the central myth of literature, in its narrative aspect, with the quest-myth. Now if we wish to see this central myth as a pattern of meaning also, we have to start with the workings of the subconscious where the epiphany originates, in other words in the dream. The human cycle of waking and dreaming corresponds closely to the natural cycle of light and darkness, and it is perhaps in this correspondence that all imaginative life begins. The correspondence is largely an antithesis: it is in daylight that man is really in the power of darkness, a prey to frustration and weakness; it is in the darkness of nature that the "libido" or conquering heroic self awakes. Hence art, which Plato called a dream for awakened minds, seems to have as its final cause the resolution of the antithesis, the mingling of the sun and the hero, the realizing of a world in which the inner desire and the outward circumstance coincide. This is the same goal, of course, that the attempt to combine human and natural power in ritual has. The social function of the arts, therefore, seems to be closely connected with visualizing the goal of work in human life. So in terms of significance, the central myth of art must be the vision of the end of social effort, the innocent world of fulfilled desires, the free human society. Once this is understood, the integral place of criticism among the other social sciences, in interpreting and systematizing the vision of the artist, will be easier to see. It is at this point that we can see how religious conceptions of the final cause of human effort are as relevant as any others to criticism.

The importance of the god or hero in the myth lies in the fact that such characters, who are conceived in human likeness and yet have more power over nature, gradually build up the vision of an omnipotent personal community beyond an indifferent nature. It is this community which the hero regularly enters in his apotheosis. The world of this apotheosis thus begins to pull away from the rotary cycle of the quest in which all triumph is temporary. Hence if we look at the quest-myth as a pattern of imagery, we see the hero's quest first of all in terms of its fulfilment. This gives us our central pattern of archetypal images, the vision of innocence which sees the world in terms of total human intelligibility. It corresponds to, and is usually found in the form of, the vision of the unfallen world or heaven in religion. We may call it the comic vision of life, in contrast to the tragic vision, which sees the quest only in the form of its ordained cycle.

We conclude with a second table of contents, in which we shall attempt to set forth the central pattern of the comic and tragic visions. One essential principle of archetypal criticism is that the individual and the universal forms of an image are identical, the reasons being too complicated for us just now. We proceed according to the general plan of the game of Twenty Questions, or, if we prefer, of the Great Chain of Being:

1. In the comic vision the *human* world is a community, or a hero who represents the wish-fulfilment of the reader. The archetype of images of symposium, communion, order, friendship and love. In the tragic vision the human world is a tyranny or anarchy, or an individual or isolated man, the leader with his back to his followers, the bullying giant of romance, the deserted or betrayed hero. Marriage or some equivalent consummation belongs to the comic vision; the harlot, witch and other varieties of Jung's "terrible mother" belong to the tragic one. All divine, heroic, angelic or other superhuman communities follow the human pattern.

2. In the comic vision the *animal* world is a community of domesticated animals, usually a flock of sheep, or a lamb, or one of the gentler birds, usually a dove. The archetype of pastoral images. In the tragic vision the animal world is seen in terms of beasts and birds of prey, wolves, vultures, serpents, dragons and the like.

3. In the comic vision the *vegetable* world is a garden, grove or park, or a tree of life, or a rose or lotus. The archetype of Arcadian images, such as that of Marvell's green world or of Shakespeare's forest comedies. In the tragic vision it is a sinister forest like the one in *Comus* or at the opening of the *Inferno* or a health or wilderness, or a tree of death.

4. In the comic vision the *mineral* world is a city, or one building or temple, or one stone, normally a glowing precious stone—in fact the whole comic series, especially the tree, can be conceived as luminous or fiery. The archetype of geometrical images: the "starlit dome" belongs here. In the tragic vision the mineral world is seen in terms of deserts, rocks and ruins, or of sinister geometrical images like the cross.

5. In the comic vision the *unformed* world is a river, traditionally fourfold, which influenced the Renaissance image of the temperate body with its four humors. In the tragic vision this world usually becomes the sea, as the narrative myth of dissolution is so often a flood myth. The combination of the sea and beast images gives us the leviathan and similar water-monsters.

Obvious as this table looks, a great variety of poetic images and forms will be found to fit it. Yeats's "Sailing to Byzantium," to take a famous example of the comic vision at random, has the city, the tree, the bird, the community of sages, the geometrical gyre and the detachment from the cyclic world. It is, of course, only the general comic or tragic context that determines the interpretation of any symbol: this is obvious with relatively neutral archetypes like the island, which may be Prospero's island or Circe's.

Our tables are, of course, not only elementary but grossly oversimplified, just as our inductive approach to the archetype was a mere hunch. The important point is not the deficiencies of either procedure, taken by itself, but the fact that, somewhere and somehow, the two are clearly going to meet in the middle. And if they do meet, the ground plan of a systematic and comprehensive development of criticism has been established.

ROLAND BARTHES

The Structuralist Activity

1964

During prolonged bouts of illness as a young man, Roland Barthes (1915–1980) read widely and deeply absorbed the works of influential thinkers as he began his lifelong work as a critic and scholar. He soon associated himself with the cutting edge of French intellectualism, and as the French philosophical tradition evolved in the middle years of the twentieth century, so too did Barthes's own thinking. His continual testing and rethinking of his own and others' ideas kept him in an uneasy relationship with the academy, which both nurtured and challenged him, and he was (and remains) widely regarded as one of the most influential theorists of the 1960s and 1970s. His work developed from structuralism and semiotics to poststructuralism while covering a wide range of topics, including literature, pop culture, and fashion.

To understand the work from Barthes's structuralist period, the first hurdle many readers must overcome is the specialized vocabulary drawn from the structural linguistic theories of Ferdinand de Saussure. One central concept is the distinction between langue, *or the full system of grammatical and syntactic rules governing a language, and* parole, *or a particular utterance spoken (or written) in the language and governed by those rules. Also key is the distinction between an actual object or idea (say, a tree or the sensation of anger) and the sound or symbol that indicates that object or idea (the spoken or written word* tree *or* anger). *Structuralists call the former the* signified *and the latter the* signifier. *The relationship between signified and signifier is arbitrary—a tree might just as well be called by some other word, and in fact it is in other languages—and exists merely because speakers of a language agree to use a particular signifier. Signified and signifier together comprise a* sign.

Barthes begins the essay that follows with the rather straightforward question, "What is structuralism?" His answer, beginning as it does by telling what structuralism isn't, may seem at first a bit oblique. He does, however, come to some ideas central to the practice of structuralist criticism. First, as the essay's title suggests, Barthes sees structuralism not as a thing or an idea or a school of thought but as an activity, *and that activity consists of two parts—analysis and synthesis. In the* analysis *phase, the structuralist breaks down a piece of discourse (whether a piece of classic or popular literature, a film, or a cultural institution such as a style of dress) into smaller, meaning-bearing units. These units range from* phonemes *(the smallest units of sound that a speaker may use to differentiate one signifier from another; note how a change of a single letter or sound can entirely change the meaning of a word) to the* mythemes *(the narrative building blocks out of which a society's myths are built).*

Structuralists such as Barthes see the grammatical and vocabulary codes we call language *as just one of many possible structures through which we organize our experience. All culture rests on a host of symbolic activities, each governed by unique codes and grammars. In the end, structuralist analysis is less interested in the particular meanings of the structures analyzed than in the ways human beings combine small units of meaning to create greater meanings in art, literature, and other cultural productions. This is where the* synthesis *phase of the structuralist activity comes in. As Barthes himself writes near the end of this essay, structuralist inquiry "highlights the strictly human process by which men give meaning to things." One who engages in such activity will understand humanity at a new level and, symbolically, become a new species of individual:* Homo significans.

WHAT IS STRUCTURALISM? Not a school, nor even a movement (at least, not yet), for most of the authors ordinarily labeled with this word are unaware of being united by any solidarity of doctrine or commitment. Nor is it a vocabulary. *Structure* is already an old word (of anatomical and grammatical provenance), today quite overworked: all the social sciences resort to it abundantly, and its use can distinguish no one, except to polemicize about the content assigned to it; *functions, forms, signs,* and *significations* are scarcely more pertinent: they are, today, words in common use from which one asks (and obtains) whatever one wants, notably the camouflage of the old determinist schema of cause and product; we must doubtless resort to pairings like those of *signifier/signified* and *synchronic/diachronic* in order to approach what distinguishes structuralism from other modes of thought: the first because it refers to the linguistic model as originated by Saussure and because, along with economics, linguistics is, in the present state of affairs, the true science of structure; the second, more decisively, because it seems to imply a certain revision of the notion of history, insofar as the idea of synchrony (although in Saussure this is a pre-eminently operational concept) accredits a certain immobilization of time, and insofar as diachrony tends to represent the historical process as a pure succession of forms. This second pairing is all the more distinctive in that the chief resistance to structuralism today seems to be of Marxist origin and in that it focuses on the notion of history (and not of structure); whatever the case, it is probably the serious recourse to the nomenclature of signification (and not to the word itself, which is, paradoxically, not at all distinctive) which we must ultimately take as structuralism's spoken sign: watch who uses *signifier* and *signified, synchrony* and *diachrony,* and you will know whether the structuralist vision is constituted.

This is valid for the intellectual metalanguage, which explicitly employs methodological concepts. But since structuralism is neither a school nor a movement, there is no reason to reduce it a priori, even in a problematical way, to the activity of philosophers; it would be better to try and find its broadest description (if not its definition) on another level than that of reflexive language. We can in fact presume that there exist certain writers, painters, musicians in whose eyes a certain exercise of structure (and no longer merely its thought) represents a distinctive experience, and that both analysts and creators must be placed under the common sign of what we might call *structural man*, defined not by his ideas or his languages, but by his imagination—in other words, by the way in which he mentally experiences structure.

So the first thing to be said is that in relation to all its users, structuralism is essentially an *activity*, i.e., the controlled succession of a certain number of mental operations: we might speak of structuralist activity as we once spoke of surrealist activity (surrealism, moreover, may well have produced the first experience of structural literature, a possibility which must some day be explored). But before seeing what these operations are, we must say a word about their goal.

The goal of all structuralist activity, whether reflexive or poetic, is to reconstruct an "object" in such a way as to manifest thereby the rules of functioning (the "functions") of this object. Structure is therefore actually a *simulacrum* of the object, but a directed, *interested* simulacrum, since the imitated object makes something appear which remained invisible or, if one prefers, unintelligible in the natural object. Structural man takes the real, decomposes it, then recomposes it; this appears to be little enough (which makes some say that the structuralist enterprise is "meaningless," "uninteresting," "useless," etc.). Yet from another point of view, this "little enough" is decisive: for between the two objects, or the two tenses, of structuralist activity, there occurs something new, and what is new is nothing less than the generally intelligible: the simulacrum is intellect added to object, and this addition has an anthropological value, in that it is man himself, his history, his situation, his freedom, and the very resistance which nature offers to his mind.

We see, then, why we must speak of a structuralist *activity*: creation or reflection are not, here, an original "impression" of the world, but a veritable fabrication of a world which resembles the primary one, not in order to copy it but to render it intelligible. Hence one might say that structuralism is essentially *an activity of imitation*, which is also why there is, strictly speaking, no *technical* difference between structuralism as an intellectual activity, on the one hand, and literature in particular, art in general, on the other: both derive from a *mimesis*, based not on the analogy of substances (as in so-called realist art), but on the analogy of functions (what Lévi-Strauss calls *homology*). When Troubetskoy reconstructs the phonetic object as a system of variations; when Dumézil elaborates a functional mythology; when Propp constructs a folk tale resulting by structuration from all the Slavic tales he has previously decomposed; when Lévi-Strauss discovers the homologic functioning of the totemic imagination, or Granger the formal rules of economic thought, or Gardin the pertinent features of prehistoric bronzes; when Richard decomposes a poem by Mallarmé into its distinctive vibrations— they are all doing nothing different from what Mondrian, Boulez, or Butor are doing when they articulate a certain object—what will be called, precisely, a *composition*—by the controlled manifestation of certain units and certain associations of these units. It is of little consequence whether the initial object submitted to the simulacrum activity is given by the world in an already assembled fashion (in the case of the structural analysis made of a constituted language or society or work) or is still dispersed (in the case of the structural "composition"); whether this initial object is drawn from a social reality or an imaginary reality. It is not the nature of the copied object which defines an art (though this is a tenacious prejudice in all realism), it is the fact that man adds to it in reconstructing it: technique is the very being of all creation. It is therefore to the degree that the goals of structuralist activity are indissolubly linked to a certain technique that structuralism exists in a distinctive fashion in relation to other modes of analysis or creation: we recompose the object in order to make certain functions appear, and it is, so to speak, the way that makes the work; this is why we must speak of the structuralist activity rather than the structuralist work.

The structuralist activity involves two typical operations: dissection and articulation. To dissect the first object, the one which is given to the simulacrum-activity, is to find in it certain mobile fragments whose differential situation engenders a certain meaning; the fragment has no meaning in itself, but it is nonetheless such that the slightest variation wrought in its configuration produces a change in the whole; a *square* by Mondrian, a *series* by Pousseur, a *versicle* of Butor's *Mobile*, the "mytheme" in Lévi-Strauss, the phoneme in the work of the phonologists, the "theme" in certain literary criticism—all these units (whatever their inner structure and their extent, quite different according to cases) have no significant existence except by their frontiers: those which separate them from other actual units of the discourse (but this is a problem of articulation) and also those which distinguish them from other virtual units, with which they form a certain class (which linguistics calls a *paradigm*); this notion of a paradigm is essential, apparently, if we are to understand the structuralist vision: the paradigm is a group, a reservoir—as limited as possible—of objects (of units) from which we summon, by an act of citation, the object or unit we wish to endow with an actual meaning; what characterizes the paradigmatic object is that it is, vis-à-vis other objects of its class, in a certain relation of affinity and of dissimilarity: two units of the same paradigm must resemble each other somewhat *in order* that the difference which separates them be indeed evident: *s* and *z* must have both a common feature (dentality) and a distinctive feature (presence or absence of sonority) so that we cannot, in French, attribute the same meaning to *poisson* and *poison*; Mondrian's squares must have both certain affinities by their shape as squares, and certain dissimilarities by their proportion and

color; the American automobiles (in Butor's *Mobile*) must be constantly regarded in the same way, yet they must differ each time by both their make
and color; the episodes of the Oedipus myth (in Lévi-Strauss's analysis) must
be both identical and varied—in order that all these languages, these works
may be intelligible. The dissection-operation thus produces an initial dispersed state of the simulacrum, but the units of the structure are not at all
anarchic: before being distributed and fixed in the continuity of the composition, each one forms with its own virtual group or reservoir an intelligent organism, subject to a sovereign motor principle: that of the least difference.

Once the units are posited, structural man must discover in them or establish for them certain rules of association: this is the activity of articulation,
which succeeds the summoning activity. The syntax of the arts and of discourse is, as we know, extremely varied; but what we discover in every work
of structural enterprise is the submission to regular constraints whose formalism, improperly indicted, is much less important than their stability; for
what is happening, at this second stage of the simulacrum-activity, is a kind
of battle against chance; this is why the constraint of recurrence of the units
has an almost demiurgic value: it is by the regular return of the units and of
the associations of units that the work appears constructed, i.e., endowed
with meaning; linguistics calls these rules of combination *forms,* and it would
be advantageous to retain this rigorous sense of an overtaxed word: form, it
has been said, is what keeps the contiguity of units from appearing as a pure
effect of chance: the work of art is what man wrests from chance. This perhaps allows us to understand on the one hand why so-called nonfigurative
works are nonetheless to the highest degree works of art, human thought
being established not by the analogy of copies and models but by the regularity of assemblages; and on the other hand why these same works appear,
precisely, fortuitous and thereby useless to those who discern in them no
form: in front of an abstract painting, Khrushchev is certainly wrong to see
only the traces of a donkey's tail whisked across the canvas; at least he knows
in his way, though, that art is a certain conquest of chance (he simply forgets
that every rule must be learned, whether one wants to apply or interpret it).

The simulacrum, thus constructed, does not render the world as it has
found it, and it is here that structuralism is important. First of all, it manifests
a new category of the object, which is neither the real nor the rational, but the
functional, thereby joining a whole scientific complex which is being developed around information theory and research. Subsequently and especially,
it highlights the strictly human process by which men give meaning to
things. Is this new? To a certain degree, yes; of course the world has never
stopped looking for the meaning of what is given it and of what it produces;
what is new is a mode of thought (or a "poetics") which seeks less to assign
completed meanings to the objects it discovers than to know how meaning is
possible, at what cost and by what means. Ultimately, one might say that the
object of structuralism is not man endowed with meanings but man fabricat-
ing meanings, as if it could not be the *content* of meanings which exhausted
the semantic goals of humanity, but only the act by which these meanings,

historical and contingent variables, are produced. *Homo significans:* such would be the new man of structural inquiry.

According to Hegel, the ancient Greek was amazed by the natural in nature; he constantly listened to it, questioned the meaning of mountains, springs, forests, storms; without knowing what all these objects were telling him by name, he perceived in the vegetal or cosmic order a tremendous shudder of meaning, to which he gave the name of a god: *Pan.* Subsequently, nature has changed, has become social: everything given to man is already human, down to the forest and the river which we cross when we travel. But confronted with this social nature, which is quite simply culture, structural man is no different from the ancient Greek: he too listens for the natural in culture, and constantly perceives in it not so much stable, finite, "true" meanings as the shudder of an enormous machine which is humanity tirelessly undertaking to create meaning, without which it would no longer be human. And it is because this fabrication of meaning is more important, to its view, than the meanings themselves, it is because the function is extensive with the works, that structuralism constitutes itself as an activity, and refers the exercise of the work and the work itself to a single identity: a serial composition or an analysis by Lévi-Strauss are not objects except insofar as they have been made: their present being *is* their past act: they are *having-been-mades;* the artist, the analyst recreates the course taken by meaning, he need not designate it: his function, to return to Hegel's example, is a *manteia;* like the ancient soothsayer, he speaks the locus of meaning but does not name it. And it is because literature, in particular, is a mantic activity that it is both intelligible and interrogating, speaking and silent, engaged in the world by the course of the meaning which it remakes with the world, but disengaged from the contingent meanings which the world elaborates: an answer to the man who consumes it yet always a question to nature, an answer which questions and a question which answers.

How then does structural man deal with the accusation of "unreality" which is sometimes flung at him? Are not forms in the world? Are not forms responsible? Was it really his Marxism that was revolutionary in Brecht? Was it not rather the decision to link to Marxism, in the theater, the placing of a spotlight or the deliberate fraying of a costume? Structuralism does not withdraw history from the world: it seeks to link to history not only certain contents (this has been done a thousand times) but also certain forms, not only the material but also the intelligible, not only the ideological but also the esthetic. And precisely because all thought about the historically intelligible is also a participation in that intelligibility, structural man is scarcely concerned to last; he knows that structuralism, too, is a certain form of the world, which will change with the world; and just as he experiences his validity (but not his truth) in his power to speak the old languages of the world in a new way, so he knows that it will suffice that a new language rise out of history, a new language which speaks *him* in his turn, for his task to be done.

Translated by Richard Howard.

JACQUES DERRIDA

Structure, Sign, and Play
in the Discourse
of the Human Sciences[1]

1966

Jacques Derrida (b. 1930) became instantly famous in American academic circles when he delivered the following article as a paper at a symposium on Structuralism held at Johns Hopkins University in 1966. In a little more than a decade, Derrida's books Of Grammatology *and* Writing and Difference, *along with other of his writings, established the widely influential but controversial literary theory known as deconstruction.*

"Structure, Sign, and Play in the Discourse of the Human Sciences" is the opening statement of the movement, which originates as a reaction to structuralism. Here Derrida attacks what he considers an intrinsic error not only in structuralism but in Western thought historically: the concept of an unshifting "center" to structures, particularly those of language, that provides for stable and reliable meanings. Derrida refutes the concept of "center" by showing the contradiction in descriptions of the defining "center" that places it both within a structure and outside the structure. Instead of achieving meaning through centeredness, Derrida asserts that words, or "signifiers," derive meaning from a complex relationship of "difference" from other words or signifiers. As a result, the meaning of a word is always deferred or postponed; if a word's meaning depends on its difference from other words, those other words also achieve their meanings from differences from other words in an indefinite chain of relationships that never arrives at the finality of a fixed and stable meaning. This explaining of signifiers by other signifiers is the process of "redoubling" mentioned at the opening of the essay. (Note: For a review of structuralist terminology, see the headnote to the essay by Roland Barthes, page 487.)

[1] "La Structure, le signe et le jeu dans le discours des sciences humaines." The text which follows is a translation of the revised version of M. Derrida's communication. The word "jeu" is variously translated here as "play," "interplay," "game," and "stake," besides the normative translation "freeplay." All footnotes to this article are additions by the translator.

Derrida coins the term différance to indicate that meaning derives from difference and is always deferred, also implying movement, or "play," which also comes to mean "game" in his nomenclature. Derrida uses the word trace (in French "imprint," "spoor," "vestige") to indicate that hidden within a sign ("occulted") is an imperceptible imprint, or trace, of the radically other that différance implies. Trace, difficult to define, is an "absent presence," which serves Derrida's argument that a sign is not a stable match of signifier with signified. Instead, signifiers in the freeplay of différance achieve meaning through the hidden trace of their opposites.

Once having exposed the error of the notion of "center," or having "deconstructed" the construct of centeredness, Derrida can also call into question traditions of thought that depend on the concept of center or presence. At the beginning of "Structure, Sign, and Play," Derrida speaks condescendingly of epistèmè, or intellectually certain knowledge. In Of Grammatology, he uses the term logocentrism, which means "Centered on the Word as Truth," to represent spuriously authoritative language. Logocentrism and epistèmè, along with similar notions that imply a stable, anchored meaning, such as "essence, consciousness, conscience, God," arise from a human need for the fact of a center. Human desire creates what Derrida calls a "transcendental signified," an illusion and not an actuality. In contradistinction to the "transcendental signified," Derrida employs the image of the Abyss, the unfathomable mystery.

Logocentrism denies freeplay by granting an unjustified privilege to one side of the dualities implied by différance. For example, the oppositions of male/female, spoken/written, present/absent, certainty/ambiguity are distorted by logocentrism into MALE/female, SPOKEN/written, PRESENT/absent, CERTAINTY/ambiguity. One goal of deconstruction is to correct the imbalance, to undermine the false authority of epistèmè. The coined term différance, for example, challenges the logocentric primacy of the spoken word. In French, différance and différence sound the same. Only the written form, différance, reveals the coined word with its deconstructionist meanings.

Derrida's ideas have occasioned much controversy and have been seen as moral anarchy, as a form of intellectual terrorism, and as an ultimate challenge to traditional theories of meaning and knowing. Yet Derrida acknowledges that humans require myths and language. His argument is pointed toward seeing language and myth as functional, however, and not as referents to an absolute. By going the full distance with his project of deconstruction, Derrida claims at the end of the essay that we may achieve a full and joyful Nietzschean affirmation as we embrace "the freeplay of the world" and thus give up sighing for a presence that does not exist.

PERHAPS SOMETHING has occurred in the history of the concept of structure that could be called an "event," if this loaded word did not entail a meaning which it is precisely the function of structural—or structuralist—thought to reduce or to suspect. But let me use the term "event" anyway, employing it with caution and as if in quotation marks. In this sense, this event will have the exterior form of a *rupture* and a *redoubling*.

It would be easy enough to show that the concept of structure and even the word "structure" itself are as old as the *epistèmè*—that is to say, as old as western science and western philosophy—and that their roots thrust deep into the soil of ordinary language, into whose deepest recesses the *epistèmè* plunges to gather them together once more, making them part of itself in a metaphorical displacement. Nevertheless, up until the event which I wish to mark out and define, structure—or rather the structurality of structure—although it has always been involved, has always been neutralized or reduced, and this by a process of giving it a center or referring it to a point of presence, a fixed origin. The function of this center was not only to orient, balance, and organize the structure—one cannot in fact conceive of an unorganized structure—but above all to make sure that the organizing principle of the structure would limit what we might call the *freeplay* of the structure. No doubt that by orienting and organizing the coherence of the system, the center of a structure permits the freeplay of its elements inside the total form. And even today the notion of a structure lacking any center represents the unthinkable itself.

Nevertheless, the center also closes off the freeplay it opens up and makes possible. *Qua* center, it is the point at which the substitution of contents, elements, or terms is no longer possible. At the center, the permutation or the transformation of elements (which may of course be structures enclosed within a structure) is forbidden. At least this permutation has always remained *interdicted*[2] (I use this word deliberately). Thus it has always been thought that the center, which is by definition unique, constituted that very thing within a structure which governs the structure, while escaping structurality. This is why classical thought concerning structure could say that the center is, paradoxically, *within* the structure and *outside* it. The center is at the center of the totality, and yet, since the center does not belong to the totality (is not part of the totality), the totality *has its center elsewhere*. The center is not the center. The concept of centered structure—although it represents coherence itself, the condition of the *epistèmè* as philosophy or science—is contradictorily coherent. And, as always, coherence in contradiction expresses the force of a desire. The concept of centered structure is in fact the concept of a freeplay based on a fundamental ground, a freeplay which is constituted upon a fundamental immobility and a reassuring certitude, which is itself beyond the reach of the freeplay. With this certitude anxiety can be mastered, for anxiety is invariably the result of a certain mode of being implicated in the game, of being caught by the game, of being as it were from the very beginning at stake in the game.[3] From the basis of what we therefore call the center (and which, because it can be either inside or outside, is as readily called the origin as the end, as readily *archè* as *telos*), the repetitions, the substitutions, the transformations, and the permutations are always *taken* from a

---

[2] *Interdite*: "forbidden," "disconcerted," "confounded," "speechless."
[3] ". . . qui naît toujours d'une certaine manière d'être impliqué dans le jeu, d'être pris au jeu, d'être comme être d'entrée de jeu dans le jeu."

history of meaning [*sens*]—that is, a history, period—whose origin may always be revealed or whose end may always be anticipated in the form of presence. This is why one could perhaps say that the movement of any archeology, like that of any eschatology, is an accomplice of this reduction of the structurality of structure and always attempts to conceive of structure from the basis of a full presence which is out of play.

If this is so, the whole history of the concept of structure, before the rupture I spoke of, must be thought of as a series of substitutions of center for center, as a linked chain of determinations of the center. Successively, and in a regulated fashion, the center receives different forms or names. The history of metaphysics, like the history of the West, is the history of these metaphors and metonymies. Its matrix—if you will pardon me for demonstrating so little and for being so elliptical in order to bring me more quickly to my principal theme—is the determination of being as *presence* in all the senses of this word. It would be possible to show that the names related to fundamentals, to principles, or to the center have always designated the constant of a presence—*eidos, archè, telos, energeia, ousia* (essence, existence, substance, subject) *aletheia,* transcendentality, consciousness, or conscience, God, man, and so forth.

The event I called a rupture, the disruption I alluded to at the beginning of this paper, would presumably have come about when the structurality of structure had to begin to be thought, that is to say, repeated, and this is why I said that this disruption was repetition in all of the senses of this word. From then on it became necessary to think the law which governed, as it were, the desire for the center in the constitution of structure and the process of signification prescribing its displacements and its substitutions for this law of the central presence—but a central presence which was never itself, which has always already been transported outside itself in its surrogate. The surrogate does not substitute itself for anything which has somehow pre-existed it. From then on it was probably necessary to begin to think that there was no center, that the center could not be thought in the form of a being-present, that the center had no natural locus, that it was not a fixed locus but a function, a sort of non-locus in which an infinite number of sign-substitutions came into play. This moment was that in which language invaded the universal problematic; that in which, in the absence of a center or origin, everything became discourse—provided we can agree on this word—that is to say, when everything became a system where the central signified, the original or transcendental signified, is never absolutely present outside a system of differences. The absence of the transcendental signified extends the domain and the interplay of signification *ad infinitum.*

Where and how does this decentering, this notion of the structurality of structure, occur? It would be somewhat naïve to refer to an event, a doctrine, or an author in order to designate this occurrence. It is no doubt part of the totality of an era, our own, but still it has already begun to proclaim itself and begun to *work.* Nevertheless, if I wished to give some sort of indication by choosing one or two "names," and by recalling those authors in whose discourses this occurrence has most nearly maintained its most radical formulation, I would probably cite the Nietzschean critique of metaphysics, the critique of the concepts of being and truth, for which were substituted the concepts of play, interpretation, and sign (sign without truth present); the Freudian critique or self-presence, that is, the critique of consciousness, of the subject, of self-identity and of self-proximity or self-possession; and, more radically, the Heideggerean destruction of metaphysics, of onto-theology, of the determination of being as presence. But all these destructive discourses and all their analogues are trapped in a sort of circle. This circle is unique. It describes the form of the relationship between the history of metaphysics and the destruction of the history of metaphysics. *There is no sense* in doing without the concepts of metaphysics in order to attack metaphysics. We have no language—no syntax and no lexicon—which is alien to this history; we cannot utter a single destructive proposition which has not already slipped into the form, the logic, and the implicit postulations of precisely what it seeks to contest. To pick out one example from many: the metaphysics of presence is attacked with the help of the concept of the *sign*. But from the moment anyone wishes to show, as I suggested a moment ago, that there is no transcendental or privileged signified and that the domain or the interplay of signification has, henceforth, no limit, he ought to extend his refusal to the concept and to the word sign itself—which is precisely what cannot be done. For the signification "sign" has always been comprehended and determined, in its sense, as sign-of, signifier referring to a signified, signifier different from its signified. If one erases the radical difference between signifier and signified, it is the word signifier itself which ought to be abandoned as a metaphysical concept. When Lévi-Strauss says in the preface to *The Raw and the Cooked*[4] that he has "sought to transcend the opposition between the sensible and the intelligible by placing [himself] from the very beginning at the level of signs," the necessity, the force, and the legitimacy of his act cannot make us forget that the concept of the sign cannot in itself surpass or bypass this opposition between the sensible and the intelligible. The concept of the sign is determined by this opposition: through and throughout the totality of its history and by its system. But we cannot do without the concept of the sign, we cannot give up this metaphysical complicity without also giving up the critique we are directing against this complicity, without the risk of erasing difference [altogether] in the self-identity of a signified reducing into itself its signifier, or, what amounts to the same thing, simply expelling it outside itself. For there are two heterogenous ways of erasing the difference between the signifier and the signified: one, the classic way, consists in reducing or deriving the signifier, that is to say, ultimately in *submitting* the sign to thought; the other, the one we are using here against the first one, consists in putting into question the system in which the preceding reduction functioned: first and foremost, the opposition between the sensible and the intelligible. The *paradox* is that the metaphysical reduction of the sign needed the opposition it was reducing. The opposition is part of the system, along

---

[4] *Le cru et le cuit* (Paris: Plon, 1964).

with the reduction. And what I am saying here about the sign can be extended to all the concepts and all the sentences of metaphysics, in particular to the discourse on "structure." But there are many ways of being caught in this circle. They are all more or less naïve, more or less empirical, more or less systematic, more or less close to the formulation or even to the formalization of this circle. It is these differences which explain the multiplicity of destructive discourses and the disagreement between those who make them. It was within concepts inherited from metaphysics that Nietzsche, Freud, and Heidegger worked, for example. Since these concepts are not elements or atoms and since they are taken from a syntax and a system, every particular borrowing drags along with it the whole of metaphysics. This is what allows these destroyers to destroy each other reciprocally—for example, Heidegger considering Nietzsche, with as much lucidity and rigor as bad faith and misconstruction, as the last metaphysician, the last "Platonist." One could do the same for Heidegger himself, for Freud, or for a number of others. And today no exercise is more widespread.

What is the relevance of this formal schéma when we turn to what are called the "human sciences"? One of them perhaps occupies a privileged place—ethnology. One can in fact assume that ethnology could have been born as a science only at the moment when a de-centering had come about: at the moment when European culture—and, in consequence, the history of metaphysics and of its concepts—had been *dislocated*, driven from its locus, and forced to stop considering itself as the culture of reference. This moment is not first and foremost a moment of philosophical or scientific discourse, it is also a moment which is political, economic, technical, and so forth. One can say in total assurance that there is nothing fortuitous about the fact that the critique of ethnocentrism—the very condition of ethnology—should be systematically and historically contemporaneous with the destruction of the history of metaphysics. Both belong to a single and same era.

Ethnology—like any science—comes about within the element of discourse. And it is primarily a European science employing traditional concepts, however much it may struggle against them. Consequently, whether he wants to or not—and this does not depend on a decision on his part—the ethnologist accepts into his discourse the premises of ethnocentrism at the very moment when he is employed in denouncing them. We ought to consider very carefully all its implications. But if nobody can escape this necessity, and if no one is therefore responsible for giving in to it, however little, this does not mean that all the ways of giving in to it are of an equal pertinence. The quality and the fecundity of a discourse are perhaps measured by the critical rigor with which this relationship to the history of metaphysics and to inherited concepts is thought. Here it is a question of a critical relationship to the language of the human sciences and a question of a critical responsibility to the discourse. It is a question of putting expressly and systematically the problem of the status of a discourse which borrows from a heritage the resources necessary for the deconstruction of that heritage itself. A problem of *economy* and *strategy*.

If I now go on to employ an examination of the texts of Lévi-Strauss as an example, it is not only because of the privilege accorded to ethnology among the human sciences, nor yet because the thought of Lévi-Strauss weighs heavily on the contemporary theoretical situation. It is above all because a certain choice has made itself evident in the work of Lévi-Strauss and because a certain doctrine has been elaborated there, and precisely in a *more or less explicit manner,* in relation to this critique of language and to this critical language in the human sciences.

In order to follow this movement in the text of Lévi-Strauss, let me choose as one guiding thread among others the opposition between nature and culture. In spite of all its rejuvenations and its disguises, this opposition is congenital to philosophy. It is even older than Plato. It is at least as old as the Sophists. Since the statement of the opposition—*physis/nomos, physis/technè*—it has been passed on to us by a whole historical chain which opposes "nature" to the law, to education, to art, to technics—and also to liberty, to the arbitrary, to history, to society, to the mind, and so on. From the beginnings of his quest and from his first book, *The Elementary Structures of Kinship,*[5] Lévi-Strauss has felt at one and the same time the necessity of utilizing this opposition and the impossibility of making it acceptable. In the *Elementary Structures,* he begins from this axiom or definition: that belongs to nature which is *universal* and spontaneous, not depending on any particular culture or on any determinate norm. That belongs to culture, on the other hand, which depends on a system of *norms* regulating society and is therefore capable of *varying* from one social structure to another. These two definitions are of the traditional type. But, in the very first pages of the *Elementary Structures,* Lévi-Strauss, who has begun to give these concepts an acceptable standing, encounters what he calls a *scandal,* that is to say, something which no longer tolerates the nature/culture opposition he has accepted and which seems to require *at one and the same time* the predicates of nature and those of culture. This scandal is the *incest-prohibition.* The incest-prohibition is universal; in this sense one could call it natural. But it is also a prohibition, a system of norms and interdicts; in this sense one could call it cultural.

> Let us assume therefore that everything universal in man derives from the order of nature and is characterized by spontaneity, that everything which is subject to a norm belongs to culture and presents the attributes of the relative and the particular. We then find ourselves confronted by a fact, or rather an ensemble of facts, which, in the light of the preceding definition, is not far from appearing as a scandal: the prohibition of incest presents without the least equivocation, and indissolubly linked together, the two characteristics in which we recognized the contradictory attributes of two exclusive orders. The prohibition of incest constitutes a rule, but a rule, alone of all the social rules, which possesses at the same time a universal character (p. 9).

[5] *Les structures élémentaires de la parenté* (Paris: Presses Universitaires de France, 1949).

Obviously there is no scandal except in the *interior* of a system of concepts sanctioning the difference between nature and culture. In beginning his
work with the *factum* of the incest-prohibition, Lévi-Strauss thus puts himself
in a position entailing that this difference, which has always been assumed to
be self-evident, becomes obliterated or disputed. For, from the moment that
the incest-prohibition can no longer be conceived within the nature/culture
opposition, it can no longer be said that it is a scandalous fact, a nucleus of
opacity within a network of transparent significations. The incest-prohibition
is no longer a scandal one meets with or comes up against in the domain of
traditional concepts; it is something which escapes these concepts and certainly precedes them—probably as the condition of their possibility. It could
perhaps be said that the whole of philosophical conceptualization, systematically relating itself to the nature/culture opposition, is designed to leave in
the domain of the unthinkable the very thing that makes this conceptualization possible: the origin of the prohibition of incest.

I have dealt too cursorily with this example, only one among so many others, but the example nevertheless reveals that language bears within itself the
necessity of its own critique. This critique may be undertaken along two tracks,
in two "manners." Once the limit of nature/culture opposition makes itself
felt, one might want to question systematically and rigorously the history of
these concepts. This is a first action. Such a systematic and historic questioning
would be neither a philological nor a philosophical action in the classic sense of
these words. Concerning oneself with the founding concepts of the whole history of philosophy, deconstituting them, is not to undertake the task of the
philologist or of the classic historian of philosophy. In spite of appearances, it
is probably the most daring way of making the beginnings of a step outside of
philosophy. The step "outside philosophy" is much more difficult to conceive
than is generally imagined by those who think they made it long ago with cav-
alier ease, and who are in general swallowed up in metaphysics by the whole
body of the discourse that they claim to have disengaged from it.

In order to avoid the possibly sterilizing effect of the first way, the other
choice—which I feel corresponds more nearly to the way chosen by Lévi-
Strauss—consists in conserving in the field of empirical discovery all these
old concepts, while at the same time exposing here and there their limits,
treating them as tools which can still be of use. No longer is any truth-value
attributed to them; there is a readiness to abandon them if necessary if other
instruments should appear more useful. In the meantime, their relative efficacy is exploited, and they are employed to destroy the old machinery to
which they belong and of which they themselves are pieces. Thus it is that
the language of the human sciences criticizes *itself*. Lévi-Strauss thinks that in
this way he can separate *method* from *truth*, the instruments of the method
and the objective signification aimed at by it. One could almost say that this
is the primary affirmation of Lévi-Strauss; in any event, the first words of the
Elementary Structures are: "One begins to understand that the distinction between state of nature and state of society (we would be more apt to say
today: state of nature and state of culture), while lacking any acceptable his-

torical signification, presents a value which fully justifies its use by modern sociology: its value as a methodological instrument."

Lévi-Strauss will always remain faithful to this double intention: to preserve as an instrument that whose truth-value he criticizes.

On the one hand, he will continue in effect to contest the value of the nature/culture opposition. More than thirteen years after the *Elementary Structures, The Savage Mind*[6] faithfully echoes the text I have just quoted: "The opposition between nature and culture which I have previously insisted on seems today to offer a value which is above all methodological." And this methodological value is not affected by its "ontological" non-value (as could be said, if this notion were not suspect here): "It would not be enough to have absorbed particular humanities into a general humanity; this first enterprise prepares the way for others . . . which belong to the natural and exact sciences: to reintegrate culture into nature, and finally, to reintegrate life into the totality of its physiochemical conditions" (p. 327).

On the other hand, still in *The Savage Mind,* he presents as what he calls *bricolage*[7] what might be called the discourse of this method. The *bricoleur,* says Lévi-Strauss, is someone who uses "the means at hand," that is, the instruments he finds at his disposition around him, those which are already there, which had not been especially conceived with an eye to the operation for which they are to be used and to which one tries by trial and error to adapt them, not hesitating to change them whenever it appears necessary, or to try several of them at once, even if their form and their origin are heterogenous—and so forth. There is therefore a critique of language in the form of *bricolage,* and it has even been possible to say that *bricolage* is the critical language itself. I am thinking in particular of the article by G. Genette, "Structuralisme et Critique littéraire," published in homage to Lévi-Strauss in a special issue of *L'Arc* (no. 26, 1965), where it is stated that the analysis of *bricolage* could "be applied almost word for word" to criticism, and especially to "literary criticism."[8]

If one calls *bricolage* the necessity of borrowing one's concepts from the texts of a heritage which is more or less coherent or ruined, it must be said that every discourse is *bricoleur.* The engineer, whom Lévi-Strauss opposes to the *bricoleur,* should be the one to construct the totality of his language, syntax, and lexicon. In this sense the engineer is a myth. A subject who would supposedly be the absolute origin of his own discourse and would supposedly construct it "out of nothing," "out of whole cloth," would be the creator of the *verbe,* the *verbe* itself. The notion of the engineer who had supposedly broken with all forms of *bricolage* is therefore a theological idea; and since Lévi-Strauss tells us elsewhere that *bricolage* is mythopoetic, the odds are that the engineer is a myth produced by the *bricoleur.* From the moment that we

---

[6] *Le pensée savage* (Paris: Plon, 1962).

[7] A *bricoleur* is a jack-of-all trades, someone who putters about with odds-and-ends, who puts things together out of bits and pieces.

[8] Reprinted in: G. Genette, *Figures* (Paris: Editions du Seuil, 1966), p. 145.

cease to believe in such an engineer and in a discourse breaking with the received historical discourse, as soon as it is admitted that every finite discourse is bound by a certain *bricolage,* and that the engineer and the scientist are also species of *bricoleurs* then the very idea of *bricolage* is menaced and the difference in which it took on its meaning decomposes.

This brings out the second thread which might guide us in what is being unraveled here.

Lévi-Strauss describes *bricolage* not only as an intellectual activity but also as a mythopoetical activity. One reads in *The Savage Mind,* "Like *bricolage* on the technical level, mythical reflection can attain brilliant and unforeseen results on the intellectual level. Reciprocally, the mythopoetical character of *bricolage* has often been noted" (p. 26).

But the remarkable endeavor of Lévi-Strauss is not simply to put forward, notably in the most recent of his investigations, a structural science or knowledge of myths and of mythological activity. His endeavor also appears—I would say almost from the first—in the status which he accords to his own discourse on myths, to what he calls his "mythologicals." It is here that his discourse on the myth reflects on itself and criticizes itself. And this moment, this critical period, is evidently of concern to all the languages which share the field of the human sciences. What does Lévi-Strauss say of his "mythologicals"? It is here that we rediscover the mythopoetical virtue (power) of *bricolage.* In effect, what appears most fascinating in this critical search for a new status of the discourse is the stated abandonment of all reference to a *center,* to a *subject,* to a privileged *reference,* to an origin, or to an absolute *archè.* The theme of this decentering could be followed throughout the "Overture" to his last book, *The Raw and the Cooked.* I shall simply remark on a few key points.

1. From the very start, Lévi-Strauss recognizes that the Bororo myth which he employs in the book as the "reference-myth" does not merit this name and this treatment. The name is specious and the use of the myth improper. This myth deserves no more than any other its referential privilege:

> In fact the Bororo myth which will from now on be designated by the name *reference-myth* is, as I shall try to show, nothing other than a more or less forced transformation of other myths originating either in the same society or in societies more or less far removed. It would therefore have been legitimate to choose as my point of departure any representative of the group whatsoever. From this point of view, the interest of the reference-myth does not depend on its typical character, but rather on its irregular position in the midst of a group. (p. 10)

2. There is no unity or absolute source of the myth. The focus or the source of the myth are always shadows and virtualities which are elusive, unactualizable, and nonexistent in the first place. Everything begins with the structure, the configuration, the relationship. The discourse on this acentric structure, the myth, that is, cannot itself have an absolute subject or an ab-

solute center. In order not to short change the form and the movement of the myth, that violence which consists in centering a language which is describing an acentric structure must be avoided. In this context, therefore it is necessary to forego scientific or philosophical discourse, to renounce the *epistèmè* which absolutely requires, which is the absolute requirement that we go back to the source, to the center, to the founding basis, to the principle, and so on. In opposition to *epistèmic* discourse, structural discourse on myths—*mythological* discourse—must itself be *mythomorphic*. It must have the form of that of which it speaks. This is what Lévi-Strauss says in *The Raw and the Cooked*, from which I would now like to quote a long and remarkable passage.

> In effect the study of myths poses a methodological problem by the fact that it cannot conform to the Cartesian principle of dividing the difficulty into as many parts as are necessary to resolve it. There exists no veritable end or term to mythical analysis, no secret unity which could be grasped at the end of the work of decomposition. The themes duplicate themselves to infinity. When we think we have disentangled them from each other and can hold them separate, it is only to realize that they are joining together again, in response to the attraction of unforeseen affinities. In consequence, the unity of the myth is only tendential and projective; it never reflects a state or a moment of the myth. An imaginary phenomenon implied by the endeavor to interpret, its role is to give a synthetic form to the myth and to impede its dissolution into the confusion of contraries. It could therefore be said that the science or knowledge of myths is *anaclastic,* taking this ancient term in the widest sense authorized by its etymology, a science which admits into its definition the study of the reflected rays along with that of the broken ones. But, unlike philosophical reflection, which claims to go all the way back to its source, the reflections in question here concern rays without any other than a virtual focus. . . . In wanting to imitate the spontaneous movement of mythical thought, my enterprise, itself too brief and too long, has had to yield to its demands and respect its rhythm. Thus is this book, on myths itself and in its own way, a myth.

This statement is repeated a little farther on (p. 20): "Since myths themselves rest on second-order codes (the first-order codes being those in which language consists), this book thus offers the rough draft of a third-order code, destined to insure the reciprocal possibility of translation of several myths. This is why it would not be wrong to consider it a myth: the myth of mythology, as it were." It is by this absence of any real and fixed center of the mythical or mythological discourse that the musical model chosen by Lévi-Strauss for the composition of his book is apparently justified. The absence of a center is here the absence of a subject and the absence of an author: "The myth and the musical work thus appear as orchestra conductors whose listeners are the silent performers. If it be asked where the real focus of the work is to be found, it must be replied that its determination is impossible. Music and mythology bring man face to face with virtual objects whose shadow alone is actual. . . . Myths have no authors" (p. 25).

Thus it is at this point that ethnographic *bricolage* deliberately assumes its mythopoetic function. But by the same token, this function makes the philosophical or epistemological requirement of a center appear as mythological, that is to say, as a historical illusion.

Nevertheless, even if one yields to the necessity of what Lévi-Strauss has done, one cannot ignore its risks. If the mythological is mythomorphic, are all discourses on myths equivalent? Shall we have to abandon any epistemological requirement which permits us to distinguish between several qualities of discourse on the myth? A classic question, but inevitable. We cannot reply—and I do not believe Lévi-Strauss replies to it—as long as the problem of the relationships between the philosopheme or the theorem, on the one hand, and the mytheme or the mythopoem(e), on the other, has not been expressly posed. This is no small problem. For lack of expressly posing this problem, we condemn ourselves to transforming the claimed transgression of philosophy into an unperceived fault in the interior of the philosophical field. Empiricism would be the genus of which these faults would always be the species. Trans-philosophical concepts would be transformed into philosophical naïvetés. One could give many examples to demonstrate this risk: the concepts of sign, history, truth, and so forth. What I want to emphasize is simply that the passage beyond philosophy does not consist in turning the page of philosophy (which usually comes down to philosophizing badly), but in continuing to read philosophers *in a certain way*. The risk I am speaking of is always assumed by Lévi-Strauss and it is the very price of his endeavor. I have said that empiricism is the matrix of all the faults menacing a discourse which continues, as with Lévi-Strauss in particular, to elect to be scientific. If we wanted to pose the problem of empiricism and *bricolage* in depth, we would probably end up very quickly with a number of propositions absolutely contradictory in relation to the status of discourse in structural ethnography. On the one hand, structuralism justly claims to be the critique of empiricism. But at the same time there is not a single book or study by Lévi-Strauss which does not offer itself as an empirical essay which can always be completed or invalidated by new information. The structural schemata are always proposed as hypotheses resulting from a finite quality of information and which are subjected to the proof of experience. Numerous texts could be used to demonstrate this double postulation. Let us turn once again to the "Overture" of *The Raw and the Cooked,* where it seems clear that if this postulation is double, it is because it is a question here of a language on language:

> Critics who might take me to task for not having begun by making an exhaustive inventory of South American myths before analyzing them would be making a serious mistake about the nature and the role of these documents. The totality of the myths of a people is of the order

of the discourse. Provided that this people does not become physically or morally extinct, this totality is never closed. Such a criticism would therefore be equivalent to reproaching a linguist with writing the grammar of a language without having recorded the totality of the words which have been uttered since that language came into existence and without knowing the verbal exchanges which will take place as long as the language continues to exist. Experience proves that an absurdly small number of sentences . . . allows the linguist to elaborate a grammar of the language he is studying. And even a partial grammar or an outline of a grammar represents valuable acquisitions in the case of unknown languages. Syntax does not wait until it has been possible to enumerate a theoretically unlimited series of events before becoming manifest, because syntax consists in the body of rules which presides over the generation of these events. And it is precisely a syntax of South American mythology that I wanted to outline. Should new texts appear to enrich the mythical discourse, then this will provide an opportunity to check or modify the way in which certain grammatical laws have been formulated, an opportunity to discard certain of them and an opportunity to discover new ones. But in no instance can the requirement of a total mythical discourse be raised as an objection. For we have just seen that such a requirement has no meaning. (pp. 15–16)

Totalization is therefore defined at one time as *useless,* at another time as *impossible.* This is no doubt the result of the fact that there are two ways of conceiving the limit of totalization. And I assert once again that these two determinations coexist implicitly in the discourses of Lévi-Strauss. Totalization can be judged impossible in the classical style: one then refers to the empirical endeavor of a subject or of a finite discourse in a vain and breathless quest of an infinite richness which it can never master. There is too much, more than one can say. But nontotalization can also be determined in another way: not from the standpoint of the concept of finitude as assigning us to an empirical view, but from the standpoint of the concept of *freeplay.* If totalization no longer has any meaning, it is not because the infinity of a field cannot be covered by a finite glance or a finite discourse, but because the nature of the field—that is, language and a finite language—excludes totalization. This field is in fact that of *freeplay,* that is to say, a field of infinite substitutions in the closure of a finite ensemble. This field permits these infinite substitutions only because it is finite, that is to say, because instead of being an inexhaustible field, as in the classical hypothesis, instead of being too large, there is something missing from it: a center which arrests and founds the freeplay of substitutions. One could say—rigorously using that word whose scandalous signification is always obliterated in French—that this movement of the freeplay, permitted by the lack, the absence of a center or origin, is the movement of *supplementarity.* One cannot determine the center, the sign which *supplements*[9] it, which takes its place in its absence—because this sign adds itself, occurs in addition, over and above, comes as a *supplement*.[10] The movement of signification adds something, which results in the fact that there is always more, but this addition is a floating one because it comes to perform a vicarious function, to supplement a lack on the part of the signified. Although Lévi-Strauss in his use of the word supplementary never emphasizes as I am doing here the two directions of meaning which are so strangely compounded within it, it is not by chance that he uses this word twice in his "Introduction to the Work of Marcel Mauss,"[11] at the point where he is speaking of the "superabundance of signifier, in relation to the signifieds to which this superabundance can refer":

> In his endeavor to understand the world, man therefore always has at his disposition a surplus of signification (which he portions out amongst things according to the laws of symbolic thought—which it is the task of ethnologists and linguists to study). This distribution of a *supplementary* allowance [*ration supplémentaire*]—if it is permissible to put it that way—is absolutely necessary in order that on the whole the available signifier and the signified it aims at may remain in the relationship of complementarity which is the very condition of the use of symbolic thought. (p. xlix)

(It could no doubt be demonstrated that this *ration supplémentaire* of signification is the origin of the *ratio* itself.) The word reappears a little farther on, after Lévi-Strauss has mentioned "this floating signifier, which is the servitude of all finite thought":

> In other words—and taking as our guide Mauss's precept that all social phenomena can be assimilated to language—we see in *mana, Wakau, oranda* and other notions of the same type, the conscious expression of a semantic function, whose role it is to permit symbolic thought to operate in spite of the contradiction which is proper to it. In this way are explained the apparently insoluble antinomies attached to this notion. . . . At one and the same time force and action, quality and state, substantive and verb; abstract and concrete, omnipresent and localized—*mana* is in effect all these things. But is it not precisely because it is none of these things that *mana* is a simple form, or more exactly, a symbol in the pure state, and therefore capable of becoming charged with any sort of symbolic content whatever? In the system of symbols constituted by all cosmologies, *mana* would simply be a *valeur symbolique zéro*, that is to say, a sign marking the necessity of a symbolic content *supplementary* [my italics] to

[9] The point being that this word, both in English and French, means "to supply a deficiency," on the one hand, and "to supply something additional," on the other.
[10] ". . . ce signe s'ajoute, vient es sus, en *supplément*."
[11] "Introduction à l'oeuvre de Marcel Mauss," in: Marcel Mauss, *Sociologie et anthropologie* (Paris: Presses Universitaires de France, 1950).

that with which the signified is already loaded, but which can take on any value required, provided only that this value still remains part of the available reserve and is not, as phonologists put it, a group-term.

Lévi-Strauss adds the note:

Linguists have already been led to formulate hypotheses of this type. For example: "A zero phoneme is opposed to all the other phonemes in French in that it entails no differential characteristics and no constant phonetic value. On the contrary, the proper function of the zero phoneme is to be opposed to phoneme absence." (R. Jakobson and J. Lutz, "Notes on the French Phonemic Pattern," *Word*, vol. 5, no. 2 [August, 1949], p. 155). Similarly, if we schematize the conception I am proposing here, it could almost be said that the function of notions like *mana* is to be opposed to the absence of signification, without entailing by itself any particular signification. (p. 1 and note)

The *superabundance* of the signifier, its *supplementary* character, is the result of a finitude, that is to say, the result of a lack which must be *supplemented*.

It can now be understood why the concept of freeplay is important in Lévi-Strauss. His references to all sorts of games, notably to roulette, are very frequent, especially in his *Conversations*,[12] in *Race and History*,[13] and in *The Savage Mind*. This reference to the game or freeplay is always caught up in a tension.

It is in tension with history, first of all. This is a classical problem, objections to which are now well worn or used up. I shall simply indicate what seems to me the formality of the problem: by reducing history, Lévi-Strauss has treated as it deserves a concept which has always been in complicity with a teleological and eschatological metaphysics, in other words, paradoxically, in complicity with that philosophy of presence to which it was believed history could be opposed. The thematic of historicity, although it seems to be a somewhat late arrival in philosophy, has always been required by the determination of being as presence. With or without etymology, and in spite of the classic antagonism which opposes these significations throughout all of classical thought, it could be shown that the concept of *epistèmè* has always called forth that of *historia*, if history is always the unity of a becoming, as tradition of truth or development of science or knowledge oriented toward the appropriation of truth in presence and self-presence, toward knowledge in consciousness-of-self.[14] History has always been conceived as the movement of a resumption of history, a diversion between two presences. But if it is

---

[12] Presumably: G. Charbonnier, *Entretiens avec Claude Lévi-Strauss* (Paris: Plon-Julliard, 1961).

[13] *Race and History* (Paris: UNESCO Publications, 1958).

[14] ". . . l'unité d'un devenir, comme tradition de la vérité dans la présence et la présence à soi, vers le savoir dans la conscience de soi."

legitimate to suspect this concept of history, there is a risk, if it is reduced without an express statement of the problem I am indicating here, of falling back into an anhistoricism of a classical type, that is to say, in a determinate moment of the history of metaphysics. Such is the algebraic formality of the problem as I see it. More concretely, in the work of Lévi-Strauss it must be recognized that the respect for structurality, for the internal originality of the structure, compels a neutralization of time and history. For example, the appearance of a new structure, of an original system, always comes about—and this is the very condition of its structural specificity—by a rupture with its past, its origin, and its cause. One can therefore describe what is peculiar to the structural organization only by not taking into account, in the very moment of this description, its past conditions: by failing to pose the problem of the passage from one structure to another, by putting history into parentheses. In this "structuralist" moment, the concepts of chance and discontinuity are indispensable. And Lévi-Strauss does in fact often appeal to them as he does, for instance, for that structure of structures, language, of which he says in the "Introduction to the Work of Marcel Mauss" that it "could only have been born in one fell swoop":

> Whatever may have been the moment and the circumstances of its appearance in the scale of animal life, language could only have been born in one fell swoop. Things could not have set about signifying progressively. Following a transformation the study of which is not the concern of the social sciences, but rather of biology and psychology, a crossing over came about from a stage where nothing had a meaning to another where everything possessed it. (p. xlvi)

This standpoint does not prevent Lévi-Strauss from recognizing the slowness, the process of maturing, the continuous toil of factual transformations, history (for example, in *Race and History*). But, in accordance with an act which was also Rousseau's and Husserl's, he must "brush aside all the facts" at the moment when he wishes to recapture the specificity of a structure. Like Rousseau, he must always conceive of the origin of a new structure on the model of catastrophe—an overturning of nature in nature, a natural interruption of the natural sequence, a brushing aside *of* nature.

Besides the tension of freeplay with history, there is also the tension of freeplay with presence. Freeplay is the disruption of presence. The presence of an element is always a signifying and substitutive reference inscribed in a system of differences and the movement of a chain. Freeplay is always an interplay of absence and presence, but if it is to be radically conceived, freeplay must be conceived of before the alternative of presence and absence; being must be conceived of as presence or absence beginning with the possibility of freeplay and not the other way around. If Lévi-Strauss, better than any other, has brought to light the freeplay of repetition and the repetition of freeplay, one no less perceives in his work a sort of ethic of presence, an ethic of nostalgia for origins, an ethic of archaic and natural innocence, of a purity of presence and self-presence in speech[15]—an ethic, nostalgia, and even remorse which he often presents as the motivation of the ethnological project when he moves toward archaic societies—exemplary societies in his eyes. These texts are well known.

As a turning toward the presence, lost or impossible, of the absent origin, this structuralist thematic of broken immediateness is thus the sad, *negative,* nostalgic, guilty, Rousseauist facet of the thinking of freeplay of which the Nietzschean *affirmation*—the joyous affirmation of the freeplay of the world and without truth, without origin, offered to an active interpretation—would be the other side. *This affirmation then determines the non-center otherwise than as loss of the center.* And it plays the game without security. For there is a *sure* freeplay: that which is limited to the *substitution* of *given and existing, present,* pieces. In absolute chance, affirmation also surrenders itself to *genetic* indetermination, to the *seminal* adventure of the trace.[16]

There are thus two interpretations of interpretation, of structure, of sign, of freeplay. The one seeks to decipher, dreams of deciphering, a truth or an origin which is free from freeplay and from the order of the sign, and lives like an exile the necessity of interpretation. The other, which is no longer turned toward the origin, affirms freeplay and tries to pass beyond man and humanism, the name man being the name of that being who, throughout the history of metaphysics or of ontotheology—in other words, through the history of all of his history—has dreamed of full presence, the reassuring foundation, the origin and the end of the game. The second interpretation of interpretation, to which Nietzsche showed us the way, does not seek in ethnography, as Lévi-Strauss wished, the "inspiration of a new humanism" (again from the "Introduction to the Work of Marcel Mauss").

There are more than enough indications today to suggest we might perceive that these two interpretations of interpretation—which are absolutely irreconcilable even if we live them simultaneously and reconcile them in an obscure economy—together share the field which we call, in such a problematic fashion, the human sciences.

For my part, although these two interpretations must acknowledge and accentuate their difference and define their irreducibility, I do not believe that today there is any question of *choosing*—in the first place because here we are in a region (let's say, provisionally, a region of historicity) where the category of choice seems particularly trivial; and in the second, because we

[15] ". . . de la présence à soi dans la parole."
[16] Tournée vers la présence, perdue ou impossible, de l'origine absente, cette thématique structuraliste de l'immédiateté rompue est donc la face triste, *négative,* nostalgique, coupable, rousseauiste, de la pensée du jeu dont *l'affirmation* nietzschéenne, l'affirmation joyeuse du jeu du monde et de l'innocence du devenir, l'affirmation d'un monde de signes sans faute, sans vérité, sans origine, offert à une interprétation active, serait l'autre face. *Cette affirmation détermine alors le* non-centre *autrement que comme perte du centre.* Et elle joue sans sécurité. Car il y a un jeu *sûr:* celui qui se limite à la *substitution* de pièces *données et existantes, présentes.* Dans le hasard absolu, l'affirmation se livre aussi à l'indétermination *génétique,* à l'aventure *séminale* de la trace.

must first try to conceive of the common ground, and the *différance* of this irreducible difference.[17] Here there is a sort of *conception, the formation, the gestation, the labor.* I employ these words, I admit, with a glance toward the business of childbearing—but also with a glance toward those who, in a company from which I do not exclude myself, turn their eyes away in the face of the as yet unnameable which is proclaiming itself and which can do so, as is necessary whenever a birth is in the offing, only under the species of the nonspecies, in the formless, mute, infant, and terrifying form of monstrosity.

Translated by Alan Bass.

---

[17] From *différer,* in the sense of "to postpone," "put off," "defer." Elsewhere Derrida uses the word as a synonym for the German *Aufschub:* "postponement," and relates to it the central Freudian concepts of *Verspätung, Nachträglichkeit,* and to the *"détours* to death" of *Beyond the Pleasure Principle* by Sigmund Freud (Standard Edition, ed. James Strachey, vol. XIX, London, 1961), Chap. V.

Adrienne Rich

When We Dead Awaken:
Writing as Re-Vision

1971

The title of Adrienne Rich's (b. 1929) essay, with its reference to Henrik Ibsen's play of the same name about the male domination of women and its pun relating revision to renewed insight, points to the heart of modern feminist literary criticism. Frankly personal and openly political, Rich traces her intellectual development from acceptance of traditional male-centered critical principles to an increasingly radical advocacy of feminist ideology. Using herself as an example, she discusses the female writer's struggle to define her own reality through conventional societal and literary structures and the restrictions such structures impose on women personally, professionally, and artistically. Her essay suggests some of the basic tenets of feminist belief: that traditionally accepted "truths" are simply codified expectations, that established political and social hierarchies do not exist as some Platonic ideal but are the creation of a male-centered culture, that individual experience—emotional and perceptual—is a legitimate means of achieving broader understanding.

Rich and other feminist poet-critics react against the idea of a universal poetic truth, arguing that what has been assumed to be "universal" is in fact an essentially male conception that often trivializes, distorts, or simply ignores central concerns of female experience and imagination. The goals of such critics are several: to nurture the development of authentic female expression based in individual experience and shared understanding, to question long-standing definitions and systems of artistic value, to create new modes of artistic and critical discourse. Like other late-twentieth-century critics, feminists see form and content as indivisible; indeed, from the most radical perspective, art is a constant struggle not only with received cultural and political formulations but with the very language that shapes our perceptions of those formulations.

Though it has precedents—including the work of Virginia Woolf (page 411)—feminist critical theory began to gain prominence around 1970, when Kate Millett's Sexual Politics, *a polemical study of male novelists, defined gender as a major literary principle and criterion. Rich's early work in fact predates Millett, and she continues to be in the vanguard of the women's movement. In the meantime, the work of feminist critics has led to interest in previously neglected women authors, to a reexamination of well-known authors such as Emily Dickinson and the Brontës, to revisions in the traditional literary canon, and to new perceptions about how literature may be studied. Feminist criticism today presents challenges to other critical approaches, demanding that assumptions and practices unquestioned for centuries be reconsidered and redefined.*

IBSEN'S *When We Dead Awaken* is a play about the use that the male artist and thinker—in the process of creating culture as we know it—has made of women, in his life and in his work; and about a woman's slow struggling awakening to the use to which her life has been put. Bernard Shaw wrote in 1900 of this play:

> [Ibsen] shows us that no degradation ever devized or permitted is as disastrous as this degradation; that through it women can die into luxuries for men and yet can kill them; that men and women are becoming conscious of this; and that what remains to be seen as perhaps the most interesting of all imminent social developments is what will happen "when we dead awaken."[1]

It's exhilarating to be alive in a time of awakening consciousness; it can also be confusing, disorienting, and painful. This awakening of dead or sleeping consciousness has already affected the lives of millions of women, even those who don't know it yet. It is also affecting the lives of men, even those who deny its claims upon them. The argument will go on whether an oppressive economic class system is responsible for the oppressive nature of male/female relations, or whether, in fact, patriarchy—the domination of males—is the original model of oppression on which all others are based. But in the last few years the women's movement has drawn inescapable and illuminating connections between our sexual lives and our political institutions. The sleepwalkers are coming awake, and for the first time this awakening has a collective reality; it is no longer such a lonely thing to open one's eyes.

Re-vision—the act of looking back, of seeing with fresh eyes, of entering an old text from a new critical direction—is for women more than a chapter in cultural history: it is an act of survival. Until we can understand the assumptions in which we are drenched we cannot know ourselves. And this drive to self-knowledge, for women, is more than a search for identity: it is part of our refusal of the self-destructiveness of male-dominated society. A radical critique of literature, feminist in its impulse, would take the work first of all as a clue to how we live, how we have been living, how we have been led to imagine ourselves, how our language has trapped as well as liberated

---

[1] G. B. Shaw, *The Quintessence of Ibsenism* (New York: Hill & Wang, 1922), p. 139. [Rich's notes.]

us, how the very act of naming has been till now a male prerogative, and how we can begin to see and name—and therefore live—afresh. A change in the concept of sexual identity is essential if we are not going to see the old political order reassert itself in every new revolution. We need to know the writing of the past, and know it differently than we have ever known it; not to pass on a tradition but to break its hold over us.

For writers, and at this moment for women writers in particular, there is the challenge and promise of a whole new psychic geography to be explored. But there is also a difficult and dangerous walking on the ice, as we try to find language and images for a consciousness we are just coming into, and with little in the past to support us. I want to talk about some aspects of this difficulty and this danger.

Jane Harrison, the great classical anthropologist, wrote in 1914 in a letter to her friend Gilbert Murray:

> By the by, about "Women," it has bothered me often—why do women never want to write poetry about Man as a sex—why is Woman a dream and a terror to man and not the other way around? ... Is it mere convention and propriety, or something deeper?[2]

I think Jane Harrison's question cuts deep into the myth-making tradition, the romantic tradition; deep into what women and men have been to each other; and deep into the psyche of the woman writer. Thinking about that question, I began thinking of the work of two twentieth-century women poets, Sylvia Plath and Diane Wakoski. It strikes me that in the work of both Man appears as, if not a dream, a fascination and a terror; and that the source of the fascination and the terror is, simply, Man's power—to dominate, tyrannize, choose, or reject the woman. The charisma of Man seems to come purely from his power over her and his control of the world by force, not from anything fertile or life-giving in him. And, in the work of both these poets, it is finally the woman's sense of *herself*—embattled, possessed—that gives the poetry its dynamic charge, its rhythms of struggle, need, will, and female energy. Until recently this female anger and this furious awareness of the Man's power over her were not available materials to the female poet, who tended to write of Love as the source of her suffering, and to view that victimization by Love as an almost inevitable fate. Or, like Marianne Moore and Elizabeth Bishop, she kept sexuality at a measured and chiseled distance in her poems.

One answer to Jane Harrison's question has to be that historically men and women have played very different parts in each others' lives. Where woman has been a luxury for man, and has served as the painter's model and the poet's muse, but also as comforter, nurse, cook, bearer of his seed, secretarial assistant, and copyist of manuscripts, man has played a quite different

---

[2] J. G. Stewart, *Jane Ellen Harrison: A Portrait from Letters* (London: Merlin, 1959), p. 140.

role for the female artist. Henry James repeats an incident which the writer Prosper Mérimée described, of how, while he was living with George Sand,

> he once opened his eyes, in the raw winter dawn, to see his companion, in a dressing-gown, on her knees before the domestic hearth, a candlestick beside her and a red *madras* round her head, making bravely, with her own hands the fire that was to enable her to sit down betimes to urgent pen and paper. The story represents him as having felt that the spectacle chilled his ardor and tried his taste; her appearance was unfortunate, her occupation an inconsequence, and her industry a reproof—the result of all which was a lively irritation and an early rupture.[3]

The specter of this kind of male judgment, along with the misnaming and thwarting of her needs by a culture controlled by males, has created problems for the woman writer: problems of contact with herself, problems of language and style, problems of energy and survival.

In rereading Virginia Woolf's *A Room of One's Own* (1929) for the first time in some years, I was astonished at the sense of effort, of pains taken, of dogged tentativeness, in the tone of that essay. And I recognized that tone. I had heard it often enough, in myself and in other women. It is the tone of a woman almost in touch with her anger, who is determined not to appear angry, who is *willing* herself to be calm, detached, and even charming in a roomful of men where things have been said which are attacks on her very integrity. Virginia Woolf is addressing an audience of women, but she is acutely conscious—as she always was—of being overheard by men: by Morgan and Lytton and Maynard Keynes and for that matter by her father, Leslie Stephen.[4] She drew the language out into an exacerbated thread in her determination to have her own sensibility yet protect it from those masculine presences. Only at rare moments in that essay do you hear the passion in her voice; she was trying to sound as cool as Jane Austen, as Olympian as Shakespeare, because that is the way the men of the culture thought a writer should sound.

No male writer has written primarily or even largely for women, or with the sense of women's criticism as a consideration when he chooses his materials, his theme, his language. But to a lesser or greater extent, every woman writer has written for men even when, like Virginia Woolf, she was supposed to be addressing women. If we have come to the point when this balance might begin to change, when women can stop being haunted, not only by

---

[3] Henry James, "Notes on Novelists," in *Selected Literary Criticism of Henry James*, Morris Shapira, ed. (London: Heinemann, 1963), pp. 157–58.

[4] *A. R., 1978:* This intuition of mine was corroborated when, early in 1978, I read the correspondence between Woolf and Dame Ethel Smyth (Henry W. and Albert A. Berg Collection, The New York Public Library, Astor, Lenox and Tilden Foundations); in a letter dated June 8, 1933, Woolf speaks of having kept her own personality out of *A Room of One's Own* lest she not be taken seriously: ". . . how personal, so will they say, rubbing their hands with glee, women always are; *I even hear them as I write.*" (Italics mine.)

"convention and propriety" but by internalized fears of being and saying themselves, then it is an extraordinary moment for the woman writer—and reader.

I have hesitated to do what I am going to do now, which is to use myself as an illustration. For one thing, it's a lot easier and less dangerous to talk about other women writers. But there is something else. Like Virginia Woolf, I am aware of the women who are not with us here because they are washing the dishes and looking after the children. Nearly fifty years after she spoke, that fact remains largely unchanged. And I am thinking also of women whom she left out of the picture altogether—women who are washing other people's dishes and caring for other people's children, not to mention women who went on the streets last night in order to feed their children. We seem to be special women here, we have liked to think of ourselves as special, and we have known that men would tolerate, even romanticize us as special, as long as our words and actions didn't threaten their privilege of tolerating or rejecting us and our work according to *their* ideas of what a special woman ought to be. An important insight of the radical women's movement has been how divisive and how ultimately destructive is this myth of the special woman, who is also the token woman. Every one of us here in this room has had great luck—we are teachers, writers, academicians; our own gifts could not have been enough, for we all know women whose gifts are buried or aborted. Our struggles can have meaning and our privileges—however precarious under patriarchy—can be justified only if they can help to change the lives of women whose gifts—and whose very being—continue to be thwarted and silenced.

My own luck was being born white and middle-class into a house full of books, with a father who encouraged me to read and write. So for about twenty years I wrote for a particular man, who criticized and praised me and made me feel I was indeed "special." The obverse side of this, of course, was that I tried for a long time to please him, or rather, not to displease him. And then of course there were other men—writers, teachers—the Man, who was not a terror or a dream but a literary master and a master in other ways less easy to acknowledge. And there were all those poems about women, written by men: it seemed to be a given that men wrote poems and women frequently inhabited them. These women were almost always beautiful, but threatened with the loss of beauty, the loss of youth—the fate worse than death. Or, they were beautiful and died young, like Lucy and Lenore. Or, the woman was like Maud Gonne, cruel and disastrously mistaken, and the poem reproached her because she had refused to become a luxury for the poet.

A lot is being said today about the influence that the myths and images of women have on all of us who are products of culture. I think it has been a peculiar confusion to the girl or woman who tries to write because she is peculiarly susceptible to language. She goes to poetry or fiction looking for *her* way of being in the world, since she too has been putting words and images together; she is looking eagerly for guides, maps, possibilities; and over and over in the "words' masculine persuasive force" of literature she comes up against something that negates everything she is about: she meets the image of Woman in books written by men. She finds a terror and a dream, she finds a beautiful pale face, she finds La Belle Dame Sans Merci, she finds Juliet or Tess or Salomé, but precisely what she does not find is that absorbed, drudging, puzzled, sometimes inspired creature, herself, who sits at a desk trying to put words together.

So what does she do? What did I do? I read the older women poets with their peculiar keenness and ambivalence: Sappho, Christina Rossetti, Emily Dickinson, Elinor Wylie, Edna Millay, H. D. I discovered that the woman poet most admired at the time (by men) was Marianne Moore, who was maidenly, elegant, intellectual, discreet. But even in reading these women I was looking in them for the same things I had found in the poetry of men, because I wanted women poets to be the equals of men, and to be equal was still confused with sounding the same.

I know that my style was formed first by male poets: by the men I was reading as an undergraduate—Frost, Dylan Thomas, Donne, Auden, Mac-Niece, Stevens, Yeats. What I chiefly learned from them was craft.[5] But poems are like dreams: in them you put what you don't know you know. Looking back at poems I wrote before I was twenty-one, I'm startled because beneath the conscious craft are glimpses of the split I even then experienced between the girl who wrote poems, who defined herself in writing poems, and the girl who was to define herself by her relationships with men. "Aunt Jennifer's Tigers" (1951), written while I was a student, looks with deliberate detachment at this split.[6]

> Aunt Jennifer's tigers stride across a screen,
> Bright topaz denizens of a world of green.
> They do not fear the men beneath the tree;
> They pace in sleek chivalric certainty.
>
> Aunt Jennifer's fingers fluttering through her wool
> Find even the ivory needle hard to pull.
> The massive weight of Uncle's wedding band
> Sits heavily upon Aunt Jennifer's hand.
>
> When Aunt is dead, her terrified hands will lie
> Still ringed with ordeals she was mastered by.
> The tigers in the panel that she made
> Will go on striding, proud and unafraid.

---

[5] *A. R., 1978:* Yet I spent months, at sixteen, memorizing and writing imitations of Millay's sonnets; and in notebooks of that period I find what are obviously attempts to imitate Dickinson's metrics and verbal compression. I knew H. D. only through anthologized lyrics; her epic poetry was not then available to me.

[6] *A. R., 1978:* Texts of poetry quoted herein can be found in A. R., *Poems Selected and New: 1950–1974* (New York: Norton, 1975).

In writing this poem, composed and apparently cool as it is, I thought I was creating a portrait of an imaginary woman. But this woman suffers from the opposition of her imagination, worked out in tapestry, and her life-style, "ringed with ordeals she was mastered by." It was important to me that Aunt Jennifer was a person as distinct from myself as possible—distanced by the formalism of the poem, by its objective, observant tone—even by putting the woman in a different generation.

In those years formalism was part of the strategy—like asbestos gloves, it allowed me to handle materials I couldn't pick up bare-handed. A later strategy was to use the persona of a man, as I did in "The Loser" (1958):

*A man thinks of the woman he once loved: first, after her wedding, and
    then nearly a decade later.*

I

I kissed you, bride and lost, and went
home from that bourgeois sacrament,
your cheek still tasting cold upon
my lips that gave you benison
with all the swagger that they knew—
as losers somehow learn to do.

Your wedding made my eyes ache; soon
the world would be worse off for one
more golden apple dropped to ground
without the least protesting sound,
and you would windfall lie, and we
forget your shimmer on the tree.

Beauty is always wasted: if
not Mignon's song sung to the deaf,
at all events to the unmoved.
A face like yours cannot be loved
long or seriously enough.
Almost, we seem to hold it off.

II

Well, you are tougher than I thought.
Now when the wash with ice hangs taut
this morning of St. Valentine,
I see you strip the squeaking line,
your body weighed against the load,
and all my groans can do no good.

Because you are still beautiful,
though squared and stiffened by the pull
of what nine windy years have done.
You have three daughters, lost a son.

I see all your intelligence
flung into that unwearied stance.

My envy is of no avail.
I turn my head and wish him well
who chafed your beauty into use
and lives forever in a house
lit by the friction of your mind.
You stagger in against the wind.

I finished college, published my first book by a fluke, as it seemed to me, and broke off a love affair. I took a job, lived alone, went on writing, fell in love. I was young, full of energy, and the book seemed to mean that others agreed I was a poet. Because I was also determined to prove that as a woman poet I could also have what was then defined as a "full" woman's life, I plunged in my early twenties into marriage and had three children before I was thirty. There was nothing overt in the environment to warn me: these were the fifties, and in reaction to the earlier wave of feminism, middle-class women were making careers of domestic perfection, working to send their husbands through professional schools, then retiring to raise large families. People were moving out to the suburbs, technology was going to be the answer to everything, even sex; the family was in its glory. Life was extremely private; women were isolated from each other by the loyalties of marriage. I have a sense that women didn't talk to each other much in the fifties—not about their secret emptinesses, their frustrations. I went on trying to write; my second book and first child appeared in the same month. But by the time that book came out I was already dissatisfied with those poems, which seemed to me mere exercises for poems I hadn't written. The book was praised, however, for its "gracefulness"; I had a marriage and a child. If there were doubts, if there were periods of null depression or active despairing, these could only mean that I was ungrateful, insatiable, perhaps a monster.

About the time my third child was born, I felt that I had either to consider myself a failed woman and a failed poet, or to try to find some synthesis by which to understand what was happening to me. What frightened me most was the sense of drift, of being pulled along on a current which called itself my destiny, but in which I seemed to be losing touch with whoever I had been, with the girl who had experienced her own will and energy almost ecstatically at times, walking around a city or riding a train at night or typing in a student room. In a poem about my grandmother I wrote (of myself): "A young girl, thought sleeping, is certified dead" ("Halfway"). I was writing very little, partly from fatigue, that female fatigue of suppressed anger and loss of contact with my own being; partly from the discontinuity of female life with its attention to small chores, errands, work that others constantly undo, small children's constant needs. What I did write was unconvincing to me; my anger and frustration were hard to acknowledge in or out of poems because in fact I cared a great deal about my husband and my children. Trying to look back and understand that time I have tried to analyze the real nature of the conflict. Most, if not all, human lives are full of fantasy—passive day-dreaming which need not be acted on. But to write poetry or fiction, or even to think well, is not to fantasize, or to put fantasies on paper. For a poem to coalesce, for a character or an action to take shape, there has to be an imaginative transformation of reality which is in no way passive. And a certain freedom of the mind is needed—freedom to press on, to enter the currents of your thought like a glider pilot, knowing that your motion can be sustained, that the buoyancy of your attention will not be suddenly snatched away. Moreover, if the imagination is to transcend and transform experience it has to question, to challenge, to conceive of alternatives, perhaps to the very life you are living at that moment. You have to be free to play around with the notion that day might be night, love might be hate; nothing can be too sacred for the imagination to turn into its opposite or to call experimentally by another name. For writing is re-naming. Now, to be maternally with small children all day in the old way, to be with a man in the old way of marriage, requires a holding-back, a putting-aside of that imaginative activity, and demands instead a kind of conservatism. I want to make it clear that I am *not* saying that in order to write well, or think well, it is necessary to become unavailable to others, or to become a devouring ego. This has been the myth of the masculine artist and thinker; and I do not accept it. But to be a female human being trying to fulfill traditional female functions in a traditional way *is* in direct conflict with the subversive function of the imagination. The word *traditional* is important here. There must be ways, and we will be finding out more and more about them, in which the energy of creation and the energy of relation can be united. But in those years I always felt the conflict as a failure of love in myself. I had thought I was choosing a full life: the life available to most men, in which sexuality, work, and parenthood could coexist. But I felt, at twenty-nine, guilt toward the people closest to me, and guilty toward my own being.

I wanted, then, more than anything, the one thing of which there was never enough: time to think, time to write. The fifties and early sixties were years of rapid revelations: the sit-ins and marches in the South, the Bay of Pigs, the early antiwar movement, raised large questions—questions for which the masculine world of the academy around me seemed to have expert and fluent answers. But I needed to think for myself—about pacifism and dissent and violence, about poetry and society, and about my own relationship to all these things. For about ten years I was reading in fierce snatches, scribbling in notebooks, writing poetry in fragments; I was looking desperately for clues, because if there were no clues then I thought I might be insane. I wrote in a notebook about this time:

> Paralyzed by the sense that there exists a mesh of relationships—
> e.g., between my anger at the children, my sensual life, pacifism, sex
> (I mean sex in its broadest significance, not merely sexual desire)—an interconnectedness which, if I could see it, make it valid,
> would give me back myself, make it possible to function lucidly and
> passionately. Yet I grope in and out among these dark webs.

I think I began at this point to feel that politics was not something "out there" but something "in here" and of the essence of my condition.

In the late fifties I was able to write, for the first time, directly about experiencing myself as a woman. The poem was jotted in fragments during children's naps, brief hours in a library, or at 3:00 A.M. after rising with a wakeful child. I despaired of doing any continuous work at this time. Yet I began to feel that my fragments and scraps had a common consciousness and a common theme, one which I would have been very unwilling to put on paper at an earlier time because I had been taught that poetry should be "universal," which meant, of course, nonfemale. Until then I had tried very much *not* to identify myself as a female poet. Over two years I wrote a ten-part poem called "Snapshots of a Daughter-in-Law" (1958–1960), in a longer looser mode than I'd ever trusted myself with before. It was an extraordinary relief to write that poem. It strikes me now as too literary, too dependent on allusion; I hadn't found the courage yet to do without authorities, or even to use the pronoun "I"—the woman in the poem is always "she." One section of it, No. 2, concerns a woman who thinks she is going mad; she is haunted by voices telling her to resist and rebel, voices which she can hear but not obey.

2.
Banging the coffee-pot into the sink
she hears the angels chiding, and looks out
past the raked gardens to the sloppy sky.
Only a week since They said: *Have no patience.*

The next time it was: *Be insatiable.*
Then: *Save yourself; others you cannot save.*
Sometimes she's let the tapstream scald her arm,
a match burn to her thumbnail,

or held her hand above the kettle's snout
right in the wooly steam. They are probably angels,
since nothing hurts her anymore, except
each morning's grit blowing into her eyes.

The poem "Orion," written five years later, is a poem of reconnection with a part of myself I had felt I was losing—the active principle, the energetic imagination, the "half-brother" whom I projected, as I had for many years, into the constellation Orion. It's no accident that the words "cold and egotistical" appear in this poem, and are applied to myself.

For back when I went zig-zagging
through tamarack pastures
you were my genius, you
my cast-iron Viking, my helmed
lion-heart king in prison.
Years later now you're young

my fierce half-brother, staring
down from that simplified west
your breast open, your belt dragged down
by an oldfashioned thing, a sword
the last bravado you won't give over
though it weighs you down as you stride

and the stars in it are dim
and maybe have stopped burning.
But you burn, and I know it;
as I throw back my head to take you in
an old transfusion happens again:
divine astronomy is nothing to it.

Indoors I bruise and blunder,
break faith, leave ill enough
alone, a dead child born in the dark.
Night cracks up over the chimney,
pieces of time, frozen geodes
come showering down in the grate.

A man reaches behind my eyes
and finds them empty
a woman's head turns away
from my head in the mirror
children are dying my death
and eating crumbs of my life.

Pity is not your forte.
Calmly you ache up there
pinned aloft in your crow's nest,
my speechless pirate!
You take it all for granted
and when I look you back

it's with a starlike eye
shooting its cold and egotistical spear
where it can do least damage.
Breathe deep! No hurt, no pardon
out here in the cold with you
you with your back to the wall.

The choice still seemed to be between "love"—womanly, maternal love, altruistic love—a love defined and ruled by the weight of an entire culture;
and egotism—a force directed by men into creation, achievement, ambition,
often at the expense of others, but justifiably so. For weren't they men, and
wasn't that their destiny as womanly, selfless love was ours? We know now
that the alternatives are false ones—that the word "love" is itself in need of
re-vision.

There is a companion poem to "Orion," written three years later, in which at last the woman in the poem and the woman writing the poem become the same person. It is called "Planetarium," and it was written after a visit to a real planetarium, where I read an account of the work of Caroline Herschel, the astronomer, who worked with her brother William, but whose name remained obscure, as his did not.

Thinking of Caroline Herschel, 1750–1848, astronomer, sister of William;
*   and others*

A woman in the shape of a monster
a monster in the shape of a woman
the skies are full of them

a woman   "in the snow
among the Clocks and instruments
or measuring the ground with poles"

in her 98 years to discover
8 comets

she whom the moon ruled
like us
levitating into the night sky
riding the polished lenses

Galaxies of women, there
doing penance for impetuousness
ribs chilled
in those spaces   of the mind

An eye,
        "virile, precise and absolutely certain"
        from the mad webs of Uranisborg

                                encountering the NOVA

every impulse of light exploding
from the core
as life flies out of us
        Tycho whispering at last
        "Let me not seem to have lived in vain"

What we see, we see
and seeing is changing

the light that shrivels a mountain
and leaves a man alive

Heartbeat of the pulsar
heart sweating through my body

The radio impulse
pouring in from Taurus

    I am bombarded yet   I stand

I have been standing all my life in the
direct path of a battery of signals
the most accurately transmitted most
untranslateable language in the universe
I am a galactic cloud so deep   so invo-
luted that a light wave could take 15
years to travel through me   And has
taken   I am an instrument in the shape
of a woman trying to translate pulsations
into images   for the relief of the body
and the reconstruction of the mind.

In closing I want to tell you about a dream I had last summer. I dreamed I was asked to read my poetry at a mass women's meeting, but when I began to read, what came out were the lyrics of a blues song. I share this dream with you because it seemed to me to say something about the problems and the future of the woman writer, and probably of women in general. The awakening of consciousness is not like the crossing of a frontier—one step and you are in another country. Much of woman's poetry has been of the nature of the blues song: a cry of pain, of victimization, or a lyric of seduction.[7] And today, such poetry by women—and prose for that matter—is charged with anger. I think we need to go through that anger, and we will betray our own reality if we try, as Virginia Woolf was trying, for an objectivity, a detachment, that would make us sound more like Jane Austen or Shakespeare. We know more than Jane Austen or Shakespeare knew: more than Jane Austen because our lives are more complex, more than Shakespeare because we know more about the lives of women—Jane Austen and Virginia Woolf included.

Both the victimization and the anger experienced by women are real, and have real sources, everywhere in the environment, built into society, language, the structures of thought. They will go on being tapped and explored by poets, among others. We can neither deny them, nor will we rest there. A new generation of women poets is already working out of the psychic energy released when women begin to move out towards what the feminist philosopher Mary Daly has described as the "new space" on the boundaries of patriarchy.[8] Women are speaking to and of women in these poems, out of a newly

[7] *A. R., 1978:* When I dreamed that dream, was I wholly ignorant of the tradition of Bessie Smith and other women's blues lyrics which transcended victimization to sing of resistance and independence?

[8] Mary Daly, *Beyond God the Father: Towards a Philosophy of Women's Liberation* (Boston: Beacon, 1973).

released courage to name, to love each other, to share risk and grief and celebration.

To the eye of a feminist, the work of Western male poets now writing reveals a deep, fatalistic pessimism as to the possibilities of change, whether societal or personal, along with a familiar and threadbare use of women (and nature) as redemptive on the one hand, threatening on the other; and a new tide of phallocentric sadism and overt woman-hating which matches the sexual brutality of recent films. "Political" poetry by men remains stranded amid the struggles for power among male groups; in condemning U.S. imperialism or the Chilean junta the poet can claim to speak for the oppressed while remaining, as male, part of a system of sexual oppression. The enemy is always outside the self, the struggle somewhere else. The mood of isolation, self-pity, and self-imitation that pervades "nonpolitical" poetry suggests that a profound change in masculine consciousness will have to precede any new male poetic—or other—inspiration. The creative energy of patriarchy is fast running out; what remains is its self-generating energy for destruction. As women, we have our work cut out for us.

TERRY EAGLETON

From *Marxism and Literary Criticism*

1976

In the preface to Marxism and Literary Criticism, *Terry Eagleton (b. 1943) writes ironically: "No doubt we shall soon see Marxist criticism comfortably wedged between Freudian and mythological approaches to literature, as yet one more stimulating academic 'approach,' one more well-tilled field of inquiry for students to tramp." He urges against such an attitude, believing it "dangerous" to the centrality of Marxism as an agent of social change. Despite his warning, however, and because of his claims for the significance of Marxist criticism, Eagleton's opening chapters, dealing with two topics central to literary criticism, are here presented for some thoughtful "tramping."*

Marxism, which in some quarters remains a pejorative term, is in fact an indispensable concern in modern intellectual history. (See the headnote to the essay by Karl Marx, page 310.) Developed primarily as a way of examining historical, economic, and social issues, Marxist doctrine does not deal explicitly with theories of literature; consequently, there is no one orthodox Marxist school (as there is an orthodox Freudianism) but rather a diversity of Marxist readings. Eagleton's own discussion partly illustrates this diversity: he uses the derogatory term "vulgar Marxism" to refer to the simplistic deterministic notion that a literary work is nothing more than the direct product of its socioeconomic base. Aware also of how Marxist theory can be perverted, Eagleton in another chapter is scornful of such politically motivated corruptions as the Stalinist doctrine of socialist realism, an extension of statist propaganda that had chilling effects on art and artists in the former Soviet Union.

Like many sophisticated Marxist critics, Eagleton stresses the complicated interrelationships between the socioeconomic base and the institutions and values (including literature) that comprise the superstructure. But precisely because those relationships are so complex, a wide variety of critical thought has been brought to bear on them. Thus, Eagleton takes as his starting point an analysis of how various Marxist critics have addressed themselves to particular questions of literary analysis. Subsequent chapters of his book, for example, explore the role that the writer plays in

advancing the cause of the working class (proletariat) and the extent to which litera-
ture is a commodity, as much the product of economic activity as the automobile.

Other problems central to Marxist critical discussions include questions such
as: What is the relationship between literature and ideology? How does literature de-
velop out of the life of a society? Are there formal laws of literature that distance it
from the forms of the material world? Is the primary function of criticism to describe,
to explain, to interpret, or to evaluate? To what extent is language separable from so-
ciety and ideology separable from language? To what extent has Marxism, itself a
body of theory, been influenced by other modern intellectual currents such as psycho-
analysis, existentialism, structuralism, and semiotics? Far from being the monolithic
dogma its detractors suggest, Marxism is a living body of thought, seeking to answer
questions such as these, which are often ignored in other approaches to literature.

1. Literature and History

Marx, Engels and Criticism

IF KARL MARX and Frederick Engels are better known for their political and
economic rather than literary writings, this is not in the least because they regarded literature as insignificant. It is true, as Leon Trotsky remarked in *Literature and Revolution* (1924), that 'there are many people in this world who
think as revolutionists and feel as philistines'; but Marx and Engels were not
of this number. The writings of Karl Marx, himself the youthful author of
lyric poetry, a fragment of verse-drama and an unfinished comic novel much
influenced by Laurence Sterne, are laced with literary concepts and allusions;
he wrote a sizeable unpublished manuscript on art and religion, and planned
a journal of dramatic criticism, a full-length study of Balzac and a treatise on
aesthetics. Art and literature were part of the very air Marx breathed, as a
formidably cultured German intellectual in the great classical tradition of his
society. His acquaintance with literature, from Sophocles to the Spanish
novel, Lucretius to potboiling English fiction, was staggering in its scope; the
German workers' circle he founded in Brussels devoted an evening a week to
discussing the arts, and Marx himself was an inveterate theatre-goer, de-
claimer of poetry, devourer of every species of literary art from Augustan
prose to industrial ballads. He described his own works in a letter to Engels
as forming an 'artistic whole', and was scrupulously sensitive to questions of
literary style, not least his own; his very first pieces of journalism argued for
freedom of artistic expression. Moreover, the pressure of aesthetic concepts
can be detected behind some of the most crucial categories of economic
thought he employs in his mature work.

Even so, Marx and Engels had rather more important tasks on their
hands than the formulation of a complete aesthetic theory. Their comments
on art and literature are scattered and fragmentary, glancing allusions rather
than developed positions. This is one reason why Marxist criticism involves
more than merely re-stating cases set out by the founders of Marxism. It also

involves more than what has become known in the West as the 'sociology of literature'. The sociology of literature concerns itself chiefly with what might be called the means of literary production, distribution and exchange in a particular society—how books are published, the social composition of their authors and audiences, levels of literacy, the social determinants of 'taste'. It also examines literary texts for their 'sociological' relevance, raiding literary works to abstract from them themes of interest to the social historian. There has been some excellent work in this field, and it forms one aspect of Marxist criticism as a whole; but taken by itself it is neither particularly Marxist nor particularly critical. It is, indeed, for the most part a suitably tamed, degutted version of Marxist criticism, appropriate for Western consumption.

Marxist criticism is not merely a 'sociology of literature', concerned with how novels get published and whether they mention the working class. Its aim is to *explain* the literary work more fully; and this means a sensitive attention to its forms, styles and meanings. But it also means grasping those forms, styles and meanings as the products of a particular history. The painter Henri Matisse once remarked that all art bears the imprint of its historical epoch, but that great art is that in which this imprint is most deeply marked. Most students of literature are taught otherwise: the greatest art is that which timelessly transcends its historical conditions. Marxist criticism has much to say on this issue, but the 'historical' analysis of literature did not of course begin with Marxism. Many thinkers before Marx had tried to account for literary works in terms of the history which produced them; and one of these, the German idealist philosopher G.W.F. Hegel, had a profound influence on Marx's own aesthetic thought. The originality of Marxist criticism, then, lies not in its historical approach to literature, but in its revolutionary understanding of history itself.

Base and Superstructure

The seeds of that revolutionary understanding are planted in a famous passage in Marx and Engels's *The German Ideology* (1845–6):

> The production of ideas, concepts and consciousness is first of all directly interwoven with the material intercourse of man, the language of real life. Conceiving, thinking, the spiritual intercourse of men, appear here as the direct efflux of men's material behaviour ... we do not proceed from what men say, imagine, conceive, nor from men as described, thought of, imagined, conceived, in order to arrive at corporeal man; rather we proceed from the really active man. .... Consciousness does not determine life: life determines consciousness.

A fuller statement of what this means can be found in the Preface to *A Contribution to the Critique of Political Economy* (1859):

In the social production of their life, men enter into definite relations
that are indispensable and independent of their will, *relations of production* which correspond to a definite stage of development of their
material productive *forces*. The sum total of these relations of production constitutes the economic structure of society, the real foundation, on which rises a legal and political superstructure and to
which correspond definite forms of social consciousness. The mode
of production of material life conditions the social, political and intellectual life process in general. It is not the consciousness of men
that determines their being, but on the contrary, their social being
that determines their consciousness.

The social relations between men, in other words, are bound up with the way
they produce their material life. Certain 'productive forces'—say, the organisation of labour in the middle ages—involve the social relations of villein to
lord we know as feudalism. At a later stage, the development of new modes
of productive organisation is based on a changed set of social relations—this
time between the capitalist class who owns those means of production, and
the proletarian class whose labour-power the capitalist buys for profit. Taken
together, these 'forces' and 'relations' of production form what Marx calls
'the economic structure of society', or what is more commonly known by
Marxism as the economic 'base' or 'infrastructure'. From this economic base,
in every period, emerges a 'superstructure'—certain forms of law and politics, a certain kind of state, whose essential function is to legitimate the
power of the social class which owns the means of economic production. But
the superstructure contains more than this: it also consists of certain 'definite
forms of social consciousness' (political, religious, ethical, aesthetic and so
on), which is what Marxism designates as *ideology*. The function of ideology,
also, is to legitimate the power of the ruling class in society; in the last analysis, the dominant ideas of a society are the ideas of its ruling class.

Art, then, is for Marxism part of the 'superstructure' of society. It is (with
qualifications we shall make later) part of a society's ideology—an element
in that complex structure of social perception which ensures that the situation in which one social class has power over the others is either seen by most
members of the society as 'natural', or not seen to all. To understand literature, then, means understanding the total social process of which it is part.
As the Russian Marxist critic Georgy Plekhanov put it: 'The social mentality
of an age is conditioned by that age's social relations. This is nowhere quite
as evident as in the history of art and literature'. Literary works are not mysteriously inspired, or explicable simply in terms of their authors' psychology.
They are forms of perception, particular ways of seeing the world; and as
such they have a relation to that dominant way of seeing the world which is
the 'social mentality' or ideology of an age. That ideology, in turn, is the
product of the concrete social relations into which men enter at a particular
time and place; it is the way those class-relations are experienced, legitimized
and perpetuated. Moreover, men are not free to choose their social relations;

they are constrained into them by material necessity—by the nature and stage of development of their mode of economic production.

To understand *King Lear, The Dunciad* or *Ulysses* is therefore to do more than interpret their symbolism, study their literary history and add footnotes about sociological facts which enter into them. It is first of all to understand the complex, indirect relations between those works and the ideological worlds they inhabit—relations which emerge not just in 'themes' and 'preoc- cupations', but in style, rhythm, image, quality and (as we shall see later) *form.* But we do not understand ideology either unless we grasp the part it plays in the society as a whole—how it consists of a definite, historically rel- ative structure of perception which underpins the power of a particular so- cial class. This is not an easy task, since an ideology is never a simple reflec- tion of a ruling class's ideas; on the contrary, it is always a complex phenomenon, which may incorporate conflicting, even contradictory, views of the world. To understand an ideology, we must analyse the precise rela- tions between different classes in a society; and to do that means grasping where those classes stand in relation to the mode of production.

All this may seem a tall order to the student of literature who thought he was merely required to discuss plot and characterization. It may seem a con- fusion of literary criticism with disciplines like politics and economics which ought to be kept separate. But it is, nonetheless, essential for the fullest expla- nation of any work of literature. Take, for example, the great Placido Gulf scene in Conrad's *Nostromo.* To evaluate the fine artistic force of this episode, as Decoud and Nostromo are isolated in utter darkness on the slowly sinking lighter, involves us in subtly placing the scene within the imaginative vision of the novel as a whole. The radical pessimism of that vision (and to grasp it fully we must, of course, relate *Nostromo* to the rest of Conrad's fiction) can- not simply be accounted for in terms of 'psychological' factors in Conrad himself; for individual psychology is also a *social* product. The pessimism of Conrad's world view is rather a unique transformation into art of an ideolog- ical pessimism rife in his period—a sense of history as futile and cyclical, of individuals as impenetrable and solitary, of human values as relativistic and irrational, which marks a drastic crisis in the ideology of the Western bour- geois class to which Conrad allied himself. There were good reasons for that ideological crisis, in the history of imperialist capitalism throughout this pe- riod. Conrad did not, of course, merely anonymously reflect that history in his fiction; every writer is individually placed in society, responding to a gen- eral history from his own particular standpoint, making sense of it in his own concrete terms. But it is not difficult to see how Conrad's personal standing, as an 'aristocratic' Polish exile deeply committed to English conservatism, in- tensified for him the crisis of English bourgeois ideology.

It is also possible to see in these terms why that scene in the Placido Gulf should be artistically fine. To write well is more than a matter of 'style'; it also means having at one's disposal an ideological perspective which can penetrate to the realities of men's experience in a certain situation. This is cer- tainly what the Placido Gulf scene does; and it can do it, not just because its author happens to have an excellent prose-style, but because his historical situation allows him access to such insights. Whether those insights are in political terms 'progressive' or 'reactionary' (Conrad's are certainly the latter) is not the point—any more than it is to the point that most of the agreed major writers of the twentieth century—Yeats, Eliot, Pound, Lawrence—are political conservatives who each had truck with fascism. Marxist criticism, rather than apologising for the fact, explains it—sees that, in the absence of genuinely revolutionary art, only a radical conservatism, hostile like Marxism to the withered values of liberal bourgeois society, could produce the most significant literature.

Literature and Superstructure

It would be a mistake to imply that Marxist criticism moves mechanically from 'text' to 'ideology' to 'social relations' to 'productive forces'. It is concerned, rather, with the *unity* of these 'levels' of society. Literature may be part of the superstructure, but it is not merely the passive reflection of the economic base. Engels makes this clear, in a letter to Joseph Bloch in 1890:

> According to the materialist conception of history, the determining element in history is *ultimately* the production and reproduction in real life. More than this neither Marx nor I have ever asserted. If therefore somebody twists this into the statement that the economic element is the *only* determining one, he transforms it into a meaningless, abstract and absurd phrase. The economic situation is the basis, but the various elements of the superstructure—political forms of the class struggle and its consequences, constitutions established by the victorious class after a successful battle, etc.—forms of law—and then even the reflexes of all these actual struggles in the brains of the combatants: political, legal, and philosophical theories, religious ideas and their further development into systems of dogma—also exercise their influence upon the course of the historical struggles and in many cases preponderate in determining their *form.*

Engels wants to deny that there is any mechanical, one-to-one correspondence between base and superstructure; elements of the superstructure constantly react back upon and influence the economic base. The materialist theory of history denies that art can *in itself* change the course of history; but it insists that art can be an active element in such change. Indeed, when Marx came to consider the relation between base and superstructure, it was art which he selected as an instance of the complexity and indirectness of that relationship:

> In the case of the arts, it is well known that certain periods of their flowering are out of all proportion to the general development of society, hence also to the material foundation, the skeletal structure, as

it were, of its organisation. For example, the Greeks compared to the moderns or also Shakespeare. It is even recognised that certain forms of art, e.g. the epic, can no longer be produced in their world epoch-making, classical stature as soon as the production of art, as such, begins; that is, that certain significant forms within the realm of the arts are possible only at an undeveloped stage of artistic development. If this is the case with the relation between different kinds of art within the realm of art, it is already less puzzling that it is the case in the relation of the entire realm to the general development of society. The difficulty consists only in the general formulation of these contradictions. As soon as they have been specified, they are already clarified.

Marx is considering here what he calls 'the unequal relationship of the development of material production . . . to artistic production'. It does not follow that the greatest artistic achievements depend upon the highest development of the productive forces, as the example of the Greeks, who produced major art in an economically undeveloped society, clearly evidences. Certain major artistic forms like the epic are only *possible* in an undeveloped society. Why then, Marx goes on to ask, do we still respond to such forms, given our historical distance from them?:

> But the difficulty lies not in understanding that the Greek arts and epic are bound up with certain forms of social development. The difficulty is that they still afford us artistic pleasure and that in a certain respect they count as a norm and as an unattainable model.

Why does Greek art still give us aesthetic pleasure? The answer which Marx goes on to provide has been universally lambasted by unsympathetic commentators as lamely inept:

> A man cannot become a child again, or he becomes childish. But does he not find joy in the child's naiveté, and must he himself not strive to reproduce its truth at a higher stage? Does not the true character of each epoch come alive in the nature of its children? Why should not the historic childhood of humanity, its most beautiful unfolding, as a stage never to return, exercise an eternal charm? There are unruly children and precocious children. Many of the old peoples belong in this category. The Greeks were normal children. The charm of their art for us is not in contradiction to the undeveloped stage of society on which it grew. (It) is its result, rather, and is inextricably bound up, rather, with the fact that the unripe social conditions under which it arose, and could alone rise, can never return.

So our liking for Greek art is a nostalgic lapse back into childhood—a piece of unmaterialist sentimentalism which hostile critics have gladly pounced on. But the passage can only be treated thus if it is rudely ripped from the context to which it belongs—the draft manuscripts of 1857, known today as the *Grundrisse*. Once returned to that context, the meaning becomes instantly apparent. The Greeks, Marx is arguing, were able to produce major art not *in spite of* but *because of* the undeveloped state of their society. In ancient societies, which have not yet undergone the fragmenting 'division of labour' known to capitalism, the overwhelming of 'quality' by 'quantity' which results from commodity-production and the restless, continual development of the productive forces, a certain 'measure' or harmony can be achieved between man and Nature—a harmony precisely dependent upon the *limited* nature of Greek society. The 'childlike' world of the Greeks is attractive because it thrives within certain measured limits—measures and limits which are brutally overridden by bourgeois society in its limitless demand to produce and consume. Historically, it is essential that this constricted society should be broken up as the productive forces expand beyond its frontiers; but when Marx speaks of 'striv(ing) to reproduce its truth at a higher stage', he is clearly speaking of the communist society of the future, where unlimited resources will serve an unlimitedly developing man.

Two questions, then, emerge from Marx's formulations in the *Grundrisse*. The first concerns the relation between 'base' and 'superstructure'; the second concerns our own relation in the present with past art. To take the second question first: how can it be that we moderns still find aesthetic appeal in the cultural products of past, vastly different societies? In a sense, the answer Marx gives is no different from the answer to the question: How is it that we moderns still respond to the exploits of, say, Spartacus? We respond to Spartacus or Greek sculpture because our own history links us to those ancient societies; we find in them an undeveloped phase of the forces which condition us. Moreover, we find in those ancient societies a primitive image of 'measure' between man and Nature which capitalist society necessarily destroys, and which socialist society can reproduce at an incomparably higher level. We ought, in other words, to think of 'history' in wider terms than our own contemporary history. To ask how Dickens relates to history is not just to ask how he relates to Victorian England, for that society was itself the product of a long history which includes men like Shakespeare and Milton. It is a curiously narrowed view of history which defines it merely as the 'contemporary moment' and relegates all else to the 'universal'. One answer to the problem of past and present is suggested by Bertolt Brecht, who argues that 'we need to develop the historical sense . . . into a real sensual delight. When our theatres perform plays of other periods they like to annihilate distance, fill in the gap, gloss over the differences. But what comes then of our delight in comparisons, in distance, in dissimilarity—which is at the same time a delight in what is close and proper to ourselves?'

The other problem posed by the *Grundrisse* is the relation between base and superstructure. Marx is clear that these two aspects of society do not form a *symmetrical* relationship, dancing a harmonious minuet hand-in-hand throughout history. Each element of a society's superstructure—art, law, politics, religion—has its own tempo of development, its own internal evolution, which is not reducible to a mere expression of the class struggle or the state of the economy. Art, as Trotsky comments, has 'a very high degree of autonomy'; it is not tied in any simple one-to-one way to the mode of production. And yet Marxism claims too that, in the last analysis, art is determined by that mode of production. How are we to explain this apparent discrepancy?

Let us take a concrete literary example. A 'vulgar Marxist' case about T.S. Eliot's *The Waste Land* might be that the poem is directly determined by ideological and economic factors—by the spiritual emptiness and exhaustion of bourgeois ideology which springs from that crisis of imperialist capitalism known as the First World War. This is to explain the poem as an immediate 'reflection' of those conditions; but it clearly fails to take into account a whole series of 'levels' which 'mediate' between the text itself and capitalist economy. It says nothing, for instance, about the social situation of Eliot himself—a writer living an ambiguous relationship with English society, as an 'aristocratic' American expatriate who became a glorified City clerk and yet identified deeply with the conservative-traditionalist, rather than bourgeois-commercialist, elements of English ideology. It says nothing about that ideology's more general forms—nothing of its structure, content, internal complexity, and how all these are produced by the extremely complex class-relations of English society at the time. It is silent about the form and language of *The Waste Land*—about why Eliot, despite his extreme political conservatism, was an *avant-garde* poet who selected certain 'progressive' experimental techniques from the history of literary forms available to him, and on what ideological basis he did this. We learn nothing from this approach about the social conditions which gave rise at the time to certain forms of 'spirituality', part-Christian, part-Buddhist, which the poem draws on; or of what role a certain kind of bourgeois anthropology (Fraser) and bourgeois philosophy (F.H. Bradley's idealism) used by the poem fulfilled in the ideological formation of the period. We are unilluminated about Eliot's social position as an artist, part of a self-consciously erudite, experimental élite with particular modes of publication (the small press, the little magazine) at their disposal; or about the kind of audience which that implied, and its effect on the poem's styles and devices. We remain ignorant about the relation between the poem and the aesthetic theories associated with it—of what role that aesthetic plays in the ideology of the time, and how it shapes the construction of the poem itself.

Any complete understanding of *The Waste Land* would need to take these (and other) factors into account. It is not a matter of *reducing* the poem to the state of contemporary capitalism; but neither is it a matter of introducing so many judicious complications that anything as crude as capitalism may to all intents and purposes be forgotten. On the contrary: all of the elements I have enumerated (the author's class-position, ideological forms and their relation to literary forms, 'spirituality' and philosophy, techniques of literary production, aesthetic theory) are directly relevant to the base/superstructure model. What Marxist criticism looks for is the unique *conjuncture* of these elements which we know as *The Waste Land*. No one of these elements can be conflated with another: each has its own relative independence. *The Waste Land* can indeed be explained as a poem which springs from a crisis of bourgeois ideology, but it has no simple correspondence with that crisis or with the political and economic conditions which produced it. (As a poem, it does not of course *know itself* as a product of a particular ideological crisis, for if it did it would cease to exist. It needs to translate that crisis into 'universal' terms—to grasp it as part of an unchanging human condition, shared alike by ancient Egyptians and modern man.) *The Waste Land*'s relation to the real history of its time, then, is highly *mediated;* and in this it is like all works of art.

Literature and Ideology

Friedrich Engels remarks in *Ludwig Feuerbach and the End of Classical German Philosophy* (1888) that art is far richer and more 'opaque' than political and economic theory because it is less purely ideological. It is important here to grasp the precise meaning for Marxism of 'ideology'. Ideology is not in the first place a set of doctrines; it signifies the way men live out their roles in class-society, the values, ideas and images which tie them to their social functions and so prevent them from a true knowledge of society as a whole. In this sense *The Waste Land* is ideological: it shows a man making sense of his experience in ways that prohibit a true understanding of his society, ways that are consequently false. All art springs from an ideological conception of the world; there is no such thing, Plekhanov comments, as a work of art entirely devoid of ideological content. But Engels' remark suggests that art has a more complex relationship to ideology than law and political theory, which rather more transparently embody the interests of a ruling class. The question, then, is what relationship art has to ideology.

This is not an easy question to answer. Two extreme, opposite positions are possible here. One is that literature is *nothing but* ideology in a certain artistic form—that works of literature are just expressions of the ideologies of their time. They are prisoners of 'false consciousness', unable to reach beyond it to arrive at the truth. It is a position characteristic of much 'vulgar Marxist' criticism, which tends to see literary works merely as reflections of dominant ideologies. As such, it is unable to explain, for one thing, why so much literature actually *challenges* the ideological assumptions of its time. The opposite case seizes on the fact that so much literature challenges the ideology it confronts, and makes this part of the definition of literary art itself. Authentic art, as Ernst Fischer argues in his significantly entitled *Art Against Ideology* (1969), always transcends the ideological limits of its time, yielding us insight into the realities which ideology hides from view.

Both of these cases seem to me too simple. A more subtle (although still incomplete) account of the relationship between literature and ideology is provided by the French Marxist theorist Louis Althusser. Althusser argues that art cannot be reduced to ideology: it has, rather, a particular *relationship* to it. Ideology signifies the imaginary ways in which men experience the real world, which is, of course, the kind of experience literature gives us too—

what it feels like to live in particular conditions, rather than a conceptual analysis of those conditions. However, art does more than just passively reflect that experience. It is held within ideology, but also manages to distance itself from it, to the point where it permits us to 'feel' and 'perceive' the ideology from which it springs. In doing this, art does not enable us to *know* the truth which ideology conceals, since for Althusser 'knowledge' in the strict sense means *scientific* knowledge—the kind of knowledge of, say, capitalism which Marx's *Capital* rather than Dickens's *Hard Times* allows us. The difference between science and art is not that they deal with different objects, but that they deal with the same objects in different ways. Science gives us conceptual knowledge of a situation; art gives us the experience of that situation, which is equivalent to ideology. But by doing this, it allows us to 'see' the nature of that ideology, and thus begins to move us towards that full understanding of ideology which is scientific knowledge.

How literature can do this is more fully developed by one of Althusser's colleagues, Pierre Macherey. In his *Pour Une Théorie de la Production Littéraire* (1966), Macherey distinguishes between what he terms 'illusion' (meaning essentially, ideology), and 'fiction'. Illusion—the ordinary ideological experience of men—is the material on which the writer goes to work; but in working on it he transforms it into something different, lends it a shape and structure. It is by giving ideology a determinate form, fixing it within certain fictional limits, that art is able to distance itself from it, thus revealing to us the limits of that ideology. In doing this, Macherey claims, art contributes to our deliverance from the ideological illusion.

I find the comments of both Althusser and Macherey at crucial points ambiguous and obscure; but the relation they propose between literature and ideology is nonetheless deeply suggestive. Ideology, for both critics, is more than an amorphous body of free-floating images and ideas; in any society it has a certain structural coherence. Because it possesses such relative coherence, it can be the object of scientific analysis; and since literary texts 'belong' to ideology, they too can be the object of such scientific analysis. A scientific criticism would seek to explain the literary work in terms of the ideological structure of which it is part, yet which it transforms in its art: it would search out the principle which both ties the work to ideology and distances it from it. The finest Marxist criticism has indeed done precisely that; Macherey's starting-point is Lenin's brilliant analyses of Tolstoy. To do this, however, means grasping the literary work as a *formal* structure; and it is to this question that we can now turn.

2. Form and Content

History and Form

In his early essay *The Evolution of Modern Drama* (1909), the Hungarian Marxist critic Georg Lukács writes that 'the truly social element in literature is the form'. This is not the kind of comment which has come to be expected of

Marxist criticism. For one thing, Marxist criticism has traditionally opposed
all kinds of literary formalism, attacking that inbred attention to sheerly technical properties which robs literature of historical significance and reduces it
to an aesthetic game. It has, indeed, noted the relationship between such critical technocracy and the behaviour of advanced capitalist societies. For another thing, a good deal of Marxist criticism has in practice paid scant attention to questions of artistic form, shelving the issue in its dogged pursuit of
political content. Marx himself believed that literature should reveal a unity
of form and content, and burnt some of his own early lyric poems on the
grounds that their rhapsodic feelings were dangerously unrestrained; but he
was also suspicious of excessively formalistic writing. In an early newspaper
article on Silesian weavers' songs, he claimed that mere stylistic exercises led
to 'perverted content', which in turn impresses the stamp of 'vulgarity' on literary form. He shows, in other words, a *dialectical* grasp of the relations in
question: form is the product of content, but reacts back upon it in a double-
edged relationship. Marx's early comment about oppressively formalistic
law in the *Rheinische Zeitung*—'form is of no value unless it is the form of its
content'—could equally be applied to his aesthetic views.

In arguing for a unity of form and content, Marx was being faithful to the
Hegelian tradition he inherited. Hegel had argued in the *Philosophy of Fine
Art* (1835) that 'every definite content determines a form suitable to it'. 'Defectiveness of form', he maintained, 'arises from defectiveness of content'. Indeed for Hegel the history of art can be written in terms of the varying relations between form and content. Art manifests different stages in the
development of what Hegel calls the 'World-Spirit', the 'Idea' or the 'Absolute'; this is the 'content' of art, which successively strives to embody itself
adequately in artistic form. At an early stage of historical development, the
World-Spirit can find no adequate formal realization: ancient sculpture, for
example, reveals how the 'Spirit' is obstructed and overwhelmed by an excess of sensual material which it is unable to mould to its own purposes.
Greek classical art, on the other hand, achieves an harmonious unity between
content and form, the spiritual and the material: here, for a brief historical
moment, 'content' finds its entirely appropriate embodiment. In the modern
world, however, and most typically in Romanticism, the spiritual absorbs the
sensual, content overwhelms form. Material forms give way before the highest development of the Spirit, which like Marx's productive forces have out-
stripped the limited classical moulds which previously contained them.

It would be mistaken to think that Marx adopted Hegel's aesthetic
wholesale. Hegel's aesthetic is idealist, drastically oversimplifying and only
to a limited extent dialectical; and in any case Marx disagreed with Hegel
over several concrete aesthetic issues. But both thinkers share the belief that
artistic form is no mere quirk on the part of the individual artist. Forms are
historically determined by the kind of 'content' they have to embody; they
are changed, transformed, broken down and revolutionized as that content
itself changes. 'Content' is in this sense prior to 'form', just as for Marxism it
is changes in a society's material 'content', its mode of production, which de-

termine the 'forms' of its superstructure. 'Form itself', Fredric Jameson has remarked in his *Marxism and Form* (1971), 'is but the working out of content in the realm of the superstructure'. To those who reply irritably that form and content are inseparable anyway—that the distinction is artificial—it is as well to say immediately that this is of course true *in practice*. Hegel himself recognized this: 'Content', he wrote, 'is nothing but the transformation of form into content, and form is nothing but the transformation of content into form'. But if form and content are inseparable in practice, they are theoretically distinct. This is why we can talk of the varying *relations* between the two.

Those relations, however, are not easy to grasp. Marxist criticism sees form and content as dialectically related, and yet wants to assert in the end the primacy of content in determining form. The point is put, tortuously but correctly, by Ralph Fox in his *The Novel and the People* (1937), when he declares that 'Form is produced by content, is identical and one with it, and, though the primacy is on the side of content, form reacts on content and never remains passive'. This dialectical conception of the form-content relationship sets itself against two opposed positions. On the one hand, it attacks that formalist school (epitomized by the Russian Formalists of the 1920s) for whom content is merely a function of form—for whom the content of a poem is selected merely to reinforce the technical devices the poem deploys. But it also criticizes the 'vulgar Marxist' notion that artistic form is merely an artifice, externally imposed on the turbulent content of history itself. Such a position is to be found in Christopher Caudwell's *Studies in a Dying Culture* (1938). In that book, Caudwell distinguishes between what he calls 'social being'—the vital, instinctual stuff of human experience—and a society's forms of consciousness. Revolution occurs when those forms, having become ossified and obsolete, are burst asunder by the dynamic, chaotic flood of 'social being' itself. Caudwell, in other words, thinks of 'social being' (*content*) as inherently formless, and of forms as inherently restrictive; he lacks, that is to say, a sufficiently dialectical understanding of the relations at issue. What he does not see is that 'form' does not merely process the raw material of 'content', because that content (whether social or literary) is for Marxism already *informed*; it has a significant structure. Caudwell's view is merely a variant of the bourgeois critical commonplace that art 'organizes the chaos of reality'. (What is the ideological significance of seeing reality as chaotic?) Fredric Jameson, by contrast, speaks of the 'inner logic of content', of which social or literary forms are transformative products.

Given such a limited view of the form-content relationship, it is not surprising that English Marxist critics of the 1930s fall often enough into the 'vulgar Marxist' mistake of raiding literary works for their ideological content and relating this directly to the class-struggle or the economy. It is against this danger that Lukács's comment is meant to warn: the true bearers of ideology in art are the very forms, rather than abstractable content, of the work itself. We find the impress of history in the literary work precisely *as literary*, not as some superior form of social documentation.

Form and Ideology

What does it mean to say that literary form is ideological? In a suggestive comment in *Literature and Revolution,* Leon Trotsky maintains that 'The relationship between form and content is determined by the fact that the new form is discovered, proclaimed and evolved under the pressure of an inner need, of a collective psychological demand which, like everything else ... has its social roots'. Significant developments in literary form, then, result from significant changes in ideology. They embody new ways of perceiving social reality and (as we shall see later) new relations between artist and audience. This is evident enough if we look at well-charted examples like the rise of the novel in eighteenth-century England. The novel, as Ian Watt has argued, reveals in its very *form* a changed set of ideological interests. No matter what content a particular novel of the time may have, it shares certain formal structures with other such works: a shifting of interest from the romantic and supernatural to individual psychology and 'routine' experience; a concept of life-like, substantial 'character'; a concern with the material fortunes of an individual protagonist who moves through an unpredictably evolving, linear narrative and so on. This changed form, Watt claims, is the product of an increasingly confident bourgeois class, whose consciousness has broken beyond the limits of older, 'aristocratic' literary conventions. Plekhanov argues rather similarly in *French Dramatic Literature and French 18th Century Painting* that the transition from classical tragedy to sentimental comedy in France reflects a shift from aristocratic to bourgeois values. Or take the break from 'naturalism' to 'expressionism' in the European theatre around the turn of the century. This, as Raymond Williams has suggested, signals a breakdown in certain dramatic conventions which in turn embody specific 'structures of feeling', a set of received ways of perceiving and responding to reality. Expressionism feels the need to transcend the limits of a naturalistic theatre which assumes the ordinary bourgeois world to be solid, to rip open that deception and dissolve its social relations, penetrating by symbol and fantasy to the estranged, self-divided psyches which 'normality' conceals. The transforming of a stage convention, then, signifies a deeper transformation in bourgeois ideology, as confident mid-Victorian notions of selfhood and relationship began to splinter and crumble in the face of growing world capitalist crises.

There is, needless to say, no simple, symmetrical relationship between changes in literary form and changes in ideology. Literary form, as Trotsky reminds us, has a high degree of autonomy; it evolves partly in accordance with its own internal pressures, and does not merely bend to every ideological wind that blows. Just as for Marxist economic theory each economic formation tends to contain traces of older, superseded modes of production, so traces of older literary forms survive within new ones. Form, I would suggest, is always a complex unity of at least three elements: it is partly shaped by a 'relatively autonomous' literary history of forms; it crystallizes out of certain dominant ideological structures, as we have seen in the case of the novel; and as we shall see later, it embodies a specific set of relations between author and audience. It is the dialectical unity between these elements that Marxist criticism is concerned to analyse. In selecting a form, then, the writer finds his choice already ideologically circumscribed. He may combine and transmute forms available to him from a literary tradition, but these forms themselves, as well as his permutation of them, are ideologically significant. The languages and devices a writer finds to hand are already saturated with certain ideological modes of perception, certain codified ways of interpreting reality; and the extent to which he can modify or remake those languages depends on more than his personal genius. It depends on whether at that point in history, 'ideology' is such that they must and can be changed.

Lukács and Literary Form

It is in the work of Georg Lukács that the problem of literary form has been most thoroughly explored. In his early, pre-Marxist work, *The Theory of the Novel* (1920), Lukács follows Hegel in seeing the novel as the 'bourgeois epic', but an epic which unlike its classical counterpart reveals the homelessness and alienation of man in modern society. In Greek classical society man is at home in the universe, moving within a rounded, complete world of immanent meaning which is adequate to his soul's demands. The novel arises when that harmonious integration of man and his world is shattered; the hero of fiction is now in search of a totality, estranged from a world either too large or too narrow to give shape to his desires. Haunted by the disparity between empirical reality and a vanished absolute, the novel's form is typically *ironic*; it is 'the epic of a world abandoned by God'.

Lukács rejected this cosmic pessimism when he became a Marxist; but much of his later work on the novel retains the Hegelian emphases of *The Theory of the Novel*. For the Marxist Lukács of *Studies in European Realism* and *The Historical Novel*, the greatest artists are those who can recapture and recreate a harmonious totality of human life. In a society where the general and the particular, the conceptual and the sensuous, the social and the individual are increasingly torn apart by the 'alienations' of capitalism, the great writer draws these dialectically together into a complex totality. His fiction thus mirrors, in microcosmic form, the complex totality of society itself. In doing this, great art combats the alienation and fragmentation of capitalist society, projecting a rich, many-sided image of human wholeness. Lukács names such art 'realism', and takes it to include the Greeks and Shakespeare as much as Balzac and Tolstoy; the three great periods of historical 'realism' are ancient Greece, the Renaissance, and France in the early nineteenth century. A 'realist' work is rich in a complex, comprehensive set of relations between man, nature and history; and these relations embody and unfold what for Marxism is most 'typical' about a particular phase of history. By the 'typical' Lukács denotes those latent forces in any society which are from a Marxist viewpoint most historically significant and progressive, which lay bare the society's inner structure and dynamic. The task of the realist writer is to flesh out these 'typical' trends and forces in sensuously realized individuals and actions; in doing so he links the individual to the social whole, and informs each concrete particular of social life with the power of the 'world-historical'—the significant movements of history itself.

Lukács's major critical concepts—'totality', 'typically', 'world-historical'—are essentially Hegelian rather than directly Marxist, although Marx and Engels certainly use the notion of 'typicality' in their own literary criticism. Engels remarked in a letter to Lassalle that true character must combine typicality with individuality; and both he and Marx thought this a major achievement of Shakespeare and Balzac. A 'typical' or 'representative' character incarnates historical forces without thereby ceasing to be richly individualized; and for a writer to dramatize those historical forces he must, for Lukács, be 'progressive' in his art. All great art is socially progressive in the sense that, whatever the author's conscious political allegiance (and in the case of Scott and Balzac it is overtly reactionary), it realizes the vital 'world-historical' forces of an epoch which make for change and growth, revealing their unfolding potential in its fullest complexity. The realist writer, then, penetrates through the accidental phenomena of social life to disclose the essences or essentials of a condition, selecting and combining them into a total form and fleshing them out in concrete experience.

Whether or not a writer can do this depends for Lukács not just on his personal skill but on his position within history. The great realist writers arise from a history which is visibly in the making; the historical novel, for example, appears as a *genre* at a point of revolutionary turbulence in the early nineteenth century, where it was possible for writers to grasp their own present as *history*—or, to put it in Lukács's phrase, to see past history as 'the pre-history of the present'. Shakespeare, Scott, Balzac and Tolstoy can produce major realist art because they are present at the tumultuous birth of an historical epoch, and so are dramatically engaged with the vividly exposed 'typical' conflicts and dynamics of their societies. It is this historical 'content' which lays the basis for their formal achievement; 'richness and profundity of created characters', Lukács claims, 'relies upon the richness and profundity of the total social process'. For the successors of the realists—for, say, Flaubert who follows Balzac—history is already an inert object, an externally given fact no longer imaginable as men's dynamic product. Realism, deprived of the historical conditions which gave it birth, splinters and declines into 'naturalism' on the one hand and 'formalism' on the other.

The crucial transition here for Lukács is the failure of the European revolutions of 1848—a failure which signals the defeat of the proletariat, seals the demise of the progressive, heroic period of bourgeois power, freezes the class-struggle and cues the bourgeoisie for its proper, sordidly unheroic task of consolidating capitalism. Bourgeois ideology forgets its previous revolutionary ideals, dehistoricizes reality and accepts society as a natural fact. Balzac depicts the last great struggles against the capitalist degradation of man, while his successors passively register an already degraded capitalist world.

This draining of direction and meaning from history results in the art we know as naturalism. By naturalism Lukács means that distortion of realism epitomized by Zola, which merely photographically reproduces the surface phenomena of society without penetrating to their significant essences. Meticulously observed detail replaces the portrayal of 'typical' features; the dialectical relations between men and their world give way to an environment of dead, contingent objects disconnected from characters; the truly 'representative' character yields to a 'cult of the average'; psychology or physiology oust history as the true determinant of individual action. It is an alienated vision of reality, transforming the writer from an active participant in history to a clinical observer. Lacking an understanding of the typical, naturalism can create no significant totality from its materials; the unified epic or dramatic actions launched by realism collapse into a set of purely private interests.

'Formalism' reacts in an opposite direction, but betrays the same loss of historical meaning. In the alienated worlds of Kafka, Musil, Joyce, Beckett, Camus, man is stripped of his history and has no reality beyond the self; character is dissolved to mental states, objective reality reduced to unintelligible chaos. As with naturalism, the dialectical unity between inner and outer worlds is destroyed, and both individual and society consequently emptied of meaning. Individuals are gripped by despair and *angst*, robbed of social relations and so of authentic selfhood; history becomes pointless or cyclical, dwindled to mere duration. Objects lack significance and become merely contingent; and so symbolism gives way to allegory, which rejects the idea of immanent meaning. If naturalism is a kind of abstract objectivity, formalism is an abstract subjectivity; both diverge from that genuinely dialectical art-form (realism) whose form mediates between concrete and general, essence and existence, type and individual.

Goldmann and Genetic Structuralism

George Lukács's chief disciple, in what has been termed the 'neo-Hegelian' school of Marxist criticism, is the Rumanian critic Lucien Goldmann. Goldmann is concerned to examine the structure of a literary text for the degree to which it embodies the structure of thought (or 'world vision') of the social class or group to which the writer belongs. The more closely the text approximates to a complete, coherent articulation of the social class's 'world vision', the greater is its validity as a work of art. For Goldmann, literary works are not in the first place to be seen as the creation of individuals, but of what he calls the 'trans-individual mental structures' of a social group — by which he means the structure of ideas, values and aspirations that group shares. Great writers are those exceptional individuals who manage to transpose into art the world vision of the class or group to which they belong, and to do this in a peculiarly unified and translucent (although not necessarily conscious) way.

Goldmann terms his critical method 'genetic structuralism', and it is important to understand both terms of that phrase. *Structuralism*, because he is less interested in the contents of a particular world vision than in the structure of categories it displays. Two apparently quite different writers may thus be shown to belong to the same collective mental structure. *Genetic,* because Goldmann is concerned with how such mental structures are historically produced—concerned, that is to say, with the relations between a world vision and the historical conditions which give rise to it.

Goldmann's work on Racine in *The Hidden God* is perhaps the most exemplary model of his critical method. He discerns in Racine's drama a certain recurrent structure of categories—God, World, Man—which alter in their 'content' and interrelations from play to play, but which disclose a particular world vision. It is the world vision of men who are lost in a valueless world, accept this world as the only one there is (since God is absent), and yet continue to protest against it—to justify themselves in the name of some absolute value which is always hidden from view. The basis of this world vision Goldmann finds in the French religious movement known as Jansenism; and he explains Jansenism, in turn, as the product of a certain displaced social group in seventeenth-century France—the so-called *noblesse de robe,* the court officials who were economically dependent on the monarchy and yet becoming increasingly powerless in the face of that monarchy's growing absolutism. The contradictory situation of this group, needing the Crown but politically opposed to it, is expressed in Jansenism's refusal both of the world and of any desire to change it historically. All of this has a 'world-historical' significance: the *noblesse de robe,* themselves recruited from the bourgeois class, represent the failure of the bourgeoisie to break royal absolutism and establish the conditions for capitalist development.

What Goldmann is seeking, then, is a set of structural relations between literary text, world vision and history itself. He wants to show how the historical situation of a social group or class is transposed, by the mediation of its world vision, into the structure of a literary work. To do this it is not enough to begin with the text and work outwards to history, or vice versa; what is required is a dialectical method of criticism which moves constantly between text, world vision and history, adjusting each to the others.

Interesting as it is, Goldmann's critical enterprise seems to me marred by certain major flaws. His concept of social consciousness, for example, is Hegelian rather than Marxist: he sees it as the direct expression of a social class, just as the literary work then becomes the direct expression of this consciousness. His whole model, in other words, is too trimly symmetrical, unable to accommodate the dialectical conflicts and complexities, the unevenness and discontinuity, which characterize literature's relation to society. It declines, in his later work *Pour une Sociologie du Roman* (1964), into an essentially mechanistic version of the base-superstructure relationship.

Pierre Macherey and 'Decentred' Form

Both Lukács and Goldmann inherit from Hegel a belief that the literary work should form a unified totality; and in this they are close to a conventional position in non-Marxist criticism. Lukács sees the work as a *constructed* totality rather than a natural organism; yet a vein of 'organistic' thinking about the art object runs through much of his criticism. It is one of the several scandalous propositions which Pierre Macherey throws out to bourgeois and neo-Hegelian criticism alike that he rejects this belief. For Macherey, a work is tied to ideology not so much by what it says as by what it does not say. It is in the significant *silences* of a text, in its gaps and absences, that the presence of ideology can be most positively felt. It is these silences which the critic must make 'speak'. The text is, as it were, ideologically forbidden to say certain things; in trying to tell the truth in his own way, for example, the author finds himself forced to reveal the limits of the ideology within which he writes. He is forced to reveal its gaps and silences, what it is unable to articulate. Because a text contains these gaps and silences, it is always *incomplete.* Far from constituting a rounded, coherent whole, it displays a conflict and contradiction of meanings; and the significance of the work lies in the difference rather than unity between these meanings. Whereas a critic like Goldmann finds in the work a central structure, the work for Macherey is always *'de-centred';* there is no central essence to it, just a continuous conflict and disparity of meanings. 'Scattered', 'dispersed', 'diverse', 'irregular': these are the epithets which Macherey uses to express his sense of the literary work.

When Macherey argues that the work is 'incomplete', however, he does not mean that there is a piece missing which the critic could fill in. On the contrary, it is in the nature of the work to be incomplete, tied as it is to an ideology which silences it at certain points. (It is, if you like, complete in its incompleteness.) The critic's task is not to fill the work in; it is to seek out the principle of its conflict of meanings, and to show how this conflict is produced by the work's relation to ideology.

To take a fairly obvious example: in *Dombey and Son* Dickens uses a number of mutually conflicting languages—realist, melodramatic, pastoral, allegorical—in his portrayal of events; and this conflict comes to a head in the famous railway chapter, where the novel is ambiguously torn between contradictory responses to the railway (fear, protest, approval, exhilaration etc.), reflecting this in a clash of styles and symbols. The ideological basis of this ambiguity is that the novel is divided between a conventional bourgeois admiration of industrial progress and a petty-bourgeois anxiety about its inevitably disruptive effects. It sympathizes with those washed-up minor characters whom the new world has superannuated at the same time as it celebrates the progressive thrust of industrial capitalism which has made them obsolete. In discovering the principle of the work's conflict of meanings, then, we are simultaneously analysing its complex relationship to Victorian ideology. . . .

MICHEL FOUCAULT

What Is an Author?

1979

Michel Foucault (1926–1984) was one of the brightest stars in the turbulent French academic and intellectual cosmos of the 1960s and 1970s. The enormous range of his theoretical interests can be surmised by browsing the titles of some of his best-known works: Madness and Civilization (1961), The Archeology of Knowledge (1972), Discipline and Punish: The Birth of the Prison (1975), The History of Sexuality (1986, published posthumously). Though his work ranged freely across the disciplinary boundaries of history, philosophy, and various social sciences, one of the principal threads that stitched together his various efforts was an abiding interest in the uses and abuses of power.

Foucault begins his essay "What Is an Author?" with the assumption that most critics already accept the much-touted "death of the author" and the idea that we should focus on the work rather than the individual who produced that work. He notes, however, that in practice the idea of the author holds considerable power and helps to regulate our perception of a particular piece of art by allowing us to classify and unify texts under the rubric of authorship. In other words, though we may claim not to base our literary judgments on authors, we still rely heavily on what Foucault calls an "author function." To explain the difference between these two concepts, he points out the distinction between William Shakespeare, the individual man who was born in Stratford and about whose biography we know relatively little, and Shakespeare the author (or rather, the "author function") whose name and image carry considerable cultural power, a power that attaches to the works attributed to him.

Furthermore, some especially influential writers and thinkers—Foucault gives among his examples Freud and Marx—become "transdiscursive," moving beyond authoring specific works to establish disciplines and perform an author function for entire fields of discourse. The essay ends with a fantasy of an intellectual world in which the author function loses its authority (note the etymological link between the words author and authority) and subjects (those who use the texts) may appropriate textual power for their own uses.

Foucault's ideas of cultural history have profoundly influenced many schools of literary criticism—among them feminist, Marxist, minority, and gay criticism—

that all seek to overcome previous exclusion from power, both political and literary. Although he was not a literary critic, Foucault's picture of cultural relativity is now ingrained in modern literary theory: many contemporary critics see a literary work not as an autonomous icon but as a reflection of a particular cultural moment.

THE COMING INTO BEING of the notion of "author" constitutes the privileged moment of *individualization* in the history of ideas, knowledge, literature, philosophy, and the sciences. Even today, when we reconstruct the history of a concept, literary genre, or school of philosophy, such categories seem relatively weak, secondary, and superimposed scansions in comparison with the solid and fundamental unit of the author and the work.

I shall not offer here a sociohistorical analysis of the author's persona. Certainly it would be worth examining how the author became individualized in a culture like ours, what status he has been given, at what moment studies of authenticity and attribution began, in what kind of system of valorization the author was involved, at what point we began to recount the lives of authors rather than of heroes, and how this fundamental category of "the-man-and-his-work criticism" began. For the moment, however, I want to deal solely with the relationship between text and author and with the manner in which the text points to this "figure" that, at least in appearance, is outside it and antecedes it.

Beckett nicely formulates the theme with which I would like to begin: "'What does it matter who is speaking,' someone said, 'what does it matter who is speaking.'" In this indifference appears one of the fundamental ethical principles of contemporary writing (*écriture*). I say "ethical" because this indifference is not really a trait characterizing the manner in which one speaks and writes, but rather a kind of immanent rule, taken up over and over again, never fully applied, not designating writing as something completed, but dominating it as a practice. Since it is too familiar to require a lengthy analysis, this immanent rule can be adequately illustrated here by tracing two of its major themes.

First of all, we can say that today's writing has freed itself from the dimension of expression. Referring only to itself, but without being restricted to the confines of its interiority, writing is identified with its own unfolded exteriority. This means that it is an interplay of signs arranged less according to its signified content than according to the very nature of the signifier. Writing unfolds like a game (*jeu*) that invariably goes beyond its own rules and transgresses its limits. In writing, the point is not to manifest or exalt the act of writing, nor is it to pin a subject within language; it is, rather, a question of creating a space into which the writing subject constantly disappears.

The second theme, writing's relationship with death, is even more familiar. This link subverts an old tradition exemplified by the Greek epic, which was intended to perpetuate the immortality of the hero: if he was willing to die young, it was so that his life, consecrated and magnified by death, might pass into immortality; the narrative then redeemed this accepted death. In another way, the motivation, as well as the theme and the pretext of Arabian narratives—such as *The Thousand and One Nights*—was also the eluding of death: one spoke, telling stories into the early morning, in order to forestall death, to postpone the day of reckoning that would silence the narrator. Scheherazade's narrative is an effort, renewed each night, to keep death outside the circle of life.

Our culture has metamorphosed this idea of narrative, or writing, as something designed to ward off death. Writing has become linked to sacrifice, even to the sacrifice of life: it is now a voluntary effacement which does not need to be represented in books, since it is brought about in the writer's very existence. The work, which once had the duty of providing immortality, now possesses the right to kill, to be its author's murderer, as in the cases of Flaubert, Proust, and Kafka. That is not all, however: this relationship between writing and death is also manifested in the effacement of the writing subject's individual characteristics. Using all the contrivances that he sets up between himself and what he writes, the writing subject cancels out the signs of his particular individuality. As a result, the mark of the writer is reduced to nothing more than the singularity of his absence; he must assume the role of the dead man in the game of writing.

None of this is recent; criticism and philosophy took note of the disappearance—or death—of the author some time ago. But the consequences of their discovery of it have not been sufficiently examined, nor has its import been accurately measured. A certain number of notions that are intended to replace the privileged position of the author actually seem to preserve that privilege and suppress the real meaning of his disappearance. I shall examine two of these notions, both of great importance today.

The first is the idea of the work. It is a very familiar thesis that the task of criticism is not to bring out the work's relationships with the author, nor to reconstruct through the text a thought or experience, but rather to analyze the work through its structure, its architecture, its intrinsic form, and the play of its internal relationships. At this point, however, a problem arises: What is a work? What is this curious unity which we designate as a work? Of what elements is it composed? Is it not what an author has written? Difficulties appear immediately. If an individual were not an author, could we say that what he wrote, said, left behind in his papers, or what has been collected of his remarks, could be called a "work"? When Sade was not considered an author, what was the status of his papers? Were they simply rolls of paper onto which he ceaselessly uncoiled his fantasies during his imprisonment?

Even when an individual has been accepted as an author, we must still ask whether everything that he wrote, said, or left behind is part of his work. The problem is both theoretical and technical. When undertaking the publication of Nietzsche's works, for example, where should one stop? Surely everything must be published, but what is "everything"? Everything that Nietzsche himself published, certainly. And what about the rough drafts for his works? Obviously. The plans for his aphorisms? Yes. The deleted passages and the notes at the bottom of the page? Yes. What if, within a work-book filled with aphorisms, one finds a reference, the notation of a meeting or of an address, or a laundry list: Is it a work, or not? Why not? And so on, ad infinitum. How can one define a work amid the millions of traces left by someone after his death? A theory of the work does not exist, and the empirical task of those who naively undertake the editing of works often suffers in the absence of such a theory.

We could go even further: Does *The Thousand and One Nights* constitute a work? What about Clement of Alexandria's *Miscellanies* or Diogenes Laertius's *Lives*? A multitude of questions arises with regard to this notion of the work. Consequently, it is not enough to declare that we should do without the writer (the author) and study the work itself. The word *work* and the unity that it designates are probably as problematic as the status of the author's individuality.

Another notion which has hindered us from taking full measure of the author's disappearance, blurring and concealing the moment of this effacement and subtly preserving the author's existence, is the notion of writing (*écriture*). When rigorously applied, this notion should allow us not only to circumvent references to the author, but also to situate his recent absence. The notion of writing, as currently employed, is concerned with neither the act of writing nor the indication—be it symptom or sign—of a meaning which someone might have wanted to express. We try, with great effort, to imagine the general condition of each text, the condition of both the space in which it is dispersed and the time in which it unfolds.

In current usage, however, the notion of writing seems to transpose the empirical characteristics of the author into a transcendental anonymity. We are content to efface the more visible marks of the author's empiricity by playing off, one against the other, two ways of characterizing writing, namely, the critical and the religious approaches. Giving writing a primal status seems to be a way of retranslating, in transcendental terms, both the theological affirmation of its sacred character and the critical affirmation of its creative character. To admit that writing is, because of the very history that it made possible, subject to the test of oblivion and repression, seems to represent, in transcendental terms, the religious principle of the hidden meaning (which requires interpretation) and the critical principle of implicit significations, silent determinations, and obscured contents (which gives rise to commentary). To imagine writing as absence seems to be a simple repetition, in transcendental terms, of both the religious principle of inalterable and yet never fulfilled tradition, and the aesthetic principle of the work's survival, its perpetuation beyond the author's death, and its enigmatic *excess* in relation to him.

This usage of the notion of writing runs the risk of maintaining the author's privileges under the protection of writing's *a priori* status: it keeps alive, in the gray light of neutralization, the interplay of those representations that formed a particular image of the author. The author's disappearance, which, since Mallarmé, has been a constantly recurring event, is subject to a series of transcendental barriers. There seems to be an important dividing line between those who believe that they can still locate today's discontinuities (*ruptures*) in the historico-transcendental tradition of the nineteenth century, and those who try to free themselves once and for all from that tradition.

It is not enough, however, to repeat the empty affirmation that the author has disappeared. For the same reason, it is not enough to keep repeating (after Nietzsche) that God and man have died a common death. Instead, we must locate the space left empty by the author's disappearance, follow the distribution of gaps and breaches, and watch for the openings that this disappearance uncovers.

First, we need to clarify briefly the problems arising from the use of the author's name. What is an author's name? How does it function? Far from offering a solution, I shall only indicate some of the difficulties that it presents.

The author's name is a proper name, and therefore it raises the problems common to all proper names. (Here I refer to Searle's analyses, among others.[1]) Obviously, one cannot turn a proper name into a pure and simple reference. It has other than indicative functions: more than an indication, a gesture, a finger pointed at someone, it is the equivalent of a description. When one says "Aristotle," one employs a word that is the equivalent of one, or a series, of definite descriptions, such as "the author of the *Analytics*," "the founder of ontology," and so forth. One cannot stop there, however, because a proper name does not have just one signification. When we discover that Rimbaud did not write *La Chasse spirituelle*, we cannot pretend that the meaning of this proper name, or that of the author, has been altered. The proper name and the author's name are situated between the two poles of description and designation: they must have a certain link with what they name, but one that is neither entirely in the mode of designation nor in that of description; it must be a *specific* link. However—and it is here that the particular difficulties of the author's name arise—the links between the proper name and the individual named and between the author's name and what it names are not isomorphic and do not function in the same way. There are several differences.

If, for example, Pierre Dupont does not have blue eyes, or was not born in Paris, or is not a doctor, the name Pierre Dupont will still always refer to the same person; such things do not modify the link of designation. The problems raised by the author's name are much more complex, however. If I discover that Shakespeare was not born in the house that we visit today, this is a modification which, obviously, will not alter the functioning of the author's name. But if we proved that Shakespeare did not write those sonnets which pass for his, that would constitute a significant change and affect the manner in which the author's name functions. If we proved that Shakespeare wrote Bacon's *Organon* by showing that the same author wrote both the

---

[1] John Searle, *Speech Acts: An Essay in the Philosophy of Language* (Cambridge, Eng.: Cambridge University Press, 1969), pp. 162–74. [Tr.]

works of Bacon and those of Shakespeare, that would be a third type of change which would entirely modify the functioning of the author's name. The author's name is not, therefore, just a proper name like the rest.

Many other facts point out the paradoxical singularity of the author's name. To say that Pierre Dupont does not exist is not at all the same as saying that Homer or Hermes Trismegistus did not exist. In the first case, it means that no one has the name Pierre Dupont; in the second, it means that several people were mixed together under one name, or that the true author had none of the traits traditionally ascribed to the personae of Homer or Hermes. To say that X's real name is actually Jacques Durand instead of Pierre Dupont is not the same as saying that Stendhal's name was Henri Beyle. One could also question the meaning and functioning of propositions like "Bourbaki is so-and-so, so-and-so, etc." and "Victor Eremita, Climacus, Anticlimacus, Frater Taciturnus, Constantine Constantius, all of these are Kierkegaard."

These differences may result from the fact than an author's name is not simply an element in a discourse (capable of being either subject or object, of being replaced by a pronoun, and the like); it performs a certain role with regard to narrative discourse, assuring a classificatory function. Such a name permits one to group together a certain number of texts, define them, differentiate them from and contrast them to others. In addition, it establishes a relationship among the texts. Hermes Trismegistus did not exist, nor did Hippocrates—in the sense that Balzac existed—but the fact that several texts have been placed under the same name indicates that there has been established among them a relationship of homogeneity, filiation, authentication of some texts by the use of others, reciprocal explication, or concomitant utilization. The author's name serves to characterize a certain mode of being of discourse: the fact that the discourse has an author's name, that one can say "this was written by so-and-so" or "so-and-so is its author," shows that this discourse is not ordinary everyday speech that merely comes and goes, not something that is immediately consumable. On the contrary, it is a speech that must be received in a certain mode and that, in a given culture, must receive a certain status.

It would seem that the author's name, unlike other proper names, does not pass from the interior of a discourse to the real and exterior individual who produced it; instead, the name seems always to be present, marking off the edges of the text, revealing, or at least characterizing, its mode of being. The author's name manifests the appearance of a certain discursive set and indicates the status of this discourse within a society and a culture. It has no legal status, nor is it located in the fiction of the work; rather, it is located in the break that founds a certain discursive construct and its very particular mode of being. As a result, we could say that in a civilization like our own there are a certain number of discourses that are endowed with the "author function," while others are deprived of it. A private letter may well have a signer—it does not have an author; a contract may well have a guarantor—it does not have an author. An anonymous text posted on a wall probably has a writer—but not an author. The author function is therefore characteristic of the mode of existence, circulation, and functioning of certain discourses within a society.

Let us analyze this "author function" as we have just described it. In our culture, how does one characterize a discourse containing the author function? In what way is this discourse different from other discourses? If we limit our remarks to the author of a book or a text, we can isolate four different characteristics.

First of all, discourses are objects of appropriation. The form of ownership from which they spring is of a rather particular type, one that has been codified for many years. We should note that, historically, this type of ownership has always been subsequent to what one might call penal appropriation. Texts, books, and discourses really began to have authors (other than mythical, "sacralized" and "sacralizing" figures) to the extent that authors became subject to punishment, that is, to the extent that discourses could be transgressive. In our culture (and doubtless in many others), discourse was not originally a product, a thing, a kind of goods; it was essentially an act—an act placed in the bipolar field of the sacred and the profane, the licit and the illicit, the religious and the blasphemous. Historically, it was a gesture fraught with risks before becoming goods caught up in a circuit of ownership.

Once a system of ownership for texts came into being, once strict rules concerning author's rights, author-publisher relations, rights of reproduction, and related matters were enacted—at the end of the eighteenth and the beginning of the nineteenth century—the possibility of transgression attached to the act of writing took on, more and more, the form of an imperative peculiar to literature. It is as if the author, beginning with the moment at which he was placed in the system of property that characterizes our society, compensated for the status that he thus acquired by rediscovering the old bipolar field of discourse, systematically practicing transgression and thereby restoring danger to a writing which was now guaranteed the benefits of ownership.

The author function does not affect all discourses in a universal and constant way, however. This is its second characteristic. In our civilization, it has not always been the same types of texts which have required attribution to an author. There was a time when the texts that we today call "literary" (narratives, stories, epics, tragedies, comedies) were accepted, put into circulation, and valorized without any question about the identity of their author; their anonymity caused no difficulties since their ancientness, whether real or imagined, as regarded as a sufficient guarantee of their status. On the other hand, those texts that we now would call scientific—those dealing with cosmology and the heavens, medicine and illnesses, natural sciences and geography—were accepted in the Middle Ages, and accepted as "true," only when marked with the name of their author. "Hippocrates said," "Pliny recounts," were not really formulas of an argument based on authority; they were the markers inserted in discourses that were supported to be received as statements of demonstrated truth.

A reversal occurred in the seventeenth or eighteenth century. Scientific discourses began to be received for themselves, in the anonymity of an established or always redemonstrable truth; their membership in a systematic ensemble, and not the reference to the individual who produced them, stood as their guarantee. The author function faded away, and the inventor's name served only to christen a theorem, proposition, particular effect, property, body, group of elements, or pathological syndrome. By the same token, literary discourses came to be accepted only when endowed with the author function. We now ask of each poetic or fictional text: From where does it come, who wrote it, when, under what circumstances, or beginning with what design? The meaning ascribed to it and the status or value accorded it depend on the manner in which we answer these questions. And if a text should be discovered in a state of anonymity—whether as a consequence of an accident or the author's explicit wish—the game becomes one of rediscovering the author. Since literary anonymity is not tolerable, we can accept it only in the guise of an enigma. As a result, the author function today plays an important role in our view of literary works. (These are obviously generalizations that would have to be refined insofar as recent critical practice is concerned.)

The third characteristic of this author function is that it does not develop spontaneously as the attribution of a discourse to an individual. It is, rather, the result of a complex operation which constructs a certain rational being that we call "author." Critics doubtless try to give this intelligible being a realistic status, by discerning, in the individual, a "deep" motive, a "creative" power, or a "design," the milieu in which writing originates. Nevertheless, these aspects of an individual which we designate as making him an author are only a projection, in more or less psychologizing terms, of the operations that we force texts to undergo, the connections that we make, the traits that we establish as pertinent, the continuities that we recognize, or the exclusions that we practice. All these operations vary according to periods and types of discourse. We do not construct a "philosophical author" as we do a "poet," just as, in the eighteenth century, one did not construct a novelist as we do today. Still, we can find through the ages certain constants in the rules of author construction.

It seems, for example, that the manner in which literary criticism once defined the author—or, rather, constructed the figure of the author beginning with existing texts and discourses—is directly derived from the manner in which Christian tradition authenticated (or rejected) the texts at its disposal. In order to "rediscover" an author in a work, modern criticism uses methods similar to those that Christian exegesis employed when trying to prove the value of a text by its author's saintliness. In *De viris illustribus*, Saint Jerome explains that homonymy is not sufficient to identify legitimately authors of more than one work: different individuals could have had the same name, or one man could have, illegitimately, borrowed another's patronymic. The name as an individual trademark is not enough when one works within a textual tradition.

How, then, can one attribute several discourses to one and the same author? How can one use the author function to determine if one is dealing with one or several individuals? Saint Jerome proposes four criteria: (1) if among several books attributed to an author one is inferior to the others, it must be withdrawn from the list of the author's works (the author is therefore defined as a constant level of value); (2) the same should be done if certain texts contradict the doctrine expounded in the author's other works (the author is thus defined as a field of conceptual or theoretical coherence); (3) one must also exclude works that are written in a difference style, containing words and expressions not ordinarily found in the writer's production (the author is here conceived as a stylistic unity); (4) finally, passages quoting statements that were made or mentioning events that occurred after the author's death must be regarded as interpolated texts (the author is here seen as a historical figure at the crossroads of a certain number of events).

Modern literary criticism, even when—as is now customary—it is not concerned with questions of authentication, still defines the author the same way: the author provides the basis for explaining not only the presence of certain events in a work, but also their transformations, distortions, and diverse modifications (through his biography, the determination of his individual perspective, the analysis of his social position, and the revelation of basic design). The author is also the principle of a certain unity of writing—all differences having to be resolved, at least in part, by the principles of evolution, maturation, or influence. The author also serves to neutralize the contradictions that may emerge in a series of texts: there must be—at a certain level of his thought or desire, of his consciousness or unconscious—a point where contradictions are resolved, where incompatible elements are at last tied together or organized around a fundamental or originating contradiction. Finally, the author is a particular source of expression that, in more or less completed forms, is manifested equally well, and with similar validity, in works, sketches, letters, fragments, and so on. Clearly, Saint Jerome's four criteria of authenticity (criteria which seem totally insufficient for today's exegetes) do define the four modalities according to which modern criticism brings the author function into play.

But the author function is not a pure and simple reconstruction made secondhand from a text given as passive material. The text always contains a certain number of signs referring to the author. These signs, well known to grammarians, are personal pronouns, adverbs of time and place, and verb conjugation. Such elements do not play the same role in discourses provided with the author function as in those lacking it. In the latter, such "shifters" refer to the real speaker and to the spatiotemporal coordinates of his discourse (although certain modifications can occur, as in the operation of relating discourses in the first person). In the former, however, their role is more complex and variable. Everyone knows that, in a novel narrated in the first person, neither the first-person pronoun nor the present indicative refers exactly either to the writer or to the moment in which he writes, but rather to an alter ego whose distance from the author varies, often changing in the course of the work. It would be just as wrong to equate the author with the real writer as to equate him with the fictitious speaker; the author function is carried out and operates in the scission itself, in this division and this distance.

One might object that this is a characteristic peculiar to novelistic or poetic discourse, a "game" in which only "quasi-discourses" participate. In fact, however, all discourses endowed with the author function do possess this plurality of self. The self that speaks in the preface to a treatise on mathematics—and that indicates the circumstances of the treatise's composition—is identical neither in its position nor in its functioning to the self that speaks in the course of a demonstration, and that appears in the form of "I conclude" or "I suppose." In the first case, the "I" refers to an individual without an equivalent who, in a determined place and time, completed a certain task; in the second, the "I" indicates an instance and a level of demonstration which any individual could perform provided that he accepted the same system of symbols, play of axioms, and set of previous demonstrations. We could also, in the same treatise, locate a third self, one that speaks to tell the work's meaning, the obstacles encountered, the results obtained, and the remaining problems; this self is situated in the field of already existing or yet-to-appear mathematical discourses. The author function is not assumed by the first of these selves at the expense of the other two, which would then be nothing more than a fictitious splitting in two of the first one. On the contrary, in these discourses the author function operates so as to effect the dispersion of these three simultaneous selves.

No doubt analysis could discover still more characteristic traits of the author function. I will limit myself to these four, however, because they seem both the most visible and the most important. They can be summarized as follows: (1) the author function is linked to the juridical and institutional system that encompasses, determines, and articulates the universe of discourses; (2) it does not affect all discourses in the same way at all times and in all types of civilization; (3) it is not defined by the spontaneous attribution of a discourse to its producer, but rather by a series of specific and complex operations; (4) it does not refer purely and simply to a real individual, since it can give rise simultaneously to several selves, to several subjects—positions that can be occupied by different classes of individuals.

Up to this point I have unjustifiably limited my subject. Certainly the author function in painting, music, and other arts should have been discussed, but even supposing that we remain within the world of discourse, as I want to do, I seem to have given the term "author" much too narrow a meaning. I have discussed the author only in the limited sense of a person to whom the production of a text, a book, or a work can be legitimately attributed. It is easy to see that in the sphere of discourse one can be the author of much more than a book—one can be the author of a theory, tradition, or discipline in which other books and authors will in their turn find a place. These authors are in a position which we shall call "transdiscursive." This is a recurring phenomenon—certainly as old as our civilization. Homer, Aristotle, and the Church Fathers, as well as the first mathematicians and the originators of the Hippocratic tradition, all played this role.

Furthermore, in the course of the nineteenth century, there appeared in Europe another, more uncommon, kind of author, whom one should confuse with neither the "great" literary authors, nor the authors of religious texts, nor the founders of science. In a somewhat arbitrary way we shall call those who belong in this last group "founders of discursivity." They are unique in that they are not just the authors of their own works. They have produced something else: the possibilities and the rules for the formation of other texts. In this sense, they are very different, for example, from a novelist, who is, in fact, nothing more than the author of his own text. Freud is not just the author of *The Interpretation of Dreams* or *Jokes and Their Relation to the Unconscious;* Marx is not just the author of the *Communist Manifesto* or *Das Kapital:* they both have established an endless possibility of discourse.

Obviously, it is easy to object. One might say that it is not true that the author of a novel is only the author of his own text; in a sense, he also, provided that he acquires some "importance," governs and commands more than that. To take a very simple example, one could say that Ann Radcliffe not only wrote *The Castles of Athlin and Dunbayne* and several other novels, but also made possible the appearance of the Gothic horror novel at the beginning of the nineteenth century; in that respect, her author function exceeds her own work. But I think there is an answer to this objection. These founders of discursivity (I use Marx and Freud as examples, because I believe them to be both the first and the most important cases) make possible something altogether different from what a novelist makes possible. Ann Radcliffe's texts opened the way for a certain number of resemblances and analogies which have their model or principle in her work. The latter contains characteristic signs, figures, relationships, and structures which could be reused by others. In other words, to say that Ann Radcliffe founded the Gothic horror novel means that in the nineteenth-century Gothic novel one will find, as in Ann Radcliffe's works, the theme of the heroine caught in the trap of her own innocence, the hidden castle, the character of the black, cursed hero devoted to making the world expiate the evil done to him, and all the rest of it.

On the other hand, when I speak of Marx or Freud as founders of discursivity, I mean that they made possible not only a certain number of analogies, but also (and equally important) a certain number of differences. They have created a possibility for something other than their discourse, yet something belonging to what they founded. To say that Freud founded psychoanalysis does not (simply) mean that we find the concept of the libido or the technique of dream analysis in the works of Karl Abraham or Melanie Klein; it means that Freud made possible a certain number of divergences—with respect to his own texts, concepts, and hypotheses—that all arise from the psychoanalytic discourse itself.

This would seem to present a new difficulty, however: is the above not true, after all, of any founder of a science, or of any author who has introduced some important transformation into a science? After all, Galileo made possible not only those discourses that repeated the laws that he had formulated, but also statements very different from what he himself had said. If Cuvier is the founder of biology or Saussure the founder of linguistics, it is not because they were imitated, nor because people have since taken up again the concept of organism or sign; it is because Cuvier made possible, to a certain extent, a theory of evolution diametrically opposed to his own fixism; it is because Saussure made possible a generative grammar radically different from his structural analyses. Superficially, then, the initiation of discursive practices appears similar to the founding of any scientific endeavor.

Still, there is a difference, and a notable one. In the case of a science, the act that founds it is on an equal footing with its future transformations; this act becomes in some respects part of the set of modifications that it makes possible. Of course, this belonging can take several forms. In the future development of a science, the founding act may appear as little more than a particular instance of a more general phenomenon which unveils itself in the process. It can also turn out to be marred by intuition and empirical bias; one must then reformulate it, making it the object of a certain number of supplementary theoretical operations which establish it more rigorously, etc. Finally, it can seem to be a hasty generalization which must be limited, and whose restricted domain of validity must be retraced. In other words, the founding act of a science can always be reintroduced within the machinery of those transformations that derive from it.

In contrast, the initiation of a discursive practice is heterogeneous to its subsequent transformations. To expand a type of discursivity, such as psychoanalysis as founded by Freud, is not to give it a formal generality that it would not have permitted at the outset, but rather to open it up to a certain number of possible applications. To limit psychoanalysis as a type of discursivity is, in reality, to try to isolate in the founding act an eventually restricted number of propositions or statements to which, alone, one grants a founding value, and in relation to which certain concepts or theories accepted by Freud might be considered as derived, secondary, and accessory. In addition, one does not declare certain propositions in the work of these founders to be false: instead, when trying to seize the act of founding, one sets aside those statements that are not pertinent, either because they are deemed inessential, or because they are considered "prehistoric" and derived from another type of discursivity. In other words, unlike the founding of a science, the initiation of a discursive practice does not participate in its later transformations.

As a result, one defines a proposition's theoretical validity in relation to the work of the founders—while, in the case of Galileo and Newton, it is in relation to what physics or cosmology *is* (in its intrinsic structure and "normativity") that one affirms the validity of any proposition that those men may have put forth. To phrase it very schematically: the work of initiators of discursivity is not situated in the space that science defines; rather, it is the science or the discursivity which refers back to their work as primary coordinates.

In this way we can understand the inevitable necessity, within these fields of discursivity, for a "return to the origin." This return, which is part of the discursive field itself, never stops modifying it. The return is not a historical supplement which would be added to the discursivity, or merely an ornament; on the contrary, it constitutes an effective and necessary task of transforming the discursive practice itself. Reexamination of Galileo's text may well change our knowledge of the history of mechanics, but it will never be able to change mechanics itself. On the other hand, reexamining Freud's texts modifies psychoanalysis itself, just as a reexamination of Marx's would modify Marxism.

What I have just outlined regarding the initiation of discursive practices is, of course, very schematic; this is true, in particular, of the opposition that I have tried to draw between discursive initiation and scientific founding. It is not always easy to distinguish between the two; moreover, nothing proves that they are two mutually exclusive procedures. I have attempted the distinction for only one reason: to show that the author function, which is complex enough when one tries to situate it at the level of a book or a series of texts that carry a given signature, involves still more determining factors when one tries to analyze it in larger units, such as groups of works or entire disciplines.

To conclude, I would like to review the reasons why I attach a certain importance to what I have said.

First, there are theoretical reasons. On the one hand, an analysis in the direction that I have outlined might provide for an approach to a typology of discourse. It seems to me, at least at first glance, that such a typology cannot be constructed solely from the grammatical features, formal structures, and objects of discourse: more likely there exist properties of relationships peculiar to discourse (not reducible to the rules of grammar and logic), and one must use these to distinguish the major categories of discourse. The relationship (or nonrelationship) with an author, and the different forms this relationship takes, constitute—in a quite visible manner—one of these discursive properties.

On the other hand, I believe that one could find here an introduction to the historical analysis of discourse. Perhaps it is time to study discourses not only in terms of their expressive value or formal transformations, but according to their modes of existence. The modes of circulation, valorization, attribution, and appropriation of discourses vary with each culture and are modified within each. The manner in which they are articulated according to social relationships can be more readily understood, I believe, in the activity of the author function and in its modifications than in the themes or concepts that discourses set in motion.

It would seem that one could also, beginning with analyses of this type, reexamine the privileges of the subject. I realize that in undertaking the internal and architectonic analysis of a work (be it a literary text, philosophical system, or scientific work), in setting aside biographical and psychological references, one has already called back into question the absolute character and founding role of the subject. Still, perhaps one must return to this question, not in order to reestablish the theme of an originating subject, but to grasp the subject's points of insertion, modes of functioning, and system of dependencies. Doing so means overturning the traditional problem, no longer raising the questions: How can a free subject penetrate the substance of things and give it meaning? How can it activate the rules of a language from within and thus give rise to the designs which are properly its own? Instead, these questions will be raised: How, under what conditions, and in what forms can something like a subject appear in the order of discourse? What place can it occupy in each type of discourse, what functions can it assume, and by obeying what rules? In short, it is a matter of depriving the subject (or its substitute) of its role as originator, and of analyzing the subject as a variable and complex function of discourse.

Second, there are reasons dealing with the "ideological" status of the author. The question then becomes: How can one reduce the great peril, the great danger with which fiction threatens our world? The answer is: one can reduce it with the author. The author allows a limitation of the cancerous and dangerous proliferation of significations within a world where one is thrifty not only with one's resources and riches, but also with one's discourses and their significations. The author is the principle of thrift in the proliferation of meaning. As a result, we must entirely reverse the traditional idea of the author. We are accustomed, as we have seen earlier, to saying that the author is the genial creator of a work in which he deposits, with infinite wealth and generosity, an inexhaustible world of significations. We are used to thinking that the author is so different from all other men, and so transcendent with regard to all languages that, as soon as he speaks, meaning begins to proliferate, to proliferate indefinitely.

The truth is quite the contrary: the author is not an indefinite source of significations which fill a work; the author does not precede the works; he is a certain functional principle by which, in our culture, one limits, excludes, and chooses; in short, by which one impedes the free circulation, the free manipulation, the free composition, decomposition, and recomposition of fiction. In fact, if we are accustomed to presenting the author as a genius, as a perpetual surging of invention, it is because, in reality, we make him function in exactly the opposite fashion. One can say that the author is an ideological product, since we represent him as the opposite of his historically real function. (When a historically given function is represented in a figure that inverts it, one has an ideological production.) The author is therefore the ideological figure by which one marks the manner in which we fear the proliferation of meaning.

In saying this, I seem to call for a form of culture in which fiction would not be limited by the figure of the author. It would be pure romanticism, however, to imagine a culture in which the fictive would operate in an absolutely free state, in which fiction would be put at the disposal of everyone and would develop without passing through something like a necessary or constraining figure. Although, since the eighteenth century, the author has played the role of the regulator of the fictive, a role quite characteristic of our era of industrial and bourgeois society, of individualism and private property, still, given the historical modifications that are taking place, it does not seem necessary that the author function remain constant in form, complexity, and even in existence. I think that, as our society changes, at the very moment when it is in the process of changing, the author function will disappear, and in such a manner that fiction and its polysemous texts will once again function according to another mode, but still with a system of constraint—one which will no longer be the author, but which will have to be determined or, perhaps, experienced.

All discourses, whatever their status, form, value, and whatever the treatment to which they will be subjected, would then develop in the anonymity of a murmur. We would no longer hear the questions that have been rehashed for so long: Who really spoke? Is it really he and not someone else? With what authenticity or originality? And what part of his deepest self did he express in his discourse? Instead, there would be other questions, like these: What are the modes of existence of this discourse? Where has it been used, how can it circulate, and who can appropriate it for himself? What are the places in it where there is room for possible subjects? Who can assume these various subject functions? And behind all these questions, we would hear hardly anything but the stirring of an indifference: What difference does it make who is speaking?

Translated by Josue V. Hatari.

PAUL DE MAN

Semiology and Rhetoric

1979

_____

Paul de Man (1919–1983) examines issues of interpretation common to New Criticism, structuralism, and deconstruction. The New Criticism he sees as reductive and compromised by inherent fallacies; and although French semiology is in his view an advance over New Criticism, de Man believes that the semiologists (or structuralists) have not been rigorous enough in their analysis of rhetoric. Because rhetoric is essential to the study of literature, he delineates an approach to rhetoric that will be appropriate to the grammatical foundations of semiology.

He defines rhetoric by alluding to Charles Sanders Peirce's distinction between grammar and rhetoric: while grammar suggests a system in which signs have a stable and explicit meaning, rhetoric requires an interpretant who reads a sign so that "one sign gives birth to another." De Man also refers to Monroe Beardsley's idea that both literary and rhetorical language are characterized by a concentrated use of implicit meanings. Finally he mentions J. L. Austin's theory of the "illocutionary act," the primary concern of which is analyzing the effect a speaker intends to achieve with a given utterance. The problem for criticism is in devising a semiology of rhetoric that will yield an instrument of investigation that is rigorous because it is based on grammar. Deconstruction will provide the means of devising such a rhetoric.

De Man demonstrates his deconstructive approach in seeking the oppositions contained in literary passages. Deconstruction is appropriate as an approach to rhetoric, he argues, because rhetoric itself deconstructs, or undermines, the grammatical stability and reliability of language. In rhetorical questions, for example, grammatical and rhetorical forms are exactly congruent; the literal and figurative meanings derived from them, however, diverge into opposites.

De Man's deconstruction of the oppositions of literal/figurative and grammatical/rhetorical leads him to discover two semiological categories of rhetoric. First is the rhetorization of grammar, as in the rhetorical question. (His example is the famous question at the end of Yeats's "Among School Children.") Second, de Man finds a grammatization of rhetoric in a passage from Proust's Swann's Way. The analysis of Proust's rhetoric reveals that the oppositions of inner/outer, reading/living,

*presence/absence, and so forth apparently develop a literary statement of the superi-
ority of metaphor (a whole equals another whole) through a strategy of metonymy
and synecdoche (a part equals a whole).*

*As is typical of much deconstruction, de Man's argument moves in deliberate
indirection, never forcing certainties but discovering and maintaining multiple possibilities. He concludes that deconstruction must ultimately merge with psycholinguistics so that our perceptions about literature will join with our understanding of
the processes of language and mind.*

To JUDGE from various recent publications, the spirit of the times is not blowing in the direction of formalist and intrinsic criticism. We may no longer be
hearing too much about relevance but we keep hearing a great deal about
reference, about the nonverbal "outside" to which language refers, by which
it is conditioned and upon which it acts. The stress falls not so much on the
fictional status of literature—a property now perhaps somewhat too easily
taken for granted—but on the interplay between these fictions and categories that are said to partake of reality, such as the self, man, society, "the
artist, his culture and the human community," as one critic puts it. Hence the
emphasis on hybrid texts considered to be partly literary and partly referential, on popular fictions deliberately aimed towards social and psychological
gratification, on literary autobiography as a key to the understanding of the
self, and so on. We speak as if, with the problems of literary form resolved
once and forever, and with the techniques of structural analysis refined to
near-perfection, we could now move "beyond formalism" towards the questions that really interest us and reap, at last, the fruits of the ascetic concentration on techniques that prepared us for this decisive step. With the internal law and order of literature well policed, we can now confidently devote
ourselves to the foreign affairs, the external politics of literature. Not only do
we feel able to do so, but we owe it to ourselves to take this step: our moral
conscience would not allow us to do otherwise. Behind the assurance that
valid interpretation is possible, behind the recent interest in writing and
reading as potentially effective public speech acts, stands a highly respectable moral imperative that strives to reconcile the internal, formal, private structures of literary language with their external, referential, and public
effects.

I want, for the moment, to consider briefly this tendency in itself, as an
undeniable and recurrent historical fact, without regard for its truth or false-
ness or for its value as desirable or pernicious. It is a fact that this sort of thing
happens, again and again, in literary studies. On the one hand, literature cannot merely be received as a definite unit of referential meaning that can be de-
coded without leaving a residue. The code is unusually conspicuous, complex, and enigmatic; it attracts an inordinate amount of attention to itself, and
this attention has to acquire the rigor of a method. The structural moment of

concentration on the code for its own sake cannot be avoided, and literature necessarily breeds its own formalism. Technical innovations in the methodical study of literature only occur when this kind of attention predominates. It can legitimately be said, for example, that, from a technical point of view, very little has happened in American criticism since the innovative works of New Criticism. There certainly have been numerous excellent books of criticism since, but in none of them have the techniques of description and interpretation evolved beyond the techniques of close reading established in the thirties and the forties. Formalism, it seems, is an all-absorbing and tyrannical muse; the hope that one can be at the same time technically original and discursively eloquent is not borne out by the history of literary criticism.

On the other hand—and this is the real mystery—no literary formalism, no matter how accurate and enriching in its analytic powers, is ever allowed to come into being without seeming reductive. When form is considered to be the external trappings of literary meaning or content, it seems superficial and expendable. The development of intrinsic, formalist criticism in the twentieth century has changed this model: form is now a solipsistic category of self-reflection, and the referential meaning is said to be extrinsic. The polarities of inside and outside have been reversed, but they are still the same polarities that are at play: internal meaning has become outside reference, and the outer form has become the intrinsic structure. A new version of reductiveness at once follows this reversal: formalism nowadays is mostly described in an imagery of imprisonment and claustrophobia: the "prison house of language," "the impasse of formalist criticism," etc. Like the grandmother in Proust's novel ceaselessly driving the young Marcel out into the garden, away from the unhealthy inwardness of his closeted reading, critics cry out for the fresh air of referential meaning. Thus, with the structure of the code so opaque, but the meaning so anxious to blot out the obstacle of form, no wonder that the reconciliation of form and meaning would be so attractive. The attraction of reconciliation is the elective breeding-ground of false models and metaphors; it accounts for the metaphorical model of literature as a kind of box that separates an inside from an outside, and the reader or critic as the person who opens the lid in order to release in the open what was secreted but inaccessible inside. It matters little whether we call the inside of the box the content or the form, the outside the meaning or the appearance. The recurrent debate opposing intrinsic to extrinsic criticism stands under the aegis of an inside/outside metaphor that is never being seriously questioned.

Metaphors are much more tenacious than facts, and I certainly don't expect to dislodge this age-old model in one short try. I merely wish to speculate on a different set of terms, perhaps less simple in their differential relationships than the strictly polar, binary opposition between inside and outside and therefore less likely to enter into the easy play of chiasmic reversals. I derive these terms (which are as old as the hills) pragmatically from the observation of developments and debates in recent critical methodology.

One of the most controversial among these developments coincides with a new approach to poetics or, as it is called in Germany, poetology, as a branch of general semiotics. In France, a semiology of literature comes about as the outcome of the long-deferred but all the more explosive encounter of the nimble French literary mind with the category of form. Semiology, as opposed to semantics, is the science or study of signs as signifiers; it does not ask what words mean but how they mean. Unlike American New Criticism, which derived the internalization of form from the practice of highly self-conscious modern writers, French semiology turned to linguistics for its model and adopted Saussure and Jakobson rather than Valéry or Proust for its masters. By an awareness of the arbitrariness of the sign (Saussure) and of literature as an autotelic statement "focused on the way it is expressed" (Jakobson) the entire question of meaning can be bracketed, thus feeling the critical discourse from the debilitating burden of paraphrase. The demystifying power of semiology, within the context of French historical and thematic criticism, has been considerable. It demonstrated that the perception of the literary dimensions of language is largely obscured if one submits uncritically to the authority of reference. It also revealed how tenaciously this authority continues to assert itself in a variety of disguises, ranging from the crudest ideology to the most refined forms of aesthetic and ethical judgment. It especially explodes the myth of semantic correspondence between sign and referent, the wishful hope of having it both ways, of being, to paraphrase Marx in *The German Ideology*, a formalist critic in the morning and a communal moralist in the afternoon, of serving both the technique of form and the substance of meaning. The results, in the practice of French criticism, have been as fruitful as they are irreversible. Perhaps for the first time since the late eighteenth century, French critics can come at least somewhat closer to the kind of linguistic awareness that never ceased to be operative in its poets and novelists and that forced all of them, including Sainte Beuve, to write their main works "contre Sainte Beuve." The distance was never so considerable in England and the United States, which does not mean, however, that we may be able, in this country, to dispense altogether with some preventative semiological hygiene.

One of the most striking characteristics of literary semiology as it is practiced today, in France and elsewhere, is the use of grammatical (especially syntactical) structures conjointly with rhetorical structures, without apparent awareness of a possible discrepancy between them. In their literary analyses, Barthes, Genette, Todorov, Greimas, and their disciples all simplify and regress from Jakobson in letting grammar and rhetoric function in perfect continuity, and in passing from grammatical to rhetorical structures without difficulty or interruption. Indeed, as the study of grammatical structures is refined in contemporary theories of generative, transformational, and distributive grammar, the study of tropes and of figures (which is how the term *rhetoric* is used here, and not in the derived sense of comment or of eloquence or persuasion) becomes a mere extension of grammatical models, a particular subset of syntactical relations. In the recent *Dictionnaire encyclopédique des sci-*

ences du langage, Ducrot and Todorov write that rhetoric has always been sat-isfied with a paradigmatic view over words (words substituting for each other), without questioning their syntagmatic relationship (the contiguity of words to each other). There ought to be another perspective, complementary to the first, in which metaphor, for example, would not be defined as a sub-stitution but as a particular type of combination. Research inspired by lin-guistics or, more narrowly, by syntactical studies, has begun to reveal this possibility—but it remains to be explored. Todorov, who calls one of his books a *Grammar of the Decameron,* rightly thinks of his own work and that of his associates as first explorations in the elaboration of a systematic grammar of literary modes, genres, and also of literary figures. Perhaps the most per-ceptive work to come out of this school, Genette's studies of figural modes, can be shown to be assimilations of rhetorical transformations or combina-tions to syntactical, grammatical patterns. Thus a recent study, now printed in *Figures III* and entitled *Metaphor and Metonymy in Proust,* shows the com-bined presence, in a wide and astute selection of passages, of paradigmatic, metaphorical figures with syntagmatic, metonymic structures. The combina-tion of both is treated descriptively and nondialectically without considering the possibility of logical tensions.

One can ask whether this reduction of figure to grammar is legitimate. The existence of grammatical structures, within and beyond the unit of the sentence, in literary texts is undeniable, and their description and classifica-tion are indispensable. The question remains if and how figures of rhetoric can be included in such a taxonomy. This question is at the core of the debate going on, in a wide variety of apparently unrelated forms, in contemporary poetics. But the historical picture of contemporary criticism is too confused to make the mapping out of such a topography a useful exercise. Not only are these questions mixed in and mixed up within particular groups or local trends, but they are often co-present, without apparent contradiction, within the work of a single author.

Neither is the theory of the question suitable for quick expository treat-ment. To distinguish the epistemology of grammar from the epistemology of rhetoric is a redoubtable task. On an entirely naïve level, we tend to conceive of grammatical systems as tending towards universality and as simply gen-erative, i.e., as capable of deriving an infinity of versions from a single model (that may govern transformations as well as derivations) without the inter-vention of another model that would upset the first. We therefore think of the relationship between grammar and logic, the passage from grammar to propositions, as being relatively unproblematic: no true propositions are con-ceivable in the absence of grammatical consistency or of controlled deviation from a system of consistency no matter how complex. Grammar and logic stand to each other in a dyadic relationship of unsubverted support. In a logic of acts rather than of statements, as in Austin's theory of speech acts, that has had such a strong influence on recent American work in literary semiology, it is also possible to move between speech acts and grammar without difficulty. The performance of what is called illocutionary acts such as ordering, questioning, denying, assuming, etc., within the language is congruent with the grammatical structures of syntax in the corresponding imperative, interrogative, negative, optative sentences. "The rules for illocutionary acts," writes Richard Ohman in a recent paper, "determine whether performance of a given act is well-executed, in just the same way as *grammatical* rules determine whether the product of a locutionary act—a sentence—is well formed. . . . But whereas the rules of grammar concern the relationships among sound, syntax, and meaning, the rules of illocutionary acts concern relationships among people."[1] And since rhetoric is then conceived exclusively as persuasion, as actual action upon others (and not as an intralinguistic figure or trope), the continuity between the illocutionary realm of grammar and the perlocutionary realm of rhetoric is self-evident. It becomes the basis for a new rhetoric that, exactly as is the case for Todorov and Genette, would also be a new grammar.

Without engaging the substance of the question, it can be pointed out, without having to go beyond recent and American examples, and without calling upon the strength of an age-old tradition, that the continuity here assumed between grammar and rhetoric is not borne out by theoretical and philosophical speculation. Kenneth Burke mentions *deflection* (which he compares structurally to Freudian displacement), defined as "any slight bias or even unintended error," as the rhetorical basis of language, and deflection is then conceived as a dialectical subversion of the consistent link between sign and meaning that operates within grammatical patterns; hence Burke's well-known insistence on the distinction between grammar and rhetoric. Charles Sanders Peirce, who, with Nietzsche and Saussure, laid the philosophical foundation for modern semiology, stressed the distinction between grammar and rhetoric in his celebrated and so suggestively unfathomable definition of the sign. He insists, as is well known, on the necessary presence of a third element, called the interpretant, within any relationship that the sign entertains with its object. The sign is to be interpreted if we are to understand the idea it is to convey, and this is so because the sign is not the thing but a meaning derived from the thing by a process here called representation that is not simply generative, i.e., dependent on a univocal origin. The interpretation of the sign is not, for Peirce, a meaning but another sign; it is a reading, not a decodage, and this reading has, in its turn, to be interpreted into another sign, and so on *ad infinitum*. Peirce calls this process by means of which "one sign gives birth to another" pure rhetoric, as distinguished from pure grammar, which postulates the possibility of unproblematic, dyadic meaning, and pure logic, which postulates the possibility of the universal truth of meanings. Only if the sign engendered meaning in the same way that the object engenders the sign, that is, by representation, would there be no need to distinguish between grammar and rhetoric.

---

[1] "Speech, Literature, and the Space in Between," *New Literary History* 4 (Autumn 1972): 50. [All notes are de Man's.]

These remarks should indicate at least the existence and the difficulty of the question, a difficulty which puts its concise theoretical exposition beyond my powers. I must retreat therefore into a pragmatic discourse and try to illustrate the tension between grammar and rhetoric in a few specific textual examples. Let me begin by considering what is perhaps the most commonly known instance of an apparent symbosis between a grammatical and a rhetorical structure, the so-called rhetorical question, in which the figure is conveyed directly by means of a syntactical device. I take the first example from the subliterature of the mass media: asked by his wife whether he wants to have his bowling shoes laced over or laced under, Archie Bunker answers with a question: "What's the difference?" Being a reader of sublime simplicity, his wife replies by patiently explaining the difference between lacing over and lacing under, whatever this may be, but provokes only ire. "What's the difference" did not ask for difference but means instead "I don't give a damn what the difference is." The same grammatical pattern engenders two meanings that are mutually exclusive: the literal meaning asks for the concept (difference) whose existence is denied by the figurative meaning. As long as we are talking about bowling shoes, the consequences are relatively trivial; Archie Bunker, who is a great believer in the authority of origins (as long, of course, as they are the right origins) muddles along in a world where literal and figurative meanings get in each other's way, though not without discomforts. But suppose that it is a *de*-bunker rather than a "Bunker," and a de-bunker of the arche (or origin), an Archie Debunker such as Nietzsche or Jacques Derrida for instance, who asks the question "What is the Difference" — and we cannot even tell from his grammar whether he "really" wants to know "what" difference is or is just telling us that we shouldn't even try to find out. Confronted with the question of the difference between grammar and rhetoric, grammar allows us to ask the question, but the sentence by means of which we ask it may deny the very possibility of asking. For what is the use of asking, I ask, when we cannot even authoritatively decide whether a question asks or doesn't ask?

The point is as follows. A perfectly clear syntactical paradigm (the question) engenders a sentence that has at least two meanings, of which the one asserts and the other denies its own illocutionary mode. It is not so that there are simply two meanings, one literal and the other figural, and that we have to decide which one of these meanings is the right one in this particular situation. The confusion can only be cleared up by the intervention of an extratextual intention, such as Archie Bunker putting his wife straight; but the very anger he displays is indicative of more than impatience; it reveals his despair when confronted with a structure of linguistic meaning that he cannot control and that holds the discouraging prospect of an infinity of similar future confusions, all of them potentially catastrophic in their consequences. Nor is this intervention really a part of the mini-text constituted by the figure which holds our attention only as long as it remains suspended and unresolved. I follow the usage of common speech in calling this semiological enigma "rhetorical." The grammatical model of the question becomes rhetorical not when we have, on the one hand, a literal meaning and on the other hand a figural meaning, but when it is impossible to decide by grammatical or other linguistic devices which of the two meanings (that can be entirely incompatible) prevails. Rhetoric radically suspends logic and opens up vertiginous possibilities of referential aberration. And although it would perhaps be somewhat more remote from common usage, I would not hesitate to equate the rhetorical, figural potentiality of language with literature itself. I could point to a great number of antecedents to this equation of literature with figure; the most recent reference would be to Monroe Beardsley's insistence in his contribution to the *Essays* to honor William Wimsatt, that literary language is characterized by being "distinctly above the norm in ratio of implicit [or, I would say rhetorical] to explicit meaning."[2]

Let me pursue the matter of the rhetorical question through one more example. Yeats's poem "Among School Children" ends with the famous line: "How can we know the dancer from the dance?" Although there are some revealing inconsistencies within the commentaries, the line is usually interpreted as stating, with the increased emphasis of a rhetorical device, the potential unity between form and experience, between creator and creation. It could be said that it denies the discrepancy between the sign and the referent from which we started out. Many elements in the imagery and the dramatic development of the poem strengthen this traditional reading; without having to look any further than the immediately preceding lines, one finds powerful and consecrated images of the continuity from part to whole that makes synecdoche into the most seductive of metaphors: the organic beauty of the tree, stated in the parallel syntax of a similar rhetorical question, or the convergence, in the dance, of erotic desire with musical form:

> O chestnut-tree, great-rooted blossomer,
> Are you the leaf, the blossom or the bole?
> O body swayed to music, O brightening glance,
> How can we know the dancer from the dance?

A more extended reading, always assuming that the final line is to be read as a rhetorical question, reveals that the thematic and rhetorical grammar of the poem yields a consistent reading that extends from the first line to the last and that can account for all details in the text. It is equally possible, however, to read the last line literally rather than figuratively, as asking with some urgency the question we asked earlier within the context of contemporary criticism: *not* that sign and referent are so exquisitely fitted to each other that all difference between them is at times blotted out but, rather, since the two essentially different elements, sign and meaning, are so intricately intertwined in the imagined "presence" that the poem addresses, how can we possibly make the distinctions that would shelter us from the error of identifying what cannot be identified? The clumsiness of the paraphrase reveals that it is not necessarily the literal reading which is simpler than the figurative one, as

---

[2] "The Concept of Literature," in *Literary Theory and Structure: Essays in Honor of William K. Wimsatt*, ed. Frank Brady, John Palmer, and Martin Price (New Haven, 1973), p. 37.

was the case in our first example; here, the figural reading, which assumes the question to be rhetorical, is perhaps naïve, whereas the literal reading leads to greater complication of theme and statement. For it turns out that the entire scheme set up by the first reading can be undermined, or deconstructed, in the terms of the second, in which the final line is read literally as meaning that, since the dancer and the dance are not the same, it might be useful, perhaps even desperately necessary—for the question can be given a ring of urgency, "Please tell me, how *can* I know the dancer from the dance"—to tell them apart. But this will replace the reading of each symbolic detail by a divergent interpretation. The oneness of trunk, leaf, and blossom, for example, that would have appealed to Goethe, would find itself replaced by the much less reassuring Tree of Life from the Mabinogion that appears in the poem "Vacillation," in which the fiery blossom and the earthly leaf are held together, as well as apart, by the crucified and castrated God Attis, of whose body it can hardly be said that it is "not bruised to pleasure soul." This hint should suffice to suggest that two entirely coherent but entirely incompatible readings can be made to hinge on one line, whose grammatical structure is devoid of ambiguity, but whose rhetorical mode turns the mood as well as the mode of the entire poem upside down. Neither can we say, as was already the case in the first example, that the poem simply has two meanings that exist side by side. The two readings have to engage each other in direct confrontation, for the one reading is precisely the error denounced by the other and has to be undone by it. Nor can we in any way make a valid decision as to which of the readings can be given priority over the other; none can exist in the other's absence. There can be no dance without a dancer, no sign without a referent. On the other hand, the authority of the meaning engendered by the grammatical structure is fully obscured by the duplicity of a figure that cries out for the differentiation that it conceals.

Yeats's poem is not explicity "about" rhetorical questions but about images or metaphors, and about the possibility of convergence between experiences of consciousness such as memory or emotions—what the poem calls passion, piety, and affection—and entities accessible to the senses such as bodies, persons, or icons. We return to the inside/outside model from which we started out and which the poem puts into question by means of a syntactical device (the question) made to operate on a grammatical as well as on a rhetorical level. The couple grammar/rhetoric, certainly not a binary opposition since they in no way exclude each other, disrupts and confuses the neat antithesis of the inside/outside pattern. We can transfer this scheme to the act of reading and interpretation. By reading we get, as we say, *inside* a text that was first something alien to us and which we now make our own by an act of understanding. But this understanding becomes at once the representation of an extra-textual meaning; in Austin's terms, the illocutionary speech act becomes a perlocutionary actual act—in Frege's terms, *Bedeutung* becomes *Sinn*. Our recurrent question is whether this transformation is semantically controlled along grammatical or along rhetorical lines. Does the metaphor of reading really unite outer meaning with inner understanding, action with reflection, into one single totality? The assertion is powerfully and suggestively made in a passage from Proust that describes the experience of reading as such a union. It describes the young Marcel, near the beginning of Combray, hiding in the closed space of his room in order to read. The example differs from the earlier ones in that we are not dealing with a grammatical structure that also functions rhetorically but have instead the representation, the dramatization, in terms of the experience of a subject, of a rhetorical structure—just as, in many other passages, Proust dramatizes tropes by means of landscapes or description of objects. The figure here dramatized is that of metaphor, an inside/outside correspondence as represented by the act of reading. The reading scene is the culmination of a series of actions taking place in enclosed spaces and leading up to the "dark coolness" of Marcel's room.

> I had stretched out on my bed, with a book, in my room which sheltered, tremblingly, its transparent and fragile coolness from the afternoon sun behind the almost closed blinds through which a glimmer of daylight had nevertheless managed to push its yellow wings, remaining motionless between the wood and the glass, in a corner, poised like a butterfly. It was hardly light enough to read, and the sensation of the light's splendor was given me only by the noise of Camus . . . hammering dusty crates; resounding in the sonorous atmosphere that is peculiar to hot weather, they seemed to spark off scarlet stars; and also by the flies executing their little concert, the chamber music of summer: evocative not in the manner of a human tune that, heard perchance during the summer, afterwards reminds you of it but connected to summer by a more necessary link: born from beautiful days, resurrecting only when they return, containing some of their essence, it does not only awaken their image in our memory; it guarantees their return, their actual, persistent, unmediated presence.
>
> The dark coolness of my room related to the full sunlight of the street as the shadow relates to the ray of light, that is to say it was just as luminous and it gave my imagination the total spectacle of the summer, whereas my senses, if I had been on a walk, could only have enjoyed it by fragments; it matched my repose which (thanks to the adventures told by my book and stirring my tranquility) supported, like the quiet of a motionless hand in the middle of a running brook the shock and the motion of a torrent of activity. [*Swann's Way*. Paris: Pléiade, 1954, p. 83.]

For our present purpose, the most striking aspect of this passage is the juxtaposition of figural and metafigural language. It contains seductive metaphors that bring into play a variety of irresistible objects: chamber music, butterflies, stars, books, running brooks, etc., and it describes these objects within dazzling fire- and water-works of figuration. But the passage also comments normatively on the best way to achieve such effects; in this sense, it is metafigural: it writes figuratively about figures. It contrasts two ways of evoking the natural experience of summer and unambiguously states its preference for one of these ways over the other: the "necessary link" that unites the buzzing of the flies to the summer makes it a much more effective symbol than the tune heard "perchance" during the summer. The preference is expressed by means of a distinction that corresponds to the difference between metaphor and metonymy, necessity and chance being a legitimate way to distinguish between analogy and contiguity. The inference of identity and totality that is constitutive of metaphor is lacking in the purely relational metonymic contact: an element of truth is involved in taking Achilles for a lion but none in taking Mr. Ford for a motor car. The passage is *about* the aesthetic superiority of metaphor over metonymy, but this aesthetic claim is made by means of categories that are the ontological ground of the metaphysical system that allows for the aesthetic to come into being as a category. The metaphor for summer (in this case, the synesthesia set off by the "chamber music" of the flies) guarantees a presence which, far from being contingent, is said to be essential, permanently recurrent and unmediated by linguistic representations or figurations. Finally, in the second part of the passage, the metaphor of presence not only appears as the ground of cognition but as the performance of an action, thus promising the reconciliation of the most disruptive of contradictions. By then, the investment in the power of metaphor is such that it may seem sacrilegious to put it in question.

Yet, it takes little perspicacity to show that the text does not practice what it preaches. A rhetorical reading of the passage reveals that the figural praxis and the metafigural theory do not converge and that the assertion of the mastery of metaphor over metonymy owes its persuasive power to the use of metonymic structures. I have carried out such an analysis in a somewhat more extended context; at this point, we are more concerned with the results than with the procedure. For the metaphysical categories of presence, essence, action, truth, and beauty do not remain unaffected by such a reading. This would become clear from an inclusive reading of Proust's novel or would become even more explicit in a language-conscious philosopher such as Nietzsche who, as a philosopher, has to be concerned with the epistemological consequences of the kind of rhetorical seductions exemplified by the Proust passage. It can be shown that the systematic critique of the main categories of metaphysics undertaken by Nietzsche in his late work, the critique of the concepts of causality, of the subject, of identity, of referential and revealed truth, etc., occurs along the same pattern of deconstruction that was operative in Proust's text; and it can also be shown that this pattern exactly corresponds to Nietzsche's description, in texts that precede *The Will to Power* by more than fifteen years, of the structure of the main rhetorical tropes. The key to this critique of metaphysics, which is itself a recurrent gesture throughout the history of thought, is the rhetorical model of the trope or, if one prefers to call it that, literature. It turns out that in these innocent-looking didactic exercises we are in fact playing for very sizeable stakes.

It is therefore all the more necessary to know what is linguistically involved in a rhetorically conscious reading of the type here undertaken on a brief fragment from a novel and extended by Nietzsche to the entire text of post-Hellenic thought. Our first examples dealing with the rhetorical questions were rhetorizations of grammar, figures generated by syntactical paradigms, whereas the Proust example could be better described as a grammatization of rhetoric. By passing from a paradigmatic structure based on substitution, such as metaphor, to a syntagmatic structure based on contingent association such as metonymy, the mechanical, repetitive aspect of grammatical forms is shown to be operative in a passage that seemed at first sight to celebrate the self-willed and autonomous inventiveness of a subject. Figures are assumed to be inventions, the products of a highly particularized individual talent, whereas no one can claim credit for the programmed pattern of grammar. Yet, our reading of the Proust passage shows that precisely when the highest claims are being made for the unifying power of metaphor, these very images rely in fact on the deceptive use of semi-automatic grammatical patterns. The deconstruction of metaphor and of all rhetorical patterns such as mimesis, paranomasis, or personification that use resemblance as a way to disguise differences, takes us back to the impersonal precision of grammar and of a semiology derived from grammatical patterns. Such a reading puts into question a whole series of concepts that underlie the value judgments of our critical discourse: the metaphors of primacy, of genetic history, and, most notably, of the autonomous power to will of the self.

There seems to be a difference, then, between what I called the rhetorization of grammar (as in the rhetorical question) and the grammatization of rhetoric, as in the readings of the type sketched out in the passage from Proust. The former end up in indetermination, in a suspended uncertainty that was unable to choose between two modes of reading, whereas the latter seems to reach a truth, albeit by the negative road of exposing an error, a false pretense. After the rhetorical reading of the Proust passage, we can no longer believe the assertion made in this passage about the intrinsic, metaphysical superiority of metaphor over metonymy. We seem to end up in a mood of negative assurance that is highly productive of critical discourse. The further text of Proust's novel, for example, responds perfectly to an extended application of this pattern: not only can similar gestures be repeated throughout the novel, at all the crucial articulations or all passages where large aesthetic and metaphysical claims are being made—the scenes of involuntary memory, the workshop of Elstir, the septette of Vinteuil, the convergence of author and narrator at the end of the novel—but a vast thematic and semiotic network is revealed that structures the entire narrative and that remained invisible to a reader caught in naïve metaphorical mystification. The whole of literature would respond in similar fashion, although the techniques and the patterns would have to vary considerably, of course, from author to author. But there is absolutely no reason why analyses of the kind here suggested for Proust would not be applicable, with proper modifications of technique, to Milton or to Dante or to Hölderlin. This will in fact be the task of literary criticism in the coming years.

It would seem that we are saying that criticism is the deconstruction of literature, the reduction to the rigors of grammar of rhetorical mystifications. And if we hold up Nietzsche as the philosopher of such a critical deconstruction, then the literary critic would become the philosopher's ally in his struggle with the poets. Criticism and literature would separate around the epistemological axis that distinguishes grammar from rhetoric. It is easy enough to see that this apparent glorification of the critic-philosopher in the name of truth is in fact a glorification of the poet as the primary source of this truth; if truth is the recognition of the systematic character of a certain kind of error, then it would be fully dependent on the prior existence of this error. Philosophers of science like Bachelard or Wittgenstein are notoriously dependent on the aberrations of the poets. We are back at our unanswered question: does the grammatization of rhetoric end up in negative certainty or does it, like the rhetorization of grammar, remain suspended in the ignorance of its own truth or falsehood?

Two concluding remarks should suffice to answer the question. First of all, it is not true that Proust's text can simply be reduced to the mystified assertion (the superiority of metaphor over metonymy) that our reading deconstructs. The reading is not "our" reading, since it uses only the linguistic elements provided by the text itself; the distinction between author and reader is one of the false distinctions that the reading makes evident. The deconstruction is not something we have added to the text but it constituted the text in the first place. A literary text simultaneously asserts and denies the authority of its own rhetorical mode, and by reading the text as we did we were only trying to come closer to being as rigorous a reader as the author had to be in order to write the sentence in the first place. Poetic writing is the most advanced and refined mode of deconstruction; it may differ from critical or discursive writing in the economy of its articulation, but not in kind.

But if we recognize the existence of such a moment as constitutive of all literary language, we have surreptitiously reintroduced the categories that this deconstruction was supposed to eliminate and that have merely been displaced. We have, for example, displaced the question of the self from the referent into the figure of the narrator, who then becomes the *signifié* of the passage. It becomes again possible to ask such naïve questions as what Proust's, or Marcel's motives may have been in thus manipulating language: was he fooling himself, or was he represented as fooling himself and fooling us into believing that fiction and action are as easy to unite, by reading, as the passage asserts? The pathos of the entire section, which would have been more noticeable if the quotation had been a little more extended, the constant vacillation of the narrator between guilt and well-being, invites such questions. They are absurd questions, of course, since the reconciliation of fact and fiction occurs itself as a mere assertion made in a text, and is thus productive of more text at the moment when it asserts its decision to escape from textual confinement. But even if we free ourselves of all false questions of intent and rightfully reduce the narrator to the status of a mere grammatical pronoun, without which the narrative could not come into being, this subject remains endowed with a function that is not grammatical but rhetorical, in that it gives voice, so to speak, to a grammatical syntagm. The term *voice*, even when used in a grammatical terminology as when we speak of the passive or interrogative voice, is, of course, a metaphor inferring by analogy the intent of the subject from the structure of the predicate. In the case of the deconstructive discourse that we call literary, or rhetorical, or poetic, this creates a distinctive complication illustrated by the Proust passage. The reading revealed a first paradox: the passage valorizes metaphor as being the "right" literary figure, but then proceeds to constitute itself by means of the epistemologically incompatible figure of metonymy. The critical discourse reveals the presence of this delusion and affirms it as the irreversible mode of its truth. It cannot pause there however. For if we then ask the obvious and simple next question, whether the rhetorical mode of the text in question is that of metaphor or metonymy, it is impossible to give an answer. Individual metaphors, such as the chiaroscuro effect or the butterfly, are shown to be subordinate figures in a general clause whose syntax is metonymic; from this point of view, it seems that the rhetoric is superseded by a grammar that deconstructs it. But this metonymic clause has as its subject a voice whose relationship to this clause is again metaphorical. The narrator who tells us about the impossibility of metaphor is himself, or itself, a metaphor, the metaphor of a grammatical syntagm whose meaning is the denial of metaphor stated, by antiphrasis, as its priority. And this subject-metaphor is, in its turn, open to the kind of deconstruction to the second degree, the rhetorical deconstruction of psycholinguistics, in which the more advanced investigations of literature are presently engaged, against considerable resistance.

We end up therefore, in the case of the rhetorical grammatization of semiology, just as in the grammatical rhetorization of illocutionary phrases, in the same state of suspended ignorance. Any question about the rhetorical mode of a literary text is always a rhetorical question which does not even know whether it is really questioning. The resulting pathos is an anxiety (or bliss, depending on one's momentary mood or individual temperament) of ignorance, not an anxiety of reference—as becomes thematically clear in Proust's novel when reading is dramatized, in the relationship between Marcel and Albertine, not as an emotive reaction to what language does, but as an emotive reaction to the impossibility of knowing what it might be up to. Literature as well as criticism—the difference between them being delusive—is condemned (or privileged) to be forever the most rigorous and, consequently, the most unreliable language in terms of which man names and transforms himself.

Stanley Fish

Is There a Text in This Class?

1980

Critics since Plato have concerned themselves with the relationship between writer and reader or with the effects of literature on its readers. As examples, recall Aristotle's definition of tragedy partly in terms of the special emotions it evokes; Longinus's definition of sublimity in terms of its unique effect on the reader; Horace's awareness of audience response as an actual determinant on composition; Wordsworth's characterization of the poet as "a man speaking to men"; and the many critics who have dealt with the function of poetry. Implicit throughout is a communication model of intersubjectivity; that is, the writer's subjectivity speaks to the reader's subjectivity through the medium of a fixed and determinate text.

Beginning in the late 1960s a number of American scholars and critics began to reexamine that communication model and to propose a closer scrutiny of what actually happens to readers, who are, after all, not merely passive receptacles. What is the reader's role in this "transaction" (as one scholar calls it)? The "reader-response" theorists may differ from one another in assumptions, methods, terminology, or conclusions, but they all deny the New Critical implication that analyses of the formal properties of a literary work ("the work itself") result in similar responses and interpretations. Indeed the history of contradiction among contending explicators tends to support that denial.

The teacher and writer who has become best known as a reader-response critic is Stanley Fish (b. 1938), who in 1967 began gradually evolving in public his own theory of interpretation. His essay, originally delivered as part of a lecture series in 1979, represents one stage in the development of his new model. Fish argues against the doctrine of the integrity of the text and regards readers as actively participating in the construction of meaning. Reading is an activity, a process; therefore, the critic's task is to analyze "the developing responses of the reader in relation to the words as they succeed one another in time." For him, the key word is "experience"; the subtitle of his Self-Consuming Artifacts (1970) is "The Experience of Seventeenth-Century Literature." In later works his discovery and rejection of the hidden formalism in his own earlier essays leads him to argue that any recognition of formal units depends on the interpretive model the reader is already familiar with;

formal units are not found in the text itself. Against the argument that the reader-response theory is solipsistic and invites anarchy, that it abandons literature to idiosyncratic and irresponsible interpretations, Fish develops the concept of interpretive communities: "The meanings and texts produced by an interpretive community are not subjective because they do not proceed from an isolated individual but from a public and conventional point of view."

In his "How I Stopped Worrying and Learned to Love Interpretation" (1980), an explanation and defense of his position as well as a rebuttal to attacks on it, Fish describes the evolution of his theory, which now subsumes both reader and text "under the larger category of interpretation." But having created a new model, he grants that the theory is still in the process of transformation, that there are many other problems yet to be dealt with.

ON THE FIRST DAY of the new semester a colleague at Johns Hopkins University was approached by a student who, as it turned out, had just taken a course from me. She put to him what I think you would agree is a perfectly straightforward question: "Is there a text in this class?" Responding with a confidence so perfect that he was unaware of it (although in telling the story, he refers to this moment as "walking into the trap"), my colleague said, "Yes; it's the *Norton Anthology of Literature*," whereupon the trap (set not by the student but by the infinite capacity of language for being appropriated) was sprung: "No, no," she said, "I mean in this class do we believe in poems and things, or is it just us?" Now it is possible (and for many tempting) to read this anecdote as an illustration of the dangers that follow upon listening to people like me who preach the instability of the text and the unavailability of determinate meanings; but in what follows I will try to read it as an illustration of how baseless this fear of these dangers finally is.

Of the charges levied against what Meyer Abrams has recently called the New Readers (Derrida, Bloom, Fish) the most persistent is that these apostles of indeterminacy and undecidability ignore, even as they rely upon, the "norms and possibilities" embedded in language, the "linguistic meanings" words undeniably have, and thereby invite us to abandon "our ordinary realm of experience in speaking, hearing, reading and understanding" for a world in which "no text can mean anything in particular" and where "we can never say just what anyone means by anything he writes." The charge is that literal or normative meanings are overriden by the actions of willful interpreters. Suppose we examine this indictment in the context of the present example. What, exactly, is the normative or literal or linguistic meaning of "Is there a text in this class?"

Within the framework of contemporary critical debate (at it is reflected in the pages, say, of *Critical Inquiry*) there would seem to be only two ways of answering this question: either there *is* a literal meaning of the utterance and we should be able to say what it is, or there are as many meanings as there are readers and no one of them is literal. But the answer suggested by my little story is that the utterance has *two* literal meanings: within the circumstances assumed by my colleague (I don't mean that he took the step of assuming them, but that he was already stepping within them) the utterance is obviously a question about whether or not there is a required textbook in this particular course; but within the circumstances to which he was alerted by his student's corrective response, the utterance is just as obviously a question about the instructor's position (within the range of positions available in contemporary literary theory) on the status of the text. Notice that we do not have here a case of indeterminacy or undecidability but of a determinacy and decidability that do not always have the same shape and that can, and in this instance do, change. My colleague was not hesitating between two (or more) possible meanings of the utterance; rather, he immediately apprehended what seemed to be an inescapable meaning, given his prestructured understanding of the situation, and then he immediately apprehended another inescapable meaning when that understanding was altered. Neither meaning was imposed (a favorite word in the anti–new-reader polemics) on a more normal one by a private, idiosyncratic interpretive act; both interpretations were a function of precisely the public and constituting norms (of language and understanding) invoked by Abrams. It is just that these norms are not embedded in the language (where they may be read out by anyone with sufficiently clear, that is, unbiased, eyes) but inhere in an institutional structure within which one hears utterances as already organized with reference to certain assumed purposes and goals. Because both my colleague and his student are situated in that institution, their interpretive activities are not free, but what constrains them are the understood practices and assumptions of the institution and not the rules and fixed meanings of a language system.

Another way to put this would be to say that neither reading of the question—which we might for convenience's sake label as "Is there a text in this class?"$_1$ and "Is there a text in this class?"$_2$—would be immediately available to any native speaker of the language. "Is there a text in this class?"$_1$ is interpretable or readable only by someone who already knows what is included under the general rubric "first day of class" (what concerns animate students, what bureaucratic matters must be attended to before instruction begins) and who therefore hears the utterance under the aegis of that knowledge, which is not applied after the fact but is responsible for the shape the fact immediately has. To someone whose consciousness is not already informed by that knowledge, "Is there a text in this class?"$_1$ would be just as unavailable as "Is there a text in this class?"$_2$ would be to someone who was not already aware of the disputed issues in contemporary literary theory. I am not saying that for some readers or hearers the question would be wholly unintelligible (indeed, in the course of this essay I will be arguing that unintelligibility, in the strict or pure sense, is an impossibility), but that there are readers and hearers from whom the intelligibility of the question would have neither of the shapes it had, in a temporal succession, for my colleague. It is possible, for example, to imagine someone who would hear or intend the question as an inquiry about the location of an object, that is, "I think I left my text in this class; have you seen it?" We would then have an "Is there a text in this class?"$_3$ and the possibility, feared by the defenders of the normative and determinate, of an endless succession of numbers, that is, of a world in which every utterance has an infinite plurality of meanings. But that is not what the example, however it might be extended, suggests at all. In any of the situations I have imagined (and in any that I might be able to imagine) the meaning of the utterance would be severely constrained, not after it was heard but in the ways in which it *could*, in the first place, be heard. An infinite plurality of meanings would be a fear only if sentences existed in a state in which they were not already embedded, and had come into view as a function of, some situation or other. That state, if it could be located, would be the normative one, and it would be disturbing indeed if the norm were free-floating and indeterminate. But there is no such state; sentences emerge only in situations, and within those situations, the normative meaning of an utterance will always be obvious or at least accessible, although within another situation that same utterance, no longer the same, will have another normative meaning that will be no less obvious and accessible. (My colleague's experience is precisely an illustration.) This does not mean that there is no way to discriminate between the meanings an utterance will have in different situations, but that the discrimination will already have been made by virtue of our being in a situation (we are never not in one) and that in another situation the discrimination will also have already been made, but differently. In other words, while at any one point it is always possible to order and rank "Is there a text in this class?"$_1$ and "Is there a text in this class?"$_2$ (because they will always have already been ranked), it will never be possible to give them an immutable once-and-for-all ranking, a ranking that is independent of their appearance or nonappearance in situations (because it is only in situations that they do or do not appear).

Nevertheless, there is a distinction to be made between the two that allows us to say that, in a limited sense, one is more normal than the other: for while each is perfectly normal in the context in which their literalness is immediately obvious (the successive contexts occupied by my colleague), as things stand now, one of those contexts is surely more available, and therefore more likely to be the perspective within which the utterance is heard, than the other. Indeed, we seem to have here an instance of what I would call "institutional nesting": if "Is there a text in this class?"$_1$ is hearable only by those who know what is included under the rubric "first day of class," and if "Is there a text in this class?"$_2$ is hearable only by those whose categories of understanding include the concerns of contemporary literary theory, then it is obvious that in a random population presented with the utterance, more people would "hear" "Is there a text in this class?"$_1$ than "Is there a text in this class?"$_2$; and, moreover, that while "Is there a text in this class?"$_1$ could be immediately hearable by someone for whom "Is there a text in this class?"$_2$ would have to be laboriously explained, it is difficult to imagine someone capable of hearing "Is there a text in this class?"$_2$ who was not already capable of hearing "Is there a text in this class?"$_1$ (One is hearable by anyone in the profession and by most students and by many workers in the book trade, and the other only by those in the profession who would not think it peculiar to find, as I did recently, a critic referring to a phrase "made popular by Lacan.") To admit as much is not to weaken my argument by reinstating the category of the normal, because the category as it appears in that argument is not transcendental but institutional; and while no institution is so universally in force and so perdurable that the meanings it enables will be normal for ever, some institutions or forms of life are so widely lived in that for a great many people the meanings they enable seem "naturally" available and it takes a special effort to see that they are the products of circumstances.

The point is an important one, because it accounts for the success with which an Abrams or an E. D. Hirsch can appeal to a shared understanding of ordinary language and argue from that understanding to the availability of a core of determinate meanings. When Hirsch offers "The air is crisp" as an example of a "verbal meaning," that is, accessible to all speakers of the language, and distinguishes what is sharable and determinate about it from the associations that may, in certain circumstances, accompany it (for example, "I should have eaten less at supper," "Crisp air reminds me of my childhood in Vermont"), he is counting on his readers to agree so completely with his sense of what that shared and normative verbal meaning is that he does not bother even to specify it; and although I have not taken a survey, I would venture to guess that his optimism, with respect to this particular example, is well founded. That is, most, if not all, of his readers immediately understand the utterance as a rough meteorological description predicting a certain quality of the local atmosphere. But the "happiness" of the example, far from making Hirsch's point (which is always, as he has recently reaffirmed, to maintain "the stable determinacy of meaning") makes mine. The obviousness of the utterance's meaning is not a function of the values its words have in a linguistic system that is independent of context; rather, it is because the words are heard as already embedded in a context that they have a meaning that Hirsch can then cite as obvious. One can see this by embedding the words in another context and observing how quickly another "obvious" meaning emerges. Suppose, for example, we came upon "The air is crisp" (which you are even now hearing as Hirsch assumes you hear it) in the middle of a discussion of music ("When the piece is played correctly the air is crisp"); it would immediately be heard as a comment on the performance by an instrument or instruments of a musical air. Moreover, it would *only* be heard that way, and to hear it in Hirsch's way would require an effort on the order of a strain. It could be objected that in Hirsch's text "The air is crisp"$_1$ has no contextual setting at all; it is merely presented, and therefore any agreement as to its meaning must be because of the utterance's acontextual properties. But there *is* a contextual setting and the sign of its presence is precisely the absence of any reference to it. That is, it is impossible even to think of a sentence independently of a context, and when we are asked to consider a sentence for which no context has been specified, we will automatically hear it in the context in which it has been most often encountered. Thus

Hirsch invokes a context by not invoking it; by not surrounding the utterance with circumstances, he directs us to imagine it in the circumstances in which it is most likely to have been produced; and to so imagine it is already to have given it a shape that seems at the moment to be the only one possible.

What conclusions can be drawn from these two examples? First of all, neither my colleague nor the reader of Hirsch's sentence is constrained by the meanings words have in a normative linguistic system; and yet neither is free to confer on an utterance any meaning he likes. Indeed, "confer" is exactly the wrong word because it implies a two-stage procedure in which a reader or hearer first scrutinizes an utterance and *then* gives it a meaning. The argument of the preceding pages can be reduced to the assertion that there is no such first stage, that one hears an utterance within, and not as preliminary to determining, a knowledge of its purposes and concerns, and that to so hear it is already to have assigned it a shape and given it a meaning. In other words, the problem of how meaning is determined is only a problem if there is a point at which its determination has not yet been made, and I am saying that there is no such point.

I am *not* saying that one is never in the position of having to self-consciously figure out what an utterance means. Indeed, my colleague is in just such a position when he is informed by his student that he has not heard her question as she intended it ("No, No, I mean in this class do we believe in poems and things, or is it just us?") and therefore must now figure it out. But the "it" in this (or any other) case is not a collection of words waiting to be assigned a meaning but an utterance whose already assigned meaning has been found to be inappropriate. While my colleague has to begin all over again, he does not have to begin from square one; and indeed he never was at square one, since from the very first his hearing of the student's question was informed by his assumption of what its concerns could possibly be. (That is why he is not "free" even if he is unconstrained by determinate meanings.) It is that assumption rather than his performance within it that is challenged by the student's correction. She tells him that he has mistaken her meaning, but this is not to say that he has made a mistake in combining her words and syntax into a meaningful unit; it is rather that the meaningful unit he immediately discerns is a function of a mistaken identification (made before she speaks) of her intention. He was prepared as she stood before him to hear the kind of thing students ordinarily say on the first day of class, and therefore that is precisely what he heard. He has not misread the text (his is not an error in calculation) but mis*pre*read the text, and if he is to correct himself he must make another (pre)determination of the structure of interests from which her question issues. This, of course, is exactly what he does and the question of how he does it is a crucial one, which can best be answered by first considering the ways in which he *didn't* do it.

He didn't do it by attending to the literal meaning of her response. That is, this is not a case in which someone who has been misunderstood clarifies her meaning by making more explicit, by varying or adding to her words in such a way as to render their sense inescapable. Within the circumstances of utterance as he has assumed them her words are perfectly clear, and what she is doing is asking him to imagine other circumstances in which the same words will be equally, but differently, clear. Nor is it that the words she does add ("No, No, I mean . . .") direct him to those other circumstances by picking them out from an inventory of all possible ones. For this to be the case there would have to be an inherent relationship between the words she speaks and a particular set of circumstances (this would be a higher level literalism) such that any competent speaker of the language hearing those words would immediately be referred to that set. But I have told the story to several competent speakers of the language who simply didn't get it, and one friend—a professor of philosophy—reported to me that in the interval between his hearing the story and my explaining it to him (and just how I was able to do that is another crucial question) he found himself asking "What kind of joke is this and have I missed it?" For a time at least he remained able only to hear "Is there a text in this class" as my colleague first heard it; the student's additional words, far from leading him to another hearing, only made him aware of his distance from it. In contrast, there are those who not only get the story but get it before I tell it; that is, they know in advance what is coming as soon as I say that a colleague of mine was recently asked, "Is there a text in this class?" Who are these people and what is it that makes their comprehension of the story so immediate and easy? Well one could say, without being the least bit facetious, that they are the people who come to hear me speak because they are the people who already know my position on certain matters (or know that I will *have* a position). That is, they hear, "Is there a text in this class?" even as it appears at the beginning of the anecdote (or for that matter as a title of an essay) in the light of their knowledge of what I am likely to do with it. They hear it coming from *me*, in circumstances which have committed me to declaring myself on a range of issues that are sharply delimited.

My colleague was finally able to hear it in just that way, as coming from me, not because I was there in his classroom, nor because the words of the student's question pointed to me in a way that would have been obvious to any hearer, but because he was able to think of me in an office three doors down from his telling students that there are no determinate meanings and that the stability of the text is an illusion. Indeed, as he reports it, the moment of recognition and comprehension consisted of his saying to himself, "Ah, there's one of Fish's victims!" He did not say this because her words identified her as such but because his ability to see her as such informed his perception of her words. The answer to the question "How did he get from her words to the circumstances within which she intended him to hear them?" is that he must already be thinking within those circumstances in order to be able to hear her words as referring to them. The question, then, must be rejected, because it assumes that the construing of sense leads to the identification of the context of utterance rather than the other way around. This does not mean that the context comes first and that once it has been identified the construing of sense can begin. This would be only to reverse the order of precedence, whereas precedence is beside the point because the two actions it would order (the identification of context and the making of sense) occur simultaneously. One does not say "Here I am in a situation; now I can begin to determine what these words mean." To be in a situation is to see the words, these or any other, as already meaningful. For my colleague to realize that he may be confronting one of my victims is *at the same time* to hear what she says as a question about his theoretical beliefs.

But to dispose of one "how" question is only to raise another: if her words do not lead him to the context of her utterance, how does he get there? Why did he think of me telling students that there were no determinate meanings and not think of someone or something else? First of all, he might well have. That is, he might well have guessed that she was coming from another direction (inquiring, let us say, as to whether the focus of this class was to be the poems and essays or our responses to them, a question in the same line of country as hers but quite distinct from it) or he might have simply been stymied, like my philosopher friend, confined, in the absence of an explanation, to his first determination of her concerns and unable to make any sense of her words other than the sense he originally made. How, then, did he do it? In part, he did it because he *could* do it; he was able to get to this context because it was already part of his repertoire for organizing the world and its events. The category "one of Fish's victims" was one he already had and didn't have to work for. Of course, *it* did not always have *him*, in that his world was not always being organized by it, and it certainly did not have him at the beginning of the conversation; but it was available to him, and he to it, and all he had to do was to recall it or be recalled to it for the meanings it subtended to emerge. (Had it not been available to him, the career of his comprehension would have been different and we will come to a consideration of that difference shortly.)

This, however, only pushes our inquiry back further. How or why was he recalled to it? The answer to this question must be probabilistic and it begins with the recognition that when something changes, not everything changes. Although my colleague's understanding of his circumstances is transformed in the course of this conversation, the circumstances are still understood to be academic ones, and within that continuing (if modified) understanding, the directions his thought might take are already severely limited. He still presumes, as he did at first, that the student's question has something to do with university business in general, and with English literature in particular, and it is the organizing rubrics associated with these areas of experience that are likely to occur to him. One of those rubrics is "what-goes-on-in-the-other-classes" and one of those other classes is mine. And so, by a route that is neither entirely unmarked nor wholly determined, he comes to me and to the notion "one of Fish's victims" and to a new construing of what his student has been saying.

Of course that route would have been much more circuitous if the category "one of Fish's victims" was not already available to him as a device for producing intelligibility. Had that device not been part of his repertoire, had he been incapable of being recalled to it because he never knew it in the first place, how would he have proceeded? The answer is that he could not have proceeded at all, which does not mean that one is trapped forever in the categories of understanding at one's disposal (or the categories at whose disposal one is), but that the introduction of new categories or the expansion of old ones to include new (and therefore newly seen) data must always come from the outside or from what is perceived, for a time, to be the outside. In the event that he was unable to identify the structure of her concerns because it had never been his (or he its), it would have been her obligation to explain it to him. And here we run up against another instance of the problem we have been considering all along. She could not explain it to him by varying or adding to her words, by being more explicit, because her words will only be intelligible if he already has the knowledge they are supposed to convey, the knowledge of the assumptions and interests from which they issue. It is clear, then, that she would have to make a new start, although she would not have to start from scratch (indeed, starting from scratch is never a possibility); but she would have to back up to some point at which there was a shared agreement as to what was reasonable to say so that a new and wider basis for agreement could be fashioned. In this particular case, for example, she might begin with the fact that her interlocutor already knows what a text is; that is, he has a way of thinking about it that is responsible for his hearing of her first question as one about bureaucratic classroom procedures. (You will remember that "he" in these sentences is no longer my colleague but someone who does not have his special knowledge.) It is that way of thinking that she must labor to extend or challenge, first, perhaps, by pointing out that there are those who think about the text in other ways, and then by trying to find a category of his own understanding which might serve as an analogue to the understanding he does not yet share. He might, for example, be familiar with those psychologists who argue for the constitutive power of perception, or with Gombrich's theory of the beholder's share, or with that philosophical tradition in which the stability of objects has always been a matter of dispute. The example must remain hypothetical and skeletal, because it can only be fleshed out after a determination of the particular beliefs and assumptions that would make the explanation necessary in the first place; for whatever they were, they would dictate the strategy by which she would work to supplant or change them. It is when such a strategy has been successful that the import of her words will become clear, not because she has reformulated or refined them but because they will now be read or heard within the same system of intelligibility from which they issue.

In short, this hypothetical interlocutor will in time be brought to the same point of comprehension my colleague enjoys when he is able to say to himself, "Ah, there's one of Fish's victims," although presumably he will say something very different to himself if he says anything at all. The difference, however, should not obscure the basic similarities between the two experiences, one reported, the other imagined. In both cases the words that are uttered are immediately heard within a set of assumptions about the direction from which they could possibly be coming, and in both cases what is required is that the hearing occur within another set of assumptions in relation to which the same words ("Is there a text in this class?") will no longer be the same. It is just that while my colleague is able to meet that requirement by calling to mind a context of utterance that is already a part of his repertoire, the repertoire of his hypothetical stand-in must be expanded to include that context so that should he some day be in an analogous situation, he would be able to call it to mind.

The distinction, then, is between already having an ability and having to acquire it, but it is not finally an essential distinction, because the routes by which that ability could be exercised on the one hand, and learned on the other, are so similar. They are similar first of all because they are similarly *not* determined by words. Just as the student's words will not direct my colleague to a context he already has, so will they fail to direct someone not furnished with that context to its discovery. And yet in neither case does the absence of such a mechanical determination mean that the route one travels is randomly found. The change from one structure of understanding to another is not a rupture but a modification of the interests and concerns that are already in place; and because they are already in place, they constrain the direction of their own modification. That is, in both cases the hearer is already in a situation informed by tacitly known purposes and goals, and in both cases he ends up in another situation whose purposes and goals stand in some elaborated relation (of contrast, opposition, expansion, extension) to those they supplant. (The one relation in which they could not stand is no relation at all.) It is just that in one case the network of elaboration (from the text as an obviously physical object to the question of whether or not the text is a physical object) has already been articulated (although not all of its articulations are in focus at one time; selection is always occurring), while in the other the articulation of the network is the business of the teacher (here the student) who begins, necessarily, with what is already given.

The final similarity between the two cases is that in neither is success assured. It was no more inevitable that my colleague tumble to the context of his student's utterance than it would be inevitable that she could introduce that context to someone previously unaware of it; and, indeed, had my colleague remained puzzled (had he simply not thought of me), it would have been necessary for the student to bring him along in a way that was finally indistinguishable from the way she would bring someone to a new knowledge, that is, by beginning with the shape of his present understanding.

I have lingered so long over the unpacking of this anecdote that its relationship to the problem of authority in the classroom and in literary criticism may seem obscure. Let me recall you to it by recalling the contention of Abrams and others that authority depends upon the existence of a determinate core of meanings because in the absence of such a core there is no normative or public way of construing what anyone says or writes, with the result that interpretation becomes a matter of individual and private construings none of which is subject to challenge or correction. In literary criticism this means that no interpretation can be said to be better or worse than any other, and in the classroom this means that we have no answer to the student who says my interpretation is as valid as yours. It is only if there is a shared basis of agreement at once guiding interpretation and providing a mechanism for deciding between interpretations that a total and debilitating relativism can be avoided.

But the point of my analysis has been to show that while "Is there a text in this class?" does not have a determinate meaning, a meaning that survives the sea change of situations, in any situation we might imagine the meaning of the utterance is either perfectly clear or capable, in the course of time, of being clarified. What is it that makes this possible, if it is not the "possibilities and norms" already encoded in language? How does communication ever occur if not by reference to a public and stable norm? The answer, implicit in everything I have already said, is that communication occurs within situations and that to be in a situation is already to be in possession of (or to be possessed by) a structure of assumptions, of practices understood to be relevant in relation to purposes and goals that are already in place; and it is within the assumption of these purposes and goals that any utterance is *immediately* heard. I stress immediately because it seems to me that the problem of communication, as someone like Abrams poses it, is a problem only because he assumes a distance between one's receiving of an utterance and the determination of its meaning—a kind of dead space when one has only the words and then faces the task of construing them. If there were such a space, a moment before interpretation began, then it would be necessary to have recourse to some mechanical and algorithmic procedure by means of which meanings could be calculated and in relation to which one could recognize mistakes. What I have been arguing is that meanings come already calculated, not because of norms embedded in the language but because language is always perceived, from the very first, within a structure of norms. That structure, however, is not abstract and independent but social; and therefore it is not a single structure with a privileged relationship to the process of communication as it occurs in any situation but a structure that changes when one situation, with its assumed background of practices, purposes, and goals, has given way to another. In other words, the shared basis of agreement sought by Abrams and others is never not already found, although it is not always the same one.

Many will find in this last sentence, and in the argument to which it is a conclusion, nothing more than a sophisticated version of the relativism they fear. It will do no good, they say, to speak of norms and standards that are context specific, because this is merely to authorize an infinite plurality of norms and standards, and we are still left without any way of adjudicating between them and between the competing systems of value of which they are functions. In short, to have many standards is to have no standards at all.

On one level this counterargument is unassailable, but on another level it is finally beside the point. It is unassailable as a general and theoretical conclusion: the positing of context- or institution-specific norms surely rules out the possibility of a norm whose validity would be recognized by everyone, no matter what his situation. But it is beside the point for any particular individual, for since everyone is situated somewhere, there is no one for whom the absence of an asituational norm would be of any practical consequence, in the sense that his performance or his confidence in his ability to perform would be impaired. So that while it is generally true that to have many standards is to have none at all, it is not true for anyone in particular (for there is no one in a position to speak "generally"), and therefore it is a truth of which one can say "it doesn't mater."

In other words, while relativism is a position one can entertain, it is not a position one can occupy. No one can *be* a relativist, because no one can achieve the distance from his own beliefs and assumptions which would result in their being no more authoritative *for him* than the beliefs and assumptions held by others, or, for that matter, the beliefs and assumptions he himself used to hold. The fear that in a world of indifferently authorized norms and values the individual is without a basis for action is groundless because no one is indifferent to the norms and values that enable his consciousness. It is in the name of personally held (in fact they are doing the holding) norms and values that the individual acts and argues, and he does so with the full confidence that attends belief. When his beliefs change, the norms and values to which he once gave unthinking assent will have been demoted to the status of opinions and become the objects of an analytical and critical attention; but that attention will itself be enabled by a new set of norms and values that are, for the time being, as unexamined and undoubted as those they displace. The point is that there is never a moment when one believes nothing, when consciousness is innocent of any and all categories of thought, and whatever categories of thought are operative at a given moment will serve as an undoubted ground.

Here, I suspect, a defender of determinate meaning would cry "solipsist" and argue that a confidence that had its source in the individual's categories of thought would have no public value. That is, unconnected to any shared and stable system of meanings, it would not enable one to transact the verbal business of everyday life; a shared intelligibility would be impossible in a world where everyone was trapped in the circle of his own assumptions and opinions. The reply to this is that an individual's assumptions and opinions are not "his own" in any sense that would give body to the fear of solipsism. That is, *he* is not their origin (in fact it might be more accurate to say that they are his); rather, it is their prior availability which delimits in advance the paths that his consciousness can possibly take. When my colleague is in the act of construing his student's question ("Is there a text in this class?"), none of the interpretive strategies at his disposal are uniquely his, in the sense that he thought them up; they follow from his preunderstanding of the interests and goals that could possibly animate the speech of someone functioning within the institution of academic America, interests and goals that are the particular property of no one in particular but which link everyone for whom their assumption is so habitual as to be unthinking. They certainly link my colleague and his student, who are able to communicate and even to reason about one another's intentions, not, however, because their interpretive efforts are constrained by the shape of an independent language but because their shared understanding of what could possibly be at stake in a classroom situation results in language appearing to them in the same shape (or successions of shapes). That shared understanding is the basis of the confidence with which they speak and reason, but its categories are their own only in the sense that as actors within an institution they automatically fall heir to the institution's way of making sense, its systems of intelligibility. That is why it is so hard for someone whose very being is defined by his position within an institution (and if not this one, then some other) to explain to someone outside it a practice or a meaning that seems to him to require no explanation, because he regards it as natural. Such a person, when pressed, is likely to say, "but that's just the way it's done" or "but isn't it obvious" and so testify that the practice of meaning in question is community property, as, in a sense, he is too.

We see then that (1) communication does occur, despite the absence of an independent and context-free system of meanings, that (2) those who participate in this communication do so confidently rather than provisionally (they are not relativists), and that (3) while their confidence has its source in a set of beliefs, those beliefs are not individual-specific or idiosyncratic but communal and conventional (they are not solipsists).

Of course, solipsism and relativism are what Abrams and Hirsch fear and what lead them to argue for the necessity of determinate meaning. But if, rather than acting on their own, interpreters act as extensions of an institutional community, solipsism and relativism are removed as fears because they are not possible modes of being. That is to say, the condition required for someone to be a solipsist or relativist, the condition of being independent of institutional assumptions and free to originate one's own purposes and goals, could never be realized, and therefore there is no point in trying to guard against it. Abrams, Hirsch, and company spend a great deal of time in a search for the ways to limit and constrain interpretation, but if the example of my colleague and his student can be generalized (and obviously I think it can be), what they are searching for is never not already found. In short, my message to them is finally not challenging, but consoling—not to worry.

Nina Baym

Melodramas of Beset Manhood

1981

When applied to a literary tradition, the word canon refers to a list of established texts, classic works with which educated readers are expected to be familiar. In its original religious usage, a canon was a list of biblical books constituting Holy Scriptures, and books in a literary canon likewise take on a quasi-religious quality of sanctified masterpieces. These are the books that are taught in schools and colleges and discussed by literary critics. Beginning about 1970, a newly prominent group of feminist critics began to ask why so few works by women were to be found in the canon of American literature. History clearly shows that women were writing, publishing, and indeed achieving celebrity as writers throughout the history of the United States, yet the books they wrote seemed seldom to achieve canonical status. In fact, as Nina Baym (b. 1936) claims in the essay that follows, it was often the very popularity of women's books that prevented the elite literary establishment from taking them seriously as "great literature." The new feminist critics refused to accept the blanket assertion that books by women tended to be less serious and of less lasting merit than those by men.

One of the principal functions of American feminist criticism, then, has been to rediscover women writers who have been forgotten. Another has been to challenge the standards of taste by which a writer becomes canonized in the national literary tradition. This second function is exemplified by Baym's essay "Melodramas of Beset Manhood." She announces her subject clearly in the first sentence when she writes, "This paper is about American literary criticism rather than American literature." Such criticism about criticism is sometimes referred to under the name of metacriticism.

Baym's primary argument is that American literature was long judged not according to its literary merit but according to its degree of "Americanness." At the same time, the most truly "American" story was supposed to be that of a hero who rejected or escaped from the oppressive bonds of society and turned on his own to the taming of the American landscape. Using numerous examples, mostly from nineteenth-century literature by men and the criticism of that literature (also by men), Baym shows how both the society escaped and the land tamed are represented *as feminine in character. Since women are unlikely to represent themselves in this negative light and tell this supposedly quintessentially American story, their works have long remained outside the mainstream canon.*

Though not practicing deconstruction here, Baym's project nonetheless shares certain qualities with that of her poststructuralist contemporaries. Like them, she questions the very mechanism by which literary hierarchies are constructed and certain texts become "privileged." This same sort of rigorous metacriticism has also proved useful for minority and gay critics, as well as others who wish to either broaden the canon or eliminate altogether the idea of the canon as a controlling force in literary education. Further discussions of canon formation, one of the major battle grounds in late twentieth-century literary criticism, may be found in the essays by Sandra M. Gilbert and Susan Gubar (page 683) and Eve Kosofsky Sedgwick (page 744).

THIS PAPER is about American literary criticism rather than American literature. It proceeds from the assumption that we never read American literature directly or freely, but always through the perspective allowed by theories. Theories account for the inclusion and exclusion of texts in anthologies, and theories account for the way we read them. My concern is with the fact that the theories controlling our reading of American literature have led to the exclusion of women authors from the canon.

Let me use my own practice as a case in point. In 1977 there was published a collection of essays on images of women in major British and American literature, to which I contributed.[1] The American field was divided chronologically among six critics, with four essays covering literature written prior to World War II. Taking seriously the charge that we were to focus only on the major figures, the four of us—working quite independently of each other—selected altogether only four women writers. Three of these were from the earliest period, a period which predates the novel: the poet Anne Bradstreet and the two diarists Mary Rowlandson and Sarah Kemble Knight. The fourth was Emily Dickinson. For the period between 1865 and 1940 no women were cited at all. The message that we—who were taking women as our subject—conveyed was clear: there have been almost no major women writers in America; the major novelists have all been men.

Now, when we wrote our essays we were not undertaking to reread all American literature and make our own decisions as to who the major authors were. That is the point: we accepted the going canon of major authors. As late as 1977, that canon did not include any women novelists. Yet, the critic who goes beyond what is accepted and tries to look at the totality of literary production in America quickly discovers that women authors have been active since the earliest days of settlement. Commercially and numerically they have probably dominated American literature since the middle of the

[1] Marlene Springer, ed., *What Manner of Woman: Essays on English and American Life and Literature* (New York: New York Univ. Press, 1977). [All notes are Baym's.]

nineteenth century. As long ago as 1854, Nathaniel Hawthorne complained to his publisher about the "damn'd mob of scribbling women" whose writings—he fondly imagined—were diverting the public from his own.

Names and figures help make this dominance clear. In the years between 1774 and 1799—from the calling of the First Continental Congress to the close of the eighteenth century—a total of thirty-eight original works of fiction were published in this country.[2] Nine of these, appearing pseudonymously or anonymously, have not yet been attributed to any author. The remaining twenty-nine are the work of eighteen individuals, of whom four are women. One of these women, Susannah Rowson, wrote six of them, or more than a fifth of the total. Her most popular work, *Charlotte* (also known as *Charlotte Temple*), was printed three times in the decade it was published, nineteen times between 1800 and 1810, and eighty times by the middle of the nineteenth century. A novel by a second of the four women, Hannah Foster, was called *The Coquette* and had thirty editions by mid-nineteenth century. *Uncle Tom's Cabin*, by a woman, is probably the all-time biggest seller in American history. A woman, Mrs. E.D.E.N. Southworth, was probably the most widely read novelist in the nineteenth century. How is it possible for a critic or historian of American literature to leave these books, and these authors, out of the picture?

I see three partial explanations for the critical invisibility of the many active women authors in America. The first is simple bias. The critic does not like the idea of women as writers, does not believe that women can be writers, and hence does not see them even when they are right before his eyes. His theory or his standards may well be nonsexist but his practice is not. Certainly, an *a priori* resistance to recognizing women authors as serious writers has functioned powerfully in the mindset of a number of influential critics. One can amusingly demonstrate the inconsistencies between standard and practice in such critics, show how their minds slip out of gear when they are confronted with a woman author. But this is only a partial explanation.

A second possibility is that, in fact, women have not written the kind of work that we call "excellent," for reasons that are connected with their gender although separable from it. This is a serious possibility. For example, suppose we required a dense texture of classical allusion in all works that we called excellent. Then, the restriction of a formal classical education to men would have the effect of restricting authorship of excellent literature to men. Women would not have written excellent literature because social conditions hindered them. The reason, though gender-connected, would not be gender per se.

The point here is that the notion of the artist, or of excellence, has efficacy in a given time and reflects social realities. The idea of "good" literature is not only a personal preference, it is also a cultural preference. We can all think of species of women's literature that do not aim in any way to achieve

[2]See Lyle Wright, *American Fiction 1774–1850* (San Marino, Calif.: Huntington Library Press, 1969).

literary excellence as society defines it: e.g., the "Harlequin Romances." Until recently, only a tiny proportion of literary women aspired to artistry and literary excellence in the terms defined by their own culture. There tended to be a sort of immediacy in the ambitions of literary women leading them to professionalism rather than artistry, by choice as well as by social pressure and opportunity. The gender-related restrictions were really operative, and the responsible critic cannot ignore them. But again, these restrictions are only partly explanatory.

There are, finally, I believe, gender-related restrictions that do not arise out of cultural realities contemporary with the writing woman, but out of later critical theories. These theories may follow naturally from cultural realities pertinent to their own time, but they impose their concerns anachronistically, after the fact, on an earlier period. If one accepts current theories of American literature, one accepts as a consequence—perhaps not deliberately but nevertheless inevitably—a literature that is essentially male. This is the partial explanation that I shall now develop.

Let us begin where the earliest theories of American literature begin, with the hypothesis that American literature is to be judged less by its form than its content. Traditionally, one ascertains literary excellence by comparing a writer's work with standards of performance that have been established by earlier authors, where formal mastery and innovation are paramount. But from its historical beginnings, American literary criticism has assumed that literature produced in this nation would have to be groundbreaking, equal to the challenge of the new nation, and completely original. Therefore, it could not be judged by referring it back to earlier achievements. The earliest American literary critics began to talk about the "most American" work rather than the "best" work because they knew no way to find out the best other than by comparing American to British writing. Such a criticism struck them as both unfair and unpatriotic. We had thrown off the political shackles of England; it would not do for us to be servile in our literature. Until a tradition of American literature developed its own inherent forms, the early critic looked for a standard of Americanness rather than a standard of excellence. Inevitably, perhaps, it came to seem that the quality of "Americanness," whatever it might be, *constituted* literary excellence for American authors. Beginning as a nationalistic enterprise, American literary criticism and theory has retained a nationalist orientation to this day.

Of course, the idea of Americanness is even more vulnerable to subjectivity than the idea of the best. When they speak of "most American," critics seldom mean the statistically most representative or most typical, the most read or the most sold. They have some qualitative essence in mind, and frequently their work develops as an explanation of this idea of "American" rather than a description and evaluation of selected authors. The predictable recurrence of the term "America" or "American" in works of literary criticism treating a dozen or fewer authors indicates that the critic has chosen his authors on the basis of their conformity to his idea of what is truly American. For examples: *American Renaissance, The Romance in America, Symbolism and*

American Literature, Form and Fable in American Fiction, The American Adam, The American Novel and Its Tradition, The Place of Style in American Literature (a subtitle), *The Poetics of American Fiction* (another subtitle). But an idea of what is American is no more than an idea, needing demonstration. The critic all too frequently ends up using his chosen authors as demonstrations of Americanness, arguing through them to his definition.

So Marius Bewley explains in *The Eccentric Design* that "for the American artist there was no social surface responsive to his touch. The scene was crude, even beyond successful satire," but later, in a concluding chapter titled "The Americanness of the American Novel," he agrees that "this 'tradition' as I have set it up here has no room for the so-called realists and naturalists."[3] F. O. Matthiessen, whose *American Renaissance* enshrines five authors, explains that "the one common denominator of my five writers, uniting even Hawthorne and Whitman, was their devotion to the possibilities of democracy."[4] The jointly written *Literary History of the United States* proclaims in its "address to the reader" that American literary history "will be a history of the books of the great and the near-great writers in a literature which is most revealing when studied as a by-product of American experience."[5] And Joel Porte announces confidently in *The Romance in America* that "students of American literature . . . have provided a solid theoretical basis for establishing that the rise and growth of fiction in this country is dominated by our authors' conscious adherence to a tradition of non-realistic romance sharply at variance with the broadly novelistic mainstream of English writing. When there has been disagreement among recent critics as to the contours of American fiction, it has usually disputed, not the existence *per se* of a romance tradition, but rather the question of which authors, themes, and stylistic strategies *deserve* to be placed with certainty at the heart of that tradition" (emphasis added).[6]

Before he is through, the critic has had to insist that some works in America are much more American than others, and he is as busy excluding certain writers as "un-American" as he is including others. Such a proceeding in the political arena would be extremely suspect, but in criticism it has been the method of choice. Its final result goes far beyond the conclusion that only a handful of American works are very good. *That* statement is one we could agree with, since very good work is rare in any field. But it is odd indeed to argue that only a handful of American works are really American.[7]

Despite the theoretical room for an infinite number of definitions of Americanness, critics have generally agreed on it—although the shifting

---

[3] Marius Bewley, *The Eccentric Design* (New York: Columbia Univ. Press, 1963), 15, 291.

[4] F. O. Matthiessen, *American Renaissance* (New York: Oxford Univ. Press, 1941), ix.

[5] Robert E. Spiller et al., eds., *Literary History of the United States* (New York: Macmillan, 1959), xix.

[6] Joel Porte, *The Romance in America* (Middletown, Conn.: Wesleyan Univ. Press, 1969), ix.

[7] A good essay on this topic is William C. Spengemann's "What Is American Literature?" *CentR*, 22 (1978), 119–38.

canon suggests that agreement may be a matter of fad rather than fixed objective qualities.[8] First, America as a nation must be the ultimate subject of the work. The author must be writing about aspects of experience and character that are American only, setting Americans off from other people and the country from other nations. The author must be writing his story specifically to display these aspects, to meditate on them, and to derive from them some generalizations and conclusions about "the" American experience. To Matthiessen the topic is the possibilities of democracy; Sacvan Bercovitch (in *The Puritan Origins of the American Self*) finds it in American identity. Such content excludes, at one extreme, stories about universals, aspects of experience common to people in a variety of times and places — mutability, mortality, love, childhood, family, betrayal, loss. Innocence versus experience is an admissible theme *only* if innocence is the essence of the American character, for example.

But at the other extreme, the call for an overview of America means that detailed, circumstantial portrayals of some aspect of American life are also, peculiarly, inappropriate: stories of wealthy New Yorkers, Yugoslavian immigrants, southern rustics. Jay B. Hubbell rather ingratiatingly admits as much when he writes, "in both my teaching and my research I had a special interest in literature as a reflection of American life and thought. This circumstance may explain in part why I found it difficult to appreciate the merits of the expatriates and why I was slow in doing justice to some of the New Critics. I was repelled by the sordid subject matter found in some of the novels written by Dreiser, Dos Passos, Faulkner, and some others."[9] Richard Poirier writes that "the books which in my view constitute a distinctive American tradition . . . resist within their pages forces of environment that otherwise dominate the world" and he distinguishes this kind from "the fiction of Mrs. Wharton, Dreiser, or Howells."[10] The *Literary History of the United States* explains that "historically, [Edith Wharton] is likely to survive as the memorialist of a dying aristocracy" (1211). And so on. These exclusions abound in all the works which form the stable core of American literary criticism at this time.

Along with Matthiessen, the most influential exponent of this exclusive Americanness is Lionel Trilling, and his work has particular applicability because it concentrates on the novel form. Here is a famous passage from his 1940 essay, "Reality in America," in which Trilling is criticizing Vernon Parrington's selection of authors in *Main Currents in American Thought*:

> A culture is not a flow, nor even a confluence; the form of its existence is struggle — or at least debate — it is nothing if not a dialectic. And in any culture there are likely to be certain artists who contain a

---

[8] See Jay B. Hubbell, *Who Are the Major American Authors?* (Durham, N.C.: Duke Univ. Press, 1972).
[9] Ibid., 335–36.
[10] Richard Poirier, *A World Elsewhere: The Place of Style in American Literature* (New York: Oxford Univ. Press, 1966), 5.

large part of the dialectic within themselves, their meaning and power lying in their contradictions; they contain within themselves, it may be said, the very essence of the culture. To throw out Poe because he cannot be conveniently fitted into a theory of American culture . . . to find his gloom to be merely personal and eccentric . . . as Hawthorne's was . . . to judge Melville's response to American life to be less noble than that of Bryant or of Greeley, to speak of Henry James as an escapist . . . this is not merely to be mistaken in aesthetic judgment. Rather it is to examine without attention and from the point of view of a limited and essentially arrogant conception of reality the documents which are in some respects the most suggestive testimony to what America was and is, and of course to get no answer from them.[11]

Trilling's immediate purpose is to exclude Greeley and Bryant from the list of major authors and to include Poe, Melville, Hawthorne, and James. We probably share Trilling's aesthetic judgment. But note that he does not base his judgment on aesthetic grounds; indeed, he dismisses aesthetic judgment with the word "merely." He argues that Parrington has picked the wrong artists because he doesn't understand the culture. Culture is his real concern.

But what makes Trilling's notion of culture more valid than Parrington's? Trilling really has no argument; he resorts to such value-laden rhetoric as "a limited and essentially arrogant conception of reality" precisely because he cannot objectively establish his version of culture over Parrington's. For the moment, there are two significant conclusions to draw from this quotation. First, the disagreement is over the nature of our culture. Second, there is no disagreement over the value of literature—it is valued as a set of "documents" which provide "suggestive testimony to what America was and is."

One might think that an approach like this which is subjective, circular, and in some sense nonliterary or even antiliterary would not have had much effect. But clearly Trilling was simply carrying on a longstanding tradition of searching for cultural essence, and his essays gave the search a decided and influential direction toward the notion of cultural essence as some sort of tension. Trilling succeeded in getting rid of Bryant and Greeley, and his choice of authors is still dominant. They all turn out—and not by accident—to be white, middle-class, male, of Anglo-Saxon derivation or at least from an ancestry which has settled in this country before the big waves of immigration which began around the middle of the nineteenth century. In every case, however, the decision made by these men to become professional authors pushed them slightly to one side of the group to which they belonged. This slight alienation permitted them to belong, and yet not to belong, to the so-called "mainstream." These two aspects of their situation—their membership in the dominant middle-class white Anglo-Saxon group, and their modest alienation from it—defined their boundaries, enabling them to "contain

[11] Lionel Trilling, *The Liberal Imagination* (New York: Anchor, 1950), 7–9.

within themselves" the "contradictions" that, in Trilling's view, constitute the "very essence of the culture." I will call the literature they produced, which Trilling assesses so highly, a "consensus criticism of the consensus."

This idea plainly excludes many groups but it might not seem necessarily to exclude women. In fact, nineteenth-century women authors were overwhelmingly white, middle-class, and anglo-Saxon in origin. Something more than what is overtly stated by Trilling (and others cited below) is added to exclude them. What critics have done is to assume, for reasons shortly to be expounded, that the women writers invariably represented the consensus, rather than the criticism of it; to assume that their gender made them part of the consensus in a way that prevented them from partaking in the criticism. The presence of these women and their works is acknowledged in literary theory and history as an impediment and obstacle, that which the essential American literature had to criticize as its chief task.

So, in his lively and influential book of 1960, *Love and Death in the American Novel*, Leslie Fiedler describes women authors as creators of the "flagrantly bad best-seller" against which "our best fictionists"—all male—have had to struggle for "their integrity and their livelihoods."[12] And, in a 1978 reader's introduction to an edition of Charles Brockden Brown's *Wieland*, Sydney J. Krause and S. W. Reid write as follows:

> What it meant for Brown personally, and belles lettres in America historically, that he should have decided to write professionally is a story unto itself. Americans simply had no great appetite for serious literature in the early decades of the Republic—certainly nothing of the sort with which they devoured . . . the ubiquitous melodramas of beset womanhood, "tales of truth," like Susanna Rowson's *Charlotte Temple* and Hannah Foster's *The Coquette*.[13]

There you see what has happened to the woman writer. She has entered literary history as the enemy. The phrase "tales of truth" is put in quotes by the critics, as though to cast doubt on the very notion that a "melodrama of beset womanhood" could be either true or important. At the same time, ironically, they are proposing for our serious consideration, as a candidate for intellectually engaging literature, a highly melodramatic novel with an improbable plot, inconsistent characterizations, and excesses of style that have posed tremendous problems for all students of Charles Brockden Brown. But, by this strategy it becomes possible to begin major American fiction historically with male rather than female authors. The certainty here that stories about women could not contain the essence of American culture means that the matter of American experience is inherently male. And this makes it highly unlikely that American women would write fiction encompassing such

---

[12] Leslie Fiedler, *Love and Death in the American Novel* (New York: Criterion Books, 1960), 93.

[13] Charles Brockden Brown, *Wieland*, ed. Sydney J. Krause and S. W. Reid (Kent, Ohio: Kent State Univ. Press, 1978), xii.

experience. I would suggest that the theoretical model of a story which may become the vehicle of cultural essence is: "a melodrama of beset manhood." This melodrama is presented in a fiction which, as we'll later see, can be taken as representative of the author's literary experience, his struggle for integrity and livelihood against flagrantly bad best-sellers written by women. Personally beset in a way that epitomizes the tensions of our culture, the male author produces his melodramatic testimony to our culture's essence—so the theory goes.

Remember that the search for cultural essence demands a relatively uncircumstantial kind of fiction, one which concentrates on national universals (if I may be pardoned the paradox). This search has identified a sort of nonrealistic narrative, a romance, a story free to catch an essential, idealized American character, to intensify his essence and convey his experience in a way that ignores details of an actual social milieu. This nonrealistic or antisocial aspect of American fiction is noted—as a fault—by Trilling in a 1947 essay, "Manners, Morals, and the Novel." Curiously, Trilling here attacks the same group of writers he had rescued from Parrington in "Reality in America." But, never doubting that his selection represents "the" American authors, he goes ahead with the task that really interests him—criticizing the culture through its representative authors. He writes:

> The novel in America diverges from its classic [i.e., British] intention which . . . is the investigation of the problem of reality beginning in the social field. The fact is that American writers of genius have not turned their minds to society. Poe and Melville were quite apart from it; the reality they sought was only tangential to society. Hawthorne was acute when he insisted that he did not write novels but romances —he thus expressed his awareness of the lack of social texture in his work. . . . In America in the nineteenth century, Henry James was alone in knowing that to scale the moral and aesthetic heights in the novel one had to use the ladder of social observation.[14]

Within a few years after publication of Trilling's essay, a group of Americanists took its rather disapproving description of American novelists and found in this nonrealism or romanticism the essentially American quality they had been seeking. The idea of essential Americanness then developed in such influential works of criticism as *Virgin Land* by Henry Nash Smith (1950), *Symbolism and American Literature* by Charles Feidelson (1953), *The American Adam* by R. W. B. Lewis (1955), *The American Novel and Its Tradition* by Richard Chase (1957), and *Form and Fable in American Fiction* by Daniel G. Hoffman (1961). These works, and others like them, were of sufficiently high critical quality, and sufficiently like each other, to compel assent to the picture of American literature that they presented. They used sophisticated New Critical close-reading techniques to identify a myth of America which

---

[14] *The Liberal Imagination*, 206.

had nothing to do with the classical fictionist's task of chronicling probable people in recognizable social situations.

The myth narrates a confrontation of the American individual, the pure American self divorced from specific social circumstances, with the promise offered by the idea of America. This promise is the deeply romantic one that in this new land, untrammeled by history and social accident, a person will be able to achieve complete self-definition. Behind this promise is the assurance that individuals come before society, that they exist in some meaningful sense prior to, and apart from, societies in which they happen to find themselves. The myth also holds that, as something artificial and secondary to human nature, society exerts an unmitigatedly destructive pressure on individuality. To depict it at any length would be a waste of artistic time; and there is only one way to relate it to the individual—as an adversary.

One may believe all this and yet look in vain for a way to tell a believable story that could free the protagonist from society or offer the promise of such freedom, because nowhere on earth do individuals live apart from social groups. But in America, given the original reality of large tracts of wilderness, the idea seems less a fantasy, more possible in reality or at least more believable in literary treatment. Thus it is that the essential quality of America comes to reside in its unsettled wilderness and the opportunities that such a wilderness offers to the individual as the medium on which he may inscribe, unhindered, his own destiny and his own nature.

As the nineteenth century wore on, and settlements spread across the wilderness, the struggle of the individual against society became more and more central to the myth; where, let's say, Thoreau could leave in Chapter I of *Walden*, Huckleberry Finn has still not made his break by the end of Chapter XLII (the conclusion) of the book that bears his name. Yet, one finds a struggle against society as early as the earliest Leatherstocking tale (*The Pioneers*, 1823). In a sense, this supposed promise of America has always been known to be delusory. Certainly by the twentieth century the myth has been transmuted into an avowedly hopeless quest for unencumbered space (*On the Road*), or the evocation of flight for its own sake (*Rabbit, Run* and *Henderson the Rain King*), or as pathetic acknowledgment of loss—e.g., the close of *The Great Gatsby* where the narrator Nick Carraway summons up "the old island here that flowered once for Dutch sailors' eyes—a fresh, green breast of the new world . . . the last and greatest of all human dreams" where man is "face to face for the last time in history with something commensurate to his capacity for wonder."

We are all very familiar with this myth of America in its various fashionings and owing to the selective vision that has presented this myth to us as the whole story, many of us are unaware of how much besides it has been created by literary Americans. Keeping our eyes on this myth, we need to ask whether anything about it puts it outside women's reach. In one sense, and on one level, the answer is no. The subject of this myth is supposed to stand for human nature, and if men and women alike share a common human nature, then all can respond to its values, its promises, and its frustrations. And in fact as a teacher I find women students responsive to the myth insofar as its protagonist is concerned. It is true, of course, that in order to represent some kind of believable flight into the wilderness, one must select a protagonist with a certain believable mobility, and mobility has until recently been a male prerogative in our society. Nevertheless, relatively few men are actually mobile to the extent demanded by the story, and hence the story is really not much more vicarious, in this regard, for women than for men. The problem is thus not to be located in the protagonist or his gender per se; the problem is with the other participants in his story—the entrammeling society and the promising landscape. For both of these are depicted in unmistakably feminine terms, and this gives a sexual character to the protagonist's story which does, indeed, limit its applicability to women. And this sexual definition has melodramatic, misogynist implications.

In these stories, the encroaching, constricting, destroying society is represented with particular urgency in the figure of one or more women. There are several possible reasons why this might be so. It seems to be a fact of life that we all—women and men alike—experience social conventions and responsibilities and obligations first in the persons of women, since women are entrusted by society with the task of rearing young children. Not until he reaches midadolescence does the male connect up with other males whose primary task is socialization; but at about this time—if he is heterosexual—his lovers and spouses become the agents of a permanent socialization and domestication. Thus, although women are not the source of social power, they are experienced as such. And although not all women are engaged in socializing the young, the young do not encounter women who are not. So from the point of view of the young man, the only kind of women who exist are entrappers and domesticators.

For heterosexual man, these socializing women are also the locus of powerful attraction. First, because everybody has social and conventional instincts; second, because his deepest emotional attachments are to women. This attraction gives urgency and depth to the protagonist's rejection of society. To do it, he must project onto the woman those attractions that he feels, and cast her in the melodramatic role of temptress, antagonist, obstacle—a character whose mission in life seems to be to ensnare him and deflect him from life's important purposes of self-discovery and self-assertion. (A Puritan would have said: from communion with Divinity.) As Richard Chase writes in *The American Novel and Its Tradition*, "The myth requires celibacy." It is partly against his own sexual urges that the male must struggle, and so he perceives the socializing and domesticating woman as a doubly powerful threat; for this reason, Chase goes on to state, neither Cooper nor "any other American novelist until the age of James and Edith Wharton" could imagine "a fully developed woman of sexual age."[15] Yet in making this statement, Chase is talking about his myth rather than Cooper's. (One should add that, for a homosexual male, the demands of society that he link himself for life to

[15] Richard Chase, *The American Novel and Its Tradition* (New York: Anchor, 1957), 55, 64.

a woman make for a particularly misogynist version of this aspect of the American myth, for the hero is propelled not by a rejected attraction, but by true revulsion.) Both heterosexual and homosexual versions of the myth co-operate with the hero's perceptions and validate the notion of woman as threat.

Such a portrayal of women is likely to be uncongenial, if not basically incomprehensible, to a woman. It is not likely that women will write books in which women play this part; and it is by no means the case that most novels by American men reproduce such a scheme. Even major male authors prominent in the canon have other ways of depicting women; e.g., Cooper's *Pathfinder* and *The Pioneers,* Hemingway's *For Whom the Bell Tolls,* Fitzgerald's *The Beautiful and Damned.* The novels of Henry James and William Dean Howells pose a continual challenge to the masculinist bias of American critical theory. And in one work—*The Scarlet Letter*—a "fully developed woman of sexual age" who is the novel's protagonist has been admitted into the canon, but only by virtue of strenuous critical revisions of the text that remove Hester Prynne from the center of the novel and make her subordinate to Arthur Dimmesdale.

So Leslie Fiedler, in *Love and Death in the American Novel,* writes this of *The Scarlet Letter:*

> It is certainly true, in terms of the plot, that Chillingworth drives the minister toward confession and penance, while Hester would have lured him to evasion and flight. But this means, for all of Hawthorne's equivocations, that the eternal feminine does not draw us on toward grace, rather that the woman promises only madness and damnation.... [Hester] is the female temptress of Puritan mythology, but also, though sullied, the secular madonna of sentimental Protestantism (236).

In the rhetorical "us" Fiedler presumes that all readers are men, that the novel is an act of communication among and about males. His characterization of Hester as one or another myth or image makes it impossible for the novel to be in any way about Hester as a human being. Giving the novel so highly specific a gender reference, Fiedler makes it inaccessible to women and limits its reference to men in comparison to the issues that Hawthorne was treating in the story. Not the least of these issues was, precisely, the human reference of a woman's tale.

Amusingly, then, since he has produced this warped reading, Fiedler goes on to condemn the novel for its sexual immaturity. *The Scarlet Letter* is integrated into Fiedler's general exposure of the inadequacies of the American male—inadequacies which, as his treatment of Hester shows, he holds women responsible for. The melodrama here is not Hawthorne's, but Fiedler's—the American critic's melodrama of beset manhood. Of course, women authors as major writers are notably and inevitably absent from Fiedler's chronicle.

In fact many books by women—including such major authors as Edith Wharton, Ellen Glasgow, and Willa Cather—project a version of the particular myth we are speaking of but cast the main character as a woman. When a woman takes the central role, it follows naturally that the socializer and domesticator will be a man. This is the situation in *The Scarlet Letter*. Hester is beset by the male reigning oligarchy and by Dimmesdale, who passively tempts her and is responsible for fathering her child. Thereafter, Hester (as the myth requires) elects celibacy, as do many heroines in versions of this myth by women: Thea in Cather's *The Song of the Lark,* Dorinda in Glasgow's *Barren Ground,* Anna Leath in Wharton's *The Reef.* But what is written in the criticism about these celibate women? They are said to be untrue to the imperatives of their gender, which require marriage, childbearing, domesticity. Instead of being read as a woman's version of the myth, such novels are read as stories of the frustration of female nature. Stories of female frustration are not perceived as commenting on, or containing, the essence of our culture, and so we don't find them in the canon.

So the role of entrapper and impediment in the melodrama of beset manhood is reserved for women. Also, the role of the beckoning wilderness, the attractive landscape, is given a deeply feminine quality. Landscape is deeply imbued with female qualities, as society is; but where society is menacing and destructive, landscape is compliant and supportive. It has the attributes simultaneously of a virginal bride and a nonthreatening mother; its female qualities are articulated with respect to a male angle of vision: what can nature do for me, asks the hero, what can it give me?

Of course, nature has been feminine and maternal from time immemorial, and Henry Nash Smith's *Virgin Land* picks up a timeless archetype in its title. The basic nature of the image leads one to forget about its potential for imbuing any story in which it is used with sexual meanings, and the gender implications of a female landscape have only recently begun to be studied. Recently, Annette Kolodny has studied the traditional canon from this approach.[16] She theorizes that the hero, fleeing a society that has been imagined as feminine, then imposes on nature some ideas of women which, no longer subject to the correcting influence of real-life experience, become more and more fantastic. The fantasies are infantile, concerned with power, mastery, and total gratification: the all-nurturing mother, the all-passive bride. Whether one accepts all the Freudian or Jungian implications of her argument, one cannot deny the way in which heroes of American myth turn to nature as sweetheart and nurture, anticipating the satisfaction of all desires through her and including among these the desires for mastery and power. A familiar passage that captures these ideas is one already quoted: Carraway's evocation of the "fresh green breast" of the new world. The fresh greenness is the virginity that offers itself to the sailors, but the breast promises maternal

---

[16] Annette Kolodny, *The Lay of the Land* (Chapel Hill: Univ. of North Carolina Press, 1975).

solace and delight. *The Great Gatsby* contains our two images of women: while Carraway evokes the impossible dream of a maternal landscape, he blames a nonmaternal woman, the socialite Daisy, for her failure to satisfy Gatsby's desires. The true adversary, of course, is Tom Buchanan, but he is hidden, as it were, behind Daisy's skirts.

I have said that women are not likely to cast themselves as antagonists in a man's story; they are even less likely, I suggest, to cast themselves as virgin land. The lack of fit between their own experience and the fictional role assigned to them is even greater in the second instance than in the first. If women portray themselves as brides or mothers it will not be in terms of the mythic landscape. If a woman puts a female construction on nature—as she certainly must from time to time, given the archetypal female resonance of the image—she is likely to write of it as more active, or to stress its destruction or violation. On the other hand, she might adjust the heroic myth to her own psyche by making nature out to be male—as, for example, Willa Cather seems to do in *O Pioneers!* But a violated landscape or a male nature does not fit the essential American pattern as critics have defined it, and hence these literary images occur in an obscurity that criticism cannot see. Thus, one has an almost classic example of the "double bind." When the woman writer creates a story that conforms to the expected myth, it is not recognized for what it is because of a superfluous sexual specialization in the myth as it is entertained in the critics' minds. (Needless to say, many male novelists also entertain this version of the myth, and do not find the masculinist bias with which they imbue it to be superfluous. It is possible that some of these novelists, especially those who write in an era in which literary criticism is a powerful influence, have formed their ideas from their reading in criticism.) But if she does not conform to the myth, she is understood to be writing minor or trivial literature.

Two remaining points can be treated much more briefly. The description of the artist and of the act of writing which emerges when the critic uses the basic American story as his starting point contains many attributes of the basic story itself. This description raises the exclusion of women to a more abstract, theoretical—and perhaps more pernicious—level. Fundamentally, the idea is that the artist writing a story of this essential American kind is engaging in a task very much like the one performed by his mythic hero. In effect, the artist writing his narrative is imitating the mythic encounter of hero and possibility in the safe confines of his study; or, reversing the temporal order, one might see that mythic encounter of hero and possibility as a projection of the artist's situation.

Although this idea is greatly in vogue at the moment, it has a history. Here, for example, is Richard Chase representing the activity of writing in metaphors of discovery and exploration, as though the writer were a hero in the landscape: "The American novel has usually seemed content to explore . . . the remarkable and in some ways unexampled territories of life in the New World and to reflect its anomalies and dilemmas. It has . . . wanted . . . to discover a new place and a new state of mind."[17] Richard Poirier takes the idea further:

> The most interesting American books are an image of the creation of America itself. . . . They carry the metaphoric burden of a great dream of freedom — of the expansion of national consciousness into the vast spaces of a continent and the absorption of those spaces into ourselves. . . . The classic American writers try through style temporarily to free the hero (and the reader) from systems, to free them from the pressures of time, biology, economics, and from the social forces which are ultimately the undoing of American heroes and quite often of their creators. . . . The strangeness of American fiction has . . . to do . . . with the environment [the novelist] tries to create for his hero, usually his surrogate.[18]

The implicit union of creator and protagonist is made specific and overt at the end of Poirier's passage here. The ideas of Poirier and Chase, and others like them, are summed up in an anthology called *Theories of American Literature,* edited by Donald M. Kartiganer and Malcolm A. Griffith.[19] The editors write, "It is as if with each new work our writers feel they must invent again the complete world of a literary form." (Yet, the true subject is not what the writers feel, but what the critics think they feel.) "Such a condition of nearly absolute freedom to create has appeared to our authors both as possibility and liability, an utter openness suggesting limitless opportunity for the imagination, or an enormous vacancy in which they create from nothing. For some it has meant an opportunity to play Adam, to assume the role of an original namer of experience" (4–5). One can see in this passage the transference of the American myth from the Adamic hero *in* the story, to the Adamic creator *of* the story, and the reinterpretation of the American myth as a metaphor for the American artist's situation.

This myth of artistic creation, assimilating the act of writing novels to the Adamic myth, imposes on artistic creation all the gender-based restrictions that we have already examined in that myth. The key to identifying an "Adamic writer" is the formal appearance, or, more precisely the *informal* appearance, of his novel. The unconventionality is interpreted as a direct representation of the open-ended experience of exploring and taming the wilderness, as well as a rejection of "society" as it is incorporated in conventional literary forms. There is no place for a woman author in this scheme. Her roles in the drama of creation are those allotted to her in a male melodrama: either she is to be silent, like nature; or she is the creator of conventional works, the spokesperson of society. What she might do as an innovator in her own right is not to be perceived.

---

[17] Chase, *American Novel,* 5.

[18] Poirier, *A World Elsewhere,* 3, 5, 9.

[19] Donald M. Kartiganer and Malcolm A. Griffith, eds., *Theories of American Literature* (New York: Macmillan, 1962).

In recent years, some refinements of critical theory coming from the Yale and Johns Hopkins and Columbia schools have added a new variant to the idea of creation as a male province. I quote from a 1979 book entitled *Home as Found* by Eric Sundquist. The author takes the idea that in writing a novel the artist is really writing a narrative about himself and proposes this addition:

> Writing a narrative about oneself may represent an extremity of Oedipal usurpation or identification, a bizarre act of self father-ing. . . . American authors have been particularly obsessed with *fathering* a tradition of their own, with becoming their "own sires." . . . The struggle . . . is central to the crisis of representation, and hence of style, that allows American authors to find in their own fantasies those of a nation and to make of those fantasies a compelling and instructive literature.[20]

These remarks derive clearly from the work of such critics as Harold Bloom, as any reader of recent critical theory will note. The point for our purpose is the facile translation of the verb "to author" into the verb "to father," with the profound gender-restrictions of that translation unacknowledged. According to this formulation, insofar as the author writes about a character who is his surrogate—which, apparently, he always does—he is trying to become his own father.

We can scarcely deny that men think a good deal about, and are profoundly affected by, relations with their fathers. The theme of fathers and sons is perennial in world literature. Somewhat more spaciously, we recognize that intergenerational conflict, usually perceived from the point of view of the young, is a recurrent literary theme, especially in egalitarian cultures. Certainly, this idea involves the question of authority, and "authority" is a notion related to that of "the author." And there is some gender-specific significance involved since authority in most cultures that we know tends to be invested in adult males. But the theory has built from these useful and true observations to a restriction of literary creation to a sort of therapeutic act that can only be performed by men. If literature is the attempt to *father* oneself by the author, then every act of writing by a woman is both perverse and absurd. And, of course, it is bound to fail.

Since this particular theory of the act of writing is drawn from psychological assumptions that are not specific to American literature, it may be argued that there is no need to confine it to American authors. In fact, Harold Bloom's *Anxiety of Influence,* defining literature as a struggle between fathers and sons, or the struggle of sons to escape from their fathers, is about British literature. And so is Edward Said's book *Beginnings,* which chronicles the history of the nineteenth-century British novel as exemplification of what he calls "filiation." His discussion omits Jane Austen, George Eliot, all three Brontë sisters, Mrs. Gaskell, Mrs. Humphrey Ward—not a sign of a woman author is found in his treatment of Victorian fiction. The result is a revisionist

[20] Eric Sundquist, *Home as Found* (Baltimore: Johns Hopkins Univ. Press, 1979), xviii–xix.

approach to British fiction that recasts it in the accepted image of the American myth. Ironically, just at the time that feminist critics are discovering more and more important women, the critical theorists have seized upon a theory that allows the women less and less presence. This observation points up just how significantly the critic is engaged in the act of *creating* literature.

Ironically, then, one concludes that in pushing the theory of American fiction to this extreme, critics have "deconstructed" it by creating a tool with no particular American reference. In pursuit of the uniquely American, they have arrived at a place where Americanness has vanished into the depths of what is alleged to be the universal male psyche. The theory of American fiction has boiled down to the phrase in my title: a melodrama of beset manhood. What a reduction this is of the enormous variety of fiction written in this country, by both women and men! And, ironically, nothing could be further removed from Trilling's idea of the artist as embodiment of a culture. As in the working out of all theories, its weakest link has found it out and broken the chain.

Umberto Eco

The Deconstruction of the Linguistic Sign

From *Semiotics and the Philosophy of Language*

1984

The prolific Italian critic and essayist Umberto Eco (b. 1932) was already well respected in academic circles when his mystery novel The Name of the Rose *(1980, translated 1983), set in a medieval monastery and with a plot revolving around scriptural and bibliographic scholarship, became a surprise bestseller. Eco's best-known academic work is principally in the field of* semiotics, *the scientific study of signs developed by nineteenth-century American philosopher Charles Sanders Peirce. Semiotics was one of the key methods that structuralists relied on to identify and analyze the rules and relations of language to achieve their goal of establishing a universal code of human communication based on linguistics. If such a venture proved successful, the study of literature might achieve the scientific validity and universal meaning critics had sought for centuries. (For more on structuralism, see the note to Roland Barthes's essay, page 487.)*

Characteristically, the excerpt reprinted here from Eco's Semiotics and the Philosophy of Language *takes a historical approach to the field. In it he demonstrates how challenges to semiotic theory have often ended up reinforcing structuralist ideas, though often giving them new names and extending them to new contexts. Various critics and revisers of the theory have, Eco writes, claimed that the notion of the sign was alternately too small and too large to be of use and have focused their energy on subdividing and analyzing different kinds of signs. Eco demonstrates his interest in the full range of semiotic possibilities, encompassing analysis of signs—both linguistic and nonlinguistic—and the contexts that give these signs their meaning and allow them to be useful for human communication. While he begins by reading modern and contemporary theorists, he also traces key elements of semiotic theory back to the Greeks, particularly Aristotle, demonstrating how ancient ideas are often renewed under new guises.*

One of the key challenges to semiotics and structuralism in the late twentieth century came from the deconstructionists. For instance, Jacques Derrida, a key figure in poststructuralist thought and the framer of deconstruction, argued in "Structure, Sign, and Play in the Discourse of the Human Sciences" (page 493) that any fixed rules and relations of language would have to assume a stability of meaning that does not and cannot exist. Rather than ignoring or dismissing such challenges to his field, Eco incorporates those elements of poststructuralist thought in which he finds value for semiotics, thus forming something of a bridge between fields that are sometimes depicted as incompatible.

1.1. Crisis of a Concept

CURRENT HANDBOOKS of semiotics provide us with different definitions of the concept of sign which are often complementary rather than contradictory. According to Peirce, a sign is "something which stands to somebody for something in some respect or capacity" (C. P. 2.228).[1] This definition is a more articulate version of the classical definition *aliquid stat pro aliquo*. When dealing with the inner structure of the sign, Saussure speaks of a twofold entity (signifier and signified). Hjelmslev's definition, which assumes the sign-function as a mutual correlation between two functives (expression-plane and content-plane), can be taken as a more rigorous development of the Saussurean concept.

However, in the same period at the turn of the century in which semiotics asserted itself as a discipline, a series of theoretical propositions concerning the death, or at least the crisis of the concept, of sign was developed. Throughout the history of Western thought, the idea of a semiotic theory—however differently defined—was always labeled as a doctrine of signs (see Jakobson 1974;[2] Rey 1973;[3] Sebeok 1976;[4] Todorov 1977[5]). The disparity of meanings attributed each time to the notion of sign calls for a rigorous critique (at least in the Kantian sense of the word 'critique'). We shall see, however, that the notion of sign had been seriously questioned in this sense since the very beginning.

In the last few years, this reasonable critical attitude seems to have generated its own mannerism. Since it is rhetorically effective to begin a course in philosophy by announcing the death of philosophy, as Freud is pronounced dead at the opening of debates on psychoanalysis, many people have deemed useful to start out in semiotics by announcing the death of the

---

[1] C.S. Peirce, *Collected Papers* (referred to as *C. P.*) (Cambridge, Mass.: Harvard University Press, 1931–58).

[2] R. Jakobson, *Coup d'oeil sur le developpement de la semiotique* (1974, Bloomington: Indiana, University Publications, 1975). English translation in R. Jakobson and M. Halle, *The Framework of Language* (Ann Arbor: University of Michigan Press, 1980).

[3] A. Rey, *Theories du signe et du sens* (Paris: Klincksiek, 1973).

[4] T.A. Sebeok, *Contributions to the Doctrine of Signs* (Bloomington: Indiana University Publications, 1976).

[5] T. Todorov, *Theories du symbole* (Paris: Seuil, 1977).

sign. This announcement is rarely prefaced by a philosophical analysis of the concept of sign or by its reexamination in terms of historical semantics. The death sentence is therefore pronounced upon an entity which, being without its identity papers, is likely to be resuscitated under a different name. . . .

1.5. The Deconstruction of the Linguistic Sign

The following critiques have characteristics in common: first, when they speak of sign in general and consider other kinds of signs, they point to the structure of the *linguistic* sign. Second, they tend to dissolve the sign into entities of greater or lesser purport.

1.5.1. *Sign vs.* Figura

As an entity, the sign is too large. Phonology's work on linguistic signifiers, seen as the result of the articulation of lesser phonological units, starts out with the Stoic's discovery of the *stoicheîa* ($\sigma\tau o\iota\chi\epsilon\hat{\iota}\alpha$), it reaches maturity with Hjelmslev's postulating the existence of *figurae,* and is crowned by Jakobson's theory of distinctive features. This theoretical achievement does not in itself question the notion of linguistic sign, but with Hjelmslev there arises the possibility of identifying *figurae* at the content level as well:

> If, for example, a mechanical inventory at a given stage of the procedure leads to a registration of the entities of content 'ram', 'ewe', 'man', 'woman', 'boy', 'girl', 'stallion', 'mare', 'sheep', 'human being', 'child', 'horse', 'he', and 'she'—then 'ram', 'ewe', 'man', 'woman', 'boy', 'girl', 'stallion', and 'mare' must be eliminated from the inventory of elements if they can be explained univocally as relational units that include only 'he' or 'she' on the one hand, and 'sheep', 'human being', 'child', 'horse', on the other. (1943:70)[6]

The discovery of a content articulation leads Hjelmslev to argue that languages cannot be described as pure sign systems:

> By the aims usually attributed to them they are first and foremost sign systems; but by their internal structure they are first and foremost something different, namely, systems of *figurae* that can be used to construct signs. The definition of a language as a sign system has thus shown itself, on closer analysis, to be unsatisfactory. It concerns only the external functions of a language, its relation to the nonlinguistic factors that surround it, but not its proper, internal functions. (Ibid., p. 47)

---

[6] L. Hjelmslev, *Omkring sprogteoriens grundlaeggelse* (Kobenhavn: Munksgaard, 1943). English translation by F.J. Whitfield, *Prolegomena to a Theory of Language* (Madison: University of Wisconsin, 1961).

The sign (or the sign-function) appears, therefore, as the manifest and recognizable end of a net of aggregations and disintegrations constantly open to further combinations. The linguistic sign is not a unit of the system of signification; it is, rather, a detectable unit in the process of communication.

Despite being invaluable for the whole development of structural semantics, Hjelmslev's proposal does not account for other kinds of signs in which it appears that the two functives are not analyzable further into *figurae*. If the cloud which announces the storm and the portrait of the Mona Lisa are to be taken as signs, there must be signs without expression *figurae*, and perhaps without content *figurae* as well. Prieto (1966)[7] has decidedly widened the field of sign analysis by showing the existence of systems without articulation, and systems which have only a first articulation. The white stick of the blind—a positive presence which constitutes itself as pertinent against the absence of the stick, as a signifier without articulations—represents blindness in general, requesting the right of way, postulating understanding on the part of bystanders. In short, it conveys a *content nebula*. As a system the stick is quite simple (presence vs. absence), but its communicational use is very complex. If the stick is not a sign, what is it, and what should it be called?

1.5.2. *Signs vs. Sentences*

In the same years which saw Hjelmslev's critique of the sign format as too broad, Buyssens maintained that the format of the sign was too minute. The semantic unit is not the sign, but something corresponding to the sentence, which Buyssens calls *sème*. The example given by Buyssens concerns street signs as well as linguistic signs. He maintains that an arrow, isolated from the context of the street sign, does not allow for the concretization of a "state of consciousness." In order to perform this function it will have to have a certain color, a certain orientation, and it will have to appear on a specific street sign, placed in a specific location. "The same thing happens with the isolated word, for instance, the word *table*. This word appeared as the potential member of different sentences in which different things are talked about" (Buyssens 1943:38).[8]

Strange opposition: Hjelmslev is uninterested in the sign because he is interested in language as an abstract system; Buyssens is uninterested in the sign because he is interested in communication as a concrete act. Obviously, the opposition extension vs. intension is in the background of this debate. Unpleasant homonymy: componential semantics will call Hjelmslev's content *figurae* (smaller than the sign) 'semes', while the tradition which developed from Buyssens (Prieto, De Mauro)[9,10] will use the term 'sème' for utterances larger than the sign.

---

[7] L. Prieto, *Messages et signaux* (Paris: Presses Universitaires de France, 1966).

[8] E. Buyssens, *Le langage et le discours* (Brussels: Office de Publicite, 1943).

[9] Prieto, *Messages et signaux*.

[10] T. De Mauro, *Senso e significato* (Bari: Adriatica, 1971).

In any case, Buyssens' seme is what others will call sentence or a performed speech act. What is surprising is the initial statement by Buyssens, according to which a sign does not have meaning. If it is true that *nominantur singularia sed universalia significantur*, one should rather say that the word *table* by itself does not name (it does not refer to) anything, but has a meaning, which Hjelmslev could have subdivided into *figurae*. Buyssens admits that this word (like the arrow) can be a potential member of different phrases. What is there, then, in the content of *table* which allows it to enter expressions such as *dinner is on the table* or *the table is made of wood*, and not in expressions such as *the table eats the fish* or *he washed his face with the dinner table*? It must be agreed, then, that precisely because of its susceptibility to analysis by content *figurae*, the word *table* must include both atomic units of content and contextual instructions ruling over the word's capacity to enter linguistic segments larger than the sign.

Prieto (1975:27)[11] clarified this apparent disagreement between Hjelmslev and Buyssens by stating that the seme (for Buyssens) is a *functional unit*, whereas the *figura* is an *economic unit*. Hjelmslev postulated the sign as a functional unit and the *figura* as an economic unit. The problem is to identify, not two, but three or more levels, where the lower level is always constituted as the economic unit of the upper level's functional unit.

Buyssens' distinction certainly anticipates, with its concreteness and complexity, all the theories opposing to the sign the speech act. However, Plato and Aristotle, the Stoics and the Sophists had already talked about the differences existing between the meaning of words and the pragmatic nature of the question, the prayer, and the order. Those who oppose a *pragmatics of discourse* to a *semantics of sign units* shift the attention from the systems of signification to the process of communication (Eco 1976);[12] but the two perspectives are actually complementary. One cannot think of the sign without seeing it in some way characterized by its contextual destiny, but at the same time it is difficult to explain why a certain speech act is understood unless the nature of the signs which it contextualizes is explained.

1.5.3. The Sign as Difference

The elements of the signifier are set into a system of oppositions in which, as Saussure explained, there are only differences. The same thing happens with the signified. In the famous example given by Hjelmslev (1943:39),[13] the difference in the content of two apparently synonymous terms, /Holz/ and /bois/, is given by the different segmentation of the continuum. The German /Holz/ encompasses everything which is not /Baum/ and is not /Wald/. The correlation between expression-plane and content-plane is also given by a difference: the sign-function exists by a dialectic of presence and absence, as a

[11] L. Prieto, *Pertinence et pratique* (Paris: Minuit, 1975).
[12] U. Eco, *A Theory of Semiotics* (Bloomington: Indiana University Press, 1976).
[13] Hjelmslev, *Omkring sprogteoriens grundlaeggelse*.

mutual exchange between two heterogeneities. Starting from this structural premise, one can dissolve the entire sign system into a net of fractures. The nature of the sign is to be found in the 'wound' or 'opening' or 'divarication' which constitutes it and annuls it at the same time.

This idea, although vigorously developed by poststructuralist thought, that of Derrida in particular, was actually developed much earlier. In the short text *De organo sive arte cogitandi,* Leibniz, searching for a restricted number of thoughts from whose combination all the others could be derived (as is the case with numbers), locates the essential combinational matrix in the opposition between God and nothing, presence and absence. The binary system of calculation is the wondrous likeness of this dialectics.

From a metaphysical perspective, it may be fascinating to see every oppositional structure as based on a constitutive difference which dissolves the different terms. Still, in order to conceptualize an oppositional system where something is perceived as absent, something else must be postulated as present, at least potentially. *The presence of one element is necessary for the absence of the other.* All observations concerning the importance of the absent element hold symmetrically for the present element as well. All observations concerning the constitutive function of difference hold for the poles from whose opposition the difference is generated. The argument is, therefore, an autophagous one. A phoneme is no doubt an abstract position within a system, and it acquires its value only because of the other phonemes to which it is opposed. Yet, for an 'emic' unit to be recognized, it must be formulated somehow as 'etic'. In other words, phonology builds up a system of oppositions in order to explain the functioning of a number of phonetic presences which, if they do not exist prior to the system, nonetheless are associated with its ghost. Without people uttering sounds, phonology could not exist, but without the system postulated by phonology, people could not distinguish between sounds. *Types* are recognized through their realizations into concrete *tokens.* One cannot speak of a form (of the expression or of the content) without presupposing a matter and linking it immediately (neither before nor after) to a substance.

1.5.4. The Predominance of the Signifier

The answer given to the preceding question could confirm a further critique of the notion of sign. If the sign can be known only through the signifier and if the signified emerges only through an act of perpetual substitution of the signifier, the semiotic chain appears to be just a 'chain of signifiers'. As such, it could be manipulated even by the unconscious (if we take the unconscious as being linguistically constituted). By the 'drift' of signifiers, other signifiers are produced. As a more or less direct consequence of these conclusions, the universe of signs and even of sentences would dissolve into discourse as an activity. This line of thought, derived from Lacan, has generated a number of varied, but essentially related, positions.

The basis for this critique is actually a misunderstanding, a wordplay. Only by substituting 'signified' every time 'signifier' appears, does the discourse of these theoreticians become comprehensible. The misunderstanding derives from the fact that every signifier can only be translated into another signifier and that only by this process of *interpretation* can one grasp the 'corresponding signified'. It must be clear, though, that in none of various displacement and condensation processes described by Freud—however multiplied and almost automatic the generative and drifting mechanisms might appear—does the interplay (even if based on assonances, alliterations, likeness of expression) fail to reverberate immediately on the aggregation of the content units, actually determining the content. In the Freudian passage from /Herr-signore/ to /Signorelli/, a series of expression differences is at work, based on identities and progressive slidings of the content. The Freudian example can, in fact, be understood only by someone who knows both German and Italian, seeing words as complete sign-functions (expression + content). A person who does not know Chinese cannot produce Freudian slips interpretable in Chinese, unless a psychoanalyst who knows Chinese demonstrates that his or her patient had displaced linguistic remembrances and that he or she unconsciously played with Chinese expressions. A Freudian slip, in order to make sense, plays on *content figurae;* if it plays only with *expression figurae* it amounts to a mechanical error (typographical or phonetic). This kind of mechanical error is likely to involve content elements only in the eye of the interpreter. But in this case it is the interpreter who must be psychoanalyzed.

1.5.5. Sign vs. Text

The so-called signifying chain produces texts which carry with them the recollection of the intertextuality which nourishes them. Texts generate, or are capable of generating, multiple (and ultimately infinite) readings and interpretations. It was argued, for instance, by the later Barthes, by the recent Derrida, and by Kristeva, that signification is to be located exclusively in the text. The text is the locus where meaning is produced and becomes productive (signifying practice). Within its texture, the signs of the dictionary (as codifying equivalences) can emerge only by a rigidification and death of all sense. This critical line takes up Buyssens' argument (communication is given only at the level of sentence), but it goes deeper. A text is not simply a communicational apparatus. It is a device which questions the previous signifying systems, often renews them, and sometimes destroys them. *Finnegans Wake*—a textual machine made to liquidate grammars and dictionaries—is exemplary in this sense, but even rhetorical figures are produced and become alive only at the textual level. The textual machine empties the terms which the literal dictionary deemed univocal and well defined, and fills them with new content figures. Yet, the production of a metaphor such as *the king of the forest* (where a figure of humanity is added to lions and an animal property reverberates on the class of kings) implies the existence of both /king/ and /lion/

as functives of two previously codified sign-functions. If signs (expressions and content) did not preexist the text, every metaphor would be equivalent simply to saying that something is something. But a metaphor says that *that* (linguistic) thing is at the same time *something else.*

The ability of the textual manifestations to empty, destroy, or reconstruct pre-existing sign-functions depends on the presence within the sign-function (that is, in the network of content figures) of a set of instructions oriented toward the (potential) production of different texts. (This concept will be further developed in 1.9.) It is in this sense that the thematization of textuality has been particularly suggestive.

1.5.6. *The Sign as Identity*

The sign is supposed to be based on the categories of 'similitude' or 'identity'. This presumed fallacy renders the sign coherent with the ideological notion of the subject. The subject as a presupposed transcendental unity which opens itself to the world (or to which the world opens) through the act of representation, as well as the subject that transfers its representations onto other subjects in the process of communication, is supposedly a philosophical fiction dominating all of the history of philosophy. Let us postpone the discussion of this objection and see now in what sense the notion of sign is seen to be coherent with the (no longer viable) notion of subject:

> Under the mask of socialization or of mechanistic realism, ideological linguistics, absorbed by the science of signs, turns the sign-subject into a center. The sign-subject becomes the beginning and the end of all translinguistic activity; it becomes closed up in itself, located in its own word, which is conceived of by positivism as a kind of 'psychism' residing in the brain. (Kristeva 1969:69)[14]

The statement above *implies the identification of the sign with the linguistic sign,* where the linguistic sign is based on the equivalence model: $p \equiv q$. In point of fact, Kristeva defines the sign as "resemblance":

> The sign brings separate instances (subject-object on one hand, subject-interlocutor on the other) back to a unified whole (a unity which presents itself as a sentence-message), replacing praxis with a single meaning, and difference with *resemblance.* . . . The relationship instituted by the sign will therefore be a *reconciliation of discrepancies,* and *identification of differences.* (Ibid., pp. 70, 84)

It seems, however, that such a criticism can apply only to a degenerate notion of linguistic sign, rooted on the equivalence model. The problem is to see whether and to what extent this notion has ever been supported by the most mature theories of signs. For instance, the notion of sign as resemblance and identity does not appear in Peirce: "A sign is something by knowing

---

[14] J. Kristeva, *Semeiotike* (Paris: Seuil, 1969).

which we know something more" (*C. P.* 8.332).[15] The sign is an instruction for interpretation, a mechanism which starts from an initial stimulus and leads to all its illative consequences. Starting from the sign, one goes through the whole semiotic process and arrives at the point where the sign becomes capable of contradicting itself (otherwise, those textual mechanisms called 'literature' would not be possible). For Peirce, the sign is a potential proposition (as even Kristeva [1974:43][16] notes). In order to comprehend this notion of sign, we need to reconsider the initial phase of its historical development. Such reconsideration requires the elimination of an embarrassing notion, that of linguistic sign. Since this notion is after all a late cultural product, we shall postpone its treatment until later.

1.6. Signs vs. Words

The term which the Western philosophical tradition has translated as *signum* was originally the Greek *sēmeîon* (σημεῖον). It appeared as a technical-philosophical term in the fifth century, with Parmenides and Hippocrates. It is often found as a synonym of *tekmérion* (τεκμήριον: proof, clue, symptom). A first distinction between the two terms appears only with Aristotle's *Rhetoric*.

Hippocrates took the notion of clue from the physicians who came before him. Alcmeon said that "the Gods have immediate knowledge of invisible and mortal things, but men must 'proceed by clues' (τεκμαίρεδδαι)" (*D. K.*, B1). The Cnidarian physicians knew the value of symptoms. Apparently, they codified them in the form of equivalences. Hippocrates maintained that the symptom is equivocal if it is not analyzed contextually, taking into account the air, the water, the environment, the general state of the body, and the regimen which is likely to modify the situation. Such a model functions as if to say: if p then q, but only with the concurrence of factors y and z. A code exists, but it is not a univocal one.

Hippocrates was not interested in linguistic signs. In any event, it appears that at the time the term 'sign' was not applied to words. A word was a *name* (*ónoma*, 'όνομα). Parmenides made use of this difference when he opposed the truth of the thought concerning Being to the illusory nature of opinions and the fallacy of sensations. Now, if representations are deceptive, names are nothing but equally deceptive levels superimposed on the objects that we think we know. *Onomázein* ('Ονομάζειν) is always used by Parmenides in order to give an arbitrary name, which is deemed to be true but does not actually correspond to the truth. The name establishes a pseudo-equivalence with reality, and in doing so it conceals it. On the other hand, Parmenides uses the term 'signs' (*sēmata*: σήματα) when he speaks of *evidence*, of an inferential principle: "That Being exists, there are signs" (*D. K.*, B8.2).

[15] Peirce, *Collected Papers*.
[16] J. Kristeva, *La revolution du langage poetique* (Paris: Seuil, 1974).

With Plato and Aristotle words are analyzed from a double point of view: (a) the difference between signifier and signified and (b) the difference between *signification* and *reference*. Signification (that is, meaning) says *what* a thing is, and in this sense it is a function performed also by single terms; in the act of reference one says, on the contrary, *that* a thing is, and in this sense reference is a function performed only by complete sentences. Throughout his whole work on logic and language, Aristotle is reluctant to use the term *sign* (*sēmeîon*) for words.

At first glance, contrary evidence is provided by the well-known page of *De Interpretatione*, 16a, where it seems that it is said that words are signs. But this page requires some careful interpretation. First, Aristotle says that both spoken and written words are *symbols* (σύμβολα) of the affections of the soul. Then he says that spoken and written words are not the same for all human beings, since (as it is restated in 16a20–30) they are posited by convention. In this sense, words are different from the sounds emitted by animals. Words are conventional and arbitrary, whereas other kinds of sounds are natural and motivated. It is evident that Aristotle reserves the term *symbol* for spoken and written words (see also Di Cesare 1981 and Lieb 1981).[17,18]

It must be noticed that *symbol* was at that time, as a philosophical term, more neutral than *sign*. The notion of sign was already introduced and discussed by the Hippocratic tratition as a precise category, whereas *symbol* was generally used as «token» or «identification mark» (see Chapter 4 of this book).

On the same page (16a.5), Aristotle says that the affections of the soul are likenesses, or images, or copies of things, and as such they cannot be studied in a logical (linguistic) framework. Therefore they will be dealt with in *De Anima*. In stressing this difference between mental images and words, he states, incidentally, that spoken and written words are signs (*sēmeîa*) of the affections of the soul. Thus *prima facie* he equates signs with symbols.

One could object that in this context *sign* is used in a metaphorical way. But one should make a more radical remark. If Aristotle was following the terminological criterion he also follows in *Rhetoric*, /signs/ still means «proof», «clue», «symptom». If this is true, he is thus saying that words (spoken or written) are the *proof* that one has something in one's mind to express; at the same time he is stating that, even though words are symptoms of mental affections, this does not mean that they have the same semiotic and psychological status of these affections.

This interpretive hypothesis is reinforced by the way in which Aristotle (16b.19ff) wonders whether verbs as *to be* or *not to be* are signs of the existence of the thing. His line of thought is the following: (a) outside the sentence, no verb can state that something really exists or actually does something;

[17] D. Di Cesare, "Il Problema logico funzionale del linguaggio in Aristotele," in *Logos Semantikos*, ed. J. Trabant (Berlin: De Gruyter; Madrid: Gredos, 1981).

[18] H.H. Lieb, "Das 'Semiotische Dreieck' bei Ogden un Richards: Eine Neuformulierung des Zeichenmodells von Aristoteles," in *Logos Semantikos*, ed. J. Trabant (Berlin: De Gruyter; Madrid: Gredos, 1981).

(b) verbs can perform this function only in a complete assertive sentence; (c) not even *to be* or *not to be,* uttered in isolation, assert the existence of something; (d) however, when they are inserted into a sentence, they are signs (or, as some translators interpret, "they are indicative of the fact") that the existence of something is asserted. Such an interpretation is confirmed by what Aristotle has previously said (16b.5ff), namely, that a verb is always the sign (or that it is indicative of the fact) that something is said or asserted of something. Aquinas, in his commentary on *De Interpretatione,* lucidly analyzes this passage. He excludes, however, a reading that could sound very attractive to a contemporary mind, that is, that the verb is the signifier of which a predication is the signified, or that the sentence that contains the verb is the vehicle of an assertive proposition. On the contrary, Aquinas chooses a more commonsensical reading: the presence of the verb within a sentence is the *proof,* the symptom that this sentence asserts the existence of something by actually predicating something of something.

Thus we are entitled to understand that, when Aristotle incidentally uses the term *sign* for words, he is simply stressing that even words can be taken as symptoms. He is not equating linguistic symbols with natural signs. He is only saying that *sometimes* symbols can be taken as proofs. But symbols are different from other natural signs because, when they function primarily as symbols (independently of their possible use as proofs), they are not based on the model of inference but on the model of equivalence. Aristotle was in fact the first to insist that linguistic terms are equivalent to their definitions and that word and definition are fully reciprocable (as we shall see in Chapter 2 of this book).

The sign makes its appearance in the *Rhetoric,* where the enthymemes are said to be derived from verisimilitudes (*eikóta:* εἰκότα) and from signs (*sēmeîa*). But the signs are divided into two logically well-differential categories. The first type of sign has a specific name, *tekmérion,* in the sense of 'evidence'. We can translate it as *necessary sign;* if one has a fever, then one is ill; if a woman has milk, then she has given birth. The necessary sign can be translated into the universal statement 'all those who have a fever are ill'. It must be noted that this statement does not establish a relation of equivalence (biconditional). One can be ill (for instance, with an ulcer) without having a fever.

The second type of sign, says Aristotle, does not have a specific name. We could call it a *weak sign:* if one has difficulty in breathing, then one has a fever. The conclusion is obviously only probable, because the difficulty in breathing could be caused by excessive physical exercise. Transformed into a premise, the sign would only give a particular affirmative: 'some people have difficulty in breathing and they have a fever' (the logical form is one of conjunction rather than implication). The weak sign is such just because the necessary sign does not establish an equivalence. A weak sign can be produced by converting the universal affirmative—into which the necessary sign has been turned—into a particular affirmative. The subordinate of 'all those who have a fever are ill' yields in terms of a logical square, 'there are some people who are ill and who have a fever', which in fact is a weak sign and permits—at most—an *induction*.

Actually, Aristotle is uneasy with these different types of signs. He knows the apodictic syllogism, but he does not know, at least not with theoretical clarity, the hypothetical syllogism, that is, the $p \supset q$ form which will be the glory of the Stoics. For this reason Aristotle traces argumentative schemes, but he does not dwell on their logical form.

Translated by Lucia Re.

ELAINE SHOWALTER

Representing Ophelia: Women, Madness, and the Responsibilities of Feminist Criticism

1985

Elaine Showalter (b. 1941) begins with two extremes of the critical problems raised by the character of Ophelia: psychoanalyst Jacques Lacan's debasing typification of her as "O-phallus," or Hamlet's lost "transcendent signifier," and the countervailing view of some feminists who want to place her at the center of the play. Showalter focuses on the issues that feminist criticism must face to achieve a satisfactory reading of Ophelia's character.

In virtually all readings before the late nineteenth century, in literary criticism, theatrical performances, and paintings, Ophelia had been shown either as a nothing, a madness without a center, as merely a foil for Hamlet, or as a Gothic, fascinating madwoman. Mid-nineteenth-century feminist criticism began to seek an understanding of Ophelia as a woman. Although Ellen Terry's performance in 1878 accorded Ophelia a realness as a normal, intelligent person destroyed by sexual intimidation, twentieth-century psychoanalytic literature, in Showalter's view, has been particularly aggressive in seeing Ophelia as an example of an inherently female mental dysfunction, from Freudian Oedipal readings, to Lacan's phallic preoccupations, to R. D. Laing's view of her as an archetype of the female schizophrenic. Stage productions influenced by psychoanalysis, from the 1930s to the present, have returned to the distortions of former times in which Ophelia is an intriguing signboard of intrinsically feminine flaws, at least as defined by a male bias.

Present-day feminist productions of Hamlet, and even rewritings of the play to show a radicalized version of Ophelia, have provided salutary counterstatements, as Showalter describes them. But although agitprop—or art used as propaganda to agitate for social reform—may be necessary in the feminist revolt against male dominance, Showalter argues that feminist criticism, to be responsible, must find a large perspective for understanding Ophelia, one that will not be distorted by the pressures of the present ideology of crisis among feminists. Instead, feminists must attend closely to past distortions and strive to "tell her story aright."

Showalter's essay shows clear parallels to those of Virginia Woolf (page 411), Adrienne Rich (page 511), and Sandra M. Gilbert and Susan Gubar (page 683). All these condemn distorted definitions of women, omission from the acknowledged histories, and denial of an equal voice for women in society as debasing and limiting, particularly for women writers. Showalter's essay, with its two-edged title, is an example of both applied criticism and an appeal for further feminist analysis.

"As a sort of a come-on, I announced that I would speak today about that piece of bait named Ophelia, and I'll be as good as my word." These are the words which begin the psychoanalytic seminar on *Hamlet* presented in Paris in 1959 by Jacques Lacan. But despite his promising come-on, Lacan was *not* as good as his word. He goes on for some 41 pages to speak about Hamlet, and when he does mention Ophelia, she is merely what Lacan calls "the object Ophelia"—that is, the object of Hamlet's male desire. The etymology of Ophelia, Lacan asserts, is "O-phallus," and her role in the drama can only be to function as the exteriorized figuration of what Lacan predictably and, in view of his own early work with psychotic women, disappointingly suggests is the phallus as transcendental signifier.[1] To play such a part obviously makes Ophelia "essential," as Lacan admits; but only because, in his words, "she is linked forever, for centuries, to the figure of Hamlet."

The bait-and-switch game that Lacan plays with Ophelia is a cynical but not unusual instance of her deployment in psychiatric and critical texts. For most critics of Shakespeare, Ophelia has been an insignificant minor character in the play, touching in her weakness and madness but chiefly interesting, of course, in what she tells us about Hamlet. And while female readers of Shakespeare have often attempted to champion Ophelia, even feminist critics have done so with a certain embarrassment. As Annette Kolodny ruefully admits: "it is after all, an imposition of high order to ask the viewer to attend to Ophelia's sufferings in a scene where, before, he's always so comfortably kept his eye fixed on Hamlet."[2]

Yet when feminist criticism allows Ophelia to upstage Hamlet, it also brings to the foreground the issues in an ongoing theoretical debate about the cultural links between femininity, female sexuality, insanity, and representation. Though she is neglected in criticism, Ophelia is probably the most frequently illustrated and cited of Shakespeare's heroines. Her visibility as a subject in literature, popular culture, and painting, from Redon who paints her drowning, to Bob Dylan, who places her on Desolation Row, to Cannon

---

[1] Jacques Lacan, "Desire and the interpretation of desire in *Hamlet*," in *Literature and Psychoanalysis: The Question of Reading: Otherwise*, ed. Shoshana Felman (Baltimore, 1982), 11, 20, 23. Lacan is also wrong about the etymology of Ophelia, which probably derives from the Greek for "help" or "succour." Charlotte M. Yonge suggested a derivation from "ophis," "serpent." See her *History of Christian Names* (1884, republished Chicago, 1966), 346–7. I am indebted to Walter Jackson Bate for this reference. [All notes are Showalter's.]

[2] Annette Kolodny, "Dancing through the minefield: some observations on the theory, practice, and politics of feminist literary criticism" (*Feminist Studies*, 6 (1980)), 7.

Mills, which has named a flowery sheet pattern after her, is in inverse relation to her invisibility in Shakespearean critical texts. Why has she been such a potent and obsessive figure in our cultural mythology? Insofar as Hamlet names Ophelia as "woman" and "frailty," substituting an ideological view of femininity for a personal one, is she indeed representative of Woman, and does her madness stand for the oppression of women in society as well as in tragedy? Furthermore, since Laertes calles Ophelia a "document in madness," does she represent the textual archetype of woman *as* madness or madness *as* woman? And finally, how should feminist criticism represent Ophelia in its own discourse? What is our responsibility towards her as character and as woman?

Feminist critics have offered a variety of responses to these questions. Some have maintained that we should represent Ophelia as a lawyer represents a client, that we should become her Horatia, in this harsh world reporting her and her cause aright to the unsatisfied. Carol Neely, for example, describes advocacy—speaking *for* Ophelia—as our proper role: "As a feminist critic," she writes, "I must 'tell' Ophelia's story."[3] But what can we mean by Ophelia's story? The story of her life? The story of her betrayal at the hands of her father, brother, lover, court, society? The story of her rejection and marginalization by male critics of Shakespeare? Shakespeare gives us very little information from which to imagine a past for Ophelia. She appears in only five of the play's twenty scenes; the preplay course of her love story with Hamlet is known only by a few ambiguous flashbacks. Her tragedy is subordinated in the play; unlike Hamlet, she does not struggle with moral choices or alternatives. Thus another feminist critic, Lee Edwards, concludes that it is impossible to reconstruct Ophelia's biography from the text: "We can imagine Hamlet's story without Ophelia, but Ophelia literally has no story without Hamlet."[4]

If we turn from American to French feminist theory, Ophelia might confirm the impossibility of representing the feminine in patriarchal discourse as other than madness, incoherence, fluidity, or silence. In French theoretical criticism, the feminine or "Woman" is that which escapes representation in patriarchal language and symbolism; it remains on the side of negativity, absence, and lack. In comparison to Hamlet, Ophelia is certainly a creature of lack. "I think nothing, my lord," she tells him in the Mousetrap scene, and he cruelly twists her words:

HAMLET: That's a fair thought to lie between maids' legs.
OPHELIA: What is, my lord?
HAMLET: Nothing.

(III.ii.117–19)

In Elizabethan slang, "nothing" was a term for the female genitalia, as in *Much Ado About Nothing*. To Hamlet, then, "nothing" is what lies between

---

[3] Carol Neely, "Feminist modes of Shakespearean criticism" (*Women's Studies,* 9 (1981)), 11.

[4] Lee Edwards, "The labors of Psyche" (*Critical Inquiry,* 6 (1979)), 36.

maids' legs, for, in the male visual system of representation and desire, women's sexual organs, in the words of the French psychoanalyst Luce Irigaray, "represent the horror of having nothing to see."[5] When Ophelia is mad, Gertrude says that "Her speech is nothing," mere "unshaped use." Ophelia's speech thus represents the horror of having nothing to say in the public terms defined by the court. Deprived of thought, sexuality, language, Ophelia's story becomes the Story of O—the zero, the empty circle of mystery of feminine difference, the cipher of female sexuality to be deciphered by feminist interpretation.[6]

A third approach would be to read Ophelia's story as the female subtext of the tragedy, the repressed story of Hamlet. In this reading, Ophelia represents the strong emotions that the Elizabethans as well as the Freudians thought womanish and unmanly. When Laertes weeps for his dead sister he says of his tears that "When these are gone,/ The woman will be out"—that is to say, that the feminine and shameful part of his nature will be purged. According to David Leverenz, in an important essay called "The Woman in *Hamlet*," Hamlet's disgust at the feminine passivity in himself is translated into violent revulsion against women, and into his brutal behavior towards Ophelia. Ophelia's suicide, Leverenz argues, then becomes "a microcosm of the male world's banishment of the female, because 'woman' represents everything denied by reasonable men."[7]

It is perhaps because Hamlet's emotional vulnerability can so readily be conceptualized as feminine that this is the only heroic male role in Shakespeare which has been regularly acted by women, in a tradition from Sarah Bernhardt to, most recently, Diane Venora, in a production directed by Joseph Papp. Leopold Bloom speculates on this tradition in *Ulysses*, musing on the Hamlet of the actress Mrs Bandman Palmer: "Male impersonator. Perhaps he was a woman? Why Ophelia committed suicide?"[8]

While all of these approaches have much to recommend them, each also presents critical problems. To liberate Ophelia from the text, or to make her its tragic center, is to re-appropriate her for our own ends; to dissolve her into a female symbolism of absence is to endorse our own marginality; to make her Hamlet's anima is to reduce her to a metaphor of male experience. I would like to propose instead that Ophelia *does* have a story of her own that feminist criticism can tell; it is neither her life story, nor her love story, nor Lacan's story, but rather the *history* of her representation. This essay tries to bring together some of the categories of French feminist thought about the

---

[5] Luce Irigaray: see *New French Feminisms*, ed. Elaine Marks and Isabelle de Courtivron (New York, 1982), 101. The quotation above, from III.ii, is taken from the Arden Shakespeare, *Hamlet*, ed. Harold Jenkins (London and New York, 1982), 295. All quotations from *Hamlet* are from this text.

[6] On images of negation and feminine enclosure, see David Wilbern, "Shakespeare's 'nothing'," in *Representing Shakespeare: New Psychoanalytic Essays*, ed. Murray M. Schwartz and Coppélia Kahn (Baltimore, 1981).

[7] David Leverenz, "The woman in *Hamlet*: an interpersonal view" (*Signs*, 4 (1978)), 303.

[8] James Joyce, *Ulysses* (New York, 1961), 76.

"feminine" with the empirical energies of American historical and critical research: to yoke French theory and Yankee knowhow.

Tracing the iconography of Ophelia in English and French painting, photography, psychiatry, and literature, as well as in theatrical production, I will be showing first of all the representational bonds between female insanity and female sexuality. Secondly, I want to demonstrate the two-way transaction between psychiatric theory and cultural representation. As one medical historian has observed, we could provide a manual of female insanity by chronicling the illustrations of Ophelia; this is so because the illustrations of Ophelia have played a major role in the theoretical construction of female insanity.[9] Finally, I want to suggest that the feminist revision of Ophelia comes as much from the actress's freedom as from the critic's interpretation.[10] When Shakespeare's heroines began to be played by women instead of boys, the presence of the female body and female voice, quite apart from details of interpretation, created new meanings and subversive tensions in these roles, and perhaps most importantly with Ophelia. Looking at Ophelia's history on and off the stage, I will point out the contest between male and female representations of Ophelia, cycles of critical repression and feminist reclamation of which contemporary feminist criticism is only the most recent phase. By beginning with these data from cultural history, instead of moving from the grid of literary theory, I hope to conclude with a fuller sense of the responsibilities of feminist criticism, as well as a new perspective on Ophelia.

"Of all the characters in *Hamlet*," Bridget Lyons has pointed out, "Ophelia is most persistently presented in terms of symbolic meanings."[11] Her behavior, her appearance, her gestures, her costume, her props, are freighted with emblematic significance, and for many generations of Shakespearean critics her part in the play has seemed to be primarily iconographic. Ophelia's symbolic meanings, moreover, are specifically feminine. Whereas for Hamlet madness is metaphysical, linked with culture, for Ophelia it is a product of the female body and female nature, perhaps that nature's purest form. On the Elizabethan stage, the conventions of female insanity were sharply defined. Ophelia dresses in white, decks herself with "fantastical garlands" of wild flowers, and enters, according to the stage directions of the "Bad" Quarto, "distracted" playing on a lute with her "hair down singing." Her speeches are marked by extravagant metaphors, lyrical free associations, and "explosive sexual imagery."[12] She sings wistful and bawdy ballads, and ends her life by drowning.

All of these conventions carry specific messages about femininity and sexuality. Ophelia's virginal and vacant white is contrasted with Hamlet's

---

[9] Sander L. Gilman, *Seeing the Insane* (New York, 1981), 126.

[10] See Michael Goldman, *The Actor's Freedom: Toward a Theory of Drama* (New York, 1975), for a stimulating discussion of the interpretative interaction between actor and audience.

[11] Bridget Lyons, "The iconography of Ophelia" (*English Literary History*, 44 (1977)), 61.

[12] See Maurice and Hanna Charney, "The language of Shakespeare's madwomen" (*Signs*, 3 (1977)), 451, 457; and Carroll Camden, "On Ophelia's madness" (*Shakespeare Quarterly* (1964)), 254.

scholar's garb, his "suits of solemn black." Her flowers suggest the discordant double images of female sexuality as both innocent blossoming and whorish contamination; she is the "green girl" of pastoral, the virginal "Rose of May" and the sexually explicit madwoman who, in giving away her wild flowers and herbs, is symbolically deflowering herself. The "weedy trophies" and phallic "long purples" which she wears to her death intimate an improper and discordant sexuality that Gertrude's lovely elegy cannot quite obscure.[13] In Elizabethan and Jacobean drama, the stage direction that a woman enters with dishevelled hair indicates that she might either be mad or the victim of a rape; the disordered hair, her offense against decorum, suggests sensuality in each case.[14] The mad Ophelia's bawdy songs and verbal license, while they give her access to "an entirely different range of experience" from what she is allowed as the dutiful daughter, seem to be her one sanctioned form of self-assertion as a woman, quickly followed, as if in retribution, by her death.[15]

Drowning too was associated with the feminine, with female fluidity as opposed to masculine aridity. In his discussion of the "Ophelia complex," the phenomenologist Gaston Bachelard traces the symbolic connections between women, water, and death. Drowning, he suggests, becomes the truly feminine death in the dramas of literature and life, one which is a beautiful immersion and submersion in the female element. Water is the profound and organic symbol of the liquid woman whose eyes are so easily drowned in tears, as her body is the repository of blood, amniotic fluid, and milk. A man contemplating this feminine suicide understands it by reaching for what is feminine in himself, like Laertes, by a temporary surrender to his own fluidity—that is, his tears; and he becomes a man again in becoming once more dry—when his tears are stopped.[16]

Clinically speaking, Ophelia's behavior and appearance are characteristic of the malady the Elizabethans would have diagnosed as female love-melancholy, or erotomania. From about 1580, melancholy had become a fashionable disease among young men, especially in London, and Hamlet himself is a prototype of the melancholy hero. Yet the epidemic of melancholy associated with intellectual and imaginative genius "curiously by-passed women." Women's melancholy was seen instead as biological, and emotional in origins.[17]

---

[13] See Margery Garber, *Coming of Age in Shakespeare* (London, 1981), 155–7; and Lyons, op. cit., 65, 70–2.

[14] On dishevelled hair as a signifier of madness or rape, see Charney and Charney, op. cit. 452–3, 457; and Allan Dessen, *Elizabethan Stage Conventions and Modern Interpreters* (Cambridge, 1984), 36–8. Thanks to Allan Dessen for letting me see advance proofs of his book.

[15] Charney and Charney, op. cit., 456.

[16] Gaston Bachelard, *L'Eau et les rêves* (Paris, 1942), 109–25. See also Brigitte Peucker, "Dröste-Hulshof's Ophelia and the recovery of voice" (*The Journal of English and Germanic Philology* (1983)), 374–91.

[17] Vieda Skultans, *English Madness: Ideas on Insanity 1580–1890* (London, 1977), 79–81. On historical cases of love-melancholy, see Michael MacDonald, *Mystical Bedlam* (Cambridge, 1982).

On the stage, Ophelia's madness was presented as the predictable outcome of erotomania. From 1660, when women first appeared on the public stage, to the beginnings of the eighteenth century, the most celebrated of the actresses who played Ophelia were those whom rumor credited with disappointments in love. The greatest triumph was reserved for Susan Mountfort, a former actress at Lincoln's Inn Fields who had gone mad after her lover's betrayal. One night in 1720 she escaped from her keeper, rushed to the theater, and just as the Ophelia of the evening was to enter for her mad scene, "sprang forward in her place . . . with wild eyes and wavering motion."[18] As a contemporary reported, "she was in truth *Ophelia herself,* to the amazement of the performers as well as of the audience—nature having made this last effort, her vital powers failed her and she died soon after."[19] These theatrical legends reinforced the belief of the age that female madness was a part of female nature, less to be imitated by an actress than demonstrated by a deranged woman in a performance of her emotions.

The subversive or violent possibilities of the mad scene were nearly eliminated, however, on the eighteenth-century stage. Late Augustan stereotypes of female love-melancholy were sentimentalized versions which minimized the force of female sexuality, and made female insanity a pretty stimulant to male sensibility. Actresses such as Mrs. Lessingham in 1772, and Mary Bolton in 1811, played Ophelia in this decorous style, relying on the familiar images of the white dress, loose hair, and wild flowers to convey a polite feminine distraction, highly suitable for pictorial reproduction, and appropriate for Samuel Johnson's description of Ophelia as young, beautiful, harmless, and pious. Even Mrs. Siddons in 1785 played the mad scene with stately and classical dignity. For much of the period, in fact, Augustan objections to the levity and indecency of Ophelia's language and behavior led to censorship of the part. Her lines were frequently cut, and the role was often assigned to a singer instead of an actress, making the mode of representation musical rather than visual or verbal.

But whereas the Augustan response to madness was a denial, the romantic response was an embrace.[20] The figure of the madwoman permeates romantic literature, from the gothic novelists to Wordsworth and Scott in such texts as "The Thorn" and *The Heart of Midlothian,* where she stands for sexual victimization, bereavement, and thrilling emotional extremity. Romantic artists such as Thomas Barker and George Shepheard painted pathetically abandoned Crazy Kates and Crazy Anns, while Henry Fuseli's "Mad Kate" is almost demonically possessed, an orphan of the romantic storm.

In the Shakespearean theater, Ophelia's romantic revival began in France rather than England. When Charles Kemble made his Paris debut as Hamlet with an English troupe in 1827, his Ophelia was a young Irish ingénue

---

[18] C. E. L. Wingate, *Shakespeare's Heroines on the Stage* (New York, 1895), 283–4, 288–9.

[19] Charles Hiatt, *Ellen Terry* (London, 1898), 11.

[20] Max Byrd, *Visits to Bedlam: Madness and Literature in the Eighteenth Century* (Columbia, 1974), xiv.

named Harriet Smithson. Smithson used "her extensive command of mime to depict in precise gesture the state of Ophelia's confused mind."[21] In the mad scene, she entered in a long black veil, suggesting the standard imagery of female sexual mystery in the gothic novel, with scattered bedlamish wisps of straw in her hair. Spreading the veil on the ground as she sang, she spread flowers upon it in the shape of a cross, as if to make her father's grave, and mimed a burial, a piece of stage business which remained in vogue for the rest of the century.

The French audiences were stunned. Dumas recalled that "it was the first time I saw in the theatre real passions, giving life to men and women of flesh and blood."[22] the 23-year-old Hector Berlioz, who was in the audience on the first night, fell madly in love, and eventually married Harriet Smithson despite his family's frantic opposition. Her image as the mad Ophelia was represented in popular lithographs and exhibited in bookshop and printshop windows. Her costume was imitated by the fashionable, and a coiffure "à la folle," consisting of a "black veil with wisps of straw tastefully interwoven" in the hair, was widely copied by the Parisian beau monde, always on the lookout for something new.[23]

Although Smithson never acted Ophelia on the English stage, her intensely visual performance quickly influenced English productions as well; and indeed the romantic Ophelia—a young girl passionately and visibly driven to picturesque madness—became the dominant international acting style for the next 150 years, from Helena Modjeska in Poland in 1871, to the 18-year-old Jean Simmons in the Laurence Olivier film of 1948.

Whereas the romantic Hamlet, in Coleridge's famous dictum, thinks too much, has an "overbalance of the contemplative faculty" and an overactive intellect, the romantic Ophelia is a girl who *feels* too much, who drowns in feeling. The romantic critics seem to have felt that the less said about Ophelia the better; the point was to *look* at her. Hazlitt, for one, is speechless before her, calling her "a character almost too exquisitely touching to be dwelt upon."[24] While the Augustans represent Ophelia as music, the romantics transform her into an *objet d'art,* as if to take literally Claudius's lament, "poor Ophelia / Divided from herself and her fair judgment, / Without the which we are pictures."

Smithson's performance is best recaptured in a series of pictures done by Delacroix from 1830 to 1850, which show a strong romantic interest in the relation of female sexuality and insanity.[25] The most innovative and influential of Delacroix's lithographs is La Mort d'Ophélie of 1843, the first of three studies. Its sensual languor, with Ophelia half-suspended in the stream as her dress slips from her body, anticipated the fascination with the erotic trance of

[21] Peter Raby, *Fair Ophelia: Harriet Smithson Berlioz* (Cambridge, 1982), 63.
[22] Ibid., 68.
[23] Ibid., 72, 75.
[24] Quoted in Camden, op. cit., 247.
[25] Raby, op. cit., 182.

the hysteric as it would be studied by Jean-Martin Charcot and his students, including Janet and Freud. Delacroix's interest in the drowning Ophelia is also reproduced to the point of obsession in later nineteenth-century painting. The English Pre-Raphaelites painted her again and again, choosing the drowning which is only described in the play, and where no actress's image had preceeded them or interfered with their imaginative supremacy.

In the Royal Academy show of 1852, Arthur Hughes's entry shows a tiny waif-life creature—a sort of Tinker Bell Ophelia—in a filmy white gown, perched on a tree trunk by the stream. The overall effect is softened, sexless, and hazy, although the straw in her hair resembles a crown of thorns. Hughes's juxtaposition of childlike femininity and Christian martyrdom was overpowered, however, by John Everett Millais's great painting of Ophelia in the same show. While Millais's Ophelia is sensuous siren as well as victim, the artist rather than the subject dominates the scene. The division of space between Ophelia and the natural details Millais had so painstakingly pursued reduces her to one more visual object; and the painting has such a hard surface, strangely flattened perspective, and brilliant light that it seems cruelly indifferent to the woman's death.

These Pre-Raphaelite images were part of a new and intricate traffic between images of women and madness in late nineteenth-century literature, psychiatry, drama, and art. First of all, superintendents of Victorian lunatic asylums were also enthusiasts of Shakespeare, who turned to his dramas for models of mental aberration that could be applied to their clinical practice. The case study of Ophelia was one that seemed particularly useful as an account of hysteria or mental breakdown in adolescence, a period of sexual instability which the Victorians regarded as risky for women's mental health. As Dr John Charles Bucknill, president of the Medico-Psychological Association, remarked in 1859, "Ophelia is the very type of a class of cases by no means uncommon. Every mental physician of moderately extensive experience must have seen many Ophelias. It is a copy from nature, after the fashion of the Pre-Raphaelite school."[26] Dr John Conolly, the celebrated superintendent of the Hanwell Asylum, and founder of the committee to make Stratford a national trust, concurred. In his *Study of Hamlet* in 1863 he noted that even casual visitors to mental institutions could recognize an Ophelia in the wards: "the same young years, the same faded beauty, the same fantastic dress and interrupted song."[27] Medical textbooks illustrated their discussions of female patients with sketches of Ophelia-like maidens.

But Conolly also pointed out that the graceful Ophelias who dominated the Victorian stage were quite unlike the women who had become the majority of the inmate population in Victorian public asylums. "It seems to be

---

[26] J. C. Bucknill, *The Psychology of Shakespeare* (London, 1859, reprinted New York, 1970), 110. For more extensive discussions of Victorian psychiatry and Ophelia figures, see Elaine Showalter, *The Female Malady: Women, Madness and English Culture* (New York, 1986).

[27] John Conolly, *Study of Hamlet* (London, 1863), 177.

supposed," he protested, "that it is an easy task to play the part of a crazy girl, and that it is chiefly composed of singing and prettiness. The habitual courtesy, the partial rudeness of mental disorder, are things to be witnessed. . . . An actress, ambitious of something beyond cold imitation, might find the contemplation of such cases a not unprofitable study."[28]

Yet when Ellen Terry took up Conolly's challenge, and went to an asylum to observe real madwomen, she found them "too *theatrical*" to teach her anything.[29] This was because the iconography of the romantic Ophelia had begun to infiltrate reality, to define a style for mad young women seeking to express and communicate their distress. And where the women themselves did not willingly throw themselves into Ophelia-like postures, asylum superintendents, armed with the new technology of photography, imposed the costume, gesture, props, and expression of Ophelia upon them. In England, the camera was introduced to asylum work in the 1850s by Dr Hugh Welch Diamond, who photographed his female patients at the Surrey Asylum and at Bethlem. Diamond was heavily influenced by literary and visual models in his posing of the female subjects. His pictures of madwomen, posed in prayer, or decked with Ophelia-like garlands, were copied for Victorian consumption as touched-up lithographs in professional journals.[30]

Reality, psychiatry, and representational convention were even more confused in the photographic records of hysteria produced in the 1870s by Jean-Martin Charcot. Charcot was the first clinician to install a fully equipped photographic atelier in his Paris hospital, La Salpêtrière, to record the performances of his hysterical stars. Charcot's clinic became, as he said, a "living theatre" of female pathology; his women patients were coached in their performances for the camera, and, under hypnosis, were sometimes instructed to play heroines from Shakespeare. Among them, a 15-year-old girl named Augustine was featured in the published volumes called *Iconographies* in every posture of *la grande hystérie*. With her white hospital gown and flowing locks, Augustine frequently resembles the reproductions of Ophelia as icon and actress which had been in wide circulation.[31]

But if the Victorian madwoman looks mutely out from men's pictures, and acts a part men had staged and directed, she is very differently represented in the feminist revision of Ophelia initiated by newly powerful and respectable Victorian actresses, and by women critics of Shakespeare. In their efforts to defend Ophelia, they invent a story for her drawn from their own experiences, grievances, and desires.

Probably the most famous of the Victorian feminist revisions of the Ophelia story was Mary Cowden Clarke's *The Girlhood of Shakespeare's Heroines*, pub-

---

[28] Ibid., 177–8, 180.

[29] Ellen Terry, *The Story of My Life* (London, 1908), 154.

[30] Diamond's photographs are reproduced in Sander L. Gilman, *The Face of Madness: Hugh W. Diamond and the Origin of Psychiatric Photography* (New York, 1976).

[31] See Georges Didi-Huberman, *L'Invention de l'hystérie* (Paris, 1982), and Stephen Heath, *The Sexual Fix* (London, 1983), 36.

lished in 1852. Unlike other Victorian moralizing and didactic studies of the female characters of Shakespeare's plays, Clarke's was specifically addressed to the wrongs of women, and especially to the sexual double standard. In a chapter on Ophelia called "The rose of Elsinore," Clarke tells how the child Ophelia was left behind in the care of a peasant couple when Polonius was called to the court at Paris, and raised in a cottage with a foster-sister and brother, Jutha and Ulf. Jutha is seduced and betrayed by a deceitful knight, and Ophelia discovers the bodies of Jutha and her still-born child, lying "white, rigid, and still" in the deserted parlor of the cottage in the middle of the night. Ulf, a "hairy loutish boy," likes to torture flies, to eat songbirds, and to rip the petals off roses, and he is also very eager to give little Ophelia what he calls a bear-hug. Both repelled and masochistically attracted by Ulf, Ophelia is repeatedly cornered by him as she grows up; once she escapes the hug by hitting him with a branch of wild roses; another time, he sneaks into her bedroom "in his brutish pertinacity to obtain the hug he had promised himself," but just as he bends over her trembling body, Ophelia is saved by the reappearance of her real mother.

A few years later, back at the court, she discovers the hanged body of another friend, who has killed herself after being "victimized and deserted by the same evil seducer." Not surprisingly, Ophelia breaks down with brain fever—a staple mental illness of Victorian fiction—and has prophetic hallucinations of a brook beneath willow trees where something bad will happen to her. The warnings of Polonius and Laertes have little to add to this history of female sexual trauma.[32]

On the Victorian stage, it was Ellen Terry, daring and unconventional in her own life, who led the way in acting Ophelia in feminist terms as a consistent psychological study in sexual intimidation, a girl terrified of her father, of her lover, and of life itself. Terry's debut as Ophelia in Henry Irving's production in 1878 was a landmark. According to one reviewer, her Ophelia was "the terrible spectacle of a normal girl becoming hopelessly imbecile as the result of overwhelming mental agony. Hers was an insanity without wrath or rage, without exaltation or paroxysms."[33] Her "poetic and intellectual performance" also inspired other actresses to rebel against the conventions of invisibility and negation associated with the part.

Terry was the first to challenge the tradition of Ophelia's dressing in emblematic white. For the French poets, such as Rimbaud, Hugo, Musset, Mallarmé and Laforgue, whiteness was part of Ophelia's essential feminine symbolism; they call her "blanche Ophélia" and compare her to a lily, a cloud, or snow. Yet whiteness also made her a transparency, an absence that took on the colors of Hamlet's moods, and that, for the symbolists like

---

[32] Mary Cowden Clarke, *The Girlhood of Shakespeare's Heroines* (London, 1852). See also George C. Gross, "Mary Cowden Clarke, *The Girlhood of Shakespeare's Heroines,* and the sex education of Victorian women" (*Victorian Studies,* 16 (1972)), 37–58, and Nina Auerbach, *Woman and the Demon* (Cambridge, Mass., 1983), 210–15.

[33] Hiatt, op. cit., 114. See also Wingate, op. cit., 304–5.

Mallarmé, made her a blank page to be written over or on by the male imagination. Although Irving was able to prevent Terry from wearing black in the mad scene, exclaiming "My God, Madam, there must be only *one* black figure in this play, and that's Hamlet!" (Irving, of course, was playing Hamlet), nonetheless actresses such as Gertrude Eliot, Helen Maude, Nora de Silva, and in Russia Vera Komisarjevskaya, gradually won the right to intensify Ophelia's presence by clothing her in Hamlet's black.[34]

By the turn of the century, there was both a male and a female discourse on Ophelia. A. C. Bradley spoke for the Victorian male tradition when he noted in *Shakespearean Tragedy* (1906) that "a large number of readers feel a kind of personal irritation against Ophelia; they seem unable to forgive her for not having been a heroine."[35] The feminist counterview was represented by actresses in such works as Helena Faucit's study of Shakespeare's female characters, and *The True Ophelia*, written by an anonymous actress in 1914, which protested against the "insipid little creature" of criticism, and advocated a strong and intelligent woman destroyed by the heartlessness of men.[36] In women's paintings of the *fin de siècle* as well, Ophelia is depicted as an inspiring, even sanctified emblem of righteousness.[37]

While the widely read and influential essays of Mary Cowden Clarke are now mocked as the epitome of naive criticism, these Victorian studies of the girlhood of Shakespeare's heroines are of course alive and well as psychoanalytic criticism, which has imagined its own prehistories of oedipal conflict and neurotic fixation; and I say this not to mock psychoanalytic criticism, but to suggest that Clarke's musings on Ophelia are a pre-Freudian speculation on the traumatic sources of a female sexual identity. The Freudian interpretation of *Hamlet* concentrated on the hero, but also had much to do with the resexualization of Ophelia. As early as 1900, Freud had traced Hamlet's irresolution to an Oedipus complex, and Ernest Jones, his leading British disciple, developed this view, influencing the performances of John Gielgud and Alec Guinness in the 1930s. In his final version of the study, *Hamlet and Oedipus*, published in 1949, Jones argued that "Ophelia should be unmistakably sensual, as she seldom is on stage. She may be 'innocent' and docile, but she is very aware of her body."[38]

In the theater and in criticism, this Freudian edict has produced such extreme readings as that Shakespeare intends us to see Ophelia as a loose woman, and that she has been sleeping with Hamlet. Rebecca West has argued that Ophelia was not "a correct and timid virgin of exquisite sensibilities," a view she attributes to the popularity of the Millais painting; but

---

[34] Terry, op. cit., 155–6.

[35] Andrew C. Bradley, *Shakespearean Tragedy* (London, 1906), 160.

[36] Helena Faucit Martin, *On Some of Shakespeare's Female Characters* (Edinburgh and London, 1891), 4, 18; and *The True Ophelia* (New York, 1914), 15.

[37] Among these paintings are the Ophelias of Henrietta Rae and Mrs F. Littler. Sarah Bernhardt sculpted a bas relief of Ophelia for the Women's Pavilion at the Chicago World's Fair in 1893.

[38] Ernest Jones, *Hamlet and Oedipus* (New York, 1949), 139.

rather "a disreputable young woman."[39] In his delightful autobiography, Laurence Olivier, who made a special pilgrimage to Ernest Jones when he was preparing his *Hamlet* in the 1930s, recalls that one of his predecessors as actor-manager had said in response to the earnest question, "Did Hamlet sleep with Ophelia?" — "In my company, always."[40]

The most extreme Freudian interpretation reads *Hamlet* as two parallel male and female psychodramas, the counterpointed stories of the incestuous attachments of Hamlet and Ophelia. As Theodore Lidz presents this view, while Hamlet is neurotically attached to his mother, Ophelia has an unresolved oedipal attachment to her father. She has fantasies of a lover who will abduct her from or even kill her father, and when this actually happens, her reason is destroyed by guilt as well as by lingering incestuous feelings. According to Lidz, Ophelia breaks down because she fails in the female developmental task of shifting her sexual attachment from her father "to a man who can bring her fulfillment as a woman."[41] We see the effects of this Freudian Ophelia on stage productions since the 1950s, where directors have hinted at an incestuous link between Ophelia and her father, or more recently, because this staging conflicts with the usual ironic treatment of Polonius, between Ophelia and Laertes. Trevor Nunn's production with Helen Mirren in 1970, for example, made Ophelia and Laertes flirtatious doubles, almost twins in their matching fur-trimmed doublets, playing duets on the lute with Polonius looking on, like Peter, Paul, and Mary. In other productions of the same period, Marianne Faithfull was a haggard Ophelia equally attracted to Hamlet and Laertes, and, in one of the few performances directed by a woman, Yvonne Nicholson sat on Laertes' lap in the advice scene, and played the part with "rough sexual bravado."[42]

Since the 1960s, the Freudian representation of Ophelia has been supplemented by an antipsychiatry that represents Ophelia's madness in more contemporary terms. In contrast to the psychoanalytic representation of Ophelia's sexual unconscious that connected her essential femininity to Freud's essays on female sexuality and hysteria, her madness is now seen in medical and biochemical terms, as schizophrenia. This is so in part because the schizophrenic woman has become the cultural icon of dualistic femininity in the mid-twentieth century as the erotomaniac was in the seventeenth and the hysteric in the nineteenth. It might also be traced to the work of R. D. Laing on female schizophrenia in the 1960s. Laing argued that schizophrenia was an intelligible response to the experience of invalidation within the family network, especially to the conflicting emotional messages and mystifying double binds experienced by daughters. Ophelia, he noted in *The Divided Self,*

---

[39] Rebecca West, *The Court and the Castle* (New Haven, 1958), 18.

[40] Laurence Olivier, *Confessions of an Actor* (Harmondsworth, 1982), 102, 152.

[41] Theodor Lidz, *Hamlet's Enemy: Madness and Myth in Hamlet* (New York, 1975), 88, 113.

[42] Richard David, *Shakespeare in the Theatre* (Cambridge, 1978), 75. This was the production directed by Buzz Goodbody, a brilliant young feminist radical who killed herself that year. See Colin Chambers, *Other Spaces: New Theatre and the RSC* (London, 1980), especially 63–7.

is an empty space. "In her madness there is no one there. . . . There is no integral selfhood expressed through her actions or utterances. Incomprehensible statements are said by nothing. She has already died. There is now only a vacuum where there was once a person."[43]

Despite his sympathy for Ophelia, Laing's readings silence her, equate her with "nothing," more completely than any since the Augustans; and they have been translated into performances which only make Ophelia a graphic study of mental pathology. The sickest Ophelias on the contemporary stage have been those in the productions of the pathologist-director Jonathan Miller. In 1974 at the Greenwich Theatre his Ophelia sucked her thumb; by 1981, at the Warehouse in London, she was played by an actress much taller and heavier than the Hamlet (perhaps punningly cast as the young actor Anton Lesser). She began the play with a set of nervous tics and tuggings of hair which by the mad scene had become a full set of schizophrenic routines—head banging, twitching, wincing, grimacing, and drooling.[44]

But since the 1970s too we have had a feminist discourse which has offered a new perspective on Ophelia's madness as protest and rebellion. For many feminist theorists, the madwoman is a heroine, a powerful figure who rebels against the family and the social order; and the hysteric who refuses to speak the language of the patriarchal order, who speaks otherwise, is a sister.[45] In terms of effect on the theater, the most radical application of these ideas was probably realized in Melissa Murray's agitprop play *Ophelia*, written in 1979 for the English women's theater group "Hormone Imbalance." In this blank verse retelling of the Hamlet story, Ophelia becomes a lesbian and runs off with a woman servant to join a guerrilla commune.[46]

While I've always regretted that I missed this production, I can't proclaim that this defiant ideological gesture, however effective politically or theatrically, is all that feminist criticism desires, or all to which it should aspire. When feminist criticism chooses to deal with representation, rather than with women's writing, it must aim for a maximum interdisciplinary contextualism, in which the complexity of attitudes towards the feminine can be analyzed in their fullest cultural and historical frame. The alternation of strong and weak Ophelias on the stage, virginal and seductive Ophelias in art, inadequate or oppressed Ophelias in criticism, tells us how these representations have overflowed the text, and how they have reflected the ideological character of their times, erupting as debates between dominant and feminist views in periods of gender crisis and redefinition. The representation of Ophelia changes independently of theories of the meaning of the play or the Prince, for it depends on attitudes towards women and madness. The decorous and pious Ophelia of the Augustan age and the postmodern schizophrenic heroine who might have

[43] R. D. Laing, *The Divided Self* (Harmondsworth, 1965), 195n.

[44] David, op. cit., 82–3; thanks to Marianne DeKoven, Rutgers University, for the description of the 1981 Warehouse production.

[45] See, for example, Hélène Cixous and Catherine Clément, *La Jeune Née* (Paris, 1975).

[46] For an account of this production, see Micheline Wandor, *Understudies: Theatre and Sexual Politics* (London, 1981), 47.

stepped from the pages of Laing can be derived from the same figure; they are both contradictory and complementary images of female sexuality in which madness seems to act as the "switching-point, the concept which allows the co-existence of both sides of the representation."[47] There is no "true" Ophelia for whom feminist criticism must unambiguously speak, but perhaps only a Cubist Ophelia of multiple perspectives, more than the sum of all her parts.

But in exposing the ideology of representation, feminist critics have also the responsibility to acknowledge and to examine the boundaries of our own ideological positions as products of our gender and our time. A degree of humility in an age of critical hubris can be our greatest strength, for it is by occupying this position of historical self-consciousness in both feminism and criticism that we maintain our credibility in representing Ophelia, and that unlike Lacan, when we promise to speak about her, we make good our word.

[47] I am indebted for this formulation to a critique of my earlier draft of this paper by Carl Friedman, at the Wesleyan Center for the Humanities, April 1984.

STEPHEN GREENBLATT

Shakespeare and the Exorcists

1985

Stephen Greenblatt (b. 1943) defines his linking of literature to history as "cultural poetics," a critical approach also called New Historicism. In cultural poetics, the critic considers literature as interactive with the social, religious, and political institutions of its time. The endeavor, in part Marxist in its attention to the ideology of power, does not usually employ, however, the Marxist dialectic of conflict between the working and ruling classes. To the New Historicist, literature both reflects and shapes ideology in a more fluid interaction than discovered in Historicism, which, in Greenblatt's opinion, erred in locating an autonomous literary text against a stable and definable historical background.

Greenblatt follows the Marxist assumption, discussed in the selections from Terry Eagleton (page 525), that the ruling class maintains power through a control of ideology. He portrays Samuel Harsnett's A Declaration of Egregious Popish Impostures, an attack on Catholic ritual, as a politically motivated support of the Protestant monarchy. Harsnett had denounced Catholic exorcism as a theatrical fraud. Greenblatt argues that Shakespeare echoes this concept in King Lear, particularly in Edgar's practice of a fraud to exorcise the plan of suicide from Gloucester's mind at the cliffs of Dover, apparently affirming in the state-sanctioned theater the ideology of exorcism as fraud.

But beyond dramatizing the official position against exorcism, Greenblatt speculates that Shakespeare undermines that ideology precisely by portraying it in the theater. All theater is known as illusion and fraudulence by the audience. A presentation of ideology in the theater makes the official position itself be seen as illusion. Greenblatt's argument parallels the theories of the contemporary French Marxist theorists Louis Althusser and Pierre Macherey that literature writes out ideology but by so doing hollows it of power. (Eagleton discusses Althusser and Macherey's theory in a section on "Literature and Ideology" in the selections from Marxism and Literary Criticism, page 534.)

Greenblatt differentiates his approach from the contrary theories of Marxism and deconstruction, but all three remove the boundary between literature and history inherent in New Criticism. The free placement of literature among all other discourse permits Greenblatt's speculation about complex kinds of interrelationship.

BETWEEN THE SPRING of 1585 and the summer of 1586, a group of English Catholic priests led by the Jesuit William Weston, alias Father Edmunds, conducted a series of spectacular exorcisms, principally in the house of a recusant gentleman, Sir George Peckham of Denham, Buckinghamshire. The priests were outlaws—by the Act of 1585 the mere presence in England of a Jesuit or seminary priest constituted high treason—and those who sheltered them were guilty of a felony, punishable by death. Yet the exorcisms, though clandestine, drew large crowds, almost certainly in the hundreds, and must have been common knowledge to hundreds more. In 1603, long after the arrest and punishment of those involved, Samuel Harsnett, then chaplain to the Bishop of London, wrote a detailed account of the cases, based upon sworn statements taken from four of the demoniacs and one of the priests. It has been recognized since the eighteenth century that Shakespeare was reading Harsnett's book, *A Declaration of Egregious Popish Impostures,* as he was writing *King Lear.*[1]

My concern is with the relation between these two texts, and I want to suggest that our understanding of this relation is greatly enhanced by the theoretical ferment that has affected (some would say afflicted) literary studies during the past decade. This claim may arouse scepticism on several counts. Source study is, as we all know, the elephants' graveyard of literary history. My own work, moreover, has consistently failed to make the move that can redeem, on these occasions, such unpromising beginnings: the move from a local problem to a universal, encompassing, and abstract problematic within which the initial concerns are situated. For me the study of the literary is the study of contingent, particular, intended, and historically embedded works; if theory inevitably involves the desire to escape from contingency into a higher realm, a realm in which signs are purified of the slime of history, then this paper is written *against* theory.[2]

But I am not convinced that theory necessarily drives toward the abstract purity of autonomous signification, and, even when it does, its influence upon the study of literature may be quite distinct from its own designs. Indeed, I believe that the most important effect of contemporary theory upon the practice of literary criticism, and certainly upon *my* practice, is to subvert the tendency to think of aesthetic representation as ultimately autonomous, separable from its cultural context and hence divorced from the social, ideological, and material matrix in which all art is produced and consumed. This subversion is true not only of Marxist theory explicity engaged in polemics

---

[1]Samuel Harsnett, *A Declaration of Egregious Popish Impostures* (London, 1603). Harsnett's influence is noted in Lewis Theobald's edition of Shakespeare, first published in 1733. On the clandestine exorcisms I am particularly indebted to D. P. Walker, *Unclean Spirits: Possession and Exorcism in France and England in the Late Sixteenth and Early Seventeenth Centuries* (Philadelphia, 1981). *King Lear* is quoted from the New Arden text, ed. Kenneth Muir (London, 1972). All other quotations from Shakespeare are taken from the Arden editions. [All notes are Greenblatt's unless otherwise noted.]

[2]For extended arguments for and against theory, see Walter Michaels and Steven Knapp, "Against theory" (*Critical Inquiry,* 8 (1982), 723–42), and the ensuing controversy in *Critical Inquiry,* 9 (1983), 725–800.

against literary autonomy, but also of deconstructionist theory, even at its most hermetic and abstract. For the undecidability that deconstruction repeatedly discovers in literary signification also calls into question the boundaries between the literary and the nonliterary. The intention to produce a work of literature does not guarantee an autonomous text, since the signifiers always exceed and thus undermine intention. This constant exceeding (which is the paradoxical expression of an endless deferral of meaning) forces the collapse of all stable oppositions, or rather compels interpretation to acknowledge that one position is always infected with traces of its radical antithesis.[3] Insofar as the absolute disjunction of the literary and the nonliterary had been the root assumption of mainstream Anglo-American criticism in the mid-twentieth century, deconstruction emerged as a liberating challenge, a salutary return of the literary text to the condition of all other texts and a simultaneous assault on the positivist certitude of the nonliterary, the privileged realm of historical fact. History cannot be divorced from textuality, and all texts can be compelled to confront the crisis of undecidability revealed in the literary text. Hence history loses its epistemological innocence, while literature loses an isolation that had come to seem more a prison than a privilege.

The problem with this theoretical liberation, in my view, is that it is forced, by definition, to discount the specific, institutional interests served both by local episodes of undecidability and contradiction and by the powerful if conceptually imperfect differentiation between the literary and the nonliterary. Deconstruction is occasionally attacked as if it were a satanic doctrine, but I sometimes think that it is not satanic enough; as John Wesley wrote to his brother, "If I have any fear, it is not of falling into hell, but of falling into nothing."[4] Deconstructionist readings lead too readily and predictably to the void; in actual literary practice the perplexities into which one is led are not moments of pure, untrammeled *aporia*[5] but localized strategies in particular historical encounters. Similarly, it is important to expose the theoretical untenability of the conventional boundaries between facts and artifacts, but the particular terms of this boundary at a specific time and place cannot simply be discarded. On the contrary, as I will try to demonstrate in some detail, these impure terms that mark the difference between the literary and the nonliterary are the currency in crucial institutional negotiations and exchange. This institutional economy is one of the central concerns of the critical method that I have called cultural poetics.

Let us return to Samuel Harsnett. The relation between *King Lear* and *A Declaration of Egregious Popish Impostures* has, as I have remarked, been known for centuries, but the knowledge has remained almost entirely inert,

---

[3] I am indebted to an important critique of Marxist and deconstructive literary theory by D. A. Miller, "Discipline in different voices: bureaucracy, police, family and *Bleak House*" (*Representations*, 1 (1983), 59–89).

[4] *John Wesley*, ed. Albert C. Outler (New York, 1964), 82.

[5] A problem arising from an awareness of opposing or incompatible views of the same theoretical matter. Systematic doubt. [Eds.]

locked in the conventional pieties of source study. From Harsnett, we are told, Shakespeare borrowed the names of the foul fiends by whom Edgar, in his disguise as the Bedlam beggar Poor Tom, claims to be possessed. From Harsnett, too, the playwright derived some of the language of madness, several of the attributes of hell, and a substantial number of colorful adjectives. These and other possible borrowings have been carefully catalogued, but the question of their significance has been not only unanswered but unmasked.[6] Until recently, the prevailing model for the study of literary sources, a model in effect parceled out between the old historicism and the new criticism, blocked such a question. As a freestanding, self-sufficient, disinterested artwork produced by a solitary genius, *King Lear* has only an accidental relation to its sources: they provide a glimpse of the "raw material" that the artist fashioned. In so far as this "material" is taken seriously at all, it is as part of the work's "historical background," a phrase that reduces history to a decorative setting or a convenient, well-lighted pigeonhole. But once the differentiations upon which this model is based begin to crumble, then source study is compelled to change its character: history cannot simply be set against literary texts as either stable antithesis or stable background, and the protective isolation of those texts gives way to a sense of their interaction with other texts and hence to the permeability of their boundaries. "When I play with my cat," writes Montaigne, "who knows if I am not a pastime to her more than she is to me?"[7] When Shakespeare borrows from Harsnett, who knows if Harsnett has not already, in a deep sense, borrowed from Shakespeare's theater what Shakespeare borrows back? Whose interests are served by the borrowing? And is there a larger cultural text produced by the exchange?

Such questions do not lead, for me at least, to the *O altitudo!*[8] of radical indeterminacy. They lead rather to an exploration of the institutional strategies in which both *King Lear* and Harsnett's *Declaration* are embedded. These strategies, I suggest, are part of an intense and sustained struggle in late sixteenth- and early seventeenth-century England to redefine the central values of society. Such a redefinition entailed a transformation of the prevailing standards of judgment and action, a rethinking of the conceptual categories by which the ruling élites constructed their world, and which they attempted

---

[6] A major exception, with conclusions different from my own, has just been published: John L. Murphy, *Darkness and Devils: Exorcism and "King Lear"* (Athens, Ohio, 1984). Murphy's fascinating study, which he kindly allowed me to read in galleys after hearing the present paper delivered as a lecture, argues that exorcism is an aspect of clandestine political and religious resistance to Queen Elizabeth's rule. See also, for interesting reflections, William Elton, *"King Lear" and the Gods* (San Marino, 1966). For useful accounts of Harsnett's relation to *Lear*, see Geoffrey Bullough (ed.), *Narrative and Dramatic Sources of Shakespeare* (London, 1975), 7, 299–302; Kenneth Muir, "Samuel Harsnett and *King Lear*" (*Review of English Studies*, 2 (1951), 11–21); Kenneth Muir (ed.), *King Lear* (London, 1972), 239–42.

[7] Michel de Montaigne, "Apology for Raymond Sebond," in *Complete Essays*, tr. Donald Frame (Stanford, 1948), 331.

[8] "Oh height beyond understanding." From Sir Thomas Browne, *Religio Medici*, First Part, Section 9. [Eds.]

to impose upon the majority of the population. At the heart of this struggle, which had as its outcome a murderous civil war, was the definition of the sacred, a definition that directly involved secular as well as religious institutions, since the legitimacy of the state rested explicitly upon its claim to a measure of sacredness. What is the sacred? Who defines and polices its boundaries? How can society distinguish between legitimate and illegitimate claims to sacred authority? In early modern England, rivalry among elites competing for the major share of authority was characteristically expressed not only in parliamentary factions but in bitter struggles over religious doctrine and practice.

Harsnett's *Declaration* is a weapon in one such struggle, the attempt by the established and state-supported Church of England to eliminate competing religious authorities by wiping out pockets of rivalrous charisma. Charisma, in Edward Shils's phrase, is "awe-arousing centrality,"[9] the sense of breaking through the routine into the realm of the "extraordinary," and hence the sense of making direct contact with the ultimate, vital sources of legitimacy, authority, and sacredness. Exorcism was for centuries one of the supreme manifestations in Latin Christianity of this charisma; "in the healing of the possessed," Peter Brown writes, "the *præsentia*[10] of the saints was held to be registered with unfailing accuracy, and their ideal power, their *potentia*,[11] shown most fully and in the most reassuring manner."[12] Reassuring, that is, not only or even primarily to the demoniac, but to the community of believers who bore witness to the ritual and indeed, through their tears and prayers and thanksgiving, participated in it. For unlike sorcery, which occurred most frequently in the dark corners of the land, in remote rural hamlets and isolated cottages, demonic possession seems largely an urban phenomenon. The devil depended upon an audience, as did the charismatic healer: the great exorcisms of the late middle ages and early Renaissance took place at the heart of cities, in cathedrals packed with spectators. They were, as voluminous contemporary accounts declare, moving testimonials to the power of the true faith. But in Protestant England of the late sixteenth century, neither the *præsentia* nor the *potentia* of the exorcist was any longer reassuring to religious authorities, and the Anglican Church had no desire to treat the urban masses to a spectacle whose edifying value had been called into question. Even relatively small assemblies, gathered far from the cities in the obscurity of private houses, had come to represent a threat.

In the *Declaration*, Harsnett specifically attacks exorcism as practiced by Jesuits, but he had earlier leveled the same charges at the Puritan exorcist John Darrell.[13] And he does so not, as we might expect, to claim a monopoly

[9] Edward Shils, *Center and Periphery: Essays in Macrosociology* (Chicago, 1975), 3. My account of institutional strategies is indebted to Shils.
[10] Presence. [Eds.]
[11] Efficacy, power. [Eds.]
[12] Peter Brown, *The Cult of the Saints: Its Rise and Function in Latin Christianity* (Chicago, 1981), 107.
[13] Samuel Harsnett, *A Discovery of the Fraudulent Practices of John Darrel* (London, 1599).

on the practice for the Anglican Church, but to expose exorcism itself as a fraud. On behalf of established religious and secular authority, Harsnett wishes, in effect, to cap permanently the great rushing geysers of charisma released in rituals of exorcism. Spiritual *potentia* will henceforth be distributed with greater moderation and control through the whole of the Anglican hierarchy, a hierarchy at whose pinnacle is placed the sole legitimate possessor of absolute charismatic authority, the monarch, supreme head of the Church in England.

The arguments that Harsnett marshalls against exorcism have a rationalistic cast that may mislead us, for despite appearances we are not dealing with an Enlightenment attempt to construct a rational faith. Harsnett denies the presence of the demonic in those whom Father Edmunds claimed to exorcize, but finds it in the exorcists themselves:

> And who was the deuil, the brocher, herald, and perswader of these vnutterable treasons, but *Weston* [*alias* Edmunds] the Iesuit, the chief plotter, and . . . all the holy Couey of the twelue deuilish comedians in their seueral turnes: for there was neither deuil, nor vrchin, nor Elfe, but themselues.[14]

Hence, writes Harsnett, the "Dialogue between *Edmunds,* & the deuil" was in reality a dialogue between "the deuil *Edmunds,* and *Edmunds* the deuil, for he played both parts himself."[15]

This strategy—the reinscription of evil onto the professed enemies of evil—is one of the characteristic operations of religious authority in the early modern period, and has its secular analogues in more recent history when famous revolutionaries are paraded forth to be tried as counterrevolutionaries. The paradigmatic Renaissance instance is the case of the *benandanti,* analyzed brilliantly by the historian Carlo Ginzburg.[16] The *benandanti* were members of a northern Italian folk cult who believed that their spirits went forth seasonally to battle with fennel stalks against their enemies, the witches. If the *benandanti* triumphed, their victory assured the peasants of good harvests; if they lost, the witches would be free to work their mischief. The Inquisition first became interested in the practice in the late sixteenth century; after conducting a series of lengthy inquiries, the Holy Office determined that the cult was demonic, and in subsequent interrogations attempted, with some success, to persuade the witch-fighting *benandanti* that they were themselves witches.

Harsnett does not hope to persuade exorcists that they are devils; he wishes to expose their fraudulence and relies upon the state to punish them. But he is not willing to abandon the demonic altogether, and it hovers in his work, half-accusation, half-metaphor, whenever he refers to Father Edmunds

---

[14] Harsnett, *Declaration,* 154–5.

[15] Ibid., 86.

[16] Carlo Ginzburg, *I benandanti: Recerche sulla stregoneria e sui culti agrari tra Cinquecento e Seicento* (Turin, 1966).

or the Pope. Satan served too important a function to be cast off lightly by the early seventeenth-century clerical establishment. The same state Church that sponsored the attacks on superstition in the *Declaration of Egregious Popish Impostures* continued to cooperate, if less enthusiastically than before, in the ferocious prosecutions of witches. These prosecutions significantly were handled by the secular judicial apparatus—witchcraft was a criminal offense like aggravated assault or murder—and hence reinforced rather than rivaled the bureaucratic control of authority. The eruption of the demonic into the human world was not denied altogether, but the problem was to be processed through the proper, secular channels. In cases of witchcraft, the devil was defeated in the courts through the simple expedient of hanging his human agents and not, as in cases of possession, compelled by a spectacular spiritual counterforce to speak out and depart.

Witchcraft, then, was distinct from possession, and though Harsnett himself is skeptical about accusations of witchcraft, his principal purpose is to expose a nexus of chicanery and delusion in the practice of exorcism.[17] By doing so he hopes to drive the practice out of society's central zone, to deprive it of its prestige and discredit its apparent efficacy. In late antiquity, as Peter Brown has demonstrated, exorcism was based upon the model of the Roman judicial system: the exorcist conducted a formal *quæstio* in which the demon, under torture, was forced to confess the truth.[18] Now, after more than a millennium, this power would once again be vested solely in the state.

Harsnett's efforts, backed by his powerful superiors, did seriously restrict the practice of exorcism. Canon 72 of the new Church Canons of 1604 ruled that henceforth no minister, unless he had the special permission of his bishop, was to attempt "upon any pretense whatsoever, whether of possession or obsession, by fasting and prayer, to cast out any devil or devils, under pain of the imputation of imposture or cozenage and deposition from the ministery."[19] Since special permission was rarely if ever granted, exorcism had, in effect, been officially halted. But it proved easier to drive exorcism from the center to the periphery than to strip it entirely of its power. Exorcism had been a process of reintegration as well as a manifestation of authority; as the ethnographer Shirokogorov observed of the shamans of Siberia, exorcists could "master" harmful spirits and restore "psychic equilibrium" to whole communities as well as to individuals.[20] The pronouncements of En-

[17] For Harsnett's comments on witchcraft, see *Declaration*, 135–6. The relation between demonic possession and witchcraft is extremely complex. John Darrell evidently had frequent recourse, in the midst of his exorcisms, to accusations of witchcraft whose evidence was precisely the demonic possessions; Harsnett remarks wryly that "Of all the partes of the tragicall Comedie acted between him and *Somers*, there was no one Scene in it, wherein M. *Darrell* did with more courage & boldnes acte his part, then in this of the discouerie of witches" (*Discovery*, 142). There is a helpful discussion of possession and witchcraft, along with an important account of Harsnett and Darrell, in Keith Thomas, *Religion and the Decline of Magic* (London, 1971).

[18] Brown, op. cit., 109–11.

[19] Thomas, op. cit., 485.

[20] S. M. Shirokogorov, *The Psycho-Mental Complex of the Tungus* (Peking and London, 1935), 265.

glish bishops could not suddenly banish from the land inner demons who stood, as Peter Brown puts it, "for the intangible emotional undertones of ambiguous situations and for the uncertain motives of refractory individuals."[21] The possessed gave voice to the rage, anxiety, and sexual frustration that built up particularly easily in the authoritarian, patriarchal, impoverished, and plague-ridden world of early modern England. The Anglicans attempted to dismantle a corrupt and inadequate therapy without effecting a new and successful cure. In the absence of exorcism, Harsnett could only offer the possessed the very slender reed of Jacobean medicine; if the recently deciphered journal of the Buckinghamshire physician, Richard Napier, is at all representative, doctors in the period struggled to treat a substantial number of cases of possession.[22] But for Harsnett the problem does not really exist, for he argues that the great majority of cases of possession are either fraudulent or subtly called into existence by the ritual designed to treat them. Eliminate the cure and you eliminate the disease. He is forced to concede that at some distant time possession and exorcism were authentic, for, after all, Jesus himself had driven a legion of unclean spirits out of a possessed man and into the Gadarene swine (Mark 5: 1–19); but the age of miracles has passed, and corporeal possession by demons is no longer possible. The spirit abroad is "the spirit of illusion."[23] Whether they profess to be Catholics or Calvinists does not matter; all modern exorcists practice the same time-honored trade: "the feate of iugling and deluding the people by counterfeyt miracles."[24] Exorcists sometimes contend, acknowledges Harsnett, that the casting out of devils is not a miracle but a wonder—"*mirandum & non miraculum*"—but "both tearmes spring from one roote of wonder or maruell: an effect which a thing strangely done doth procure in the minds of the beholders, as being aboue the reach of nature and reason."[25]

The significance of exorcism, then, lies not in any intrinsic quality of the ritual nor in the precise character of the marks of possession; it lies entirely in the impression made upon the spectators. It may appear that the exorcist and the possessed are utterly absorbed in their terrifying confrontation, but in the midst of the sound and fury—"crying, gnashing of teeth, wallowing, foaming, extraordinarie and supernaturall strength, and supernaturall knowledge"[26]— the real object of the performers' attention is the crowd of beholders.

To counter these effects, Harsnett needed an analytical tool that would enable him to demystify exorcism, to show his readers why the ritual could be so empty and yet so powerful, why beholders could be induced to believe that they were witnessing the ultimate confrontation of good and evil, why a few miserable shifts could produce the experience of horror and wonder. He finds that tool in *theater*.

[21] Brown, op. cit., 110.
[22] Michael MacDonald, *Mystical Bedlam* (Cambridge, 1981).
[23] Harsnett, *Declaration*, A3r.
[24] Harsnett, *Discovery*, A2r.
[25] Ibid., A4r–v.
[26] Ibid., 29.

In the most powerful artistic practice of his age, Harsnett claims to reveal the analytical key to disclosing the degradation of the ancient spiritual practice: exorcisms are stage plays fashioned by cunning clerical dramatists and performed by actors skilled in improvisation. Harsnett first used this theatrical analysis in his attack on Darrell, but it was not until three years later, in his polemic against the Jesuit exorcists, that he worked out its implications in detail.[27] In the account presented in the *Declaration of Egregious Popish Impostures*, some of the participants are self-conscious professionals, like Father Edmunds and his cohorts; others (mostly impressionable young serving women and unstable, down-at-heel young gentlemen) are amateurs cunningly drawn into the demonic stage business. Those selected to play the possessed are in effect taught their roles without realizing at first that they *are* roles.

The priests begin by talking conspicuously about the way successful exorcisms abroad had taken place, and describing in lurid detail the precise symptoms of the possessed. They then await occasions upon which to improvise: a serving man, "beeing pinched with penurie, & hunger, did lie but a night, or two, abroad in the fieldes, and beeing a melancholicke person, was scared with lightning, and thunder, that happened in the night, & loe, an euident signe, that the man was possessed";[28] a dissolute young gentleman "had a spice of the *Hysterica passio*" or, as it is popularly called, "the Moother,"[29] and that too is a sign of possession. An inflamed toe, a pain in the side, a fright taken from the sudden leaping of a cat, a fall in the kitchen, an intense depression following the loss of a beloved child—all are occasions for the priests to step forward and detect the awful presence of the demonic, whereupon the young "scholers," as Harsnett wryly terms the naive performers, "*frame* themselues iumpe and fit vnto the Priests humors, to mop, mow, iest, raile, raue, roare, commend & discommend, and as the priests would have them, vpon fitting occasions (according to the differences of times, places, and commers in) in all things to play the deuils accordinglie."[30]

The theatricality of exorcism, to which the *Declaration* insistently calls attention, has been repeatedly noted by modern ethnographers who do not share Harsnett's reforming zeal or his sense of outrage. In an illuminating study of possession among the Ethiopians of Gondar, Michel Leiris notes that the healer carefully instructs the *zar*, or spirit, who has seized upon someone, how to behave: the types of cries appropriate to the occasion, the expected violent contortions, the "decorum," as Harsnett would put it, of the trance state.[31] The treatment is in effect an initiation into the performance of the

---

[27] D. P. Walker suggests that the attack on the Jesuits is a screen for an attack on the more politically sensitive nonconformists; in early seventeenth-century England, when in doubt it was safer to attack a Catholic.

[28] Harsnett, *Declaration*, 24.

[29] Ibid., 25. See Edmund Jorden, *A Briefe Discourse of a Disease Called the Suffocation of the Mother* (London, 1603).

[30] Harsnett, *Declaration*, 38.

[31] Michel Leiris, *La Possession et ses aspects théâtraux chez les Ethiopiens de Gondar* (Paris, 1958).

symptoms, which are then cured precisely because they conform to the stereotype of the healing process. One must not conclude, writes Leiris, that there are no "real"—that is, sincerely experienced—cases of possession, for many of the patients (principally young women and slaves) seem genuinely ill, but at the same time there are no cases that are exempt from artifice.[32] Between authentic possession, spontaneous and involuntary, and inauthentic possession, simulated to provide a show or extract some material or moral benefit, there are so many subtle shadings that it is impossible to draw a firm boundary.[33] Possession in Gondar *is* theater, but theater that cannot confess its own theatrical nature, for this is not "theater played" (*théâtre joué*) but "theater lived" (*théâtre vécu*), lived not only by the spirit-haunted actor but by the audience. Those who witness a possession may at any moment be themselves possessed, and even if they are untouched by the *zar*, they remain participants rather than passive spectators. For the theatrical performance is not shielded from them by an impermeable membrane; possession is extraordinary but not marginal, a heightened but not separate state. In possession, writes Leiris, the collective life itself takes the form of theater.[34]

Precisely those qualities that fascinate and charm the ethnographer disgust the embattled Harsnett: where the former can write of "authentic" possession, in the unspoken assurance that none of his readers actually believes in the existence of "*zars*," the latter, granted no such assurance and culturally threatened by the alternative vision of reality, struggles to prove that possession is by definition inauthentic; where the former sees a complex ritual integrated into the social process, the latter sees "a *Stygian* comedy to make silly people afraid";[35] where the former sees the theatrical expression of collective life, the latter sees the theatrical promotion of specific and malevolent institutional interests. And where Leiris's central point is that possession is a theater that does not confess its own theatricality, Harsnett's concern is to enforce precisely such a confession: the last 102 pages of the *Declaration of Egregious Popish Impostures* reprint the "severall Examinations, and confessions of the parties pretended to be possessed, and dispossessed by *Weston* the Iesuit, and his adherents: set downe word for worde as they were taken vpon oath before her Maiesties Commissioners for causes Ecclesiasticall."[36] These transcripts prove, according to Harsnett, that the solemn ceremony of exorcism is a "play of sacred miracles," a "wonderful pageant," a "deuil Theater."[37]

The force of this confession, for Harsnett, is to demolish exorcism. Theater is not the disinterested expression of the popular spirit, but the indelible mark of falsity, tawdriness, and rhetorical manipulation. And these sinister qualities are rendered diabolical by that which so appeals to Leiris:

[32] Ibid., 27–8.
[33] Ibid., 94–5.
[34] Ibid., 96.
[35] Harsnett, *Declaration*, 69.
[36] Ibid., 172.
[37] Ibid., 2, 106.

exorcism's cunning concealment of its own theatricality. The spectators do not know that they are responding to a powerful if sleazy tragicomedy; hence their tears and joy, their transports of "commiseration and compassion,"[38] are rendered up, not to a troupe of acknowledged players, but to seditious Puritans or to the supremely dangerous Catholic Church. The theatrical seduction is not, for Harsnett, merely a Jesuitical strategy; it is the essence of the Church itself: Catholicism is a "Mimick superstition."[39]

Harsnett's response is to try to compel the Church to become the theater, just as Catholic clerical garments—the copes and albs and amices and stoles that were the glories of medieval textile crafts—were sold during the Reformation to the players. When an actor in a history play took the part of an English bishop, he could conceivably have worn the actual robes of the character he was representing. Far more is involved here than thrift: the transmigration of a single ecclesiastical cloak from the vestry to the wardrobe may stand as an emblem of the more complex and elusive institutional exchanges that are my subject: a sacred sign, designed to be displayed before a crowd of men and women, is emptied, made negotiable, traded from one institution to another. Such exchanges are rarely so tangible; they are not usually registered in inventories, not often sealed with a cash payment. Nonetheless they occur constantly, for it is precisely through the process of institutional negotiation and exchange that differentiated expressive systems, distinct cultural discourses, are fashioned. We may term such fashioning cultural poesis; the sale of clerical garments is an instance of the ideological labor that such poesis entails. What happens when the piece of cloth is passed from the church to the playhouse? A consecrated object is reclassified, assigned a cash value, transferred from a sacred to a profane setting, deemed suitable to be staged. The theater company is willing to pay for the object not because it contributes to naturalistic representation but because it still bears a symbolic value, however attenuated. On the bare Elizabethan stage, costumes were particularly important—companies were willing to pay more for a good costume than for a good play—and that importance in turn reflected culture's fetishistic obsession with clothes as a mark of status and degree. And if for the theater the acquisition of clerical garments was a significant appropriation of symbolic power, why would the Church part with that power? Because selling Catholic vestments to the players was a form of symbolic aggression: a vivid, wry reminder that Catholicism, as Harsnett puts it, is "the Pope's playhouse."[40]

This blend of appropriation and aggression is similarly at work in the transfer of possession and exorcism from sacred to profane representation. Hence the *Declaration* takes pains to identify exorcism not merely with "the

---

[38] Ibid., 74.

[39] Ibid., 20. This argument has the curious effect of identifying all exorcisms, including those conducted by nonconformist preachers, with the Pope. On attacks on the Catholic Church as a theater, see Jonas Barish, *The Antitheatrical Prejudice* (Berkeley, 1981), 66–131 *passim*.

[40] Harsnett, *Discovery*, A3ʳ.

theatrical"—a category that scarcely exists for Harsnett—but with the actual theater; at issue is not so much a metaphorical concept as a functioning institution. For if Harsnett can drive exorcism into the theater—if he can show that the stately houses in which the rituals were performed were playhouses, that the sacred garments were what he calls a "lousie holy wardrop,"[41] that the terrifying writhings were simulations, that the uncanny signs and wonders were contemptible stage tricks, that the devils were the "cassiered woodden-beaten" Vices from medieval drama,[42] and that the exorcists were "vagabond players, that coast from Towne to Towne"[43]—then the ceremony and everything for which it stands will, as far as he is concerned, be emptied out. And, with this emptying out, Harsnett will have driven exorcism from the center to the periphery—in the case of London, quite literally to the periphery, where increasingly stringent urban regulation had already driven the public playhouses.

It is in this symbolically charged zone of pollution, disease, and licentious entertainment that Harsnett seeks to situate the practice of exorcism.[44] What had once occurred in solemn glory at the very center of the city would now be staged alongside the culture's other vulgar spectacles and illusions. Indeed the sense of the theater's tawdriness, marginality, and emptiness—the sense that everything the players touch is thereby rendered hollow—underlies Harsnett's analysis not only of exorcism but of the entire Catholic Church. Demonic possession is a particularly attractive cornerstone for such an analysis, not only because of its histrionic intensity but because the theater itself is by its very nature bound up with possession. Harsnett did not have to believe that the cult of Dionysus out of which the Greek drama evolved was a cult of possession; even the ordinary and familiar theater of his own time depended upon the apparent transformation of the actor into the voice, the actions, and the face of another.

With his characteristic opportunism and artistic self-consciousness, Shakespeare in his first known play, *The Comedy of Errors* (1590), was already toying with the connection between theater, illusion, and spurious possession. Antipholus of Syracuse, accosted by his twin's mistress, imagines that he is encountering the devil: "Satan avoid I charge thee tempt me not" (IV.iii.46). The Ephesian Antipholus's wife, Adriana, dismayed by the apparently mad behavior of her husband, images that the devil has possessed him, and she dutifully calls in an exorcist: "Good Doctor Pinch, you are a conjurer; / Establish him in his true sense again" (IV.iv.45–6). Pinch begins the solemn ritual:

---

[41] Ibid., 78.
[42] Ibid., 114–15.
[43] Ibid., 149.
[44] Harsnett was not, of course, alone. See, for example, John Gee: "The Jesuits being or having Actors of such dexterity, I see no reason but that they should set up a company for themselves, which surely will put down The Fortune, Red-Bull, Cock-pit, and Globe" (*New Shreds of the Old Snare* (London, 1624)). I owe this reference, along with powerful reflections on the significance of the public theater's physical marginality, to Steven Mullaney.

> I charge thee, Satan, hous'd within this man,
> To yield possession to my holy prayers,
> And to thy state of darkness hie thee straight;
> I conjure thee by all the saints in heaven.
>
> (IV.iv.52–5)

only to be interrupted with a box on the ears from the outraged husband: "Peace, doting wizard, peace; I am not mad." For the exorcist, such denials only confirm the presence of an evil spirit: "the fiend is strong within him" (IV.iv.105). At the scene's end, Antipholus is dragged away to be "bound and laid in some dark room."

The false presumption of demonic possession in *The Comedy of Errors* is not the result of deception; it is an instance of what one of Shakespeare's sources calls a "suppose"—an attempt to make sense of a series of bizarre actions gleefully generated by the comedy's screwball coincidences. Exorcism is the kind of straw people clutch at when the world seems to have gone mad. In *Twelfth Night*, written some ten years later, Shakespeare's view of exorcism, though still comic, has darkened. Possession now is not a mistaken "suppose" but a fraud, a malicious practical joke played upon Malvolio. "Pray God he be not bewitched" (III.iv.102), Maria piously intones at the sight of the cross-gartered, leering gull, and when he is out of earshot Fabian laughs, "If this were played upon a stage now, I could condemn it as an improbable fiction" (III.iv.128–9).[45] The theatrical self-consciousness is intensified when Feste the clown is brought in to conduct a mock-exorcism; "I would I were the first that ever dissembled in such a gown" (IV.ii.5–6), he remarks sententiously as he disguises himself as Sir Topas the curate. If the gibe had a specific reference for the play's original audience, it would be to the Puritan Darrell who had only recently been convicted of dissembling in the exorcism of William Sommers of Nottingham. Now, the scene would suggest, the tables are being turned on the self-righteous fanatic. "Good Sir Topas," pleads Malvolio, "do not think I am mad. They have laid me here in hideous darkness." "Fie, thou dishonest Satan!" Feste replies. "I call thee by the most modest terms, for I am one of those gentle ones that will use the devil himself with courtesy" (IV.ii.29–34).

By 1600 then Shakespeare had clearly marked out possession and exorcism as frauds, so much so that in *All's Well That Ends Well*, a few years later, he could casually use the term "exorcist" as a synonym for illusion-monger: "Is there no exorcist / Beguiles the truer office of mine eyes?" cries the King of France when Helena, whom he thought dead, appears before him: "Is't real that I see?" (V.iii.298–300). When in 1603 Harsnett was whipping exorcism toward the theater, Shakespeare was already at the entrance to the Globe to welcome it.

Given Harsnett's frequent expressions of the "anti-theatrical prejudice," this welcome may seem strange, but in fact nothing in the *Declaration of Egre-*

---

[45] This sentiment could serve as the epigraph to both of Harsnett's books on exorcism; it is the root perception from which most of Harsnett's rhetoric grows.

gious Popish Impostures necessarily implies hostility to the theater as a professional institution. It was Darrell, and not Harsnett, who represented an implacable threat to the theater, for where the Anglican polemicist saw the theatrical in the demonic the Puritan polemicist saw the demonic in the theatrical: "The Devil," wrote Stephen Gosson, "is the efficient cause of plays."[46] Harsnett's work attacks a form of theater that pretends that it is not entertainment but sober reality; hence his polemic virtually depends upon the existence of an officially designated commercial theater, marked off openly from all other forms and ceremonies of public life precisely by virtue of its freely acknowledged fictionality. Where there is no pretense to truth, there can be no *imposture:* it is this argument that permits so ontologically anxious a figure as Sir Philip Sidney to defend poetry—"Now for the poet, he nothing affirms, and therefore never lieth."[47]

In this spirit Puck playfully defends *A Midsummer Night's Dream:*

If we shadows have offended,
Think but this, and all is mended,
That you have but slumber'd here
While these visions did appear.
And this weak and idle theme,
No more yielding but a dream.

(V.i.409–14)

With a similarly frank admission of illusion Shakespeare can open the theater to Harsnett's polemic. Indeed, as if Harsnett's momentum carried *him* into the theater along with the fraud he hotly pursues, Shakespeare in *King Lear* stages not only exorcism, but Harsnett *on* exorcism:

Five fiends have been in poor Tom at once; as Oberdicut, of lust; Hoberdidance, prince of dumbness; Mahu, of stealing; Modo, of murder; Flibbertigibbet, of mopping and mowing; who since possesses chambermaids and waiting-women.[48]

(IV.i.57–62)

Those in the audience who had read Harsnett's book or heard of the notorious Buckinghamshire exorcisms would recognize in Edgar's lines an odd, joking allusion to the chambermaids, Sara and Friswood Williams, and the

---

[46] Stephen Gosson, *Plays Confuted in Five Actions* (London, c. 1582), cited in E. K. Chambers, *The Elizabethan Stage* (Oxford, 1923), 215.

[47] Philip Sidney, *The Defense of Poesie* (1583), in *Literary Criticism: Plato to Dryden*, ed. Allan H. Gilbert (Detroit, 1962), 439.

[48] These lines were included in the Quarto but omitted from the Folio. For the tangled textual history, see Michael J. Warren, "Quarto and Folio *King Lear*, and the interpretation of Albany and Edgar," in David Bevington and Jay L. Halio (eds), *Shakespeare: Pattern of Excelling Nature* (Newark, Del., 1978), 95–107; Steven Urkowitz, *Shakespeare's Revision of "King Lear"* (Princeton, 1980); and Gary Taylor, "The war in *King Lear*" (*Shakespeare Survey*, 33 (1980)), 27–34. Presumably, by the time the Folio appeared, the point of the allusion to Harsnett would have been lost, and the lines were dropped.

waiting woman, Ann Smith, principal actors in Father Edmund's "Devil Theater." The humor of the anachronism here is akin to the Fool's earlier quip, "This prophecy Merlin shall make; for I live before his time" (III.ii.95–6); both are bursts of a cheeky self-consciousness that dares deliberately to violate the historical setting in order to remind the audience of the play's conspicuous doubleness, its simultaneous distance and contemporaneity.

A Declaration of Egregious Popish Impostures supplies Shakespeare not only with an uncanny anachronism but with the model of Edgar's histrionic disguise. For it is not the *authenticity* of the demonology that the playwright finds in Harsnett—the usual reason for authorial recourse to a specialized source (as, for example, to a military or legal handbook)—but rather the inauthenticity of a theatrical role. Shakespeare appropriates for Edgar, then, a documented fraud, complete with an impressive collection of what the *Declaration* calls "uncouth non-significant names"[49] that have been made up to sound exotic and that carry with them a faint but ineradicable odor of spuriousness.

In Sidney's *Arcadia*, which provided the outline of the Gloucester subplot, the good son, having escaped his father's misguided attempt to kill him, becomes a soldier in another land and quickly distinguishes himself. Shakespeare insists not only on Edgar's perilous fall from his father's favor but upon his marginalization: Edgar becomes the possessed Poor Tom, the outcast with no possibility of working his way back in toward the center. "My neighbours," writes John Bunyan in the 1660s, "were amazed at this my great conversion from prodigious profaneness to something like a moral life; and truly so well they might for this my conversion was as great as for a Tom of Bethlem to become a sober man."[50] Of course, Edgar is only a pretend Tom o'Bedlam and hence can return to the community when it is safe to do so; but the force of Harsnett's argument is to make mimed possession even more marginal and desperate than the real thing.

Indeed, Edgar's desperation is bound up with the stress of "counterfeiting," a stress he has already noted in the presence of the mad and ruined Lear and now, in the lines I have just quoted, feels still more intensely in the presence of his blinded and ruined father. He is struggling with the urge to stop playing or, as he puts it, with the feeling that he "cannot daub it further" (IV.i.51). Why he does not simply reveal himself to Gloucester at this point is entirely unclear. "And yet I must" is all he says of his continued disguise, as he recites the catalog of devils and leads his despairing father off to Dover Cliff.[51]

The subsequent episode—Gloucester's suicide attempt—deepens the play's brooding upon spurious exorcism. "It is a good *decorum* in a Come-

[49] Harsnett, *Declaration*, 46.

[50] John Bunyan, *Grace Abounding to the Chief of Sinners*, ed. Roger Sharrock (Oxford, 1966), 15.

[51] Edgar's later explanation—that he feared for his father's ability to sustain the shock of an encounter—is, like so many explanations in *King Lear*, too little, too late. On this characteristic belatedness as an element of the play's greatness, see Stephen Booth, *"King Lear," "Macbeth," Indefinition, and Tragedy* (New Haven, 1983).

die," writes Harsnett, "To giue us emptie names for things, and to tell us of strange Monsters within, where there be none";[52] so too the "Miracle-minter," Father Edmunds, and his fellow exorcists manipulate their impressionable gulls: "The priests doe report often in their patients hearing the dreadful formes, similitudes, and shapes, that the deuils vse to depart in out of those possessed bodies . . . : and this they tell with so graue a countenance, pathetical termes, and accommodate action, as it leaues a very deepe impression in the memory, and fancie of their actors."[53] Thus by the power of theatrical suggestion, the anxious subjects on whom the priests work their charms come to believe that they too have witnessed the devil depart in grotesque form from their own bodies, whereupon the priests turn their eyes heavenward and give thanks to the Blessed Virgin. In much the same manner Edgar persuades Gloucester that he stands on a high cliff, and then, after his credulous father has flung himself forward, Edgar switches roles and pretends that he is a bystander who has seen a demon depart from the old man:

> As I stood here below methought his eyes
> Were two full moons; he had a thousand noses,
> Horns whelk'd and wav'd like the enridged sea:
> It was some fiend; therefore, thou happy father,
> Think that the clearest Gods, who make them honours
> Of men's impossibilities, have preserved thee.
>
> (IV.vi.69–74)

Edgar tries to create in Gloucester an experience of awe and wonder so intense that it can shatter his suicidal despair and restore his faith in the benevolence of the gods: "Thy life's a miracle," he tells his father.[54] For Shakespeare, as for Harsnett, this miracle-minting is the product of specifically histrionic manipulations; the scene at Dover is simultaneously a disenchanted analysis of religious and of theatrical illusions. Walking about on a perfectly flat stage, Edgar does to Gloucester what the theater usually does to the audience: he persuades his father to discount the evidence of his senses—"Methinks the ground is even"—and to accept a palpable fiction: "Horrible steep." But the audience at a play, of course, never absolutely accepts such fictions: we enjoy being brazenly lied to, we welcome for the sake of pleasure what we know to be untrue, but we withhold from the theater the simple assent that we grant to everyday reality. And we enact this withholding when, depending on the staging, either we refuse to believe that Gloucester is on a cliff above Dover beach or we realize that what we thought was a cliff (in the convention of theatrical representation) is in reality flat ground.

Hence, in the midst of Shakespeare's demonstration of the convergence of exorcism and theater, we return to the difference that enables *King Lear* to borrow comfortably from Harsnett: the theater elicits from us complicity

---

[52] Harsnett, *Declaration*, 142.

[53] Ibid., 142–3.

[54] On the production of "counterfeit miracles" in order to arouse awe and wonder, see especially Harsnett, *Discovery*, "Epistle to the reader."

rather than belief. Demonic possession is responsibly marked out for the audience as a theatrical fraud, designed to gull the unsuspecting: monsters such as the fiend with the thousand noses are illusions most easily imposed on the old, the blind, and the despairing; evil comes not from the mysterious otherworld of demons but from this world, the world of court and family intrigue. In *King Lear* there are no ghosts, as there are in *Richard III, Julius Caesar*, or *Hamlet;* no witches, as in *Macbeth;* no mysterious music of departing demons, as in *Antony and Cleopatra.*

King Lear is haunted by a sense of rituals and beliefs that are no longer efficacious, that have been *emptied out.* The characters appeal again and again to the pagan gods, but the gods remain utterly silent.[55] Nothing answers to human questions but human voices; nothing breeds about the heart but human desires; nothing inspires awe or terror but human suffering and human depravity. For all the invocation of the gods in *King Lear*, it is quite clear that there are no devils.

Edgar is no more possessed than the sanest of us, and we can see for ourselves that there was no demon standing by Gloucester's side. Likewise Lear's madness does not have a supernatural origin; it is linked, as in Harsnett, to *hysterica passio,* exposure to the elements, and extreme anguish, and its cure comes at the hands not of an exorcist but of a doctor. His prescription involves neither religious rituals (as in Catholicism) nor fasting and prayer (as in Puritanism), but tranquillized sleep:

> Our foster-nurse of nature is repose,
> The which he lacks; that to provoke in him,
> Are many simples operative, whose power
> Will close the eye of anguish.

(IV.iv.12–15)[56]

King Lear's relation to Harsnett's book, then, is essentially one of reiteration, a reiteration that signals a deeper and unexpressed institutional exchange. The official church dismantles and cedes to the players the powerful mechanisms of an unwanted and dangerous charisma; in return, the players confirm the charge that those mechanisms are theatrical and hence illusory. The material structure of Elizabethan and Jacobean public theaters heightened this confirmation, since, unlike medieval drama with its fuller integration into society, Shakespeare's drama took place in carefully demarcated playgrounds. *King Lear* offers then a double corroboration of Harsnett's arguments: within the play, Edgar's possession is clearly designated as a fiction, while the play itself is bounded by the institutional signs of fictionality: the wooden walls of the play space, payment for admission, known actors playing the parts, applause, the dances that followed the performance.

---

[55] Words, signs, gestures that claim to be in touch with super-reality, with absolute goodness and absolute evil, are exposed as vacant—illusions manipulated by the clever and imposed upon the gullible.

[56] This is, in effect, Edmund Jorden's prescription for cases such as Lear's.

The theatrical confirmation of the official position is neither superficial nor unstable. And yet, I want now to suggest, Harsnett's arguments are alienated from themselves when they make their appearance on the Shakespearean stage. This alienation may be set in the context of a more general observation: the closer Shakespeare seems to a source, the more faithfully he reproduces it on stage, the more devastating and decisive his transformation of it. Let us take, for a small, initial instance, Shakespeare's borrowing from Harsnett of the unusual adjective "corky"—i.e., sapless, dry, withered. The word appears in the *Declaration* in the course of a sardonic explanation of why, despite the canonists' declaration that only old women are to be exorcized, Father Edmunds and his crew have a particular fondness for tying in a chair and exorcizing young women. Along with more graphic sexual innuendoes, Harsnett observes that the theatrical role of a demonic requires "certain actions, motions, distortions, writhings, tumblings, and turbulent passions . . . not to be performed but by suppleness of sinewes. . . . It would (I feare mee) pose all the cunning Exorcists, that are this day to be found, to teach an old corkie woman to writhe, tumble, curvet, and fetch her morice gamboles."[57]

Now Shakespeare's eye was caught by the word "corkie," and he reproduces it in a reference to old Gloucester. But what had been a flourish of Harsnett's typically bullying comic style becomes part of the horror of an almost unendurable scene, a scene of torture that begins when Cornwall orders his servant to take the captive Gloucester and "Bind fast his corky arms" (III.vii.29). The note of bullying humor is still present in the word, but it is present in the character of the torturer.

This one-word instance of repetition as transvaluation may suggest in the tiniest compass what happens to Harsnett's work in the course of *Lear*. The *Declaration*'s arguments are loyally reiterated but in a curiously divided form. The voice of skepticism is assimilated to Cornwall, to Goneril, and above all to Edmund, whose "naturalism" is exposed as the argument of the younger and illegitimate son bent on displacing his legitimate older brother and eventually on destroying his father. The fraudulent possession and exorcism are given to the legitimate Edgar, who is forced to such shifts by the nightmarish persecution directed against him. Edgar adopts the role of Poor Tom not out of a corrupt will to deceive, but out of a commendable desire to survive. Modu, Mabu, and the rest are fakes, exactly as Harsnett said they were, but they are the venial sins of a will to endure. And even "venial sins" is too strong: they are the clever inventions that enable a decent and unjustly persecuted man to live. Similarly, there is no grotesque monster standing on the cliff with Gloucester—there isn't even any cliff—but Edgar, himself hunted down like an animal, is trying desperately to save his father from suicidal despair.

All of this has an odd and unsettling resemblance to the situation of the Jesuits in England, if viewed from an unofficial perspective. The resemblance does not necessarily resolve itself into an allegory in which Catholicism is

[57] Harsnett, *Declaration*, 23.

revealed to be the persecuted, legitimate elder brother forced to defend himself by means of theatrical illusions against the cold persecution of his skeptical bastard brother Protestantism. But the possibility of such a radical undermining of the orthodox position exists, and not merely in the cool light of your own historical distance. In 1610 a company of traveling players in Yorkshire included *King Lear* and *Pericles* in a repertoire that included a "St Christopher Play" whose performance came to the attention of the Star Chamber. The plays were performed in the manor house of a recusant couple, Sir John and Lady Julyan Yorke, and the players themselves and their organizer, Sir Richard Cholmeley, were denounced for recusancy by their Puritan neighbor, Sir Posthumus Hoby.[58] It is difficult to resist the conclusion that someone in Stuart Yorkshire believed that, despite its apparent staging of a fraudulent possession, *King Lear* was not hostile, was strangely sympathetic even, to the situation of persecuted Catholics. At the very least, we may suggest, the current of sympathy is enough to undermine the intended effect of Harsnett's *Declaration:* an intensified adherence to the central system of official values. In Shakespeare, the realization that demonic possession is a theatrical imposture leads not to a clarification—the clear-eyed satisfaction of the man who refuses to be gulled—but to a deeper uncertainty, a loss of moorings, in the face of evil.

"Let them anatomize Regan," Lear raves, "see what breeds about her heart. Is there any cause in nature that makes these hard hearts?" (III.vi.74–6). We know that there is no cause *beyond* nature; the voices of evil in the play—"Thou, Nature, art my goddess"; "What need one?"; "Bind fast his corky arms"—come from the unpossessed. Does it make it any better to know this? Is it a relief to understand that the evil was not visited upon the characters by demonic agents but released from the structure of the family and the state by Lear himself?

Edgar's pretended demonic possession, by ironic contrast, is of the homiletic variety; the devil compels him to acts of self-punishment, the desperate masochism of the very poor, but not to acts of viciousness. On the contrary, like the demoniacs in Harsnett's contemptuous account who praise the Mass and the Catholic Church, Poor Tom gives a highly moral performance:

> Take heed o' th'foul fiend. Obey thy parents; keep thy word justly; swear not; commit not with man's sworn spouse; set not thy sweet heart on proud array. Tom's a-cold. (III.iv.78–81)

Is it a relief to know that Edgar is only miming this little sermon?

All attempts by the characters to explain or relieve their sufferings through the invocation of transcendent forces are baffled. Gloucester's belief in the influence of "These late eclipses in the sun and moon" (I.ii.100) is decisively dismissed, even if the spokesman for the dismissal is the villainous Edmund. Lear's almost constant appeals to the gods

[58] On the Yorkshire performance, see Murphy, op. cit., 93–118.

> O Heavens,
> If you do love old men, if your sweet sway
> Allow obedience, if you yourselves are old,
> Make it your cause; send down and take my part!
>
> (II.iv.187–90)

are constantly left unanswered. The storm in the play seems to several characters to be of more than natural intensity, and Lear above all tries desperately to make it *mean* something (a symbol of his daughters' ingratitude, a
punishment for evil, a sign from the gods of the impending universal judgment); but the thunder refuses to speak. When Albany calls Goneril a "devil"
and a "fiend" (IV.ii.59,66), we know that he is not identifying her as a supernatural being—it is impossible, in this play, to witness the eruption of the
denizens of hell into the human world—just as we know that Albany's
prayer for "visible spirits" to be sent down by the heavens "to tame these vile
offences" (IV.ii.46–7) will be unanswered.

In *King Lear*, as Harsnett says of the Catholic Church, "neither God,
Angel, nor devil can be gotten to speake."[59] For Harsnett this silence beto-
kens a liberation from lies; we have learned, as the last sentence of his tract
puts it, "to loath these despicable Impostures and returne vnto the truth."[60]
But for Shakespeare the silence leads to the desolation of the play's close:

> Lend me a looking-glass;
> If that her breath will mist or stain the stone,
> Why, then she lives.
>
> (V.iii.260–2)

The lines give voice to a hope by which the audience has been repeatedly
tantalized: a hope that Cordelia will not die, that the play will build toward a
revelation powerful enough to justify Lear's atrocious suffering, that we
are in the midst of what the Italians called a *tragedia di fin lieto*, that is, a
play where the villains absorb the tragic punishment while the good are
wondrously restored.[61] Shakespeare in effect invokes the conventions of
this genre, only to insist with appalling finality that Cordelia is "dead as
earth."

In the wake of Lear's first attempt to see some sign of life in Cordelia,
Kent asks, "Is this the promis'd end?" Edgar echoes the question, "Or image
of that horror?" And Albany says, "Fall and cease." By itself Kent's question
has an oddly literary quality, as if he were remarking on the end of the play,
either wondering what kind of ending this is or implicitly objecting to the
disastrous turn of events. Edgar's response suggests that the "end" is the end
of the world, the Last Judgment, here experienced not as a "promise"—the

---

[59] Harsnett, *Declaration*, 169.

[60] Ibid., 171.

[61] In willing this disenchantment against the evidence of our senses, we pay tribute to
the theater. Harsnett has been twisted around to make this tribute possible.

punishment of the wicked, the reward of the good—but as a "horror." But, like Kent, Edgar is not certain about what he is seeing: his question suggests that he may be witnessing not the end itself but a possible "image" of it, while Albany's enigmatic "Fall and cease" empties even that image of significance. The theatrical means that might have produced a "counterfeit miracle" out of this moment are abjured; there will be no imposture, no histrionic revelation of the supernatural.

Lear repeats this miserable emptying out of the redemptive hope in his next lines:

> This feather stirs; she lives! if it be so,
> It is a chance which does redeem all sorrows
> That ever I have felt.

> (V.iii.264–6)

Deeply moved by the sight of the mad king, a nameless gentleman had earlier remarked, "Thou hast one daughter, / who redeems nature from the general curse / Which twain have brought her to" (IV.vi.202–4). Now, in Lear's words, this vision of universal redemption through Cordelia is glimpsed again, intensified by the King's own conscious investment in it. What would it mean to "redeem" Lear's sorrows? To buy them back from the chaos and brute meaninglessness they now seem to signify, to reward the king with a gift so great that it outweighs the sum of misery in his entire long life, to reinterpret his pain as the necessary preparation—the price to be paid—for a consummate bliss. In the theater such reinterpretation would be represented by a spectacular turn in the plot—a surprise unmasking, a sudden reversal of fortunes, a resurrection—and this dramatic redemption, however secularized, would almost invariably recall the consummation devoutly wished by centuries of Christian believers. This consummation had in fact been represented again and again in medieval resurrection plays which offered the spectators ocular proof that Christ had risen.[62] Despite the pre-Christian setting of Shakespeare's play, Lear's craving for just such proof—"This feather stirs; she lives!"—would seem to evoke precisely this theatrical and religious tradition, only in order to reveal itself, C. L. Barber's acute phrase, as "post-Christian."[63] *If it be so:* Lear's sorrows are not redeemed; nothing can turn them into joy, but the forlorn hope of an impossible redemption persists, drained of its institutional and doctrinal significance, empty and vain, cut off even from a theatrical realization but, like the dream of exorcism, ineradicable.

The close of *King Lear* in effect acknowledges that it can never satisfy this dream, but the acknowledgment must not obscure the fact that the play itself

---

[62] O. B. Hardison, Jr., *Christian Rite and Christian Drama in the Middle Ages: Essays in the Origin and Early History of Modern Drama* (Baltimore, 1965), esp. 220–52.

[63] C. L. Barber, "The family in Shakespeare's development: tragedy and sacredness," in *Representing Shakespeare: New Psychoanalytic Essays,* ed. Murray M. Schwartz and Coppélia Kahn (Baltimore, 1980), 196.

has generated the craving for such satisfaction. That is, Shakespeare does not simply inherit and make use of an anthropological given; rather, at the moment when the official religious and secular institutions were, for their own reasons, abjuring the rituals they themselves had once fostered, Shakespeare's theater moves to appropriate this function. On stage the ritual is effectively contained in the ways we have examined, but Shakespeare intensifies as theatrical experience the need for exorcism, and his demystification of the practice is not identical in its interest to Harsnett's.

Harsnett's polemic is directed toward a bracing anger against the lying agents of the Catholic Church and a loyal adherence to the true, established Church of England. He writes as a representative of that true Church, and this institutional identity is reinforced by the secular institutional imprimatur on the confessions that are appended to the text. The joint religious and secular apparatus works to strip away imposture and discover the hidden reality which is, Harsnett says, the theater. Shakespeare's play dutifully reiterates this discovery: when Lear thinks he has found in Poor Tom "the thing itself," "unaccommodated man," he has in fact found a man playing a theatrical role. But if false religion is theater, and if the difference between true and false religion is the presence of theater, what happens when this difference is enacted in the theater?

What happens, as we have already begun to see, is that the official position is *emptied out,* even as it is loyally confirmed. This "emptying out" bears a certain resemblance to Brecht's "alienation effect," and still more to Althusser and Macherey's "internal distantiation." But the most fruitful terms for describing the felt difference between Shakespeare's art and the religious ideology to which it gives voice are to be found, I think, within the theological system to which Harsnett adhered. What is the status of the Law, asks Hooker, after the coming of Christ? Clearly the Saviour effected the "evacuation of the Law of Moses." But did that abolition mean "that the very name of Altar, of Priest, of Sacrifice itself, should be banished out of the world"? No, replies Hooker, even after evacuation, "the words which were do continue; the only difference is, that whereas before they had a literal, they now have a metaphorical use, and are as so many notes of remembrance unto us, that what they did signify in the letter is accomplished in the truth."[64] Both exorcism and Harsnett's own attack on exorcism undergo a comparable process of evacuation and transformed reiteration in *King Lear.* Whereas before they had a literal, they now have a literary use, and are as so many notes of remembrance unto us, that what they did signify in the letter is accomplished — with a drastic swerve from the sacred to the secular — in the theater.

Edgar's possession is a theatrical performance, exactly in Harsnett's terms, but there is no saving institution, purged of theater, against which it

---

[64] Hooker, *Laws of Ecclesiastical Polity,* IV.xi.10. This truth, which is the triumph of the metaphorical over the literal, confers upon the Church the liberty to use certain names and rites, even though they have been abolished. For the entire passage from Hooker, see Appendix. I am indebted for the reference to Richard Hooker to John Coolidge.

may be set, nor is there a demonic institution which the performance may be shown to serve. On the contrary, Edgar's miming is a response to a free-floating, contagious evil more terrible than anything Harsnett would allow. For Harsnett the wicked are corrupt individuals in the service of a corrupt Church; in *King Lear* there are neither individuals nor institutions adequate to contain the released and enacted wickedness; the force of evil in the play is larger than any local habitation or name. In this sense, Shakespeare's tragedy reconstitutes as theater the demonic principle demystified by Harsnett. Edgar's fraudulent, histrionic performance is a response to this principle: evacuated rituals, drained of their original meaning, are preferable to no rituals at all.

Shakespeare does not counsel, in effect, that one accept as true the fraudulent institution for the sake of the dream of a cure—the argument of the Grand Inquisitor. He writes for the greater glory and profit of the theater, a fraudulent institution that never pretends to be anything but fraudulent, an institution that calls forth what is not, that signifies absence, that transforms the literal into the metaphorical, that evacuates everything it represents. By doing so the theater makes for itself the hollow round space within which it survives. The force of *King Lear* is to make us love the theater, to seek out its satisfactions, to serve its interests, to confer upon it a place of its own, to grant it life by permitting it to reproduce itself over generations. Shakespeare's theater has outlived the institutions to which it paid homage, has lived to pay homage to other, competing institutions which in turn it seems to represent and empty out. This complex, limited institutional independence, this marginal and impure autonomy, arises not out of an inherent, formal self-reflexiveness but out of the ideological matrix in which Shakespeare's theater is created and recreated.

There are, of course, further institutional strategies that lie beyond a love for the theater. In a move that Ben Jonson rather than Shakespeare seems to have anticipated, the theater itself comes to be emptied out in the interests of reading. In the argument made famous by Charles Lamb and Coleridge, and reiterated by Bradley, theatricality must be discarded to achieve absorption, and Shakespeare's imagination yields forth its sublime power not to a spectator but to one who, like Keats, sits down to reread *King Lear*. Where institutions like the King's Men had been thought to generate their texts, now texts like *King Lear* appear to generate their institutions. The commercial contingency of the theater gives way to the philosophical necessity of literature.

Why has our culture embraced *King Lear*'s massive display of mimed suffering and fraudulent exorcism? Because the judicial torture and expulsion of evil have for centuries been bound up with the display of power at the center of society. Because we no longer believe in the magical ceremonies through which devils were once made to speak and were driven out of the bodies of the possessed. Because the play recuperates and intensifies our need for these ceremonies, even though we do not believe in them, and performs them, carefully marked out for us as frauds, for our continued consumption. Because, with our full complicity, Shakespeare's company and scores of companies that followed have catered profitably to our desire for spectacular impostures.

And also, perhaps, because the Harsnetts of the world would free us from the oppression of false belief only in order to reclaim us more firmly for the official state Church, and the "solution"—confirmed by the rechristening, as it were, of the devil as the Pope—is hateful. Hence we embrace an alternative that seems to confirm the official line and thereby to take its place in the central system of values, yet that works at the same time to unsettle all official lines.[65] Shakespeare's theater empties out the center that it represents, and in its cruelty—Edmund, Goneril, Regan, Cornwall, Gloucester, Cordelia, Lear: all dead as earth—paradoxically creates in us the intimation of a fullness that we can only savor in the conviction of its irremediable loss:

> we that are young
> Shall never see so much, nor live so long.

Appendix

Hooker, *Laws of Ecclesiastical Polity:* "They which honour the Law as an image of the wisdom of God himself, are notwithstanding to know that the same had an end in Christ. But what? Was the Law so abolished with Christ, that after his ascension the office of Priests became immediately wicked, and the very name hateful, as importing the exercise of an ungodly function? No, as long as the glory of the Temple continued, and till the time of that final desolation was accomplished, the very Christian Jews did continue with their sacrifices and other parts of legal service. That very Law therefore which our Saviour was to abolish, did not *so soon* become unlawful to be observed as some imagine; nor was it afterwards unlawful *so far*, that the very name of Altar, of Priest, of Sacrifice itself, should be banished out of the world. For though God do now hate sacrifice, whether it be heathenish or Jewish, so that we cannot have the same things which they had but with impiety; yet unless there be some greater let than the only evacuation of the Law of Moses, the names themselves may (I hope) be retained without sin, in respect of that proportion which things established by our Saviour have unto them which by him are abrograted. And so throughout all the writings of the ancient Fathers we see that the words which were do continue; the only difference is, that whereas before they had a literal, they now have a metaphorical use, and are as so many notes of remembrance unto us, that what they did signify in the letter is accomplished in the truth. And as no man can deprive the Church of this liberty, to use names whereunto the Law was accustomed, so neither are we generally forbidden the use of things which the Law hath; though it neither command us any particular rite, as it did the Jews a number, and the weightiest which it did command them are unto us in the Gospel prohibited." (IV.xi.10)

[65] Roland Barthes, *Mythologies,* tr. Annette Lavers (New York, 1972), 135.

Barbara Johnson

A Hound, a Bay Horse, and a Turtle Dove: Obscurity in Walden

From A World of Difference

1987

In 1896 the eminent American critic James Russell Lowell said of Henry David Thoreau, "He had none of the artist in him which controls a great work of art to the serene balance of completeness"—a severe formalist appraisal that found agreement among numerous later critics. Much attention has been paid, for instance, to a particular passage in Thoreau's Walden in which he introduces the symbolic triad of a hound, a bay horse, and a turtle dove, symbols that the formalists fault for their frustrating obscurity. But deconstructive criticism rejects the formalist insistence on unity and "the serene balance of completeness," preferring instead to see gaps, undecidability, and a play of signifiers. When the prominent American deconstructionist Barbara Johnson (b. 1947) turns her attention to this passage from Thoreau, she finds gold where the formalists had seen only lead.

The following essay in applied deconstruction largely avoids the usual French vocabulary in its challenge of earlier formalist critiques of Walden. Johnson asserts that the formalist objections to the passage result from a misconceived attempt to find a stable match of symbol with meaning, as she puts it "to fill these enigmatic symbols with interpretive content." Despite Thoreau's refusal to articulate a particular "interpretive content," various critics have used his biography and other writings to posit specific meanings for the hound, the horse, and the dove. In fact, Johnson locates the value of the passage for readers in the very lack of one-to-one correspondence between any of these symbols and an actual person or event in Thoreau's life.

Instead of being the stable, clear symbols formalists seek, Johnson sees them as catachresis—a type of metaphor in which the symbolic term (in formalist terminology, the "vehicle") does not substitute for any literal object (the "tenor"). For deconstructionists, no symbol, and for that matter no utterance of any sort, can ever have a single or stable meaning, a one-to-one correspondence with the thing named. What Thoreau then does is to exploit and foreground this inevitable undecidability, bring-

ing readers face to face with the emptiness of his symbols. For Johnson, the genius of this passage of Walden *lies in the fact that it forces each of us to recognize the emptiness of the symbols, attempt to fill them in for ourselves, and finally recognize that our own attempts must be equally unstable.*

THE EXPERIENCE OF READING Thoreau's *Walden* is often a disconcerting one. The very discrepancy between the laconic, concrete chapter titles and the long, convoluted sentences of the text alerts the reader to a process of level-shifting that delights and baffles—indeed, that delights because it baffles. Consider, for example, the following passage:

> I sometimes despair of getting anything quite simple and honest done in this world by the help of men. They would have to be passed through a powerful press first, to squeeze their old notions out of them, so that they would not soon get upon their legs again; and then there would be some one in the company with a maggot in his head, hatched from an egg deposited there nobody knows when, for not even fire kills these things, and you would have lost your labor. Nevertheless, we will not forget that some Egyptian wheat was handed down to us by a mummy.[1]

It is difficult to read this passage without doing a double take. The logical seriousness of the style of "Nevertheless, we will not forget . . ." in no way prepares the reader for the sudden appearance of wheat in a mummy. The passage shifts with unruffled rapidity from abstract generalization to dead figure ("squeeze their old notions out of them") to a soon-to-awaken figure hidden in a cliché ("maggot in the head") to mininarrative ("deposited there nobody knows when") to folk wisdom ("Not even fire kills these things") to counterclaim ("Nevertheless, we will not forget . . ."). By the time one reaches the mummy, one no longer knows what the figure stands for, whether it, like the mummy, is dead or alive, or even when the boundaries of the analogy (if it *is* an analogy) lie.

It is paradoxical that a writer who constantly exhorts us to "Simplify, simplify" should also be the author of some of the most complex and difficult paragraphs in the English language. What is it about this seemingly simple account of life in the woods that so often bewilders the reader, making him, in Emerson's words, "nervous and wretched to read it"?

In an article entitled *"Walden's* False Bottoms," Walter Benn Michaels amply demonstrates the book's capacity to engender nervousness as he details the long history of readers' attempts to cope with *Walden's* obscurity, first by attributing it to Thoreau's alleged "want of continuity of mind" (James Russell Lowell), then by subsuming it under the larger patterns of

---

[1] Henry David Thoreau, *Walden, or, Life in the Woods* (New York: Signet, 1960), p. 22. All page references to *Walden* are to this edition. [All notes are Johnson's.]

Walden's literary unity (Matthiessen, Anderson), then by considering it as a challenge to the reader's ability to read figuratively (Cavell, Buell). Walter Benn Michaels ends his own account of the undecidability of *Walden*'s contradictions by saying, "It's heads I win, tails you lose. No wonder the game makes us nervous."[2]

The passage through which I would like to gain access to one of the principal difficulties of *Walden*'s game is precisely a passage about losing. It is one of the most often-discussed passages in the book, a fact that is in itself interesting and instructive. The passage stands as an isolated paragraph, seemingly unrelated to what precedes or follows:

> I long ago lost a hound, a bay horse, and a turtle dove, and am still
> on their trail. Many are the travellers I have spoken concerning
> them, describing their tracks and what calls they answered to. I have
> met one or two who had heard the hound, and the tramp of the
> horse, and even seen the dove disappear behind a cloud, and they
> seemed as anxious to recover them as if they had lost them them-
> selves. (P. 16)

It should come as no surprise that the hound, the bay horse, and the turtle dove are almost universally seen as symbols by Thoreau's readers. The questions asked of this passage are generally, What do the three animals symbolize? and Where did the symbols come from? The answers to these questions are many and varied: for T. M. Raysor, the animals represent the "gentle boy" Edmund Sewall, Thoreau's dead brother John, and the woman to whom he unsuccessfully proposed marriage, Ellen Sewall; for Francis H. Allen, the symbols represent "the vague desires and aspirations of man's spiritual nature"; for John Burroughs, they stand for the "fine effluence" that for Thoreau constitutes "the ultimate expression of fruit of any created thing." Others have seen in the symbols "a mythical record of [Thoreau's] disappointments" (Emerson), a "quest . . . for an absolutely satisfactory condition of friendship" (Mark Van Doren), the "wildness that keeps man in touch with nature, intellectual stimulus, and purification of spirit" (Frank Davidson), and a "lost Eden" (Alfred Kazin). Sources for Thoreau's symbols are said to be found in such diverse texts as Voltaire's *Zadig* (Edith Peairs), the "Chinese Four Books," that Thoreau edited for *The Dial*, an old English ballad, an Irish folk tale, and a poem by Emerson.[3]

The sense shared by all readers that the hound, the bay horse and the turtle dove *are* symbols, but that what they symbolize is unclear, is made explicit in the following remarks by Stanley Cavell:

---

[2] Walter Benn Michaels, "*Walden's* False Bottoms," *Glyph* 1: *Johns Hopkins Textual Studies* (Baltimore: Johns Hopkins University Press, 1977), pp. 132–49.

[3] For detailed bibliographical information on these and other readings of the passage, see *The Annotated Walden*, ed. Philip Van Doren Stern (New York: Clarkson N. Potter, 1970), pp. 157–58, and *The Variorum Walden*, ed. Walter Harding (New York: Twayne, 1962), pp. 270–72.

> I have no new proposal to offer about the literary or biographical sources of those symbols. But the very obviousness of the fact that they are symbols, and function within a little myth, seems to me to tell us what we need to know. The writer comes to us from a sense of loss; the myth does not contain more than symbols because it is no set of desired things he has lost, but a connection with things, the track of desire itself.[4]

The notion that what is at stake here is not any set of lost *things* but rather the very fact of *loss* seems to find confirmation in the replies that Thoreau himself gave on two different occasions to the question of the passage's meaning. In a letter to B. B. Wiley, dated April 26, 1857, he writes:

> How shall we account for our pursuits if they are original? We get the language with which to describe our various lives out of a common mint. If others have their losses, which they are busy repairing, so have I *mine,* & their hound & horse may *perhaps* be the symbols of some of them. But also I have lost, or am in danger of losing, a far finer & more etherial treasure, which commonly no loss of which they are conscious will symbolize—this I answer hastily & with some hesitation, according as I now understand my own words. (*Annotated Walden,* pp. 157–58)

And on another occasion, as the *Variorum* tells it:

> Miss Ellen Watson, in "Thoreau Visits Plymouth" . . . , reports that when Thoreau visited Plymouth, Mass., a year or two after the publication of *Walden,* he met there "Uncle Ed" Watson who asked him what he meant when he said he lost "a hound, a horse, and a dove." Thoreau replied, "Well, Sir, I suppose we have all our losses." "That's a pretty way to answer a fellow," replied Uncle Ed. (P. 270)

Most readers have shared Uncle Ed's disappointment at this answer that seems no answer at all. The editors of the *Annotated* and *Variorum Waldens* both conclude their surveys of the literature on the subject in a similar way:

> In conclusion, however, it should be pointed out that there is no unanimity on interpretation of these symbols and the individual critic is left free to interpret as he wishes. (*Variorum,* p. 272)

> Since there is no clear explanation, each reader will have to supply his own. (*Annotated Walden,* p. 158)

In attempting to fill these enigmatic symbols with interpretive content, most readers have assumed that the hound, the bay horse, and the turtle dove were figurative containers or concrete vehicles into which some deeper, higher, or more abstract meanings could be made to fit. This is what the business of interpreting symbols is all about. In cases like the present, where

---

[4] Stanley Cavell, *The Senses of Walden* (San Francisco: North Point, 1981), p. 51.

there exists no unanimity or clarity about the symbols' meanings, readers tend to believe *not* that there is something inadequate about the way they are asking the question, but that each individual becomes "free" to settle on an answer for himself.

Before going back to attempt a different type of analysis of this passage, I would like first to quote in its entirety the paragraph that immediately precedes the hound-horse-dove passage in the text:

> In any weather, at any hour of the day or night, I have been anxious to improve the nick of time, and notch it on my stick too; to stand on the meeting of two eternities, the past and the future, which is precisely the present moment; to toe that line. You will pardon some obscurities, for there are more secrets in my trade than in most men's, and yet not voluntarily kept, but inseparable from its very nature. I would gladly tell all that I know about it, and never paint "No Admittance" on my gate.
>
> I long ago lost a hound, a bay horse, and a turtle dove, and am still on their trail. Many are the travellers I have spoken concerning them, describing their tracks and what calls they answered to. I have met one or two who had heard the hound, and the tramp of the horse, and even seen the dove disappear behind a cloud, and they seemed as anxious to recover them as if they had lost them themselves. (P. 16)

There appears at first sight to be no relation between these two paragraphs. Yet the very abruptness of the transition, the very discrepancy of rhetorical modes, may perhaps indicate that the first paragraph consists of a set of instructions about how to read the second. It is surely no accident that one of the most enigmatic passages in *Walden* should be placed immediately after the sentence "You will pardon some obscurities." If the secret identities of the hound, the horse, and the dove are never to be revealed, it is not, says Thoreau, that they are being *voluntarily* withheld. Such secrets are simply inseparable from the nature of my trade—that is, writing. "I would gladly tell all that I know about it, and never paint 'No Admittance' on my gate." But all I *know* about it is not all there *is* about it. You are not being forcibly or gently kept away from a knowledge I possess. The gate is wide open, and that is why the path is so obscure. The sign "obscurity" is pointing directly at the symbols, making the sentence read, "I long ago lost an X, a Y, and a Z," and you are supposed to recognize them not as obscure symbols, but as symbols standing for the obscure, the lost, the irretrievable.

But yet, we insist, your X, Y, and Z are so *particular*—so houndlike, so horselike, so birdlike. If they merely symbolize the lost object as such, why do we hear the baying of the hound and the tramp of the horse? Why do those fellow travellers give us such precise reports?

Ah, but you see, Thoreau might answer, the symbols *are* symbols, after all. What is lost is always intensely particular. Yet it is known only in that it is lost—lost in one of the two eternities between which we clumsily try to toe the line.

To follow the trail of what is lost is possible only, it seems, if the loss is maintained in a state of transference from traveller to traveller, so that each takes up the pursuit as if the loss were his own. Loss, then, ultimately belongs to an other; the losses we treat as our own are perhaps losses of which we never had conscious knowledge ourselves. "If others have their losses, which they are busy repairing, so have I *mine,* & their hound & horse may *perhaps* be the symbols of some of them. But also I have lost, or am in danger of losing, a far finer & more etherial treasure, which commonly no loss *of which they are conscious* will symbolize."

Walden's great achievement is to wake us up to our own lost losses, to make us participate in the transindividual movement of loss in its infinite particularity, urging us passionately to follow the tracks of we know not quite what, as if we had lost it, or were in danger of losing it, ourselves.

In order to communicate the irreducibly particular yet ultimately unreadable nature of loss, Thoreau has chosen to use three symbols that clearly *are* symbols but that do not really symbolize anything outside themselves. They are figures for which no literal, proper term can be substituted. They are, in other words, catachreses—"figures of abuse," figurative substitutes for a literal term that does not exist. Like the "legs" and "arms" of our favorite recliner, Thoreau's hound, horse, and dove belong to a world of homely figurative richness, yet the impersonal literality they seem to presuppose is nowhere to be found. The structure of catachretic symbolism is thus the very structure of transference and loss. Through it Thoreau makes us see that every lost object is always, in a sense, a catachresis, a figurative substitute for nothing that ever could be literal.

It could be said that Nature itself is for Thoreau a catachretic symbol that enables him to displace his discourse without filling in its symbolic tenor. But in order to analyze a more particular aspect of the way in which Thoreau's catachretic rhetoric creates obscurity in *Walden,* let us first look at a more traditional and semantically "full" use of nature imagery: the *analogies* drawn between natural objects and human predicaments.

I begin with a somewhat atypically explicit analogy:

> One day . . . I saw a striped snake run into the water, and he lay on the bottom, apparently without inconvenience, as long as I staid there, or more than a quarter of an hour; perhaps because he had not yet fairly come out of the torpid state. It appears to me that for a like reason men remain in their present low and primitive condition; but if they should feel the influence of the spring of springs arousing them, they would of necessity rise to a higher and more ethereal life. (P. 33)

No rhetorical strategy could be more classical than this weaving of analogy between the natural and the human worlds. It is the mark of the moralist, the evangelist, the satirist, and the lyric poet, all of which Thoreau indeed is.

From the New Testament to Aesop and Swedenborg, the natural world has been a source of figures of the preoccupations and foibles of man. As Emerson puts it in his own essay on Nature:

> The memorable words of history and the proverbs of nations consist usually of a natural fact, selected as a picture or parable of a moral truth. Thus; A rolling stone gathers no moss; A bird in hand is worth two in the bush; A cripple in the right way will beat a racer in the wrong; Make hay while the sun shines; 'Tis hard to carry a full cup even; Vinegar is the son of wine; The last ounce broke the camel's back; Long-lived trees make roots first;—and the like. In their primary sense these are trivial facts, but we repeat them for the value of their analogical import. What is true of proverbs, is true of all fables, parables, and allegories.[5]

Yet although Thoreau draws on many centuries of analogical writing, there is a subtle difference in his rhetorical use of nature, and it is the specificity of that difference that I would like to attempt to identify in conclusion. The difference begins to become perceptible in the following examples:

> Why has man rooted himself thus firmly in the earth, but that he may rise the same proportion into the heavens above?—for the nobler plants are valued for the fruit they bear at last in the air and light, far from the ground, and are not treated like the humbler esculents, which, though they may be biennials, are cultivated only till they have perfected their root, and often cut down at top for this purpose, so that most would not know them in their flowering season. (P. 15)

> We don garment after garment, as if we grew like exogenous plants by addition without. Our outside and often thin and fanciful clothes are our epidermis or false skin, which partakes not of our life, and may be stripped off here and there without fatal injury; our thicker garments, constantly worn, are our cellular integument, or cortex; but our shirts are our liber or true bark, which cannot be removed without girdling and so destroying the man. (P. 21)

In both these examples, what begins as a fairly routine analogy tends, in the course of its elaboration, to get wildly out of hand. The fascination with the vehicle as an object of attention in its own right totally eclipses the original anthropomorphic tenor. Words like "esculents," "biennials," "cortex," and "liber" pull away from their subordinate, figurative status and begin giving information about themselves, sidetracking the reader away from the original thrust of the analogy. In the first example, what begins as an opposition between nobler and humbler men and plants collapses as it is revealed that the humbler plants are humble only because they are never *allowed* to

[5] Ralph Waldo Emerson, *Selected Prose and Poetry* (New York: Holt, Rinehart, and Winston, 1964), p. 20.

flower. In the second example, the hierarchy of integuments ends by privileging not the skin but the shirt as that part of a man that cannot be removed without destroying him. In an effort to show that man is confused about where his inside ends and his outside begins, Thoreau resorts to a logic of tree growth which entirely takes over as the exogenous striptease procedes.

It is perhaps in the "Bean-field" chapter that the rhetorical rivalries between the literal and the figurative, the tenor and the vehicle, become most explicit. On the one hand, Thoreau writes, "I was determined to know beans," and goes on to detail the hours of hoeing and harvesting, listing the names of weeds and predators, and accounting for outgo and income down to the last half penny. And on the other, he admits that "some must work in fields if only for the sake of tropes and expression, to serve a parable-maker one day." He speaks of sowing the seeds of sincerity, truth, simplicity, faith, and innocence, asking, "Why concern ourselves so much about our beans for seed, and not be concerned at all about a new generation of men?"

The perverse complexity of *Walden*'s rhetoric is intimately related to the fact that it is never possible to be sure what the rhetorical status of any given image is. And this is because what Thoreau has done in moving to Walden Pond is to move *himself,* literally, into the world of his own figurative language. The literal woods, pond, and bean field still assume the same classical rhetorical guises in which they have always appeared, but they are suddenly readable in addition as the nonfigurative ground of a naturalist's account of life in the woods. The ground has shifted, but the figures are still figures. When is it that we decide that Thoreau never lost that hound, that horse, and that dove? It is because we can never be absolutely sure, that we find ourselves forever on their trail.

Walden is obscure, therefore, to the extent that Thoreau has *literally* crossed over into the very parable he is writing, where *reality itself* has become a catachresis, both ground and figure at once, and where, he tells us, "if you stand right fronting and face to face with a fact, you will see the sun glimmer on both its surfaces, as if it were a cimeter, and feel its sweet edge dividing you through the heart and marrow."

Shoshana Felman

The Case of Poe

1987

The application of psychoanalytic theory to literature has been an important branch
of twentieth-century criticism, beginning with and most often referring to the
founder of psychoanalysis, Sigmund Freud. (See his essay, "The Theme of the Three
Caskets," page 394.) In the essay that follows, however, Shoshana Felman demonstrates that psychoanalytic criticism can move usefully beyond its original source.
She first discusses the critical history surrounding the works of Edgar Allan Poe, focusing on two major critical studies, both of which she finds inadequate because they
seek to psychoanalyze the author based on his stories and poems. This trend in
Freudian criticism is problematic because it fails to consider the text as literature and
also leads to conclusions that are overly speculative. Recognizing these shortcomings, Felman is one of the group of psychoanalytic critics who take as their model the
work not of Freud but of other psychoanalysts.

   French psychoanalyst Jacques Lacan became well known in the 1950s for his
reinterpretation of Freud and his use of principles from structuralist linguistics to
bolster his belief that language plays a central role in the development of the conscious and the unconscious mind. In 1956, Lacan conducted a year-long seminar on
Poe's story "The Purloined Letter," the report of which appears as the first essay in
Lacan's influential Ecrits. Emphasizing Poe's story and not his biography, Lacan argues that the letter of the story's title acts as a signifier with shifting meanings. (For
a discussion of the signified/signifier relationship, see the introductory note to
Roland Barthes, page 487.) First, the letter signifies an illicit romance; second it signifies to the Minister an instrument of power to use against the queen; third, it becomes a much-desired object for the police. Finally, when Dupin finds the letter and
returns it to the queen, it now signifies that an "analyst"—a detective in Poe's
usage, but a psychoanalyst in Lacan's—has triumphed.

   As Felman points out, Lacan's application of ideas from structuralist linguistics
to psychoanalysis suggests important possibilities for literary criticism. To begin
with, in keeping with dominant models of twentieth-century criticism, Lacan focuses
his attention on the text and not the author, thus overcoming the problems of previous analyses of Poe's work. Felman also points out how Lacan's methodology goes be-

yond the straightforward application of psychoanalysis to literature and shows that psychoanalysis and literature are joined in a more multidirectional relationship. The most wide-ranging of Felman's conclusions is that psychoanalytic critics need to be aware "that there is more than one way to implicate psychoanalysis in literature; that how to implicate psychoanalysis in literature is itself a question for interpretation." In this way, the field of psychoanalytic criticism can remain vital and flexible and not bound forever to a static interpretation of the works of Sigmund Freud.

LACAN'S FIRST COLLECTION of published essays, the *Ecrits,* opens with a chapter entitled "The Seminar on *The Purloined Letter.*" This so-called "Seminar" is the written account of a year-long course devoted to the exploration of a short literary text, one of Edgar Allan Poe's *Extraordinary Tales,* "The Purloined Letter." The Seminar was offered to trainees in psychoanalysis. Why did Lacan choose to devote a whole year of teaching to this tale? What is the significance of the strategic decision to place this "Seminar" at the opening of the *Ecrits,* as a key work in Lacan's endeavor?

I will approach these questions indirectly, by meditating first on the "case of Poe" in the literary investigations of psychology and psychoanalysis before Lacan. I will then attempt to analyze both the difference that Lacan has made in the psychoanalytical approach to reading and the way in which the lesson Lacan derived from Poe is a lesson in psychoanalysis.

To account for poetry in psychoanalytical terms has traditionally meant to analyze poetry as a symptom of a particular poet. I would here like to reverse this approach, and to analyze a particular poet as a symptom of poetry.

Perhaps no poet has been so highly acclaimed and, at the same time, so violently disclaimed as Edgar Allan Poe. One of the most controversial figures on the American literary scene, "perhaps the most thoroughly misunderstood of all American writers,"[1] "a stumbling block for the judicial critic,"[2] no other poet in the history of criticism has engendered so much disagreement and so many critical contradictions. It is my contention that this critical disagreement is itself symptomatic of a *poetic effect,* and that the critical contradictions to which Poe's poetry has given rise are themselves indirectly significant of the nature of poetry.

---

[1] "Although Poe was not the social outcast Baudelaire conceived him to be, he was, and still is, perhaps the most thoroughly misunderstood of all American writers." Floyd Stovall, *Edgar Poe the Poet: Essays New and Old on the Man and His Work* (Charlottesville: University of Virginia Press, 1969). [All notes are Felman's.]

[2] T. S. Eliot's famous statement on Poe in his study, "From Poe to Valéry," *Hudson Review,* Autumn 1949; reprinted in *The Recognition of Edgar Allan Poe: Selected Criticism since 1829,* ed. Eric W. Carlson (Ann Arbor: University of Michigan Press, 1966), p. 205. This collection of critical essays will hereafter be cited as *Recognition,* with individual essays abbreviated as follows: P. P. Cooke, "Edgar A. Poe" (1848); T. S. Eliot, "From Poe to Valéry" (1949); T. W. Higginson, "Poe" (1879); Aldous Huxley, "Vulgarity in Literature" (1931); J. R. Lowell, "Edgar Allan Poe" (1845); C. M. Rourke, "Edgar Allan Poe" (1931); G. B. Shaw, "Edgar Allan Poe" (1909); Edmund Wilson, "Poe at Home and Abroad" (1926); Ivor Winters, "Edgar Allan Poe: A Crisis in American Obscurantism" (1937).

The Poe-etic Effect:
A Literary Case History

No other poet has been so often referred to as a "genius," in a sort of common consensus shared even by his detractors. Joseph Wood Krutch, whose study tends to belittle Poe's stature and to disparage the value of his artistic achievement, nevertheless entitles his monographer *Edgar Allan Poe: A Study in Genius*.[3] So do many other critics, who acknowledge and assert Poe's "genius" in the very titles of their essays.[4] "It happens to us but few times in our lives," writes Thomas Wentworth Higginson, "to come consciously into the presence of that extraordinary miracle we call genius. Among the many literary persons whom I have happened to meet . . . there are not half a dozen who have left an irresistible sense of this rare quality; and among these few, Poe."[5] The English poet Swinburne speaks of "the special quality of [Poe's] strong and delicate genius"; the French poet Mallarmé describes his translations of Poe as "a monument to the genius who . . . exercised his influence in our country"; and the American poet James Russell Lowell, one of Poe's harshest critics, who, in his notorious versified verdict, judged Poe's poetry to include "two fifths sheer fudge," nonetheless asserts, "Mr. Poe has that indescribable something which men have agreed to call *genius*. . . . Let talent writhe and contort itself as it may, it has no such magnetism. Larger of bone and sinew it may be, but the wings are wanting."[6]

However suspicious and unromantic the critical reader might wish to be with respect to "that indescribable something which men have agreed to call genius," it is clear that Poe's poetry produces what might be called a *genius effect*: the impression of some undefinable but compelling force to which the reader is subjected. To describe "this power, *which is felt*,"[7] as one reader puts it, Lowell speaks of "magnetism"; other critics speak of "magic." "Poe," writes Bernard Shaw, "constantly and inevitably produced magic where his greatest contemporaries produced only beauty."[8] T. S. Eliot quite reluctantly agrees: "Poe had, to an exceptional degree, the feeling for the incantatory element in poetry, of that which may, in the most nearly literal sense, be called 'the magic of verse.'"[9]

---

[3] J. W. Krutch, *Edgar Allan Poe: A Study in Genius* (New York: Knopf, 1926).

[4] J. M. S. Robertson, "The Genius of Poe," *Modern Quarterly*, 3 (1926); Camille Mauclair, *Le Génie d'Edgar Poe* (Paris, 1925); John Dillon, *Edgar Allan Poe: His Genius and His Character* (New York, 1911); John R. Thompson, *The Genius and Character of Edgar Allan Poe* (privately printed, 1929); Jeannet A. Marks, *Genius and Disaster: Studies in Drugs and Genius* (New York, 1925); Jean A. Alexander, "Affidavits of Genius: French Essays on Poe," *Dissertation Abstracts*, 22 (September 1961).

[5] Higginson, "Poe," *Recognition*, p. 67.

[6] Swinburne, letter to Sara Sigourney Rice, 9 November 1875, *Recognition*, p. 63. Mallarmé, "Scolies," in *Oeuvres complètes*, ed. H. Mondor and G. Jean-Aubry (Paris: Pléiade, 1945), p. 223; my translation. Lowell, "Edgar Allan Poe," *Recognition*, p. 11.

[7] Cooke, quoting Elizabeth Barrett, in "Edgar A. Poe," *Recognition*, p. 23; original italics.

[8] Shaw, "Edgar Allan Poe," *Recognition*, p. 98.

[9] Eliot, "From Poe to Valéry," *Recognition*, p. 209.

Poe's "magic" is thus ascribed to the ingenuity of his versification, to his exceptional technical virtuosity. And yet the word *magic,* "in the most nearly literal sense," means much more than just the intellectual acknowledgment of an outstanding technical skill; it connotes the effective action of something that exceeds both the understanding and the control of the person who is subjected to it; it connotes a force to which the reader has no choice but to submit. "No one could tell us what it is," writes Lowell, still in reference to Poe's genius, "and yet there is none who is not inevitably aware of . . . its power" (p. 11). "Poe," said Shaw, "inevitably produced magic." Something about Poe's poetry is experienced as inevitable, unavoidable (and not just as irresistible). What is more, once this poetry is read, its inevitability is there to stay; it becomes lastingly inevitable: "it will stick to the memory of every one who reads it," writes P. Pendleton Cooke (p. 23). And Eliot: "Poe is the author of a few . . . short poems . . . which do somehow stick in the memory" (pp. 207–208).

This is why Poe's poetry can be defined, and indeed has been, as a poetry of influence par excellence, in the sense emphasized by Harold Bloom: "to inflow," or to have power over another. The case of Poe in literary history could in fact be accounted for as an extreme and complex case of "the anxiety of influence," of the anxiety unwittingly provoked by the "influence" irresistibly emanating from this poetry. What is unique, however, about Poe's influence, as about the magic of his verse, is the extent to which its action is unaccountably insidious, exceeding the control, the will, and the awareness of those who are subjected to it. Eliot writes:

> Poe's influence is . . . puzzling. In France the influence of his poetry and of his poetic theories has been immense. In England and America it seems almost negligible. . . . And yet one cannot be sure that one's own writing has *not* been influenced by Poe. (p. 205; original italics)

Studying Poe's influence on Baudelaire, Mallarmé, and Valéry, Eliot goes on to comment:

> Here are three literary generations, representing almost exactly a century of French poetry. Of course, these are poets very different from each other. . . . But I think we can trace the development and descent of one particular theory of the nature of poetry through these three poets and it is a theory which takes its origin in the theory . . . of Edgar Poe. And the impression we get of the influence of Poe is the more impressive, because of the fact that Mallarmé, and Valéry in turn, did not merely derive from Poe through Baudelaire: each of them subjected himself to that influence directly, and has left convincing evidence of the value which he attached to the theory and practice of Poe himself. (p. 206; original italics)

Curiously enough, while Poe's worldwide importance and effective influence is beyond question, critics nonetheless continue to protest and to proclaim, as loudly as they can, that Poe is unimportant, that Poe is *not* a major poet. Taxing Poe with "vulgarity," Aldous Huxley argues:

> Was Edgar Allan Poe a major poet? It would surely never occur to any English-speaking critic to say so. And yet, in France, from 1850 till the present time, the best poets of each generation—yes, and the best critics, too; for, like most excellent poets, Baudelaire, Mallarmé, Paul Valéry are also admirable critics—have gone out of their way to praise him. . . . We who are speakers of English . . . , we can only say, with all due respect, that Baudelaire, Mallarmé, and Valéry were wrong and that Poe is not one of our major poets. (*Recognition*, p. 160)

Poe's detractors seem to be unaware, however, of the paradox that underlies their enterprise: it is by no means clear why anyone should take the trouble to write—at length—about a writer of no importance. Poe's most systematic denouncer, Ivor Winters, thus writes:

> The menace lies not, primarily, in his impressionistic admirers among literary people of whom he still has some, even in England and in America, where a familiarity with his language ought to render his crudity obvious, for these individuals in the main do not make themselves permanently very effective: it lies rather in the impressive body of scholarship. . . . When a writer is supported by a sufficient body of such scholarship, a very little philosophical elucidation will suffice to establish him in the scholarly world as a writer whose greatness is self-evident. (*Recognition*, p. 177)

The irony here is that, in writing his attack on Poe, what the attacker is in fact doing is adding still another study to the bulk of "the impressive body of scholarship" in which, in his own terms, "the menace lies"; so that, paradoxically enough, through Winters' study, the menace—that is, the possibility of taking Poe's "greatness as a writer" as "self-evident"—will indeed increase. I shall argue that, regardless of the value-judgment it may pass on Poe, this impressive bulk of Poe scholarship, the very quantity of the critical literature to which Poe's poetry has given rise, is itself an indication of its effective poetic power, of the strength with which it drives the reader to an *action*, compels him to a *reading act*. The elaborate written denials of Poe's value, the loud and lengthy negations of his importance, are therefore very like psychoanalytical negations. It is clear that if Poe's text in effect were unimportant, it would not seem so important to proclaim, argue, and prove that he is unimportant. The fact that it so much *matters* to proclaim that Poe *does not matter* is but evidence of the extent to which Poe's poetry is, in effect, a poetry that matters.

Poe might thus be said to have a *literary case history*, most revealing in that it incarnates, in its controversial forms, the paradoxical nature of a strong poetic effect: the very poetry that, more than any other, is experienced as *irresistible* has also proved to be, in literary history, the poetry most *re-sisted*, the one that, more than any other, has provoked resistances.

This apparent contradiction, which makes of Poe's poetry a unique case in literary history, clearly partakes of the paradoxical nature of an *analytical effect*. The enigma it presents us with is the enigma of the analytical par excellence, as stated by Poe himself, whose amazing intuitions of the nature of what he calls "analysis" are strikingly similar to the later findings of psychoanalysis: "The mental features discoursed of as the analytical are, in themselves, but little susceptible of analysis. We appreciate them only in their effects."[10]

Because of the very nature of its strong effects, of the reading-acts that it provokes, Poe's text (and not just Poe's biography of his personal neurosis) is clearly an analytical case in the history of literary criticism, a case that suggests something crucial to understand in psychoanalytic terms. It is therefore not surprising that Poe has been repeatedly singled out for psychoanalytical research, has persistently attracted the attention of psychoanalytic critics.

The Psychoanalytical Approaches

The best-known and most influential psychoanalytic studies of Poe are the 1926 study by Joseph Wood Krutch and the 1933 study by Marie Bonaparte, *Edgar Poe: Etude psychanalytique.*[11] Through a brief summary of the psychoanalytic issues raised by these two works, I will attempt to analyze the methodological presuppositions guiding their approaches (their "application" of psychoanalysis), in order to compare them later to Lacan's strikingly different approach in his methodologically unprecedented "Seminar on *The Purloined Letter*," published in 1966.[12]

Joseph Wood Krutch: Ideological Psychology, or the Approach of Normative Evaluation

For Krutch, Poe's text is nothing other than an accurate transcription of a severe neurosis, a neurosis whose importance and significance for "healthy" people is admittedly unclear. Poe's "position as the first of the great neurotics has never been questioned," writes Krutch ambiguously. And less ambiguously, in reply to some admiring French definitions of that position: "Poe 'first inaugurated the poetic conscience' only if there is no true poetry except

[10] "The Murders in the Rue Morgue," in *Edgar Allan Poe: Selected Writings,* ed. David Galloway (New York: Penguin, 1967), p. 189; hereafter cited as *Poe.*

[11] Bonaparte, *Edgar Poe* (Paris: Denöel et Steele, 1933). English edition: *Life and Works of Edgar Allan Poe,* trans. John Rodker (London: Imago, 1949). All references to Marie Bonaparte will be to the English editions.

[12] Lacan, "Le Séminaire sur *La Lettre volée,*" in *Ecrits* (Paris: Seuil, 1966); first translated by Jeffrey Mehlman in "French Freud," *Yale French Studies,* 48 (1972). All references here to Lacan's Poe Seminar are to the *Yale French Studies* translation.

the poetry of morbid sensibility." Since Poe's works, according to Krutch, "bear no conceivable relation . . . to the life of any people, and it is impossible to account for them on the basis of any social or intellectual tendencies or as the expression of the spirit of any age" (p. 210), the only possible approach is a biographical one, and "any true understanding" of the work is contingent upon a diagnosis of Poe's nervous malady. Krutch thus diagnoses in Poe a pathological condition of sexual impotence, the result of a fixation on his mother, and explains Poe's literary drive as a desire to compensate for, on the one hand, the loss of social position of which his foster father had deprived him, through the acquisition of literary fame and, on the other hand, his incapacity to have normal sexual relations, through the creation of a fictional world of horror and destruction where he found refuge. Poe's fascination with logic would thus be merely an attempt to prove himself rational when he felt he was going insane; and his critical theory merely an attempt to justify his peculiar artistic practice.

The obvious limitations of such a psychoanalytic approach were very sharply and accurately pointed out by Edmund Wilson in his essay "Poe at Home and Abroad." Krutch, argues Wilson, seriously misunderstands and undervalues Poe's writings, in

> complacently caricaturing them—as the modern school of social psychological biography, of which Mr. Krutch is a typical representative, seems inevitably to tend to caricature the personalities of its subjects. We are nowadays being edified by the spectacle of some of the principal ornaments of the human race exhibited exclusively in terms of their most ridiculous manias, their most disquieting neurosis, and their most humiliating failures. (*Recognition*, p. 144)

It is, in other words, the reductionist, stereotypical simplification under which Krutch subsumes the complexities of Poe's art and life that renders this approach inadequate:

> Mr. Krutch quotes with disapproval the statement of President Hadley of Yale, in explaining the refusal of the Hall of Fame to accept Poe among its immortals: "Poe wrote like a drunkard and a man who is not accustomed to pay his debts"; and yet Mr. Krutch himself . . . is almost as unperceptive when he tells us, in effect, that Poe wrote like a dispossessed Southern gentleman and a man with a fixation on his mother. (p. 145)

Subscribing to Wilson's criticism, I would like to indicate briefly some further limitations in this type of psychoanalytic approach to literature. Krutch himself, in fact, points out some of the limits of his method in his conclusion:

> We have, then, traced Poe's art to an abnormal condition of the nerves and his critical ideas to a rationalized defense of the limitations of his own taste. . . . The question whether or not the case of

Poe represents an exaggerated example of the process by which all creation is performed is at best an open question. The extent to which all imaginative works are the result of the unfulfilled desires which spring from either idiosyncratic or universally human maladjustments to life is only beginning to be investigated, and with it is linked the related question of the extent to which all critical principles are at bottom the systematized and rationalized expression of instinctive tastes which are conditioned by causes often unknown to those whom they affect. The problem of finding an answer to these questions . . . is the one distinctly new problem which the critic of today is called upon to consider. He must, in a word, endeavor to find the relationship which exists between psychology and aesthetics. (pp. 234–35)

This, indeed, is the real question, the real challenge that Poe as poet (and not as psychotic) presents to the psychoanalytic critic. But this is precisely the question that is never dealt with in Krutch's study. Krutch discards the question by saying that "the present state of knowledge is not such as to enable" us to give any answers. This remark, however, presupposes that the realm of aesthetics, of literature and art, might not itself contain some knowledge about, precisely, "the relationship between psychology and aesthetics"; it presupposes knowledge as a given, external to the literary object and imported into it, and not as a result of a reading-process, that is, of the critic's work upon and with the literary text. It presupposes, furthermore, that a critic's task is not to question but to answer, and that a question that cannot be answered, can also therefore not be asked; that to raise a question, to articulate its thinking power, is not itself a fruitful step that takes some work, some doing, into which the critic could perhaps be guided by the text.

Thus, in claiming that he has traced "Poe's art to an abnormal condition of the nerves," and that Poe's "criticism falls short of psychological truth," Krutch believes that his own work is opposed to Poe's as health is opposed to sickness, as normality is opposed to abnormality, as truth is opposed to delusion. But this ideologically determined, clear-cut opposition between health and sickness is precisely one that Freud's discovery fundamentally unsettles, deconstructs. In tracing Poe's "critical ideas to a rationalized defense of the limitations of his own taste," Krutch is unsuspicious of the fact that his own critical ideas about Poe could equally be so traced; that his doctrine, were it true, could equally apply to his own critical enterprise; that if psychoanalysis indeed puts rationality as such in question, it also by the same token puts itself in question.

Krutch, in other words, reduces not just Poe but analysis itself into an ideologically biased and psychologically opinionated caricature, missing totally (as is most often the case with "Freudian" critics) the radicality of Freud's psychoanalytic insights: their self-critical potential, their power to return upon themselves and to unseat the critic from any guaranteed, authoritative stance of truth. Krutch's approach does not, then, make sophisticated use of psychoanalytic insights, nor does it address the crucial question of the relationship between psychology and aesthetics, nor does it see that the crux of this question is not so much in the interrogation of whether or not all artists are necessarily pathological, but of what it is that makes of art—not of the artist—an object of *desire* for the public; of what it is that makes for art's effect, for the compelling power of Poe's poetry over its readers. The question of what makes poetry lies, indeed, not so much in what it was that made Poe write, but in what it is that makes us read him[13] and that ceaselessly drives so many people to write about him.

Marie Bonaparte: The Approach of Clinical Diagnosis

In contrast to Krutch's claim that Poe's works are only meaningful as the expression of morbidity, bearing "no conceivable relation . . . to the life of any people," Marie Bonaparte, although in turn treating Poe's works as nothing other than the recreations of his neuroses, tries to address the question of Poe's power over his readers through her didactic explanation of the relevancy, on the contrary, of Poe's pathology to "normal" people: the pathological tendencies to which Poe's text gives expression are an exaggerated version of drives and instincts universally human, which normal people have simply repressed more successfully in their childhood. What fascinates readers in Poe's texts is precisely the unthinkable and unacknowledged but strongly felt community of these human sexual drives.

If Marie Bonaparte, unlike Krutch, thus treats Poe with human sympathy, suspending the traditional puritan condemnation and refraining from passing judgment on his "sickness," she nonetheless, like Krutch, sets out primarily to diagnose that sickness and trace the poetry to it. Like Krutch, she comes up with a clinical portrait of the artist that, in claiming to account for the poetry, once again verges on caricature:

> If Poe was fundamentally necrophilist, as we saw, Baudelaire is revealed as a declared sadist; the former preferred dead prey or prey mortally wounded . . . ; the latter preferred live prey and killing. . . .
>
> How was it then, that despite these different sex lives, Baudelaire the sadist recognized a brother in the necrophilist Poe? . . .
>
> This particular problem raises that of the general relation of sadism to necrophilia and cannot be resolved except by an excursus into the theory of instincts. (p. 680)

Can poetry thus be clinically diagnosed? In setting out to expose didactically the methods of psychoanalytic interpretation, Bonaparte's pioneering book at

---

[13] Edmund Wilson: "The recent revival of interest in Poe has brought to light a good deal of new information and supplied us for the first time with a serious interpretation of his personal career, but it has so far entirely neglected to explain why we should still want to read him" (*Recognition,* p. 142).

the same time exemplifies the very naiveté of competence, the distinctive professional crudity of what has come to be the classical psychoanalytic treatment of literary texts. Eager to point out the resemblances between psychoanalysis and literature, Bonaparte, like most psychoanalytic critics, is totally unaware of the differences between the two: unaware of the fact that the differences are as important and as significant for understanding the meeting-ground as are the resemblances, and that those differences also have to be accounted for if poetry is to be understood in its own right. Bonaparte, paradoxically enough but in a manner symptomatic of the whole tradition of applied psychoanalysis, thus remains blind to the very specificity of the object of her research.

It is not surprising that this blind nondifferentiation or confusion of the poetic and the psychotic has unsettled sensitive readers, and that various critics have protested against this all too crude equation of poetry with sickness. The protestations, however, most often fall into the same ideological trap as the psychoanalytical studies they oppose: taking for granted the polarity of sickness versus health, of normality versus abnormality, they simply trace Poe's art (in opposition, so they think, to the psychoanalytic claim) to normality as opposed to abnormality, to sanity as opposed to insanity, to the history of ideas rather than that of sexual drives, to a conscious project as opposed to an unconscious one. Camille Mauclair insists upon the fact that Poe's texts are "constructed objectively by a will absolutely in control of itself," and that genius of that kind is "always sane."[14] For Allen Tate,

> The actual emphases Poe gives the perversions are richer in philosophical implication than his psychoanalytic critics have been prepared to see . . . Poe's symbols refer to a known tradition of thought, an intelligible order, apart from what he was as a man, and are not merely the index to a compulsive neurosis . . . the symbols . . . point towards a larger philosophical dimension. (*Recognition*, p. 239)

For Floyd Stovall, the psychoanalytic studies "are not literary critiques at all, but clinical studies of a supposed psychopathic personality":

> I believe the critic should look within the poem or tale for its meaning, and that he should not, in any case, suspect the betrayal of the author's unconscious self until he has understood all that his conscious self has contributed. To affirm that a work of imagination is only a report of the unconscious is to degrade the creative artist to the level of an amanuensis.
>
> I am convinced that all of Poe's poems were composed with conscious art. (p. 183) . . .

---

[14] Mauclair, *Le Génie d'Edgar Poe*; quoted in *Poe*, p. 24.

"The Raven," and with certain necessary individual differences every other poem Poe wrote, was the product of conscious effort by a healthy and alert intelligence. (p. 186)

It is obvious that this conception of the mutual exclusiveness, of the clear-cut opposition between conscious art and the unconscious, is itself naive and oversimplified. Nonetheless, Stovall's critique of applied psychoanalysis is relevant to the extent that the psychoanalytic explanation, in pointing exclusively to the author's unconscious sexual fantasies, indeed does not account for Poe's outstanding conscious art, for his poetic mastery and his technical and structural self-control. As do its opponents, so does applied psychoanalysis itself fail precisely to account for the dynamic interaction between the unconscious and the conscious elements of art.

If the thrust of the discourse of applied psychoanalysis is, in tracing poetry to a clinical reality, to reduce the poetic to a "cause" outside itself, the crucial limitation of this process of reduction is that the cause, while it may be necessary, is by no means a sufficient one. "Modern psychiatry," judiciously writes David Galloway, "may greatly aid the critic of literature, but . . . it cannot thus far explain why other men, suffering from deprivations or fears or obsessions similar to Poe's, failed to demonstrate his particular creative talent. Though no doubt Marie Bonaparte was correct in seeing Poe's own art as a defense against madness, we must be wary of identifying the necessity for this defense, in terms of Poe's own life, with the success of this defense, which can only be measured in his art."[15]

That the discourse of applied psychoanalysis is limited precisely in that it does not account for Poe's poetic genius is in fact the crucial point made by Freud himself in his prefatory note to Marie Bonaparte's study:

In this book my friend and pupil, Marie Bonaparte, has shown the light of psychoanalysis on the life and work of a great writer with pathologic trends.

Thanks to her interpretative effort, we now realize how many of the characteristics of Poe's works were conditioned by his personality, and can see how that personality derived from intense emotional fixations and painful infantile experiences. *Investigations such as this do not claim to explain creative genius,* but they do reveal the factors which awake it and the sort of subject matter it is destined to choose.

No doubt, Freud's remarkable superiority over most of his disciples—including Marie Bonaparte—proceeds from his acute awareness of the very limitations of his method, an awareness that in his followers seems most often not to exist.

[15] Galloway, Introduction to *Poe,* pp. 24–25.

I would like here to raise a question that has, amazingly enough, never been asked as a serious question: Is there a way around Freud's perspicacious reservation, warning us that studies like those of Bonaparte "do not claim to explain creative genius"? Is there, in other words, a way—a different way—in which psychoanalysis *can* help us to account for poetic genius? Is there an alternative to applied psychoanalysis?—an alternative that would be capable of touching, in a psychoanalytic manner, upon the very specificity of what constitutes the poetic?

Lacan: The Approach of Textual Problematization

"The Purloined Letter," as is well known, is the story of the double theft of a compromising letter, originally sent to the queen. Surprised by the unexpected entrance of the king, the queen leaves the letter on the table in full view of any visitor, where it is least likely to appear suspicious and therefore to attract the king's attention. Enter the Minister D who, observing the queen's anxiety and the play of glances between her and the unsuspicious king, analyzes the situation, figures out, recognizing the addressor's handwriting, what the letter is about, and steals it—by substituting for it another letter he takes from his pocket—under the very eyes of the challenged queen, who can do nothing to prevent the theft without provoking the king's suspicions. The queen then asks the prefect of police to search the minister's apartment and person for the letter. The prefect uses every conceivable secret-police technique to search every conceivable hiding place on the minister's premises, but to no avail.

Having exhausted his resources, the prefect consults Auguste Dupin, the famous "analyst," as Poe calls him (i.e., an amateur detective who excels in solving problems by means of deductive logic), to whom he tells the whole story. (It is, in fact, from this narration of the prefect of police to Dupin and in turn reported by the first-person narrator, Dupin's friend, who is also present, that we, the readers, learn the story.)

On a second encounter, Dupin, to the great surprise of the prefect and of the narrator, produces the purloined letter out of his drawer and hands it to the prefect in return for a large amount of money. The prefect leaves, and Dupin explains to the narrator how he found the letter: he deduced that the minister, knowing that his premises would be thoroughly combed by the police, had concluded that the best principle of concealment would be to leave the letter in the open, in full view; the letter would not be discovered precisely because it would be too self-evident. On this assumption, Dupin called on the minister in his apartment and, glancing around, soon located the letter carelessly hanging from the mantelpiece in a card rack. A little later, a disturbance in the street provoked by a man in Dupin's employ drew the minister to the window, at which moment Dupin quickly replaced the letter with a facsimile.

What Lacan is concerned with at this point of his research is the psycho-analytic problematics of the "repetition compulsion,"[16] as elaborated in Freud's speculative *Beyond the Pleasure Principle*. The thrust of Lacan's endeavor, with respect to Poe, is thus to point out the way in which the story's plot, its sequence of events (as, for Freud, the sequence of events in a life-story), is contingent on, overdetermined by, a principle of repetition that governs it and inadvertently structures its dramatic and ironic impact. "There are two scenes," remarks Lacan, "the first of which we shall straight-way designate the primal scene ... since the second may be considered its repetition in the very sense we are considering today" (p. 41). The primal scene takes place in the queen's boudoir: it is the theft of the letter from the queen by the minister; the second scene—its repetition—is the theft of the letter from the minister by Dupin.

What constitutes repetition for Lacan, however, is not the mere thematic resemblance of the double theft, but the whole structural situation in which the repeated theft takes place: in each case, the theft is the outcome of an intersubjective relationship between three terms; in the first scene, the three participants are the king, the queen, and the minister; in the second, the three participants are the police, the minister, and Dupin. In much the same way as Dupin takes the place of the minister in the first scene (the place of the letter's robber), the minister in the second scene takes the place of the queen in the first (the dispossessed possessor of the letter); whereas the police, for whom the letter remains invisible, take the place formerly occupied by the king. The two scenes thus mirror each other, in that they dramatize the repeated exchange of "three glances, borne by three subjects, incarnated each time by different characters." What is repeated, in other words, is not a psychological act committed as a function of the individual psychology of a character, but three functional *positions in a structure* which, determining three different viewpoints, embody three different relations to the act of seeing—of seeing, specifically, the purloined letter.

> The first is a glance that sees nothing: the King and the Police.
>
> The second, a glance which sees that the first sees nothing and deludes itself as to the secrecy of what it hides: the Queen, then the Minister.
>
> The third sees that the first two glances leave what should be hidden exposed to whomever would seize it: the Minister, and finally Dupin. (p. 44)

I have devised the following diagram as an attempt to schematize Lacan's analysis and to make explicit the synchronic, structural perceptions he proposes of the temporal, diachronic unfolding of the drama.

---

[16] For a remarkable analysis of the way repetition is enacted in the problematics of reading set in motion by Lacan's text, see Barbara Johnson's "The Frame of Reference: Poe, Lacan, Derrida," in *The Critical Difference: Essays in the Rhetoric of Contemporary Criticism* (Baltimore: Johns Hopkins University Press, 1980).

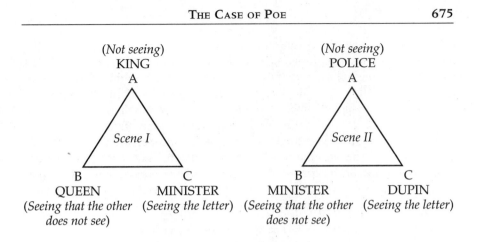

(*Not seeing*)
KING
A

Scene I

B   C
QUEEN   MINISTER
(*Seeing that the other*   *Seeing the letter*)
does not see)

(*Not seeing*)
POLICE
A

Scene II

B   C
MINISTER   DUPIN
(*Seeing that the other*   *Seeing the letter*)
does not see)

Although Lacan does not elaborate upon the possible ramifications of this structure, the diagram is open to a number of terminological translations, reinterpreting it in the light of Freudian and Lacanian concepts. Here are two such possible translations:

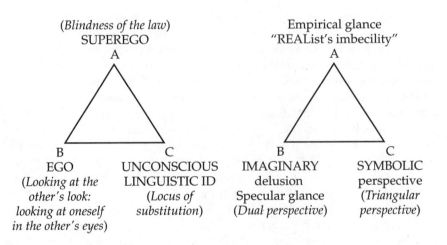

(*Blindness of the law*)
SUPEREGO
A

B   C
EGO   UNCONSCIOUS
(*Looking at the*   LINGUISTIC ID
other's look: (*Locus of*
looking at oneself   *substitution*)
in the other's eyes)

Empirical glance
"REAList's imbecility"
A

B   C
IMAGINARY   SYMBOLIC
delusion   perspective
Specular glance   (*Triangular*
(*Dual perspective*)   *perspective*)

"What interests us today," insists Lacan,

> is the manner in which the subjects relay each other in their displacement during the intersubjective repetition.
> We shall see that their displacement is determined by the place which a pure signifier—the purloined letter—comes to occupy in their trio. And that is what will confirm for us its status as repetition automatism. (p. 45)

The purloined letter, in other words, becomes itself—through its insistence in the structure—a symbol or a signifier of the unconscious, to the extent that it is destined "to signify the annulment of what it signifies"—the necessity of its own repression, of the repression of its message: "It is not only the meaning but the text of the message which it would be dangerous to place in circulation" (p. 56). But in much the same way as the repressed *returns* in the *symptom*, which is its repetitive symbolic substitute, the purloined letter ceaselessly returns in the tale—as a signifier of the repressed—through its repetitive displacements and replacements. "This is indeed what happens in the repetition compulsion," says Lacan (p. 60). Unconscious desire, once repressed, survives in displaced symbolic media that govern the subject's life and actions without his ever being aware of their meaning or of the repetitive pattern they structure:

> If what Freud discovered and rediscovers with a perpetually increasing sense of shock has a meaning, it is that the displacement of the signifier determines the subjects in their acts, in their destiny, in their refusals, in their blindnesses, in their end and in their fate, their innate gifts and social acquisitions notwithstanding, without regard for character or sex, and that, willingly or not, everything that might be considered the stuff of psychology, kit and caboodle, will follow the path of the signifier. (p. 60)

In what sense, then, does the second scene in Poe's tale, while repeating the first scene, nonetheless differ from it? In the sense, precisely, that the second scene, through the repetition, allows for an understanding, for an *analysis* of the first. This analysis through repetition is to become, in Lacan's ingenious reading, no less than an *allegory of psychoanalysis*. The intervention of Dupin, who restores the letter to the queen, is thus compared to the intervention of the analyst, who rids the patient of the symptom. The analyst's effectiveness, however, does not spring from his intellectual strength but—insists Lacan—from his position in the repetitive structure. By virtue of his occupying the third position—that is, the *locus* of the unconscious of the subject as a place of substitution of letter for letter (of signifier for signifier)—the analyst, through transference, allows at once for a repetition of the trauma and for a symbolic substitution, and thus effects the drama's denouement.

It is instructive to compare Lacan's study of the psychoanalytical repetition compulsion in Poe's text to Marie Bonaparte's study of Poe's repetition compulsion through his text. Although the two analysts study the same author and focus on the same psychoanalytic concept, their approaches are strikingly different. To the extent that Bonaparte's study of Poe has become a classic, a model of applied psychoanalysis, I would like, in pointing out the differences in Lacan's approach, to suggest the way in which those differences at once put in question the traditional approach and offer an alternative to it.

1. *What does a repetition compulsion repeat? Interpretation of difference as opposed to interpretation of identity.* For Marie Bonaparte, what is compulsively repeated through the variety of Poe's texts is the same unconscious fantasy: Poe's sadonecrophiliac desire for his dead mother. For Lacan, what is re-

peated in the text is not the content of a fantasy but the symbolic displacement of a signifier through the insistence of a signifying chain; repetition is not of *sameness* but of *difference*, not of independent terms or of analogous themes but of a structure of differential interrelationships,[17] in which what *returns* is always *other*. Thus, the triangular structure repeats itself only through the difference of the characters who successively come to occupy the three positions; its structural significance is perceived only *through* this difference. Likewise, the significance of the letter is situated in its displacement, that is, in its repetitive movements toward a different place. And the second scene, being, for Lacan, an allegory of analysis, is important not just in that it *repeats* the first scene, but in the way this repetition (like the transferential repetition of a psychoanalytical experience) *makes a difference:* brings about a solution to the problem. Thus, whereas Bonaparte analyzes repetition as the insistence of identity, for Lacan any possible insight into the reality of the unconscious is contingent on a perception of repetition, not as a confirmation of identity, but as the insistence of the indelibility of a difference.

2. *An analysis of the signifier as opposed to an analysis of the signified.* In the light of Lacan's reading of Poe's tale as itself an allegory of the psychoanalytic reading, it might be illuminating to define the difference in approach between Lacan and Bonaparte in terms of the story. If the purloined letter can be said to be a sign of the unconscious, for Bonaparte the analyst's task is to uncover the letter's content, which she believes—as do the police—to be hidden somewhere in the real, in some secret biographical depth. For Lacan, on the other hand, the analyst's task is not to read the letter's hidden referential content, but to situate the superficial indication of its textual movement, to analyze the paradoxically invisible symbolic evidence of its displacement, its structural insistence, in a signifying chain. "There is such a thing," writes Poe, "as being too profound. Truth is not always in a well. In fact, as regards the most important knowledge, I do believe she is invariably superficial."[18] Espousing Poe's insight, Lacan makes the principle of symbolic evidence the guideline for an analysis not of the signified but of the signifier—for an analysis of the unconscious (the repressed) not as hidden but on the contrary as *exposed*—in language—through a significant (rhetorical) displacement.

This analysis of the signifier, the model of which can be found in Freud's interpretation of dreams, is nonetheless a radical reversal of the traditional

---

[17] "Need we emphasize the similarity of these two sequences? Yes, for the resemblance we have in mind is not a simple collection of traits chosen only in order to delete their difference. And it would not be enough to retain those common traits at the expense of the others for the slightest truth to result. It is rather the intersubjectivity in which the two actions are motivated that we wish to bring into relief, as well as the three terms through which it structures them. The special status of these terms results from their corresponding simultaneously to the three logical moments through which the decision is precipitated and to the three places it assigns to the subjects among whom it constitutes a choice. . . . Thus three moments, structuring three glances, borne by three subjects, incarnated each time by different characters." "Seminar on *The Purloined Letter,*" pp. 43–44.

[18] "The Murders in the Rue Morgue," *Poe,* p. 204.

expectations involved in the common psychoanalytical approach to literature and its invariable search for hidden meanings. Indeed, not only in Lacan's reading of "The Purloined Letter" subversive of the traditional model of psychoanalytic reading: it is, in general, a type of reading that is methodologically unprecedented in the history of literary criticism. The history of reading has accustomed us to the assumption—usually unquestioned—that reading is finding meaning, that interpretation can dwell only on the meaningful. Lacan's analysis of the signifier opens up a radically new assumption, an assumption that is an insightful logical and methodological consequence of Freud's discovery: that what *can* be read (and perhaps what *should* be read) is not just meaning but the lack of meaning; that significance lies not just in consciousness but, specifically, in its disruption; that the signifier can be analyzed in its effect without its signified being known; that the lack of meaning—the discontinuity in conscious understanding—can and should be interpreted as such, without necessarily being transformed into meaning. "Let's take a look," writes Lacan:

> We shall find illumination in what at first seems to obscure matters: the fact that the tale leaves us in virtually total ignorance of the sender, no less than of the contents, of the letter. (p. 57)
>
> The signifier is not functional. . . . We might even admit that the letter has an entirely different (if no more urgent) meaning for the Queen than the one understood by the Minister. The sequence of events would not be noticeably affected, not even if it were strictly incomprehensible to an uninformed reader. (p. 56)
>
> But that this is the very effect of the unconscious in the precise sense that we teach that the unconscious means that man is inhabited by the signifier. (p. 66)

Thus, for Lacan, what is analytical par excellence is not (as is the case for Bonaparte) the readable but the unreadable and the effects of the unreadable. What calls for analysis is the insistence of the unreadable in the text.

Poe, of course, had said it all in his comment on the nature of what he too—amazingly enough, before the fact—called "the analytical": "The mental features discoursed of as the analytical are, in themselves, but little susceptible of analysis. We appreciate them only in their effects." But, oddly enough, what Poe himself had said so strikingly about the analytical had itself remained totally unanalyzed, indeed unnoticed, by psychoanalytic scholars before Lacan, perhaps because it, too, according to its own analytical logic, had been "a little too self-evident" to be perceived.

3. *A textual as opposed to a biographical approach.* The analysis of the signifier implies a theory of textuality for which Poe's biography, or his so-called sickness, or his hypothetical personal psychoanalysis, become irrelevant. The presupposition—governing enterprises like that of Marie Bonaparte—that poetry can be interpreted only as autobiography is obviously limiting and limited. Lacan's textual analysis for the first time offers a psychoanalytical al-

ternative to the previously unquestioned and thus seemingly exclusive biographical approach.

4. *The analyst/author relation: a subversion of the master/slave pattern and of
the doctor/patient opposition.* Let us remember how many readers were unsettled by the humiliating and sometimes condescending psychoanalytic emphasis on Poe's "sickness," as well as by an explanation equating the poetic
with the psychotic. There seemed to be no doubt in the minds of psychoanalytic readers that if the reading situation could be assimilated to the psychoanalytic situation, the poet was to be equated with the sick patient, with the
analysand on the couch. Lacan's analysis, however, subverts not only this
clinical status of the poet, but along with it the "bedside" security of the interpreter. If Lacan is not concerned with Poe's sickness, he is quite concerned
nonetheless with the figure of the poet in the tale, and with the hypotheses
made about his specific competence and incompetence. Both the minister
and Dupin are said to be poets, and it is their *poetic* reasoning that the prefect
fails to understand and that thus enables both to outsmart the police.
"D———, I presume, is not altogether a fool," comments Dupin early in the
story, to which the prefect of police replies:

> "Not altogether a fool . . . but then he's a poet, which I take to be
> only one remove from a fool."
> "True," said Dupin, after a long and thoughtful whiff from his
> meerschaum, "although I have been guilty of certain doggerel my-
> self." (p. 334)

A question Lacan does not address could be raised by emphasizing still another point that would normally tend to pass unnoticed, since, once again, it
is both so explicit and so ostentatiously insignificant: Why does Dupin say
that he too is *guilty* of poetry? In what way does the status of the poet involve
guilt? In what sense can we understand the guilt of poetry?

Dupin, then, draws our attention to the fact that both he and the minister
are poets, a qualification to which the prefect is condescending. Later, when
Dupin explains to the narrator the prefect's defeat, he again insists upon the
prefect's blindness to a logic or to a "principle of concealment" which has to
do with poets and thus (it might be assumed) is specifically poetic:

> This functionary has been thoroughly mystified; and the remote
> source of his defeat lies in the supposition that the Minister is a fool,
> because he has acquired renown as a poet. All fools are poets; this
> the Prefect feels; and he is merely guilty of a *non distributio medii* in
> thence inferring that all poets are fools. (pp. 341–342)

In Baudelaire's translation of Poe's tale into French, the word *fool* is rendered,
in its strong, archaic sense, as *fou*, "mad." Here, then, is Lacan's paraphrase
of this passage in the story:

> After which, a moment of derision [on Dupin's part] at the Prefect's
> error in deducing that because the Minister is a poet, he is not far

from being mad, an error, it is argued, which would consist . . . simply in a false distribution of the middle term, since it is far from following from the fact that all madmen are poets.

Yes indeed. But we ourselves are left in the dark as to the poet's superiority in the art of concealment. (p. 52)

Both this passage in the story and this comment by Lacan seem to be marginal, incidental. Yet the hypothetical *relationship between poetry and madness* is significantly relevant to the case of Poe and to the other psychoanalytical approaches we have been considering. Could it not be said that the error of Marie Bonaparte (who, like the prefect, engages in a search for hidden meaning) lies precisely in the fact that, like the prefect once again, she simplistically equates the poetic with the psychotic, and so, blinded by what she takes to be the poetic *incompetence,* fails to see or understand the specificity of poetic *competence*? Many psychoanalytic investigations diagnosing the poet's sickness and looking for his poetic secret in his person (as do the prefect's men) are indeed very like police investigations; and like the police in Poe's story, they fail to find the letter, fail to see the textuality of the text.

Lacan, of course, does not say all this—this is not what is at stake in his analysis. All he does is open up still another question where we believed we had come into possession of some sort of answer:

Yes indeed. But we ourselves are left in the dark as to the poet's superiority in the art of concealment.

This seemingly lateral question, asked in passing and left unanswered, suggests, however, the possibility of a whole different focus or perspective of interpretation in the story. If "The Purloined Letter" is specifically the story of "the poet's superiority in the art of concealment," then it is not just an allegory of psychoanalysis but also, at the same time, an allegory of poetic writing. And Lacan is himself a poet to the extent that a thought about poetry is what is superiorly concealed in his Seminar.

In Lacan's interpretation, however, the poet's superiority can only be understood as the structural superiority of the third position with respect to the letter: the minister in the first scene, Dupin in the second, both poets. But the third position is also—this is the main point of Lacan's analysis—the position of the analyst. It follows that, in Lacan's approach, the status of the poet is no longer that of the sick patient but, if anything, that of the analyst. If the poet is still the object of the accusation of being a fool, his folly—if it does exist (which remains an open question)—would at the same time be the folly of the analyst. The clear-cut opposition between madness and health, or between doctor and patient, is unsettled by the odd functioning of the purloined letter of the unconscious, which no one can possess or master. "There is no metalanguage," says Lacan: there is no language in which interpretation can itself escape the effects of the unconscious; the interpreter is no more immune than the poet to unconscious delusions and errors.

5. *Implication, as opposed to application, of psychoanalytic theory.* Lacan's approach no longer falls into the category of what has been called "applied psychoanalysis," since the concept of application implies a relation of exteriority between the applied science and the field it is supposed, unilaterally, to inform. Since, in Lacan's analysis, Poe's text serves to reinterpret Freud just as Freud's text serves to interpret Poe; since psychoanalytic theory and the literary text mutually inform—and displace—each other; since the very position of the interpreter—of the analyst—turns out to be not outside but inside the text, there is no longer a clear-cut opposition or a well-defined border between literature and psychoanalysis: psychoanalysis can be intraliterary just as much as literature is intrapsychoanalytic. The methodological stake is no longer that of the *application* of psychoanalysis *to* literature but, rather, of their *interimplication in* each other.

If I have dealt at length with Lacan's innovative contribution and with the different methodological example of his approach, it is not so much to set this example up as a new model for imitation, but rather to indicate the way in which it suggestively invites us to go beyond itself (as it takes Freud beyond itself), the way in which it opens up a whole new range of as yet untried possibilities for the enterprise of reading. Lacan's importance in my eyes does not, in other words, lie specifically in any new dogma his "school" may propose, but in his outstanding demonstration that *there is more than one way* to implicate psychoanalysis in literature; that *how to* implicate psychoanalysis in literature is itself a question for interpretation, a challenge to the ingenuity and insight of the interpreter, and not a *given* that can be taken in any way for granted; that what is of analytical relevance in a text is not necessarily and not exclusively "the unconscious of the poet," let alone his sickness or his problems in life; that to situate in a text the analytical as such—to situate the object of analysis or the textual point of its implication—is not necessarily to recognize a *known,* to find an answer, but also, and perhaps more challengingly, to locate an *unknown,* to find a question.

The Poe-etic Analytical

Let us now return to the crucial question we left in suspension earlier, after having raised it by reversing Freud's reservation concerning Marie Bonaparte's type of research: Can psychoanalysis give us an insight into the specificity of the poetic? We can now supplement this question with a second one: where can we situate the analytical with respect to Poe's poetry?

The answers to these questions might be sought in two directions. (1) In a direct reading of a poetic text by Poe, trying to locate in the poem itself a signifier of poeticity and to analyze its functioning and its effects; to analyze, in other words, how poetry as such works through signifiers (to the extent that signifiers, as opposed to meanings, are always signifiers of the unconscious); (2) in an analytically informed reading of literary history itself, since

its treatment of Poe obviously constitutes a literary *case history*. Such a reading has never, to my knowledge, been undertaken with respect to any writer:
never has literary history itself been viewed as an analytical object, as a subject for a psychoanalytic interpretation.[19] And yet it is overwhelmingly obvious, in a case like Poe's, that the discourse of literary history itself points to
some unconscious determinations that structure it but of which it is not
aware. What is the unconscious of literary history? Can the question of *the
guilt of poetry* be relevant to that unconscious? Could literary history be in
any way considered a repetitive unconscious *transference* of the guilt of poetry?

Literary history, or more precisely the critical discourse surrounding
Poe, is indeed one of the most visible ("self-evident") effects of Poe's poetic
signifier, of his text. Now, how can the question of the peculiar effect of Poe
be dealt with analytically? My suggestion is: by locating what seems to be
unreadable or incomprehensible in this effect; by situating the most prominent discrepancies or discontinuities in the overall critical discourse concerning Poe, the most puzzling critical contradictions, and by trying to interpret
those contradictions as symptomatic of the unsettling specificity of the Poe-
etic effect, as well as of the contingence of such an effect on the unconscious.

According to its readers' contradictory testimonies, Poe's poetry, let it be
recalled, seemed to be at once the most *irresistible* and the most *resisted* poetry
in literary history. Poe is felt to be at once the most unequaled master of conscious art *and* the most tortuous unconscious case, as such doomed to remain
"the perennial victim of the *idée fixe*, and of amateur psychoanalysis."[20] Poetry, I would thus argue, is precisely the effect of a deadly struggle between
consciousness and the unconscious; it has to do with resistance and with
what can neither be resisted nor escaped. Poe is a symptom of poetry to the
extent that poetry is both what most resists a psychoanalytical interpretation
and what most depends on psychoanalytical effects.

But this, paradoxically enough, is what poetry and psychoanalysis have
in common. They both exist only insofar as they resist our reading. When
caught in the act, both are always already, once again, purloined.

---

[19] I have attempted, however, an elementary exploration of such an approach with respect to Henry James in my essay, "Turning the Screw of Interpretation," in *Writing and
Madness: Literature/Philosophy/Psychoanalysis* (Ithaca: Cornell University Press, 1985).
[20] The formula is David Galloway's (*Poe*, p. 24).

Sandra M. Gilbert

and

Susan Gubar

Tradition and the Female Talent: Modernism and Masculinism

From *No Man's Land*

1988

In an influential 1981 article, feminist critic Elaine Showalter (see her essay on Hamlet's Ophelia, page 615) described two modes of writing that exemplified the poles of contemporary feminist criticism. The first, which she called the feminist critique, *seeks to expose the portrayals of stereotyped female characters and sexist attitudes in male-authored texts. The second, which Showalter named* gynocritics, *focuses on establishing and critiquing the tradition of female-authored texts, many of which have been ignored by the most influential traditions of literary scholarship. "Tradition and the Female Talent" by Sandra M. Gilbert (b. 1936) and Susan Gubar (b. 1944) draws from both of these types of feminist criticism for its central argument.*

In keeping with the tradition of the feminist critique, the authors point out the sexist assumptions and character portrayals of a number of influential male authors and critics of the early twentieth century. (The portion of the essay excerpted here contains several examples of this method, but even more appear in the section not reprinted.) While the essay most explicitly responds to T. S. Eliot's "Tradition and the Individual Talent" (page 404), it also confronts directly several other male modernists whose works demonstrate sexist bias. Moreover, the essay is a fine example of gynocriticism, in that it helps to establish more fully the influence of women writers in both the British and American traditions. Significantly, Gilbert and Gubar do not see the female tradition as separate and parallel to the better-established male tradition. Rather, they seek to describe the ways in which female authors profoundly affected their better-known male contemporaries and influenced subsequent generations of women writers.

New York natives Gilbert and Gubar rose to prominence in feminist literary critical circles with the publication of Madwoman in the Attic *(1979), their study of nineteenth-century woman authors. They have remained significant contributors to a critical tradition also exemplified in this volume by Virginia Woolf (page 411), Adrienne Rich (page 511), Showalter, and Nina Baym (page 586). Some have claimed that their continuing collaboration itself exemplifies the cooperative spirit of feminism at its best.*

Towards the end of the eighteenth century a change came about which, if I were re-writing history, I should describe more fully and think of greater importance than the Crusades or the Wars of the Roses. The middle-class woman began to write.

—Virginia Woolf[1]

The fact that the recognised heads of literature in the Homeric age were the nine muses . . . throws back the suggestion of female authorship to a very remote period. . . . If the truth were known, we might very likely find that it was man rather than woman who has been the interloper in the domain of literature.

—Samuel Butler

In the nineteenth century men were confident, the women were not, but in the twentieth century the men have no confidence.

—Dashiell Hammett to Gertrude Stein

The existing monuments form an ideal order among themselves, which is modified by the introduction of the new (the really new) work of art among them.

—T. S. Eliot

ON DECEMBER 30, 1927, Max Beerbohm wrote Virginia Woolf a strangely ambiguous fan letter. Praising her criticism for its likeness to her father's work—"if he had been a 'Georgian' and a woman, just so would he have written"—he went on quite unexpectedly to attack her fiction: "Your novels beat me—black and blue. I retire howling, aching, sore; full, moreover, of an acute sense of disgrace. I return later, I re-submit myself to the discipline. No use: I am carried out half-dead."[2] What was bothering the incomparable

---

[1] Epigraphs: Woolf, *A Room of One's Own*, p. 68; Butler, *The Authoress of the Odyssey*, with a new introduction by David Grene (1897; Chicago: University of Chicago Press, 1967), p. 13; Stein, *Everybody's Autobiography* (1937; New York: Vintage, 1973), p. 5; Eliot, "Tradition and the Individual Talent," in *Selected Essays of T. S. Eliot* (1919; New York: Harcourt, 1950), p. 5. Further references to this essay will be to this edition, and page numbers will appear in the text. [All notes are Gilbert's and Gubar's.]

[2] Beerbohm's letter to Woolf is held in the Robert H. Taylor Collection of the Firestone Library at Princeton University. This remarkable letter will be quoted in full in Sir Rupert Hart-Davis's forthcoming *Letters of Max Beerbohm* [1989].

Max? Certainly, in the context of his admiration for *The Common Reader* ("a book which I have read twice and rate above any modern book of criticism"), his somewhat paranoid association of Woolf's novels with bondage and discipline seems inexplicable, almost bizarre.

To be sure, Beerbohm goes on in the same letter to provide an explanation of his pain which would appear to suggest that his quarrel with Leslie Stephen's daughter is part of a larger generational conflict in the world of letters. "I don't really, insidious though you are, believe in your Cambridge argument that a new spirit exacts a new method . . . of narration," he explains, identifying himself with "Homer's and Thackeray's method, and Tolstoi's and Tom's, Dick's, Chaucer's, Maupassant's, and Harry's," all presumably methods grounded in the modes and manners of traditional realism. In other words, he sets himself, as a late Victorian man of letters, against Woolf, as a representative of Cambridge/Bloomsbury modernism. "You may be right in thinking that we are 'on the verge of one of the great ages of English literature'," he admits, but adds, "I believe that ten years hence and one hundred years hence fictional narrative will be thriving only in the old method about which I have been so stodgy and so longsome. . . ." Despite this explanation, Beerbohm's description of the effect Woolf's novels have on him, together with his list of the Toms, Dicks, and Harrys who constitute his literary patrilineage, implies that more than a conflict of cohorts is being enacted here. Curiously enough, moreover, the rhetoric of his letter echoes a story he had published seven years earlier, a story about a specifically literary battle not between the generations but between the sexes. Indeed, Beerbohm's image of a generational struggle may mask a more profound sexual-literary struggle dramatized not only in his fiction but also in the fiction of many of his contemporaries, a struggle associated with the more general battle of the sexes we have already discussed.

"The Crime," which was included in Beerbohm's *And Even Now* (1920), describes the acute "sense of disgrace" experienced by a nameless narrator who impetuously flings a woman writer's novel into a fireplace but cannot seem to burn the book up. Vacationing in a rented cottage in a remote county, this solitary man of letters compares himself at the outset of the story to "Lear in the hovel on the heath."[3] Idly looking for something to read, he picks up the latest novel by a well-known woman writer whom he has met and been daunted by on several occasions: "She had a sisterly, brotherly way. . . . But I was conscious that my best, under her eye, was not good . . . she said for me just what I had tried to say, and proceeded to show me just why it was wrong" (247). In fact, he reminisces, his few conversations with her led him to speculate on the "'sex war'" that, "we are often told[,] is to be one of the features of the world's future—women demanding the right to do men's work, and men refusing, resisting, counter-attacking" (248). Although he claims that he himself has never had his "sense of fitness jarred, not a spark of animosity

---

[3] "The Crime," in Beerbohm, *And Even Now* (London: Heinemann, 1920), p. 246. Subsequent references will be to this edition, and page numbers will be included in the text.

roused" by most feminist demands, he confesses that he is disturbed by the idea of a woman practicing the art of writing. More specifically, he admits that he is bothered if a woman is "an habitual, professional author, with a passion for her art, and a fountain-pen and an agent, and sums down in advance of royalties on sales in Canada and Australia" (248–49).

But the novelist whose book Beerbohm's man of letters picks up in his country cottage is emphatically all these things and, worse still, her work, as its jacket copy suggests, is characterized by "immense vitality," "intense vitality"; her newest novel, say the critics, is "A book that will live" (247). Furthermore, when he begins reading this book, he soon discovers that the novel is itself a *Kunstlerroman* about a successful woman of letters, a mother who sits "writing in a summer-house at the end of a small garden," her pen traveling "rapidly across the foolscap" (249). He feels "exquisite satisfaction," therefore, when he discovers that, following "an impulse . . . almost before I was conscious of it" (250), he has committed the heinous crime of flinging his landlord's copy of this woman's book into the fire, where it stands for a moment gloriously glowing. But although at first "little tongues of bright colour" (251) leaping from the binding let him exult that "I had scored . . . perfectly" against this "Poor woman!," he soon discovers to his dismay that the text itself refuses to be burnt. Enacting a cross between a ritual rape and a sacrificial burning at the stake, this increasingly obsessed narrator "rakes" the book "fore and aft" with a poker, "carve[s]" it into sections, "subdivide[s] it, spread[s] it, redistribute[s] it" (251–52). Yet still its intense and immense vitality proclaims that "It [is] a book that would live—do what one might" (252), while fragments of its sentences haunt and taunt him—"'lways loathed you, bu'" for instance. Finally, then, Beerbohm's disgraced man of letters has to concede that his female antagonist has "scored again." Not only has he been unable to destroy her book in "the yawning crimson jaws" of his hearth, her book has itself damped his flames. As his fire goes "darkly, dismally, gradually quite out" (252), he is left alone in a small and chilly room, as dispossessed as a parodic Lear confined to the prison of his consciousness.

Beerbohm's story is, of course, a masterfully comical satire on the futile rage with which men of letters greeted female literary achievement. At the same time, it is also, as the author's own letter to Virginia Woolf suggests, an enactment of that futile rage. Like Beerbohm himself, the narrator of "The Crime" admires his literary woman's "creative work immensely—but only in a bemused and miserable manner." Like Beerbohm, too, he tries to "resubmit himself to the discipline" of reading her text, but ends up experiencing "an acute sense of disgrace." Again, like Beerbohm, he finds the woman novelist's methods "insidious." And, like Beerbohm, he is beaten "black and blue." What the juxtaposition of the letter and the story demonstrates, therefore, is that the existence of a tradition of "habitual, professional" women authors made for a battle of the sexes over the province and provenance of literature, a battle which—like the more general battle over votes and rights—men felt they were losing in the years when Beerbohm wrote.

That Beerbohm was no noncombatant in the war between men and women which had been gathering force since the late nineteenth century is manifest in *Zuleika Dobson* (1906), that ultimate comedy of the femme fatale. Zuleika's narcissistic female charm, after all, causes all the youth of Oxford simultaneously to immolate themselves in the allegorically significant river Isis on the day Judas's boating crew is supposed to bump the crew of Magdalene. Even the dandy Duke of Dorset, a consummate poet in ancient and modern languages, must unwillingly submit to the sorcery of a "She-Wizard" whose conjuring tricks include the Demon Egg-Cup, the Magic Cannister, and the Blazing Ball of Worsted, and Zuleika's beauty is so threatening that, when she comes to town, the grim Roman Emperors whose busts grace Oxford sweat and weep.[4] Always masking his masculinist anxieties with elegant irony, Beerbohm nevertheless understood the deeply dialectical relationship in which men and women found themselves by the fin de siècle, a relationship that was unprecedented in literary history, as Virginia Woolf herself pointed out.

Eight years after Beerbohm wrote "The Crime," Woolf observed, in a passage from *A Room of One's Own* which we have used as an epigraph here, that "Toward the end of the eighteenth century a change came about which, if I were rewriting history, I should describe more fully and think of greater importance than the Crusades or the War of the Roses. The middle-class woman began to write" (68). Earlier, moreover, in just the year when Beerbohm wrote "The Crime," Woolf had analyzed the empowering implications of the entrance of women into literary history, noting in a letter to *The New Statesman* that "the seventeenth century produced more remarkable women than the sixteenth, the eighteenth than the seventeenth, and the nineteenth than all three put together[.] When I compare the Duchess of Newcastle with Jane Austen, the matchless Orinda with Emily Brontë, Mrs. Haywood with George Eliot, Aphra Behn with Charlotte Brontë, Jane Gray with Jane Harrison, the advance in intellectual power seems to me not only sensible but immense."[5] Describing the evolution of a tradition of immense and intense vitality, Woolf's statement almost seems to gloss the dilemma Beerbohm dramatizes in "The Crime." Moreover, the implicit dialogue between Beerbohm and Woolf that we have traced here seems itself to gloss the asymmetrical responses of men and women of letters to the strong new presence of women in the literary marketplace. For, when the middle-class woman began not only to enter the professions but specifically to enter the profession of letters, both sexes reacted with powerful but different changes in their views of the world and themselves.

How did male reactions inflect the engendering of literary history in the twentieth century? To begin with—and most dramatically—writers like

---

[4] Beerbohm, *Zuleika Dobson; Or, An Oxford Love Story* (New York: Heritage, 1960).

[5] Woolf, "Response to 'Affable Hawk' [Desmond MacCarthy]," in *The New Statesman*, 2 October 1920; reprinted in Virginia Woolf, *Women and Writing*, ed. Michele Barrett (New York: Harcourt, 1979), pp. 55–56.

James in America and Wilde in England could not help noticing that theirs was among the earliest generations to have female precursors. But what did it mean for such men to have to confront not only the commercial successes of, say, Harriet Beecher Stowe in America and Mary Elizabeth Braddon in England, but also the cultural achievements of, say, George Eliot, Elizabeth Barrett Browning, and Charlotte Brontë in England? Where literary men had traditionally looked for inspiration to the idealized mother or mistress whom convention metaphorized as a muse, turn-of-the-century and twentieth-century men of letters suffered from a disquieting intimation that the goddesses of literature, like the literary women male readers now encountered in increasing numbers, might reserve creative power for themselves. Worse still, these men feared that real-life "sisters of the sacred well" might go beyond what Milton had magisterially defined as "denial vain, and coy excuse" to produce texts that would eclipse or actually obliterate male efforts.[6] The literally castrating "Mommy" of Edward Albee's *The American Dream* may indeed be linked to the literarily castrating female precursor whose rivalrous descendants had to brag *"Who's Afraid of Virginia Woolf?"*

But perhaps even more important, because for late nineteenth- and early twentieth-century literary sons the Oedipal struggle against the father was in some sense doomed from the start, this historical change reinforced the feeling of belatedness—the anxiety about the originatory power of the father—upon which, as Harold Bloom has shown, literary men had already been brooding for several centuries. Where the male precursor had had an acquiescent mother-muse, his heir now confronted rebellious ancestresses and ambitious female peers, literary women whose very existence called the concept of the willing muse into question. Moreover, where the male precursor had himself been an adequate inheritor, capable of articulating a mature authority sufficient to the demands of his lineage, the modernist often felt that, as Wyndham Lewis put it in 1921, his culture was characterized by "a sort of No Man's Land atmosphere" and that, except for a marginalized elite, "[t]there is no mature authority."[7] Thus, what Matthew Arnold called in "The Scholar Gypsy" "this strange disease of modern life" (l. 203) became a literary disease with the "feminine, chattering, canting age" that Basil Ransom had excoriated in *The Bostonians*. At the same time, however, the very dis-ease fostered by this unprecedented cultural crisis worked paradoxically to the advantage of many literary men: as the richness of the (male) modernist tradition attests, for many male writers Beerbohm's futile rage became fertile rage, fueling the innovations of the avant garde in order to ward off the onslaughts of women. . . .

[6] "Lycidas," lines 15, 18. Harold Bloom, of course, discusses the relationship between the (female) muse and the (male) poet extensively throughout *The Anxiety of Influence* (New York: Oxford, 1973) and its companion volumes.
[7] Lewis, "The Children of the New Epoch," *The Tyro* I (April 1921): 3; reprinted in *Wyndham Lewis on Art: Collected Writings 1913–1956*, ed. Walter Michel and C. J. Fox (New York: Funk & Wagnalls, 1969), p. 195. We are grateful to Elyse Blankley for bringing this remark to our attention.

Of course, as John Guillory has demonstrated, T. S. Eliot's elevation of "an alternative canon," based on "his preference for the Metaphysicals and Dryden over Spenser and Milton, for the Jacobean dramatists over Shakespeare, and his rejection of virtually all Romantic and Victorian poetry," must be seen as a consequence of this influential poet-critic's own sense of belatedness toward the male tradition fathered by Milton and continued in the nineteenth century.[8] At the same time, however, such a consecration of an "orthodox" tradition, and particularly such a yearning for a Golden Age before "the dissociation of sensibility set in" (64) as well as a desire to learn "how to see the world as the Christian Fathers saw it" (291), erases the history associated with the entrance of women into the literary marketplace. Moreover, the Eliotian theory (propounded in "Tradition and the Individual Talent") that poetry involves "an escape from emotion" and "an escape from personality" constructs an implicitly masculine aesthetic of hard, abstract, learned verse that is opposed to the aesthetic of soft, effusive, personal verse supposedly written by women and Romantics (10). Thus in Eliot's critical writing women are implicitly devalued and the Romantics are in some sense feminized as Buckley hinted they had been by Tennyson, but Tennyson himself becomes part of a contaminated and metaphorically emasculated century.

In different ways, e. e. cummings, Ezra Pound, Wallace Stevens, and William Carlos Williams made statements which elaborate the sexual assumptions that shaped Eliot's thinking. In a meditation on "the Cambridge ladies who live in furnished souls," cummings connects mediocre women with dead gods and dull Victorians, declaring that these women are "unbeautiful and have comfortable minds," and suggesting that the worse thing about them is that "they believe in Christ and Longfellow, both dead."[9] In a frequently cited discussion of creativity in verse, Pound claimed that "Poetry speaks phallic direction," and, as Hugh Kenner notes, reflected "on a career of driving ideas into 'the great passive vulva of London.'"[10] In "A High-Toned Old Christian Woman," a poem that is less sexually graphic but has equally masculinist overtones, Wallace Stevens observes with patronizing aplomb that "Poetry is the supreme fiction, madame," adding that "fictive things / Wink as they will. Wink most when widows wince."[11] More explicitly, Williams produced in *Imaginations* (1970) a strikingly sexualized definition of the distinction between "good" and "bad" poetry: "What is good poetry made of," he asks, and answers "Of rats and snails and puppy-dog's tails," and then he adds "What is bad poetry made of," and he answers "Of sugar and spice and everything nice, / That is what bad poetry is made of."[12]

[8] Guillory, "The Ideology of Canon Formation: T. S. Eliot and Cleanth Brooks," *Critical Inquiry* 10 (1983):179. Further references are included in the text.

[9] cummings, *Complete Poems 1913–1962* (New York: Harcourt, 1972), p. 70.

[10] Pound quoted in Hugh Kenner, *The Pound Era* (Berkeley: University of California Press, 1971), pp. 104 and 256.

[11] Stevens, "A High-Toned Old Christian Woman," *The Collected Poems of Wallace Stevens* (New York: Knopf, 1954), p. 59.

[12] Williams, *Imaginations,* ed. Webster Schott (New York: New Directions, 1970), p. 169.

Though such American New Critics as John Crowe Ransom and R. P. Blackmur may not have so overtly sexualized "good" and "bad" poetry, their attempts at evaluation and canonization seem to have been motivated by a nostalgia as strong as Eliot's for the lost powers of "the Christian Fathers," and implicitly for the male strength associated with bygone male sexual hierarchies, a nostalgia which no doubt caused Ransom to refer to Emily Dickinson as "a little home-keeping person" and Blackmur to say, just as patronizingly, that she "wrote indefatigably, as some women cook or knit. Her gift for words and the cultural predicament of her time drove her to poetry instead of antimacassars."[13] To poet-critics from Lawrence, Eliot, Pound, and Williams to Ransom and Blackmur, a literary landscape populated by women, whether they were scribblers, mentors, or great artists, may have seemed like a no man's land, a wasted and wasting country that left them with what Beerbohm called "an acute sense of disgrace."

Indeed, the acute sense of disgrace we associate with such a waste land may arise from the fact that, as much as the industrial revolution and the fall of God, the rise of the female imagination was a central problem for the twentieth-century male imagination. Thus when we focus not only on women's increasingly successful struggle for autonomy in the years from, say, 1880 to 1920, but also on their increasingly successful production of literary texts throughout the nineteenth and twentieth centuries, we find ourselves confronting an entirely different modernism. And it is a modernism constructed not just against the grain of Victorian male precursors, not just in the shadow of a shattered God, but as an integral part of a complex response to *female* precursors and contemporaries. Indeed, it is possible to hypothesize that a reaction-formation against the rise of literary women became not just a theme in modernist writing but a motive for modernism. Even the establishment of a supposedly anti-establishment avant garde can be seen as part of this phenomenon, for the twin strategies of excavation and innovation deployed in experimental works like *The Cantos* (1917–69), *The Waste Land,* and *Ulysses* reconstitute the hierarchies implicit in what T. S. Eliot called in "Tradition and the Individual Talent" "the mind of Europe" (6). . . . As we shall argue in chapter five, the excavation of that mind's fragments functions simultaneously to counter and to recover the noble fatherhood of precursors from Homer to Dante and Shakespeare, while the linguistic innovation associated with the avant garde—the use of puns, allusions, phrases in foreign languages, arcane and fractured forms—functions to occult language so that only an initiated elite can participate in the community of high culture. A few women like Gertrude Stein and Djuna Barnes did intermittently join such a community, but by and large it remained (and may have been unconsciously designed as) a men's club. It is not surprising, therefore, that on his first read-

---

[13] Ransom, "Emily Dickinson: A Poet Restored," in *Emily Dickinson: A Collection of Critical Essays,* ed. Richard B. Sewall (Englewood Cliffs, New Jersey: Prentice-Hall, 1963), p. 89; Blackmur is quoted in Reeves, "Introduction," *Selected Poems of Emily Dickinson* (New York: Macmillan, 1960), p. 119.

ing of *The Waste Land* Joyce noted that T. S. Eliot's masterpiece "ends [the] idea of poetry for ladies," which was, after all, no more than what Hulme had called "roses, roses all the way."[14]

The need somehow to "end . . . poetry for ladies" did not end with modernists, for more recently some literary men seem to have felt as strongly as Harold Stearns did in 1922 that they were living in an age of "extraordinary feminization." Describing the Statue of Liberty, Robert Lowell characterizes the spirit of his society as militant and female: noting "the thrilling, chilling silver of your laugh, / the hysterical digging of your accursed spur," he apostrophizes her as an "Amazon, gazing on me, pop-eyed, cool, / ageless, not holding back your war-whoop."[15] Indeed, from James Thurber to Norman Mailer, William Gass, Anthony Burgess, Leroi Jones, and Edward Albee, from Theodore Roethke to John Berryman and Lowell himself, many postmodernist men of letters continued to define their artistic integrity in opposition to either the literary incompetence or the aesthetic hysteria they associated with women.

In "Here Lies Miss Groby" (1942), for instance, Thurber protested against what Ann Douglas has called "the feminization of American culture" by satirizing the high school English teacher who has traditionally been a literary culture bearer. His Miss Groby is presented as a classic battle axe of a schoolmarm who "crucifie[d] sentences" by parsing them on the blackboard, who never "saw any famous work of literature from far enough away to know what it meant," who was so preoccupied with counting that she "would have got an enormous thrill out of Wordsworth's famous lines about Lucy if they had been written" so that Lucy was "Fair as a star when ninety-eight / Are shining in the sky," and who causes the young Thurber to become so obsessed with finding an example of the "Thing Contained for the Container" that he imagines a woman saying to her husband " 'Get away from me or I'll hit you with the milk.' "[16] An antisentimental, bluestocking heiress of the tradition exemplified by Twain's sentimental Emmeline Grangerford, Miss Groby leaves her ex-pupil "tossing and moaning" (39) over her destruction of literary values and her deconstruction of good writing. And thus, though she is not herself a writer, this Miss Groby resembles the stereotypical Mrs. Grundy, whose moralistic strictures contaminate social as well as literary structures.

Where Thurber is genial and comic about his high school English teacher, many of his descendants are far more scornful about the virtually sexual incapacity of women writers. As usual, Norman Mailer—whose *The Prisoner of Sex* was written to counter Kate Millett's attack on him in *Sexual Politics*—is among the most belligerent of these postmodernists. In *Advertisements for Myself* (1959), he makes what he calls a "terrible confession":

[14] Quoted in Richard Ellmann, *James Joyce* (New York: Oxford University Press, 1959), p. 510.

[15] Lowell, "Statue of Liberty," *History* (New York: Farrar, Straus, 1973), p. 147.

[16] Thurber, *Thurber Carnival*, pp. 38–39.

I have nothing to say about any of the talented women who write today. . . . I can only say that the sniffs I get from the ink of women are always fey, old-hat . . . too dykily psychotic, crippled creepish, fashionable, frigid . . . or else bright and stillborn. Since I've never been able to read Virginia Woolf, and am sometimes willing to believe it can conceivably be my fault, this verdict may be taken as the twisted tongue of a soured taste, at least by those readers who do not share with me the ground of departure—that a good novelist can do without everything but the remnant of his balls.[17]

Gass and Burgess have also made comparable remarks, with Gass declaring that women writers "lack that blood-congested genital drive which energizes every great style," and Burgess complaining that Jane Austen's work "lacks a strong male thrust."[18] At the same time, despite such efforts to represent women writers as metaphorically castrated, it seems significant that Baraka's Lena the Hyena, the villainess of *Dutchman,* is a woman *poet* and that the reiterated refrain of Albee's Martha is "Who's Afraid of Virginia Woolf?"

To be sure, Roethke, Berryman, and Lowell would seem to be considerably less virulent than, say, Mailer. Yet even when these literary men celebrate female contemporaries and precursors, they tend to single out a token woman for attention, or to qualify in one text the compliment expressed in another. Roethke, for example, writes with admiration about Louise Bogan, Berryman with reverence for Anne Bradstreet, and Lowell with adulation about Elizabeth Bishop. But each has also made critical gestures that suggest some measure of hostility toward literary women. Reviewing Louise Bogan, Roethke prefaces his praise for her with an attack on women poets:

Two of the charges most frequently levelled against poetry by women are lack of range—in subject matter, in emotional tone—and lack of sense of humor. And one could, in individual instances among writers of real talent, add other aesthetic and moral shortcomings: the spinning-out; the embroidering of trivial themes; a concern for the mere surfaces of life—that special province of the feminine talent in prose—hiding from the real agonies of the spirit; refusing to face up to what existence is; lyric or religious posturing; running between the boudoir and the altar, stamping a tiny foot against God; or lapsing into sententiousness that implies the author has reinvented integrity; carrying on excessively about Fate, about time; lamenting the lot of the woman; caterwauling; writing the same poem about fifty times, and so on.[19]

[17] Mailer, *Advertisements for Myself* (New York: Berkeley, 1966), pp. 434–35.

[18] Burgess, "The Book Is Not for Reading," *New York Times Book Review,* 4 December 1966, pp. 1, 74, and Gass, on Mailer's *Genius and Lust, New York Times Book Review,* 24 October 1976, p. 2.

[19] Roethke, "The Poetry of Louise Bogan," *On the Poet and His Craft: Selected Prose of Theodore Roethke,* ed. Ralph J. Mills, Jr. (Seattle: University of Washington Press, 1965), pp. 133–34.

Similarly, despite his *Homage to Mistress Anne Bradstreet* (1956), John Berryman explains in *The Dream Songs* (1969) that

Them lady poets must not marry, pal.
Miss Dickinson—fancy in Amherst bedding her.
Fancy a lark with Sappho,
a tumble in the bushes with Miss Moore,
a spoon with Emily, while Charlotte glare.
Miss Bishop's too noble-O.

and adds in the next stanza that "Sylvia Plath is not. / She—she her credentials / has handed in, leaving alone two tots / and widower to what he makes of it— / surviving guy."[20] Finally, though Lowell pays tribute to Jean Stafford and Elizabeth Bishop and though he wrote a preface to the American edition of *Ariel*, he makes a similar but nastier statement about the dead Plath, noting in "Sylvia Plath" that because female English majors now say "*I am Sylvia,* / I hate marriage, I must hate babies . . . sixty thousand American infants a year, / U. I. D., Unexplained Infant Deaths, / born physically whole and hearty, refuse to live." These dead babies, asserts Lowell, are the consequence of the pernicious influence wielded by Plath's "*Miniature mad talent*": "Sylvia the expanding torrent of your attack."[21]

Earlier, in the dazzling prose memoir "91 Revere Street" that he embedded in *Life Studies* (1959), Lowell had sardonically remembered his family's dislike of their literary ancestress Amy Lowell and obviously relished repeating one of "Commander Billy's" "tiresome, tasteless harangues" against the authoress of "Patterns": "Remember Amy Lowell, that cigar-chawing, guffawing, senseless and meterless, multimillionheiress, heavyweight mascot on a floating fortress. Damn the *Patterns*! Full speed ahead on a cigareeto!" (38). In a manner closer to his critique of Plath, moreover, Lowell addressed a poem to Adrienne Rich in which, though he conceded that "Your groundnote is joy," he asked, "disabled veteran, how long will you bay with the hounds / and beat time with crutches?" (154).[22]

In addition, and more notoriously, after he had left Elizabeth Hardwick, Lowell versified a number of painful passages from her letters in an act of usurpation comparable to Williams's quotation of Marcia Nardi's letters in *Paterson* or, for that matter, to Berryman's impersonation of Anne Bradstreet. Of course, like Williams and Berryman, Lowell might be said to have been

[20] Berryman, 187 ("Them lady poets") in *The Dream Songs* (New York: Farrar, Straus, 1974), p. 206.

[21] Lowell, "Sylvia Plath," *History*, p. 135.

[22] For Lowell on Amy Lowell, see *Life Studies and For the Union Dead* (New York: Noonday, 1967), p. 38; on Rich, see *History*, p. 154. Also worth considering in this context is Auden's famous introduction to Adrienne Rich's *A Change of Worlds* (1951), vol. 48 in the Yale Younger Poets series: her poems, he says, "are neatly and modestly dressed, speak quietly but do not mumble, respect their elders but are not cowed by them, and do not tell fibs" (p. 11); as well as Randall Jarrell's observation about Rich's *The Diamond Cutters* (1955) that the "poet whom we see behind" these poems "cannot help seeming to us a sort of princess in a fairy tale" (Jarrell, "Five Poets," *Yale Review* 46:1 [Autumn 1956]:100).

offering an expiatory homage to Hardwick in these poems, for just as Nardi's letters portray Williams as culpable and Berryman's poem depicts Bradstreet as admirable, Hardwick's words reveal both Lowell's guilt and her strength. Yet, like Williams, Lowell also humiliates the woman whose painted sentences he exhibits to public view and, like Berryman—who stresses Bradstreet's suffering sense that "a male great pestle smashes / small women swarming toward the mortar's rim in vain"—he manages to speak patronizingly about Hardwick even while he speaks through and as her.[23] Clearly, for writers in the 1950s, 1960s, and 1970s, the literary "woman question" was still so urgent that many of the strongest male artists continued to find their own voices by entering into an explicit or implicit dialogue with women. Recently, for instance, the British novelist D. M. Thomas became notorious for his controversial appropriation, in *The White Hotel,* of Dina Pronicheva's account of her experience at Babi Yar.[24] But perhaps more to the point in terms of the battle of the sexes is another of Lowell's poems: that the "almost impotent almost faithful" speaker of Lowell's "Loser" has a wife who sits all night "reading Simone de Beauvoir till day" suggests this male poet's own consciousness of the implications of the revitalized women's liberation movement.[25]

Throughout the century, then, men of letters persistently expressed feelings of loss and anger, feelings that the mother-muse had abandoned them. Indeed, as the Oedipal paradigm through which Harold Bloom has analyzed literary history dissolved into a far more complicated complex, they ever more deeply understood the ramifications of what women also, though very differently, experienced: the incontrovertible fact that the once willing muse had now become self-willing and, they feared, self-willed. Experiencing themselves as belated, stranded, and "suffocating" on the territory that a play by Harold Pinter called *No Man's Land* (1975), they insisted, with Pinter's bleakly drifting anti-hero Spooner, that "I'm a friend of the arts, particularly the art of poetry, and a guide to the young. I keep open house. Young poets come to me. They read me their verses. . . . Women are admitted; some of whom are also poets. Some are not." But then they admit their fear that "Some of the men are not. Most of the men are not."[26] Thus, the muse had to be reconstructed either as a passive woman or, more radically, as an empowering and empowered man. In Dylan Thomas's surrealistic "Ballad of the Long-legged Bait," for instance, she is "A girl alive with . . . hooks through her lips" whom a fisherman, in an allegory of creativity, throws to the "swift flood."[27] And in Ezra Pound's "Sage Homme," a comic comment on *The*

[23] For Lowell's use of Hardwick's letters, see *The Selected Poems of Robert Lowell* (New York: Farrar, Straus, 1976): "Voices," p. 223; "Records," p. 226; "In the Mail," p. 229; "Exorcism," p. 230; "The Couple," p. 231; and "Christmas," p. 237.

[24] For a discussion of this from the point of view of a holocaust scholar, see Alvin H. Rosenfeld, *Imagining Hitler* (Bloomington: Indiana University Press, 1985), p. 57.

[25] Lowell, "Loser," *History,* p. 182.

[26] Pinter, *No Man's Land* (New York: Grove, 1975), pp. 36, 18.

[27] Thomas, "The Ballad of the Long-legged Bait," *The Collected Poems of Dylan Thomas* (New York: New Directions, 1957), p. 167.

Waste Land, Milton's maternal muse becomes a transsexual Sire, suggesting that the modernist poet may be in a double bind. Because he no longer has a suitable female muse, he might construct a male surrogate for her. But, as "Sage Homme" hints, such a figure seems at best comic and at worst perverse, indeed potentially capable of inducing a kind of homophobic panic:

> These are the poems of Eliot
> By the Uranian Muse begot;
> A Man their Mother was,
> A Muse their Sire.

> How did the printed Infancies result
> From Nuptuals thus doubly difficult?

> If you must needs enquire
> Know diligent Reader
> That on each Occasion
> Ezra performed the Caesarean Operation.[28]

Pound's redefinition of the engendering of male creativity certainly helps explain why and how *The Waste Land* ended the "idea of poetry for ladies," but, more, it functions as an acknowledgment that, for both sexes, the shock of the new—and specifically the new world of women's words—required shocking sociocultural redefinitions. T. S. Eliot himself may not have understood the radical implications of the relationship between tradition and the individual talent that he described in 1919 in *The Egoist* (a journal, incidentally, which began its career as a suffrage periodical called *The Freewoman* and then *The New Freewoman*). But Eliot's theory that new works of art alter not only our sense of the past but also our sense of what art might *be* actually seems to reflect the sexual crisis that underlies modernism. For inevitably, the "ideal order" of patriarchal literary history was radically "modified by the introduction of the new (the really new) work of art"—and, as Woolf remarked, that "really new work" was women's work.

---

[28] Pound, "Sage Homme," *The Letters of Ezra Pound, 1907–1941,* ed. D. D. Paige (New York: Harcourt, 1950), p. 170. The "Uranian Muse" might be an allusion to the male homosexuals Edward Carpenter associates with the "third sex" and calls "Uranians" or "Urnings" in *The Intermediate Sex: A Study of Some Transitional Types of Men and Women* (London: G. Allen and Unwin, 1908) and *Intermediate Types among Primitive Folk: A Study in Social Evolution* (London: G. Allen, 1914).

Henry Louis Gates, Jr.

The Trope of the Talking Book

From *The Signifying Monkey*

1988

In The Signifying Monkey, *Henry Louis Gates, Jr. (b. 1950) advances a theory of the relationship of black vernacular English to the African American literary tradition. Signifyin(g), which Gates spells with parentheses to indicate a particular meaning, is a rhetorical device of black English in which the true meaning of a statement is hidden, creating a "double-voice." Gates cites as an example of signifyin(g) the hymn title "Steal Away to Jesus," which when used among slaves might carry a hidden meaning of "Go to a religious meeting forbidden by the plantation owners." The double meaning in signifyin(g) takes on many forms and uses: concealment of true meaning, bragging, baiting, indirect criticism, seduction, play, and, finally, a self-reflexive commentary upon itself.*

Gates sees Esu and the Monkey, two trickster figures from African myths but widely dispersed with the slaves, as source figures of the double-voice. Myths of Esu and the Monkey portray them as a duality of law versus speaking, of the literal versus the figurative, of determinacy versus indeterminacy in interpretation. The double-voice of signifyin(g) is a mythic heritage of African American culture.

The trope of the Talking Book draws from this vernacular tradition of signifyin(g). African American writing is double-voiced in the metaphor of texts that "talk" to other texts, both black and white. Gates posits that the Talking Book is the fundamental trope of African American writing and the defining principle of narrative voice in black fiction. He traces the trope through five African American texts published by 1815. Generally the issues are of movement from spoken to written language, from African languages to English, and from an illiteracy associated with subhuman status to literate membership in the human community. The problems of finding a voice to constitute black identity in an alien culture continues in the twentieth century in Zora Neale Hurston's Their Eyes Were Watching God, *in Ishmael Reed's* Mumbo Jumbo, *and in Alice Walker's* The Color Purple.

696

While arguing that African American writers portray a "black essentialism"
and also establish intertextuality with American literature more generally, Gates is
also very much in the mainstream of contemporary literary theory. He develops his
argument in the terminology of contemporary literary theory, with his play on the
words "signifyin(g)" and structuralist "signifying," in the deconstructionist con-
cern with "figuration" and tropes, and in the interest in discovering a distinctive lib-
erating voice within a minority group.

[A] disingenuous and unmanly *Position* had been formed; and privately
(*and as it were in the dark*) handed to and again, which is this, that the
Negro's, though in their Figure they carry some resemblances of Manhood, yet are indeed *no Men.* . . .

    [The] consideration of the shape and figure of our *Negro's* Bodies,
their Limbs and Members; their Voice and Countenance, in all things
according with other Mens; together with their *Risibility* and *Discourse*
(Man's *peculiar* Faculties) should be sufficient Conviction. How should
they otherwise be capable of *Trades,* and other no less Manly im-
ployments; as also of *Reading and Writing* . . . were they not truly
Men?

                               — Morgan Godwyn, 1680[1]

Let us to the Press Devoted Be,
Its *Light* will *Shine* and *Speak Us Free.*

                               — David Ruggles, 1835

I

THE LITERATURE of the slave, published in English between 1760 and 1865, is
the most obvious site to excavate the origins of the Afro-American literary
tradition. Whether our definition of *tradition* is based on the rather narrow
lines of race or nationality of authors, upon shared themes and narrated
stances, or upon repeated and revised tropes, it is to the literature of the
black slave that the critic must turn to identify the beginning of the Afro-
American literary tradition.

    "The literature of the slave" is an ironic phrase, at the very least, and is
an oxymoron at its most literal level of meaning. "Literature," as Samuel
Johnson used the term, denoted an "acquaintance with 'letters' or books," according to the *Oxford English Dictionary.* It also connoted "polite or humane
learning" and "literary culture." While it is self-evident that the ex-slave who
managed (as Frederick Douglass put it) to "steal" some learning from his or

---

[1] Morgan Godwyn, *The Negro's and Indians' Advocate . . . in Our Plantation* (1680), cited in
Frances Smith Foster, *Witnessing Slavery: The Development of Antebellum Slave Narratives*
(Westport, Conn.: Greenwood, 1979), pp. 7–9. [All notes are Gates's.]

her master and the master's texts, was bent on demonstrating to a skeptical public an acquaintance with letters or books, we cannot honestly conclude that slave literature was meant to exemplify either polite or humane learning or the presence in the author of literary culture. Indeed, it is more accurate to argue that the literature of the slave consisted of texts that represent impolite learning and that these texts collectively railed against the arbitrary and inhumane learning which masters foisted upon slaves to reinforce a perverse fiction of the "natural" order of things. The slave, by definition, possessed at most a liminal status within the human community.[2] To read and to write was to transgress this nebulous realm of liminality. The slave's texts, then, could not be taken as specimens of a black literary culture. Rather, the texts of the slave could only be read as testimony of defilement: the slave's *representation* and reversal of the master's attempt to transform a human being into a commodity, and the slave's simultaneous verbal witness of the possession of a humanity shared in common with Europeans. The chiasmus, perhaps the most commonly used rhetorical figure in the slave narratives and throughout subsequent black literature, is figured in the black vernacular tradition by tropes of the crossroads, that liminal space where Esu resides. The slave wrote not primarily to demonstrate humane letters, but to demonstrate his or her own membership in the human community.

This intention cannot be disregarded as a force extraneous to the production of a text, a common text that I like to think of as the text of blackness. If we recall Ralph Ellison's apt phrase by which he defines what I am calling tradition, "a sharing of that 'concord of sensibilities' which the group *expresses*," then what I wish to suggest by the text of blackness is perhaps clearer. Black writers to a remarkable extent have created texts that express the broad "concord of sensibilities" shared by persons of African descent in the Western hemisphere. Texts written over two centuries ago address what we might think of as common subjects of condition that continue to be strangely resonant, and relevant, as we approach the twenty-first century. Just as there are remarkably few literary traditions whose first century's existence is determined by texts created by slaves, so too are there few traditions that claim such an apparent unity from a fundamental political condition represented for over two hundred years in such strikingly similar patterns and details.

Has a common experience, or, more accurately, the shared sense of a common experience, been largely responsible for the sharing of this text of blackness? It would be foolish to say no. Nevertheless, shared experience of black people vis-à-vis white racism is not sufficient evidence upon which to argue that black writers have shared patterns of representation of their common subject for two centuries—unless one wishes to argue for a genetic theory of literature, which the biological sciences do not support. Rather, shared modes of figuration result only when writers read each other's texts and

2My understanding of *liminality* arises from Robert Pelton's usages in *The Trickster in West Africa* and from Houston Baker's novel usage as taken from Victor Turner's work. See Baker's *Blues, Ideology, and Afro-American Literature: A Vernacular Theory* (1985).

seize upon topoi and tropes to revise in their own texts. This form of revision is a process of grounding and has served to create curious formal lines of continuity between the texts that together comprise the shared text of blackness, the discrete chapters of which scholars are still establishing.

What seems clear upon reading the texts created by black writers in English or the critical texts that responded to these black writings is that the production of literature was taken to be the central arena in which persons of African descent could, or could not, establish and redefine their status within the human community. Black people, the evidence suggests, had to represent themselves as "speaking subjects" before they could even begin to destroy their status as objects, as commodities, within Western culture. In addition to all of the myriad reasons for which human beings write books, this particular reason seems to have been paramount for the black slave. At least since 1600, Europeans had wondered aloud whether or not the African "species of men," as they most commonly put it, could ever create formal literature, could ever master the arts and sciences. If they could, then, the argument ran, the African variety of humanity and the European variety were fundamentally related. If not, then it seemed clear that the African was destined by nature to be a slave.

Determined to discover the answer to this crucial quandary, several Europeans and Americans undertook experiments in which young African slaves were tutored and trained along with white children. Phillis Wheatley was merely one result of such an experiment. Francis Williams, a Jamaican who took the B.A. at Cambridge before 1750; Jacobus Capitein, who earned several degrees in Holland; Wilhelm Amo, who took the doctorate degree in philosophy at Halle; and Ignatius Sancho, who became a friend of Laurence Sterne's and who published a volume of *Letters* in 1782, are just a few of the black subjects of such experiments. The published writings of these black men and one woman, who wrote in Latin, Dutch, German, and English, were seized upon both by pro- and anti-slavery proponents as proof that their arguments were sound.

So widespread was the debate over "the nature of the African" between 1730 and 1830 that not until the Harlem Renaissance would the work of black writers be as extensively reviewed as it was in the eighteenth century. Phillis Wheatley's list of reviewers includes Voltaire, Thomas Jefferson, George Washington, Samuel Rush, and James Beatty, to list only a few. Francis Williams's work was analyzed by no less than David Hume and Immanuel Kant. Hegel, writing in the *Philosophy of History* in 1813, used the absence of writing of Africans as the sign of their innate inferiority. The list of commentators is extensive, amounting to a "Who's Who" of the French, English, and American Enlightenment.

Why was the creative writing of the African of such importance to the eighteenth century's debate over slavery? I can briefly outline one thesis. After Descartes, reason was privileged, or valorized, over all other human characteristics. Writing, especially after the printing press became so widespread, was taken to be the visible sign of reason. Blacks were reasonable, and hence "men," if — and only if — they demonstrated mastery of "the arts and sciences," the eighteenth century's formula for writing. So, while the

Enlightenment is famous for establishing its existence upon man's ability to reason, it simultaneously used the absence and presence of reason to delimit and circumscribe the very humanity of the cultures and people of color which Europeans had been "discovering" since the Renaissance. The urge toward the systematization of all human knowledge, by which we characterize the Englightenment, in other words led directly to the relegation of black people to a lower rung on the Great Chain of Being, an eighteenth-century metaphor that arranged all of creation on the vertical scale from animals and plants and insects through man to the angels and God himself. By 1750, the chain had become individualized; the human scale rose from "the lowliest Hottentot" (black South Africans) to "glorious Milton and Newton." If blacks could write and publish imaginative literature, then they could, in effect, take a few giant steps up the Chain of Being, in a pernicious game of "Mother, May I?" The Rev. James W. C. Pennington, an ex-slave who wrote a slave narrative and who was a prominent black abolitionist, summarized this curious idea in his prefatory note to Ann Plato's 1841 book of essays, biographies, and poems: "The history of the arts and sciences is the history of individuals, of individual nations." Only by publishing books such as Plato's, he argues, can blacks demonstrate "the fallacy of that stupid theory, *that nature has done nothing but fit us for slaves, and that art cannot unfit us for slavery!*"[3]

Not a lot changed, then, between Phillis Wheatley's 1773 publication of her *Poems* (complete with a prefatory letter of authenticity signed by eighteen of "the most respectable characters in Boston") and Ann Plato's, except that by 1841 Plato's attestation was supplied by a black person.[4] What we might think of as the black text's mode of being, however, remained pretty much the same during these sixty-eight years. What remained consistent was that black people could become speaking subjects only by inscribing their voices in the written word. If this matter of recording an authentic black voice in the text of Western letters was of widespread concern in the eighteenth century, then how did it affect the production of black texts, if indeed it affected them at all? It is not enough simply to trace a line of shared argument as context to show that blacks regarded this matter as crucial to their tasks; rather evidence for such a direct relationship of text to context must be found in the black texts themselves.

The most salient indication that this idea informed the writing of black texts is found in a topos that appears in five black texts published in English

---

[3] James W. C. Pennington, "To the Reader," in Ann Plato, *Essays; Including Biographies and Miscellaneous Pieces, in Prose and Poetry* (Hartford: for the author, 1841), pp. xviii, xx.

[4] On April 30, 1773, Mrs. Susanna Wheatley wrote to the Countess of Huntington to thank her for granting permission to her slave, Phillis, to dedicate her forthcoming volume of poems to this distinguished humanitarian. Since Phillis Wheatley sailed to England in May of 1773, and because the book was published in London before she returned to Boston in late July, we must conclude that the certificate of attestation was signed well before Susanna Wheatley sent the manuscript to the countess. See Sarah D. Jackson, "Letters of Phillis Wheatley and Susanna Wheatley," *Journal of Negro History* LVII, no. 2 (April 1972): 214–15; and William H. Robinson, *Phillis Wheatley in the Black American Beginnings* (Detroit: Broadside Press, 1975), pp. 15–18. See also "To the Publick," in *Poems on Various Subjects, Religious and Moral,* by Phillis Wheatley, Negro Servant to Mr. John Wheatley, of Boston, in New England (London: A. Bell, 1773).

by 1815. This topos assumed such a central place in the black use of figurative language that we can call it a trope. It is the trope of the Talking Book, which first occurred in a 1770 slave narrative and was then revised in other slave narratives published in 1785, 1787, 1789, and 1815. Rebecca Jackson refigures this trope in her autobiographical writings, written between 1830 and 1832 but not published until 1981. Jackson's usage serves as a critique of her black male antecedents' usages because she refigures the trope in terms of male domination of a female's voice and her quest for literacy. (I analyze Jackson's revision in Chapter 7.) Not only does this shared but revised trope argue forcefully that blacks were intent on placing their individual and collective voices in the text of Western letters, but also that even the earliest writers of the Anglo-African tradition read each other's texts and grounded these texts in what soon became a tradition.

The trope of the Talking Book is the ur-trope of the Anglo-African tradition. Bakhtin's metaphor of double-voiced discourse, figured most literally in representational sculptures of Esu and implied in the Signifying Monkey's function as the rhetoric of a vernacular literature, comes to bear in black texts through the trope of the Talking Book. In the slave narratives discussed in this chapter, making the white written text speak with a black voice is the initial mode of inscription of the metaphor of the double-voiced. In Zora Neale Hurston, the concept of voice is complex, oscillating as representation among direct discourse, indirect discourse, and a unique form of free indirect discourse that serves to privilege the speaking voice. In Ishmael Reed's novel, Mumbo Jumbo, the double-voiced text emerges as the text of ultimate critique and revision of the rhetorical strategies at work in the canonical texts of the tradition. Finally, in Alice Walker's The Color Purple, the double-voiced text assumes the form of the epistolary novel in which revision manifests itself as a literal representation of a protagonist creating her self by finding her voice, but finding this voice in the act of writing. The written representation of this voice is a rewriting of the speaking voice that Hurston created for her protagonist in Their Eyes Were Watching God. Walker, in this brilliant act of grounding herself in the tradition by Signifyin(g) upon Hurston's rhetorical strategy, tropes Hurston's trope by "capping" (metalepsis) and inverts Hurston's effect of creating an invisible writing that speaks, by creating an invisible speaking voice that can only write!

The explication of the trope of the Talking Book enables us to witness the extent of intertextuality and presupposition at work in the first discrete period in Afro-American literary history. But it also reveals, rather surprisingly, that the curious tension between the black vernacular and the literate white text, between the spoken and the written word, between the oral and the printed forms of literary discourse, has been represented and thematized in black letters at least since slaves and ex-slaves met the challenge of the Elightenment to their humanity by literally writing themselves into being through carefully crafted representation in language of the black self.

Literacy, the very literacy of the printed book, stood as the ultimate parameter by which to measure the humanity of authors struggling to define an

African self in Western letters. It was to establish a collective black voice through the sublime example of an individual text, and thereby to register a black presence in letters, that most clearly motivated black writers, from the Augustan Age to the Harlem Renaissance. Voice and presence, silence and absence, then, have been the resonating terms of a four-part homology in our literary tradition for well over two hundred years.

The trope of the Talking Book became the first repeated and revised trope of the tradition, the first trope to be Signified upon. The paradox of representing, of containing somehow, the oral within the written, precisely when oral black culture was transforming itself into a written culture, proved to be of sufficient concern for five of the earliest black autobiographers to repeat the same figure of the Talking Book that fails to speak, appropriating the figure accordingly with embellished rhetorical differences. Whereas James Gronniosaw, John Marrant, and John Jea employ the figure as an element of plot, Ottobah Cugoano and Olaudah Equiano, with an impressive sense of their own relation to these earlier texts, bracket the tale in ways that direct attention to its status as a figure. The tension between the spoken and the written voice, for Cugoano and Equiano, is a matter they problematize as a rhetorical gesture, included in the text for its own sake, voicing, as it were, for the black literary tradition a problematic of speaking and writing. Jea's use of this curious figure has become decadent in the repetition, with the deus ex machina here represented literally as God in the text in this primal, or supernatural, scene of instruction.

This general question of the voice in the text is compounded in any literature, such as the Afro-American literary tradition, in which the oral and the written literary traditions comprise separate and distinct discursive universes which, on occasion, overlap, but often do not. Precisely because successive Western cultures have privileged written art over oral or musical forms, the writing of black people in Western languages has, at all points, remained political, implicitly or explicitly, regardless of its intent or its subject. Then, too, since blacks began to publish books they have been engaged in one form of direct political dialogue or another, consistently up to the present. The very proliferation of black written voices, and the concomitant political import of them, led fairly rapidly in our literary history to demands both for the coming of a "black Shakespeare or Dante," as one critic put it in 1925, and for an authentic black printed voice of deliverance, whose presence would, by definition, put an end to all claims of the black person's subhumanity. In the black tradition, writing became the visible sign, the commodity of exchange, the text and technology of reason.

II

The first text in which the trope of the Talking Book appears is James Albert Ukawsaw Gronniosaw's first edition of *A Narrative of the Most Remarkable Particulars in the Life of James Albert Ukawsaw Gronniosaw, An African Prince, As*

Related by Himself. Gronniosaw's narrative of enslavement and delivery had by 1811 been published in seven editions, including American editions in 1774 and 1810 and a Dublin edition in 1790. In 1840 another edition was published simultaneously in London, Manchester, and Glasgow. It is this edition to which I refer.[5]

Reading and writing were of signal import to the shaping of Gronniosaw's text, as presences and absences refigured throughout his twenty-four-page narrative. While the 1770 edition says in its subtitle that Gronniosaw "related" his tale "himself," the 1774 edition, reprinted at Newport, Rhode Island, claims that his narrative was "written by himself." When referred to in editions subsequent to 1840, "related" or "dictated" replace "written by himself." It is the narrator's concern with literacy that is of most interest to our argument here.

Gronniosaw's curious narrative has not enjoyed a wide reading among critics, or at least has not engendered many critical readings, unlike the works of his eighteenth-century colleagues John Marrant and Olaudah Equiano. What we know of him stems only from his slave narrative, generally thought to be the second example of the genre, after the 1760 *Narrative of the Uncommon Sufferings and Surprising Deliverance of Briton Hammon, A Negro Man.* While the two texts are narratives of bondage and deliverance, and while they both use the figure of the "return to my Native Land," Gronniosaw's more clearly inaugurates the genre of the slave narrative, from its "I was born" opening sentence to the use of literacy training as a repeated figure that functions to unify the structure of his tale.[6]

Who does Gronniosaw claim to be? He states that he was born "in the city of Bournou," which is the "chief city" of the Kingdom of Zaara. Gronniosaw's mother was the oldest daughter of "the reigning King of Zaara," and he was the youngest of six children. Gronniosaw stresses his intimate relationship with his mother, and to a lesser extent with his maternal grandfather, but rarely mentions his father, who we presume was not born to royalty but wed royalty. Gronniosaw's identification of himself in his narrative's title as "an African Prince" helps to explain the significance of this rhetorical gesture. Gronniosaw, by representing himself as a prince, implicitly tied his narrative to the literary tradition of the "Noble Savage" and to its subgenre, the "Noble Negro."[7]

Gronniosaw, in other words, represents himself as no mere common Negro slave, but as one nurtured, indulged, and trained in the manner of royalty everywhere. Faced with what must have seemed a deafening silence

---

[5] For a full list of this book's editions, see Janheinz Jahn and Claus Peter Dressler, *Biography of Creative African Writing* (Millwood, N.Y.: Kraus-Thomson Organization, 1975), p. 135. The 1770 edition was published by S. Hazard, with an introduction by W. Shirley. The 1770 edition consists of forty-nine pages, but the 1840 edition that I am using has twenty-nine pages.

[6] Briton Hammon, *Narrative . . .* (Boston: Green & Russell, 1760), p. 14; Gronniosaw, p. 17.

[7] See Wylie Sypher, *Guinea's Captive Kings: British Anti-Slavery Literature of the XVIIIth Century* (Chapel Hill: University of North Carolina Press, 1942), pp. 103–55.

in black literary antecedents, Gronniosaw turned to the fictions of the Noble Savage to ground his text within a tradition. He also turned to the tradition of the Christian confession, referring to the import of works of Bunyan and Baxter upon his quest to learn the identity of "some great Man of Power," as he proudly tells us. Gronniosaw, in other words, represents himself as an ebony admixture of Oronooko and the Lord's questing Pilgrim.[8]

One of the ironies of representation of the Noble Savage is that he or she is rendered noble through a series of contrasts with his or her black country-men. Oronooko bears aquiline features, has managed through some miracu-lous process to straighten his kinky hair, and speaks French fluently, among other languages. Oronooko, in other words, looks like a European, speaks like a European, and thinks and acts like a European—or, more properly, like a European king. Unlike the conventions of representing most other Noble Savage protagonists, then, Oronooko and his fellow black princes-in-bondage are made noble by a dissimilarity with their native countrymen. He is the exception, and not in any way the rule. Several Africans gained notori-ety in eighteenth-century England and France by claiming royal lineage, even attending performances of *Oronooko* on stage, weeping loudly as they were carried from the theater.

Gronniosaw seized upon this convention of Noble Savage literature, but with a critical difference. To ground himself in the tradition of Bunyan, Gron-niosaw figures his sense of difference as the only person in his grandfather's kingdom who understood, "from my infancy," that "some great Man of Power . . . resided above the sun, moon, and stars, the objects of our [African] worship." Gronniosaw's salient sign of difference is his inherent knowledge that there existed one God, rather than the many worshipped by all and sundry in the Kingdom of Zaara.[9]

The youngest prince's noble beliefs led, as we might suspect, to an es-trangement from his brothers and sisters and even, eventually, from his fa-ther, his grandfather, and his devoted mother. Gronniosaw represents his discourse with his mother as follows:

> My dear mother, said I, pray tell me who is the great Man of Power that makes the thunder. She said that there was no power but the sun, moon, and stars; that they made all our country. I then inquired how all our people came. She answered me, from one another; and so carried me to many generations back. Then, says I, who made the *first man*, and who made the first cow, and the first lion, and where does the fly come from, as no one can make him? My mother seemed in great trouble; for she was apprehensive that my senses were impaired, or that I was foolish. My father came in, and seeing her in grief, asked the cause; but when she related our conversation to him, he was exceedingly angry with me, and told me that he

---

[8]Gronniosaw, p. 11.
[9]Ibid., p. 3.

would punish me severely if ever I was so troublesome again; so
that I resolved never to say anthing more to her. But I grew unhappy
in myself.[10]

Gronniosaw tells us that "these wonderful impressions" were unique in all of
the Kingdom of Zaara, a situation "which affords me matter of admiration
and thankfulness." But his alienation increased to such an uncomfortable extent that when "a merchant from the Gold Coast" offered to take the young
man to a land where he "should see houses with wings to them walk upon
the water" and "see the white folks," he beseeched of his parents the freedom
to leave. The only family tie that he regretted severing was with his sister
Logwy, who was "quite white and fair, with fine light hair, though my father
and mother were black."

Gronniosaw's affection for his "white" sister is one of three curious figures that he uses to represent his inherent difference from other black people.
On one occasion, he describes "the devil" as "a black man" who "lives in
hell," while he by contrast seeks to be washed clean of the blackness of sin.
Moreover, the woman ordained by God for him to marry turns out to be
white, echoing his bond with his "white" sister. Gronniosaw's color symbolism privileges whiteness, as we shall see, at the expense of his blackness.[11]

The young prince, of course, was traded into slavery and sailed to "Bar-
badoes," where he was purchased by a Mr. Vanhorn of New York. His subsequent adventures, motivated by a desire to live among the "holy" inhabitants
of England ("because the authors of the books that had been given me were
Englishmen"), took him to "St. Domingo," "Martinco," "Havannah," and
then to London and Holland, only to return to marry and raise a family in
England. The remainder of his *Narrative* depicts the economic hardships he
suffers from racism and from evil people generally, and his fervent devotion
to the principles of Christian dogma.[12]

What concerns us about Gronniosaw's *Narrative* is his repeated references
to reading and writing. His second master in New York, a Mr. Freeland-
house, and his wife "put me to school," he writes, where he "learnt to read
pretty well." His master and mistress, wishing to help him overcome his spiritual dilemma about the nature of this one God ("the Author of all my comforts") whom he discovered at New York, gave him copies of "John Bunyan
on the Holy War" and "Baxter's 'Call to the Unconverted.'" As an example
of the "much persecution" that he received from "the sailors," Gronniosaw
writes, "I cannot help mentioning one circumstance that hurt me more than
all the rest."[13] Even this scene of cruelty turns upon the deprivation of a book:

I was reading a book that I was very fond of, and which I frequently
amused myself with, when this person snatched it out of my hand,

[10] Ibid., pp. 4–5.
[11] Ibid., pp. 3, 5, 9.
[12] Ibid., p. 14.
[13] Ibid., pp. 10, 11, 13.

and threw it into the sea. But, which was very remarkable, he was the first that was killed in our engagement. I do not pretend to say that this happened because he was not my friend; but I thought it was a very awful providence, to see how the enemies of the Lord were cut off.[14]

It is his ability to read and write and speak the Word of the Lord which motivates Gronniosaw's prilgrimage to England, as it did for Phillis Wheatley, to "find out Mr. [George] Whitefield." Since Gronniosaw informs his readers late in his text that he "could not read English," and since he describes his eloquent discourse on religion with "thirty-eight ministers, every Tuesday, for seven weeks together" in Holland, and since his two masters at New York bore Dutch names, it is probable that he was literate in Dutch.[15] By the age of "sixty," which W. Shirley in his "Preface" estimates to be his age at the time of publication, he spoke fluent English, in which, like Caliban, he learned first "to curse and swear surprisingly."[16]

If Gronniosaw, like Caliban, first learned the master's tongue to curse and swear, he quickly mended his ways. Indeed, almost from the beginning of his capture, Gronniosaw seems to have been determined to allow nothing to come between his desire to know the name of the Christian God and its fulfillment. Gronniosaw represents this desire within an extended passage in which he uses the trope of the Talking Book. He first describes his pleasure at disregarding the principal material sign of his African heritage, an extensive gold chain which must have been remarkably valuable judging by its description:

> When I left my dear mother, I had a large quantity of gold about me, as is the custom of our country. It was made into rings, and they were linked one into another, and formed into a *kind of chain*, and so put round my neck, and arms, and legs, and a large piece hanging at one ear, almost in the shape of a pear. I found all this troublesome, and was glad when my new master [a Dutch captain of a ship] took it from me. I was now washed, and clothed in the Dutch or English manner.[17]

Gronniosaw admits to being glad when his royal chain, a chain of gold that signified his cultural heritage, was removed from him, to be replaced, after a proverbial if secular baptism by water, with the "Dutch or English" clothing of a ship's crew. That which signified his African past, a veritable signifying chain, Gronniosaw eagerly abandons, just as he longs to abandon the language that his European captors "did not understand."

---

[14] Ibid., p. 15.
[15] Ibid., pp. 17, 21. George Whitefield, a central figure of the Protestant Great Awakening of the eighteenth century, appears frequently in black texts published before 1800. Gronniosaw, Wheatley, and Equiano, among others, refer to him or depict him as a character in their narratives.
[16] Ibid., pp. 8, 9, 19.
[17] Ibid., p. 8 (emphasis added).

Gronniosaw's signifying gold chain is an ironic prefigurement of Brother Tarp's link to *his* cultural heritage, a prison gang, in *Invisible Man*. When Tarp tells Ellison's narrator that his chain "had a whole lot of signifying wrapped up in it" and that "it might help you remember what we're really fighting against," we not only recall Gronniosaw's willingness to relinquish his signifying chain, but we also begin to understand why. Gronniosaw has absolutely no desire to "remember what we're really fighting against." As Tarp continues, such a signifying chain "signifies a heap more" than the opposition between "*yes* and *no*" that it connotes, on a first level of meaning, for the escaped prisoner. These significations are what Gronniosaw seeks to forget.[18]

If Gronniosaw willingly abandons his signifying chain of gold, then he is also willing to discard that chain of signifiers that comprised whatever African discourse he used to greet his Dutch enslavers. He represents this desire in the black tradition's first use of the trope of the Talking Book, which follows the unchaining ceremony in the same paragraph:

> [My master] used to read prayers in public to the ship's crew every Sabbath day; and when I first saw him read, I was never so surprised in my life, as when I saw the book talk to my master, for I thought it did, as I observed him to look upon it, and move his lips. I wished it would do so with me. As soon as my master had done reading, I followed him to the place where he put the book, being mightily delighted with it, and when nobody saw me, I opened it, and put my ear down close upon it, in great hopes that it would say something to me; but I was very sorry, and greatly disappointed, when I found that it would not speak. This thought immediately presented itself to me, that every body and every thing despised me because I was black.[19]

What can we say of this compelling anecdote? The book had no voice for Gronniosaw; it simply refused to speak to him, or with him. For Gronniosaw, the book—or, perhaps I should say, the very concept of "book"—constituted a silent primary text, a text, however, in which the black man found no echo of his own voice. The silent book did not reflect or acknowledge the black presence before it. The book's rather deafening silence renames the received tradition in European letters that the mask of blackness worn by Gronniosaw and his countrymen was a trope of absence.

Gronniosaw can speak to the text only if the text first speaks to him. The text does not, not even in the faintest whisper, a decibel level accounted for by the black man's charming gesture of placing his "ear down close upon it." Gronniosaw cannot address the text because the text will not address Gronniosaw. The text does not recognize his presence, and so refuses to share its secrets or decipher its coded message. Gronniosaw and the text are silent; the

---

[18] Ralph Ellison, *Invisible Man* (New York: Random House, 1982), p. 293. See the epigraph to Chapter 3.

[19] Gronniosaw, p. 8.

"dialogue" that he records having observed between the book and his master eludes him. To explain the difference between his master's relations to this text and the slave's relation to the same text, Gronniosaw seizes upon one explanation, and only one: the salient difference was his blackness, the very blackness of silence.

Gronniosaw explains the text's silence by resorting to an oxymoronic figure in which voice and presence, (black) face and absence are conflated. Perhaps a more accurate description of the figure is that Gronniosaw conflates an oral figure (voice) with a visual figure (his black face). In other words, Gronniosaw's explanation of the silence of the text allows for no other possibility but one; and it, he tells us, suggested itself on the spot: "This thought immediately presented itself to me, that every body and every thing despised me because I was black."

Gronniosaw's conflation of the senses, of the oral and the visual—the book refused to speak to me because my face was black—was a curiously arbitrary choice for figural substitution. After all, a more "natural" explanation might have been that the book refused to speak to him because he could not speak Dutch, especially if we remember that this scene occurs on the ship that transports the newly captured slave from the Gold Coast to Barados, the ship's destination. This more logical or natural explanation, however, did not apparently occur to the African. Rather, the curse of silence that the text yielded could only be accounted for by the curse of blackness that God had ostensibly visited upon the dusky sons of Ham. The text's voice, for Gronniosaw, presupposed a face; and a black face, in turn, presupposed the text's silence since blackness was a sign of absence, the remarkably ultimate absence of face *and* voice. Gronniosaw could achieve no recognition from this canonical text of Western letters—either the Bible or a prayer book—because the text could not see him or hear him. Texts can only address that which they can see. Cognition, or the act of knowing as awareness and judgment, presupposes the most fundamental form of recognition in Gronniosaw's text. It was his black face that interrupted this most basic, if apparently essential, mode of recognition, thereby precluding communication.

This desire for recognition of his self in the text of Western letters motivates Gronniosaw's creation of a text, in both a most literal and a most figurative manner. Literally, this trope of the (non-) Talking Book becomes the central scene of instruction against which this black African's entire autobiography must be read. The text refuses to speak to Gronniosaw, so some forty-five years later Gronniosaw writes a text that speaks his face into existence among the authors and texts of the Western tradition. As I have shown above, no less than five subsequent scenes of instruction (in a twenty-four-page text) are represented in the *Narrative* through tropes of reading and writing, including and curious scene in which Gronniosaw (with admirable control if obvious pleasure) explains to us that the white man who "snatched" his favorite book from his hands and "threw it into the sea" proved to be "the first that was killed in our [first military] engagement." Gronniosaw represents a sixty-year life in a brief text that depends for the shape of its rhetorical strategy on six tropes of reading and writing. Gronniosaw narrates a text, the rhetorical patterning of his autobiography forces us to conclude, to satisfy the desire created when his first master's seminal text, the prayer book, refuses to address him. Gronniosaw, in other words, narrates a text that simultaneously voices, contains, and reflects the peculiar contours of his (black) face. Given the fact that by 1770 only four black people are thought to have published books in Western languages (Juan Latino, Jacobus Capitein, Wilhelm Amo, and Briton Hammon), Gronniosaw's gesture was a major one, if its motivation as inscribed in his central trope is ironic.[20]

But is his a black face as voiced in his text? When I wrote above that the ship captain's text and its refusal to speak to the slave motivated the slave to seek recognition in other Western texts (as figured in his several scenes of literacy instruction), I argued that this motivation was both literal and metaphorical. By metaphorical, I mean that the face of the author at sixty is fundamentally altered from that (black) African face that the adolescent Gronniosaw first presented in his encounter with his first Western text. Gronniosaw is a careful narrator and is especially careful to state what he means. We recall that the trope of the Talking Book occurs in the same paragraph as his description of his eager abandonment of the gold chain that signifies his African heritage. Indeed, he presents his face before the captain's speaking text only after he has been "washed, and clothed in the Dutch or English manner." The text represents this procedure as if it were a rite of baptism, but a secular or cultural cleansing or inundation that obliterates (or is meant to obliterate) the traces of an African past that Gronniosaw is eager to relinquish, as emblematized in his gold chain: "I found all this troublesome, and was glad when my new master took it from me."

In the sentence immediately following this one, Gronniosaw tells us, "My master grew fond of me, and I loved him exceedingly," unlike the mutual disdain and mistrust that had obtained between him and his first master and his partner. We recall that it was the first master who, along with his partner, had persuaded the unhappy adolescent to leave the Kingdom of Bournou to seek the land of "the white folks," where "houses with wings to them walk upon the water." His second master "grew fond" of the "new" Gronniosaw, the Gronniosaw who had willingly submitted to being "washed, and clothed in the Dutch or English manner." His old master had related to an "old" Gronniosaw, an unregenerated (black) African Gronniosaw whose alienation from his traditional belief system and from most of the members of his family had, in retrospect, persuaded him to seek "the white folks" in the first place. Gronniosaw, in other words, was now capable of being regarded "fondly" by his second master because he was no longer the pure cultural African that he was when enticed to leave his village.[21]

---

[20] I say forty-five years later because W. Shirley, the author of the "Preface" to Gronniosaw's *Narrative*, deduces that he was "about fifteen years old" when "James Albert left his native country," and that at the time of publication, "He now appears to be turned of sixty."

[21] See Gronniosaw, pp. 8, 10, 11, 14, 15, 19, 21.

If he was, at this point in his *Narrative,* no longer the African that he once was, he was not yet the Anglo-African that he would become and that he so wished to be. "Clothes," and, we might add, a good washing, "do not make the man," the captain's text in its silent eloquence informs the new Gronniosaw. He was merely an African, sans signifying chain, cloaked in European garb. His dress may have been appropriately European, but his face retained the blackness of his willingly abandoned African brothers. Gronniosaw, as he placed his ear close upon the text, was a third term, neither fish nor fowl. No longer the unadulterated African, he was not yet the European that he would be. The text of Western letters could not accommodate his liminal status and therefore refused to speak to him, because Gronniosaw was not yet *this* while clearly he was no longer *that.* It was not enough, the text in its massive silence informed him, to abandon his signifying gold chain in order to be able to experience the sublime encounter with the European text's chain of signifiers. Much more washing and reclothing would be demanded of him to make the text speak.

Forty-five years later, Gronniosaw registered his presence and figured the contours of his face in the text of his autobiography. At sixty, he was fluent in two European languages, Dutch and English; he was a freed man; he was sufficiently masterful of the "Calvinist" interpretation of Christianity to discourse "before thirty-eight [Dutch] ministers every Tuesday, for seven weeks together, and they were all very well satisfied"; and he was the husband of an English wife and the father of both her child (by an English first marriage) and their "mulatto" children. The Christian text that had once refused to acknowledge him he had by sixty mastered sufficiently not only to "satisfy" and "persuade" others by his eloquence "that I was what I pretended to be," but also to interweave within the fabric of his autobiographical text the warp and the woof of Protestant Christianity and the strange passage from black man to white. The presence found in Gronniosaw's own text is generated by the voice, and face, of assimilation. What is absent, of course, is the African's black mask of humanity, a priceless heritage discarded as readily as was a priceless gold chain. Indeed, Gronniosaw's text is free of what soon became in the slave narratives the expected polemic against the ungodly enslavement of blacks. It is also free of descriptions of any other black characters, except for the "old black servant that lived in the [Vanhorn] family," and his reference to "a black man called the devil." It was the "old black servant" who taught Gronniosaw about the devil's identity and who, we presume (along with other servants), taught him to curse. No longer could Gronniosaw claim that "every body and every thing despised me because I was black."

In its trope of the Talking Book, Gronniosaw's important text in the history of black letters Signifies upon three texts of the Western tradition. I shall defer the revelation of the third text to my discussion of Ottobah Cugoano's revision of the trope of the Talking Book, for it is Cugoano's 1787 slave narrative that reveals the ultimate textual source of this figure for these black narrators. Here, however, let us briefly examine the other two.

The first text is that of Willem Bosman, entitled *A New and Accurate Description of the Coast of Guinea*, which I discussed briefly in Chapter 1. Bosman's account of his travels in Africa was published in Dutch in 1704 and in English at London in 1705. By 1737, four Dutch editions had been published, as well as translations in French, German, and English. In 1752, an Italian translation appeared. At least two more English editions have been published in this century.[22]

Bosman was the Dutch "Chief Factor" at the Fort of Elmira, on the coast of West Africa (popularly called Guinea at the time) in what is now Ghana. Bosman is thought to have been the "second most important Dutch official on the coast of Guinea from about 1688 to 1702." Bosman's "Letter X" is devoted to "the Religion of the *Negroes*" at "Guinea," another name for the "Gold Coast" that appears in Gronniosaw's *Narrative*. Indeed, it is probable that Gronniosaw's Dutch ship captain set sail from the Fort of Elmira. It is just as probable that Gronniosaw and Bosman were at Elmira within twenty-three years of each other, if W. Shirley's estimate of Gronniosaw's age in 1770 is correct. If he has underestimated Gronniosaw's age, then it is conceivable that the two men could have been at Elmira's at the same time. What is more probable is that Gronniosaw knew Bosman's Dutch text, especially "Letter X."[23]

Bosman's "Letter X," according to Robert D. Richardson, has had an extraordinary influence on the development of the concept of fetishism in modern anthropology, by way of Pierre Bayle's *Historical and Critical Dictionary* (1697, 1734–1738) and Charles de Brosses's *Du culte des dieux fétiches* (1760), the latter of which asserted the theory that fetishism, as practiced by blacks in West Africa, was the most fundamental form of religious worship. Auguste Comte's declaration that a "primary, fetishistic, or theological stage" was central to the development of a society depended on de Brosses's 1760 theory of fetishism. Bosman's observations, then, have proven to be central to the discourse on religion so fundamental to the development of anthropology in this century.[24]

Bosman's letter begins with an assertion that "all the Coast *Negroes* believe in one true God, to whom they attribute the Creation of the World." This claim, of course, at first appears to be at odds with Gronniosaw's claim that he alone of all the people in the Kingdom of Zaara held this belief. But

---

[22] Willem Bosman, *A New and Accurate Description of the Coast of Guinea* (1705; New York: Barnes and Noble, 1967). These facts, as well as the biographical description that follows, are taken from Robert D. Richardson's headnote to his reprinting of "Letter X" in *The Rise of Modern Mythology, 1680–1860*, ed. by Burton Feldman and Robert D. Richardson (Bloomington: Indiana University Press, 1972), pp. 41–42. All subsequent citations refer to this edition.

[23] Elmira Fort (or "Castle") was the site of Jacobus Capitein's departure from Africa and his subsequent return. Capitein was one of the African children chosen to be educated in Europe as an experiment to ascertain the black's "capacity" for "progress" and "elevation." Feldman and Richardson, *The Rise of Modern Mythology*, p. 42.

[24] Margaret T. Hodgen, *Early Anthropology in the Sixteenth and Seventeenth Centuries* (Philadelphia: University of Pennsylvania Press, 1964), p. 491; Feldman and Richardson, *The Rise of Modern Mythology*, p. 42.

Bosman quickly adds that for this belief in the one *God* the coastal blacks "are not obliged to themselves nor the Tradition of their Ancestors." Rather, the source of this notion is "their daily conversation with the *Europeans,* who from time to time have continually endeavoured to emplant this notion in them." The initial sense of difference that Gronniosaw strives so diligently to effect between himself and his African kinsmen (his monotheism as opposed to their polytheism) is prefigured in Bosman's second paragraph.[25]

What is even more relevant here is that Bosman's account of the Ashanti people's myth of creation turns upon an opposition between gold, on one hand, and "Reading and Writing," on the other. As Bosman recounts this fascinating myth:

> [A] great part of the *Negroes* believe that man was made by *Anansie,* that is, a great Spider: the rest attribute the Creation of Man to God, which they assert to have happened in the following manner: They tell us, that in the beginning God created Black as well as White Men; thereby not only hinting but endeavouring to prove that their race was as soon in the World as ours; and to bestow a yet greater Honour on themselves, they tell us that God having created these two sorts of Men, offered two sorts of Gifts, *viz,* Gold, and the Knowledge of Arts of Reading and Writing, giving the Blacks, the first Election, who chose Gold, and left the Knowledge of Letters to the White. God granted their Request, but being incensed at their Avarice, resolved that the Whites should for ever be their Masters, and they obliged to wait on them as their Slaves.[26]

Gold, spake God to the African, or the arts of Western letters—*choose!* The African, much to his regret, elected gold and was doomed by his avarice to be a slave. As a footnote to Bosman's first edition tells us, the African's avarice was an eternal curse, and his punishment was the doom of never mastering the Western arts and letters.

If the African at the Creation was foolish enough to select gold over reading and writing, Gronniosaw, African man but European-in-the-making, would not repeat that primal mistake. Gronniosaw eschewed the temptation of his gold chain and all that it signified, and sought a fluency in Western languages through which he could remake the features, and color, of his face.

If Gronniosaw echoes Bosman, probably self-consciously, then he also echoes Kant, probably not aware of Kant's 1764 German text. Writing in *Observations on the Feelings of the Beautiful and Sublime,* Kant prefigures Gronniosaw's equation of his black skin with the text's refusal to speak to him. Kant, drawing upon Hume's note on blacks in "Of National Characters," argues that "So fundamental is the difference between these two races of man, [that] it appears to be as great in regard to mental capacities as in color." Two

[25] Feldman and Richardson, *The Rise of Modern Mythology,* p. 44.
[26] Ibid., pp. 44–45.

pages later, responding to a black man's comment to Jean Baptiste Labat about male-female relations in Europe, Kant points to this supposedly natural relationship between blackness and intelligence: "And it might be that there was something in this which perhaps deserved to be considered; but in short, this fellow was quite black from head to foot, a clear proof that what he said was stupid."[27] Gronniosaw, after Kant, presupposes a natural relationship between blackness and being "despised" by "every body and every thing," including the Dutch ship captain's silent primary text. To undoing this relationship Gronniosaw devoted his next forty-five years, until he was fully able to structure the events of his life into a pattern that speaks quite eloquently, if ironically, to readers today.

III

The Narrative of the Lord's Wonderful Dealings with John Marrant, A Black is not properly a slave narrative, though it is usually described as such. Rather, it is an Indian captivity tale, a genre that was extraordinarily popular in the eighteenth century. Of the narratives that comprise this genre, John Marrant's was "one of the three most popular stories of Indian captivity, surpassed in number of editions only by those of Peter Williamson (1757) and Mary Jemison (1784)." Marrant's *Narrative*, which he "related" to the Rev. William Aldridge, was published in 1785 at London. Four successive editions followed in the same year, including the fourth and fifth editions "with additions." A sixth edition (1788) was followed by a 1790 Dublin edition, an 1802 London edition, three Halifax editions (1808, 1812, 1813), an 1815 Leeds edition, a Welsh translation (Caerdydd, 1818), and an 1820 edition published at Middletown, Connecticut. By 1835, Marrant's book had been printed no less than twenty times.[28]

Marrant's text was narrated to William Aldridge, who states in his "Preface" that he has "always preserved *Mr.* Marrant's ideas, tho' I could not his language," assuring Marrant's readers, however, that "no more alterations . . . have been made, than were thought necessary," whatever this might mean. Marrant's text states in its first sentence that he was "born June 15th, 1755, in New York," of free black parents. Marrant was never a slave, and he narrated his story with almost no references to black people

[27] Immanuel Kant, *Observations on the Feelings of the Beautiful and the Sublime*, trans. by John T. Goldthwait (Berkeley: University of California Press, 1960), pp. 111, 113.

[28] For a full discussion of the Indian captivity tales, and a selection of some of the most gripping of the genre, see Richard Van Der Beets, *Held Captive by Indians* (Knoxville: University of Tennessee Press, 1973). See Van Der Beets, p. 177; and Dorothy B. Porter, "Early American Negro Writings: A Bibliographical Study," *Papers of the Bibliographical Society of America* 39 (Fourth Quarter 1943): 247–51. Throughout I am citing a reprinting of the London edition of 1788. John Marrant, *A Narrative of the Lord's Wonderful Dealings with John Marrant, A Black (Now Gone to Preach the Gospel in Nova-Scotia) Born in New-York, North-America, Taken Down from his own Relation, arranged, corrected and published by the Rev. Mr. Aldridge* (London: Gilbert and Plummer, 1788), reprinted in Van Der Beets, *Held Captive by Indians*, pp. 178–201.

outside of his family. Marrant experienced a profound religious conversion, which soon alienated him from his two sisters and one brother, and eventually even from his mother, just as Gronniosaw's religious stirrings alienated him from his African family. Like Gronniosaw, Marrant was heavily influenced by the Rev. George Whitefield, cofounder with John Wesley of Methodism. Alienated from his family, Marrant "went over the fence, about half a mile from our house [in Charleston, South Carolina], which divided the inhabited and cultivated parts of the country from the wilderness." It is in this "wilderness" (which he calls "the desart") that the recently converted Christian is tried sorely in his capture by Cherokee Indians.[29]

Marrant's text is remarkable in its depiction of "the Lord's wonderful Dealings" with his convert, including Marrant's "singular deliverance" from "a violent storm," during which he was "washed overboard" three times, only to be "tossed upon deck again" each time: "he who heard Jonah's prayer, did not shut out mine." The sales of Marrant's *Narrative* were no doubt influenced by both his Christian piety and his remarkable imagination for scenes of deliverance. But it is his reworking of Gronniosaw's trope of the Talking Book which is of interest to us here.

Marrant, like Gronniosaw, was fifteen when captured. Wandering through the wilderness, Marrant encountered an Indian "fortification," protected by strategically placed "guards." The Cherokee guard politely informed him that he must be put to death for venturing onto Cherokee land. A resident judge next sentenced Marrant to death, an excruciating execution by fire. About to be executed, Marrant began to pray, politely if enthusiastically reminding the Lord that he had delivered "the three children in the fiery furnace" and "Daniel in the lion's den," and asking if perhaps his servant John might be delivered in such fashion. At "about the middle of my prayer," Marrant states, "the Lord impressed a strong desire upon my mind to turn into their language, and pray in their tongue." It is this divinely inspired fluency in Cherokee which, Marrant continues, "wonderfully affected the people" gathered around to watch him slowly roast. The executioner, "savingly converted to God," interrupted the proceedings to take the black captive off for an audience with the king.[30]

In an audience before the king, however, Marrant's gift of tongues backfired, and he was sentenced to die once again for being a "witch." Marrant's account of these events contains his revision, or curious inversion, of the trope of the Talking Book:

> At this instant the king's eldest daughter came into the chamber, a person about 19 years of age, and stood at my right-hand. I had a Bible in my hand, which she took out of it, and having opened it, she kissed it, and seemed much delighted with it. When she had put it

[29] Van Der Beets, p. 185.
[30] Ibid., p. 190.

into my hand again, the king asked me what it was? and I told him, the name of my God was recorded there; and, after several questions, he bid me read it, which I did, particularly the 53d chapter of Isaiah, in the most solemn manner I was able; and also the 26 chapter of Matthew's Gospel; and when I pronounced the name of Jesus, the particular effect it had upon me was observed by the king. When I had finished reading, he asked me why I read those names with so much reverence? I told him, because the Being to whom those names belonged made heaven and earth, and I and he; this he denied. I then pointed to the sun, and asked him who made the sun, and moon, and stars, and preserved them in their regular order? He said there was a man in their town that did it. I laboured as much as I could to convince him to the contrary. His daughter took the book out of my hand a second time; she opened it, and kissed it again; her father bid her give it to me, which she did; but said, with much sorrow, the book would not speak to her. The executioner then fell upon his knees, and begged the king to let me go to prayer, which being granted, we all went upon our knees, and now the Lord displayed his glorious power. In the midst of the prayer some of them cried out, particularly the king's daughter, and the man who ordered me to be executed, and several others seemed under deep conviction of sin: This made the king very angry; he called me a witch, and commanded me to be thrust into the prison, and to be executed the next morning. This was enough to make me think, as old Jacob once did, "All these things are against me"; for I was dragged away, and thrust into the dungeon with much indignation; but God, who never forsakes his people, was with me.[31]

Marrant is saved from this second sentence of execution, he informs us a paragraph later, by curing the king's ill daughter through prayer. After he prayed three times, "the Lord appeared most lovely and glorious; the king himself was awakened, and [I] set at Liberty."[32]

What is so striking about Marrant's Signifyin[g] revision of Gronniosaw's trope is that he inverts Gronniosaw's opposition of blackness and the silence of the text. Rather, in this Kingdom of the Cherokee, it is only the black man who can make the text speak. The king's daughter, representing the Cherokee people, says "with much sorrow" that "the book would not speak to her." Marrant's capacity to make the text speak leads directly to his second condemnation for being a witch. Only by making the Lord himself appear, "most lovely and glorious," does Marrant escape the sentence of death. If in Gronniosaw's trope voice presupposes a white or assimilated face, in Marrant's text voice presupposes both a black face and an even more

[31] Ibid., pp. 191–92.
[32] Ibid., p. 193.

luminous presence, the presence of God himself. This scene, we shall see, is refigured in John Jea's revision of the trope of the Talking Book.

If Marrant Signifies upon Gronniosaw by substituting the oppositions of black/Cherokee and Christian/non-Christian for black illiterate African/white literate European, what has become of Gronniosaw's "signifying chain"? Marrant does not disappoint us; the chain is inverted as well, although it is still made of gold. And, like Gronniosaw, Marrant by contiguity in his narration associates the golden chain with his own mastery of language, the Cherokee language. Marrant's figure of the golden chain does not appear until the penultimate sentence in the two-and-one-half-page paragraph in which the Talking Book episode occurs. In this sentence, Marrant informs us that it is the Cherokee king who owns the gold "chain and bracelets," and as we might suspect, it is John Marrant, literate[33] black man from another world, who has the power over the king to command him to put them on, or take them off, "like a child": "The King would take off his golden garments, his chain and bracelets, like a child, if I objected to them and lay them aside."[34] It is Marrant, master of the text and its presences, of its voice and letters, who, for reasons never stated in his text, can force the king to "lay" his golden chain "aside," like Gronniosaw, who eagerly lays his golden chain aside in the very first attempt to shed his African identity. But Marrant is not only the king's master because of his mastery of the English text of the Bible; he soon becomes master of the King's language as well. In the paragraph's final sentence, following immediately upon the unchaining episode, Marrant tells us, "Here I learnt to speak their tongue in the highest stile." Marrant's fluency in Cherokee, inspired by God in the first instance to save him from an initial death decree, now enables him to live with the Cherokee in "perfect liberty." If Gronniosaw's golden chains signified his royal heritage, now Marrant's power of articulation leads to his fullest transformation; from "poor condemned prisoner," the "new" Marrant is "treated like a prince."[35] Marrant, in other words, has turned Gronniosaw's trope of the Talking Book inside out, reversing Gronniosaw's figures of the text that refuses to speak, the golden chain, and the movement from prince to commoner, detail by detail. Marrant wrestles from Gronniosaw a space for his own representation of a black pious life, with a Signifyin(g) revision of his only truly antecedent text and of its central trope.

For all of his apparent piety, then, Marrant seems to have been concerned to use the text of his sole predecessor in the Anglo-African tradition as a model to be revised. Marrant's revision inaugurates the black tradition of English literature, not because he was its first author but because he was the tradition's first revisionist. My idea of tradition, in part, turns upon this

---

[33] Marrant tells us in the third sentence of the *Narrative's* first paragraph that he "went to school" in St. Augustine, where he learned "to read and spell." Ibid., p. 180.

[34] Ibid., p. 193.

[35] Ibid.

definition of texts read by an author and then Signified upon in some formal way, as an implicit commentary on grounding and on satisfactory models of representation—in this instance, a mode of representation of the black pious pilgrim who descends into a chaotic wilderness of sin, is captured, suffers through several rather unbelievable trials of faith, then emerges whole and cleansed and devout.

But of what sort is Marrant's mode of Signifyin(g) upon Gronniosaw's *Narrative*? Marrant's revision is an excellent example of "capping," which is the black vernacular equivalent of metalepsis. Marrant is capping upon Gronniosaw's trope because his revision seeks to reverse the received trope by displacement and substitution. All of the key terms of Gronniosaw's trope are present in Marrant's revision, but the "original" pattern has been re-arranged significantly. (I put quotes around "original" because, as we shall see below, Gronniosaw also revised the trope from another text.) Gone is Gronniosaw's ironic claim of difference from all other black people. Although Marrant, as I stated earlier, is not concerned in this text at least to speak to the perilous condition of black bondsmen or even the marginally free, he does claim that his belief in the true God is unlike the beliefs of his kinsmen. Marrant implies that the degree of his faith alienates him from the religious beliefs of his family (and vice versa), so he takes leave for the wilderness, encountering trials and tribulations akin to those of Bunyan's Pilgrim. Nevertheless, there is a major difference between what Bosman called "fetishism" and Christianity (Gronniosaw's difference) and the *kinds* of Christianity (Marrant's difference).

Marrant, moreover, also rejects what we might think of as Gronniosaw's claim of the whiteness of the text. Instead of retaining Gronniosaw's op-positions between black/white, literate/illiterate, presence/absence, speak-ing/silence, European/African, and naked/clothed, Marrant substitutes Christian/non-Christian, Black/Cherokee, English language/Cherokee lan-guage, and so on. Gone is Gronniosaw's problematic desire to redress the ab-sence of the voice in the text, which he somehow attributes to his physical and, as it were, metaphysical blackness, and to which he responds by narrat-ing a text of a life that charts his pilgrimage to the shrines of European cul-ture. Instead, Marrant restructures the trope such that it is the Cherokee who assume the perilous burdens of negation. Marrant's difference, then, emerges in contrast with other people of color, or a people of another color, rather then primarily from a claimed difference from other black people, despite the fact that the families of both narrators believe them to be "crazy" and as "un-stable as water," as Marrant admits.[36]

Whereas Gronniosaw attributes the burden of his rejection by the text to his blackness, Marrant creates a narrative in which the black controls the voice in the text, a literally bilingual voice that speaks in fluent English and, with God's initial help and the supplement of the Indians, in fluent Chero-kee. Whereas Gronniosaw depicts the motivation of his plot and of its

[36] Ibid., pp. 181, 185.

writing as the desire to make the text respond to his presence and address him, Marrant in marked contrast displaces that desire upon the Cherokee, a desire that he, and the good Lord, manipulate miraculously. It is Marrant who is the text's ventriloquist; it is Marrant who emerges fully in control.

It is also Marrant who controls the Cherokee king's signifying chain, which Marrant can force him to remove at will, "like a child." Marrant controls the golden chain because he controls the text's chain of signifiers in a manner that Gronniosaw, the African prince, only wishes to do. Marrant's trope reverses Gronniosaw's trope of absence by transforming it into a trope of his presence and divine presence, at the expense, of course, of the unfortunate Cherokee. If we can say that Gronniosaw puts his blackness under erasure, then Marrant puts the Cherokee King under erasure at will, by commanding him to put on or remove the king's ultimate sign of authority, his golden ornaments. Marrant's revision of Gronniosaw is one of the black tradition's earliest examples of Signifyin(g) as capping.

IV

John Stuart was a black man who wrote letters. He was concerned to influence certain powerful members of English society about "the evil and wicked traffic of the slavery and commerce of the human species," as part of the title of his book would read. Accordingly, he wrote twice to the Prince of Wales and apparently once to Edmund Burke, King George III, and Granville Sharp. The point of this correspondence was to convince these gentlemen that human bondage was a form of oppression that militated against "the natural liberties of Men," as he wrote to King George. Such "abandoned wickedness" struck at the moral fabric of a kingdom dedicated to the rights of man. To outline his argument more forcefully, he wrote, he enclosed with three of his letters a copy of the 148-page book that he had published in 1787. Lest they be confused about its author's relation to the signature on each of the letters, Stuart added that John Stuart was in fact "He whose African Name is the title of the book."[37]

John Stuart was the English name that Quobna Ottobah Cugoano apparently adopted in London. But in 1787 he published his major argument against human slavery under a version of his Ghanaian name, Ottobah Cugoano.[38] Ottobah Cugoano was born about 1757, near Ajumako in what is now Ghana. Cugoano was a member of the "Fantee" (Fanti) people. If not born to royalty like Gronniosaw, his family did enjoy an intimate association

---

[37] These letters are reprinted in Paul Edward's edition of *Thoughts and Sentiments on the Evil and Wicked Traffic of the Slavery and Commerce of the Human Species, Humbly Submitted to the Inhabitants of Great-Britain, by Ottobah Cugoano, a Native of Africa* (1787; London: Dawsons of Pall Mall, 1969), pp. xix–xxiii. This prefatory matter is hereafter referred to as Edwards, while Cugoano's text is referred to as Cugoano.

[38] Cugoano used his full name in his edited and revised 1791 edition. See Edwards, pp. xi–xii.

with royalty; his father "was a companion to the chief," and Cugoano was a companion of the chief's nephew. In 1770, at about the age of thirteen, Cugoano was captured, sold into slavery, and taken to Grenada.[39]

At Grenada, the young slave was purchased by "a gentleman coming to England," who "took me for his servant." Thus was he "delivered from Grenada, and that horrid brutal slavery" in 1772. Cugoano became a freedman, and at least by 1786 emerged as a leader of the "black poor" of London. Cugoano was also a close friend of Olaudah Equiano, whom I shall discuss below, and of Scipione Piattoli, a member of the Polish patriotic movement led by King Stanislaw II. Cugoano, then, was a major black public figure in England at least between 1786 and 1791.[40]

It was at the height of his authority that he published his *Thoughts and Sentiments* in 1787. Cugoano's book is an impassioned and extended argument for the abolition of slavery, not primarily an autobiography. While the genre of the slave narrative is characterized by both polemics and autobiography ("my bondage and my freedom," as Frederick Douglass put it in his 1855 narrative), Cugoano leans heavily toward the side of the polemic. Cugoano, in fact, wrestles in his text with several other eighteenth-century authors of works about slavery, some named and some unnamed, including James Tobin's *Cursory Remarks upon the Reverend Mr. Ramsay's Essay* (London, 1785), James Ramsay's *Essay on the Treatment and Conversion of the African Slaves in the British Sugar Colonies* (London, 1784), Anthony Benezet's *Some Historical Account of Guinea* (London, 1771), Patrick Gordon's *The Geography of England* (London, 1744) and *Geography Anatomized* (London, 1693), Gordon Turnbull's *An Apology for Slavery* (London, 1786), and David Hume's 1754 version of his well-known essay "Of National Characters," among other texts. Cugoano's *Thoughts and Sentiments*, in other words, is constructed as a response to the eighteenth century's major treatises on African enslavement.

Cugoano, early in his text, accounts for his literacy and for his familiarity with the works of Europeans on slavery:

> After coming to England, and seeing others write and read, I had a strong desire to learn, and getting what assistance I could, I applied myself to learn reading and writing, which soon became my recreation, pleasure, and delight; and when my master perceived that I could write some, he sent me to a proper school for that purpose to learn. Since, I have endeavoured to improve my mind in reading, and have sought to get all the intelligence I could, in my situation in life, towards the state of my brethren and countrymen in complexion, and of the miserable situation of those who are barbarously sold into captivity, and unlawfully held in slavery.[41]

[39] Cugoano, p. 6. All biographical details come from Edwards's "Introduction" to the 1969 edition of Cugoano's *Thoughts and Sentiments* and from Cugoano's biographical note printed on p. iv of his text. See Cugoano, p. 12, and Edwards, p. iv.

[40] Edwards, pp. v–vii.

[41] Cugoano, pp. 12–13.

Cugoano describes for his readers how he learned to read and write and also how he knows so very much about the literature of slavery. The representation of the scene of instruction of the black author's literacy became, after Cugoano, a necessary principle of structure of virtually all of the slave narratives published between 1789 and 1865. Cugoano's, however, is the first instance of associating the mastery of letters with freedom. Indeed, Cugoano, like Job Ben Solomon in 1731, suggests that he virtually "wrote" his way from bondage to freedom.[42] Cugoano also acknowledges that despite the brutality of his enslavement, it did enable him to learn about "principles" and the Christian religion "unknown to the people of my native country":

> [One] great duty I owe to Almighty God . . . that, although I have been brought away from my native country, . . . I have both obtained liberty; and acquired the great advantages of some little learning, in being able to read and write, and, what is still infinitely of greater advantage, I trust, to know something of *Him who is that God whose providence rules over all.*[43]

"In this respect," Cugoano continues, "I am highly indebted to many of the good people of England for learning and principles unknown to the people of my native country." Despite this appreciation, however, Cugoano is not the pious pilgrim that Marrant is; rather, he is determined to show that slavery is both a defilement of sacred writ and contrary to the secular notion of liberty to which all Englishmen are heir.

If Cugoano claims to have read the major texts on slavery, he also implies that he has read the works of Gronniosaw and Marrant. Cugoano effectively makes his two predecessors in the Anglo-African tradition characters in his text, just as both Gronniosaw and Marrant do with the Rev. Mr. Whitefield. Cugoano cites Gronniosaw and Marrant as examples of blacks who managed to "get their liberty" and who were able "eventually [to] arrive at some knowledge of the Christian religion, and the great advantages to it." Of Gronniosaw, Cugoano writes:

> Such was the case of Ukawsaw Gronniosaw, an African prince, who lived in England. He was a long time in a state of great poverty and distress, and must have died at one time for want, if a good and charitable attorney had not supported him. He was long after in a very poor state, but he would not have given his faith in the Christian religion, in exchange for all the kingdoms of Africa, if they could have been given to him, in place of his poverty, for it.[44]

[42] On the relationship between freedom and literacy, see Robert Burns Stepto, *From Behind the Veil: A Study of Afro-American Narrative* (Urbana: University of Illinois Press, 1979), pp. 3–32. On Job Ben Solomon, see Douglass Grant, *The Fortunate Slave: An Illustration of African Slavery in the Early Eighteenth Century* (London: Oxford University Press, 1968).
[43] Cugoano, p. 13.
[44] Ibid., p. 22.

Cugoano knew his Gronniosaw, as his final sentence ironically suggests, for Gronniosaw, seeking to become a "man of parts and learning," wanted no parts of Africa, not even his gold chain.

And what of John Marrant? Cugoano compares him favorably with Gronniosaw:

> And such was A. Morrant [sic] in America. When a Boy, he could stroll away into a desart, and prefer the society of wild beasts to the absurd Christianity of his mother's house. He was conducted to the king of the Cherokees, who, in a miraculous manner, was induced by him to embrace the Christian faith. This Morrant was in the British service last war, and his royal convert, the king of the Cherokee Indians, accompanied General Clinton at the siege of Charles Town.[45]

Cugoano recapitulates the import of Marrant's text by focusing on the miracle of the Talking Book and of God emerging from the text. He does so as a delayed preface to his own revision of the trope of the Talking Book.

Fifty-odd pages after introducing Gronniosaw and Marrant, Cugoano represents his own revision of the trope of the text that speaks. He does so in a most enterprising manner, as the climax of a narrative of "the base perfidy and bloody treachery of the Spaniards" in their treatment of the Native Americans. His revision is contained in a tale embedded within Cugoano's larger narrative of actions "so very disgraceful to human nature," occasioned by the "barbarous inhuman Europeans" as they conquered and enslaved the peoples of Africa, Mexico, and Peru. As we shall see, Marrant's supplement of the Cherokee in his revision presents Cugoano the occasion to relate a longer tale.[46]

Cugoano is recounting his version of "the base treacherous bastard Pizarra" (Pizarro), who stood "at the head of the Spanish banditti of miscreant depredators," and his brutal slaughter of "the Peruvian empire" and of "the noble Atahualpa, the great Inca or Lord of that empire." At this point in the story, "Pizarra" has deceived Atahualpa into believing that his was "an embassy of peace from a great monarch." Atahualpa, not trusting the Spaniards but afraid of their overwhelming military superiority, and "thinking to appease them by complying with their request, relied on Pizarra's feigned pretensions of friendship." Cugoano narrates the subsequent events:

> As [Atahualpa] approached near the Spanish quarters the arch fanatic Father Vincente Valverde, chaplain to the expedition, advanced with a crucifix in one hand and a breviary in the other, and began with a long discourse, pretending to explain some of the general doctrines of Christianity . . . ; and that the then Pope, Alexander, by donation, had invested their master as the sole

[45] Ibid., p. 23.
[46] Ibid., pp. 77, 78.

Monarch of all the New World ... [Atahualpa] observed [in re-
sponse] that he was Lord of the dominions over which he reigned by
hereditary succession; and, said, that he could not conceive how a
foreign priest should pretend to dispose of territories which did not
belong to him, and that if such a preposterous grant had been made,
he, who was the rightful possessor, refused to confirm it; that he had
no inclination to renounce the religious institutions established by
his ancestors; nor would he forsake the service of the Sun, the immortal divinity whom he and his people revered, in order to worship the God of the Spaniards, who was subject to death; and that
with respect to other matters, he had never heard of them before,
and did not then understand their meaning. And he desired to know
where Valverde had learned things so extraordinary. In this book,
replied the fanatic Monk, reaching out his breviary. The Inca opened
it eagerly, and turning over the leaves, lifted it to his ear: This, says
he, is silent; it tells me nothing; and threw it with disdain to the
ground. The enraged father of ruffians, turning toward his countrymen, the assassinators, cried out, to arms, Christians, to arms; the
word of God is insulted; avenge this profanation on these impious
dogs.[47]

The Spaniards, we know, slaughtered the Incas and captured Atahualpa, de-
ceiving him a second time before murdering him brutally.

If Cugoano's narrative of Atahualpa and the Talking Book retains Marrant's substitution of the Indian supplicant before the text, he too inverts its
meaning by having the noble Indian disdainfully throw the silent book to the
ground. A text which contained no voice had no significance for Atahualpa;
its silent letters were dead. Unlike Marrant's Cherokee king, the king of the
Incas was not awed by Friar Vincente's silent text, even if it refused to address him just as it had done the princess of the Cherokee. Our sympathies
remain with Atahualpa in Cugoano's narration of the tale, just as Cugoano
intended. Indeed, the magical speaking text has been perverted by the Spanish friar, in a prefiguring of Father John's climactic pronouncement rendered
near the end of Jean Toomer's *Cane* (1923):

O th sin th white folks 'mitted
when they made th Bible lie.[48]

The Spaniards used the breviary as the justification of their "rights" to someone else's lands. Cugoano has revised Marrant's trope by transforming it into
an allegory of evil—the evils of colonization, to be sure, but also the evils of
the abuses of biblical exegesis.

Just as Marrant had revised Gronniosaw's scene of instruction by rearranging its salient details into an allegory of the Lord's "Wonderful Deal-

[47] Ibid., pp. 78–81.
[48] Jean Toomer, *Cane* (New York: Harper & Row, 1969), p. 237.

ings," Cugoano has revised Marrant by using the trope as the climax of a tale-within-a-tale, but at the European's expense. Gronniosaw's trope reveals him to be a would-be European, a white-man-in-the-making who not unimportantly encounters his text during the dread Middle Passage, a most appropriate locale because he too is in "middle passage" from the African prince he once was to the Christian pilgrim he soon would be. Marrant, on the other hand, amounts to a substituted white man in the presence of the Cherokee, because it is he, and only he, who controls the voices and presences of the white man's holy text. Cugoano, unlike his two black predecessors in the tradition, writes primarily to indict a perverted economic and moral order, rather than either to exemplify the living wonders of Protestant Christianity or to fashion in public an articulated life. Rather, he writes to chart a freed slave's remarkably extensive knowledge of the sheer horrors attendant upon human slavery. Ironically, he succeeds at turning the trope of the Talking Book back upon itself, thereby underscoring the nobility of the Inca, and simultaneously showing the perversity of a "civilization" which justifies even murder and pillage through the most sacred of written words. Cugoano, like Caliban, masters the master's tongue only to curse him more satisfactorily. The sort of Signifyin(g) in which Cugoano is engaged partakes of metaphor (or its extended form, allegory) tinged throughout with irony. In the Afro-American tradition, Cugoano's revision is an instance of extended "Naming," which has the same import as "calling out of one's name."

If Cugoano retains Marrant's Indians, what has happened to the golden chain? There is no chain, but Cugoano does not disappoint us. The figure of gold comes to bear in his account of the Spaniards' second deceit of Atahualpa. After they captured the king, the Spaniards imprisoned him. Expecting an execution, Atahualpa attempted to escape death by offering to his captors to fill his prison "apartment," which Cugoano tells us measured twenty-two feet by sixteen feet, with "vessels of gold as high as he could reach." Eagerly, the Spaniards accepted this proposal, and dutifully the Incas filled the apartment to the appointed mark. Cugoano narrates the tales's conclusion:

> The gold was accordingly collected from various parts with the greatest expedition by the Inca's obedient and loving subjects, who thought nothing too much for his ransom and life; but, after all, poor Atahualpa was cruelly murdered, and his body burnt by a military inquisition, and his extensive and rich dominions devoted to destruction and ruin by these merciless depredators.[49]

The power of the speaking text that gives Marrant the power to "unchain" the king of the Cherokee is not represented in Cugoano's revision because the Spaniards' breviary has no power over the Inca king. Only the guns of the Spaniards have power, a power of negation which is the objective counterpart of the Spaniards' deceitful words. Only their word is necessary to extract from

[49]Cugoano, p. 81.

Atahualpa all of the gold needed to fill his prison apartment. The Spaniards exchange their sacred oath, sworn no doubt on their sacred breviary, for the Inca's gold. Cugoano makes of the gold chain of Gronniosaw and Marrant the perverted booty gained by the immoral use of European words.

Cugoano's use of the tale-within-a-tale serves to emphasize that the Talking Book is a trope, rather than a quaint experience encountered by the narrator on his road from slavery to salvation. Cugoano, in other words, calls attention to the figurative nature of the trope itself instead of drawing upon it as an element in his primary narrative line. This bracketing of the trope of the Talking Book calls attention to the author's rhetorical strategies, to his control over his materials. Cugoano, we recall, is the only writer of the three; both Gronniosaw and Marrant dictated their tales to the people who edited them. Cugoano's bracketed tale of Atahualpa reflects a borrowing of the story from another text, which turns out not to be the text of either Gronniosaw or Marrant. Rather, Cugoano, who gives no citation for the original, points to the "original" source of the trope, which Gronniosaw and Marrant could also possibly have been revising.

Cugoano is revising the story of Atahualpa as he probably encountered it in an English translation of the event, or nonevent, as we shall see. His careful use of detail would suggest that he has followed closely another text. I am not certain which text this might be, but the most well-known account presents the trope only to claim that it never "really" happened, that it is a fiction, a myth propagated by "historians." Not only does the book not speak, but the depiction of these uncited histories is of a nonevent, something created for narrative purposes rather than an element of history necessarily incorporated into a full reconstruction of whatever occurred just before the Spaniards slaughtered the Incas.

It turns out that the story of Atahualpa and Friar Vincente de Valverde was published by Gracilasso de la Vega, the Inca, in 1617. Gracilasso published the story in his *Historia General del Perú*, which is Part II of his *Commentarios reales del Perú*, a work translated by Sir Paul Rycaut into English and published in 1688 as *The Royal Commentaries of Peru*.[50] According to Gracilasso's "true account," the exchange of speeches between the Spaniards and Atahualpa was problematical from the start because of difficulties of translation. Felipillo, the interpreter, apparently spoke a dialect different from that spoken by Atahualpa. Frustrated by these difficulties, they finally resort to *quipus* (a mode of writing using knots as signs) instead of word exchanges, but to no avail. As we might expect, one of the most problematical areas of mutual understanding apparently was the matter of the authority of the texts the Spaniards cited to justify their desire to colonize the Incas. Gracilasso's refutation of the Talking Book incident follows:

[50] Gracilasso de la Vega, *The Royal Commentaries of Peru*, Part II, *General History of Peru*, trans. by Sir Paul Rycaut (London: Miles Flesher, 1688), pp. 456–57. The Spanish edition is entitled El Ynca Gracilasso de la Vega, *Historia General del Perú* (Córdoba, 1617), p. 20. José Piedra located this source, and I am especially indebted to him for sharing it with me.

And here it is to be noted, that it is not true that some Historians report of Atahualpa, that he should say, "You believe that Christ is
God and that he died: I adore the Sun and the Moon, which are immortal: And who taught you, that your God created the Heaven and
the Earth?" to which Valverde made answer, "This book hath taught
it to us:" Then the King took it in his hand, and opening the Leaves,
laid it to his Ear; and not hearing it speak to him, he threw it upon
the ground. Upon which, they say, that the Friar starting up, ran
to his Companions, crying out, that the Gospel was despised and
trampled under foot; Justice and Revenge upon those who contemn
our Law and refuse our Friendship.[51]

Regardless of what Atahualpa might have said, Rycaut's 1688 translation
could have been Cugoano's source, and Marrant's, since they both read English, unlike Gronniosaw. Cugoano, however, was familiar with Marrant's
revision and seems to have decided to use the "original" version as a way of
stepping around Marrant. What seems clear from this is that, as early in the
Anglo-African tradition as 1787, black texts were already "mulatto" texts,
with complex double, or two-toned, literary heritages. The split between influence of form and influence of content, which I have suggested is the import of Ralph Ellison's statements about his own literary ancestry, would
seem to have obtained as early as 1787.

V

Two years later, in 1789, Cugoano's friend Olaudah Equiano published his
slave narrative, *The Interesting Narrative of the Life of Olaudah Equiano*.[52]
Equiano's *Narrative* was so richly structured that it became the prototype of
the nineteenth-century slave narrative, best exemplified in the works of Frederick Douglas, William Wells Brown, and Harriet Jacobs. It was Equiano
whose text served to create a model that other ex-slaves would imitate. From
his subtitle, "Written by Himself" and a signed engraving of the black author
holding an open text (the Bible) in his lap, to more subtle rhetorical strategies
such as the overlapping of the slave's arduous journey to freedom and his simultaneous journey from orality to literacy, Equiano's strategies of self-
presentation and rhetorical representation heavily informed, if not determined, the shape of black narrative before 1865.

Equiano's two-volume work was exceptionally popular. Eight editions
were printed in Great Britain during the author's lifetime, and a first American edition appeared in New York in 1791. By 1837, another eight editions

---

[51] Gracilasso, *General History of Peru*, pp. 456–57.

[52] Olaudah Equiano, *The Interesting Narrative of the Life of Olaudah Equiano, or Gustavus
Vassa, the African, Written by Himself*, 2 vols. (London: the author, 1789). I shall be using Paul
Edwards's 1969 edition of Equiano's first edition, published at London by Dawsons and
hereafter referred to as Equiano.

had appeared, including an abridgment in 1829. Three of these editions were published together with Phillis Wheatley's *Poems*. Dutch and German translations were published in 1790 and 1791.[53]

Equiano told a good story, and he even gives a believable account of cultural life among the Igbo peoples of what is now Nigeria. The movement of his plot, then, is from African freedom, through European enslavement, to Anglican freedom. Both his remarkable command of narrative devices and his detailed accounts of his stirring adventures no doubt combined to create a readership broader than that enjoyed by any black writer before 1789. When we recall that his adventures include service in the Seven Years War with General Wolfe in Canada and Admiral Boscawen in the Mediterranean, voyages to the Arctic with the 1772–73 Phipps expedition, six months among the Miskito Indians in Central America, and "a grand tour of the Mediterranean as personal servant to an English gentleman," it is clear that this ex-slave was one of the most well-traveled people in the world when he decided to write a story of his life.[54]

Like his friend Cugoano, Equiano was extraordinarily well read, and, like Cugoano, he borrowed freely from other texts, including Constantine Phipp's *A Journal of a Voyage Towards the North Pole* (London, 1774), Anthony Benezet's *Some Historical Account of Guinea* (London, 1771), and Thomas Clarkson's *An Essay on the Slavery and Commerce of the Human Species* (London, 1785). He also paraphrased frequently, especially would-be "direct" quotations from Milton, Pope, and Thomas Day.[55] Nevertheless, Equiano was an impressively self-conscious writer and developed two rhetorical strategies that would come to be utilized extensively in the nineteenth-century slave narratives: the trope of chiasmus, and the use of two distinct voices to distinguish, through rhetorical strategies, the simple wonder with which the young Equiano approached the New World of his captors and a more eloquently articulated voice that he employs to describe the author's narrative present. The interplay of these two voices is only as striking as Equiano's overarching plot-reversal pattern, within which all sorts of embedded reversal tales occur. Both strategies combine to make Equiano's text a representation of becoming, of a development of a self that not only has a past and a present but which speaks distinct languages at its several stages which culminate in the narrative present. Rarely would a slave narrator match Equiano's mastery of self-representation.[56]

Equiano refers to his literacy training a number of times. Richard Baker, an American boy on board the ship that first took Equiano to England, was, Equiano tells us, his "constant companion and instructor," and "interpreter."

---

[53] Paul Edwards's excellent "Introduction" to the 1969 edition is the source of these data on Equiano's editions as well as Equiano's place of origins, hereafter referred to as Edwards. See Edwards, pp. v, vii–ix.

[54] Edwards, p. v.

[55] Ibid., pp. xlv–liii.

[56] See ibid., pp. lxvii–lxix.

At Guernsey, his playmate Mary's mother "behaved to me with great kindness and attention; and taught me every thing in the same manner as she did her own child, and indeed in every way treated me as such."[57] Within a year, he continues,

> I could now speak English tolerably well, and I perfectly understood everything that was said. I not only felt myself quite easy with these new countrymen, but relished their society and manners. I no longer looked upon them as spirits, but as men superior to us; and I therefore had the stronger desire to resemble them, to imbibe their spirit, and imitate their manners. I therefore embraced every occasion of improvement, and every new thing that I observed I treasured up in my memory. I had long wished to be able to read and write; and for this purpose I took every opportunity to gain instruction, but had made as yet very little progress. However, when I went to London with my master, I had soon an opportunity of improving myself, which I gladly embraced. Shortly after my arrival, he sent me to wait upon the Miss Guerins, who had treated me with such kindness when I was there before; and they sent me to school.[58]

Equiano also used the sea as an extension school, as he did on the "Aetna fireship":

> I now became the captain's steward, in such situation I was very happy: for I was extremely well treated by all on board; and I had leisure to improve myself in reading and writing. The latter I had learned a little of before I left the Namur, as there was a school on board.[59]

Equiano, in short, leaves a trail of evidence to prove that he was fully capable of writing his own life's story. Despite these clues, however, at least the reviewer for *The Monthly Review* wondered aloud about the assistance of "some English writer" in the production of his text.[60]

Equiano uses the trope of the Talking Book in his third chapter, in which he describes his voyages from Barbados to Virginia and on to England. It is on this voyage that he begins to learn English. Equiano uses the trope as a climax of several examples sprinkled throughout the early pages of this chapter of sublime moments of cross-cultural encounters experienced by the wide-eyed boy. His encounters with a watch and a portrait are among the first items on his list:

> The first object that engaged my attention was a watch which hung on the chimney, and was going. I was quite surprised at the noise it

[57] Equiano, Vol. I, pp. 98, 109.
[58] Ibid., pp. 132–33.
[59] Ibid., pp. 151–52.
[60] *Monthly Review* (June 1789): 551.

made, and was afraid it would tell the gentleman any thing I might
do amiss: and when I immediately after observed a picture hanging
in the room, which appeared constantly to look at me, I was still
more affrighted, having never seen such things as these before. At
one time I thought it was something relative to magic; and not seeing it move I thought it might be some way the whites had to keep
their great men when they died, and offer them libations as we used
to do our friendly spirits.[61]

When he sees snow for the first time, he thinks it is salt. He concludes just before introducing as a separate paragraph the Talking Book scene, "I was astonished at the wisdom of the white people in all things I saw."[62]

Equiano returns to Gronniosaw's use of the trope for its details and
refers to gold only implicitly, in his reference to the "watch which hung on
the chimney." The trope is presented in a self-contained paragraph, which
does not refer directly either to the paragraph that precedes it or to the one
that follows. Nevertheless, the trope culminates the implicit list of wonder-
ments that the young African experiences at the marvels of the West. As
Equiano narrates:

I had often seen my master and Dick employed in reading; and I had
a great curiosity to talk to the books, as I thought they did; and so to
learn how all things had a beginning: for that purpose I have often
taken up a book, and have talked to it, and then put my ears to it,
when alone, in hopes it would answer me; and I have been very
much concerned when I found it remained silent.[63]

A watch, a portrait, a book that speaks: these are the elements of wonder that
the young African encounters on his road to Western culture. These are the
very signs through which Equiano represents the difference in subjectivity
that separates his, now lost, African world from the New World of "white
folks" that has been thrust upon him.

Significantly, Equiano endows each of these objects with his master's
subjectivity. The portrait seems to be watching him as he moves through the
room. The watch, he fears, can see, hear, and speak, and appears to be quite
capable of and willing to report his actions to his sleeping master once he
awakes. The watch is his master's surrogate overseer, standing in for the
master as an authority figure, even while he sleeps. The painting is also a surrogate figure of the master's authority, following his movements silently as
he walks about the room. The book that speaks to "my master and Dick" is a
double sign of subjectivity, since Equiano represents its function as one that
occurs in dialogue between a human being and its speaking pages. What can

[61] Equiano, Vol. I, pp. 92–93.
[62] Ibid., pp. 104, 106.
[63] Ibid., pp. 106–7.

we make of these elements that comprise Equiano's list of the salient signs of difference?

While dramatizing rather effectively the sensitive child's naiveté and curiosity, and his ability to interpret the culture of the Europeans from a distinctly African point of reference, Equiano is contrasting his earlier self with the self that narrates his text. This, certainly, is essential to his apparent desire to represent in his autobiography a dynamic self that once was "like that" but is now "like this." His ability to show his readers his own naiveté, rather than merely to tell us about it or to claim it, and to make this earlier self the focus of his readers' sympathy and amusement, are extraordinarily effective rhetorical strategies that serve to heighten our identification with the openly honest subject whose perceptions these were and who has remembered them for us to share. But Equiano is up to much more. Under the guise of the representation of his naive self, he is naming or reading Western culture closely, underlining relationships between subjects and objects that are implicit in commodity cultures. Watches do speak to their masters, in a language that has no other counterpart in this culture, and their language frequently proves to be the determining factor in the master's daily existence. The narrative past and the narrative present through which the narrator's consciousness shifts so freely and tellingly are symbolized by the voice that the young Equiano attributes to the watch. Portraits, moreover, do stare one in the face as one moves about within a room. They are also used as tokens of the immortality of their subjects, commanding of their viewers symbolic "libations," which the young Equiano "thought it might." Portraits are would-be tropes against the subject's mortality, just as Equiano imagined them to be. Books, finally, do speak to Europeans, and not to the Africans of the eighteenth century. The book recognizes "my master and Dick," acknowledging both their voices and their faces by engaging in a dialogue with them; neither the young African's voice nor his face can be recognizable to the text, because his countenance and discourse stand in Western texts as signs of absence, of the null and void. The young Equiano has read these texts closely, and rather tellingly, while the older Equiano represents this reading at a double-voiced level, allowing his readers to engage this series of encounters on both a manifest and a latent level of meaning.

But what can we make of the shift of tenses (from "had" to "have," for example) in Equiano's passage on the Talking Book? One key to reading this shift of tenses within the description itself is Equiano's endowment of these objects of Western culture with the master's subjectivity. Equiano, the slave, enjoys a status identical to that of the watch, the portrait, and the book. He is the master's object, to be used and enjoyed, purchased, sold, or discarded, just like a watch, a portrait, or a book. By law, the slave has no more and no less rights than do the other objects that the master collects and endows with his subjectivity. Of course the book does not speak to him. Only subjects can endow an object with subjectivity; objects, such as a slave, possess no inherent subjectivity of their own. Objects can only reflect the subjectivity of the subject, like a mirror does. When Equiano, the object, attempts to speak to the book, there follows only the deafening silence that obtains between two lifeless objects. Only a subject can speak. Two mirrors can only reflect each other, in an endless pattern of voided repetition. But they cannot speak to each other, at least not in the language of the master. When the master's book looks to see whose face is behind the voice that Equiano speaks, it can only see an absence, the invisibility that dwells in an unattended looking-glass.

Through the act of writing alone, Equiano announces and preserves his newly found status as a subject. It is he who is the master of his text, a text that speaks volumes of experience and subjectivity. If once he too was an object, like a watch, a portrait, or a book, now he has endowed himself with his master's culture's ultimate sign of subjectivity, the presence of a voice which is the signal feature of a face. The shift in verb tenses creates irony, because we, his readers, know full well by this moment within the narrative that Equiano the narrator no longer speaks to texts that cannot see his face or that, therefore, refuse to address him. Equiano the author is a speaking subject, "just like" his master. But he is not "just like" his master and never can be in a culture in which the blackness of his face signifies an absence. Nevertheless, Equiano's use of shifting tenses serves to represent the very movement that he is experiencing (in a Middle Passage, as was Gronniosaw) as he transforms himself from African to Anglo-African, from slave to potential freedman, from an absence to a presence, and indeed from an object to a subject.

If the master's voice endows his objects with reflections of his subjectivity, then the representation, in writing, of the master's voice (and this process of endowment or reflection of subjectivity) serves to enable the object to remake himself into a subject. Equiano's shift in tenses enables his readers to observe him experiencing the silent text, within a narrative present that has been inscribed within a passage from his past; but it also serves, implicitly, to represent the difference between the narrator and this character of his (past) self, a difference marked through verb tense as the difference between object and subject. The process by which the master endows his commodities with the reflection of subjectivity, as figured in the African's readings of the watch, the portrait, and the book, is duplicated by Equiano's narrator's account of his own movement from slave-object to author-subject. The shift of tenses is Equiano's grammatical analogue of this process of becoming—of becoming a human being who reads differently from the child, of becoming a subject by passing a test (the mastery of writing) that no object can pass, and of becoming an author who represents, under the guise of a series of naive readings, an object's "true" nature by demonstrating that he can now read these objects in both ways, as he once did in the Middle Passage but also as he does today. The narrator's character of himself, of course, reads on a latent level of meaning; the first test of subjectivity is to demonstrate the ability to read on a manifest level. By revising the trope of the Talking Book, and by shifting from present to past and back to present, Equiano the author is able to read these objects simultaneously on both levels and to demonstrate his true mastery of the text of Western letters and the text of his verbal representation of his past and present selves.

What does this complex mode of representation suggest about Equiano's revisionary relationship to his friend and companion Cugoano? Cugoano had left Equiano very little room in which to maneuver, both by implicitly naming the "original" of the Anglo-African tradition's central trope and then by representing it as a fiction of a fiction, as a story about a story. Cugoano's bracketed narrative of Atahualpa calls attention to itself by removing it from the linear flow of the rest of his narrative, in a manner not found in the usages of either Gronniosaw or Marrant. By 1787, then, the trope could not be utilized without a remarkable degree of self-consciousness. So Cugoano engages in two maximal signs of self-consciousness: he uses the trope as an allegory of storytelling, allowing the characters even to speak in direct discourse, and simultaneously names its source, which is Gronniosaw and Marrant in one line of descent and an Inca historian in another line of descent. Equiano could not, as Gronniosaw and Marrant had done, simply make the trope a part of a linear narrative. So he subordinates it to a list of latent readings of the "true" nature of Western culture and simultaneously allows it to function as an allegory of his own act of fashioning an Anglo-African self out of words. Equiano's usage amounts to a fiction about the making of a fiction. His is a Signifyin(g) tale that Signifies upon the Western order of things, of which his willed black present self is the ironic double. If Cugoano names the trope, Equiano names his relation to Western culture through the trope. But he also, through his brilliant revision, names his relation to his three antecedent authors as that of the chain of narrators, a link, as it were, between links.

VI

The final revision of the trope of the Talking Book is that of John Jea. Jea revises the trope extensively in his autobiography, *The Life, History, and Unparalleled Sufferings of John Jea*. Jea enjoys a rare distinction in the Anglo-African tradition: he is one of the few, if not the only black poet before this century who published both an autobiography and a work of imaginative literature. Despite this unique place in black letters, however, both of Jea's works had been lost until they were accidentally uncovered in 1983. Neither work appears in any of the standard bibliographies of black poetry or autobiography.[64]

---

[64] John Jea, *The Life, History, and Unparalleled Sufferings of John Jea, the African Preacher. Compiled and Written by Himself* (Portsea, Eng.: for the author, 1815?). Jea wrote a number of religious poems, which he called hymns. In 1816, he collected these and published them in a volume that also includes hymns written by other authors. This extraordinarily rare and interesting volume was discovered in the summer of 1983. See Henry Louis Gates, Jr., *The Collected Works of John Jea, African Preacher* (New York: Oxford University Press, forthcoming).

We do not yet know very many of the particulars of Jea's life, beyond those narrated in his autobiography. He tells us that he, "the subject of this narrative," was born in "Old Callabar, in Africa, in the year 1773." Jea tells his readers that he, his parents, and his brothers and sisters "were stolen" from Africa, and taken to New York. His master and mistress, Oliver and Angelika Triehuen, were Dutch. Jea's narrative is an account of the arduous labors forced upon the slaves of the Triehuens, and of his rescue by God and Christianity, despite the most severe beatings by his master whenever Jea succeeded in attending any sort of religious gathering. Eventually, Jea is freed and becomes an itinerant preacher, whose travels take him to Boston, New Orleans, the "East Indies," South America, Holland, France, Germany, Ireland, and England. Jea's travels, replete with "surprising deliverances" effected by Divine Providence, make for fascinating reading, but what is of most interest here are his rhetorical strategies.

The discovery of Jea's narrative enables us to gain a much better understanding than was possible before of the formal development of strategies of self-presentation that obtain in the slave narratives published between 1760 and 1865. Jea's text stands as something of a missing link in the chain of black narrators, because his is one of the few black autobiographies published between 1800 and 1830, by which date the structure of the slave narratives becomes fairly fixed. Jea's text, for instance, is replete with animal metaphors drawn upon to describe the life of the slave. These metaphors are much less common in the narratives published in the eighteenth century than they are in those published after 1830. Jea's text, moreover, is explicitly concerned with literacy as the element that enables the slave to reverse his or her status, from a condition of slave/animal to that of articulate subject. Jea is also explicitly concerned to be a voice for the abolition of slavery, an institution that he repeatedly claims to be at odds with the divine order. Finally, Jea's narrative, as full of italicized citations from the Bible as it is of antislavery sentiment, helps us to understand how the "sacred life of the troubled Christian" that had been Gronniosaw's and Marrant's concern to express, was readily used as a model to transform black autobiography into a fundamentally secular narrative mode after 1830, in which the slave-subject apparently feels no need to justify his or her rights to freedom by calling upon the Lord and his scriptures. Jea's is the last of the great black "sacred" slave autobiographies. After his text, slave narrators generally relegate the sacred to a tacit presence, while the secular concern with abolition becomes predominant.

Jea introduces two major revisions of the slave narrative structure that he received from the eighteenth century. These include the visual representation of the text's subject, which prefaces his text, and the trope of the Talking Book. As Equiano had done twenty-six years before him, Jea prefaces his text with his own image, but an image represented both in profile and in silhouette. Jea's representation of himself in shadow draws attention primarily to his "African" features, especially to his "Bantu" nose, his thick lips, and his "Ibo" forehead, unlike the engravings of Phillis Wheatley and Equiano, which call attention to the assimilated presence of a subject who is Anglo-African, a hybrid third term meant to mediate between the opposites signified by "African" and "Anglo-Saxon." Jea's choice of representation of himself, while common among other Protestant ministers who published autobiographies contemporaneous with Jea's, is the negative, if you will, of the positive image selected by Wheatley and Equiano. Jea reverses the convention of self-presentation by employing the silhouette to underscore a literal blackness of the subject, represented as black upon black.[65]

But even more curious for the purposes of this chapter is Jea's revision of the trope of the Talking Book, which he also seeks to make literal. By this I mean that Jea—like both Gronniosaw and Marrant before him—uses the trope of the Talking Book as an element in a larger linear narrative, unlike Cugoano, who brackets the trope by making it a narrative-within-a-narrative, and unlike Equiano, who utilizes it as a signal element in his "list of differences" that separated the African from the European. Equiano succeeds in calling attention to the figurative uses he is making of the trope through several rhetorical devices, especially by a shift of verb tenses that serves to remind his readers that he, the author and subject of his narrative, is now able to make the text speak in his own tongue, and that this Equiano, the author, is not the same Equiano we overhear speaking to a silent text. Jea, like Marrant and Gronniosaw, also makes this scene a part of his linear plot development, but with one major difference: he reads the trope literally as "the word made flesh," then uses this curious event to claim that it alone led to his true manumission, a psychological manumission that necessarily follows the legal manumission he had achieved by undergoing baptism.

Jea's account of the Talking Book unfolds over five pages of his text. Unlike the texts of his antecedents, it is not readily available, only three copies being registered in England and in the United States. Because it is so rare, and more especially because it does not summarize well, I have decided to reprint it as follows below. It occurs in Jea's narrative immediately after he tells us that he "ran from" his last human master's house "to the house of God, [and] was baptized unknown to him." (Jea tells us later that "It was a law of the state of the city of New York, that if any slave could give a satisfactory account of what he knew of the word of the Lord on his soul, he was free from slavery." This process was responsible for "releasing some thousands of us poor black slaves from the galling chains of slavery.")[66] Jea's text follows:

But my master strove to baffle me, and to prevent me from understanding the Scriptures: so he used to tell me that there was a time to every purpose under the sun, to do all manner of work, that slaves

---

[65] See *Periodical Accounts, Relative to the Baptist Missionary Society* (Dunstable, 1806), Vol. 3; and the silhouettes of Petumber Singee and Krishno Presaud, Indian preachers of the Gospel. David Dabydeen pointed out this reference to me.

[66] Jea, *The Life*, p. 39.

were in duty bound to do whatever their masters commanded them, whether it was right or wrong; so that they must be as obedient to a hard spiteful master as to a good one. He then took the Bible and showed it to me, and said that the book talked with him. Thus he talked with me endeavouring to convince me that I ought not to leave him, although I had received my full liberty from the magistrates, and was fully determined, by the grace of God, to leave him; yet he strove to the uttermost to prevent me; but thanks be to God, his strivings were all in vain.

My master's sons also endeavoured to convince me, by their reading in the behalf of their father, for it surprised me much, how they could take that blessed book into their hands, and to be so superstitious as to want to make me believe that the book did talk with them; so that every opportunity when they were out of the way, I took the book, and held it up to my ears, to try whether the book would talk with me or not, but it proved to be all in vain, for I could not hear it speak one word, which caused me to grieve and lament, that after God had done so much for me as he had, in pardoning my sins, and blotting out my iniquities and transgressions, and making me a new creature, the book would not talk with me; but the Spirit of the Lord brought this passage of Scripture to my mind, where Jesus Christ says, "Whatsoever, ye shall ask the Father in my name, ye shall receive. Ask in faith nothing doubting: for according unto your faith it shall be unto you. For unto him that believeth, all things are possible." Then I began to ask God in faithful and fervent prayer, as the Spirit of the Lord gave me utterance, begging earnestly of the Lord to give me the knowledge of his word, that I might be enabled to understand it in its pure light, and be able to speak it in the Dutch and English languages, that I might convince my master that he and his sons had not spoken to me as they ought, when I was their slave.

Thus I wrestled with God by faithful and fervent prayer, for five or six weeks, like Jacob of old, Gen. xxxii. 24. Hosea vii. 4. My master and mistress, and all people, laughed me to scorn, for being such a fool, to think that God would hear my prayer and grant unto me my request. But I gave God no rest day or night, and I was so earnest, that I can truly say, I shed as many tears for this blessing, as I did when I was begging God to grant me the pardon and forgiveness of my sins. During the time I was pouring out my supplications and prayers unto the Lord, my hands were employed, labouring for the bread that perisheth, and my heart within me still famishing for the word of God; as spoken in the Scriptures, "There shall be a famine in the land; not a famine of bread, nor of water, but of the word of God." And thus blessed be the Lord, that he sent a famine into my heart, and caused me to call upon him by his Spirit's assistance, in the time of my trouble.

The Lord heard my groans and cries at the end of six weeks, and sent the blessed angel of the covenant to my heart and soul, to release me from all my distress and troubles, and delivered me from all mine enemies, which were ready to destroy me; thus the Lord was pleased in his infinite mercy, to send an angel, in a vision, in shining raiment, and his countenance shining as the sun, with a large Bible in his hands, and brought it unto me, and said, "I am come to bless thee, and to grant thee thy request," as you read in the Scriptures. Thus my eyes were opened at the end of six weeks, while I was praying, in the place where I slept; although the place was as dark as a dungeon, I awoke, as the Scripture saith, and found it illuminated with the light of the glory of God, and the angel standing by me, with the large book open, which was the Holy Bible, and said unto me, "Thou has desired to read and understand this book, and to speak the language of it both in English and in Dutch; I will therefore teach thee, and now read"; and then he taught me to read the first chapter of the gospel according to St. John; and when I had read the whole chapter, the angel and the book were both gone in the twinkling of an eye, which astonished me very much, for the place was dark immediately; being about four o'clock in the morning in the winter season. After my astonishment had a little subsided, I began to think whether it was a fact that an angel had taught me to read, or only a dream; for I was in such a strait, like Peter was in the prison, when the angel smote him on the side, and said unto Peter, "Arise, Peter, and take thy garment, and spread it around thee, and follow me." And Peter knew not whether it was a dream or not; and when the angel touched him the second time, Peter arose, took his garment, folded it around him, and followed the angel, and the gates opened unto him of their own accord. So it was with me when the room was darkened again, that I wondered within myself whether I could read or not, but the Spirit of the Lord convinced me that I could; I went out of the house to a secret place, and there rendered thanksgivings and praises unto God's holy name, for his goodness in showing me to read his holy word, to understand it, and to speak it, both in the English and Dutch languages.

I tarried at a distance from the house, blessing and praising God, until the dawning of the day, and by that time the rest of the slaves were called to their labour; they were all very much surprised to see me there so early in the morning, rejoicing as if I had found a pearl of great price, for they used to see me very sad and grieved on other mornings, but now rejoicing, and they asked me what was the reason of my rejoicing more now than at other times, but I answered I would not tell them. After I had finished my day's work I went to the minister's house, and told him that I could read, but he doubted greatly of it, and said unto me, "How is it possible that you can read? For when you were a slave your master would not suffer any one, whatever, to come near you to teach you, nor any of the slaves, to read; and it is not long since you had your liberty, not long enough to learn to read." But I told him, that the Lord had learnt me to read last night. He said it was impossible. I said, "Nothing is impossible with God, for all things are possible with him; but the thing impossible with man is possible with God: for he doth with the host of heaven, and with the inhabitants of the earth, as he pleaseth, and there is none that can withstay his hand, nor dare to say what dost thou? And so did the Lord with me as it pleased him, in shewing me to read his word, and to speak it, and if you have a large Bible, as the Lord showed me last night, I can read it." But he said, "No, it is not possible that you can read." This grieved me greatly, with caused me to cry. His wife then spoke in my behalf, and said unto him, "You have a large Bible, fetch it, and let him try and see whether he can read it or not, and you will then be convinced." The minister then brought the Bible to me, in order that I should read; and as he opened the Bible for me to read, it appeared unto me, that a person said, "That is the place, read it." Which was the first chapter of the gospel of St. John, the same the Lord had taught me to read. So I read to the minister; and he said to me, "You read very well and very distinct"; and asked me who had learnt me. I said the Lord had learnt me last night. He said that it was impossible; but, if it were so, he should find it out. On saying this he went and got other books, to see whether I could read them; I tried, but could not. He then brought a spelling book, to see if I could spell; but he found to his great astonishment, that I could not. This convinced him and his wife that it was the Lord's work, and it was marvellous in their eyes.

This caused them to spread a rumour all over the city of New York, saying, that the Lord had worked great miracles on a poor black man. The people flocked from all parts to know whether it was true or not; and some of them took me before the magistrates, and had me examined concerning the rumour that was spread abroad, to prevent me, if possible, from saying the Lord had taught me to read in one night, in about fifteen minutes; for they were afraid that I should teach the other slaves to call upon the name of the Lord, as I did aforetime, and that they should come to the knowledge of the truth.

The magistrates examined me strictly, to see if I could read, as the report states; they brought a Bible for me to read in, and I read unto them the same chapter the Lord had taught me, as before-mentioned, and they said I read very well and very distinct, and asked me who had taught me to read. I still replied, that the Lord had taught me. They said that it was impossible; but brought forth spelling and other books, to see if I could read them, or whether I could spell, but they found to their great surprise, that I could not read other books, neither could I spell a word; when they said, it was the work of the Lord, and a very great miracle indeed; whilst others exclaimed and said that it was not right that I should have my liberty. The magistrates said that it was right and just that I should have my liberty, for they believed that I was of God, for they were persuaded that no man could read in such a manner, unless he was taught of God.

From that hour, in which the Lord taught me to read, until the present, I have not been able to read in any book, nor any reading whatever, but such as contain the word of God.[67]

What are we to make of Jea's fantastic revision of the trope of the Talking Book? Where are the golden chains that appear in Gronniosaw, Marrant, and Cugoano? Whereas Equiano's self-reflexive strategy of representing the trope makes his chain the very chain of narrators whom he is revising, Jea's chains are the "chains of sin," which he has carefully elaborated upon before he tells us of the Talking Book:

[Unless] you improve your advantages, you had better be a slave in any dark part of the world, than a neglecter of the gospel in this highly favoured land; recollect also that even here you might be a slave of the most awful description: — a slave to your passions — a slave to the world — a slave to sin — a slave to satan — a slave to hell — and, unless you are made free by Christ, through the means of the gospel, you will remain in captivity, tied and bound in the *chains* of your sin, till at last you will be bound hand and foot, and cast into utter darkness, there shall be weeping and gnashing of teeth forever.[68]

Jea reverses the semantic associations of "slave" and "chains," making his condition the metaphor of the human condition. It is clear early on in his text, then, that this Christian life of a slave bears a relationship to other lives as the part stands for the whole. Jea, as I hope to show, has much in mind in his revisions of the contents of the trope of the Talking Book.

Let us be clear about Jea's chain: while nominally freed by the laws of New York because he was baptized and because he "could give a satisfactory account of what he knew of the work of the Lord on his soul," it was not until he demonstrated his ability to "read" the first chapter of the Gospel of John, "very well and distinct" as Jea tells us twice, that his rights to "liberty" were confirmed by "the magistrates" of New York because he had been "taught of God." Jea, in other words, literally reads his way out of slavery, just as Job Ben Solomon in 1731 had literally written his way out of bondage. Whereas Gronniosaw, Marrant, Cugoano, and Equiano had represented a truly cultural or metaphysical manumission through the

[67] Ibid., pp. 33–38.
[68] Ibid., p. 9 (emphasis added).

transference afforded by the trope of the Talking Book, Jea, on the surface at least, erases this received trope by literalizing it to a degree that most narrators would not dream of attempting before Jea's usage and especially afterward.

Jea attempts to ground his representation of this miracle by carefully selecting concrete details of the event to share with his readers. He names the text that the angel teaches him to read; he adds that the event occurs just before dawn, "being about four o'clock in the morning," and that the entire reading lesson unfolded "in about fifteen minutes." Jea also gives his readers a fairly precise account of events that led to the angel's appearance, and of his actions immediately before and after this supernatural visitation. Finally, he tells us three times that his request of God and God's gift in return was to "read," "understand," and "speak the language" of this chapter of the Bible in both "the English and Dutch languages." Jea's desire, satisfied by divine intervention when all other merely mortal avenues had been closed off by the evils of slavery, was for a bilingual facility with the text of God, a facility that he is able to demonstrate upon demand of the skeptical. It is the mastery of the text of God, alone of all other texts, which leads directly to his legal manumission.

It is not an arbitrary text that the angel (or God) selects for the black slave's mastery. Rather, it is the Gospel of John. Let us recall its opening verse: "In the beginning was the World, and the Word was with God, and the Word was God." Jea's "mastery" of reading is centered upon the curious sentence of the New Testament which explicitly concerns the nature of "the Word," upon the logos, speech or the word as reason. And let us recall the first chapter's final verse: "And he saith unto him, Verily, verily, I say unto you, Hereafter ye shall see heaven open, and the angels of God ascending and descending upon the Son of man." Jea takes these framing verses of this major text and represents its wonders in the most literal manner possible, by having "heaven open" and an angel both descend and then ascend, but also by literally dramatizing the text's first verse, that "the Word" is the beginning, and is with God in the beginning, and indeed "was God." Only God, epitome and keeper of the Word, can satisfy the illiterate slave's desire to know this Word, "in the English and Dutch languages," because all human agencies are closed off to him by slavery. God-in-the-text, then, emerges from the text, and rewards his servant's unusual plea with its fulfillment at its most literal level. While we, his readers, find Jea's account of his literacy training to be allegorical at best, he does not seek to emphasize the event as figurative; on the contrary, by making it one more element in his linear narration (albeit a crucial one), and by representing it as the event that leads directly to his attainment of legal liberty, Jea disregards the strategies of revision drawn upon by Cugoano and Equiano (both of whom call attention to its figurative properties, as we have seen) and attempts to represent the several literal and figurative elements of the received trope as if they all happened. This is what I mean when I say that Jea literalizes the trope, that he erases its figurative properties by expanding its compacted denotations and connotations into a five-page account of the event that transforms his life in a most fundamental way.

But Jea's revision does more than make the trope literal. His revision names the trope and all of the transferences that we have seen to be at work in his antecedent narrators' revisions. His naming of the trope, moreover, is the event that, at last, enables him to tell *his* name, a name that he places in his title and that the text of his life elaborates upon in some detail. Jea's concern with naming is explicitly stated in the Wesley hymn that appears on the last page of his narrative, as an afterthought or coda. In two of the hymn's five stanzas, Wesley addresses the significance of naming explicitly and provocatively:

> I need not tell thee who I am;
>   My misery and sin declare:
> Thyself has call'd me by my name;
>   Look on thy hands, and read it there:
> But who, I ask thee, who art thou?
>   Tell me thy Name, and tell me now. . . .
>
> Wilt thou not yet to me reveal
>   Thy new, unutterable Name?
> Tell me, I still beseech thee, tell;
>   To know it now, resolv'd I am:
> Wrestling I will not let thee go,
>   Till I thy name, thy Nature know.

Through a long dark night of the soul, like Jacob with the angel, the subject of the hymn wrestles with "the God-man" only to learn His name. In one's name is one's "Nature," the hymn says, arguing for a natural relationship between signs and what they signify. Jea inscribes his name in his autobiographical text, so that his readers can also know his name and thereby know his nature and that of the black slaves for whom he stands as the part stands for the whole.

What are the names he gives to the trope through his revision? Jea shows us that the trope of the Talking Book figures the difference that obtains in Western culture between the slave and the free, between African and European, between non-Christian and Christian. His revision tells us that true freedom, in the life of the slave, turns upon the mastery of Western letters or, more properly, upon the mastery inherent in the communion of the subject with the logos, in both its most literal and most figurative forms. He tells us that in literacy was to be found the sole sign of difference that separated chattel property from human being. And he tells us that this figure, as encoded in the tropes that he received from Gronniosaw, Marrant, Cugoano, and Equiano, was not merely a figure, but a figure of a figure, literacy being Western culture's trope of dominance over the peoples of color it had "discovered," colonized, and enslaved since the fifteenth century. Jea's revision also tells us that the trope, all along, has been one of presence, the presence of the human voice necessary for the black slave narrator effectively to transform himself—and to represent this transformation—from silent object to speaking subject, in the form of a life containable in autobiography.

Jea's revision also addresses the complex matter of the distance that separates the oral from the written. Just as what I am calling the trope of the Talking Book in fact is more properly the trope of the un-Talking Book, in which the canceled presence of an opposite term is enunciated by the silence or absence of the text, so too is Jea's literacy a canceled presence because he can only read one chapter of one book, albeit a major chapter of a major book. Indeed it is not clear if Jea could read or write at all; despite the claim of his text's title that the autobiography has been "Compiled and Written by Himself," Jea tells us near the end of his tale (p. 95), "My dear reader, I would now inform you, that I have stated this in the best manner I am able, for I cannot write, therefore it is not so correct as if I had been able to have written it myself." Jea, in other words, can only make the text speak, as it were, by memorization rather than by the true mastery of its letters. His is the oral reading and writing of memory, of the sort practiced by the Yoruba *babalawo*. (Jea's birthplace of "Old Callabar," we recall, is in the east of Nigeria, where similar modes of narration would have obtained even in the eighteenth century.) Jea's is at best an ironic mode of reading. Like Gronniosaw and Marrant before him, never is he able to write his life, only to write it by oral narration. Jea is the third-term resolution between the illiterate slave and the fully literate European.

After Jea's revision, or erasure as I am thinking of it, the trope of the Talking Book disappears from the other slave narratives published in the nineteenth century. No longer is this sign of the presence of literacy, and all that this sign connotes in the life of the black slave, available for revision after Jea has erased its figurative properties by his turn to the supernatural. Rather, the trope of the Talking Book now must be displaced in a second-order revision in which the absence and presence of the speaking voice is refigured as the absence and presence of the written voice. Jea's scene of instruction, or midnight dream of instruction (did it actually happen, he wonders aloud as his readers wonder, or was it "only a dream?"), represents the dream of freedom as the dream of literacy, a dream realized as if by a miracle of literacy. Jea's dream is, as I have stated, composed of elements common to the usages of his black antecedents, but the central content of the trope has been expanded disproportionately from its figurative associations to its most literal level, wherein an angel teaches the slave how to read and thus escape the clutches of the devil that keeps the slave in chains. Equiano's angel was a young white boy; Frederick Douglass's guardian angel was the white woman married to his master. Many of the post-1830 slave narrators' guardian angels are also white women or children, related directly or indirectly by a marriage bond to the master.

These representations of the mastery of letters (literally, the A B C's) are clearly transferences and displacements of the dream of freedom figured for the tradition by Jea's text, again, in the most literal way. Whereas Jea's Signifyin(g) relation to Gronniosaw, Marrant, Cugoano, and Equiano is defined by a disproportionate expansion and elaboration upon the contents of their tropes, to such an extent that we are led to conclude that these narrators could have saved themselves loads of trouble had they only prayed to God intensely for six weeks to make the text speak, Jea's revision erased the trope (or Signified upon it by reducing it to the absurd) for the slave narrators who follow him in the tradition. They no longer can revise the trope merely by displacing or condensing its contents. Rather, Jea's supernatural naming demands that a completely new trope be figured to represent what Jea's revision has made unrepresentable without some sort of censorship, if the narrator is to be believed and believable as one who is capable of, and entitled to, the enjoyment of the secular idea of liberty that obtains in a text of a life such as Frederick Douglass's. Because Douglass and his black contemporaries wish to write their way to a freedom epitomized by the abolition movement, they cannot afford Jea's luxury of appealing, in his representation of his signal scene of instruction, primarily to the Christian converted. Douglass and his associates long for a secular freedom now. They can ill afford to represent even their previous selves—the earlier self that is transformed, as we read their texts, into the speaking subjects who obviously warrant full equality with white people—as so naive as to believe that books speak when their masters speak to them. Instead, the post-Jea narrators refigure the trope of the Talking Book by the secular equation of the mastery of slavery through the "simple" mastery of letters. Their dream of freedom, figured primarily in tropes of writing rather than speaking, constitutes a displacement of the eighteenth-century trope of the Talking Book, wherein the presence of the human voice in the text is only implied by its absence as we read these narratives and especially their tropes of writing (as Robert Stepto has so ably done) against the trope that we have been examining here.[69]

These narrators, linked by revision of a trope into the very first black chain of signifiers, implicitly Signify upon another chain, the metaphorical Great Chain of Being. Blacks were most commonly represented on the chain either as the lowest of the human races or as first cousin to the ape. Since writing, according to Hume, was the ultimate sign of difference between animal and human, these writers implicitly were Signifyin(g) upon the figure of the chain itself, simply by publishing autobiographies that were indictments of the received order of Western culture of which slavery, to them, by

---

[69] See Stepto, *From Behind the Veil*, chapter 1.

definition stood as the most salient sign. The writings of Gronniosaw, Marrant, Equiano, Cugoano, and Jea served as a critique of the sign of the Great Chain of Being and the black person's figurative place on the chain. This chain of black signifiers, regardless of their intent or desire, made the first political gesture in the Anglo-African literary tradition "simply" by the act of writing, a collective act that gave birth to the black literary tradition and defined it as the other's chain, the chain of black being as black people themselves would have it. Making the book speak, then, constituted a motivated, and political, engagement with and condemnation of Europe's fundamental figure of domination, the Great Chain of Being.

The trope of the Talking Book is not a trope of the presence of voice at all, but of its absence. To speak of a silent voice is to speak in an oxymoron. There is no such thing as a silent voice. Furthermore, as Juliet Mitchell has put the matter, there is something untenable about the attempt to represent what is not there, to represent what is *missing* or absent. Given that this is what these five black authors are seeking to do, we are justified in wondering aloud if the sort of subjectivity that they seek can be realized through a process that is so very ironic from the outset. Indeed, how can the black subject posit a full and sufficient self in a language in which blackness is a sign of absence?

The modes of revision of one trope that are charted in this chapter, a trope fundamental to the slave narratives in one form or another between 1770 and 1865, attest to the sort of shared, if altered, patterns of representation that serve to define a literary tradition. One could easily write an account of the shaping of the Afro-American tradition, from Briton Hammon's 1760 narrative to Alice Walker's *The Color Purple,* simply by explicating the figures used to represent the search of the black subject for a textual voice. In the three remaining chapters of this book, I wish to explore this matter of voicing and its various representations, first (Chapter 5) in Zora Neale Hurston's use of free indirect discourse in *Their Eyes Were Watching God,* a text whose central theme is the quest of a silent black woman both to find a voice and then to share it in loving dialogue with a friend (Phoeby) and a lover (Tea Cake), a process that turns upon the literal and figurative (or, more properly, the white and the black vernacular usages) of "Signifyin(g)." In Chapter 6 I wish to explicate the doubling of voices as the undergirding rhetorical strategy through which Ishmael Reed critiques and revises the black fiction tradition by an extended Signifyin(g) riff. Finally, concluding in Chapter 7, I wish to demonstrate how Alice Walker's Signification consists of a rewriting of the speakerly strategies of narration at work in Hurston's use of free indirect discourse, by turning to the epistolary novel and representing a subject who *writes* herself to a personal freedom and to a remarkable level of articulation in the dialect voice in which Hurston's protagonist *speaks.*

Typology of the Trope of the Talking Book*

	Chain	Status	Alienated from family	"Dutch or English"	Scene	Geo. Whitfield	Book
Gronniosaw	Gold	Slave prince	X	X	Middle passage	X	Bible
Marrant	Gold	Free prince	X		Moment of execution	X	Bible
Cugoano	Gold	Inca chief			Moment of confrontation		Breviary
Equiano	Gold (watch)	Slave			Middle passage		Bible
Jea	Sin	Slave to sin; slave	X	X	Dark night of the soul	X	Bible

*I would like to thank Elizabeth Petrino, who prepared this chart.

Eve Kosofsky Sedgwick

From *Epistemology of the Closet*

1990

Before the middle of the 1980s, Eve Sedgwick (b. 1950) saw her work as based in the
field of feminist criticism. But she became increasingly interested in the emerging
area of homosexual theory and gay and lesbian studies, and with the publication of
Between Men: English Literature and Male Homosocial Desire (1985), she became one of the leading voices in American gay criticism. The work that followed, including Epistemology of the Closet (1990) and Tendencies (1993), has kept her a
central figure in the growing gay studies movement and has often provided an illuminating mix of theory and textual criticism.

In the selection that follows, Sedgwick begins her look at the relationship between gay studies and canon formation by pointing out the example of Herman
Melville's Billy Budd and Oscar Wilde's Dorian Gray. Despite remarkable similarities — structural, aesthetic, and historical — between the two novels, they are seldom
seen as belonging to a single tradition. This, Sedgwick asserts, is because canons
have traditionally been defined by rigid boundaries of nationalities and historical periods, while disallowing groupings by other categories, including (though certainly
not restricted to) the common content of homosexual and homosocial desire to be
found in key texts from supposedly separate traditions. The very existence of canons,
she suggests, helps to limit the permissible readings of texts by preemptively placing
them within a particular tradition.

Of course, recent work in a number of critical fields, most notably feminist criticism, has challenged the master canons of Anglo-American literature. See, for example, the essays in this volume by Nina Baym (page 586) and Sandra M. Gilbert
and Susan Gubar (page 683). There have been numerous attempts both to widen the
canon by making it more inclusive and to destroy entirely the notion of a canon —
either way creating more room for the reading and study of once marginalized texts
and authors. But the position of gay studies on the canon is necessarily complicated.
For, unlike women and ethnic minorities who can make convincing claims for having
been excluded from the master canon, gay male authors cannot. In fact, as Sedgwick
notes, many of the central texts in the Anglo-American literary tradition were written by gay men and/or inscribe homosexual and homosocial themes, as the examples

of Billy Budd and Dorian Gray *illustrate. What has been missing from the canon is not homosexuals but homosexuality. The very existence of a canon based on national and historical boundaries asks us to focus on particular features of a text and, not incidentally, to ignore those features (such as the sexuality of the author) that might disturb orthodox ideas about literary history and literary genius.*

Axiom 6: The relation of gay studies to debates on the literary canon is, and had best be, tortuous.

EARLY ON IN THE WORK ON *Epistemology of the Closet,* in trying to settle on a literary text that would provide a first example for the kind of argument I meant the book to enable, I found myself circling around a text of 1891, a narrative that in spite of its relative brevity has proved a durable and potent centerpiece of gay male intertextuality and indeed has provided a durable and potent physical icon for gay male desire. It tells the story of a young Englishman famous for an extreme beauty of face and figure that seems to betray his aristocratic origin—an origin marked, however, also by mystery and class misalliance. If the gorgeous youth gives his name to the book and stamps his bodily image on it, the narrative is nonetheless more properly the story of a male triangle: a second, older man is tortured by a desire for the youth for which he can find no direct mode of expression, and a third man, emblem of suavity and the world, presides over the dispensation of discursive authority as the beautiful youth murders the tortured lover and is himself, in turn, by the novel's end ritually killed.

But maybe, I thought, one such text would offer an insufficient basis for cultural hypothesis. Might I pick two? It isn't yet commonplace to read *Dorian Gray* and *Billy Budd* by one another's light, but that can only be a testimony to the power of accepted English and American literary canons to insulate and deform the reading of politically important texts. In any gay male canon the two contemporaneous experimental works must be yoked together as overarching gateway texts of our modern period, and the conventionally obvious differences between them of style, literary positioning, national origin, class ethos, structure, and thematics must cease to be taken for granted and must instead become newly salient in the context of their startling erotic congruence. The book of the beautiful male English body foregrounded on an international canvas; the book of its inscription and evocation through a trio of male figures—the lovely boy, the tormented desirer, the deft master of the rules of their discourse; the story in which the lover is murdered by the boy and the boy is himself sacrificed; the deftly magisterial recounting that finally frames, preserves, exploits, and desublimates the male bodily image: *Dorian Gray* and *Billy Budd* are both that book.

The year 1891 is a good moment to which to look for a cross-section of the inaugural discourses of modern homo/heterosexuality—in medicine and psychiatry, in language and law, in the crisis of female status, in the career of imperialism. *Billy Budd* and *Dorian Gray* are among the texts that have set the terms for a modern homosexual identity. And in the Euro-American culture of this past century it has been notable that foundational texts of modern gay culture—*A la recherche du temps perdu* and *Death in Venice,* for instance, along with *Dorian Gray* and *Billy Budd*—have often been the identical texts that mobilized and promulgated the most potent images and categories for (what is now visible as) the canon of homophobic mastery.

Neither *Dorian Gray* nor *Billy Budd* is in the least an obscure text. Both are available in numerous paperback editions, for instance; and, both conveniently short, each differently canonical within a different national narrative, both are taught regularly in academic curricula. As what they are taught, however, and as what canonized, comes so close to disciplining the reading permitted of each that even the contemporaneity of the two texts (*Dorian Gray* was published as a book the year *Billy Budd* was written) may startle. That every major character in the archetypal American "allegory of good and evil" is English; that the archetypal English fin-de-siècle "allegory of art and life" was a sufficiently American event to appear in a Philadelphia publisher's magazine nine months before it became a London book—the canonic regimentation that effaces these international bonds has how much the more scope to efface the intertext and the intersexed. How may the strategy of a new canon operate in this space?

Contemporary discussions of the question of the literary canon tend to be structured either around the possibility of change, of rearrangement and reassignment of texts, within one overarching master-canon of literature— the strategy of adding Mary Shelley to the Norton Anthology—or, more theoretically defensible at the moment, around a vision of an exploding master-canon whose fracture would produce, or at least leave room for, a potentially infinite plurality of mini-canons, each specified as to its thematic or structural or authorial coverage: francophone Canadian or Inuit canons, for instance; clusters of magical realism or national allegory; the blues tradition; working-class narrative; canons of the sublime or the self-reflexive; Afro-Caribbean canons; canons of Anglo-American women's writing.

In fact, though, the most productive canon effects that have been taking place in recent literary studies have occurred, not from within the mechanism either of the master-canon or of a postfractural plurality of canons, but through an interaction between these two models of the canon. In this interaction the new pluralized mini-canons have largely failed to dislodge the master-canon from its empirical centrality in such institutional practices as publishing and teaching, although they have made certain specific works and authors newly available for inclusion in the master-canon. Their more important effect, however, has been to challenge, if not the empirical centrality, then the conceptual anonymity of the master-canon. The most notorious instance of this has occurred with feminist studies in literature, which by on the one hand confronting the master-canon with alternative canons of women's literature, and on the other hand reading rebelliously within the master-canon, has not only somewhat rearranged the table of contents for the master-canon but, more important, given it a title. If it is still in important respects *the* master-canon it nevertheless cannot now escape naming itself with every syllable also *a* particular canon, a canon of mastery, in this case of men's mastery over, and over against, women. Perhaps never again need women — need, one hopes, anybody — feel greeted by the Norton Anthology of mostly white men's Literature with the implied insolent salutation, "I'm nobody. Who are you?"

This is an encouraging story of female canon-formation, working in a sort of pincers movement with a process of feminist canon-*naming*, that has been in various forms a good deal told by now. How much the cheering clarity of this story is indebted, however, to the scarifying coarseness and visibility with which women and men are, in most if not all societies, distinguished publicly and once and for all from one another emerges only when attempts are made to apply the same model to that very differently structured though closely related form of oppression, modern homophobia. It is, as we have seen, only recently — and, I am arguing, only very incompletely and raggedly, although to that extent violently and brutally — that a combination of discursive forces have carved out, for women and for men, a possible though intensively proscribed homosexual identity in Euro-American culture. To the extent that such an identity is traceable, there is clearly the possibility, now being realized within literary criticism, for assembling alternative canons of lesbian and gay male writing *as* minority canons, as a literature of oppression and resistance and survival and heroic making. This modern view of lesbians and gay men as a distinctive minority population is of course importantly anachronistic in relation to earlier writing, however; and even in relation to modern writing it seems to falter in important ways in the implicit analysis it offers of the mechanisms of homophobia and of same-sex desire. It is with these complications that the relation between lesbian and gay literature as a minority canon, and the process of making salient the homosocial, homosexual, and homophobic strains and torsions in the already existing master-canon, becomes especially revealing.

It's revealing only, however, for those of us for whom relations within and among canons are active relations of thought. From the keepers of a dead canon we hear a rhetorical question — that is to say, a question posed with the arrogant intent of maintaining ignorance. Is there, as Saul Bellow put it, a Tolstoi of the Zulus? Has there been, ask the defenders of a mono-cultural curriculum, not intending to stay for an answer, has there ever yet been a Socrates of the Orient, an African-American Proust, a female Shakespeare? However assaultive or fatuous, in the context of the current debate the question has not been unproductive. To answer it in good faith has been to broach inquiries across a variety of critical fronts: into the canonical or indeed world-historic texts of non-Euro-American cultures, to begin with, but also into the nonuniversal functions of literacy and the literary, into the contingent and uneven secularization and sacralization of an aesthetic realm, into the relations of public to private in the ranking of genres, into the cult of the individual author and the organization of liberal arts education as an expensive form of masterpiece theatre.

Moreover, the flat insolent question teases by the very difference of its resonance with different projects of inquiry: it stimulates or irritates or reveals differently in the context of oral or written cultures; of the colonized or the colonizing, or cultures that have had both experiences; of peoples concentrated or in diaspora; of traditions partially internal or largely external to a dominant culture of the latter twentieth century.

From the point of view of this relatively new and inchoate academic presence, then, the gay studies movement, what distinctive soundings are to be reached by posing the question our way—and staying for an answer? Let's see how it sounds.

> Has there ever been a gay Socrates?
> Has there ever been a gay Shakespeare?
> Has there ever been a gay Proust?

Does the Pope wear a dress? If these questions startle, it is not least as tautologies. A short answer, though a very incomplete one, might be that not only have there been a gay Socrates, Shakespeare, and Proust but that their names are Socrates, Shakespeare, Proust; and, beyond that, legion—dozens or hundreds of the most centrally canonic figures in what the monoculturalists are pleased to consider "our" culture, as indeed, always in different forms and senses, in every other.

What's now in place, in contrast, in most scholarship and most curricula is an even briefer response to questions like these: Don't ask. Or, less laconically: You shouldn't know. The vast preponderance of scholarship and teaching, accordingly, even among liberal academics, does simply neither ask nor know. At the most expansive, there is a series of dismissals of such questions on the grounds that:

1. Passionate language of same-sex attraction was extremely common during whatever period is under discussion—and therefore must have been completely meaningless. Or
2. Same-sex genital relations may have been perfectly common during the period under discussion—but since there was no language about them, *they* must have been completely meaningless. Or
3. Attitudes about homosexuality were intolerant back then, unlike now—so people probably didn't do anything. Or
4. Prohibitions against homosexuality didn't exist back then, unlike now—so if people did anything, it was completely meaningless. Or
5. The word "homosexuality" wasn't coined until 1869—so everyone before then was heterosexual. (Of course, heterosexuality has always existed.) Or
6. The author under discussion is certified or rumored to have had an attachment to someone of the other sex—so their feelings about people of their own sex must have been completely meaningless. Or (under a perhaps somewhat different rule of admissible evidence)

7. There is no actual proof of homosexuality, such as sperm taken from the body of another man or a nude photograph with another woman—so the author may be assumed to have been ardently and exclusively heterosexual. Or (as a last resort)

8. The author or the author's important attachments may very well have been homosexual—but it would be provincial to let so insignificant a fact make any difference at all to our understanding of any serious project of life, writing, or thought.

These responses reflect, as we have already seen, some real questions of sexual definition and historicity. But they only reflect them and don't reflect *on* them: the family resemblance among this group of extremely common responses comes from their closeness to the core grammar of *Don't ask; You shouldn't know.* It didn't happen; it doesn't make any difference; it didn't mean anything; it doesn't have interpretive consequences. Stop asking just here; stop asking just now; we know in advance the kind of difference that could be made by the invocation of *this* difference; it makes no difference; it doesn't mean. The most openly repressive projects of censorship, such as William Bennett's literally murderous opposition to serious AIDS education in schools on the grounds that it would communicate a tolerance for the lives of homosexuals, are, through this mobilization of the powerful mechanism of the open secret, made perfectly congruent with the smooth, dismissive knowingness of the urbane and the pseudo-urbane.

And yet the absolute canonical centrality of the list of authors about whom one might think to ask these questions—What was the structure, function, historical surround of same-sex love in and for Homer or Plato or Sappho? What, then, about Euripides or Virgil? If a gay Marlowe, what about Spenser or Milton? Shakespeare? Byron? But what about Shelley? Montaigne, Leopardi . . . ? Leonardo, Michelangelo, but . . . ? Beethoven? Whitman, Thoreau, Dickinson (Dickinson?), Tennyson, Wilde, Woolf, Hopkins, but Brontë? Wittgenstein, but . . . Nietzsche? Proust, Musil, Kafka, Cather, but . . . Mann? James, but . . . Lawrence? Eliot? but . . . Joyce? The very centrality of this list and its seemingly almost infinite elasticity suggest that no one *can* know *in advance* where the limits of a gay-centered inquiry are to be drawn, or where a gay theorizing of and through even the hegemonic high culture of the Euro-American tradition may need or be able to lead. The emergence, even within the last year or two, of nascent but ambitious programs and courses in gay and lesbian studies, at schools including those of the Ivy League, may now make it possible for the first time to ask these difficult questions from within the very heart of the empowered cultural institutions to which they pertain, as well as from the marginal and endangered institutional positions from which, for so long, the most courageous work in this area has emanated.

Furthermore, as I have been suggesting, the violently contradictory and volatile energies that every morning's newspaper proves to us are circulating even at this moment, in our society, around the issues of homo/heterosexual definition show over and over again how preposterous is anybody's urbane pretense at having a clear, simple story to tell about the outlines and meanings of what and who are homosexual and heterosexual. To be gay, or to be potentially classifiable as gay—that is to say, *to be sexed or gendered*—in this system is to come under the radically overlapping aegises of a universalizing discourse of acts or bonds and at the same time of a minoritizing discourse of kinds of persons. Because of the double binds implicit in the space overlapped by universalizing and minoritizing models, the stakes in matters of definitional control are extremely high.

Obviously, this analysis suggests as one indispensable approach to the traditional Euro-American canon a pedagogy that could treat it neither as something quite exploded nor as something quite stable. A canon seen to be genuinely unified by the maintenance of a particular tension of homo/heterosexual definition can scarcely be dismantled; but neither can it ever be treated as the repository of reassuring "traditional" truths that could be made matter for any settled consolidation or congratulation. Insofar as the problematics of homo/heterosexual definition, in an intensely homophobic culture, are seen to be precisely internal to the central nexuses of that culture, this canon must always be treated as a loaded one. Considerations of the canon, it becomes clear, while vital in themselves cannot take the place of questions of pedagogic relations within and around the canon. Canonicity itself then seems the necessary wadding of pious obliviousness that allows for the transmission from one generation to another of texts that have the potential to dismantle the impacted foundations upon which a given culture rests.

GEORGE P. LANDOW

From *Hypertext: The Convergence of Contemporary Critical Theory and Technology*

1992

―――――――――
―――――――――

It has long been recognized that the reading and writing of literature is not indepen-
dent of technological influences, from the printing press to television and a host of
other developments large and small. The work of George Landow (b. 1940) represents
one of the newest fields emerging within literary theory, the study of the ways in
which computers and other electronic technologies affect the practice of reading and
writing. In this excerpt from Hypertext, *Landow concerns himself with the conver-*
gence of key elements of late twentieth-century literary theory with developments in
computer science. He notes remarkable similarities between the ideas of theorists in
the two fields who often work in complete ignorance of one another, and he suggests
that the discourse of literacy has undergone a paradigm shift*—one of those rare,*
important moments in which an entire field begins to reconsider its most fundamen-
tal assumptions.

According to Landow, the poststructuralist work of such thinkers as Barthes,
Derrida, and Foucault (see their essays on pages 487, 493, and 544) is unable to
reach more than theoretical status as long as the authors are unable to conceive of a
type of writing that is not bound to the technologies of traditional print media. But
though the poststructuralist theorists and experimental postmodern writers them-
selves may not have known of the newly developing technologies in the computer
world, their ideas are often fully embodied in the reading and writing of hypertext
and hypermedia (the electronic documents that Landow defines as "nonsequential
writing"). Landow cites, for instance, the degree to which James Joyce's Ulysses *re-*
lies on intertextuality, drawing from and making oblique reference to a number of ex-
ternal sources. He explains how hypertext links can be used to make explicit these
textual bonds merely suggested in traditional print. Likewise, since hypertext allows
readers to choose their own paths and move easily among any number of linked docu-
ments, the single, authoritative center to a discourse becomes destabilized, much as
Derrida claims it could in "Structure, Sign, and Play in the Discourse of Human

Sciences." With the coming of hypertext, then, a great deal of power has shifted from author to reader, just as Barthes, Foucault, and others had posited, though they had not known of a mechanism to carry out this project.

Much of Landow's article is speculative. It was published at a time when sophisticated hypertext systems were only recently commercially available and readily usable by nonspecialists. The now-massive hypermedia World Wide Web was tiny and virtually unknown outside of computer science circles, and even most educated readers were not familiar with the idea that an alternative to linear, print text was becoming available. With rapid developments making hypertext (and related computer technologies) ever more available and user friendly, within only a few years of Landow's publishing this piece many readers and writers were putting into practice on a daily basis what he could only speculate about in 1992.

Hypertextual Derrida, Poststructuralist Nelson?

WHEN DESIGNERS of computer software examine the pages of *Glas* or *Of Grammatology,* they encounter a digitalized, hypertextual Derrida; and when literary theorists examine *Literary Machines,* they encounter a deconstructionist or poststructuralist Nelson. These shocks of recognition can occur because over the past several decades literary theory and computer hypertext, apparently unconnected areas of inquiry, have increasingly converged. Statements by theorists concerned with literature, like those by theorists concerned with computing, show a remarkable convergence. Working often, but not always, in ignorance of each other, writers in these areas offer evidence that provides us a way into the contemporary *episteme* in the midst of major changes. A paradigm shift, I suggest, has begun to take place in the writings of Jacques Derrida and Theodor Nelson, of Roland Barthes and Andries van Dam. I expect that one name in each pair will be unknown to most of my readers. Those working in computing will know well the ideas of Nelson and van Dam; those working in literary and cultural theory will know equally well the ideas of Derrida and Barthes.[1] All four, like many others who write on hypertext or literary theory, argue that we must abandon conceptual systems founded upon ideas of center, margin, hierarchy, and linearity and replace them with ones of multilinearity, nodes, links, and networks. Almost all parties to this paradigm shift, which marks a revolution in human thought, see electronic writing as a direct response to the strengths and weaknesses of the printed book. This response has profound implications for literature, education, and politics.

The many parallels between computer hypertext and critical theory have many points of interest, the most important of which, perhaps, lies in the fact

---

[1] Here, right at the beginning, let me assure my readers that although I urge that Barthes and Derrida relate in interesting and important ways to computer hypertext, I do not take them—or semiotics and poststructuralism, or, for that matter, structuralism—to be essentially the same. [All notes are Landow's.]

that critical theory promises to theorize hypertext and hypertext promises to embody and thereby test aspects of theory, particularly those concerning textuality, narrative, and the roles or functions of reader and writer. Using hypertext, critical theorists will have, or now already have, a new laboratory, in addition to the conventional library of printed texts, in which to test their ideas. Most important, perhaps, an experience of reading hypertext or reading with hypertext greatly clarifies many of the most significant ideas of critical theory. As J. David Bolter points out in the course of explaining that hypertextuality embodies poststructuralist conceptions of the open text, "what is unnatural in print becomes natural in the electronic medium and will soon no longer need saying at all, because it can be shown."[2]

The Definition of Hypertext and Its History as a Concept

In *S/Z*, Roland Barthes describes an ideal textuality that precisely matches that which has come to be called computer hypertext—text composed of blocks of words (or images) linked electronically by multiple paths, chains, or trails in an open-ended, perpetually unfinished textuality described by the terms *link, node, network, web,* and *path:* "In this ideal text," says Barthes, "the networks [*réseaux*] are many and interact, without any one of them being able to surpass the rest; this text is a galaxy of signifiers, not a structure of signifieds; it has no beginning; it is reversible; we gain access to it by several entrances, none of which can be authoritatively declared to be the main one; the codes it mobilizes extend *as far as the eye can reach,* they are indeterminable . . . ; the systems of meaning can take over this absolutely plural text, but their number is never closed, based as it is on the infinity of language" (emphasis in original).[3]

Like Barthes, Michel Foucault conceives of text in terms of network and links. In *The Archeology of Knowledge,* he points out that the "frontiers of a book are never clear-cut," because "it is caught up in a system of references to other books, other texts, other sentences: it is a node within a network . . . [a] network of references."[4] Like almost all structuralists and poststructuralists, Barthes and Foucault describe text, the world of letters, and the power and status relations they involve in terms shared by the field of computer hypertext.

Hypertext, a term coined by Theodor H. Nelson in the 1960s, refers also to a form of electronic text, a radically new information technology, and a mode of publication. "By 'hypertext,'" Nelson explains, "I mean *nonsequential writing*—text that branches and allows choices to the reader, best read at an

---

[2] J. David Bolter, *Writing Space* (Hillsdale, N.J.: Lawrence Erlbaum, 1990), 143.

[3] Roland Barthes, *S/Z* (Paris: Éditions du Seuil, 1970), 11–12; *S/Z*, trans. Richard Miller (New York: Hill and Wang, 1974), 5–6. Subsequent references are to the English translation.

[4] Michel Foucault, *The Archeology of Knowledge,* trans. A. M. Sheridan Smith (New York: Harper Colophon, 1976), 23.

interactive screen. As popularly conceived, this is a series of text chunks connected by links which offer the reader different pathways."[5] Hypertext, as the term will be used in the following pages, denotes text composed of blocks of text—what Barthes terms a *lexia*—and the electronic links that join them. *Hypermedia* simply extends the notion of the text in hypertext by including visual information, sound, animation, and other forms of data. Since hypertext, which links a passage of verbal discourse to images, maps, diagrams, and sound as easily as to another verbal passage, expands the notion of text beyond the solely verbal, I do not distinguish between hypertext and hypermedia. *Hypertext* denotes an information medium that links verbal and nonverbal information. In the following pages, I shall use the terms *hypermedia* and *hypertext* interchangeably. Electronic links connect lexias "external" to a work—say, commentary on it by another author or parallel or contrasting texts—as well as within it and thereby create text that is experienced as nonlinear, or, more properly, as multilinear or multisequential. Although conventional reading habits apply within each lexia, once one leaves the shadowy bounds of any text unit, new rules and new experience apply.

The standard scholarly article in the humanities or physical sciences perfectly embodies the underlying notions of hypertext as multisequentially read text. For example, in reading an article on, say, James Joyce's *Ulysses*, one reads through what is conventionally known as the main text, encounters a number or symbol that indicates the presence of a foot- or endnote, and leaves the main text to read that note, which can contain a citation of passages in *Ulysses* that supposedly support the argument in question or information about the scholarly author's indebtedness to other authors, disagreement with them, and so on. The note can also summon up information about sources, influences, and parallels in other literary texts. In each case, the reader can follow the link to another text indicated by the note and thus move entirely outside the scholarly article itself. Having completed reading the note or having decided that it does not warrant a careful reading at the moment, one returns to the main text and continues reading until one encounters another note, at which point one again leaves the main text.

This kind of reading constitutes the basic experience and starting point of hypertext. Suppose now that one could simply touch the page where the symbol of a note, reference, or annotation appeared, and thus instantly bring into view the material contained in a note or even the entire other text—here all of *Ulysses*—to which that note refers. Scholarly articles situate themselves within a field of relations, most of which the print medium keeps out of sight and relatively difficult to follow, because in print technology the referenced (or linked) materials lie spatially distant from the references to them. Electronic hypertext, in contrast, makes individual references easy to follow and the entire field of interconnections obvious and easy to navigate. Changing the ease with which one can orient oneself within such a context and pursue

---

[5] Theodor H. Nelson, *Literary Machines* (Swarthmore, Pa.: self-published, 1981), 0/2. Pagination begins with each section or chapter; thus 0/2 = prefatory matter, page 2/.

individual references radically changes both the experience of reading and ultimately the nature of that which is read. For example, if one possessed a hypertext system in which our putative Joyce article was linked to all the other materials it cited, it would exist as part of a much larger system, in which the totality might count more than the individual document; the article would now be woven more tightly into its context than would a printed counterpart.

As this scenario suggests, hypertext blurs the boundaries between reader and writer and therefore instantiates another quality of Barthes's ideal text. From the vantage point of the current changes in information technology, Barthes's distinction between readerly and writerly texts appears to be essentially a distinction between text based on print technology and electronic hypertext, for hypertext fulfills

> the goal of literary work (of literature as work) [which] is to make the reader no longer a consumer, but a producer of the text. Our literature is characterized by the pitiless divorce which the literary institution maintains between the producer of the text and its user, between its owner and its customer, between its author and its reader. This reader is thereby plunged into a kind of idleness—he is intransitive; he is, in short, *serious:* instead of functioning himself, instead of gaining access to the magic of the signifier, to the pleasure of writing, he is left with no more than the poor freedom either to accept or reject the text: reading is nothing more than a *referendum.* Opposite the writerly text, then, is its countervalue, its negative, reactive value: what can be read, but not written: the *readerly.* We call any readerly text a classic text. (S/Z, 4)

Compare the way the designers of Intermedia, one of the most advanced hypertext systems thus far developed, describe the active reader that hypertext requires and creates:

> Both an author's tool and a reader's medium, a hypertext document system allows authors or groups of authors to *link* information together, create *paths* through a corpus of related material, *annotate* existing texts, and create notes that point readers to either bibliographic data or the body of the referenced text. . . . Readers can browse through linked, cross-referenced, annotated texts in an orderly but nonsequential manner.[6]

To get an idea of how hypertext produces Barthes's readerly text, let us examine how you, the reader of this book, would read it in a hypertext version. In the first place, instead of encountering it in a paper copy, you would begin to read it on a computer screen. Contemporary screens, which have neither the portability nor the tactility of printed books, make the act of

---

[6] Nicole Yankelovich, Norman Meyrowitz, and Andries van Dam, "Reading and Writing the Electronic Book," *IEEE Computer* 18 (October 1985): 18.

reading somewhat more difficult. For people like me who do a large portion of their reading reclining on a bed or couch, screens also appear less convenient. At the same time, reading on Intermedia, the hypertext system with which I work, offers certain important compensations. Reading an Intermedia version of this book, for example, you could change the size and even style of font to make reading easier. Although you could not make such changes permanently in the text as seen by others, you could make them whenever you wished.

More important, since you would read this hypertext book on a large two-page graphics monitor, you would have the opportunity to place several texts next to one another. Thus, upon reaching the first note in the main text, which follows the passage just quoted from *S/Z*, you would activate the hypertext equivalent of a reference mark (button, link marker), and this action would bring the endnote into view. A hypertext version of a note differs from that in a printed book in several ways. First, it links directly to the reference symbol and does not reside in some sequentially numbered list at the rear of the main text. Second, once opened and either superimposed upon the main text or placed along side it, it appears as an independent, if connected, document in its own right and not as some sort of subsidiary, supporting, possibly parasitic text.

The note in question contains the following information: "Roland Barthes, *S/Z*, trans. Richard Miller (New York: Hill and Wang, 1974), 5–6." A hypertext lexia equivalent to this note could include this same information, or, more likely, take the form of the quoted passage, a longer section or chapter, or the entire text of Barthes's work. Furthermore, that passage could in turn link to other statements by Barthes of similar import, comments by students of Barthes, and passages by Derrida and Foucault that also concern this notion of the networked text. As a reader, you would have to decide whether to return to my argument, pursue some of the connections I have suggested by links, or, using other capacities of the system, search for connections I had not suggested. The multiplicity of hypertext, which appears in multiple links to individual blocks of text, calls for an active reader.

In addition, a full hypertext system, unlike a book and unlike some of the first approximations of hypertext currently available (HyperCard, Guide), offers the reader and writer the same environment. Therefore, by opening the text-processing program, or editor, as it is known, you can take notes, or you can write against my interpretations, against my text. Although you cannot change my text, you can write a response and then link it to my document. You thus have read the readerly text in two ways not possible with a book: You have chosen your reading path—and since you, like all readers, will choose individualized paths, the hypertext version of this book might take a very different form in your reading, perhaps suggesting the values of alternate routes and probably devoting less room in the main text to quoted passages. You might also have begun to take notes or produce responses to the text as you read, some of which might take the form of texts that either support or contradict interpretations proposed in my texts.

Other Convergences: Intertextuality,
Multivocality, and Decenteredness

Like Barthes, Foucault, and Mikhail Bakhtin, Jacques Derrida continually uses the terms *link (liaison), web (toile), network (réseau)*, and *interwoven (s'y tissent)*, which cry out for hypertextuality;[7] but in contrast to Barthes, who emphasizes the readerly text and its nonlinearity, Derrida emphasizes textual openness, intertextuality, and the irrelevance of distinctions between inside and outside a particular text. These emphases appear with particular clarity when he claims that "like any text, the text of 'Plato' couldn't not be involved, at least in a virtual, dynamic, lateral manner, with all the worlds that composed the system of the Greek language" (129). Derrida in fact here describes extant hypertext systems in which the active reader in the process of exploring a text, probing it, can call into play dictionaries with morphological analyzers that connect individual words to cognates, derivations, and opposites. Here again something that Derrida and other critical theorists describe as part of a seemingly extravagant claim about language turns out precisely to describe the new economy of reading and writing with electronic virtual, rather than physical, forms.

Derrida properly acknowledges (in advance, one might say) that a new, freer, richer form of text, one truer to our potential experience, perhaps to our actual if unrecognized experience, depends upon discrete reading units. As he explains, in what Gregory Ulmer terms "the fundamental generalization of his writing,"[8] there also exists "the possibility of disengagement and citational graft which belongs to the structure of every mark, spoken and written, and which constitutes every mark in writing before and outside of every horizon of semiolinguistic communication. . . . Every sign, linguistic or nonlinguistic, spoken or written . . . can be *cited*, put between quotation marks." The implication of such citability and separability appears in the fact, crucial to hypertext, that, as Derrida adds, "in so doing it can break with every given context, engendering an infinity of new contexts in a manner which is absolutely illimitable."[9]

Like Barthes, Derrida conceives of text as constituted by discrete reading units. Derrida's conception of text relates to his "methodology of decomposition" that might transgress the limits of philosophy. "The organ of this new philosopheme," as Gregory Ulmer points out, "is the mouth, the mouth that bites, chews, tastes. . . . The first step of decomposition is the bite" (57). Derrida, who describes text in terms of something close to Barthes's lexias,

---

[7] See, for example, Jacques Derrida, *La Dissémination* (Paris: Éditions de Seuil, 1972), 71, 108, 172, 111; *Dissemination*, trans. Barbara Johnson (Chicago: University of Chicago Press, 1981), 96, 63, 98, 149. Subsequent references are to the English translation.

[8] Gregory L. Ulmer, *Applied Grammatology: Post(e)-Pedagogy from Jacques Derrida to Joseph Beuys* (Baltimore: Johns Hopkins University Press, 1985), 58.

[9] Jacques Derrida, "Signature Event Context," *Glyph 1: Johns Hopkins Textual Studies* (Baltimore: Johns Hopkins University Press, 1977), 185. Quoted by Ulmer, *Applied Grammatology*, 58–59.

explains in *Glas* that "the object of the present work, its style too, is the 'mourceau,'" which Ulmer translates as "bit, piece, morsel, fragment; musical composition; snack, mouthful." This *mourceau*, adds Derrida, "is always detached, as its name indicates and so you do not forget it, with the teeth," and these teeth, Ulmer explains, refer to "quotation marks, brackets, parentheses: when language is cited (put between quotation marks), the effect is that of releasing the grasp or hold of a controlling context" (58).

Derrida's groping for a way to foreground his recognition of the way text operates in a print medium—he is, after all, the fierce advocate of writing as against orality—shows the position, possibly the dilemma, of the thinker working with print who sees its shortcomings but for all his brilliance cannot think his way outside this *mentalité*. Derrida, the experience of hypertext shows, gropes toward a new kind of text: he describes it, he praises it, but he can present it only in terms of the devices—here those of punctuation—associated with a particular kind of writing. As the Marxists remind us, thought derives from the forces and modes of production, though, as we shall see, few Marxists or Marxians ever directly confront the most important mode of literary production—that dependent upon the *techne* of writing and print.

From this Derridean emphasis upon discontinuity comes the conception of hypertext as a vast assemblage, what I have elsewhere termed the *metatext* and what Nelson calls the "docuverse." Derrida in fact employs the word *assemblage* for cinema, which he perceives as a rival, an alternative, to print. Ulmer points out that "the gram or trace provides the 'linguistics' for collage/montage" (267), and he quotes Derrida's use of *assemblage* in *Speech and Phenomena*: "The word 'assemblage' seems more apt for suggesting that the kind of bringing-together proposed here has the structure of an interlacing, a weaving, or a web, which would allow the different threads and different liens of sense or force to separate again, as well as being ready to bind others together."[10] To carry Derrida's instinctive theorizing of hypertext further, one may also point to his recognition that such a montagelike textuality marks or foregrounds the writing process and therefore rejects a deceptive transparency.

Hypertext and Intertextuality

Hypertext, which is a fundamentally intertextual system, has the capacity to emphasize intertextuality in a way that page-bound text in books cannot. As we have already observed, scholarly articles and books offer an obvious example of *explicit* hypertextuality in nonelectronic form. Conversely, any work of literature—which for the sake of argument and economy I shall here confine in a most arbitrary way to mean "high" literature of the sort we read and teach in universities—offers an instance of *implicit* hypertext in nonelectronic form. Again, take Joyce's *Ulysses* as an example. If one looks, say, at the Nau-

---

[10]Jacques Derrida, *Speech and Phenomena*, trans. David B. Allison (Evanston, Ill.: Northwestern University Press, 1973), 131.

sicaa section, in which Bloom watches Gerty McDowell on the beach, one notes that Joyce's text here "alludes" or "refers" (the terms we usually employ) to many other texts or phenomena that one can treat as texts, including the Nausicaa section of the *Odyssey*, the advertisements and articles in the women's magazines that suffuse and inform Gerty's thoughts, facts about contemporary Dublin and the Catholic Church, and material that relates to other passages within the novel. Again, a hypertext presentation of the novel links this section not only to the kinds of materials mentioned but also to other works in Joyce's career, critical commentary, and textual variants. Hypertext here permits one to make explicit, though not necessarily intrusive, the linked materials that an educated reader perceives surrounding it.

Thaïs Morgan suggests that intertextuality, "as a structural analysis of texts in relation to the larger system of signifying practices or uses of signs in culture," shifts attention from the triad constituted by author/work/tradition to another constituted by text/discourse/culture. In so doing, "intertextuality replaces the evolutionary model of literary history with a structural or synchronic model of literature as a sign system. The most salient effect of this strategic change is to free the literary text from psychological, sociological, and historical determinisms, opening it up to an apparently infinite play of relationships."[11] Morgan well describes a major implication of hypertext (and hypermedia) intertextuality: such opening up, such freeing one to create and perceive interconnections, obviously occurs. Nonetheless, although hypertext intertextuality would seem to devalue any historic or other reductionism, it in no way prevents those interested in reading in terms of author and tradition from doing so. Experiments thus far with Intermedia, HyperCard, and other hypertext systems suggest that hypertext does not necessarily turn one's attention away from such approaches. What is perhaps most interesting about hypertext, though, is not that it may fulfill certain claims of structuralist and poststructuralist criticism but that it provides a rich means of testing them.

Hypertext and Multivocality

In attempting to imagine the experience of reading and writing with (or within) this new form of text, one would do well to pay heed to what Mikhail Bakhtin has written about the dialogic, polyphonic, multivocal novel, which he claims "is constructed not as the whole of a single consciousness, absorbing other consciousness as objects into itself, but as a whole formed by the interaction of several consciousnesses, none of which entirely becomes an object for the other."[12] Bakhtin's description of the polyphonic literary form presents the Dostoevskian novel as a hypertextual fiction in which the individual voices take the form of lexias.

---

[11] Thaïs E. Morgan, "Is There an Intertext in This Text?: Literary and Interdisciplinary Approaches to Intertextuality," *American Journal of Semiotics* 3 (1985): 1–2.

[12] Mikhail Bakhtin, *Problems of Dostoevsky's Poetics*, ed. and trans. Caryl Emerson (Minneapolis: University of Minnesota Press, 1984), 18.

If Derrida illuminates hypertextuality from the vantage point of the "bite" or "bit," Bakhtin illuminates it from the vantage point of its own life and force—its incarnation or instantiation of a voice, a point of view, a Rortyian conversation.[13] Thus, according to Bakhtin, "in the novel itself, non-participating 'third persons' are not represented in any way. There is no place for them, compositionally or in the larger meaning of the work" (*Problems*, 18). In terms of hypertextuality this points to an important quality of this information medium: hypertext does not permit a tyrannical, univocal voice. Rather the voice is always that distilled from the combined experience of the momentary focus, the lexia one presently reads, and the continually forming narrative of one's reading path.

Hypertext and De-centering

As readers move through a web or network of texts, they continually shift the center—and hence the focus or organizing principle—of their investigation and experience. Hypertext, in other words, provides an infinitely re-centerable system whose provisional point of focus depends upon the reader, who becomes a truly active reader in yet another sense. One of the fundamental characteristics of hypertext is that it is composed of bodies of linked texts that have no primary axis of organization. In other words, the metatext or document set—the entity that describes what in print technology is the book, work, or single text—has no center. Although this absence of a center can create problems for the reader and the writer, it also means that anyone who uses hypertext makes his or her own interests the de facto organizing principle (or center) for the investigation at the moment. One experiences hypertext as an infinitely de-centerable and re-centerable system, in part because hypertext transforms any document that has more than one link into a transient center, a directory document that one can employ to orient oneself and to decide where to go next.

Western culture imagined such quasi-magical entrances to a networked reality long before the development of computing technology. Biblical typology, which played such a major role in English culture during the seventeenth and nineteenth centuries, conceived sacred history in terms of types and shadows of Christ and his dispensation.[14] Thus, Moses, who existed in his own right, also existed as Christ, who fulfilled and completed the

---

[13] I am thinking of Richard Rorty's description of edifying philosophy as a conversation: "To see keeping a conversation going as a sufficient aim of philosophy, to see wisdom as consisting in the ability to sustain a conversation, is to see human beings as generators of new descriptions rather than beings one hopes to be able to describe accurately. To see the aim of philosophy as truth—namely, the truth about the terms which provide ultimate commensuration for all human inquiries and activities—is to see human beings as objects rather than subjects, as existing *en-soi* rather than as both *pour-soi* and *en-soi*, as both described objects and describing subjects" (*Philosophy and the Mirror of Nature* [Princeton: Princeton University Press, 1979], 378). To a large extent, Rorty can be thought of as the philosopher of hypertextuality.

[14] George P. Landow, *Victorian Types, Victorian Shadows: Biblical Typology and Victorian Literature, Art, and Thought* (Boston: Routledge and Kegan Paul, 1980).

prophet's meaning. As countless seventeenth-century and Victorian sermons, tracts, and commentaries demonstrate, any particular person, event, or phenomenon acted as a magical window into the complex semiotic of the divine scheme for human salvation. Like the biblical type, which allows significant events and phenomena to participate simultaneously in many realities or levels of reality, the individual lexia inevitably provides a way into the network of connections. Given that evangelical Protestantism in America preserves and extends these traditions of biblical exegesis, one is not surprised to discover that some of the first applications of hypertext involved the Bible and its exegetical tradition.[15]

Not only do lexia work much in the manner of types, they also become Borgesian Alephs, points in space that contain all other points, because from the vantage point each provides one can see everything else—if not exactly simultaneously, then a short way distant, one or two jumps away, particularly in systems that have full text searching. Unlike Jorge Luis Borges's Aleph, one does not have to view it from a single site, neither does one have to sprawl in a cellar resting one's head on a canvas sack.[16] The hypertext document becomes a traveling Aleph.

Such capacity has an obvious relation to the ideas of Derrida, who emphasizes the need to shift vantage points by de-centering discussion. As Derrida points out in "Structure, Sign, and Play in the Discourse of the Human Sciences," the process or procedure he calls de-centering has played an essential role in intellectual change. He says, for example, that "ethnology could have been born as a science only at the moment when a de-centering had come about: at the moment when European culture—and, in consequence, the history of metaphysics and of its concepts—had been *dislocated,* driven from its locus, and forced to stop considering itself as the culture of reference."[17] Derrida makes no claim that an intellectual or ideological center is in any way bad, for, as he explains in response to a query from Serge Doubrovsky, "I didn't say that there was no center, that we could get along without the center. I believe that the center is a function, not a being—a reality, but a function. And this function is absolutely indispensable" (271).

[15] Examples include *GodSpeed Instant Bible Search Program,* from Kingdom Age Software in San Diego, California, and the Dallas Seminary CD-Word Project, which builds upon Guide, a hypertext system developed by OWL (Office Workstations Limited) International. See Steven J. DeRose, "Biblical Studies and Hypertext," in *Hypermedia and Literary Studies,* ed. Paul Delany and George P. Landow (Cambridge: MIT Press, 1991), 185–204.

[16] Jorge Luis Borges, "The Aleph," in *The Aleph and Other Stories, 1933–1969,* trans. Norman Thomas di Giovanni (New York: Bantam, 1971), 13: "In that single gigantic instant I saw millions of acts both delightful and awful; not one of them amazed me more than the fact that all of them occupied the same point in space, without overlapping or transparency. What my eyes beheld was simultaneous, but what I shall now write down will be successive, because language is successive.... The Aleph's diameter was probably little more than an inch, but all space was there, actual and undiminished. Each thing (a mirror's face, let us say) was infinite things, since I saw it from every angle of the universe."

[17] Jacques Derrida, "Structure, Sign, and Play in the Discourse of the Human Sciences," in *The Structuralist Controversy: The Languages of Criticism and the Sciences of Man* (Baltimore: Johns Hopkins University Press, 1972), 251.

All hypertext systems permit the individual reader to choose his or her own center of investigation and experience. What this principle means in practice is that the reader is not locked into any kind of particular organization or hierarchy. Experiences with Intermedia reveal that for those who choose to organize a session on the system in terms of authors—moving, say, from Keats to Tennyson—the system represents an old-fashioned, traditional, and in many ways still useful author-centered approach. On the other hand, nothing constrains the reader to work in this manner, and readers who wish to investigate the validity of period generalizations can organize their sessions in terms of such periods by using the Victorian and Romantic overviews as starting or midpoints while yet others can begin with ideological or critical notions, such as feminism or the Victorian novel. In practice most readers employ the materials developed at Brown University as a text-centered system, since they tend to focus upon individual works, with the result that even if they begin sessions by entering the system to look for information about an individual author, they tend to spend most time with lexias devoted to specific texts, moving between poem and poem (Swinburne's "Laus Veneris" and Keats's "La Belle Dame Sans Merci" or works centering on Ulysses by Joyce, Tennyson, and Soyinka) and between poem and informational texts ("Laus Veneris" and files on chivalry, medieval revival, courtly love, Wagner, and so on).

HOMI K. BHABHA

The Postcolonial and the Postmodern: The Question of Agency

From *Locations of Culture*

1994

———————

Born in Bombay and educated in both India and England, Homi Bhabha (b. 1949) was exposed early to the conflicts and congruencies of culture that characterize both colonized and colonizing peoples. He is well known for his work in the field of cultural criticism known as postcolonial studies. As the name implies, postcolonial criticism tends to focus on works produced in those portions of the world that were once part of the large European colonial empires that reached their height in the nineteenth century. For Bhabha, though, the notion of postcoloniality encompasses more than this and has significance even for peoples who were never colonized in the most traditional sense of the word. The breadth of his interest and diversity of what he would include under the rubric of "postcolonial" is suggested in the following excerpt, which touches on race and ethnicity, gender, sexuality, and even the threat of AIDS, as well as the more central postcolonial concerns of nation and identity.

    Like many postmodern critics, Bhabha begins with the importance of subject positions. Each of us, the theory goes, occupies a subject position comprised of such factors as our race, class, gender, age, nationality, religion, state of health, and so forth. These factors are major determinants not only in our lifestyles but in our behavior toward others, our thinking patterns, and our very concept of ourselves. Bhabha, however, is not content with a static conception of the subject position and its impact on human behavior (thus, ultimately, on the formation of culture). For him, subjectivity and culture are always moving targets, evolving as different cultures and peoples negotiate with one another in a complex and ever-shifting world. His interest in "cultural hybridities" keeps him focused on the interstices, or the in-between, of the many cultures that collide for all of us in daily life.

    In the following excerpt, though he refers to many cultures, texts, and subjectivities, he focuses most closely on two books. Toni Morrison's Beloved *is the story of an African American slave driven to infanticide in an attempt to save her daughter from the terrors and indignities that have plagued her own life. Nadine Gordimer's* My Son's Story *depicts the struggles of a mulatto (or, in the language of South Africa, "coloured") woman who feels herself to live forever in a "halfway be-tween . . . not defined" world. Bhabha finds these novels and these characters partic-ularly revealing because their problems transcend any static conception of culture. For them, as for Bhabha, culture and identity are shifting and difficult to articulate. They therefore foreground the condition of all humanity: we must all perform our identities and define ourselves out of the places where cultures come into contact and often into conflict.*

A boundary is not that at which something stops but, as the Greeks recognized, the boundary is that from which *something begins its pres-encing.*

— Martin Heidegger, 'Building, dwelling, thinking'

Border Lives: The Art of the Present

IT IS THE TROPE of our times to locate the question of culture in the realm of the *beyond*. At the century's edge, we are less exercised by annihilation—the death of the author—or epiphany—the birth of the 'subject'. Our existence today is marked by a tenebrous sense of survival, living on the borderlines of the 'present', for which there seems to be no proper name other than the cur-rent and controversial shiftiness of the prefix 'post': *postmodernism, postcolo-nialism, postfeminism. . . .*

The 'beyond' is neither a new horizon, nor a leaving behind of the past. . . . Beginnings and endings may be the sustaining myths of the middle years; but in the *fin de siècle,* we find ourselves in the moment of transit where space and time cross to produce complex figures of difference and identity, past and present, inside and outside, inclusion and exclusion. For there is a sense of disorientation, a disturbance of direction, in the 'beyond': an ex-ploratory, restless movement caught so well in the French rendition of the words *au-delà*—here and there, on all sides, *fort/da,* hither and thither, back and forth.[1]

The move away from the singularities of 'class' or 'gender' as primary conceptual and organizational categories, has resulted in an awareness of the subject positions—of race, gender, generation, institutional location, geopo-litical locale, sexual orientation—that inhabit any claim to identity in the modern world. What is theoretically innovative, and politically crucial, is the need to think beyond narratives of originary and initial subjectivities and to

---

[1] For an interesting discussion of gender boundaries in the *fin de siècle,* see E. Showalter, *Sexual Anarchy: Gender and Culture in the Fin de Siècle* (London: Bloomsbury, 1990), especially 'Borderlines', pp. 1–18. [All notes are Bhabha's.]

focus on those moments or processes that are produced in the articulation of cultural differences. These 'in-between' spaces provide the terrain for elaborating strategies of selfhood—singular or communal—that initiate new signs of identity, and innovative sites of collaboration, and contestation, in the act of defining the idea of society itself.

It is in the emergence of the interstices—the overlap and displacement of domains of difference—that the intersubjective and collective experiences of *nationness*, community interest, or cultural value are negotiated. How are subjects formed 'in-between', or in excess of, the sum of the 'parts' of difference (usually intoned as race/class/gender, etc.)? How do strategies of representation or empowerment come to be formulated in the competing claims of communities where, despite shared histories of deprivation and discrimination, the exchange of values, meanings and priorities may not always be collaborative and dialogical, but may be profoundly antagonistic, conflictual and even incommensurable?

The force of these questions is borne out by the 'language' of recent social crises sparked off by histories of cultural difference. Conflicts in South Central Los Angeles between Koreans, Mexican-Americans and African-Americans focus on the concept of 'disrespect'—a term forged on the borderlines of ethnic deprivation that is, at once, the sign of racialized violence and the symptom of social victimage. In the aftermath of the *Satanic Verses* affair in Great Britain, Black and Irish feminists, despite their different constituencies, have made common cause against the 'racialization of religion' as the dominant discourse through which the State represents their conflicts and struggles, however secular or even 'sexual' they may be.

Terms of cultural engagement, whether antagonistic or affiliative, are produced performatively. The representation of difference must not be hastily read as the reflection of *pre-given* ethnic or cultural traits set in the fixed tablet of tradition. The social articulation of difference, from the minority perspective, is a complex, on-going negotiation that seeks to authorize cultural hybridities that emerge in moments of historical transformation. The 'right' to signify from the periphery of authorized power and privilege does not depend on the persistence of tradition; it is resourced by the power of tradition to be reinscribed through the conditions of contingency and contradictoriness that attend upon the lives of those who are 'in the minority'. The recognition that tradition bestows is a partial form of identification. In restaging the past it introduces other, incommensurable cultural temporalities into the invention of tradition. This process estranges any immediate access to an originary identity or a 'received' tradition. The borderline engagements of cultural difference may as often be consensual as conflictual; they may confound our definitions of tradition and modernity; realign the customary boundaries between the private and the public, high and low; and challenge normative expectations of development and progress.

I wanted to make shapes or set up situations that are kind of open. . . . My work has a lot to do with a kind of fluidity, a movement back and forth, not making a claim to any specific or essential way of being.[2]

Thus writes Renée Green, the African-American artist. She reflects on the need to understand cultural difference as the production of minority identities that 'split'—are estranged unto themselves—in the act of being articulated into a collective body:

> Multiculturalism doesn't reflect the complexity of the situation as I face it daily. . . . It requires a person to step outside of him/herself to actually see what he/she is doing. I don't want to condemn well-meaning people and say (like those T-shirts you can buy on the street) 'It's a black thing, you wouldn't understand.' To me that's essentialising blackness.[3]

Political empowerment, and the enlargement of the multiculturalist cause, come from posing questions of solidarity and community from the interstitial perspective. Social differences are not simply given to experience through an already authenticated cultural tradition; they are the signs of the emergence of community envisaged as a project—at once a vision and a construction—that takes you 'beyond' yourself in order to return, in a spirit of revision and reconstruction, to the political *conditions* of the present:

> Even then, it's still a struggle for power between various groups within ethnic groups about what's being said and who's saying what, who's representing who? What is a community anyway? What is a black community? What is a Latino community? I have trouble with thinking of all these things as monolithic fixed categories.[4]

If Renée Green's questions open up an interrogatory, interstitial space between the act of representation—who? what? where?—and the presence of community itself, then consider her own creative intervention within this in-between moment. Green's 'architectural' site-specific work, *Sites of Genealogy* (Out of Site, The Institute of Contemporary Art, Long Island City, New York), displays and displaces the binary logic through which identities of difference are often constructed—Black/White, Self/Other. Green makes a metaphor of the museum building itself, rather than simply using the gallery space:

> I used architecture literally as a reference, using the attic, the boiler room, and the stairwell to make associations between certain binary divisions such as higher and lower and heaven and hell. The stairwell became a liminal space, a pathway between the upper and

---

[2] Renée Green interviewed by Elizabeth Brown, from catalogue published by Allen Memorial Art Museum, Oberlin College, Ohio.

[3] Interview conducted by Miwon Kwon for the exhibition 'Emerging New York Artists', Sala Mendonza, Caracas, Venezuela (xeroxed manuscript copy).

[4] Ibid., p. 6.

lower areas, each of which was annotated with plaques referring to blackness and whiteness.[5]

The stairwell as liminal space, in-between the designations of identity, becomes the process of symbolic interaction, the connective tissue that constructs the difference between upper and lower, black and white. The hither and thither of the stairwell, the temporal movement and passage that it allows, prevents identities at either end of it from settling into primordial polarities. This interstitial passage between fixed identifications opens up the possibility of a cultural hybridity that entertains difference without an assumed or imposed hierarchy:

> I always went back and forth between racial designations and designations from physics or other symbolic designations. All these things blur in some way. . . . To develop a genealogy of the way colours and noncolours function is interesting to me.[6]

'Beyond' signifies spatial distance, marks progress, promises the future; but our intimations of exceeding the barrier or boundary—the very act of going *beyond*—are unknowable, unrepresentable, without a return to the 'present' which, in the process of repetition, becomes disjunct and displaced. The imaginary of spatial distance—to live somehow beyond the border of our times—throws into relief the temporal, social differences that interrupt our collusive sense of cultural contemporaneity. The present can no longer be simply envisaged as a break or a bonding with the past and the future, no longer a synchronic presence: our proximate self-presence, our public image, comes to be revealed for its discontinuities, its inequalities, its minorities. Unlike the dead hand of history that tells the beads of sequential time like a rosary, seeking to establish serial, causal connections, we are now confronted with what Walter Benjamin describes as the blasting of a monadic moment from the homogenous course of history, 'establishing a conception of the present as the "time of the now"'.[7]

If the jargon of our times—postmodernity, postcoloniality, postfeminism—has any meaning at all, it does not lie in the popular use of the 'post' to indicate sequentiality—*after*-feminism; or polarity—*anti*-modernism. These terms that insistently gesture to the beyond, only embody its restless and revisionary energy if they transform the present into an expanded and ex-centric site of experience and empowerment. For instance, if the interest in postmodernism is limited to a celebration of the fragmentation of the 'grand narratives' of postenlightenment rationalism then, for all its intellectual excitement, it remains a profoundly parochial enterprise.

[5] Renée Green in conversation with Donna Harkavy, Curator of Contemporary Art at the Worcester Museum.

[6] Ibid.

[7] W. Benjamin, 'Theses on the philosophy of history', in his *Illuminations* (London: Jonathan Cape, 1970), p. 265.

The wider significance of the postmodern condition lies in the awareness that the epistemological 'limits' of those ethnocentric ideas are also the enunciative boundaries of a range of other dissonant, even dissident histories and voices — women, the colonized, minority groups, the bearers of policed sexualities. For the demography of the new internationalism is the history of postcolonial migration, the narratives of cultural and political diaspora, the major social displacements of peasant and aboriginal communities, the poetics of exile, the grim prose of political and economic refugees. It is in this sense that the boundary becomes the place from which *something begins its presencing* in a movement not dissimilar to the ambulant, ambivalent articulation of the beyond that I have drawn out: 'Always and ever differently the bridge escorts the lingering and hastening ways of men to and fro, so that they may get to other banks. . . . The bridge *gathers* as a passage that crosses.'[8]

The very concepts of homogenous national cultures, the consensual or contiguous transmission of historical traditions, or 'organic' ethnic communities — *as the grounds of cultural comparativism* — are in a profound process of redefinition. The hideous extremity of Serbian nationalism proves that the very idea of a pure, 'ethnically cleansed' national identity can only be achieved through the death, literal and figurative, of the complex interweavings of history, and the culturally contingent borderlines of modern nationhood. This side of the psychosis of patriotic fervour, I like to think, there is overwhelming evidence of a more transnational and translational sense of the hybridity of imagined communities. Contemporary Sri Lankan theatre represents the deadly conflict between the Tamils and the Sinhalese through allegorical references to State brutality in South Africa and Latin America; the Anglo-Celtic canon of Australian literature and cinema is being rewritten from the perspective of Aboriginal political and cultural imperatives; the South African novels of Richard Rive, Bessie Head, Nadine Gordimer, John Coetzee, are documents of a society divided by the effects of apartheid that enjoin the international intellectual community to meditate on the unequal, asymmetrical worlds that exist elsewhere; Salman Rushdie writes the fabulist historiography of post-Independence India and Pakistan in *Midnight's Children* and *Shame,* only to remind us in *The Satanic Verses* that the truest eye may now belong to the migrant's double vision; Toni Morrison's *Beloved* revives the past of slavery and its murderous rituals of possession and self-possession, in order to project a contemporary fable of a woman's history that is at the same time the narrative of an affective, historic memory of an emergent public sphere of men and women alike.

What is striking about the 'new' internationalism is that the move from the specific to the general, from the material to the metaphoric, is not a smooth passage of transition and transcendence. The 'middle passage' of contemporary culture, as with slavery itself, is a process of displacement and disjunction that does not totalize experience. Increasingly, 'national' cultures

---

[8] M. Heidegger, 'Building, dwelling, thinking', in *Poetry, Language, Thought* (New York: Harper & Row, 1971), pp. 152–3.

are being produced from the perspective of disenfranchised minorities. The most significant effect of this process is not the proliferation of 'alternative histories of the excluded' producing, as some would have it, a pluralist anarchy. What my examples show is the changed basis for making international connections. The currency of critical comparativism, or aesthetic judgement, is no longer the sovereignty of the national culture conceived as Benedict Anderson proposes as an 'imagined community' rooted in a 'homogeneous empty time' of modernity and progress. The great connective narratives of capitalism and class drive the engines of social reproduction, but do not, in themselves, provide a foundational frame for those modes of cultural identification and political affect that form around issues of sexuality, race, feminism, the lifeworld of refugees or migrants, or the deathly social destiny of AIDS.

The testimony of my examples represents a radical revision in the concept of human community itself. What this geopolitical space may be, as a local or transnational reality, is being both interrogated and reinitiated. Feminism, in the 1990s, finds its solidarity as much in liberatory narratives as in the painful ethical position of a slavewoman, Morrison's Sethe, in *Beloved*, who is pushed to infanticide. The body politic can no longer contemplate the nation's health as simply a civic virtue; it must rethink the question of rights for the entire national, and international, community, from the AIDS perspective. The Western metropole must confront its postcolonial history, told by its influx of postwar migrants and refugees, as an indigenous or native narrative *internal to its national identity;* and the reason for this is made clear in the stammering, drunken words of Mr. 'Whisky' Sisodia from *The Satanic Verses:* 'The trouble with the Engenglish is that their hiss hiss history happened overseas, so they dodo don't know what it means.'[9]

Postcoloniality, for its part, is a salutary reminder of the persistent 'neocolonial' relations within the 'new' world order and the multinational division of labour. Such a perspective enables the authentication of histories of exploitation and the evolution of strategies of resistance. Beyond this, however, postcolonial critique bears witness to those countries and communities—in the North and the South, urban and rural—constituted, if I may coin a phrase, 'otherwise than modernity'. Such cultures of a postcolonial *contra-modernity* may be contingent to modernity, discontinuous or in contention with it, resistant to its oppressive, assimilationist technologies; but they also deploy the cultural hybridity of their borderline conditions to 'translate', and therefore reinscribe, the social imaginary of both metropolis and modernity. Listen to Guillermo Gomez-Peña, the performance artist who lives, amongst other times and places, on the Mexico/US border:

hello America
this is the voice of *Gran Vato Charollero*
broadcasting from the hot deserts of Nogales, Arizona

[9] S. Rushdie, *The Satanic Verses* (London: Viking, 1988), p. 343.

zona de libre cogercio
2000 megaherz en todas direciones

you are celebrating Labor Day in Seattle
while the Klan demonstrates
against Mexicans in Georgia
ironia, 100% ironia[10]

Being in the 'beyond', then, is to inhabit an intervening space, as any dictionary will tell you. But to dwell 'in the beyond' is also, as I have shown, to be part of a revisionary time, a return to the present to redescribe our cultural contemporaneity; to reinscribe our human, historic commonality; *to touch the future on its hither side.* In that sense, then, the intervening space 'beyond', becomes a space of intervention in the here and now. To engage with such invention, and intervention, as Green and Gomez-Peña enact in their distinctive work, requires a sense of the new that resonates with the hybrid chicano aesthetic of *'rasquachismo'* as Tomas Ybarra-Frausto describes it:

> the utilization of available resources for syncretism, juxtaposition, and integration. *Rasquachismo* is a sensibility attuned to mixtures and confluence... a delight in texture and sensuous surfaces... self-conscious manipulation of materials or iconography... the combination of found material and satiric wit... the manipulation of *rasquache* artifacts, code and sensibilities from both sides of the border.[11]

The borderline work of culture demands an encounter with 'newness' that is not part of the continuum of past and present. It creates a sense of the new as an insurgent act of cultural translation. Such art does not merely recall the past as social cause or aesthetic precedent; it renews the past, refiguring it as a contingent 'in-between' space, that innovates and interrupts the performance of the present. The 'past-present' becomes part of the necessity, not the nostalgia, of living.

Pepon Osorio's *objets trouvés* of the Nuyorican (New York/Puerto Rican) community—the statistics of infant mortality, or the silent (and silenced) spread of AIDS in the Hispanic community—are elaborated into baroque allegories of social alienation. But it is not the high drama of birth and death that captures Osorio's spectacular imagination. He is the great celebrant of the migrant act of survival, using his mixed-media works to make a hybrid cultural space that forms contingently, disjunctively, in the inscription of signs of cultural memory and sites of political agency. *La Cama (The Bed)* turns the highly decorated four-poster into the primal scene of lost-and-found childhood memories, the memorial to a dead nanny Juana, the *mise-en-scène* of the eroticism of the 'emigrant' everyday. Survival, for Osorio, is

[10] G. Gomez-Peña, *American Theatre,* vol. 8, no. 7, October 1991.
[11] T. Ybarra-Frausto, 'Chicano movement/chicano art,' in I. Karp and S.D. Lavine (eds.) (Washington and London: Smithsonian Institution Press, 1991), pp. 133–4.

working in the interstices of a range of practices: the 'space' of installation, the spectacle of the social statistic, the transitive time of the body in performance.

Finally, it is the photographic art of Alan Sekula that takes the borderline condition of cultural translation to its global limit in *Fish Story*, his photographic project on harbours: 'the harbour is the site in which material goods appear in bulk, in the very flux of exchange'.[12] The harbour and the stockmarket become the *paysage moralisé* of a containerized, computerized world of global trade. Yet, the non-synchronous time-space of transnational 'exchange', and exploitation, is embodied in a navigational allegory:

> Things are more confused now. A scratchy recording of the Norwegian national anthem blares out from a loudspeaker at the Sailor's Home on the bluff above the channel. The container ship being greeted flies a Bahamian flag of convenience. It was built by Koreans working long hours in the giant shipyards of Ulsan. The underpaid and the understaffed crew could be Salvadorean or Filipino. Only the Captain hears a familiar melody.[13]

Norway's nationalist nostalgia cannot drown out the babel on the bluff. Transnational capitalism and the impoverishment of the Third World certainly create the chains of circumstance that incarcerate the Salvadorean or the Filipino/a. In their cultural passage, hither and thither, as migrant workers, part of the massive economic and political diaspora of the modern world, they embody the Benjaminian 'present': that moment blasted out of the continuum of history. Such conditions of cultural displacement and social discrimination—where political survivors become the best historical witnesses—are the grounds on which Frantz Fanon, the Martinican psychoanalyst and participant in the Algerian revolution, locates an agency of empowerment:

> As soon as I *desire* I am asking to be considered. I am not merely here-and-now, sealed into thingness. I am for somewhere else and for something else. I demand that notice be taken of my *negating activity* [my emphasis] insofar as I pursue something other than life; insofar as I do battle for the creation of a human world—that is a world of reciprocal recognitions.

> I should constantly remind myself that the real *leap* consists in introducing invention into existence.
>
>   In the world in which I travel, I am endlessly creating myself. And it is by going beyond the historical, instrumental hypothesis that I will initiate my cycle of freedom.[14]

---

[12] A. Sekula, *Fish Story*, manuscript, p. 2.

[13] Ibid., p. 3.

[14] F. Fanon, *Black Skin, White Masks*, Introduction by H. K. Bhabha (London: Pluto, 1986), pp. 218, 229, 231.

Once more it is the desire for recognition, 'for somewhere else and for something else' that takes the experience of history *beyond* the instrumental hypothesis. Once again, it is the space of intervention emerging in the cultural interstices that introduces creative invention into existence. And one last time, there is a return to the performance of identity as iteration, the recreation of the self in the world of travel, the resettlement of the borderline community of migration. Fanon's desire for the recognition of cultural presence as 'negating activity' resonates with my breaking of the time-barrier of a culturally collusive 'present'.

Unhomely Lives: The Literature of Recognition

Fanon recognizes the crucial importance, for subordinated peoples, of asserting their indigenous cultural traditions and retrieving their repressed histories. But he is far too aware of the dangers of the fixity and fetishism of identities within the calcification of colonial cultures to recommend that 'roots' be struck in the celebratory romance of the past or by homogenizing the history of the present. The negating activity is, indeed, the intervention of the 'beyond' that establishes a boundary: a bridge, where 'presencing' begins because it captures something of the estranging sense of the relocation of the home and the world—the unhomeliness—that is the condition of extra-territorial and cross-cultural initiations. To be unhomed is not to be homeless, nor can the 'unhomely' be easily accommodated in that familiar division of social life into private and public spheres. The unhomely moment creeps up on you stealthily as your own shadow and suddenly you find yourself with Henry James's Isabel Archer, in *The Portrait of a Lady*, taking the measure of your dwelling in a state of 'incredulous terror'.[15] And it is at this point that the world first shrinks for Isabel and then expands enormously. As she struggles to survive the fathomless waters, the rushing torrents, James introduces us to the 'unhomeliness' inherent in that rite of extra-territorial and cross-cultural initiation. The recesses of the domestic space become sites for history's most intricate invasions. In that displacement, the borders between home and world become confused; and, uncannily, the private and the public become part of each other, forcing upon us a vision that is as divided as it is disorienting.

Although the 'unhomely' is a paradigmatic colonial and post-colonial condition, it has a resonance that can be heard distinctly, if erratically, in fictions that negotiate the powers of cultural difference in a range of transhistorical sites. You have already heard the shrill alarm of the unhomely in that moment when Isabel Archer realizes that her world has been reduced to one high, mean window, as her house of fiction becomes 'the house of darkness, the house of dumbness, the house of suffocation'.[16] If you hear it thus at

[15] H. James, *The Portrait of a Lady* (New York: Norton, 1975), p. 360.
[16] Ibid., p. 361.

the Palazzo Roccanera in the late 1870s, then a little earlier in 1873 on the outskirts of Cincinnati, in mumbling houses like 124 Bluestone Road, you hear the undecipherable language of the black and angry dead; the voice of Toni Morrison's *Beloved*, 'the thoughts of the women of 124, unspeakable thoughts, unspoken'.[17] More than a quarter of a century later in 1905, Bengal is ablaze with the Swadeshi or Home Rule movement when 'home-made Bimala, the product of the confined space', as Tagore describes her in *The Home and the World*, is aroused by 'a running undertone of melody, low down in the bass . . . the true manly note, the note of power'. Bimala is possessed and drawn forever from the zenana, the secluded women's quarters, as she crosses that fated verandah into the world of public affairs—'over to another shore and the ferry had ceased to ply'.[18] Much closer to our own times in contemporary South Africa, Nadine Gordimer's heroine Aila in *My Son's Story* emanates a stilling atmosphere as she makes her diminished domesticity into the perfect cover for gun-running: suddenly the home turns into another world, and the narrator notices that 'It was as if everyone found that he had unnoticingly entered a strange house, *and it was hers. . . .* '[19]

The historical specificities and cultural diversities that inform each of these texts would make a global argument purely gestural; in any case, I shall only be dealing with Morrison and Gordimer in any detail. But the 'unhomely' does provide a 'non-continuist' problematic that dramatizes—in the figure of woman—the ambivalent structure of the civil State as it draws its rather paradoxical boundary between the private and the public spheres. If, for Freud, the *unheimlich* is 'the name for everything that ought to have remained . . . secret and hidden but has come to light', then Hannah Arendt's description of the public and private realms is a profoundly unhomely one: 'it is the distinction between things that should be hidden and things that should be shown', she writes, which through their inversion in the modern age 'discovers how rich and manifold the hidden can be under conditions of intimacy'.[20]

This logic of reversal, that turns on a disavowal, informs the profound revelations and reinscriptions of the unhomely moment. For what was 'hidden from sight' for Arendt, becomes in Carole Pateman's *The Disorder of Women* the 'ascriptive domestic sphere' that is *forgotten* in the theoretical distinctions of the private and public spheres of civil society. Such a forgetting—or disavowal—creates an uncertainty at the heart of the generalizing subject of civil society, compromising the 'individual' that is the support for its universalist aspiration. By making visible the forgetting of the 'unhomely' moment in civil society, feminism specifies the patriarchal, gendered nature of civil society and disturbs the symmetry of private and public which is now

---

[17] T. Morrison, *Beloved* (London: Chatto & Windus, 1987), pp. 198–9.

[18] R. Tagore, *The Home and the World* (Harmondsworth: Penguin, 1985), pp. 70–1.

[19] N. Gordimer, *My Son's Story* (London: Bloomsbury, 1990), p. 249.

[20] S. Freud, 'The uncanny', Standard Edition XVII, p. 225; H. Arendt, *The Human Condition* (Chicago: Chicago University Press, 1958), p. 72.

shadowed, or uncannily doubled, by the difference of genders which does not neatly map on to the private and the public, but becomes disturbingly supplementary to them. This results in redrawing the domestic space as the space of the normalizing, pastoralizing, and individuating techniques of modern power and police: the personal-*is*-the-political; the world-*in*-the-home.

The unhomely moment relates the traumatic ambivalences of a personal, psychic history to the wider disjunctions of political existence. Beloved, the child murdered by her own mother, Sethe, is a daemonic, belated repetition of the violent history of black infant deaths, during slavery, in many parts of the South, less than a decade after the haunting of 124 Bluestone Road. (Between 1882 and 1895 from one-third to a half of the annual black mortality rate was accounted for by children under five years of age.) But the memory of Sethe's act of infanticide emerges through 'the holes—the things the fugitives did not say; the questions they did not ask . . . the unnamed, the unmentioned'.[21] As we reconstruct the narrative of child murder through Sethe, the slave mother, who is herself the victim of social death, the very historical basis of our ethical judgement undergoes a radical revision.

Such forms of social and psychic existence can best be represented in that tenuous survival of literary language itself, which allows memory to speak:

> while knowing Speech can (be) at best, a shadow echoing
> the silent light, bear witness
> To the truth, it is not . . .

W. H. Auden wrote those lines on the powers of *poesis* in *The Cave of Making*, aspiring to be, as he put it, 'a minor Atlantic Goethe'.[22] And it is to an intriguing suggestion in Goethe's final 'Note on world literature' (1830) that I now turn to find a comparative method that would speak to the 'unhomely' condition of the modern world.

Goethe suggests that the possibility of a world literature arises from the cultural confusion wrought by terrible wars and mutual conflicts. Nations

> could not return to their settled and independent life again without noticing that they had learned many foreign ideas and ways, which they had unconsciously adopted, and come to feel here and there previously unrecognized spiritual and intellectual needs.[23]

Goethe's immediate reference is, of course, to the Napoleonic wars and his concept of 'the feeling of neighbourly relations' is profoundly Eurocentric, extending as far as England and France. However, as an Orientalist who read Shakuntala at seventeen years of age, and who writes in his autobiography of

---

[21] Morrison, *Beloved*, p. 170.

[22] W. H. Auden, 'The cave of making', in his *About the House* (London: Faber, 1959), p. 20.

[23] *Goethe's Literary Essays*, J. E. Spingarn (ed.) (New York: Harcourt, Brace, 1921), pp. 98–9.

the 'unformed and overformed'[24] monkey god Hanuman, Goethe's speculations are open to another line of thought.

What of the more complex cultural situation where 'previously unrecognized spiritual and intellectual needs' emerge from the imposition of 'foreign' ideas, cultural representations, and structures of power? Goethe suggests that the 'inner nature of the whole nation as well as the individual man
works all unconsciously'.[25] When this is placed alongside his idea that the
cultural life of the nation is 'unconsciously' lived, then there may be a sense
in which world literature could be an emergent, prefigurative category that
is concerned with a form of cultural dissensus and alterity, where non-
consensual terms of affiliation may be established on the grounds of historical trauma. The study of world literature might be the study of the way in
which cultures recognize themselves through their projections of 'otherness'.
Where, once, the transmission of national traditions was the major theme of a
world literature, perhaps we can now suggest that transnational histories of
migrants, the colonized, or political refugees—these border and frontier conditions—may be the terrains of world literature. The centre of such a study
would neither be the 'sovereignty' of national cultures, nor the universalism
of human culture, but a focus on those 'freak social and cultural displacements' that Morrison and Gordimer represent in their 'unhomely' fictions.
Which leads us to ask: can the perplexity of the unhomely, intrapersonal
world lead to an international theme?

If we are seeking a 'worlding' of literature, then perhaps it lies in a critical act that attempts to grasp the sleight of hand with which literature conjures with historical specificity, using the medium of psychic uncertainty,
aesthetic distancing, or the obscure signs of the spirit-world, the sublime and
the subliminal. As literary creatures and political animals we ought to concern ourselves with the understanding of human action and the social world
as a moment when *something is beyond control, but it is not beyond accommoda-
tion.* This act of writing the world, of taking the measure of its dwelling, is
magically caught in Morrison's description of her house of fiction—art as
'the fully realized presence of a haunting'[26] of history. Read as an image that
describes the relation of art to social reality, my translation of Morrison's
phrase becomes a statement on the political responsibility of the critic. For
the critic must attempt to fully realize, and take responsibility for, the unspoken, unrepresented pasts that haunt the historical present.

Our task remains, however, to show how historical agency is transformed through the signifying process; how the historical event is represented in a discourse that is *somehow beyond control.* This is in keeping with
Hannah Arendt's suggestion that the author of social action may be the ini-
tiator of its unique meaning, but as agent he or she cannot control its outcome. It is not simply what the house of fiction contains or 'controls' *as*

[24] *The Autobiography of Goethe,* J. Oxenford (ed.) (London: Henry G. Bohn, 1948), p. 467.
[25] Goethe, 'Note on world literature', p. 96.
[26] T. Morrison, *Honey and Rue* programme notes, Carnegie Hall Concert, January 1991.

content. What is just as important is the metaphoricity of the houses of racial memory that both Morrison and Gordimer construct—those subjects of the narrative that mutter or mumble like 124 Bluestone Road, or keep a still silence in a 'grey' Cape Town suburb.

Each of the houses in Gordimer's *My Son's Story* is invested with a specific secret or a conspiracy, an unhomely stirring. The house in the ghetto is the house of the collusiveness of the coloureds in their antagonistic relations to the blacks; the lying house is the house of Sonny's adultery; then there is the silent house of Aila's revolutionary camouflage; there is also the nocturnal house of Will, the narrator, writing of the narrative that charts the phoenix rising in his home, while the words must turn to ashes in his mouth. But each 'unhomely' house marks a deeper historical displacement. And that is the condition of being 'coloured' in South Africa, or as Will describes it, 'halfway between . . . being not defined—and it was this lack of definition in itself that was never to be questioned, but observed like a taboo, something which no one, while following, could ever admit to'.[27]

This halfway house of racial and cultural origins bridges the 'in-between' diasporic origins of the coloured South African and turns it into the symbol for the disjunctive, displaced everyday life of the liberation struggle: 'like so many others of this kind, whose families are fragmented in the diaspora of exile, code names, underground activity, people for whom a real home and attachments are something for others who will come after'.[28]

Private and public, past and present, the psyche and the social develop an interstitial intimacy. It is an intimacy that questions binary divisions through which such spheres of social experience are often spatially opposed. These spheres of life are linked through an 'in-between' temporality that takes the measure of dwelling at home, while producing an image of the world of history. This is the moment of aesthetic distance that provides the narrative with a double edge, which like the coloured South African subject represents a hybridity, a difference 'within', a subject that inhabits the rim of an 'in-between' reality. And the inscription of this borderline existence inhabits a stillness of time and a strangeness of framing that creates the discursive 'image' at the crossroads of history and literature, bridging the home and the world.

Such a strange stillness is visible in the portrait of Aila. Her husband Sonny, now past his political prime, his affair with his white revolutionary lover in abeyance, makes his first prison visit to see his wife. The wardress stands back, the policeman fades, and Aila emerges as an unhomely presence, on the opposite side from her husband and son:

> but through the familiar beauty there was a vivid strangeness. . . . It was as if some chosen experience had seen in her, as a painter will in his subject, what she was, what was there to be discovered. In

---

[27] Gordimer, *My Son's Story,* pp. 20–1.
[28] Ibid., p. 21.

Lusaka, in secret, in prison—who knows where—she had sat for her hidden face. *They had to recognise her.*[29]

Through this painterly distance a vivid strangeness emerges; a partial or double 'self' is framed in a climactic political moment that is also a contingent historical event—'some chosen experience . . . who knows where . . . or what there was to be discovered'.[30] They had to recognize her, but *what* do they recognize in her?

Words will not speak and the silence freezes into the images of apartheid: identity cards, police frame-ups, prison mug-shots, the grainy press pictures of terrorists. Of course, Aila is not judged, nor is she judgemental. Her revenge is much wiser and more complete. In her silence she becomes the unspoken 'totem' of the taboo of the coloured South African. She displays the unhomely world, 'the halfway between . . . not defined' world of the coloured as the 'distorted place and time in which they—all of them—Sonny, Aila, Hannah—lived'.[31] The silence that doggedly follows Aila's dwelling now turns into an image of the 'interstices', the in-between hybridity of the history of sexuality and race.

> The necessity for what I've done—She placed the outer edge of each hand, fingers extended and close together, as a frame on either sides of the sheets of testimony in front of her. And she placed herself before him, to be judged by him.[32]

Aila's hidden face, the outer edge of each hand, these small gestures through which she speaks describe another dimension of 'dwelling' in the social world. Aila as coloured woman defines a boundary that is at once inside and outside, the insider's outsideness. The stillness that surrounds her, the gaps in her story, her hesitation and passion that speak between the self and its acts—these are moments where the private and public touch in contingency. They do not simply transform the content of political ideas; the very 'place' from which the political is spoken—the public sphere itself, becomes an experience of liminality which questions, in Sonny's words, what it means to speak 'from the centre of life'.[33]

The central political preoccupation of the novel—till Aila's emergency—focuses on the 'loss of absolutes', the meltdown of the cold war, the fear 'that if we can't offer the old socialist paradise in exchange for the capitalist hell here, we'll have turned traitor to our brothers'.[34] The lesson Aila teaches requires a movement away from a world conceived in binary terms, away from a notion of the people's aspirations sketched in simple black and white. It also requires a shift of attention from the political as a pedagogical,

[29] Ibid., p. 230.
[30] Ibid.
[31] Ibid., p. 241.
[32] Ibid.
[33] Ibid.
[34] Ibid., p. 214.

ideological practice to politics as the stressed necessity of everyday life—politics as a performativity. Aila leads us to the unhomely world where, Gordimer writes, the banalities are enacted—the fuss over births, marriages, family affairs with their survival rituals of food and clothing.[35] But it is precisely in these banalities that the unhomely stirs, as the violence of a racialized society falls most enduringly on the details of life: where you can sit, or not; how you can live, or not; what you can learn, or not; who you can love, or not. Between the banal act of freedom and its historic denial rises the silence: 'Aila emanated a stilling atmosphere; the parting jabber stopped. It was as if everyone found he had unnoticingly entered a strange house, and it was hers; she stood there.'[36]

In Aila's stillness, its obscure necessity, we glimpse what Emmanuel Levinas has magically described as the twilight existence of the aesthetic image—art's image as 'the very event of obscuring, a descent into night, an invasion of the shadow'.[37] The 'completion' of the aesthetic, the distancing of the world in the image, is precisely not a transcendental activity. The image—or the metaphoric, 'fictional' activity of discourse—makes visible 'an interruption of time by a movement going on on the hither side of time, in its interstices'.[38] The complexity of this statement will become clearer when I remind you of the stillness of time through which Aila surreptitiously and subversively interrupts the ongoing presence of political activity, using her interstitial role, her domestic world to both 'obscure' her political role and to articulate it the better. Or, as Beloved, the continual eruption of 'undecipherable languages' of slave memory obscures the historical narrative of infanticide only to articulate the unspoken: that ghostly discourse that enters the world of 124 'from the outside' in order to reveal the transitional world of the aftermath of slavery in the 1870s, its private and public faces, its historical past and its narrative present.

The aesthetic image discloses an ethical time of narration because, Levinas writes, 'the real world appears in the image as it were between parentheses'.[39] Like the outer edges of Aila's hands holding her enigmatic testimony, like 124 Bluestone Road which is a fully realized presence haunted by undecipherable languages, Levinas's parenthetical perspective is also an ethical view. It effects an 'externality of the inward' as the very enunciative position of the historical and narrative subject, 'introducing into the heart of subjectivity a radical and anarchical reference to the other which in fact constitutes the inwardness of the subject'.[40] Is it not uncanny that

---

[35] Ibid., p. 243.

[36] Ibid., p. 249.

[37] E. Levinas, 'Reality and its shadow', in Collected Philosophical Papers (Dordrecht: Martinus Nijhoff, 1987), pp. 1–13.

[38] Ibid.

[39] Ibid., pp. 6–7.

[40] Robert Bernasconi quoted in 'Levinas's ethical discourse, between individuation and universality', in Re-Reading Levinas, R. Bernasconi and S. Critchley, (eds.) (Bloomington: Indiana University Press, 1991), p. 90.

Levinas's metaphors for this unique 'obscurity' of the image should come from those Dickensian unhomely places—those dusty boarding schools, the pale light of London offices, the dark, dank second-hand clothes shops?

For Levinas the 'art-magic' of the contemporary novel lies in its way of 'seeing inwardness from the outside', and it is this ethical-aesthetic positioning that returns us, finally, to the community of the unhomely, to the famous opening lines of *Beloved:* '124 was spiteful. The women in the house knew it and so did the children.'

It is Toni Morrison who takes this ethical and aesthetic project of 'seeing inwardness from the outside' furthest or deepest—right into Beloved's naming of her desire for identity: 'I want you to touch me on my inside part and call me my name.'[41] There is an obvious reason why a ghost should want to be so realized. What is more obscure—and to the point—is how such an inward and intimate desire would provide an 'inscape' of the memory of slavery. For Morrison, it is precisely the signification of the historical and discursive boundaries of slavery that are the issue.

Racial violence is invoked by historical dates—1876, for instance—but Morrison is just a little hasty with the events 'in-themselves', as she rushes past 'the true meaning of the Fugitive Bill, the Settlement Fee, God's Ways, antislavery, manumission, skin voting'.[42] What has to be endured is the knowledge of doubt that comes from Sethe's eighteen years of disapproval and a solitary life, her banishment in the unhomely world of 124 Bluestone Road, as the pariah of her postslavery community. What finally causes the thoughts of the women of 124 'unspeakable thoughts to be unspoken' is the understanding that the victims of violence are themselves 'signified upon': they are the victims of projected fears, anxieties and dominations that do not originate within the oppressed and will not fix them in the circle of pain. The stirring of emancipation comes with the knowledge that the racially supremacist belief 'that under every dark skin there was a jungle' was a belief that grew, spread, touched every perpetrator of the racist myth, turned them mad from their own untruths, and was then expelled from 124 Bluestone Road.

But before such an emancipation from the ideologies of the master, Morrison insists on the harrowing ethical repositioning of the slave mother, who must be the enunciatory site for seeing the inwardness of the slave world from the outside—when the 'outside' is the ghostly return of the child she murdered; the double of herself, for 'she is the laugh I am the laugher I see her face which is mine'.[43] What could be the ethics of child murder? What historical knowledge returns to Sethe, through the aesthetic distance or 'obscuring' of the event, in the phantom shape of her dead daughter Beloved?

In her fine account of forms of slave resistance in *Within the Plantation Household*, Elizabeth Fox-Genovese considers murder, self-mutilation and

41 Morrison, *Beloved*, p. 116.
42 Ibid., p. 173.
43 Ibid., p. 213.

infanticide to be the core psychological dynamic of all resistance. It is her
view that 'these extreme forms captured the essence of the slave woman's
self-definition'.[44] Again we see how this most tragic and intimate act of violence is performed in a struggle to push back the boundaries of the slave
world. Unlike acts of confrontation against the master or the overseer which
were resolved within the household context, infanticide was recognized as
an act against the system and at least acknowledged the slavewoman's legal
standing in the public sphere. Infanticide was seen to be an act against the
master's property—against his surplus profits—and perhaps that, Fox-
Genovese concludes, 'led some of the more desperate to feel that, by killing an
infant they loved, they would be in some way reclaiming it as their own'.[45]

Through the death and the return of Beloved, precisely such a reclamation takes place: the slave mother regaining through the presence of the
child, the property of her own person. This knowledge comes as a kind of
self-love that is also the love of the 'other': Eros and Agape together. It is an
ethical love in the Levinasian sense in which the 'inwardness' of the subject is
inhabited by the 'radical and anarchical reference to the other'. This knowledge is visible in those intriguing chapters[46] which lay over each other,
where Sethe, Beloved, and Denver perform a fugue-like ceremony of claiming and naming through intersecting and interstitial subjectivities: 'Beloved,
she my daughter'; 'Beloved is my sister'; 'I am Beloved and she is mine.' The
women speak in tongues, from a space 'in-between each other' which is a
communal space. They explore an 'interpersonal' reality: a social reality that
appears within the poetic image as if it were in parentheses—aesthetically
distanced, held back, and yet historically framed. It is difficult to convey the
rhythm and the improvization of those chapters, but it is impossible not to
see in them the healing of history, a community reclaimed in the making of a
name. We can finally ask ourselves:

Who is Beloved?

Now we understand: she is the daughter that returns to Sethe so that her
mind will be homeless no more.

Who is Beloved?

Now we may say: she is the sister that returns to Denver, and brings hope of
her father's return, the fugitive who died in his escape.

Who is Beloved?

Now we know: she is the daughter made of murderous love who returns to
love and hate and free herself. Her words are broken, like the lynched people
with broken necks; disembodied, like the dead children who lost their rib-

---

[44] E. Fox-Genovese, *Within the Plantation Household* (Chapel Hill, N.C.: University of
North Carolina Press, 1988), p. 329.
[45] Ibid., p. 324.
[46] Morrison, *Beloved*, Pt. II, pp. 200–17.

bons. But there is no mistaking what her live words say as they rise from the dead despite their lost syntax and their fragmented presence.

My face is coming   I have to have it   I am looking for the join
I am loving my face so much   I want to join   I am loving my
face so much   my dark face is close to me   I want to join.[47]

Looking for the Join

To end, as I have done, with the nest of the phoenix, not its pyre is, in another way, to return to my beginning in the *beyond*. If Gordimer and Morrison describe the historical world, forcibly entering the house of art and fiction in order to invade, alarm, divide and dispossess, they also demonstrate the contemporary compulsion to move beyond; to turn the present into the 'post'; or, as I said earlier, to touch the future on its hither side. Aila's in-between identity and Beloved's double lives both affirm the borders of culture's insurgent and interstitial existence. In that sense, they take their stand with Renée Green's pathway between racial polarities; or Rushdie's migrant history of the English written in the margins of satanic verses; or Osorio's bed—*La Cama*—a place of dwelling, located between the unhomeliness of migrancy and the baroque belonging of the metropolitan, New York/Puerto-Rican artist.

When the public nature of the social event encounters the silence of the word it may lose its historical composure and closure. At this point we would do well to recall Walter Benjamin's insight on the disrupted dialectic of modernity: 'Ambiguity is the figurative appearance of the dialectic, the law of the dialectic at a standstill.'[48] For Benjamin that stillness is Utopia; for those who live, as I described it, 'otherwise' than modernity but not outside it, the Utopian moment is not the necessary horizon of hope. I have ended this argument with the woman framed—Gordimer's Aila—and the woman renamed—Morrison's Beloved—because in both their houses great world events erupted—slavery and apartheid—and their happening was turned, through that peculiar obscurity of art, into a second coming.

Although Morrison insistently repeats at the close of *Beloved*, 'This is not a story to pass on,' she does this only in order to engrave the event in the deepest resources of our amnesia, of our unconsciousness. When historical visibility has faded, when the present tense of testimony loses its power to arrest, then the displacements of memory and the indirections of art offer us the image of our psychic survival. To live in the unhomely world, to find its ambivalencies and ambiguities enacted in the house of fiction, or its sundering and splitting performed in the work of art, is also to affirm a profound desire for social solidarity: 'I am looking for the join . . . I want to join . . . I want to join.'

---

[47] Ibid., p. 213.
[48] W. Benjamin, *Charles Baudelaire: A Lyric Poet in the Era of High Capitalism* (London: NLB, 1973), p. 171.

FURTHER READING

General

Abrams, M. H. *Doing Things with Texts: Essays in Criticism and Critical Theory,* 1989.
———. *The Mirror and the Lamp,* 1953.
Adams, Hazard. *The Interests of Criticism,* 1969.
Atkins, J. W. H. *English Literary Criticism* (3 vols.), 1943–1951.
Auerbach, Erich. *Mimesis,* 1953.
Beardsley, Monroe. *Aesthetics: Problems in the Philosophy of Criticism,* 1958.
Booth, Wayne B. *Critical Understanding,* 1979.
Buckley, Vincent. *Poetry and Morality,* 1959.
Collingwood, R. G. *The Principles of Art,* 1938.
Crane, Ronald S. *The Languages of Criticism and the Structure of Poetry,* 1953.
———, ed. *Critics and Criticism: Ancients and Moderns,* 1952.
Daiches, David. *Critical Approaches to Literature,* 1956.
Empson, William. *The Structure of Complex Words,* 1989.
Gardner, Helen. *The Business of Criticism,* 1959.
Goodman, Paul. *The Structure of Literature,* 1954.
Graff, Gerald. *Professing Literature: An Institutional History,* 1987.
Greene, Theodore M. *The Arts and the Art of Criticism,* 1940.
Kermode, Frank. *An Appetite for Poetry,* 1989.
Kramer, Victor A. *American Critics at Work: Examinations of Contemporary Literary Theories,* 1984.
Langer, Suzanne K. *Feeling and Form,* 1953.
Lentricchia, Frank. *After the New Criticism,* 1980.
Levin, Harry. *The Contexts of Criticism,* 1963.
Muller, Herbert. *Science and Criticism: The Humanist Tradition,* 1943.
Olsen, Stein Haugon. *The End of Literary Theory,* 1987.
Pepper, Stephen C. *The Basis of Criticism in the Arts,* 1945.
Pritchard, John P. *Criticism in America,* 1956.
Said, Edward W. *The World, the Text, and the Critic,* 1983.
Thorpe, James, ed. *Relations of Literary Study,* 1967.
Trilling, Lionel. *The Liberal Imagination,* 1953.
Warren, Alba, Jr. *English Poetic Theory, 1825–1865,* 1950.
Watson, George. *The Literary Critics,* 1962.
Wellek, Rene. *Concepts of Criticism,* 1963.
———. *A History of Modern Criticism, 1700–1950* (4 vols.), 1955–1965.
Wellek, Rene, and Austin Warren. *Theory of Literature,* 1949.

Wimsatt, William K., and Cleanth Brooks. *Literary Criticism: A Short History*, 1957.

General Critical Theory Websites

Voice of the Shuttle
<http://humanitas.ucsb.edu/shuttle/theory.html>
The University of California, Santa Barbara, has compiled one of the most thorough lists of links on all schools of criticism. The hundreds of links are arranged chronologically from the classical age to the present.

Contemporary Philosophy, Critical Theory, and Postmodern Thought
<http://www.cudenver.edu/~mryder/itc_data/postmodern.html>
This site rivals *Voice of the Shuttle* for sheer number of links. The University of Colorado at Denver has organized these myriad links by resources, related sites, readings, and theorist. A page that lists many links on semiotics can be found here.

Critical Inquiry
<http://www2.uchicago.edu/jnl-crit-inq/main.html>
Critical Inquiry, published quarterly by University of Chicago Press, has been called "the best of the academic journals" by the *Times Literary Supplement*. *Critical Inquiry* provides a forum for critical exchange and scholarly debate in all areas of the arts and humanities, but the essays are appropriate for the general reader who is interested in contemporary cultural issues.

CTHEORY
<http://www.ctheory.com/>
CTHEORY is an international journal of theory, technology, and culture. Articles, interviews, and key book reviews in contemporary discourse are published weekly.

Theory.org
<http://www.leeds.ac.uk/ics/theory-r.htm>
Theory.org, an e-journal created by David Gauntlett and hosted by the Institute of Communication Studies, focuses on the relationship between the mass media, identities, and gender.

Humanitas
<http://www.nhumanities.org/hum.htm>
The journal *Humanitas* seeks to sponsor a spirit of open inquiry—a willingness to challenge cherished doctrines and look beyond conventional categories of thought. *Humanitas* explores issues of moral and social philosophy, epistemology, and aesthetics and the relations among them, such as the moral and cultural conditions of knowledge.

Jouvert: A Journal of Postcolonial Studies
<http://152.1.96.5/jouvert/>
Jouvert is a multidisciplinary journal published three times a year by North
    Carolina State University. It offers articles in postcolonial theory, litera-
    ture, history, arts, and politics.

Cyberspace, Hypertext, and Critical Theory
<http://www.stg.brown.edu/projects/hypertext/landow/cspace/cspaceov
    .html>
This collection of interlinked materials began as an Intermedia Internet proj-
    ect that supported courses taught at Brown University. The great major-
    ity of the materials collected here, which number more than 7,000 docu-
    ments and images, consists mainly of student projects from George
    Landow's courses on hypertext, literary theory, and cyberspace.

Plato

The Dialogues of Plato, translated by Benjamin Jowett, 4th ed. (4 vols.), 1953.
Else, Gerald F. *Plato and Aristotle on Poetry*, 1986.
Grube, G. M. A. *The Greek and Roman Critics*, 1965.
Gulley, Norman. *Plato's Theory of Knowledge*, 1962.
Havelock, Eric. *Preface to Plato*, 1963.
Lodge, Rupert C. *Plato's Theory of Art*, 1953.
Oates, Whitney J. *Plato's View of Art*, 1972.
Shorey, Paul. *What Plato Said*, 1933.
Taylor, A. E. *Plato*, 1929.

Related Internet Link

Plato and His Dialogues
<http://phd.evansville.edu/plato.htm>
This site, created by a French scholar, Bernard Suzanne, and sponsored by
    Anthony Beavers at the University of Evansville, includes a short biogra-
    phy of Plato, a list of his works, a brief history of the interpretation of his
    dialogues, and links that will interest serious researchers.

Aristotle

Brunius, Teddy. *Imagination and Katharsis*, 1966.
Butcher, S. H. *Aristotle's Theory of Poetry and Fine Art*, 4th ed., 1923.
Bywater, Ingram. *Aristotle on the Art of Poetry*, 1909.
Cooper, Lane. *The Poetics of Aristotle: Its Meaning and Influence*, 1923.
Else, Gerald F. *Aristotle's Poetics: The Argument*, 1957.
Grube, G. M. A. *The Greek and Roman Critics*, 1965.
Lucas, F. L. *Tragedy in Relation to Aristotle's "Poetics,"* 1928.
Olson, Elder, ed. *Aristotle's Poetics and English Literature*, 1965.

Related Internet Link

The Works of Aristotle
<http://libertyonline.hypermall.com/Aristotle/Default.htm>
Created by Jawaid Bazyar at *Liberty Online,* this site includes the texts of Aristotle's *Poetics, Rhetoric,* and other writings.

Longinus

Atkins, J. W. H. *Literary Criticism in Antiquity* (vol. 2), 1934.
Brody, Jules. *Boileau and Longinus,* 1958.
Grube, G. M. A. *The Greek and Roman Critics,* 1965.
Henn, T. R. *Longinus and English Criticism,* 1934.
Monk, S. H. *The Sublime: A Study of Critical Theories in Eighteenth-Century England,* 1935.
Tate, Allen. "Longinus and the New Criticism," in *Lectures in Criticism,* edited by Elliott Coleman, 1949.

Related Internet Link

"Sacred Ambivalence: Mimetology in Aristotle, Horace, and Longinus"
<http://www.humnet.ucla.edu/humnet/anthropoetics/ap0101/schneid
    .htm>
In this essay published by *Anthropoetics: The Electronic Journal of Generative Anthropology,* Matthew Schneider at Chapman University discusses three of the classical age's most influential philosophers.

Horace

Brink, C. O. *Horace on Poetry,* 1963.
Campbell, A. Y. *Horace: A New Interpretation,* 1924.
Goad, Caroline. *Horace in the English Literature of the Eighteenth Century,* 1918.
Grube, G. M. A. *The Greek and Roman Critics,* 1965.
Herrick, Marvin T. *The Fusion of Horatian and Aristotelian Literary Criticism,* 1946.
Saintonge, P. F., and others. *Horace: Three Phases of His Influence,* 1936.
Showerman, Grant. *Horace and His Influence,* 1922.

Related Internet Link

Selections from Horace's *Odes*
<http://www.uky.edu/ArtsSciences/Classics/horawill.html>
The University of Kentucky provides a short biography, an annotated bibliography, and translations of Horace's *Odes* by Steven Willett as part of a larger website called *Materials for the Study of Women and Gender in the Ancient World.*

Dante

Alighieri, Dante. *The Divine Comedy,* translated and with a commentary by Charles S. Singleton, 1970–1975.
Dunbar, Helen Flanders. *Symbolism in Medieval Thought,* 1929.
Hollander, Robert. *Allegory in Dante's Commedia,* 1969.
Jackson, W. W. *The Banquet* in *Dante's Convivio,* 1909.
Kirkpatrick, Robin. *Dante's Paradiso and the Limitations of Modern Criticism: A Study of Style and Poetic Theory,* 1978.
Toynbee, Paget Jackson. *Dante in English Literature from Chaucer to Cary,* 1909.

Related Internet Link

Digital Dante
<http://www.ilt.columbia.edu/projects/dante/index.html>
The Institute for Learning Technologies at Columbia University created this extensive site on Dante, which includes Internet resources, maps, a bibliography, links to Dante's works, scholar's works, useful classics, and a section on recent news.

Sidney

Baldwin, C. S. *Renaissance Literary Theory and Practice,* 1938.
Clark, Donald L. *Rhetoric and Poetic in the Renaissance,* 1939.
Hall, Vernon, Jr. *Renaissance Literary Criticism: A Study of Its Social Content,* 1959.
Myrick, K. O. *Sir Phillip Sidney as a Literary Craftsman,* 1935.
Robinson, Forrest. *The Shape of Things Unknown: Sidney's Apology and Its Philosophical Tradition,* 1972.
Spingarn, Joel E. *A History of Literary Criticism in the Renaissance,* 1908.
Wallace, M. W. *The Life of Sir Phillip Sidney,* 1915.

Related Internet Link

Sir Phillip Sidney, 1554–1586
<http://www.luminarium.org/renlit/sidney.htm>
Part of *Luminarium*'s site on sixteenth-century Renaissance English literature, this page on Sir Phillip Sidney offers quotes, a biography, links to Sidney's works, related essays and articles, and additional resources.

Dryden

Bredvold, Louis I. *The Intellectual Milieu of John Dryden,* 1934.
Eliot, T. S. *John Dryden: The Poet, the Dramatist, the Critic,* 1966.

Hume, Robert D. *Dryden's Criticism,* 1970.

Huntley, Frank L. *The Unity of Dryden's Dramatic Criticism,* 1944.

Jenson, H. James. *A Glossary of John Dryden's Critical Terms,* 1969.

Pechter, Edward. *Dryden's Classical Theory of Literature,* 1975.

Swendenberg, H. T. *The Theory of the Epic in England, 1650–1800,* 1944.

Watson, George, ed. *John Dryden: Of Dramatic Poesy and Other Critical Essays* (2 vols.), 1962.

Related Internet Link

Selected Poetry and Prose of John Dryden (1631–1700)

<http://library.utoronto.ca/www/utel/rp/authors/dryden.html>

The second version of *Representative Poetry On-line,* hosted by the University of Toronto, includes more than 2,000 English poems by 310 poets from the early medieval period to the beginning of the twentieth century. Here you can find more than twenty poems by Dryden and his prose piece, *An Essay of Dramatic Poesy.*

Pope

Edwards, Thomas R. *This Dark Estate: A Reading of Pope,* 1963.

Empson, William. "'Wit' in the *Essay on Criticism,*" *Hudson Review* 2, 1950.

Fenner, Arthur, Jr. "The Unity of Pope's Essay on Criticism," *Philological Quarterly* 39, 1960.

Hooker, E. N. "Pope on Wit: The Essay on Criticism," *Hudson Review* 2, 1950.

Root, Robert K. *The Poetical Career of Pope,* 1938.

Stack, Frank. *Pope and Horace: Studies in Imitation,* 1985.

Warren, Austin. *Alexander Pope as Critic and Humanist,* 1929.

Related Internet Link

Selected Poetry and Prose of Alexander Pope

<http://library.utoronto.ca/www/utel/rp/authors/pope.html>

The second version of *Representative Poetry On-line,* hosted by the University of Toronto, includes more than 2,000 English poems by 310 poets from the early medieval period to the beginning of the twentieth century. A few of the documents you will find include *An Essay on Criticism, An Essay on Man, The Rape of the Lock,* and the preface to Pope's translation of *The Iliad.*

Johnson

Bate, Walter J. *The Achievement of Samuel Johnson,* 1955.

Bosker, A. *Literary Criticism in the Age of Johnson,* 1930.

Brown, Joseph E. *The Critical Opinions of Samuel Johnson*, 1926.

Fussell, Paul. *Samuel Johnson and the Life of Writing*, 1986.

Hagstrum, Jean. *Samuel Johnson's Literary Criticism*, 1952.

Keast, W. R. "The Theoretical Foundations of Johnson's Criticism," in *Critics and Criticism*, edited by R. S. Crane, 1952.

Sherbo, Arthur. *Johnson, Editor of Shakespeare*, 1956.

Related Internet Link

Samuel Johnson

<http://andromeda.rutgers.edu/~jlynch/Johnson/>

This thoroughly researched page, created and maintained by Jack Lynch at Rutgers University, includes electronic texts to many works by Johnson, a guide for beginners, scholarship, and more.

Kant

Cassier, H. W. *Commentary on Kant's Critique of Judgement*, 1983.

Cohen, Ted, and Paul Guyer, eds. *Essays in Kant's Aesthetics*, 1982.

Coleman, Francis, X. J. *The Harmony of Reason: A Study in Kant's Aesthetics*, 1974.

Guyer, Paul. *Kant and the Claims of Taste*, 1979.

Richardson, Robert Allan. *Aesthetics and Freedom: A Critique of Kant's Analysis of Beauty*, 1969.

Rogerson, Kenneth F. *Kant's Aesthetics: The Roles of Form and Expression*, 1986.

Schaper, Eva. *Studies in Kant's Aesthetics*, 1979.

Related Internet Link

Immanuel Kant: Links

<http://comp.uark.edu/~rlee/semiau96/kantlink.html>

The University of Arkansas provides over eighty links to Kant-related sites, including writing by and about Kant.

Wordsworth

Hefferman, J. A. *Wordsworth's Theory of Poetry*, 1969.

Jones, H. J. F. *The Egotistical Sublime: A History of Wordsworth's Imagination*, 1954.

Lucas, F. L. *The Decline and Fall of the Romantic Ideal*, 1936.

Peacock, Markham L., Jr. *Critical Opinions of William Wordsworth*, 1950.

Thorpe, C. D. "The Imagination: Coleridge versus Wordsworth," *Philosophical Quarterly* 18, 1939.

Wlecke, Albert O. *Wordsworth and the Sublime*, 1973.

Related Internet Link

Complete Poetical Works of William Wordsworth
<http://www.cc.columbia.edu/acis/bartleby/wordsworth/index.html>
Project Bartleby, named after Melville's stubborn scrivener, promises accurate
    editions, free public access, careful, well-researched selections, and state-
    of-the-art presentation of more than twenty authors.

Coleridge

Baker, James V. *The Sacred River: Coleridge's Theory of Imagination,* 1957.
Christensen, Jerome. *Coleridge's Blessed Machine of Language,* 1981.
Fogle, Richard H. *The Idea of Coleridge's Criticism,* 1962.
McKenzie, Gordon. *Organic Unity in Coleridge,* 1939.
Read, Herbert. *Coleridge as Critic,* 1948.
Richards, I. A. *Coleridge on Imagination,* 1950.
Wheeler, Kathleen M. *Sources, Processes, and Methods in Coleridge's "Biographia
    Literaria,"* 1980.

Related Internet Link

S. T. Coleridge
<http://www.lib.virginia.edu/etext/stc/Coleridge/stc.html>
As part of their British poetry archive, the University of Virginia offers links
    to Coleridge's poetry, literary theory and criticism, a time line, a critical
    essay on the conversation poems, and more.

Keats

Bate, Walter, J. *Negative Capability,* 1939.
D'Avanzo, Mario L. *Keats' Metaphors for the Poetic Imagination,* 1967.
Ende, Stuart A. *Keats and the Sublime,* 1976.
Thekla, Sister. *The Disinterested Heart: The Philosophy of John Keats,* 1973.
Thorpe, Clarence D. *The Mind of John Keats,* 1926.
Trilling, Lionel, ed. *The Selected Letters of John Keats,* 1951.
Ward, Aileen. *John Keats: The Making of a Poet,* 1986.

Related Internet Link

Poetical Works of John Keats
<http://www.cc.columbia.edu/acis/bartleby/keats/index.html>
Project Bartleby, named after Melville's stubborn scrivener, promises accurate
    editions, free public access, careful, well-researched selections, and state-
    of-the-art presentation of more than twenty authors.

Shelley

Barrell, Joseph. *Shelley and the Thought of His Time,* 1967.

Bloom, Harold. *Shelley's Mythmaking,* 1959.

Damm, Robert F. *A Tale of Human Power: Art and Life in Shelley's Poetic Theory,* 1970.

Grabo, Carl H. *The Magic Plant: The Growth of Shelley's Thought,* 1936.

Notopoulos, James A. *The Platonism of Shelley,* 1969.

Schulze, Earl J. *Shelley's Theory of Poetry: A Reappraisal,* 1966.

Shawcross, John, ed. *Shelley's Literary and Philosophical Criticism,* 1909.

Solve, Melvin T. *Shelley: His Theory of Poetry,* 1927.

Wright, John W. *Shelley's Myth of Metaphor,* 1970.

Related Internet Link

Complete Poetical Works of Percy Bysshe Shelley
<http://www.cc.columbia.edu/acis/bartleby/shelley/index.html>
Project Bartleby, named after Melville's stubborn scrivener, promises accurate
editions, free public access, careful, well-researched selections, and state-
of-the-art presentation of more than twenty authors.

Marx

Ahearn, Edward. *Marx and Modern Fiction,* 1989.

Berlin, Isaiah. *Karl Marx: His Life and Environment,* 1996.

Demetz, Peter. *Marx, Engels, and the Poets: Origins of Marxist Literary Criticism,*
1967.

Foucault, Michel. *Remarks on Marx,* 1991.

Lifshitz, Mikhail. *The Philosophy of Art of Karl Marx,* 1933, 1973.

Marx, Karl, and Friedrich Engels. *Marx and Engels on Literature and Art,* 1973.

Mazlish, Bruce. *The Meaning of Karl Marx,* 1984.

Related Internet Link

Cultural Logic
<http://eserver.org/clogic/>
Cultural Logic is a biannual, interdisciplinary journal that publishes essays,
poetry, and reviews (books, films, and other media) by writers working
within the Marxist tradition.

Nietzsche

Donadio, Stephen. *Nietzsche, Henry James, and the Artistic Will,* 1976.

Gilman, Sander L. *Nietzschean Parody: An Introduction to Reading Nietzsche,*
1976.

Jaspers, Karl. *Nietzsche: An Introduction to the Understanding of His Philosophical Activity*, 1965.

Ludovici, Anthony. *Nietzsche and Art*, 1912.

Megill, Allan. *Prophets of Extremity: Nietzsche, Heidegger, Foucault, Derrida*, 1985.

Nehamas, Alexander. *Nietzsche: Life as Literature*, 1985.

Related Internet Link

The Nietzsche Page

<http://www.usc.edu/~douglast/nietzsche.html>

Written and designed by Douglas Thomas at the University of Southern California, this page is set up to help facilitate the study of Nietzsche's works by providing scholars with an online reference for contemporary scholarship. It includes links to articles, discussion boards, societies and organizations, and other Nietzsche websites.

Arnold

Anderson, W. D. *Matthew Arnold and the Classical Tradition*, 1965.

Boutellier, Victor N. *Imginative Reason: The Continuity of Arnold's Critical Effort*, 1977.

Brown, E. K. *Arnold: A Study in Conflict*, 1948.

Carroll, Joseph. *The Cultural Theory of Matthew Arnold*, 1982.

Eells, J. S. *The Touchstones of Matthew Arnold*, 1955.

Robbins, William. *The Ethical Idealism of Matthew Arnold*, 1959.

Trilling, Lionel. *Matthew Arnold*, 1955.

Related Internet Link

Selected Prose and Poetry of Matthew Arnold (1822–1888)

<http://library.utoronto.ca/www/utel/rp/authors/arnold.html>

The second version of *Representative Poetry On-line,* hosted by the University of Toronto, includes more than 2,000 English poems by 310 poets from the early medieval period to the beginning of the twentieth century. Here you can find links to 29 poems by Arnold and his prose piece, *The Function of Criticism at the Present Time.*

Pater

Buckler, William E. *Walter Pater: The Critic as Artist of Ideas*, 1987.

Child, Ruth C. *The Aesthetic of Walter Pater*, 1940.

Crinkley, Richmond. *Walter Pater: Humanist*, 1970.

Eliot, T. S. "Arnold and Pater," in *Selected Essays*, 1932.

Hough, Graham. *The Last Romantics*, 1949.

McKenzie, Gordon. *The Literary Character of Walter Pater*, 1967.
Ward, Anthony. *Walter Pater: The Idea in Nature*, 1966.
Young, Helen H. *The Writings of Walter Pater*, 1933.

Related Internet Link

"Art vs. Aestheticism: The Case of Walter Pater."
<http://www.cycad.com/cgi-bin/Upstream/People/Kimball/pater.html>
An online journal that prides itself on independent thinking, *Upstream* printed
    this review of Denis Donoghue's book *Walter Pater: Lover of Strange Souls*.

James

Andreas, Osborn. *Henry James and the Expanding Horizon*, 1948.
Beach, Joseph Warren. *The Method of Henry James* (enlarged ed.), 1954.
Daugherty, Sarah B. *The Literary Criticism of Henry James*, 1981.
Edel, Leon, ed. *The Prefaces of James*, 1931.
Hughes, Herbert L. *Theory and Practice in Henry James*, 1969.
Miller, James E., Jr. *Theory of Fiction: Henry James*, 1972.
Roberts, Morris. *Henry James' Criticism*, 1929.
Veeder, William. "Image as Argument: Henry James and the Style of Criticism," *Henry James Review* 6, 1985.

Related Internet Link

The Henry James Scholar's Guide to Web Sites
<http://www.newpaltz.edu/~hathaway/>
Richard Hathaway's comprehensive site on Henry James includes many electronic versions of James's novels, links to articles by and about James, an online discussion group, conferences, movie reviews, and other nineteenth-century American writers.

Wilde

Behrendt, Patricia F. *Oscar Wilde: Eros and Aesthetics*, 1991.
Buckler, William E. "Wilde's 'Trumpet Against the Gate of Dullness': 'The Decay of Lying,'" *English Literature in Transition* 33, 1990.
Freedman, Jonathan, ed. *Oscar Wilde: A Collection of Critical Essays*, 1995.
Gagnier, Regina. *Critical Essays on Oscar Wilde*, 1991.
Gide, Andre. *Oscar Wilde: A Study*, 1975.
Murray, Isobel M. *Oscar Wilde*, 1989.
Small, Ian. "Semiotics and Oscar Wilde's Account of Art," *British Journal of Aesthetics*, 1985.
Wilde, Oscar. *The Artist as Critic: Critical Writings of Oscar Wilde*, 1968.

Related Internet Link

The World-Wide Wilde Web
<http://www.showgate.com/tots/gross/wildeweb.html>
A handy guide to Wilde and his works, this site contains a biography, a
   collection of Wilde wit, a comprehensive bibliography of works
   about Wilde, a listing of works by Wilde, photographs, and other literary
   sites.

Tolstoy

Duffield, Holley Gene, and Manuel Bilsky, eds. *Tolstoy and the Critics*, 1965.
Farrell, James T. *Literature and Morality*, 1947.
Flaccus, Louis W. *Artists and Thinkers*, 1967.
Maude, Aylmer. *Tolstoy on Art and Its Critics*, 1925.
Simmons, Ernest J. *Leo Tolstoy*, 1946.
Spence, Gordon W. *Tolstoy the Ascetic*, 1968.
Steiner, George, *Tolstoy or Dostoevsky, an Essay in the Old Criticism*, 1959.

Related Internet Link

Tolstoy Studies Journal
<http://www.utoronto.ca/tolstoy/>
The *Tolstoy Studies Journal* includes a review of current literary criticism, links
   to related journals, Tolstoy images, a Tolstoy library, and other sites
   around the world.

Freud

Bowie, Malcolm. *Psychoanalysis and the Future of Theory*, 1994.
Freud, Sigmund. *The Standard Edition of the Complete Psychological Works*,
   1940–1968.
Gilman, Sander L., ed. *Introducing Psychoanalytic Theory*, 1982.
Hoffman, Frederick J. *Freudianism and the Literary Mind*, 1977.
Jones, Ernest. *Hamlet and Oedipus*, 1949.
Kofmar, Sarah. *The Childhood of Art: An Interpretation of Freud's Aesthetics*,
   1988.
Kris, Ernst. *Psychoanalytical Explorations in Art*, 1952.
Rimmon-Kenan, Shlomith. *Discourse in Psychoanalysis and Literature*, 1987.
Thomas, Ronald R. *Dreams of Authority: Freud and the Fictions of the Uncon-
   scious*, 1990.
Trilling, Lionel. "Freud and Literature," in *The Liberal Imagination*, 1953.

Related Internet Link

Freudian Links
<http://www.mii.kurume-u.ac.jp/~leuers/Freud.htm>
Kurume University in Japan organizes their links by these topics: email forums, journals, papers, bibliographies, and other websites.

Eliot

Allan, Mowbray. *T. S. Eliot's Impersonal Theory of Poetry*, 1974.
Freed, Lewis. *T. S. Eliot: Aesthetics and History*, 1962.
Frye, Northrop. *T. S. Eliot*, 1963.
Lucy, Sean. *T. S. Eliot and the Idea of Tradition*, 1960.
Matthiessen, F. O. *The Achievement of T. S. Eliot*, 3rd ed., 1958.
Menand, Louis. *Discovering Modernism: T. S. Eliot and His Context*, 1987.

Related Internet Link

T. S. Eliot
<http://www.cc.columbia.edu/acis/bartleby/eliot/index.html>
Project Bartleby, named after Melville's stubborn scrivener, promises accurate editions, free public access, careful, well-researched selections, and state-of-the-art presentation of more than twenty authors.

Woolf

Bell, Quentin. *Virginia Woolf: A Biography*, 1972.
Majumdar, Robin. *Virginia Woolf: An Annotated Bibliography of Criticism*, 1976.
Marcus, Jane. *New Feminist Essays on Virginia Woolf*, 1981.
——. *Virginia Woolf and the Language of Patriarchy*, 1987.
Marder, Herbert. *Feminism and Art: A Study of Virginia Woolf*, 1968.
Rosenman, Ellen Bayuk. *A Room of One's Own: Women Writers and the Politics of Creativity*, 1995.
Woolf, Virginia. *The Essays of Virginia Woolf*, 1986.
——. *A Room of One's Own*, 1929.

Related Internet Link

Welcome to VWW: Virginia Woolf Web
<http://www.aianet.ne.jp/~orlando/VWW/english.html>
With more than one hundred links to biographies of Woolf, her works, modernism, the Bloomsbury group, and more, this is a good site to begin Internet research.

Bakhtin

Bakhtin, Mikhail. *Art and Answerability: Early Philosophical Essays,* 1990.
————. *The Dialogic Imagination: Four Essays,* 1981.
————. *Rabelais and His World,* 1968.
————. *Speech Genres, and Other Essays,* 1987.
Holquist, Michael. *Dialogism: Bakhtin and His World,* 1990.
Richter, David. "Dialogism and Poetry," *Studies in the Literary Imagination,* Spring 1990.
Todorov, Tzvetan. *Mikhail Bakhtin: The Dialogical Principle,* 1985.

Related Internet Link

The Bakhtin Centre
<http://hippo.shef.ac.uk/uni/academic/A-C/bakh/bakhtin.html>
The Bakhtin Centre's homepage offers many resources to anyone interested in the Russian philosopher including an analytical database of primary and secondary documents and links to other Bakhtin sites around the world.

Ransom

Brooks, Cleanth. *Modern Poetry and the Tradition,* 1939.
Krieger, Murray. *The New Apologists for Poetry,* 1956.
Magner, James E. *John Crowe Ransom: Critical Principles and Preoccupations,* 1971.
Quinlan, Kieran. *John Crowe Ransom's Secular Faith,* 1989.
Ransom, John Crowe. *The New Criticism,* 1941.
————. *The World's Body,* 1938.
Stewart, John L. *John Crowe Ransom,* 1962.
Young, Thomas D., ed. *The New Criticism and After,* 1976.

Related Internet Link

John Crowe Ransom Papers
<http://www.library.vanderbilt.edu/speccol/ransom.html>
The Jean and Alexander Heard Library at Vanderbilt University houses what is probably the largest single collection of Ransom material in one repository. Their website offers a detailed biography and a guide to their collection.

Brooks

Brooks, Cleanth. "Irony as a Principle of Structure," from *Literary Opinion in America,* edited by M. D. Zabel, 1951.
———. *Modern Poetry and the Tradition,* 1939.
———. *The Well Wrought Urn,* 1947.
Cutrer, Thomas W. *Parnassus on the Mississippi,* 1984.
Krieger, Murray. *The New Apologists for Poetry,* 1956.
Ransom, John Crowe. *The New Criticism,* 1941.
Simpson, Louis R. *The Possibilities of Order: Cleanth Brooks and His Work,* 1976.
Tate, Allen. *The Man of Letters in the Modern World,* 1955.
Wimsatt, W. K. *The Verbal Icon,* 1954.

Related Internet Link

Understanding Poetry: An Anthology for College Students
<http://dept.english.upenn.edu/~afilreis/50s/understanding-poetry.html>
Part of Al Filreis's site on American literature and culture of the 1950s, this page contains excerpts from Cleanth Brooks and Robert Penn Warren's textbook *Understanding Poetry: An Anthology for College Students* (1950).

Frye

Bodkin, Maud. *Archetypal Patterns in Poetry,* 1963.
Campbell, Joseph. *The Hero with a Thousand Faces,* 1949.
Denham, Robert D. *Northrop Frye: An Enumerative Bibliography,* 1974.
Frye, Northrop. *Anatomy of Criticism,* 1957.
———. *The Great Code: The Bible in Literature,* 1983.
Kermode, Frank. *Puzzles and Epiphanies,* 1962.
Krieger, Murray, ed. *Northrop Frye in Modern Criticism: Selected Papers from the English Institute,* 1966.
Murray, Henry A., ed. *Myth and Myth-Making,* 1960.
Seboek, Thomas, ed. *Myth, A Symposium,* 1955.
Slote, Bernice, ed. *Myth and Symbol,* 1963.
Wheelwright, Philip. *The Burning Fountain,* 1954.

Related Internet Link

The Age of Simulation
<http://www.transparencynow.com/introfry2.htm>
This essay, titled "Northrop Frye, Simulation, and the Creation of a 'Human World,'" is part of a series of essays hosted by Transparency Now, an organization whose mission is "to make things clear."

Barthes

Barthes, Roland. *Critical Essays*, 1972.
———. *S/Z*, 1974.
———. *Writing Degree Zero*, 1968.
Culler, Jonathan. *Structuralist Poetics: Structuralism, Linguistics, and the Study of Literature*, 1975.
Kurzweil, Edith. *The Age of Structuralism*, 1980.
Lavers, Annette. *Roland Barthes: Structuralism and After*, 1982.
Lentricchia, Frank. *After the New Criticism*, 1980.
Petit, Philip. *The Concept of Structuralism: A Critical Analysis*, 1977.
Scholes, Robert. *Structuralism in Literature: An Introduction*, 1974.

Related Internet Link

Roland Barthes: *Mythologies* (1957)
<http://orac.sund.ac.uk/~os0tmc/myth.htm>
This site contains a series of lectures written by Tony McNeill at the University of Sunderland in Great Britain. Recommendations for further reading are listed at the end.

Derrida

Culler, Jonathan. *Framing the Sign: Criticism and Its Institutions*, 1989.
———. *On Deconstruction: Theory and Criticism in the 1970s*, 1982.
Derrida, Jacques. *Of Grammatology*, 1976.
———. *Writing and Difference*, 1978.
Ellis, John M. *Against Deconstruction*, 1989.
Hartman, Geoffrey. *Saving the Test: Literature/Derrida/Philosophy*, 1981.
Leitch, Vincent B. *Deconstructive Criticism: An Advanced Introduction*, 1983.
Macksey, Richard, and Eugenio Donato, eds. *The Structuralist Controversy*, 1970.
Norris, Christopher. *Deconstruction, Theory and Practice*, 1982.

Related Internet Link

Derridian Links
<http://www.mii.kurume-u.ac.jp/~leuers/Derrida.htm>
Compiled by Timothy Leuer, this page is designed to be a fast reference tool and contains few images. The links are arranged in the following sections: email forums, journals, paper snippets, websites, bibliographies, and courses.

Rich

Auerbach, Nina. *Communities of Women*, 1978.
Bernikow, Louise. *Among Women*, 1980.

Daly, Mary. *Beyond God the Father,* 1973.

Kolodny, Annette. "Dancing through the Minefield: Some Observations on the Theory, Practice and Politics of a Feminist Literary Theory," *Feminist Studies* 6, 1981.

Millett, Kate. *Sexual Politics,* 1969.

Moers, Ellen. *Literary Women,* 1976.

Ratcliffe, Krista. *Anglo-American Feminist Challenges to the Rhetorical Traditions: Virginia Woolf, Mary Daly, and Adrienne Rich,* 1995.

Rich, Adrienne. *On Lies, Secrets, and Silence,* 1979.

Templeton, Alice. *The Dream and the Dialogue: Adrienne Rich's Feminist Poetics,* 1995.

Related Internet Link

The Dream of an Artist's Language
<http://www.hotink.com/8797.html>
In this excerpt from her letter to the National Endowment for the Arts, Rich explains her reasons for refusing to accept the National Medal for the Arts in 1997. The site links to her poem "For the Record" and to the full text of her letter at the *Los Angeles Times Book Review.*

Eagleton

Avron, Henri. *Marxist Aesthetics,* 1970.

Baxandall, Lee. *Marxism and Aesthetics,* 1968.

Caudwell, Christopher. *Illusion and Reality: A Study of the Sources of Poetry,* 1947.

Demetz, Peter. *Marx, Engels and the Poets: Origins of Marxist Literary Criticism,* 1967.

Eagleton, Terry. *Criticism and Ideology: A Study in Marxist Literary Theory,* 1978.

———. *The Significance of Theory,* 1990.

Jameson, Fredric. *Marxism and Form,* 1971.

Lukacs, Georg. *Realism in Our Time: Literature and the Class Struggle,* 1964.

Williams, Raymond. *Marxism and Literature,* 1977.

Related Internet Link

Some Terry Eagleton Links
<http://elo.helsinki.fi/~kniemela/eaglelinks.html>
Kyösti Niemelä at the University of Helsinki has compiled these Eagleton-related links, which include articles by and about Eagleton and reviews of his books.

Foucault

Abrams, M. H. "The Deconstructive Angel," *Critical Inquiry* 3, 1977.

Caws, Peter. *Structuralism: The Art of the Intelligible,* 1988.

Dreyfus, Hubert L., and Paul Rabinow. *Michel Foucault: Beyond Structuralism and Hermeneutics*, 1983.

Foucault, Michel. *The Foucault Reader*, 1984.

———. *Power/Knowledge*, 1980.

Girard, Rene. *Deceit, Desire, and the Novel: The Self and Other in Literary Structure*, 1965.

Greimas, A. J. *Structural Semantics: An Attempt at a Method*, 1984.

Searle, John. *Speech Acts*, 1969.

Related Internet Link

Welcome to the World of Michel Foucault
<http://www.csun.edu/~hfspc002/foucault.home.html>
This Foucault page at California State University, Northridge, offers a genealogy, discussion lists, online essays by, about, or influenced by Foucault, and many more links.

de Man

Bloom, Harold. *Agon: Towards a Theory of Revisionism*, 1982.

———. *Deconstruction and Criticism*, 1979.

———. *A Map of Misreading*, 1975.

de Man, Paul. *Allegories of Reading*, 1979.

———. *Blindness and Insight: Essays in the Rhetoric of Contemporary Criticism*, 1971.

Donoghue, Denis. "The Strange Case of Paul de Man," *New York Review of Books*, June 29, 1989.

Eagleton, Terry. "The Paul de Man Affair," *The Times Literary Supplement*, May 26–June 1, 1989.

Miller, J. Hillis. *The Ethics of Reading: Kant, de Man, Eliot, Trollope, James and Benjamin*, 1987.

Waters, Lindsay, and Wlad Godzich, eds. *Reading de Man Reading*, 1989.

Related Internet Link

Paul de Man Bibliography
<http://sun3.lib.uci.edu/~scctr/Wellek/deman/>
This bibliography compiled by Eddie Yeghiayan, a librarian at the University of California, Irvine, is arranged chronologically by year of publication.

Fish

Bleich, David. *Readings and Feelings: An Introduction to Subjective Criticism*, 1975.

Fish, Stanley. *Change, Rhetoric, and the Practice of Theory in Literary and Legal Studies*, 1989.

———. *Surprised by Sin*, 1967.

Holland, Norman N. *The Dynamics of Literary Response*, 1968.

Iser, Wolfgang. *The Act of Reading*, 1978.

McGuire, Richard L. *Passionate Attention*, 1973.

Rosenblatt, Louise. *The Reader, the Text, the Poem*, 1978.

Slatoff, Walter, J. *With Respect to Readers*, 1970.

Related Internet Link

"'There Is No Such Thing as Free Speech': An Interview with Stanley Fish"
<http://www.lib.latrobe.edu.au/AHR/archive/Issue-February-1998/fish.html>
From the *Australian Humanities Review,* a peer-reviewed interdisciplinary electronic journal, this interview by Peter Lowe and Annemarie Jonson focuses on Fish's theories about speech.

Baym

Baym, Nina. *Feminism and American Literary History*, 1992.

———. *Woman's Fiction: A Guide to Novels by and about Women in America*, 1978.

Ezell, Margaret J. M. "The Myth of Judith Shakespeare: Creating the Canon of Women's Literature," *New Literary History* 21, 1990.

McConnell-Ginet, Sally, Ruth Borker, and Nelly Furman, eds. *Women and Language in Literature and Society*, 1980.

Robinson, Lillian S. "Canon Fathers and Myth Universe," *Left Politics and the Literary Profession*, 1990.

Related Internet Link

Nina Baym
<http://www.english.uiuc.edu/baym/>
The University of Urbana–Champaign, where Baym is the Swanlund Endowed Chair, hosts her homepage, which links to seven online essays.

Eco

Culler, Jonathan. *The Pursuit of Signs: Semiotics, Literature, Deconstruction*, 1981.

Eco, Umberto. *The Search for the Perfect Language*, 1995.

———. *Semiotics and the Philosophy of Language*, 1984.

———. *A Theory of Semiotics*, 1975.

Kristeva, Julia. *Essays in Semiotics,* 1971.
Sebeok, Thomas, ed. *Approaches to Semiotics,* 1964.

Related Internet Link

"A Conversation on Information: An Interview with Umberto Eco"
<http://www.cudenver.edu/~mryder/itc data/eco/eco.html>
In this lengthy interview from February 1995, Eco discussed how computer
    technology and the Internet have changed his role as an author and liter-
    ary researcher.

Showalter

Felman, Shoshana. "Rereading Femininity," *Yale French Studies* 62, 1981.
Fetterley, Judith. *The Resisting Reader: A Feminist Approach to American Fiction,*
    1978.
Kolodny, Annette. "Some Notes on Defining a 'Feminist Literary Criticism,'"
    Critical Inquiry 2, 1975.
Mitchell, Juliet. *Psychoanalysis and Feminism,* 1974.
Showalter, Elaine. *The Female Malady: Women, Madness, and English Culture
    1830–1980,* 1986.
————. *The New Feminist Criticism: Essays on Women, Literature and Theory,*
    1985.
————. *Sexual Anarchy: Gender and Culture at the Fin de Siècle,* 1990.

Related Internet Link

"Plague of the Millennium"
<http://www.princetoninfo.com/hysteria.html>
This feature profile covers various topics, from the hate mail and threats
    Showalter has received from fringe groups, to her recent work uncover-
    ing the roots of six seemingly unrelated contemporary maladies: chronic
    fatigue syndrome, Gulf War syndrome, recovered memories of sexual
    abuse, multiple personality disorder, Satanic ritual abuse, and alien ab-
    duction.

Greenblatt

Bercovitch, Sacvan, and Myra Jehlen, eds. *Ideology and Classic American Litera-
    ture,* 1986.
Greenblatt, Stephen. *The Power of Forms in the English Renaissance,* 1982.
————. *Renaissance Self-Fashioning: From More to Shakespeare,* 1980.
Leverenz, David. *Manhood in the American Renaissance,* 1989.

Reynolds, David S. *Beneath the American Renaissance: The Subversive Imagination in the Age of Emerson and Melville*, 1989.

Thomas Brook. *The New Historicism and Other Old-Fashioned Topics*, 1991.

Vesser, H. Aram., ed. *The New Historicism*, 1989.

Related Internet Link

Stephen Jay Greenblatt
<http://sun3.lib.uci.edu/~scctr/hri/editing/greenblatt.html>
This biliography compiled by Eddie Yeghiayan, a librarian at the University of California, Irvine, is arranged chronologically by year of publication.

Johnson

Abrams, M. H. "The Deconstructive Angel," *Critical Inquiry* 3, 1977.

Arac, Jonathan, and Barbara Johnson, eds. *Consequences of Theory* (Selected Papers from the English Institute, 1987–88, New Series, No. 14), 1991.

Bloom, Harold, et al. *Deconstruction and Criticism*, 1979.

Derrida, Jacques. *Of Grammatology*, 1976.

———. *Writing and Difference*, 1978.

Johnson, Barbara. *The Critical Difference: Essays in the Contemporary Rhetoric of Reading*, 1980.

———. *The Feminist Difference: Literature, Psychoanalysis, Race, and Gender*, 1998.

———. *The Wake of Deconstruction* (The Bucknell Lectures in Literary Theory, Vol. 11), 1994.

Related Internet Link

Deconstruction: Some Assumptions
<http://www.brocku.ca/english/courses/4F70/deconstruction.html>
These introductory notes, written by John Lye for his classes at Brock University, include a quote by Barbara Johnson about Derrida and deconstructive reading.

Felman

Felman, Shoshana. *Jacques Lacan and the Adventure of Insight: Psychoanalysis in Contemporary Culture*, 1987.

———. *Literature and Psychoanalysis: The Question of Reading: Otherwise*, 1982.

Felman, Shoshana, and Dori Laub. *Testimony: Crises of Witnessing in Literature, Psychoanalysis, and History*, 1991.

Grosz, Elizabeth. *Jacques Lacan: A Feminist Introduction*, 1990.

Kris, Ernst. *Psychoanalytic Explorations in Art*, 1952.

MacCannell, Juliet Flower. *Figuring Lacan: Criticism and the Cultural Unconscious*, 1986.

Wilden, Anthony. *The Language of the Self: The Function of Language in Psychoanalysis*, 1968.

Related Internet Link

"Forms of Judicial Blindness, or The Evidence of What Cannot Be Seen: Traumatic Narratives and Legal Repetitions in the O. J. Simpson Case and in Tolstoy's *The Kreutzer Sonata*"
<http://www2.uchicago.edu/jnl-crit-inq/v23/v23n4.felman.html>
In this long excerpt published by *Critical Inquiry*, Felman attempts to illuminate legal obscurities with literary insights and to reflect on ambiguities the O. J. Simpson trial has left by using textual issues that turn out to be quite relevant.

Gilbert and Gubar

Beauvoir, Simone de. *The Second Sex*, 1972.

Felman, Shoshana. "Rereading Femininity," *Yale French Studies* 62, 1981.

Gilbert, Sandra, and Susan Gubar. *The Madwoman in the Attic: The Woman Writer and the Nineteenth-Century Literary Imagination*, 1979.

———. *No Man's Land*, 1988.

Kahn, Coppelia, and Gayle Greene, eds. *Making a Difference: Feminist Literary Criticism*, 1985.

Moi, Toril. *Sexual/Textual Politics: Feminist Literary Theory*, 1985.

Related Internet Links

"What Ails Feminist Criticism?"
<http://www2.uchicago.edu/jnl-crit-inq/gubar.html>
Susan Gubar's article appeared in the spring 1999 volume of *Critical Inquiry*.

Sandra Gilbert
<http://wwwenglish.ucdavis.edu/Faculty/gilbert/gilbert.htm>
This page is part of the English Department website at the University of California, Davis, where Gilbert is a professor. It includes a biography and outlines her major works.

Gates

African and African American Literature. Special topic issue of *PMLA*, January 1990.

Baker, Houston A., Jr. *Afro-American Literary Study in the 1990s*, 1989.

———. *The Journey Back*, 1980.

Braxton, Joanne M., and Adree Nicola McLaughlin. *Wild Women in the Whirl-wind: Afra-American Culture and the Contemporary Literary Renaissance,* 1989.

Gates, Henry Louis, Jr. *The Signifying Monkey,* 1988.

Pryse, Marjorie, and Hortense J. Spiller, eds. *Conjuring: Black Women, Fiction, and Literary Tradition,* 1985.

Wall, Cheryl A., ed. *Changing Our Own Words: Essays on Criticism, Theory, and Writing by Black Women,* 1989.

Related Internet Link

Colored People
<http://www.booknotes.org/authors/10279.htm>
In a conversation with Brian Lamb, host of C-SPAN's show *Booknotes*, Gates touched on topics ranging from his mother and his childhood in West Virginia to his new book, *Colored People: A Memoir.*

Sedgwick

Butler, Judith. *Gender Trouble: Feminism and the Subversion of Identity,* 1990.

Foucault, Michel. *The History of Sexuality,* 1980.

Kauffman, Linda, ed. *Gender and Theory: Dialogues on Feminist Criticism,* 1985.

Rich, Adrienne. "Compulsory Heterosexuality and Lesbian Existence," *Women, Sex, and Sexuality,* edited by Catharine Stimpson and Ethel Spector Person, 1980.

Sedgwick, Eve Kosofsky. *Between Men: English Literature and Male Homosocial Desire,* 1986.

———. *Epistemology of the Closet,* 1990.

Related Internet Link

"Sedgwick Sense and Sensibility: An Interview with Eve Kosofsky Sedg-wick"
<http://www.arts.ucsb.edu/~tvc/v09/interviews/v09int.sedg.html>
In this interview, Sedgwick talked about her book *Epistemology of the Closet,* her first volume of poetry *Fat Art, Thin Art,* and her ongoing obsession with performative utterances.

Landow

Aarseth, Espen, J. *Cybertext: Perspectives on Ergodic Literature,* 1997.

Delany, Paul, and George Landow, eds. *Hypermedia and Literary Studies,* 1991.

Landow, George P. *Hyper/Text/Theory,* 1994.

————. *Hypertext 2.0: The Convergence of Contemporary Critical Theory and Technology,* 1997.

Lanham, Richard A. *The Electronic Word: Democracy, Technology, and the Arts,* 1995.

Snyder, Ilana. *Hypertext: The Electronic Labyrinth,* 1997.

Related Internet Link

"Hypertext 2.0: An Interview with George Landow"
<http://www.altx.com/int2/george.landow.html>

Alt-X Online Publishing Network, an e-zine that publishes cutting-edge fiction, criticism, and hypertext articles, hosts this interview with George Landow on the expanded version of his book *Hypertext: The Convergence of Contemporary Critical Theory and Technology.* Note: Depending on your browser, the words on the screen might be too light to read. If so, highlight the entire text, and it will become visible.

Bhabha

Bhabha, Homi K. *The Location of Culture,* 1994.

Bhabha, Homi K., ed. *Nation and Narration,* 1990.

Geertz, Clifford. *The Interpretation of Cultures: Selected Essays,* 1973.

Said, Edward W. *Culture and Imperialism,* 1993.

Spivak, Gayatri Chakravorty. "How to Read a 'Culturally Different' Book," *Colonial Discourse/Postcolonial Theory,* 1994.

White, Hayden. *Tropics of Discourse: Essays in Cultural Criticism,* 1978.

Related Internet Link

Homi K. Bhabha: An Overview
<http://www.stg.brown.edu/projects/hypertext/landow/post/poldiscourse/bhabha/bhabha1.html>

Benjamin Graves, a student at Brown University, wrote this page on Bhabha's essay "The Commitment to Theory" as a link to his homepage, *Political Discourse: Theories of Colonialism and Postcolonialism.*

Acknowledgments *(continued from page iv)*

Nina Baym. "Melodramas of Beset Manhood." From *American Quarterly,* Vol. 33.2 (Summer 1981): 123–39. Copyright © 1981. Reprinted by permission of The Johns Hopkins University Press.

Homi K. Bhabha. "The Postcolonial and the Postmodern: The Question of Agency." From *Locations of Culture* by Homi K. Bhabha, pp. 171–97. Copyright © 1994 by Homi K. Bhabha. Reprinted by permission of Routledge Ltd.

Cleanth Brooks. "Keats's Sylvan Historian: History without Footnotes." From *The Well Wrought Urn,* copyright 1947 and renewed 1975 by Cleanth Brooks. Reprinted by permission of Harcourt Brace & Company.

Paul de Man. "Semiology and Rhetoric." From *Diacritics,* 3:3, 1973. Copyright © 1973. Reprinted by permission of The Johns Hopkins University Press.

Jacques Derrida. "Structure, Sign, and Play in the Discourse of the Human Sciences." From *The Structuralist Controversy,* edited by Richard Macksey and Eugenio Donato. Copyright © 1972. Reprinted by permission of The Johns Hopkins University Press.

Terry Eagleton. "Marxism and Literary Criticism (Chapters 1–2)." From *Marxism and Literary Criticism.* © 1976 by Terry Eagleton. Used by permission of the Regents of the University of California and the University of California Press.

Umberto Eco. Excerpts from pp. 14–15, 20–29 in *Semiotics and the Philosophy of Language* by Umberto Eco. Copyright © 1986 by Umberto Eco. Reprinted by permission of Indiana University Press.

T. S. Eliot. "Tradition and the Individual Talent." From *Selected Essays* by T. S. Eliot. Copyright © 1950 by Harcourt Brace & Company and renewed 1978 by Esme Valerie Eliot. Reprinted by permission of Harcourt Brace & Company and Faber & Faber Ltd.

Shoshana Felman. "The Case of Poe: Applications/Implications of Psychoanalysis." From *Jacques Lacan and the Adventure of Insight: Psychoanalysis in Contemporary Culture* by Shoshana Felman. Copyright © 1987 by the President and Fellows of Harvard College. Reprinted by permission of the publisher, Harvard University Press.

Stanley Fish. "Is There a Text in This Class?" Excerpt from pp. 303–21 in *Is There a Text in This Class? The Authority of Interpretive Communities* by Stanley Fish. Copyright © 1980 by the President and Fellows of Harvard College. Reprinted by permission of Harvard University Press.

Michael Foucault. "What Is an Author?" From *Textual Strategies: Perspectives in Post-Structuralist Criticism,* translated and edited from the French by Josue V. Harari. Copyright © 1979 by Cornell University. Used by permission of the publisher, Cornell University Press.

Sigmund Freud. "The Theme of the Three Caskets." Copyrights, The Institute of Psycho-Analysis and The Hogarth Press for permission to quote from *The Standard Edition of the Complete Psychological Works of Sigmund Freud,* translated and edited by James Strachey.

Northrop Frye. "The Archetypes of Literature." From *Fables of Identity* by Northrop Frye. Copyright © 1963 by Harcourt Brace Jovanovich, Inc. Reprinted by permission.

Henry Louis Gates, Jr. "The Trope of the Talking Book." From pp. 127–69 in *The Signifying Monkey: A Theory of African-American Literary Criticism* by Henry Louis Gates, Jr. Copyright © 1988 by Henry Louis Gates, Jr. Reprinted by permission of Oxford University Press, Inc.

Sandra M. Gilbert and Susan Gubar. "Tradition and the Female Talent." Excerpts from pp. 125–31, 154–62 (Chapter 3) in *No Man's Land: The Place of the Woman Writer in the Twentieth Century,* vol. 1: *The War of the Words,* by Sandra

M. Gilbert and Susan Gubar. Copyright © 1988 by Sandra M. Gilbert and
    Susan Gubar. Reprinted by permission of Yale University Press.
Stephen Greenblatt. "Shakespeare and the Exorcists." From *Shakespeare and the
    Question of Theory,* edited by Patricia Parker and Geoffrey Hartman. Re-
    printed by permission of Methuen & Co.
Horace. "Epistle to the Pisones/The Art of Poetry." Translated by Norman J. De-
    Witt. Copyright © 1961 by Norman J. DeWitt; used by permission of Mrs.
    Norman J. DeWitt. First published in *Drama Survey* I, 2 (October 1961).
Barbara Johnson. "A Hound, a Bay Horse, and a Turtle Dove: Obscurity in
    Walden." From pp. 149–70 in *Psychoanalysis and the Question of the Text* by the
    English Institute. Originally titled "The Frame of Reference: Poe, Lacan, Der-
    rida." Copyright © 1978 by the English Institute. Reprinted by permission of
    The Johns Hopkins University Press.
Immanuel Kant. "Analytic of the Beautiful." Excerpts from pp. 44–46, 51, 78–84 in
    Critique of Judgment, translated by Werner S. Pluhar. Copyright © 1987 by
    Hackett Publishing Company. Reprinted by permission of Hackett Publish-
    ing Company. All rights reserved.
John Keats. Letters 43, 45, 62, and 118 from *The Letters of John Keats: 1814–1821,*
    edited by Hyder E. Rollins. Copyright © 1958 by the President and Fellows
    of Harvard College. Reprinted by permission of Harvard University Press.
George P. Landow. Excerpt from pp. 2–18 in *Hypertext: The Convergence of Con-
    temporary Critical Theory and Technology* by George P. Landow. Copyright
    © 1992 by George P. Landow. Reprinted by permission of The Johns Hop-
    kins University Press.
Karl Marx. Excerpts from "The Premises of the Materialist Method" and "Artistic
    Talent under Communism" in *Karl Marx: Selected Writings,* edited by David
    McLellan. Copyright © 1977 by David McLellan. Reprinted by permission of
    Oxford University Press (UK).
Friedrich Nietzsche. Excerpt from "The Birth of Tragedy" in *The Basic Writings of
    Nietzsche* by Friedrich Nietzsche, translated by Walter Kaufmann. Copyright
    © 1967 by Walter Kaufmann. Copyright © renewed 1994 by Mrs. Hazel
    Kaufmann. Reprinted by permission of Random House, Inc.
Plato: *"The Republic*: Book X" and "The Ion." From *The Dialogues of Plato,* trans-
    lated by Benjamin Jowett, 4th revised edition. Oxford University Press, 1953.
    Reprinted by permission of Oxford University Press.
John Crowe Ransom. "Criticism as Pure Speculation." Excerpt from pp. 41–62
    in *The Intent of the Critic,* edited by Donald A. Stauffer. Copyright © 1941,
    © renewed 1969 by Princeton University Press. Reprinted with permission
    of Princeton University Press.
Adrienne Rich. "When We Dead Awaken: Writing as Re-Vision." From *On Lies,
    Secrets, and Silence: Selected Prose 1966–1978* by Adrienne Rich. Copyright
    © 1979 by W. W. Norton & Company, Inc. Poems noted in this essay —
    "Aunt Jennifer's Tigers" © 1993, 1951; "The Loser" © 1993, 1967, 1963; lines
    from "Snapshots of a Daughter-in-Law" © 1993, 1967, 1963; "Orion" © 1993;
    and "Planetarium" © 1993 (all © by Adrienne Rich) — are from *Collected Early
    Poems: 1950–1970* by Adrienne Rich. All selections reprinted by permission of
    W. W. Norton & Company, Inc.
Eva Kosofsky Sedgwick. Excerpt from "Introduction: Axiomatic." From *Episte-
    mology of the Closet* by Eve Kosofsky Sedgwick. Copyright © 1990 by The Re-
    gents of the University of California. Reprinted by permission of the Univer-
    sity of California Press.
Elaine Showalter. "Representing Ophelia: Women, Madness, and the Responsi-
    bilities of Feminist Criticism." From *Shakespeare and the Question of Theory,*
    edited by Patricia Parker and Geoffrey Hartman. Reprinted by permission of
    Methuen & Co.

Virginia Woolf. "Shakespeare's Sister." Excerpt from *A Room of One's Own* by Virginia Woolf. Copyright © 1929 by Harcourt Brace & Company and renewed 1957 by Leonard Woolf. Reprinted by permission of the publisher.

William Wordsworth. "Preface to *Lyrical Ballads*." From *Wordsworth's Literary Criticism*, edited by Nowell C. Smith. Henry Frowde, Oxford University Press, 1905. Reprinted by permission of Oxford University Press.

INDEX